Psychopathology

Psychopathology

History, Diagnosis, and Empirical Foundations

Third Edition

W. EDWARD CRAIGHEAD,

DAVID J. MIKLOWITZ, AND

LINDA W. CRAIGHEAD

EDITORS

WILEY

Published by Jossey-Bass
A Wiley Brand
One Montgomery Street, Suite 1000, San Francisco, CA 94104-4594—www.josseybass.com

Jossey-Bass books and products are available through most bookstores. To contact Jossey-Bass directly call our Customer Care Department within the U.S. at 800-956-7739, outside the U.S. at 317-572-3986, or fax 317-572-4002.

Wiley publishes in a variety of print and electronic formats and by print-on-demand. Some material included with standard print versions of this book may not be included in e-books or in print-on-demand. If this book refers to media such as a CD or DVD that is not included in the version you purchased, you may download this material at **http://booksupport.wiley.com**. For more information about Wiley products, visit **www.wiley.com**.

Library of Congress Cataloging-in-Publication Data

Names: Craighead, W. Edward, author. | Miklowitz, David Jay, 1957- author. |
    Craighead, Linda W., author.
Title: Psychopathology : history, diagnosis, and empirical foundations /
    W. Edward Craighead, David J. Miklowitz, Linda W. Craighead.
Description: Third edition. | Hoboken : Wiley, 2017. | Revised edition of
    Psychopathology, [2013] | Includes bibliographical references and index.
Identifiers: LCCN 2016033868| ISBN 9781119221739 (hardback) | ISBN
    9781119221746 (Adobe PDF) | ISBN 9781119221753 (epub)
Subjects: LCSH: Psychology, Pathological. | BISAC: PSYCHOLOGY /
    Psychopathology / General.
Classification: LCC RC454 .C73 2017 | DDC 616.89—dc23 LC record
    available at https://lccn.loc.gov/2016033868

Cover Design: Wiley
Cover Image: © Malcolm MacGregor/Getty Images, Inc.

Printed in the United States of America

THIRD EDITION

HB Printing   10 9 8 7 6 5 4 3 2

Contents

Preface

This book provides a basic description and evaluation of clinical theory and research regarding psychopathology. It is intended primarily as an advanced text for psychopathology courses taught to graduate students in clinical, counseling, and school psychology, as well as neuroscience, psychiatry, and social work. Some instructors may find it appropriate for an upper-level undergraduate course in abnormal psychology or psychopathology. This book also provides updated and refresher materials for mental health professionals engaged in assessment, diagnosis, and treatment of psychological disorders.

The first edition of this book emerged from our many discussions regarding how best to provide reading materials for the graduate psychopathology course when we were all professors at the University of Colorado, Boulder. From time to time different faculty members had been called upon to teach this course, and each time this occurred we had lengthy discussions about the most appropriate reading lists and books. In addition to the standard materials regarding psychopathology, we wanted to include clinically relevant materials that focused on vulnerability and stress, genetic markers, human development, affective neuroscience, translational research, and empirically supported treatments including efficacy and effectiveness outcomes. We faced repeated difficulties in assembling such materials and requesting readings from colleagues around the world. We concluded that it was an appropriate time to ask several of our clinical science colleagues to help us create a resource that would incorporate these current and critical areas of interest. We asked them to provide a broad range of information drawn from psychopathology and related basic research for each disorder, so the reader would have a 35- to 45-page comprehensive view of each of the topics. Although we have now moved to other universities and venues for our work, we believe there is still a need in the psychopathology area for an integrative set of reading materials. In order to reflect enormous changes in psychopathology research, we have updated, revised, and produced this third edition of the book.

The initial version of the *DSM-5* was published in May 2013, and this edition of the book is organized around the disorders as defined in *DSM-5*. Nevertheless, most of the relevant psychopathology literature is based on earlier editions of the *DSM*. Additional *DSM-5*–based psychopathology research will supply the basis of future editions. Furthermore, psychopathology research is beginning to take a somewhat different focus. Future books on this topic may present a quite different organizational structure, perhaps surrounding constructs underlying *DSM* categories of psychopathology (see the National Institute of Mental Health [NIMH], at https://www.nimh.nih.gov/research-priorities/rdoc).

Historical Perspective

Although descriptions of psychopathological disorders, at least on a nonscientific basis, have existed for hundreds of years, the first modern attempts to classify behaviors, thoughts, biology, and feelings within a formal classification system are usually attributed to the prominent German psychiatrist Emil Kraepelin, who did most of his work at the end of the 19th century. Psychology emerged as a discipline at about that same time, and except for learning disabilities and a few of the childhood disorders, psychology was largely unconcerned with psychopathology. It was a half-century later that psychiatry (via the American Psychiatric Association [APA]) offered the first full-scale and systematic modern classification manual—the *Diagnostic and Statistical Manual of Mental Disorders*—in 1952. As Lilienfeld, Smith, and Watts note in the first chapter in this book, this diagnostic manual has undergone extensive revision and reorganization over the past half-century.

In order to understand the slow development of psychology's role in the evolution of theories and research in psychopathology, it is important to have at least a glimpse of the history of professional developments within psychology. By the time of World War I (1914–1918), psychologists had emerged on mental health teams as professionals who primarily conducted formal clinical assessments. Psychologists' activities proliferated during World War I, though the emphasis remained on assessment. Psychologists had originally focused primarily on intellectual assessment, but during World War I this focus shifted to include assessment of personality, largely in order to assess and predict what is now known as posttraumatic stress disorder. Between World War I and World War II, clinical psychology continued to emphasize the development of intelligence tests and assessments of intelligence, but the discipline also began in earnest to develop instruments and methods to assess personality. It was only during World War II and subsequent years that psychologists began conducting psychotherapy on more than a minimal basis, initially under the supervision of psychiatrists and only later, during the 1960–1970 era, as independent professionals. This movement toward broader involvement in clinical, counseling, and school intervention brought with it an interest in psychopathology as well as psychotherapy. A number of theoretical and practical developments (ranging from insurance reimbursement for clinical practice to National Institutes of Health funding for research) contributed to wide-scale acceptance of the *DSM* classification system, even though this framework has been associated with much controversy, as will be evident throughout this book.

During the preceding professional developments, it was psychiatrists who first directed and led most mental health teams in child hygiene clinics and community mental health centers. Psychologists only gradually became genuinely concerned with more broadly defined psychopathology and its assessment as they became involved in the delivery of therapeutic services. The field of psychopathology has thus emerged over the past five decades to reflect advances in psychology, psychiatry, and neuroscience. There have been very few books since Maher's *Principles of Psychopathology* (1968) that have provided extensive, comprehensive, and scientifically based overviews of theories and empirical foundations of psychopathology at the graduate level. It is our hope that this tightly coordinated book will be a step toward filling that vacuum.

This book begins with a chapter that picks up where the preceding brief historical review leaves off, as Lilienfeld, Smith, and Watts present an overview of the major issues that arise in the study of psychopathology at an advanced level. This introductory chapter is followed by overviews of most of the major clinical disorders. In order to ensure consistency in the material presented in each chapter, we asked the authors to follow a specific format, though some chapter topics and their associated research fit less easily within that format than others. The general outline for each chapter is as follows: (a) a description of the diagnostic criteria for each disorder examined in the chapter, including a brief history and a case example; (b) prevalence and epidemiological findings; (c) empirical foundations of each disorder, including findings regarding behavioral, cognitive, emotional, and neurobiological factors; (d) assessment of each disorder, including interviews, clinical rating scales, self-reports, and neurobiological assessments; (e) a brief description and evaluation of the current interventions for each disorder; and (f) a summary and discussion of future directions. We greatly appreciate the willingness of the authors to adhere to this uniform outline. This approach improved our ability to provide consistent coverage across disorders, which makes this volume particular suitable for coursework. It also makes it easier for readers to find the needed information when using this volume as a reference or resource book. Based on feedback from professors who use this book as a text and reviewers of the prior editions, and in order to better match an academic semester, this third edition has been reduced to 15 chapters.

Following a long tradition that dates back to Freud's view of the centrality of anxiety in psychopathology, the *DSM* traditional anxiety disorders are presented first. These include social anxiety disorder, including avoidant personality disorder (discussed by Ledley, Erwin, Morrison, and Heimberg in Chapter 2); panic disorder (Arch, Kirk, and Craske, Chapter 3); and generalized anxiety disorder (Rowa, Waechter, Hood, and Antony, Chapter 4). Both obsessive-compulsive and related disorders (Abramowitz and Blakey, Chapter 5) and posttraumatic stress disorder (PTSD) (Resick, Monson, and LoSavio, Chapter 6), which were formerly treated as subtypes of anxiety disorders, are given separate diagnostic status in *DSM-5* and therefore separate chapters here. This book then continues with two chapters related to what have previously been labeled mood disorders: major depressive and persistent depressive disorder (W. E. Craighead, Klein, Gillespie, Ritschel, and Phillips, Chapter 7) and bipolar disorders (Miklowitz and Johnson, Chapter 8). Sleep-wake disorders, discussed by Dong, Kanady, and Harvey in Chapter 9, are important dysregulations in their own right, but are also particularly important as they relate to mood disorders. Chapter 10, by Ryan, Trotman, Mittal, Tessner, and Walker, provides a thorough discussion of schizophrenia and the psychotic spectrum disorders. Chapter 11, by Ray, Courtney, Green, and Bacio, reports on substance-related disorders, with a focus on alcohol. Just as with mood disorders in Chapter 7, Chapter 12 (L. W. Craighead, Martinez, Klump, Lock, and Kirz), reporting on eating disorders, combines and updates two chapters from the previous edition (on binge eating and bulimia and on anorexia). The remainder of the book presents chapters on sexual dysfunction, by Meston and Stanton (Chapter 13); borderline personality disorder, by Hooley and Masland (Chapter 14); and key developments in the assessment, etiology, and treatment of psychopathy, by Vitale and Newman (Chapter 15), As is apparent from this list, the chapter authors were chosen because of their and their colleagues' and students' major contributions to our knowledge of psychopathology; this is also apparent in the materials included in each chapter.

References

American Psychiatric Association. (1952). *Diagnostic and statistical manual of mental disorders* (1st ed.). Washington, DC: Author.

American Psychiatric Association. (2013). *Diagnostic and statistical manual of mental disorders* (5th ed.). Washington, DC: Author.

Maher, B. (1968). *Principles of psychopathology: An experimental approach.* New York: McGraw-Hill.

Acknowledgments

A very large number of people have contributed to the development and publication of this book. First, we acknowledge our own mentors: Leonard Ullmann and Gordon Paul (WEC), Michael Goldstein (DJM), and Alan Kazdin and Carolyn Sherif (LWC) are greatly appreciated. Colleagues, students, and friends who have contributed to our understanding of psychopathology, assessment, and interventions are just too numerous to mention, but fortunately they know who they are. We are especially appreciative to the Craighead and Miklowitz families for their support and caring while we completed this project. Specifically, we thank Ben, Wade (along with Tara and Sawyer), and Daniel Craighead and Margaret Craighead Shuster (along with Justin, Lily, and Zoey Shuster), and Mary Yaeger and Ariana Miklowitz.

We would like to thank our staff members, especially Lara Alexander, Valeria Tretyak, and Sean Carey. Both have been very helpful, efficient, and punctual in their assistance during the many phases of the development of this edition of the book.

We would also like to thank the Fuqua Family Foundations and the Mary and John Brock Foundation for their continued support of the Emory CAMP program. Their support contributed to the completion of this book.

We cannot imagine a better editor than Wiley's Patricia Rossi, who has been of great help from our very earliest conceptualization of the first edition right through the production of this third edition. She has been involved in every phase of its production, and in this process we have come to appreciate her insights and professional expertise in every phase of the editing process. It is a pleasure to work with such a talented person and genuinely fine human being. We also appreciate the help of the other cooperative and helpful people at John Wiley & Sons.

Finally, we would like to express our gratitude to the authors of the various chapters in this book. Each chapter's author team includes at least one of the established international leaders studying the topic. Coauthors were carefully chosen in their areas of expertise. As planned, the chapters reflect not only the contributions of the authors but also detailed reviews of the larger literature pertinent to each disorder. Thus, the reader can enjoy the detailed review of the psychopathology of the disorder in each chapter as well as the interesting commentary and thoughts about future directions for research and clinical issues from the perspective of individuals who are intimately involved in ongoing clinical psychopathology research. Our hope is that this will inform readers and also stimulate the thinking of developing research investigators and students to inspire them to ask important questions regarding psychopathology. These outstanding scholars, in composite, have done what no one individual (or even three) can do today—namely, provide a thorough and comprehensive summary of the current state of knowledge regarding psychopathology.

List of Contributors

Jonathan S. Abramowitz, PhD
University of North Carolina at
Chapel Hill
Chapel Hill, NC

Martin M. Antony, PhD
Ryerson University
Toronto, Ontario, Canada

Joanna J. Arch, PhD
University of Colorado, Boulder
Boulder, CO

Guadalupe A. Bacio, PhD
University of California, Los Angeles
Los Angeles, CA

Shannon M. Blakey, MS
University of North Carolina at
Chapel Hill
Chapel Hill, NC

Kelly E. Courtney, MA
University of California, Los Angeles
Los Angeles, CA

Linda W. Craighead, PhD
Emory University
Atlanta, GA

W. Edward Craighead, PhD
Emory University
Atlanta, GA

Michelle G. Craske, PhD
University of California, Los Angeles
Los Angeles, California

Lu Dong, PhD, MHS
University of California, Berkeley
Berkeley, California

Brigette A. Erwin, PhD
The Anxiety and OCD Center
Exton, PA

Charles F. Gillespie, MD, PhD
Emory University
Atlanta, GA

ReJoyce Green, BA
University of California, Los Angeles
Los Angeles, California

Allison G. Harvey, PhD
University of California, Berkeley
Berkeley, CA

Richard G. Heimberg, PhD
Temple University
Philadelphia, PA

Heather K. Hood, PhD
Homewood Health Centre
Guelph, Ontario, Canada

Jill M. Hooley, DPhil
Harvard University
Cambridge, MA

Sheri L. Johnson, PhD
University of California, Berkeley
Berkeley, CA

Jennifer C. Kanady, MA
University of California, Berkeley
Berkeley, CA

Alex Kirk, MA
University of Colorado, Boulder
Boulder, CO

Nina Kirz, MD
Stanford University
Stanford, CA

Daniel N. Klein, PhD
Stony Brook University
Stony Brook, NY

Kelly L. Klump, PhD
Michigan State University
East Lansing, MI

Deborah Roth Ledley, PhD
Children's Center for OCD and Anxiety
Plymouth Meeting, PA

Scott O. Lilienfeld, PhD
Emory University
Atlanta, GA

James Lock, MD, PhD
Stanford University
Stanford, CA

Stefanie T. LoSavio, PhD
Duke University
Durham, NC

Margaret A. Martinez, MA
Emory University
Atlanta, GA

Sara R. Masland, MA
Harvard University
Cambridge, MA

Cindy M. Meston, PhD
University of Texas at Austin
Austin, TX

David J. Miklowitz, PhD
University of California, Los Angeles
Los Angeles, CA

Vijay A. Mittal, PhD
Northwestern University
Evanston, IL

Candice M. Monson, PhD
Ryerson University
Toronto, Ontario, Canada

Amanda S. Morrison, PhD
Stanford University
Stanford, CA

Joseph P. Newman, PhD
University of Wisconsin, Madison
Madison, WI

Katherine E. Phillips, BS
Emory University
Atlanta, GA

Lara A. Ray, PhD
University of California, Los Angeles
Los Angeles, CA

Patricia A. Resick, PhD, ABPP
Duke University
Durham, NC

Lorie A. Ritschel, PhD
University of North Carolina at Chapel
    Hill
Chapel Hill, GA

Karen Rowa, PhD
McMaster University
Hamilton, Ontario, Canada

Arthur T. Ryan, PhD
Emory University
Atlanta, GA

Sarah Francis Smith, PhD
Emory University
Atlanta, GA

Amelia M. Stanton, BA
University of Texas at Austin
Austin, TX

Kevin D. Tessner, PhD
Erie VA Medical Center
Erie, PA

Hanan D. Trotman, PhD
Mercer University
Atlanta, GA

Jennifer E. Vitale, PhD
Hampden-Sydney College
Hampden-Sydney, VA

Stephanie Waechter, PhD
St. Joseph's Healthcare Hamilton
Hamilton, Ontario, Canada

Elaine F. Walker, PhD
Emory University
Atlanta, GA

Ashley L. Watts, MA
Emory University
Atlanta, GA

Psychopathology

Chapter 1

Diagnosis

Conceptual Issues and Controversies

SCOTT O. LILIENFELD, SARAH FRANCIS SMITH, AND ASHLEY L. WATTS

Psychiatric diagnosis is fundamental to the understanding of mental illness. Without it, the study, assessment, and treatment of psychopathology would be in disarray. In this chapter, we examine (a) the raison d'être underlying psychiatric diagnosis, (b) widespread misconceptions regarding psychiatric classification and diagnosis, (c) the present system of psychiatric classification and its strengths and weaknesses, and (d) fruitful directions for improving this system.

A myriad of forms of abnormality are housed under the exceedingly broad umbrella of mental disorders. Indeed, the current psychiatric classification system, as described in the *Diagnostic and Statistical Manual of Mental Disorders (DSM-5)*, contains well over 300 diagnoses (American Psychiatric Association [APA], 2013). In addition, Chapter V of the International Classification of Diseases, 10th edition (ICD-10), contains approximately 100 diagnoses housed within 26 categories (World Health Organization, 1992). The enormous heterogeneity of psychopathology makes a formal system of organization imperative. Just as in the biological sciences, where Linnaeus's hierarchical taxonomy categorizes fauna and flora, and in chemistry, where Mendeleev's periodic table orders the elements, a psychiatric classification system helps to organize the bewildering subforms of abnormality. Such a system, if effective, permits us to parse the variegated universe of psychological disorders into more homogeneous, and ideally more clinically meaningful, categories.

From the practitioner's initial inchoate impression that a patient's behavior is aberrant to his or her later and better-elaborated case conceptualization, diagnosis plays an integral role in the clinical process. Indeed, the essential reason for initiating assessment and treatment is often the observer's sense that "something is just not quite right" about the person. Meehl (1973) commented that the mental health professional's core task is to answer the question: "What does this person have, or what befell him, that makes him different from those who have not developed clinical psychopathology?" (p. 248). Therein lies the basis for psychiatric diagnosis.

1

General Terminological Issues

Before proceeding, a bit of terminology is in order. It is crucial at the outset to distinguish two frequently confused terms: classification and diagnosis. A system of *classification* is an overarching taxonomy of mental illness, whereas *diagnosis* is the act of placing an individual, based on a constellation of signs (observable indicators, like crying in a depressed patient) or symptoms (subjective indicators, like feelings of guilt in a depressed patient), or both, into a category within that taxonomy. Classification is a prerequisite for diagnosis.

Another key set of terminological issues concerns the distinctions among syndrome, disorder, and disease. As Kazdin (1983) observed, we can differentiate among these three concepts based on our levels of understanding of their pathology—the underlying pathophysiology that may accompany the condition—and etiology, that is, causation (Gough, 1971; Lilienfeld, Waldman, & Israel, 1994).

At the lowest rung of the hierarchy of understanding there are *syndromes*, which are typically constellations of signs and symptoms that co-occur across individuals (*syndrome* means "running together" in Greek). In classical syndromes, neither pathology nor etiology is well understood, nor is the syndrome's causal relation to other conditions established. Antisocial personality disorder is a relatively clear example of a syndrome because its signs (e.g., the use of an alias) and symptoms (e.g., lack of remorse) tend to covary across individuals. Nevertheless, its pathology and etiology are largely unknown, and its causal relation to other conditions is poorly understood (Lykken, 1995). In contrast, some authors (e.g., Lilienfeld, 2013; but see Lynam & Miller, 2012) argue that psychopathic personality (psychopathy) may not be a classical syndrome. These researchers contend that psychopathy is instead a configuration of several largely independent constructs, such as boldness, coldness, and disinhibition, that come together in an interpersonally malignant fashion (Patrick, Fowles, & Krueger, 2009; see also Vitale & Newman, Chapter 15, in this book).

In other cases, syndromes may also constitute groupings of signs and symptoms that exhibit minimal covariation across individuals but that point to an underlying etiology (Lilienfeld et al., 1994). For example, Gerstmann's syndrome in neurology (Benton, 1992) is marked by four major features: agraphia (inability to write), acalculia (inability to perform mental computation), finger agnosia (inability to differentiate among fingers on the hand), and left-right disorientation. Although these indicators are negligibly correlated across individuals in the general population, they co-occur dependably following certain instances of parietal lobe damage.

At the second rung of the hierarchy of understanding there are *disorders*, which are syndromes that cannot be readily explained by other conditions. For example, in the present diagnostic system, obsessive-compulsive disorder (OCD) can be diagnosed only if its symptoms (e.g., recurrent fears of contamination) and signs (e.g., recurrent hand washing) cannot be accounted for by a specific phobia (e.g., irrational fear of dirt). Once we rule out other potential causes of OCD symptoms, such as specific phobia, anorexia nervosa, and trichotillomania (compulsive hair pulling), we can be reasonably certain that an individual exhibiting marked obsessions or compulsions, or both, suffers from a well-defined disorder (APA, 2000, p. 463).

At the third and highest rung of the hierarchy of understanding there are *diseases*, which are disorders in which pathology and etiology are reasonably well understood (Kazdin, 1983; McHugh & Slavney, 1998). Sickle-cell anemia is a prototypical disease because its pathology (crescent-shaped erythrocytes containing hemoglobin S) and etiology (two autosomal recessive alleles) have been conclusively identified (Sutton, 1980). For other conditions that approach the status of bona fide diseases, such as Alzheimer's disease, the primary pathology (senile plaques, neurofibrillary tangles, and granulovacuolar degeneration) has been identified, while their etiology is evolving but incomplete (Selkoe, 1992).

With the possible exception of Alzheimer's disease and a handful of other organic conditions, the diagnoses in our present system of psychiatric classifications are almost exclusively syndromes or, in rare cases, disorders (Kendell & Jablensky, 2003). This fact is a sobering reminder that the pathology in most cases of psychopathology is largely unknown, and their etiology is poorly understood (Kendler, 2005; Kendler, Zachar, & Craver, 2011). Therefore, although we genuflect to hallowed tradition in this chapter by referring to the major entities within the current psychiatric classification system as mental "disorders," readers should bear in mind that few are disorders in the strict sense of the term.

Functions of Psychiatric Diagnosis

Diagnosis serves three principal functions for practitioners and researchers alike. We discuss each in turn.

DIAGNOSIS AS COMMUNICATION

Diagnosis furnishes a convenient vehicle for communication about an individual's condition. It allows professionals to be reasonably confident that when they use a diagnosis (such as persistent depressive disorder or borderline personality disorder) to describe a patient, other professionals will recognize it as referring to the same condition. Moreover, a diagnosis distills relevant information, such as frantic efforts to avoid abandonment and chronic feelings of emptiness, in a shorthand form that aids in other professionals' understanding of a case. Blashfield and Burgess (2007) described this role as "information retrieval." Just as botanists use the name of a species to summarize distinctive features of a specific plant, psychologists and psychiatrists rely on a diagnosis to summarize distinctive features of a specific mental disorder (Blashfield & Burgess, 2007). Diagnoses succinctly convey important information about a patient to clinicians, investigators, family members, managed care organizations, and others.

ESTABLISHING LINKAGES WITH OTHER DIAGNOSES

Psychiatric diagnoses are organized within the overarching nosological structure of other diagnoses. Nosology is the branch of science that deals with the systematic classification of diseases. Within this system, most diagnostic categories are arranged in relation to other conditions; the nearer in the network two conditions are, the more closely related they ostensibly are as disorders. For example, social anxiety disorder (social phobia) and specific phobia are both classified as anxiety disorders in the *Diagnostic and Statistical Manual of Mental Disorders* (*DSM-5*; APA, 2013), and are presumably more closely linked etiologically than are social anxiety disorder and narcissistic personality disorder, the latter of which is classified as a personality disorder in *DSM-5*. Thus, diagnoses help to locate the patient's presenting problems within the context of both more and less related diagnostic categories.

PROVISION OF SURPLUS INFORMATION

Perhaps most important, a diagnosis helps us to learn new things; it affords us surplus information that we did not have previously. Among other things, a diagnosis allows us to generate predictions regarding case trajectory. As Goodwin and Guze (1996) noted, perhaps hyperbolically, "diagnosis is prognosis" (Kendler, 1980). The diagnostic label of bipolar I disorder describes a distinctive constellation of indicators (e.g., one or more manic or mixed episodes) that discriminates the course, rate of recovery, and treatment response from such related conditions as major depression and bipolar II disorder, the latter of which is marked by one or more episodes of hypomania and disabling depression. But a valid diagnosis does considerably more than predict prognosis. Robins and Guze's (1970) landmark article delineated formal criteria for ascertaining whether a diagnosis is valid. *Validity* refers to the extent to which a diagnosis measures what it purports to measure. More colloquially, validity is truth in advertising: A valid diagnosis is true to its name in that it correlates in expected directions with external criteria. Specifically, Robins and Guze outlined four requirements for the validity of psychiatric diagnoses. According to them, a valid diagnosis offers the following:

1. Clinical description, including symptomatology, demographics, precipitants, and differences from seemingly related disorders. The last-named task of distinguishing a diagnosis from similar diagnoses is called *differential diagnosis*.
2. Laboratory research, including data from psychological, biological, and laboratory tests.
3. Natural history, including course and outcome.
4. Family studies, especially studies examining the prevalence of a disorder in the first-degree relatives of probands—that is, individuals identified as having the diagnosis in question.

As a further desideratum, some authors have suggested that a valid diagnosis should ideally be able to predict the individual's response to treatment (Waldman, Lilienfeld, & Lahey, 1995). Nevertheless, this criterion should probably not be mandatory given that the treatment of a condition bears no necessary implications for its etiology. For example, although both schizophrenia and nausea induced by food poisoning generally respond to psychopharmacological agents that block the action of the neurotransmitter dopamine, these two conditions spring from entirely distinct causal mechanisms. Some authors (e.g., Ross & Pam, 1996) have invoked the felicitous phrase *ex juvantibus* reasoning (reasoning backward from what works) to describe the error of inferring a disorder's etiology from its treatment. Headaches, as the hoary example goes, are not caused by a deficiency of aspirin in the bloodstream, and similarly, bipolar I disorder is not caused by a lithium deficiency.

There is reasonably strong evidence that diagnoses of many mental disorders fulfill Robins and Guze's (1970) criteria for validity. When these criteria are met, the diagnosis offers additional information about the patient, information that was not available before this diagnosis was made. For example, if we correctly diagnose a patient with schizophrenia, we have learned that this patient

- Is likely to exhibit psychotic symptoms that are not solely a consequence of a severe mood disturbance, such as major depressive disorder.
- Has a higher than expected likelihood of exhibiting abnormalities on several laboratory measures, including indices of sustained attention, smooth pursuit eye tracking, and detection of biological motion (Kim, Park, & Blake, 2011).
- Has a higher than average probability of having close biological relatives with schizophrenia and schizophrenia-spectrum disorders, such as schizotypal and paranoid personality disorders.
- Is likely to exhibit a chronic course, with few or no periods of entirely normal functioning, but approximately a 30% chance of overall improvement.
- Is likely to respond positively to medications that block the action of dopamine, although this is most likely to be the case for the positive symptoms (e.g., delusions, hallucinations) but not the negative symptoms (e.g., anhedonia, loss of motivation) of the disorder (Subotnick et al., 2011).

Andreasen (1995) extended the Robins and Guze (1970) framework to incorporate indicators from molecular genetics, neurochemistry, and functional and structural brain imaging as additional validating indicators for psychiatric diagnoses (Kendell & Jablensky, 2003). Her friendly amendment to the Robins and Guze criteria allows us to use endophenotypic indicators to assist in the validation of a diagnosis. Endophenotypes are typically biomarkers or laboratory indicators, that is, "measurable components unseen by the unaided eye along the pathway between disease and distal genotype" (Gottesman & Gould, 2003, p. 636; Gottesman & McGue, 2015; Waldman, 2005). They are often contrasted with exophenotypes, the traditional signs and symptoms of a disorder.

We can view the process of validating psychiatric diagnoses within the overarching framework of construct validity (Cronbach & Meehl, 1955; Loevinger, 1957; Messick, 1995; but see Borsboom, Cramer, Kievit, Zand Scholten, & Franic, 2009, for a different perspective on construct validity), which refers to the extent to which a measure assesses a hypothesized attribute of individuals. As Morey (1991) noted, psychiatric classification systems are collections of hypothetical constructs; thus, the process of validating psychiatric diagnoses is also a process of construct validation. More broadly, we can conceptualize most or even all psychiatric diagnoses as open concepts (Meehl, 1977, 1990). Open concepts are marked by (a) fuzzy boundaries, (b) a list of indicators (signs and symptoms) that are indefinitely extendable, and (c) an unclear inner nature.

Recalling that psychiatric diagnoses are open concepts helps us to avoid the perils of premature reification of diagnostic entities (Faust & Miner, 1986). For example, the present diagnostic criteria for schizophrenia are not isomorphic with the construct of schizophrenia; they are merely fallible, albeit somewhat valid, indicators of this construct. Yet, the past few decades have occasionally witnessed a troubling tendency to reify and deify the categories within the current classification system, with some authors regarding them as fixed Platonic essences rather than as rough approximations to the true state of nature (Ghaemi, 2003; Kendler, 2005; Michels, 1984). This error is manifested, for example, when journal or grant reviewers criticize researchers for examining alternative operationalizations of mental disorders that depart from those in the current diagnostic manual (see the section "Psychiatric Classification from *DSM-I* to the Present," later in this chapter). It is also manifested by the common error of referring to measures of certain psychiatric conditions as "gold standards" (see Skeem & Cooke, 2010, for a discussion of this tendency in the field of psychopathy). This phrasing is erroneous in view of the fact that all signs and symptoms of psychopathology are at present fallible—in that they are necessarily imperfect indicators of the constructs of interest—and provisional.

In a classic article, Cronbach and Meehl (1955) adopted from neopositivist philosophers of science the term *nomological network* to designate the system of lawful relationships conjectured to hold between theoretical entities (states, structures, events, dispositions) and observable indicators. They selected the network metaphor to emphasize the structure of such systems in which the nodes of the network, representing the postulated theoretical entities, are connected by the strands of the network, representing the lawful relationships hypothesized to hold among the entities (Garber & Strassberg, 1991).

For Cronbach and Meehl (1955), construct validation is a progressive and never-ending process of testing the links between hypothesized strands of the nomological network, especially those that connect latent constructs, which include psychiatric diagnoses (e.g., schizophrenia and major depression), to manifest indicators, which include the external criteria (e.g., laboratory tests and family history) laid out by Robins and Guze (1970). The more such construct-to-manifest indicator links are corroborated, the more certain we can be that our conception of the diagnosis in question is accurate. From this perspective, the approach to diagnostic validation outlined by Robins and Guze is merely one specific instantiation of construct validation.

One limitation of the Robins and Guze (1970) approach to construct validation is its exclusive emphasis on external validation, that is, the process of ascertaining the construct's associations with correlates that lie outside the construct itself. As Skinner (1981, 1986; also Loevinger, 1957) observed, internal validation, ascertaining the construct's inner structure, is also a key component of construct validation. Internal validation can help investigators to test hypotheses regarding a construct's homogeneity (versus heterogeneity) and factor structure (Waldman et al., 1995). For example, if analyses suggest that a diagnosis consists of multiple subtypes that are largely or entirely statistically independent, the validity of the diagnosis would be called into question. Alternatively, factorial validity (i.e., the extent to which the factor structure of a diagnosis comports with theoretical predictions) can inform debates regarding the validity of a diagnosis. For example, factor analyses of attention-deficit/hyperactivity disorder (ADHD) generally support the separation of inattention from impulsivity and hyperactivity, as implied by the *DSM* criteria for this disorder (Martel, Von Eye, & Nigg, 2010).

In summary, valid psychiatric diagnoses serve three primary functions:

1. They summarize distinctive features of a disorder and thereby allow professionals to communicate clearly with one another.
2. They place each diagnosis under the umbrella structure of other diagnoses. This nosological framework links one diagnosis to both more and less related diagnoses.
3. They provide practitioners and researchers with surplus information regarding a diagnosed patient's clinical profile, laboratory findings, natural history, family history, and possible response to treatment; they may also offer information regarding endophenotypic indicators.

Misconceptions Regarding Psychiatric Diagnosis

Beginning psychology graduate students and many among the general public hold a plethora of misconceptions regarding psychiatric diagnosis; we examine five such misconceptions here. Doing so will also permit us to introduce a number of key principles of psychiatric diagnosis. As we will discover, refuting each misconception regarding psychiatric diagnosis affirms at least one important principle.

MISCONCEPTION #1: MENTAL ILLNESS IS A MYTH

The person most closely associated with this position is the late psychiatrist Thomas Szasz (1960), who argued famously for over 40 years that the term *mental illness* is a false and misleading metaphor (Schaler, 2004). For Szasz, individuals whom psychologists and psychiatrists term mentally ill actually suffer from problems in living (i.e., difficulties in adjusting their behaviors to the demands of society). Moreover, Szasz contended that mental health professionals often apply the mental illness label to nonconformists who jeopardize the status quo (Sarbin, 1969; Szasz, 1960). This label serves as a convenient justification for forcing maladjusted, malcontented, and maverick members of society to comply with prevailing societal norms.

Specifically, Szasz maintained that medical disorders can be clearly recognized by a lesion to the anatomical structure of the body, but that the disorder concept cannot be imported to the mental realm because there is no such lesion to indicate deviation from the norm. According to him only the body can become diseased, so mentally ill people do not suffer from an illness akin to a medical disorder.

It is undeniable that psychiatric diagnoses are sometimes misapplied. Nevertheless, this legitimate pragmatic concern must be logically separated from the question of whether the mental illness concept itself exists (Wakefield, 1992). We should recall the logical principle of *abusus non tollit usum* (abuse does not take away use): Historical and sociological misuses of a concept do not negate its validity.

Wakefield (1992) and others (e.g., Kendell, 1975) have observed that the Szaszian argument is problematic on several fronts. Among other problems, it assumes that medical disorders are in every case traceable to discernible lesions in an anatomical structure, and that all lesions give rise to medical disorders. Yet identifiable lesions cannot be found in certain clear-cut medical diseases—such as trigeminal neuralgia and senile pruritis—and certain identifiable lesions, such as albinism, are not regarded as medical disorders (Kendell, 1975; Wakefield, 1992). Szasz's assertion that identifiable lesions are essentially synonymous with medical disorders is false; therefore, his corollary argument that mental disorders cannot exist because they are not invariably associated with identifiable lesions is similarly false.

MISCONCEPTION #2: PSYCHIATRIC DIAGNOSIS IS MERELY PIGEONHOLING

According to this criticism, when we diagnose people with a mental disorder, we deprive them of their uniqueness: we imply that all people within the same diagnostic category are alike in all important respects.

To the contrary, a psychiatric diagnosis does nothing of the sort; it implies only that all people with that diagnosis are alike in at least one important way, namely, that they display the signs and symptoms of that condition. In this respect, psychiatric diagnosis is no different from medical diagnosis. Physicians understand that all patients with essential hypertension are linked by high blood pressure, but can differ in myriad other ways. Similarly, psychologists and psychiatrists are well aware that even within a given diagnostic category, such as schizophrenia or bipolar I disorder, people differ dramatically in their race and cultural background, personality traits, co-occurring psychological conditions, interests, and cognitive skills (APA, 2013).

MISCONCEPTION #3: PSYCHIATRIC DIAGNOSES ARE UNRELIABLE

Reliability refers to the consistency of a diagnosis. As many textbooks in psychometrics remind us, reliability is a prerequisite for validity but not vice versa. Just as a bathroom scale cannot validly measure weight if it yields dramatically different weight estimates for the same person over brief periods of time, a diagnosis cannot validly measure a mental disorder if it yields dramatically different scores on measures of psychopathology across times, situations, and raters.

Because validity is not a prerequisite for reliability, extremely high reliability can exist without validity. A researcher who based diagnoses of schizophrenia on patients' heights would end up with extremely reliable but entirely invalid diagnoses of schizophrenia.

There are three major subtypes of reliability. Contrary to popular (mis)conception, these subtypes are frequently discrepant with one another, so high levels of reliability for one metric do not necessary imply high levels for the others.

Test-retest reliability refers to the stability of a diagnosis following a relatively brief time interval, typically about a month. In other words, after a short time lapse, will patients receive the same diagnoses? Note that we wrote *brief* and *short* in the previous sentences; marked changes following lengthy time lapses, such as several years, may reflect genuine changes in patient status rather than the measurement error associated with test-retest unreliability.

In general, we assess test-retest reliability using either a Pearson correlation coefficient or, more rigorously, an intraclass correlation coefficient. Intraclass correlations tend to provide the most stringent estimates of test-retest reliability because, in contrast to Pearson correlations, they are influenced not merely by the rank ordering and differences among people's scores, but by their absolute magnitude.

Our evaluation of the test-retest reliability of a diagnosis hinges on our conceptualization of the disorder. We should anticipate high test-retest reliability only for diagnoses that are traitlike, such as personality disorders, or that tend to be chronic (long-lasting), such as schizophrenia. In contrast, we should not necessarily anticipate high levels of test-retest reliability for diagnoses that tend to be episodic (intermittent), such as major depression.

Internal consistency refers to the extent to which the signs and symptoms comprising a diagnosis hang together—that is, correlate highly with one another. We generally assess internal consistency using such metrics as coefficient alpha (Cronbach, 1951), or the mean inter-item correlation. Cronbach's alpha can overestimate the homogeneity of a diagnosis, however, if the relevant diagnosis contains numerous signs and symptoms, because this statistic is affected by test length (Schmidt, Le, & Ilies, 2003; Sijtsma, 2009). We should anticipate high levels of internal consistency for most conditions in the current classification system given that most are syndromes, most of which are constellations of signs and symptoms that covary across people.

Interrater reliability is the degree to which two or more observers, such as different psychologists or psychiatrists, agree on the diagnosis of a set of individuals. High interrater reliability is a prerequisite for all psychiatric diagnoses, because different observers must agree on the presence or absence of a condition before valid research on that condition can proceed.

Many early studies of psychiatric diagnosis operationalized interrater reliability in terms of percentage agreement, that is, the proportion of cases on which two or more raters agree on the presence or absence of a given diagnosis. Nevertheless, measures of percentage agreement tend to overestimate interrater reliability. Here's why: Imagine two diagnosticians working in a setting (e.g., an outpatient phobia clinic) in which the base rate (prevalence) of the diagnosis of specific phobia is 95%. The finding that they agree with each other on the diagnosis of specific phobia 95% of the time would hardly be impressive and could readily be attributed to chance. As a consequence, most investigators today operationalize interrater reliability in terms of the kappa coefficient, which assesses the degree to which raters agree on a diagnosis after correcting for chance, with chance being the base rate of the disorder in question. Nevertheless, the kappa coefficient often provides a conservative estimate of interrater reliability, as the correction for chance sometimes penalizes raters for their independent expertise (Meyer, 1997).

Many laypersons and even political pundits believe that psychiatric diagnoses possess low levels of reliability, especially interrater reliability. This perception is probably fueled by high-profile media coverage of dueling expert witnesses in criminal trials in which one expert diagnoses a defendant as schizophrenic, for example, and another diagnoses him as normal. After the widely publicized 1982 trial of John Hinckley, who was acquitted on the basis of insanity for his attempted assassination of then-president Ronald Reagan, political commentator George Will maintained (on national television) that the disagreements among expert witnesses regarding Hinckley's diagnosis merely bore out what most people already knew: that psychiatric diagnosis is wildly unreliable (Lilienfeld, 1995).

Yet there is a straightforward explanation for such disagreement: Given the adversarial nature of our legal system, the prosecution and defense typically go out of their way to find expert witnesses who will support their point of view. This inherently antagonistic arrangement virtually guarantees that the interrater reliabilities of experts in criminal trials will be modest at best.

Certainly, the interrater reliability of psychiatric diagnoses is far from perfect. Yet for most major mental disorders, such as schizophrenia, mood disorders, anxiety disorders, and alcohol use disorder (alcoholism), interrater reliabilities are typically about as high—with intraclass correlations between raters of 0.8 or above, out of a maximum of 1.0—as those for most well-established medical disorders (Lobbestael, Leurgans, & Arntz, 2011; Matarazzo, 1983). Still, the picture is not entirely rosy. For many personality disorders, in particular, interrater reliabilities tend to be considerably lower than for other conditions (Maffei et al., 1997; Zimmerman, 1994), probably because most of these disorders comprise highly inferential constructs (e.g., lack of empathy) that raters find difficult to assess during the course of brief interviews.

Misconception #4: Psychiatric Diagnoses Are Invalid

From the standpoint of Szasz (1960) and other critics of psychiatric diagnosis (Eysenck, Wakefield, & Friedman, 1983), psychiatric diagnoses are largely useless because they do not provide us with new information. According to them, diagnoses are merely descriptive labels for behaviors we do not like. Even the most recent director of the National Institute of Mental Health, psychiatrist Thomas Insel (2013), stated that the major problem with the *DSM* was its "lack of validity." In this regard, Millon (1975) proposed a helpful distinction between psychiatric labels and diagnoses; a label simply describes behaviors, whereas a diagnosis helps to explain them.

When it comes to a host of informal "pop psychology" labels, like sexual addiction, Peter Pan syndrome, codependency, shopping disorder, Internet addiction, road rage disorder, and the relatively new "condition" of affluenza (a sense of malaise, anxiety, and unfulfillment supposedly stemming from excessive materialism; James, 2007), Szasz and his fellow critics probably have a point. Most of these labels merely describe collections of socially problematic behavior and do not provide us with much, if any, new information (McCann, Shindler, & Hammond, 2003; Smith, Winiarski, & Lilienfeld, 2015). The same may hold for some personality disorders in the current classification system. For example, the diagnosis of dependent personality disorder, which has been retained in *DSM-5* (APA, 2013), arguably appears to do little more than describe ways in which people are pathologically dependent on others, such as relying excessively on others for reassurance and expecting others to make everyday life decisions for them.

Yet, as we have already seen, many psychiatric diagnoses, such as schizophrenia, bipolar I disorder, and panic disorder, do yield surplus information (Robins & Guze, 1970; Waldman et al., 1995) and, therefore, possess adequate levels of validity. Nevertheless, because construct validation, like all forms of theory testing in science, is a never-ending process, the validity of these diagnoses is likely to improve over time with subsequent revisions to the present classification system.

MISCONCEPTION #5: PSYCHIATRIC DIAGNOSES STIGMATIZE PEOPLE, AND OFTEN RESULT IN SELF-FULFILLING PROPHECIES

According to advocates of labeling theory, including Szasz (1960), Sarbin (1969), and Scheff (1975), psychiatric diagnoses produce adverse effects on labeled individuals. They argue that diagnostic labels not only stigmatize patients, but also frequently become self-fulfilling prophecies, leading observers to interpret ambiguous and relatively mild behaviors (e.g., occasional outbursts of anger) as reflecting serious mental illness.

A sensational 1973 and widely cited (over 3,100 citations as of this writing) study by Rosenhan appeared to offer impressive support for labeling theory. Rosenhan, along with seven other normal individuals, posed as pseudopatients (fake patients) in 12 U.S. psychiatric hospitals (some of the pseudopatients presented at more than one hospital). They informed the admitting psychiatrist only that they were hearing a voice saying, "empty," "hollow," and "thud." All were promptly admitted to the hospital and remained there for an average of 3 weeks, despite displaying no further symptoms or signs of psychopathology. In 11 of these 12 cases, they were discharged with diagnoses of schizophrenia in remission (the 12th pseudopatient was discharged with a diagnosis of manic depression in remission).

Rosenhan (1973) noted that the hospital staff frequently interpreted pseudopatients' innocuous behaviors, such as note taking, as indicative of abnormality. In case summaries, these staff also construed entirely run-of-the-mill details of pseudopatients' life histories, such as emotional conflicts with parents during adolescence, as consistent with their present illness. These striking results led Rosenhan to conclude that psychiatric labels color observers' perceptions of behavior, often to the point that they can no longer distinguish mental illness from normality.

Even today, some writers interpret Rosenhan's findings as a resounding affirmation of labeling theory (e.g., Slater, 2004; but see Spitzer, Lilienfeld, & Miller, 2005, for a critique of Slater, 2004). Yet, the evidence for labeling theory is less impressive than it appears. As Spitzer (1975) observed, the fact that all 12 of Rosenhan's pseudopatients were released with diagnoses in remission (meaning showing no indications of illness) demonstrates that the psychiatrists who treated them were in all cases able to distinguish mental illness from normality. Spitzer went further, demonstrating in a survey of psychiatric hospitals that in-remission diagnoses of previously psychotic patients are exceedingly infrequent, showing that the psychiatrists in Rosenhan's study successfully made an extremely rare judgment with perfect consensus.

Although *incorrect* psychiatric diagnoses can engender stigma, at least in the short run (Harris, Milich, Corbitt, Hoover, & Brady, 1992; Milich, McAninich, & Harris, 1992), there is scant evidence to support the popular claim that correctly applied psychiatric diagnoses do so. The lion's share of the research suggests that stigma is a consequence not of diagnostic labels, but rather of disturbed and sometimes disturbing behavior that precedes labeling (Link & Cullen, 1990; Ruscio, 2004). For example, within 30 minutes or less, children begin to react negatively to children with attention-deficit/hyperactivity disorder (ADHD) who have joined their peer group (Milich et al., 1992; Pelham & Bender, 1982).

Contrary to the tenets of labeling theory, there is evidence that accurate psychiatric diagnoses sometimes reduce stigma, because they provide observers with at least a partial explanation for otherwise inexplicable behaviors (Ruscio, 2004). For example, adults tend to evaluate intellectually disabled children more positively when these children are labeled as mentally retarded than when they are not (Seitz & Geske, 1976), and peers rate the essays of children with ADHD more positively when these children are labeled with ADHD than when they are not (Cornez-Ruiz & Hendricks, 1993).

What Is Mental Disorder?

Our discussion up to this point presupposes that the boundaries of the higher-order concept of "disorder," including mental disorder, are clear-cut or at least reasonably well delineated.[1] To develop a classification system of disorders, one must first be able to ascertain whether a given condition is or is not a disorder. Yet the answer to the question of how best to define disorder, including mental disorder, remains elusive (Gorenstein, 1992). The issues here are of more than academic interest, because each revision of psychiatry's diagnostic manual has been marked by contentious disputes regarding whether such conditions as ADHD, premenstrual dysphoric disorder, and, more recently, binge eating disorder, attenuated psychosis syndrome, and hypersexual disorder are genuine disorders (Frances & Widiger, 2012; Wakefield, 1992). The fact that homosexuality was removed from the formal psychiatric classification system in 1974 by a majority vote of the membership of the American Psychiatric Association (Bayer & Spitzer, 1982) further demonstrates that these debates are frequently resolved more by group consensus than by scientific research.

Here we evaluate several influential attempts to delineate the boundaries of disorder. As we will discover, each approach has its limitations but each captures something important about the concept of disorder. As we will also discover, these approaches differ in the extent to which they embrace an essentialist as opposed to a nominalist view of disorder (Ghaemi, 2003; Scadding, 1996). Advocates of an essentialist view (Widiger & Trull, 1985) believe that all disorders share some essence or underlying property, whereas advocates of a nominalist view (Lilienfeld & Marino, 1995, 1999; Rosenhan & Seligman, 1995) believe that the higher-order concept of disorder is a social construction that groups together a variety of largely unrelated conditions for the purposes of social or semantic convenience.

STATISTICAL MODEL

Advocates of a statistical model, such as Cohen (1981), equate disorder with statistical rarity. According to this view, disorders are abnormal because they are infrequent in the general population. This definition accords with findings that many mental disorders are indeed rare; schizophrenia, for example, is found in about 1% of the population across much of the world (APA, 2013).

Yet, a purely statistical model falls short on at least three grounds. First, it offers no guidance for where to draw cutoffs between normality and abnormality. In many cases, these cutoffs are scientifically arbitrary. Second, it is silent on the crucial question of which

---

[1] In our discussion of the definition of disorder, we use the term *disorder*, including mental disorder, generically to refer to all medical and psychological conditions and do not distinguish disorder from disease (Wakefield, 1992).

dimensions are relevant to abnormality. As a consequence, a statistical model misclassifies high scores on certain adaptive dimensions (like intelligence, creativity, and altruism) as inherently abnormal. Moreover, it does not explain why high scores on certain dimensions (e.g., anxiety) but not on others (e.g., hair length) are pertinent to psychopathology. Third, by definition a statistical model assumes that all common conditions are normal (Wakefield, 1992). Yet the common cold is still an illness despite its essentially 100% lifetime prevalence in the population, and the Black Death (bubonic plague) was still an illness in the mid-1300s despite wiping out approximately one third of the European population.

SUBJECTIVE DISTRESS MODEL

Proponents of a subjective distress model maintain that the core feature distinguishing disorder from nondisorder is psychological pain. This model unquestionably contains a large kernel of truth; many serious mental illnesses (such as major depression, obsessive-compulsive disorder, generalized anxiety disorder, and gender identity disorder) are marked by considerable distress, even anguish.

The subjective distress model also falls short of an adequate definition of mental illness, because it fails to distinguish ego-dystonic conditions (those that conflict with one's self-concept) from ego-syntonic conditions (those that are consistent with one's self-concept). Although most mental disorders (such as major depression and generalized anxiety disorder) are typically ego-dystonic, some (such as antisocial personality disorder and bipolar I disorder, at least in its manic phase) are largely or entirely ego-syntonic, because individuals with these conditions frequently see little or nothing wrong with their behavior. They experience little or no distress in conjunction with their condition, and frequently seek treatment only when that is demanded by courts or significant others, or when their condition is complicated by a secondary condition that generates interpersonal difficulties (e.g., alcohol use disorder). Moreover, approximately half of patients with schizophrenia and other severe psychotic conditions are afflicted with anosognosia, meaning that they are unaware of the fact that they are ill (Amador & Paul-Odouard, 2000).

BIOLOGICAL MODEL

Proponents of a biological model (Kendell, 1975) contend that disorder can be defined in terms of a biological or evolutionary disadvantage to the organism, such as reduced lifespan or fitness (i.e., the ability to pass on genes to subsequent generations). Indeed, some mental disorders are associated with biological disadvantages; for example, major depression is associated with a dramatically increased risk for completed suicide (Joiner, 2006), and between 5% and 10% of patients with anorexia nervosa eventually die from complications due to starvation (Goodwin & Guze, 1996).

A biological model, however, also falls prey to numerous counterexamples. For example, being a soldier in frontline combat is not a disorder despite its average adverse effect on longevity and fitness. Nor is priesthood an illness even though it is associated with lower direct evolutionary fitness. Conversely, some relatively mild psychological conditions, such as specific phobia, are probably not associated with decreased longevity or fitness, yet are still mental disorders.

NEED FOR TREATMENT

One parsimonious definition is simply that disorders are a heterogeneous class of conditions all characterized by a perceived need for medical intervention on the part of health (including mental health) professionals (Kraupl Taylor, 1971). Like other definitions, this definition captures an important truth: many or most mental disorders, such as schizophrenia, bipolar I disorder, and obsessive-compulsive disorder, are indeed viewed by society as necessitating treatment. Nevertheless, this definition also falls victim to counterexamples. For example, pregnancy clearly is associated with a perceived need for medical intervention, yet it is not regarded as a disorder.

HARMFUL DYSFUNCTION

In an effort to remedy the shortcomings of extant models of disorder, Wakefield (1992) proposed a hybrid definition that incorporates both essentialist and nominalist features.

According to Wakefield, all disorders, including all mental disorders, are harmful dysfunctions: socially devalued (harmful) breakdowns of evolutionarily selected systems (dysfunctions). For example, according to Wakefield, panic disorder is a mental disorder because it (a) is negatively valued by society and often by the individual afflicted with it, and (b) reflects the activation of the fight-flight system in situations for which that system was not evolutionary selected, namely those in which objective danger is absent. In other words, panic attacks are false alarms (Barlow, 2001). Wakefield's operationalization of disorder has its strengths; for example, it acknowledges (correctly) that most and perhaps all disorders are viewed negatively by others. The concept of disorder, including mental disorder, is clearly associated with social values. As Wakefield (1992) noted, however, social devaluation is not sufficient to demarcate disorder from nondisorder, claims by Szasz (1960) to the contrary. For example, rudeness, laziness, slovenliness, and even racism are viewed negatively by society, but are not disorders (for a dissenting view regarding racism, see Poussaint, 2002). Therefore, Wakefield contends that something else is necessary to distinguish disorder from nondisorder, namely evolutionary dysfunction.

Nevertheless, the dysfunction component of Wakefield's analysis appears to fall prey to counterexamples. In particular, many medical disorders appear to be adaptive defenses against threat or insult. For instance, the symptoms of influenza (flu), such as vomiting, coughing, sneezing, and fever, are all adaptive efforts to expel an infectious agent rather than failures or breakdowns in an evolutionarily selected system (Lilienfeld & Marino, 1999; Neese & Williams, 1994). Such counterexamples appear to falsify the harmful dysfunction analysis. Similarly, many psychological conditions appear to be adaptive reactions to perceived threat. For example, in contrast to other forms of specific phobia, blood/injection/injury phobia is marked by a coordinated set of dramatic parasympathetic reactions—especially rapid decreases in heart rate and blood pressure—that were almost surely evolutionarily selected to minimize blood loss (Barlow, 2001). Although these responses may not be especially adaptive in the early 21st century, they were adaptive prior to the advent of Band-Aids, tourniquets, and anticoagulants (Lilienfeld & Marino, 1995).

ROSCHIAN ANALYSIS

An alternative approach to defining disorder, Roschian analysis, is radically different. According to a Roschian analysis, the attempt to define disorder explicitly is sure to fail because disorder is intrinsically undefinable (Gorenstein, 1992). Drawing on the work of cognitive psychologist Eleanor Rosch (Rosch, 1973; Rosch & Mervis, 1975), advocates of a Roschian analysis contend that the concept of mental disorder lacks defining (i.e., singly necessary and jointly sufficient) features and possesses intrinsically fuzzy boundaries. In this respect, mental disorder is similar to many other concepts. For example, the concept of a chair lacks strictly defining features (e.g., a human-made object with four legs that someone can sit on does not succeed as a defining feature, because one can sit on a table and many chairs do not have four legs) and displays unclear boundaries. In addition, the concept of mental disorder, like many other concepts, is organized around a prototype that shares all the features of the category. Just as certain chairs (e.g., a typical office chair) are more chairlike than others (e.g., a beanbag), certain mental disorders (e.g., schizophrenia, panic disorder) are more disorder-like than others (e.g., hypersexual disorder, premenstrual dysphoric disorder). Not surprisingly, it is at the fuzzy boundaries of disorder where controversies concerning whether a psychological condition is really a disorder most frequently arise. According to the Roschian analysis, these controversies are not only inevitable but are also unresolvable by scientific data.

Even if the Roschian analysis is correct (for criticisms of this approach, see Cooper, 2011; Wakefield, 1999; and Widiger, 1997), it would not imply that specific mental disorders themselves are not amenable to scientific inquiry. As Gorenstein (1992) noted, the concept of a drug is inherently undefinable; there are no scientific criteria for deciding whether caffeine, nicotine, and many other widely used but addictive substances are drugs. Yet, this problem has not stopped psychopharmacologists from studying specific drugs' properties, modes of action, or behavioral effects. Nor should the absence of an explicit definition of mental disorder preclude psychopathology researchers from investigating the diagnosis, etiology, treatment, and prevention of schizophrenia, major depression, panic disorder, and other conditions.

Psychiatric Classification From *DSM-I* to the Present

Prior to the 1950s, the state of psychiatric classification in the United States was largely disorganized, as no standard system was in place for operationalizing specific mental disorders. Indeed, prior to World War I, there was scant interest in developing a systematic classification of mental disorders (Grob, 1991), and even after World War I, it took over three decades to put in place a consensual system of classification. As a consequence, what one diagnostician meant by major depression might bear minimal correspondence to what another diagnostician meant by the same term.

DSM-I AND *DSM-II*

This situation gradually began to change in 1918, when the U.S. Bureau of the Census released the *Statistical Manual for the Use of Institutions of the Insane*, which divided mental disorders (largely psychoses) into 22 groups; this manual was revised 10 times through 1942 (Grob, 1991). It was not until 1952, however, that the American Psychiatric Association released the first edition of its *Diagnostic and Statistical Manual of Mental Disorders*, abbreviated as *DSM-I* (APA, 1952). Although *DSM-I* was a slim 132 pages in length, it was a landmark. For the first time, it offered reasonably clear, albeit brief, descriptions of major psychiatric diagnoses, thereby facilitating interrater reliability among clinicians and researchers. Here, for example, is the description for "Manic Depressive Reaction, Depressed type" (later to be called major depression) in *DSM-I*:

> Here will be classified those cases with outstanding depression of mood and with mental and motor retardation and inhibition; in some cases there is much uneasiness and apprehension. Perplexity, stupor or agitation may be prominent symptoms, and may be added to the diagnosis as manifestations. (APA, 1952, p. 25)

DSM-II appeared 16 years later (APA, 1968) and was similar in approach and scope to *DSM-I*, although it provided somewhat greater detail concerning the signs and symptoms of many diagnoses.

Despite their strengths, *DSM-I* and *DSM-II* suffered from several notable weaknesses, three of which we discuss here:

1. The interrater reliabilities of many of their diagnoses were still problematic, probably because these manuals consisted of global and often vague descriptions of mental illnesses that necessitated considerable subjective judgment on the part of diagnosticians. For example, returning to the description of manic depressive reaction, depressed type, *DSM-I* is silent on what qualifies as "outstanding depression," and how much motor retardation and inhibition are necessary for the diagnosis.

2. *DSM-I* and *DSM-II* were not theoretically agnostic. In particular, they were influenced by psychoanalytic concepts of mental disorders and often made references to defense mechanisms and other concepts derived from Freudian theory. As a consequence, diagnosticians whose orientation was not psychoanalytic, such as behaviorists, cognitive behaviorists, or humanistic-existential psychologists, found these classification systems difficult to use. Interestingly, a recent effort to revive psychoanalytic conceptions within psychiatric diagnosis has emerged in the form of the *Psychodynamic Diagnostic Manual* (Alliance of Psychoanalytic Organizations, 2006), which conceptualizes mental disorders largely in terms of psychodynamic concepts, such as unconscious drives and defense mechanisms. Nevertheless, this manual appears to have exerted little impact outside of psychoanalytic circles.

   DSM-I and *DSM-II* also conceptualized mental disorders largely from the perspective of psychiatrist Adolf Meyer (1866–1950), who regarded most forms of psychopathology as aberrant reactions to life events (Lief, 1948), hence the use of the term *reaction* in the diagnosis of manic depressive reaction, depressed type, and many other *DSM-I* and *DSM-II* diagnoses. Nevertheless, this assumption was based more on plausible theoretical conjecture than on evidence.

3. Despite their Meyerian emphasis, *DSM-I* and *DSM-II* focused almost exclusively on patients' mental disorders per se, and largely neglected to consider contextual factors, such as co-occurring medical conditions, life stressors, and adaptive functioning, which can play key roles in the etiology and maintenance of psychopathology.

DSM-III AND BEYOND

Largely in response to these criticisms, the American Psychiatric Association, with the late psychiatrist Robert Spitzer at the helm, released *DSM-III* in 1980. As most historians of psychiatric classification and diagnosis now recognize, *DSM-III* was an important revision of the diagnostic manual; it represented a radical change in thinking and approach from all that came before, and has provided the template for all that has come since (Klerman, 1984; Mayes & Horwitz, 2005), including the newest revision, *DSM-5* (APA, 2013). In this respect, it was every bit as much a landmark, if not more, than was *DSM-I*. Coming in at a hefty 494 pages, a nearly fourfold increase from *DSM-II*, *DSM-III* not only dramatically increased the coverage of mental disorders—from 163 to 224—but also presented far more detailed guidelines for establishing diagnoses than did its predecessors. The operational and philosophical approach of *DSM-III* is often termed neo-Kraepelinian (Compton & Guze, 1995) because it followed in the footsteps of the great German psychiatrist Emil Kraepelin (1856–1926), who grouped and differentiated psychological conditions on the basis on their signs, symptoms, and natural histories. By and large, this neo-Kraepelinian approach has been carried over in the development of *DSM-5*.

Diagnostic Criteria, Algorithms, Hierarchical Exclusion Rules, and a Multiaxial Approach

In accord with its neo-Kraepelinian emphasis, *DSM-III* instituted several major changes in psychiatric classification and diagnosis. First and foremost, *DSM-III* introduced (a) standardized diagnostic criteria and (b) algorithms, or decision rules, for each diagnosis. For a number of major disorders, the interrater reliability and validity of the proposed *DSM-III* criterion sets were pilot-tested in systematic field trials. Rather than merely describing each diagnosis as *DSM-I* and *DSM-II* had done, *DSM-III* explicitly delineated the signs and symptoms comprising each diagnosis and the method by which these signs and symptoms needed to be combined to establish each diagnosis. In these respects, it was influenced heavily by the pioneering efforts of the St. Louis group at Washington University (including Robins, Guze, Winokur, and other giants of descriptive psychopathology), who had introduced preliminary diagnostic criteria and algorithms for 14 major mental disorders in the early 1970s (the "Feighner criteria"; see Feighner et al., 1972). Another major precursor of *DSM-III* was the Research Diagnostic Criteria (RDC), which expanded the Feighner criteria by adding criteria for several other disorders (Spitzer, Endicott, & Robins, 1978).

As an example of *DSM-III*'s highly structured approach to diagnosis, we can examine its criteria for a major depressive episode (MDE). To meet diagnostic criteria for MDE, *DSM-III* required that clients (a) experience "dysphoric mood or loss of interest or pleasure in all or almost all activities" (p. 213; with dysphoric mood described in terms of seven symptoms, including depression, hopelessness, and irritability), and (b) experience at least four of eight signs and symptoms, such as poor appetite, insomnia, loss of energy, and difficulty thinking and concentrating, nearly every day for at least a 2-week period. Compare the specificity of these criteria with the skimpy and highly impressionistic description in *DSM-I* presented earlier.

DSM-III also outlined hierarchical exclusion rules for many diagnoses; such rules prevent clinicians and researchers from making these diagnoses if other diagnoses can account for the clinical picture. For example, *DSM-III* forbade clinicians and researchers from making a diagnosis of major depressive episode if the episode was superimposed on schizophrenia, a schizophreniform disorder, or a paranoid disorder, or if it appeared to be due to either an organic mental disorder (e.g., hypothyroidism) or uncomplicated bereavement (a prolonged grief reaction). Among other things, hierarchical exclusion rules remind diagnosticians to "think organic": that is, to rule out potential physical causes of mental disorders before diagnosing them (Morrison, 1997; Schildkrout, 2011).

DSM-III's use of diagnostic criteria, algorithms, and hierarchical exclusion rules has been maligned by many commentators as the "Chinese menu" approach to diagnosis (choose three from column A, two from column B, four from column C). Despite these criticisms, there is evidence that this approach markedly decreased the subjectivity of diagnostic decision making and increased the interrater reliabilities of many diagnoses (Spitzer, Forman, & Nee, 1979). However, some authors argue that these increases were exaggerated by *DSM-III*'s proponents (Kirk & Kutchins, 1992).

The interrater reliability of *DSM* diagnoses has also been enhanced by the development of structured and semistructured diagnostic interviews, such as the Structured Clinical Interview for DSM (SCID; First, Spitzer, Gibbon, & Williams, 2002), which are coordinated explicitly around *DSM* criteria. These interviews consist of standardized questions—to be read verbatim by interviewers—and required and suggested follow-up probes with which to assess specific diagnostic criteria. For example, the SCID provides the following question to assess the criterion of current, unexpected panic attacks in the *DSM-IV* diagnosis of panic disorder: "Have you ever had a panic attack, when you suddenly felt frightened or anxious or suddenly developed a lot of physical symptoms?" If the respondent replies yes, the SCID instructs the interviewer to ask, "Have these attacks ever come on completely out of the blue—in situations where you didn't expect to be nervous or uncomfortable?" (First et al., 2002).

Finally, *DSM-III* adopted a multiaxial approach to diagnosis, which was dropped from *DSM-5* (APA, 2013) but had been retained in somewhat different form in ICD-10 (Michels et al., 1996). In a multiaxial approach, clients are described along a series of axes (that is, dimensions). A multiaxial approach encourages clinicians to adopt a more holistic approach to diagnosis by considering variables in addition to the individuals' mental disorders. In *DSM-III* (and its revision), the first two axes are restricted to mental illnesses (with Axis I containing major mental disorders, such as schizophrenia and major depression, and Axis II containing personality disorders and mental retardation, the latter now termed intellectual disability in *DSM-5*), and the last three axes assess other dimensions (e.g., medical conditions, life stressors, global adaptive functioning) often relevant to psychological adjustment.

Nevertheless, *DSM-5* jettisoned the multiaxial system of its predecessors, largely in response to the fact that the rationale for the Axis I–Axis II distinction was never grounded in high-quality scientific evidence (Harkness & Lilienfeld, 1997). As discussed later, there is increasing evidence that some Axis I conditions, including mood and anxiety disorders, are underpinned by dimensions (e.g., high levels of negative emotionality) similar or identical to those that underpin many Axis II conditions. Moreover, there is little or no compelling evidence for a qualitative (black-and-white) difference between Axis I and Axis II conditions.

Theoretical Agnosticism

In sharp contrast to its predecessors, *DSM-III* was agnostic with respect to etiology (with the principal exception of one diagnosis, posttraumatic stress disorder, which required the presence of a traumatic event ostensibly tied to the resulting symptoms of the disorder). In particular, *DSM-III* assiduously shunned concepts, such as defense mechanisms, that were tied to psychoanalysis or other specific theoretical orientations. By doing so, it permitted practitioners and researchers of varying persuasions to use the manual with equal ease and comfort. It also facilitated scientific progress by allowing researchers to pit differing theoretical orientations against each other to determine which offers the most scientifically supported etiological explanations for specific disorders (Wakefield, 1998).

DSM-III-R AND DSM-IV

DSM-III–Revised (*DSM-III-R*), which appeared in 1987, and *DSM-IV*, which appeared in 1994 (and in an expanded text revision in 2000, which with minor exceptions was identical to *DSM-IV* in its diagnostic criteria), retained all the major features and innovations of *DSM-III* (APA, 1987, 1994, 2000). Nevertheless, the manual's developers continued to increase the *DSM*'s coverage of psychopathology; *DSM-IV*, which was 943 pages long, contained 374 diagnoses (APA, 2000).

DSM-III-R and *DSM-IV* gradually moved away from a monothetic approach to diagnosis, emphasized in much of *DSM-III*, toward a polythetic approach. In a monothetic approach, the signs and symptoms are singly necessary and jointly sufficient for a diagnosis. In contrast, in a polythetic approach the signs and symptoms are neither necessary nor sufficient for a diagnosis.

The potential disadvantage of a polythetic approach is extensive heterogeneity at the symptom and (perhaps) etiological levels. In *DSM-IV*, for example, 256 different symptom combinations are compatible with a diagnosis of borderline personality disorder. It is implausible that the etiologies of all of these combinations are similar, let alone identical. It is even possible for two people to meet criteria for obsessive-compulsive personality disorder yet share no criteria (Widiger, 2007). Nevertheless, many scholars argue that the potential disadvantage of symptomatic heterogeneity is outweighed by the higher inter-rater reliability of the polythetic approach (Widiger, Frances, Spitzer, & Williams, 1991). In a monothetic approach, a disagreement about the presence or absence of only one criterion necessarily leads to a disagreement about the presence or absence of the diagnosis. In contrast, in a polythetic approach, such disagreement often has no impact on levels of agreement about the presence or absence of the diagnosis, because raters can still agree on the presence or absence of the diagnosis even if they disagree on one or more of the specific criteria.

The shift toward a polythetic approach is also an implicit nod to the finding that few, if any, signs and symptoms of psychopathology are pathognomonic. A pathognomonic indicator is one that can be used by itself to establish the presence or absence of a disorder. For example, Koplik's spots—tiny spots in the mouth that look much like grains of sand surrounded by red rings—are essentially pathognomonic for measles. A sign or symptom can in principle be one-way pathognomonic, meaning that it is a perfect inclusion test (the sign's or symptom's presence always indicates the presence of the disorder), or two-way pathognomonic, meaning that it is both a perfect inclusion test and a perfect exclusion test (the sign's or symptom's presence always indicates the presence of the disorder, and the sign's or symptom's absence always indicates the absence of the disorder). With the possible exception of certain organic brain disorders, no *DSM* diagnoses boast a one-way, let alone a two-way, pathognomonic indicator. *DSM-III-R* and *DSM-IV* also witnessed a relaxation of many, though not all, of *DSM-III*'s hierarchical exclusion rules (Pincus, Tew, & First, 2004). This change largely reflected the paucity of research evidence concerning the causal primacy of certain disorders above others. In addition, many of these exclusion rules proved difficult to apply in practice, because they required subjective and highly inferential judgments of causal primacy on the part of diagnosticians.

Finally, *DSM-IV* added an appendix for culture-bound syndromes, recognizing the fact that some conditions vary, or at least vary markedly in their expression, across cultures (Draguns & Tanaka-Matsumi, 2003). Most of these culture-bound syndromes are widely known in non-Western cultures, although their etiology and relation to conditions diagnosed in Western cultures are poorly understood. For example, *koro*, an epidemic condition observed in parts of China and Malaysia, is marked by abrupt and intense fears that the penis (in men) or vulva or breasts (in women) are receding into the body. Still other culture-bound syndromes appear to be variants of diagnoses that we readily recognize in Western culture. For example, *taijin kyofusho*, common in Japan, refers to a fear of offending others by one's appearance, body odor, nonverbal behavior, and so on. It may be a subspecies of social phobia that is especially prevalent in cultures, especially in Asia, that stress group harmony above individual autonomy (Kleinknecht, Dinnel, Tanouye-Wilson, & Lonner, 1994).

DSM-5

Following the publication of *DSM-IV* in 1994 and its text revision in 2000, a great deal of data accumulated regarding the prevalence and correlates of various *DSM* diagnoses. In an effort to accommodate these new data, *DSM-5*, spearheaded by psychiatrists David Kupfer and Darrel Regier, was published in May 2013 (APA, 2013), amid a host of controversies. By and large, *DSM-5* retained most of the major categories of *DSM-IV* but, as noted earlier, dropped the multiaxial system. In addition, one goal of *DSM-5* was to stem the tide of the perceived proliferation of new diagnoses by relying on rigorous validity data for potential new conditions. As will be discussed later, however, *DSM-5* has already been widely criticized on a number of grounds, including its decision to lower the threshold for several diagnostic categories (Batstra & Frances, 2012a). Moreover, others have charged that the field trials for *DSM-5* were inadequate, focusing largely on clinical feasibility and interrater reliability, with scant examination of the validity of new diagnostic categories or the potential effects of alterations in extant categories on the prevalence of *DSM* disorders (Frances & Widiger, 2012).

Although *DSM-5* is now the predominant system of psychiatric classification in the world, Chapter V of ICD-10 (World Health Organization, 1992) is an increasingly influential alternative; indeed, as of the fall of 2015, an ICD-10 diagnosis has been required by most insurers for reimbursement for mental health services. ICD-11 is under construction as of this writing. Although there is substantial overlap in diagnostic coverage between the two systems, ICD-10 consists of clinical prototypes, much as did *DSM-I* and *DSM-II* (Goldberg, 2012). Therefore, its diagnoses may hinge more on clinical judgment than do those of *DSM-5*. Despite their similarities, many *DSM* and ICD categories differ in non-trivial ways, with only one condition (transient tic disorder) being identical in its criteria (First, 2009). In a study of over 1,300 patients using earlier (*DSM-IV*) criteria, the concordance between ICD-10 and *DSM-IV* ranged from only 33% for substance abuse to 87% for dysthymic disorder (which is similar to persistent depressive disorder in *DSM-5*); we are unaware of comparable comparisons between ICD-10 and *DSM-5*.

Criticisms of the Current Classification System

Recent versions of the diagnostic manual, from *DSM-III* through *DSM-5*, have helped to place the field of psychopathology on firmer scientific grounds, largely because they have established reasonably reliable operationalizations for most mental disorders and furthered the development of standardized instruments, such as structured psychiatric interviews, to assess these disorders. The theoretical agnosticism of recent *DSMs* has also facilitated research comparing the scientific support for competing theoretical conceptualizations of psychopathology (Wakefield, 1998). Despite the undeniable advances of *DSM-III* and its progeny, many critics have argued that these manuals are scientifically problematic in several respects. Here we examine four key criticisms of the *DSM-5* classification system, many of which also applied to *DSM-III*, *DSM-III-R*, and *DSM-IV*: comorbidity, medicalization of normality, neglect of the attenuation paradox, and unsupported retention of a categorical model.[2]

COMORBIDITY

DSM-5, like *DSM-III* and its other progeny, is marked by high levels of co-occurrence and covariation among many of its diagnostic categories, a phenomenon known, perhaps misleadingly, as *comorbidity* (Caron & Rutter, 1991; Lilienfeld et al., 1994; Pincus et al., 2004). We say misleadingly because it is premature in most cases to assume that comorbidity reflects the overlap among etiologically distinct conditions, as opposed to slightly different variants of the same underlying condition (Drake & Wallach, 2007). Although comorbidity is frequent among all mental disorders, it is especially rampant among personality disorders (Widiger & Rogers, 1989). In one analysis based on multiple sites, patients who met criteria for one personality disorder on average met criteria for

---

[2] One frequent criticism of the *DSM* revision process (e.g., Caplan, 1995) that we do not discuss at length here is the reliance on committee consensus in settling on both (a) the inclusion and exclusion of specific disorders from the manual and (b) the diagnostic criteria for specific disorders, largely because we find this criticism to be without substantial merit. Although expert consensus inevitably introduces subjective and political considerations into the diagnostic revision process (Ghaemi, 2003; Kirk & Kutchins, 1992) and has almost certainly resulted in flawed decisions, it is almost surely superior to a system in which one appointed expert adjudicates scientifically complex disputes without the benefit of input from other experts. As Widiger and Clark (2000) observed, "no diagnostic manual can be constructed without a group of fallible persons interpreting the results of existing research" (p. 948). To paraphrase Winston Churchill's famous wisecrack about democracy, the *DSM* revision process is probably the worst system possible except for every other system.

approximately two additional personality disorders—with 10% meeting criteria for four or more personality disorders (Stuart et al., 1998). One patient in a research study met criteria for all 10 *DSM* personality disorders (Widiger et al., 1998).

The extent of comorbidity among mental disorders, including personality disorders, is often underestimated in routine clinical practice (Zimmerman & Mattia, 2000), in part because of a phenomenon known as diagnostic overshadowing. *Diagnostic overshadowing* refers to the tendency for a more florid disorder to draw attention away from less florid co-occurring disorders, thereby leading diagnosticians to either overlook them or attribute them to the more florid disorder. For example, the dramatic symptoms of borderline personality disorder frequently lead clinicians to underdiagnose commonly co-occurring but less salient conditions, such as narcissistic and dependent personality disorders (Garb, 1998). The full extent of comorbidity among personality disorders typically becomes evident only when structured and semistructured diagnostic interviews, which force assessors to inquire about all diagnostic criteria, are administered (Zimmerman & Mattia, 2000).

There are multiple potential explanations for comorbidity—some primarily substantive, others primarily methodological (for reviews, see Cramer, Waldorp, van der Maas, & Borsboom, 2010; Klein & Riso, 1993; and Lilienfeld, 2003). On the substantive front, one disorder (e.g., generalized anxiety disorder) may predispose to another disorder (e.g., dysthymic disorder), the two disorders may mutually influence each other, or both disorders may be slightly different expressions (*formes frustes*) of the same latent liability, such as neuroticism or negative emotionality. On the methodological front, comorbidity may result from overlapping diagnostic criteria or from clinical selection bias (du Fort, Newman, & Bland, 1993), that is, the tendency for psychiatric patients with one disorder, such as alcohol use disorder, to seek treatment only when they develop a co-occurring disorder, such as major depression. Comorbidity can also arise from Berksonian bias (Berkson, 1946), a selection bias resulting from the tendency of people with multiple conditions to be selected for research. For example, individuals with both specific phobia and major depression, most of whom are experiencing intense distress, may be more likely to volunteer for research on anxiety disorders than are people with specific phobia alone, who often exhibit relatively mild impairment. In addition, comorbidity can be produced by "logical errors" (Guilford, 1936), that is, mistakes stemming from the tendency of diagnosticians to assume that two largely unrelated conditions are correlated.

Whatever its causes, extensive comorbidity is potentially problematic for the *DSM*, because an ideal classification system yields largely mutually exclusive categories with few overlapping cases (Lilienfeld, VanValkenburg, Larntz, & Akiskal, 1986; Sullivan & Kendler, 1998). As a consequence, such comorbidity may suggest that the current classification system is attaching multiple labels to differing manifestations of the same underlying condition. Defenders of the current classification system are quick to point out that high levels of comorbidity are also prevalent in organic medicine, and often indicate that certain conditions (e.g., diabetes) increase individuals' risk for other conditions (e.g., blindness), a phenomenon that Kaplan and Feinstein (1974) termed *pathogenetic comorbidity*. Nevertheless, in stark contrast to organic medicine, in which the causal pathways contributing to pathogenetic comorbidity are often well understood, the causal pathways contributing to pathogenetic comorbidity in the domain of psychopathology generally remain unknown.

MEDICALIZATION OF NORMALITY

A number of critics have raised concerns that recent *DSM*s, *DSM-5* in particular, have overmedicalized normality (Frances, 2013; Sommers & Satel, 2005). They have done so, these authors contend, in two ways: (1) by increasing the number of diagnoses and (2) by lowering the threshold for a number of extant diagnoses. In this way, recent *DSM*s, including *DSM-5*, may risk opening the floodgates to a pathologizing of largely normative behaviors, emotions, and thoughts. Probably the most vocal critic in this regard has been psychiatrist Allen Frances, who was the principal architect of *DSM-IV*. In a number of publications, Frances and others have decried *DSM-5*'s apparently lowered diagnostic thresholds for a number of conditions, as well as its introduction of new and largely unvalidated disorders (Batstra & Frances, 2012a; Frances, 2013).

Historically, one dramatic change from *DSM-I* to *DSM-IV* was the massive increase in the sheer number of diagnoses, a trend potentially reversed by *DSM-5*. Some critics have argued that this increase reflects the tendency for successive editions of the *DSM* to expand their range of coverage into new and largely uncharted waters (Houts, 2001). Many of these novel diagnoses, which describe relatively mild problems, may be of questionable validity. For example, the new *DSM-5* diagnosis of disruptive mood dysregulation disorder, which is intended to capture many cases of what some authors believe to be pediatric bipolar disorder, has been harshly criticized by Frances (2012) and others for "turn[ing] temper tantrums into a mental disorder" (see Dobbs, 2012). Another potential example is the *DSM-5* category of minor neurocognitive disorder, which some authors contend may unduly pathologize mild forgetfulness and other largely normative cognitive problems often associated with aging.

As Wakefield (2001) noted, however, there is little evidence that *DSM* actually expanded its range of coverage from *DSM-III* to *DSM-IV*. Although it is unclear at present, the same conclusion may hold for *DSM-5*. As Wakefield observed, most increases in the number of diagnoses across previous *DSM*s, and since then possibly stabilized by *DSM-5*, reflect an increased splitting of broader diagnoses into progressively narrower subtypes.

The distinction between splitting and lumping derives from biological taxonomy (Mayr, 1982) and refers to the difference between two classificatory styles: the tendency to subdivide broad and potentially heterogeneous categories into narrower and presumably more homogeneous categories (splitting) or the tendency to combine narrow and presumably more homogeneous categories into broad and potentially heterogeneous categories (lumping). For example, given evidence that bipolar I disorder and bipolar II disorder are related (although by no means identical) conditions with relatively similar family histories, laboratory correlates, prognoses, and treatment responses, should we keep these diagnoses separate or combine them into a more encompassing, albeit more heterogeneous, category? In the case of autism and allied conditions, the developers of *DSM-5* elected to embrace a lumping approach, combining several conditions, such as autistic disorder, Asperger's disorder, and childhood disintegrative disorder, into the broader domain of what is now termed autism spectrum disorder. Nevertheless, some authors have argued that this change will incorrectly exclude children with milder forms of autism spectrum conditions from the *DSM* (McPartland, Reichow, & Volkmar, 2012).

The splitting preferences of the architects of *DSM-III*, *DSM-III-R*, and *DSM-IV* in particular have been widely maligned (Houts, 2001). Herman van Praag (2000) even humorously "diagnosed" the *DSM*'s predilection for splitting as the disorder of "nosologomania" (also see Ghaemi, 2003). Nevertheless, a preference for splitting is defensible from the standpoint of research and nosological revision. A key point is that the relation between splitting and lumping is asymmetrical: If we begin by splitting diagnostic categories, we can always lump them later if research demonstrates that they are essentially identical according to the Robins and Guze (1970) criteria for validity. Yet, if we begin by lumping, it will often be difficult or impossible to split later. As a consequence, we may overlook potentially crucial distinctions among etiologically separable subtypes that bear differing implications for treatment and prevention.

At the same time, it is unclear whether *DSM-5*'s new diagnoses, such as disruptive mood regulation disorder, reflect merely a splitting of the diagnostic pie into narrower slices or an actual enlargement of the pie. If the latter, *DSM-5* may risk extending the umbrella of pathology to relatively mild and normative problems.

As noted earlier, a second way in which recent *DSM*s, including *DSM-5*, may over-medicalize normality is by lowering the threshold for a number of conditions (Batstra & Frances, 2012a; Frances & Widiger, 2012). For example, by increasing the age of onset from 7 to 12 years of age and decreasing the proportion of symptoms for the diagnosis, *DSM-5* appears to have made it easier to meet criteria for ADHD (Batstra & Frances, 2012b). Even more controversial was the decision in *DSM-5* to remove the bereavement criterion for major depression, allowing individuals to be diagnosed with this condition as soon as 2 weeks following the death of a loved one (APA, 2013).

We believe the concerns of Frances and others regarding the potential overmedicalization of normality are important and worth raising. Nevertheless, the ultimate question is whether the changes in *DSM-5* increase or decrease the construct validity of the resultant disorders, not whether they alter the prevalence of individuals diagnosed with these disorders (cf. Batstra & Frances, 2012a). The answer to the latter question will surely vary by disorder, and at present awaits clarification in light of future research.

NEGLECT OF THE ATTENUATION PARADOX

Much of the impetus behind *DSM-III* was the laudable attempt to increase the reliability of psychiatric diagnosis and, thereby, place the fields of psychiatry and clinical psychology on firmer scientific footing. The importance of the reliability of diagnostic categories continues to be recognized in *DSM-5*. Nevertheless, reliability is only a means to an end, namely validity; moreover, as noted earlier, validity is limited not by reliability per se, but by its square root (Meehl, 1986). Therefore, diagnoses of even modest reliability can, in principle, achieve high levels of validity.

Ironically, efforts to achieve higher reliability, especially internal consistency, can sometimes produce decreases in validity, a phenomenon that Loevinger (1957) referred to as the *attenuation paradox* (also see Clark & Watson, 1995). This paradox can result when an investigator uses a narrowly circumscribed pool of items to capture a broad and multifaceted construct. In such a case, the measure of the construct may exhibit high internal consistency yet low validity, because it does not adequately tap the full breadth and richness of the construct.

Some authors have argued that this state of affairs occurred with several *DSM* diagnoses. Putting it a bit differently, they have suggested that *DSM-III* and its descendants sacrificed validity at the altar of reliability (Vaillant, 1984). For example, the current *DSM* diagnosis of antisocial personality disorder (ASPD) is intended to assess the core interpersonal and affective features of psychopathic personality (psychopathy) delineated by Cleckley (1941), Karpman (1948), and others. Indeed, the accompanying text of *DSM-5* even refers misleadingly to ASPD as synonymous with psychopathy (APA, 2013, p. 659). Because the developers of *DSM-III* (APA, 1980) were concerned that the personality features of psychopathy—such as guiltlessness, callousness, and self-centeredness—were difficult to assess reliably, they opted for a diagnosis emphasizing overt and easily agreed on antisocial behaviors—such as vandalism, stealing, and physical aggression (Hare, 2003; Lilienfeld, 1994). These changes may have resulted in a diagnosis with greater internal consistency and interrater reliability than the more traditional construct of psychopathy (although evidence for this possibility is lacking). Nevertheless, they may have also resulted in a diagnosis with lower validity, because the *DSM* diagnosis of ASPD largely fails to assess the personality features central to psychopathy (Lykken, 1995; Skeem, Polaschek, Patrick, & Lilienfeld, 2011). Indeed, accumulating evidence suggests that measures of ASPD are less valid for predicting a number of theoretically meaningful variables—including laboratory indicators—than are measures of psychopathy (Hare, 2003; also see Vaillant, 1984, for a discussion of the reliability trade-off in the case of the *DSM-III* diagnosis of schizophrenia).

UNSUPPORTED RETENTION OF A CATEGORICAL MODEL

Technically, the *DSM* is agnostic on the question of whether psychiatric diagnoses are truly categories in nature, or what Meehl (Meehl & Golden, 1982) termed *taxa*, as opposed to continua, or *dimensions*. Taxa differ from normality in kind, whereas dimensions differ in degree. Pregnancy is a taxon, as a woman cannot be slightly pregnant; in contrast, height is almost always a dimension (although certain rare taxonic conditions, like hormonal abnormalities, can lead to heights that differ qualitatively from the general population). The opening pages of *DSM-IV* state: "There is no assumption that each category of mental disorder is a completely discrete entity with absolute boundaries dividing it from other mental disorders or from no mental disorder" (p. xxxi). Yet at the measurement level, the *DSM* embraces an exclusively categorical model, classifying individuals as either meeting criteria for a disorder or not meeting them. In a highly contentious move, *DSM-5* passed on an opportunity to embrace a dimensional model of personality disorders, leaving the current categorical model in place and relegating a proposed dimensional alternative to Section III of the manual (devoted to provisional criterion sets meriting future consideration).

The *DSM* categorical model is problematic for at least two reasons. First, there is growing evidence from taxometric analyses (Meehl & Golden, 1982)—namely, those that allow researchers to ascertain whether a single observed distribution is decomposable into multiple independent distributions—that many or even most *DSM* diagnoses are underpinned by dimensions rather than taxa (Kendell & Jablensky, 2003), with schizophrenia and schizophrenia-spectrum disorders being notable probable exceptions (Lenzenweger & Korfine, 1992). This is particularly true for most personality disorders (Cloninger, 2009; Trull & Durrett, 2005), including antisocial personality disorder (Marcus, Lilienfeld, Edens, & Poythress, 2006). Even many or most other mental disorders—such as major depression (Slade & Andrews, 2005), social anxiety disorder

(Kollman, Brown, Liverant, & Hofmann, 2006), and ADHD (Marcus, Norris, & Coccaro, 2012)—appear to be dimensional as opposed to taxonic in structure.

Second, setting aside the ontological issue of taxonicity versus dimensionality, there is good evidence that measuring most disorders (especially personality disorders) dimensionally by using the full range of scores almost always results in higher correlations with external validating variables than does measuring them categorically in an all-or-none fashion (Craighead, Sheets, Craighead, & Madsen, 2011; Markon, Chmielewski, & Miller, 2011; Ullrich, Borkenau, & Marneros, 2001). Such findings are not surprising given that artificial dichotomization of variables almost always results in a loss of information and, hence, statistical power (Cohen, 1983; MacCallum, Zhang, Preacher, & Rucker, 2002).

The *DSM*: *Quo Vadis*?

In some respects, *DSM-III-R* and *DSM-IV* were disappointments, as they did not resolve many of the serious problems endemic to *DSM-III* (Ghaemi, 2003). If anything, comorbidity in *DSM-III-R* and *DSM-IV* mushroomed, due to the dismantling of many hierarchical exclusion rules (Lilienfeld & Waldman, 2004). Moreover, some diagnostic categories of questionable validity (e.g., dependent personality disorder) remained. It is too early to tell whether *DSM-5* will help to resolve these and other problems. *DSM-5* presents both challenges and opportunities: challenges because many conceptual and methodological quandaries regarding psychiatric diagnosis remain unresolved, and opportunities because a new manual opens the door for novel approaches to the classification of psychopathology.

With these considerations in mind, we sketch out two promising future directions for psychiatric diagnosis: adoption of a dimensional approach and the incorporation of endophenotypic markers into psychiatric diagnosis (see Widiger & Clark, 2000, for other proposals for *DSM-5* and future *DSM*s).

A DIMENSIONAL APPROACH

The accumulating evidence for the dimensionality of many psychiatric conditions, particularly personality disorders, has led many authors to suggest replacing or at least supplementing the *DSM* with a set of dimensions derived from the basic science of personality (Krueger et al., 2011; Widiger & Clark, 2000). One early candidate for a dimensional model is the *five-factor model* (FFM; Goldberg, 1993), which consists of five major dimensions that have emerged repeatedly in factor analyses of omnibus (broad) measures of personality: extraversion, neuroticism, agreeableness, conscientiousness, and openness to experience (the FFM, incidentally, can easily be recalled using the waterlogged mnemonics of OCEAN or CANOE). These five dimensions also contain lower-order facets that provide a fine-grained description of personality; for example, the FFM dimension of extraversion contains facets of warmth, gregariousness, assertiveness, excitement seeking, and so on (Costa & McCrae, 1992).

The framers of *DSM-5* considered a dimensional model for personality disorders influenced substantially by research on the FFM, and by the work of Harkness and his colleagues (see Harkness & McNulty, 1994), which has yielded a somewhat similar set of five dimensions that bears greater relevance to psychopathology. In this model, five broad dimensions of antagonism, detachment, negative affectivity (similar to but broader than neuroticism), disinhibition, and psychoticism are used to describe all personality variation in the abnormal range. Nevertheless, this bold proposal was ultimately vetoed by the American Psychiatric Association board of trustees, in part because its clinical feasibility was deemed to be insufficiently demonstrated. As noted earlier, however, these dimensions appear in Section III of *DSM-5*, in an effort to encourage further research with an eye toward *DSM-6*. In addition, research on the correlates of a self-report measure of these dimensions, the Personality Inventory for *DSM-5* (PID-5), is beginning to accumulate (e.g., Fossati et al., in press; Thomas et al., 2012).

In addition to concerns about its clinical feasibility, there are other potential objections to a dimensional model. For example, there is disagreement regarding both the precise nature and the number of the personality dimensions to be used, with some authors advocating for alternative (e.g., three-dimensional) models. Another objection derives from the often-neglected distinction between basic tendencies and characteristic adaptations in personality psychology (Harkness & Lilienfeld, 1997; McCrae & Costa, 1995). Basic tendencies are core personality traits, whereas characteristic adaptations are the behavioral manifestations of these traits. A large body of personality research suggests that basic tendencies can often be expressed in a wide variety of different characteristic adaptations depending on the upbringing, interests, cognitive skills, and other personality traits of the individual. For example, the scores of firefighters on a well-validated measure of the personality trait of sensation seeking (a construct closely related to, although broader than, risk taking) are significantly higher than those of college students, but comparable to those of incarcerated prisoners (Zuckerman, 1994). This finding dovetails with the notion that the same basic tendency, in this case sensation seeking, can be expressed in either socially constructive or destructive outlets, depending on yet unidentified moderating influences.

The distinction between basic tendencies and characteristic adaptations implies that personality dimensions may never be sufficient to capture the full variance in personality disorders. This is because these dimensions (basic tendencies) do not adequately assess many key aspects of psychopathological functioning, many of which can be viewed as maladaptive characteristic adaptations (Sheets & Craighead, 2007). This theoretical conjecture is corroborated by findings that the FFM dimensions do not account for a sizable chunk of variance in many *DSM* personality disorders. For example, in one study the correlations between FFM prototype scores of *DSM* personality disorders (derived from expert ratings of the FFM facets most closely associated with each disorder) and structured interview-based measures of these disorders were high for some disorders (e.g., avoidant personality disorder, $r = .67$) and modest or even negligible for others (e.g., obsessive-compulsive disorder, $r = .13$) (Miller, Reynolds, & Pilkonis, 2004). The latter finding may reflect the fact that some obsessive-compulsive traits—such as perfectionism—may be adaptive in certain settings and, therefore, may not lead inevitably to personality pathology. Moreover, Skodol et al. (2005) reported that the dimensions of the Schedule for Nonadaptive and Adaptive Personality (SNAP; Clark, 1993)—a measure that assesses many pathological behaviors associated with personality disorders—displayed incremental validity above and beyond the FFM dimensions in distinguishing among *DSM* personality disorders (also see Reynolds & Clark, 2001). This finding suggests that the FFM overlooks crucial distinctions captured by the SNAP, perhaps in part because the SNAP assesses not only basic tendencies but also the maladaptive characteristic adaptations of many personality disorders (Lilienfeld, 2005).

The findings reviewed here imply that a dimensional model may be useful in capturing core features of many *DSM* personality disorders. Nevertheless, they raise the possibility that personality dimensions may not be sufficient by themselves to capture personality pathology, because they cannot tell us whether individuals' behavioral adaptations to these dimensions are adaptive or maladaptive, nor can they express the phenotypic (behavioral) manifestations these adaptations have assumed.

RESEARCH DOMAIN CRITERIA

Despite their noteworthy research achievements, the *DSM* and ICD have not borne witness to clear-cut reductions in the morbidity or mortality related to major mental disorders (Insel, 2009). Furthermore, many, and arguably most, *DSM* and ICD categories appear to lack treatment utility: different diagnoses are often not linked to differential recommendations for evidence-based interventions. Indeed, interventions are often the same for different diagnoses; for example, selective serotonin reuptake inhibitors appear to be efficacious for a broad class of conditions, including a number of mood, anxiety, and eating disorders. All of these anomalies have led many scholars to contend that the *DSM*-ICD approach has not "carved nature at its joints" and that a system more closely tied to psychobiological systems is more likely to yield fruit (Lilienfeld & Treadway, 2016).

In this vein, the National Institute of Mental Health (NIMH) launched the Research Domain Criteria (RDoC) in 2009 as a research program that might ultimately provide an alternative to the *DSM*, ICD, and similar diagnostic manuals. As of this writing, RDoC is more of an envisioned research approach than a proposed system in its own right. Nevertheless, its long-term goal is to identify well-established psychobiological systems that undergird psychopathology (Morris & Cuthbert, 2012), along with promising markers of these systems. Examples of such systems include negative valence systems (e.g., acute threat), positive valence systems (e.g., approach), and cognitive systems (e.g., working memory). In turn, each of these systems can be measured using indicators at different levels of analysis, including observable behavior, self-report indices, laboratory measures, and brain imaging findings (Insel et al., 2010; Sanislow et al., 2010). Ultimately, such a system could supplement or even supplant the extant *DSM* system, but as of this writing, progress along these lines remains preliminary. In contrast to the *DSM*, which adopts a categorical system for measurement purposes, RDoC embraces a dimensional system, although it does not preclude the existence of taxa.

RDoC was substantially informed by the endophenotype approach to psychopathology research, which, as noted earlier, strives to identify promising markers of mental disorders that lie "beneath the skin" (Andreasen, 1995; Waldman, 2005). RDoC goes beyond these approaches, however, in shifting the focus from mental disorders themselves to neural circuitry putatively associated with risk for these disorders. Nevertheless, with the exception of certain sleep disorders (e.g., narcolepsy), endophenotypic markers have thus far been excluded from *DSM* diagnostic criterion sets, which consist almost entirely of the classical signs and symptoms of disorders (exophenotypes). This omission is noteworthy, because endophenotypes may lie closer to the etiology of many disorders than do exophenotypes. This situation may change in coming years with accumulating evidence from studies of biochemistry, brain imaging, and performance on laboratory tasks; this evidence holds the promise of identifying more valid markers of certain mental disorders (Patrick & Hajcak, 2016; Widiger & Clark, 2000). Nevertheless, at least two potential obstacles confront the use of endophenotypic markers in psychiatric diagnosis and the RDoC initiative more broadly, the first conceptual and the second empirical. First, the widespread assumption that endophenotypic markers are more closely linked to underlying etiological processes than exophenotypic markers (Kihlstrom, 2002) is just that: an assumption. For example, the well-replicated finding that diminished amplitude of the P300 (a brain event–related potential appearing approximately 300 milliseconds following stimulus onset) is dependably associated with externalizing disorders—such as conduct disorder and substance dependence (Patrick et al., 2006)—could reflect the fact that P300 is merely a sensitive indicator of attention. As a consequence, diminished P300 amplitude, as well as several other event-related potential findings, such as diminished error-related negativity (see Olvet & Hajcak, 2008), could be a downstream consequence of the inattention and low levels of motivation often associated with externalizing disorders (Lilienfeld & Treadway, 2016). This possibility would not necessarily negate the incorporation of P300 amplitude into diagnostic criterion sets, although it could raise questions concerning its specificity to externalizing disorders, let alone specific externalizing disorders.

Second, no endophenotypic markers yet identified are close to serving as inclusion tests for their respective disorders. Even smooth pursuit eye movement dysfunction, which is perhaps the most dependable biological marker of schizophrenia, is present only in anywhere from 40% to 80% of patients with schizophrenia, so it would miss many individuals with the disorder. It may come closer, however, to serving as a good exclusion test, as it is present in only about 10% of normal individuals (Clementz & Sweeney, 1990; Keri & Janka, 2004). Thus, although endophenotypic markers may eventually add to the predictive efficiency of some diagnostic criterion sets, they are likely to be fallible indicators, just as traditional signs and symptoms are. These markers also hold out the hope of assisting in the identification of more etiologically pure subtypes of disorders; for example, schizophrenia patients with abnormal smooth pursuit eye movements may prove to be separable in important ways from other patients with this disorder. Alternatively, and broadly consistent with the RDoC approach, such markers may be more helpful in assessing individual differences in neural circuits, such as those relevant to threat systems, than in identifying DSM and ICD disorders themselves. Such individual differences might in turn eventually inform the selection of the most efficacious treatment. In the next decade, we should have a better gauge of this approach's scientific status and its promise for informing psychiatric classification and diagnosis.

Summary and Future Directions

We conclude this chapter with 10 take-home messages:

1. A systematic system of psychiatric classification is a prerequisite for psychiatric diagnosis.
2. Psychiatric diagnoses serve important, even essential, communicative functions.

3. A valid psychiatric diagnosis gives us new information—for example, it tells about the diagnosed individual's probable family history, performance on laboratory tests, natural history, and perhaps response to treatment—and it also distinguishes that person's diagnosis from other, related diagnoses.

4. The claim that mental illness is a myth rests on a misunderstanding of the role of lesions in medical disorders.

5. Prevalent claims to the contrary, psychiatric diagnoses often achieve adequate levels of reliability and validity, and do not typically pigeonhole or stigmatize individuals when correctly applied.

6. There is no clear consensus on the correct definition of mental disorder, and some authors have suggested that the higher-order concept of mental disorder is intrinsically undefinable. Even if true, this should have no effect on the scientific investigation, assessment, or treatment of specific mental disorders (e.g., schizophrenia, panic disorder), which undeniably exist.

7. Early versions of the diagnostic manual (*DSM-I* and *DSM-II*) were problematic because they provided clinicians and researchers with minimal guidance for establishing diagnoses and required high levels of subjective judgment and clinical inference.

8. *DSM-III*, which appeared in 1980, helped to alleviate this problem by providing diagnosticians with explicit diagnostic criteria, algorithms (decision rules), and hierarchical exclusion criteria, leading to increases in the reliability of many psychiatric diagnoses.

9. The current classification system, *DSM-5*, is a clear advance over *DSM-I* and *DSM-II*. Nevertheless, from initial reports, *DSM-5* continues to be plagued by a variety of problems, especially extensive comorbidity, reliable diagnoses that are nevertheless of questionable validity, and retention of a categorical model in the absence of compelling scientific evidence. ICD-10 is an alternative to *DSM-5* used in many parts of the world; many of its diagnoses overlap substantially with those of *DSM-5*, although there are noteworthy differences for others.

10. Fruitful potential directions for psychiatric classification include the development of a dimensional model of personality to replace or supplement the existing categorical system of personality disorders, and the adoption of a system based on neural circuitry tied to risk for psychopathology, consistent with the recently launched NIMH RDoC initiative.

References

Alliance of Psychoanalytic Organizations. (2006). *Psychodynamic diagnostic manual.* Silver Spring, MD: Author.

Amador, X. F., & Paul-Odouard, R. (2000). Defending the Unabomber: Anosognosia in schizophrenia. *Psychiatric Quarterly, 71,* 363–371.

American Psychiatric Association. (1952). *Diagnostic and statistical manual of mental disorders.* Washington, DC: Author.

American Psychiatric Association. (1968). *Diagnostic and statistical manual of mental disorders* (2nd ed.). Washington, DC: Author.

American Psychiatric Association. (1980). *Diagnostic and statistical manual of mental disorders* (3rd ed.). Washington, DC: Author.

American Psychiatric Association. (1987). *Diagnostic and statistical manual of mental disorders* (3rd ed., rev.). Washington, DC: Author.

American Psychiatric Association. (1994). *Diagnostic and statistical manual of mental disorders* (4th ed.). Washington, DC: Author.

American Psychiatric Association. (2000). *Diagnostic and statistical manual of mental disorders* (4th ed., text rev.). Washington, DC: Author.

American Psychiatric Association. (2013). *Diagnostic and statistical manual of mental disorders* (5th ed.). Washington, DC: Author.

Andreasen, N. C. (1995). The validation of psychiatric diagnosis: New models and approaches. *American Journal of Psychiatry, 152,* 161–162.

Barlow, D. H. (2001). *Anxiety and its disorders: The nature and treatment of anxiety and panic* (2nd ed.). New York, NY: Guilford Press.

Batstra, L., & Frances, A. (2012a). Diagnostic inflation: Causes and a suggested cure. *Journal of Nervous and Mental Disease, 200,* 474–479.

Batstra, L., & Frances, A. (2012b). Holding the line against diagnostic inflation in psychiatry. *Psychotherapy and Psychosomatics, 81,* 5–10.

Bayer, R., & Spitzer, R. L. (1982). Edited correspondence on the status of homosexuality in DSM-III. *Journal of the History of the Behavioral Sciences, 18,* 32–52.

Benton, A. L. (1992). Gerstmann's syndrome. *Archives of Neurology, 49,* 445–447.

Berkson, J. (1946). Limitations of the application of fourfold table analysis to hospital data. *Biometrics Bulletin, 2,* 47–53.

Blashfield, R., & Burgess, D. (2007). Classification provides an essential basis for organizing mental disorders. In S. O. Lilienfeld & W. T. O'Donohue (Eds.), *The great ideas of clinical science: 17 Principles that every mental professional should understand* (pp. 93–118). New York, NY: Routledge.

Borsboom, D., Cramer, A. O., Kievit, R. A., Zand Scholten, A., & Franic, S. (2009). The end of construct validity. In R. W. Lissitz (Ed.), *The concept of validity: Revisions, new directions, and applications* (pp. 135–170). Charlotte, NC: Information Age Publishing.

Caplan, P. J. (1995). *They say you're crazy: How the world's most powerful psychiatrists decide who's normal.* Reading, MA: Addison-Wesley.

Caron, C., & Rutter, M. (1991). Comorbidity in child psychopathology: Concepts, issues and research strategies. *Journal of Child Psychology and Psychiatry, 32,* 1063–1080.

Clark, L. A. (1993). *Manual for the Schedule for Nonadaptive and Adaptive Personality (SNAP).* Minneapolis: University of Minnesota Press.

Clark, L. A., & Watson, D. (1995). Constructing validity: Basic issues in objective scale development. *Psychological Assessment, 7,* 309–319.

Cleckley, H. (1941). *The mask of sanity.* St. Louis, MO: Mosby.

Clementz, B. A., & Sweeney, J. A. (1990). Is eye movement dysfunction a biological marker for schizophrenia? A methodological review. *Psychological Bulletin, 108,* 77–92.

Cloninger, C. R. (2009). Foreword. In W. O'Donohue, K. A. Fowler, & S. O. Lilienfeld (Eds.), *Personality disorders: Toward the DSM-V* (pp. vii–xv). Los Angeles, CA: Sage.

Cohen, H. (1981). The evolution of the concept of disease. In A. L. Caplan, H. T. Engelhardt, Jr., & J. J. McCartney (Eds.), *Concepts of health and disease: Interdisciplinary perspectives* (pp. 209–220). Reading, MA: Addison-Wesley.

Cohen, J. (1983). The cost of dichotomization. *Applied Psychological Measurement, 7,* 249–253.

Compton, W. M., & Guze, S. B. (1995). The neo-Kraepelinian revolution in psychiatric diagnosis. *European Archives of Psychiatry and Clinical Neuroscience, 245*, 196–201.

Cooper, R. (2011). Mental health and disorder. In H. T. Have, R. Chadwick, & E. M. Meslin (Eds.), *The Sage handbook of health care ethics* (pp. 251–260). London, England: Sage.

Cornez-Ruiz, S., & Hendricks, B. (1993). Effects of labeling and ADHD behaviors on peer and teacher judgments. *Journal of Educational Research, 86*, 349–355.

Costa, P. T., Jr., & McCrae, R. R. (1992). *Revised NEO Personality Inventory (NEO-PI-R) and NEO Five-Factor Inventory (NEO-FFI) professional manual.* Odessa, FL: Psychological Assessment Resources.

Craighead, W. E., Sheets, E. S., Craighead, L. W., & Madsen, J. W. (2011). Recurrence of MDD: A prospective study of personality pathology and cognitive distortions. *Personality Disorders: Theory, Research, and Treatment, 2*, 83–97.

Cramer, A. O., Waldorp, L. J., van der Maas, H. L., & Borsboom, D. (2010). Comorbidity: A network perspective. *Behavioral and Brain Sciences, 33*, 137–150.

Cronbach, L. J. (1951). Coefficient alpha and the internal structure of tests. *Psychometrika, 16*, 297–335.

Cronbach, L. J., & Meehl, P. E. (1955). Construct validity in psychological tests. *Psychological Bulletin, 52*, 281–302.

Dobbs, D. (2012, December 7). The new temper tantrum disorder. *Slate.* Retrieved from http://www.slate.com/articles/double_x/doublex/2012/12/disruptive_mood_dysregulation_disorder_in_dsm_5_criticism_of_a_new_diagnosis.html

Draguns, J. G., & Tanaka-Matsumi, J. (2003). Assessment of psychopathology across and within cultures: Issues and findings. *Behaviour Research and Therapy, 41*, 755–776.

Drake, R. E., & Wallach, M. A. (2007). Is comorbidity a psychological science? *Clinical Psychology: Science and Practice, 14*, 20–22.

du Fort, G. G., Newman, S. C., & Bland, R. C. (1993). Psychiatric comorbidity and treatment seeking: Sources of selection bias in the study of clinical populations. *Journal of Nervous and Mental Disease, 181*, 467–474.

Eysenck, H. J., Wakefield, J., & Friedman, A. (1983). Diagnosis and clinical assessment: The DSM-III. *Annual Review of Psychology, 34*, 167–193.

Faust, D., & Miner, R. A. (1986). The empiricist in his new clothes: DSM-III in perspective. *American Journal of Psychiatry, 143*, 962–967.

Feighner, J., Robins, E., Guze, S., Woodruff, R., Winokur, G., & Munoz, R. (1972). Diagnostic criteria for use in psychiatric research. *Archives of General Psychiatry, 26*, 57–63.

First, M. B. (2009). Summaries of the DSM-V research planning conferences. Retrieved from www.psych.org/MainMenu/ Research/DSMIV/DSMV/DSM RevisionActivities/ ResearchPlanningatHigher Magnification.aspx

First, M. B., Spitzer, R. L., Gibbon, M., & Williams, J.B.W. (2002). *Structured clinical interview for DSM-IV-TR Axis I Disorders, Research Version, Patient Edition.* New York, NY: Biometrics Research, New York State Psychiatric Institute.

Fossati, A., Somma, A., Borroni, S., Maffei, C., Markon, K. E., & Krueger, R. F. (in press). A head-to-head comparison of the Personality Inventory for DSM-5 (PID-5) with the Personality Diagnostic Questionnaire-4 (PDQ-4) in predicting the general level of personality pathology among community dwelling subjects. *Journal of Personality Disorders.*

Frances, A. J. (2012, December 2). The DSM-5 is not a bible: Ignore its ten worst changes. *Psychology Today.* Retrieved from http://www.psychologytoday.com/blog/dsm5-in-distress/201212/dsm-5-is-guide-not-bible-ignore-its-ten-worst-changes

Frances, A. J. (2013). *Saving normal: An insider's look at what caused the epidemic of mental illness and how to cure it.* New York, NY: HarperCollins.

Frances, A. J., & Widiger, T. (2012). Psychiatric diagnosis: Lessons from the *DSM-IV* past and cautions for the DSM-5 future. *Annual Review of Clinical Psychology, 8*, 109–130.

Garb, H. N. (1998). *Studying the clinician: Judgment research and psychological assessment.* Washington, DC: American Psychological Association.

Garber, J., & Strassberg, Z. (1991). Construct validity: History and application to developmental psychopathology. In W. M. Grove & D. Cicchetti (Eds.), *Personality and psychopathology* (pp. 218–258). Minneapolis: University of Minnesota Press.

Ghaemi, N. (2003). *The concepts of psychiatry: A pluralistic approach to the mind and mental illness.* Baltimore, MD: Johns Hopkins University Press.

Goldberg, D. P. (2012). Comparison between ICD and DSM diagnostic systems for mental disorders.

In E. Sorel (Ed.), *21st century global mental health* (pp. 37–53). Burlington, MA: Jones & Bartlett Learning.

Goldberg, L. R. (1993). The structure of phenotypic personality traits. *American Psychologist*, *48*, 266–275.

Goodwin, D. W., & Guze, S. B. (1996). *Psychiatric diagnosis* (5th ed.). New York, NY: Oxford University Press.

Gorenstein, E. E. (1992). *The science of mental illness*. San Diego, CA: Academic Press.

Gottesman, I. I., & Gould, T. D. (2003). The endophenotype concept in psychiatry: Etymology and strategic intentions. *American Journal of Psychiatry*, *160*, 636–645.

Gottesman, I. I., & McGue, M. (2015). Endophenotype. In R. Cautin & S. O. Lilienfeld (Eds.), *The encyclopedia of clinical psychology*. Chichester, England: Wiley. Retrieved from http://onlinelibrary.wiley.com/doi/10.1002/9781118625392.wbecp423/abstract;jsessionid=A5F00C051923257412DB666CC4525BE3.f04t02?userIsAuthenticated=false&deniedAccessCustomisedMessage=

Gough, H. (1971). Some reflections on the meaning of psychodiagnosis. *American Psychologist*, *26*, 160–167.

Grob, G. N. (1991). Origins of DSM-I: A study in appearance and reality. *American Journal of Psychiatry*, *148*, 421–431.

Guilford, J. P. (1936). *Psychometric methods*. New York, NY: McGraw-Hill.

Hare, R. D. (2003). *Manual for the Revised Psychopathy Checklist* (2nd ed.). Toronto, ON: Multi-Health Systems.

Harkness, A. R., & Lilienfeld, S. O. (1997). Individual differences science for treatment planning: Personality traits. *Psychological Assessment*, *9*, 349–360.

Harkness, A. R., & McNulty, J. L. (1994). The Personality Psychopathology Five (PSY-5): Issue from the pages of a diagnostic manual instead of a dictionary. In S. Strack & M. Lorr (Eds.), *Differentiating normal and abnormal personality* (pp. 291–315). New York, NY: Springer.

Harris, M. J., Milich, R., Corbitt, E. M., Hoover, D. W., & Brady, M. (1992). Self-fulfilling effects of stigmatizing information on children's social interactions. *Journal of Personality and Social Psychology*, *63*, 41–50.

Houts, A. C. (2001). The diagnostic and statistical manual's new white coat and circularity of plausible dysfunctions: Response to Wakefield, part 1. *Behaviour Research and Therapy*, *39*, 315–345.

Insel, T. R. (2009). Translating scientific opportunity into public health impact: A strategic plan for research on mental illness. *Archives of General Psychiatry*, *66*, 128–133.

Insel, T. (2013, April 29). Director's blog: Transforming diagnosis. *National Institute of Mental Health*. Retrieved from http://www.nimh.nih.gov/about/director/2013/transforming-diagnosis.shtml

Insel, T., Cuthbert, B., Garvey, M., Heinssen, R., Kozak, M., Pine, D. S., … Wang, P. (2010). Research Domain Criteria (RDoC): Developing a valid diagnostic framework for research on mental disorders. *American Journal of Psychiatry*, *167*, 748–751.

James, O. (2007). *Affluenza—a contagious middle class virus causing depression, anxiety, addiction and ennui*. London, England: Random House.

Joiner, T. (2006). *Why people die by suicide*. Cambridge, MA: Harvard University Press.

Kaplan, M. H., & Feinstein, A. R. (1974). The importance of classifying initial co-morbidity in evaluating the outcome of diabetes mellitus. *Journal of Chronic Diseases*, *27*, 387–404.

Karpman, B. (1948). The myth of the psychopathic personality. *American Journal of Psychiatry*, *104*, 523–524.

Kazdin, A. E. (1983). Psychiatric diagnosis, dimensions of dysfunction, and child behavior therapy. *Behavior Therapy*, *14*, 73–99.

Kendell, R., & Jablensky, A. (2003). Distinguishing between the validity and utility of psychiatric diagnoses. *American Journal of Psychiatry*, *160*, 4–12.

Kendell, R. E. (1975). The concept of disease and its implications for psychiatry. *British Journal of Psychiatry*, *127*, 305–315.

Kendler, K. S. (1980). The nosologic validity of paranoia (simple delusional disorder): A review. *Archives of General Psychiatry*, *37*, 699–706.

Kendler, K. S. (2005). Toward a philosophical structure for psychiatry. *American Journal of Psychiatry*, *162*, 433–440.

Kendler, K. S., Zachar, P., & Craver, C. (2011). What kinds of things are psychiatric disorders? *Psychological Medicine*, *41*, 1143–1150.

Keri, S., & Janka, Z. (2004). Critical evaluation of cognitive dysfunctions as endophenotypes of schizophrenia. *Acta Psychiatrica Scandinavica*, *110*, 83–91.

Kihlstrom, J. F. (2002). To honor Kraepelin…: From symptoms to pathology in the diagnosis of mental illness. In L. Beutler & M. Malik (Eds.), *Rethinking the DSM: A psychological perspective* (pp. 279–303). Washington, DC: American Psychological Association.

Kim, J., Park, S., & Blake, R. (2011). Perception of biological motion in schizophrenia and healthy individuals: A behavioral and fMRI study. *PloS One, 6*(5), e19971.

Kirk, S. A., & Kutchins, H. (1992). *The selling of DSM: The rhetoric of science in psychiatry.* New York, NY: Aldine de Gruyter.

Klein, D., & Riso, L. P. (1993). Psychiatric disorders: Problems of boundaries and comorbidity. In C. G. Costello (Ed.), *Basic issues in psychopathology* (pp. 19–66). New York, NY: Guilford Press.

Kleinknecht, R. A., Dinnel, D. L., Tanouye-Wilson, S., & Lonner, W. J. (1994). Cultural variation in social anxiety and phobia: A study of *taijin kyofusho. Behavioral Therapist, 17*(8), 175–178.

Klerman, G. (1984). The advantages of DSM-III. *American Journal of Psychiatry, 141*, 539–542.

Kollman, D. M., Brown, T. A., Liverant, G. I., & Hofmann, S. G. (2006). A taxometric investigation of the latent structure of social anxiety disorder in outpatients with anxiety and mood disorders. *Depression and Anxiety, 23*, 190–199.

Kraupl Taylor, F. (1971). A logical analysis of medicophysiological concept of disease. *Psychological Medicine, 1*, 356–364.

Krueger, R. F., Eaton, N. R., Clark, L. A., Watson, D., Markon, K. E., Derringer, J., … Livesley, W. J. (2011). Deriving an empirical structure of personality pathology for DSM-5. *Journal of Personality Disorders, 25*, 170–191.

Lenzenweger, M. F., & Korfine, L. (1992). Confirming the latent structure and base rate of schizotypy: A taxometric analysis. *Journal of Abnormal Psychology, 101*, 567–571.

Lief, A. A. (Ed.). (1948). *The commonsense psychiatry of Dr. Adolf Meyer: Fifty-two selected papers.* New York, NY: McGraw-Hill.

Lilienfeld, S. O. (1994). Conceptual problems in the assessment of psychopathy. *Clinical Psychology Review, 14*, 17–38.

Lilienfeld, S. O. (1995). *Seeing both sides: Classic controversies in abnormal psychology.* Pacific Grove, CA: Brooks/Cole.

Lilienfeld. S. O. (2003). Comorbidity between and within childhood externalizing and internalizing disorders: Reflections and directions. *Journal of Abnormal Child Psychology, 31*, 285–291.

Lilienfeld, S. O. (2005). Longitudinal studies of personality disorders: Four lessons from personality psychology. *Journal of Personality Disorders, 19*, 547–556.

Lilienfeld, S. O. (2013). Is psychopathy a syndrome? Commentary on Marcus, Fulton, and Edens. *Personality Disorders: Theory, Practice, and Research, 4*(1), 85–86.

Lilienfeld, S. O., & Marino, L. (1995). Mental disorder as a Rochian concept: A critique of Wakefield's "harmful dysfunction" analysis. *Journal of Abnormal Psychology, 104*, 411–420.

Lilienfeld, S. O., & Marino, L. (1999). Essentialism revisited: Evolutionary theory and the concept of a mental disorder. *Journal of Abnormal Psychology, 108*, 400–411.

Lilienfeld, S. O., & Treadway, M. T. (2016). Clashing diagnostic approaches: DSM-ICD versus RDoC. *Annual Review of Clinical Psychology, 12*, 435–463.

Lilienfeld, S. O., Van Valkenburg, C., Larntz, K., & Akiskal, H. S. (1986). The relationship of histrionic personality to antisocial personality and somatization disorders. *American Journal of Psychiatry, 143*, 718–722.

Lilienfeld, S. O., & Waldman, I. D. (2004). Comorbidity and Chairman Mao. *World Psychiatry, 3*, 26–27.

Lilienfeld, S. O., Waldman, I. D., & Israel, A. C. (1994). A critical note on the use of the term and concept of "comorbidity" in psychopathology research. *Clinical Psychology: Science and Practice, 1*, 71–83.

Link, B. G., & Cullen, F. T. (1990). The labeling theory of mental disorder: A review of the evidence. *Research in Community and Mental Health, 6*, 75–105.

Lobbestael, J., Leurgans, M., & Arntz, A. (2011). Inter-rater reliability of the Structured Clinical Interview for DSM-IV Axis I disorders (SCID I) and Axis II disorders (SCID II). *Clinical Psychology & Psychotherapy, 18*, 75–79.

Loevinger, J. (1957). Objective tests as instruments of psychological theory. *Psychological Reports, 3*, 635–694.

Lykken, D. T. (1995). *The antisocial personalities.* Hillsdale, NJ: Erlbaum.

Lynam, D. R., & Miller, J. D. (2012). Fearless dominance and psychopathy: A response to Lilienfeld et al. *Personality Disorders: Theory, Research, and Treatment*, *3*, 341–353.

MacCallum, R. C., Zhang, S., Preacher, K. J., & Rucker, D. D. (2002). On the practice of dichotomization of quantitative variables. *Psychological Methods*, *7*, 19–40.

Maffei, C., Fossati, A., Agostoni, I., Barraco, A., Bagnato, M., Namia, C., … Petrachi, M. (1997). Interrater reliability and internal consistency of the Structured Clinical Interview for DSM-IV Axis II personality disorders (SCID-II), version 2.0. *Journal of Personality Disorders*, *11*, 279–284.

Marcus, D. K., Lilienfeld, S. O., Edens, J. F., & Poythress, N. G. (2006). Is antisocial personality disorder continuous or categorical? A taxometric analysis. *Psychological Medicine*, *36*, 1571–1581.

Marcus, D. K., Norris, A. L., & Coccaro, E. F. (2012). The latent structure of attention deficit/hyperactivity disorder in an adult sample. *Journal of Psychiatric Research*, *46*, 782–789.

Markon, K. E., Chmielewski, M., & Miller, C. J. (2011). The reliability and validity of discrete and continuous measures of psychopathology: A quantitative review. *Psychological Bulletin*, *137*, 856–879.

Martel, M. M., Von Eye, A., & Nigg, J. T. (2010). Revisiting the latent structure of ADHD: Is there a "g" factor? *Journal of Child Psychology and Psychiatry*, *51*, 905–914.

Matarazzo, J. D. (1983). The reliability of psychiatric and psychological diagnosis. *Clinical Psychology Review*, *3*, 103–145.

Mayes, R., & Horwitz, A. V. (2005). DSM-III and the revolution in the classification of mental illness. *Journal of the History of the Behavioral Sciences*, *41*, 249–267.

Mayr, E. (1982). *The growth of biological thought: Diversity, evolution, and inheritance*. Cambridge, MA: Belknap Press.

McCann, J. T., Shindler, K. L., & Hammond, T. R. (2003). The science and pseudoscience of expert testimony. In S. O. Lilienfeld, J. M. Lohr, & S. J. Lynn (Eds.), *Science and pseudoscience in contemporary clinical psychology* (pp. 77–108). New York, NY: Guilford Press.

McCrae, R. R., & Costa, P. T. (1995). Trait explanations in personality psychology. *European Journal of Personality*, *9*, 231–252.

McHugh, P. R., & Slavney, P. R. (1998). *The perspectives of psychiatry* (2nd ed.). Baltimore, MD: Johns Hopkins University Press.

McPartland, J. C., Reichow, B., & Volkmar, F. R. (2012). Sensitivity and specificity of proposed DSM-5 diagnostic criteria for autism spectrum disorder. *Journal of the American Academy of Child & Adolescent Psychiatry*, *51*, 368–383.

Meehl, P. E. (1973). Why I do not attend case conferences. In P. E. Meehl (Ed.), *Psychodiagnosis: Selected papers* (pp. 225–302). Minneapolis: University of Minnesota Press.

Meehl, P. E. (1977). Specific etiology and other forms of strong influence: Some quantitative meanings. *Journal of Medicine and Philosophy*, *2*, 33–53.

Meehl, P. E. (1986). Diagnostic taxa as open concepts: Metatheoretical and statistical questions about reliability and construct validity in the grand strategy of nosological revision. In T. Millon & G. L. Klerman (Eds.), *Contemporary directions in psychopathology: Toward the DSM-IV* (pp. 215–231). New York, NY: Guilford Press.

Meehl, P. E. (1990). Schizotaxia as an open concept. In A. I. Rabin, R. Zucker, R. Emmons, & S. Frank (Eds.), *Studying persons and lives* (pp. 248–303). New York, NY: Springer.

Meehl, P. E., & Golden, R. (1982). Taxometric methods. In P. C. Kendall & J. N. Butcher (Eds.), *Handbook of research methods in clinical psychology* (pp. 127–181). New York, NY: Wiley.

Messick, S. (1995). Validity of psychological assessment: Validation of inferences from persons' responses and performances as scientific inquiry into score meaning. *American Psychologist*, *50*, 741–749.

Meyer, G. J. (1997). Assessing reliability: Critical corrections for a critical examination of the Rorschach Comprehensive System. *Psychological Assessment*, *9*, 480–489.

Michels, R. (1984). A debate on DSM-III: First rebuttal. *American Journal of Psychiatry*, *141*, 548–553.

Michels, R., Siebel, U., Freyberger, H. J., Stieglitz, R. D., Schaub, R. T., & Dilling, H. (1996). The multiaxial system of ICD-10: Evaluation of a preliminary draft in a multicentric field trial. *Psychopathology*, *29*, 347–356.

Milich, R., McAninich, C. B., & Harris, M. J. (1992). Effects of stigmatizing information on children's peer relations: Believing is seeing. *School Psychology Review*, *21*, 399–408.

Miller, J. D., Reynolds, S. K., & Pilkonis, P. A. (2004). The validity of the five-factor model prototypes for personality disorders in two clinical samples. *Psychological Assessment, 16*, 310–322.

Millon, T. (1975). Reflections on Rosenhan's "On being sane in insane places." *Journal of Abnormal Psychology, 84*, 456–461.

Morey, L. C. (1991). Classification of mental disorders as a collection of hypothetical constructs. *Journal of Abnormal Psychology, 100*, 289–293.

Morris, S. E., & Cuthbert, B. N. (2012). Research Domain Criteria: Cognitive systems, neural circuits, and dimensions of behavior. *Dialogues in Clinical Neuroscience, 14*, 29–37.

Morrison, J. (1997). *When psychological problems mask medical disorders: A guide for psychotherapists.* New York, NY: Guilford Press.

Neese, R., & Williams, G. (1994). *Why we get sick.* New York, NY: Vintage.

Olvet, D. M., & Hajcak, G. (2008). The error-related negativity (ERN) and psychopathology: Toward an endophenotype. *Clinical Psychology Review, 28*, 1343–1354.

Patrick, C. J., Bernat, E., Malone, S. M., Iacono, W. G., Krueger, R. F., & McGue, M. K. (2006). P300 amplitude as an indicator of externalizing in adolescent males. *Psychophysiology, 43*, 84–92.

Patrick, C. J., Fowles, D. C., & Krueger, R. F. (2009). Triarchic conceptualization of psychopathy: Developmental origins of disinhibition, boldness, and meanness. *Development and Psychopathology, 21*(3), 913–938.

Patrick, C. J., & Hajcak, G. (2016). RDoC: Translating promise into progress. *Psychophysiology, 53*, 415–424.

Pelham, W. E., & Bender, M. E. (1982). Peer relationships in hyperactive children: Description and treatment. In K. D. Gadow & I. Bialer (Eds.), *Advances in learning and behavioral disabilities* (Vol. 1, pp. 365–436). Greenwich, CT: JAI Press.

Pincus, H. A., Tew, J. D., & First, M. B. (2004). Psychiatric comorbidity: Is more less? *World Psychiatry, 3*, 18–23.

Pouissant, A. F. (2002). Is extreme racism a mental illness? Point-counterpoint. *Western Journal of Medicine, 176*, 4.

Reynolds, S. K., & Clark, L. A. (2001). Predicting personality disorder dimensions from domains and facets of the five-factor model. *Journal of Personality, 69*, 199–222.

Robins, E., & Guze, S. B. (1970). Establishment of diagnostic validity in psychiatric illness: Its application to schizophrenia. *American Journal of Psychiatry, 126*, 983–987.

Rosch, E. R. (1973). Natural categories. *Cognitive Psychology, 4*, 328–350.

Rosch, E. R., & Mervis, C. B. (1975). Family resemblances: Studies in the internal structure of categories. *Cognitive Psychology, 7*, 573–605.

Rosenhan, D. L. (1973). On being sane in insane places. *Science, 179*, 250–258.

Rosenhan, D. L., & Seligman, M. E. (1995). *Abnormal psychology.* New York, NY: W. W. Norton.

Ross, C., & Pam, A. (1996). *Pseudoscience in biological psychiatry: Blaming the body.* New York, NY: Wiley.

Ruscio, J. (2004). Diagnoses and the behaviors they denote: A critical evaluation of the labeling theory of mental illness. *Scientific Review of Mental Health Practice, 3*(1), 5–22.

Sanislow, C. A., Pine, D. S., Quinn, K. J., Kozak, M. J., Garvey, M. A., Heinssen, R. K., … Cuthbert, B. N. (2010). Developing constructs for psychopathology research: Research Domain Criteria. *Journal of Abnormal Psychology, 119*, 631–639.

Sarbin, T. R. (1969). On the distinction between social roles and social types, with special reference to the hippie. *American Journal of Psychiatry, 125*, 1024–1031.

Scadding, J. G. (1996). Essentialism and nominalism in medicine: Logic of diagnosis in disease terminology. *Lancet, 348*, 594–596.

Schaler, J. A. (Ed.). (2004). *Szasz under fire: The psychiatric abolitionist faces his critics.* Chicago, IL: Open Court.

Scheff, T. (Ed.). (1975). *Labeling madness.* Englewood Cliffs, NJ: Prentice Hall.

Schildkrout, B. (2011). *Unmasking psychological symptoms: How therapists can learn to recognize the psychological presentation of medical disorders.* Hoboken, NJ: Wiley.

Schmidt, F. L., Le, H., & Ilies, R. (2003). Beyond alpha: An empirical examination of the effects of different sources of measurement error on reliability estimates for measures of individual differences constructs. *Psychological Methods, 8*, 206–224.

Seitz, S., & Geske, D. (1976). Mothers' and graduate trainees' judgments of children: Some effects of labeling. *American Journal of Mental Deficiency, 81*, 362–370.

Selkoe, D. J. (1992). Aging brain, aging mind. *Scientific American, 267*, 134–142.

Sheets, E., & Craighead, W. E. (2007). Toward an empirically based classification of personality pathology. *Clinical Psychology: Science and Practice, 14*, 77–93.

Sijtsma, K. (2009). On the use, the misuse, and the very limited usefulness of Cronbach's alpha. *Psychometrika, 74*, 107–120.

Skeem, J. L., & Cooke, D. J. (2010). One measure does not a construct make: Directions toward reinvigorating psychopathy research—reply to Hare and Neumann (2010). *Psychological Assessment, 22*, 455–459.

Skeem, J. L., Polaschek, D. L., Patrick, C. J., & Lilienfeld, S. O. (2011). Psychopathic personality bridging the gap between scientific evidence and public policy. *Psychological Science in the Public Interest, 12*, 95–162.

Skinner, H. A. (1981). Toward the integration of classification theory and methods. *Journal of Abnormal Psychology, 90*, 68–87.

Skinner, H. A. (1986). Construct validation approach to psychiatric classification. In T. Millon & G. L. Klerman (Eds.), *Contemporary directions in psychopathology: Toward the* DSM-IV (pp. 307–330). New York, NY: Guilford Press.

Skodol, A. E., Oldham, J. M., Bender, D. S., Dyck, I. R., Stout, R. L., Morey, L. C., ... Gunderson, J. C. (2005). Dimensional representations of DSM-IV personality disorders: Relationships to functional impairment. *American Journal of Psychiatry, 162*(10), 1919–1925.

Slade, T., & Andrews, G. (2005). Latent structure of depression in a community sample: A taxometric analysis. *Psychological Medicine, 35*, 489–497.

Slater, L. (2004). *Opening Skinner's box: Great psychological experiments of the 20th century.* New York, NY: W. W. Norton.

Smith, S. F., Winiarski, D. A., & Lilienfeld, S. O. (2015). Pop psychology diagnoses. In R. L. Cautin & S. O. Lilienfeld (Eds.), *Encyclopedia of clinical psychology.* Chichester, England: Wiley.

Sommers, C. H., & Satel, S. (2005). *One nation under therapy: How the helping culture is eroding self-reliance.* New York, NY: St. Martin's.

Spitzer, R. L. (1975). On pseudoscience, logic in remission, and psychiatric diagnosis: A critique of Rosenhan's "On being sane in insane places." *Journal of Abnormal Psychology, 84*, 442–452.

Spitzer, R. L., Endicott, J., & Robins, E. (1978). Research Diagnostic Criteria: Rationale and reliability. *Archives of General Psychiatry, 35*(6), 773–782.

Spitzer, R. L., Forman, J.B.W., & Nee, J. (1979). DSM-III field trials. *American Journal of Psychiatry, 136*, 815–820.

Spitzer, R. L., Lilienfeld, S. O., & Miller, M. B. (2005). Rosenhan revisited: The scientific credibility of Lauren Slater's pseudopatient diagnosis study. *Journal of Nervous and Mental Disease, 193*, 734–739.

Stuart, S., Pfohl, B., Battaglia, M., Bellodi, L., Grove, W., & Cadoret, R. (1998). The cooccurrence of DSM-III-R personality disorders. *Journal of Personality Disorders, 12*, 302–315.

Subotnik, K. L., Nuechterlein, K. H., Ventura, J., Gitlin, M. J., Marder, S., Mintz, J., ... Singh, I. R. (2011). Risperidone nonadherence and return of positive symptoms in the early course of schizophrenia. *American Journal of Psychiatry, 168*(3), 286–292.

Sullivan, P. F., & Kendler, K. S. (1998). The genetic epidemiology of smoking. *Nicotine and Tobacco Research, 1*, S51–S57.

Sutton, E. H. (1980). *An introduction to human genetics.* Philadelphia, PA: Saunders College.

Szasz, T. (1960). The myth of mental illness. *American Psychologist, 15*, 113–118.

Thomas, K. M., Yalch, M. M., Krueger, R. F., Wright, A.G.C., Markon, K. E., & Hopwood, C. J. (2012). The convergent structure of DSM-5 personality trait facets and five-factor model trait domains. *Assessment.* Advance online publication. doi: 10.1177/1073191112457589

Trull, T. J., & Durrett, C. A. (2005). Categorical and dimensional models of personality disorder. *Annual Review of Clinical Psychology, 1*, 355–380.

Ullrich, S., Borkenau, P., & Marneros, A. (2001). Personality disorders in offenders: Categorical versus dimensional approaches. *Journal of Personality Disorders, 15*, 442–449.

Vaillant, G. E. (1984). The disadvantages of DSM-III outweigh its advantages. *American Journal of Psychiatry, 14*, 542–545.

van Praag, H. M. (2000). Nosologomania: A disorder of psychiatry. *World of Biological Psychiatry, 1*, 151–158.

Wakefield, J. C. (1992). The concept of mental disorder: On the boundary between biological facts and social values. *American Psychologist, 47*, 373–388.

Wakefield, J. C. (1998). The DSM's theory-neutral nosology is scientifically progressive: Response to

Follette and Houts. *Journal of Consulting and Clinical Psychology, 66*, 846–852.

Wakefield, J. C. (1999). Evolutionary versus prototype analyses of the concept of disorder. *Journal of Abnormal Psychology, 108*, 374–399.

Wakefield, J. C. (2001). The myth of DSM's invention of new categories of disorder: Houts's diagnostic discontinuity thesis disconfirmed. *Behaviour Research and Therapy, 39*, 575–624.

Waldman, I. D. (2005). Statistical approaches to complex phenotypes: Evaluating neuropsychological endophenotypes of attention-deficit/hyperactivity disorder. *Biological Psychiatry, 57*, 1347–1356.

Waldman, I. D., Lilienfeld, S. O., & Lahey, B. B. (1995). Toward construct validity in the childhood disruptive behavior disorders: Classification and diagnosis in DSM-IV and beyond. In T. H. Ollendick & R. J. Prinz (Eds.), *Advances in clinical child psychology* (Vol. 17, pp. 323–363). New York, NY: Plenum Press.

Widiger, T. A. (1997). The construct of mental disorder. *Clinical Psychology: Science and Practice, 4*, 262–266.

Widiger, T. A. (2007). Alternatives to DSM-IV: Axis II. In W. O'Donohue, K. A. Fowler, & S. O. Lilienfeld (Eds.), *Personality disorders: Toward the DSM-V* (pp. 21–40). Thousand Oaks, CA: Sage.

Widiger, T. A., & Clark, L. A. (2000). Toward DSM-V and the classification of psychopathology. *Psychological Bulletin, 126*, 946–963.

Widiger, T. A., Frances, A. J., Pincus, H. A., Ross, R., First, M. B., & Davis, W. W. (Eds.). (1998). DSM-IV *sourcebook* (Vol. 4). Washington, DC: American Psychiatric Press.

Widiger, T. A., Frances, A. J., Spitzer, R. L., & Williams, J.B.W. (1991). The DSM-III-R personality disorders: An overview. *American Journal of Psychiatry, 145*, 786–795.

Widiger, T. A., & Rogers, J. H. (1989). Prevalence and comorbidity of personality disorders. *Psychiatric Annals, 19*, 132–136.

Widiger, T. A., & Trull, T. (1985). The empty debate over the existence of mental illness: Comments on Gorenstein. *American Psychologist, 40*, 468–470.

World Health Organization. (1992). Mental and behavioural disorders. In *International statistical classification of diseases and related health problems* (chap. V). Geneva, Switzerland: Author.

Zimmerman, M. (1994). Diagnosing personality disorders. *Archives of General Psychiatry, 51*, 225–245.

Zimmerman, M., & Mattia, J. I. (2000). Principal and additional *DSM-IV* disorders for which outpatients seek treatment. *Psychiatric Services, 51*, 1299–1304.

Zuckerman, M. (1994). *Behavioral expressions and biosocial bases of sensation seeking.* New York, NY: Cambridge University Press.

Chapter 2

Social Anxiety Disorder

Deborah Roth Ledley, Brigette A. Erwin, Amanda S. Morrison, and Richard G. Heimberg

In this chapter, we review the most current knowledge on the nature and treatment of social anxiety disorder (SAD). We begin by briefly describing the symptoms of SAD and its prevalence. We then outline several factors that might contribute to both the development and the maintenance of this common and highly impairing disorder. Finally, assessment and treatment strategies are reviewed.

Description of the Disorder: Symptoms and Diagnostic Criteria

Individuals with *social anxiety disorder* (SAD) show "marked fear or anxiety about one or more social situations in which the individual is exposed to possible scrutiny by others" (*DSM-5*; American Psychiatric Association [APA], 2013, p. 202, Criterion A). The *DSM-5* further specifies that the individual with social anxiety "fears that he or she will act in a way or show anxiety symptoms that will be negatively evaluated (i.e., will be humiliating or embarrassing; will lead to rejection or offend others)" (Criterion B, p. 202). This newly written criterion emphasizes the importance of fear of negative evaluation in social anxiety, which was not explicitly included in previous versions of the *DSM*.

The *DSM-5* diagnostic criteria also state that social situations almost always provoke fear or anxiety (Criterion C) and that these situations are avoided or endured with great distress (Criterion D). Interestingly, about 50% of adults with SAD experience panic attacks in anticipation of or when exposed to social or performance situations, and the presence of panic attacks may be listed as a diagnostic specifier (APA, 2013). Epidemiological data suggest that individuals with SAD who experience situational panic attacks exhibit greater fear and avoidance of social situations and more impairment than individuals who do not have this experience (Potter et al., 2014). Although children do not typically describe experiencing panic attacks in social situations, their anxiety tends to manifest as crying, tantrums, freezing, clinging, shrinking, or failing to speak in social situations.

The *DSM-5* also states that the fear or anxiety is out of proportion to the actual threat posed by the social situation and to the sociocultural context (Criterion E). In earlier versions of the *DSM*, there was a requirement that individuals 18 years of age and over recognize their anxiety as excessive or unreasonable. This requirement has been eliminated in the *DSM-5*, with that judgment now made by the clinician, taking into account the fact that individuals with social anxiety often exhibit poor insight. For example, a high school student with social anxiety might avoid the school cafeteria because she is convinced that everyone is looking at her as she selects her lunch and finds a seat. Without treatment, she might be unable to recognize that most of her fellow students are simply focusing on eating their own lunches and speaking to their friends.

To receive a diagnosis of SAD, the fear or anxiety must have lasted for 6 months or more (Criterion F), to rule out transient social anxiety that might occur at times of life transition (e.g., moving to a new city, starting college) or as a normal part of child development. The fear, anxiety, or avoidance must cause significant impairment in functioning (Criterion G). As with other diagnostic criteria, SAD cannot be diagnosed if the symptoms are better explained by use of a substance (Criterion H), the symptoms of another mental disorder (Criterion I), or a medical condition (Criterion J). However, if the anxiety symptoms are related to a medical condition, a diagnosis of SAD may be given if they are clearly excessive, as judged by comparison to other persons with the medical condition.

The generalized subtype of social anxiety disorder, which was defined by a fear of most social situations, has been removed from the *DSM-5*, largely because most individuals with SAD fear numerous social situations. The *DSM-5* now lists a different specifier in the diagnostic criteria for SAD—performance only—assigned to individuals whose anxiety is limited to public speaking or performing in public (e.g., playing a musical instrument). This specifier will be much less frequently used, and its utility remains to be evaluated.

It is important to note that "social anxiety disorder" has become the preferred name for the disorder in the *DSM-5*, rather than "social phobia," the preferred name in earlier editions of the *DSM*. This choice was made because experts in the field were concerned that the term *social phobia* did not adequately capture the impairing nature of this disorder (see Heimberg, Hofmann, et al., 2014). SAD is associated with significant impairment in social, educational, and occupational functioning (Acarturk, de Graaf, van Straten, ten Have, & Cuijpers, 2008), and brings with it a substantial economic and societal burden (Acarturk et al., 2009; Patel, Knapp, Henderson, & Baldwin, 2002). Individuals with SAD are also less likely to be married than individuals without SAD, have fewer friends, and are less likely to be involved in clubs and activities (see Alden, Regambal, & Plasencia, 2014, for a review).

Alden and Taylor (2004) introduced the concept of a "self-perpetuating interpersonal cycle" (p. 860) that describes the interpersonal difficulties experienced by individuals with SAD. They posit that socially anxious people go into social interactions expecting negative evaluation, and therefore behave in ways that "'pull' on other people … to evoke responses that maintain … social assumptions" (p. 858). There are numerous ways in which socially anxious individuals can exert this pull on others. First, individuals with SAD rely on safety behaviors, which are typically defined as actions perceived by an individual as necessary to prevent the occurrence of a feared outcome (Salkovskis, 1991; Wells et al., 1995; see Piccirillo, Dryman, & Heimberg, in press, for a review). For example, if an individual with SAD fears that his voice will shake when he speaks, he might speak very softly or not speak at all. Although these safety behaviors are intended to prevent feared outcomes (in this example, being judged badly for the tone of his voice), they often backfire, increasing the likelihood that he will sound odd and that, more broadly, people will not want to talk to him again. Second, individuals with SAD may distance themselves emotionally from others, engaging in less self-disclosure than nonanxious people (e.g., see Alden & Bieling, 1998). When they do engage in self-disclosure, socially anxious individuals tend to have difficulty describing emotional experiences (Turk, Heimberg, Luterek, Mennin, & Fresco, 2005). Furthermore, patients with SAD often describe fearing that if people "really got to know them," they would ultimately reject them. This kind of core belief is likely related to attachment patterns that have their origins in early childhood. Specifically, individuals with SAD tend to exhibit insecure, fearful attachment patterns (Eng, Heimberg, Hart, Schneier, & Liebowitz, 2001; Wenzel, 2002). Not surprisingly, they tend to be more dependent in their relationships than individuals without SAD (Davila & Beck, 2002), and this dependency takes a toll on their significant others (see Zaider, Heimberg, & Iida, 2010).

As noted above, individuals with SAD also exhibit significant impairment in the workplace. They also have lower levels of educational attainment than individuals without the disorder (see Himle et al., 2014) and, following from this, it is not surprising that SAD is also associated with reduced income and higher rates of unemployment (Himle et al., 2014). When people with SAD are employed, their productivity and job performance is rated more poorly than that of people without the disorder. Stein and Kean (2000) reported that 20% of individuals with SAD have turned down a job offer or promotion that was offered to them because of their social fears. Clinically, we often see clients who are underemployed given their training, education, or intelligence (e.g., a lawyer working as a paralegal), or clients who have stepped off their career track completely due to fear of job interviews, making presentations at meetings, or feeling uncomfortable with the day-to-day socializing that occurs in the workplace.

Prevalence and Epidemiological Factors

Findings from the National Comorbidity Survey Replication indicate that SAD is one of the most prevalent psychiatric disorders in the United States, with a lifetime prevalence of 12.1% and a 1-year prevalence of 6.8% (Kessler, Berglund, et al., 2005; Kessler, Chiu, Demler, Merikangas, & Walters, 2005). A recent study by Bandelow and Michaelis (2015) reports similarly high prevalence rates (13.0% lifetime; 8.0% 12-month). However, lower prevalence rates were reported in the National Epidemiologic Survey on Alcohol and Related Conditions (Grant et al., 2005; 5.0% lifetime; 2.8% 12-month) and in the European Study of the Epidemiology of Mental Disorders (ESEMeD) (Alonso, Lépine, & ESEMeD 2000 Scientific Committee, 2007; 2.8% lifetime; 1.6% 12-month). Even with these divergent findings, it is important to note that across all of these studies, anxiety disorders are consistently shown to be the most prevalent psychiatric disorders, with as much as one third of the population affected during their lifetimes (see Bandelow & Michaelis, 2015).

Hofmann, Asnaani, and Hinton (2010) examined cultural differences in prevalence rates of SAD. Although rates similar to those in the United States have been found in South American countries, prevalence rates are far lower in Asian countries, at less than 1% for 1-year prevalence. Interestingly, Asian race/ethnicity is associated with low prevalence in American samples as well. In American samples, being Hispanic or black is also associated with lower risk compared to being non-Hispanic white. Hofmann et al. write that "it remains uncertain to what extent these differences ... reflect genuine differences in psychopathology, or whether they are due to insufficient consideration of cultural aspects of the *DSM* criteria, the assessment instruments, or the influence of features associated with race and culture" (p. 1118).

With respect to differences in psychopathology, consider the example of *taijin kyofusho* (TKS). This variant of SAD is particularly prevalent in Japanese and Korean cultures, although it does occur in the United States as well (Choy, Schneier, Heimberg, Oh, & Liebowitz, 2008). In contrast to the common presentation of SAD, in which individuals typically fear embarrassing themselves, those with TKS worry about embarrassing another person. For example, an individual with TKS might be so concerned about embarrassing others with his body odor that he avoids most social situations. If we screen for SAD in our typical ways, we might miss this unique but highly impairing variant of the disorder, perhaps explaining why rates of SAD are so low in Asian populations. Now that fear of offending others is explicitly included in the diagnostic criteria for SAD (APA, 2013), it will be interesting to see if the rates of co-occurrence of SAD and TKS will be increased.

The mean age of onset for SAD ranges from 13 to 20 years old (Hazen & Stein, 1995), but many patients recall having struggled all of their lives with shyness and fear of negative evaluation. In epidemiological studies, the disorder has been found to be more common in women than in men (Bandelow & Michaelis, 2015; Magee, Eaton, Wittchen, McGonagle, & Kessler, 1996), with gender differences emerging in adolescence (Ranta, Kaltiala-Heino, Rantanen, Tuomisto, & Marttunen, 2007). Men tend to take longer than women to seek treatment (Wang et al., 2007), but men tend to slightly outnumber women in clinical samples (Chapman, Mannuzza, & Fyer, 1995; Stein, 1997). This discrepancy is frequently explained by reference to cultural norms for social behavior. The cost of not pursuing treatment may be higher for men, who are typically expected to be outgoing and assertive compared with women, for whom it is more acceptable to be shy and reticent (Weinstock, 1999; see also McLean & Anderson, 2009).

SAD is associated with a high degree of Axis I comorbidity. Acarturk et al. (2008), using data from a community-based survey, reported that 66.2% of respondents with SAD also met criteria for an additional psychological disorder. Given the relatively early onset of SAD, it is not surprising that the onset of SAD typically predates the onset of comorbid conditions. This chronology suggests that SAD may be a risk factor for the development of other psychiatric disorders (Magee et al., 1996; Schneier, Johnson, Hornig, Liebowitz, & Weissman, 1992).

SAD most frequently co-occurs with other anxiety disorders, particularly generalized anxiety disorder (see Szafranski, Talkovsky, Farris, & Norton, 2014, for a review). Major depressive disorder is also very common among individuals with SAD (Szafranski et al., 2014). Data from both epidemiological and clinical samples suggest that over one third of individuals currently diagnosed with SAD report having experienced a major depressive episode at some time in their lives. Individuals who have both SAD and depression have an earlier age of onset of their depression, a greater number of depressive episodes, episodes of longer duration, and more suicidal ideation compared to individuals with depression alone (see Dalrymple & Zimmerman, 2011). The co-occurrence of SAD and depression is also associated with greater impairment than either disorder alone (Dalrymple &

Zimmerman, 2011; Erwin, Heimberg, Juster, & Mindlin, 2002). Specifically, these individuals are less likely to marry, attend college, or maintain stable employment.

Studies have also examined whether comorbid depression negatively affects the outcome of treatment for SAD. Some studies suggest that patients with comorbid depression make as much improvement during treatment as patients without depression (Erwin et al., 2002; LeMoult, Rowa, Antony, Chudzick, & McCabe, 2014; Marom, Gilboa-Schechtman, Aderka, Weizman, & Hermesh, 2009), with two studies showing that they did end treatment with more severe social anxiety symptoms, but simply because they began treatment with more severe symptoms (Erwin et al., 2002; LeMoult et al., 2014). Other studies, however, suggest that higher levels of depressive symptoms are associated with poorer outcome and higher rates of attrition (Chambless, Tran, & Glass, 1997; Ledley et al., 2005; Tillfors, Furmark, Carlbring, & Andersson, 2015). This pattern of depression interfering with SAD treatment outcome has recently been observed in two large studies (with around 1,000 patients each), one in adults (Kelly, Jakubovski, & Bloch, 2015) and one in youth (Hudson et al., 2015). Only one study has examined long-term maintenance of gains in patients with SAD and comorbid depression (Marom et al., 2009). Although patients with comorbid depression did just as well as patients without depression during acute treatment for SAD, depression was associated with poorer maintenance of gains 1 year later.

It is interesting to examine what happens to depressive symptoms when social anxiety is the focus of treatment. Addressing this issue is important for designing treatments for comorbid groups because it is unclear whether depression remits with successful treatment of SAD or whether depression-specific interventions need to be added to treatments for this comorbid group. Erwin et al. (2002) demonstrated that scores on a measure of depression were substantially reduced after cognitive-behavioral group therapy for SAD. However, this question was examined in greater depth in a study by Moscovitch, Hofmann, Suvak, and In-Albon (2005). Their data showed that improvement in depression (which was not a target of treatment) was fully mediated by improvement in social anxiety. However, improvement in social anxiety was not mediated by improvement in depression. In other words, patients' moods improved because their social anxiety improved. It is important to point out that the sample of patients in this study who had both clinically significant SAD and depression was quite small. Furthermore, studies have not yet examined the efficacy of treatments designed specifically for patients with SAD and comorbid depression. Such treatments might be necessary and beneficial for a subset of comorbid patients who have particularly severe symptoms.

SAD is also frequently comorbid with substance use disorders, with most research attention paid to alcohol use disorders. Approximately 48% of individuals with a lifetime diagnosis of SAD also meet criteria for a lifetime diagnosis of alcohol use disorder (Grant et al., 2005). The 12-month prevalence of alcohol use disorder among individuals with SAD is 13.1% (Grant et al., 2005), compared to only 8.5% in the general population (Grant et al., 2004). As with depression, individuals with both SAD and an alcohol use disorder are more impaired than individuals with a sole diagnosis of SAD, at least in part because of high rates of other comorbidities that occur in this group. Schneier et al. (2010) reported that individuals with comorbid SAD and alcohol dependence had a mean of 4.6 additional disorders, almost twice the number seen in individuals with either SAD or alcohol dependence.

Onset of SAD typically predates onset of alcohol dependence (Black et al., 2015), suggesting that SAD is a risk factor for alcohol problems. One study using a nonclinical sample suggests that fear of scrutiny (i.e., fear of being observed by others) is the unique aspect of social anxiety that places people at risk for the later development of alcohol use disorders (Buckner & Schmidt, 2009). Some studies have also looked at the function of alcohol use in socially anxious individuals. One study found that alcohol use prior to a speech reduced anxiety and blushing during the speech (Stevens, Cludius, Bantin, Hermann, & Gerlach, 2014), and another found that drinking was associated with less post-event processing 4 days after a conversation with a member of the opposite sex, but only for socially anxious women (Battista, Pencer, & Stewart, 2014). Although there are few studies that actually administer alcohol prior to or during a socially stressful task, those available point to the reinforcing effects of alcohol use for socially anxious individuals.

Individuals with comorbid SAD and alcohol dependence report very low rates of treatment seeking (Schneier et al., 2010), and research on how to best treat this group has been sparse. Most studies of treatment for SAD exclude patients with substance use problems or make no mention of current substance use at all. There have been some recent efforts to develop and test treatments for this complex and impaired group. Kushner and colleagues (2013) studied individuals with SAD who were in a residential alcohol treatment program. Treatment with cognitive-behavioral therapy (CBT) designed to lower social anxiety and to explore and weaken the links between social anxiety and motivation to drink was associated with reduced drinking 4 months posttreatment (as compared to a progressive muscle relaxation control), but CBT showed only a slight advantage over the control treatment for anxiety reduction. Courbasson and Nishikawa (2010) conducted a pilot study looking at the effect of cognitive-behavioral group therapy modified to address both social anxiety and substance use. They reported a significant decrease in social anxiety, but no change in alcohol expectancies.

We have previously proposed combining motivational enhancement therapy for alcohol use disorder and CBT for SAD and have outlined the treatment's efficacy in a case report (Buckner, Ledley, Heimberg, & Schmidt, 2008). A trial is currently ongoing, called the Combined Alcohol Social Phobia (CASP) Trial Protocol (Baillie et al., 2013, see also Stapinski et al., 2015), comparing a combined CBT and motivational interviewing protocol to treatment as usual for alcohol use disorders. The findings from this large, randomized trial will be an important contribution to this very inconclusive body of research.

Researchers have also begun to examine cannabis use in patients with SAD (Buckner, Heimberg, Matthews, & Silgado, 2012; Buckner, Heimberg, & Schmidt, 2011; Buckner, Heimberg, Schneier, et al., 2012; Buckner, Schmidt, et al., 2008). Epidemiological studies show that SAD is more strongly related to cannabis dependence than to cannabis abuse (Buckner, Heimberg, Schneier, et al., 2012), that SAD almost always comes before cannabis use, and that individuals with this comorbidity experience greater impairment than individuals with either disorder alone. Tepe, Dalrymple, and Zimmerman (2012) reported that individuals with comorbid SAD and cannabis use disorders are also more likely to have lifetime diagnoses of posttraumatic stress disorder, specific phobias, and other substance use disorders than individuals with either disorder alone, giving further support to the impairment likely seen in this group. Further research is needed to understand this comorbid combination, as well as how to treat it.

SAD is also highly comorbid with avoidant personality disorder (APD), with a median of 60% of individuals with generalized SAD (as defined by earlier versions of the *DSM*) meeting criteria for APD (Heimberg, 1996). This is not surprising given the considerable overlap in the criteria for these two disorders. *DSM-5* defines APD as "a pervasive pattern of social inhibition, feelings of inadequacy, and hypersensitivity to negative evaluation, beginning by early adulthood, and present in a variety of contexts" (APA, 2013, p. 672). Genetic and family studies suggest that SAD and APD are strongly related (Isomura et al., 2015; Torvik et al., 2016). When researchers have tried to determine what might differentiate these two disorders, nothing terribly clear emerges. It has been proposed that APD might be associated with greater personality dysfunction (Eikenaes, Hummelen, Abrahamsen, Andrea, & Wilberg, 2013) or a greater degree of emotional guardedness (Marques et al., 2012) than SAD. The most parsimonious description of the relationship between SAD and APD, however, may be that they are not different disorders and that APD represents the most severely impaired persons with SAD (Chambless, Fydrich, & Rodebaugh, 2008; Heimberg, Holt, et al., 1993; see Reich, 2014, for a review).

Following from this, individuals with both generalized SAD and APD tend to be more depressed and to have greater functional impairment and reduced quality of life compared to individuals with SAD alone (Cox, Pagura, Stein, & Sareen, 2009; Huppert, Strunk, Ledley, Davidson, & Foa, 2008; Marques et al., 2012), In one study, these differences were no longer evident when severity of social anxiety was controlled (Chambless et al., 2008). With regard to treatment outcome, some studies have found that clients with generalized SAD with and without comorbid APD make similar gains (Brown, Heimberg, & Juster, 1995; Hofmann, Newman, Becker, Taylor, & Roth, 1995; Hope, Herbert, & White, 1995), although others have found comorbid APD to be associated with poorer treatment response (Chambless et al., 1997; Feske, Perry, Chambless, Renneberg, & Goldstein, 1996).

Biological, Psychological, Behavioral, and Environmental and Sociocultural Factors

SAD is caused by multiple biological and psychosocial factors and is associated with both biological and psychological dysfunction. In this section, these etiological factors are reviewed.

BIOLOGICAL FACTORS

Genetics appear to be important in the development of SAD. Family studies have shown higher rates of SAD in the relatives of individuals with the disorder than in the relatives of people without the disorder (see Tillfors, 2004, for a review), and this suggests that SAD is moderately heritable (Stein, Gelernter, & Smoller, 2004). Generalized SAD demonstrates stronger familial aggregation than nongeneralized SAD (Mannuzza et al., 1995; Stein et al., 1998). Twin studies also support a modest role of genetics in the heritability of SAD and social anxiety–related symptoms, including behavioral inhibition and fear of negative evaluation (see Stein & Gelernter, 2014). Both twin studies and genetic linkage studies suggest that SAD and panic disorder might share common susceptibility genes (see Stein & Gelernter, 2014). This is an interesting finding given that these two disorders are frequently comorbid and share many clinical features (as we have already noted, about half of adults with SAD experience panic attacks in response to social or performance situations).

Given the complexity of psychiatric disorders, it is unlikely that a single gene or group of genes that leads to the transmission of a specific anxiety disorder will be identified. Rather, researchers believe that "some underlying behavioral trait (e.g., behavioral inhibition or neuroticism) is thought to be genetically transmitted, contributing to spectrums of psychopathology" (Stein & Stein, 2008, p. 1118). The research is this area is still inconclusive. However, specific genetic variations have been found that are related to neuroticism, introversion/extraversion, behaviorally inhibited temperament, shyness in children, and increased activation of the amygdala and insula on exposure to emotional faces (see Stein & Gelernter, 2014; Stein & Stein, 2008, for reviews), all relevant to the pathology seen in SAD.

With respect to neurobiology, several brain regions have been implicated in SAD. The amygdala, which forms and stores emotional memories, is part of the brain's fear pathway. Individuals with SAD show greater activation of the amygdala in response to threatening faces, with greater magnitude of activation associated with severity of SAD (Phan, Fitzgerald, & Nathan, 2006). A study by Furmark and colleagues (2002) showed that successful treatment of SAD by either CBT or the selective serotonin reuptake inhibitor (SSRI) citalopram was associated with decreased blood flow to the amygdala during a public speaking task.

The insula is the part of the brain associated with interoceptive awareness. Studies have shown increased activity in the insula when individuals with SAD are presented with socially relevant stimuli like negative facial expressions or social transgressions (see Syal & Stein, 2014, for a review). Findings from studies of the fusiform cortex have been complex. This brain region is associated with facial recognition. As reviewed by Syal and Stein (2014), some studies in individuals with SAD have shown increased activation in this area, but others have shown decreased activation when presented with a range of facial stimuli. Interestingly, hypoactivation of this area has also been seen in individuals with Asperger's syndrome (Deeley et al., 2007), a disorder marked by poor social connectedness. Individuals with SAD can, at times, home in on social stimuli in order to gain support for their negative beliefs (e.g., focusing on the one person in the audience who is dozing off during a presentation; see the study by Veljaca & Rapee, 1998). At many other times, individuals with SAD shift their attention away from faces, as we see in the case of averted eye contact (which is also seen in autism spectrum disorder; APA, 2013). These mixed research findings might be capturing the complexities of this disorder.

Finally, recent research has examined the role of the prefrontal cortex, the seat of planning, problem solving, and most relevant to SAD—social behavior and emotion regulation. Studies have shown that the same socially relevant stimuli that lead to activation of the amygdala also lead to activation of the prefrontal cortex (see Syal & Stein, 2014, for a review). This suggests that once fear is activated by the amygdala, individuals with SAD process this information in a different way than individuals without the disorder do. Goldin, Manber-Ball, Werner, Heimberg, and Gross (2009) examined cognitive reappraisals of negative self-beliefs among individuals with SAD and healthy controls.

Although individuals with SAD were able to reappraise their negative self-beliefs, it was a much more effortful task for them than for control individuals, and this difficulty was manifest in relatively delayed recruitment of brain areas related to cognitive control (e.g., the dorsolateral and ventrolateral prefrontal cortex), among others. Treatment of SAD with CBT resulted in earlier recruitment of the prefrontal cortex compared to a wait-list control (Goldin et al., 2013).

For many years, researchers have examined the neurotransmitters that might be implicated in SAD. Serotonin has been implicated, but its role is unclear. In challenge studies, when individuals with SAD are given agents that release or mimic serotonin, they experience an increase in anxiety (e.g., Mathew, Coplan, & Gorman, 2001; Potts, Book, & Davidson, 1996). Nevertheless, the SSRIs, which make available greater levels of serotonin in the synaptic cleft, have been shown in numerous studies to *reduce* anxiety (Stein & Stahl, 2000). One plausible explanation for the inconsistency of this evidence is that increased levels of serotonin may have different short-term versus long-term effects. This conclusion is supported by clinical evidence that when patients begin taking SSRIs, they frequently experience an initial increase in anxiety, followed by improvement in their anxiety symptoms (Stein & Stahl, 2000).

Dopamine may also play a role in SAD, as suggested by a number of lines of evidence. First, the monoamine oxidase inhibitors (which work on both the dopaminergic and serotonin systems) are efficacious in the treatment of SAD (Blanco et al., 2003), whereas the tricyclic antidepressants (which work on the serotonin and norepinephrine systems) are not (Simpson et al., 1998). Second, low dopamine transporter density has been found in individuals with SAD (Tilhonen et al., 1997). Third, higher than expected rates of SAD are seen in individuals with Parkinson's disease. The drugs used to treat Parkinson's disease facilitate dopamine transmission (Stein, Heuser, Juncos, & Uhde, 1990). Finally, low dopamine receptor binding potential in the striatum region of the brain has also been found in individuals with SAD (Schneier et al., 2000). Interestingly, this same deficit has been found in animals with subordinate social status, which have been used as models for human SAD (see Schneier et al., 2000).

More recently, researchers have turned their attention to the role of oxytocin. Oxytocin is a neuropeptide that is associated with social approach behavior and bonding. Research suggests that impairments in the oxytocin system might play a role in SAD, as well as other disorders characterized by deficits in the formation of social bonds (including autism spectrum disorder and postpartum depression; see Heinrichs, Chen, & Domes, 2012, for a review). It is also possible that oxytocin could serve as a novel treatment or adjunct to more commonly used treatments for SAD (e.g., Guastella, Howard, Dadds, Mitchell, & Carson, 2009; Labuschagne et al., 2010).

PSYCHOLOGICAL FACTORS: COGNITIVE-BEHAVIORAL MODELS OF THE MAINTENANCE OF SAD

Several cognitive-behavioral models have been posited to explain the self-sustaining nature of SAD. According to these models, beliefs that social situations are inherently dangerous and that people are inherently critical, along with behavioral avoidance and physiological symptoms, are the crucial structures that maintain social anxiety. Several models have been put forth (e.g., Alden & Taylor, 2010; Beck & Emery, 1985; Clark

& Wells, 1995; Hofmann, 2007; Kimbrel, 2008; Leary & Jongman-Sereno, 2014; Moscovitch, 2009; Rapee & Heimberg, 1997; Stopa, 2009). Many of these models are summarized and compared by Wong, Gordon, and Heimberg (2014). The model proposed by Rapee and Heimberg (1997), updated to incorporate subsequent research (Heimberg, Brozovich, & Rapee, 2014), will be the current focus.

The development and maintenance of social anxiety is accounted for by both fear of evaluation and negative imagery of the self and others. The core feature of social anxiety disorder was traditionally thought to be fear of negative evaluation by others. However, Weeks and colleagues (2008; see Weeks & Howell, 2014, for a review) have recently demonstrated that the core feature of social anxiety disorder is more accurately described as fear of any evaluation, either negative or positive. Fear of evaluation develops out of beliefs that social and performance situations are dangerous and that other people are critical.

Rapee and Heimberg (1997) proposed that, upon entering a social or performance situation, persons with SAD allocate their attention first to the audience, bringing to such situations certain cognitive biases resulting in the prediction that they will fall short of the perceived standards of the audience. For example, persons with social anxiety are more likely than those low in social anxiety to report that most people are inherently critical of others, such that they will be judged negatively (Leary, Kowalski, & Campbell, 1988). In addition, persons with SAD formulate a mental representation of the self as seen by others, engaging in negative self-imagery such that their self-image is from this presumed critical observer's perspective (Hackman, Surawy, & Clark, 1998). These findings are consistent with the theory that persons with social anxiety disorder view social interactions as inherently competitive (Trower & Gilbert, 1989).

Information extracted from the individuals' initial impressions of the audience's reaction are combined with information from past similar situations and internal (e.g., heart palpitations) and external cues to make an assessment of how the audience is likely to view them. That is, persons with SAD constantly monitor their behavior and the behavior of others to determine whether there is any potential for evaluation. Similarly, when persons with SAD perform well, they are likely to avoid similar subsequent situations since they believe that they will have to meet similar or even increasingly positive expectations. Consistent with evolutionary theories of the etiology of social anxiety disorder (Gilbert, 2014; Gilboa-Schechtman, Shachar, & Helpman, 2014), persons with social anxiety disorder are also hypothesized to both avoid drawing attention to themselves and to work to maintain low social status, so that they can avoid either losing or having to engage in conflict in order to defend higher social status, consistent with the notion of fear of positive evaluation.

Ironically, the allocation of attentional resources to multiple factors (i.e., monitoring the environment for evidence of evaluation, monitoring performance for evidence of inadequacy, attending to thoughts about being evaluated), in addition to attending to the social or performance task at hand, may increase the probability of a poor performance. For persons with SAD, evidence confirming their poor performance will be weighted more heavily than evidence to the contrary. For example, sweating, losing one's train of thought, or a brief response given by a conversation partner will be interpreted as confirmatory evidence of negative evaluation. Such perceived evaluation is likely projected to future catastrophic outcomes such as social rejection, being professionally discredited, or extreme loneliness.

Thoughts such as these provide the content for post-event processing (PEP; Brozovich & Heimberg, 2008; Clark & Wells, 1995), the biased, distorted, and ruminative cognitive process that contributes consistently to the maintenance of SAD and that links one occurrence of a feared social situation to the next.

Another prominent cognitive-behavioral model of social anxiety disorder put forth by Clark and Wells (1995) differs from the Rapee and Heimberg model in several important ways (as reviewed by Schultz & Heimberg, 2008). First, Clark and Wells posit that the attention of the person with social anxiety disorder is largely focused on internal symptoms of anxiety, which are then used to support the belief that others are indeed evaluating them negatively. Rapee and Heimberg (1997) posit a similar internal focus of attention but further assert that the attention of the person with social anxiety disorder is split between this internal focus and an external search for indicators of evaluation. A second difference between these two theoretical models is that Clark and Wells suggest that subtle avoidance behaviors, such as conversing but remaining passive in the conversation, play a central role in the maintenance of social anxiety disorder. Rapee and Heimberg maintain that all unhelpful anxiety management strategies, ranging from subtle to complete avoidance, all contribute to the maintenance of the disorder.

PSYCHOLOGICAL FACTORS: IMPAIRMENTS IN INFORMATION PROCESSING

Three kinds of bias in information processing have been studied in individuals with SAD: biases of attention, biases in judgment and interpretation, and biases of memory and imagery.

Attentional Bias

Attentional bias refers to the idea that people attend preferentially to information in the environment that they find particularly relevant. For example, when engaged in public speaking, a socially anxious person tends to notice the one bored-looking person in the audience rather than the 99 others who might appear more interested. Two types of attentional bias have been considered in the context of anxiety, namely, orienting biases toward threat (or hypervigilance for detecting threat) and difficulties disengaging attention from threat (or difficulty shifting attention away from threat once attention has been captured). Either way, it is hypothesized that maintaining attention on social threat–relevant information to the exclusion of more neutral or positive social information makes the person more prone to social anxiety.

Research examining attentional bias has made use of a number of experimental methodologies, the foremost of which have included the emotional Stroop and dot-probe paradigms. In the emotional Stroop task, participants are shown socially threatening and neutral words printed in various colors and asked to respond by naming the color as quickly as possible, rather than reading the word. Slowed response suggests that the content of the word has captured participants' attention, making it more difficult to quickly report the color. In the dot-probe paradigm, participants are shown two stimuli (e.g., words or faces), one neutral and one emotionally valenced. These stimuli are presented briefly, followed by a dot or other probe stimulus appearing in place of one of the stimuli. If participants respond more quickly to the probe displayed in the same location as the emotionally valenced stimulus, compared to their response when the probe is displayed in the location of the neutral stimulus, they may be attending preferentially to that stimulus instead of looking away from it or focusing on the neutral stimulus.

Although emotional Stroop studies have consistently shown slowed color naming of social threat–related information among people with SAD (e.g., Mattia, Heimberg, & Hope, 1993), researchers have noted several shortcomings of the task. For example, slowed color naming of social threat words could indicate biased attention or cognitive avoidance (de Ruiter & Brosschot, 1994). Likewise, findings from studies using the dot-probe task have been criticized in recent years. Early studies using the dot-probe task supported attentional bias toward threat, as individuals with SAD were faster than nonclinical control participants to identify the probe when it appeared in the same location as the threat stimulus compared to when it appeared in the same location as the neutral stimulus (e.g., Asmundson & Stein, 1994; for a meta-analysis, see Bar-Haim, Lamy, Pergamin, Bakermans-Kranenburg, & van IJzendoorn, 2007). More recently, however, researchers have noted a number of reports of biased attention *away* from threat (i.e., faster responses to probes following the neutral relative to social threat stimulus; see Bögels & Mansell, 2004) or null results (e.g., Heeren, Mogoaşe, McNally, Schmitz, & Philippot, 2015) in those with SAD. Indeed, a recent review of the literature concluded that findings of an attentional bias toward threat in those with SAD are relatively uncommon (Van Bockstaele et al., 2014). Finally, a number of studies have criticized the use of the dot-probe task, given its poor psychometric properties (e.g., Schmukle, 2005).

Before we discuss recent advances in this research area, it is interesting to consider whether attentional bias has a causal effect on anxiety. In other words, if we can train people to attend to neutral rather than threat information, will this help to alleviate their anxiety? Early studies of such cognitive bias modification of attention (CBM-A) procedures were supportive of this theory (i.e., Amir, Weber, Beard, Bomyea, & Taylor, 2008; Amir et al., 2009; Heeren, Peschard, & Philippot, 2012; Schmidt, Richey, Buckner, & Timpano, 2009). More recently, studies have failed to replicate these findings, and although a recent meta-analysis indicated a small but significant effect of CBM-A compared to control training procedures on posttreatment social anxiety, this effect had disappeared at the 4-month follow-up (Heeren, Mogoaşe, Philippot, & McNally, 2015).

In response to these complex findings, investigators have turned to fine-tuning conceptualizations and assessments of attentional bias. One way they have done this is by situating the finding of attentional bias toward threat within a broader literature that has documented, with psychometrically sound tasks, an association between heightened anxiety and difficulties with the effortful or deliberate control of attention (e.g., Derryberry & Reed, 2002; for a review, see Eysenck, Derakshan, Santos, & Calvo, 2007). Anxious individuals are thought to have difficulty inhibiting or shifting attention away from any salient, task-irrelevant stimulus, including stimuli that are neutral in valence. Social threat represents just one, particularly salient, type of stimulus. Indeed, several studies in nonclinical samples of socially anxious individuals indicate difficulties with the executive control of attention (Moriya & Sugiura, 2012; Moriya & Tanno, 2008; Morrison & Heimberg, 2013), which supports the notion that discrepant findings in the attentional bias literature may be due largely to unreliability of measures.

In a different vein, researchers have begun to consider that the degree and type of threat-related attentional bias may vary considerably between and within people with SAD. Price, Tone, and Anderson (2011) found that individuals with SAD who exhibited a general pretreatment attentional bias *away* from threat fared worse in CBT than those who exhibited a general pretreatment bias *toward* threat (the purported "bad" variant of attentional bias). This suggests that attentional bias is not uniform across individuals with SAD. It also supports the finding that traditional CBM-A, which trains attention away from threat, may be effective only for those with SAD who exhibit a bias toward threat (Kuckertz et al., 2014). Attentional bias may also vary within the same person over time. Although not yet tested in SAD, attentional bias in individuals with spider phobia has been found to be dynamic rather than static during the course of a dot-probe task, with the most harmful type of bias being one with drastic fluctuations in attentional bias toward *and* away from threat (Zvielli, Bernstein, & Koster, 2015). This finding fits nicely within the framework that suggests that poor control over attention, rather than strict biases toward threat, may characterize anxious individuals.

If we conclude that individuals with SAD tend to either over- or underattend to social threat–relevant information in their environments, and that they have difficulty controlling the focus of their attention, it is important to consider how these patterns relate to difficulties with social relationships. It seems reasonable to conclude from the available literature that many socially anxious individuals go into social interactions looking for cues that support the expectation that they will be evaluated. Such hypervigilance for threat may lead the socially anxious person to notice relatively harmless cues. For example, an interaction partner might furrow his brow during a brief moment of disagreement. Whereas this cue might go unnoticed by a non-socially anxious person, a socially anxious person might be apt to notice it *and* to perceive that he or she is acting in a socially unacceptable manner.

Furthermore, avoiding threat information or having difficulty controlling attention can negatively affect social interactions. If someone looks away from a conversation partner, he or she may miss out on important social cues that would make the conversation flow well. These might include positive cues like the other person's smiling or nodding that would indicate to the socially anxious individual that he or she is doing well in the interaction. By looking away or having difficulty concentrating, socially anxious individuals might come across to others as bored, disinterested, or socially unskilled, potentially sabotaging a newly forming relationship. In established relationships, poor eye contact may make the nonanxious member of the dyad wonder if the anxious person is not being open or honest. Taken together, this seemingly simple protective stance can put a strain on the quality of both new and established interpersonal relationships.

Judgment and Interpretation Bias

As we have repeatedly noted, socially anxious individuals approach social situations expecting negative evaluation from others. Research on judgment and interpretation bias provides further support for this notion. First, socially anxious individuals tend to be their own worst critics. Numerous studies have shown that socially anxious individuals (e.g., Rapee & Hayman, 1996), as well as those with SAD (e.g., Alden & Wallace, 1995; Rapee & Lim, 1992; Stopa & Clark, 1993), judge themselves more negatively than they judge others and also judge themselves more negatively than they are judged by others. Furthermore, individuals with SAD are more likely than nonclinical controls to assume that other people interpret physical symptoms that they exhibit (like blushing, shaking, or sweating) as signs of an intense anxiety problem or some other psychiatric disorder, rather than some more benign explanation, such as being hot, cold, or tired (Roth, Antony,

& Swinson, 2001). Given that socially anxious individuals judge themselves so harshly, it is not at all surprising that they enter social situations assuming that others will do the same (or worse).

Numerous studies have shown that individuals with SAD overestimate the probability of negative outcomes in social situations and greatly overestimate the cost of these outcomes (Foa, Franklin, Perry, & Herbert, 1996; Gilboa-Schechtman, Franklin, & Foa, 2000). Individuals with SAD tend to interpret both ambiguous social events (e.g., those not obviously positively or negatively valenced; Amir, Foa, & Coles, 1998) and mildly negative social events (Stopa & Clark, 2000) as extremely negative and catastrophic. At the same time, they tend to negatively interpret positive social information (Alden, Taylor, Mellings, & Laposa, 2008) and fail to accept others' positive reactions at face value (Vassilopoulos & Banerjee, 2010). When interpretation bias is inferred from relatively automatic processes, such as event-related brain potentials, socially anxious individuals also appear to lack the positive or nonthreat interpretation bias that is typical of nonanxious individuals (Moser, Hajcak, Huppert, Foa, & Simons, 2008).

As with attentional bias toward threat, research on interpretation biases has been concerned with whether such biases *cause* anxiety. To address this question, researchers have turned to cognitive bias modification of interpretations (CBM-I). Repeated training to make benign interpretations of ambiguous scenarios has resulted in reduced threat interpretations and reduced social anxiety in individuals with high social anxiety (Beard & Amir, 2008) and in individuals with SAD (Amir & Taylor, 2012). Most recently, an internet-based application of CBM-I has shown the potential to reduce threat interpretations and anxiety symptoms in individuals with SAD (Brettschneider, Neumann, Berger, Renneberg, & Boettcher, 2015), although controlled studies are needed, given that a control CBM-I condition (i.e., training to generate 50% positive and 50% negative interpretations) was as efficacious as the active condition in reducing anxiety (but not interpretation bias) in an internet-based study in a mixed anxiety sample (Salemink, Kindt, Rienties, & van den Hout, 2014).

Again, it is interesting to consider how bias relates to difficulties with social relationships. The literature on judgment and interpretation bias suggests that socially anxious individuals routinely put themselves into no-win situations. Almost any socially relevant information, whether it is negative, ambiguous, or positive, is perceived negatively and interpreted as costly, undoubtedly affecting the quality of social interactions. Taken together, these studies highlight why it is so compelling for socially anxious individuals to simply avoid social situations. To this point, laboratory studies of judgment and interpretation bias have generally involved asking participants what kind of judgments they would make if certain experiences happened to them (e.g., seeing a table of people laughing as you walk by). Basically, socially anxious individuals assume that they would make negative and costly judgments in these hypothetical situations. Researchers have not examined how individuals with SAD think about their own contributions to the development and maintenance of relationships. We do know that individuals with SAD have a difficult time with self-disclosure, and as noted earlier, our patients often express fears that people would reject them if they really got to know them. An interesting question is whether individuals with the disorder overestimate the probability that people will judge them negatively if they share relatively benign attributes about themselves (like being shy), and overestimate the cost of such self-disclosures (like being rejected). Certainly, this kind of bias might underlie difficulties with self-disclosure, thereby sabotaging the formation of new relationships and the maintenance of existing ones.

Memory and Imagery Biases

Research on memory bias focuses on whether socially anxious individuals preferentially remember socially threatening information relative to neutral information or information that is threatening but lacking in personal salience (see Coles & Heimberg, 2002, and Morrison, Gordon, & Heimberg, 2013, for reviews). In general, studies on memory bias have been inconsistent. In studies of explicit memory, or conscious, effortful retrieval of previously learned information, most studies have found no evidence of preferential recall or recognition of social threat in individuals with SAD (e.g., Rapee, McCallum, Melville, Ravenscroft, & Rodney, 1994). An explicit bias is more likely observed when the encoding stimuli have personal relevance. For example, Lundh and Öst (1996) asked participants to rate faces as critical or accepting; individuals with SAD subsequently recognized more critical than accepting faces, whereas the opposite was true for controls.

Similarly, most studies of implicit memory, or retrieval of information that is learned as an unintended effect of experience and is tested indirectly, have revealed no evidence of a bias for social threat information (e.g., Lundh & Öst, 1997). The only two studies that have produced evidence of a bias have used versions of the white noise paradigm (e.g., Amir, Foa, & Coles, 2000), suggesting that more research is needed before conclusions can be drawn.

It has also been suggested that individuals with SAD may preferentially remember autobiographical social events, but studies in this area have also been inconsistent. Few studies that have used relatively objective outcome measures (e.g., number of memories recalled) have found evidence of a bias. One exception was a study by Wenzel and Cochran (2006), who found that richer retrieval cues, namely negative cognitions related to social anxiety, resulted in retrieval of more anxiety-related memories and faster retrieval of these memories for individuals with SAD compared to nonanxious individuals. In contrast to studies with objective measures, studies that have assessed subjective aspects of the memories, such as associated emotions or memory content, have largely supported an autobiographical memory bias. In one study (Erwin, Heimberg, Marx, & Franklin, 2006), individuals with SAD responded to memories of stressful social events with symptoms of hyperarousal and avoidance, whereas control participants did not. In another study, individuals high in social anxiety recalled more negative and social anxiety-related memories than individuals low in social anxiety when cued by emotion words and when asked to recall "self-defining memories" (Krans, de Bree, & Bryant, 2014). Clearly this area of research deserves further attention, but empirical support thus far suggests that rich, personally relevant cues and assessment of the subjective content of memories are necessary preconditions for observing an autobiographical memory bias for threat in social anxiety.

A related area is involuntary memory, or memories of personal events that come to mind with no preceding attempt at retrieval (Berntsen, 1996). Much of this literature has focused on the study of mental imagery and visual memories. As a whole, these studies suggest that individuals with SAD experience repetitive, intrusive, negative, and biased visual memories of themselves in social situations. Hackmann et al. (1998) asked patients to recall a recent social situation in which they felt anxious and to describe the image that they had of themselves during it. Compared to nonclinical controls, individuals with

SAD were more likely to report having a clear, negative self-image that felt like a very accurate depiction of how they were coming across at the time of the event. Hackmann, Clark, and McManus (2000) asked patients if they associated this negative self-image with a particular event. Indeed, most could recall a specific past event in which they felt embarrassed and humiliated, with the image clearly connected to the most negative aspects of this recalled event. This finding fits nicely with the study by Erwin et al. (2006) on autobiographical memories in SAD. In that study, a majority of patients with SAD recalled having experienced a socially stressful life event, like feeling humiliated after a poor public performance or being rejected by a potential romantic interest. These memories were accompanied by such significant symptoms of avoidance and hyperarousal that patients would have met criteria for posttraumatic stress disorder (PTSD) had these events qualified as PTSD Criterion A events. It is likely that the patients in this study had negative self-images related to these socially stressful life events, just as the patients in the studies conducted by Clark's group did.

A number of studies have also examined imagery perspective. There are two perspectives from which to recall visual memories of social events—either the observer perspective, in which people see themselves through the eyes of others (as if they are viewing themselves on videotape), or the field perspective, in which people recall situations as viewed through their own eyes. Socially anxious individuals are more likely to take an observer perspective when remembering themselves in social situations. In contrast, individuals without the disorder tend to take the field perspective. In other words, when socially anxious individuals look back on social situations, they tend to remember them from the perspective of how they *think* they were viewed by others (e.g., Coles, Turk, & Heimberg, 2002; Coles, Turk, Heimberg, & Fresco, 2001; Hackmann et al., 1998; Wells, Clark, & Ahmad, 1998), rather than based on what actually occurred in the social situation. The problem with this information is that it is terribly biased, always in the negative direction. The bias comes about because socially anxious individuals believe that they know what other people are thinking about them. Unfortunately, as is often discussed in therapy, human beings are not mind readers, and so we can never know how others truly perceive us (unless we are told directly, which rarely occurs!). Holding the belief that we have access to what others think of us causes socially anxious individuals to come away from situations remembering themselves in a very negative light, undoubtedly affecting their willingness to enter similar situations in the future.

As with attentional bias and interpretation bias, there is support for the idea that negative self-imagery contributes causally to the maintenance of social anxiety. In several studies, researchers have trained participants to hold either a negative or a benign self-image in mind while engaging in a social task. Negative self-imagery elicited higher self-reported anxiety in individuals with SAD (Hirsch, Clark, Mathews, & Williams, 2003); individuals with high social anxiety (Hirsch, Meynen, & Clark, 2004); and even nonanxious individuals (Hirsch, Mathews, Clark, Williams, & Morrison, 2006; Makkar & Grisham, 2011). Indeed, a recent systematic review concluded that the effects of negative self-imagery on anxiety were similarly deleterious across the social anxiety spectrum (Ng, Abbott, & Hunt, 2014). Therefore, it appears that it is the greater *prevalence* of negative self-imagery among socially anxious individuals that contributes to the maintenance of anxiety. Moreover, socially anxious individuals appear to spontaneously regulate negative self-imagery in maladaptive ways, such as through suppression, whereas low anxiety individuals tend to make greater use of adaptive strategies, such as altering the content of their images (Moscovitch, Chiupka, & Gavric, 2013).

Hirsch, Clark, and Mathews (2006) proposed that different kinds of cognitive biases interact with one another and are best understood in this way rather than in isolation. Thus far, research has shown support for the effects of negative imagery on interpretation biases, interpretation biases on memory biases, and interpretation biases on attentional biases. For example, socially anxious participants were faster to retrieve negative autobiographical memories when they held a negative self-image in mind (Stopa & Jenkins, 2007). Participants in a negative interpretation bias induction condition also produced more negative self-related images than did participants in a positive bias induction condition (Hirsch, Mathews, & Clark, 2007). This trend in information processing research is likely to continue to grow, and the connections among attentional bias, interpretation and judgment bias, and memory and imagery biases will be better understood.

ENVIRONMENTAL AND SOCIOCULTURAL FACTORS

Ollendick and Benoit (2012) point out that SAD originates from a "delicate interplay of parent and child influences" (p. 82). They suggest that five factors, in particular, are important to consider: temperamental characteristics, parental anxiety, attachment processes, information processing biases (which we have just discussed), and parenting practices.

The temperament that has been most studied in relation to anxiety is the highly reactive or "behaviorally inhibited" temperament (see Kagan, 1994). Behavioral inhibition is the temperamental tendency to display restraint, fearfulness, or withdrawal when faced with unfamiliar people, situations, and objects (Kagan, Reznick, & Snidman, 1988). A robust body of research performed over several decades suggests that behaviorally inhibited temperament is a specific risk factor for SAD (see Hirshfeld-Becker, Micco, Wang, & Hennin, 2014). It is important to note, however, that all behaviorally inhibited children do not go on to develop SAD—only about one fourth to one third do (see Ollendick & Benoit, 2012). This suggests the interplay of other factors in the development of SAD.

Clearly, parental anxiety plays an important role. Children have been found to be at increased risk of developing anxiety disorders, and SAD in particular, when their parents are anxious or when their parents have clinically significant panic disorder with agoraphobia or SAD (see Ollendick & Benoit, 2012). These findings fit well with studies that show that socially anxious children tend to grow up in homes with low levels of family sociability. Growing up with extremely shy parents can have a number of consequences. First, while growing up, children do not see their parents participating in strong, positive interpersonal relationships of their own (e.g., Bögels, van Oosten, Muris, & Smulders, 2001; Bruch, Heimberg, Berger, & Collins, 1989). Similarly, they see their parents reacting anxiously in a variety of social situations. One study observed mothers and their 10-week-old babies during an interaction with a stranger (Murray, Cooper, Creswell, Schofield, & Sack, 2007). During this interaction, mothers with SAD exhibited more anxiety and were also less encouraging of their baby's interactions with the stranger than were mothers with generalized anxiety disorder or nonanxious mothers. This study suggests that offspring of socially anxious mothers might begin to learn about (and even imitate) social anxiety from a very young age. A little later on in life, shy parents are less likely to facilitate peer interactions for their children (e.g., Caster, Inderbitzen, & Hope, 1999). During the early years, parents are not only involved in planning playdates with other parents but are also socializing during these playdates. In the study by Bögels et al. (2001), the finding that greater levels of social anxiety in children were associated with greater levels of social anxiety in parents was actually carried by the levels of social anxiety experienced by mothers. This is not surprising, given that it is mothers who tend to be more involved in the day-to-day social lives of their children. By the time children of socially anxious parents reach adolescence and can be more socially independent, it is quite likely that the usual anxieties of adolescence combined with lack of experience could make social interactions difficult to tolerate.

Theorists have also asked about the role of early attachment to parents. They posit that people develop schemas for understanding their social world via these earliest interpersonal relationships. The quality of these relationships is thought to affect personality development and the quality of relationships later in life (e.g., Bowlby, 1982; see also Greenberg, 1999). Attachment theorists have long distinguished between secure and insecure attachment relationships (see Dozier, Stovall, & Albus, 1999). It is thought that securely attached children have parents who are attentive and responsive, whereas insecurely attached children have parents who are rejecting and undependable. Shyness and social anxiety during childhood are related to insecure attachment patterns during infancy (see Bohlin, Hagekull, & Rydell, 2000; LaFreniere & Sroufe, 1985). When asked to recall their early childhood, shy adults tend to report having had parents who were rejecting and lacking in warmth (Schlette et al., 1998). Researchers have also examined adult attachment patterns, since the way that we relate to one another as adults likely has its roots in the early parent-child relationship. Relationships have been found between SAD in adulthood and insecure attachment patterns (e.g., Eng, Heimberg, et al., 2001; Mickelson, Kessler, & Shaver, 1997).

As children grow older, their relationships to their peers become increasingly important and further set the groundwork for the quality of their later relationships. Socially anxious children are more likely than nonanxious children to experience negative peer relations, most notably peer neglect (La Greca, Dandes, Wick, Shaw, & Stone, 1988; Strauss, Lahey, Frick, Frame, & Hynd, 1988), which exacerbates and maintains social anxiety (see also Rubin & Mills, 1988; Vernberg, Abwender, Ewell, & Beery, 1992).

The association between social anxiety and peer victimization, including teasing, is demonstrated in two prospective studies (Siegel, La Greca, & Harrison, 2009; Storch, Masia-Warner, Crisp, & Klein, 2005) and many retrospective studies (McCabe, Antony, Summerfeldt, Liss, & Swinson, 2003; McCabe, Miller, Laugesen, Antony, & Young, 2010; Roth, Coles, & Heimberg, 2002). The relationship between social anxiety and peer victimization is bidirectional, such that peer victimization was both a predictor and consequence of social anxiety (Siegel et al., 2009; Crawford & Manassis, 2011; Erath, Flanagan, & Bierman, 2007; Storch et al., 2005). McCabe and colleagues (2003) found that recalled childhood teasing was much more strongly related to adult SAD than to adult obsessive-compulsive disorder or panic disorder. A higher frequency of recalled childhood teasing was associated with greater severity of adult social anxiety symptoms (McCabe et al., 2010).

Recalled teasing in the social domain (e.g., being teased about looking shy or appearing nervous) was more strongly related to psychological distress during adulthood than recalled teasing in other domains, such as appearance or academics (Storch et al., 2005; see also McCabe et al., 2010). Recalled childhood teasing was also related to greater early adulthood impairment in interpersonal functioning, specifically less comfort with intimacy and closeness, less ability to trust and depend on others, as well as a greater degree of worry about being unloved or abandoned in relationships (Ledley et al., 2006).

Rose and Abramson (1992) proposed that repeated childhood emotional maltreatment may lead to a negative inferential style, since children are likely to attribute the maltreatment to stable and global negative characteristics of the self. Similarly, the emotional maltreatment found in childhood peer victimization may lead to the development of a negative inferential style, interpersonal deficits, and hopelessness regarding one's ability to change negative events (Ledley et al., 2006).

Parenting style also plays an important role in the development of SAD. However, the research in this area is somewhat murky. On the one hand, SAD has been associated with controlling, overprotective, and critical parenting (see Bruch, Heimberg, et al., 1989; Caster et al., 1999). On the other hand, parents who are warm and accommodating have been found to exacerbate avoidant behavior in their inhibited children (Kagan, Arcus, & Snidman, 1993). It is quite possible that both of these scenarios exist and that these extremes of parenting (too much accommodation and warmth or too much criticism and lack of help) are poor fits for children at risk for SAD.

This delicate interplay of parent and child factors is clearly observed in clinical practice. Typically, we see children and adolescents who could be described as behaviorally inhibited since infancy. Parents recall them being nervous around new people, but also reactive to new toys, foods, and routines. The families we see in clinical practice often have at least one parent who describes himself or herself as socially anxious, and many of the families describe themselves as quite insular, often doing things only within the nuclear or extended family. It is interesting to see parents who show both ends of the parenting style spectrum, sometimes within a single day! Although parents of socially anxious children tend to want to protect them from feeling anxious and uncomfortable, they might also get angry after a time and criticize their children for looking anxious (which might of course arouse the parents' own concern about negative evaluation from others). If parents' instinct is to avoid anxiety, they will in turn facilitate avoidance of social situations for their children. Therefore, their children will never learn that they can cope with anxiety, nor that their anxiety will habituate with repeated exposure to a feared situation. Furthermore, they never see that social interactions are usually quite pleasant and rewarding, increasing the likelihood of continued avoidance into adolescence and adulthood.

Assessment of Social Anxiety Disorder

SAD may be evaluated by means of various clinical interviews, rating scales, and self-report measures. In addition, session-by-session measures can be used to assess treatment-related change. In this section, neurobiological assessment will also be briefly reviewed. In research settings, this mode of assessment can be used to examine changes in brain activity that occur with treatment for SAD.

CLINICAL INTERVIEWS

In research settings, semistructured diagnostic interviews are used to establish diagnoses and, in some cases, to rate the severity of diagnoses (McNeil & Quentin, 2014). Semistructured interviews present the assessor with a set of questions to guide decisions about the presence or absence of *DSM* diagnoses, but also allow the assessor sufficient flexibility to gain a clear understanding of the patient's primary concerns. Semistructured interviews may greatly reduce the rates of false negatives in the diagnosis of SAD (Zimmerman & Mattia, 1999). In anxiety disorder research settings, the Structured Clinical Interview for DSM-IV-TR Axis I Disorders–Patient Edition (SCID-I/P; First, Spitzer, Gibbon, & Williams, 2002) and the most recent *DSM-5* research version (SCID-5-RV; First, Williams, Karg, Spitzer, 2015), along with the Anxiety Disorders Interview Schedule for DSM-IV (ADIS-IV; Brown, DiNardo, & Barlow, 1994) and the most recent Anxiety and Related Disorders Interview Schedule for DSM-5 (ADIS-5; Brown & Barlow, 2014) are the most commonly used instruments. Because *DSM-5* was recently published, the available psychometric data are from the *DSM-IV* versions of these instruments. However, since the *DSM-5* revisions to SAD were relatively straightforward, the psychometric data should be expected to maintain relevance.

An advantage of the SCID is that it can be completed in a relatively brief and efficient manner. It includes screening questions for each diagnosis that allow clinicians to skip sections that do not seem relevant to a given patient and to skip particular sections once they have ascertained that criteria for the given disorder are not met. A disadvantage of the SCID is that it does not cue clinicians to gather additional data on a patient's difficulties beyond *DSM* criteria, and such data may reduce false negatives (Dalrymple & Zimmerman, 2008). Thus, the information gathered during the SCID is not sufficiently detailed for use in treatment planning (Hart, Jack, Turk, & Heimberg, 1999).

In contrast, the ADIS includes numerous questions that go beyond *DSM* criteria, items that query triggers of anxiety (e.g., feared social and performance situations) and reactions to these triggers (e.g., avoidance and experience of situationally cued panic attacks). Also queried are specific behaviors, thoughts, the scope of avoidance, and past history of social anxiety symptoms. These additional questions mean that the ADIS can sometimes be lengthy to administer, but also that it provides valuable information for treatment planning. The ADIS also allows the clinician to assign a clinical severity rating (CSR) for each diagnosis. The CSR has clear utility in research and clinical settings. This rating of symptom severity facilitates treatment planning, provides an estimate of treatment length, and allows for assessment of improvement over the course of treatment. The psychometric properties of the ADIS have been examined in a clinical sample of individuals with anxiety disorders. In 362 patients with mixed diagnoses, Brown, Di Nardo, Lehman, and Campbell (2001) reported a kappa of .77 for a primary diagnosis of SAD using the lifetime version of the ADIS-IV.

CLINICAL RATING SCALES

The most commonly used clinician-administered measure of social anxiety is the Liebowitz Social Anxiety Scale (LSAS; Liebowitz, 1987), and it will be our focus here (another clinician-administered measure, the Brief Social Phobia Scale, is not reviewed here, but information about it is available from Davidson et al., 1991, 1997). The LSAS has 24 items, 11 pertaining to social interaction situations (e.g., meeting strangers) and 13 pertaining to performance situations (e.g., making a presentation to a small group). Each item is rated according to the degree to which the patient has feared and avoided specific situations over the past week. The LSAS is unique because it assesses specific situations, whereas other measures of social anxiety assess symptomatology (Beard et al., 2011; Heeren, Maurage, et al., 2012). The LSAS includes numerous subscales, but its total score is most commonly used in research. The LSAS has strong convergent validity and adequate discriminant validity, and is sensitive to treatment change (Adler et al., 2009; Book, Thomas, Randall, & Randall, 2008; Fresco et al., 2001; Heimberg et al., 1999). It is also a highly reliable measure, with reported Cronbach's alphas of .95 and .96 for the LSAS total score (Fresco et al., 2001; Heimberg et al., 1999). A self-report version (LSAS-SR) correlates highly with the original interviewer-rated version and demonstrates strong psychometric properties (Fresco et al., 2001; Rytwinski et al., 2009). A version of the LSAS has been developed for use with children and adolescents and also has strong psychometric properties (LSAS-CA; Masia-Warner et al., 2003).

The LSAS is also an excellent clinical tool. Because it gathers information on the various social and performance situations that patients fear and avoid, it can be used for treatment planning (e.g., creating a hierarchy of feared situations) and to assess improvement over the course of treatment (e.g., Heimberg et al., 1998; Liebowitz et al., 1999). A score of 30 discriminates patients with social anxiety disorder from normal controls with good specificity and sensitivity (Mennin et al., 2002; Rytwinski et al., 2009.

SELF-REPORT MEASURES

Numerous self-report measures are available to assess social anxiety symptoms. Common self-report measures for SAD in adults include the Social Interaction Anxiety Scale (SIAS; Mattick & Clarke, 1998); the Social Phobia Scale (SPS; Mattick & Clarke, 1998); the Brief Fear of Negative Evaluation scale (BFNE; Leary, 1983); the Social Phobia Inventory (SPIN; Connor et al., 2000); and the Social Phobia and Anxiety Inventory (SPAI; Turner, Beidel, Dancu, & Stanley, 1989). Each of these measures assesses slightly different aspects of social anxiety disorder. All can be used to establish severity of social anxiety at pretreatment, to assess treatment-related change in symptoms, and for treatment planning. For a detailed and thoughtful review of considerations in the evaluation of self-report measures for social anxiety in adults, see Fernandez, Piccirillo, and Rodebaugh (2014). For a review of measures for use with children and adolescents, see Herbert, Brandsma, and Fischer (2014).

The SIAS measures anxiety that is experienced in dyads and groups (sample items: "I feel I will say something embarrassing when talking," and "I have difficulty making eye contact with others"). The SPS measures anxiety in situations in which the person may be observed critically by others (sample items: "I get nervous that people are staring at me as I walk down the street," and "I worry I might do something to attract the attention of other people"). Both the SIAS and the SPS have been shown to be reliable instruments for the assessment of social anxiety disorder and to possess a high degree of convergent validity with other indices of social anxiety and avoidance (Brown et al., 1997; Habke, Hewitt, Norton, & Asmundson, 1997; Heimberg, Mueller, Holt, Hope, &

Liebowitz, 1992; Mattick & Clarke, 1998; Peters, 2000). Rodebaugh, Woods, and Heimberg (2007) found that the three reverse-scored items of the SIAS related more strongly to the personality trait of extraversion than to social anxiety and that eliminating them to produce a 17-item version of the SIAS (SIAS-Straightforward or SIAS-S) results in a more valid measure of social interaction anxiety, with excellent psychometric properties in undergraduate and clinical samples. This concern is not relevant to the SPS, which includes no reverse-scored items.

The 12-item BFNE assesses a core concern experienced by individuals with social anxiety—fear of negative evaluation (sample item: "I am frequently afraid of other people noticing my shortcomings"). Rodebaugh and colleagues (2004) and Weeks and colleagues (2005) demonstrated that the four reversed-scored items on the BFNE were less related to measures of social anxiety than the straightforwardly worded items were and that those were adversely influenced by the respondents' level of education. As with the SIAS, both sets of investigators concluded that the BFNE is most valid when only the eight straightforwardly worded items are used (BFNE-S). The BFNE-S has been shown to have strong psychometric properties in undergraduate samples (Rodebaugh et al., 2004) and clinical samples (Weeks et al., 2005).

The 17-item Social Phobia Inventory (SPIN; Antony, Coons, McCabe, Ashbaugh, & Swinson, 2006; Connor et al., 2000) assesses three theoretical components of social anxiety: subjective fear, avoidance behavior, and physiological symptoms. The SPIN has demonstrated good reliability, significant correlations with related measures, and the ability to discriminate between clients with social anxiety disorder and those with other anxiety disorders. A three-item version of the SPIN, the Mini-SPIN, has also shown substantial utility as a screening device for social anxiety disorder in both general health care settings (Connor, Kobak, Churchill, Katzelnick, & Davidson, 2001) and anxiety specialty clinic settings (Weeks, Spokas, & Heimberg, 2007; de Lima Osório, Crippa, & Loureiro, 2010).

The Social Phobia and Anxiety Inventory (SPAI; Turner et al., 1989) queries somatic, cognitive, and behavioral responses to social and performance situations. It also queries situations commonly feared by individuals with panic disorder and agoraphobia. It consists of 45 items, but because some require multiple responses, respondents actually answer a total of 109 items. These items yield three subscales: a social phobia subscale, an agoraphobia subscale, and a derived difference (or total) score. The SPAI has been shown to be a valid scale, has demonstrated adequate reliability and good test-retest reliability (Herbert, Bellack, & Hope, 1991; Turner et al., 1989), and is sensitive to treatment-related change (Beidel, Turner, & Cooley, 1993; Taylor, Woody, McLean, & Koch, 1997). Most recently, Roberson-Nay, Strong, Nay, Beidel, and Turner (2007) developed an abbreviated 23-item version of the SPAI with excellent psychometric properties in a sample of college students (Schry, Roberson-Nay, & White, 2012).

SESSION-BY-SESSION ASSESSMENT

As noted earlier, the measures that are commonly used with socially anxious patients are all useful in assessing treatment-related change. A specific measure has been developed to assess session-by-session change over the course of treatment for SAD. The Social Anxiety Session Change Index (SASCI; Hayes, Miller, Hope, Heimberg, & Juster, 2008) is a four-item scale that is completed prior to each treatment session to assess the progress the patient believes he or she has made since beginning treatment. Hayes and colleagues (2008) found the scale to be a valid measure with good internal consistency. Furthermore, the SASCI is sensitive to symptom improvement and is associated with changes in the BFNE and in clinician-rated improvement. Its strong psychometric properties, along with its brevity and ease of scoring, make the SASCI an excellent choice for assessing session-by-session change over the course of treatment for SAD.

Depending on the clinical profile of individual patients, additional measures can be administered on a weekly basis to gather important information and to aid in treatment planning. As an example, patients with co-occurring depression can complete the Beck Depression Inventory–II (Beck, Steer, & Brown, 1996). Those with co-occurring alcohol use can complete the Alcohol Use Disorders Identification Test (Saunders, Aasland, Babor, de la Fuente, & Grant, 1993). Both of these measures are brief enough to be completed prior to each treatment session. Idiographically designed self-monitoring forms in which patients record aspects of their anxiety and behavior in feared social situations are also extremely useful in the treatment of SAD.

NEUROBIOLOGICAL ASSESSMENT

As was mentioned earlier, imaging studies have been used to examine neurobiological changes in brain activity as a result of treatment (e.g., Furmark et al., 2002; Goldin et al., 2013). Although neurobiological assessments are not routinely used with patients with SAD, they may have utility in the future, as suggested by two preliminary studies. Doehrmann et al. (2013) demonstrated that whole-brain responses to angry versus neutral faces at baseline significantly predicted response to CBT for SAD. Goldin et al. (2014) demonstrated that changes from baseline to posttreatment in neural responses when asked to reappraise criticism from others predicted unique variance in CBT-related reductions in social anxiety.

Treatment

This section discusses both psychological and biological interventions in the treatment of SAD. In the section on psychological interventions, focus will be placed on the use of cognitive-behavioral therapy in the treatment of SAD. In the section on biological interventions, focus will be placed on the use of SSRIs and SNRIs; novel treatments will also be reviewed.

PSYCHOLOGICAL INTERVENTIONS

As described previously, the experience of social anxiety occurs along three domains. Cognitive symptoms of anxiety describe the negative internal dialogue experienced by socially anxious individuals in anticipation of social situations, during these situations, and even while processing these situations once they have occurred (i.e., post-event processing). For example, an individual with SAD might have thoughts like, "I am a loser,"

"They can see my hands shake and will know I am anxious," "She'll never want to date me," or "I won't get the job." Thoughts like these contain errors of logic, causing socially anxious individuals to judge their performance as poor regardless of its actual quality (Hope, Heimberg, & Turk, 2010).

Behavioral symptoms of anxiety refer to avoidance mechanisms that persons with SAD employ in anxiety-provoking situations. Avoidance may take a variety of forms, such as choosing not to enter a situation at all, or engaging in safety behaviors that make entering a situation tolerable but prevent the person from being fully present in that situation. As an example of the latter, a socially anxious individual might go to parties, but she might spend the whole time speaking only to people she already knows, saying as little as possible, and drinking alcohol to ease her anxiety symptoms. As already noted, these safety behaviors often do not result in the desired outcomes and may increase the likelihood of coming across badly.

Finally, physical symptoms of anxiety such as blushing, stammering, shaking, or sweating (Amies, Gelder, & Shaw, 1983; Solyom, Ledwidge, & Solyom, 1986) are commonly experienced by persons with SAD (Heimberg et al., 1990). Persons with SAD focus on their physical symptoms, overestimate the visibility of these symptoms to others (Bruch, Gorsky, Collins, & Berger, 1989), gauge the approval of others by the level of anxiety they experience, and view their symptoms as evidence of failure. Safety behaviors are often employed to mask physical symptoms (e.g., gripping a glass very tightly with both hands at a cocktail party so no one will notice the hands are shaking), but as noted, these strategies often do not result in the desired outcome (Piccirillo et al., in press).

As the cognitive, behavioral, and physiological symptoms of anxiety elevate, they are interpreted as further evidence of how one's appearance and behavior are perceived by others. Cycling back, a more negative estimation of how the audience sees the person is made, and the cognitive, behavioral, and physiological symptoms of anxiety worsen. This "vicious cycle" of social anxiety increases the probability that the person with SAD will judge the social situation as a failure. A collection of similar experiences has further negative impact, as it may strengthen maladaptive beliefs and lower expectations for success in future situations.

The cognitive-behavioral models of SAD have directly informed the treatment of SAD, and the psychological intervention that has gained the most empirical support for the treatment of SAD is CBT. One widely used CBT protocol for SAD (Hope et al., 2010) includes three primary components (exposure, cognitive restructuring, and homework assignments), which are designed to treat the symptoms of social anxiety that maintain the disorder. In-session exposures are cognitive-behavioral exercises designed to help patients face social and performance situations in which they experience distress or that they are likely to avoid. Cognitive restructuring helps patients to become more aware of their dysfunctional thoughts and to examine and reframe these thoughts. Cognitive restructuring also helps patients to challenge biases, assumptions, and beliefs, which allows them to view the world in a more accurate way so that they do not expect failure in every social situation. As interpretations become more adaptive, patients are more likely to attend to their social performance and to the feedback from others participating in the situation. Greater attentiveness in social and performance situations will be associated with increasingly adaptive thoughts and beliefs and reductions in post-event processing. Exposure and cognitive restructuring homework is assigned so that patients apply what they have learned in therapy to in vivo situations. Homework compliance is associated with improved outcome in CBT for SAD (Leung & Heimberg, 1996).

One of the most widely investigated treatment programs for SAD is cognitive-behavioral group therapy (CBGT). CBGT, as originally developed by Heimberg's group (see Heimberg & Becker, 2002), is typically administered to groups of five or six patients in 12 weekly, 2.5-hour-long sessions. During the first two sessions, patients are educated about social anxiety and are taught cognitive restructuring skills. During session three, in-session exposures are initiated. These exposures are tailored to target each patient's unique concerns and are preceded and followed by therapist-directed cognitive restructuring exercises. At the end of each session, patients are assigned homework that typically consists of in vivo exposure, with patient-directed pre- and postexposure cognitive restructuring. As treatment proceeds, patients confront increasingly anxiety-provoking situations and are helped to explore the core beliefs that underlie their difficulties with social anxiety. Multiple studies by Heimberg's group (Heimberg et al., 1990, 1998; Hope, Heimberg, & Bruch, 1995; Liebowitz et al., 1999) and others (Chambless et al., 1997; Edelman & Chambless, 1995; Gelernter et al., 1991; Woody, Chambless, & Glass, 1997) support the efficacy of CBGT. CBGT has also been shown to have good long-term efficacy (Heimberg, Salzman, Holt, & Blendell, 1993) and is associated with significant improvements in quality of life (Eng, Coles, Heimberg, & Safren, 2001, 2005; Safren, Heimberg, Brown, & Holle, 1997). Other group treatments based on CBGT (e.g., Foa, Franklin, & Kozak, 2001; Franklin, Jaycox, & Foa, 1999), have also been shown to be efficacious (Davidson et al., 2004). A recently completed trial of CBGT in comparison to mindfulness-based stress reduction (MBSR) and a wait-list control showed positive outcomes across a variety of outcomes and maintenance of gains at 1-year follow-up for both treatments (Goldin et al., 2016). A meta-analysis of controlled trials of multiple variants of CBGT suggests that it is as efficacious as individual CBT or pharmacotherapy for SAD (Barkowski et al., 2016).

Although group treatment certainly holds appeal for the treatment of SAD, it can be logistically difficult to implement, particularly in clinical settings in which it can take a long time to gather a sufficient number of appropriate patients to form a group. CBGT has been adapted to a manualized, individual CBT format (Hope et al., 2010), which has been shown to be more efficacious than a wait-list control condition (Goldin et al., 2012; Ledley et al., 2009). In addition, Ledley and colleagues and Goldin and colleagues found high protocol adherence, little attrition, and significant improvement on both self-report and clinician-administered measures of social anxiety among patients treated with individual CBT.

Clark and colleagues have developed an individual cognitive therapy (CT) based on Clark and Wells's (1995) cognitive model of SAD. Consistent with Clark and Wells's theoretical assumption that attention is largely focused on internal symptoms of anxiety and that safety behaviors play a central role in the maintenance of SAD, CT teaches patients to reduce safety behaviors and to shift attention externally, with the goals of helping patients to gather more accurate information about how they are evaluated by others and reframe their distorted self-image. CT employs specific strategies to facilitate external focus of attention, such as video feedback, which provides patients a source of external information and allows comparison of predicted and actual performance (Clark et al., 2003). When compared with exposure and progressive muscle relaxation (i.e., applied relaxation), CT was more efficacious at posttreatment (Clark et al., 2006) and at 5-year follow-up (Mörtberg, Clark, & Bejerot, 2011). CT was also more efficacious than interpersonal psychotherapy in the treatment of SAD (Stangier, Schramm, Heidenreich, Berger, & Clark, 2011). When compared with manualized psychodynamic therapy, CT was more efficacious at posttreatment (Leichsenring et al., 2013) but results were relatively equivalent at 2-year follow-up (Leichsenring et al., 2014).

Several meta-analyses suggest significant effects of individual CBT (e.g., Mayo-Wilson et al., 2014). Although most meta-analyses suggest no difference in efficacy between group and individual treatment for SAD (e.g., Barkowski et al., 2016; Powers, Sigmarsson, & Emmelkamp, 2008), the meta-analysis by Aderka (2009) of a small sample of studies conducted between 2000 and 2006 suggested that individual treatments resulted in larger effect sizes and lower attrition rates than group treatments. In the network meta-analysis conducted by Mayo-Wilson et al. (2014), only individual CBT was superior to both wait-list and placebo controls. CBGT was superior only to wait-list controls, but individual and group CBT did not differ from each other. Based on these findings, the United Kingdom's National Institute for Health and Care Excellence (2013) recommends individual CBT over CBGT (or pharmacological treatment) as the first-line treatment of SAD in adults.

Several recent studies have provided encouraging evidence in support of the generalizability and transportability of group CBT (Gaston, Abbott, Rapee, & Neary, 2006; McEvoy, 2007; McEvoy, Nathan, Rapee, & Campbell, 2012), including evidence in support of a recently developed imagery-enhanced variant (McEvoy, Erceg-Hurn, Saulsman, & Thibodeau, 2015), as well as evidence in support of individual CBT (Lincoln et al., 2003) for SAD in private practice and community settings. Effect sizes in community settings were comparable to those reported in laboratory studies and meta-analyses. Comparable effect sizes in community settings are particularly encouraging given the fact that clinical trials are often conducted in university or medical school research settings, manualized treatment protocols are used and monitored for adherence, and strict exclusion criteria may be employed in clinical trials (Lincoln et al., 2003). Furthermore, these encouraging findings were demonstrated despite the fact that patients from the community had more severe symptoms, more comorbid disorders, and lower educational attainment than the patients from the research clinic (McEvoy et al., 2012).

BIOLOGICAL INTERVENTIONS

Medications are frequently used to treat SAD. The first-line pharmacological treatments for SAD are the SSRIs and the serotonin-norepinephrine reuptake inhibitors (SNRIs) (Blanco, Bragdon, Schneier, & Liebowitz, 2013). The Food and Drug Administration has approved four medications for the treatment of SAD: paroxetine, sertraline, extended release fluvoxamine (all SSRIs), and extended release venlafaxine (an SNRI). These medications tend to yield moderate effect sizes with mild side effects and low risk of overdose and are the most efficacious for the treatment of disorders frequently comorbid with SAD, including major depressive disorder and other anxiety disorders. Several controlled studies and meta-analyses support their efficacy (see Blanco et al., 2013; Hedges, Brown, Shwalb, Godfrey, & Larcher, 2007) and suggest no significant differences in efficacy between SSRIs and SNRIs (Hansen et al., 2008). The SSRI fluoxetine appears to be less efficacious in the treatment of SAD than the other SSRIs and SNRIs (Clark et al., 2003; Kobak, Greist, Jefferson, & Katzelnick, 2002). Although less well studied, venlafaxine has surpassed a pill placebo in reducing social anxiety symptoms (e.g., Liebowitz, Gelenberg, & Munjack, 2005; Liebowitz, Mangano, Bradwejn, & Asnis, 2005) and has efficacy comparable to paroxetine (Liebowitz, Gelenberg, et al., 2005).

Benzodiazepines have also been studied as treatments for SAD. Though studies with clonazepam have yielded very positive results (e.g., Davidson, Potts, et al., 1993), studies of alprazolam have been less promising (e.g., Gelernter et al., 1991). Bromazepam has been reported to be efficacious in the treatment of SAD (Versiani, Nardi, Figueira, Mendlowicz, & Marques, 1997). Benzodiazepines are frequently prescribed and are useful on an as-needed basis for less frequent high-anxiety situations. In addition, benzodiazepines can be a useful adjunct during the initial 4 to 6 weeks of adjustment to an SSRI or SNRI. Because of their abuse potential and sometimes problematic withdrawal effects (e.g., rebound anxiety on withdrawal from alprazolam), benzodiazepines must be administered with adequate supervision and avoided in patients with a history of substance abuse. In addition, benzodiazepines can cause sedation and impair cognition, which can interfere with performance and they are associated with falls in the elderly.

Monoamine oxidase inhibitors (MAOIs), such as phenelzine, were the first medications studied for the treatment of SAD and were found to be very efficacious (e.g., Blanco et al., 2010; Gelernter et al., 1991; Heimberg et al., 1998). However, patients who take them must adhere to strict dietary restrictions, avoiding any foods, beverages, and medications containing tyramine. Failure to adhere to this dietary regimen can lead to a sudden surge in blood pressure, with potentially serious effects. Given this risk, MAOIs are typically used only *after* other medications (e.g., SSRIs, benzodiazepines, venlafaxine, etc.) have proven ineffective for a given patient.

Three classes of medication have shown promise in the treatment of SAD, but require more research. Two controlled trials found D-cycloserine (DCS), a partial NMDA receptor agonist, an efficacious adjunct to brief exposure therapy for public speaking fears among patients with SAD (Guastella et al., 2008; Hofmann et al., 2006), with a particularly positive effect on anxiety reduction and performance appraisal immediately after exposure exercises (Guastella et al., 2008). This interesting finding suggests that DCS may enhance the efficacy of the exposure component of CBT. However, when employed as an adjunct to a full 12-week course of CBT, DCS was not associated with better response or remission rates (Hofmann et al., 2013). Second, in small clinical trials, the atypical antipsychotics olanzapine (Barnett, Kramer, Casat, Connor, & Davidson, 2002); quetiapine (Schutters, van Megan, & Westenberg, 2005; Vaishnavi, Alamy, Zhang, Connor, & Davidson, 2007); and risperidone (Simon et al., 2006) were efficacious for the treatment of SAD. Given the potential side effects of these medications, including weight gain and metabolic syndrome, larger trials are needed to confirm their efficacy. In clinical practice, the atypical antipsychotics are typically prescribed as adjuncts to SSRIs. Clinical trials are necessary to confirm the utility of this practice. Finally, a placebo-controlled trial of the anticonvulsant gabapentin (Pande et al., 1999) and two randomized, double-blind trials of its successor, pregabalin (Feltner, Liu-Dumaw, Schweizer, & Bielski, 2011; Pande et al., 2004) found these drugs to be more efficacious than a placebo.

Meta-analyses suggest effects of pharmacological treatments that range from equivalent to CBT (Gould, Buckminster, Pollack, Otto, & Yap, 1997) to superior to CBT

(Fedoroff & Taylor, 2001) for SAD. The effects of pharmacotherapy may be achieved more rapidly (Heimberg et al., 1998); however, CBT may offer greater protection against relapse (Liebowitz et al., 1999). Studies that have combined CBT with medication have produced mixed results (see Blanco et al., 2010; Blomhoff et al., 2001; Davidson et al., 2004).

Summary and Future Directions

Great progress has been made in understanding the nature of the impairments observed in SAD, advancing hypotheses regarding factors that might have contributed to these impairments, and developing and testing treatments. There is, however, still much to be done. One essential goal is for researchers to come to a clearer understanding of the nature of the social relationships of individuals with SAD. Beginning with children, it is important to elucidate not only why socially anxious individuals have fewer relationships than their less anxious counterparts, but also what occurs within relationships that leads to dissatisfaction and other difficulties. As we gain a clearer understanding of the nature of these impairments, new components of treatment can be developed (e.g., Alden & Taylor, 2011). It will also be important to maintain a focus on how biases inherent in SAD (e.g., interpretation biases, exaggeration of probability and cost, biased self-image) negatively affect relationships and how best to correct these biases (e.g., conducting exposures without the use of safety behaviors or using video feedback for those who have the most negatively biased self-perceptions), thereby reducing social anxiety symptoms. This is a strategy that has been fruitful in past research (Rodebaugh & Rapee, 2005; Wells et al., 1995).

Current psychosocial and pharmacological treatments yield excellent results, but further efforts should be made to optimize outcomes (see Ledley & Heimberg, 2005). These might include development of new pharmacological agents, new ways of using existing agents (e.g., combining medications to enhance outcomes), promulgation of new guidelines for action when a first-line agent does not work (e.g., increasing the dose or switching to a new agent; see Pollack et al., 2014), and matching agents with particular symptom profiles. It is also important to explore how best to combine pharmacological and psychosocial treatments. Previous research has found no consistent advantage of combining medication and CBT, but the two treatments were always administered concurrently. Combined treatments might work better if they were sequenced—for example, adding CBT to medication once the drug has had a chance to take effect—or if the second-administered treatment were reserved only for those who had not shown adequate improvements on the first-administered treatment.

With psychosocial treatments, another important agenda is to learn more about treatment of patients with comorbid conditions, particularly depression and alcohol use disorders. These disorders often co-occur with SAD, but comorbid patients are typically excluded from treatment studies. Thus, we know little about how they fare in standard treatment for SAD. We know even less about modifications to treatment that might improve outcomes for these particularly impaired groups.

Finally, future research should focus on making empirically supported treatments more available to individuals with SAD. Despite extensive research on the utility of CBT and SSRIs for SAD, psychodynamic therapy and benzodiazepines are still among the most commonly used treatments for this impairing disorder (see Keller, 2003). We must educate the public about SAD and treatments for it, taking into account that a common barrier to treatment is that individuals with SAD fear what others think about them (Olfson et al., 2000). Knowing that some individuals with SAD will never seek professional help (Kessler, Stein, & Berglund, 1998), we must develop interventions that appeal to this population, and a strong tool in this effort may be the Internet. Recent studies have shown that internet-based CBT with minimal therapist contact is effective in reducing social anxiety compared to wait-list groups, may be as effective as face-to-face treatment, demonstrates maintenance of gains at follow-up, and is as or more cost effective than face-to-face treatment (see review by Andersson, Rozental, Rück, & Carlbring, 2015). Of course, it is also essential that we disseminate empirically supported treatments for SAD to clinicians in the community. Such efforts should include explorations into the best ways to train clinicians to use such protocols effectively.

References

Acarturk, C., de Graaf, R., van Straten, A., ten Have, M., & Cuijpers, P. (2008). Social phobia and number of social fears, and their association with comorbidity, health-related quality of life and help seeking. *Social Psychiatry and Psychiatric Epidemiology, 43*, 273–279. doi: 10.1007/s00127-008-0309-1

Acarturk, C., Smit, F., de Graaf, R., van Straten, A., ten Have, M., & Cuijpers, P. (2009). Economic costs of social phobia: A population-based study. *Journal of Affective Disorders, 115*, 421–429. doi: 10.1016/j.jad.2008.10.008

Aderka, I. M. (2009). Factors affecting treatment efficacy in social phobia: The use of video feedback and individual vs. group formats. *Journal of Anxiety Disorders, 23*, 12–17. doi: 10.1016/j.janxdis.2008.05.003

Adler, L. A., Liebowitz, M., Kronenberger, W., Qiao, M., Rubin, R., Hollandbeck, M., … Durell, T. (2009). Atomoxetine treatment in adults with attention-deficit/hyperactivity disorder and comorbid social anxiety disorder. *Depression and Anxiety, 26*, 212–221. doi: 10.1002/da.20549

Alden, L. E., & Bieling, P. (1998). Interpersonal consequences of the pursuit of safety. *Behaviour Research and Therapy, 36*, 53–64. doi: 10.1016/S0005-7967(97)00072-7

Alden, L. E., Regambal, M. J., & Plasencia, L. (2014). Relational processes in social anxiety disorder. In J. W. Weeks (Ed.), *The Wiley-Blackwell handbook of social anxiety disorder* (pp. 159–181). Chichester, England: Wiley.

Alden, L. E., & Taylor, C. T. (2004). Interpersonal processes in social phobia. *Clinical Psychology Review, 24*, 857–882. doi: 10.1016/j.cpr.2004.07.006

Alden, L. E., & Taylor, C. T. (2010). Interpersonal processes in social anxiety disorder. In J. G. Beck (Ed.), *Interpersonal processes in the anxiety disorders* (pp. 125–152). Washington, DC: American Psychological Association.

Alden, L. E., & Taylor, C. T. (2011). Relational treatment strategies increase social approach behaviors in patients with generalized social anxiety disorder. *Journal of Anxiety Disorders, 25*, 309–318. doi: 10.1016/j.janxdis.2010.10.003

Alden, L. E., Taylor, C. T., Mellings, T. M., & Laposa, J. M. (2008). Social anxiety and the interpretation of positive social events. *Journal of Anxiety Disorders, 22*, 577–590. doi: 10.1016/j.janxdis.2007.05.007

Alden, L. E., & Wallace, S. T. (1995). Social phobia and social appraisal in successful and unsuccessful social interactions. *Behaviour Research and Therapy, 33*, 497–505. doi: 10.1016/0005-7967(94)00088-2

Alonso, J., Lépine, J. P., & ESEMeD 2000 Scientific Committee. (2007). Overview of key data from the European Study of the Epidemiology of Mental Disorders (ESEMeD). *Journal of Clinical Psychiatry, 68* (Suppl. 2), 3–9.

American Psychiatric Association. (2013). *Diagnostic and statistical manual of mental disorders* (5th ed.). Washington, DC: Author.

Amies, P. L., Gelder, M. G., & Shaw, P. M. (1983). Social phobia: A comparative clinical study. *British Journal of Psychiatry, 142*, 174–179.

Amir, N., Beard, C., Taylor, C. T., Klumpp, H., Elias, J., Burns, M., & Chen, X. (2009). Attention training in individuals with generalized social phobia: A randomized controlled trial. *Journal of Consulting and Clinical Psychology, 77*, 961–973. doi: 10.1037/a0016685

Amir, N., Foa, E. B., & Coles, M. E. (1998). Negative interpretation bias in social phobia. *Behaviour Research and Therapy, 36*, 959–970.

Amir, N., Foa, E. B., & Coles, M. E. (2000). Implicit memory bias for threat-relevant information in generalized social phobia. *Journal of Abnormal Psychology, 109*, 713–720. doi: 10.1037/0021-843X.109.4.713

Amir, N., & Taylor, C. T. (2012). Interpretation training in individuals with generalized social anxiety disorder: A randomized controlled trial. *Journal of Consulting and Clinical Psychology, 80*, 497–511. doi: 10.1037/a0026928

Amir, N., Weber, G., Beard, C., Bomyea, J., & Taylor, C. T. (2008). The effect of a single-session attention modification program on response to a public-speaking challenge in socially anxious individuals. *Journal of Abnormal Psychology, 117*, 860–868. doi: 10.1037/a0013445

Andersson, G., Rozental, A., Rück, C., & Carlbring, P. (2015). Guided internet-delivered CBT: Can it really be as good as seeing a therapist? *The Behavior Therapist, 38*, 123–126.

Antony, M. M., Coons, M. J., McCabe, R. E., Ashbaugh, A., & Swinson, R. P. (2006). Psychometric properties of the Social Phobia Inventory: Further evaluation. *Behaviour Research and Therapy*, *44*, 1177–1185. doi: 10.1016/j.brat.2005.08.013

Asmundson, G.J.G., & Stein, M. B. (1994). Selective processing of social threat in patients with generalized social phobia: Evaluation using a dot-probe paradigm. *Journal of Anxiety Disorders*, *8*, 107–117. doi: 10.1016/0887-6185(94)90009-4

Baillie, A. J., Sannibale, C., Stapinski, L. A., Teesson, M., Rapee, R. M. & Haber, P. S. (2013). An investigator-blinded, randomized study to compare the efficacy of combined CBT for alcohol use disorders and social anxiety disorder versus CBT focused on alcohol alone in adults with comorbid disorders: The Combined Alcohol Social Phobia (CASP) trial protocol. *BMC Psychiatry*, *13*, 199. doi: 10.1186/1471-244X-13-199

Bandelow, B., & Michaelis, S. (2015). Epidemiology of anxiety disorders in the 21st century. *Dialogues in Clinical Neuroscience*, *17*, 327–335.

Bar-Haim, Y., Lamy, D., Pergamin, L., Bakermans-Kranenburg, M. J., & van IJzendoorn, M. H. (2007). Threat-related attentional bias in anxious and nonanxious individuals: A meta-analytic study. *Psychological Bulletin*, *133*, 1–24. doi: 10.1037/0033-2909.133.1.1

Barkowski, S., Schwartze, D., Strauss, B., Burlingame, G. M., Barth, J., & Rosendahl, J. (2016). Efficacy of group psychotherapy for social anxiety disorder: A meta-analysis of randomized-controlled trials. *Journal of Anxiety Disorders*, *39*, 44–64. doi: 10.1016/j.janxdis.2016.02.005

Barnett, S. D., Kramer, M. L., Casat, C. D., Connor, K. M., & Davidson, J. R. (2002). Efficacy of olanzapine in social anxiety disorder: A pilot study. *Journal of Psychopharmacology*, *16*, 365–368. doi: 10.1177/026988110201600412

Battista, S., Pencer, A., & Stewart, S. H. (2014). Drinking and thinking: Alcohol effects on post-event processing in social anxious individuals. *Cognitive Therapy and Research*, *38*, 33–42. doi: 10.1007/s10608-013-9574-8

Beard, C., & Amir, N. (2008). A multi-session interpretation modification program: Changes in interpretation and social anxiety symptoms. *Behaviour Research and Therapy*, *46*, 1135–1141. doi: 10.1016/j.brat.2008.05.012

Beard, C., Rodriguez, B. F., Moitra, E., Sibrava, N., Weisberg, R. B., & Keller, M. B. (2011). Psychometric properties of the Liebowitz Social Anxiety Scale (LSAS) in a longitudinal study of African Americans with anxiety disorders. *Journal of Anxiety Disorders*, *25*, 722–726. doi: 10.1016/j.janxdis.2011.03.009

Beck, A. T., & Emery, G. (with Greenberg, R. L.). (1985). *Anxiety disorders and phobias: A cognitive perspective*. New York, NY: Basic Books.

Beck, A. T., Steer, R. A., & Brown, G. K. (1996). *Beck Depression Inventory manual* (2nd ed.). San Antonio, TX: Psychological Corporation.

Beidel, D. C., Turner, S. M., & Cooley, M. R. (1993). Assessing reliable and clinically significant change in social phobia: Validity of the Social Phobia and Anxiety Inventory. *Behaviour Research and Therapy*, *31*, 149–158. doi: 10.1016/0005-7967(93)90033-Q

Berntsen, D. (1996). Involuntary autobiographical memories. *Applied Cognitive Psychology*, *10*, 435–454. doi: 10.1002/(SICI)1099-0720(199610)10:5<435::AID-ACP408>3.0.CO;2-L

Black, J. J., Clark, D. B., Martin, C. S., Kim, K. H., Blaze, T. J., Creswell, K. G., & Chung, T. (2015). Course of alcohol symptoms and social anxiety disorder from adolescence to young adulthood. *Alcoholism, Clinical and Experimental Research*, *39*, 1008–1015. doi: 10.1111/acer.12711

Blanco, C., Bragdon, L. B., Schneier, F. R., & Liebowitz, M. R. (2013). The evidence-based pharmacotherapy of social anxiety disorder. *International Journal of Neuropsychopharmacology*, *16*, 235–249. doi: 10.1017/S1461145712000119

Blanco, C., Heimberg, R. G., Schneier, F. R., Fresco, D. M., Chen, H., Turk, C., ... Liebowitz, M. R. (2010). A placebo-controlled trial of phenelzine, cognitive behavioral group therapy, and their combination for social anxiety disorder. *Archives of General Psychiatry*, *67*, 286–295. doi: 10.1001/archgenpsychiatry.2010.11

Blanco, C., Schneier, F. R., Schmidt, A., Blanco-Jerez, C.-R., Marshall, R. D., Sanchez-Lacày, A., & Liebowitz, M. R. (2003). Pharmacological treatment of social anxiety disorder: A meta-analysis. *Depression and Anxiety*, *18*, 29–40. doi: 10.1002/da.10096

Blomhoff, S., Haug, T. T., Hellstrom, K., Holme, I., Humble, M., Madsbu, H. P., & Wold, J. E. (2001). Randomised controlled general practice trial of sertraline, exposure therapy and combined treatment in generalized social phobia. *British Journal of Psychiatry*, *179*, 23–30. doi: 10.1192/bjp.179.1.23

Bögels, S. M., & Mansell, W. (2004). Attention processes in the maintenance and treatment of social phobia: Hypervigilance, avoidance and self-focused attention. *Clinical Psychology Review, 24*, 827–856. doi: 10.1016/j.cpr.2004.06.005

Bögels, S. M., van Oosten, A., Muris, P., & Smulders, D. (2001). Familial correlates of social anxiety in children and adolescents. *Behaviour Research and Therapy, 39*, 273–287. doi: 10.1016/S0005-7967(00)00005-X

Bohlin, G., Hagekull, B., & Rydell, A.-M. (2000). Attachment and social functioning: A longitudinal study from infancy to middle childhood. *Social Development, 9*, 24–39. doi: 10.1111/1467-9507.00109

Book, S. W., Thomas, S. E., Randall, P. K., & Randall, C. L. (2008). Paroxetine reduces social anxiety in individuals with a co-occurring alcohol use disorder. *Journal of Anxiety Disorders, 22*, 310–318. doi: 10.1016/j.janxdis.2007.03.001

Bowlby, J. (1982). *Attachment and loss* (Vol. *1*). London, England: Hogarth Press.

Brettschneider, M., Neumann, P., Berger, T., Renneberg, B., & Boettcher, J. (2015). Internet-based interpretation bias modification for social anxiety: A pilot study. *Journal of Behavior Therapy and Experimental Psychiatry, 49*, 21–29. doi: 10.1016/j.jbtep.2015.04.008

Brown, E. J., Heimberg, R. G., & Juster, H. R. (1995). Social phobia subtype and avoidant personality disorder: Effect on severity of social phobia, impairment, and outcome of cognitive-behavioral treatment. *Behavior Therapy, 26*, 467–486. doi: 10.1016/S0005-7894(05)80095-4

Brown, E. J., Turovsky, J., Heimberg, R. G., Juster, H. R., Brown, T. A., & Barlow, D. H. (1997). Validation of the Social Interaction Anxiety Scale and the Social Phobia Scale across the anxiety disorders. *Psychological Assessment, 9*, 21–27. doi: 10.1037/1040-3590.9.1.21

Brown, T. A., & Barlow, D. H. (2014). *Anxiety and Related Disorders Interview Schedule for DSM-5(ADIS-5)–Lifetime Version*. New York, NY: Oxford University Press

Brown, T. A., DiNardo, P. A., & Barlow, D. H. (1994). *Anxiety Disorders Interview Schedule for DSM-IV (ADIS-IV)*. New York, NY: Oxford University Press.

Brown, T. A., Di Nardo, P. A., Lehman, C. L., & Campbell, L. A. (2001). Reliability of *DSM-IV* anxiety and mood disorders: Implications for the classification of emotional disorders. *Journal of Abnormal Psychology, 110*, 49–58. doi: 10.1037/0021-843X.110.1.49

Brozovich, F., & Heimberg, R. G. (2008). An analysis of post-event processing in social anxiety disorder. *Clinical Psychology Review, 28*, 891–903. doi: 10.1016/j.cpr.2008.01.002

Bruch, M. A., Gorsky, J. M., Collins, T. M., & Berger, P. A. (1989). Shyness and sociability reexamined: A multicomponent analysis. *Journal of Personality and Social Psychology, 57*, 904–915. doi: 10.1037/0022-3514.57.5.904

Bruch, M. A., Heimberg, R. G., Berger, P., & Collins, T. M. (1989). Social phobia and perceptions of early parental and personal characteristics. *Anxiety Research, 2*, 57–65. doi: 10.1080/08917778908249326

Buckner, J. D., Heimberg, R. G., Matthews, R. A., & Silgado, J. (2012). Marijuana-related problems and social anxiety: The role of marijuana behaviors in social situations. *Psychology of Addictive Behaviors, 26*, 151–156. doi: 10.1037/a0025822

Buckner, J. D., Heimberg, R. G., & Schmidt, N. B. (2011). Social anxiety and marijuana-related problems: The role of social avoidance. *Addictive Behaviors, 36*, 129–132. doi: 10.1016/j.addbeh.2010.08.015

Buckner, J. D., Heimberg, R. G., Schneier, F., Liu, S., Wang, S., & Blanco, C. (2012). The relationship between cannabis use disorders and social anxiety disorder in the National Epidemiologic Study of Alcohol and Related Conditions (NESARC). *Drug and Alcohol Dependence, 124*, 128–134. doi: 10.1016/j.drugalcdep.2011.12.023

Buckner, J. D., Ledley, D. R., Heimberg, R. G., & Schmidt, N. B. (2008). Treating comorbid social anxiety and alcohol use disorders: Combining motivation enhancement therapy with cognitive-behavioral therapy. *Clinical Case Studies, 7*, 208–223. doi: 10.1177/1534650107306877

Buckner, J. D., & Schmidt, N. B. (2009). Understanding social anxiety as a risk for alcohol use disorders: Fear of scrutiny, not social interaction fears, prospectively predicts alcohol use disorders. *Journal of Psychiatric Research, 43*, 477–483. doi: 10.1016/j.jpsychires.2008.04.012

Buckner, J. D., Schmidt, N. B., Lang, A. R., Small, J., Schlauch, R. C., & Lewinsohn, P. M. (2008). Specificity of social anxiety disorder as a risk factor for alcohol and cannabis dependence. *Journal of Psychiatric Research*, *42*, 230–239. doi: 10.1016/ j.jpsychires.2007.01.002

Caster, J. B., Inderbitzen, H. M., & Hope, D. (1999). Relationship between youth and parent perceptions of family environment and social anxiety. *Journal of Anxiety Disorders*, *13*, 237–251. doi: 10.1016/S0887-6185(99)00002-X

Chambless, D. L., Fydrich, T., & Rodebaugh, T. L. (2008). Generalized social phobia and avoidant personality disorder: Meaningful distinction or useless duplication? *Depression and Anxiety*, *25*, 8–19. doi: 10.1002/da.20266

Chambless, D. L., Tran, G. Q., & Glass, C. R. (1997). Predictors of response to cognitive-behavioral group therapy for social phobia. *Journal of Anxiety Disorders*, *11*, 221–240. doi: 10.1016/ S0887-6185(97)00008-x

Chapman, T. F., Mannuzza, S., & Fyer, A. J. (1995). Epidemiology and family studies in social phobia. In R. G. Heimberg, M. R. Liebowitz, D. A. Hope, & F. R. Schneier (Eds.), *Social phobia: Diagnosis, assessment, and treatment* (pp. 21–40). New York, NY: Guilford Press.

Choy, Y., Schneier, F. R., Heimberg, R. G., Oh, K.-S., & Liebowitz, M. R. (2008). Features of the offensive subtype of *Taijin-Kyofu-Sho* in U.S. and Korean patients with DSM-IV social anxiety disorder. *Depression and Anxiety*, *25*, 230–240. doi: 10.1002/da.20295

Clark, D. M., Ehlers, A., Hackmann, A., McManus, F., Fennell, M., Grey, N., … Wild, J. (2006). Cognitive therapy versus exposure and applied relaxation in social phobia: A randomized controlled trial. *Journal of Consulting and Clinical Psychology*, *74*, 568–578. doi: 10.1037/0022-006X.74.3.568

Clark, D. M., Ehlers, A., McManus, F., Hackmann, A., Fennell, M., Campbell, H., … Louis, B. (2003). Cognitive therapy versus fluoxetine in generalized social phobia: A randomized placebo-controlled trial. *Journal of Consulting and Clinical Psychology*, *71*, 1058–1067. doi: 10.1037/0022-006X.71.6.1058

Clark, D. M., & Wells, A. (1995). A cognitive model of social phobia. In R. G. Heimberg, M. R. Liebowitz, D. A. Hope, & F. R. Schneier (Eds.), *Social phobia: Diagnosis, assessment, and treatment* (pp. 69–93). New York, NY: Guilford Press.

Coles, M. E., & Heimberg, R. G. (2002). Memory biases in the anxiety disorders: Current status. *Clinical Psychology Review*, *22*, 587–627. doi: 10.1016/ S0272-7358(01)00113-1

Coles, M. E., Turk, C. L., & Heimberg, R. G. (2002). The role of memory perspective in social phobia: Immediate and delayed memories for role-played situations. *Behavioural and Cognitive Psychotherapy*, *30*, 415–425. doi: 10.1017/S1352465802004034

Coles, M. E., Turk, C. L., Heimberg, R. G., & Fresco, D. M. (2001). Effects of varying levels of anxiety within social situations: Relationship to memory perspective and attributions in social phobia. *Behaviour Research and Therapy*, *39*, 651–665. doi: 10.1016/ S0005-7967(00)00035-8

Connor, K. M., Davidson, J.R.T., Churchill, E., Sherwood, A., Foa, E. B., & Weisler, R. H. (2000). Psychometric properties of the Social Phobia Inventory (SPIN): A new self-rating scale. *British Journal of Psychiatry*, *176*, 379–386. doi: 10.1192/ bjp.176.4.379

Connor, K. M., Kobak, K. A., Churchill, E., Katzelnick, D., & Davidson, J.R.T. (2001). Mini-SPIN: A brief screening assessment for generalized social anxiety disorder. *Depression and Anxiety*, *14*, 137–140. doi: 10.1002/da.1055

Courbasson, C. M., & Nishikawa, Y. (2010). Cognitive behavioral group therapy for patients with co-existing social anxiety disorder and substance use disorders: A pilot study. *Cognitive Therapy and Research*, *34*, 82–91. doi: 10.1007/s10608-008 -9216-8

Cox, B. J., Pagura, J., Stein, M. B., & Sareen, J. (2009). The relationship between generalized social phobia and avoidant personality disorder in a national mental health survey. *Depression and Anxiety*, *26*, 354–362. doi: 10.1002/da.20475

Crawford, M., & Manassis, K. (2011). Anxiety, social skills, friendship quality, and peer victimization: An integrated model. *Journal of Anxiety Disorders*, *25*, 924–931. doi: 10.1016/j.janxdis.2011.05.005

Dalrymple, K. L., & Zimmerman, M. (2008). Screening for social fears and social anxiety disorder in psychiatric outpatients. *Comprehensive Psychiatry*, *49*, 399–406.

Dalrymple, K. L., & Zimmerman, M. (2011). Age of onset of social anxiety disorder in depressed outpatients. *Journal of Anxiety Disorders*, *25*(1), 131–137.

Davidson, J. R., Foa, E. B., Huppert, J. D., Keefe, F. J., Franklin, M. E., Compton, J. S., … Gadde, K. M. (2004). Fluoxetine, comprehensive cognitive behavioral therapy, and placebo in generalized social phobia. *Archives of General Psychiatry*, *61*, 1005–1013. doi: 10.1001/archpsych.61.10.1005

Davidson, J.R.T., Miner, C. M., De Veaugh-Geiss, J., Tupler, L. A., Colket, J. T., & Potts, N. L. S. (1997). The Brief Social Phobia Scale: A psychometric evaluation. *Psychological Medicine*, *27*, 161–166. doi: 10.1017/S0033291796004217

Davidson, J.R.T., Potts, N.L.S., Richichi, E. A., Ford, S. M., Krishnan, R. R., Smith, R. D., & Wilson, W. (1991). The Brief Social Phobia Scale. *Journal of Clinical Psychiatry*, *52*, 48–51.

Davidson, J.R.T., Potts, N., Richichi, E., Krishnan, R., Ford, S. M., Smith, R., & Wilson, W. H. (1993). Treatment of social phobia with clonazepam and placebo. *Journal of Clinical Psychopharmacology*, *13*, 423–428. doi: 10.1097/00004714-199312000 -00008

Davila, J., & Beck, J. G. (2002). Is social anxiety associated with impairment in close relationships? A preliminary investigation. *Behavior Therapy*, *33*, 427–446. doi: 10.1016/S0005-7894(02)80037-5

de Lima Osório, F., Crippa, J. A., & Loureiro, S. R. (2010). Further study of the psychometric qualities of a brief screening tool for social phobia (MINI-SPIN) applied to clinical and nonclinical samples. *Perspectives in Psychiatric Care*, *46*, 266–278. doi: 10.1111/j.1744-6163.2010.00261.X

de Ruiter, C., & Brosschot, J. F. (1994). The emotional Stroop interference effect in anxiety: Attentional bias or cognitive avoidance? *Behaviour Research and Therapy*, *32*, 315–319. doi: 10.1016/ 0005-7967(94)90128-7

Deeley, Q., Daly, E. M., Surguladze, S., Page, L., Toal, F., Robertson, D., … Murphy, D. G. (2007). An event related functional magnetic resonance imaging study of facial emotion processing in Asperger syndrome. *Biological Psychiatry*, *62*, 207–217. doi: 10.1016/j.biopsych.2006.09.037

Derryberry, D., & Reed, M. A. (2002). Anxiety-related attentional biases and their regulation by attentional control. *Journal of Abnormal Psychology*, *111*, 225–236. doi: 10.1037/0021-843X.111.2.225

Doehrmann, O., Ghosh, S. S., Polli, F. E., Reynolds, G. O., Horn, F., Keshavan, A., … Gabrieli, J. D. (2013). Predicting treatment response in social anxiety disorder from functional magnetic resonance imaging. *JAMA Psychiatry*, *70*, 87–97. doi: 10.1001/ 2013.jamapsychiatry.5

Dozier, M., Stovall, K. C., & Albus, K. E. (1999). Attachment and psychopathology in adulthood. In J. Cassidy & P. R. Shaver (Eds.), *Handbook of attachment: Theory, research, and clinical applications* (pp. 497–519). New York, NY: Guilford Press.

Edelman, R. E., & Chambless, D. L. (1995). Adherence during session and homework in cognitive-behavioral group treatment of social phobia. *Behaviour Research and Therapy*, *33*, 537–577. doi: 10.1016/0005-7967(94)00068-U

Eikenaes, I., Hummelen, B., Abrahamsen, G., Andrea, H., & Wilberg, T. (2013). Personality functioning in patients with avoidant personality disorder and social phobia. *Journal of Personality Disorders*, *27*, 746–763. doi: 10.1521/pedi_2013_27_109.

Eng, W., Coles, M. E., Heimberg, R. G., & Safren, S. A. (2001). Quality of life following cognitive behavioral treatment for social anxiety disorder: Preliminary findings. *Depression and Anxiety*, *13*, 192–193. doi: 10.1002/da.1037

Eng, W., Coles, M. E., Heimberg, R. G., & Safren, S. A. (2005). Domains of life satisfaction in social anxiety disorder: Relation to symptoms and response to cognitive-behavioral therapy. *Journal of Anxiety Disorders*, *19*, 143–156. doi: 10.1016/j.janxdis .2004.01.007

Eng, W., Heimberg, R. G., Hart, T. A., Schneier, F. R., & Liebowitz, M. R. (2001). Attachment in individuals with social anxiety disorder: The relationship among adult attachment styles, social anxiety and depression. *Emotion*, *1*, 365–380. doi: 10.1037/1528 -3542.1.4.365

Erath, S. A., Flanagan, K. S., & Bierman, K. B. (2007). Social anxiety and peer relations in early adolescence: Behavioral and cognitive factors. *Journal of Abnormal Child Psychology*, *35*, 405–416. doi: 10.1007/s10802-007-9099-2

Erwin, B. A., Heimberg, R. G., Juster, H. R., & Mindlin, M. (2002). Comorbid anxiety and mood disorders among persons with social anxiety disorder. *Behaviour Research and Therapy*, *40*, 19–35. doi: 10.1016/S0005-7967(00)00114-5

Erwin, B. A., Heimberg, R. G., Marx, B. P., & Franklin, M. E. (2006). Traumatic and socially stressful life events among persons with social anxiety disorder. *Journal of Anxiety Disorders*, *20*, 896–914. doi: 10.1016/j.janxdis.2005.05.006

Eysenck, M. W., Derakshan, N., Santos, R., & Calvo, M. G. (2007). Anxiety and cognitive performance: Attentional control theory. *Emotion*, *7*, 336–353. doi: 10.1037/1528-3542.7.2.336

Fedoroff, I. C., & Taylor, S. (2001). Psychological and pharmacological treatments of social phobia: A meta-analysis. *Journal of Clinical Psychopharmacology*, *21*, 311–323. doi: 10.1097/00004714-200106000-00011

Feltner, D. E., Liu-Dumaw, M., Schweizer, E., & Bielski, R. (2011). Efficacy of pregabalin in generalized social anxiety disorder: Results of a double-blind, placebo-controlled, fixed-dose study. *International Clinical Psychopharmacology*, *26*, 213–220. doi: 10.1097/YIC.0b013e32834519bd

Fernandez, K. C., Piccirillo, M. L., & Rodebaugh, T. L. (2014). Self-report assessment: The status of the field and room for improvement. In J. W. Weeks (Ed.), *The Wiley-Blackwell handbook of social anxiety disorder* (pp. 292–319). Chichester, England: Wiley-Blackwell.

Feske, U., Perry, K. J., Chambless, D. L., Renneberg, B., & Goldstein, A. J. (1996). Avoidant personality disorder as a predictor for treatment outcome among generalized social phobics. *Journal of Personality Disorders*, *10*(2), 174–184.

First, M. B., Spitzer, R. L., Gibbon, M., & Williams, J. (2002). *Structured Clinical Interview for DSM-IV-TR Axis I Disorders–Patient Edition (SCID-I/P)*. New York, NY: Biometrics Research Department.

First, M. B., Williams, J.B.W., Karg, R. S., & Spitzer, R. L. (2015). *Structured Clinical Interview for DSM-5–Research Version (SCID-5-RV)*. Arlington, VA: American Psychiatric Association Publishing.

Foa, E. B., Franklin, M. E., & Kozak, M. J. (2001). Social phobia: An information processing perspective. In S. G. Hofmann & P. M. DiBartolo (Eds.), *From social anxiety to social phobia: Multiple perspectives* (pp. 268–280). Needham, MA: Allyn & Bacon.

Foa, E. B., Franklin, M. E., Perry, K. J., & Herbert, J. D. (1996). Cognitive biases in generalized social phobia. *Journal of Abnormal Psychology*, *105*, 433–439. doi: 10.1037/0021-843X.105.3.433

Franklin, M. E., Jaycox, L. H., & Foa, E. B. (1999). Social phobia: Social skills training. In M. Hersen & A. Bellack (Eds.), *Handbook of comparative interventions for adult disorders* (2nd ed., pp. 317–339). New York, NY: Wiley.

Fresco, D. M., Coles, M. E., Heimberg, R. G., Liebowitz, M. R., Hami, S., Stein, M. B., & Goetz, D. (2001). The Liebowitz Social Anxiety Scale: A comparison of the psychometric properties of self-report and clinician-administered formats. *Psychological Medicine*, *31*, 1025–1035. doi: 10.1017/S0033291701004056

Furmark, T., Tillfors, M., Marteinsdottir, I., Fischer, H., Pissiota, A., Långström, B., & Fredrikson, M. (2002). Common changes in cerebral blood flow in patients with social phobia treated with citalopram or cognitive-behavioral therapy. *Archives of General Psychiatry*, *59*, 425–433. doi: 10.1001/archpsych.59.5.425

Gaston, J. E., Abbott, M. J., Rapee, R. M., & Neary, S. A. (2006). Do empirically supported treatments generalize to private practice? A benchmark study of a cognitive-behavioural group treatment programme for social phobia. *British Journal of Clinical Psychology*, *45*, 33–48. doi: 10.1348/014466505X35146

Gelernter, C. S., Uhde, T. W., Cimbolic, P., Arnkoff, D. B., Vittone, B. J., & Tancer, M. E. (1991). Cognitive-behavioral approaches and pharmacological treatments of social phobia: A controlled study. *Archives of General Psychiatry*, *48*, 938–945. doi: 10.1001/archpsyc.1991.01810340070009

Gilbert, P. (2014). Evolutionary models: Practical and conceptual utility for the treatment and study of social anxiety disorder. In J. W. Weeks (Ed.), *The Wiley-Blackwell handbook of social anxiety disorder* (pp. 24–52). Chichester, England: Wiley-Blackwell.

Gilboa-Schechtman, E., Franklin, M. E., & Foa, E. B. (2000). Anticipated reactions to social events: Differences among individuals with generalized social phobia, obsessive compulsive disorder, and nonanxious controls. *Cognitive Therapy and Research*, *24*, 731–746. doi: 10.1023/A:1005595513315

Gilboa-Schechtman, E., Shachar, I., & Helpman, L. (2014). Evolutionary perspective on social anxiety. In S. G. Hofmann, & P. M. DiBartolo (Eds.). *Social anxiety: Clinical, developmental, and social perspectives* (3rd ed., pp. 599–622). Waltham, MA: Academic Press.

Goldin, P. R., Manber-Ball, T., Werner, K., Heimberg, R., & Gross, J. J. (2009). Neural mechanisms of cognitive reappraisal of negative self-beliefs in social anxiety disorder. *Biological Psychiatry*, *66*, 1091–1099. doi: 10.1016/j.biopsych.2009.07.014

Goldin, P. R., Morrison, A., Jazaieri, H., Brozovich, F., Heimberg, R. G., & Gross, J. J. (2016). Group CBT versus MBSR for social anxiety disorder: A randomized controlled trial. *Journal of Consulting and Clinical Psychology*, *84*, 427–437.

Goldin, P. R., Ziv, M., Jazaieri, H., Hahn, K., Heimberg, R., & Gross, J. J. (2013). Impact of cognitive-behavioral therapy for social anxiety disorder on the neural dynamics of cognitive reappraisal of negative self-beliefs: Randomized clinical trial. *JAMA Psychiatry*, *70*, 1048–1056. doi: 10.1001/jamapsychiatry.2013.234

Goldin, P. R., Ziv, M., Jazaieri, H., Weeks, J., Heimberg, R. G., & Gross, J. J. (2014). Impact of cognitive-behavioral therapy for social anxiety disorder on the neural bases of emotional reactivity to and regulation of social evaluation. *Behaviour Research and Therapy*, *62*, 97–106. doi: 10.1016/.2014.08.005

Goldin, P. R., Ziv, M., Jazaieri, H., Werner, K., Kraemer, H., Heimberg, R. G., & Gross, J. J. (2012). Cognitive reappraisal self-efficacy mediates the effects of individual cognitive-behavioral therapy for social anxiety disorder in a randomized controlled trial. *Journal of Consulting and Clinical Psychology*, *80*, 1034–1040.

Gould, R. A., Buckminster, S., Pollack, M. H., Otto, M. W., & Yap, L. (1997). Cognitive-behavioral and pharmacological treatment for social phobia: A meta-analysis. *Clinical Psychology: Science and Practice*, *4*, 291–306. doi: 10.1111/j.1468-2850.1997.tb00123.x

Grant, B. F., Hasin, D. S., Blanco, C., Stinson, F. S., Chou, S. P., Goldstein, R. B., ... Huang, B. (2005). The epidemiology of social anxiety disorder in the United States: Results from the National Epidemiologic Survey on Alcohol and Related Conditions. *Journal of Clinical Psychiatry*, *66*, 1351–1361. doi: 10.4088/JCP.v66n1102

Grant, B. F., Stinson, F. S., Dawson, D. A., Chou, S. P., Ruan, J., & Pickering, R. P. (2004). Co-occurrence of 12–month alcohol and drug use disorders and personality disorders in the United States: Results from the National Epidemiologic Survey on Alcohol and Related Conditions. *Archives of General Psychiatry*, *61*, 362–368. doi: 10.1001/archpsyc.61.4.361

Greenberg, M. T. (1999). Attachment and psychopathology in childhood. In J. Cassidy & P. R. Shaver (Eds.), *Handbook of attachment: Theory, research, and clinical applications* (pp. 469–496). New York, NY: Guilford Press.

Guastella, A. J., Howard, A. L., Dadds, M. R., Mitchell, P., & Carson, D. S. (2009). A randomized controlled trial of intranasal oxytocin as an adjunct to exposure therapy for social anxiety disorder. *Psychoneuroendocrinology*, *34*, 917–923. doi: 10.1016/j.psyneuen.2009.01.005

Guastella, A. J., Richardson, R., Lovibond, P. F., Rapee, R. M., Gaston, J. E., Mitchell, P., & Dadds, M. R. (2008). A randomized controlled trial of D-cycloserine enhancement of exposure therapy for social anxiety disorder. *Biological Psychiatry*, *63*, 544-549. doi: 10.1016/j.biopsych.2007.11.011

Habke, A. M., Hewitt, P. L., Norton, R., & Asmundson, G. (1997). The Social Phobia and Social Interaction Anxiety Scales: An exploration of the dimensions of social anxiety and sex differences in the structure and relations and pathology. *Journal of Psychopathology and Behavioral Assessment*, *19*, 21–39. doi: 10.1007/BF02263227

Hackmann, A., Clark, D. M., & McManus, F. (2000). Recurrent images and early memories in social phobia. *Behaviour Research and Therapy*, *38*, 601–610. doi: 10.1016/S0005-7967(99)00161-8

Hackmann, A., Surawy, C., & Clark, D. M. (1998). Seeing yourself through others' eyes: A study of spontaneously occurring images in social phobia. *Behavioral and Cognitive Psychotherapy*, *26*, 3–12. doi: 10.1017/S1352465898000022

Hansen, R. A., Gaynes, B. N., Gartlehner, G., Moore, C. G., Tiwari, R., & Lohr, K. N. (2008). Efficacy and tolerability of second-generation antidepressants in social anxiety disorder. *International Clinical Psychopharmacology*, *23*, 170–179. doi: 10.1176/appi.ps.59.10.1121

Hart, T. A., Jack, M. S., Turk, C. L., & Heimberg, R. G. (1999). Issues for the measurement of social phobia. In H.G.M. Westenberg & J. A. den Boer (Eds.), *Social phobia: Recent trends and progress* (pp. 133–155). Amsterdam, Netherlands: Syn-Thesis.

Hayes, S. A., Miller, N. A., Hope, D. A., Heimberg, R. G., & Juster, H. R. (2008). Assessing client progress session-by-session: The Social Anxiety Session Change Index. *Cognitive and Behavioral Practice*, *15*, 203–211. doi: 10.1016/j.cbpra.2007.02.010

Hazen, A. L., & Stein, M. B. (1995). Clinical phenomenology and comorbidity. In M. B. Stein (Ed.), *Social phobia: Clinical and research perspectives* (pp. 3–41). Washington, DC: American Psychiatric Press.

Hedges, D. W., Brown, B. L., Shwalb, D. A., Godfrey, K., & Larcher, A. M. (2007). The efficacy of selective serotonin reuptake inhibitors in adult social anxiety disorder: A meta-analysis of double-blind, placebo-controlled trials. *Journal of Psychophar-macology*, *21*, 102–111. doi: 10.1177/0269881106065102

Heeren, A., Maurage, P., Rossignol, M., Vanhaelen, M., Peschard, V., Eeckhout, C., & Philippot, P. (2012). Self-report version of the Liebowitz Social Anxiety Scale: Psychometric properties of the French version. *Canadian Journal of Behavioural Science*, *44*, 99–107. doi: 10.1037/a0026249

Heeren, A., Mogoaşe, C., McNally, R. J., Schmitz, A., & Philippot, P. (2015). Does attention bias modification improve attentional control? A double-blind randomized experiment with individuals with social anxiety disorder. *Journal of Anxiety Disorders*, *29*, 35–42. doi: 10.1016/j.janxdis.2014.10.007

Heeren, A., Mogoaşe, C., Philippot, P., & McNally, R. J. (2015). Attention bias modification for social anxiety: A systematic review and meta-analysis. *Clinical Psychology Review*, *40*, 76–90. doi: 10.1016/j.cpr.2015.06.001

Heeren, A., Peschard, V., & Philippot, P. (2012). The causal role of attentional bias for threat cues in social anxiety: A test on a cyber-ostracism task. *Cognitive Therapy and Research*, *36*, 512–521. doi: 10.1007/s10608-011-9394-7

Heimberg, R. G. (1996). Social phobia, avoidant personality disorder, and the multiaxial conceptualization of interpersonal anxiety. In P. Salkovskis (Ed.), *Trends in cognitive and behavioural therapies* (pp. 43–62). Chichester, England: Wiley.

Heimberg, R. G., & Becker, R. E. (2002). *Cognitive-behavioral group therapy for social phobia: Basic mechanisms and clinical strategies*. New York, NY: Guilford Press.

Heimberg, R. G., Brozovich, F. A., & Rapee, R. M. (2014). A cognitive-behavioral model of social anxiety disorder. In S. G. Hofmann, & P. M. DiBartolo (Eds.), *Social anxiety: Clinical, developmental, and social perspectives* (3rd ed., pp. 705–728). Waltham, MA: Academic Press. doi: 10.1016/B978-0-12-394427-6.00024-8

Heimberg, R. G., Dodge, C. S., Hope, D. A., Kennedy, C. R., Zollo, L., & Becker, R. E. (1990). Cognitive behavioral group treatment of social phobia: Comparison to a credible placebo control. *Cognitive Therapy and Research*, *14*, 1–23. doi: 10.1007/BF01173521

Heimberg, R. G., Hofmann, S. G., Liebowitz, M. R., Schneier, F. R., Smits, J.A.J., Stein, M. B., ... Craske, M. G. (2014). Social anxiety disorder in DSM-5. *Depression and Anxiety*, *31*, 472–479. doi: 10.1002/da.22231

Heimberg, R. G., Holt, C. S., Schneier, F. R., Spitzer, R. L., & Liebowitz, M. R. (1993). The issue of subtypes in the diagnosis of social phobia. *Journal of Anxiety Disorders*, *7*, 249–269. doi: 10.1016/0887-6185(93)90006-7

Heimberg, R. G., Horner, K. J., Juster, H. R., Safren, S. A., Brown, E. J., Schneier, F. R., & Liebowitz, M. R. (1999). Psychometric properties of the Liebowitz Social Anxiety Scale. *Psychological Medicine*, *29*, 199–212. doi: 10.1017/S0033291798007879

Heimberg, R. G., Liebowitz, M. R., Hope, D. A., Schneier, F. R., Holt, C. S., Welkowitz, L. A., ... Klein, D. F. (1998). Cognitive-behavioral group treatment versus phenelzine in social phobia: 12-week outcome. *Archives of General Psychiatry*, *55*, 1133–1141. doi: 10.1001/archpsyc.55.12.1133

Heimberg, R. G., Mueller, G. P., Holt, C. S., Hope, D. A., & Liebowitz, M. R. (1992). Assessment of anxiety in social interaction and being observed by others: The Social Interaction Anxiety Scale and the Social Phobia Scale. *Behavior Therapy*, *23*, 53–73. doi: 10.1016/S0005-7894(05)80308-9

Heimberg, R. G., Salzman, D., Holt, C. S., & Blendell, K. (1993). Cognitive behavioral group treatment of social phobia: Effectiveness at 5-year follow-up. *Cognitive Therapy and Research*, *17*, 325–339. doi: 10.1007/BF01177658

Heinrichs, M., Chen, F. S. & Domes, G. (2012). Oxytocin. In S. G. Hofmann (Ed.), *Psychobiological approaches for anxiety disorders: Treatment combination strategies* (pp. 123–143). Chichester, England: Wiley-Blackwell.

Herbert, J. D., Bellack, A. S., & Hope, D. A. (1991). Concurrent validity of the Social Phobia and Anxiety Inventory. *Journal of Psychopathology and Behavioral Assessment*, *13*, 357–369. doi: 10.1007/BF00960447

Herbert, J. D., Brandsma, L. L., & Fischer, L. (2014). Assessment of social anxiety and social phobia. In S. G. Hofmann, & P. M. DiBartolo (Eds.). *Social anxiety: Clinical, developmental, and social perspectives* (3rd ed., pp. 46–94). Waltham, MA: Academic Press.

Himle, J. A., Weaver, A., Bybee, D., O'Donnell, L., Vlnka, S., Laviolette, W., ... Levine, D. S. (2014). A comparison of unemployed job-seekers with and without social anxiety. *Psychiatric Services*, *65*, 924–930. doi: 10.1176/appi.ps.201300201

Hirsch, C., Clark, D. M., & Mathews, A. (2006). Imagery and interpretations in social phobia: Support for the combined cognitive biases hypothesis. *Behavior Therapy, 37,* 223–236. doi: 10.1016/j.beth.2006.02.001

Hirsch, C. R., Clark, D. M., Mathews, A., & Williams, R. (2003). Self-images play a causal role in social phobia. *Behaviour Research and Therapy, 41,* 909–921. doi: 10.1016/S0005-7967(02)00103-1

Hirsch, C. R., Mathews, A., & Clark, D. M. (2007). Inducing an interpretation bias changes self-imagery: A preliminary investigation. *Behaviour Research and Therapy, 45,* 2173–2181. doi: 10.1016/j.brat.2006.11.001

Hirsch, C. R., Mathews, A., Clark, D. M., Williams, R., & Morrison, J. A. (2006). The causal role of negative imagery in social anxiety: A test in confident public speakers. *Journal of Behavior Therapy and Experimental Psychiatry, 37,* 159–170. doi: 10.1016/j.jbtep.2005.03.003

Hirsch, C. R., Meynen, T., & Clark, D. M. (2004). Negative self-imagery in social anxiety contaminates social interactions. *Memory, 12,* 496–506. doi: 10.1080/09658210444000106

Hirshfeld-Becker, D. R., Micco, J. A, Wang, C. H. & Hennin, A. (2014). Behavioral inhibition: A discrete precursor to social anxiety disorder? In J. W. Weeks (Ed.), *The Wiley-Blackwell handbook of social anxiety disorder* (pp. 133–158). Chichester, England: Wiley-Blackwell.

Hofmann, S. G. (2007). Cognitive factors that maintain social anxiety disorder: A comprehensive model and its treatment implications. *Cognitive Behaviour Therapy, 36,* 193–209. doi: 10.1080/16506070701421313

Hofmann, S., Asnaani, A., & Hinton, D. (2010). Cultural aspects in social anxiety and social anxiety disorder. *Depression and Anxiety, 27,* 1117–1127. doi: 10.1002/da.20759

Hofmann, S. G., Meuret, A. E., Smits, J.A.J., Simon, N. M., Pollack, M. H., Eisenmenger, K., ... Otto, M. W. (2006). Augmentation of exposure therapy with D-cycloserine for social anxiety disorder. *Archives of General Psychiatry, 63,* 298–304. doi: 10.1001/archpsyc.63.3.298

Hofmann, S. G., Newman, M. G., Becker, E., Taylor, C. B., & Roth, W. T. (1995). Social phobia with and without avoidant personality disorder: Preliminary behavior therapy outcome findings. *Journal of Anxiety Disorders, 9,* 427–438. doi: 10.1016/0887-6185(95)00022-G

Hofmann, S. G., Smits, J.A.J., Rosenfield, D., Simon, N., Otto, M. W., Meuret, A. E., ... Pollack, M. H. (2013). D-cycloserine as an augmentation strategy with cognitive-behavioral therapy for social anxiety disorder. *American Journal of Psychiatry, 170,* 751–758. doi: 10.1176/appi.ajp.2013.12070974

Hope, D. A., Heimberg, R. G., & Bruch, M. A. (1995). Dismantling cognitive-behavioral group therapy for social phobia. *Behaviour Research and Therapy, 33,* 637–650. doi: 10.1016/0005-7967(95)00013-N

Hope, D. A., Heimberg, R. G., & Turk, C. L. (2010). *Managing social anxiety: A cognitive-behavioral approach (client workbook)* (2nd ed.). New York, NY: Oxford University Press.

Hope, D. A., Herbert, J. D., & White, C. (1995). Diagnostic subtype, avoidant personality disorder, and efficacy of cognitive behavioral group therapy for social phobia. *Cognitive Therapy and Research, 19,* 399–417. doi: 10.1007/BF02230408

Hudson, J. L., Rapee, R. M., Lyneham, H. J., McLellan, L. F., Wuthrich, V. M., & Schniering, C. A. (2015). Comparing outcomes for children with different anxiety disorders following cognitive behavioural therapy. *Behaviour Research and Therapy, 72,* 30–37. doi: 10.1016/j.brat.2015.06.007

Huppert, J. D., Strunk, D. R., Ledley, D. R., Davidson, J.R.T., & Foa, E. B. (2008). Generalized social anxiety disorder and avoidant personality disorder: Structural analysis and treatment outcome. *Depression and Anxiety, 25,* 441–448. doi: 10.1002/da.20349

Isomura, K., Boman, M., Ruck, C., Serlachius, E., Larsson, H., Lichtenstein, P., & Mataix-Cols. (2015). Population-based, multi-generational family clustering study of social anxiety disorder and avoidant personality disorder. *Psychological Medicine, 45,* 1581–1589. doi: 10.1017/S0033291714002116

Kagan, J. (1994). *The nature of the child.* New York, NY: Basic Books.

Kagan, J., Arcus, D., & Snidman, N. (1993). The idea of temperament: Where do we go from here? In R. Plomin & G. E. McClearn (Eds.), *Nature, nurture & psychology* (pp. 197–210). Washington, DC: American Psychological Association. doi: 10.1037/10131-009

Kagan, J., Reznick, J. S., & Snidman, N. (1988). Biological bases of childhood shyness. *Science, 240,* 167–171. doi: 10.1126/science.3353713

Keller, M. B. (2003). The lifelong course of social anxiety disorder: A clinical perspective. *Acta*

Psychiatrica Scandinavica, 108(Suppl. 417), 85–94. doi: 10.1034/j.1600-0447.108.s417.6.x

Kelly, J. M., Jakubovski, E., & Bloch, M. H. (2015). Prognostic subgroups for remission and response in the Coordinated Anxiety Learning and Management (CALM) trial. *Journal of Clinical Psychiatry, 76,* 267–278. doi: 10.4088/JCP.13m08922.

Kessler, R. C., Berglund, P. D., Demler, O., Olga, J. R., Merikangas, K. R., & Walters, E. E. (2005). Lifetime prevalence and age-of-onset distributions of DSM-IV disorders in the National Comorbidity Survey Replication. *Archives of General Psychiatry, 62,* 593–602. doi: 10.1001/archpsyc.62.6.593

Kessler, R. C., Chiu, W. T., Demler, O., Merikangas, K., & Walters, E. E. (2005). Prevalence, severity, and comorbidity of 12-month DSM-IV disorders in the National Comorbidity Survey Replication. *Archives of General Psychiatry, 62,* 617–627. doi: 10.1001/archpsyc.62.6.617

Kessler, R. C., Stein, M. B., & Berglund, P. (1998). Social phobia subtypes in the National Comorbidity Survey. *American Journal of Psychiatry, 155,* 613–619. doi: 10.1176/ajp.155.5.613

Kimbrel, N. A. (2008). A model of the development and maintenance of generalized social phobia. *Clinical Psychology Review, 28,* 592–612. doi: 10.1016/j.cpr.2007.08.003

Kobak, K. A., Greist, J. H., Jefferson, J. W., & Katzelnick, D. J. (2002). Fluoxetine in social phobia: A double-blind, placebo-controlled pilot study. *Journal of Clinical Psychopharmacology, 22,* 257–262. doi: 10.1097/00004714-200206000-00005

Krans, J., de Bree, J., & Bryant, R. A. (2014). Autobiographical memory bias in social anxiety. *Memory, 22,* 890–897. doi: 10.1080/096.58211.2013.844261

Kuckertz, J. M., Gildebrant, E., Liliequist, B., Karlström, P., Väppling, C., Bodlund, O., … Carlbring, P. (2014). Moderation and mediation of the effect of attention training in social anxiety disorder. *Behaviour Research and Therapy, 53,* 30–40. doi: 10.1016/j.brat.2013.12.003

Kushner, M. G., Maurer, E. W., Thuras, P., Donahue, C., Frye, B., Menary, K. R., … Van Demark, J. (2013). Hybrid cognitive behavioral therapy versus relaxation training for co-occurring anxiety and alcohol disorder: A randomized clinical trial. *Journal of Consulting and Clinical Psychology, 81,* 429–442. doi: 10.1037/a0031301

Labuschagne, I., Phan, K. L., Wood, A., Angstadt, M., Chua, P., Heinrichs, M., … Nathan, P. J. (2010).

Oxytocin attenuates amygdala reactivity to fear in generalized social anxiety disorder. *Neuropsychopharmacology, 35,* 2403–2413. doi: 10.1038/npp.2010.123

LaFreniere, P. J., & Sroufe, L. A. (1985). Profiles of peer competence in the preschool: Interrelations between measures, influence of social ecology, and relation to attachment history. *Developmental Psychology, 21,* 56–69. doi: 10.1037/0012-1649.21.1.56

La Greca, A. M., Dandes, S. K., Wick, P., Shaw, K., & Stone, W. L. (1988). Development of the Social Anxiety Scale for Children: Reliability and concurrent validity. *Journal of Clinical Child Psychology, 17,* 84–91. doi: 10.1207/s15374424jccp 1701_11

Leary, M. R. (1983). A brief version of the Fear of Negative Evaluation Scale. *Personality and Social Psychology Bulletin, 9,* 371–375. doi: 10.1177/0146167283093007

Leary, M. R., & Jongman-Sereno, K. P. (2014). Social anxiety as an early warning system: A refinement and extension of the self-presentation theory of social anxiety. In S. G. Hofmann & P.M. DiBartolo (Eds.), *Social anxiety: Clinical, developmental, and social perspectives* (3rd ed., pp. 579–597). Waltham, MA: Academic Press.

Leary, M. R., Kowalski, R. M., & Campbell, C. D. (1988). Self-presentational concerns and social anxiety: The role of generalized impression expectancies. *Journal of Research in Personality, 22,* 308–321. doi: 10.1016/0092-6566(88)90032-3

Ledley, D. R., & Heimberg, R. G. (2005). Social anxiety disorder. In M. M. Antony, D. R. Ledley, & R. G. Heimberg (Eds.), *Improving outcomes and preventing relapse in cognitive behavioral therapy* (pp. 38–76). New York, NY: Guilford Press.

Ledley, D. R., Heimberg, R. G., Hope, D. A., Hayes, S. A., Zaider, T. I., Van Dyke, M., … Fresco, D. M. (2009). Efficacy of a manualized and workbook-driven individual treatment for social anxiety disorder. *Behavior Therapy, 40,* 414–424. doi: 10.1016/j.beth.2008/.12.001

Ledley, D. R., Huppert, J. D., Foa, E. B., Davidson, J.R.T., Keefe, F. J., & Potts, N.L.S. (2005). The impact of depressive symptoms on the treatment of generalized social anxiety disorder. *Depression and Anxiety, 22,* 161–167. doi: 10.1002/da.20121

Ledley, D. R., Storch, E. A., Coles, M. E., Heimberg, R. G., Moser, J., & Bravata, E. A. (2006). The relationship between childhood teasing and later interpersonal functioning. *Journal of Psychopathology and Behavioral Assessment*, *28*, 33–40. doi: 10.1007/s10862-006-4539-9

Leichsenring, F., Salzer, S., Beutel, M. E., Herpertz, S., Hiller, W., Hoyer, J., … Leibing, E. (2013). Psychodynamic therapy and cognitive-behavioral therapy in social anxiety disorder: A multicenter randomized controlled trial. *American Journal of Psychiatry*, *170*, 759–767. doi: 10.1176/appi.ajp.2013.12081125. Erratum in: *American Journal of Psychiatry*, 2013, 170, 1373.

Leichsenring, F., Salzer, S., Beutel, M. E., Herpertz, S., Hiller, W., Hoyer, J., … Leibing, E. (2014). Long-term outcome of psychodynamic therapy and cognitive-behavioral therapy in social anxiety disorder. *American Journal of Psychiatry*, *171*, 1074–1082. doi: 10.1176/appi.ajp.2014.13111514.

LeMoult, J., Rowa, K., Antony, M. M., Chudzik, S., & McCabe, R. E. (2014). Impact of comorbid depression on cognitive behavioral group treatment for social anxiety disorder. *Behaviour Change*, *31*, 53–64. doi: 10.1017/bec.2013.32

Leung, A. W., & Heimberg, R. G. (1996). Homework compliance, perceptions of control, and outcome of cognitive-behavioral treatment of social phobia. *Behaviour Research and Therapy*, *34*, 423–432. doi: 10.1016/0005-7967(96)00014-9

Liebowitz, M. (1987). Social phobia. *Modern Problems of Pharmacopsychiatry*, *22*, 141–173.

Liebowitz, M. R., Gelenberg, A. J., & Munjack, D. (2005). Venlafaxine extended release vs. placebo and paroxetine in social anxiety disorder. *Archives of General Psychiatry*, *62*, 190–198. doi: 10.1001/archpsyc.62.2.190

Liebowitz, M. R., Heimberg, R. G., Schneier, F. R., Hope, D. A., Davies, S., Holt, C. S., … Klein, D. F. (1999). Cognitive-behavioral group therapy versus phenelzine in social phobia: Long term outcome. *Depression and Anxiety*, *10*, 89–98. doi: 10.1002/(SICI)1520-6394(1999)10:3<89::AID-DA1>3.0.CO;2-5

Liebowitz, M. R., Mangano, R. M., Bradwejn, J., & Asnis, G. (2005). A randomized controlled trial of venlafaxine extended release in generalized social anxiety disorder. *Journal of Clinical Psychiatry*, *66*, 238–247. doi: 10.4088/JCP.v66n0213

Lincoln, T. M., Rief, W., Hahlweg, K., Frank, M., von Witzleben, I., Schroeder, B., & Fiegenbaum, W. (2003). Effectiveness of an empirically supported treatment for social phobia in the field. *Behaviour Research and Therapy*, *41*, 1251–1269. doi: 10.1016/S000

Lundh, L. G., & Öst, L.-G. (1996). Recognition bias for critical faces in social phobics. *Behaviour Research and Therapy*, *34*, 787–794. doi: 10.1016/0005-7967(96)00035-6

Lundh, L. G., & Öst, L.-G. (1997). Explicit and implicit memory bias in social phobia: The role of subdiagnostic type. *Behaviour Research and Therapy*, *35*, 305–317. doi: 10.1016/S0005-7967(96)00122-2

Magee, W. J., Eaton, W. W., Wittchen, H.-U., McGonagle, K. A., & Kessler, R. C. (1996). Agoraphobia, simple phobia, and social phobia in the National Comorbidity Survey. *Archives of General Psychiatry*, *53*, 159–168. doi: 10.1001/archpsyc.1996.01830020077009

Makkar, S. R., & Grisham, J. R. (2011). Social anxiety and the effects of negative self-imagery on emotion, cognition, and post-event processing. *Behaviour Research and Therapy*, *49*, 654–664. doi: 10.1016/j.brat.2011.07.004

Mannuzza, S., Schneier, F. R., Chapman, T. F., Liebowitz, M. R., Klein, D. F., & Fyer, A. J. (1995). Generalized social phobia: Reliability and validity. *Archives of General Psychiatry*, *52*(3), 230–237.

Marom, S., Gilboa-Schechtman, E., Aderka, I. M., Weizman, A., & Hermesh, H. (2009). Impact of depression on treatment effectiveness and gains maintenance in social phobia: A naturalistic study of cognitive behavior group therapy. *Depression and Anxiety*, *26*, 289–300. doi: 10.1002/da.20390

Marques, L., Porter, E., Keshaviah, A., Pollack, M. H., Van Ameringen, M., Stein, M. B., & Simon, N. M. (2012). Avoidant personality disorder in individuals with generalized social anxiety disorder: What does it add? *Journal of Anxiety Disorders*, *26*, 665–672. doi: 10.1016/j.janxdis.2012.05.004

Masia-Warner, C., Storch, E. A., Pincus, D. B., Klein, R. G., Heimberg, R. G., & Liebowitz, M. R. (2003). The Liebowitz Social Anxiety Scale for Children and Adolescents: An initial psychometric investigation. *Journal of the American Academy of Child & Adolescent Psychiatry*, *42*, 1076–1084. doi: 10.1097/01.CHI.0000070249.24125.89

Mathew, S. J., Coplan, J. D., & Gorman, J. M. (2001). Neurobiological mechanisms of social anxiety disorder. *American Journal of Psychiatry*, *158*, 1558–1567. doi: 10.1176/appi.ajp.158.10.1558

Mattia, J. I., Heimberg, R. G., & Hope, D. A. (1993). The revised Stroop color-naming task in social phobics. *Behaviour Research and Therapy*, *31*, 305–313. doi: 10.1016/0005-7967(93)90029-T

Mattick, R. P., & Clarke, J. C. (1998). Development and validation of measures of social phobia scrutiny fear and social interaction anxiety. *Behaviour Research and Therapy*, *36*, 455–470. doi: 10.1016/S0005-7967(97)10031-6

Mayo-Wilson, E., Dias, S., Mavranezouli, I., Kew, K., Clark, D. M., Ades, A. E., & Pilling, S. (2014). Psychological and pharmacological interventions for social anxiety disorder in adults: A systematic review and network meta-analysis. *Lancet Psychiatry*, *1*, 368–376. doi: 10.1016/S2215-0366(14)70329-3

McCabe, R. E., Antony, M. M., Summerfeldt, L. J., Liss, A., & Swinson, R. P. (2003). Preliminary examination of the relationship between anxiety disorders in adults and self-reported history of teasing or bullying experiences. *Cognitive Behaviour Therapy*, *32*, 187–193. doi: 10.1080/16506070310005051

McCabe, R. E., Miller, J. L., Laugesen, N., Antony, M. M., & Young, L. (2010). The relationship between anxiety disorders in adults and recalled childhood teasing. *Journal of Anxiety Disorders*, *24*, 238–243. doi: 10.1016/j.janxdis.2009.11.002

McEvoy, P. M. (2007). Effectiveness of cognitive behavioural group therapy for social phobia in a community clinic: A benchmarking study. *Behaviour Research and Therapy*, *45*, 3030–3040. doi: 10.1016/j.brat.2007.08.002

McEvoy, P., Erceg-Hurn, D., Saulsman, L., & Thibodeau, M. (2015). Imagery enhancements increase the effectiveness of cognitive behavioural group therapy for social anxiety disorder: A benchmarking study. *Behaviour Research and Therapy*, *65*, 42–51. doi: 10.1016/j.brat.2014.12.011

McEvoy, P. M., Nathan, P., Rapee, R. M., & Campbell, B.N.C. (2012). Cognitive behavioural group therapy for social phobia: Evidence of transportability to community clinics. *Behaviour Research and Therapy*, *50*, 258–265. doi: 10.1016/j.brat.2012.01.009

McLean, C. P., & Anderson, E. R. (2009). Brave men and timid women? A review of the gender differences in fear and anxiety. *Clinical Psychology Review*, *29*, 496–505. doi: 10.1016/j.cpr.2009.05.003

McNeil, D. W., & Quentin, L. L. (2014). Clinical interviews: Empirical overview and procedural recommendations. In J. W. Weeks (Ed.), *The Wiley-Blackwell handbook of social anxiety disorder* (pp. 271–291). Chichester, England: Wiley-Blackwell.

Mennin, D. S., Fresco, D. M., Heimberg, R. G., Schneier, F. R., Davies, S. O., & Liebowitz, M. R. (2002). Screening for social anxiety disorder in the clinical setting: Using the Liebowitz Social Anxiety Scale. *Journal of Anxiety Disorders*, *16*, 661–673. doi: 10.1016/S0887-6185(02)00134-2

Mickelson, K. D., Kessler, R. C., & Shaver, P. R. (1997). Adult attachment in a nationally representative sample. *Journal of Personality and Social Psychology*, *73*, 1092–1106. doi: 10.1037/0022-3514.73.5.1092

Moriya, J., & Sugiura, Y. (2012). Impaired attentional disengagement from stimuli matching the contents of working memory in social anxiety. *PloS One*, e47221. doi: 10.1371/journal.pone.0047221

Moriya, J., & Tanno, Y. (2008). Relationships between negative emotionality and attentional control in effortful control. *Personality and Individual Differences*, *44*, 1348–1355. doi: 10.1016/j.paid.2007.12.003

Morrison, A. S., Gordon, D., & Heimberg, R. G. (2013). Anxiety disorders. In M. D. Robinson, E. R. Watkins, & E. Harmon-Jones (Eds.), *Guilford handbook of cognition and emotion* (pp. 421–442). New York, NY: Guilford Press.

Morrison, A. S., & Heimberg, R. G. (2013). Attentional control mediates the effect of social anxiety on positive affect. *Journal of Anxiety Disorders*, *27*, 56–67. doi: 10.1016/j.janxdis.2012.10.002

Mörtberg, E., Clark, D. M., & Bejerot, S. (2011). Intensive group cognitive therapy and individual cognitive therapy for social phobia: Sustained improvement at 5-year follow-up. *Journal of Anxiety Disorders*, *25*, 994–1000. doi: 10.1016/j.janxdis.2011.06.007

Moscovitch, D. A. (2009). What is the core fear in social phobia? A new model to facilitate individualized case conceptualization and treatment. *Cognitive and Behavioral Practice*, *16*, 123–134. doi: 10.1016/j.cbpra.2008.04.002

Moscovitch, D. A., Chiupka, C. A., & Gavric, D. L. (2013). Within the mind's eye: Negative mental imagery activates different emotion regulation strategies in high versus low socially anxious individuals. *Journal of Behavior Therapy and Experimental Psychiatry*, *44*, 426–432. doi: 10.1016/j.jbtep.2013.05.002

Moscovitch, D. A., Hofmann, S. G., Suvak, M. K., & In-Albon, T. (2005). Mediation of changes in anxiety and depression during treatment of social phobia. *Journal of Consulting and Clinical Psychology*, *73*, 945–952. doi: 10.1037/0022-006X.73.5.945

Moser, J. S., Hajcak, G., Huppert, J. D., Foa, E. B., & Simons, R. F. (2008). Interpretation bias in social anxiety as detected by event-related brain potentials. *Emotion, 8,* 693–700. doi: 10.1037/a0013173

Murray, L., Cooper, P., Creswell, C., Schofield, E., & Sack, C. (2007). The effects of maternal social phobia on mother-infant interactions and infant social responsiveness. *Journal of Child Psychology and Psychiatry, 48,* 45–52. doi: 10.1111/j.1469-7610.2006.01657.x

National Institute for Health and Care Excellence. (2013). Social anxiety disorder: Recognition, assessment and treatment. Retrieved from https://www.nice.org.uk/guidance/cg159

Ng, A. S., Abbott, M. J., & Hunt, C. (2014). The effect of self-imagery on symptoms and processes in social anxiety: A systematic review. *Clinical Psychology Review, 34,* 620–633. doi: 10.1016/j.cpr.2014.09.003

Olfson, M., Guardino, M., Struening, E., Schneier, F. R., Hellman, F., & Klein, D. F. (2000). Barriers to treatment of social anxiety. *American Journal of Psychiatry, 157,* 521–527. doi: 10.1176/appi.ajp.157.4.521

Ollendick, T. H., & Benoit, K. (2012). A parent-child interactional model of social anxiety disorder in youth. *Clinical Child and Family Psychology Review, 15,* 81–91. doi: 10.1007/s10567-011-0108-1

Pande, A. C., Davidson, J. R., Jefferson, J. W., Janney, C. A., Katzelnick, D. J., Weisler, R. H., … Sutherland, S. M. (1999). Treatment of social phobia with gabapentin: A placebo-controlled study. *Journal of Clinical Psychopharmacology, 19,* 341–348. doi: 10.1097/00004714-199908000-00010

Pande, A. C., Feltner, D. E., Jefferson, J. W., Davidson, J. R., Pollack, M., Stein, M. B., … Werth, J. L. (2004). Efficacy of the novel anxiolytic pregabalin in social anxiety disorder: A placebo-controlled, multicenter study. *Journal of Clinical Psychopharmacology, 24,* 141–149. doi: 10.1097/01.jcp.0000117423.05703.e7

Patel, A., Knapp, M., Henderson, J., & Baldwin, D. (2002). The economic consequences of social phobia. *Journal of Affective Disorders, 68*(2–3), 221–233. doi: 10.1016/S0165-0327(00)00323-2

Peters, L. (2000). Discriminant validity of the Social Phobia and Anxiety Inventory (SPAI), the Social Phobia Scale (SPS) and the Social Interaction Anxiety Scale (SIAS). *Behaviour Research and Therapy, 38,* 943–950. doi: 10.1016/S0005-7967(99)00131-X

Phan, K., Fitzgerald, D., & Nathan, P. (2006). Association between amygdala hyperactivity to harsh faces and severity of social anxiety in generalized social phobia. *Biological Psychiatry, 59,* 424–429. doi: 10.1016/j.biopsych.2005.08.012

Piccirillo, M. L., Dryman, M. T., & Heimberg, R. G. (in press). Safety behaviors in adults with social anxiety: review and future directions. *Behavior Therapy.* doi: 10.1016/j.beth.2015.11.005

Pollack, M. H., Van Ameringen, M., Simon, N. M., Worthington, J. W., Hoge, E. A., Keshaviah, A., & Stein, M. B. (2014). A double-blind randomized controlled trial of augmentation and switch strategies for refractory social anxiety disorder. *American Journal of Psychiatry, 171,* 44–53. doi: 10.1176/appi.ajp.2013.12101353

Potter, C. M., Wong, J., Heimberg, R. G., Blanco, C., Liu, S.-M., Wang, S., & Schneier, F. R. (2014). Situational panic attacks in social anxiety disorder. *Journal of Affective Disorders, 167,* 1–7. doi: 10.1016/j.jad.2014.05.044

Potts, N.L.S., Book, S., & Davidson, J.R.T. (1996). The neurobiology of social phobia. *International Clinical Psychopharmacology, 11*(Suppl. 3), 43–48. doi: 10.1097/00004850-199606003-00008

Powers, M. B., Sigmarsson, S. R., & Emmelkamp, P.M.G. (2008). A meta-analytic review of psychological treatments for social anxiety disorder. *International Journal of Cognitive Therapy, 1,* 94–113. doi: 10.1521/ijct.2008.1.2.94

Price, M., Tone, E. B., & Anderson, P. L. (2011). Vigilant and avoidant attention biases as predictors of response to cognitive behavioral therapy for social phobia. *Depression and Anxiety, 28,* 349–353. doi: 10.1002/da.20791

Ranta, K., Kaltiala-Heino, R., Rantanen, P., Tuomisto, M. T., & Marttunen, M. (2007). Screening social phobia in adolescents from general population: The validity of the Social Phobia Inventory (SPIN) against a clinical interview. *European Psychiatry, 22,* 244–251. doi: 10.1016/j.eurpsy.2006.12.002

Rapee, R. M., & Hayman, K. (1996). The effects of video feedback on the self-evaluation of performance in socially anxious subjects. *Behaviour Research and Therapy, 34,* 315–322. doi: 10.1016/0005-7967(96)00003-4

Rapee, R. M., & Heimberg, R. G. (1997). A cognitive-behavioral model of anxiety in social phobia. *Behaviour Research and Therapy, 35,* 741–756. doi: 10.1016/S0005-7967(97)00022-3

Rapee, R. M., & Lim, L. (1992). Discrepancy between self- and observer ratings of performance in social phobics. *Journal of Abnormal Psychology, 101,* 728–731. doi: 10.1037/0021-843X.101.4.728

Rapee, R. M., McCallum, S. L., Melville, L. F., Ravenscroft, H., & Rodney, J. M. (1994). Memory bias in social phobia. *Behaviour Research and Therapy, 32,* 89–99. doi: 10.1016/0005-7967(94)90087-6

Reich, J. (2014). Avoidant personality disorder and its relationship to social phobia. In S. Hofmann & P. M. DiBartolo (Eds.), *Social anxiety: Clinical, developmental, and social perspectives* (3rd ed., pp. 27–44). Waltham, MA: Academic Press.

Roberson-Nay, R., Strong, D. R., Nay, W. T., Beidel, D. C., & Turner, S. M. (2007). Development of an abbreviated Social Phobia and Anxiety Inventory using item response theory: The SPAI-23. *Psychological Assessment, 19,* 133–145. doi: 10.1037/1040-3590.19.1.133

Rodebaugh, T. L., & Rapee, R. M. (2005). Those who think they look worst respond best: Self-observer discrepancy predicts response to video feedback following a speech task. *Cognitive Therapy and Research, 29,* 705–715. doi: 10.1007/s10608-005-9634-9

Rodebaugh, T. L., Woods, C. M., & Heimberg, R. G. (2007). The reverse of social anxiety is not always the opposite: The reverse-scored items of the Social Interaction Anxiety Scale do not belong. *Behavior Therapy, 38,* 192–206. doi: 10.1016/j.beth.2006.08.001

Rodebaugh, T. L., Woods, C. M., Thissen, D. M., Heimberg, R. G., Chambless, D. L., & Rapee, R. M. (2004). More information from fewer questions: The factor structure and item properties of the original and Brief Fear of Negative Evaluation scale. *Psychological Assessment, 16,* 169–181. doi: 10.1037/1040-3590.16.2.169

Rose, D. T., & Abramson, L. Y. (1992). Developmental predictors of depressive cognitive style: Research and theory. In D. Chicetti & S. Toth (Eds.), *Rochester symposium of developmental psychopathology* (Vol. 4, pp. 323–349). Rochester, NY: University of Rochester Press.

Roth, D. A., Antony, M. M., & Swinson, R. P. (2001). Interpretations for anxiety symptoms in social phobia. *Behaviour Research and Therapy, 39,* 129–138. doi: 10.1016/S0005-7967(99)00159-X

Roth, D. A., Coles, M., & Heimberg, R. G. (2002). The relationship between memories for childhood teasing and anxiety and depression in adulthood. *Journal of Anxiety Disorders, 16,* 151–166. doi: 10.1016/S0887-6185(01)00096-2

Rubin, K. H., & Mills, R.S.L. (1988). The many faces of social isolation in childhood. *Journal of Consulting and Clinical Psychology, 56,* 916–924. doi: 10.1037/0022-006X.56.6.916

Rytwinski, N. K., Fresco, D. M., Heimberg, R. G., Coles, M. E., Liebowitz, M. R., Cissell, S., ... Hofmann, S. G. (2009). Screening for social anxiety disorder with the self-report version of the Liebowitz Social Anxiety Scale. *Depression and Anxiety, 26,* 34–38. doi: 10.1002/da.20503

Safren, S. A., Heimberg, R. G., Brown, E. J., & Holle, C. (1997). Quality of life in social phobia. *Depression and Anxiety, 4,* 126–133. doi: 10.1002/(SICI)1520-6394(1996)4:3<126::AID-DA5>3.0.CO;2-E

Salemink, E., Kindt, M., Rienties, H., & van den Hout, M. (2014). Internet-based cognitive bias modification of interpretations in patients with anxiety disorders: A randomized controlled trial. *Journal of Behavior Therapy and Experimental Psychiatry, 45,* 186–195. doi: 10.1016/j.btep.2013.10.005

Salkovskis, P. M. (1991). The importance of behaviour in the maintenance of anxiety and panic: A cognitive account. *Behavioural Psychotherapy, 19,* 6–19. doi: 10.1017/S0141347300011472

Saunders, J. B., Aasland, O. G., Babor, T. F., de la Fuente, J. R., & Grant, M. (1993). Development of the Alcohol Use Disorders Identification Test (AUDIT): WHO collaborative project on early detection of persons with harmful alcohol consumption–II. *Addiction, 88,* 791–804. doi: 10.1111/j.1360-0443.1993.tb02093.x

Schlette, P., Brändström, S., Eisemann, M., Sigvardsson, S., Nylander, P.-O., Adolfsson, R., & Perris, C. (1998). Perceived parental rearing behaviours and temperament and character in healthy adults. *Personality and Individual Differences, 24,* 661–668. doi: 10.1016/S0191-8869(97)00229-8

Schmidt, N. B., Richey, J. A., Buckner, J. D., & Timpano, K. R. (2009). Attention training for generalized social anxiety disorder. *Journal of Abnormal Psychology, 118,* 5–14. doi: 10.1037/a0013643

Schmukle, S. C. (2005). Unreliability of the dot probe task. *European Journal of Personality, 19,* 595–605. doi: 10.1002/per.554

Schneier, F. R., Foose, T. E., Hasin, D. S., Heimberg, R. G., Liu, S.-M., Grant, B. F., & Blanco, C. (2010). Social anxiety disorder and alcohol use disorder comorbidity in the National Epidemiologic

Survey on Alcohol and Related Conditions. *Psychological Medicine*, *40*, 977–988. doi: 10.1017/S0033291709991231

Schneier, F. R., Johnson, J., Hornig, C. D., Liebowitz, M. R., & Weissman, M. M. (1992). Social phobia: Comorbidity and morbidity in an epidemiologic sample. *Archives of General Psychiatry*, *49*, 282–288. doi: 10.1001/archpsyc.1992.01820040034004

Schneier, F. R., Liebowitz, M. R., Abi-Dargham, A., Zea-Ponce, Y., Lin, S.-H., & Laruelle, M. (2000). Low dopamine D_2 receptor binding potential in social phobia. *American Journal of Psychiatry*, *157*, 457–459. doi: 10.1176/appi.ajp.157.3.457

Schry, A. R., Roberson-Nay, R., & White, S. W. (2012). Measuring social anxiety in college students: A comprehensive evaluation of the psychometric properties of the SPAI-23. *Psychological Assessment*, *24*, 846–854.

Schultz, L. T., & Heimberg, R. G. (2008). Attentional focus in social anxiety disorder: Potential for interactive processes. *Clinical Psychology Review*, *28*, 1206–1221. doi: 10.1016/j.cpr.2008.04.003

Schutters, S. I., van Megan, H. J., & Westenberg, H. G. (2005). Efficacy of quetiapine in generalized social anxiety disorder: Results from an open-label study. *Journal of Clinical Psychiatry*, *66*, 540–542. doi: 10.4088/JCP.v66n0420b

Siegel, R., La Greca, A. M., & Harrison, H. M. (2009). Peer victimization and social anxiety in adolescents: Prospective and reciprocal relationships. *Journal of Youth and Adolescence*, *38*, 1096–1109. doi: 10.1007/s10964-009-9392-1

Simon, N. M., Hoge, E. A., Fischmann, D., Worthington, J. J., Christian, K. M., Kinrys, G., & Pollack, M. H. (2006). An open-label trial of risperidone augmentation for refractory anxiety disorders. *Journal of Clinical Psychiatry*, *67*, 381–385. doi: 10.4088/JCP.v67n0307

Simpson, H. B., Schneier, F. R., Campeas, R., Marshall, R. D., Fallon, B. A., Davies, S., … Liebowitz, M. R. (1998). Imipramine in the treatment of social phobia. *Journal of Clinical Psychopharmacology*, *18*, 132–135. doi: 10.1097/00004714-199804000-00005

Solyom, L., Ledwidge, B., & Solyom, C. (1986). Delineating social phobia. *British Journal of Psychiatry*, *149*(4), 464–470.

Stangier, U., Schramm, E., Heidenreich, T., Berger, M., & Clark, D. (2011). Cognitive therapy vs interpersonal psychotherapy in social anxiety disorder: A randomized controlled trial. *Archives of General Psychiatry*, *68*, 692–700. doi: 10.1001/archgenpsychiatry.2011.67

Stapinski, L. A., Rapee, R. M., Sannibale, C., Teeson, M., Haber, P. S., & Baillie, A. J. (2015). The clinical and theoretical basis for integrated cognitive behavioral treatment of comorbid social anxiety and alcohol use disorders. *Cognitive and Behavioral Practice*, *22*, 504–521. doi: 10.1016/j.cbpra.2014.05.004

Stein, D. J., & Stahl, S. (2000). Serotonin and anxiety: Current models. *International Clinical Psychopharmacology*, *15*(Suppl. 2), S1–S6.

Stein, M. B. (1997). Phenomenology and epidemiology of social phobia. *International Clinical Psychopharmacology*, *12*(Suppl. 6), S23–S26. doi: 10.1097/00004850-199710006-00005

Stein, M. B., Chartier, M. J., Hazen, A. L., Kozak, M. V., Tancer, M. E., Lander, S., … Walker, J. R. (1998). A direct-interview family study of generalized social phobia. *American Journal of Psychiatry*, *155*, 90–97. doi: 10.1176/ajp.155.1.90

Stein, M. B., & Gelernter, J. (2014). Genetic factors in social anxiety disorder. In J. W. Weeks (Ed.), *The Wiley Blackwell handbook of social anxiety disorder* (pp. 53–66). Chichester, England: Wiley.

Stein, M. B., Gelernter, J., & Smoller, J. W. (2004). Genetic aspects of social anxiety and related traits. In B. Bandelow & D. J. Stein (Eds.), *Social anxiety disorder: More than shyness* (pp. 197–214). New York, NY: Marcel Dekker.

Stein, M. B., Heuser, I. J., Juncos, J. L., & Uhde, T. W. (1990). Anxiety disorders in patients with Parkinson's disease. *American Journal of Psychiatry*, *147*, 217–220. doi: 10.1176/ajp.147.2.217

Stein, M. B., & Kean, Y. (2000). Disability and quality of life in social phobia: Epidemiologic findings. *American Journal of Psychiatry*, *157*, 1606–1613. doi: 10.1176/appi.ajp.157.10.1606

Stein, M. B., & Stein, D. J. (2008). Social anxiety disorder. *Lancet*, *371*, 1115–1125. doi: 10.1016/S0140-6736(08)60488-2

Stevens, S., Cludius, B., Banti, T., Hermann, C., & Gerlach A. (2014). Influence of alcohol on social anxiety: An investigation of attentional, physiological and behavioral effects. *Biological Psychology*, *96*, 126–133. doi: 10.1016/j.biopsycho.2013.12.004

Stopa, L. (2009). Why is the self important in understanding and treating social phobia? *Cognitive Behaviour Therapy*, *38*, 48–54. doi: 10.1080/16506070902980737

Stopa, L., & Clark, D. M. (1993). Cognitive processes in social phobia. *Behaviour Research and Therapy, 31,* 255–267. doi: 10.1016/0005-7967(93)90024-O

Stopa, L., & Clark, D. M. (2000). Social phobia and interpretation of social events. *Behaviour Research and Therapy, 38,* 273–283. doi: 10.1016/S0005-7967(99)00043-1

Stopa, L., & Jenkins, A. (2007). Images of the self in social anxiety: Effects on the retrieval of autobiographical memories. *Journal of Behavior Therapy and Experimental Psychiatry, 38,* 459–473. doi: 10.1016/j.jbtep.2007.08.006

Storch, E. A., Masia-Warner, C., Crisp, H., & Klein, R. G. (2005). Peer victimization and social anxiety in adolescence: A prospective study. *Aggressive Behavior, 31,* 437–452. doi: 10.1002/ab.20093

Strauss, C. C., Lahey, B. B., Frick, P., Frame, C. L., & Hynd, G. W. (1988). Peer social status of children with social anxiety disorders. *Journal of Consulting and Clinical Psychology, 56,* 137–141. doi: 10.1037/0022-006X.56.1.137

Syal, S. & Stein, D. J. (2014). The social neuroscience of social anxiety disorder. In J. W. Weeks (Ed.), *The Wiley-Blackwell handbook of social anxiety disorder* (pp. 67–89). Chichester, England: Wiley-Blackwell.

Szafranski, D. D., Talkovsky, A. M., Farris, S. G., & Norton, P .J. (2014). Comorbidity: Social anxiety disorder and psychiatric comorbidity are not shy to co-occur. In J. W. Weeks (Ed.), *The Wiley-Blackwell handbook of social anxiety disorder* (pp. 201–222). Chichester, England: Wiley-Blackwell.

Taylor, S., Woody, S., McLean, P. D., & Koch, W. J. (1997). Sensitivity of outcome measures for treatments of generalized social phobia. *Assessment, 4,* 181–191. doi: 10.1177/107319119700400207

Tepe, E., Dalrymple, K., & Zimmerman, M. (2012). The impact of comorbid cannabis use disorders on the clinical presentation of social anxiety disorder. *Journal of Psychiatric Research, 46,* 50–56. doi: 10.1016/j.jpsychires.2011.09.021

Tilhonen, J., Kuikka, J., Bergstrom, K., Lepola, U., Koponen, H., & Leinonen, E. (1997). Dopamine reuptake site densities in patients with social phobia. *American Journal of Psychiatry, 154,* 239–242. doi: 10.1176/ajp.154.2.239

Tillfors, M. (2004). Why do some individuals develop social phobia? A review with emphasis on the neurobiological influences. *Nordic Journal of Psychiatry, 58,* 267–276. doi: 10.1080/08039480410005774

Tillfors, M., Furmark, T., Carlbring, P., & Andersson, G. (2015). Risk profiles for poor treatment response to internet-delivered CBT in people with social anxiety disorder. *Journal of Anxiety Disorders, 33,* 103–109.

Torvik, F. A., Welander-Vatn, A., Ystrom, E., Knudsen, G. P., Czajkowski, N., Kendler, K. S., & Reichborn-Kjennerud, T. (2016). Longitudinal associations between social anxiety disorder and avoidant personality disorder: A twin study. *Journal of Abnormal Psychology, 125,* 114–124. doi: 10.1037/abn0000124

Trower, P., & Gilbert, P. (1989). New theoretical conceptions of social anxiety and social phobia. *Clinical Psychology Review, 9,* 19–35. doi: 10.1016/0272-7358(89)90044-5

Turk, C. L., Heimberg, R. G., Luterek, J. A., Mennin, D. S., & Fresco, D. M. (2005). Emotion dysregulation in generalized anxiety disorder: A comparison with social anxiety disorder. *Cognitive Therapy and Research, 29,* 89–106. doi: 10.1007/s10608-005-1651-1

Turner, S. M., Beidel, D. C., Dancu, C. V., & Stanley, M. A. (1989). An empirically derived inventory to measure social fears and anxiety: The Social Phobia and Anxiety Inventory. *Psychological Assessment, 1,* 35–40. doi: 10.1037/1040-3590.1.1.35

Vaishnavi, S., Alamy, S., Zhang, W., Connor, K. M., & Davidson, J.R.T. (2007). Quetiapine as monotherapy for social anxiety disorder: A placebo-controlled study. *Progress in Neuro-Psychopharmacology and Biological Psychiatry, 31,* 1464–1469. doi: 10.1016/j.pnpbp.2007.06.027

Van Bockstaele, B., Verschuere, B., Tibboel, H., De Houwer, J., Crombez, G., & Koster, E. (2014). A review of current evidence for the causal impact of attentional bias on fear and anxiety. *Psychological Bulletin, 140,* 682–721. doi: 10.1037/a0034834

Vassilopoulos, S. P., & Banerjee, R. (2010). Social interaction anxiety and the discounting of positive interpersonal events. *Behavioural and Cognitive Psychotherapy, 38,* 597–609. doi: 10.1017/S135246581000433

Veljaca, K. A., & Rapee, R. M. (1998). Detection of negative and positive audience behaviours by socially anxious subjects. *Behaviour Research and Therapy, 36,* 311–321. doi: 10.1016/s0005-7967(98)00016-3

Vernberg, E. M., Abwender, D. A., Ewell, K. K., & Beery, S. H. (1992). Social anxiety and peer relationships in early adolescence: A prospective analysis.

Journal of Clinical Child Psychology, 21, 189–196. doi: 10.1207/s15374424jccp2102_11

Versiani, M., Nardi, A. E., Figueira, I., Mendlowicz, M., & Marques, C. (1997). Double-blind placebo controlled trials with bromazepam. *Jornal Brasileiro de Psiquiatria, 46,* 167–171.

Wang, P. S., Angermeyer, M., Guilherme, B., Bruffaerts, R., Chiu, W. T., De Girolamo, G., ... Bedirhan Ustun, T. (2007). Delay and failure in treatment seeking after first onset of mental disorders in the World Health Organization's World Mental Health Survey Initiative. *World Psychiatry, 6,* 177–185.

Weeks, J. W., Heimberg, R. G., Fresco, D. M., Hart, T. A., Turk, C. L., Schnieier, F. R., & Liebowitz, M. R. (2005). Empirical validation and psychometric evaluation of the Brief Fear of Negative Evaluation Scale in patients with social anxiety disorder. *Psychological Assessment, 17,* 179–190. doi: 10.1037/1040-3590.17.2.179

Weeks, J. W., Heimberg, R. G., Rodebaugh, T. L., & Norton, P. J. (2008). Exploring the relationship between fear of positive evaluation and social anxiety. *Journal of Anxiety Disorders, 22,* 386–400. doi: 10.1016/j.janxdis.2007.04.009

Weeks, J. W., & Howell, A. N. (2014). Fear of positive evaluation: The neglected fear domain in social anxiety. In J. W. Weeks (Ed.), *The Wiley-Blackwell handbook of social anxiety disorder* (pp. 433–453). Chichester, England: Wiley.

Weeks, J. W., Spokas, M. E., & Heimberg, R. G. (2007). Psychometric evaluation of the Mini–Social Phobia Inventory (Mini-SPIN) in a treatment-seeking sample. *Depression and Anxiety, 24,* 382–391. doi: 10.1002/da.20250

Weinstock, L. S. (1999). Gender differences in the presentation and management of social anxiety disorder. *Journal of Clinical Psychiatry, 60*(Suppl. 9), 9–13.

Wells, A., Clark, D. M., & Ahmad, S. (1998). How do I look with my mind's eye? Perspective taking in social phobic imagery. *Behaviour Research and Therapy, 36,* 631–634. doi: 10.1016/S0005-7967(98)00037-0

Wells, A., Clark, D. M., Salkovskis, P., Ludgate, J., Hackmann, A., & Gelder, M. (1995). Social phobia: The role of in-situation safety behaviors in maintaining anxiety and negative beliefs. *Behavior Therapy, 26,* 153–161. doi: 10.1016/S0005-7894(05)80088-7

Wenzel, A. (2002). Characteristics of close relationships in individuals with social phobia: A preliminary comparison with nonanxious individuals. In J. H. Harvey & A. Wenzel (Eds.), *Maintaining and enhancing close relationships: A clinician's guide* (pp. 199–213). Mahwah, NJ: Erlbaum.

Wenzel, A., & Cochran, C. (2006). Autobiographical memories prompted by automatic thoughts in panic disorder and social phobia. *Cognitive Behaviour Therapy, 35,* 129–137. doi: 10.1080/16506070600583130

Wong, J., Gordon, E. A., & Heimberg, R. G. (2014). Cognitive-behavioral models of social anxiety disorder. In J. W. Weeks (Ed.), *The Wiley-Blackwell handbook of social anxiety disorder* (pp. 3–23). Chichester, England: Wiley.

Woody, S. R., Chambless, D. L., & Glass, C. R. (1997). Self-focused attention in the treatment of social phobia. *Behaviour Research and Therapy, 35,* 117–129. doi: 10.1016/S0005-7967(96)00084-8

Zaider, T. I., Heimberg, R. G., & Iida, M. (2010). Anxiety disorders and intimate relationships: A study of daily processes in couples. *Journal of Abnormal Psychology, 119,* 163–173. doi: 10:1037/a0018473

Zimmerman, M., & Mattia, J. I. (1999). Psychiatric diagnosis in clinical practice: Is comorbidity being missed? *Comprehensive Psychiatry, 40,* 182–191. doi: 10.1016/S0010-440X(99)90001-9

Zvielli, A., Bernstein, A., & Koster, E.H.W. (2015). Temporal dynamics of attentional bias. *Clinical Psychological Science, 3,* 772–778. doi: 10.1177/2167702614551572

Chapter 3

Panic Disorder

Joanna J. Arch, Alex Kirk, and Michelle G. Craske

The purpose of this chapter is to offer an up-to-date review on the nature, etiology, assessment, and treatment of panic disorder. The chapter aims to integrate a substantial body of previous research on panic disorder with the most recent advances in the field.

Panic Disorder

A *panic attack* is an abrupt surge of intense fear or discomfort that is diagnosed by the presence of 4 or more of 13 physical and cognitive symptoms: palpitations, pounding heart, or accelerated heart rate; sweating; trembling or shaking; sensations of shortness of breath or smothering; feeling of choking; chest pain or discomfort; nausea or abdominal distress; feeling dizzy, unsteady, lightheaded, or faint; chills or heat sensations; paresthesias (numbness or tingling sensations); derealization (feelings of unreality) or depersonalization (being detached from oneself); fear of losing control or going crazy; and fear of dying (American Psychiatric Association [APA], 2013). The sudden, abrupt surge of intense fear or discomfort peaks within minutes, as opposed to gradually building anxious arousal. This abrupt surge can occur from an anxious or calm baseline state. A *full-blown* panic attack is defined as four or more symptoms, whereas *limited symptom* attacks are defined as fewer than four symptoms.

Panic disorder is characterized by repeated unexpected panic attacks, i.e. attacks that occur without an obvious trigger, "out of the blue," plus at least 1 month of persistent worry or concern about the recurrence of panic or its consequences, or a significant, maladaptive behavioral change related to the attacks. These behavioral changes may include avoidance of activities in which panic attacks are expected to occur, particularly physiologically arousing activities such as exercise, saunas, scary movies, sex, unfamiliar places, and so forth, or use of safety behaviors, such as frequent attendance at medical facilities for fear of a medical problem. Panic attacks often, but not always, occur within the context of *agoraphobia*—marked fear or anxiety about situations from which escape might be difficult or in which help might be unavailable in the event of panic-like or other incapacitating symptoms (e.g., loss of bowel control or a sense of falling). A diagnosis of agoraphobia requires fear of at least two of the following situations: public transportation (e.g., traveling in automobiles, buses, trains, ships, or planes), open spaces (e.g., parking lots, marketplaces, or bridges), enclosed places (e.g., shops, theaters, or cinemas), standing in line or being in a crowd, and being outside of the home alone.

Panic attacks commonly occur within the context of any of the anxiety disorders, as well as substance use disorders and other psychiatric conditions. Panic attacks are also a marker of psychopathology, predictive of the onset of a variety of disorders as well as their course and severity (Batelaan et al., 2012; Kircanski, Craske, Epstein, & Wittchen, 2009). Consequently, panic attack can be added as a specifier for any *DSM-5* diagnosis. What distinguishes panic attacks associated with other *DSM-5* disorders (outside of panic disorder) is that they are *expected* or *confined* to the context of that disorder, e.g., panic attacks occur only when recovering from the effects of alcohol in an alcohol use disorder, or when encountering trauma cues in posttraumatic stress disorder, or when speaking publicly in social anxiety disorder. Furthermore, in those disorders, the panic attacks themselves are rarely the focus of concern. In contrast, within *panic disorder*, the panic attacks occur unexpectedly (repeatedly), although expected attacks can occur as well, and the focus of concern is on the physical and mental consequences of the panic attacks themselves. In addition, panic attacks may also occur in the *absence* of psychiatric disorder; thus, nearly one third of the 22% of adults in the National Comorbidity Survey Replication who reported having had at least one panic attack in their lifetime did not meet the criteria for any other *DSM-IV* diagnosis (Kessler et al., 2006).

Panic attacks are characterized by a unique action tendency: specifically, urges to escape and, less often, urges to fight. In other words, panic attacks represent activation of the fight-flight system. Accordingly, panic attacks usually involve elevated autonomic nervous system arousal, needed to support such fight-flight reactivity. Furthermore, perceptions of imminent threat, such as death, loss of control, or social ridicule, frequently accompany the fight-flight response. However, the urgency to escape, autonomic arousal, and perception of threat are not present in every self-reported occurrence of panic. For example, data gathered from ambulatory (portable) devices have found sympathetic nervous system activation during reported panic attacks (Wilkinson et al., 1998), although nonactivation has also been documented (for about 40% of self-reported panic attacks; see Margraf, Taylor, Ehlers, Roth, & Agras, 1987; Taylor et al., 1986). Severe panic attacks are more autonomically based (Margraf et al., 1987). Self-reported panic in the absence of actual autonomic activation is assumed to reflect anticipatory anxiety versus true panic (Barlow, Brown, & Craske, 1994). Another discordant example occurs when perceptions of loss of control, dying, or going crazy are refuted, despite the report of intense fear and arousal. This has been termed *noncognitive* panic (Kircanski et al., 2009; Rachman, Lopatka, & Levitt, 1988). It has been reported that up to 30% of people who experience panic attacks do so without reported fear of dying, losing control, or going crazy (Chen, Tsuchiya, Kawakami, & Furukawa, 2009).

A subset of individuals who have panic disorder also experience *nocturnal* panic attacks. Nocturnal panic refers to waking from sleep in a state of panic with symptoms that are very similar to panic attacks that occur during wakeful states (Craske & Barlow, 1989). Nocturnal panic does *not* refer to waking from sleep and panicking after a lapse of waking time, or nighttime arousals induced by nightmares or environmental stimuli (such as unexpected noises). Also, nocturnal panic is distinct from sleep terrors and sleep apnea (see Craske & Tsao, 2005, for a review). Although epidemiological studies have not been conducted, surveys of select clinical groups suggest that nocturnal panic is relatively common among individuals with panic disorder, with 44% to 71% reporting nocturnal panic at least once, and 30% to 45% reporting repeated nocturnal panics (Craske & Barlow, 1989; Mellman & Uhde, 1989; Singareddy & Uhde, 2009).

Panic disorder was first regarded as a diagnostic entity with the publication 33 years ago of the *DSM-III* (APA, 1980). Prior to that time, panic attacks were viewed as symptoms of a general neurosis, although accounts of clinically similar syndromes had appeared much earlier. These were labeled *soldier's heart* (Wooley, 1982), *neurocirculatory asthenia* (Wheeler, White, Reed, & Cohen, 1950), and *effort syndrome* (Nixon, 1993). In the *DSM-III*, agoraphobia was considered a separate disorder, which might or might not be associated with panic attacks. Observations of clinical samples by Klein (1981) and others (Craske & Barlow, 1988; Turner, Williams, Beidel, & Mezzich, 1986) suggested that agoraphobia generally developed following panic attacks, and this led to a redefinition of agoraphobia as a secondary response to panic attacks in *DSM-III-R* (APA, 1987; Barlow, 2002) through *DSM-IV-TR* (APA, 1994). In *DSM-5*, panic disorder and agoraphobia are once again considered two distinct, although highly comorbid, disorders. This change was made in recognition of the substantial number of individuals, albeit possibly more in the community than in clinical settings, who exhibit the full features of agoraphobia but do not report ever having had a full-blown panic attack or panic-like symptoms (Wittchen, Gloster, Beesdo-Baum, Fava, & Craske, 2010). The 13 symptoms of a panic attack remained unchanged from *DSM-IV* to *DSM-5*, although recognition has been given to some culture-specific symptoms that may be associated with panic attacks: for example, uncontrollable crying or sore neck. However, these culture-specific symptoms do not count toward having the required 4 of the 13 standard panic attack symptoms.

As noted earlier, greater recognition has been given in *DSM-5* to the notion that panic attacks may occur in the context of any anxiety disorder: a panic attack specifier may be applied to any diagnosis.

CASE EXAMPLE

Sandy is a 30-year-old Caucasian mother of a 5-year-old and a 3-year-old, who lives with her husband of 6 years. For the past 2 years, she has been chronically anxious and panic-stricken. Her panic attacks are described as intolerable and increasing in frequency. Her first panic attack occurred 3 years ago, just after the birth of her second child. She recalls suddenly experiencing strong sensations of lightheadedness and weakness when she was at home alone with her newborn and 2-year-old child. Convinced that she was about to pass out, she immediately lay down. The feelings passed within a few minutes, but Sandy remained very concerned that she would pass out. This concern was particularly worrisome since Sandy feared what would happen to her children if she lost consciousness. She felt anxious for a day or so but then forgot about the feelings until a few weeks later when again, at home alone with her children, she was overcome with even stronger sensations of lightheadedness, weakness, and a cold sweat. She became very afraid, especially for her children, and called her husband, who left work to be with her. A visit to her primary care doctor the next day did not reveal any medical explanations for the symptoms. Nonetheless, Sandy began to pay close attention to her physical state and became very anxious about her husband's upcoming business trip. While her husband was away, she panicked daily, each time phoning her mother, who would come over to look after the children while Sandy lay down until the feelings subsided. From that time onward, Sandy was very anxious about being alone with her children.

Currently Sandy has panic attacks in many situations. She describes them as intense feelings of lightheadedness, weakness, a sense of unreality and detachment, a racing heart, nausea, and fears of losing consciousness. The lightheadedness and unreality scare her the most, for fear of passing out and leaving her children unattended. Consequently, Sandy is now sensitive to anything that produces lightheadedness and feelings of unreality, such as standing quickly from a seated position, heat, the semiconsciousness that occurs just before falling asleep, bright lights, alcohol, and drugs. Even though she has a prescription for Klonopin (a high-potency benzodiazepine), she rarely uses medication because of her fear of feeling "weird" and unable to take care of her children. She wants to be as alert as possible at all times, but she keeps the Klonopin with her in the event that she has no other escape route. She has become very sensitive to her body in general—anything that feels a little different than usual scares her. Even coffee, which she used to enjoy, is distressing to her now because it has agitating effects and makes her heart race. She was never a big exerciser, but to think of exerting herself is now also scary. She reports that she is constantly waiting for the next panic attack to occur. She avoids being alone with her children, and also avoids situations where she thinks she is more likely to pass out, such as driving, being in restaurants, and being long distances from home. She avoids crowds and large groups as well, partly because of the feeling of too much stimulation and partly because she is afraid she might panic in front of others. In general, she prefers to be with her husband or her mother.

Sandy's reliance on her husband and mother has strained those relationships. Her husband is frustrated with Sandy's behavior and the restrictions it has placed on his own life: he no longer goes on business trips, he spends every free moment with Sandy and the children, and sometimes he has to leave work to come home because Sandy's mother is not available to be with her. Similarly, while her mother offers to help as much as possible, she also feels that Sandy's reliance upon her is too much.

Sandy describes how weak and scared she is now—quite different from how she used to be. The only other incident that has any similarity to her current panic attacks occurred in her late teens when she smoked marijuana. Sandy recalls being very scared of the feeling of losing control and the sense that she would never return to reality. She has not taken drugs since then. Otherwise she has no history of serious medical conditions or any previous psychological treatment. Sandy was shy as a young child and throughout her teens. However, her social anxiety improved throughout her 20s to the point that, up until the onset of her panic attacks, she was mostly very comfortable around people. Since the onset of her panic attacks, she has become concerned that others will notice that she appears different or strange. However, her social anxiety is limited to panic attacks and does not reflect a broader social phobia.

At least once a week Sandy wakes abruptly in the middle of the night with a panic attack, feeling short of breath and scared. Consequently, her sleep is restless. Sandy worries about what will happen to her children if she loses consciousness, and what will happen to them in the long term if she continues to panic. She has some difficulty concentrating, but in general she functions well when she feels safe—that is, when her mother or husband is nearby. She sometimes becomes depressed about her panic and the limitations on her independence. She occasionally has times of feeling hopeless about the future, doubting if she will ever be able to get back to feeling the way she did before these attacks began.

Prevalence and Epidemiology of Panic Disorder

According to the National Comorbidity Survey Replication (NCS-R), prevalence estimates for panic disorder are 2.4% (12-month), 4.7% (lifetime), and 6.8% (lifetime morbid risk) (Kessler, Berglund, et al., 2005; Kessler, Chiu, Demler, Merikangas, & Walters, 2005; Kessler, Petukhova, Sampson, Zaslavsky, & Wittchen, 2012). These rates are higher than estimates from the Ukraine (Bromet et al., 2005), Japan (Kawakami et al., 2005), Germany (Goodwin, Fergusson, & Horwood, 2005), and Greece (Skapinakis et al., 2013, though prevalence in that study was assessed over only a 1-week period), but commensurate with the Netherlands (Batelaan et al., 2012). While data from the United States suggest increased prevalence over the past two decades (Kessler, Berglund, et al., 2005), these data from other countries raise the possibility that the range in prevalence rates reflects differences in diagnostic methodology as well as variations in diagnostic criteria.

Individuals with agoraphobia who are seeking treatment almost always report a history of panic that preceded development of their avoidance behavior (Wittchen, Reed, & Kessler, 1998); however, epidemiological data indicate relatively high rates for agoraphobia without a history of panic disorder: 0.8% to 1.7% in the prior 12 months (Kessler, Berglund, et al., 2005; Kessler et al., 2012) and 1.4% lifetime prevalence (Kessler, Chiu, et al., 2005). The more recent data still indicate that agoraphobia without a history of panic disorder occurs at roughly one third the rate of panic disorder. The discrepancy between the clinical and epidemiological data may occur because individuals who panic are more likely to seek help (Boyd, 1986).

Rarely does the diagnosis of panic disorder, with or without agoraphobia, occur in isolation. Data from the NCS-R show that 93.7% of individuals with panic disorder, with or without agoraphobia, have at least one other mental or chronic physical disorder (Gadermann, Alonso, Vilagut, Zaslavsky, & Kessler, 2012). These same data further suggest that those with panic disorder meet the criteria for an average of 4.5 additional (mental or physical) disorders. Commonly co-occurring Axis I conditions include specific phobias, social phobia, dysthymia, generalized anxiety disorder, major depressive disorder, and substance abuse (e.g., Brown, Campbell, Lehman, Grisham, & Mancill, 2001, found such co-occurring conditions in 60% of those studied; Brown, Antony, & Barlow, 1995, in 51% of those studied, and Kessler et al., 2006, found them in 83% of their panic disorder sample). Also, from 25% to 60% of persons with panic disorder meet criteria for a current comorbid personality disorder, mostly avoidant or dependent personality disorders (e.g., Chambless & Renneberg, 1988).

The modal age of onset for panic disorder is early adulthood, between the ages of 21 and 23, although there is significant variability in onset period (Kessler et al., 2006, 2012). In fact, a substantial proportion of adolescents report panic attacks; 13- to 17-year-olds show a 2.3% and 2.7% 12-month prevalence of panic disorder and agoraphobia, respectively (Kessler et al., 2012). Subsequent research from the Netherlands Study of

Depression and Anxiety (NESDA) has proposed a bimodal distribution for onset, at ages 17 and 39, with a single mean of age 25 (Tibi et al., 2013). Treatment is usually sought at a much later age, around 34 years (e.g., Noyes et al., 1986). The overall ratio of adult females to males with panic disorder is approximately 2:1 (Kessler et al., 2006, 2012) although the ratio shifts dramatically in the direction of female predominance as the level of agoraphobia worsens (e.g., Thyer, Himle, Curtis, Cameron, & Nesse, 1985).

Panic disorder in children and adolescents tends to be chronic and comorbid with other anxiety, mood, and disruptive disorders (Biederman, Faraone, Marrs, & Moore, 1997), with onset reported as early as 6 years old (Moreau, Weissman, & Warner, 1989). While the physiological symptoms of panic attacks tend to be similar for children and adolescents and for adults, adolescents are more likely than children to report a fear of going crazy (Doerfler, Connor, Volungis, & Toscano, 2007). This may corroborate earlier work by Nelles and Barlow (1988), who proposed that the interpretation of physiological symptoms may distinguish child from adolescent panic, whereby children are more likely to apply external explanations for panic and adolescents are more likely to apply internal explanations (such as "I'm going crazy").

Most individuals with panic disorder, with or without agoraphobia, (approximately 72%; Craske, Miller, Rotunda, & Barlow, 1990) report identifiable stressors around the time of their first panic attack. These include interpersonal stressors and stressors related to physical well-being, such as negative drug experiences, disease, or death in the family (e.g., Pollard, Pollard, & Corn, 1989; Roy-Byrne, Geraci, & Uhde, 1986). However, another study suggests that stressors experienced by those with panic disorder may not differ in number but are rated as more distressing than stressors reported by adults without a history of panic disorder or any other psychological disorder (Rapee, Litwin, & Barlow, 1990). Approximately one half report having experienced panicky feelings at some time before their first full panic attack, suggesting that onset may be either insidious or acute (Craske et al., 1990).

Finally, panic disorder, particularly in combination with agoraphobia, tends to be highly chronic (Bruce et al., 2005), displaying only modest decreases in severity over a 14-year follow-up (Ramsawh, Raffa, Edelen, Rende, & Keller, 2009) in a sample of treatment-seeking, middle-aged adults (who received at least some treatment, though not necessarily evidence-based treatment). Further, panic disorder entails severe financial and interpersonal costs. Individuals with panic disorder overutilize medical resources compared to the general public (Marciniak et al., 2005) or other primary care patients (Roy-Byrne et al., 1999). Even with or following pharmacological treatment, only a minority of patients remit without subsequent relapse ($\approx$30%), although a similar proportion (25% to 35%) experience notable improvement, albeit with a waxing and waning course (Katschnig & Amering, 1998; Roy-Byrne & Cowley, 1995). Nonetheless, the prognosis for panic disorder (in the absence of agoraphobia) is more positive than that for generalized anxiety disorder or social anxiety disorder (Bruce et al., 2005).

Psychological Models and Empirical Data on Panic Disorder

This discussion of psychological models and empirical data is organized around the behavioral, cognitive, and emotional features of panic disorder.

BEHAVIORAL FEATURES OF PANIC DISORDER

The behavioral features of panic disorder involve maladaptive behaviors related to the panic attacks. These can include avoidance of situations in which panic attacks are expected to occur, avoidance of activities that induce panic-like sensations, safety behaviors, and experiential avoidance.

Avoidance of Particular Situations

Avoidance of situations in which panic attacks are expected to occur may warrant a diagnosis of agoraphobia. However, agoraphobia pertains to fear and situational avoidance for reasons beyond the occurrence of panic attacks: namely, fear and avoidance of panic-like symptoms or other incapacitating symptoms. Thus, the person with agoraphobia may fear and avoid situations for reasons related *or* unrelated to panic attacks. Individuals with panic disorder vary widely in their degree of agoraphobia (Craske & Barlow, 1988); some manifest few or no agoraphobic symptoms, whereas others spend years as virtual prisoners in their own homes. Still others limit themselves to a safety zone of a few blocks or miles around their homes and do not venture beyond its radius, unaccompanied or at all (Barlow, 2002). In general, evidence suggests that agoraphobia tends to increase the severity of panic disorder (Kessler et al., 2006) and the severity of comorbid conditions (Pané-Farré et al., 2013).

What accounts for these wide discrepancies in the development of agoraphobia among individuals with panic disorder? Although agoraphobia tends to increase as history of panic lengthens (Kikuchi et al., 2005; Pané-Farré et al., 2013), a significant proportion of individuals panic for many years without developing agoraphobia (Wittchen et al., 2010). Individuals with both agoraphobia and panic disorder do not differ from individuals with only panic disorder in terms of fears of dying, going crazy, or losing control (Cox, Endler, & Swinson, 1995), although they show significantly more impairments overall (see Wittchen et al., 2010) and greater distress regarding the social consequences of panicking (Amering et al., 1997; de Jong & Bouman, 1995; Nay, Brown, & Roberson-Nay, 2013).

Occupational status also predicts agoraphobia, accounting for 18% of the variance: "the more one is forced to leave the house by means of employment, the less one is likely to suffer from agoraphobia" (de Jong & Bouman, 1995, p. 197). But perhaps the strongest predictor of agoraphobia is gender. Agoraphobia without panic is even more female dominated than panic disorder (see Wittchen et al., 2010), and female preponderance increases with agoraphobia severity (e.g., Thyer et al., 1985). Socialized sex role expectations and behaviors may contribute to these effects, as socialization may reinforce activity, independence, and confrontation of feared stimuli and situations to a greater extent in boys than in girls (see Craske, 2003). Given the direct relevance of avoidance behaviors for the development of agoraphobia, the clinical implications are clear.

Interoceptive Avoidance

Strong sensitivity to and avoidance of the internal bodily symptoms associated with anxiety and panic is known as *interoceptive avoidance* (Bouton, Mineka, & Barlow, 2001; Rapee, Craske, & Barlow, 1995; White & Barlow, 2002). Behavioral manifestations include actions intended to minimize exposure to situations, substances, or activities that reproduce bodily sensations associated with symptoms of anxiety and/or panic attacks. Common examples include avoiding exercise, sex, caffeine, alcohol, saunas, wearing a necktie, watching arousing or scary movies, or situations that may produce anger. Assessing the specific interoceptive cues and situations that panic disorder patients avoid is central to treatment.

Safety Behaviors

Safety behaviors are "behaviors which are intended to avoid *disaster*" (Salkovskis, Clark, Hackmann, Wells, & Gelder, 1999, p. 573; emphasis in original). A more recent definition defines safety behaviors as "dysfunctional emotion regulation strategies ... [that] can be differentiated from adaptive coping both by the situation in which they occur," a situation of "overrated or no real threat," and by their function, "preventing feared outcomes that are unlikely to happen" (Helbig-Lang & Petermann, 2010, pp. 220–221). Within panic disorder, they are behaviors that help individuals feel more protected and secure in the event of a panic attack (White & Barlow, 2002). Examples include checking to make sure that a bathroom or hospital is close by, taking one's pulse rate whenever cardiac concerns arise, and carrying a cell phone, religious symbols, smelling salts, a special "safe" object, food, or drink. Perhaps the most common safety behavior is carrying antianxiety medication; some people even find carrying empty pill bottles sufficient to prevent attacks. Another widespread behavior is bringing along or checking on the location of a safe person, often a spouse, whose presence provides a sense of reassurance that facilitates venturing out to places that otherwise would be avoided. The "safe" person is generally considered to be such because he or she knows about the patient's panic attacks and can assist if the panic attack becomes overwhelming (White & Barlow, 2002).

When individuals with panic disorder enact safety behaviors, they seek objects, persons, and situations that signal safety against having a panic attack; thus, the safe objects, persons, and situations themselves are referred to as "safety signals"—cues that signal safety. An extensive animal literature (see Hermans, Craske, Mineka, & Lovibond, 2006) demonstrates that the presence of safety signals functions as a conditioned inhibitor that interferes with extinction. Though somewhat limited methodologically, a few treatment studies indicate that exposure therapy targeting reductions of safety behaviors and signals is more successful than exposure therapy alone (Salkovskis et al., 1999; Telch, Sloan, & Smits, 2000, as cited in Powers, Smits, & Telch, 2004). Also, the mere availability of safety signals rather than the actual use of them disrupted fear extinction in exposure treatment for claustrophobia (Powers, Smits, & Telch, 2004). Hence, safety behaviors may reduce anxiety in the short term but likely serve to maintain panic disorder in the long term by preventing the disconfirmation of the patient's catastrophic predictions about panic (Salkovskis et al., 1999) and/or the extinction of the conditioned response (see Hermans et al., 2006). Based on these findings, a recent cognitive-behavioral therapy (CBT) trial for anxiety disorders (with 44% of the subjects having a primary diagnosis of panic disorder, that is, the disorder causing the most distress) targeted the elimination of safety behaviors, and demonstrated promising results (Schmidt et al., 2012).

Recently, however, several investigations have challenged this view by showing that the "judicious use" of safety behaviors does not impede exposure outcomes among undergraduates (Levy & Radomsky, 2014; Rachman, Shafran, Radomsky, & Zysk, 2011; van den Hout, Engelhard, Toffolo, & van Uijen, 2011), and in one case, unexpectedly improved outcomes (Sy, Dixon, Lickel, Nelson, & Deacon, 2011). This hypothesis has not yet been confirmed in a panic disorder sample but is intriguing in that it contradicts previous studies of safety behavior utilization, which show detrimental effects on anxiety or panic outcomes following exposure (see Helbig-Lang & Petermann, 2010; Helbig-Lang et al., 2014).

Experiential Avoidance

Experiential avoidance occurs when a person is "unwilling to remain in contact with particular private experiences [e.g., bodily sensations, emotions, thoughts, memories, behavioral predispositions] and takes steps to alter the form or frequency of these events and the contexts" in which they occur (Hayes, Wilson, Giffore, Follette, & Strosahl, 1996, p. 1154). The types of avoidance discussed thus far, particularly interoceptive avoidance, also may be characterized as experiential avoidance. In addition, any form of distraction from anxiety- and panic-related symptoms falls into this category. Distraction behaviors can include watching TV, playing video games, and eating, among others. From an experiential avoidance perspective, distraction often represents an unwillingness to experience anxiety- and fear-related thoughts and emotions. Whether distraction interferes with exposure therapy for anxiety is a subject of debate (see, e.g., Devilly, 2001a and 2001b versus Lipke, 2001; Podină, Koster, Philippot, Dethier, & David, 2013; see also Rodriguez & Craske, 1993). However, several controlled, empirical studies (e.g., Rodriguez & Craske, 1995; Telch et al., 2004) have found that distraction occurring in the context of exposure therapy generally results in less effective fear reduction. Further, a meta-analysis of exposure for specific phobia found that distraction was inferior to uninstructed exposure but superior to focused exposure (deliberately attending to the feared stimulus or to the internal anxiety and fear produced by the exposure; Podină et al., 2013). However, the exclusive focus on specific phobia and the lack of differentiating internal focus from external focus in comparison to distracted or uninstructed exposure, means that further study in the context of panic disorder is needed.

Experiential avoidance also includes avoidance and suppression of anxiety- and panic-related cognitions, such as, "I'm having a heart attack." Evidence generally suggests that such thought suppression has a negative impact. That is, thought suppression and to some extent emotion suppression have been shown to be relatively counterproductive, facilitating the return of the very thought or emotional arousal one hoped to avoid (e.g., Lambert, Hu, Magee, Beadel, & Teachman, 2014; Richards & Gross, 2000; Wenzlaff & Wegner, 2000).

Researchers of experiential avoidance argue that psychopathology in general, including panic disorder, is caused and maintained by experiential avoidance. In other words, psychopathology stems from an unwillingness to experience whatever thoughts, feelings, memories, and so forth appear in the present (e.g., Eifert & Forsyth, 2005; Hayes et al., 1996; Hayes, Levin, Plumb-Vilardaga, Villatte, & Pistorello, 2013). Acceptance (of anxiety- and panic-related thoughts, feelings, and sensations) is promoted over direct modification and change (Eifert & Forsyth, 2005; Hayes et al., 2013; Hayes, Luoma, Bond, Masuda, & Lillis, 2006; Hayes, Strosahl, & Wilson, 1999). In support of this view, correlational evidence demonstrates that panickers report higher experiential avoidance and lack of emotional clarity and acceptance than nonpanickers do (Tull & Roemer, 2007). Further, instructions to notice and *accept* symptoms of induced panic—the opposite of experiential avoidance—resulted in lower fear and avoidance among panic disorder patients (Levitt, Brown, Orsillo, & Barlow, 2004) and high anxiety sensitivity individuals (Eifert & Heffner, 2003) than did instructions to suppress (Levitt et al., 2004) or control symptoms (Eifert & Heffner, 2003). Nonetheless, experiential avoidance has been criticized for a lack of definitional clarity and unclear incremental validity (Chawla & Ostafin, 2007). Recent work, however, has led to improved definition and measurement of experiential avoidance (Bond et al., 2011; Gámez et al., 2014; Gámez, Chmielewski, Kotov, Ruggero, & Watson, 2011; Wolgast, Lundh, & Viborg, 2013) and evidence of incremental validity in accounting for panic-related worries and disability in panic disorder (Kämpfe et al., 2012) and in moderating the relationship between anxiety sensitivity and perceived stress (Bardeen, Fergus, & Orcutt, 2013). In accounting for the etiology and maintenance of panic disorder, reducing experiential avoidance represents a promising approach for which additional research is needed.

COGNITIVE FEATURES OF PANIC DISORDER

Persons with panic disorder have strong beliefs and fears of physical or mental harm arising from bodily sensations that are associated with panic attacks (e.g., Chambless, Caputo, Bright, & Gallagher, 1984; Sandin, Sánchez-Arribas, Chorot, & Valiente, 2015). They are more likely to interpret bodily sensations in a catastrophic fashion (Clark et al., 1988), and to attend more to words that represent physical threat, such as *disease* and *fatality* (e.g., Asmundson, Sandler, Wilson, & Walker, 1992; De Cort et al., 2013); catastrophe words, such as *death* and *insane* (e.g., Maidenberg, Chen, Craske, Bohn, & Bystritsky, 1996); and (what patients believed was real) heartbeat information (Kroeze & van den Hout, 2000). Further, adults with panic disorder show greater anxiety responses to panic words relative to adults with mixed anxiety disorders and healthy controls (De Cort et al., 2013). A more recent effort (De Cort, Hermans, Spruyt, Griez, & Schruers, 2008), however, failed to establish that panic-specific words resulted in greater attentional bias among people with panic disorder compared to other anxiety disorders. More work is needed to establish content and disorder specificity of attentional biases toward panic-related threat.

Individuals with panic disorder are more likely to fear procedures that elicit bodily sensations similar to the ones experienced during panic attacks, including benign cardiovascular, respiratory, and audiovestibular exercises and inductions (Jacob, Furman, Clark, & Durrant, 1992; Kaplan et al., 2012; Zarate, Rapee, Craske, & Barlow, 1988), and carbon dioxide inhalations compared to patients with other anxiety disorders (e.g., Rapee, Brown, Antony, & Barlow, 1992; see Vickers, Jafarpour, Mofidi, Rafat, & Woznica, 2012) or healthy controls (e.g., Gorman et al., 1994; Zvolensky & Eifert, 2001). Indeed, even in interoceptive conditioning studies using healthy participants, a suffocation-focused interpretation of a carbon dioxide inhalation task can significantly induce fear symptoms relative to neutral and non-panic-focused control conditions (De Cort, Grieze, Büchler, & Schruers, 2012). Patients with panic disorder fear signals that ostensibly reflect heightened arousal and false physiological feedback (Craske & Freed, 1995; Craske, Lang, et al., 2002; Ehlers, Margraf, Roth, Taylor, & Birbaumer, 1988). Findings are not fully consistent, however, as patients with panic disorder did not differ from patients with social phobia in response to an epinephrine challenge (Veltman, van Zijderveld, Tilders, & van Dyck, 1996).

In addition, direct manipulation of appraisals can affect level of distress over physical symptoms. For example, persons with panic disorder and nonclinical panickers report significantly less fear and panic during laboratory-based panic provocation procedures, such as hyperventilation and carbon dioxide inhalation, when they perceive that the procedure is safe and/or controllable (e.g., Rapee, Mattick, & Murrell, 1986; Sanderson, Rapee, & Barlow, 1989), when accompanied by a safe person (Carter, Hollon, Carson, & Shelton, 1995), or after cognitive-behavioral treatment that reduces fears of bodily sensations (Craske, Lang, Aikins, & Mystkowski, 2005; Schmidt, Trakowski, & Staab, 1997). However, manipulations of predictability and controllability did not significantly affect frequency of panic responses among panic disorder patients in an epinephrine challenge study (Veltman, van Zijderveld, van Dyck, & Bakker, 1998).

Individuals with panic disorder sometimes demonstrate memory abnormalities, although results have been varied and contradictory at times. A comprehensive early meta-analysis (Mitte, 2008) clarified that anxiety disorders and high anxiety—including panic disorder—do not affect implicit memory or recognition abilities. However, anxiety was associated with a memory bias toward recalling threat-related information, with no differences between individuals with high anxiety and those with anxiety disorders. A modest memory recall bias toward threat is consistent with the attentional biases toward threat observed in panic disorder and other anxiety disorders. A more recent study also documented *nonverbal* memory and visuoconstructive ability impairments in panic disorder relative to healthy controls, independent of benzodiazepine use (Deckersbach, Moshier, Tuschen-Caffier, & Otto, 2011). Finally, a recent meta-analysis showed that, among 10 studies investigating memory deficits in individuals with panic disorder specifically, seven found such deficits when compared to healthy controls (Alves, Pereira, Machado, Nardi, & Oliveira e Silva, 2013). These included difficulties in visual memory tasks (Lucas, Telch, & Bigler, 1991), spatial memory (Boldrini et al., 2005), free recall and cued recall (Airaksinen, Larsson, & Forsell, 2005), short-term memory for numbers and words (Gordeev, 2008), and working memory (Castillo, Coy, Shejet, Duran, & Cabrera, 2010). However, most of these studies were small, indicating that further investigation is needed.

Other studies have looked at dual-task versus single-task memory in panic disorder patients, and compared deficits in panic disorder to other anxiety disorders. Among inpatients with severe panic disorder (without co-occurring current or past disorders), Lautenbacher and colleagues (Lautenbacher, Spernal, & Kreig, 2002) found attentional deficits within a dual-task paradigm for divided attention, but not within a single-task paradigm for selective attention. These deficits also were evident among individuals with severe depression (without co-occurring disorders) but not among healthy controls, suggesting that these two severe patient groups show similar deficits in tasks with a high attentional load. The meta-analysis by Alves et al. (2013) discussed above investigated eight studies on attentional issues in individuals with panic disorder, with three of the eight reporting deficits when compared to healthy controls. Whereas two showed panic disorder–specific problems in selective attention (Castillo et al., 2010; Gordeev, 2008), the third (Lautenbacher et al., 2002) contradicted these results by finding no differences in selective attention tasks.

Studies utilizing event-related brain potential electroencephalogram (EEG) methodologies provide a more precise understanding of the time course of panic-related attentional and memory abnormalities. In contrast to healthy controls, panic patients failed to modulate prefrontal event-related brain potentials when responding to words with different affective connotations in a memory recognition task (Windmann, Sakhavat, & Kutas, 2002). The effect was found in the latency range of responding (300–500 milliseconds), which generally assumes greater influence of autonomic rather than controlled memory processes, but not at later processing stages (700+ milliseconds). Hence, the authors suggest that patients may "adopt conscious strategies to minimize the impact of these early processing abnormalities on overt behaviors" (p. 357). On a cautionary note, half of the patients had mild depression, making it unclear whether the results were due to panic- or depression-related functioning (or to both). In a related set of findings, Pauli and colleagues (Pauli, Amrhein, Muhlberger, Dengler, & Wiedemann, 2005) found that panic patients—but not healthy controls—showed early enhanced brain potentials (at 100–200 and 200–400 milliseconds) in response to panic-related words. The authors concluded that panic disorder may be characterized by an early, largely automatic processing bias toward panic-related stimuli. A review of EEG findings in individuals with panic disorder suggests that most changes are evident in the frontal and temporal cortexes (de Carvalho et al., 2013). Specifically, adults with panic disorder show increased right frontal hemisphere activation, which could reflect a more acute emotional response in response to fear stimuli. Such a response may indeed be associated with negative emotionality and subsequent behavioral avoidance systems.

Whereas event-related brain potential studies help identify the timing of cognitive processing abnormalities, functional magnetic resonance imaging (fMRI) brain imaging studies reveal their location and functional relationships. Previous fMRI studies of visual exposure to physical threat and neutral words find that individuals with panic disorder showed greater left posterior cingulate and dorsolateral prefrontal cortex activity during threat words relative to healthy controls (see de Carvalho et al., 2010; Maddock, Buonocore, Kile, & Garrett, 2003). Maddock and colleagues (2003) associated these regions with emotion and verbal memory processing, consistent with the notion of greater processing of threat-related words in panic disorder (though memory for threat words was not tested directly). In an fMRI study of neuroanatomical correlates of the Stroop task across panic disorder, obsessive-compulsive disorder, and hypochondriasis patient groups (van den Heuvel et al., 2005), panic disorder patients showed activation patterns similar to hypochondriacal patients. Both displayed increased ventral and dorsal brain region activation, suggesting increased unconscious emotional processing as well as increased cognitive elaboration.

EMOTIONAL FEATURES OF PANIC DISORDER

The temperament variable most associated with anxiety disorders, including panic disorder, is *neuroticism* (Eysenck, 1967; Gray, 1982; Longley, Watson, Noyes, & Yoder, 2006), or proneness to experience negative emotions in response to stressors. A closely linked construct is *negative affectivity*, or the tendency to experience an array of negative emotions across a variety of situations, even in the absence of objective stressors (Watson & Clark, 1984). Structural analyses confirm that negative affect is a higher-order factor that distinguishes individuals with anxiety and/or depressive disorders from controls with no mental disorder. The anxiety disorders load differentially on negative affectivity, with more pervasive anxiety disorders such as generalized anxiety disorder loading more heavily, panic disorder loading at an intermediate level, and social anxiety disorder loading the least (Brown, Chorpita, & Barlow, 1998).[1] Lower-order factors further discriminate among the anxiety disorders, with fear of fear being the factor that discriminates panic disorder from other anxiety disorders (Brown et al., 1998; Zinbarg & Barlow, 1996).

Longitudinal prospective evidence for the role of neuroticism in predicting the onset of panic disorder is relatively limited. However, neuroticism was found to predict the onset of panic *attacks* (Hayward, Killen, Kraemer, & Taylor, 2000; Schmidt, Lerew, & Jackson, 1997, 1999), and emotional reactivity at age 3 was a significant variable in the classification of panic disorder in 18- to 21-year-old males (Craske, Poulton, Tsao, & Plotkin, 2001). Ongoing studies, such as the Northwestern/UCLA Youth Emotion Project (Zinbarg et al., 2010), are currently evaluating the relationships among neuroticism, various other risk factors, and panic disorder.

Interaction with Environmental Factors

Environmental factors interact with biologically and genetically-related temperamental factors to increase (or decrease) risk for anxiety disorders, including panic disorder. Early deficient caregiving and/or parenting likely relate more to risk for psychopathology in general, whereas abuse and especially childhood experiences with illness may relate to panic disorder more specifically. Depending on their nature, life stressors can play a more general or specific role in the etiology and maintenance of panic disorder. We review each environmental factor in turn.

EARLY CAREGIVING AND INFANT ATTACHMENT

Emerging research supports the hypothesis that early experiences related to infant care may play an important role in buffering or facilitating later proneness toward anxiety. Specifically, early experiences with prediction and control may be associated with the development of adaptive emotional regulatory capacities in the face of negative stressors. In this context, prediction refers to a contingency (cause-effect) awareness of events in the environment, as well as outcome prediction by virtue of one's own responding, and control refers to control over emotions and outcomes via one's own attention and behaviors (see Craske, 2003). Evidence (e.g., Papousek & Papousek, 2002; Rochat & Striano, 1999) supports the assertion that parental monitoring and reactivity to infant signals enable infants to learn contingency-response relationships and hence a sense of predictability. Initially, a sense of predictability may develop from the relationship between an infant's cues and the caretaker's response. Later, this may transfer to contingency knowledge of the relationship between an infant's own behaviors and responses (see Craske, 2003). According to attachment pioneer Bowlby (1969, 1980), caregiver responses that are characterized by unpredictability and unresponsiveness may lead to anxious attachment in which the child is chronically insecure and apprehensive. In support, a recent

---

[1] Specific phobias were not assessed, but by being most circumscribed, they would be hypothesized to load the least on negative affectivity.

meta-analysis of both longitudinal and cross-sectional studies showed a moderate relationship ($r = .3$) between early insecure attachment (particularly ambivalent attachment) and the development of anxiety disorders and symptoms in childhood and adolescence (Colonnesi et al., 2011).

This work, however, remains limited by the fact that experimentally manipulating predictability and control for extended periods of time in infant humans is not ethically possible. Hence, the most compelling evidence of the causal effects of prolonged lack of predictability and control in infants comes from research with rhesus monkeys. Mineka, Gunnar, and Champoux (1986) demonstrated that infant rhesus monkeys who were granted control over toys and food habituated more quickly to novel stimuli, demonstrated more exploratory behavior in a novel playroom, and demonstrated enhanced coping responses during separation from peers compared to infants without control (but with equal exposure) over toys and food. Mineka and Cook (1986) concluded that experiences with mastery and control buffer the effects of stressful experiences.

PARENTING

In addition to infant attachment, general parental styles across situations may contribute to children's trait anxiety, whereas situationally specific parental behaviors may contribute to the development of particular anxiety disorders (Craske, 1999). Although many previous studies examining these hypotheses are fraught with methodological difficulties, more recent studies on parent-child interactions have been more informative.

One line of studies examines children's perceptions of their parents' behavior. Generally, children of anxious parents view their families as more conflictual, less independent, less cohesive, and more controlling than children with healthy, nonanxious parents do (see Whaley, Pinto, & Sigman, 1999). In addition, children with anxiety disorders view their families as less independence promoting than nonanxious children do. Another study demonstrated that perceptions of low maternal caring and overprotectiveness were highest among children with anxiety disorders, slightly lower among high trait anxious children, and lowest among low trait anxious children (Bennet & Stirling, 1998). Still another found that children's self-perceived competence mediated the relation between child-reported maternal overcontrol and child-reported anxiety (Affrunti & Ginsburg, 2012). However, a study of 7- to 13-year-old children referred to mental health clinics and their parents (Gere, Villabø, Torgersen, & Kendall, 2012) found that the presence of child behavior symptoms accounted for the relationship between parental protectiveness and child anxiety symptoms, suggesting that parental overprotectiveness may stem from other child symptoms. These studies, however, are limited by reliance on self-report measures and cross-sectional designs (see Craske, 2003; Wood, McLeod, Sigman, Hwang, & Chu, 2003).

A longitudinal study found a bidirectional pattern whereby mothers' anxious parenting and adolescents' anxiety influenced one another. Adolescents' perception of maternal anxious parenting (overprotection and high anxiety expression) predicted their own self-reported anxiety 12 months later, whereas mother-reported adolescent anxiety predicted adolescents' perception of maternal anxious parenting 12 months later (Rapee, 2009). Again, however, this study relied on self-reported anxiety, and recent work has shown that mother-child agreement on (reported) child anxiety symptoms is influenced by the presence of maternal worry and depression (Affrunti & Woodruff-Borden, 2015).

A more reliable body of research relies on behavioral coding of observed parent-child interactions. Fortunately, the findings generally converge with the self-report data. Whaley and Sigman (Moore, Whaley, & Sigman, 2004; Whaley et al., 1999) found that in comparison with nonanxious control mothers, anxious mothers were observed to criticize and catastrophize more, and to display less warmth and autonomy granting toward their children. Maternal behaviors predicted children's anxiety levels, and children's anxiety levels predicted maternal autonomy granting (Whaley et al., 1999). Finally, mothers of anxiety-disordered children, regardless of their own anxiety status, displayed less warmth and autonomy granting (Moore et al., 2004). These combined findings support an interactive model in which parenting behaviors predict offspring anxiety, and offspring anxiety molds parenting behaviors. A descriptive review by Wood et al. (2003) concluded that observed parental control during parent-child interactions (defined as overprotectiveness, excessive regulation of activities, routines, and decision making) consistently predicted child shyness and childhood anxiety disorders, a finding confirmed by a more recent meta-analysis (McLeod, Wood, & Weisz, 2007). The meta-analysis concluded that parenting accounted for only modest (4%) variance in child anxiety on average, but certain parenting domains had greater influence. Specifically, autonomy granting was especially important—accounting for 18% of the variance in child anxiety—whereas parental warmth was not strongly associated with child anxiety. More recently, Schneider et al. (2009) used observational coding to compare mothers with panic disorder to nonanxious mothers and found that mothers with panic disorder were more verbally controlling and more conflictual with their children, regardless of the children's anxiety status. This finding remained after controlling for parental depression, which may indicate a specific manner in which mothers with panic disorder interact with their children. However, in this study other independent disorders of the mother were not considered (e.g., depression without comorbid panic disorder or other anxiety disorders).

Overall, however, the extent to which negative, intrusive, or overinvolved parenting styles are anxiety-specific remains debatable. Hudson and Rapee (2001) observed that mothers of anxious children were more negative, overinvolved, and intrusive than mothers of nonanxious control children, (e.g., Hibbs, Hamburger, Kruesi, & Lenane, 1993); but see Stubbe, Zahner, Goldstein, and Leckman (1993) for the opposite finding. That study failed to find a difference in maternal behaviors toward children with anxiety disorders versus children with oppositional disorders. Similarly, as noted, another study showed that parental overprotectiveness is more influenced by child behavior problems than by child anxiety symptoms (Gere et al., 2012). In a longitudinal investigation using observational coding, Schwartz et al. (2012) demonstrated that greater parental aggression predicted higher adolescent anxiety *and* depression symptoms over the course of 2.5 years. Thus, maladaptive parental behaviors such as overinvolvement and aggression may characterize parents of children with significant psychopathology or distress rather than children with anxiety disorders or panic disorder in particular.

A rare experimental study of parental modeling among older youth demonstrated that when young adolescents (mean age of 12 years) observed their parent escape a voluntary 3-minute hyperventilation (which produces panic-like symptoms), they were more likely to escape themselves, relative to adolescents who observed their parent complete the hyperventilation (Bunaciu et al., 2014). This study is particularly interesting given its focus on a pubertal stage of youth, which, as the authors note, is a developmental stage that predicts the development of panic-related problems. Thus, the role of vicarious learning in fear panic-related symptoms via parental modeling of avoidance and escape from panic-relevant sensations and/or contexts represents a promising pathway for further research.

The vast majority of studies have focused on the influence of maternal behaviors and symptoms on childhood anxiety, reflecting samples made up only or largely of mothers; in contrast, the influence of paternal behaviors and symptoms has received less attention. Yet in one study, the offspring (mean age of 14 years) of a clinical sample of fathers and mothers treated for panic disorder and/or depression 10 years earlier demonstrated that paternal panic disorder predicted higher rates of panic disorder, agoraphobia, obsessive-compulsive disorder, and multiple anxiety disorders at similar or higher rates than maternal panic disorder (Hirshfeld-Becker et al., 2012), suggesting the importance of including fathers in parenting studies on panic disorder. Thus, given the seeming importance of both maternal and paternal behaviors in influencing offspring's risk for panic disorder, research is now needed to demonstrate the direct causal links and specificity of parental behaviors that confer such risk.

CHILDHOOD EXPERIENCES WITH ILLNESS AND ABUSE

Childhood experience with medical illness, personally or via observing others, may increase the risk for the subsequent development of anxiety disorders in general and panic disorder in particular. Experience with personal respiratory disturbance and parental illness in childhood predicted panic disorder onset at ages 18 or 21 in a large, longitudinal sample (Craske et al., 2001). This finding is consistent with multiple reports of more respiratory disease and disturbance in the history of panic disorder patients compared to other anxiety-disordered patients (Goodwin & Pine, 2002; Verburg, Griez, Meijer, & Pols, 1995). Further, one study found that first-degree relatives of panic disorder patients had a significantly higher prevalence of chronic obstructive respiratory disease and asthma than did first-degree relatives of patients with other anxiety disorders (van Beek, Schruers, & Griez, 2005). A review of the literature (Grassi et al., 2013) found that adults with panic disorder, relative to healthy controls, evidenced baseline respiratory abnormalities that reflected a state of chronic hyperventilation (independent of state anxiety levels) as well as greater respiration variability and irregularity. Additional research now needs to examine whether such respiratory abnormalities are present, and whether they increase the short- or long-term risk for panic disorder, among the offspring of parents with panic disorder.

Childhood experiences of sexual and physical abuse may also prime panic disorder. Retrospective reports of childhood abuse were associated with panic disorder onset at ages 16 to 21 in a longitudinal analysis of New Zealanders from birth to age 21 (Goodwin et al., 2005), a finding consistent with multiple cross-sectional studies in both clinical and community samples (e.g., Kessler, Davis, & Kendler, 1997; Stein et al., 1996). The link with childhood abuse was stronger for panic disorder than for other anxiety disorders such as social phobia (Safren, Gershuny, Marzol, Otto, & Pollack, 2002; Stein et al., 1996) and obsessive-compulsive disorder (Stein et al., 1996). Further, a gene by environment interaction study indicated that childhood maltreatment mediated the relationship between the serotonin transporter gene promoter polymorphism (5-HTTLPR) and anxiety sensitivity, which is implicated in the etiology of panic disorder (Stein, Schork, & Gelernter, 2008). However, more recent data from the National Comorbidity Survey (Kessler et al., 1997) and National Comorbidity Survey Replication (NCS-R; Cougle, Timpano, Sachs-Ericsson, Keough, & Riccardi, 2010) demonstrated a relationship between childhood sexual abuse and panic disorder as well as multiple other psychiatric disorders (social anxiety disorder, generalized anxiety disorder, and posttraumatic stress disorder in the latter study). Similarly, in the NCS-R study, neglect-related parenting was associated with slightly elevated risk for all mood and anxiety disorders (including panic disorder), again suggesting a lack of specificity to panic disorder (Nickerson, Bryant, Aderka, Hinton, & Hofmann, 2013). Thus, the extent to which childhood abuse or neglect uniquely predicts panic disorder remains debatable. In addition, some studies found an association between panic disorder and exposure to violence between other family members, usually interparental violence (e.g., Bandelow et al., 2002), whereas the most recent study did not (Goodwin et al., 2005). Retrospective reporting of childhood abuse or neglect in all of these studies, however, limits their findings.

STRESS

The relationship between external aversive events, also known as stressful events, and panic disorder has several facets. First, temperamental vulnerabilities, such as neuroticism, may contribute to more frequent and more potent stressful life events (Craske, 2003). Second, stressful life events may precipitate initial panic attacks and contribute to their repeated occurrence over time: As described earlier, a large percentage of individuals with panic disorder report the presence of identifiable stressors around the time of the first panic attack (Craske et al., 1990; Pollard et al., 1989; Roy-Byrne et al., 1986; although see Rapee, Litwin, & Barlow, 1990 for somewhat different findings). As alluded to earlier, significant childhood adversity and stressful life events are both associated with increased risk for anxiety disorders as well as other psychopathology (Brown, Harris, & Eales, 1993; Kessler et al., 1997). In addition, variations in anxiety symptom levels over time are influenced by life stress and other environmental factors (Mackinnon, Henderson, & Andrews, 1990). Life stressors over multiple months and years predicted later anxious and depressive symptoms in adult (Cohen, McGowan, Fooskas, & Rose, 1984) though not adolescent samples (Cohen, Burt, & Bjork, 1987; Rueter, Scaramella, Wallace, & Conger, 1999). Recently, however, self-reported history of traumatic event exposure among adolescents was found to predict panic symptoms outside the laboratory and greater anxious and fearful responses to an in-session hyperventilation task (Hawks, Blumenthal, Feldner, Leen-Feldner, & Jones, 2011). For panic disorder specifically, potentially traumatic events are more influential in leading to the disorder when they occur during childhood rather than adulthood (Zlotnick et al., 2008).

A stress-diathesis perspective would hypothesize that stressful life events interact with preexisting vulnerabilities to produce panic attacks and panic disorder. For example, autonomic instability (e.g., the tendency to experience cardiac symptoms and shortness of breath) may develop into full-blown panic when instances occur in threatening contexts or following life stressors, when the sensations are more likely to be perceived as threatening (Craske, 1999). According to Bouton et al. (2001), high anxiety can elevate the likelihood of panic attacks. Stressful life events may elevate levels of anxiety, particularly in vulnerable individuals, which in turn increases the risk for panic. From a related perspective, a study of Russian individuals examined the interaction of anxiety sensitivity, or the tendency to interpret anxiety symptoms as dangerous and threatening, and recent exposure to stressful life events (Zvolensky, Kotov, Antipova, & Schmidt, 2005). Beyond levels of negative affect, high levels of stressful life events interacted with a subscale of anxiety sensitivity (the physical concerns subscale) to predict panic attacks in the past week and agoraphobic avoidance. These findings are consistent with a stress-diathesis model; however, the notion of stress-diathesis does not offer specificity in the etiology of panic disorder relative to other anxiety disorders.

Looking beyond the infant attachment period, the death of a parent or loss of a loved one may threaten attachment and, thus, might be expected to hold specificity as a risk factor for panic disorder. Again, however, the specificity to panic disorder remains dubious; earlier parental loss, for example, is associated with greater risk for all anxiety and mood disorders rather than panic disorder specifically (Nickerson et al., 2013). A study comparing Korean adults with panic disorder and healthy controls (Choe et al., 2013) found that the number of separation-related life events (e.g., death of a loved one, divorce) interacted with the presence of serotonergic gene polymorphisms (5-HTTLPR S/S homozygotes) to predict current panic disorder status and harm avoidance. If replicated, this finding suggests that loss-related life stressors activate genetic vulnerabilities in a manner that can increase risk for panic disorder. However, the lack of a psychiatric control group obscures whether this interaction also predicts other forms of psychopathology or panic disorder specifically.

Biological Features of Panic Disorder

Investigations into the genetic and neurobiological underpinnings of panic disorder have greatly expanded over the past decade. In this section, we offer an updated account of the complex biological factors that contribute to elevated risk for and maintenance of panic disorder.

GENETICS

According to family studies, the heritability of panic disorder accounts for approximately 30% to 40% of the variance in panic disorder (Hettema, Neale, & Kendler, 2001; López-Solà et al., 2014). Even though heritability studies of anxiety disorders often rely on poorly validated lifetime diagnostic instruments (e.g., the Diagnostic Interview Schedule), two broad but distinct genetic factors have been identified. The first factor is defined by high loadings for generalized anxiety disorder and major depression, but only moderate loadings for panic disorder (Mineka, Watson, & Clark, 1998) and agoraphobia (Kendler, Neale, Kessler, Heath, & Eaves, 1993). The trait of neuroticism loads heavily on this first factor and roughly half of the variance in neuroticism is accounted for by genetic factors (Lake, Eaves, Maes, Heath, & Martin, 2000). Twin studies provide evidence that symptoms of panic or fear (i.e., breathlessness, heart pounding) may be additionally explained by a second genetic factor (e.g., a second source of genetic variance), which is distinct from general symptoms of anxiety and depression (Kendler et al., 1993) and, at least in females, from neuroticism (Martin, Jardine, Andrews, & Heath, 1988). Support for these two broad diatheses, one focused on general anxiety and depression symptoms and the other focused on fear and panic symptoms, exists in analyses of the Vietnam Era Twin Registry (Scherrer et al., 2000).

In addition, recent advances in molecular genetics have begun to illuminate a complex interplay of more specific chromosomal regions, genes, and alleles that may be related to panic disorder. Previously, panic disorder phenotype transmission has been linked to numerous chromosomal regions; however, few of these are actually shared across samples (Sakolsky, McCracken, & Nurmi, 2012). Further, although many of these associations have been found for panic disorder specifically, they may be relevant for the transmission of high trait anxiety or anxiety disorders more broadly.

Somewhat better progress has been made on linking panic disorder to specific genetic polymorphisms. Broadly, the gene polymorphism 5-HTTLPR—a promoter region on the serotonin transporter gene—has been a target of investigation across the mood and anxiety disorders, with mixed findings. For example, a meta-analysis of 10 studies investigating 5-HTTLPR polymorphism in individuals with and without panic disorder found no significant association between 5-HTTLPR and panic disorder (Blaya, Salum, Lima, Leistner-Segal, & Manfro, 2007), whereas a more recent study (Lonsdorf et al., 2009) found strong associations between bi- and triallelic 5-HTTLPR polymorphisms and panic disorder symptoms assessed dimensionally (rather than categorically as is typically done). Further, several meta-analyses found strong associations between 5-HTTLPR and neuroticism measured by the NEO Personality Inventory (Munafò, Freimer, et al., 2008; Schinka, Busch, & Robichaux-Keene, 2004; Sen, Burmeister, & Ghosh, 2004), which is implicated in risk for panic disorder and anxiety disorders more generally. One study (Agorastos et al., 2014) suggests that adults with the short/short 5-HTTLPR genotype show blunted autonomic reactivity when confronted by panic-like arousal (induced by cholecystokinin tetrapeptide), compared to adults with the long/long 5-HTTLPR genotype. Although this study did not focus on individuals with panic disorder, results point toward a potential genetic vulnerability associated with hyporeactivity and hyperreactivity to interoceptive, panic-like sensations. Similarly, a meta-analysis has shown an association between the 5-HTTLPR genotype and increased acute HPA-axis and cortisol reactivity among adults with the short/short relative to the short/long or long/long 5-HTTLPR genotype (Miller, Wankerl, Stalder, Kirschbaum, & Alexander, 2013). Thus, the short/short 5-HTTLPR genotype appears to confer risk for stress sensitivity and vulnerability to psychological disorders in general, rather than to panic disorder in particular.

A study based on the stress-diathesis model (Gunthert et al., 2007) showed that elevated anxiety in response to daily stressors (e.g., self-reported via daily diary over 2 months, 1 year apart) varied as a function of 5-HTTLPR genotype. A meta-analysis of neuroimaging studies found associations between 5-HTTLPR and brain activity in the amygdala, a region involved in anxiety (Munafò, Brown, & Hariri, 2008). The authors concluded that the 5-HTTLPR gene locus could account for up to 10% of phenotypic variance in amygdala activation. However, a later study examining physiological and affective responses to a carbon dioxide challenge (an acute panicogenic stressor) in a high and low neuroticism sample failed to find group differences in reactivity based on the 5-HTTLPR genotype (Verschoor & Markus, 2012). Further, an investigation of people with panic disorder, social anxiety disorder, or both, failed to find an association with 5-HTTLPR but did find a panic disorder–specific association with SLC6A4, the serotonin transporter gene on which the 5-HTTLPR polymorphism region is located (Strug et al., 2010). Additional research has found that the 5-HTTLPR genotype does not by itself strongly predict panic disorder, but does predict it when coupled with certain life stressors such as early separation events (Choe et al., 2013). In summary, the association between 5-HTTLPR genotypes and panic disorder is complex and requires additional investigation to elucidate the currently mixed findings. Nonetheless, multiple studies suggest that 5-HTTLPR genotypes may be relevant for understanding dimensional expressions of panic disorder, as well as daily anxiety reactivity and neural regions linked to anxiety.

A range of various other genetic loci have been investigated in panic disorder. Association and linkage studies, for example, implicate the adenosine receptor gene in panic disorder and anxiety sensitivity (Deckert et al., 1998; Gajewska et al., 2013; Hamilton et al., 2004). Recently, a variant of the adenosine receptor gene, particularly the T-allele, was found to indicate risk for panic disorder, especially with agoraphobia (Hohoff et al., 2010). However, the T-allele was also associated with anxiety-related harm-avoidance personality traits in healthy individuals, suggesting that it may be more relevant for understanding panic disorder risk dimensionally rather than categorically. Additionally, a susceptibility locus for panic disorder has been mapped to chromosome 7p14–q15 (e.g., Logue, Vieland, Goedken, & Crowe, 2003). An allele of the neuropeptide S receptor gene, located on chromosome 7, was linked in a sample of Japanese men to panic disorder but was not linked to schizophrenia or attention-deficit/hyperactivity disorder (Okamura et al., 2007). A more recent study found a female-specific effect, linking the neuropeptide S receptor gene to panic disorder (compared to healthy controls) and to anxiety sensitivity and heightened physiological arousal during a stressful behavioral avoidance task (Domschke et al., 2011). This study also found the neuropeptide S allele to predict decreased anterior cingulate cortex activity, which had been previously linked to panic disorder (e.g., Pillay, Gruber, Rogowska, Simpson, & Todd, 2006). Another investigation found a gender-specific effect relating the angiotensin converting enzyme gene (located on chromosome 17) to panic disorder only in males (Bandelow et al., 2010). Many of these findings await further replication and elucidation. In addition, more recent research has found that an interaction between the neuropeptide S receptor TT genotype and the adenosinergic system potentially mediates affect-modulated startle response in humans (Domschke et al., 2012).

Additionally, the Val158Met polymorphism of the catechol-O-methyltransferase (COMT) gene—involved in dopamine regulation in the prefrontal cortex as well as other subcortical regions—has been associated with alterations in fear arousal and emotion regulation (e.g., Olsson et al., 2005) and has been implicated in panic disorder susceptibility in several independent samples (Maron, Hettema, & Shlik, 2010). More precisely, a meta-analysis found that the COMT Val158Met polymorphism corresponded with panic disorder in Caucasian samples with a trend toward correspondence in Asian samples, though effects in both groups were specific to females (Domschke, Deckert, O'Donovan, & Glatt, 2007). Thus, the polymorphism demonstrated both ethnicity and sex-specific effects. However, a more recent meta-analysis (Gatt, Burton, Williams, & Schofield, 2015) found that this polymorphism was implicated in multiple psychiatric disorders and thus is not specific to panic disorder. Additional COMT gene variants await exploration. Other, lesser known candidate genes are also being investigated for their link to panic disorder (e.g., Erhardt et al., 2012; see also Gatt et al., 2015).

Recently, the role of microRNAs, which repress gene expression, has gained attention in understanding phenotypic expression. For example, several studies (Muiños-Gimeno et al., 2011; Hommers et al., 2015) have found preliminary evidence for microRNAs that affected expression of candidate genes implicated in panic disorder. Thus, further research on microRNA regulation of genetic pathways in panic disorder is indicated.

BASIC NEUROCIRCUITRY

Neural Networks Involving the Amygdala

Current neural models focus on the role of the amygdala and related structures as central to the dysfunctional anxiety evaluation and response system in panic disorder (Gorman, Kent, Sullivan, & Coplan, 2000; Kim, Dager, & Lyoo, 2012). The amygdala serves as a mediator of input from the environment (via the thalamus and sensory cortex) and stored experience (via the frontal cortex and hippocampus), which then triggers anxiety and panic response by activating brain regions involved in panic symptoms, including the hypothalamus (HPA axis and autonomic system), locus coeruleus (heart rate and blood pressure), and parabrachial nucleus (changes in respiration; see Roy-Byrne, Craske, & Stein, 2006). Research on patients with panic disorder has found alterations in the amygdala and associated structures consistent with this model, including reduced volume in the amygdala (see Del Casale et al., 2013; Kim et al., 2012); decreased cerebral glucose metabolism in amygdala, hippocampus, thalamus, brain stem (Sakai et al., 2005), right middle temporal gyrus, right caudate body, and left posterior cingulate gyrus (Kang et al., 2012); and lowered levels of creatine and phosphocreatine metabolites in the right medial temporal lobe (Atmaca, Yildirim, Gurok, Akyol, & Koseoglu, 2012; Massana et al., 2002), in resting states. In addition, while some evidence points to decreased volume in the left temporal lobe (e.g., Uchida et al., 2003), other research shows no difference in this brain region for individuals with panic disorder relative to healthy controls (e.g., Del Casale et al., 2013). Evidence also points to the role of the anterior cingular cortex, insula, and midbrain periaqueductal gray in the pathophysiology of experimentally induced panic attacks and panic disorder (Graeff & Del-Ben, 2008). Many of these findings occur in various combinations within other anxiety disorders, such as social anxiety and posttraumatic stress disorder (Kent & Rauch, 2003), indicating that they are not necessarily specific to panic disorder.

One neural pathway possibly associated with the onset of panic disorder exists between the ventromedial prefrontal cortex (vmPFC) and the amygdala (Johnson, Federici, & Shekhar, 2014). Evidence suggests that the vmPFC may be underactive in panic disorder, resulting in diminished inhibitory inputs to the amygdala and subcortical panic-generation regions within the perifornical hypothalamus and dorsal periaqueductal gray (Johnson et al., 2014). Indeed, a review and a meta-analysis by de Carvalho and colleagues (2010, 2013) suggest that most studies investigating the neural underpinnings of panic disorder show inhibitory deficits of the prefrontal cortex when modulating amygdala activity.

GABA/Benzodiazepine System

Another neurological system potentially implicated in the pathophysiology of panic disorder is the γ-aminobutyric acid (GABA) neuronal system. Some studies demonstrate that patients with panic disorder exhibit low baseline GABA levels in the occipital cortex (Goddard et al., 2001) and, following acute benzodiazepine administration, show blunted benzodiazepine sensitivity (Roy-Byrne, Cowley, Greenblatt, Shader, & Hommer, 1990) and GABA neuronal responses (Goddard et al., 2004). In contrast, a more recent study found no deficits in GABA within the occipital cortex for individuals with panic disorder (Long et al., 2013) but, rather, decreased GABA in the anterior cingulate and medial prefrontal cortex. However, sample sizes were small, suggesting the need for further investigation and replication. Potentially elucidating these findings, several studies (Bremner et al., 2000; Malizia et al., 1998), but not all studies (Brandt et al., 1998), have found lowered benzodiazepine receptor density in amygdala and perihippocampal areas and in frontocortical areas more generally (by a mean of –13%; Nikolaus, Antke, Beu, & Muller, 2011) in patients with panic disorder relative to healthy controls. However, GABA abnormalities have also been found in patients with other psychological disorders such as depression (Mohler, 2012) and alcohol dependency (Xuei et al., 2010), suggesting once again that these findings may not necessarily be specific to panic disorder.

HPA Axis and Autonomic Nervous System Functioning

Dysregulation of the autonomic nervous system and HPA axis has been hypothesized to be central to panic disorder. Thus, significant research has been conducted in this area, although findings are sometimes contradictory. Abelson and colleagues (Abelson, Khan, Liberzon, & Young, 2007) reexamined four HPA studies from their laboratory and concluded that experimental contexts that are novel, uncontrollable, or threatening produce elevated HPA responses in panic disorder patients relative to healthy controls and account for disparate findings from previous studies. In other words, they found consistent evidence that individuals with panic disorder show elevated HPA reactivity to specific environmental cues, rather than elevated HPA responding in general (i.e., at baseline). The same effect has been observed with measures of the time course of startle eyeblink responding (which is mediated by the amygdala; Anders, Martin, Erb, Grodd, & Birbaumer, 2004): baseline startle was enhanced in participants with panic disorder relative to controls, but the groups showed otherwise equivalent patterns of responding to approaching shock (Grillon, Ameli, Goddard, Woods, & Davis, 1994). Since baseline represents a state of anticipation about upcoming experimental procedures, the results are interpreted as elevated emotional reactivity to stressful conditions in general versus exaggerated responding to explicit threat cues (Grillon, 2002). Thus, once again, relative to healthy controls, adults with panic disorder have difficulty distinguishing threat cues from safety cues, and thus fear becomes generalized more to the threat context than to the specific threat cue (e.g., Lissek et al., 2009, 2010). Similarly, investigations of autonomic state, such as galvanic skin response, heart rate, respiration, and skin temperature, generally indicate that persons with panic disorder show an elevated response to experimental *contexts* (a context or situation in which threat *may* be present) versus explicit threat stimuli (the threat itself) (e.g., Roth et al., 1992).

However, recent research indicates that the general versus explicit threat distinction may not be completely consistent, and that HPA axis dysregulation in panic disorder patients can alternatively manifest as *dampened* response to threat. In a series of German experiments employing the Trier Social Stress Test (TSST), panic disorder patients lacked a salivary and plasma cortisol response to the TSST (an acute social performance stressor) compared to healthy controls, even though they had the same heart rate elevation (Petrowski, Herold, Joraschky, Wittchen, & Kirschbaum, 2010; Petrowski, Wintermann, Kirschbaum, & Bornstein, 2013) and no differences in basal cortisol or cortisol awakening responses (Petrowski et al., 2010). Other studies show mixed results for blunted response in panic disorder relative to healthy controls (Jezova, Vigas, Hlavacova, & Kukumberg, 2010; van Duinen, Schruers, Maes, & Griez, 2007); however, these additional studies are limited by very small samples ($ns = 9$ to 16 per group, depending on the study). In sum, findings suggest hypocortisol responsiveness to acute (physiological and external) threat among panic disorder patients. Further, a more recent study indicates that different markers of HPA axis activation—cortisol and ACTH—may be decoupled in panic disorder (Petrowski, Wintermann, Kirschbaum, & Bornstein, 2012). Thus, abnormalities in panic disorder may be evident further downstream in the HPA system, or in the communication and responsiveness of the various elements within the system.

HPA axis dysfunction also has been examined for structural abnormality. An MRI study found that patients with panic disorder evidenced significantly lower pituitary gland volume than healthy controls, and that panic disorder patients with agoraphobia had significantly smaller pituitary glands than those without agoraphobia (Kartalci et al., 2011). Further, pituitary volume was linked to severity and duration of panic disorder. Though this structural difference is consistent with a malfunctioning neuroendocrine system, hormone levels were not directly assessed.

Heart rate variability and specifically cardiac vagal tone, the high-frequency component of heart rate variability, have emerged as popular means of assessing parasympathetic responding. High cardiac vagal tone[2] is hypothesized to facilitate the organism's capacity for quick, precise cardiac and behavioral adaptations to changes in internal states and environmental circumstances, whereas low vagal tone limits such flexible responding (Porges, 1992). Panic disorder has been linked to abnormal heart rate variability and vagal tone, but it is unclear whether these findings are specific to panic disorder or characteristic of anxiety or emotional disorder patients more generally. On one hand, compared to nonpanic controls, multiple heart rate variability abnormalities (involving both high- and low-frequency spectral power) have been found in panic disorder samples during both nonpanic and panicogenic conditions (Friedman & Thayer, 1998; Friedman, Thayer, & Borkovec, 1993). Finally, heart rate variability increases in response to CBT but not in response to SSRI medication treatment for panic disorder (Garakani et al., 2009). That stated, heart rate variability abnormalities have also been found among adults with other anxiety disorders outside of panic disorder (e.g., Cohen et al., 1998, 2000; Hoehn-Saric, McLeod, & Hipsley, 1995; Pittig, Arch, Lam, & Craske, 2013; Thayer, Friedman, Borkovec, Johnsen, & Molina, 2000). Thus, it remains unclear whether a distinct pattern of heart rate variability abnormalities characterizes panic disorder or whether similar abnormalities generalize across the anxiety disorders. More important, multiple well-controlled studies have failed to find heart rate variability differences in panic disorder patients versus healthy controls (Asmundson & Stein, 1994;

---

[2] Heart rate in humans is regulated by the sinoatrial node (SA), the natural pacemaker of the heart, located in the muscle fibers of the right atrial chamber. The SA is enervated by the sympathetic and parasympathetic branches of the autonomic nervous system, both of which modulate the regular rhythm set by the SA. The vagus, the 10th cranial nerve, serves as the principal source of parasympathetic communication between the SA and the central nervous system (Porges, 2003).

Slaap et al., 2004), or they have shown that heart rate variability differences disappeared after accounting for psychotropic medication use (Licht, de Geus, van Dyck, & Penninx, 2009; although see Pittig et al., 2013, for the opposite finding). Differences in time of testing, environmental and psychological conditions surrounding testing (e.g., Abelson et al., 2007), methods of recording and analysis, and subject demographic factors such as age, fitness, and illness duration and severity (e.g., Ito et al., 1999) likely account for these inconsistencies, with the bulk of the evidence pointing to the presence of heart rate variability abnormalities across the anxiety disorders.

Researchers also have focused on assessing sympathetic nervous system functioning in panic disorder. Evaluations of sympathetic nervous system functioning over extended periods of time in the natural environment have yielded mixed results. Some report no baseline differences between a panic disorder sample and nonanxious controls in terms of respiratory and cardiovascular functioning (Clark et al., 1990; Shear et al., 1992), whereas others find differences (Anastasiades, Clark, Salkovskis, & Middleton, 1990; Bystritsky, Craske, Maidenberg, Vapnik, & Shapiro, 1995), including in the dysfunctional baroreflex regulation of sympathetic nerve activity (Shioiri et al., 2005). Differences in the contextual threat value of the studies (anticipating and experiencing stressful stimuli versus resting) perhaps account for these seemingly contradictory findings (see Abelson et al., 2007). Further, Alvarenga and colleagues (Alvarenga, Richards, Lambert, & Esler, 2006) measured cardiac sympathetic nervous tone during resting baseline via rates of cardiac noradrenaline spillover and found no differences between individuals with and without panic disorder. Rather, they found reductions in measures of the noradrenaline transporter among panic disorder patients, suggesting impaired neuronal uptake of noradrenaline in panic disorder. Interestingly, Middleton and Ashby (1995) found that panic disorder treatment in the form of CBT or imipramine increased plasma noradrenaline, suggesting that noradrenaline-associated dysregulations may be modifiable via treatment.

The vast majority of studies (e.g., Brambilla, Perna, Garberi, Nobile, & Bellodi, 1995; Charney, Woods, Krystal, Nagy, & Heninger, 2007) have shown that patients with panic disorder display blunted growth hormone responses to clonidine, an alpha2-adrenoreceptor partial agonist. However, Abelson and colleagues (Abelson, Curtis, & Uhde, 2005) measured growth hormone secretion over a 24-hour period and found no differences between panic patients and nonpatients, suggesting that growth hormone *circadian* patterns and basal activity are normal in panic disorder. Hence, growth hormone abnormalities in panic disorder may be evidenced only in specific activation paradigms, most consistently with clonidine. These combined findings have been interpreted as consistent with subsensitivity in postsynaptic alpha2-adrenoreceptor in response to excessive central noradrenergic outflow.

In sum, the contradictory and inconsistent findings in the physiological literature on panic disorder may stem from differences in contextual, methodological, and sample demographic factors. Nonetheless, numerous studies suggest abnormalities in HPA and autonomic nervous system functioning; their influence on cardiac and respiratory functioning may account, at least partially, for the cardiac and respiration-focused symptoms that characterize panic disorder. Future studies should systematically investigate the effect of treatment (behavioral and pharmacological) on the physiology of panic disorder.

Etiological Models of Panic Disorder

Barlow (2002; Barlow, Chorpita, & Turovsky, 1996) characterizes panic attacks as false alarms, in which a fight-or-flight response is triggered in the absence of threatening stimuli. While some research finds no association between somatic symptoms or sensations and panic disorder (Moreno-Peral et al., 2014), alarms in the form of panic attacks occur relatively commonly in the general population (e.g., Norton, Cox, & Malan, 1992; Wittchen & Essau, 1991). This finding begs this question: What accounts for the difference between the majority of individuals who display little to no distress over panic attacks versus the minority who develop panic disorder?

As described earlier, neuroticism is viewed as a higher-order factor characteristic of all anxiety disorders, with fear of fear being more singular to panic disorder. The construct of fear of fear overlaps with the construct of anxiety sensitivity, or the belief that anxiety and its associated symptoms may cause deleterious physical, social, and psychological consequences that extend beyond any immediate physical discomfort during an episode of anxiety or panic (Reiss, Peterson, Gursky, & McNally, 1986). Anxiety sensitivity is elevated across most anxiety disorders (Wheaton, Deacon, McGrath, Berman, & Abramowitz, 2012), but it is particularly elevated in panic disorder (e.g., Taylor, Koch, & McNally, 1992; Zinbarg & Barlow, 1996), especially on the physical concerns subscale (Zinbarg & Barlow, 1996; Zinbarg, Barlow, & Brown, 1997; Wheaton et al., 2012; Olthuis, Watt, & Stewart, 2014). That is, beliefs that physical symptoms of anxiety are harmful seem to be particularly relevant to panic disorder and appear to be mediated by catastrophic misinterpretations about physiological sensations (Sandin et al., 2015).

Anxiety sensitivity may be acquired insidiously from a lifetime of direct aversive experiences (such as a personal history of significant illness or injury), vicarious observations (such as exposure to significant illnesses or death among family members, or to family members who display fear of body sensations through hypochondriasis), or informational transmissions (such as parental overprotectiveness regarding physical well-being; Craske & Rowe, 1997). In support, Watt, Stewart, and colleagues (Stewart et al., 2001; Watt, Stewart, & Cox, 1998) reported that levels of anxiety sensitivity in young adulthood were positively correlated with (retrospectively reported) learning experiences related to anxiety symptoms in the form of parental reinforcement (instrumental learning) and parental modeling (vicarious learning) that such symptoms were to be feared. In addition, similar results have been found in the adolescent literature, with findings that when parents model or encourage fearful or distressing responses to symptoms that can be triggered by or contribute to anxiety, such as dizziness, racing heart, shortness of breath, and nausea, it predicts the development of panic symptomatology for youth high in anxiety sensitivity (Knapp, Frala, Blumenthal, Badour, & Leen-Feldner, 2013). Unfortunately, data from all of these studies are retrospective and thus vulnerable to biased recall.

Anxiety sensitivity is posited to be a risk factor for panic disorder because it primes reactivity to bodily sensations. Consistent with this view is the finding that anxiety sensitivity predicts subjective distress and reported symptoms in response to procedures that induce strong physical sensations, such as carbon dioxide inhalation (Blechert, Wilhelm, Meuret, Wilhelm, & Roth, 2013; Forsyth, Palav, & Duff, 1999), balloon inflation (Messenger & Shean, 1998), and hyperventilation (Sturges, Goetsch,

Ridley, & Whittal, 1998), in nonclinical samples, even after controlling for the effects of trait anxiety (Rapee & Medoro, 1994). Further, Blechert and colleagues (2013) found that relative to those with low anxiety sensitivity, young adults with high anxiety sensitivity showed respiratory abnormalities during carbon dioxide (CO_2) inhalation, particularly during a second CO_2 task, suggesting that respiratory abnormalities are common and may be conditionable. In addition, several longitudinal studies indicate that high scores on the Anxiety Sensitivity Index predict the onset of panic attacks over 1- to 4-year intervals in adolescents (Hayward et al., 2000), college students (Maller & Reiss, 1992), and community samples with specific phobias or no anxiety disorders (Ehlers, 1995), as well as during an acute military stressor (basic training) (Schmidt et al., 1997, 1999). The predictive relationship remains after controlling for prior depression (Hayward et al., 2000) and history of panic attacks and trait anxiety (Schmidt et al., 1997, 1999). Nonetheless, Bouton et al. (2001) argue that the relationship between anxiety sensitivity and panic attacks in these studies is relatively small, is not exclusive to panic, and is weaker than the relationship between panic and general neuroticism. Furthermore, these studies have not evaluated prediction of full panic disorder as opposed to panic attacks.

Two other models offer accounts for the persistence of fear of bodily sensations. The first model, put forth primarily by Clark (1986, 1988, 1996), is cognitive in nature. Clark and others (e.g., Salkovskis, 1988) argue that catastrophic misappraisals of bodily sensations, including misinterpretation of panic- and anxiety-related bodily sensations as signs of imminent death, craziness, loss of control, and so forth, are central to the development and maintenance of panic disorder. As reviewed earlier, there is extensive evidence that persons with panic disorder judge certain bodily sensations to be detrimental. However, Bouton et al. (2001) take issue with Clark's cognitive misappraisal model for multiple reasons, including that the model cannot account for panic attacks that lack conscious cognitive appraisal (e.g., nocturnal panic) without becoming untestable. They also note that although catastrophic cognitions often occur in panic patients, they do not necessarily play a causal role in panic disorder. Finally, Bouton et al. critique the cognitive model for not specifying how and when such cognitions are acquired and for whom and under what circumstances they become catastrophic.

The second model was initially put forth by Eysenck more than four decades ago (Eysenck, 1960; Eysenck & Rachman, 1965), then expanded by Goldstein and Chambless (1978), and more recently brought up to date by Bouton et al. (2001). This model emphasizes interoceptive fear conditioning, or the process by which low-level somatic sensations of arousal or anxiety (e.g., elevated heart rate or perspiration) become conditioned stimuli due to their association with intense fear, pain, or distress (Razran, 1961). In the context of panic disorder, the result is that early somatic components of the anxiety response come to elicit significant bursts of anxiety or panic. An extensive body of experimental literature attests to the robustness of interoceptive conditioning (e.g., Dworkin & Dworkin, 1999; Acheson, Forsyth, & Moses, 2012), particularly with regard to early interoceptive drug onset cues becoming conditioned stimuli for larger drug effects (e.g., Sokolowska, Siegel, & Kim, 2002). In addition, interoceptive conditioned responses are not dependent on conscious awareness of triggering cues (Razran, 1961) and are observed even under anesthesia in animals (e.g., Shibuki, Hamamura, & Yagi, 1984; Uno, 1970) and humans (e.g., Block, Ghoneim, Fowles, Kumar, & Pathak, 1987). Within this model, slight changes in relevant bodily functions that are not consciously recognized may elicit conditioned fear and panic due to previous pairings with the terror of panic (Bouton et al., 2001). Nevertheless, some researchers argue that the acquisition of interoceptive conditioned responding requires conscious awareness (e.g., Lovibond & Shanks, 2002).

Expanding on Eysenck's view, Bouton et al. (2001) argue that the similarity between conditioned and unconditioned stimuli creates very strong, easily conditioned responses, as occurs when initial bodily symptoms of panic (conditioned stimulus) signal the rest of the panic attack (unconditioned stimulus). Drawing on the extensive animal and human learning literature, they explain that interoceptive cues do not always produce conditioned panic, owing to factors such as the presence of safety signals and context effects (e.g., performance in one context does not always generalize to performance in another context). In addition, they cite evidence from Öhman and Mineka (2001) and others (e.g., LeDoux, 1996) to argue against the notion that conditioning necessarily involves propositional knowledge and cognitive awareness. Rather, Bouton et al. (2001) argue that catastrophic misappraisals may accompany panic attacks because they are part of the range of responses linked to panic or because they have been encouraged or reinforced. Such thoughts may become conditioned stimuli that trigger anxiety or they may simply be part of the conditioned response to anxiety- and panic-related cues.

Related work demonstrates that panic disorder patients show impaired safety learning (Schroijen et al., 2015), including reporting higher expectancies of danger in the presence of safety cues but equal expectancies in the presence of danger cues (Lissek et al., 2009). Further, panic disorder patients show greater generalization of fear responding, as reflected by enhanced startle blink EMG responses, greater electrodermal activity, and more pronounced respiration in response to multiple generalization tasks with varying intensities (Lissek et al., 2010). A recent laboratory conditioning study by Schroijen et al. (2015) demonstrated that the interoceptive fear learning and generalization is modulated by stimulus intensity (which is typically high in panic disorder), and that impaired discriminatory learning is closely linked to fear generalization. In summary, evidence shows that panic disorder is characterized by impaired discriminative learning between safety and danger cues, which creates a context in which fear conditioning more readily occurs and generalizes.

Assessment of Panic Disorder

Fortunately, a wide range of tools and approaches are available for the assessment of panic disorder. In this section, we highlight commonly used and up-and-coming instruments across the domains of semistructured clinical interviews; dimensional clinical rating scales; self-report and behavioral measures; behavioral approach tests; ongoing, repeated assessment; and neurobiological assessment.

INTERVIEWS

An in-depth interview is the first step in establishing diagnostic and behavioral-cognitive profiles. The value of structured interviews lies in their contribution to differential diagnosis and interrater reliability. Several semistructured and fully structured interviews exist. The Schedule for Schizophrenia and Affective Disorders–Lifetime Version (anxiety modified) produces reliable diagnoses for most of the anxiety disorders (generalized anxiety disorder and simple phobia being the exceptions; Mannuzza et al., 1989), as does the Structured Clinical Interview for DSM-IV, which covers all of the mental disorders (First, Spitzer, Gibbon, & Williams, 1994). However, the semistructured interview that most specifically focuses on assessment and differential diagnosis among the anxiety disorders is the Anxiety Disorders Interview Schedule (ADIS; DiNardo, Brown, & Barlow, 1994), which has been updated for *DSM-5* (Brown & Barlow, 2014). In addition to its primary focus on anxiety disorders, the ADIS-5 evaluates mood disorders and somatoform disorders, as well as screens for psychotic and drug conditions. Differential diagnosis among the anxiety disorders is sometimes difficult because, as described earlier, panic is a ubiquitous phenomenon (Craske et al., 2010), occurring across a wide variety of emotional disorders. It is not uncommon for persons with specific phobias, generalized anxiety disorder, obsessive-compulsive disorder, and posttraumatic stress disorder to report panic attacks. Hence, the ADIS-5 facilitates a reliable method of gathering information to make differential diagnoses among the anxiety disorders and also provides the information to distinguish between clinical and subclinical presentations of a disorder. Interrater agreement using the ADIS for DSM-IV (which is very similar to the ADIS-5 due to minimal changes among the descriptions of anxiety disorders) ranges from satisfactory to excellent for the various anxiety disorders (Brown, Di Nardo, Lehman, & Campbell, 2001).

CLINICAL RATING SCALES

The Panic Disorder Severity Scale (PDSS; Houck, Spiegel, Shear, & Rucci, 2002; Shear et al., 1997, 2001) is a well-validated, seven-item measure designed to efficiently assess the severity of panic disorder symptoms. In addition to providing a dimensional severity rating, a cutoff score of 8 on the PDSS identifies patients with panic disorder with high sensitivity (83%) and acceptable specificity (64%) (Shear et al., 2001). The PDSS is available in both interview-administered (Shear et al., 1997, 2001) and self-report (Houck et al., 2002) versions.

Although the PDSS has been employed with increasing frequency (see, e.g., Barlow, Gorman, Shear, & Woods, 2000), clinical severity ratings (CSRs) of distress and disablement (0 = not at all, 8 = extreme) have been more commonly used as dimensional ratings for panic disorder and other anxiety disorders. A CSR is based on the information gathered from the diagnostic interview; a rating of 4 or higher indicates that the individual meets diagnostic criteria for a given disorder and evidences clinically significant distress and/or disablement stemming from that disorder. With proper clinician training procedures, adequate reliabilities have been demonstrated for CSRs based on the ADIS-IV interview (Brown, Di Nardo, et al., 2001).

Building on the success of these earlier scales, the *DSM-5* Anxiety Disorders Subgroup preliminarily validated a promising new 10-item dimensional rating scale for panic disorder and a separate scale for agoraphobia (LeBeau et al., in press). The new scales are consistent with the revisions to the *DSM*, and are consistent in form and content across the anxiety disorders.

SELF-REPORT AND BEHAVIORAL MEASURES

Several standardized self-report inventories provide useful information for treatment planning, as well as being sensitive markers of therapeutic change. The Anxiety Sensitivity Index (Reiss et al., 1986) and the multidimensional Anxiety Sensitivity Index–3 (Taylor et al., 2007) have received wide acceptance as trait measures of threatening beliefs about bodily sensations. Both display good psychometric properties, and the former tends to discriminate panic disorder from other types of anxiety disorders (e.g., Taylor et al., 1992; Telch, Shermis, & Lucas, 1989). More specific information about which particular bodily sensations are feared the most, and what specific misappraisals occur most often, can be obtained from the Body Sensations Questionnaire and Agoraphobic Cognitions Questionnaire (Chambless et al., 1984). Extensive psychometric and clinical research indicates that these questionnaires show strong psychometric properties (Arrindell, 1993; Chambless et al., 1984), discriminate between individuals with panic and agoraphobia and people with other anxiety disorders (Chambless & Gracely, 1989), and are sensitive to change following treatment (Chambless et al., 1984). Fears of interoceptive stimuli (e.g., caffeine, exercise) can be measured by the Albany Panic and Phobia Questionnaire, which has shown good internal validity and adequate test-retest reliability (Rapee et al., 1995). The Mobility Inventory for Agoraphobia (Chambless, Caputo, Jasin, Gracely, & Williams, 1985) lists agoraphobic situations that are rated based on degree of avoidance when alone and when accompanied. This instrument is useful for establishing in vivo exposure hierarchies. Newman and colleagues (Newman, Holmes, Zuellig, Kachin, & Behar, 2006) developed the Panic Disorder Self-Report (PDSR), a self-report diagnostic measure based on *DSM-IV* panic disorder criteria. The PDSR demonstrates excellent sensitivity and specificity in diagnosing panic disorder, strong agreement with a structured diagnostic interview, good retest reliability, and convergent and discriminant validity (Newman et al., 2006). Finally, the Panic Disorder Screener (PADIS) was developed as a way to identify panic disorder in community settings and to assess symptom severity (Batterham, Mackinnon, & Christensen, 2015). The PADIS shows adequate validity and reliability as a measurement tool in both research and clinical settings.

BEHAVIORAL TESTS

The behavioral test is a useful measure of degree of avoidance of specific situations. Behavioral approach tests can be standardized or individually tailored. The standardized behavioral test for agoraphobia usually involves walking or driving a particular route, such as a 1-mile loop around the clinic setting. Anxiety levels are rated at regular intervals, and actual distance walked or driven is measured. The disadvantage is that the specific task may not be relevant to all clients. More useful clinically are individually tailored behavioral tasks that usually entail attempts at three to five individualized situations that are somewhat to extremely difficult for the client. These might include driving two exits on a freeway, waiting in a bank line, or shopping in a local supermarket for 15 minutes. The therapist assesses the client's maximum levels of anxiety and degree of approach (i.e., refused task, attempted but escaped from task, or completed task) for each situation. Though informative for clinical practice, such individualized tasks confound between-subject comparisons for research purposes. Standardized behavioral tests for individuals with panic disorder target interoceptive sensations and typically include exercises such as spinning, running in place, and hyperventilating. As with the behavioral tests for agoraphobia, anxiety levels are recorded continuously along with the duration for which the client continued each exercise.

Standardized and individually tailored behavioral tests are susceptible to demand biases for fear and avoidance prior to treatment and for improvement after treatment (Borkovec, Weerts, & Bernstein, 1977). However, behavioral tests are an important supplement to self-report of agoraphobic avoidance because clients tend to underestimate what they can actually achieve (Craske, Rapee, & Barlow, 1988). In addition, behavioral tests often reveal information of which the individual is not fully aware, but that is important for treatment planning. For example, the safety-seeking behavior of remaining close to supports such as railings or walls may not be apparent until observing the client walk through a shopping mall.

ONGOING ASSESSMENT

Self-monitoring is a very important part of assessment and treatment for panic disorder and agoraphobia. Retrospective recall of past episodes of panic and anxiety, especially when made under anxious conditions, may inflate estimates of panic frequency and intensity (Margraf et al., 1987; Rapee, Craske, & Barlow, 1990). Moreover, such inflation may contribute to apprehension about future panic. Thus, to the degree that ongoing self-monitoring yields more accurate, less inflated estimates, it is a therapeutic tool (see Craske & Tsao, 1999, for a comprehensive review of self-monitoring for panic and anxiety). Also, ongoing self-monitoring is believed to contribute to increased objective self-awareness, which is essential to cognitive-behavioral therapy approaches.

To assess the course and rate of change in treatment, as well as to investigate the mechanisms or mediators by which a given treatment exerts its effects (see Kraemer, Wilson, Fairburn, & Agras, 2002), it is important to conduct psychometrically sound assessment of anxiety symptoms during treatment. Ongoing, session-by-session measures, also known as *process measures*, can be administered to patients at regular intervals during treatment to assess changes in panic symptomology. The Anxiety Sensitivity Index (Reiss et al., 1986; Taylor et al., 2007) is one example of an appropriate symptom process measure for treatment of panic disorder. Finally, particularly at treatment follow-up, assessments may benefit from including broader quality of life (QOL) measures that capture the wider impact of panic disorder treatment. For example, the Quality of Life Inventory (Frisch, Cornell, Villanueva, & Retzlaff, 1992) assesses 17 domains, including the quality of a client's family relationships and friendships and his or her sense of meaning and life direction, whereas the frequently used, well-validated 36-Item Short Form Health Survey (SF-36; Ware, 1993) assesses physical functioning, mental health, social functioning, vitality, and general health. These QOL measures, however, are quite general; panic- and anxiety-specific measures of QOL have not yet been developed.

NEUROBIOLOGICAL ASSESSMENT

A medical evaluation is generally recommended because several medical conditions should be ruled out before assigning the diagnosis of panic disorder and agoraphobia.

These include thyroid conditions, caffeine or amphetamine intoxication, drug withdrawal, or pheochromocytoma (a rare adrenal gland tumor). Furthermore, certain medical conditions can exacerbate panic disorder and agoraphobia, although panic and agoraphobia are likely to continue even when such conditions are under medical control. Mitral valve prolapse, asthma, allergies, and hypoglycemia fall into this category. These medical conditions exacerbate panic disorder and agoraphobia to the extent that they elicit the types of physical sensations that are feared. For example, mitral valve prolapse sometimes produces the sensation of a heart flutter, asthma produces shortness of breath, and hypoglycemia produces dizziness and weakness.

Ongoing physiological measures are not very practical tools for clinicians, but can provide important information. In particular, the discrepancy described earlier between reports of symptoms and actual physiological arousal can serve as a therapeutic demonstration of the role of attention and appraisal in symptom production. Similarly, actual recordings provide data to disconfirm misappraisals such as, "My heart feels like its going so fast that it will explode," or "I'm sure my blood pressure is so high that I could have a stroke at any minute." Finally, baseline levels of physiological functioning, which are sometimes dysregulated in anxious individuals, may be sensitive measures of treatment outcome (e.g., Craske et al., 2005).

Treatment of Panic Disorder

This section addresses the prevention of panic disorder as well as psychological and biological modes of treatment.

PSYCHOLOGICAL

The most widely studied and validated psychotherapeutic treatment for panic disorder is cognitive-behavioral therapy (CBT) in its various forms. The two major forms of CBT have been Barlow and Craske's panic control treatment (PCT; Barlow, Craske, Cerny, & Klosko, 1989), and Clark's cognitive therapy for panic disorder (Clark, 1986). Both treatments emphasize using components of psychoeducation about panic to correct misconceptions regarding panic symptoms, cognitive restructuring to identify and correct distortions in thinking, and interoceptive exposure to feared bodily sensations (e.g., palpitations, dyspnea, dizziness) and in vivo exposure to feared situations (e.g., unfamiliar areas, driving) to obtain corrective information that disconfirms fearful misappraisals and eventually lessens fear responding. Breathing retraining as a means of helping patients to cope with panic and anxiety is sometimes included. Although PCT and Clark's cognitive therapy for panic disorder have not been directly compared, the major difference lies in the reliance of PCT on both cognitive and conditioning models, with behavioral exposure functioning as a primary agent of therapeutic change. In Clark's approach, cognitive models are more central and behavioral exposure serves as a vehicle for cognitive change.

Results for both of these forms of CBT typically yield panic-free rates in the range of 70% to 80% of those treated and high end-state rates (i.e., within normative ranges of functioning) in the range of 50% to 70% (e.g., Barlow et al., 1989; Clark et al., 1994). Two meta-analyses reported very large effect sizes of 1.55 and 0.90 for CBT for panic disorder (Mitte, 2005; Sanchez-Meca, Rosa-Alcazar, Marin-Martinez, & Gomez-Conesa, 2010). Similarly robust findings emerge from a meta-analysis of CBT in real-world clinic settings (e.g., effectiveness studies), including for panic disorder (Stewart & Chambless, 2009), and from a meta-analysis of the effects of CBT on improving quality of life (pre- to posttreatment for panic disorder; $g = .46$; Hofmann, Wu, & Boettcher, 2014). Another meta-analysis demonstrated that CBT for panic disorder was superior to placebo (e.g., pill placebo or nondirected-supportive therapy) (Hofmann & Smits, 2008). Benefits generally are maintained over follow-up intervals for as long as 2 years (Craske, Brown, & Barlow, 1991). This contrasts with the higher relapse rates typically found with medication approaches to the treatment of panic disorder, particularly the use of high-potency benzodiazepines (e.g., Gould, Otto, & Pollack, 1995).

That stated, a recent comprehensive review that integrated multiple stringent criteria to assess CBT response rates (Loerinc et al., 2015) concluded that the response rate for panic disorder was 53% at posttreatment and 59% at follow-up—lower than typically reported rates. Further, an earlier analysis of individual profiles over time also suggested a less optimistic picture, in that one third of clients who were panic-free 24 months after CBT had experienced a panic attack in the preceding year, and 27% had sought additional treatment for panic over that same interval of time (Brown & Barlow, 1995). Nevertheless, this approach to analysis did not take into account the general trend toward continuing improvement over time. Thus, CBT is a well-studied and relatively efficacious treatment for panic disorder, but there is room for improvement (see Loerinc et al., 2015). One approach to improving long-term response rates involves monthly "booster," or "maintenance," CBT sessions. A recent investigation (White et al., 2013), for example, demonstrated that following acute CBT for panic disorder (11 sessions), panic disorder patients randomized to 9 monthly maintenance CBT sessions showed substantially lower relapse rates over a 21-month follow-up than did patients who were simply assessed and not offered maintenance sessions (5% versus 18%). Thus, monthly maintenance sessions offer a promising and straightforward approach to improving outcomes following CBT for panic disorder.

The effectiveness of CBT extends to patients who experience nocturnal panic attacks (Craske et al., 2005). Also, CBT has proven very helpful in lowering relapse rates upon discontinuation of high-potency benzodiazepines (e.g., Otto, McHugh, et al., 2010). Moreover, treatment is effective even when there is comorbidity. Indeed, initial studies indicated that comorbidity did not reduce the effectiveness of CBT for panic disorder (e.g., Brown et al., 1995; McLean, Woody, Taylor, & Koch, 1998). More recent studies suggest that comorbid depression only slightly reduced the effectiveness of CBT for panic disorder (Emmrich et al., 2012), whereas comorbid personality disorders moderately reduced effectiveness (Telch, Kamphuis, & Schmidt, 2011). In addition, CBT results in improvements in comorbid conditions (e.g., Brown et al., 1995; Tsao, Mystkowski, Zucker, & Craske, 2005). In other words, co-occurring symptoms of depression and other anxiety disorders tend to improve after CBT for panic disorder. However, a study assessing patients 2 years after treatment showed that the benefits for comorbid conditions can lessen over time (Brown et al., 1995). Nonetheless, the general finding of improvement in comorbidity suggests the value of remaining focused on panic disorder treatment even when comorbidity is present, since the comorbidity will be benefited as well (for at least up to 1 year). In fact, preliminary evidence suggests that *simultaneously* addressing panic disorder along with comorbidity (using CBT, tailored to each disorder) may be less effective than remaining focused on panic disorder (Craske et al., 2007), although this finding is in need of replication.

Generally, CBT for agoraphobia involves more situational exposure than CBT for panic disorder alone. Randomized controlled studies of CBT for agoraphobia generally yield slightly less effective results than CBT for panic disorder with no or minimal agoraphobia (e.g., Williams & Falbo, 1996). Moreover, greater agoraphobic avoidance represents one of the only consistent predictors of worse outcomes in the context of CBT for panic disorder and agoraphobia (Porter & Chambless, 2015). Nonetheless, the trends suggest continuing improvement over time after CBT has ended (see Loerinc et al., 2015). Furthermore, Fava, Zielezny, Savron, and Grandi (1995) found that only 18.5% of their panic-free clients relapsed over a period of 5 to 7 years after exposure-based treatment for agoraphobia. Some research suggests that the trend for improvement after acute treatment is facilitated by involvement of significant others in every aspect of treatment (e.g., Cerny, Barlow, Craske, & Himadi, 1987). An intensive 8-day treatment using a sensation-focused PCT approach was developed for individuals with moderate to severe agoraphobia, and initial results are promising (Morissette, Spiegel, & Heinrichs, 2005).

Attempts have been made to dismantle the different components of CBT for panic and agoraphobia. The results are somewhat complex and to some extent depend on the samples used (e.g., mild versus severe levels of agoraphobia), the exact comparisons made, and the outcomes assessed. However, a meta-analysis of 42 panic disorder treatment studies (Sanchez-Meca et al., 2010) concluded that the combination of exposure, relaxation, and breathing retraining resulted in the highest effect size ($d = 1.84$), followed by exposure alone ($d = 1.53$). Further, in vivo exposure led to larger gains than imaginal or mixed exposure (e.g., use of more than one exposure approach). However, the cognitive therapy component may be effective even when conducted in full isolation from exposure and behavioral procedures (e.g., Salkovskis, Clark, & Hackmann, 1991). Despite this, many studies find that cognitive therapy does not improve outcome when added to in vivo exposure treatment for agoraphobia (e.g., van den Hout, Arntz, & Hoekstra, 1994; see Craske, 1999; Longmore & Worrell, 2007). In support, meta-analyses have found no differences between CBT and behavioral therapies in the treatment of panic disorder (Chambless & Peterman, 2004) or have found an advantage for exposure alone or for CBT combinations that include exposure over cognitive therapy alone (Sanchez-Meca et al., 2010). The finding that exposure alone represents a highly effective treatment for panic disorder, combined with the evidence that cognitive components generally do not increase the efficacy of exposure therapy (Sanchez-Meca et al., 2010), have led some to conclude that cognitive components (e.g., cognitive restructuring) are unnecessary (Longmore & Worrell, 2007), although the debate continues (Hofmann, 2008). Further, growing evidence suggests that exposure represents the most powerful component of CBT for panic disorder. A large study in primary care demonstrated that strong utilization of the *non*exposure components of CBT resulted in *worse* outcomes (Craske et al., 2006). Another large trial of CBT for panic disorder with agoraphobia showed that exposure evidenced a dose-response effect in reducing agoraphobic avoidance (Gloster et al., 2011), suggesting that exposure led directly to agoraphobia improvement. Further, the same CBT for panic disorder trial (Gloster et al., 2011) demonstrated superior outcomes when in vivo exposure was conducted *during* sessions (outside the therapy room) than when therapists planned the in vivo exposure exercises in session but then assigned them for homework. This finding supports the central importance of exposure in CBT by linking in-session completion of exposure exercises (which presumably were completed at a higher rate than in the condition in which exposure was merely assigned for homework) to better outcomes. Relatedly, an earlier study found that breathing retraining and interoceptive exposure did not improve outcome beyond in vivo exposure alone for agoraphobia (de Beurs, van Balkom, Lange, Koele, & van Dyke, 1995). In summary, although more dismantling research is needed, extant evidence suggests that the exposure component of CBT plays a strongly efficacious role.

Group formats appear to be nearly as effective as individual treatment formats for CBT for panic and agoraphobia (Néron, Lacroix, & Chaput, 1995; Sharp, Power, & Swanson, 2004). Although group formats are highly effective, individual formats may be superior at posttreatment (Sharp et al., 2004) or at reducing co-occurring depression and general anxiety symptoms in the long term (Néron et al., 1995). Current findings warrant more direct comparisons between group and individual formats before firm conclusions can be drawn.

Most of the panic disorder treatment studies described in the previous sections averaged around 11 to 12 treatment sessions. Four to 6 sessions of PCT also are effective (Craske, Maidenberg, & Bystritsky, 1995; Roy-Byrne et al., 2005), although the results are not as strong as those typically seen with 11 or 12 treatment sessions. However, studies have demonstrated equally effective results when delivering CBT for panic disorder across the standard 12 sessions versus approximately 6 sessions (Clark et al., 1999), good results following 5-session CBT (Otto et al., 2012), and good effectiveness with intensive CBT over 2 days (e.g., Deacon & Abramowitz, 2006).

Self-directed treatments, with minimal direct therapist contact, are very beneficial to highly motivated and educated clients (e.g., Ghosh & Marks, 1987; Gould & Clum, 1995; Gould, Clum, & Shapiro, 1993). Computer-assisted and internet versions of CBT are effective for panic disorder (e.g., Richards, Klein, & Carlbring, 2003). Internet-based CBT for panic disorder has shown effectiveness similar to face-to-face CBT across multiple studies (e.g., Bergström et al., 2010; Kiropoulos et al., 2008), albeit possibly lower quality of life improvements (Hofmann et al., 2014). For professional-assisted online CBT, delivery by psychologists led to better results than delivery by primary care physicians (Shandley et al., 2008). Moreover, findings from computerized programs for emotional disorders in general indicate that such treatments are more acceptable and enjoyable when they are combined with therapist involvement (e.g., Carlbring, Ekselius, & Andersson, 2003).

The theorized role of experiential avoidance as a risk and maintenance factor for panic disorder has led to the development of acceptance-based behavioral treatments for anxiety disorders. One of the most prominent of the new therapies is acceptance and commitment therapy (ACT; Hayes, Strosahl, & Wilson, 1999, 2012). Eifert and Forsyth (2005) developed an ACT-based treatment manual for anxiety disorders, including panic disorder. Arch, Eifert, et al. (2012) compared ACT with traditional CBT for heterogeneous anxiety disorders (42% of patients had principal panic disorder), demonstrating equivalent outcomes for both treatments at posttreatment. Importantly, both treatments utilized behavioral exposure (which has not been used in all ACT studies and here was framed in a manner consistent with ACT). At 12-month follow-up, ACT demonstrated lower diagnostic severity and lower experiential avoidance among completers, and CBT demonstrated higher quality of life. Thus, preliminary evidence suggests that ACT is an efficacious treatment for anxiety disorders.

Regarding panic disorder–specific ACT studies, Meuret, Twohig, Rosenfield, Hayes, and Craske (2012) demonstrated the feasibility of combining 4 sessions of ACT with 6 subsequent sessions of exposure therapy for panic disorder, with preliminary pre-/posttreatment efficacy on the order of large effect sizes. More recently, Gloster and colleagues (2015) conducted a small randomized clinical trial focused on adults with panic disorder and/or agoraphobia with prior unsuccessful evidence-based treatment, e.g., treatment-resistant patients with an average of 42 previous sessions of (traditional) CBT (88%) and/or medication (33%) for panic disorder. Patients were randomized to 8 twice-weekly sessions of ACT or a wait-list with delayed treatment. At posttreatment, those receiving ACT reported medium to large effect size gains on primary outcomes over the wait-list group, and continued to improve over the 6-month follow-up. Thus, although additional panic disorder–specific studies are needed, ACT appears to offer a promising approach for the treatment of panic disorder—perhaps particularly for treatment-resistant patients.

Mindfulness meditation, in which mindfulness states are intentionally cultivated, represents the central skill taught in the 8-week mindfulness-based stress reduction (MBSR) group intervention designed by Kabat-Zinn (1990).[3] Building on the success of an earlier nonrandomized study of MBSR for panic disorder and generalized anxiety disorder (Kabat-Zinn et al., 1992; Miller, Fletcher, & Kabat-Zinn, 1995), two randomized trials of MBSR for mixed anxiety disorders have been completed. In the first study (Vøllestad, Sivertsen, & Nielsen, 2011), MBSR completers (50% with principal panic disorder) improved significantly on all outcomes compared to wait-list controls, with moderate to large effect size improvements on measures of anxiety and depression maintained through 6-month follow-up. In the second study (Arch et al., 2013), veterans with anxiety disorders (31% with principal panic disorder) showed large equivalent improvements in principal disorder severity following adapted MBSR or CBT. However, CBT resulted in superior improvements on anxious arousal, whereas adapted MBSR resulted in superior improvements in worry and comorbid emotional disorders (though baseline differences complicated the latter findings). These initial studies demonstrate the preliminary efficacy of MBSR for anxiety disorders; clearly more randomized trial work is needed to test MBSR's efficacy for panic disorder specifically and in comparison to CBT. A related intervention, mindfulness-based cognitive therapy (Segal, Williams, & Teasdale, 2002), was shown to serve as a successful adjunct to medication in a pre-post study for Korean adults with panic disorder (Kim et al., 2010). Though the study was very small ($n = 23$) and nonrandomized, these participants had not sufficiently responded to medication after 6+ months (and thus might be classified as treatment resistant), and they were followed for a full year after MBCT, suggesting the value of further investigating MBCT for panic disorder.

Two additional treatment developments merit attention. First, there is longstanding and growing interest in the potential benefit of physical exercise for the treatment of anxiety

---

[3] Although scientifically defining the construct of mindfulness has been challenging, it is thought to involve the cultivation of concentration, attention, and nonjudgmental acceptance toward whatever one is experiencing in the present moment (Bishop et al., 2004).

disorders (e.g., Powers, Asmundson, & Smits, 2015; Stonerock et al., 2015). Examining its potential for the treatment of panic disorder specifically, Hovland and colleagues (2013), in a small trial, compared CBT to physical exercise (three times a week) for adults with panic disorder, and found that CBT outperformed physical exercise. More recent work preliminarily shows that physical exercise assigned in the context of CBT treatment for panic disorder boosts CBT's efficacy (Gaudlitz, Plag, Dimeo, & Ströhle, 2015). Thus, exercise appears better as an adjunct to CBT.

Capnometry-assisted respiratory training (CART), a treatment developed by Meuret and colleagues (Meuret, Wilhelm, Ritz, & Roth, 2008; Meuret, Rosenfield, Hofmann, Seidel, & Bhaskara, 2010), appears to offer a more promising stand-alone treatment for panic disorder. CART helps patients with panic disorder learn how to breathe in a manner that reduces the chronic hyperventilation or hypocapnia (abnormally low levels of carbon dioxide, or CO_2) that characterizes this disorder. In CART, patients practice breathing exercises, paced by audio tones, at home twice per day, while connected to a respiratory feedback device that monitors their respiration rate and end-tidal CO_2. At the end of the paced breathing period, they continue breathing without the pacing tones while aiming to maintain the same end-tidal CO_2 and respiration rate as before. In an initial trial (Meuret et al., 2010), CART improved panic disorder symptoms to an extent similar to cognitive therapy results, and functioned via the unique mechanism of normalizing respiration. This promising approach warrants further investigation.

BIOLOGICAL (MEDICATIONS)

Based on 19 placebo-controlled, randomized clinical trials (Roy-Byrne & Cowley, 2002), selective serotonin reuptake inhibitors (SSRIs) are the medication treatment of choice for panic disorder. Meta-analyses and reviews have reported medium to large effect sizes compared to placebo (e.g., Bakker, van Balkom, & Spinhoven, 2002; Mitte, 2005). The majority of trials have been short-term, although several have examined and confirmed longer-term efficacy up to 1 year.

Benzodiazepines are effective agents for panic disorder as well. They work rapidly, within days to 1 week, and are even better tolerated than the very tolerable SSRI class of agents. They are limited by their risk of physiological dependence and withdrawal and by the risk of abuse (Roy-Byrne & Cowley, 2002), and thus, prescribing trends have shifted away from them in recent years (e.g., Berney, Halperin, Tango, Daeniker-Dayer, & Schulz, 2007). However, a recent meta-analysis (Offidani, Guidi, Tomba, & Fava, 2013) found that benzodiazepines were more effective than antidepressant medication (e.g., tricyclics, SSRIs) in reducing the number of panic attacks, and resulted in fewer side effects and less (premature) discontinuation.

Numerous studies show clearly that discontinuation of medication results in relapse in a significant proportion of patients, with placebo-controlled discontinuation studies showing rates between 25% and 50% within 6 months, depending on study design (Roy-Byrne & Cowley, 2002). In addition, SSRIs, serotonin-norepinephrine reuptake inhibitors (SNRIs), and benzodiazepines are associated with a time-limited withdrawal syndrome (considerably worse for the benzodiazepines), which itself may serve as an interoceptive stimulus that promotes or contributes to panic disorder relapse.

In terms of comparison between pharmacological and psychological approaches, a meta-analysis of 21 randomized trials involving over 1,700 patients with panic disorder with or without agoraphobia clearly showed that combined treatment with antidepressants and psychotherapy (behavioral, CBT, and other) was superior to antidepressants alone and to psychotherapy alone in the acute phase (Furukawa, Watanabe, & Churchill, 2006). After treatment discontinuation, however, combined treatment was superior to medication only but did not differ from psychotherapy alone, and specifically CBT alone. Similarly, a more recent meta-analysis showed that CBT plus pharmacotherapy (e.g., combined treatment) was superior to CBT plus placebo at posttreatment but not at 6-month follow-up (Hofmann, Sawyer, Korten, & Smits, 2009), confirming the short-term advantage but lack of long-term advantage for combined treatment. Following medication discontinuation, other studies show that the combination of medication and CBT fares worse than CBT alone (and worse than CBT plus placebo, see Barlow et al., 2000), suggesting the possibility that state- or context-dependent learning in the presence of medication may have attenuated the new learning that occurs during CBT (Otto, Pollack, & Sabatino, 1996; Otto, Smits, & Reese, 2005). Thus, once medication is discontinued, having received combined treatment may reduce the long-term effectiveness of CBT. Further, naturalistic use of SSRIs in the context of CBT for panic disorder has been associated with worse outcomes (e.g., Arch & Craske, 2007). Finally, a recent meta-analysis demonstrated a significant advantage for CBT alone over medication alone in the treatment of panic disorder, of moderate effect size (Roshanaei-Moghaddam et al., 2011).

Findings from the combination of fast-acting anxiolytics, especially the high-potency benzodiazepines, with behavioral treatments for panic disorder with agoraphobia are contradictory (e.g., Marks et al., 1993; Wardle et al., 1994). Nevertheless, several studies reliably show detrimental effects from chronic, naturalistic use of benzodiazepines on short-term and long-term outcome from CBT for panic or agoraphobia (e.g., Fava et al., 2001; Otto et al., 1996; van Balkom, de Beurs, Koele, Lange, & van Dyck, 1996; and Westra, Stewart, & Conrad, 2002, for as-needed benzodiazepine use). Specifically, there is evidence for more attrition, poorer memory for CBT-related psychoeducational materials, poorer outcome, and greater relapse when cognitive-behavioral therapy is conducted in the context of chronic, naturalistic use of benzodiazepines. In summary, because medication may reduce the long-term effectiveness of CBT and often requires continual use to prevent relapse, CBT alone represents the most cost-effective (in group format; Gould et al., 1995) and durable first-line treatment for panic disorder.

PREVENTION

Prevention for high-risk samples might halt the development of panic disorder as well as prevent the development of other psychological disorders, since people who report panic attacks are at risk for other psychological problems, including other anxiety disorders, depression, and substance abuse (e.g., Warren & Zgourides, 1988). Moreover, comorbid diagnoses such as depressive disorders (e.g., Roy-Byrne et al., 2000) and substance abuse (e.g., Marshall, 1997) are believed to sometimes develop as a direct function of having panic disorder.

In addition, prevention using a brief cognitive-behavioral intervention is likely to be highly cost efficient. Cognitive-behavioral therapy is among the least expensive treatments for panic disorder (Gould et al., 1995). Prevention may cut indirect costs as well, given that people with panic disorder are heavy users of the medical system (e.g., Roy-Byrne et al., 1999). However, research on prevention is limited.

At least two studies (Marchand et al., 2012; Swinson, Soulios, Cox, & Kuch, 1992) have briefly intervened with patients seeking care at emergency rooms for panic attacks or non-cardiac chest pain, with the goal of preventing future panic attacks and panic disorder. One study (Swinson et al., 1992) demonstrated that a single session of psychoeducation plus self-exposure instructions resulted in significantly fewer panic attacks (through 6-month follow-up) than psychoeducation plus reassurance instructions. However, diagnostic evaluations and independent assessments were not conducted. A more rigorous study (Lessard et al., 2012) found that pharmacotherapy, a single session of CBT, or seven sessions of CBT were all more effective than usual care at reducing panic disorder severity (but not agoraphobia or daily interference) at posttreatment, and did not differ from one another.

Gardenswartz and Craske (2001) conducted a selective/indicated prevention study that targeted panic disorder. College students reporting at least one panic attack in the past year and at least moderate anxiety sensitivity (as assessed by the Anxiety Sensitivity Index) were randomized to either a 5-hour, group cognitive-behavioral workshop modified from empirically supported cognitive-behavioral treatment for panic disorder (Barlow & Cerny, 1988), or a wait-list control group. Six months later, 13.6% of the individuals in the control group developed panic disorder, as opposed to only 1.8% of individuals in the workshop group. Among non-treatment-seeking university students with elevated anxiety sensitivity, Keough and Schmidt (2012) compared a single 50-minute session of psychoeducation and interoceptive exposure to a general health training matched for time and therapist contact. Relative to health training, the single psychoeducation and exposure session reduced anxiety sensitivity; improvements were maintained through 6-month follow-up, suggesting the efficacy of very brief CBT-based interventions for reducing anxiety sensitivity. Similarly, Meulenbeek and colleagues (2009, 2010) designed a 16-hour CBT group intervention aimed at preventing severe panic disorder in individuals with subclinical and mild panic disorder. Relative to wait-list control, the intervention led to moderate to large effect size improvements in panic disorder symptoms and diagnostic status, maintained through 6-month follow-up (Meulenbeek et al., 2010). In summary, extant studies demonstrate the promise of early intervention and prevention efforts for panic disorder.

Summary and Future Directions

As the many studies discussed in this chapter attest, panic disorder enjoys the position as the most researched anxiety disorder. The outgrowth of this intensive research includes an emerging understanding of the interplay between environmental and individual factors in shaping risk for panic disorder, converging evidence on the neurocircuitry of fear and panic, an integration of the latest advances in learning theory into models of etiology and maintenance, and the development of effective cognitive-behavioral and pharmacological treatments. Nevertheless, despite a proliferation of studies and technological advances in methodology, there remain areas in which the research is contradictory, including several areas of panic-related molecular genetics as well as panic-related psychophysiology.

Looking toward the future, multiple new and continuing areas of investigation will likely attract increasing attention from researchers and clinicians alike. One rapidly expanding research area involves the interaction of genetic and environmental factors in increasing the risk for panic disorder. Future studies may range from investigating the separate and interactive effects of high genetic risk with known environmental risk factors, to linking our emerging understanding of parent and child interactions in the etiology and maintenance of anxiety disorders to specific genetic risk factors (i.e., familial/environmental by individual by genetics interactions). Additional potentially emerging areas include associations between in utero, birth-related, and early childhood trauma and genetics in increasing risk for panic disorder, and for other forms of psychopathology.

Regarding the underlying theoretical account of exposure treatment for panic disorder and other anxiety disorders, empirical evidence has increasingly shown that the traditional emotional processing theory is not well supported (Craske et al., 2008, 2014; Craske, Liao, Brown, & Vervliet, 2012). The success of exposure-based therapy appears to stem rather from the strength of learned nonthreat associations and the likelihood of their recall within the real-world contexts in which feared stimuli are reencountered. We have outlined the implications of this theoretical shift for the treatment of panic disorder (Arch & Craske, 2011), including violating patient expectancies regarding predicted negative outcomes, conducting exposures in multiple real-world contexts during treatment, weaning safety signals, integrating multiple excitors, scheduling treatment booster sessions at increasing time intervals from treatment, and perhaps developing safety recall cues that can be drawn upon in daily life. Recent empirical research further explores the implications of this theoretical shift for panic disorder (e.g., Meuret, Seidel, Rosenfield, Hofmann, & Rosenfield, 2012), and we expect additional work in this area in the future.

In the realm of treatment, the augmentation of exposure therapy for anxiety disorders with D-cycloserine (DCS) represents one potential pathway. DCS enhances extinction learning by serving as a partial agonist of an extinction-related receptor in the basolateral amygdala (see Norberg, Krystal, & Tolin, 2008). One small, randomized study (Otto, Tolin, et al., 2010) demonstrated that DCS improved outcomes of brief CBT for panic disorder at posttreatment and 1-month follow-up. Although another study showed advantages of DSC over placebo among patients with more severe panic disorder, the groups were not equal in severity at baseline (Siegmund et al., 2011). DCS-enhanced CBT, therefore, may represent a promising path to improving CBT outcomes with medication, but research with larger samples and longer follow-ups are now needed, particularly since a Cochrane review of 21 studies found no evidence of benefit for DCS augmentation of CBT for anxiety disorders in general (Ori et al., 2015).

Treatment mediation and moderation studies comparing acceptance and mindfulness treatments to traditional CBT for anxiety disorders (e.g., Arch, Wolitzky-Taylor, Eifert, & Craske, 2012; Wolitzky-Taylor, Arch, Rosenfield, & Craske, 2012) represent another important recent development; such studies illuminate how each treatment works and for whom. Many moderator studies to date, however, have been plagued by low power and weak statistical tests of moderation (Schneider, Arch, & Wolitzky-Taylor, 2015), demonstrating that more robust investigations are now needed. Mindfulness strategies

(Treanor, 2011) and ACT (Meuret, Twohig, et al., 2012) have been proposed as potentially powerful ways to enhance exposure therapy for anxiety disorders, including panic disorder; these hypotheses await further testing in randomized trials. Finally, interest in experiential avoidance and mindfulness should continue to spawn new self-report and behavioral measures to assess and validate these constructs. Several such self-measures have already emerged (e.g., Bond et al., 2011; K. W. Brown & Ryan, 2003; Gámez et al., 2011; Hayes et al., 2004).

With the emergence of new treatments and the existence of proven, effective ones (e.g., CBT), it is important to consider that treatments are only as effective as the patients and clinicians who know about and use them. Despite the existence for over a decade of effective cognitive-behavioral treatments, the vast majority of individuals with panic disorder never receive CBT (even if they seek psychiatric treatment, see Wolitzky-Taylor, Zimmermann, Arch, De Guzman, & Lagomasino, 2015) or any other form of treatment (Johnson & Coles, 2013). In fact, many individuals with panic disorder are never treated by mental health professionals, but nearly 85% initially seek medical help for their symptoms (Katerndahl & Realini, 1997). Hence, researchers have begun adapting treatment models to the medical locations in which most (help-seeking) panic disorder patients are seen: primary care and emergency room settings (Craske, Roy-Byrne, et al., 2002). The most recent of these treatment models trains non–mental health professionals, such as primary care nurses, to conduct therapy (e.g., Roy-Byrne et al., 2010). A multisite panic disorder treatment study conducted in a primary care setting demonstrated that an enhanced CBT and medication-based intervention was more effective than usual care (Roy-Byrne et al., 2005), a finding that was recently replicated across multiple anxiety disorder groups, including panic disorder (Craske et al., 2011; Roy-Byrne et al., 2010). Given the significant unmet needs of medical patients for recognition and treatment of panic disorder and the success of these early trials, future work in this direction is needed.

Regarding our neurobiological understanding of panic disorder, neuroimaging has highlighted low levels of activation in the ventral medial prefrontal cortex (vmPFC), which may result in lessened inhibitory influences upon the amygdala (Johnson et al., 2014). This pattern is not specific to panic disorder but is also observed in posttraumatic stress disorder (Milad et al., 2009) and obsessive-compulsive disorder (Milad et al., 2013). Thus, rather than representing a neural signature of panic disorder, hypoactivation of the vmPFC is more likely to represent an underlying construct that is shared across these disorders, such as elevated threat sensitivity. Whether a unique neural signature exists for panic disorder awaits considerably larger scale investigation across multiple disorders associated with elevated threat sensitivity. Furthermore, studies to date have generally focused on generic threat relevant stimuli or fear conditioning to neutral stimuli to establish the neural correlates of panic disorder. The neural correlates of fear of bodily sensations—the hallmark feature of panic disorder—may elucidate more specific neural pathways. Aside from issues of specificity, neural activation may be a useful tool for personalizing treatment approach, should certain neural features differentially moderate outcomes from one treatment approach (e.g., exposure therapy) over another (e.g., mindfulness or pharmacotherapy). Again, larger scale studies will be needed to investigate neural predictors of treatment response.

Finally, given the enormous financial, quality of life, familial, and societal costs of panic disorder (e.g., Ettigi, Meyerhoff, Chirban, Jacobs, & Wilson, 1997; Greenberg et al., 1999;

Katerndahl & Realini, 1997), efforts toward early detection and prevention of panic disorder will continue to demand the attention of researchers, mental health professionals, and policy makers. Significant strides have been made in the identification of general risk and buffering factors in the development of anxiety disorders (see Zucker & Craske, 2001). Individuals at risk may be defined broadly (e.g., females, high neurotics, or people in high-stress situations) or more narrowly (e.g., children of parents with anxiety disorders or individuals with disorder-specific genetic profiles or high anxiety sensitivity, chronic somatic illness, or subthreshold panic attacks) (Batelaan et al., 2010; Craske & Zucker, 2001). Similarly, prevention and early detection efforts can be directed broadly through mass media or school-based programs, or more specifically toward individuals at risk for anxiety disorders (selective prevention) or individuals with subclinical anxiety symptoms (indicated prevention). Greater attention is currently needed to identify the most effective timing for prevention efforts, the buffers that prevent high-risk or symptomatic individuals from developing full-blown anxiety disorders, and whether prevention efforts are better directed at broad vulnerability to anxiety or vulnerability to specific anxiety disorders (Zucker & Craske, 2001).

References

Abelson, J. L., Curtis, G. C., & Uhde, T. W. (2005). Twenty-four hour growth hormone secretion in patients with panic disorder. *Psychoneuroendocrinology, 30*, 72–79.

Abelson, J. L., Khan, S., Liberzon, I., & Young, E. A. (2007). HPA axis activity in patients with panic disorder: Review and synthesis of four studies. *Depression and Anxiety, 24*(1), 66–76.

Acheson, D. T., Forsyth, J. P., & Moses, E. (2012). Interoceptive fear conditioning and panic disorder: The role of conditioned stimulus-unconditioned stimulus predictability. *Behavior Therapy, 43*(1), 174–189.

Affrunti, N. W., & Ginsburg, G. S. (2012). Maternal overcontrol and child anxiety: The mediating role of perceived competence. *Child Psychiatry & Human Development, 43*(1), 102–112.

Affrunti, N. W., & Woodruff-Borden, J. (2015). The effect of maternal psychopathology on parent–child agreement of child anxiety symptoms: A hierarchical linear modeling approach. *Journal of Anxiety Disorders, 32*, 56–65.

Agorastos, A., Kellner, M., Stiedl, O., Muhtz, C., Becktepe, J. S., Wiedemann, K., & Demiralay, C. (2014). The 5-HTTLPR genotype modulates heart rate variability and its adjustment by pharmacological panic challenge in healthy men. *Journal of Psychiatric Research, 50*, 51–58.

Airaksinen, E., Larsson, M., & Forsell, Y. (2005). Neuropsychological functions in anxiety disorders in population-based samples: Evidence of episodic memory dysfunction. *Journals of Psychiatric Research, 39*(2), 207–214.

Alvarenga, M. E., Richards, J. C., Lambert, G., & Esler, M. D. (2006). Psychophysiological mechanisms in panic disorder: A correlative analysis of noradrenaline spillover, neuronal noradrenaline reuptake, power spectral analysis of heart rate variability, and psychological variables. *Psychosomatic Medicine, 68*, 8–16.

Alves, M. R., Pereira, V. M., Machado, S., Nardi, A. E., & Oliveira e Silva, A. C. (2013). Cognitive functions in patients with panic disorder: A literature review. *Revista Brasileira de Psiquiatria, 35*(2), 193–200.

American Psychiatric Association. (1980). *Diagnostic and statistical manual of mental disorders* (3rd ed.). Washington, DC: Author.

American Psychiatric Association. (1987). *Diagnostic and statistical manual of mental disorders* (3rd ed., rev.). Washington, DC: Author.

American Psychiatric Association. (1994). *Diagnostic and statistical manual of mental disorders* (4th ed.). Washington, DC: Author.

American Psychiatric Association. (2013). *Diagnostic and statistical manual of mental disorders* (5th ed.). Washington, DC: Author.

Amering, M., Katschnig, H., Berger, P., Windhaber, J., Baischer, W., & Dantendorfer, K. (1997). Embarrassment about the first panic attack predicts agoraphobia in panic disorder patients. *Behaviour Research and Therapy, 35*, 517–521.

Anastasiades, P., Clark, D. M., Salkovskis, P. M., & Middleton, H. (1990). Psychophysiological responses in panic and stress. *Journal of Psychophysiology, 4*(4), 331–338.

Anders, S., Martin, L., Erb, M., Grodd, W., & Birbaumer, N. (2004). Brain activity underlying emotional valence and arousal: A response-related fMRI study. *Human Brain Mapping, 23*, 200–209.

Arch, J. J., Ayers, C. A., Baker, A., Almklov, E., Dean, D. J., & Craske, M. G. (2013). Randomized clinical trial of adapted mindfulness based stress reduction versus group cognitive behavioral therapy for heterogeneous anxiety disorders. *Behaviour Research and Therapy, 51*(4–5), 185–196.

Arch, J. J., & Craske, M. G. (2007). Implications of naturalistic use of pharmacotherapy in CBT treatment of panic disorder. *Behaviour Research and Therapy, 45*(7), 1435–1447.

Arch, J. J., & Craske, M. G. (2011). Addressing relapse in cognitive behavioral therapy for panic disorder: Methods for optimizing long-term treatment outcomes. *Cognitive and Behavioral Practice, 18*, 306–315.

Arch, J. J., Eifert, G. H., Davies, C., Plumb, J. C., Rose, R. D., & Craske, M. G. (2012). Randomized clinical trial of cognitive behavioral therapy versus acceptance and commitment therapy for the treatment of mixed anxiety disorders. *Journal of Consulting and Clinical Psychology, 80*(5), 750–765.

Arch, J. J., Wolitzky-Taylor, K. B., Eifert, G. H., & Craske, M. G. (2012). Longitudinal treatment mediation of traditional cognitive behavioral therapy and acceptance and commitment therapy for anxiety disorders. *Behaviour Research and Therapy*, *50*(7–8), 469–478.

Arrindell, W. A. (1993). The fear of fear concept: Stability, retest artifact and predictive power. *Behaviour Research and Therapy*, *31*, 139–148.

Asmundson, G. J., Sandler, L. S., Wilson, K. G., & Walker, J. R. (1992). Selective attention toward physical threat in patients with panic disorder. *Journal of Anxiety Disorders*, *6*, 295–303.

Asmundson, G. J., & Stein, M. B. (1994). Vagal attenuation in panic disorder: An assessment of parasympathetic nervous system function and subjective reactivity to respiratory manipulations. *Psychosomatic Medicine*, *56*, 187–193.

Atmaca, M., Yildirim, H., Gurok, M. G., Akyol, M., & Koseoglu, F. (2012). Hippocampal neurochemical pathology in patients with panic disorder. *Psychiatry Investigation*, *9*(2), 161–165.

Bakker, A., van Balkom, A. J. L. M., & Spinhoven, P. (2002). SSRIs vs. TCAs in the treatment of panic disorder: A meta-analysis. *Acta Psychiatrica Scandinavica*, *106*, 163–167.

Bandelow, B., Saleh, K., Pauls, J., Domschke, K., Wedekind, D., & Falkai, P. (2010). Insertion/deletion polymorphism in the gene for angiotensin converting enzyme (ACE) in panic disorder: A gender-specific effect? *World Journal of Biological Psychiatry*, *11*(1), 66–70.

Bandelow, B., Spath, C., Tichaner, G. A., Brooks, A., Hajak, G., & Ruther, E. (2002). Early traumatic life events, parental attitudes, family history, and birth risk factors in patients with panic disorder. *Comprehensive Psychiatry*, *43*, 269–278.

Bardeen, J. R., Fergus, T. A., & Orcutt, H. K. (2013). Experiential avoidance as a moderator of the relationship between anxiety sensitivity and perceived stress. *Behavior Therapy*, *44*(3), 459–469.

Barlow, D. H. (2002). *Anxiety and its disorders: The nature and treatment of anxiety and panic* (2nd ed.). New York, NY: Guilford Press.

Barlow, D. H., Brown, T. A., & Craske, M. G. (1994). Definitions of panic attacks and panic disorder in the *DSM-IV*: Implications for research. *Journal of Abnormal Psychology*, *103*, 553–564.

Barlow, D. H., & Cerny, J. A. (1988). *Psychological treatment of panic*. New York, NY: Guilford Press.

Barlow, D. H., Chorpita, B. P., & Turovsky, J. (1996). Fear, panic, anxiety, and disorders of emotion. In D. A. Hope (Ed.), *Perspectives on anxiety, panic,*

and fear (The 43rd Annual Nebraska Symposium on Motivation), (pp. 251–328). Lincoln: University of Nebraska Press.

Barlow, D. H., Craske, M. G., Cerny, J. A., & Klosko, J. S. (1989). Behavioral treatment of panic disorder. *Behavior Therapy*, *20*(2), 261–282.

Barlow, D. H., Gorman, J. M., Shear, M. K., & Woods, S. W. (2000). Cognitive-behavioral therapy, imipramine, or their combination for panic disorder. *JAMA*, *283*(19), 2529–2536.

Batelaan, N. M., Rhebergen, D., de Graaf, R., Spijker, J., Beekman, A. T., & Penninx, B. W. (2012). Panic attacks as a dimension of psychopathology: Evidence for associations with onset and course of mental disorders and level of functioning. *Journal of Clinical Psychiatry*, *73*, 1195–1202.

Batelaan, N., Smit, F., de Graaf, R., van Balkom, A., Vollebergh, W., & Beekman, A. (2010). Identifying target groups for the prevention of anxiety disorders in the general population. *Acta Psychiatrica Scandinavica*, *122*(1), 56–65.

Batterham, P. J., Mackinnon, A. J., & Christensen, H. (2015). The Panic Disorder Screener (PADIS): Development of an accurate and brief population screening tool. *Psychiatry Research*, *228*(1), 72–76.

Bennet, A., & Stirling, J. (1998). Vulnerability factors in the anxiety disorders. *British Journal of Medical Psychology*, *71*, 311–321.

Bergström, J., Andersson, G., Ljótsson, B., Rück, C., Andreewitch, S., Karlsson, A., … Lindefors, N. (2010). Internet-versus group-administered cognitive behaviour therapy for panic disorder in a psychiatric setting: A randomised trial. *BMC Psychiatry*, *10*(1), 54.

Berney, P., Halperin, D., Tango, R., Daeniker-Dayer, I., & Schulz, P. (2007). A major change of prescribing pattern in absence of adequate evidence: Benzodiazepines versus newer antidepressants in anxiety disorders. *Psychopharmacology Bulletin*, *41*(3), 39–47.

Biederman, J., Faraone, S. V., Marrs, A., & Moore, P. (1997). Panic disorder and agoraphobia in consecutively referred children and adolescents. *Journal of the American Academy of Child & Adolescent Psychiatry*, *36*, 214–223.

Bishop, S. R., Lau, M., Shapiro, S., Carlson, L., Anderson, N. D., Carmody, J., … Devins, G. (2004). Mindfulness: A proposed operational definition. *Clinical Psychology: Science and Practice*, *11*(3), 230–241.

Blaya, C., Salum, G. A., Lima, M. S., Leistner-Segal, S., & Manfro, G. G. (2007). Lack of association between the serotonin transporter promoter polymorphism (5-HTTLPR) and panic disorder: A systematic review and meta-analysis. *Behavioral and Brain Functions, 3*, 41.

Blechert, J., Wilhelm, F. H., Meuret, A. E., Wilhelm, E. M., & Roth, W. T. (2013). Experiential, autonomic, and respiratory correlates of CO_2 reactivity in individuals with high and low anxiety sensitivity. *Psychiatry Research, 209*(3), 566–573.

Block, R. I., Ghoneim, M. M., Fowles, D. C., Kumar, V., & Pathak, D. (1987). Effects of a subanesthetic concentration of nitrous oxide on establishment, elicitation, and semantic and phonemic generalization of classically conditioned skin conductance responses. *Pharmacology Biochemistry & Behavior, 28*, 7–14.

Boldrini, M., Del Pace, L., Placidi, G. P., Keilp, J., Ellis, S. P., Signori, S., ... Cappa, S. F. (2005). Selective cognitive deficits in obsessive-compulsive disorder compared to panic disorder with agoraphobia. *Acta Psychiatrica Scandinavica, 111*(2), 150–158.

Bond, F. W., Hayes, S. C., Baer, R. A., Carpenter, K. M., Guenole, N., Orcutt, H. K., ... Zettle, R. D. (2011). Preliminary psychometric properties of the Acceptance and Action Questionnaire–II: A revised measure of psychological inflexibility and experiential avoidance. *Behavior Therapy, 42*(4), 676–688.

Borkovec, T. D., Weerts, T. C., & Bernstein, D. A. (1977). Assessment of anxiety. In A. R. Ciminero, K. S. Calhoun, & H. E. Adams (Eds.), *Handbook of behavioral assessment* (pp. 367–428). New York, NY: Wiley.

Bouton, M. E., Mineka, S., & Barlow, D. H. (2001). A modern learning theory perspective on the etiology of panic disorder. *Psychological Review, 108*, 4–32.

Bowlby, J. (1969). Disruption of affectional bonds and its effects on behavior. *Canada's Mental Health Supplement, 59*, 12.

Bowlby, J. (1980). By ethology out of psycho-analysis: An experiment in interbreeding. *Animal Behaviour, 28*, 649–656.

Boyd, J. H. (1986). Use of mental health services for the treatment of panic disorder. *American Journal of Psychiatry, 143*, 1569–1574.

Brambilla, F., Perna, G., Garberi, A., Nobile, P., & Bellodi, L. (1995). Alpha2-adrenergic receptor sensitivity in panic disorder: I. GH response to GHRH and clonidine stimulation in panic disorder. *Psychoneuroendocrinology, 20*, 1–9.

Brandt, C. A., Meller, J., Keweloh, L., Hoschel, K., Staedt, J., Munz, D., & Stoppe, G. (1998). Increased benzodiazepine receptor density in the prefrontal cortex in patients with panic disorder. *Journal of Neural Transmission, 105*, 1325–1333.

Bremner, J. D., Innis, R. B., White, T., Masahiro, F., Silbersweig, D., Goddard, A. W., & Charney, D. S. (2000). SPECT [I-123] iomazenil measurement of the benzodiazepine receptor in panic disorder. *Biological Psychiatry, 47*, 96–106.

Bromet, E. J., Gluzman, S. F., Paniotto, V. I., Webb, C. P. M., Tintle, N. L., Zakhozha, V., ... Schwartz, J. E. (2005). Epidemiology of psychiatric and alcohol disorders in Ukraine: Findings from the Ukraine World Mental Health Survey. *Social Psychiatry and Psychiatric Epidemiology, 40*, 681–690.

Brown, G. W., Harris, T. O., & Eales, M. J. (1993). Aetiology of anxiety and depressive disorders in an inner-city population: II. Comorbidity and adversity. *Psychological Medicine, 23*, 155–165.

Brown, K. W., & Ryan, R. M. (2003). The benefits of being present: Mindfulness and its role in psychological well-being. *Journal of Personality and Social Psychology, 84*, 822–848.

Brown, T. A., Antony, M. M., & Barlow, D. H. (1995). Diagnostic comorbidity in panic disorder: Effect on treatment outcome and course of comorbid diagnoses following treatment. *Journal of Consulting and Clinical Psychology, 63*, 408–418.

Brown, T. A., & Barlow, D. H. (1995). Long-term outcome in cognitive behavioral treatment of panic disorder: Clinical predictors and alternative strategies for assessment. *Journal of Consulting and Clinical Psychology, 63*, 754–765.

Brown, T. A., & Barlow, D. H. (2014). *Anxiety Disorders Interview Schedule for DSM-5 (ADIS-5)–Adult Version*. Oxford, England: Oxford University Press.

Brown, T. A., Campbell, L. A., Lehman, C. L., Grisham, J. R., & Mancill, R. B. (2001). Current and lifetime comorbidity of the *DSM-IV* anxiety and mood disorders in a large clinical sample. *Journal of Abnormal Psychology, 110*, 585–599.

Brown, T. A., Chorpita, B. F., & Barlow, D. H. (1998). Structural relationships among dimensions of the *DSM-IV* anxiety and mood disorders and dimensions of negative affect, positive affect, and autonomic arousal. *Journal of Abnormal Psychology, 107*, 179–192.

Brown, T. A., Di Nardo, P. A., Lehman, C. L., & Campbell, L. A. (2001). Reliability of *DSM-IV* anxiety and mood disorders: Implications for the classification of emotional disorders. *Journal of Abnormal Psychology*, *110*, 49–58.

Bruce, S. E., Yonkers, K. A., Otto, M. W., Eisen, J. L., Weisberg, R. B., Pagano, M., ... Keller, M. B. (2005). Influence of psychiatric comorbidity on recovery and recurrence in generalized anxiety disorder, social phobia, and panic disorder: A 12-year prospective study. *American Journal of Psychiatry*, *162*, 1179–1187.

Bunaciu, L., Leen-Feldner, E. W., Blumenthal, H., Knapp, A. A., Badour, C. L., & Feldner, M. T. (2014). An experimental test of the effects of parental modeling on panic-relevant escape and avoidance among early adolescents. *Behavior Therapy*, *45*(4), 517–529.

Bystritsky, A., Craske, M., Maidenberg, E., Vapnik, T., & Shapiro, D. (1995). Ambulatory monitoring of panic patients during regular activity: A preliminary report. *Biological Psychiatry*, *38*, 684–689.

Carlbring, P., Ekselius, L., & Andersson, G. (2003). Treatment of panic disorder via the Internet: A randomized trial of CBT vs. applied relaxation. *Journal of Behavior Therapy and Experimental Psychiatry*, *34*, 129–140.

Carter, M. M., Hollon, S. D., Carson, R., & Shelton, R. C. (1995). Effects of a safe person on induced distress following a biological challenge in panic disorder with agoraphobia. *Journal of Abnormal Psychology*, *104*, 156–163.

Castillo, E. P., Coy, P. E. C., Shejet, F. O., Duran, E. T., & Cabrera, D. M. (2010). Evaluación de funciones cognitivas: Atención y memoria en pacientes con trastorno de pánico. *Salud Mental*, *33*(6), 481–488.

Cerny, J. A., Barlow, D. H., Craske, M. G., & Himadi, W. G. (1987). Couples treatment of agoraphobia: A two-year follow-up. *Behavior Therapy*, *18*, 401–415.

Chambless, D. L., Caputo, G. C., Bright, P., & Gallagher, R. (1984). Assessment of fear of fear in agoraphobics: The Body Sensations Questionnaire and the Agoraphobic Cognitions Questionnaire. *Journal of Consulting and Clinical Psychology*, *52*, 1090–1097.

Chambless, D. L., Caputo, G. C., Jasin, S. E., Gracely, E. J., & Williams, C. (1985). The Mobility Inventory for Agoraphobia. *Behaviour Research and Therapy*, *23*, 35–44.

Chambless, D. L., & Gracely, E. J. (1989). Fear of fear and the anxiety disorders. *Cognitive Therapy and Research*, *13*, 19–20.

Chambless, D. L., & Peterman, M. (2004). Evidence on cognitive-behavioral therapy for generalized anxiety disorder and panic disorder: The second decade. In R. L. Leahy (Ed.), *Contemporary cognitive therapy: Theory, research, and practice* (pp. 86–115), New York, NY: Guilford Press.

Chambless, D. L., & Renneberg, B. (1988, September). Personality disorders of agoraphobics. Paper presented at the World Congress of Behavior Therapy, Edinburgh, Scotland.

Charney, D. S., Woods, S., Krystal, J. H., Nagy, L., & Heninger, G. (2007). Noradrenergic neuronal dysregulation in panic disorder: The effects of intravenous yohimbine and clonidine in panic disorder patients. *Acta Psychiatrica Scandinavica*, *86*(4), 273–282.

Chawla, N., & Ostafin, B. (2007). Experiential avoidance as a functional dimensional approach to psychopathology: An empirical review. *Journal of Clinical Psychology*, *63*(9), 871–890.

Chen, J., Tsuchiya, M., Kawakami, N., & Furukawa, T. A. (2009). Non-fearful vs. fearful panic attacks: A general population study from the National Comorbidity Survey. *Journal of Affective Disorders*, *112*(1–3), 273–278.

Choe, A. Y., Kim, B., Lee, K. S., Lee, J. E., Lee, J. Y., Choi, T. K., & Lee, S. H. (2013). Serotonergic genes (5-HTT and HTR1A) and separation life events: Gene-by-environment interaction for panic disorder. *Neuropsychobiology*, *67*(4), 192–200.

Clark, D. B., Taylor, C. B., Hayward, C., King, R., Margraf, J., Ehlers, A., ... Stewart, A. W. (1990). Motor activity and tonic heart rate in panic disorder. *Psychiatry Research*, *32*, 45–53.

Clark, D. M. (1986). A cognitive approach to panic. *Behaviour Research and Therapy*, *24*, 461–470.

Clark, D. M. (1988). A cognitive model of panic attacks. In S. Rachman & J. D. Maser (Eds.), *Panic: Psychological perspectives* (pp. 71–89). Hillside, NJ: Erlbaum.

Clark, D. M. (1996). Panic disorder: From theory to therapy. In P. M. Salkovskis (Ed.), *Frontiers of cognitive therapy* (pp. 318–344). New York, NY: Guilford Press.

Clark, D. M., Salkovskis, P. M., Gelder, M., Koehler, C., Martin, M., Anastasiades, P., ... Jeavons, A. (1988). Tests of a cognitive theory of panic. In I. Hand & H.-U. Wittchen (Eds.), *Panic and phobias II: Treatments and variables affecting course and outcome* (pp. 71–90). Berlin, Germany: Springer-Verlag.

Clark, D. M., Salkovskis, P. M., Hackmann, A., Middleton, H., Anastasiades, P., & Gelder, M. (1994). A comparison of cognitive therapy, applied relaxation, and imipramine in the treatment of panic disorder: A randomized controlled trial. *British Journal of Psychiatry*, *164*, 759–769.

Clark, D. M., Salkovskis, P. M., Hackmann, A., Wells, A., Ludgate, J., & Gelder, M. (1999). Brief cognitive therapy for panic disorder: A randomized controlled trial. *Journal of Consulting and Clinical Psychology*, *67*, 583–589.

Cohen, H., Benjamin, J., Geva, A. B., Matar, M. A., Kaplan, Z., & Kotler, M. (2000). Autonomic dysregulation in panic disorder and in post-traumatic stress disorders: Application of power spectrum analysis of heart rate variability at rest and in response to recollection of trauma or panic attacks. *Psychiatry Research*, *96*, 1–13.

Cohen, H., Matar, A. M., Kaplan, Z., Miodownik, H., Cassuto, Y., & Kotler, M. (1998). Analysis of heart rate variability in post-traumatic stress disorder patients: At rest and in response to a trauma-related reminder. *Biological Psychiatry*, *44*, 1054–1059.

Cohen, L., McGowan, J., Fooskas, S., & Rose, S. (1984). Positive life events and social support and the relationship between life stress and psychological disorder. *American Journal of Community Psychology*, *12*, 567–587.

Cohen, L. H., Burt, C. E., & Bjork, J. P. (1987). Life stress and adjustment: Effects of life events experienced by young adolescents and their parents. *Developmental Psychology*, *23*, 583–592.

Colonnesi, C., Draijer, E. M., Stams, G. J. J., Van der Bruggen, C. O., Bögels, S. M., & Noom, M. J. (2011). The relation between insecure attachment and child anxiety: A meta-analytic review. *Journal of Clinical Child & Adolescent Psychology*, *40*(4), 630–645.

Cougle, J. R., Timpano, K. R., Sachs-Ericsson, N., Keough, M. E., & Riccardi, C. J. (2010). Examining the unique relationships between anxiety disorders and childhood physical and sexual abuse in the National Comorbidity Survey Replication. *Psychiatry Research*, *177*(1–2), 150.

Cox, B. J., Endler, N. S., & Swinson, R. P. (1995). An examination of levels of agoraphobic severity in panic disorder. *Behaviour Research and Therapy*, *33*, 57–62.

Craske, M. G. (1999). *Anxiety disorders: Psychological approaches to theory and treatment*. Boulder, CO: Westview.

Craske, M. G. (2003). *Origins of phobias and anxiety disorders: Why more women than men?* Oxford, England: Elsevier.

Craske, M. G., & Barlow, D. H. (1988). A review of the relationship between panic and avoidance. *Clinical Psychology Review*, *8*, 667–685.

Craske, M. G., & Barlow, D. H. (1989). Nocturnal panic. *Journal of Nervous and Mental Disease*, *177*, 160–167.

Craske, M. G., Brown, T. A., & Barlow, D. H. (1991). Behavioral treatment of panic disorder: A two-year follow-up. *Behavior Therapy*, *22*, 289–304.

Craske, M. G., Farchione, T. J., Allen, L. B., Barrios, V., Stoyanova, M., & Rose, R. (2007). Cognitive behavioral therapy for panic disorder and comorbidity: More of the same or less of more? *Behaviour Research and Therapy*, *45*(6), 1095–1109.

Craske, M. G., & Freed, S. (1995). Expectations about arousal and nocturnal panic. *Journal of Abnormal Psychology*, *104*, 567–575.

Craske, M. G., Kircanski, K., Epstein, A., Wittchen, H.-U., Pine, D. S., Lewis-Fernández, R., & Hinton, D. (2010). Panic disorder: A review of DSM-IV panic disorder and proposals for DSM-V. *Depression and Anxiety*, *27*(2), 93–112.

Craske, M. G., Kircanski, K., Zelikowsky, M., Mystkowski, J., Chowdhury, N., & Baker, A. (2008). Optimizing inhibitory learning during exposure therapy. *Behaviour Research and Therapy*, *46*(1), 5–27. doi: 10.1016/j.brat.2007.10.003

Craske, M. G., Lang, A. J., Aikins, D., & Mystkowski, J. L. (2005). Cognitive behavioral therapy for nocturnal panic. *Behavior Therapy*, *36*, 43–54.

Craske, M. G., Lang, A. J., Rowe, M., DeCola, J. P., Simmons, J., Mann, C., … Bystritsky, A. (2002). Presleep attributions about arousal during sleep: Nocturnal panic. *Journal of Abnormal Psychology*, *111*, 53–62.

Craske, M. G., Liao, B., Brown, L., & Vervliet, B. (2012). Role of inhibition in exposure therapy. *Journal of Experimental Psychopathology*, *3*(3), 322–345.

Craske, M. G., Maidenberg, E., & Bystritsky, A. (1995). Brief cognitive-behavioral versus non-directive therapy for panic disorder. *Journal of Behavior Therapy and Experimental Psychiatry*, *26*, 113–120.

Craske, M. G., Miller, P. P., Rotunda, R., & Barlow, D. H. (1990). A descriptive report of features of initial unexpected panic attacks in minimal and extensive avoiders. *Behaviour Research and Therapy*, *28*(5), 395–400.

Craske, M. G., Niles, A. N., Burklund, L. J., Wolitzky-Taylor, K. B., Plumb, J. C., Arch, J. J., … Lieberman, M. D. (2014). Randomized controlled trial of cognitive behavioral therapy and acceptance and commitment therapy for social phobia: Outcomes and moderators. *Journal of Consulting and Clinical Psychology, 82*(6), 1034–1048.

Craske, M. G., Poulton, R., Tsao, J. C. I., & Plotkin, D. (2001). Paths to panic disorder/agoraphobia: An exploratory analysis from age 3 to 21 in an unselected birth cohort. *Journal of the American Academy of Child & Adolescent Psychiatry, 40*, 556–563.

Craske, M. G., Rapee, R. M., & Barlow, D. H. (1988). The significance of panic-expectancy for individual patterns of avoidance. *Behavior Therapy, 19*, 577–592.

Craske, M. G., & Rowe, M. K. (1997). Nocturnal panic. *Clinical Psychology: Science & Practice, 4*, 153–174.

Craske, M. G., Roy-Byrne, P., Stein, M. B., Donald-Sherbourne, C., Bystritsky, A., Katon, W., & Sullivan G. (2002). Treating panic disorder in primary care: A collaborative care intervention. *General Hospital Psychiatry, 24*(3), 148–155.

Craske, M. G., Roy-Byrne, P., Stein, M. B., Sullivan, G., Hazlett-Stevens, H., Bystritsky, A., & Sherbourne, C. (2006). CBT intensity and outcome for panic disorder in a primary care setting. *Behavior Therapy, 37*, 112–119.

Craske, M. G., Stein, M. B., Sullivan, G., Sherbourne, C., Bystritsky, A., Rose, R. D., … Roy-Byrne, P. (2011). Disorder-specific impact of coordinated anxiety learning and management treatment for anxiety disorders in primary care. *Archives of General Psychiatry, 68*(4), 378–387. doi: 10.1001/archgenpsychiatry.2011.25

Craske, M. G., & Tsao, J. C. I. (1999). Self-monitoring with panic and anxiety disorders. *Psychological Assessment, 11*, 466–479.

Craske, M. G., & Tsao, J. C. I. (2005). Assessment and treatment of nocturnal panic attacks. *Sleep Medicine Reviews, 9*, 173–184.

Craske, M. G., & Zucker, B. G. (2001). Prevention of anxiety disorders: A model for intervention. *Applied and Preventive Psychology, 10*(3), 155–175.

de Beurs, E., van Balkom, A. J., Lange, A., Koele, P., & van Dyke, R. (1995). Treatment of panic disorder with agoraphobia: Comparison of fluvoxamine, placebo, and psychological panic management combined with exposure and of exposure in vivo alone. *American Journal of Psychiatry, 152*, 683–691.

de Carvalho, M. R., Dias, G. P., Cosci, F., de-Melo-Neto, V. L., Bevilaqua, M. C., Gardino, P. F., & Nardi, A. E. (2010). Current findings of fMRI in panic disorder: Contributions for the fear neurocircuitry and CBT effects. *Expert Review of Neurotherapeutics, 10*(2), 291–303.

de Carvalho, M. R., Velasques, B. B., Cagy, M., Marques, J. B., Teixeira, S., Nardi, A. E., … Ribeiro, P. (2013). Electroencephalographic findings in panic disorder. *Trends in Psychiatry and Psychology, 35*(4), 238–251.

De Cort, K., Griez, E., Büchler, M., & Schruers, K. (2012). The role of "interoceptive" fear conditioning in the development of panic disorder. *Behavior Therapy, 43*(1), 203–215.

De Cort, K., Hermans, D., Noortman, D., Arends, W., Griez, E. J., & Schruers, K. R. (2013). The weight of cognitions in panic: The link between misinterpretations and panic attacks. *PLoS One, 8*(8), e70315.

De Cort, K., Hermans, D., Spruyt, A., Griez, E., & Schruers, K. (2008). A specific attentional bias in panic disorder? *Depression and Anxiety, 25*(11), 951–955.

de Jong, G. M., & Bouman, T. K. (1995). Panic disorder: A baseline period; Predictability of agoraphobic avoidance behavior. *Journal of Anxiety Disorders, 9*, 185–199.

Deacon, B., & Abramowitz, J. (2006). A pilot study of two-day cognitive-behavioral therapy for panic disorder. *Behaviour Research and Therapy, 44*, 807–817.

Deckersbach, T., Moshier, S., Tuschen-Caffier, B., & Otto, M. W. (2011). Memory dysfunction in panic disorder: An investigation of the role of chronic benzodiazepine use. *Depression and Anxiety, 28*(11), 999–1007.

Deckert, J., Nothen, M. M., Franke, P., Delmo, C., Fritze, J., Knapp, M., … Propping, P. (1998). Systematic mutation screening and association study of the A1 and A2a adenosine receptor genes in panic disorder suggest a contribution of the A2a gene to the development of disease. *Molecular Psychiatry, 3*, 81–85.

Del Casale, A., Serata, D., Rapinesi, C., Kotzalidis, G. D., Angeletti, G., Tatarelli, R., … Girardi, P. (2013). Structural neuroimaging in patients with panic disorder: Findings and limitations of recent studies. *Psychiatria Danubina, 25*(2), 108–114.

Devilly, G. J. (2001a). Effect size and methodological rigor in EMDR: A reply to Lipke's (2001) comment. *Behavior Therapist, 24*, 195–196.

Devilly, G. J. (2001b). The influence of distraction during exposure and researcher allegiance during outcome trials. *Behavior Therapist, 24*, 18–21.

DiNardo, P. A., Brown, T. A., & Barlow, D. H. (1994). *Anxiety Disorders Interview Schedule for DSM-IV: Clinician's manual.* New York, NY: Graywind.

Doerfler, L. A., Connor, D. F., Volungis, A. M., & Toscano, P. F., Jr. (2007). Panic disorder in clinically referred children and adolescents. *Child Psychiatry & Human Development, 38*(1), 57–71.

Domschke, K., Deckert, J., O'Donovan, M. C., & Glatt, S. J. (2007). Meta-analysis of COMT val158met in panic disorder: Ethnic heterogeneity and gender specificity. *American Journal of Medical Genetics Part B: Neuropsychiatric Genetics, 144*(5), 667–673.

Domschke, K., Klauke, B., Winter, B., Gajewska, A., Herrmann, M. J., Warrings, B., ... Deckert, J. (2012). Modification of caffeine effects on the affect-modulated startle by neuropeptide S receptor gene variation. *Psychopharmacology, 222*(3), 533–541.

Domschke, K., Reif, A., Weber, H., Richter, J., Hohoff, C., Ohrmann, P., ... Deckert, J. (2011). Neuropeptide S receptor gene—converging evidence for a role in panic disorder. *Molecular Psychiatry, 16*(9), 938–948.

Dworkin, B. R., & Dworkin, S. (1999). Heterotopic and homotopic classical conditioning of the baroreflex. *Integrative Physiological & Behavioral Science, 34*, 158–176.

Ehlers, A. (1995). A 1-year prospective study of panic attacks: Clinical course and factors associated with maintenance. *Journal of Abnormal Psychology, 104*, 164–172.

Ehlers, A., Margraf, J., Roth, W. T., Taylor, C. B., & Birbaumer, N. (1988). Anxiety induced by false heart rate feedback in patients with panic disorder. *Behaviour Research and Therapy, 26*, 1–11.

Eifert, G. H., & Forsyth, J. P. (2005). *Acceptance and commitment therapy for anxiety disorders: A practitioner's treatment guide to using mindfulness, acceptance, and values-based behavior change strategies.* Oakland, CA: New Harbinger.

Eifert, G. H., & Heffner, M. (2003). The effects of acceptance versus control contexts on avoidance of panic-related symptoms. *Journal of Behavioral Therapy and Experimental Psychiatry, 34*, 293–312.

Emmrich, A., Beesdo-Baum, K., Gloster, A. T., Knappe, S., Höfler, M., Arolt, V., ... Wittchen, H.-U. (2012). Depression does not affect the treatment outcome of CBT for panic and agoraphobia: Results from a multicenter randomized trial. *Psychotherapy and Psychosomatics, 81*(3), 161–172.

Erhardt, A., Schumacher, A. N., Czamara, D., Karbalai, N., Müller-Myhsok, B., Mors, O., ... Binder, E. B. (2012). Replication and meta-analysis of TMEM132D gene variants in panic disorder. *Translational Psychiatry, 2*, e156.

Ettigi, P., Meyerhoff, A. S., Chirban, J. T., Jacobs, R. J., & Wilson, R. R. (1997). The quality of life and employments in panic disorder. *Journal of Nervous and Mental Disease, 185*, 368–372.

Eysenck, H. J. (Ed.). (1960). *Behavior therapy and the neuroses.* Oxford, England: Pergamon Press.

Eysenck, H. J. (1967). *The biological basis of personality.* Springfield, IL: C. C. Thomas.

Eysenck, H. J., & Rachman, S. (1965). *The causes and cures of neurosis.* London, England: Routledge & Kegan Paul.

Fava, G. A., Rafanelli, C., Grandi, S., Conti, S., Ruini, C., Mangelli, L., ... Belluardo, P. (2001). Long-term outcome of panic disorder with agoraphobia treated by exposure. *Psychological Medicine, 31*, 891–898.

Fava, G. A., Zielezny, M., Savron, G., & Grandi, S. (1995). Long-term effects of behavioural treatment for panic disorder with agoraphobia. *British Journal of Psychiatry, 166*, 87–92.

First, M. B., Spitzer, R. L., Gibbon, M., & Williams, J. B. W. (1994). *Structured clinical interview for Axis I DSM-IV disorders.* New York, NY: Biometric Research Department, New York State Psychiatric Institute.

Forsyth, J. P., Palav, A., & Duff, K. (1999). The absence of relation between anxiety sensitivity and fear conditioning using 20% versus 13% CO_2-enriched air as unconditioned stimuli. *Behaviour Research and Therapy, 37*, 143–153.

Friedman, B. H., & Thayer, J. F. (1998). Autonomic balance revisited: Panic anxiety and heart rate variability. *Journal of Psychosomatic Research, 44*, 133–151.

Friedman, B. H., Thayer, J. F., & Borkovec, T. D. (1993). Heart rate variability in generalized anxiety disorder [abstract]. *Psychophysiology, 30*(Suppl.), S28.

Frisch, M. B., Cornell, J., Villanueva, M., & Retzlaff, P. J. (1992). Clinical validation of the Quality of Life Inventory: A measure of life satisfaction for use in treatment planning and outcome assessment. *Psychological Assessment, 4*, 92–101.

Furukawa, T. A., Watanabe, N., & Churchill, R. (2006). Psychotherapy plus antidepressant for panic disorder with or without agoraphobia: Systematic review. *British Journal of Psychiatry, 188*, 305–312.

Gadermann, A. M., Alonso, J., Vilagut, G., Zaslavsky, A. M., & Kessler, R. C. (2012). Comorbidity and disease burden in the National Comorbidity Survey Replication (NSC-R). *Depression and Anxiety, 29*, 797–806.

Gajewska, A., Blumenthal, T. D., Winter, B., Hermann, M. J., Conzelmann, A., Mühlberger, A., …Domschke, K. (2013). Effects of ADORA2A gene variation and caffeine on prepulse inhibition: A multi-level risk model of anxiety. *Progress in Neuro-Psychopharmacology & Biological Psychiatry, 40*(1), 115–121.

Gámez, W., Chmielewski, M., Kotov, R., Ruggero, C., Suzuki, N., & Watson, D. (2014). The Brief Experiential Avoidance Questionnaire: Development and initial validation. *Psychological Assessment, 26*(1), 35–45.

Gámez, W., Chmielewski, M., Kotov, R., Ruggero, C., & Watson, D. (2011). Development of a measure of experiential avoidance: The Multidimensional Experiential Avoidance Questionnaire. *Psychological Assessment, 23*(3), 692–713.

Garakani, A., Martinez, J. M., Aaronson, C. J., Voustianiouk, A., Kaufmann, H., & Gorman, J. M. (2009). Effect of medication and psychotherapy on heart rate variability in panic disorder. *Depression and Anxiety, 26*(3), 251–258.

Gardenswartz, C. A., & Craske, M. G. (2001). Prevention of panic disorder. *Behavior Therapy, 32*(4), 725–737.

Gatt, J. M., Burton, K. L., Williams, L. M., & Schofield, P. R. (2015). Specific and common genes implicated across major mental disorders: A review of meta-analysis studies. *Journal of Psychiatry Research, 60*, 1–13.

Gaudlitz, K., Plag, J., Dimeo, F., & Ströhle, A. (2015). Aerobic exercise training facilitates the effectiveness of cognitive behavioral therapy in panic disorder. *Depression and Anxiety, 32*(3), 221–228.

Gere, M. K., Villabø, M. A., Torgersen, S., & Kendall, P. C. (2012). Overprotective parenting and child anxiety: The role of co-occurring child behavior problems. *Journal of Anxiety Disorders, 26*(6), 642–649.

Ghosh, A., & Marks, I. M. (1987). Self-treatment of agoraphobia by exposure. *Behavior Therapy, 18*, 3–16.

Gloster, A. T., Sonntag, R., Hoyer, J., Meyer, A. H., Heinze, S., Ströhle, A., …Wittchen, H.-U. (2015). Treating treatment-resistant patients with panic disorder and agoraphobia using psychotherapy: A randomized controlled switching trial. *Psychotherapy and Psychosomatics, 84*(2), 100–109.

Gloster, A. T., Wittchen, H.-U., Einsle, F., Lang, T., Helbig-Lang, S., Fydrich, T., …Arolt, V. (2011). Psychological treatment for panic disorder with agoraphobia: A randomized controlled trial to examine the role of therapist-guided exposure in situ in CBT. *Journal of Consulting and Clinical Psychology, 79*(3), 406–420. doi: 10.1037/a0023584

Goddard, A. W., Mason, G. F., Almai, A., Rothman, D. L., Behar, K. L., Petroff, O. A. C., …Krystal, J. H. (2001). Reductions in occipital cortex GABA levels in panic disorder detected with 1h-magnetic resonance spectroscopy. *Archives of General Psychiatry, 58*, 556–561.

Goddard, A. W., Mason, G. F., Appel, M., Rothman, D. L., Gueorguieva, R., Behar, K. L., …Krystal, J. H. (2004). Impaired GABA neuronal response to acute benzodiazepine administration in panic disorder. *American Journal of Psychiatry, 161*, 2186–2193.

Goldstein, A. J., & Chambless, D. L. (1978). A reanalysis of agoraphobia. *Behavior Therapy, 9*, 47–59.

Goodwin, R. D., Fergusson, D. M., & Horwood, L. J. (2005). Childhood abuse and familial violence and the risk of panic attacks and panic disorder in young adulthood. *Psychological Medicine, 35*, 881–890.

Goodwin, R. D., & Pine, D. S. (2002). Respiratory disease and panic attacks among adults in the United States. *Chest, 122*(2), 645–650.

Gordeev, S. A. (2008). Cognitive functions and the state of nonspecific brain systems in panic disorder. *Neuroscience and Behavioral Physiology, 38*(7), 707–714.

Gorman, J. M., Kent, J. M., Sullivan, G. M., & Coplan, J. D. (2000). Neuroanatomical hypothesis of panic disorder, revised. *American Journal of Psychiatry, 157*, 493–505.

Gorman, J. M., Papp, L. A., Coplan, J. D., Martinez, J. M., Lennon, S., Goetz, R. R., …Klein, D. F. (1994). Anxiogenic effects of CO_2 and hyperventilation in patients with panic disorder. *American Journal of Psychiatry, 151*(4), 547–553.

Gould, R. A., & Clum, G. A. (1995). Self-help plus minimal therapist contact in the treatment of panic disorder: A replication and extension. *Behavior Therapy, 26*, 533–546.

Gould, R. A., Clum, G. A., & Shapiro, D. (1993). The use of bibliotherapy in the treatment of panic: A preliminary investigation. *Behavior Therapy, 24,* 241–252.

Gould, R. A., Otto, M. W., & Pollack, M. H. (1995). A meta-analysis of treatment outcome for panic disorder. *Clinical Psychology Review, 15,* 819–844.

Graeff, F. G., & Del-Ben, C. M. (2008). Neurobiology of panic disorder: From animal models to brain neuroimaging. *Neuroscience & Biobehavioral Reviews, 32*(7), 1326–1335.

Grassi, M., Caldirola, D., Vanni, G., Guerriero, G., Piccinni, M., Valchera, A., & Perna, G. (2013). Baseline respiratory parameters in panic disorder: A meta-analysis. *Journal of Affective Disorders, 146*(2), 158–173.

Gray, J. A. (1982). *The neuropsychology of anxiety: An enquiry into the functions of the septo-hippocampal system.* New York, NY: Oxford University Press.

Greenberg, P. E., Sisitsky, T., Kessler, R. C., Finkelstein, S. N., Berndt, E. R., Davidson, J. R. T., … Fyer, A. J. (1999). The economic burden of anxiety disorders in the 1990s. *Journal of Clinical Psychiatry, 60,* 427–435.

Grillon, C. (2002). Startle reactivity and anxiety disorders: Aversive conditioning, context, and neurobiology. *Biological Psychiatry, 52,* 958–975.

Grillon, C., Ameli, R., Goddard, A., Woods, S. W., & Davis, M. (1994). Baseline and fear-potentiated startle in panic disorder patients. *Biological Psychiatry, 35,* 431–439.

Gunthert, K. C., Conner, T. S., Armeli, S., Tennen, H., Covault, J., & Kranzler, H. R. (2007). Serotonin transporter gene polymorphism (5-HTTLPR) and anxiety reactivity in daily life: A daily process approach to gene-environment interaction. *Psychosomatic Medicine, 69*(8), 762–768.

Hamilton, S. P., Slager, S. L., De Leon, A. B., Heiman, G. A., Klein, D. F., Hodge, S. E., … Knowles, J. A. (2004). Evidence for genetic linkage between a polymorphism in the adenosine 2A receptor and panic disorder. *Neuropsychopharmacology, 29,* 558–565.

Hawks, E., Blumenthal, H., Feldner, M. T., Leen-Feldner, E. W., & Jones, R. (2011). An examination of the relation between traumatic event exposure and panic-relevant biological challenge responding among adolescents. *Behavior Therapy, 42*(3), 427–438.

Hayes, S. C., Levin, M. E., Plumb-Vilardaga, J., Villatte, J. L., & Pistorello, J. (2013). Acceptance and commitment therapy and contextual behavioral science: Examining the progress of a distinctive model of behavioral and cognitive therapy. *Behavior Therapy, 44*(2), 180–198.

Hayes, S. C., Luoma, J. B., Bond, F. W., Masuda, A., & Lillis, J. (2006). Acceptance and commitment therapy: Model, processes and outcomes. *Behaviour Research and Therapy, 44,* 1–25.

Hayes, S. C., Strosahl, K. D., & Wilson, K. G. (1999). *Acceptance and commitment therapy: An experiential approach to behavior change.* New York, NY: Guilford Press.

Hayes, S. C., Strosahl, K. D., & Wilson, K. G. (2012). *Acceptance and commitment therapy: The process and practice of mindful change* (2nd ed.). New York, NY: Guilford Press.

Hayes, S. C., Strosahl, K., Wilson, K. G., Bissett, R. T., Pistorello, J., Toarmino, D., … McCurry, S. M. (2004). Measuring experiential avoidance: A preliminary test of a working model. *Psychological Record, 54*(4), 553–578.

Hayes, S. C., Wilson, K. G., Giffore, E. V., Follette, V. M., & Strosahl, K. (1996). Experiential avoidance and behavioral disorders: A functional dimensional approach to diagnosis and treatment. *Journal of Consulting and Clinical Psychology, 64,* 1152–1168.

Hayward, C., Killen, J. D., Kraemer, H. C., & Taylor, C. B. (2000). Predictors of panic attacks in adolescents. *Journal of the American Academy of Child & Adolescent Psychiatry, 39,* 207–214.

Helbig-Lang, S., & Petermann, F. (2010). Tolerate or eliminate? A systematic review on the effects of safety behavior across anxiety disorders. *Clinical Psychology: Science and Practice, 17*(3), 218–233.

Helbig-Lang, S., Richter, J., Lang, T., Gerlach, A. L., Fehm, L., Alpers, G. W., … Wittchen, H.-U. (2014). The role of safety behaviors in exposure-based treatment for panic disorder and agoraphobia: Associations to symptom severity, treatment course, and outcome. *Journal of Anxiety Disorders, 28*(8), 836–844.

Hermans, D., Craske, M. G., Mineka, S., & Lovibond, P. F. (2006). Extinction in humans. *Biological Psychiatry, 60,* 361–368.

Hettema, J. M., Neale, M. C., & Kendler, K. S. (2001). A review and meta-analysis of the genetic epidemiology of anxiety disorders. *American Journal of Psychiatry, 158*(10), 1568–1578.

Hibbs, E. D., Hamburger, S. D., Kruesi, M. J. P., & Lenane, M. (1993). Factors affecting expressed emotion in parents of ill and normal children. *American Journal of Orthopsychiatry*, *63*, 103–112.

Hirshfeld-Becker, D. R., Micco, J. A., Henin, A., Petty, C., Faraone, S. V., Mazursky, H., … Biederman, J. (2012). Psychopathology in adolescent offspring of parents with panic disorder, major depression, or both: A 10-year follow-up. *Psychopathology*, *169*(11).

Hoehn-Saric, R., McLeod, D. R., & Hipsley, P. (1995). Is hyperarousal essential to obsessive-compulsive disorder? Diminished physiologic flexibility, but not hyperarousal, characterizes patients with obsessive-compulsive disorder. *Archives of General Psychiatry*, *52*, 688–693.

Hofmann, S. G. (2008). Common misconceptions about cognitive mediation of treatment change: A commentary to Longmore and Worrell (2007). *Clinical Psychology Review*, *28*, 67–70.

Hofmann, S. G., Sawyer, A. T., Korten, A. E., & Smits, J. A. J. (2009). Is it beneficial to add pharmacotherapy to cognitive-behavioral therapy when treating anxiety disorders? A meta-analytic review. *International Journal of Cognitive Therapy*, *2*(2), 160–175.

Hofmann, S. G., & Smits, J. A. J. (2008). Cognitive-behavioral therapy for adult anxiety disorders: A meta-analysis of randomized placebo-controlled trials. *Journal of Clinical Psychiatry*, *69*(4), 621–632.

Hofmann, S. G., Wu, J. Q., & Boettcher, H. (2014). Effect of cognitive-behavioral therapy for anxiety disorders on quality of life: A meta-analysis. *Journal of Consulting and Clinical Psychology*, *82*(3), 375.

Hohoff, C., Mullings, E. L., Heatherley, S. V., Freitag, C. M., Neumann, L. C., Domschke, K., … Deckert, J. (2010). Adenosine A2A receptor gene: Evidence for association of risk variants with panic disorder and anxious personality. *Journal of Psychiatric Research*, *44*(14), 930–937.

Hommers, L., Raab, A., Bohl, A., Weber, H., Scholz, C. J., Erhardt, A., … Kalisch, R. (2015). MicroRNA hsa-miR-4717-5p regulates RGS2 and may be a risk factor for anxiety-related traits. *American Journal of Medical Genetics Part B: Neuropsychiatric Genetics*, *168*(4), 296–306.

Houck, P. R., Spiegel, D. A., Shear, M. K., & Rucci, P. (2002). Reliability of the self-report version of the Panic Disorder Severity Scale. *Depression and Anxiety*, *15*(4), 183–185.

Hovland, A., Nordhus, I. H., Sjøbø, T., Gjestad, B. A., Birknes, B., Martinsen, E. W., … Pallesen, S. (2013). Comparing physical exercise in groups to group

cognitive behaviour therapy for the treatment of panic disorder in a randomized controlled trial. *Behavioural and Cognitive Psychotherapy*, *41*(4), 408–432.

Hudson, J., & Rapee, R. (2001). Parent–child interactions and anxiety disorders: An observational study. *Behaviour Research and Therapy*, *39*, 1411–1427.

Ito, T., Inoue, Y., Sugihara, T., Yamada, H., Katayama, S., & Kawahara, R. (1999). Autonomic function in the early stage of panic disorder: Power spectral analysis of heart rate variability. *Psychiatry and Clinical Neurosciences*, *53*(6), 667–672.

Jacob, R. G., Furman, J. M., Clark, D. B., & Durrant, J. D. (1992). Vestibular symptoms, panic, and phobia: Overlap and possible relationships. *Annals of Clinical Psychiatry*, *4*, 163–174.

Jezova, D., Vigas, M., Hlavacova, N., & Kukumberg, P. (2010). Attenuated neuroendocrine response to hypoglycemic stress in patients with panic disorder. *Neuroendocrinology*, *92*(2), 112–119.

Johnson, E. M., & Coles, M. E. (2013). Failure and delay in treatment-seeking across anxiety disorders. *Community Mental Health Journal*, *49*(6), 668–674.

Johnson, P. L., Federici, L. M., & Shekhar, A. (2014). Etiology, triggers and neurochemical circuits associated with unexpected, expected, and laboratory-induced panic attacks. *Neuroscience & Biobehavioral Reviews*, *46*(3), 429–454.

Kabat-Zinn, J. (1990). *Full catastrophe living: Using the wisdom of your body and mind to face stress, pain, and illness*. New York, NY: Delta.

Kabat-Zinn, J., Massion, A. O., Kristeller, J., Peterson, L. G., Fletcher, K. E., Pbert, L., … Santorelli, S. F. (1992). Effectiveness of a meditation-based stress reduction program in the treatment of anxiety disorders. *American Journal of Psychiatry*, *149*, 936–943.

Kämpfe, C. K., Gloster, A. T., Wittchen, H.-U., Helbig-Lang, S., Lang, T., Gerlach, A. L., … Deckert, J. (2012). Experiential avoidance and anxiety sensitivity in patients with panic disorder and agoraphobia: Do both constructs measure the same? *International Journal of Clinical and Health Psychology*, *12*(1), 5–22.

Kang, E. H., Park, J. E., Lee, K. H., Cho, Y. S., Kim, J. J., & Yu, B. H. (2012). Regional brain metabolism and treatment response in panic disorder patients: An [18F]FDG-PET study. *Neuropsychobiology*, *66*(2), 106–111.

Kaplan, J. S., Arnkoff, D. B., Glass, C. R., Tinsley, R., Geraci, M., Hernandez, E., … Carlson, P. J. (2012).

Avoidant coping in panic disorder: A yohimbine biological challenge study. *Anxiety, Stress, & Coping*, *25*(4), 425–442.

Kartalci, S., Dogan, M., Unal, S., Ozcan, A. C., Ozdemir, S., & Atmaca, M. (2011). Pituitary volume in patients with panic disorder. *Progress in Neuro-Psychopharmacology and Biological Psychiatry*, *35*(1), 203–207.

Katerndahl, D. A., & Realini, J. P. (1997). Quality of life and panic-related work disability in subjects with infrequent panic and panic disorder. *Journal of Clinical Psychiatry*, *58*, 153–158.

Katschnig, H., & Amering, M. (1998). The long-term course of panic disorder and its predictors. *Journal of Clinical Psychopharmacology*, *18*(Suppl. 2), 6S–11S.

Kawakami, N., Takeshima, T., Ono, Y., Uda, H., Hata, Y., Nakane, Y., … Kikkawa, T. (2005). Twelve-month prevalence, severity, and treatment of common mental disorders in communities in Japan: Preliminary finding from the World Mental Health Japan Survey 2002–2003. *Psychiatry and Clinical Neurosciences*, *59*, 441–452.

Kendler, K. S., Neale, M. C., Kessler, R. C., Heath, A. C., & Eaves, L. J. (1993). Major depression and phobias: The genetic and environmental sources of comorbidity. *Psychological Medicine*, *23*, 361–371.

Kent, J. M., & Rauch, S. L. (2003). Neurocircuitry of anxiety disorders. *Current Psychiatry Report*, *5*, 266–273.

Keough, M. E., & Schmidt, N. B. (2012). Refinement of a brief anxiety sensitivity reduction intervention. *Journal of Consulting and Clinical Psychology*, *80*(5), 766–772.

Kessler, R. C., Berglund, P., Demler, O., Jin, R., Merikangas, K. R., & Walters, E. E. (2005). Lifetime prevalence and age-of-onset distributions of DSM-IV disorders in the National Comorbidity Survey Replication. *Archives of General Psychiatry*, *62*, 593–602.

Kessler, R. C., Chiu, W. T., Demler, O., Merikangas, K. R., & Walters, E. E. (2005). Prevalence, severity, and comorbidity of 12-month DSM-IV disorders in the National Comorbidity Survey Replication. *Archives of General Psychiatry*, *62*, 617–627.

Kessler, R. C., Chiu, W. T., Jin, R., Ruscio, A. M., Shear, K., & Walters, E. E. (2006). The epidemiology of panic attacks, panic disorder, and agoraphobia in the National Comorbidity Survey Replication. *Archives of General Psychiatry*, *63*(4), 415–424.

Kessler, R. C., Davis, C. G., & Kendler, K. S. (1997). Childhood adversity and adult psychiatric disorder in the U.S. National Comorbidity Survey. *Psychological Medicine*, *27*, 1101–1119.

Kessler, R. C., Petukhova, M., Sampson, N. A., Zaslavsky, A., & Wittchen, H.-U. (2012). Twelve-month and lifetime prevalence and lifetime morbid risk of anxiety and mood disorders in the United States. *International Journal of Methods in Psychiatric Research*, *21*(3), 169–184.

Kikuchi, M., Komuro, R., Hiroshi, O., Kidani, T., Hanaoka, A., & Koshino, Y. (2005). Panic disorder with and without agoraphobia: Comorbidity within a half-year of the onset of panic disorder. *Psychiatry and Clinical Neurosciences*, *58*, 639–643.

Kim, B., Lee, S. H., Kim, Y. W., Choi, T. K., Yook, K., Suh, S. Y., … Yook, K. H. (2010). Effectiveness of a mindfulness-based cognitive therapy program as an adjunct to pharmacotherapy in patients with panic disorder. *Journal of Anxiety Disorders*, *24*(6), 590–595.

Kim, J. E., Dager, S. R., & Lyoo, K. (2012). The role of the amygdala in the pathophysiology of panic disorder: Evidence from neuroimaging studies. *Biology of Mood & Anxiety Disorders*, *2*, 20.

Kircanski, K., Craske, M. G., Epstein, A. M., & Wittchen, H.-U. (2009). Subtypes of panic attacks: A critical review of the empirical literature. *Depression and Anxiety*, *26*, 878–887.

Kiropoulos, L. A., Klein, B., Austin, D. W., Gilson, K., Pier, C., Mitchell, J., & Ciechomski, L. (2008). Is internet-based CBT for panic disorder and agoraphobia as effective as face-to-face CBT? *Journal of Anxiety Disorders*, *22*(8), 1273–1284.

Klein, D. F. (1981). Anxiety reconceptualized. In D. F. Klein & J. G. Rabkin (Eds.), *Anxiety: New research and changing concepts* (pp. 235–262). New York, NY: Raven.

Knapp, A. A., Frala, J., Blumenthal, H., Badour, C. L., & Leen-Feldner, E. W. (2013). Anxiety sensitivity and childhood learning experiences: Impacts on panic symptoms among adolescents. *Cognitive Therapy and Research*, *37*, 1151–1159.

Kraemer, H. C., Wilson, T., Fairburn, C. G., & Agras, W. S. (2002). Mediators and moderators of treatment effects in randomized clinical trials. *Archives of General Psychiatry*, *59*(10), 877–883.

Kroeze, S., & van den Hout, M. A. (2000). Selective attention for cardiac information in panic patients. *Behaviour Research and Therapy*, *38*, 63–72.

Lake, R. I. E., Eaves, L. J., Maes, H. H. M., Heath, A. C., & Martin, N. G. (2000). Further evidence against the environmental transmission of individual differences in neuroticism from a collaborative study of 45,850 twins and relatives of two continents. *Behavior Genetics*, *30*, 223–233.

Lambert, A. E., Hu, Y., Magee, J. C., Beadel, J. R., & Teachman, B. A. (2014). Thought suppression across time: Change in frequency and duration of thought recurrence. *Journal of Obsessive-Compulsive and Related Disorders*, *3*(1), 21–28.

Lautenbacher, S., Spernal, J., & Krieg, J.-C. (2002). Divided and selective attention in panic disorder: A comparative study of patients with panic disorder, major depression and healthy controls. *European Archives of Psychiatry and Clinical Neuroscience*, *252*, 210–213.

LeBeau, R. T., Glenn, D. E., Hanover, L. N., Beesdo-Baum, K., Wittchen, H.-U., & Craske, M. G. (In press). Preliminary assessment of a dimensional approach to measuring anxiety for DSM-5. *International Journal of Methods in Psychiatric Research*.

LeDoux, J. E. (1996). *The emotional brain: The mysterious underpinnings of emotional life*. New York, NY: Simon & Schuster.

Lessard, M. J., Marchand, A., Pelland, M. È., Belleville, G., Vadeboncoeur, A., Chauny, J. M., … Lavoie, K. L. (2012). Comparing two brief psychological interventions to usual care in panic disorder patients presenting to the emergency department with chest pain. *Behavioural and Cognitive Psychotherapy*, *40*(2), 129.

Levitt, J. T., Brown, T. A., Orsillo, S. M., & Barlow, D. H. (2004). The effects of acceptance versus suppression of emotion on subjective and psychophysiological response to carbon dioxide challenge in patients with panic disorder. *Behavior Therapy*, *35*(4), 747–766.

Levy, H. C., & Radomsky, A. S. (2014). Safety behaviour enhances the acceptability of exposure. *Cognitive Behaviour Therapy*, *43*(1), 83–92.

Licht, C. M. M., de Geus, E. J. C., van Dyck, R., & Penninx, B. W. J. H. (2009). Association between anxiety disorders and heart rate variability in the Netherlands Study of Depression and Anxiety (NESDA). *Psychosomatic Medicine*, *71*(5), 508–518. doi: 10.1097/PSY.0b013e3181a292a6

Lipke, H. (2001). Response to Devilly's (2001) claims on distraction and exposure. *Behavior Therapist*, *24*(9), 195.

Lissek, S., Rabin, S., Heller, R. E., Lukenbaugh, D., Geraci, M., Pine, D. S., & Grillon, C. (2010). Overgeneralization of conditioned fear as a pathogenic marker of panic disorder. *American Journal of Psychiatry*, *167*(1), 47.

Lissek, S., Rabin, S. J., McDowell, D. J., Dvir, S., Bradford, D. E., Geraci, M., … Grillon, C. (2009). Impaired discriminative fear-conditioning resulting from elevated fear responding to learned safety cues among individuals with panic disorder. *Behaviour Research and Therapy*, *47*(2), 111–118.

Loerinc, A. G., Meuret, A. E., Twohig, M. P., Rosenfield, D., Bluett, E. J., & Craske, M. G. (2015). Response rates for CBT for anxiety disorders: Need for standardized criteria. *Clinical Psychology Review*, *42*, 72–82.

Logue, M. W., Vieland, V. J., Goedken, R. J., & Crowe, R. R. (2003). Bayesian analysis of a previously published genome screen for panic disorder reveals new and compelling evidence for linkage to chromosome 7. *American Journal of Medical Genetics Part B: Neuropsychiatric Genetics*, *121*(1), 95–99.

Long, Z., Medlock, C., Dzemidzic, M., Shin, Y. W., Goddard, A. W., & Dydak, U. (2013). Decreased GABA levels in anterior cingulate cortex/medial prefrontal cortex in panic disorder. *Progress in Neuro-Psychopharmacology & Biological Psychiatry*, *44*, 131–135.

Longley, S. L., Watson, D., Noyes, R., & Yoder, K. (2006). Panic and phobic anxiety: Associations among neuroticism, physiological hyperarousal, anxiety sensitivity, and three phobias. *Journal of Anxiety Disorders*, *20*, 718–739.

Longmore, R. J., & Worrell, M. (2007). Do we need to challenge thoughts in cognitive behavioral therapy? *Clinical Psychology Review*, *27*, 173–187.

Lonsdorf, T. B., Rück, C., Bergström, J., Andersson, G., Öhman, A., Schalling, M., & Lindefors, N. (2009). The symptomatic profile of panic disorder is shaped by the 5-HTTLPR polymorphism. *Progress in Neuro-Psychopharmacology and Biological Psychiatry*, *33*(8), 1479–1483.

López-Solà, C., Fontenelle, L. F., Alonso, P., Caudras, D., Foley, D. L., Pantelis, C., … Harrison, B. J. (2014). Prevalence and heritability of obsessive-compulsive spectrum and anxiety disorder symptoms: A survey of the Australian Twin Registry. *American Journal of Medical Genetics Part B: Neuropsychiatric Genetics*, *165B*(4), 314–325.

Lovibond, P. F., & Shanks, D. R. (2002). The role of awareness in Pavlovian conditioning: Empirical evidence and theoretical implications. *Journal of Experimental Psychology: Animal Behavior Processes, 28*, 3–26.

Lucas, J. A., Telch, M. J., & Bigler, E. D. (1991). Memory functioning in panic disorder: A neuropsychological perspective. *Journal of Anxiety Disorders, 5*(1), 1–20.

Mackinnon, A. J., Henderson, A. S., & Andrews, G. (1990). Genetic and environmental determinants of the lability of trait neuroticism and the symptoms of anxiety and depression. *Psychological Medicine, 20*, 581–591.

Maddock, R. J., Buonocore, M. H., Kile, S. J., & Garrett, A. S. (2003). Brain regions showing increased activation by threat-related words in panic disorder. *NeuroReport, 14*, 325–328.

Maidenberg, E., Chen, E., Craske, M., Bohn, P., & Bystritsky, A. (1996). Specificity of attentional bias in panic disorder and social phobia. *Journal of Anxiety Disorders, 10*, 529–541.

Malizia, A. L., Cunningham, V. J., Bell, C. J., Liddle, P. F., Jones, T., & Nutt, D. J. (1998). Decreased brain GABA(A)-benzodiazepine receptor binding in panic disorder: Preliminary results from a quantitative PET study. *Archives of General Psychiatry, 55*, 715–720.

Maller, R. G., & Reiss, S. (1992). Anxiety sensitivity in 1984 and panic attacks in 1987. *Journal of Anxiety Disorders, 6*, 241–247.

Mannuzza, S., Fyer, A. J., Martin, L. Y., Gallops, M. S., Endicott, J., Gorman, J. M., ... Klein, D. F. (1989). Reliability of anxiety assessment: I. Diagnostic agreement. *Archives of General Psychiatry, 46*, 1093–1101.

Marchand, A., Belleville, G., Fleet, R., Dupuis, G., Bacon, S. L., Poitras, J., ... Lavoie, K. L. (2012). Treatment of panic in chest pain patients from emergency departments: Efficacy of different interventions focusing on panic management. *General Hospital Psychiatry, 34*(6), 671–680.

Marciniak, M. D., Lage, M. J., Dunayevich, E., Russell, J. M., Bowman, L., Landbloom, R. P., & Levine, L. R. (2005). The cost of treating anxiety: The medical and demographic correlates that impact total medical costs. *Depression and Anxiety, 21*(4), 178–184.

Margraf, J., Taylor, C. B., Ehlers, A., Roth, W. T., & Agras, W. S. (1987). Panic attacks in the natural environment. *Journal of Nervous and Mental Disease, 175*, 558–565.

Marks, I. M., Swinson, R. P., Basoglu, M., Kuch, K., Noshirvani, H., O'Sullivan, G., ... Sengun, S. (1993). "Alprazolam and exposure alone and combined in panic disorder with agoraphobia: A controlled study in London and Toronto": Reply. *British Journal of Psychiatry, 162*, 790–794.

Maron, E., Hettema, J., & Shlik, J. (2010). Advances in molecular genetics of panic disorder. *Molecular Psychiatry, 15*(7), 681–701.

Marshall, J. R. (1997). Alcohol and substance abuse in panic disorder: Discussion. *Journal of Clinical Psychiatry, 58*, 46–50.

Martin, N. G., Jardine, R., Andrews, G., & Heath, A. C. (1988). Anxiety disorders and neuroticism: Are there genetic factors specific to panic? *Acta Psychiatrica Scandinavica, 77*, 698–706.

Massana, G., Gasto, C., Junque, C., Mercader, J. M., Gomez, B., Massana, J., ... Salamero, M. (2002). Reduced levels of creatine in the right medial temporal lobe region of panic disorder patients detected with (1)H magnetic resonance spectroscopy. *Neuroimage, 16*(pt. 1), 836–842.

McLean, P. D., Woody, S., Taylor, S., & Koch, W. J. (1998). Comorbid panic disorder and major depression: Implications for cognitive-behavioral therapy. *Journal of Consulting and Clinical Psychology, 66*(2), 240–247.

McLeod, B. D., Wood, J. J., & Weisz, J. R. (2007). Examining the association between parenting and childhood anxiety: A meta-analysis. *Clinical Psychology Review, 27*(2), 155–172.

Mellman, T. A., & Uhde, T. W. (1989). Sleep panic attacks: New clinical findings and theoretical implications. *American Journal of Psychiatry, 146*(9), 1204–1207.

Messenger, C., & Shean, G. (1998). The effects of anxiety sensitivity and history of panic on reactions to stressors in a non-clinical sample. *Journal of Behavior Therapy, 29*, 279–288.

Meulenbeek, P., Willemse, G., Smit, F., Smits, N., van Balkom, A., Spinhoven, P., & Cuijpers, P. (2009). Effects and feasibility of a preventive intervention in sub-threshold and mild panic disorder: Results of a pilot study. *BMC Research Notes, 2*(1), 4.

Meulenbeek, P., Willemse, G., Smit, F., van Balkom, A., Spinhoven, P., & Cuijpers, P. (2010). Early intervention in panic: Pragmatic randomised controlled trial. *British Journal of Psychiatry, 196*(4), 326–331.

Meuret, A. E., Rosenfield, D., Hofmann, S. G., Seidel, A., & Bhaskara, L. (2010). Respiratory and cognitive mediators of treatment change in panic disorder: Evidence for intervention specificity. *Journal of Consulting and Clinical Psychology, 78*(5), 691–704.

Meuret, A. E., Seidel, A., Rosenfield, B., Hofmann, S. G., & Rosenfield, D. (2012). Does fear reactivity during exposure predict panic symptom reduction? *Journal of Consulting and Clinical Psychology, 80*(5), 773.

Meuret, A. E., Twohig, M. P., Rosenfield, D., Hayes, S. C., & Craske, M. G. (2012). Brief acceptance and commitment therapy and exposure for panic disorder: A pilot study. *Cognitive and Behavioral Practice, 19*(4), 606–618. doi: 10.1016/j.cbpra.2012.05.004

Meuret, A. E., Wilhelm, F. H., Ritz, T., & Roth, W. T. (2008). Feedback of end-tidal pCO_2 as a therapeutic approach for panic disorder. *Journal of Psychiatric Research, 42*, 560–568.

Middleton, H. C., & Ashby, M. (1995). Clinical recovery from panic disorder is associated with evidence of changes in cardiovascular regulation. *Acta Psychiatrica Scandinavica, 91*, 108–113.

Milad, M. R., Furtak, S. C., Greenberg, J. L., Keshaviah, A., Im, J. J., Falkenstein, M. J., ... & Wilhelm, S. (2013). Deficits in conditioned fear extinction in obsessive-compulsive disorder and neurobiological changes in the fear circuit. *JAMA Psychiatry, 70*(6), 608–618.

Milad, M. R., Pitman, R. K., Ellis, C. B., Gold, A. L., Shin, L. M., Lasko, N. B., ... Rauch, S. L. (2009). Neurobiological basis of failure to recall extinction memory in posttraumatic stress disorder. *Biological Psychiatry, 66*(12), 1075–1082.

Miller, J. J., Fletcher, K., & Kabat-Zinn, J. (1995). Three-year follow-up and clinical implications of a mindfulness meditation-based stress reduction intervention in the treatment of anxiety disorders. *General Hospital Psychiatry, 17*, 192–200.

Miller, R., Wankerl, M., Stalder, T., Kirschbaum, C., & Alexander, N. (2013). The serotonin transporter gene-linked polymorphic region (5-HTTLPR) and cortisol stress reactivity: A meta-analysis. *Molecular Psychiatry, 18*(9), 1018–1024.

Mineka, S., & Cook, M. (1986). Immunization against the observational conditioning of snake fear in rhesus monkeys. *Journal of Abnormal Psychology, 95*, 307–318.

Mineka, S., Gunnar, M., & Champoux, M. (1986). Control and early socioemotional development: Infant rhesus monkeys reared in controllable versus uncontrollable environments. *Child Development, 57*, 1241–1256.

Mineka, S., Watson, D., & Clark, L. A. (1998). Comorbidity of anxiety and unipolar mood disorders. *Annual Review of Psychology, 49*, 377–412.

Mitte, K. (2005). A meta-analysis of the efficacy of psycho- and pharmacotherapy in panic disorder with and without agoraphobia. *Journal of Affective Disorders, 88*, 27–45.

Mitte, K. (2008). Memory bias for threatening information in anxiety and anxiety disorders: A meta-analytic review. *Psychological Bulletin, 134*(6), 886–911.

Mohler, H. (2012). The GABA system in anxiety and depression and its therapeutic potential. *Neuropharmacology, 62*(1), 42–53.

Moore, P. S., Whaley, S. E., & Sigman, M. (2004). Interactions between mothers and children: Impacts of maternal and child anxiety. *Journal of Abnormal Psychology, 113*, 471–476.

Moreau, D. L., Weissman, M., & Warner, V. (1989). Panic disorder in children at high risk for depression. *American Journal of Psychiatry, 146*(8), 1059–1060.

Moreno-Peral, P., Conejo-Cerón, S., Motrico, E., Rodríguez-Morejón, A., Fernández, A., García-Campayo, J., ... Bellón, J. Á. (2014). Risk factors for the onset of panic and generalised anxiety disorders in the general adult population: A systematic review of cohort studies. *Journal of Affective Disorders, 168*, 337–348.

Morissette, S. B., Spiegel, D. A., & Heinrichs, N. (2005). Sensation-focused intensive treatment for panic disorder with moderate to severe agoraphobia. *Cognitive and Behavioral Practice, 12*, 17–29.

Muiños-Gimeno, M., Espinosa-Parrilla, Y., Guidi, M., Kagerbauer, B., Sipilä, T., Maron, E., ... Estivill, X. (2011). Human microRNAs miR-22, miR-138-2, miR-148a, and miR-488 are associated with panic disorder and regulate several anxiety candidate genes and related pathways. *Biological Psychiatry, 69*(6), 526–533.

Munafò, M. R., Brown, S. M., & Hariri, A. R. (2008). Serotonin transporter (5-HTTLPR) genotype and amygdala activation: A meta-analysis. *Biological Psychiatry, 63*(9), 852–857.

Munafò, M. R., Freimer, N. B., Ng, W., Ophoff, R., Veijola, J., Miettunen, J., ... Flint, J. (2008). 5-HTTLPR genotype and anxiety-related personality traits: A meta-analysis and new data. *American Journal of Medical Genetics Part B: Neuropsychiatric Genetics, 150*(2), 271–281.

Nay, W., Brown, R., & Roberson-Nay, R. (2013). Longitudinal course of panic disorder with and without agoraphobia using the National Epidemiologic Survey on Alcohol and Related Conditions (NESARC). *Psychiatry Research, 208*(1), 54–61.

Nelles, W. B., & Barlow, D. H. (1988). Do children panic? *Clinical Psychology Review, 8*(4), 359–372.

Néron, S., Lacroix, D., & Chaput, Y. (1995). Group vs. individual cognitive behaviour therapy in panic disorder: An open clinical trial with a six month follow-up. *Canadian Journal of Behavioural Science, 27*, 379–392.

Newman, M. G., Holmes, M., Zuellig, A. R., Kachin, K. E., & Behar, E. (2006). The reliability and validity of the Panic Disorder Self-Report: A new diagnostic screening measure of panic disorder. *Psychological Assessment, 18*, 49–61.

Nickerson, A., Bryant, R. A., Aderka, I. M., Hinton, D. E., & Hofmann, S. G. (2013). The impacts of parental loss and adverse parenting on mental health: Findings from the National Comorbidity Survey-Replication. *Psychological Trauma: Theory, Research, Practice, and Policy, 5*(2), 119.

Nikolaus, S., Antke, C., Beu, M., & Muller, H.-W. (2011). Cortical GABA, striatal dopamine and midbrain serotonin as the key players in compulsive and anxiety disorders—results from in vivo imaging studies. *Reviews in the Neurosciences, 21*(2), 119–140.

Nixon, P. G. (1993). The grey area of effort syndrome and hyperventilation: From Thomas Lewis to today. *Journal of the Royal College of Physicians of London, 27*, 377–383.

Norberg, M. M., Krystal, J. H., & Tolin, D. F. (2008). A meta-analysis of D-cycloserine and the facilitation of fear extinction and exposure therapy. *Biological Psychiatry, 63*(12), 1118–1126.

Norton, G. R., Cox, B. J., & Malan, J. (1992). Nonclinical panickers: A critical review. *Clinical Psychology Review, 12*, 121–139.

Noyes, R., Crowe, R. R., Harris, E. L., Hamra, B. J., McChesney, C. M., & Chaudhry, D. R. (1986). Relationship between panic disorder and agoraphobia: A family study. *Archives of General Psychiatry, 43*, 227–232.

Offidani, E., Guidi, J., Tomba, E., & Fava, G. A. (2013). Efficacy and tolerability of benzodiazepines versus antidepressants in anxiety disorders: A systematic review and meta-analysis. *Psychotherapy and Psychosomatics, 82*(6), 355–362.

Öhman, A., & Mineka, S. (2001). Fears, phobias, and preparedness: Toward an evolved module of fear and fear learning. *Psychological Review, 108*, 483–522.

Okamura, N., Hashimoto, K., Iyo, M., Shimizu, E., Dempfle, A., Friedel, S., & Reinscheid, R. K. (2007). Gender-specific association of a functional coding polymorphism in the neuropeptide S receptor gene with panic disorder but not with schizophrenia or attention-deficit/hyperactivity disorder. *Progress in Neuro-Psychopharmacology and Biological Psychiatry, 31*(7), 1444–1448.

Olsson, C. A., Anney, R. J., Lotfi-Miri, M., Byrnes, G. B., Williamson, R., & Patton, G. C. (2005). Association between the COMT Val158Met polymorphism and propensity to anxiety in an Australian population-based longitudinal study of adolescent health. *Psychiatric Genetics, 15*(2), 109.

Olthuis, J. V., Watt, M. C., & Stewart, S. H. (2014). Anxiety Sensitivity Index (ASI-3) subscales predict unique variance in anxiety and depressive symptoms. *Journal of Anxiety Disorders, 28*(2), 115–124.

Ori, R., Amos, T., Bergman, H., Soares-Weiser, K., Ipser, J. C., & Stein, D. J. (2015). Augmentation of cognitive and behavioural therapies (CBT) with d-cycloserine for anxiety and related disorders. *Cochrane Database of Systematic Reviews, 2015*(5).

Otto, M. W., McHugh, R. K., Simon, N. M., Farach, F. J., Worthington, J. J., & Pollack, M. H. (2010). Efficacy of CBT for benzodiazepine discontinuation in patients with panic disorder: Further evaluation. *Behaviour Research and Therapy, 48*(8), 720–727.

Otto, M. W., Pollack, M. H., & Sabatino, S. A. (1996). Maintenance of remission following cognitive behavior therapy for panic disorder: Possible deleterious effects of concurrent medication treatment. *Behavior Therapy, 27*(3), 473–482.

Otto, M. W., Smits, J. A. J., & Reese, H. E. (2005). Combined psychotherapy and pharmacotherapy for mood and anxiety disorders in adults: Review and analysis. *Clinical Psychology: Science and Practice, 12*, 72–86.

Otto, M. W., Tolin, D. F., Nations, K. R., Utschig, A. C., Rothbaum, B. O., Hofmann, S. G., & Smits, J. A. (2012). Five sessions and counting: Considering ultra-brief treatment for panic disorder. *Depression and Anxiety, 29*(6), 465–470.

Otto, M. W., Tolin, D. F., Simon, N. M., Pearlson, G. D., Basden, S., Meunier, S. A., ... Pollack, M. H. (2010). Efficacy of D-cycloserine for enhancing response to cognitive-behavior therapy for panic disorder. *Biological Psychiatry, 67*(4), 365–370.

Pané-Farré, C. A., Fenske, K., Stender, J. P., Meyer, C., John, U., Rumpf, H. J., ... Hamm, A. O. (2013). Sub-threshold panic attacks and agoraphobic avoidance increase comorbidity of mental disorders: Results from an adult general population sample. *Journal of Anxiety Disorders, 27*(5), 485–493.

Papousek, H., & Papousek, M. (2002). Intuitive parenting. In M. H. Bornstein (Ed.), *Handbook of parenting: Vol. 2. Biology and ecology of parenting* (2nd ed., pp. 183–203). Mahwah, NJ: Erlbaum.

Pauli, P., Amrhein, C., Muhlberger, A., Dengler, W., & Wiedemann, G. (2005). Electrocortical evidence for an early abnormal processing of panic-related words in panic disorder patients. *International Journal of Psychophysiology, 57*, 33–41.

Petrowski, K., Herold, U., Joraschky, P., Wittchen, H.-U., & Kirschbaum, C. (2010). A striking pattern of cortisol non-responsiveness to psychosocial stress in patients with panic disorder with concurrent normal cortisol awakening responses. *Psychoneuroendocrinology, 35*(3), 414.

Petrowski, K., Wintermann, G. B., Kirschbaum, C., & Bornstein, S. R. (2012). Dissociation between ACTH and cortisol response in DEX-CRH test in patients with panic disorder. *Psychoneuroendocrinology, 37*(8), 1199–1208.

Petrowski, K., Wintermann, G. B., Schaarschmidt, M., Bornstein, S. R., & Kirschbaum, C. (2013). Blunted salivary and plasma cortisol response in patients with panic disorder under psychosocial stress. *International Journal of Psychophysiology, 88*(1), 35–39.

Pillay, S. S., Gruber, S. A., Rogowska, J., Simpson, N., & Todd, D. A. (2006). fMRI of fearful facial affect recognition in panic disorder: The cingulate gyrus-amygdala connection. *Journal of Affective Disorders, 94*, 173–181.

Pittig, A., Arch, J. J., Lam, C. W. R., & Craske, M. G. (2012). Heart rate and heart rate variability in panic, social anxiety, obsessive-compulsive, and generalized anxiety disorders at baseline and in response to relaxation and hyperventilation. *International Journal of Psychophysiology, 87*(1), 19–27.

Podină, I. R., Koster, E. H., Philippot, P., Dethier, V., & David, D. O. (2013). Optimal attentional focus during exposure in specific phobia: A meta-analysis. *Clinical Psychology Review, 33*(8), 1172–1183.

Pollard, C. A., Pollard, H. J., & Corn, K. J. (1989). Panic onset and major events in the lives of agoraphobics:

A test of contiguity. *Journal of Abnormal Psychology, 98*, 318–321.

Porges, S. W. (1992). Autonomic regulation and attention. In B. A. Campbell, H. Hayne, & R. Richardson (Eds.), *Attention and information processing in infants and adults* (pp. 201–223). Hillsdale, NJ: Erlbaum.

Porges, S. W. (2003). The polyvagal theory: Phylogenetic contributions to social behavior. *Physiology & Behavior, 79*, 503–513.

Porter, E., & Chambless, D. L. (2015). A systematic review of predictors and moderators of improvement in cognitive-behavioral therapy for panic disorder and agoraphobia. *Clinical Psychology Review, 42*, 179–192.

Powers, M. B., Asmundson, G. J., & Smits, J. A. (2015). Exercise for mood and anxiety disorders: The state-of-the science. *Cognitive Behaviour Therapy, 44*(4), 237–239.

Powers, M. B., Smits, J. A. J., & Telch, M. J. (2004). Disentangling the effects of safety behavior utilization and safety-behavior availability during exposure based treatments: A placebo-controlled trial. *Journal of Consulting and Clinical Psychology, 72*, 448–454.

Rachman, S., Lopatka, C., & Levitt, K. (1988). Experimental analyses of panic: II. Panic patients. *Behaviour Research and Therapy, 26*, 33–40.

Rachman, S., Shafran, R., Radomsky, A. S., & Zysk, E. (2011). Reducing contamination by exposure plus safety behaviour. *Journal of Behavior Therapy and Experimental Psychiatry, 42*(3), 397–404.

Ramsawh, H. J., Raffa, S. D., Edelen, M., Rende, R., & Keller, M. B. (2009). Anxiety in middle adulthood: Effects of age and time on the 14-year course of panic disorder, social phobia and generalized anxiety disorder. *Psychological Medicine, 39*(4), 615–624.

Rapee, R. M. (2009). Early adolescents' perceptions of their mother's anxious parenting as a predictor of anxiety symptoms 12 months later. *Journal of Abnormal Child Psychology, 37*(8), 1103–1112.

Rapee, R. M., Brown, T. A., Antony, M. M., & Barlow, D. H. (1992). Response to hyperventilation and inhalation of 5.5% carbon dioxide-enriched air across the *DSM-III-R* anxiety disorders. *Journal of Abnormal Psychology, 101*, 538–552.

Rapee, R. M., Craske, M. G., & Barlow, D. H. (1990). Subject-described features of panic attacks using self-monitoring. *Journal of Anxiety Disorders, 4*, 171–181.

Rapee, R. M., Craske, M. G., & Barlow, D. H. (1995). Assessment instrument for panic disorder that includes fear of sensation-producing activities: The Albany Panic and Phobia Questionnaire. *Anxiety, 1,* 114–122.

Rapee, R. M., Litwin, E. M., & Barlow, D. H. (1990). Impact of life events on subjects with panic disorder and on comparison subjects. *American Journal of Psychiatry, 147,* 640–644.

Rapee, R. M., Mattick, R., & Murrell, E. (1986). Cognitive mediation in the affective component of spontaneous panic attacks. *Journal of Behavior Therapy & Experimental Psychiatry, 17,* 245–253.

Rapee, R. M., & Medoro, L. (1994). Fear of physical sensations and trait anxiety as mediators of the response to hyperventilation in nonclinical subjects. *Journal of Abnormal Psychology, 103,* 693–699.

Razran, G. (1961). The observable unconscious and the inferable conscious in current Soviet psychophysiology: Interoceptive conditioning, semantic conditioning, and the orienting reflex. *Psychological Review, 69,* 81–150.

Reiss, S., Peterson, R. A., Gursky, D. M., & McNally, R. J. (1986). Anxiety sensitivity, anxiety frequency and the predictions of fearfulness. *Behaviour Research and Therapy, 24,* 1–8.

Richards, J., Klein, B., & Carlbring, P. (2003). Internet-based treatment for panic disorder. *Cognitive Behaviour Therapy, 32,* 125–135.

Richards, J. M., & Gross, J. J. (2000). Emotion regulation and memory: The cognitive costs of keeping one's cool. *Journal of Personality and Social Psychology, 79,* 410–424.

Rochat, P., & Striano, T. (1999). Social-cognitive development in the first year. In P. Rochat (Ed.), *Early social cognition: Understanding others in the first months of life* (pp. 3–34). Mahwah, NJ: Erlbaum.

Rodriguez, B. I., & Craske, M. G. (1993). The effects of distraction during exposure to phobic stimuli. *Behaviour Research and Therapy, 31,* 549–558.

Rodriguez, B. I., & Craske, M. G. (1995). Does distraction interfere with fear reduction during exposure? A test among animal-fearful subjects. *Behavior Therapy, 26,* 337–349.

Roshanaei-Moghaddam, B., Pauly, M. C., Atkins, D. C., Baldwin, S. A., Stein, M. B., & Roy-Byrne, P. (2011). Relative effects of CBT and pharmacotherapy in depression versus anxiety: Is medication somewhat better for depression, and CBT somewhat better for anxiety? *Depression and Anxiety, 28,* 560–567.

Roth, W. T., Margraf, J., Ehlers, A., Taylor, C. B., Maddock, R. J., Davies, S., & Agras, W. S. (1992). Stress test reactivity in panic disorder. *Archives of General Psychiatry, 49*(4), 301–310.

Roy-Byrne, P. P., & Cowley, D. S. (1995). Course and outcome in panic disorder: A review of recent follow-up studies. *Anxiety, 1,* 151–160.

Roy-Byrne, P. P., & Cowley, D. S. (2002). Pharmacologic treatments for panic disorder, generalized anxiety disorder, specific phobia and social anxiety disorders. In P. E. Nathan & J. M. Gorman (Eds.), *A guide to treatments that work* (2nd ed., pp. 337–365). New York, NY: Oxford University Press.

Roy-Byrne, P. P., Cowley, D. S., Greenblatt, D. J., Shader, R. I., & Hommer, D. (1990). Reduced benzodiazepine sensitivity in panic disorder. *Archives of General Psychiatry, 47,* 534–538.

Roy-Byrne, P. P., Craske, M. G., & Stein, M. B. (2006). Panic disorder. *Lancet, 368*(9540), 1023–1032.

Roy-Byrne, P. P., Craske, M. G., Stein, M. B., Sullivan, G., Bystritsky, A., Katon, W., … Sherbourne, C. D. (2005). A randomized effectiveness trial of cognitive-behavioral therapy and medication for primary care treatment of panic disorder. *Archives of General Psychiatry, 62,* 290–298.

Roy-Byrne, P. P., Craske, M. G., Sullivan, G., Rose, R. D., Edlund, M. J., Lang, A., … Stein, M. B. (2010). Delivery of evidence-based treatment for multiple anxiety disorders in primary care: A randomized controlled trial. *JAMA, 19*(303), 1921–1928.

Roy-Byrne, P. P., Geraci, M., & Uhde, T. W. (1986). Life events and the onset of panic disorder. *American Journal of Psychiatry, 143,* 1424–1427.

Roy-Byrne, P. P., Stang, P., Wittchen, H.-U., Ustun, B., Walters, E. E., & Kessler, R. C. (2000). Lifetime panic-depression comorbidity in the National Comorbidity Survey: Association with symptoms, impairment, course and help-seeking. *British Journal of Psychiatry, 176,* 229–235.

Roy-Byrne, P. P., Stein, M. B., Russo, J., Mercier, E., Thomas, R., McQuaid, J., … Sherbourne, C. D. (1999). Panic disorder in the primary care setting: Comorbidity, disability, service utilization, and treatment. *Journal of Clinical Psychiatry, 60,* 492–499.

Rueter, M. A., Scaramella, L., Wallace, L. E., & Conger, R. D. (1999). First onset of depressive or anxiety disorders predicted by the longitudinal course of internalizing symptoms and parent–adolescent disagreements. *Archives of General Psychiatry, 56,* 726–732.

Safren, S. A., Gershuny, B. S., Marzol, P., Otto, M. W., & Pollack, M. H. (2002). History of childhood abuse in panic disorder, social phobia, and generalized anxiety disorder. *Journal of Nervous and Mental Disease, 190,* 453–456.

Sakai, Y., Kumano, H., Nishikawa, M., Sakano, Y., Kaiya, H., Imabayashi, E., … Kuboki, T. (2005). Cerebral glucose metabolism associated with a fear network in panic disorder. *Neuroreport, 16*(9), 927–931.

Sakolsky, D. J., McCracken, J. T., & Nurmi, E. L. (2012). Genetics of pediatric anxiety disorders. *Child & Adolescent Psychiatric Clinics of North America, 21*(3), 479–500.

Salkovskis, P. M. (1988). Phenomenology, assessment, and the cognitive model of panic. In S. Rachman & J. D. Maser (Eds.), *Panic: Psychological perspectives* (pp. 111–136). Hillsdale, NJ: Erlbaum.

Salkovskis, P. M., Clark, D. M., & Hackmann, A. (1991). Treatment of panic attacks using cognitive therapy without exposure or breathing retraining. *Behaviour Research and Therapy, 29,* 161–166.

Salkovskis, P. M., Clark, D. M., Hackmann, A., Wells, A., & Gelder, M. G. (1999). An experimental investigation of the role of safety behaviours in the maintenance of panic disorder with agoraphobia. *Behaviour Research and Therapy, 37,* 559–574.

Sanchez-Meca, J., Rosa-Alcazar, A. I., Marin-Martinez, F., & Gomez-Conesa, A. (2010). Psychological treatment of panic disorder with or without agoraphobia: A meta-analysis. *Clinical Psychology Review, 30*(1), 37–50. doi: 10.1016/j.cpr.2009.08.011

Sanderson, W. C., Rapee, R. M., & Barlow, D. H. (1989). The influence of an illusion of control on panic attacks induced via inhalation of 5.5% carbon dioxide-enriched air. *Archives of General Psychiatry, 46,* 157–162.

Sandin, B., Sánchez-Arribas, C., Chorot, P., & Valiente, R. M. (2015). Anxiety sensitivity, catastrophic misinterpretations and panic self-efficacy in the prediction of panic disorder severity: Towards a tripartite cognitive model of panic disorder. *Behaviour Research and Therapy, 67,* 30–40.

Scherrer, J. F., True, W. R., Xian, H., Lyons, M. J., Eisen, S. A., Goldberg, J., … Tsuang, M. T. (2000). Evidence for genetic influences common and specific to symptoms of generalized anxiety and panic. *Journal of Affective Disorders, 57,* 25–35.

Schinka, J. A., Busch, R. M., & Robichaux-Keene, N. (2004). A meta-analysis of the association between the serotonin transporter gene polymorphism (5-HTTLPR) and trait anxiety. *Molecular Psychiatry, 9*(2), 197–202.

Schmidt, N. B., Buckner, J. D., Pusser, A., Woolaway-Bickel, K., Preston, J. L., & Norr, A. (2012). Randomized controlled trial of false safety behavior elimination therapy: A unified cognitive behavioral treatment for anxiety psychopathology. *Behavior Therapy, 43*(3), 518–532.

Schmidt, N. B., Lerew, D. R., & Jackson, R. J. (1997). The role of anxiety sensitivity in the pathogenesis of panic: Prospective evaluation of spontaneous panic attacks during acute stress. *Journal of Abnormal Psychology, 106,* 355–364.

Schmidt, N. B., Lerew, D. R., & Jackson, R. J. (1999). Prospective evaluation of anxiety sensitivity in the pathogenesis of panic: Replication and extension. *Journal of Abnormal Psychology, 108,* 532–537.

Schmidt, N. B., Trakowski, J. H., & Staab, J. P. (1997). Extinction of panicogenic effects of a 35% CO_2 challenge in patients with panic disorder. *Journal of Abnormal Psychology, 106,* 630–638.

Schneider, R. L., Arch, J. J., & Wolitzky-Taylor, K. B. (2015). The state of personalized treatment for anxiety disorders: A systematic review of treatment moderators. *Clinical Psychology Review, 38,* 39–54.

Schneider, S., Houweling, J. E., Gommlich-Schneider, S., Klein, C., Nündel, B., & Wolke, D. (2009). Effect of maternal panic disorder on mother–child interaction and relation to child anxiety and child self-efficacy. *Archives of Women's Mental Health, 12*(4), 251–259.

Schroijen, M., Pappens, M., Schruers, K., Van den Bergh, O., Vervliet, B., & Van Diest, I. (2015). Generalization of fear to respiratory sensations. *Behavior Therapy, 46*(5), 611–626.

Schwartz, O. S., Dudgeon, P., Sheeber, L. B., Yap, M. B., Simmons, J. G., & Allen, N. B. (2012). Parental behaviors during family interactions predict changes in depression and anxiety symptoms during adolescence. *Journal of Abnormal Child Psychology, 40*(1), 59–71.

Segal, Z. V., Williams, J. M., & Teasdale, J. D. (2002). *Mindfulness-based cognitive therapy for depression: A new approach to preventing relapse.* New York, NY: Guilford Press.

Sen, S., Burmeister, M., & Ghosh, D. (2004). Meta-analysis of the association between a serotonin transporter promoter polymorphism (5-HTTLPR) and anxiety-related personality traits. *American Journal of Medical Genetics Part B: Neuropsychiatric Genetics, 127*(1), 85–89.

Shandley, K., Austin, D. W., Klein, B., Pier, C., Schattner, P., Pierce, D., & Wade, V. (2008). Therapist-assisted, internet-based treatment for panic disorder: Can general practitioners achieve comparable patient outcomes to psychologists? *Journal of Medical Internet Research, 10*(2), e14. doi: 10.2196/jmir.1033

Sharp, D., Power, K., & Swanson, V. (2004). A comparison of the efficacy and acceptability of group versus individual cognitive behaviour therapy in the treatment of panic disorder and agoraphobia in primary care. *Clinical Psychology & Psychotherapy, 11*(2), 73–82.

Shear, M. K., Brown, T. A., Barlow, D. H., Money, R., Sholomskas, D. E., Woods, S. W., … Papp, L. A. (1997). Multicenter collaborative panic disorder severity scale. *American Journal of Psychiatry, 154*(11), 1571–1575.

Shear, M. K., Polan, J. J., Harshfield, G., Pickering, T., Mann, J. J., Frances, A., & James, G. (1992). Ambulatory monitoring of blood pressure and heart rate in panic patients. *Journal of Anxiety Disorders, 6*(3), 213–221.

Shear, M. K., Rucci, P., Williams, J., Frank, E., Grochocinski, V., Vander Bilt, J., Houck, P., & Wang, T. (2001). Reliability and validity of the Panic Disorder Severity Scale: Replication and extension. *Journal of Psychiatric Research, 35*(5), 293–296.

Shibuki, K., Hamamura, M., & Yagi, K. (1984). Conditioned heart rate response: Testing under anaesthesia in rats. *Neuroscience Research, 1*, 373–378.

Shioiri, T., Kojima, M., Toshihiro, H., Kitamura, H., Tanaka, A., Yoshizawa, M., … Someya, T. (2005). Dysfunctional baroreflex regulation of sympathetic nerve activity in remitted patients with panic disorder: A new methodological approach. *European Archives of Psychiatry and Clinical Neuroscience, 255*, 293–298.

Siegmund, A., Golfels, F., Finck, C., Halisch, A., Räth, D., Plag, J., & Ströhle, A. (2011). D-cycloserine does not improve but might slightly speed up the outcome of in-vivo exposure therapy in patients with severe agoraphobia and panic disorder in a randomized double blind clinical trial. *Journal of Psychiatric Research, 45*(8), 1042–1047.

Singareddy, R., & Uhde, T. W. (2009). Nocturnal sleep panic and depression: Relationship to subjective sleep in panic disorder. *Journal of Affective Disorders, 112*(1–3), 262–266.

Skapinakis, P., Bellos, S., Koupidis, S., Grammatikopoulos, I., Theodorakis, P. N., & Mavreas, V. (2013). Prevalence and sociodemographic associations of common mental disorders in a nationally representative sample of the general population of Greece. *BMC Psychiatry, 13.* doi: 10.1186/1471-244X-13-163

Slaap, B. R., Nielen, M. M., Boshuisen, M. L., van Roon, A. M., & den Boer, J. A. (2004). Five-minute recordings of heart rate variability in obsessive-compulsive disorder, panic disorder and healthy volunteers. *Journal of Affective Disorders, 78*, 141–148.

Sokolowska, M., Siegel, S., & Kim, J. A. (2002). Intra-administration associations: Conditional hyperalgesia elicited by morphine onset cues. *Journal of Experimental Psychology: Animal Behavior Processes, 28*, 309–320.

Stein, M. B., Schork, N. J., & Gelernter, J. (2008). Gene-by-environment (serotonin transporter and childhood maltreatment) interaction for anxiety sensitivity, an intermediate phenotype for anxiety disorders. *Neuropsychopharmacology, 33*(2), 321–329.

Stein, M. B., Walker, J. R., Anderson, G., Hazen, A. L., Ross, C. A., Eldridge, G., … Forde, D. R. (1996). Childhood physical and sexual abuse in patients with anxiety disorders and a community sample. *American Journal of Psychiatry, 153*, 275–277.

Stewart, R. E., & Chambless, D. L. (2009). Cognitive-behavioral therapy for adult anxiety disorders in clinical practice: A meta-analysis of effectiveness studies. *Journal of Consulting and Clinical Psychology, 77*(4), 595.

Stewart, S. H., Taylor, S., Jang, K. L., Cox, B. J., Watt, M. C., Fedoroff, I. C., & Borger, S. C. (2001). Causal modeling of relations among learning history, anxiety sensitivity, and panic attacks. *Behaviour Research and Therapy, 39*(4), 443–456.

Stonerock, G. L., Hoffman, B. M., Smith, P. J., & Blumenthal, J. A. (2015). Exercise as treatment for anxiety: Systematic review and analysis. *Annals of Behavioral Medicine, 49*(4), 1–15.

Strug, L. J., Suresh, R., Fyer, A. J., Talati, A., Adams, P. B., Li, W., … Weissman, M. M. (2010). Panic disorder is associated with the serotonin transporter gene (SLC6A4) but not the promoter region (5-HTTLPR). *Molecular Psychiatry, 15*(2), 166–176.

Stubbe, D. E., Zahner, G. E. P., Goldstein, M. J., & Leckman, J. F. (1993). Diagnostic specificity of a brief measure of expressed emotion: A community study of children. *Journal of Child Psychology and Psychiatry, 34*, 139–154.

Sturges, L. V., Goetsch, V. L., Ridley, J., & Whittal, M. (1998). Anxiety sensitivity and response to hyperventilation challenge: Physiologic arousal, interoceptive acuity, and subjective distress. *Journal of Anxiety Disorders, 12*, 103–115.

Swinson, R. P., Soulios, C., Cox, B. J., & Kuch, K. (1992). Brief treatment of emergency room patients with panic attacks. *American Journal of Psychiatry, 149*, 944–946.

Sy, J. T., Dixon, L. J., Lickel, J. J., Nelson, E. A., & Deacon, B. J. (2011). Failure to replicate the deleterious effects of safety behaviors in exposure therapy. *Behaviour Research and Therapy, 49*(5), 305–314.

Taylor, C. B., Sheikh, J., Agras, W. S., Roth, W. T., Margraf, J., Ehlers, A., … Gossard, D. (1986). Ambulatory heart rate changes in patients with panic attacks. *American Journal of Psychiatry, 143*, 478–482.

Taylor, S., Koch, W. J., & McNally, R. J. (1992). How does anxiety sensitivity vary across the anxiety disorders? *Journal of Anxiety Disorders, 6*, 249–259.

Taylor, S., Zvolensky, M. J., Cox, B. J., Deacon, B., Heimberg, R. G., Ledley, D. R., … Cardenas, S. J. (2007). Robust dimensions of anxiety sensitivity: Development and initial validation of the Anxiety Sensitivity Index–3. *Psychological Assessment, 19*(2), 176.

Telch, M. J., Kamphuis, J. H., & Schmidt, N. B. (2011). The effects of comorbid personality disorders on cognitive behavioral treatment for panic disorder. *Journal of Psychiatric Research, 45*(4), 469–474.

Telch, M. J., Shermis, M. D., & Lucas, J. A. (1989). Anxiety sensitivity: Unitary personality trait or domain-specific appraisals? *Journal of Anxiety Disorders, 3*, 25–32.

Telch, M. J., Sloan, T., & Smits, J. (2000, November). *Safety-behavior fading as a maintenance treatment for panic disorder.* Symposium presentation at the Annual Meeting of the Association for Advancement of Behavior Therapy, New Orleans, LA.

Telch, M. J., Valentiner, D. P., Ilai, D., Young, P. R., Powers, M. B., & Smits, J. A. J. (2004). Fear activation and distraction during the emotional processing of claustrophobic fear. *Journal of Behavior Therapy and Experimental Psychiatry, 35*, 219–232.

Thayer, J. F., Friedman, B. H., Borkovec, T. D., Johnsen, B. H., & Molina, S. (2000). Phasic heart period reactions to cued threat and nonthreat stimuli in generalized anxiety disorder. *Psychophysiology, 37*, 361–368.

Thyer, B. A., Himle, J., Curtis, G. C., Cameron, O. G., & Nesse, R. M. (1985). A comparison of panic disorder and agoraphobia with panic attacks. *Comprehensive Psychiatry, 26*, 208–214.

Tibi, L., van Oppen, P., Aderka, I. M., van Balkom, A. J., Batelaan, N. M., Spinhoven, P., … Anholt, G. E. (2013). Examining determinants of early and late age at onset in panic disorder: An admixture analysis. *Journal of Psychiatric Research, 47*, 1870–1875.

Treanor, M. (2011). The potential impact of mindfulness on exposure and extinction learning in anxiety disorders. *Clinical Psychology Review, 31*(4), 617–625.

Tsao, J. C. I., Mystkowski, J. L., Zucker, B. G., & Craske, M. G. (2005). Impact of cognitive-behavioral therapy for panic disorder on comorbidity: A controlled investigation. *Behaviour Research and Therapy, 43*, 959–970.

Tull, M. T., & Roemer, L. (2007). Emotion regulation difficulties associated with the experience of uncued panic attacks: Evidence of experiential avoidance, emotional nonacceptance, and decreased emotional clarity. *Behavior Therapy, 38*(4), 378–391.

Turner, S. M., Williams, S. L., Beidel, D. C., & Mezzich, J. E. (1986). Panic disorder and agoraphobia with panic attacks: Covariation along the dimensions of panic and agoraphobic fear. *Journal of Abnormal Psychology, 95*, 384–388.

Uchida, R. R., Del-Ben, C. M., Santos, A. C., Araujo, D., Crippa, J. A., Guiamaraes, F. S., … Graeff, F. G. (2003). Decreased left temporal lobe volume of panic patients measured by magnetic resonance imaging. *Brazilian Journal of Medical and Biological Research, 36*, 925–929.

Uno, T. (1970). The effects of awareness and successive inhibition on interoceptive and exteroceptive conditioning of the galvanic skin response. *Psychophysiology, 7*, 27–43.

van Balkom, A. J., de Beurs, E., Koele, P., Lange, A., & van Dyck, R. (1996). Long-term benzodiazepine use is associated with smaller treatment gain in panic disorder with agoraphobia. *Journal of Nervous and Mental Disease*, *184*(2), 133–135.

van Beek, N., Schruers, K. R. J., & Griez, E. J. L. (2005). Prevalence of respiratory disorders in first-degree relatives of panic disorder patients. *Journal of Affective Disorders*, *87*, 337–340.

van den Heuvel, O. A., Veltman, D. J., Groenewegen, H. J., Witter, M. P., Merkelbach, J., Cath, D. C., … van Dyck, R. (2005). Disorder-specific neuro-anatomical correlates of attentional bias in obsessive-compulsive disorder, panic disorder, and hypochondriasis. *Archives of General Psychiatry*, *62*, 922–933.

van den Hout, M., Arntz, A., & Hoekstra, R. (1994). Exposure reduced agoraphobia but not panic, and cognitive therapy reduced panic but not agoraphobia. *Behaviour Research and Therapy*, *32*, 447–451.

van den Hout, M., Engelhard, I. M., Toffolo, M. B. J., & van Uijen, S. L. (2011). Exposure plus response prevention versus exposure plus safety behaviours in reducing feelings of contamination, fear, danger and disgust: An extended replication of Rachman, Shafran, Radomsky & Zysk (2011). *Journal of Behavior Therapy and Experimental Psychiatry*, *42*(3), 364–370. doi: 10.1016/j.jbtep.2011.02.009

van Duinen, M. A., Schruers, K. R., Maes, M., & Griez, E. J. (2007). CO_2 challenge induced HPA axis activation in panic. *International Journal of Neuro-Psychopharmacology*, *10*(6), 797–804.

Veltman, D. J., van Zijderveld, G., Tilders, F. J. H., & van Dyck, R. (1996). Epinephrine and fear of bodily sensations in panic disorder and social phobia. *Journal of Psychopharmacology*, *10*, 259–265.

Veltman, D. J., van Zijderveld, G. A., van Dyck, R., & Bakker, A. (1998). Predictability, controllability, and fear of symptoms of anxiety in epinephrine-induced panic. *Biological Psychiatry*, *44*, 1017–1026.

Verburg, K., Griez, E., Meijer, J., & Pols, H. (1995). Respiratory disorders as a possible predisposing factor for panic disorder. *Journal of Affective Disorders*, *33*, 129–134.

Verschoor, E., & Markus, C. R. (2012). Physiological and affective reactivity to a 35% CO(2) inhalation challenge in individuals differing in the 5-HTTLPR genotype and trait neuroticism. *European Neuropsychopharmacology*, *22*(8), 546–554.

Vickers, K., Jafarpour, S., Mofidi, A., Rafat, B., & Woznica, A. (2012). The 35% carbon dioxide test in stress and panic research: Overview of effects and integration of findings. *Clinical Psychology Review*, *32*(3), 153–164.

Vøllestad, J., Sivertsen, B., & Nielsen, G. H. (2011). Mindfulness-based stress reduction for patients with anxiety disorders: Evaluation in a randomized controlled trial. *Behaviour Research and Therapy*, *49*(4), 281–288.

Wardle, J., Hayward, P., Higgitt, A., Stabl, M., Blizard, R., & Gray, J. (1994). Effects of concurrent diazepam treatment on the outcome of exposure therapy in agoraphobia. *Behaviour Research and Therapy*, *32*, 203–215.

Ware, J. E. (1993). *SF-36 health survey manual and interpretation guide*. Boston, MA: Health Institute, New England Medical Center.

Warren, R., & Zgourides, G. (1988). Panic attacks in high school students: Implications for prevention and intervention. *Phobia Practice and Research Journal*, *1*, 97–113.

Watson, D., & Clark, L. A. (1984). Negative affectivity: The disposition to experience aversive emotional states. *Psychological Bulletin*, *96*, 465–490.

Watt, M. C., Stewart, S. H., & Cox, B. J. (1998). A retrospective study of the learning history origins of anxiety sensitivity. *Behaviour Research and Therapy*, *36*, 505–525.

Wenzlaff, R. M., & Wegner, D. M. (2000). Thought suppression. *Annual Review of Psychology*, *51*, 59–91.

Westra, H. A., Stewart, S. H., & Conrad, B. E. (2002). Naturalistic manner of benzodiazepine use and cognitive behavioral therapy outcome in panic disorder with agoraphobia. *Journal of Anxiety Disorders*, *16*, 233–246.

Whaley, S. E., Pinto, A., & Sigman, M. (1999). Characterizing interactions between anxious mothers and their children. *Journal of Consulting and Clinical Psychology*, *67*, 826–836.

Wheaton, M. G., Deacon, B. J., McGrath, P. B., Berman, N. C., & Abramowitz, J. S. (2012). Dimensions of anxiety sensitivity in the anxiety disorders: Evaluation of the ASI-3. *Journal of Anxiety Disorders*, *26*(3), 401–408.

Wheeler, E. O., White, P. D., Reed, E. W., & Cohen, M. E. (1950). Neurocirculatory asthenia, anxiety neurosis, effort syndrome, neurasthenia: A 20 year follow-up study of 173 patients. *Journal of the American Medical Association, 142*, 878–889.

White, K. S., & Barlow, D. H. (2002). Panic disorder and agoraphobia. In D. H. Barlow (Ed.), *Anxiety and its disorders: The nature and treatment of anxiety and panic* (pp. 328–379). New York, NY: Guilford Press.

White, K. S., Payne, L. A., Gorman, J. M., Shear, M. K., Woods, S. W., Saksa, J. R., & Barlow, D. H. (2013). Does maintenance CBT contribute to long-term treatment response of panic disorder with or without agoraphobia? A randomized controlled clinical trial. *Journal of Consulting and Clinical Psychology, 81*(1), 47.

Wilkinson, D. J., Thompson, J. M., Lambert, G. W., Jennings, G. L., Schwarz, R. G., Jefferys, D., … Esler, M. D. (1998). Sympathetic activity in patients with panic disorder at rest, under laboratory mental stress, and during panic attacks. *Archives of General Psychiatry, 55*, 511–520.

Williams, S. L., & Falbo, J. (1996). Cognitive and performance-based treatments for panic attacks in people with varying degrees of agoraphobic disability. *Behaviour Research and Therapy, 34*(3), 253–264.

Windmann, S., Sakhavat, Z., & Kutas, M. (2002). Electrophysiological evidence reveals affective evaluation deficits early in stimulus processing in patients with panic disorder. *Journal of Abnormal Psychology, 111*, 357–369.

Wittchen, H.-U., & Essau, C. A. (1991). The epidemiology of panic attacks, panic disorder and agoraphobia. In J. R. Walker, G. R. Norton, & C. A. Ross (Eds.), *Panic disorder and agoraphobia* (pp. 103–149). Monterey, CA: Brooks/Cole.

Wittchen, H.-U., Gloster, A. T., Beesdo-Baum, K., Fava, G. A., & Craske, M. G. (2010). Agoraphobia: A review of the diagnostic classificatory position and criteria. *Depression and Anxiety, 27*, 113–133.

Wittchen, H.-U., Reed, V., & Kessler, R. C. (1998). The relationship of agoraphobia and panic in a community sample of adolescents and young adults. *Archives of General Psychiatry, 55*, 1017–1024.

Wolgast, M., Lundh, L. G., & Viborg, G. (2013). Experiential avoidance as an emotion regulatory function: An empirical analysis of experiential avoidance in relation to behavioral avoidance, cognitive reappraisal, and response suppression. *Cognitive Behaviour Therapy, 42*(3), 224–232.

Wolitzky-Taylor, K. B., Arch, J. J., Rosenfield, D., & Craske, M. G. (2012). Moderators and non-specific predictors of treatment outcome for anxiety disorders: A comparison of cognitive behavioral therapy to acceptance and commitment therapy. *Journal of Consulting and Clinical Psychology, 80*(5), 786–799.

Wolitzky-Taylor, K., Zimmermann, M., Arch, J. J., De Guzman, E., & Lagomasino, I. (2015). Has evidence-based psychosocial treatment for anxiety disorders permeated usual care in community mental health settings? *Behaviour Research and Therapy, 72*, 9–17.

Wood, J., McLeod, B., Sigman, M., Hwang, W., & Chu, B. (2003). Parenting and childhood anxiety: Theory, empirical findings, and future directions. *Journal of Child Psychology and Psychiatry and Allied Disciplines, 44*, 134–151.

Wooley, C. F. (1982). Jacob Mendez DaCosta: Medical teacher, clinician, and clinical investigator. *American Journal of Cardiology, 50*, 1145–1148.

Xuei, X., Flury-Wetherill, L., Dick, D., Goate, A., Tischfield, J., Nurnberger, J., Jr., … Edenberg, H. J. (2010). GABRR1 and GABRR2, encoding the GABA-A receptor subunits ρ1 and ρ2, are associated with alcohol dependence. *American Journal of Medical Genetics Part B: Neuropsychiatric Genetics, 153*(2), 418–427.

Zarate, R., Rapee, R. M., Craske, M. G., & Barlow, D. H. (1988). *Response-norms for symptom induction procedures*. Poster presented at the 22nd Annual AABT Convention, New York, NY.

Zinbarg, R. E., & Barlow, D. H. (1996). Structure of anxiety and the anxiety disorders: A hierarchical model. *Journal of Abnormal Psychology, 105*, 184–193.

Zinbarg, R. E., Barlow, D. H., & Brown, T. A. (1997). Hierarchical structural and general factor saturation of the anxiety sensitivity index: Evidence and implications. *Psychological Assessment, 9*, 277–284.

Zinbarg, R. E., Mineka, S., Craske, M. G., Griffith, J. W., Sutton, J., Rose, R. D., … Waters, A. M. (2010). The Northwestern-UCLA youth emotion project:

Associations of cognitive vulnerabilities, neuroticism and gender with past diagnoses of emotional disorders in adolescents. *Behaviour Research and Therapy, 48*(5), 347–358.

Zlotnick, C., Johnson, J., Kohn, R., Vicente, B., Rioseco, P., & Saldivia, S. (2008). Childhood trauma, trauma in adulthood, and psychiatric diagnoses: Results from a community sample. *Comprehensive Psychiatry, 49*(2), 163–169.

Zucker, B. G., & Craske, M. G. (2001). Prevention of anxiety disorders: A model for intervention. *Applied & Preventive Psychology, 10*, 155–175.

Zvolensky, M. J., & Eifert, G. H. (2001). A review of psychological factors/processes affecting anxious responding during voluntary hyperventilation and inhalations of carbon dioxide-enriched air. *Clinical Psychology Review, 21*(3), 375–400.

Zvolensky, M. J., Kotov, R., Antipova, A. V., & Schmidt, N. B. (2005). Diathesis stress model for panic-related distress: A test in a Russian epidemiological sample. *Behaviour Research and Therapy, 43*, 521–532.

Chapter 4

Generalized Anxiety Disorder

KAREN ROWA, STEPHANIE WAECHTER, HEATHER K. HOOD,
AND MARTIN M. ANTONY

*G*eneralized anxiety disorder (GAD) is characterized by excessive worry about a variety of topics. Until the publication of the revision of the third edition of the *Diagnostic and Statistical Manual of Mental Disorders* (*DSM-III-R*; American Psychiatric Association [APA], 1987), the diagnostic features of this disorder were not well established, and GAD was essentially a residual diagnostic category for individuals with persistent anxiety whose symptoms did not meet criteria for another anxiety disorder. Since the publication of *DSM-III-R* and in each subsequent edition of the *DSM*, the key feature of GAD has been chronic and excessive worry, and GAD is no longer considered a residual category. However, problems with unreliability in the diagnostic criteria, as well as considerable revisions from one version of *DSM* to the next, have taken their toll on the empirical status of knowledge regarding this disorder. Changing criteria have made it difficult for researchers to identify the essential biological and psychological underpinnings of GAD. Until recently, treatment efforts were restricted by the inherent instability of the core features of this disorder. Now, however, GAD has finally begun to receive the research emphasis it deserves, and studies have built a more stable foundation of theory and knowledge regarding the nature and phenomenology of this disorder.

Symptoms and Diagnostic Criteria

The central feature of GAD according to the *Diagnostic and Statistical Manual of Mental Disorders, Fifth Edition* (*DSM-5*; APA, 2013) is excessive worry, occurring on more days than not, about a number of events, activities, or topics. Worry must persist for at least 6 months, and can involve a wide variety of topics such as work or school, finances, health, safety, and minor matters. Interestingly, the worries typically seen in GAD are indistinguishable in content from those reported by nonclinical samples (Becker, Goodwin, Hölting, Hoyer, & Margraf, 2003), although they are distinguishable from cognitions seen in panic disorder (Breitholtz, Johansson, & Öst, 1999) and social anxiety disorder (Hoyer, Becker, & Roth, 2001), and appear to be more future oriented than worries found in other anxiety disorders (Dugas, Gagnon, Ladouceur, & Freeston, 1998). However, the features that seem to best distinguish the worries found in GAD from normal worries include increased frequency and intensity, and the individual's perceived inability to control the worry (Craske, Rapee, Jackel, & Barlow, 1989). As a result of such findings, difficulty controlling the worry was added as a diagnostic criterion in *DSM-IV* (APA, 1994) and remains in *DSM-5*.

In addition to the presence of uncontrollable and persistent worry, the diagnosis of GAD requires the presence of at least three out of six symptoms reflecting physiological or psychological arousal that accompany the worry. These include feeling keyed up, restless, or on edge; difficulty concentrating or having one's mind go blank due to worry; disrupted sleep due to worry; muscle tension; irritability; and fatigue. *DSM-5* requires that a diagnosis of GAD not be made if the worry is better explained by another mental disorder. In addition, because worry is a particularly common feature of depressive disorders, bipolar and related disorders, and psychotic disorders, *DSM-5* states (in the text, rather than the official criteria) that GAD should not be diagnosed if excessive worry occurs only during the course of a disorder from one of these three categories. In other words, to establish a comorbid diagnosis of GAD with depression, bipolar disorder, or a psychotic disorder, the presence of excessive worry should predate the onset of the other condition or continue to be present even during periods of remission from the other disorder (e.g., Uher, Payne, Pavlova, & Perlis, 2014).

As with other diagnoses, the worry and associated symptoms of GAD must lead to significant distress or impairment in a person's life. Further, the symptoms must not be better accounted for by another disorder (e.g., fear of negative evaluation in social anxiety disorder), by another medical condition, or by the use of a substance.

HISTORICAL PERSPECTIVES ON DIAGNOSTIC CRITERIA FOR GAD

Prior to 1980, generalized anxiety disorder symptoms would have likely been subsumed under the broad categories of anxiety reaction (*DSM-I*; APA, 1952) and anxiety neurosis (*DSM-II*; APA, 1968). The diagnosis of GAD was first introduced in *DSM-III* (APA, 1980). To meet criteria for GAD according to the *DSM-III*, three of the following four symptoms needed to be met for at least 1 month: (1) symptoms reflecting startle, tension, and restlessness; (2) symptoms reflecting autonomic hyperactivity; (3) symptoms of anxious apprehension (e.g., worry, rumination); and (4) symptoms of hypervigilance. Thus, according to this diagnostic scheme, worry could be part of the diagnostic picture, but did not need to be present to meet criteria for a diagnosis of GAD. Further, according to *DSM-III*, GAD could be diagnosed only if all other anxiety disorders were ruled out, and none of the anxiety disorders could be diagnosed if another more pervasive problem had been diagnosed (e.g., a depressive or psychotic disorder). Thus, GAD was truly a residual category. The 1-month symptom duration also meant that a broader range of symptom presentations were able to meet criteria because of the inclusion of symptoms of a short duration. Accordingly, the reliability of this diagnostic category was poor (Di Nardo, O'Brien, Barlow, Waddell, & Blanchard, 1983). Changes in the *DSM-III-R* attempted to rectify some of the difficulties with the original diagnostic criteria for GAD, though these changes led to only a small increase in the reliability of the diagnosis (Di Nardo, Moras, Barlow, Rapee, & Brown, 1993). It was in the *DSM-III-R* that for the first time, worry became the central feature of GAD, with excessive worry about at least two life circumstances having to be present. Further, symptoms had to be present for at least 6 months, raising the stringency for meeting criteria for GAD. Although establishing a minimum 6-month duration of symptoms appeared to be a reasonable strategy for increasing the meaningfulness of the diagnosis, more recent research questions whether this duration is necessary (Lee et al., 2009).

DSM-III-R also addressed some of the hierarchical rule-outs that had contributed to GAD's residual status: for example, it allowed the diagnosis of GAD even in the presence of another disorder (except for a mood disorder), as long as the GAD symptoms were not better accounted for by the other disorder. Despite these changes, the associated symptoms of GAD remained somewhat problematic, with the list of possible associated symptoms being too broad (6 out of 18 associated symptoms were required for a GAD diagnosis in *DSM-III-R*). Subsequent research provided useful suggestions for further revision to identify the most relevant associated symptoms. For example, Marten and colleagues (1993) found that symptoms of autonomic arousal (e.g., palpitations) were the least reliable in distinguishing individuals with GAD from nonanxious controls, and therefore these symptoms were removed in *DSM-IV*. More recently, studies have provided additional clarity on the symptoms most distinctively associated with GAD (Aldao, Mennin, Linardatos, & Fresco, 2010).

Prevalence and Epidemiological Factors

It has been difficult to establish prevalence estimates for GAD due to the shifts in diagnostic criteria. The first prevalence estimates based on *DSM-III-R* criteria came from the National Comorbidity Survey. This study found that GAD was relatively rare in terms of current prevalence (1.6%), but was more common (approximately 5%) when lifetime prevalence was examined (Wittchen, Zhao, Kessler, & Eaton, 1994). The replication of the National Comorbidity Survey suggested a lifetime prevalence of GAD of 5.7% (Kessler et al., 2005). Rates of GAD in primary care appear to be even higher. A review of prevalence rates in primary care indicate a median point prevalence of this disorder of 5.8%, suggesting that people with GAD may be more likely to seek medical attention than individuals with other disorders and are therefore more highly represented in primary care settings than in the general population (Roy-Byrne & Wagner, 2004).

In the replication of the National Comorbidity Survey, the median age of onset of GAD was 31 (Kessler et al., 2005). In a study of individuals who presented at an anxiety disorders clinic, mean age of onset was substantially lower at 21 (Brown, Campbell, Lehman, Grisham, & Mancill, 2001). Studies suggest that earlier onset of this disorder is associated with higher levels of symptom severity, comorbidity, and vulnerability to other disorders (Campbell, Brown, & Grisham, 2003).

Studies of the long-term course of GAD suggest that it is a chronic and relapsing disorder with some fluctuation in course. A 5-year follow-up of clients with GAD found that only 18% of these clients achieved full remission at the follow-up assessment compared to 45% of clients with panic disorder (Woodman, Noyes, Black, Schlosser, & Yagla, 1999). A recent 5-year prospective study found that the probability of full remission at some point over the 5 years was 38% and the probability of partial remission was 47%, with accompanying high levels of relapse (Yonkers, Dyck, Warshaw, & Keller, 2000). Results from a longitudinal study of individuals with GAD in primary care revealed a chronic course of illness, in which many individuals experienced periods of symptom improvement or recovery over a 2-year follow-up, with most experiencing a subsequent recurrence of symptoms (Rodriguez et al., 2006). In this study, predictors of chronicity included being female, having greater comorbidity (especially depression and the anxiety disorders), and demonstrating more severe psychosocial impairment. Other predictors of a negative clinical course appear to be certain comorbid disorders (Bruce et al., 2005), such as Cluster B or C personality disorders (Ansell et al., 2011; Yonkers et al., 2000). Decreased life satisfaction and difficult family relationships are also associated with a more severe clinical course (Yonkers et al., 2000).

GAD appears to be more common in women than men, with some estimates indicating that women are almost twice as likely to meet diagnostic criteria for GAD at some time in their lives (McLean, Asnaani, Litz, & Hofmann, 2011). Importantly, these gender differences are associated with different patterns of comorbidity and disability. In one study, men with GAD had higher rates of comorbid alcohol and substance use, whereas women with GAD had higher rates of comorbid mood and anxiety disorders and a greater degree of disability (Vesga-López et al., 2008). One explanation for this gender difference is that women may use less effective strategies to manage worry. One study found that women were more likely than men to use thought suppression and to have a more negative problem orientation in response to worry (Robichaud, Dugas, & Conway, 2003). Other hypotheses suggest that there is a complex, bidirectional interaction of genetic vulnerabilities, such as higher trait anxiety and negative affectivity, with environmental factors, such as gender role socialization, that increases the likelihood that women will develop problems with anxiety and worry (for a review, see McLean & Anderson, 2009).

Minimal research has examined differences in symptom presentation across different ethnic or cultural groups. Theories of the impact of sociocultural factors on the onset of psychological disorders suggest that some racial or ethnic groups may have a greater vulnerability to developing psychological symptoms owing to their differential exposure to stressful events, lower socioeconomic position, and culturally specific beliefs about coping (Dohrenwend & Dohrenwend, 1969). Some studies have found no differences in GAD symptoms across ethnic groups (Ghafoori, Barragan, Tohidian, & Palinkas, 2012), while others show higher endorsement of GAD symptoms by Caucasian individuals (Asnaani, Richey, Dimaite, Hinton, & Hofmann, 2010). Other studies indicate that the content and severity of worry domains are not uniform across ethnic groups. For example, Scott, Eng, and Heimberg (2002) found that African American individuals reported less worry than Asian or Caucasian individuals on the topics of self-confidence, future goals, work competence, and relationship stability. Asian individuals reported more worry than the other groups on future goals, and African Americans reported the most frequent worry about financial issues, despite similar levels of socioeconomic status across the groups.

Although GAD was once considered a minor disorder, the significant impairment associated with it is now well established. Individuals with GAD have functional impairment similar to that of individuals with major depression, and the impairment is worse for those with both conditions (Wittchen, 2002). Some individuals with GAD report severe disability across domains, but particularly in the area of romantic relationships (Henning, Turk, Mennin, Fresco, & Heimberg, 2007). Compared to individuals without GAD, people with GAD also report higher work absences and more health care visits (Toghanian, DiBonaventura, Järbrink, & Locklear, 2014). In addition, compared to nonanxious controls, individuals with GAD report significantly lower overall quality of life and life satisfaction on a wide range of indices, including self-esteem, work, health, and social relationships (Henning et al., 2007).

Comorbidity

Even though GAD was once conceptualized as a "residual disorder" that was most likely a secondary problem, research suggests that a principal diagnosis of GAD is common and that numerous other psychiatric problems often co-occur with it. For example, data from the first National Comorbidity Survey found that 80% of respondents with a principal diagnosis of GAD also had a comorbid mood disorder (Judd et al., 1998). A 32-year longitudinal study found that the onset of GAD was as likely to precede the onset of a major depressive episode as follow it, suggesting that GAD is not simply a secondary condition (Moffitt et al., 2007). Research regarding the comorbidity of GAD, using *DSM-IV* criteria, suggests that a current principal diagnosis of GAD is highly comorbid with other disorders, including panic disorder with or without agoraphobia (41%), social phobia (42%), and major depressive disorder (MDD) (29%) (Brown et al., 2001). Comorbidity rates are even higher when lifetime diagnoses are studied. High rates of comorbidity in GAD are associated with high levels of trait anxiety and negative affect, variables that are consistently elevated in GAD patients (Chambers, Power, & Durham, 2004). In addition, rates of personality disorders are also elevated in individuals with GAD, including avoidant (26%), paranoid (10%), and schizotypal (10%) personality disorders (Brawman-Mintzer et al., 1993). The authors also found that anxiety symptoms per se did not contribute to personality disorder symptoms, suggesting that other variables in these patients (e.g., interpersonal sensitivity) may explain the high comorbidity rates with personality disorders (Mavissakalian, Hamann, Haidar, & de Groot, 1995).

Prospective studies find that rates of comorbidity increased over a 4-year follow-up period for individuals with GAD, and that this comorbidity had negative implications for the likelihood of remission from GAD symptoms (Bruce, Machan, Dyck, & Keller, 2001). Importantly, comorbidity rates appear to diminish with successful treatment (Newman, Przeworski, Fisher, & Borkovec, 2010).

Biological, Psychological, Behavioral, and Environmental Factors

To understand the psychopathology of generalized anxiety disorder, one needs to view it from a biopsychosocial perspective. The following sections review research findings on the neurobiology and psychophysiology of GAD and the social and psychological correlates of this disorder.

Neurobiology

Studies on the neurobiology of generalized anxiety disorder are limited, and no integrated neurobiological theory of the development of the disorder has been put forth. However, studies do implicate certain brain regions and neurotransmitters in understanding this disorder (see Sinha, Mohlman, & Gorman, 2004). A number of neurotransmitter systems have been studied in GAD, each of which has previously been implicated in fear and anxiety. One such neurotransmitter is gamma-aminobutyric acid (GABA). Hypotheses involving GABA in GAD revolve around GABA's inhibitory role in the brain, aiding inhibition of subcortical circuits that are stimulated by threat (Thayer & Lane, 2000). It is thought that individuals with GAD and other anxiety disorders may have decreased GABA activity (Friedman, 2007), which leads to less inhibition of these threat-activated structures. Further, individuals with GAD may also have reduced benzodiazepine receptor sensitivity, which contributes to anxiety because the binding of a benzodiazepine receptor actually facilitates GABA binding, which then inhibits excitatory responses in the brain (Sinha et al., 2004). Research to support these ideas includes the findings that (a) GABA receptors appear to be densely congregated in brain areas implicated in fear and anxiety, such as the frontal cortex, hippocampus, and amygdala (Petrovich & Swanson, 1997); (b) binding of a benzodiazepine to its receptor appears to increase the ability of GABA receptors to bind with available GABA (Goddard & Charney, 1997); and (c) benzodiazepines appear to be an effective treatment for GAD (reviewed later in this chapter).

Norepinephrine has also been implicated in GAD; however, data regarding the role of norepinephrine in GAD are mixed. Norepinephrine is the primary neurotransmitter in the sympathetic nervous system, which is the system responsible for the fight-or-flight response. Studies have demonstrated that norepinephrine levels are elevated in certain other anxiety disorders (e.g., Ballenger, 2001), raising the possibility that norepinephrine may also be elevated in GAD. However, other studies have been equivocal (see Sinha et al., 2004). To date, the majority of studies that have examined the role of norepinephrine in GAD have found no differences between clinical and control groups, despite the use of various methodologies and biological challenges (Kalk, Nutt, & Lingford-Hughes, 2011).

Serotonin (5-HT) is also broadly implicated across the anxiety disorders, with studies suggesting that low levels of serotonin or serotonin receptor dysfunction, particularly in the midbrain region, are linked with increased anxiety (Nikolaus, Antke, Beu, & Müller, 2010). However, studies of serotonin in GAD have also yielded inconclusive results. Some studies have found that serotonin agonists lead to increased anxiety in GAD (Germine, Goddard, Woods, Charney, & Heninger, 1992).

Cholecystokinin (CCK) has been linked to the panic attacks sometimes seen in GAD. One study found that a CCK agonist induced panic attacks in 71% of participants with GAD as compared to 14% of control participants (Brawman-Mintzer et al., 1997). However, studies have failed to find an anxiolytic effect of CCK receptor antagonists (Adams, Pyke, Costa, & Cutler, 1995).

Cortisol levels, which suggest increased functioning of the limbic-hypothalamic-pituitary-adrenal (LHPA) axis, are also hallmark biochemical markers of stress and anxiety. Some evidence of overproduction of cortisol in GAD exists, though research findings are not consistent (Tiller, Biddle, Maguire, & Davies, 1988). A recent study provided evidence implicating hyperactivity of the hypothalamic-pituitary-adrenal (HPA) axis in GAD, in which elevated salivary cortisol levels were significantly reduced following selective serotonin reuptake inhibitor (SSRI) treatment for GAD, and reduced cortisol was associated with lower reported anxiety (Lenze et al., 2011). There tends to be a more consistent relationship in older adults between GAD symptom severity and elevated cortisol levels, perhaps due to age-associated alterations in the HPA axis (Mantella et al., 2008).

There have been few neuroimaging studies completed in GAD. Those that have been completed suggest larger amygdala volumes in children with GAD (De Bellis et al., 2000), and in adults, larger superior temporal gyrus volumes (De Bellis et al., 2002), lower metabolic rates in the basal ganglia (Wu et al., 1991), and hypermetabolism in the prefrontal cortex (Wu et al., 1991). Recent studies have also identified decreased hypothalamus volumes as a possible risk factor for lifetime GAD. For example, Hettema and colleagues (2012) collected neuroimaging data from a small sample of female monozygotic twin pairs and found that lifetime GAD diagnosis and genetic risk for internalizing disorders significantly predicted smaller left hippocampal volumes. Other studies have noted decreased bilateral hippocampal volumes among individuals with GAD (Terlevic et al., 2013). Structural and functional neuroanatomical studies have identified increased amygdala volumes among individuals with GAD compared to healthy controls, and disrupted connectivity of the amygdala with other cortical and subcortical regions involved in anticipatory anxiety and emotional processing of threat (Etkin, Prater, Hoeft, Menon, & Schatzberg, 2010).

In a study of adolescents with GAD, neuroimaging revealed greater activation in response to angry faces in the right ventrolateral prefrontal cortex, but this activation had a negative relationship with subjective anxiety levels. This finding is inconsistent with other imaging studies, which have found a positive relationship between anxiety levels and prefrontal cortex activation (Monk et al., 2006). To explain this discrepancy, the authors postulated that activation in the prefrontal cortex may play a compensatory function, helping to regulate activation in subcortical structures. In support of this hypothesis, a follow-up study by Monk et al. (2008) found that adolescents with GAD showed hyperactivation of the right amygdala in response to masked angry faces compared to healthy controls. Further, functional connectivity between the right amygdala and the right ventrolateral prefrontal cortex was weaker in the GAD group, suggesting that the ventrolateral prefrontal cortex in GAD individuals may be less effective at downregulating the amygdala response to threatening emotional stimuli.

Studies have also noted a similar inhibitory role of the prefrontal cortex in adults with GAD, particularly in the anterior cingulate cortex, a region of the medial prefrontal cortex. For example, Tromp et al. (2012) found structural abnormalities in the connectivity of the anterior cingulate cortex and the amygdala. Further, two studies have found that pretreatment activity in the anterior cingulate cortex was associated with better response to an 8-week trial of venlafaxine for patients with GAD (Nitschke et al., 2009; Whalen et al., 2008). Taken together, these studies suggest that the anterior cingulate cortex and the amygdala may be integral to understanding the emotional processing deficits seen in GAD.

PSYCHOPHYSIOLOGY

Chronic worry is also associated with reduced autonomic variability during stressful tasks. This recent focus on the inhibitory function of the parasympathetic nervous system has helped in understanding central nervous system functioning in GAD. Earlier studies tended to focus more exclusively on the excitation end of the equation (Friedman, 2007).

However, as Friedman (2007) points out, physiological variability is actually the most effective way that organisms can maintain stability of their systems. The more variability an organism can show in responding to threat cues (a sympathetic system function) and recovering from threat cues (a parasympathetic system function), the more able to adapt to the environment the organism is likely to be. Thus, autonomic rigidity is thought to lead to less adaptive behavioral and emotional responses to stressful events in comparison to an adaptive system where a more flexible autonomic system can help a person organize his or her physiological responses (Porges, 1995). Thus, autonomic rigidity may play an important role in maintaining GAD.

The most commonly used marker of autonomic rigidity is lower levels of heart rate variability in response to various stressors. Research suggests that individuals with GAD demonstrate lower heart rate variability during periods of worry and rest, decreased parasympathetic activity during periods of worry and rest (Thayer, Friedman, & Borkovec, 1996), and impaired habituation of heart rate activity to neutral words (Thayer, Friedman, Borkovec, Molina, & Johnsen, 2000). Although there is evidence that all anxiety disorders are characterized by reduced baseline heart rate variability compared to healthy controls, heart rate variability is associated with symptom severity only in GAD (Pittig, Arch, Lam, & Craske, 2013). This finding may suggest that decreased heart rate variability reflects a shared biological dysfunction across anxiety disorders, but the specific manifestation of this feature may vary across disorders. However, autonomic rigidity in worry has not been consistently demonstrated, with one study finding no evidence for autonomic rigidity as measured by heart rate variability during periods of relaxation, nonstressful cognitive tasks, worry, and negative imagery (Davis, Montgomery, & Wilson, 2002). Thus, more research is still necessary to fully understand the rigidity of the physiological system underlying GAD.

In summary, neurobiological indices suggest that individuals with GAD have a dys-regulated central nervous system that may take longer to recover from a stressor than individuals without GAD. Further, the suppressed and rigid autonomic activity that is associated with worry may have implications for the maintenance of worry, providing individuals with short-term avoidance of physiological responses to stress, but impairing long-term adaptation to these stressors. These ideas will be discussed more thoroughly in the following sections (see, especially, the section on avoidance theories of worry). However, there still exist many inconsistencies across studies on the neurobiology of GAD, and further research is necessary to aid in the development of a more coherent understanding of the neurobiology of GAD.

COGNITIVE AND BEHAVIORAL CORRELATES OF GAD

Life Events

A small body of research has investigated the role that stressful life events might play in the development of chronic worry and GAD. An early study found that the presence of at least one stressful life event defined as unexpected, negative, and very important was associated with an increased risk of developing GAD symptoms (Blazer, Hughes, & George, 1987). This association was even more dramatic for men who had experienced more than four stressful life events; these men had a risk of GAD that was over eight times greater than men reporting zero to three life events. In addition, stressful life events appear to predict relapse in previously remitted GAD patients, although specific worry themes were not strongly related to the likelihood of relapse (Francis, Moitra, Dyck, & Keller, 2012). It appears that stressful life events may be a general risk factor for the development and relapse of a depressive or anxiety disorder, perhaps because stressful life events alter the stress response and, consequently, activity of the HPA axis, creating a vulnerability to psychopathology (Faravelli et al., 2012).

Problem-Solving Ability

Researchers have also questioned the association between chronic, elevated worry and problem-solving ability in understanding GAD. Worrying has been conceptualized as an attempt to anticipate or solve real-life problems (Tallis, Davey, & Capuzzo, 1994), and worry frequency is related to constructive, problem-focused coping (Davey, Hampton, Farrell, & Davidson, 1992). However, at some point, the worry process as constructive problem solving breaks down. Davey et al. (1992) hypothesized that pathological worry may be associated with either poor problem-solving ability or poor confidence in problem solving, which would prevent individuals from reaching acceptable solutions to perceived problems, leading to further worry.

Interestingly, individuals with chronic worry do not have deficits in problem-solving ability (Dugas, Freeston, & Ladouceur, 1997), but do hold a negative problem orientation in response to problems (Belzer, D'Zurilla, & Maydeu-Olivares, 2002). Negative problem orientation refers to dysfunctional attitudes (e.g., low confidence) about one's own ability to solve problems. Individuals with GAD tend to have a more negative problem orientation than individuals with other anxiety disorders (Ladouceur et al., 1999) and controls (Dugas, Gagnon, et al., 1998). In a sample of individuals with mood and anxiety disorders, Fergus, Valentiner, Wu, and McGrath (2015) showed that negative problem orientation was more strongly associated with worry than other mood and anxiety symptoms. Negative problem orientation, together with intolerance of uncertainty, were also the strongest predictors of worry severity, and differentiated individuals with moderate and severe GAD symptoms from those with mild GAD symptoms (Dugas et al., 2007). Further, manipulating problem-solving confidence through false feedback has been found to result in higher anxiety and personal worry (Davey, Jubb, & Cameron, 1996). This study lends credence to the notion that low problem-solving confidence may play a causal role in determining subsequent levels of worry.

Results for problem-solving ability in relation to orientation are similar to those found when examining the relationship between time management and worry. Worry has been found to have no relationship with time management behaviors (e.g., setting goals, employing organizational skills), but does have a negative relationship with time structure and purpose (e.g., possessing the notion that one's time use has a purpose, being present-focused, demonstrating persistence when completing tasks) (Kelly, 2003). Thus, pathological worry as seen in GAD is likely influenced by the thoughts and feelings individuals have toward their problem-solving abilities and the perception that they are not using their time for a purpose.

Studies have also examined the strategies people with GAD use in response to their chronic worry. Similar to strategies used by individuals with other anxiety disorders, individuals with GAD reported a greater use of worry (e.g., thinking about more minor problems) and punishment (e.g., shouting at oneself) strategies than did nonanxious controls, and less use of distraction (e.g., thinking about something else) and social control (e.g., talking to a friend) strategies (Coles & Heimberg, 2005). Chronic worriers also appear to catastrophize about positive aspects of their lives as well as hypothetical situations (Davey & Levy, 1998).

Probability Overestimation and Catastrophizing

Excessive worry, the defining feature of GAD, is essentially a cognitive phenomenon. Adults with GAD (Provencher, Freeston, Dugas, & Ladouceur, 2000) and childhood worriers (Suarez & Bell-Dolan, 2001) exhibit cognitive errors that include probability overestimation (thinking a feared consequence is more likely to occur than it really is) and catastrophizing (assuming that an outcome will be much less manageable than it actually is). Estimates of the cost of one's worry are related to worry severity, such that greater cost estimates are linked with greater worry severity (Berenbaum, Thompson, & Pomerantz, 2007).

Information Processing Biases in Worry

Individuals with GAD pay greater attention to threatening stimuli, preferentially encode this information, interpret ambiguous stimuli as threatening, and have biases in memory for threatening events. Through such processes, individuals have greater access to frightening and threatening information, leading to increased states of anxiety. Thus, these attentional biases are hypothesized to play a potential causal role in the development of anxiety disorders (see Van Bockstaele et al., 2014, for a review). A meta-analysis examining threat-related attentional biases in anxiety found that the anxiety disorders, including GAD, are characterized by heightened attentional and memory biases for threat (Bar-Haim, Lamy, Pergamin, Bakermans-Kranenburg, & van IJzendoorn, 2007). Importantly, these biases are robust across a variety of experimental paradigms, age groups, and stimuli that require conscious processing and that are presented subliminally. Specific characteristics of these attentional biases include selective attention toward, difficulty disengaging from, and attentional avoidance of threatening stimuli (Cisler & Koster, 2010).

Research using the emotional Stroop paradigm has provided evidence for a cognitive bias in GAD (Mogg & Bradley, 2005). In the emotional Stroop paradigm, participants are presented with threatening and neutral words presented in different colors. Participants are asked to quickly name the color of the word, while ignoring the meaning of the word. The inability to ignore the meaning of the word (thus suggesting preferential encoding of threat meanings) is deduced from slower color naming. Individuals with GAD appear to have difficulty with the Stroop task, taking longer to name the colors of threatening words (e.g., "disgrace") than nonthreatening words (e.g., "carpet") (Mathews & MacLeod, 1985). This result is consistent when stimuli involve general threat words (Martin, Williams, & Clark, 1991), when stimuli are relevant to the participant's idiosyncratic concerns (Mathews & Klug, 1993), and when stimuli are general emotional words, including positive emotional words (Becker, Rinck, Margraf, & Roth, 2001). Further, the Stroop effect is also seen when word stimuli are masked: that is, when words are followed by a masking stimulus designed to restrict the participant's conscious awareness of the word (Bradley, Mogg, Millar, & White, 1995). This attentional bias appears to be modifiable by treatment, such that color-naming interference in GAD participants is ameliorated by cognitive-behavioral therapy (CBT; Mogg, Bradley, Millar, & White, 1995).

The visual dot-probe task is another paradigm for studying attentional biases in GAD. Individuals are asked to respond to a probe stimulus (e.g., a small dot) presented on a screen. Just prior to this probe stimulus, participants are presented with stimuli on the screen, one of which is the experimental stimulus (e.g., a threatening word or face). If participants respond more quickly to a probe stimulus that appears in the same spot as the threatening stimulus, it is assumed that the participant was attending to that threat cue, and is therefore demonstrating an attentional bias for the threat cue. Individuals with GAD demonstrate an attentional bias on this task in response to threat words (MacLeod, Mathews, & Tata, 1986), negative words (Mogg, Bradley, & Williams, 1995), emotional faces (Bradley, Mogg, White, Groom, & de Bono, 1999), and aversive pictures (MacNamara & Hajcak, 2010). Further, this bias is also demonstrated when stimuli are masked, suggesting that the processing of threat cues may not be at a conscious level (Mogg, Bradley, Millar, et al., 1995). Individuals with GAD were more likely to look at threat faces rather than neutral faces in a visual probe task than were nonanxious controls and individuals with depression (Mogg, Millar, & Bradley, 2000).

Individuals with GAD also appear to interpret ambiguous stimuli in a negative or threatening manner. For example, when presented with a number of homophones with both a threatening and nonthreatening meaning (e.g., "die" versus "dye") and asked to write out these words, individuals with GAD tend to write down a greater proportion of the threatening spellings of these words than do control participants (Mogg, Baldwin, Brodrick, & Bradley, 2004). Similarly, when GAD participants are presented with sentences that have a threatening or nonthreatening interpretation and are then asked to pick out recognized sentences whose meaning has been clarified by context, they have better recognition for the sentences that were given a threatening meaning by context compared to those given a nonthreatening meaning (Eysenck, Mogg, May, Richards, & Mathews, 1991).

Biases in memory for threatening cues have also been studied in GAD. Researchers have hypothesized that individuals with GAD would demonstrate better memory for threatening than nonthreatening stimuli, and also that compared to control participants, they would demonstrate enhanced memory for threatening stimuli. Support for memory biases in GAD is not as consistent as the support for other types of cognitive biases. Generally, individuals with GAD do not appear to preferentially recall more threatening stimuli (e.g., Becker, Roth, Andrich, & Margraf, 1999), though there are exceptions to these findings. For example, memory biases in GAD tend to be more pronounced when the stimulus words are ideographically selected and more personally relevant to the participant (Coles, Turk, & Heimberg, 2007).

However, several studies have found an implicit memory bias in GAD such that threatening information may be preferentially activated in individuals with GAD even when stimuli are not consciously perceived. For example, MacLeod and McLaughlin (1995) presented threatening and nonthreatening words to individuals with GAD and nonanxious controls, and then asked these participants to identify briefly presented words. Individuals with GAD were more readily able to identify the threatening words. Although there is other evidence for an implicit memory bias in GAD, results are still equivocal (for a review, see MacLeod & Rutherford, 2004).

Clearly, individuals with GAD demonstrate a number of biases for threat-relevant information, and these biases may be an important aspect of the development and maintenance of this disorder. What is still unclear is the relationship between these cognitive biases and the physiology of GAD. One would assume that preferentially encoding threat information would lead to sympathetic arousal, but as reviewed earlier, individuals with GAD do not demonstrate such arousal. In addition, the mechanisms underlying these attentional biases are not fully understood. Various models propose that attentional biases are mediated by impairment in the attentional control system, inappropriate use of emotion regulation strategies, specific neural mechanisms (e.g., activation in the amygdala and prefrontal cortex), and stage of information processing (for a review, see Cisler & Koster, 2010). Although each of these mediating variables accounts for some facets of the observed attentional biases, a comprehensive model incorporating these aspects has yet to be tested. A comprehensive model would help to guide studies of the mechanisms of action of CBT and possibly identify specific treatment targets.

Avoidance Theories of Worry

Researchers have proposed that individuals engage in worry to cope with perceived threat (see Borkovec, Alcaine, & Behar, 2004). The cognitive avoidance theory of worry proposes that worry is an attempt at cognitive avoidance, which is similar in function to the behavioral avoidance seen in many types of anxiety disorders. In other words, the verbal activity of worry distracts individuals from the full experience of fear (e.g., feared imagery, sensations of arousal, etc.) and other negative emotional states. Evidence for the notion of worry as cognitive avoidance stems from a number of lines of research. Studies suggest that worry is primarily a verbal and linguistic activity rather than an imagery-based process (Behar, Zuellig, & Borkovec, 2005). Further, worry tends to be less concrete and more abstract (Stöber, 1998) than other types of thought, making it less likely to activate emotional processing. Verbal recounting of feared material is thought to produce less sympathetic nervous system response than imagining feared images. Thus, worry in the face of perceived threat would be negatively reinforced because it allows a person to experience a reduction in distress and arousal in the short term when confronted by a stressful trigger (e.g., a deadline at work or a family member's illness).

College students who meet diagnostic criteria for GAD report more use of worry to distract themselves from emotional topics than do control participants (Borkovec & Roemer, 1995). For example, an individual with GAD might worry about a number of topics (e.g., work, finances, relationships) to avoid confronting in depth the emotions associated with his or her most feared scenario (e.g., an ill parent dying). People with GAD report higher levels of experiential avoidance than do control individuals (Roemer, Salters, Raffa, & Orsillo, 2005), and self-reported worriers avoid anxiety-provoking images even when instructed to attend to them (Laguna, Ham, Hope, & Bell, 2004). Worrying appears to provide only short-term benefit, and is associated with increased arousal in the long term (Wells & Papageorgiou, 1995). Borkovec et al. (2004) suggest that worrying may ultimately interfere with emotional processing of stressful stimuli. Thus, just as situational avoidance provides only short-term but not long-term reduction in anxiety, worry does the same.

In partial support of this cognitive avoidance model of worry, Stapinski, Abbott, and Rapee (2010) found that individuals instructed to worry in response to an anxiety-provoking trigger maintained threat expectancies and decreased perceptions of control compared to those who used imaginal processing or relaxation/distraction. However, contrary to predictions, worry did not reduce physiological arousal relative to imaginal processing or relaxation, as denoted by increased skin conductance. In addition, there was no long-term maintenance of worry among those in the worry condition, suggesting that worry is not necessarily a self-perpetuating process and the effects of worry may be short-term.

Newman and Llera (2011) proposed an extension and modification of the cognitive avoidance theory that focuses on experiential avoidance in GAD. Specifically, their contrast avoidance model draws on evidence that worry does not necessarily enable avoidance of negative emotional experiences; instead, individuals with GAD use worry to avoid sharp increases in negative emotions, also known as negative contrast (Llera & Newman, 2010). They posited that the chronic distress associated with worry helps individuals prepare for negative events and precludes an increase in distress should the negative outcome occur. Further, the positive contrast between anxiety-related distress and relief is heightened when the anticipated negative outcome fails to occur. Evidence for this model comes from Llera and Newman (2014), who asked participants with GAD and nonanxious controls to worry or relax prior to exposure to emotional film clips. Both self-reported emotional changes and skin conductance changes were collected. The worry condition resulted in higher negative emotionality compared to baseline for all participants, which remained during the film clips. In contrast, low emotion during relaxation and neutral inductions led to sharp increases in negative emotionality for all participants in response to the film clips. Importantly, GAD participants reported that the worry condition helped them to cope with the film clips, while the controls reported the opposite. Although this model requires further empirical support, it appears to provide a synthesis of the extant literature.

Intolerance of Uncertainty

Dugas, Buhr, and Ladouceur (2004) have proposed that a central difficulty in GAD involves an individual's tendency to react negatively to uncertain or ambiguous situations, sometimes preferring a negative outcome to an uncertain one. They suggest that intolerance of uncertainty is a cognitive filter through which a person with GAD views his or her world. Because many events and situations are characterized by uncertainty, the outcome of having this filter is an enhanced likelihood of worrying.

Intolerance of uncertainty is increasingly being recognized as a transdiagnostic feature across anxiety and mood disorders. In a recent study comparing intolerance of uncertainty across diagnostic groups, individuals with GAD, social anxiety disorder (SAD), obsessive-compulsive disorder (OCD), and major depressive disorder (MDD) reported significantly greater intolerance of uncertainty compared to undergraduate and community samples, though there were no differences among the clinical groups (Carleton, Mulvogue, et al., 2012). This study suggests that intolerance of uncertainty may represent a vulnerability factor for mood and anxiety symptoms. A taxometric analysis indicated that intolerance of uncertainty is not a categorical variable that differentiates diagnostic groups, but rather a continuous variable that appears to be present in varying degrees in the general population (e.g., community members; Carleton, Weeks, et al., 2012). These data are consistent with the interpretation that intolerance of uncertainty may be an underlying vulnerability factor for the development of psychopathology.

Studies suggest that intolerance of uncertainty is related to worry in nonclinical participants (Freeston, Rhéaume, Letarte, Dugas, & Ladouceur, 1994) and is elevated in individuals with GAD (Dugas, Gagnon, et al., 1998). Although some studies indicate that elevated levels of intolerance of uncertainty are specific to GAD (e.g., Dugas, Marchand, & Ladouceur, 2005), this is likely an artifact of the measures used to assess intolerance of uncertainty. For example, a meta-analysis found that intolerance of uncertainty was more strongly related to GAD when using a definition of intolerance of uncertainty developed specifically for GAD, and similarly associated with OCD, MDD, and GAD when using an OCD-specific definition (Gentes & Ruscio, 2011). Carleton, Mulvogue, et al. (2012) found that self-reported intolerance of uncertainty in individuals with GAD did not differ from that of individuals with other emotional disorders (e.g., social anxiety disorder, obsessive-compulsive disorder, or depression).

Experimental manipulation of intolerance of uncertainty has shown that increasing participants' level of intolerance of uncertainty leads to increased catastrophic worrying and low mood (Meeten, Dash, Scarlet, & Davey, 2012). Further, time-series analyses of the temporal sequence of change in CBT for GAD found that, for the majority of participants, changes in intolerance of uncertainty preceded changes in time spent worrying (Dugas, Langlois, Rhéaume, & Ladouceur, 1998). Thus, evidence is accumulating to suggest that intolerance of uncertainty may play a causal role in the development or exacerbation of pathological worry in GAD.

Researchers have also studied the relationship between intolerance of uncertainty and other variables demonstrated to be important in understanding GAD. For example, intolerance of uncertainty and negative problem orientation both contribute to the prediction of worry in nonclinical (Dugas et al., 1997) and clinical (Dugas et al., 2007) samples. Intolerance of uncertainty has also been linked to an information processing bias, such that participants high in intolerance of uncertainty recalled a greater proportion of words involving uncertainty (e.g., "inconclusive" and "unclear") and were more concerned about ambiguous situations than participants low in intolerance of uncertainty (Dugas, Hedayati, et al., 2005). In a replication and extension of this study, Koerner and Dugas (2008) found that individuals high in intolerance of uncertainty were more likely to make negative appraisals of ambiguous scenarios than those low in intolerance of uncertainty, even after controlling for gender, low mood, and GAD severity. Further, negative appraisals mediated the relationship between intolerance of uncertainty and worry, and, conversely, worry was a partial mediator of the relationship between intolerance of uncertainty and negative appraisals. This indicates that intolerance of uncertainty represents a cognitive vulnerability for the development of mood and anxiety symptoms only when other cognitive biases are present. Although it is not clear how these cognitive biases develop, Dugas et al. (2004) theorized that intolerance of uncertainty might affect people's perception of their problem-solving abilities, such that they feel less capable of effectively solving problems as they arise, leading to pathological worry instead of problem solutions.

Metacognition and GAD

Wells (e.g., Wells, 1999) has proposed a metacognitive model of GAD that involves positive and negative beliefs about worry, as well as two types of worry content. Metacognition refers to the act of thinking about one's thought processes. Wells (1999) suggests that it is not typical worry per se that is the most significant problem in GAD, but rather the way one thinks about and reacts to this typical worry. Type 1 worry refers to this so-called typical worry—worry triggered by everyday events (e.g., worries about health, safety, or relationships). Type 2 worry consists of worry about these cognitive processes, or in other words, *worry about worry*. In this model, Wells proposes that positive beliefs that a person holds about worry (e.g., "Worry will help me cope") cause a person to actively select worry as a coping strategy when faced with some sort of stressor. As a result, Type 1 worry is activated. In some circumstances, the process of worry is terminated by a felt sense that the person will be able to cope with the particular stressor. However, if this felt sense is *not* achieved, Type 2 beliefs about worry might be activated. These might include beliefs that worry is uncontrollable and/or beliefs that worrying might have negative mental or physical consequences for an individual. The activation of Type 2 worry is thought to produce excessive levels of anxiety, as well as to lead to unhelpful behavioral coping and thought control strategies, such that Type 2 worries cannot be disconfirmed and the worry cycle is maintained. For example, an increase in anxiety interferes with a person's ability to achieve a felt sense that he or she can cope, so the person begins to avoid feared situations as a means of coping. Unfortunately, avoidance of the situations that trigger worry does not allow the person to experience disconfirmatory information about the impact of worry on his or her functioning.

Studies confirm that individuals hold both positive and negative beliefs about worrying. For example, Davey, Tallis, and Capuzzo (1996) found that individuals' beliefs about worrying clustered into three factors representing negative consequences (i.e., worry disrupting performance, worry exaggerating the problem, and worry causing emotional distress), and two factors representing positive consequences (i.e., worry as motivation and worry as helping analytical thinking). Cartwright-Hatton and Wells (1997) developed the Meta-Cognitions Questionnaire, and found that three subscales uniquely predicted worry: positive beliefs about worry, negative beliefs about the controllability of thoughts, and cognitive confidence (i.e., lack of confidence in one's cognitive skills). In a case study of CBT for an individual with GAD, modifying positive beliefs about worry led to positive treatment outcomes (Borkovec, Hazlett-Stevens, & Diaz, 1999). Although it is clear that positive beliefs about worry are an important aspect of GAD, they are not the most robust predictor of GAD severity (Dugas et al., 2007) and they are not considered unique to GAD (Penney, Mazmanian, & Rudanycz, 2013).

In contrast, negative beliefs that worry is uncontrollable or dangerous appear to be central to the maintenance of GAD symptoms. Studies have provided support for the presence of Type 2 worry and its unique association with pathological worry, even when Type 1 worries and trait anxiety are controlled (Wells & Carter, 1999). For example, Ruscio and Borkovec (2004) compared the appraisals of worry following a stressor task by high worriers with and without GAD. They found that individuals with GAD were more likely to endorse beliefs that worry was uncontrollable and dangerous, and reported lower confidence in their cognitive abilities. However, the groups did not differ in their positive beliefs about worry. In a follow-up study with a nonclinical sample, negative beliefs about the uncontrollability and dangerousness of worry, but not positive beliefs about worry, mediated the relationship between trait worry and GAD symptoms (Penney et al., 2013). These results suggest that individuals with high trait worry who perceive their worry as dangerous or uncontrollable are more likely to experience GAD. There is also evidence of the specificity of meta-worry to GAD. Individuals with GAD scored higher on measures of meta-worry than did nonclinical control participants and nonworried anxious controls (Davis & Valentiner, 2000), as well as individuals with social phobia, panic disorder, depression (Wells & Carter, 2001), and OCD (Barahmand, 2009). Clearly, the role of metacognitive factors in GAD has provided a useful way of understanding why individuals with GAD routinely choose worry as a coping strategy.

EMOTIONAL CORRELATES

Individuals with GAD may have difficulties with emotion regulation (Mennin, Heimberg, Turk, & Fresco, 2005). More specifically, individuals with GAD may experience more intense emotions; have more difficulty naming, understanding, and accepting emotions (especially negative emotions); and demonstrate difficulty regulating negative emotions that do occur (Mennin et al., 2005). Although each of these emotion regulation deficits appears to be present in other disorders, heightened intensity of emotion is a particularly strong predictor of GAD, differentiating GAD from social anxiety and major depressive disorder and suggesting that there may be some disorder specificity in emotion regulation deficits (Mennin, Holaway, Fresco, Moore, & Heimberg, 2007).

Individuals with GAD report being more fearful of depression and having more intense emotions than do individuals with social phobia and nonanxious controls (Turk, Heimberg, Luterek, Mennin, & Fresco, 2005). In an experimental study in which fear of anxiety was manipulated, nonclinical participants in the increased fear of anxiety condition reported significantly greater worry following an anxiety-provoking task than those in the decreased fear of anxiety group (Buhr & Dugas, 2009). Fear of anxiety has been shown to predict worry over and above other variables associated with worry, including avoidance and intolerance of uncertainty (Buhr & Dugas, 2012). Further, self-reported worry has been associated with general and specific emotion regulation deficits, including deficits in the ability to engage in goal-directed activity when distressed, control over impulses, acceptance of emotions, clarity of emotional state, and access to self-regulation strategies, even when controlling for general negative affect (Salters-Pedneault, Roemer, Tull, Rucker, & Mennin, 2006). Mennin et al. (2005) found that students who endorsed criteria for GAD on a questionnaire had a stronger physiological reaction to a mood induction than did controls, and reported more difficulty accepting and influencing their emotional state than controls. Thus, there is preliminary evidence that emotion regulation deficits may be an important variable for understanding the chronic worry seen in GAD.

Individuals with GAD may also find their worry process affected by preexisting negative emotional states. Davey and colleagues (e.g., Startup & Davey, 2001, 2003) found evidence for a "mood-as-input" approach to understanding perseverative, catastrophic worry like that found in GAD. They suggest that individuals who have pathological worry use rules in order to decide when to stop worrying. The stop rules they have identified are (a) "feel like continuing," which is when individuals continue to try to solve a problem until they do not feel like continuing to work on it, and (b) "as many as can," which is when individuals persist with problem-solving attempts until they feel they have generated as many possible responses as they possibly can (Davey, 2006). When the "as many as can" stop rule is paired with negative mood, the person is unlikely to feel that he or she has generated as many possible responses as possible after reasonable effort, leading to perseveration on a given task. In applying this specifically to pathological worry, Davey

(2006) suggests that worriers are likely candidates for perseveration. He notes that worriers are often in a negative mood state, the task of worrying has no obvious end point, and worriers often apply an "as many as can" rule to determine when to stop worrying. Thus, this model predicts that pathological worriers will frequently be subject to entering an iterative worry cycle that is not easily exited.

This group of researchers has provided empirical support for the assertion that a negative mood induction actually increased the number of catastrophizing steps individuals made when asked to worry about a particular topic. Worriers who were asked to use an "as many as can" stop rule generated more catastrophizing steps than nonworriers (Startup & Davey, 2001). In a sample of worriers, the interaction of negative mood and increased responsibility yielded greater catastrophizing, suggesting that levels of inflated responsibility may be one reason worriers use an "as many as can" stop rule (Startup & Davey, 2003).

Research has investigated differences between worry and related symptoms such as rumination and obsessions. Worry and rumination both involve repetitive, negative thinking and are correlated in nonclinical (Fresco, Frankel, Mennin, Turk, & Heimberg, 2002) and clinical (Segerstrom, Tsao, Alden, & Craske, 2000) samples. On a measure assessing nine ways in which these cognitive processes might differ, seven significant differences emerged between ruminative and worrisome thoughts (Watkins, Moulds, & Mackintosh, 2005). For example, worries were reported as having a longer duration, the content of worries was associated more strongly with future events and less with past events, worries were rated as more disturbing and less realistic, and worries were associated with greater feelings of insecurity. More recent research suggests that worry is related to both anxious and depressive symptoms, whereas rumination is more uniquely associated with depression (Hong, 2007). There is also evidence for physiological differences in the manifestation of worry and rumination, with worry, but not rumination, having a strong negative relationship with heart rate variability across emotional contexts (Aldao, Mennin, & McLaughlin, 2013). Thus, although worry and rumination share core features, they appear to be functionally different constructs.

Research also suggests that worry and obsessional thinking are similar but distinct processes. Comer, Kendall, Franklin, Hudson, and Pimentel (2004) concluded that worrisome thoughts can be best differentiated from obsessions by the presence of an identifiable trigger, less mental imagery, and metacognitive beliefs about the dangerousness and uncontrollability of worry. Langlois, Freeston, and Ladouceur (2000) found that nonclinical participants rated their worrisome thoughts as being more realistic, less ego dystonic, more persistent, and more verbally oriented than obsessions. Thus, although similarities exist between worry and related symptoms such as rumination and obsessions, worry appears to be a distinct cognitive phenomenon.

Environmental and Family Factors

Environmental and family factors appear to play a number of roles in the development, phenomenology, and maintenance of generalized anxiety disorder. For example, among individuals with a propensity to worry, actual situations of enhanced risk appear to trigger a tendency to overestimate the likelihood of risk associated with a task (Constans, 2001).

Factors related to family environment and parenting styles may also be relevant for understanding GAD. Critically, most studies on this topic have relied on self-report or retrospective reports of family environments, which may be affected by bias. Despite this limitation, results converge to suggest that people with GAD may have experienced unpleasant, negative, and rejecting family environments. For example, a study of self-reported parenting styles and GAD symptoms found a relationship between perceived parental alienation and rejection on the one hand and GAD symptoms in a sample of community adolescents on the other (Hale, Engels, & Meeus, 2006). Further, college students who endorsed criteria for GAD on a questionnaire also endorsed less secure attachment to their parents than did control participants (Eng & Heimberg, 2006). A recent longitudinal study found a bidirectional relationship between perceived father-adolescent attachment relationships and GAD symptoms, but a unidirectional relationship for the mother-adolescent attachment relationship, with GAD symptoms leading to a lower-quality relationship (van Eijck, Branje, Hale, & Meeus, 2012). Although this study relies on adolescents' self-reported GAD symptoms and perceived attachment, it suggests that the effects of attachment are more nuanced than previously believed.

Other researchers have argued that interpersonal problems, in general, may play a causal role in the development of GAD. For example, Crits-Christoph, Gibbons, Narducci, Schamberger, and Gallop (2005) have emphasized the high frequency of interpersonal themes in worry content and biases to social threat cues in GAD. Those with GAD show more parent-child boundary problems than do individuals without GAD (Cassidy & Shaver, 1999). Drawing from these ideas, these investigators examined the change in interpersonal problems across the course of brief psychodynamic treatment for GAD and found that changes in self-reported interpersonal problems were significantly related to improvements in worry symptoms. Similarly, Borkovec, Newman, Pincus, and Lytle (2002) found that participants in a CBT trial for GAD demonstrated interpersonal difficulties at posttreatment, and that these difficulties were associated with fewer gains and improvements across follow-up. However, other research suggests that interpersonal problems in GAD may be more focused, with no evidence of disrupted peer relationships in a college sample who endorsed criteria for GAD on a questionnaire (Eng & Heimberg, 2006). The role of interpersonal difficulties in GAD, therefore, is not clearly understood, including whether interpersonal difficulties are a cause or a consequence of excessive worry and anxiety.

Assessment

As noted earlier, the inherent instability in the diagnostic criteria for GAD has made it difficult to reliably diagnose and assess these disorders. As diagnostic criteria have become more stable, reliable means of assessing GAD and chronic worry have also become more available; however, reliably assessing for GAD still presents challenges. For example, the *DSM-5* field trials had clinicians conduct diagnostic interviews with patients based on checklists of the *DSM-5* criteria. The results of the field trial showed low interrater reliability for GAD (kappa = 0.2; Clarke et al., 2013). It has been suggested that a comprehensive assessment of GAD should examine the following: worry, beliefs about worry, intolerance of uncertainty, anxiety, associated features (e.g., tension), comorbid symptoms, goals and areas of behavioral inactivation, and emotional avoidance (Roemer & Medaglia, 2001). In this section, we review several useful tools for the assessment of GAD according to *DSM-5* criteria.

ANXIETY AND RELATED DISORDERS INTERVIEW SCHEDULE FOR *DSM-5* (ADIS-5)

The ADIS-5 (Brown & Barlow, 2014) is a clinician-administered semistructured interview that provides *DSM-5* diagnostic information about a range of psychological problems, including anxiety disorders, obsessive-compulsive and related disorders, trauma- and stressor-related disorders, mood disorders, somatic symptom disorders, and substance use disorders. Screening questions are provided for other conditions, including impulse control disorders, hoarding disorder, eating disorders, attention deficit disorder, dissociative disorders, and psychotic disorders. Depending on the version of the ADIS-5 used (standard versus lifetime version), current and lifetime diagnoses can be assigned. Clinicians require extensive training in the administration of this interview, and the interview duration can be lengthy, particularly for the lifetime version (i.e., several hours). Despite these drawbacks to use in everyday practice, the ADIS-5 has the benefit of providing clear questions to help determine the presence or absence of GAD and common comorbid disorders.

Although there have been no published investigations of the reliability of the ADIS-5, its precursor, the ADIS-IV (Brown, DiNardo, & Barlow, 2004), has demonstrated good reliability. Gordon and Heimberg (2011) examined the reliability and validity of particular features of GAD assessed using the ADIS-IV. Interrater reliability was strongest when assessing excessiveness and uncontrollability of worry, interference, and severity of fatigue, but was lowest when evaluating subjective distress. The authors concluded that GAD can be reliably diagnosed using the ADIS-IV, though there are limitations with the reliability of certain features of the disorder. Because of the overlap in diagnostic criteria for GAD from *DSM-IV* to *DSM-5*, these findings on reliability may also apply to the ADIS-5.

STRUCTURED CLINICAL INTERVIEW FOR DSM-5 (SCID-5)

The SCID-5 (First, Williams, Karg, & Spitzer, 2015) is also a clinician-administered semistructured interview that provides diagnostic decisions about a wide range of psychiatric disorders. Two versions are available—a clinician version (SCID-5-CV) and a research version (SCID-5-RV). The clinician version was designed for use in clinical settings and has a less extensive coverage of disorders. Extensive training is required to administer the SCID-5, and administration can be lengthy, especially for the research version. There have been no published investigations of the reliability of the SCID-5 to date.

SELF-REPORT MEASURES

Self-report measures of GAD have been developed for a number of purposes, including assessing the presence of diagnostic criteria, the severity of worry, and the range and content of worry topics. Further, there are a number of self-report measures designed to measure constructs thought to be important in the theoretical understanding of this disorder (e.g., measures of intolerance of uncertainty and meta-worry). In this section, we briefly review some of the most often used self-report measures of worry and GAD. It is notable that some of these measures (e.g., GADQ-IV; GAD-7) are based on *DSM-IV* criteria.

Generalized Anxiety Disorder Questionnaire

The Generalized Anxiety Disorder Questionnaire for DSM-IV (GADQ-IV; Newman et al., 2002) is an efficient and useful tool for assessing the presence of the GAD diagnostic criteria, especially when it is not practical to use a semistructured interview. It is a brief and simple measure to administer and score, making it a popular tool in research involving analogue samples. Most questions involve yes or no responses, two questions involve a severity scale, and one question is open-ended, asking for a list of frequent worries. Thus, the GADQ-IV provides both diagnostic and content-related information about a person's symptoms. The psychometric properties of this measure are quite strong, as it has demonstrated good test-retest reliability and good convergence with diagnoses made using the ADIS-IV (Newman et al., 2002). Because diagnostic criteria for GAD are essentially unchanged in the *DSM-5*, the GADQ-IV may be used for assessing GAD based on *DSM-5* criteria.

Generalized Anxiety Disorder 7-Item Scale

The Generalized Anxiety Disorder 7-Item Scale (GAD-7; Spitzer, Kroenke, Williams, & Löwe, 2006) is a brief, self-report screening measure of *DSM-IV* GAD diagnosis and symptom severity, intended for use in primary care settings. Individuals rate how often over the past 2 weeks they have been bothered by symptoms, using a scale of 0 (not at all) to 3 (nearly every day), with total scores ranging from 0 to 21. According to the development and validation study (Spitzer et al., 2006), a total score of 10 or greater provides the optimal cut score for identifying cases of GAD. Further, the GAD-7 provides an index of symptom severity, with cases identified as mild (5–9), moderate (10–14), or severe (15–21). The scale has good psychometric properties (Spitzer et al., 2006).

Self-Report Measures of Worry Severity and Worry Content

The Penn State Worry Questionnaire (PSWQ; Meyer, Miller, Metzger, & Borkovec, 1990) is a brief self-report measure that was designed to measure a person's tendency to worry excessively, without assessing the content of the worry. It is a widely used measure that has demonstrated strong psychometric properties (see Roemer, 2001, for a review). In contrast, the Worry Domains Questionnaire (WDQ; Tallis, Eysenck, & Mathews, 1992) provides an assessment of the content of worry. More specifically, it assesses the degree to which a person worries about relationships, lack of confidence, the future, work, and finances. Its psychometric properties are also strong (Roemer, 2001). The content of worry can also be assessed with the Anxious Thoughts Inventory (AnTI; Wells, 1994), which assesses social worry, health worry, and meta-worry.

Self-Report Measures of Theoretical Constructs Relevant to GAD

Several other self-report measures assess theoretical constructs believed to be important in understanding a person's GAD symptoms. For example, metacognitions about worry can be assessed by the Metacognitions Questionnaire (MCQ; Cartwright-Hatton &

Wells, 1997), and its 30-item short form, the MCQ-30 (Wells & Cartwright-Hatton, 2004). This measure assesses positive beliefs about worry, the belief that worry is dangerous and harmful, lack of confidence in one's cognitive functioning, negative consequences or fears about worrying, and the degree to which an individual monitors his or her thinking. It has demonstrated good internal consistency and test-retest reliability (Cartwright-Hatton & Wells, 1997), and individuals with GAD score higher on this measure than do those with other anxiety disorders or related conditions (Wells & Carter, 2001). Positive beliefs about worry can be assessed using the Why Worry Scale and Why Worry Scale–II (Freeston et al., 1994). Both negative and positive beliefs about worry can be ascertained using the Consequences of Worrying Scale (Davey, Tallis, et al., 1996).

As described earlier, intolerance of uncertainty has been proposed to be an important construct in understanding the development and maintenance of worry. The Intolerance of Uncertainty Scale (Freeston et al., 1994) consists of statements describing how one might react to uncertainties (e.g., "I always want to know what the future has in store for me"), and respondents indicate how characteristic each statement is of them. This measure has demonstrated good psychometric properties (see Roemer, 2001). A 12-item short form of the Intolerance of Uncertainty Scale has been developed that appears to retain the strong psychometric properties of the longer version (Carleton, Norton, & Asmundson, 2007; Hale et al., 2015).

ONGOING ASSESSMENT AND FOLLOW-UP

Assessment should not end after establishing a diagnosis and understanding the features of the disorder at hand. All of the above-cited assessment tools can be used at any stage of contact, therapy, or follow-up. Indeed, it may be most beneficial to use a complement of diagnostic and descriptive tools in ongoing assessments to have a thorough understanding of the course of a person's symptoms and diagnosis. For example, follow-up studies of the outcome of interventions often assess diagnostic status (using, e.g., the SCID, ADIS, or GADQ-IV), worry severity (e.g., the PSWQ), as well as other constructs of interest to the particular study. In addition, ongoing assessment often involves the assessment of more general constructs such as functional impairment due to anxiety symptoms, disability, interpersonal functioning, and quality of life.

Treatment

There has been considerable interest in finding effective psychological or biological interventions for generalized anxiety disorder. Results are encouraging, though further research and refinements in treatment options are necessary. We review the state of both psychological and biological interventions for GAD in the following section.

PSYCHOLOGICAL INTERVENTIONS

Research on the efficacy of psychological treatments for generalized anxiety disorder has expanded considerably in the last decade with theoretical advances in the understanding of GAD and pathological worry. Given this improved understanding, several newer treatments derived from various models of GAD have been developed (for a review, see Behar, DiMarco, Hekler, Mohlman, & Staples, 2009). Although each treatment approach attempts to target the precise mechanisms relevant to its respective theoretical models, most of these approaches are derivatives of previous cognitive-behavioral protocols for treating GAD. Indeed, cognitive-behavioral therapy (CBT) for GAD is the best-studied psychological intervention for this disorder and has shown good outcomes in the few randomized controlled trials that have been completed. It is with traditional CBT interventions that this review begins.

COGNITIVE-BEHAVIORAL THERAPY

Although different CBT protocols contain somewhat different components, the most commonly used components are psychoeducation, relaxation training, monitoring of cues and triggers for worry, imaginal exposure, in vivo exposure (if necessary), and cognitive restructuring (for a review, see Ouimet, Covin, & Dozois, 2012). Psychoeducation involves providing information about GAD, worry, and anxiety. Further, individuals are provided with an overview of the rationale for CBT. Relaxation training can involve a number of strategies, including progressive muscle relaxation and breathing techniques. Monitoring forms are used to identify environmental triggers for worry and anxiety, to record the content of worries, and to become aware of behavioral and physiological consequences of worry. Imaginal and in vivo exposure techniques are used in a CBT protocol when relevant for a client's symptoms. For example, if someone is avoiding reading the newspaper for fear that it will trigger unwanted worries about world events, exposure to reading news stories would likely be an important component of treatment. Imaginal exposure (repeated exposure to catastrophic images and fears) is used to help individuals become more comfortable with the content of their most feared consequences. Cognitive restructuring is the process by which individuals challenge their fearful thoughts and learn to consider realistic alternatives.

In a number of investigations, CBT has proven superior to wait-list controls and nonspecific alternative treatments (Mitte, 2005; Ouimet et al., 2012); a meta-analysis also showed that the effects of CBT are similar to pharmacological interventions (Mitte, 2005). To isolate the effects of CBT on worry, the core symptom of GAD, a meta-analysis examined only those studies using the PSWQ as an outcome measure and found that effect sizes for CBT interventions were large ($g = -1.15$) when compared to nonspecific or no-treatment control conditions (Covin, Ouimet, Seeds, & Dozois, 2008). This meta-analysis found that the effects of CBT were moderated by age, with younger age groups responding more strongly to CBT than older cohorts, although the effect sizes were in the large range across age groups. In meta-analyses comparing CBT with pharmacological interventions, effect sizes for CBT and pharmacotherapy are similar, although there appears to be an advantage for CBT for long-term maintenance of treatment gains (Gould, Otto, Pollack, & Yap, 1997) and for patient acceptability and tolerability (Mitte, 2005). CBT has also been found useful in helping individuals discontinue their benzodiazepine use (Gosselin, Ladouceur, Morin, Dugas, & Baillargeon, 2006). CBT appears to be effective not only for decreasing symptoms of worry, anxiety, and depression but also for decreasing related symptoms such as insomnia (Bélanger, Morin, Langlois, & Ladouceur, 2004) and improving quality of life (Hofmann, Wu, & Boettcher, 2014).

Studies have also investigated the specific components of CBT protocols. For example, a study by Arntz (2003) compared applied relaxation to cognitive strategies. Both treatments were effective across a number of outcome measures, with an initial follow-up advantage for relaxation lost at 6-month follow-up. Both treatments appeared to be effective at 6-month follow-up, with just over half of the sample demonstrating a strong outcome on measures of anxiety. In another study, problem-solving training (which is often used in CBT protocols for GAD) was compared to imaginal exposure, and again both treatment components yielded significant improvements on a variety of symptom measures (Provencher, Dugas, & Ladouceur, 2004).

In a meta-analysis, Hanrahan, Field, Jones, and Davey (2012) found large effect sizes for the efficacy of cognitive therapy in reducing worry at posttreatment and 12-month follow-up. Although there was some conceptual overlap in terms of the treatment comparison groups (i.e., cognitive and cognitive-behavioral treatments were not isolated), this meta-analysis suggests that treatment models targeting cognitive variables, such as intolerance of uncertainty and meta-worry, can be effective in treating the core symptoms of GAD. Despite these successes, more work is needed to understand the individual differences and treatment-specific variables affecting outcomes in order to enhance treatment efficacy.

Recent Advances in CBT for GAD

As reviewed earlier in this chapter, there is considerable evidence that GAD is characterized by heightened levels of intolerance of uncertainty. Accordingly, treatment protocols that have been developed to specifically target intolerance of uncertainty have produced encouraging results. In an initial study of this protocol, 26 individuals with GAD were assigned to active treatment or a delayed treatment condition. Treatment was a modification of a CBT protocol that targeted intolerance of uncertainty, positive and negative beliefs about worry, negative problem-solving orientation, and cognitive avoidance. This protocol led to significant and lasting improvements on GAD diagnostic status and associated symptoms (Ladouceur et al., 2000). Positive outcomes are seen whether this treatment is offered in group formats (Dugas et al., 2003) or individual formats (Dugas et al., 2010). Interestingly, CBT targeting intolerance of uncertainty resulted in similar posttreatment improvements in worry compared to applied relaxation, but the gains were maintained only in the CBT condition (Dugas et al., 2010), indicating that the effects of CBT are more durable than effects of applied relaxation.

Therapy based on Wells's metacognitive theory of GAD (Wells, 1995) has also demonstrated positive results. This treatment focuses on modifying individuals' negative beliefs about the uncontrollability of worry, negative beliefs about the danger of worry, and positive beliefs about the utility of worry (Wells, 2006). A meta-analysis, which included five studies with GAD patients, found that metacognitive therapies were more effective than wait-list control conditions across mood and anxiety disorders (Normann, van Emmerik, & Morina, 2014). An open trial of metacognitive therapy for GAD found strong effect sizes on measures of worry, anxiety, and depression, and recovery rates remained strong at 12-month follow-up (Wells & King, 2006). A pilot randomized controlled trial found metacognitive therapy for GAD to be superior to applied relaxation at posttreatment and follow-up (Wells et al., 2010). When directly compared, CBT targeting metacognition and CBT targeting intolerance of uncertainty both produced significant and lasting improvements in GAD symptoms. However, the therapy derived from Wells's metacognitive model produced significantly greater reductions on all measures (van der Heiden, Muris, & van der Molen, 2012).

Another modification of a traditional CBT protocol for GAD has involved the incorporation of mindfulness and acceptance strategies into therapy. This change is based on evidence that individuals with GAD may be using worry to avoid negative emotional experiences. The inclusion of mindfulness and acceptance strategies encourages a client to accept his or her emotional experience and to move toward valued goals rather than engage in typical worry-related behaviors. This approach derives from acceptance-based therapies developed by Hayes, Strosahl, and Wilson (1999) and Linehan (1993). Case studies (e.g., Fresco, Mennin, Heimberg, & Ritter, 2013), open trials (Roemer & Orsillo, 2007), and randomized controlled trials (Roemer, Orsillo, & Salters-Pedneault, 2008) suggest that the incorporation of these strategies shows promise for individuals with GAD. Clients in these studies specifically acknowledged the mindfulness and acceptance elements of therapy as beneficial.

In addition, augmenting CBT with motivational interviewing (MI), which is a client-centered approach focused on facilitating a client's own motivation for change, appears to reduce treatment resistance (Aviram & Westra, 2011) and enhance efficacy (Westra, Arkowitz, & Dozois, 2009). A recent randomized controlled trial compared 15 sessions of traditional CBT with a 15-session integrated protocol (4 sessions of MI and 11 sessions of MI-enhanced CBT) (Westra, Constantino, & Antony, 2016) for individuals with GAD. Although treatment outcomes were similar immediately after treatment, the MI plus CBT showed more change (more reduction in worry and general distress) at 12-month follow up. These results suggest that augmenting CBT with MI approaches may result in better long-term outcomes for individuals with GAD.

In summary, CBT has been shown to be an effective intervention for individuals with GAD, demonstrating superiority to results for wait-list controls and alternative therapies. It is still unclear which components of the CBT protocol are the most useful, and whether new variants can outperform standard CBT in randomized controlled trials. However, despite the benefits accrued by CBT, outcome data continue to be modest and large percentages of clients continuing to experience significant symptoms at posttreatment and follow-up. Thus, more work is necessary to identify the elements needed for an optimal psychological intervention for GAD.

BIOLOGICAL INTERVENTIONS

Recent revisions to clinical practice guidelines recommend that selection of treatment approach be based on the client's preference, as there is no conclusive evidence that biological or psychological interventions for GAD are superior to one another (National Institute for Health and Clinical Excellence, 2011). Conclusions about effective pharmacological interventions for GAD are limited by several factors. Most studies have examined benzodiazepines as a treatment for GAD, with only a handful of more recent studies investigating the utility of antidepressants and other medications for this condition. Further, most randomized controlled trials limit the comorbid psychological conditions that study participants can have. They tend to include only "pure GAD" cases. As noted earlier, GAD is highly comorbid with other disorders, making it difficult to find these pure cases and further limiting the generalizability of study results to the treatment of individuals with more complicated diagnostic profiles. The lack of consistent diagnostic criteria for GAD has also hampered our knowledge of effective pharmacological interventions, as many medication trials have used *DSM-III* or *DSM-III-R* criteria. The response of GAD to placebo appears to be particularly high (e.g., greater than 40%; Schweizer & Rickels, 1997), making it more difficult to find active pharmacological agents that can demonstrate significantly better effects than this. Despite these limitations, there is an accumulating body of research on pharmacological agents for GAD (for a review, see Baldwin, Waldman, & Allgulander, 2011).

Research generally supports the effectiveness of benzodiazepines when compared to placebo for GAD (see Anderson & Palm, 2006), although initial benefits were not maintained in some studies (e.g., Pourmotabbed, McLeod, Hoehn-Saric, Hipsley, & Greenblatt, 1996). Benzodiazepines appear to reduce symptoms of worry, tension, and concentration in addition to the somatic features of GAD. A meta-analysis of studies comparing pharmacotherapy (usually benzodiazepines) to CBT concluded that the two interventions appear to be similarly effective (Mitte, 2005). However, due to concerns about the development of potential tolerance, dependence, and withdrawal symptoms, recommendations have been made to prescribe benzodiazepines only under limited circumstances, such as for short-term treatment (i.e., less than 4 weeks), as an adjunct to antidepressant medication, or in cases of severe, treatment-resistant GAD symptoms (Baldwin et al., 2011).

In reviews of pharmacotherapy for GAD, SSRIs are identified as a first-line therapy (see Baldwin et al., 2011). More specifically, approved medications include paroxetine, sertraline, and escitalopram, with each medication demonstrating efficacy compared to pill placebo (Lenze et al., 2009). Escitalopram may also be more efficacious than paroxetine (Baldwin, Huusom, & Maehlum, 2006), may be better tolerated than paroxetine (Bielski, Bose, & Chang, 2005), and is more effective than placebo in preventing relapse after successful pharmacotherapy of GAD symptoms (Allgulander, Florea, & Huusom, 2006). Further, a small pilot study presented preliminary evidence that escitalopram may provide additional benefits to partial responders and nonresponders following a course of CBT for GAD (Schneier, Belzer, Kishon, Amsel, & Simpson, 2010).

Agents other than SSRIs have been studied in GAD. Although there is consistent evidence that buspirone, a partial agonist of the presynaptic serotonin receptors, is an effective medication, demonstrating a moderate effect size in a recent meta-analysis (Mitte, Noack, Steil, & Hautzinger, 2005), it appears to be less well tolerated in clinical practice (see Anderson & Palm, 2006) and less effective than SSRI treatments (Egger & Hebert, 2011). Studies suggest that the serotonin-norepinephrine reuptake inhibitor venlafaxine is also effective for GAD, demonstrating a moderate effect size across studies (Mitte et al., 2005) and showing effects similar to paroxetine (Kim et al., 2006). This medication has also demonstrated effectiveness over longer treatment trials (Gelenberg et al., 2000). However, some authors argue that it should remain a second-line treatment for GAD due to concerns about its safety in overdose and cardiac implications (see Anderson & Palm, 2006). The serotonin-norepinephrine reuptake inhibitor duloxetine has also been shown as an effective treatment (e.g., Hartford et al., 2007).

Recent evidence is emerging for the efficacy of alternative psychotropic treatment approaches. For example, pregabalin, an analogue of the neurotransmitter GABA, has been demonstrated in several randomized controlled trials to be an efficacious treatment for GAD. A meta-analysis of seven randomized controlled trials found small to moderate effect sizes for pregabalin compared to placebo, and the effect was more pronounced for reducing psychological distress relative to somatic symptoms of GAD (Boschen, 2011). A recent study investigated pregabalin as an adjunctive therapy for individuals with GAD who had not fully responded to other pharmacotherapy, and found better outcomes for the pregabalin group compared to the placebo group (Rickels et al., 2012). Currently, however, limited evidence is available comparing pregabalin to other active pharmacological or psychological treatments for GAD.

Second-generation antipsychotic medications have failed to demonstrate consistent efficacy as an augmentation treatment for treatment-refractory GAD (Lalonde & Van Lieshout, 2011). However, based on a limited number of controlled trials, quetiapine monotherapy appears to be more effective than placebo in producing clinically significant improvement in GAD symptoms (Baldwin et al., 2011; Lalonde & Van Lieshout, 2011). Unfortunately, patients treated with quetiapine are more likely to report significant side effects, such as weight gain, and to discontinue treatment (Lalonde & Van Lieshout, 2011), calling into question the clinical utility of antipsychotic medications as stand-alone or adjunctive treatments for GAD.

Summary and New Directions

Generalized anxiety disorder is a prevalent, chronic, and debilitating disorder. Unfortunately, research on this condition has suffered due to the unreliable and changing diagnostic status of GAD. Compared to criteria for other anxiety disorders, the criteria used to diagnose GAD dramatically fluctuated across earlier editions of the *DSM*. There is still debate about the essential criteria and duration of symptoms that would be optimal to achieve greater reliability of diagnosis. For example, several studies suggest that the 6-month minimum duration of excessive worry and anxiety may not be necessary and will miss a small, but significant, number of individuals who present with all the other symptoms of GAD for a shorter duration (e.g., Angst et al., 2006). Thus, the first challenge in the field appears to be to address the diagnostic criteria of GAD to ensure that these criteria are capturing the essence of this disorder but are not so restrictive as to exclude clinically meaningful cases of the disorder.

Additional work needs to be done to improve reliability. Although interrater reliability estimates for GAD on the SCID-IV and ADIS-IV were adequate, they fell below those for other psychological disorders. Studies suggest that the source of diagnostic unreliability was often that GAD was assigned at a threshold level in some instances and labeled as a subthreshold constellation of symptoms in other instances (Brown et al., 2001). This suggests that, once again, the essential features and duration of this disorder require further clarification.

More optimistically, the identification of excessive worry as the essential feature of GAD has led to a proliferation of theorizing and research on this disorder over the past two decades. Our understanding of the psychopathology of excessive worry and GAD is quite strong, with a number of complementary theories regarding the development and maintenance of GAD being extensively studied by numerous research groups. These research groups, each with its own ideas about the central issues in GAD, appear to have been able to incorporate others' ideas into their own understanding of the disorder. For example, more recent ideas about intolerance of uncertainty and meta-worry blend nicely with earlier theories of worry as a means of emotional avoidance (Borkovec et al., 2004). As the field continues to progress, it will be interesting to see whether differing theoretical positions will continue to converge or will become increasingly divergent. It will also be interesting to see whether neuroanatomical, physiological, and other biological studies will be consistent with the growing information on the psychology of GAD, as well as add to our understanding of the essential components and processes of pathological worry.

Although existing theories of GAD and worry are complementary, there is less convergence in terms of identifying the essential components of a CBT program for GAD. Different review articles and chapters recommend different CBT strategies for treating GAD. Ongoing research is focusing on multiple new components of psychotherapy for GAD, with minimal overlap with earlier components. Dismantling studies have yet to suggest exactly what therapists should be doing with their GAD clients. Furthermore, although CBT has been shown to be an efficacious therapy for GAD, effectiveness data are still needed. Thus, it is clear that much work is needed to allow a better understanding of how to best treat GAD from a psychological perspective.

Similarly, much work remains to be done to understand how best to utilize biological treatments for GAD. Although recommendations exist for first- and second-line pharmacological treatments for GAD, progress in this area has been hampered by shifts in diagnostic criteria, by a focus on benzodiazepines as a first-line treatment, and by selecting individuals for medication trials who do not represent a typical individual with GAD. With the continued consistency of diagnostic criteria, it is hoped that some of these hurdles can be overcome to allow researchers to investigate new and potentially useful medications. Research has begun to examine the effectiveness of treatments adjunctive to SSRIs (e.g., Bandelow et al., 2010), but further research is warranted. Further understanding of the biological, biochemical, and neuroanatomical aspects of GAD will also help in understanding the types of pharmacological agents that might best help individuals with GAD.

It is clear that GAD has enormous personal and societal costs for afflicted individuals. Thus, effective treatment programs need to be balanced with research on the prevention of the onset or exacerbation of symptoms. We know that GAD shares a genetic diathesis with depression (Roy, Neale, Pedersen, Mathe, & Kendler, 1995), that anxiety disorders run in families (Merikangas, Avenevoli, Dierker, & Grillon, 1999), and that specific life events are associated with heightened symptoms of generalized anxiety (e.g., the postpartum period; Wenzel, Haugen, Jackson, & Robinson, 2003). Prevention efforts need to make use of such information to target higher risk populations before symptoms become debilitating.

References

Adams, J. B., Pyke, R. E., Costa, J., & Cutler, N. R. (1995). A double-blind, placebo-controlled study of a CCK-B receptor antagonist, CI-988, in patients with generalized anxiety disorder. *Journal of Clinical Psychopharmacology, 15*, 428–434.

Aldao, A., Mennin, D. S., Linardatos, E., & Fresco, D. M. (2010). Differential patterns of physical symptoms and subjective processes in generalized anxiety disorder and unipolar depression. *Journal of Anxiety Disorders, 24*, 250–259.

Aldao, A., Mennin, D. S., & McLaughlin, K. A. (2013). Differentiating worry and rumination: Evidence from heart rate variability during spontaneous regulation. *Cognitive Therapy and Research, 37*, 613–619.

Allgulander, C., Florea, I., & Huusom, A. K. T. (2006). Prevention of relapse in generalized anxiety disorder by escitalopram treatment. *International Journal of Neuropsychopharmacology, 9*, 495–505.

American Psychiatric Association. (1952). *Diagnostic and statistical manual of mental disorders*. Washington, DC: Author.

American Psychiatric Association. (1968). *Diagnostic and statistical manual of mental disorders* (2nd ed.). Washington, DC: Author.

American Psychiatric Association. (1980). *Diagnostic and statistical manual of mental disorders* (3rd ed.). Arlington, VA: Author.

American Psychiatric Association. (1987). *Diagnostic and statistical manual of mental disorders* (3rd ed., rev.). Arlington, VA: Author.

American Psychiatric Association. (1994). *Diagnostic and statistical manual of mental disorders* (4th ed.). Arlington, VA: Author.

American Psychiatric Association. (2013). *Diagnostic and statistical manual of mental disorders* (5th ed.). Washington, DC: Author.

Anderson, I. M., & Palm, M. E. (2006). Pharmacological treatments for worry: Focus on generalized anxiety disorder. In G. C. L. Davey & A. Wells (Eds.), *Worry and its psychological disorders: Theory, assessment, and treatment* (pp. 305–334). Chichester, England: Wiley.

Angst, J., Gamma, A., Bienvenu, O. J., Eaton, W. W., Ajdacic, V., Eich, D., & Rössler, W. (2006). Varying temporal criteria for generalized anxiety disorder: Prevalence and clinical characteristics in a young age cohort. *Psychological Medicine, 36*, 1283–1292.

Ansell, E. B., Pinto, A., Edelen, M. O., Markowitz, J. C., Sanislow, C. A., Yen, S., … Gunderson, J. G. (2011). The association of personality disorders with the prospective 7-year course of anxiety disorders. *Psychological Medicine, 41*, 1019–1028.

Arntz, A. (2003). Cognitive therapy versus applied relaxation as a treatment of generalized anxiety disorder. *Behaviour Research and Therapy, 41*, 633–646.

Asnaani, A., Richey, J. A., Dimaite, R., Hinton, D. E., & Hofmann, S. G. (2010). A cross-ethnic comparison of lifetime prevalence rates of anxiety disorders. *Journal of Nervous and Mental Disease, 198*, 551–555.

Aviram, A., & Westra, H. A. (2011). The impact of motivational interviewing on resistance in cognitive behavioural therapy for generalized anxiety disorder. *Psychotherapy Research, 21*, 698–708.

Baldwin, D. S., Huusom, A. K. T., & Maehlum, E. (2006). Escitalopram and paroxetine in the treatment of generalized anxiety disorder: Randomized, placebo-controlled, double-blind study. *British Journal of Psychiatry, 189*, 264–272.

Baldwin, D. S., Waldman, S., & Allgulander, C. (2011). Evidence-based pharmacological treatment of generalized anxiety disorder. *International Journal of Neuropsychopharmacology, 14*, 697–710.

Ballenger, J. C. (2001). Treatment of anxiety disorders to remission. *Journal of Clinical Psychiatry, 62*, 5–9.

Bandelow, B., Chouinard, G., Bobes, J., Ahokas, A., Eggens, I., Liu, S., & Eriksson, H. (2010). Extended-release quetiapine fumarate (quetiapine XR): A once-daily monotherapy effective in generalized anxiety disorder. Data from a randomized, double-blind, placebo- and active-controlled study. *International Journal of Neuropsychopharmacology, 13*, 305–320.

Bar-Haim, Y., Lamy, D., Pergamin, L., Bakermans-Kranenburg, M., & van IJzendoorn, M. H. (2007). Threat-related attentional bias in anxious and nonanxious individuals: A meta-analytic study. *Psychological Bulletin, 133*, 1–24.

Barahmand, U. (2009). Meta-cognitive profiles in anxiety disorders. *Psychiatry Research, 169*, 240–243.

Becker, E. S., Goodwin, R., Hölting, C., Hoyer, J., & Margraf, J. (2003). Content of worry in the community: What do people with generalized anxiety disorder or other disorders worry about? *Journal of Nervous and Mental Disease, 191,* 688–691.

Becker, E. S., Rinck, M., Margraf, J., & Roth, W. T. (2001). The emotional Stroop effect in anxiety disorders: General emotionality or disorder specificity? *Journal of Anxiety Disorders, 15,* 147–159.

Becker, E. S., Roth, W. T., Andrich, M., & Margraf, J. (1999). Explicit memory in anxiety disorders. *Journal of Abnormal Psychology, 108,* 153–163.

Behar, E., DiMarco, I. D., Hekler, E. B., Mohlman, J., & Staples, A. M. (2009). Current theoretical models of generalized anxiety disorder (GAD): Conceptual review and treatment implications. *Journal of Anxiety Disorders, 23,* 1011–1023.

Behar, E., Zuellig, A. R., & Borkovec, T. D. (2005). Thought and imaginal activity during worry and trauma recall. *Behavior Therapy, 36,* 157–168.

Bélanger, L., Morin, C. M., Langlois, F., & Ladouceur, R. (2004). Insomnia and generalized anxiety disorder: Effects of cognitive behavior therapy for GAD on insomnia patients. *Journal of Anxiety Disorders, 18,* 561–571.

Belzer, K. D., D'Zurilla, T. J., & Maydeu-Olivares, A. (2002). Social problem solving and trait anxiety as predictors of worry in a college student population. *Personality and Individual Differences, 33,* 573–585.

Berenbaum, H., Thompson, R. J., & Pomerantz, E. M. (2007). The relation between worrying and concerns: The importance of perceived probability and cost. *Behaviour Research and Therapy, 45,* 301–311.

Bielski, R. J., Bose, A., & Chang, C. (2005). A double-blind comparison of escitalopram and paroxetine in the long-term treatment of generalized anxiety disorder. *Annals of Clinical Psychiatry, 17,* 65–69.

Blazer, D., Hughes, D., & George, L. K. (1987). Stressful life events and the onset of a generalized anxiety syndrome. *American Journal of Psychiatry, 144,* 1178–1183.

Borkovec, T. D., Alcaine, O., & Behar, E. (2004). Avoidance theory of worry and generalized anxiety disorder. In R. G. Heimberg, C. L. Turk, & D. S. Mennin (Eds.), *Generalized anxiety disorder: Advances in research and practice* (pp. 77–108). New York, NY: Guilford Press.

Borkovec, T. D., Hazlett-Stevens, H., & Diaz, M. L. (1999). The role of positive beliefs about worry in generalized anxiety disorder and its treatment. *Clinical Psychology & Psychotherapy, 6,* 126–138.

Borkovec, T. D., Newman, M. G., Pincus, A. L., & Lytle, R. (2002). A component analysis of cognitive-behavioral therapy for generalized anxiety disorder and the role of interpersonal problems. *Journal of Consulting and Clinical Psychology, 70,* 288–298.

Borkovec, T. D., & Roemer, L. (1995). Perceived functions of worry among generalized anxiety disorder subjects: Distraction from more emotional topics? *Journal of Behavior Therapy and Experimental Psychiatry, 26,* 25–30.

Boschen, M. J. (2011). A meta-analysis of the efficacy of pregabalin in the treatment of generalized anxiety disorder. *Canadian Journal of Psychiatry, 56,* 558–566.

Bradley, B. P., Mogg, K., Millar, N., & White, J. (1995). Selective processing of negative information: Effects of clinical anxiety, concurrent depression, and awareness. *Journal of Abnormal Psychology, 104,* 532–536.

Bradley, B. P., Mogg, K., White, J., Groom, C., & de Bono, J. (1999). Attentional bias for emotional faces in generalised anxiety disorder. *British Journal of Clinical Psychology, 38,* 267–278.

Brawman-Mintzer, O., Lydiard, R. B., Bradwejn, J., Villarreal, G., Knapp, R., Emmanuel, N., ... Ballenger, J. C. (1997). Effects of the cholecystokinin agonist pentagastrin in patients with generalized anxiety disorder. *American Journal of Psychiatry, 154,* 700–702.

Brawman-Mintzer, O., Lydiard, B., Emmanuel, N., Payeur, R., Johnson, M., Roberts, J., ... Ballenger, J. C. (1993). Psychiatric comorbidity in patients with generalized anxiety disorder. *American Journal of Psychiatry, 150,* 1216–1218.

Breitholtz, E., Johansson, B., & Öst, L. G. (1999). Cognitions in generalized anxiety disorder and panic disorder patients: A prospective approach. *Behaviour Research and Therapy, 37,* 533–544.

Brown, T. A., & Barlow, D. H. (2014). *Anxiety Disorders Interview Schedule for DSM-5 (ADIS-5)–Adult Version.* Oxford, England: Oxford University Press.

Brown, T. A., Campbell, L. A., Lehman, C. L., Grisham, J. R., & Mancill, R. B. (2001). Current and lifetime comorbidity of the *DSM-IV* anxiety and mood disorders in a large clinical sample. *Journal of Abnormal Psychology, 110,* 585–599.

Brown, T. A., DiNardo, P. A., & Barlow, D. H. (2004). *Anxiety Disorders Interview Schedule for DSM-IV (ADIS-IV).* New York, NY: Oxford University Press.

Bruce, S. E., Machan, J. T., Dyck, I., & Keller, M. B. (2001). Infrequency of "pure" GAD: Impact of psychiatric comorbidity on clinical course. *Depression and Anxiety, 14,* 219–225.

Bruce, S. E., Yonkers, K. A., Otto, M. W., Eisen, J. L., Weisberg, R. B., Pagano, M., ... Keller, M. B. (2005). Influence of psychiatric comorbidity on recovery and recurrence in generalized anxiety disorder, social phobia, and panic disorder: A 12-year prospective study. *American Journal of Psychiatry, 162,* 1179–1187.

Buhr, K., & Dugas, M. J. (2009). The role of fear of anxiety and intolerance of uncertainty in worry: An experimental manipulation. *Behaviour Research and Therapy, 47,* 215–223.

Buhr, K., & Dugas, M. J. (2012). Fear of emotions, experiential avoidance, and intolerance of uncertainty in worry and generalized anxiety disorder. *International Journal of Cognitive Therapy, 5,* 1–17.

Campbell, L. A., Brown, T. A., & Grisham, J. R. (2003). The relevance of age of onset to the psychopathology of generalized anxiety disorder. *Behavior Therapy, 34,* 31–48.

Carleton, R. N., Mulvogue, M. K., Thibodeau, M. A., McCabe, R. E., Antony, M. M., & Asmundson, G. J. G. (2012). Increasingly certain about uncertainty: Intolerance of uncertainty across anxiety and depression. *Journal of Anxiety Disorders, 26,* 468–479.

Carleton, R. N., Norton, M. A. P., & Asmundson, G. J. G. (2007). Fearing the unknown: A short version of the Intolerance of Uncertainty Scale. *Journal of Anxiety Disorders, 21,* 105–117.

Carleton, R. N., Weeks, J. W., Howell, A. N., Asmundson, G. J. G., Antony, M. M., & McCabe, R. E. (2012). Assessing the latent structure of the intolerance of uncertainty construct: An initial taxometric analysis. *Journal of Anxiety Disorders, 26,* 150–157.

Cartwright-Hatton, S., & Wells, A. (1997). Beliefs about worry and intrusions: The Meta-Cognitions Questionnaire and its correlates. *Journal of Anxiety Disorders, 11,* 279–296.

Cassidy, J. A., & Shaver, P. R. (Eds.). (1999). *Handbook of attachment: Theory, research, and clinical applications.* New York, NY: Guilford Press.

Chambers, J. A., Power, K. G., & Durham, R. C. (2004). The relationship between trait vulnerability and anxiety and depressive diagnoses at long-term follow-up of generalized anxiety disorder. *Journal of Anxiety Disorders, 18,* 587–607.

Cisler, J. M., & Koster, E. H. W. (2010). Mechanisms of attentional biases towards threat in anxiety disorders: An integrative review. *Clinical Psychology Review, 30,* 203–216.

Clarke, D. E., Narrow, W. E., Regier, D. A., Kuramoto, S. J., Kupfer, D. J., Kuhl, E. A., ... Kraemer, H. C. (2013). DSM-5 field trials in the United States and Canada: Part I. Study design, sampling strategy, implementation, and analytic approaches. *American Journal of Psychiatry, 170*(1), 43–58.

Coles, M. E., & Heimberg, R. G. (2005). Thought control strategies in generalized anxiety disorder. *Cognitive Therapy and Research, 29,* 47–56.

Coles, M. E., Turk, C. L., & Heimberg, R. G. (2007). Memory bias for threat in generalized anxiety disorder: The potential importance of stimulus relevance. *Cognitive Behaviour Therapy, 36,* 65–73.

Comer, J. S., Kendall, P. C., Franklin, M. E., Hudson, J. L., & Pimentel, S. S. (2004). Obsessing/worrying about the overlap between obsessive-compulsive disorder and generalized anxiety disorder in youth. *Clinical Psychology Review, 24,* 663–683.

Constans, J. I. (2001). Worry propensity and the perception of risk. *Behaviour Research and Therapy, 39,* 721–729.

Covin, R., Ouimet, A. J., Seeds, P. M., & Dozois, D. J. A. (2008). A meta-analysis of CBT for pathological worry among clients with GAD. *Journal of Anxiety Disorders, 22,* 108–116.

Craske, M. G., Rapee, R. M., Jackel, L., & Barlow, D. H. (1989). Qualitative dimensions of worry in DSM-III-R generalized anxiety disorder subjects and nonanxious controls. *Behaviour Research and Therapy, 27,* 397–402.

Crits-Christoph, P., Gibbons, M. B. C., Narducci, J., Schamberger, M., & Gallop, R. (2005). Interpersonal problems and the outcome of interpersonally oriented psychodynamic treatment of GAD. *Psychotherapy: Theory, Research, Practice, and Training, 42,* 211–224.

Davey, G. C. L. (2006). A mood-as-input account of perseverative worrying. In G. C. L. Davey & A. Wells (Eds.), *Worry and its psychological disorders: Theory, assessment, and treatment* (pp. 217–238). Chichester, England: Wiley.

Davey, G. C. L., Hampton, J., Farrell, J., & Davidson, S. (1992). Some characteristics of worrying: Evidence for worrying and anxiety as separate constructs. *Personality and Individual Differences, 13,* 133–147.

Davey, G. C. L., Jubb, M., & Cameron, C. (1996). Catastrophic worrying as a function of changes in problem-solving confidence. *Cognitive Therapy and Research, 20*, 333–344.

Davey, G. C. L., & Levy, S. (1998). Catastrophic worrying: Personal inadequacy and a perseverative iterative style as features of the catastrophizing process. *Journal of Abnormal Psychology, 107*, 576–586.

Davey, G. C. L., Tallis, F., & Capuzzo, N. (1996). Beliefs about the consequences of worrying. *Cognitive Therapy and Research, 20*, 499–520.

Davis, M., Montgomery, I., & Wilson, G. (2002). Worry and heart rate variables: Autonomic rigidity under challenge. *Journal of Anxiety Disorders, 16*, 639–659.

Davis, R. N., & Valentiner, D. P. (2000). Does meta-cognitive theory enhance our understanding of pathological worry and anxiety? *Personality and Individual Differences, 29*, 513–526.

De Bellis, M. D., Casey, B. J., Dahl, R. E., Birmaher, B., Williamson, D. E., Thomas, K. M., ... Ryan, N. D. (2000). A pilot study of amygdala volumes in pediatric generalized anxiety disorder. *Biological Psychiatry, 48*, 51–57.

De Bellis, M. D., Keshavan, M. S., Shifflett, H., Iyengar, S., Dahl, R. E., Axelson, D. A., ... Ryan, N. D. (2002). Superior temporal gyrus volumes in pediatric generalized anxiety disorder. *Biological Psychiatry, 51*, 553–562.

Di Nardo, P., Moras, K., Barlow, D. H., Rapee, R. M., & Brown, T. A. (1993). Reliability of DSM-III anxiety disorder categories. *Archives of General Psychiatry, 50*, 251–256.

Di Nardo, P. A., O'Brien, G. T., Barlow, D. H., Waddell, M. T., & Blanchard, E. B. (1983). Reliability of DSM-III anxiety disorder categories using a new structured interview. *Archives of General Psychiatry, 40*, 1070–1074.

Dohrenwend, B. P., & Dohrenwend, B. S. (1969). *Social status and psychological disorder: A causal inquiry*. New York, NY: Wiley.

Dugas, M. J., Brillon, P., Savard, P., Turcotte, J., Gaudet, A., Ladouceur, R., ... Gervais, N. J. (2010). A randomized clinical trial of cognitive-behavioral therapy and applied relaxation for adults with generalized anxiety disorder. *Behavior Therapy, 41*, 46–58.

Dugas, M. J., Buhr, K., & Ladouceur, R. (2004). The role of intolerance of uncertainty in etiology and maintenance. In R. G. Heimberg, C. L. Turk, & D. S. Mennin (Eds.), *Generalized anxiety disorder:*

Advances in research and practice (pp. 143–163). New York, NY: Guilford Press.

Dugas, M. J., Freeston, M. H., & Ladouceur, R. (1997). Intolerance of uncertainty and problem orientation in worry. *Cognitive Therapy and Research, 21*, 593–606.

Dugas, M. J., Gagnon, F., Ladouceur, R., & Freeston, M. H. (1998). Generalized anxiety disorder: A preliminary test of a conceptual model. *Behaviour Research and Therapy, 36*, 215–226.

Dugas, M. J., Hedayati, M., Karavidas, A., Buhr, K., Francis, K., & Phillips, N. A. (2005). Intolerance of uncertainty and information processing: Evidence of biased recall and interpretation. *Cognitive Therapy and Research, 29*, 57–70.

Dugas, M. J., Ladouceur, R., Léger, E., Freeston, M. H., Langlois, F., Provencher, M. D., & Boisvert, J. M. (2003). Group cognitive-behavioral therapy for generalized anxiety disorder: Treatment outcome and long-term follow-up. *Journal of Consulting and Clinical Psychology, 71*, 821–825.

Dugas, M. J., Langlois, F., Rhéaume, J., & Ladouceur, R. (1998, November). Intolerance of uncertainty and worry: Investigating causality. In J. Stöber (Chair), *Worry: New findings in applied and clinical research*. Symposium presented at the annual meeting of the Association for the Advancement of Behavior Therapy, Washington, DC.

Dugas, M. J., Marchand, A., & Ladouceur, R. (2005). Further validation of a cognitive-behavioral model of generalized anxiety disorder: Diagnostic and symptom specificity. *Journal of Anxiety Disorders, 19*, 329–343.

Dugas, M. J., Savard, P., Gaudet, A., Turcotte, J., Laugesen, N., Robichaud, M., ... Koerner, N. (2007). Can the components of a cognitive model predict the severity of generalized anxiety disorder? *Behavior Therapy, 38*, 169–178.

Egger, J. F., & Hebert, C. (2011). Buspirone: Anxiolytic, antidepressant, or neither? *Psychiatric Annals, 41*, 166–175.

Eng, W., & Heimberg, R. G. (2006). Interpersonal correlates of generalized anxiety disorder: Self versus other perception. *Journal of Anxiety Disorders, 20*, 380–387.

Etkin, A., Prater, K. E., Hoeft, F., Menon, V., & Schatzberg, A. F. (2010). Failure of anterior cingulate activation and connectivity with the amygdala during implicit regulation of emotional processing in generalized anxiety disorder. *American Journal of Psychiatry, 167*, 545–554.

Eysenck, M. W., Mogg, K., May, J., Richards, A., & Mathews, A. (1991). Bias in interpretation of ambiguous sentences related to threat in anxiety. *Journal of Abnormal Psychology, 100*, 144–150.

Faravelli, C., Sauro, C. L., Godini, L., Lelli, L., Benni, L., Pietrini, F., ... Ricca, V. (2012). Childhood stressful events, HPA axis and anxiety disorders. *World Journal of Psychiatry, 22*, 13–25.

Fergus, T. A., Valentiner, D. P., Wu, K. D., & McGrath, P. B. (2015). Examining the symptom-level specificity of negative problem orientation in a clinical sample. *Cognitive Behaviour Therapy, 44*, 153–161.

First, M. B., Williams, J. B. W., Karg, R. S., & Spitzer, R. L. (2015). *Structured Clinical Interview for DSM-5–Research Version (SCID-5-RV)*. Arlington, VA: American Psychiatric Association.

Francis, J. L., Moitra, E., Dyck, I., & Keller, M. B. (2012). The impact of stressful life events on relapse of generalized anxiety disorder. *Depression and Anxiety, 29*, 386–391.

Freeston, M. H., Rhéaume, J., Letarte, H., Dugas, M. J., & Ladouceur, R. (1994). Why do people worry? *Personality and Individual Differences, 17*, 791–802.

Fresco, D. M., Frankel, A. N., Mennin, D. S., Turk, C. L., & Heimberg, R. G. (2002). Distinct and overlapping features of rumination and worry: The relationship of cognitive production to negative affective states. *Cognitive Therapy and Research, 26*, 179–188.

Fresco, D. M., Mennin, D. S., Heimberg, R. G., & Ritter, M. (2013). Emotion regulation therapy for generalized anxiety disorder. *Cognitive and Behavioral Practice, 20*, 282–300.

Friedman, B. H. (2007). An autonomic flexibility-neurovisceral integration model of anxiety and cardiac vagal tone. *Biological Psychiatry, 74*, 185–199.

Gelenberg, A. J., Lydiard, R. B., Rudolph, R. L., Aguiar, L., Haskins, J. T., & Salinas, E. (2000). Efficacy of venlafaxine extended-release capsules in nondepressed outpatients with generalized anxiety disorder: A 6-month randomized controlled trial. *JAMA, 283*, 3082–3088.

Gentes, E. L., & Ruscio, A. M. (2011). A meta-analysis of the relation of intolerance of uncertainty to symptoms of generalized anxiety disorder, major depressive disorder, and obsessive-compulsive disorder. *Clinical Psychology Review, 31*, 923–933.

Germine, M., Goddard, A. W., Woods, S. W., Charney, D. S., & Heninger, G. R. (1992). Anger and anxiety responses to m-chlorophenylpiperazine in generalized anxiety disorder. *Biological Psychiatry, 32*, 457–461.

Ghafoori, B., Barragan, B., Tohidian, N., & Palinkas, L. (2012). Racial and ethnic differences in symptom severity of PTSD, GAD, and depression in trauma-exposed, urban, treatment-seeking adults. *Journal of Traumatic Stress, 25*, 106–110.

Goddard, A. W., & Charney, D. S. (1997). Toward an integrated neurobiology of panic disorder. *Journal of Clinical Psychiatry, 58*, 4–12.

Gordon, D., & Heimberg, R. G. (2011). Reliability and validity of DSM-IV generalized anxiety disorder features. *Journal of Anxiety Disorders, 25*, 813–821.

Gosselin, P., Ladouceur, R., Morin, C. M., Dugas, M. J., & Baillargeon, L. (2006). Benzodiazepine discontinuation among adults with GAD: A randomized trial of cognitive-behavioral therapy. *Journal of Consulting and Clinical Psychology, 74*, 908–919.

Gould, R. A., Otto, M. W., Pollack, M. H., & Yap, L. (1997). Cognitive behavioral and pharmacological treatment of generalized anxiety disorder: A preliminary meta-analysis. *Behavior Therapy, 28*, 285–305.

Hale, W. W., Engels, R., & Meeus, W. (2006). Adolescent's perceptions of parenting behaviors and its relationship to adolescent generalized anxiety disorder symptoms. *Journal of Adolescence, 29*, 407–417.

Hale, W., Richmond, M., Bennett, J., Berzins, T., Fields, A., Weber, D., ... Osman, A. (2015). Resolving uncertainty about the Intolerance of Uncertainty Scale–12: Application of modern psychometric strategies. *Journal of Personality Assessment, 98*, 200–208.

Hanrahan, F., Field, A. P., Jones, F., & Davey, G. C. (2012). A meta-analysis of cognitive therapy for worry in generalized anxiety disorder. *Clinical Psychology Review, 33*, 120–132.

Hartford, J., Kornstein, S., Liebowitz, M., Pigott, T., Russell, J., Detke, M., ... Erickson, J. (2007). Duloxetine as an SNRI treatment for generalized anxiety disorder: Results from a placebo and active-controlled trial. *International Clinical Psychopharmacology, 22*, 167–174.

Hayes, S. C., Strosahl, K. D., & Wilson, K. G. (1999). *Acceptance and commitment therapy: An experiential approach to behavior change*. New York, NY: Guilford Press.

Henning, E. R., Turk, C. L., Mennin, D. S., Fresco, D. M., & Heimberg, R. G. (2007). Impairment and quality of life in individuals with generalized anxiety disorder. *Depression and Anxiety, 24,* 342–349.

Hettema, J. M., Kettenmann, B., Ahluwalia, V., McCarthy, C., Kates, W. R., Schmitt, J. E., ... Fatouros, P. (2012). Pilot multimodal twin imaging study of generalized anxiety disorder. *Depression and Anxiety, 29,* 202–209.

Hofmann, S. G., Wu, J. Q., & Boettcher, H. (2014). Effect of cognitive-behavioral therapy for anxiety disorders on quality of life: A meta-analysis. *Journal of Consulting and Clinical Psychology, 82,* 375–391.

Hong, R. Y. (2007). Worry and rumination: Differential associations with anxious and depressive symptoms and coping behavior. *Behaviour Research and Therapy, 45,* 277–290.

Hoyer, J., Becker, E. S., & Roth, W. T. (2001). Characteristics of worry in GAD patients, social phobics, and controls. *Depression and Anxiety, 13,* 89–96.

Judd, L. L., Kessler, R. C., Paulus, M. P., Zeller, P. V., Wittchen, H.-U., & Kunovac, J. L. (1998). Comorbidity as a fundamental feature of generalized anxiety disorder: Results from the National Comorbidity Study (NCS). *Acta Psychiatrica Scandinavica, 98,* 6–11.

Kalk, N. J., Nutt, D. J., & Lingford-Hughes, A. (2011). The role of central noradrenergic dysregulation in anxiety disorders: Evidence from clinical studies. *Journal of Psychopharmacology, 25,* 3–16.

Kelly, W. E. (2003). No time to worry: The relationship between worry, time structure, and time management. *Personality and Individual Differences, 35,* 1119–1126.

Kessler, R. C., Berglund, P., Demler, O., Jin, R., Merikangas, K. R., & Walters, E. E. (2005). Lifetime prevalence and age-of-onset distributions of DSM-III-R disorders in the National Comorbidity Survey replication. *Archives of General Psychiatry, 62,* 593–602.

Kim, T., Pae, C., Yoon, S., Bahk, W., Jun, T., Rhee, W., & Chae, J. (2006). Comparison of venlafaxine extended release versus paroxetine for treatment of patients with generalized anxiety disorder. *Psychiatry and Clinical Neurosciences, 60,* 347–351.

Koerner, N., & Dugas, M. J. (2008). An investigation of appraisals in individuals vulnerable to excessive worry: The role of intolerance of uncertainty. *Cognitive Therapy and Research, 32*(5), 619–638.

Ladouceur, R., Dugas, M. J., Freeston, M. H., Léger, E., Gagnon, E., & Thibodeau, N. (2000). Efficacy of a new cognitive-behavioral treatment for generalized anxiety disorder: Evaluation in a controlled clinical trial. *Journal of Consulting and Clinical Psychology, 68,* 957–964.

Ladouceur, R., Dugas, M. J., Freeston, M. H., Rhéaume, J., Blais, F., Boisvert, J., ... Thibodeau, N. (1999). Specificity of generalized anxiety disorder symptoms and processes. *Behavior Therapy, 30,* 191–207.

Laguna, L. B., Ham, L. S., Hope, D. A., & Bell, C. (2004). Chronic worry as avoidance of arousal. *Cognitive Therapy and Research, 28,* 269–281.

Lalonde, C. D., & Van Lieshout, R. J. (2011). Treating generalized anxiety disorder with second generation antipsychotics: A systematic review and meta-analysis. *Journal of Clinical Psychopharmacology, 31,* 326–333.

Langlois, F., Freeston, M. H., & Ladouceur, R. (2000). Differences and similarities between obsessive intrusive thoughts and worry in a non-clinical population: Study 1. *Behaviour Research and Therapy, 38,* 157–173.

Lee, S., Tsang, A., Ruscio, A. M., Haro, J. M., Stein, D. J., Alonso, J., ... Kessler, R. C. (2009). Implications of modifying the duration requirement of generalized anxiety disorder in developed and developing countries. *Psychological Medicine, 39,* 1163–1176.

Lenze, E. J., Mantella, R. C., Shi, P., Goate, A. M., Nowotny, P., Butters, M. A., ... Rollman, B. L. (2011). Elevated cortisol in older adults with generalized anxiety disorder is reduced by treatment: A placebo-controlled evaluation of escitalopram. *American Journal of Geriatric Psychiatry, 19,* 482–490.

Lenze, E. J., Rollman, B. L., Shear, M. K., Dew, M. A., Pollock, B. G., Ciliberti, C., ... Reynolds, C. F. (2009). Escitalopram for older adults with generalized anxiety disorder: A randomized controlled trial. *JAMA, 301,* 295–303.

Linehan, M. M. (1993). *Cognitive-behavioral treatment of borderline personality disorder.* New York, NY: Guilford Press.

Llera, S. J., & Newman, M. G. (2010). Effects of worry on physiological and subjective reactivity to emotional stimuli in generalized anxiety disorder and nonanxious control participants. *Emotion, 10,* 640–650.

Llera, S. J., & Newman, M. G. (2014). Rethinking the role of worry in generalized anxiety disorder: Evidence supporting a model of emotional contrast avoidance. *Behavior Therapy, 45*(3), 283–299.

MacLeod, C., Mathews, A., & Tata, P. (1986). Attentional bias in emotional disorders. *Journal of Abnormal Psychology, 95*, 15–20.

MacLeod, C., & McLaughlin, K. (1995). Implicit and explicit memory bias in anxiety: A conceptual replication. *Behaviour Research and Therapy, 33*, 1–14.

MacLeod, C., & Rutherford, E. (2004). Information-processing approaches: Assessing the selective functioning of attention, interpretation, and retrieval. In R. G. Heimberg, C. L. Turk, & D. S. Mennin (Eds.), *Generalized anxiety disorder: Advances in research and practice* (pp. 109–142). New York, NY: Guilford Press.

MacNamara, A., & Hajcak, G. (2010). Distinct electrocortical and behavioral evidence for increased attention to threat in generalized anxiety disorder. *Depression and Anxiety, 27*, 234–243.

Mantella, R. C., Butters, M. A., Amico, J. A., Mazumdar, S., Rollman, B. L., Begley, A. E., ... Lenze, E. J. (2008). Salivary cortisol is associated with diagnosis and severity of late-life generalized anxiety disorder. *Psychoneuroendocrinology, 33*, 773–781.

Marten, P. A., Brown, T. A., Barlow, D. H., Borkovec, T. D., Shear, M. K., & Lydiard, R. B. (1993). Evaluation of the ratings comprising the associated symptom criterion of DSM-III-R generalized anxiety disorder. *Journal of Nervous and Mental Disease, 181*, 676–682.

Martin, M., Williams, R., & Clark, D. (1991). Does anxiety lead to selective processing of threat-related information? *Behaviour Research and Therapy, 29*, 147–160.

Mathews, A., & Klug, F. (1993). Emotionality and interference with color-naming in anxiety. *Behaviour Research and Therapy, 31*, 57–62.

Mathews, A., & MacLeod, C. (1985). Selective processing of threat cues in anxiety states. *Behaviour Research and Therapy, 23*, 563–569.

Mavissakalian, M. R., Hamann, M. S., Haidar, S. A., & de Groot, C. M. (1995). Correlates of DSM-III personality disorder in generalized anxiety disorder. *Journal of Anxiety Disorders, 9*, 103–115.

McLean, C. P., & Anderson, E. R. (2009). Brave men and timid women? A review of the gender differences in fear and anxiety. *Clinical Psychology Review, 29*, 496–505.

McLean, C. P., Asnaani, A., Litz, B. T., & Hofmann, S. G. (2011). Gender differences in anxiety disorders: Prevalence, course of illness, comorbidity and burden of illness. *Journal of Psychiatric Research, 45*, 1027–1035.

Meeten, F., Dash, S. R., Scarlet, A. L. S., & Davey, G. C. L. (2012). Investigating the effect of intolerance of uncertainty on catastrophic worrying and mood. *Behaviour Research and Therapy, 50*, 690–698.

Mennin, D. S., Heimberg, R. G., Turk, C. L., & Fresco, D. M. (2005). Preliminary evidence for an emotion dysregulation model of generalized anxiety disorder. *Behaviour Research and Therapy, 43*, 1281–1310.

Mennin, D. S., Holaway, R. M., Fresco, D. M., Moore, M. T., & Heimberg, R. G. (2007). Delineating components of emotion and its dysregulation in anxiety and mood psychopathology. *Behavior Therapy, 38*, 284–302.

Merikangas, K. R., Avenevoli, S., Dierker, L., & Grillon, C. (1999). Vulnerability factors among children at risk for anxiety disorders. *Society for Biological Psychiatry, 99*, 172–179.

Meyer, T. J., Miller, M. L., Metzger, R. L., & Borkovec, T. D. (1990). Development and validation of the Penn State Worry Questionnaire. *Behaviour Research and Therapy, 28*, 487–495.

Mitte, K. (2005). Meta-analysis of cognitive-behavioral treatments for generalized anxiety disorder: A comparison with pharmacotherapy. *Psychological Bulletin, 131*, 785–795.

Mitte, K., Noack, P., Steil, R., & Hautzinger, M. (2005). A meta-analytic review of the efficacy of drug treatment in generalized anxiety disorder. *Psychopharmacology, 176*, 141–150.

Moffitt, T. E., Harrington, H., Caspi, A., Kim-Cohen, J., Goldberg, D., Gregory, A. M., & Poulton, R. (2007). Depression and generalized anxiety disorder: Cumulative and sequential comorbidity in a birth cohort followed prospectively to age 32 years. *Archives of General Psychiatry, 64*, 651–660.

Mogg, K., Baldwin, D. S., Brodrick, P., & Bradley, B P. (2004). Effect of short-term SSRI treatment on cognitive bias in generalized anxiety disorder. *Psychopharmacology, 176*, 466–470.

Mogg, K., & Bradley, B. P. (2005). Attentional bias in generalized anxiety disorder versus depressive disorder. *Cognitive Therapy and Research, 29*, 29–45.

Mogg, K., Bradley, B. P., Millar, N., & White, J. (1995). A follow-up study of cognitive bias in generalized anxiety disorder. *Behaviour Research and Therapy, 33*, 927–935.

Mogg, K., Bradley, B. P., & Williams, R. (1995). Attentional bias in anxiety and depression: The role of awareness. *British Journal of Clinical Psychology, 34*, 17–36.

Mogg, K., Millar, N., & Bradley, B. P. (2000). Biases in eye movements to threatening facial expressions in generalized anxiety disorder and depressive disorder. *Journal of Abnormal Psychology, 109*, 695–704.

Monk, C. S., Nelson, E. E., McClure, E. B., Mogg, K., Bradley, B. P., Leibenluft, E., ... Pine, D. S. (2006). Ventrolateral prefrontal cortex activation and attentional bias in response to angry faces in adolescents with generalized anxiety disorder. *American Journal of Psychiatry, 163*, 1091–1097.

Monk, C. S., Telzer, E. H., Mogg, K., Bradley, B. P., Mai, X., Louro, H. M. C., ... Pine, D. S. (2008). Amygdala and ventrolateral prefrontal cortex activation to masked angry faces in children and adolescents with generalized anxiety disorder. *Archives of General Psychiatry, 65*, 568–576.

National Institute for Health and Clinical Excellence. (2011). *Generalised anxiety disorder and panic disorder (with or without agoraphobia) in adults: Management in primary, secondary and community care.* Manchester, England: Author.

Newman, M. G., & Llera, S. J. (2011). A novel theory of experiential avoidance in generalized anxiety disorder: A review and synthesis of research supporting a contrast avoidance model of worry. *Clinical Psychology Review, 31*, 371–382.

Newman, M. G., Przeworski, A., Fisher, A. J., & Borkovec, T. D. (2010). Diagnostic comorbidity in adults with generalized anxiety disorder: Impact of comorbidity on psychotherapy outcome and impact of psychotherapy on comorbid diagnoses. *Behavior Therapy, 41*, 59–72.

Newman, M. G., Zuellig, A. R., Kachin, K. E., Constantino, M. J., Przeworski, A., Erickson, T., & Cashman-McGrath, L. (2002). Preliminary reliability and validity of the Generalized Anxiety Disorder Questionnaire–IV: A revised self-report diagnostic measure of generalized anxiety disorder. *Behavior Therapy, 33*, 215–233.

Nikolaus, S., Antke, C., Beu, M., & Müller, H. (2010). Cortical GABA, striatal dopamine and midbrain serotonin as the key players in compulsive and anxiety disorders—results from in vivo imaging studies. *Reviews in the Neurosciences, 21*, 119–139.

Nitschke, J. B., Sarinopoulos, I., Oathes, D. J., Johnstone, T., Whalen, P. J., Davidson, R. J., & Kalin, N. H. (2009). Anticipatory activation in the amygdala and anterior cingulate in generalized anxiety disorder and prediction of treatment response. *American Journal of Psychiatry, 166*, 302–310.

Normann, N., van Emmerik, A. A., & Morina, N. (2014). The efficacy of metacognitive therapy for anxiety and depression: A meta-analytic review. *Depression and Anxiety, 31*, 402–411.

Ouimet, A. J., Covin, R., & Dozois, D. J. A. (2012). Generalized anxiety disorder. In P. Sturmey & M. Hersen (Eds.), *Handbook of evidence-based practice in clinical psychology: Vol. 2. Adult disorders* (pp. 651–679). Hoboken, NJ: Wiley.

Penney, A. M., Mazmanian, D., & Rudanycz, C. (2013). Comparing positive and negative beliefs about worry in predicting generalized anxiety disorder symptoms. *Canadian Journal of Behavioural Science, 45*, 34–41. doi: 10.1037/a0027623

Petrovich, G. D., & Swanson, L. W. (1997). Projections from the lateral part of the central amygdalar nucleus to the postulated fear conditioning circuit. *Brain Research, 763*, 247–254.

Pittig, A., Arch, J. J., Lam, C. W. R., & Craske, M. G. (2013). Heart rate and heart rate variability in panic, social anxiety, obsessive-compulsive, and generalized anxiety disorders at baseline and in response to relaxation and hyperventilation. *International Journal of Psychophysiology, 87*, 19–27. doi: 10.1016/j.ijpsycho.2012.10.012

Porges, S. W. (1995). Orienting in a defensive world: Mammalian modifications of our evolutionary heritage. *A polyvagal theory. Psychophysiology, 32*, 301–318.

Pourmotabbed, T., McLeod, D. R., Hoehn-Saric, R., Hipsley, P., & Greenblatt, D. J. (1996). Treatment, discontinuation, and psychomotor effects of diazepam in women with generalized anxiety disorder. *Journal of Clinical Psychopharmacology, 16*, 202–207.

Provencher, M. D., Dugas, M. J., & Ladouceur, R. (2004). Efficacy of problem-solving training and cognitive exposure in the treatment of generalized anxiety disorder: A case replication series. *Cognitive and Behavioural Practice, 11*, 404–414.

Provencher, M. D., Freeston, M. H., Dugas, M. J., & Ladouceur, R. (2000). Catastrophizing assessment of worry and threat schemata among worriers. *Behavioral and Cognitive Psychotherapy*, *28*, 211–224.

Rickels, K., Shiovitz, T. M., Ramey, T. S., Weaver, J. J., Knapp, L. E., & Miceli, J. J. (2012). Adjunctive therapy with pregabalin in generalized anxiety disorder patients with partial response to SSRI or SNRI treatment. *International Clinical Psychopharmacology*, *27*, 142–150.

Robichaud, M., Dugas, M. J., & Conway, M. (2003). Gender differences in worry and associated cognitive-behavioral variables. *Journal of Anxiety Disorders*, *17*, 501–516.

Rodriguez, B. F., Weisberg, R. B., Pagano, M. E., Bruce, S. E., Spencer, M. A., Culpepper, L., & Keller, M. B. (2006). Characteristics and predictors of full and partial recovery from generalized anxiety disorder in primary care patients. *Journal of Nervous and Mental Disease*, *194*, 91–97.

Roemer, L. (2001). Measures for generalized anxiety disorder. In M. M. Antony, S. M. Orsillo, & L. Roemer (Eds.), *Practitioner's guide to empirically based measures of anxiety* (pp. 197–210). New York, NY: Springer.

Roemer, L., & Medaglia, E. (2001). Generalized anxiety disorder: A brief overview and guide to assessment. In M. M. Antony, S. M. Orsillo, & L. Roemer (Eds.), *Practitioner's guide to empirically based measures of anxiety* (pp. 189–195). New York, NY: Springer.

Roemer, L., & Orsillo, S. M. (2007). An open trial of an acceptance-based behavior therapy for generalized anxiety disorder. *Behavior Therapy*, *38*, 72–85.

Roemer, L., Orsillo, S. M., & Salters-Pedneault, K. (2008). Efficacy of an acceptance-based behavior therapy for generalized anxiety disorder: Evaluation in a randomized controlled trial. *Journal of Consulting and Clinical Psychology*, *76*, 1083–1089.

Roemer, L., Salters, K., Raffa, S. D., & Orsillo, S. M. (2005). Fear and avoidance of internal experiences in GAD: Preliminary tests of a conceptual model. *Cognitive Therapy and Research*, *29*, 71–88.

Roy, M., Neale, M. C., Pedersen, N. L., Mathe, A. A., & Kendler, K. S. (1995). A twin study of generalized anxiety disorder and major depression. *Psychological Medicine*, *25*, 1037–1049.

Roy-Byrne, P., & Wagner, A. (2004). Primary care perspectives on generalized anxiety disorder. *Journal of Clinical Psychiatry*, *65*(Suppl. 13), 20–26.

Ruscio, A. M., & Borkovec, T. D. (2004). Experience and appraisal of worry among high worriers with and without generalized anxiety disorder. *Behaviour Research and Therapy*, *42*(12), 1469–1482.

Salters-Pedneault, K., Roemer, L., Tull, M. T., Rucker, L., & Mennin, D. S. (2006). Evidence of broad deficits in emotion regulation associated with chronic worry and generalized anxiety disorder. *Cognitive Therapy and Research*, *30*, 469–480.

Schneier, F. R., Belzer, K. D., Kishon, R., Amsel, L., & Simpson, H. B. (2010). Escitalopram for persistent symptoms of generalized anxiety disorder after CBT: A pilot study. *Journal of Nervous and Mental Disease*, *198*, 458–461.

Schweizer, E., & Rickels, K. (1997). Placebo response in generalized anxiety: Its effect on the outcome of clinical trials. *Journal of Clinical Psychiatry*, *58*, 30–38.

Scott, E. L., Eng, W., & Heimberg, R. G. (2002). Ethnic differences in worry in a nonclinical population. *Depression and Anxiety*, *15*, 79–82.

Segerstrom, S. C., Tsao, J. C. I., Alden, L. E., & Craske, M. G. (2000). Worry and rumination: Repetitive thought as a concomitant and predictor of negative mood. *Cognitive Therapy and Research*, *24*, 671–688.

Sinha, S. S., Mohlman, J., & Gorman, J. M. (2004). Neurobiology. In R. G. Heimberg, C. L. Turk, & D. S. Mennin (Eds.), *Generalized anxiety disorder: Advances in research and practice* (pp. 187–216). New York, NY: Guilford Press.

Spitzer, R. L., Kroenke, K., Williams, J. B. W., & Löwe, B. (2006). A brief measure for assessing generalized anxiety disorder: The GAD-7. *Archives of Internal Medicine*, *166*, 1092–1097.

Stapinski, L. A., Abbott, M. J., & Rapee, R. M. (2010). Evaluating the cognitive avoidance model of generalised anxiety disorder: Impact of worry on threat appraisal, perceived control and anxious arousal. *Behaviour Research and Therapy*, *48*, 1032–1040.

Startup, H. M., & Davey, G. C. L. (2001). Mood as input and catastrophic worrying. *Journal of Abnormal Psychology*, *110*, 83–96.

Startup, H. M., & Davey, G. C. L. (2003). Inflated responsibility and the use of stop rules for catastrophic worrying. *Behaviour Research and Therapy*, *41*, 495–503.

Stöber, J. (1998). Worry, problem elaboration and suppression of imagery: The role of concreteness. *Behaviour Research and Therapy*, *36*, 751–756.

Suarez, L., & Bell-Dolan, D. (2001). The relationship of child worry to cognitive biases: Threat interpretation and likelihood of event occurrence. *Behavior Therapy*, *32*, 425–442.

Tallis, F., Davey, G. C. L., & Capuzzo, N. (1994). The phenomenology of non-pathological worry: A preliminary investigation. In G. C. L. Davey & F. Tallis (Eds.), *Worrying: Perspectives on theory, assessment, and treatment* (pp. 61–89). Chichester, England: Wiley.

Tallis, F., Eysenck, M., & Mathews, A. (1992). A questionnaire for the measurement of nonpathological worry. *Personality and Individual Differences*, *13*, 161–168.

Terlevic, R., Isola, M., Ragogna, M., Meduri, M., Canalaz, F., Perini, L., … Brambilla, P. (2013). Decreased hypothalamus volumes in generalized anxiety disorder but not in panic disorder. *Journal of Affective Disorders*, *146*, 390–394. doi: 10.1016/j.jad .2012.09.024

Thayer, J. F., Friedman, T., & Borkovec, T. D. (1996). Autonomic characteristics of generalized anxiety disorder and worry. *Biological Psychiatry*, *39*, 255–266.

Thayer, J. F., Friedman, T., Borkovec, T. D., Molina, S., & Johnsen, B. H. (2000). Phasic heart period reactions to cued threat and non-threat stimuli in generalized anxiety disorder. *Psychophysiology*, *37*, 361–368.

Thayer, J. F., & Lane, R. D. (2000). A model of neurovisceral integration in emotion regulation and dysregulation. *Journal of Affective Disorders*, *61*, 201–216.

Tiller, J. W., Biddle, N., Maguire, K. P., & Davies, B. M. (1988). The dexamethasone suppression test and plasma dexamethasone in generalized anxiety disorder. *Biological Psychiatry*, *23*, 261–270.

Toghanian, S., DiBonaventura, M., Järbrink, K., & Locklear, J. C. (2014). Economic and humanistic burden of illness in generalized anxiety disorder: An analysis of patient survey data in Europe. *Clinicoeconomics and Outcomes Research*, *6*, 151–163.

Tromp, D. P., Grupe, D. W., Oathes, D. J., McFarlin, D. R., Hernandez, P. J., Kral, T. R., … Nitschke, J. B. (2012). Reduced structural connectivity of a major frontolimbic pathway in generalized anxiety disorder. *Archives of General Psychiatry*, *69*, 925–934.

Turk, C. L., Heimberg, R. G., Luterek, J. A., Mennin, D. S., & Fresco, D. M. (2005). Emotion dysregulation in generalized anxiety disorder: A comparison with social anxiety disorder. *Cognitive Therapy and Research*, *29*, 89–106.

Uher, R., Payne, J. L., Pavlova, B., & Perlis, R. H. (2014). Major depressive disorder in DSM-5: Implications for clinical practice and research of changes from DSM-IV. *Depression and Anxiety*, *31*, 459–471.

Van Bockstaele, B., Verschuere, B., Tibboel, H., De Houwer, J., Crombez, G., & Koster, E. H. (2014). A review of current evidence for the causal impact of attentional bias on fear and anxiety. *Psychological Bulletin*, *140*, 682–721.

van der Heiden, C., Muris, P., & van der Molen, H. T. (2012). Randomized controlled trial on the effectiveness of metacognitive therapy and intolerance-of-uncertainty therapy for generalized anxiety disorder. *Behaviour Research and Therapy*, *50*, 100–109.

van Eijck, F. E. A. M., Branje, S. J. T., Hale, W. W., & Meeus, W. H. J. (2012). Longitudinal associations between perceived parent-adolescent attachment relationship quality and generalized anxiety disorder symptoms in adolescence. *Journal of Abnormal Child Psychology*, *40*, 871–883.

Vesga-López, O., Schneier, F. R., Wang, S., Heimberg, R. G., Liu, S., Hasin, D. S., & Blanco, C. (2008). Gender differences in generalized anxiety disorder: Results from the National Epidemiologic Survey on Alcohol and Related Conditions (NESARC). *Journal of Clinical Psychiatry*, *69*, 1606–1616.

Watkins, E., Moulds, M., & Mackintosh, B. (2005). Comparisons between rumination and worry in a non-clinical population. *Behaviour Research and Therapy*, *43*, 1577–1585.

Wells, A. (1994). A multi-dimensional measure of worry: Development and preliminary validation of the Anxious Thoughts Inventory. *Anxiety, Stress, and Coping*, *6*, 280–299.

Wells, A. (1995). Meta-cognition and worry: A cognitive model of generalised anxiety disorder. *Behavioural and Cognitive Psychotherapy*, *23*, 301–320.

Wells, A. (1999). A metacognitive model and therapy for generalized anxiety disorder. *Clinical Psychology & Psychotherapy*, *6*, 86–95.

Wells, A. (2006). The metacognitive model of worry and generalised anxiety disorder. In G. C. L. Davey & A. Wells (Eds.), *Worry and its psychological disorders: Theory, assessment, and treatment* (pp. 179–200). Chichester, England: Wiley.

Wells, A., & Carter, K. (1999). Preliminary tests of a cognitive model of generalized anxiety disorder. *Behaviour Research and Therapy*, *37*, 585–594.

Wells, A., & Carter, K. (2001). Further tests of a cognitive model of generalized anxiety disorder: Metacognitions and worry in GAD, panic disorder, social phobia, depression, and nonpatients. *Behavior Therapy, 32*, 85–102.

Wells, A., & Cartwright-Hatton, S. (2004). A short form of the Metacognitions Questionnaire: Properties of the MCQ-30. *Behaviour Research and Therapy, 42*, 385–396.

Wells, A., & King, P. (2006). Metacognitive therapy for generalized anxiety disorder: An open trial. *Journal of Behavior Therapy and Experimental Psychiatry, 37*, 206–212.

Wells, A., & Papageorgiou, C. (1995). Worry and the incubation of intrusive images following stress. *Behaviour Research and Therapy, 33*, 579–583.

Wells, A., Welford, M., King, P., Papageorgiou, C., Wisely, J., & Mendel, E. (2010). A pilot randomized trial of metacognitive therapy vs applied relaxation in the treatment of adults with generalized anxiety disorder. *Behaviour Research and Therapy, 48*, 429–434.

Wenzel, A., Haugen, E. N., Jackson, L. C., & Robinson, K. (2003). Prevalence of generalized anxiety at eight weeks postpartum. *Archives of Women's Mental Health, 6*(1), 43–49. doi: 10.1007 /s00737-002-0154-2

Westra, H. A., Arkowitz, H., & Dozois, D. J. A. (2009). Adding a motivational interviewing pretreatment to cognitive behavioral therapy for generalized anxiety disorder: A preliminary randomized controlled trial. *Journal of Anxiety Disorders, 23*, 1106–1117.

Westra, H. A., Constantino, M. J., & Antony, M. M. (2016). Integrating motivational interviewing with cognitive-behavioral therapy for severe generalized anxiety disorder: An allegiance-controlled randomized clinical trial. *Journal of Consulting and Clinical Psychology, 84*(9), 768–782. doi: 10.1037/ ccp0000098

Whalen, P. J., Johnstone, T., Somerville, L. H., Nitschke, J. B., Polis, S., Alexander, A. L., … Kalin, N. H. (2008). A functional magnetic resonance imaging predictor of treatment response to venlafaxine in generalized anxiety disorder. *Biological Psychiatry, 63*, 858–863.

Wittchen, H.-U. (2002). Generalized anxiety disorder: Prevalence, burden, and cost to society. *Depression and Anxiety, 16*, 162–171.

Wittchen, H.-U., Zhao, S., Kessler, R. C., & Eaton, W. W. (1994). DSM-III-R generalized anxiety disorder in the National Comorbidity Survey. *Archives of General Psychiatry, 51*, 355–364.

Woodman, C. L., Noyes, R., Jr., Black, D., Schlosser, S., & Yagla, S. (1999). A 5-year follow-up study of generalized anxiety disorder and panic disorder. *Journal of Nervous and Mental Disease, 187*, 3–9.

Wu, J. C., Buchsbaum, M. S., Hershey, T. G., Hazlett, E., Sicotte, N., & Johnson, J. C. (1991). PET in generalized anxiety disorder. *Biological Psychiatry, 29*, 1181–1199.

Yonkers, K. A., Dyck, I. R., Warshaw, M., & Keller, M. B. (2000). Factors predicting the clinical course of generalized anxiety disorder. *British Journal of Psychiatry, 176*, 544–549.

Chapter 5

Obsessive-Compulsive and Related Disorders

JONATHAN S. ABRAMOWITZ AND SHANNON M. BLAKEY

Obsessive-compulsive disorder (OCD) is one of the most devastating psychological disorders. Its symptoms often interfere with work or school, with interpersonal relationships, and with activities of daily living (e.g., watching television, child care). Moreover, the psychopathology of OCD is among the most complex of the psychological disorders. Sufferers appear to struggle against seemingly ubiquitous unwanted thoughts, doubts, and urges that, while senseless on the one hand, are perceived as signs of danger on the other. The wide array of symptoms and intricate associations between behavioral and cognitive symptoms can perplex even the most experienced of clinicians. This chapter describes the nature of OCD symptoms, the leading explanatory theories, and the empirically supported approaches to assessment and treatment.

The Nature of OCD: Diagnostic Criteria

Obsessive-compulsive disorder (OCD) is defined by the presence of *obsessions* or *compulsions* that produce significant distress and cause noticeable interference with various aspects of role functioning (e.g., academic or occupational functioning) (American Psychiatric Association [APA], 2013). The *DSM-5* diagnostic criteria appear in Table 5.1. *Obsessions* are intrusive thoughts, ideas, images, impulses, or doubts that the person experiences as senseless and that evoke anxiety. Examples include unwanted ideas of germs and contamination, unwanted doubts that one has been negligent, and unacceptable thoughts of a violent, sexual, or blasphemous nature. *Compulsions* are urges to perform overt (e.g., checking, washing) or mental (e.g., praying) rituals in response to obsessions or to reduce anxiety or distress. The person typically perceives these compulsive rituals as senseless or excessive.

Traditionally, OCD has been considered an anxiety disorder because its cardinal features are anxiety and fear, and efforts to control and escape from anxiety and fear. In *DSM-5*, however, OCD has been removed from the anxiety disorders and is now the flagship diagnosis for a new diagnostic category: obsessive-compulsive and related disorders (OCRDs). Other conditions in this category include body dysmorphic disorder, hair pulling disorder (aka trichotillomania), skin picking disorder, and hoarding disorder.

TABLE 5.1   **Clinical Features of Obsessive-Compulsive Disorder**

Diagnosis requires either obsessions or compulsions, or both:

Obsessions are recurrent, persistent thoughts, urges, or images that are intrusive and unwanted, which the individual tries to ignore, suppress, or neutralize.

Compulsions are repetitive behaviors or mental acts that are intended to prevent or reduce anxiety or distress or to prevent a dreaded event that the person feels driven to do, either to neutralize an obsession or prevent an event, even though the behaviors or mental acts are not reasonably related to the obsession or are excessive.

In addition, the obsessions and compulsions must be time-consuming (more than an hour a day) and cause distress or impairment, not be due to other substances or medical conditions, and not be better explained by other mental conditions.

Specifiers:

Note if good/fair insight (recognition that beliefs probably not true), poor insight (believed to be probably true), or absent insight/delusional (believed to be definitely true).

Note if tic-related (current or past history of a tic disorder).

Source: Based on *DSM-5*.

Signs and Symptoms of OCD

A multifaceted condition, OCD involves not only different types of symptoms but also different thematic variations within each symptom. This section describes the primary symptoms of the disorder, along with a number of other conditions that have been grouped together with OCD.

OBSESSIONS

As mentioned previously, obsessions are thoughts, images, impulses, doubts, and ideas that are experienced as unwanted, persistent, and intrusive; anxiety- or guilt-provoking; or repugnant and senseless (APA, 2013). Although highly individualized, the general themes of obsessions can be organized into categories such as contamination; guilt and responsibility for harm (to self or others); uncertainty; taboo thoughts about sex, violence, and blasphemy; and the need for order and symmetry. Most patients evince multiple obsessional themes and forms, and sometimes there are shifts in the content of these phenomena.

Unlike other types of repetitive thoughts, obsessions are experienced as *unwanted* or *uncontrollable* in that they *intrude* into consciousness (often triggered by something in the environment). The content of obsessions is also *incongruent* with the individual's belief system and is not the type of thought the person would expect of himself or herself. Finally, obsessions are *resisted*; that is, they are accompanied by the sense that they must be "dealt with," neutralized, or altogether avoided. The motivation to resist is activated by the fear that if action is not taken, disastrous consequences may occur. Table 5.2 presents examples of common obsessions observed in people with OCD.

TABLE 5.2   Examples of Obsessions Reported by Clinic Patients with OCD

Category	Example
Contamination	What if I get rabies from driving over a dead animal on the street?
	I used a public bathroom; what if I have someone else's germs on me?
Responsibility for harm or mistakes	By mistake, I might have kissed someone other than my spouse without realizing it.
	What if I left the door unlocked and someone will break into my home?
	What if I called my friend a racial slur without realizing it?
	What if I hit someone with my car without realizing it?
Symmetry/order	Odd numbers are incorrect.
	The books must be evenly placed on the shelf or else I will have bad luck.
Unacceptable thoughts with immoral, sexual, or violent content	Image of Jesus with an erection on the Cross.
	Image of my grandparents having sex.
	Thought about stabbing my husband in his sleep.

COMPULSIONS

Compulsive rituals are the most conspicuous features of OCD and often the most func-tionally impairing. They typically belong to the following categories: decontamination (washing/cleaning), checking (including asking others for reassurance), repeating rou-tine activities (e.g., going back and forth through a doorway), ordering and arranging, and mental rituals. Compulsions are senseless and excessive, and often need to be per-formed according to rules. They are also intentional, in contrast to mechanical or robotic repetitive behaviors such as tics. Finally, rituals in OCD are performed to reduce dis-tress, in contrast to repetitive behaviors in addictive or impulse-control disorders (e.g., sexual addiction, trichotillomania), which are carried out because they produce pleasure, distraction, or gratification (APA, 2013).

In most instances, compulsive rituals are performed to reduce obsessional anxiety about particular feared consequences that the individual can articulate. Examples include exces-sively checking appliances to reduce fears of electrical fires and excessive cleaning to avoid a feared sickness. In other cases, patients have difficulty articulating the presence of obsessionally feared consequences, and instead perform rituals to reduce feelings of anxiety or to achieve a feeling of completeness. Table 5.3 presents examples of common compulsive rituals observed in people with OCD.

As Table 5.3 shows, compulsions can be overt or covert. Additional examples of covert (mental) rituals include repetition of "safe" phrases or prayers in a specific manner, and mentally checking ("analyzing" or "reviewing") one's previous conversations to be sure one has not said anything offensive. In response to their obsessional fears, most people with OCD also deploy strategies that do not meet *DSM* criteria for compulsions (i.e., the strategies are not rule-bound or repeated over and over). Examples include purposeful distraction and thought suppression. Such rituals can take infinitely diverse forms, and

TABLE 5.3   Examples of Compulsive Rituals Reported by Clinic Patients with OCD

Category	Example
Decontamination	Hand washing for 45 minutes in response to using the bathroom.
	Wiping down all objects brought into the house for fear of germs from recently applied pesticides on an adjacent lawn.
Checking	Driving back to recheck that no accidents were caused at the intersection.
	Returning home after seeing a fire engine to make sure the house wasn't on fire.
Repeating routine activities	Going through a doorway over and over to prevent bad luck.
	Retracing one's steps to make sure that no mistakes were made.
Ordering/arranging	Saying the word "left" whenever one hears the word "right."
	Rearranging the books on the bookshelf until they are "just right."
Mental rituals	Canceling a bad thought by thinking of a good thought.
	Excessive praying to prevent feared disastrous consequences.

some may be remarkably subtle. Functionally, however, all of these behaviors serve to neutralize obsessional thoughts or fears. The following examples illustrate neutralization strategies.

- One man gripped the steering wheel tightly when he had distressing thoughts of driving his car into opposing traffic.
- A woman with obsessional thoughts of her child drowning tried to suppress and dismiss such images when they came to mind (thought suppression).
- A woman with obsessions about harming her husband confessed these thoughts to him whenever they came to her mind. She explained, "If I tell my husband that I'm thinking about hurting him, he'll be ready to stop me if I start to act."

Many individuals with OCD also engage in repeated attempts to gain ultimate certainty that obsessional doubts are invalid. Such attempts to gain assurances might be overt (e.g., asking questions, checking the Internet) or covert (checking one's body for signs of sexual arousal in response to inappropriate stimuli), although the most straightforward style is asking similar questions over and over.

AVOIDANCE

Avoidance behavior is present in most people with OCD and is intended to prevent obsessional fears and compulsive urges altogether. The aim of avoidance in some cases might be to thwart specific consequences such as contamination or illness, whereas in other instances avoidance is focused on preventing obsessional thoughts from occurring in the first place. For example, one woman avoided using knives because they evoked thoughts and fears of impulsively stabbing her children. Other patients engage in avoidance so they do not have to carry out tedious compulsive rituals. For instance, a young man with obsessional fears of contamination from his family's home computer (because it had been used to view pornography) engaged in elaborate and time-consuming compulsive cleaning and showering rituals. During the morning and afternoon he avoided the computer room so that he would not have to perform these rituals during the day. In the evening, however, he relaxed his avoidance and allowed himself to enter the room and become contaminated knowing that he could "work in" his ritualistic showering before bedtime.

Subtypes and Dimensions of OCD

Although there are grounds for conceptualizing OCD as a single disorder, research has identified four reliable and valid OCD symptom dimensions (Abramowitz et al., 2010; McKay et al., 2004). These include (a) contamination (contamination obsessions and decontamination rituals), (b) responsibility for harm and mistakes (aggressive obsessions and checking rituals), (c) incompleteness (obsessions about order or exactness and arranging rituals), and (d) unacceptable taboo violent, sexual, or blasphemous thoughts with mental rituals.

Poor Insight

As is shown in Table 5.1, the *DSM-5* criteria for OCD include the specifiers "good or fair insight," "poor insight," and "absent insight" to denote the degree to which the person views his or her obsessional fears and compulsive behavior as reasonable. Although most people with OCD recognize that their obsessions and compulsions are senseless and excessive, there is a continuum of insight, with 4% of patients convinced that their symptoms are realistic (i.e., they have poor or absent insight; Foa & Kozak, 1995). Poorer insight appears to be associated with religious obsessions, fears of mistakes, and aggressive obsessional impulses (Tolin, Abramowitz, Kozak, & Foa, 2001).

Tic-Related OCD

The *DSM-5* criteria also denote a subtype of OCD in which the individual has a history of tic disorders, such as Tourette's syndrome. While the data are inconclusive, this putative variant of OCD appears to run in families and to involve an early onset and male predominance. The patient's obsessions typically concern symmetry and exactness, and their compulsions often involve ordering and arranging.

Interpersonal Aspects of OCD

OCD frequently has a negative impact on the sufferer's interpersonal relationships—such as those with a romantic partner, spouse, or other family members. In turn, dysfunctional relationship patterns can promote the maintenance of OCD symptoms so that a vicious cycle develops. For example, a partner or spouse might inadvertently behave in ways that maintain OCD symptoms by helping with compulsive rituals and avoidance behavior out of love, care, and concern for the sufferer (i.e., *symptom accommodation*). OCD symptoms also create relationship distress and conflict, which exacerbate the anxiety and obsessional symptoms. In this section we discuss these patterns and their effects on OCD symptoms.

Symptom Accommodation

Accommodation occurs when a friend or relative participates in the loved one's rituals, facilitates avoidance strategies, assumes daily responsibilities for the sufferer, or helps to resolve problems that have resulted from the patient's obsessional fears and compulsive urges. The accommodation might occur at the request (or demand) of the individual with OCD, who deliberately tries to involve loved ones to help with controlling his or her anxiety. In other instances, loved ones voluntarily accommodate because they feel the need to empathize with their suffering partners and do not wish to see them become highly anxious. Table 5.4 shows examples of accommodation behaviors we have observed in our work with couples in which one partner has OCD.

Conceptually, because avoidance and compulsive rituals prevent the natural extinction of obsessional fear and ritualistic urges, accommodation by a relative or close friend perpetuates OCD symptoms. For instance, consider a woman with obsessional fears of acting on unwanted impulses to molest her newborn infant, who requests that her husband change and bathe their newborn child. By engaging in this behavior by himself (i.e., by accommodating his wife's OCD symptoms), he prevents his wife from learning that she is unlikely to act on her unwanted obsessional thoughts. Furthermore, she misses the opportunity to learn that she could manage the temporary anxiety that accompanies her repugnant obsessions. Indeed, researchers have found that family accommodation predicts an attenuated response to cognitive-behavioral treatment for OCD (Steketee & Van Noppen, 2003).

Relationship Conflict

Relationship stress and conflict also play an important role in the maintenance of OCD. Couples in which one partner suffers with OCD often report problems with interdependency, unassertiveness, and avoidant communication patterns that foster stress and conflict. In all likelihood, OCD symptoms and relationship distress influence each other, rather

TABLE 5.4   Examples of Family Accommodation Behaviors in OCD

OCD Symptom	Partner Accommodation Behavior
Contamination and washing symptoms	Washing or cleaning for the patient
	Doing extra laundry
	Avoiding contaminated stimuli
Obsessional doubting and compulsive checking	Assisting with checking rituals
	Providing reassurance
	Helping the patient avoid ambiguous situations that might trigger doubts
Violent, sexual, and religious obsessions	Providing reassurance
	Helping with avoidance of stimuli that trigger obsessional thoughts
	Helping with praying or interpreting Bible passages or religious doubts
Ordering and symmetry ("not just right") obsessions and compulsions	Checking to make sure things are in order or arranged properly
	Repeating answers until they are just right

than one exclusively leading to the other. For example, a husband's contentious relationship with his wife might contribute to overall anxiety and uncertainty that develops into his obsessional doubting. His excessive checking, reassurance seeking, and overly cautious actions could also lead to frequent disagreements and relationship conflict. Particular aspects of a relationship that might increase distress and contribute to OCD maintenance include poor problem-solving skills, hostility, and criticism. Moreover, criticism, hostility, and emotional overinvolvement are associated with premature treatment discontinuation and symptom relapse (Chambless & Steketee, 1999).

OBSESSIVE-COMPULSIVE RELATED DISORDERS

In *DSM-5*, OCD has been removed from its traditional categorization among the anxiety disorders, and placed in a new category of putatively similar obsessive-compulsive and related disorders (OCRDs), which includes body dysmorphic disorder, hoarding disorder, skin picking disorder, and hair pulling disorder (trichotillomania). This change has been criticized on conceptual, practical, and empirical grounds as we briefly describe next (for a more thorough discussion, see Abramowitz & Jacoby, 2015).

One impetus for the creation of the OCD-related disorders category in *DSM-5* is the fact that the disorders of this group all involve repetitive thoughts or behaviors. Repetitive behaviors are indeed present in both OCD and the OCRDs—for example, trichotillomania (now called hair pulling disorder in *DSM-5*) and excessive skin picking. Whereas compulsive rituals in OCD are performed in response to obsessional fear and they function as an escape from distress, hair pulling and skin picking are not triggered by obsessions or fear, and do not function to reduce fears of negative consequences (e.g., Stanley, Swann, Bowers, & Davis, 1992). Although individuals with these problems may experience guilt, shame, and anxiety associated with their repetitive behaviors, this is not the same as obsessional fear.

Body Dysmorphic Disorder (BDD)

Both BDD and OCD can involve intrusive, distressing thoughts concerning one's appearance, and repeated checking might be observed in both disorders. However, the focus of BDD symptoms is limited to one's appearance, whereas people with OCD also tend to have other obsessions. Nevertheless, similar psychological treatments can be effective for both conditions.

Hoarding

Once considered to be a symptom of OCD, hoarding is now understood as a separate problem. Indeed, many individuals with hoarding do not meet diagnostic criteria for OCD (Pertusa et al., 2010), and hoarding symptoms are no more prevalent in patients with OCD than in patients with other psychological disorders (Abramowitz, Wheaton, & Storch, 2008). Hoarding also differs from other OCD symptom domains and does not fit into conceptual frameworks for understanding OCD (Rachman, Elliot, Shafran, & Radomsky, 2009). Hoarding typically involves thoughts about acquiring and maintaining possessions, thoughts that are not particularly intrusive or unwanted; in fact, these thoughts are generally emotionally positive or neutral and thus do not meet criteria for obsessions (Rachman et al., 2009). It is also difficult to conceptualize excessive saving as

compulsive or ritualistic, and this behavior does not result in an escape from (or neutralization of) obsessional anxiety in the way that checking or washing compulsions do
(Rachman et al., 2009).

OBSESSIVE-COMPULSIVE PERSONALITY DISORDER (OCPD)

OCPD involves the presence of personality traits such as excessive perfectionism, inflexibility, and need for control that negatively impact interpersonal relationships, occupational
functioning, or other important domains of an individual's life. Individuals with this condition often maintain strict principles and are intolerant of others who do not conform to
their standards. Historically, clinical opinion has proposed a special relationship between
OCPD and OCD, which can be traced back to Freud's anecdotal account of the "Rat Man,"
who was described as having both conditions. Similarities between OCD and OCPD can
sometimes be observed, such as excessive list making and arranging. However, the functional roles of these symptoms are notably distinct in each syndrome. The experience of
individuals with OCPD is *ego-syntonic* in that they consider their behaviors and urges
as rational and appropriate. In contrast, the obsessive thoughts experienced by individuals with OCD are *ego-dystonic* in that they are experienced as unwanted, upsetting, and
personally repugnant. People with OCD harming obsessions may feel compelled to write
down everything they have done during a day in order to reassure themselves that they have
not caused a catastrophe, whereas an individual with OCPD may believe that making lists
of daily activities maximizes efficiency and ensures that no details are overlooked.

Although distinct, OCD and OCPD may co-occur. Comorbidity estimates have suggested that between 23% and 32% of OCD patients also display one or more symptoms
of OCPD, and some studies have suggested that comorbid OCPD is associated with poorer
treatment outcome for OCD (Eisen, Mancebo, Chiappone, Pinto, & Rasmussen, 2008).
However, OCPD has also been found to co-occur with a variety of other anxiety disorders
as well as depression (Dowson & Grounds, 1995). In addition, other personality disorders,
such as avoidant and dependent personality disorder, have been estimated to co-occur with
OCD at least as frequently as OCPD, if not more so (Pfohl & Blum, 1991), suggesting the
lack of a unique relationship between OCD and OCPD.

Prevalence and Epidemiology of OCD

Once considered a rare condition, OCD is now known to be among the most common
psychological disorders. Data consistently show that the prevalence and course of OCD
are similar cross-culturally and worldwide.

PREVALENCE

The lifetime prevalence of OCD has been estimated at between 0.7% and 2.9% (e.g.,
Kessler et al., 2005) and there is a slight preponderance of females (Rasmussen & Eisen,
1992a). The disorder typically begins by age 25, although childhood or adolescence onset
is not rare. Mean onset age is earlier in males (about 21 years) than in females (22 to
24 years) (Rasmussen & Eisen, 1992b).

COURSE

OCD is a chronic condition with a low rate of spontaneous remission. Left untreated, symptoms fluctuate, with worsening during periods of increased life stress. Fortunately, more patients now receive effective treatments than ever before, leading to increased rates of symptom remission. Full recovery, however, is the exception rather than the rule.

Psychological Models

Early conceptualizations of OCD were dominated by the Freudian psychoanalytic tradition—the disorder was viewed as arising from unconscious conflicts Those from the behavioral tradition, however, rejected psychoanalytic approaches because of the lack of scientific validity, and instead relied on empirically demonstrable principles of learning and conditioning to explain the problem. Cognitive theorists later considered the need to incorporate the role of one's thinking (whether normal and abnormal) in understanding the OCD, leading to contemporary cognitive-behavioral conceptualizations.

LEARNING MODELS

Behavioral (conditioning) models of OCD are based on Mowrer's (1960) two-stage theory of fear acquisition and maintenance. In the first stage (classical conditioning), a previously neutral stimulus (the conditioned stimulus, or CS) is paired with an aversive stimulus (the unconditioned stimulus, or UCS; e.g., a traumatic experience), so that the CS comes to elicit a conditioned fear response, or CR. As a result, situations (e.g., driving, using the bathroom); objects (e.g., door handles, knives); and thoughts, images, doubts, or impulses (e.g., thoughts of harm) that pose no objective threat come to evoke obsessional fear.

In the second stage (operant conditioning), avoidance behaviors develop as a means of reducing anxiety; avoidance is negatively reinforced by the immediate (albeit temporary) reduction in distress it engenders. Compulsive rituals, which develop as an escape behavior from obsessional fear when avoidance is impossible, are also negatively reinforced in this way. Avoidance and escape behaviors, however, prevent the natural extinction of obsessional fears, and thereby maintain such fear.

Although the conditioning explanation has fallen out of favor as an explanation for the *development* of OCD symptoms, operant conditioning (negative reinforcement) does appear to play a role in the *maintenance* of OCD symptoms. Experimental research, for example, has repeatedly found that compulsive behavior leads to anxiety reduction (e.g., Hodgson & Rachman, 1972). Overall, then, negative reinforcement provides an empirically valid explanation for the *persistence* of compulsive rituals and avoidance behavior in OCD.

COGNITIVE DEFICIT MODELS

Memory

Some theorists have proposed that OCD symptoms arise from abnormally functioning cognitive processes, such as memory. Compulsive checking, for example, could develop as a consequence of not being able to remember whether one has locked the door, and so on. Research, however, has found no evidence of a memory deficit in OCD (e.g., Abramovitch, Abramowitz, & Mittleman, 2013; Woods, Vevea, Chambless, & Bayen, 2002). In fact, patients appear to have a selectively *better* memory for OCD-related information relative to non-OCD-relevant stimuli (Radomsky, Rachman, & Hammond, 2001).

Reality Monitoring

It has also been proposed that OCD is related to problems with *reality monitoring*—the ability to discriminate between memories of *actual* versus *imagined* events. Compulsive checking, for example, could be prompted by difficulties discerning whether an action (e.g., locking the door) was really carried out or merely imagined. Across a series of studies addressing this issue, however, no differences in reality monitoring between OCD patients and control groups were found (Woods et al., 2002).

Inhibitory Deficits

The intrusive and repetitive quality of obsessions has led some researchers to hypothesize that OCD is characterized by deficits in cognitive inhibition—the ability to dismiss extraneous mental stimuli. Studies examining recall and recognition suggest that people with OCD have more difficulty forgetting negative material and material related to their obsessional fears relative to other sorts of material.

Synthesis

Cognitive deficit models of OCD have a number of limitations. First, they do not account for the heterogeneity of OCD symptoms (e.g., why do some people have washing compulsions while others have checking rituals?). Second, they do not account for the fact that similar mild cognitive deficits have been found in many psychological disorders. Thus, if cognitive deficits play a causal role in OCD, it is most likely to be a nonspecific vulnerability factor, as opposed to a specific cause (e.g., Abramovitch et al., 2013).

COGNITIVE-BEHAVIORAL MODELS

The most promising psychological model of OCD is the cognitive-behavioral model, which is based on Beck's (1976) cognitive theory that emotional disturbance is brought about not by situations and stimuli themselves, but by how one makes sense out of such situations or stimuli. Accordingly, obsessions and compulsions are thought to arise from specific sorts of dysfunctional beliefs, with the strength of these beliefs influencing the person's degree of insight into his or her OCD symptoms. In particular, the cognitive-behavioral model of OCD is based on the finding that unwanted intrusive thoughts (i.e., thoughts, images, and impulses that intrude into consciousness) are a normal experience (e.g., Rachman & de Silva, 1978). These normal intrusions are postulated to develop into clinical obsessions when they are appraised as significant and harmful. To illustrate, consider an intrusive thought to push an innocent person in front of traffic. Most people experiencing such an intrusion would regard it as an insignificant cognitive event. Such an intrusion, however, could develop into a clinical obsession if the person appraises it as having serious consequences; for example: "If I think about it, I might lose control and do it," or "I must take extra precautions to ensure that it doesn't happen." Such appraisals evoke distress and motivate attempts to suppress or remove the unwanted intrusion (e.g., by replacing it with a "good" thought), or prevent any harmful events associated with it (e.g., by avoidance of busy street corners).

According to this model, compulsive rituals and avoidance represent efforts to remove intrusions and prevent feared consequences. Salkovskis (1996) advanced two reasons that compulsions and avoidance become persistent and excessive. First, they are negatively reinforced by their ability to reduce distress (as in the learning model). Second, they prevent people from learning that their appraisals of intrusions are exaggerated and unrealistic. That is, performing the ritual robs the person of the opportunity to discover that the anticipated negative outcome would most likely not have occurred in the first place. If the individual avoids obsessional triggers, there is no opportunity to learn that distressing obsessional thoughts do not pose danger.

The cognitive-behavioral model has a good deal of empirical support (e.g., Clark, 2004). Psychometric research indicates that there are three principal domains of dysfunctional beliefs (shown in Table 5.5) associated with OCD symptoms (e.g., Wheaton, Abramowitz, Berman, Riemann, & Hale, 2010), and laboratory experiments have demonstrated that inducing such beliefs influences dysfunctional appraisals and exacerbates obsessional symptoms (e.g., Rassin, Merckelbach, Muris, & Spaan, 1999). Longitudinal prospective research has also found that these types of beliefs confer vulnerability to the onset or worsening of obsessive-compulsive symptoms under certain conditions (e.g., Abramowitz, Khandher, Nelson, Deacon, & Rygwall, 2006).

Implications

The cognitive-behavioral model implies that a successful treatment for OCD symptoms must accomplish two things: (1) the correction of maladaptive beliefs and appraisals that lead to obsessional fear, and (2) the termination of avoidance and compulsive rituals that prevent the self-correction of maladaptive beliefs and extinction of anxiety. In short, the task of cognitive behavior therapy (CBT) for OCD is to foster an evaluation of obsessional stimuli as nonthreatening and therefore not demanding of further action. Patients must come to understand their problem not in terms of the risk of feared consequences, but in

TABLE 5.5 Domains of Dysfunctional Beliefs in OCD

Belief	Description
Inflated responsibility/ overestimation of threat	Belief that one has the power to cause and/or the duty to prevent negative outcomes
	Belief that negative events are likely and would be unmanageable
Exaggeration of the importance of thoughts and need to control thoughts	Belief that the mere presence of a thought indicates that the thought is significant
	Belief that complete control over one's thoughts is both necessary and possible
Perfectionism/intolerance of uncertainty	Belief that mistakes and imperfection are intolerable
	Belief that it is necessary and possible to be 100% certain that negative outcomes will not occur

terms of how they are thinking and behaving in response to stimuli that objectively pose a low risk of harm.

Neurobiological Models of OCD

Neurobiological models of OCD focus on putative neurochemical abnormalities and structural or functional brain dysfunctions. Such models became fashionable in the 1980s with the *DSM-III*'s "medicalization" of psychiatric nomenclature. The availability of neuroimaging technology in the 1980s also made it easier to examine the brains of people with OCD. To date, however, as described in this section, neurobiological research has generally failed to deliver a conceptually coherent or empirically stable biological model of this condition.

SEROTONIN HYPOTHESIS

The serotonin hypothesis proposes that obsessions and compulsions arise from abnormalities in this neurotransmitter system, specifically a hypersensitivity of the postsynaptic serotonergic receptors (Zohar & Insel, 1987). Three lines of evidence are cited to support the serotonin hypothesis: medication outcome studies, biological marker studies, and biological challenge studies in which OCD symptoms are evoked using serotonin agonists and antagonists. The most consistent findings come from the pharmacotherapy literature, which suggests that selective serotonin reuptake inhibitor (SSRI) medications (e.g., fluoxetine) are more effective than medications with other mechanisms of action (e.g., imipramine) in reducing OCD symptoms. In contrast, studies of biological markers—such as blood and cerebrospinal fluid levels of serotonin metabolites—have provided inconclusive results regarding a relationship between serotonin and OCD (e.g., Insel, Mueller, Alterman, Linnoila, & Murphy, 1985). Similarly, results from studies using the pharmacological challenge paradigm are largely incompatible with the serotonin hypothesis (Hollander et al., 1992).

STRUCTURAL MODELS

Structural models hypothesize that OCD is caused by neuroanatomical and functional abnormalities in particular areas of the brain, specifically the orbitofrontal-subcortical circuits, which are thought to connect brain regions involved in processing information with those involved in the initiation of behavioral responses. The classical conceptualization of this circuitry consists of a direct and an indirect pathway. The direct pathway projects from the cerebral cortex to the striatum to the internal segment of the globus pallidus/substantia nigra pars reticulata complex, then to the thalamus and back to the cortex. The indirect pathway is similar, but projects from the striatum to the external segment of the globus pallidus to the subthalamic nucleus before returning to the common pathway. Overactivity of the direct circuit is thought to give rise to OCD symptoms.

Structural models of OCD are derived from neuroimaging studies in which activity levels in specific brain areas are compared between people with and without the condition.

Investigations using positron-emission tomography (PET) have found increased glucose utilization in the orbitofrontal cortex (OFC), caudate, thalamus, prefrontal cortex, and anterior cingulate among patients with OCD compared to nonpatients (e.g., Baxter et al., 1988). Studies using single-photon emission computed tomography (SPECT) have reported decreased blood flow to the OFC, caudate, various areas of the cortex, and thalamus in OCD patients compared to nonpatients (for a review see Whiteside, Port, & Abramowitz, 2004). Finally, studies comparing individuals with OCD to healthy controls using magnetic resonance spectroscopy (MRS) have reported decreased levels of various markers of neuronal viability in the left and right striatum and in the medial thalamus (e.g., Fitzgerald, Moore, Paulson, Stewart, & Rosenberg, 2000). Although findings vary across studies, a meta-analysis of 10 PET and SPECT studies found that relative to healthy individuals, those with OCD evince more activity in the orbital gyrus and the head of the caudate nucleus (Whiteside et al., 2004).

EVALUATION OF BIOLOGICAL MODELS

One limitation of biological models is that no explanation has been offered for how neurotransmitter or neuroanatomical abnormalities translate into OCD symptoms (e.g., why does hypersensitivity of postsynaptic receptors cause obsessional thoughts or compulsive rituals?). In addition, biological models are unable to explain (a) why OCD symptoms are generally constrained to the particular themes discussed earlier, and (b) why someone would experience one type of obsession (e.g., contamination) but not another (e.g., sexual). A third problem with biological models is their logical (as opposed to empirical) basis. Since the serotonin hypothesis *originated from* the findings of preferential efficacy of serotonergic medication (SSRIs) over nonserotonergic antidepressants (e.g., imipramine), the assertion that the effectiveness of SSRIs supports the serotonin hypothesis is circular. Further still, there is a logical fallacy in deriving etiological models from treatment results. This fallacy is best illustrated with the following example: "When I use steroid cream, my rash goes away. Therefore, the reason I got the rash in the first place was that my steroid level was too low." Evidence from controlled studies of differences in serotonergic functioning between individuals with and without OCD is especially inconsistent, so there is actually little convincing evidence that OCD is caused by an abnormally functioning serotonin system. A final problem with biological models is that they are based on correlational studies, which cannot address (a) whether true abnormalities exist and (b) whether the observed relationships are causal.

Assessment

There are no biological tests for OCD. The presence and severity of the disorder must be assessed using a clinical interview or self-report questionnaire. A number of such instruments have been developed to aid in making the diagnosis and measuring severity. In addition to conducting a diagnostic assessment, it is important to understand the patient-specific parameters of obsessions and compulsions so that effective psychological treatment can be tailored individually.

DIAGNOSTIC INTERVIEWS

The Structured Clinical Interview for DSM-5 Disorders (SCID-5; First, Williams, Karg, & Spitzer, 2016); the Mini International Neuropsychiatric Interview (MINI; Sheehan et al., 1998); and the Anxiety and Related Disorders Interview Schedule for DSM-5 (ADIS-5; Brown & Barlow, 2014) all assess the cardinal features of OCD. The ADIS provides the most detail about OCD symptoms, assessing their severity using dimensional rating scales.

CLINICIAN-RATED SEVERITY SCALES

The Yale-Brown Obsessive Compulsive Scale (Y-BOCS; Goodman et al., 1989a, 1989b) is the most widely used clinician-rated measure of OCD. It contains three parts: first, the interviewer provides definitions of obsessions and compulsions to help in identifying these symptoms. Second, using a symptom checklist of over 50 common obsessions and compulsions, the interviewer asks the patient to indicate whether each symptom is currently present, is absent, or was present only in the past. The clinician and patient then generate a list of the three most severe obsessions, compulsions, and OCD-related avoidance behaviors. The third section is a 10-item severity scale that assesses the (a) time spent with, (b) interference from, (c) distress associated with, (d) efforts to resist, and (e) ability to control obsessions (items 1–5) and compulsions (items 6–10). Each item is rated on a scale from 0 (no symptoms) to 4 (extremely severe), and scores on the 10 items are summed to produce a total score ranging from 0 to 40. In most instances, scores of 0 to 7 represent subclinical OCD symptoms, those from 8 to 15 represent mild symptoms, scores of 16 to 23 relate to moderate symptoms, scores from 24 to 31 suggest severe symptoms, and scores of 32 to 40 imply extreme symptoms.

The Y-BOCS is sensitive to multiple aspects of OCD severity independent of the *number* or *types* of different obsessions and compulsions. A limitation, however, is that the symptom checklist contains some items that are not genuine obsessions or compulsions (e.g., hair pulling). Research indicates that the Y-BOCS possesses adequate reliability, validity, and sensitivity to treatment (Taylor, Thordarson, & Sochting, 2002). Conelea, Freeman, and Garcia (2012) have described ways to use the Y-BOCS that are consistent with recent conceptualizations of the links between obsessions and compulsions.

The Brown Assessment of Beliefs Scale (BABS; Eisen et al., 1998) is a 7-item interview assessing the degree of insight into the senselessness of OCD symptoms. The individual's main obsessional fear (e.g., "If I do not perform a prayer ritual, my mother will die") is rated along the following parameters of insight: (1) conviction (that the belief is accurate), (2) perception of others' views (about the fear's accuracy), (3) explanation for any difference between the patient's and others' views of the belief, (4) whether the person could be convinced that the belief is wrong (i.e., fixity), (5) attempts to disprove beliefs, (6) whether the person recognizes that the belief has a psychological cause, and (7) an optional item assessing delusions of reference. Each item is rated from 0 to 4, with higher scores indicating poorer insight; the first six items are summed to create a total score (range, 0 to 24). The seventh item is not included in the total score because referential thinking is characteristic of some disorders but not others. The BABS has strong internal consistency ($\alpha = .87$), strong interrater and test-retest reliability, and good convergent and discriminant validity.

SELF-REPORT MEASURES

An array of self-report and interview measures has been developed to assess OC symptoms. These include the Obsessive Compulsive Inventory (OCI) and its revision (OCI-R; Foa et al., 2002), the Padua Inventory (PI; Sanavio, 1988) and its revision (PI-R; Burns, Keortge, Formea, & Sternberger, 1996), and the Vancouver Obsessive Compulsive Inventory (VOCI; Thordarson et al., 2004). These instruments measure the wide range of possible obsessions and compulsions and generally contain items assessing *specific* and *quintessential* types of obsessions and compulsions (e.g., "I feel that there are good and bad numbers"; Foa et al., 2002). The items are rated on a Likert-type scale of agreement, personal relevance, or associated distress.

Although widely used, many self-report measures of OCD have drawbacks that detract from their ability to provide a time-efficient, empirically consistent, and conceptually clear assessment of OCD symptom severity. One limitation is that relative to respondents with fewer (or more circumscribed) types of obsessions and compulsions, those with multiple types of symptoms will endorse a greater number of scale items, and therefore (all else being equal) obtain more severe scores. Thus, many OCD symptom measures confound severity with the range of symptoms present. Actual OCD severity, however, is independent of the number of different types of symptoms reported (e.g., McKay et al., 2004). For example, one patient might be singly obsessed with contamination yet be severely impaired by fear, avoidance, and compulsive washing rituals, whereas another patient might have sexual, religious, and violent obsessions, as well as mental rituals, yet experience only mild fear, avoidance, and impairment.

The heterogeneous and idiosyncratic nature of obsessions and compulsions also challenges authors of self-report scales to pick and choose which symptoms to include in scale items (a scale including items to match all possible OCD symptoms would be extremely long, and many items would not apply to any given respondent). As a result, respondents whose obsessions and compulsions happen to match those chosen by scale authors to be represented by items on the measure will appear more severe than those whose symptoms do not match. For example, the PI-R contains an abundance of items related to obsessions about harm; thus individuals with more harming obsessions (as opposed to symmetry obsessions, which are not assessed on the PI-R) will have higher scores than those with fewer harming obsessions. Often, obsessions that are *uncommon* (e.g., obsessional fear of developing schizophrenia) and rituals that are *covert* (e.g., mental rituals) are underrepresented on self-report measures. Thus, such scales also confound severity with the level of obscurity of the respondent's obsessions and compulsions.

Another limitation is that existing self-report measures of OCD contain a one-dimensional assessment of severity. For example, on the VOCI, respondents indicate how much each symptom-based item is "true of you" (e.g., "not at all" to "very much"). Similarly, on the OCI-R, respondents rate their level of "distress" associated with 18 different types of obsessions and compulsions. OCD symptom severity, however, is multidimensional; it consists of parameters such as distress, functional interference, and the frequency or duration of obsessions and compulsions. The use of a single rating of item relevance, severity, or distress might account for the fact that some existing self-report measures of OCD symptoms show strong correlations with measures of general anxiety and depression.

A fourth weakness of existing self-report OCD measures is that these instruments assess obsessions separately from compulsions, thus treating these symptoms as disconnected phenomena. As indicated earlier, however, structural analyses indicate that OCD psychopathology does not distill neatly into obsessions and compulsions, but rather into dimensions characterized by both obsessions *and* compulsions. Relatedly, avoidance behavior is not adequately captured on most OCD self-report measures. The general failure to account for avoidance, however, leads to underestimating OCD symptom severity because avoidance is often used in place of compulsive rituals to reduce obsessional anxiety (e.g., avoiding public bathrooms in place of lengthy compulsive washing rituals). Thus, individuals with OCD who do not endorse many compulsions might have severe avoidance strategies that, while an important (and functionally debilitating) element of their OCD symptom picture, are not captured on existing rating scales. Finally, with the exception of the PI and PI-R, self-report OCD measures include items assessing hoarding, which appears to be distinct from OCD. As a result, these measures are inconsistent with the most up-to-date, empirically derived structural framework of OCD symptoms. Moreover, such measures are likely to overestimate OC symptom severity among individuals with hoarding behaviors.

To address many of the aforementioned limitations, Abramowitz et al. (2010) developed the Dimensional Obsessive-Compulsive Scale (DOCS), a 20-item self-report measure that assesses the severity of the four most consistently replicated OCD symptom dimensions (which correspond to four DOCS subscales): (1) contamination, (2) responsibility for harm and mistakes, (3) symmetry/ordering, and (4) unacceptable thoughts. To accommodate the heterogeneity of OCD symptoms and the presence of obsessions and rituals within each symptom dimension, each subscale begins with a description of the symptom dimension along with examples of representative obsessions and rituals. The examples clarify the form and function of each dimension's fundamental obsessional fears, compulsive rituals, and avoidance behaviors. Within each symptom dimension, five items (rated 0 to 4) assess the following parameters of severity (over the past month): (1) time occupied by obsessions and rituals, (2) avoidance behavior, (3) associated distress, (4) functional interference, and (5) difficulty disregarding the obsessions and refraining from the compulsions. The DOCS subscales have excellent reliability in clinical samples ($\alpha = .94$ to $.96$) and the measure converges well with other measures of OCD symptoms (Abramowitz et al., 2010).

FUNCTIONAL ASSESSMENT

Functional assessment is the compiling of detailed patient-specific information about the antecedents and consequences of target behaviors and emotions, usually for the purposes of developing a treatment plan. Behavioral or cognitive-behavioral theory dictates what information is collected and how it is organized to form a conceptualization of the problem that will drive therapeutic intervention (usually cognitive-behavioral treatment). We provide a framework for the functional assessment of OCD in the following paragraphs.

Assessment of Obsessional Stimuli

This assessment includes compiling a comprehensive list of the external and internal stimuli that evoke obsessional fear. External triggers include objects, situations, places, and the like that give rise to obsessional thinking and urges to ritualize (e.g., trash cans, hammers, religious icons, the number 666, locking doors, and schoolyards). Examples of questions to elicit this information include:

- What kinds of situations make you feel anxious?
- What kinds of things do you avoid?
- What triggers you to want to do rituals?

Internal obsessional stimuli include recurring ideas, images, doubts, and impulses that the individual finds unwanted, upsetting, immoral, repulsive, or otherwise unacceptable (i.e., obsessional thoughts). Examples include thoughts of bacteria, ideas of harming loved ones, unwanted sexual or blasphemous images, doubts about completing paperwork incorrectly, and impulses to harm babies. Examples of questions to elicit this information include:

- What intrusive thoughts do you have that trigger anxiety?
- What thoughts do you try to avoid, resist, or dismiss?

It is similarly important to obtain information about the cognitive basis of the individual's obsessional anxiety (i.e., the feared consequences). For example, what does the person fear if exposed to obsessional stimuli? Examples of questions to elicit feared consequences include:

- What is the worst thing you imagine happening if you are exposed to _____ [obsessional trigger]?
- What do you think might happen if you don't do your _____ rituals?

The cognitive-behavioral model proposes that misinterpretations of unwanted thoughts, impulses, and images give rise to OCD symptoms. Therefore, assessment should include identification of mistaken beliefs about the presence and meaning of such stimuli. For example, "Thinking about molesting a child could lead me to actually become a child molester," "God will punish me for thinking immoral thoughts," and "I'm a pervert if I have unwanted thoughts about sex." Examples of questions to elicit this information include:

- What do you think it means that you have this thought?
- What will happen if you think this thought too much?
- Why do you try to avoid or dismiss these thoughts?

Some individuals with OCD fear that if obsessional anxiety is evoked, anxiety and related bodily sensations will persist indefinitely or spiral out of control. For example, "If I don't arrange the pictures on the wall perfectly, I will always feel that things aren't just right." Questions to help elicit these types of cognitions include:

- Do you worry that you will become anxious and that the anxiety will never go away?
- What might happen to you if you remained anxious for long periods of time?

Two self-report questionnaires, the Obsessive Beliefs Questionnaire (OBQ) and the Interpretation of Intrusions Inventory (III), have been developed to systematically measure a range of pertinent OCD-related beliefs and misinterpretations (Frost & Steketee, 2002).

These psychometrically validated instruments are useful to include in the functional assessment to augment interview data.

Assessment of Avoidance and Compulsive Rituals

The cognitive-behavioral model proposes that avoidance and compulsive behavior maintain obsessional fear. It is, therefore, necessary to include such behaviors in a functional assessment. Most individuals with OCD avoid obsessional stimuli in order to reduce anxiety over feared disasters. Examples include avoidance of certain people (e.g., religious leaders), places (e.g., cemeteries), situations (e.g., being the last one to leave the house), and words (e.g., "murder"). Examples of questions to elicit this information include:

- What situations do you avoid because of obsessional fear?
- Can you ever confront this situation?
- How does avoiding _____ make you feel more comfortable?

If avoidance is impossible, compulsive behaviors are performed to escape from distress or reduce the probability of feared consequences. In addition to gathering detailed information about all rituals (e.g., cleaning, checking, repeating actions, arranging objects, and asking for reassurance), subtle mini rituals such as wiping, using special soaps, and brief checks must be assessed. The cognitive motivation of all rituals should also be clarified as well (e.g., checking to prevent a break-in, using a certain soap to target certain contaminants). Examples of questions to elicit this information include:

- What do you do when you can't avoid _____ [insert situation]?
- Tell me about the strategies or rituals you use to reduce obsessional fear of _____ [insert obsessional fear]?
- How does doing this ritual reduce your discomfort?
- What might happen if you didn't engage in this ritual?

Mental rituals are often overlooked in the functional assessment of OCD because they are not directly observable. Thus, it is important to ascertain any cognitive strategies the patient uses in response to obsessional stimuli. Examples include thinking "good" thoughts, repeating mantras in a certain way, excessively mentally reviewing one's own actions to gain assurance, and habitual thought suppression and mental distraction. As with overt rituals, it is necessary to ascertain the cognitive links between mental rituals and the obsessional thoughts. For example, repeating the phrase "God is good" to avoid punishment for having blasphemous thoughts, and suppression of sexual thoughts to prevent acting inappropriately. Examples of questions to elicit this information include:

- What kinds of mental strategies do you use to dismiss unwanted thoughts?
- What might happen if you didn't use the strategy?

Self-Monitoring

Self-monitoring of rituals and avoidance behavior is an excellent tool for collecting real-time data on OCD symptoms. A log sheet can be given to the patient on which he or she records the (a) date, (b) time, (c) obsessional thought or stimulus that triggers anxiety, (d) level of anxiety on a 0 to 10 scale, and (e) ritual or avoidance behavior employed. Self-monitoring helps both the clinician and the patient gain an accurate picture of OCD symptom severity and the functional relationship between obsessions and compulsions. It also helps the patient identify obsessions and rituals that he or she might not be aware of.

Case Conceptualization

The main value of a functional assessment is that it yields information from which to synthesize a case conceptualization. The case conceptualization is an individualized blueprint of OCD symptoms and is derived by listing (a) the situations and thoughts that trigger obsessional fear, (b) the associated cognitive variables (i.e., dysfunctional beliefs and appraisals), and (c) avoidance and compulsive rituals. Next, using the cognitive-behavioral model of OCD (as discussed previously) as a framework, links between these phenomena are sketched as shown in Figure 5.1. The individual in this case had obsessional fears of contamination along with decontamination rituals.

Psychological Treatment

Cognitive behavior therapy (CBT), a set of techniques derived from the cognitive-behavioral theoretical model described earlier, is considered the most effective approach to the psychological treatment of OCD. Two specific CBT methods have been examined in clinical studies: behavior therapy by exposure and response prevention (ERP) and cognitive therapy (CT). This section provides a concise description of these procedures and reviews research substantiating their effectiveness. Detailed guidelines for planning and implementing CBT techniques are provided in various treatment manuals (e.g., Abramowitz & Jacoby, 2014).

EXPOSURE AND RESPONSE PREVENTION

Exposure and response prevention (ERP) entail confrontation with stimuli that provoke obsessional fear, but that objectively pose a low risk of harm. Exposure can occur in the form of repeated actual encounters with the feared situations (situational or in vivo exposure), or in the form of imagined confrontation with the feared disastrous consequences of confronting these situations (imaginal exposure). For example, an individual with obsessional fears of causing fires would be asked to practice leaving the home without checking to make sure appliances were turned off properly for situational exposure. She would also practice imaginal exposure to thoughts of possibly having caused a fire and being held responsible. A patient with fears of contaminating his mother might be asked to touch objects that he considers unclean—a trash can, his genitals, a neighbor's pet—before handling objects that belong to his mother—for situational exposure. He would then confront thoughts of his mother coming down with a serious illness as a result of his carelessness with these perceived contaminants.

As might be anticipated, initiating exposure tasks evokes the patient's anxiety. Patients are encouraged to engage in such tasks completely, and to allow themselves to experience this obsessional distress without resisting the feelings of anxiety. Over time, the anxiety

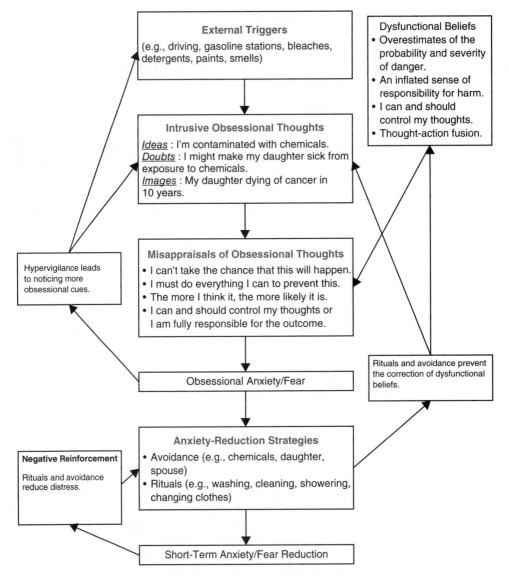

FIGURE 5.1   Case Conceptualization of an Individual with OCD

(and associated physiological responding) naturally subsides—a process called *habituation*. With each repetition of the exposure task, habituation occurs more rapidly. Moreover, by engaging in exposures without ritualizing, patients have the opportunity to learn that feared outcomes are less likely or less severe than they had anticipated.

The response prevention component of ERP entails refraining from compulsive rituals and other subtle avoidance behaviors that serve as an escape from obsessive fear. Response prevention helps to prolong exposure and to facilitate the eventual extinction of obsessional anxiety. In the previous examples, the first patient might practice refraining from any strategies she typically uses to reassure herself that no fires will have occurred, such as returning home to check, or asking neighbors to check. The second patient would be instructed to refrain from decontamination rituals such as washing or cleaning.

The Delivery of ERP

The way ERP is delivered can vary widely. One format that has been found to produce particularly potent effects includes a few hours of assessment and treatment planning followed by 15 (daily or twice-weekly) treatment sessions, lasting about 90 minutes each (Abramowitz, Foa, & Franklin, 2003). When pragmatic concerns render intensive regimens impractical, conducting the treatment sessions on a weekly basis works very well for individuals with less severe OCD (Warren & Thomas, 2001). Self-supervised exposure homework practice should be assigned for completion between sessions. It is important that home-based self-supervised exposure exercises (as with therapist-supervised exposure) last long enough for the patient to learn either that anxiety dissipates (i.e., habituation occurs) or that he or she can tolerate the anxiety.

A course of ERP ordinarily begins with the assessment of obsessions, compulsive rituals, avoidance strategies, and anticipated consequences of confronting feared situations. Information gathered during the assessment sessions is then used to plan the specific exposure exercises that will be pursued. Importantly, the term *response prevention* does not imply that the therapist physically restrains the patient from performing rituals. Instead, the therapist must convince patients to resist their own urges to carry out these behaviors. The therapist must also provide a cogent rationale for how exposure and response prevention will be helpful in reducing OCD. This rationale must motivate the patient to tolerate the distress that typically accompanies therapy. The treatment rationale also lets the patient know that this distress is temporary and that it usually subsides with repeated practice, although learning how to tolerate anxiety is an important part of long-term success with ERP.

The exposure exercises in ERP might begin with moderately distressing situations, stimuli, and images, and progress to the most distressing situations, although progressing in such a hierarchy-driven manner is not essential. On the one hand, beginning with less anxiety-evoking exposure tasks might increase the likelihood that the patient will learn to manage his or her distress. This also increases confidence in the treatment. On the other hand, by completing more difficult exposures early on, patients might learn quickly that they are better at coping with anxiety than they had thought. At the end of each treatment session, the therapist instructs the patient to continue that session's exposure for several hours and in different environmental contexts without the therapist. Exposure to the most anxiety-evoking situations—which must be faced—is completed during the middle of the treatment program (as opposed to waiting until the very end). This allows the patient ample opportunity to repeat such exposures in different contexts to allow generalization of treatment effects. During later sessions, the therapist emphasizes the importance of generalization and of the individual continuing to apply the ERP procedures learned during treatment.

Mechanisms of Change

Foa and Kozak (1986) hypothesized that ERP produces its effects by correcting patients' overestimates of danger that underlie obsessional anxiety. These authors point to three requirements for a successful outcome with ERP. First, physiological arousal and subjective fear must be evoked during exposure. Second, the fear responses must gradually diminish during the exposure session in the absence of compulsive rituals (within-session habituation). Third, the initial fear response at the beginning of each exposure session should decline across sessions (between-sessions habituation).

More recently, Craske and colleagues (2008) have emphasized the role of inhibitory learning in exposure-based therapy. According to this approach, original fear-based associations (e.g., floors are dangerous) are neither *corrected* nor *replaced* during exposure, but rather new safety-based associations (e.g., floors are generally safe) are formed, and they compete with the fear-based associations. The aim of ERP for OCD, then, is to help the patient develop this new learning and then enhance the recall of the new associations relative to the older, threat-based associations (Abramowitz & Arch, 2014; Craske et al., 2008).

Several dismantling studies have examined the individual effects of exposure and response prevention techniques (e.g., Foa, Steketee, Grayson, Turner, & Lattimer, 1984), finding that whereas exposure produces the greatest effects on obsessional anxiety, response prevention produces the greatest reduction of compulsive rituals. Nevertheless, there is an additive effect of combining the two techniques: using both exposure and response prevention is more effective than using either of these components alone (Foa et al., 1984).

The Efficacy of ERP

The numerous trials evaluating the effects of ERP for OCD consistently show that patients who receive and complete this intervention attain clinically significant and durable improvement. Average improvement rates are typically from 50% to 70% in these studies (Olatunji, Davis, Powers, & Smits, 2012). A review of 16 trials (involving 756 patients) indicated that ERP was substantially more effective than comparison treatments (e.g., relaxation, anxiety management training, waiting list, medication), above and beyond the effects of nonspecific factors such as the therapeutic relationship and spontaneous improvement. Moreover, the effects of ERP are not limited to highly selected research samples or to treatment as delivered in specialty clinics. Effectiveness studies conducted with nonresearch patients (e.g., Franklin, Abramowitz, Foa, Kozak, & Levitt, 2000) show that over 80% of patients who complete ERP achieve clinically significant improvement. While ERP is effective for most people with OCD, about 20% do not respond and about 25% to 30% drop out of therapy.

COGNITIVE THERAPY

The basis of cognitive therapy (CT) for OCD is the rational and evidence-based challenging and correction of faulty and dysfunctional thoughts and beliefs that underlie emotional distress. As has been discussed, individuals with OCD hold characteristic faulty beliefs that lead to obsessive fear. It is these beliefs that are targeted in CT, including overestimates of the probability and severity of danger and misinterpretations of intrusive thoughts as having implications for responsibility for harm.

Delivery of CT

Cognitive therapy typically begins with the therapist presenting a rationale for treatment that incorporates the notion that intrusive obsessional thoughts are normal experiences and not harmful or significant. The patient is then socialized to the cognitive-behavioral framework for understanding OCD, as discussed earlier in this chapter. A central aim of CT is therefore to reduce obsessional fear and the need for compulsive rituals by helping the patient correct dysfunctional thinking and behavioral responses to obsessional stimuli (situations, thoughts, images) so that such situations no longer require avoidance and intrusive thoughts are no longer perceived as needing to be controlled or neutralized via rituals.

Various CT techniques are used to help patients identify and correct their erroneous appraisals, such as didactic presentation of educational material, Socratic dialogue, and cognitive restructuring aimed at helping patients recognize and remedy dysfunctional thinking patterns. Behavioral experiments, in which patients enter situations that exemplify their fears, are often used to facilitate the acquisition of corrective information about the realistic risks associated with obsessional fears. For a detailed manual describing the use of CT techniques for OCD, see Wilhelm and Steketee (2006).

CT Versus ERP

A handful of studies have addressed the relative efficacy of CT and ERP by directly comparing variants of the two interventions. Although most of these studies have found that these treatments produced equivalent effects, methodological problems prevent definitive conclusions. In earlier studies, for example, both ERP and CT yielded minimal improvements in OCD symptoms. The efficacy of ERP was likely attenuated by the lack of therapist-supervised exposure, and CT programs were likely enhanced by the use of supervised behavioral experiments, which mimic the effects of exposure. Vogel, Stiles, and Götestam (2004), however, found that the inclusion of CT was useful in reducing dropout from ERP. Thus, there are likely benefits to incorporating CT techniques along with ERP; perhaps CT techniques improve the acceptability of ERP.

Biological Treatment

Biological treatments for OCD include medications and certain types of neurosurgeries. This section provides an overview of these approaches.

SEROTONIN REUPTAKE INHIBITORS

Pharmacotherapy using selective serotonin reuptake inhibitor (SSRI) medication is the most widely used treatment for OCD. The specific agents in this class of drugs include fluoxetine, paroxetine, sertraline, citalopram, and fluvoxamine. Clomipramine, a tricyclic medication that also possesses serotonergic properties, is also used in the treatment of OCD. Problems with the serotonin hypothesis (as discussed earlier in this chapter) notwithstanding, it is this model that provides the rationale for the use of serotonergic medications to treat OCD. On average, serotonin medications produce a 20% to 40% reduction in obsessions and compulsions (Rauch & Jenike, 1998). The major strengths of a pharmacological approach to treating OCD include the convenience and the requirement of little effort on the patient's part. Limitations include the relatively modest improvement and likelihood of residual symptoms, high rate of nonresponse (40% to 60% of patients do not show any favorable response), and the prospect of unpleasant side effects (which can often be stabilized, however, by adjusting the dose). Moreover, once SSRIs are terminated, OCD symptoms typically return rapidly (Pato, Zohar-Kadouch, Zohar, & Murphy, 1988).

NEUROSURGICAL TREATMENT

Although they have received little in the way of controlled empirical evaluation, four neurosurgical procedures have been reported with OCD patients: (1) subcaudate tractotomy, (2) limbic leucotomy, (3) cingulotomy, and (4) capsulotomy. These operations involve severing interconnections between areas of the brain's frontal lobes and the limbic system. Surgical procedures are recommended only in cases where severe and unmanageable OCD and depressive symptoms persist despite adequate trials of all other available treatments; the risks of neurosurgery include permanent alterations in cognitive functioning and personality. Although clinical improvement has been observed in some cases, it remains unknown why these procedures are successful for only a subset of OCD patients (Jenike, 2000). There is also an increased risk of suicide following failure with this approach.

Summary and Future Directions

Few syndromes in psychopathology have generated as much curiosity and clinical exploration as has OCD. Since the 1970s, research on OCD has increased exponentially, leading to a clearer understanding of the heterogeneity of the disorder, its boundaries with other syndromes, and the development of increasingly sophisticated theoretical models of etiology and maintenance. Perhaps most important, research has led to advances in treatment; and whereas the first-line therapies (ERP and serotonergic medication) are not entirely effective for every patient, they have transformed OCD from an unmanageable lifetime affliction into a treatable problem that need not reduce quality of life.

Despite the aforementioned advances, a number of unresolved disagreements concerning OCD have emerged. Differences, for example, have surfaced over phenomenological issues, etiological models, and approaches to treatment. These disagreements occur predominantly along disciplinary lines between biologically oriented and cognitive-behaviorally oriented schools of thought. Biologically inclined theorists view OCD as a medical condition involving abnormal neurological or neurotransmitter-based processes, whereas psychosocial formulations emphasize the role of learning and dysfunctional cognitions. Yet, because of the relative insularity within each camp, theoretical conjecture and empirical findings from within different approaches are typically addressed toward distinct and narrow audiences. Clinicians, researchers, and students with broad interests are hindered from gaining a clear understanding of the diverse (and sometimes polarized) perspectives. Most likely, the etiology of OCD involves a complex interaction of both biological and environmental factors.

We presently stand at a time when we can look to the past and to the future with hope. In looking back, we can be glad that the days are gone when individuals with OCD had little hope of receiving the help that they needed, or worse, underwent years of ineffective treatment with false hopes of improvement. Today, we can see that there are treatments that are useful and oftentimes highly effective. We can also see that there is energetic disagreement among experts in the OCD research communities, and it is the sort of disagreement that can lead to productive outcomes, fruitful debate, and more refined care of individuals with OCD. Although cognitive-behavioral treatments can be highly effective, one challenge for the future involves helping patients without good access to this therapy. Other challenges include helping individuals with motivational problems, and those with families and other social circles that reinforce OCD symptoms, to enter and succeed with treatment. In looking forward, we can also hope that investigators with differing backgrounds and research agendas will engage with one another as they pursue their own work, so that at the close of this century we will have an understanding of OCD that integrates the best methods of behavioral science with the best methods of neurochemistry and neurophysiology.

References

Abramovitch, A., Abramowitz, J. S., & Mittleman, A. (2013). The neuropsychology of adult obsessive-compulsive disorder: A meta-analysis. *Clinical Psychology Review, 33,* 1163–1171. doi: 10.1016/j.cpr.2013.09.004

Abramowitz, J. S., & Arch, J. J. (2014). Strategies for improving long-term outcomes in cognitive behavioral therapy for obsessive-compulsive disorder: Insights from learning theory. *Cognitive and Behavioral Practice, 21,* 20–31. doi: 10.1016/j.cbpra.2013.06.004

Abramowitz, J. S., Deacon, B., Olatunji, B., Wheaton, M. G., Berman, N., Losardo, D., … Hale, L. (2010). Assessment of obsessive-compulsive symptom dimensions: Development and evaluation of the Dimensional Obsessive-Compulsive Scale. *Psychological Assessment, 22,* 180–198. doi: 10.1037/a0018260

Abramowitz, J. S., Foa, E. B., & Franklin, M. E. (2003). Exposure and ritual prevention for obsessive-compulsive disorder: Effects of intensive versus twice-weekly sessions. *Journal of Consulting and Clinical Psychology, 71,* 394–398. doi: 10.1037/0022-006X.71.2.394

Abramowitz, J. S., & Jacoby, R. J. (2014). *Obsessive-compulsive disorder in adults.* Boston, MA: Hogrefe.

Abramowitz, J. S., & Jacoby, R. J. (2015). Obsessive-compulsive related disorders: A critical review of the new diagnostic class. *Annual Review of Clinical Psychology, 11,* 165–186. doi: 10.1146/annurev-clinpsy-032813-153713.

Abramowitz, J. S., Khandher, M., Nelson, C., Deacon, B. J., & Rygwall, R. (2006). The role of cognitive factors in the pathogenesis of obsessive-compulsive symptoms: A prospective study. *Behaviour Research and Therapy, 44,* 1361–1374. doi: 10.1016/j.brat.2005.09.011

Abramowitz, J., Wheaton, M., & Storch, A. (2008). The status of hoarding as a symptom of obsessive-compulsive disorder. *Behaviour Research and Therapy, 46,* 1026–1033. doi: 10.1016/j.brat.2008.05.006

American Psychiatric Association. (2013). *Diagnostic and statistical manual of mental disorders* (5th ed.). Washington, DC: Author.

Baxter, L. R., Jr., Schwartz, J. M., Mazziotta, J. C., Phelps, M. E., Pahl, J. J., Guze, B. H., & Fairbanks, L. (1988). Cerebral glucose metabolic rates in nondepressed patients with obsessive-compulsive disorder. *American Journal of Psychiatry, 145,* 1560–1563.

Beck, A. T. (1976). *Cognitive therapy of the emotional disorders.* New York, NY: International Universities Press.

Brown, T. A., & Barlow, D. H. (2014). *Anxiety Disorders Interview Schedule for DSM-5 (ADIS-5)–Adult Version.* Oxford, England: Oxford University Press.

Burns, G. L., Keortge, S. G., Formea, G. M., & Sternberger, L. G. (1996). Revision of the Padua Inventory for obsessive compulsive disorder symptoms: Distinctions between worry, obsessions, and compulsions. *Behaviour Research and Therapy, 34,* 163–173. doi: 10.1016/0005-7967(95)00035-6

Chambless, D. L., & Steketee, G. (1999). Expressed emotion and behavior therapy outcome: A prospective study with obsessive-compulsive and agoraphobic outpatients. *Journal of Consulting and Clinical Psychology, 67,* 658–665. doi: 10.1037//0022-006X.67.5.658

Clark, D. A. (2004). *Cognitive-behavioral therapy for OCD.* New York, NY: Guilford Press.

Conelea, C. A., Freeman, J. B., & Garcia, A. M. (2012). Integrating behavioral theory with OCD assessment using the Y-BOCS/CY-BOCS symptom checklist. *Journal of Obsessive-Compulsive and Related Disorders, 1,* 112–118.

Craske, M. G., Kircanski, K., Zelikowsky, M., Mystkowski, J., Chowdhury, N., & Baker, A. (2008). Optimizing inhibitory learning during exposure therapy. *Behaviour Research and Therapy, 46,* 5–27.

Dowson, J. H., & Grounds, A. T. (1995). *Personality disorders: Recognition and clinical management.* Cambridge, England: Cambridge University Press.

Eisen, J. L., Mancebo, M. C., Chiappone, K. L., Pinto, A., & Rasmussen, S. A. (2008). Obsessive-compulsive personality disorder. In J. A. Abramowitz, D. McKay, & S. Taylor (Eds.), *Clinical handbook of obsessive-compulsive disorder and related problems* (pp. 316–333). Baltimore, MD: Johns Hopkins University Press.

Eisen, J. L., Phillips, K. A., Baer, L., Beer, D. A., Atala, K. D., & Rasmussen, S. A. (1998). The Brown Assessment of Beliefs Scale: Reliability and validity. *American Journal of Psychiatry, 155,* 102–108.

First, M. B., Williams, J., Karg, R., & Spitzer, R. (2015). *Structured Clinical Interview for DSM-5.* Arlington, VA: American Psychiatric Association.

Fitzgerald, K. D., Moore, G. J., Paulson, L. A., Stewart, C. M., & Rosenberg, D. R. (2000). Proton spectroscopic imaging of the thalamus in treatment-naive pediatric obsessive-compulsive disorder. *Biological Psychiatry*, *47*, 174–182. doi: 10.1016/S0006-3223(99)00286-3

Foa, E. B., Huppert, J. D., Leiberg, S., Langner, R., Kichic, R., Hajcak, G., & Salkovskis, P. M. (2002). The Obsessive-Compulsive Inventory: Development and validation of a short version. *Psychological Assessment*, *14*, 485–496. doi: 10.1037/1040-3590.14.4.485

Foa, E. B., & Kozak, M. J. (1986). Emotional processing of fear: Exposure to corrective information. *Psychological Bulletin*, *99*, 20–35. doi: 10.1037//0033-2909.99.1.20

Foa, E. B., & Kozak, M. J. (1995). DSM-IV field trial: Obsessive-compulsive disorder. *American Journal of Psychiatry*, *152*, 90–96.

Foa, E. B., Steketee, G, Grayson, J., Turner, R., & Lattimer, P. (1984). Deliberate exposure and blocking of obsessive-compulsive rituals: Immediate and long-term effects. *Behavior Therapy*, *15*, 450–472. doi: 10.1016/S0005-7894(84)80049-0

Franklin, M., Abramowitz, J., Foa, E., Kozak, M., & Levitt, J. (2000). Effectiveness of exposure and ritual prevention for obsessive-compulsive disorder: Randomized compared with nonrandomized samples. *Journal of Consulting and Clinical Psychology*, *68*, 594–602. doi: 10.1037//0022-006X.68.4.594

Frost, R. O., & Steketee, S. (2002). *Cognitive approaches to obsessions and compulsions: Theory, assessment, and treatment.* Oxford, England: Elsevier.

Goodman, W. K., Price, L. H., Rasmussen, S. A., Mazure, C., Delgado, P., Heninger, G. R., & Charney, D. (1989a). The Yale-Brown Obsessive Compulsive Scale: Validity. *Archives of General Psychiatry*, *46*, 1012–1016. doi: 10.1001/archpsyc.1989.01810110054008

Goodman, W. K., Price, L. H., Rasmussen, S. A., Mazure, C., Fleischmann, R. L., Hill, C. L., … Charney, D. (1989b). The Yale-Brown Obsessive Compulsive Scale: Development, use, and reliability. *Archives of General Psychiatry*, *46*, 1006–1011. doi: 10.1001/archpsyc.1989.01810110048007

Hodgson, R., & Rachman, S. (1972). The effects of contamination and washing in obsessional patients. *Behaviour Research and Therapy*, *10*, 111–117. doi: 10.1016/S0005-7967(72)80003-2

Hollander, E., DeCaria, C. M., Nitescu, A., Gully, R., Suckow, R. F., Cooper, T. B., … Liebowitz, M. R. (1992). Serotonergic function in obsessive-compulsive disorder: Behavioral and neuroendocrine responses to oral m-chlorophenylpiperazine and fenfluramine in patients and healthy volunteers. *Archives of General Psychiatry*, *49*, 21–28. doi: 10.1001/archpsyc.1992.01820010021003

Insel, T. R., Mueller, E. A., Alterman, I., Linnoila, M., & Murphy, D. L. (1985). Obsessive-compulsive disorder and serotonin: Is there a connection? *Biological Psychiatry*, *20*, 1174–1188. doi: 10.1016/0006-3223(85)90176-3

Jenike, M. (2000). Neurosurgical treatment of obsessive-compulsive disorder. In W. Goodman, J. Maser, & M. V. Rudorfer (Eds.), *Obsessive-compulsive disorder* (pp. 457–482). Mahwah, NJ: Erlbaum.

Kessler, R., Berglund, P., Demler, O., Jin, R., Merikangas, K., & Walters, E. (2005). Lifetime prevalence and age-of-onset distributions of DSM-IV disorders in the National Comorbidity Survey Replication. *Archives of General Psychiatry*, *62*, 593–602. doi: 10.1001/archpsyc.62.6.593

McKay, D., Abramowitz, J. S., Calamari, J. E., Kyrios, M., Radomsky, A. S., Sookman, D., … Wilhelm, S. (2004). A critical evaluation of obsessive-compulsive disorder subtypes: Symptoms versus mechanisms. *Clinical Psychology Review*, *24*, 283–313. doi: 10.1016/j.cpr.2004.04.003

Mowrer, O. (1960). *Learning theory and behavior.* New York, NY: Wiley.

Olatunji, B. O., Davis, M. L., Powers, M. B., & Smits, J.A.J. (2012). Cognitive-behavioral therapy for obsessive-compulsive disorder: A meta-analysis of treatment outcome and moderators. *Journal of Psychiatric Research. Advance online publication.* doi: 10.1016/j.jpsychires.2012.08.020

Pato, M. T., Zohar-Kadouch, R., Zohar, J., & Murphy, D. L. (1988). Return of symptoms after discontinuation of clomipramine in patients with obsessive-compulsive disorder. *American Journal of Psychiatry*, *145*, 1521–1525.

Pertusa, A., Frost, R. O., Fullana, M. A., Samuels, J. F., Steketee, G., Tolin, D. F., … Mataix-Cols, D. (2010). Refining the diagnostic boundaries of compulsive hoarding: A critical review. *Clinical Psychology Review*, *30*, 371–386. doi: 10.1016/j.cpr.2010.01.007

Pfohl, B., & Blum, N. (1991). Obsessive-compulsive personality disorder: A review of available data and recommendations for DSM-IV. *Journal of Personality Disorders, 5*, 363–375. doi: 10.1521/pedi.1991.5.4.363

Rachman, S., & de Silva, P. (1978). Abnormal and normal obsessions. *Behaviour Research and Therapy, 16*, 233–248. doi: 10.1016/0005-7967(78)90022-0

Rachman, S., Elliot, C. M., Shafran, R., & Radomsky, A. S. (2009). Separating hoarding from OCD. *Behaviour Research and Therapy, 47*, 520–522. doi: 10.1016/j.brat.2009.02.014

Radomsky, A. S., Rachman, S., & Hammond, D. (2001). Memory bias, confidence and responsibility in compulsive checking. *Behaviour Research and Therapy, 39*, 813–822. doi: 10.1016/S0005-7967(00)00079-6

Rasmussen, S. A., & Eisen, J. L. (1992a). The epidemiology and clinical features of obsessive-compulsive disorder. *Psychiatric Clinics of North America, 15*, 743–758.

Rasmussen, S. A., & Eisen, J. L. (1992b). The epidemiology and differential diagnosis of obsessive-compulsive disorder. *Journal of Clinical Psychiatry, 53*, 4–10. doi: 10.1007/978-3-642-77608-3_1

Rassin, E., Merckelbach, H., Muris, P., & Spaan, V. (1999). Thought-action fusion as a causal factor in the development of intrusions. *Behaviour Research and Therapy, 37*, 231–237. doi: 10.1016/S0005-7967(98)00140-5

Rauch, S., & Jenike, M. (1998). Pharmacological treatment of obsessive compulsive disorder. In P. E. Nathan & J. M. Gorman (Eds.), *A guide to treatments that work* (345–360). London, England: Oxford University Press.

Salkovskis, P. (1996). Cognitive-behavioral approaches to the understanding of obsessional problems. In R. Rapee (Ed.), *Current controversies in the anxiety disorders* (pp. 103–133). New York, NY: Guilford Press.

Sanavio, E. (1988). Obsessions and compulsions: The Padua Inventory. *Behaviour Research and Therapy, 26*, 169–177. doi: 10.1016/0005-7967(88)90116-7

Sheehan, D., Lecrubier, Y., Harnett-Sheehan, K., Amoriam, P., Janavs, J., Weiller, E., … Dunbar, G. (1998). The Mini International Neuropsychiatric Interview (M.I.N.I.): The development and validation of a structured diagnostic interview for DSM-IV and ICD-10. *Journal of Clinical Psychiatry, 59*(Suppl. 20), 22–33.

Stanley, M., Swann, A., Bowers, T., & Davis, M. (1992). A comparison of clinical features in trichotillomania and obsessive-compulsive disorder. *Behaviour Research and Therapy, 30*, 39–44. doi: 10.1016/0005-7967(92)90094-W

Steketee, G., & Van Noppen, B. (2003). Family approaches to treatment for obsessive-compulsive disorder. *Brazilian Journal of Psychiatry, 25*(1), 43–50.

Taylor, S., Thordarson, D., & Sochting, I. (2002). Obsessive-compulsive disorder. In M. Antony & D. H. Barlow (Eds.), *Handbook of assessment and treatment planning for psychological disorders* (pp. 182–214). New York, NY: Guilford Press.

Thordarson, D. S., Radomsky, A. S., Rachman, S., Shafran, R., Sawchuk, C. N., & Hakstian, A. (2004). The Vancouver Obsessional Compulsive Inventory (VOCI). *Behaviour Research and Therapy, 42*, 1289–1314. doi: 10.1016/j.brat.2003.08.007

Tolin, D. F., Abramowitz, J. S., Kozak, M. J., & Foa, E. B. (2001). Fixity of belief, perceptual aberration, and magical ideation in obsessive-compulsive disorder. *Journal of Anxiety Disorders, 15*, 501–510. doi: 10.1016/S0887-6185(01)00078-0

Vogel, P. A., Stiles, T. C., & Götestam, K. G. (2004). Adding cognitive therapy elements to exposure therapy for obsessive compulsive disorder: A controlled study. *Behavioural and Cognitive Psychotherapy, 32*, 275–290. doi: 10.1017/S1352465804001353

Warren, R., & Thomas, J. C. (2001). Cognitive-behavior therapy of obsessive-compulsive disorder in private practice: An effectiveness study. *Journal of Anxiety Disorders, 15*, 277–285. doi: 10.1016/S0887-6185(01)00063-9

Wheaton, M. G., Abramowitz, J. S., Berman, N. C., Riemann, B. C., & Hale, L. R. (2010). The relationship between obsessive beliefs and symptom dimensions in obsessive-compulsive disorder. *Behavior Research and Therapy, 48*, 949–954. doi: 10.1016/j.brat.2010.05.027

Whiteside, S. P., Port, J. D., & Abramowitz, J. S. (2004). A meta-analysis of functional neuroimaging in obsessive-compulsive disorder. *Psychiatry*

Research: Neuroimaging, 132, 69–79. doi: 10.1016/j.pscychresns.2004.07.001

Wilhelm, S., & Steketee, G. (2006). *Cognitive therapy for obsessive-compulsive disorder: A guide for professionals.* Oakland, CA: New Harbinger.

Woods, C. M., Vevea, J. L., Chambless, D. L., & Bayen, U. J. (2002). Are compulsive checkers impaired in memory? A meta-analytic review.

Clinical Psychology: Science and Practice, 9, 353–366. doi: 10.1093/clipsy/9.4.353

Zohar, J., & Insel, T. R. (1987). Obsessive-compulsive disorder: Psychobiological approaches to diagnosis, treatment, and pathophysiology. *Biological Psychiatry, 22,* 667–687. doi: 10.1016/0006-3223(87)90199-5

Chapter 6

Posttraumatic Stress Disorder

PATRICIA A. RESICK, CANDICE M. MONSON, AND STEFANIE T. LoSAVIO

Prior to the publication of the third edition of the *Diagnostic and Statistical Manual of Mental Disorders* (*DSM-III*; American Psychiatric Association [APA]) in 1980, the condition we now know as *posttraumatic stress disorder* (PTSD) went by many names, such as "traumatic neurosis," "gross stress reaction," "war neurosis," and "combat fatigue" (Monson, Friedman, & La Bash, 2014). Following the return of thousands of veterans from Vietnam, many of whom exhibited difficulties adjusting back to civilian life, along with the rise of the women's movement, which heightened consciousness of the effects of sexual and physical victimization (e.g., rape trauma syndrome, battered women's syndrome), the modern diagnosis became known as posttraumatic stress disorder (PTSD). Over the past three decades, the study of PTSD has evolved through a large body of research that has established the reliability and validity of the diagnosis; associated biological, cognitive, affective, perceptual, and behavioral characteristics; and a number of highly effective treatments.

For students of psychopathology, it should be pointed out that PTSD contrasts to most other disorders in that it is a disorder of nonrecovery. PTSD is one of the few disorders in which researchers and clinicians can pinpoint the genesis of the disorder and can study risk and resilience factors as people grapple with some of life's worst events. Prospective studies can be mounted from the time of a traumatic event, and in some cases before exposure, to study how people react and recover. The strongest emotions, biological reactions, thoughts, and escape-and-avoidance behaviors occur during and soon after the traumatic event. Those who are eventually diagnosed with PTSD do not typically develop greater symptoms over time; rather, they stall out in their recovery. Those who do *not* go on to have PTSD, in contrast, continue to recover over the months after the event has occurred (Gutner, Rizvi, Monson, & Resick, 2006; Rothbaum, Foa, Riggs, & Walsh, 1992). This chapter provides an overview of this recovery process with regard to symptoms comprising the disorder; its epidemiology and comorbidity factors; the biological, cognitive, emotional, and behavioral components of the disorder; assessment; and treatment.

Symptoms and Diagnostic Criteria

Posttraumatic stress disorder (PTSD) and acute stress disorder are among the only disorders in our current classification system that require an identifiable external event as a precursor to the disorder's existence. The *Diagnostic and Statistical Manual of Mental Disorders, Fifth Edition* (*DSM-5*; APA, 2013) was unveiled in May 2013, and with this new edition, the symptoms of PTSD were modified for the first time since the *DSM-III-R* (APA, 1987). Furthermore, the biggest change may be the move of PTSD out of the anxiety disorders section and into a chapter on stress and trauma disorders. This move could change the focus of mechanisms research from considering PTSD from a fear circuitry model to including top-down cognitive models and greater focus on other emotions such as guilt, anger, shame, and sadness. Research is ongoing comparing the old and new criteria for PTSD. Given the relative recency of the change in diagnostic criteria, much of the research presented in this chapter is based on the *DSM-IV* (APA, 1994) PTSD diagnosis, unless otherwise noted.

According to the *DSM-5*, in order for a diagnosis of PTSD to be considered, an individual must have experienced, witnessed, or learned about the traumatic event of a loved one, or have experienced repeated exposure to the aftermath of traumas, such as the experiences of first responders (Criterion A). In addition to exposure to a Criterion A event, an individual must also be experiencing a qualifying number of symptoms in each of four clusters of symptoms: intrusion, avoidance, negative alterations in cognitions and mood, and alterations in arousal and reactivity (Criteria B, C, D, and E, respectively). Namely, an individual must exhibit at least one of the intrusion (Criterion B) symptoms, which include persistent and distressing memories of the trauma, recurrent distressing nightmares about the traumatic event, dissociative reactions (e.g., flashbacks), and intense psychological or physiological responses when exposed to cues (internal or external) that resemble the trauma. The individual must also exhibit at least one of the avoidance (Criterion C) symptoms: effortful avoidance of internal cues and efforts to avoid external reminders of the trauma like places, people, or situations. These symptoms reflect strategies that individuals use in order to reduce coming into contact with events, places, thoughts, or emotions that remind them of the traumatic event. In addition, the individual must exhibit two or more of the negative cognitions and mood (Criterion D) symptoms; these symptoms reflect the range of affect, from numbing and amnesia (and inability to have positive feelings) to strong negative emotions such as guilt, anger, or fear; distorted self-blame or erroneous blame of others who did not cause or intend the event; and negative beliefs about self, others, and the world as a consequence of the traumatic event. The individual must also meet at least two of the arousal and reactivity (Criterion E) symptoms, which include sleep difficulties, concentration impairment, exaggerated startle response, and hypervigilance, but also irritable or aggressive behaviors and reckless or self-destructive behavior. All the symptoms of PTSD must have started or worsened after the traumatic event. However, it is important to recognize that such an assessment may be difficult, especially in cases in which the trauma occurred in the distant past or in the presence of a comorbid mood disorder.

The required number of symptoms from the four clusters must be present concurrently for at least 1 month in order to receive a diagnosis of PTSD, and they must be perceived as distressing or causing functional impairment. Furthermore, a diagnosis of PTSD with delayed expression can be made in cases in which the diagnostic threshold is not met or exceeded until at least 6 months after the traumatic event. Cases of true delayed onset are extremely rare and are more likely to occur as reactivation or exacerbation of prior symptoms or just failing to meet criteria earlier versus later (e.g., Andrews, Brewin,

Philpott, & Stewart, 2007). That is, it is highly unlikely that an individual will be completely symptom-free following a trauma only to be diagnosed with PTSD at a later time.

The *DSM-5* specifies two (unrelated) subtypes that can be identified. The first is a subtype for children younger than 6 years of age. This subtype takes into account the differences in presentation of PTSD in the very young (Scheeringa, Myers, Putnam, & Zeanah, 2012; Scheeringa, Zeanah, & Cohen, 2011). For example, young children do not display as many avoidance and negative alterations in cognitions and mood symptoms as adults; therefore, the required number of symptoms for diagnosis among young children across these two clusters is reduced. Additionally, symptoms in this subtype are more behaviorally anchored (e.g., children may present with social withdrawal rather than feelings of detachment, or with constriction of play instead of diminished interest in activities). The second subtype is PTSD with prominent dissociative symptoms. This subtype is for individuals who meet full criteria for PTSD and also experience either persistent or frequent experiences of depersonalization or derealization. The dissociative subtype was added to *DSM-5* in the face of mounting evidence that those with severe PTSD and dissociative responses are qualitatively different from those with severe PTSD without dissociation (e.g., Griffin, Resick, & Mechanic, 1997; Lanius, Brand, Vermetten, Frewen, & Spiegel, 2012; Wolf et al., 2012).

As noted earlier, the current diagnostic criteria for PTSD represent a change from the criteria of the *DSM-IV*. The *DSM-IV* specified that an event is considered traumatic if it involved actual or threatened death, serious injury, or threat to physical integrity (Criterion A1). Furthermore, at the time of the event, the individual must have responded with intense fear, helplessness, or horror (Criterion A2). However, based on empirical research that suggests limited utility to the A2 criterion (e.g., Friedman, Resick, Bryant, & Brewin, 2011), the *DSM-5* eliminates A2 as a criterion. In the *DSM-5*, it is also not sufficient to be exposed to events on television or learn about events to others who are unknown to the person. Another change in the *DSM-5* involves expanding the number of domains of PTSD symptoms. What were previously 17 symptoms organized into three clusters (i.e., reexperiencing symptoms, avoidance and numbing symptoms, and physiological hyperarousal symptoms) are now 20 symptoms categorized into the four domains discussed earlier. New symptoms were added to *DSM-5* (e.g., cognitions and negative emotions; reckless or self-destructive behaviors), while some other symptoms were reformulated. Finally, the two aforementioned PTSD subtypes are new to *DSM-5* as well. One of the most important changes from the *DSM-IV* was moving PTSD out of the anxiety disorders to a chapter with other trauma-related disorders, to move it away from being conceptualized as a fear-based disorder.

CASE EXAMPLE

Anne was a 30-year-old woman who presented for treatment wanting help to manage "anger and anxiety." She lived alone and, with the exception of two female friends, had no significant social relationships. She further reported that she had not had any romantic relationships during her adult life. She had been unemployed for the past 3 months, having been fired from her last job due to "anger problems." She was currently supporting herself with savings, which were quickly waning; however, she expressed ambivalence about finding another job because, she stated, she "didn't like being around most people."

During a standard intake interview, Anne, with much trepidation, acknowledged that she had been raped more than 10 years earlier. She stated that she had not told anyone about this previously. The rape occurred when she was out on a first date with a man she knew casually from one of her college classes. After dinner, he suggested a walk on the beach, during which he became sexually suggestive and began to fondle her. Anne reported that she initially resisted his advances but he became more aggressive and eventually physically restrained her, pinning her down with his body and covering her mouth with his hand. Anne remarked that she "shut down" and felt numb all over during the rape. Immediately afterward, the man told her that she "just got what she wanted" and that if she told anyone about what occurred, he would deny it. He further said that since he was a popular person on campus, everyone would believe him and think that she was "easy." Anne remembered returning to her dormitory room, where she immediately showered and then told everyone that she wasn't feeling well so that she could stay alone in her room for several days.

Anne reported that since then she had thought about the rape every day, often with perseveration about how she might have prevented it or how she might get revenge against the rapist. She frequently had nightmares about being restrained and would wake up in a sweat. In addition, she frequently exhibited a generalized response of anger toward men and reported feeling suspicious of all men, with only a few exceptions. She stated that she felt "men were only after one thing" and were "manipulators and liars." Because of this, Anne reported that she avoided all social situations because she did not want to interact with men on a social level. When she couldn't avoid it (e.g., family weddings), she would feel extreme anxiety and would often respond to fairly innocuous comments (e.g., "You look nice tonight") with an outburst of anger. She reported that she had gained the reputation of being the black sheep of the family as a result. She further stated that because the rape occurred on a beach, she had not been to a beach since because she feared it would bring up memories too intense to manage.

Anne reported that prior to the rape she had had good peer relationships, and stated that she had many life goals, including a career in journalism. She stated that after the rape she lost interest in her goals and in being with others, and barely graduated from college. She spent most of her time alone. Anne described feeling angry a good portion of the day and said that she felt she had a "short fuse"; many things irritated her that would not irritate others. Throughout her adult life she had held a string of temporary jobs, mostly as a receptionist, and would often get terminated due to complaints from customers that she was rude. She stated that she often slept only 3 to 4 hours a night and would wake up feeling frightened from her nightmares. When this occurred, she would go around her apartment to check the locks on the windows and doors because she felt unsafe and was worried that an intruder would break in. She stated that she often had intrusive images of the rapist's face, and when this happened, she would have panic-like symptoms and be "filled with rage and self-loathing."

Prevalence and Epidemiological Factors

Large, nationally representative, epidemiological studies estimating the prevalence of trauma exposure and PTSD have not yet been reported based on *DSM-5* criteria. Thus, the following estimates are based on *DSM-IV* criteria, and *DSM-5* findings are noted when available.

Results from several epidemiological studies indicate that experiencing a traumatic event in one's life is the rule rather than the exception. For example, in an examination of the prevalence and effects of trauma in individuals from the National Comorbidity Survey, Kessler, Sonnega, Bromet, Hughes, and Nelson (1995) found that approximately 60.7% of men and 51.2% of women had experienced at least one trauma in their lifetime. In comparison with women, men were more likely to report experiencing a physical attack, being threatened with a weapon, being in an accident, or witnessing a trauma. Women were more likely to report rape, molestation, neglect, or physical abuse. Furthermore, Norris (1992) has highlighted the significance of motor vehicle accidents (MVAs) in terms of both prevalence and rates of PTSD. Approximately 23% of the population is estimated to experience at least one MVA in their lifetime, and the incidence of PTSD from MVAs is estimated at 12%.

As noted earlier, most individuals exhibit PTSD symptoms immediately following trauma exposure. For example, 2 weeks after a sexual assault, 80% to 94% of victims would meet *DSM-IV* criteria for PTSD if not for the duration requirement; however, 3 months after the rape, the rates of PTSD drop to approximately 50% (Gutner et al., 2006; Rothbaum & Foa, 1993). These statistics suggest that perhaps the important question to ask is not, "Who develops PTSD?" but rather, "Who fails to recover following a traumatic event?" Events considered to be more heterogeneous in terms of severity and less personal—such as accidents or natural disasters—are associated with lower rates of PTSD than sexual assault (Kessler et al., 1995).

In terms of prevalence, epidemiological studies suggest that less than 7% of the population will have had PTSD at some point in their lifetime (Kessler et al., 2005). Rates of PTSD are significantly higher among war veterans (Dohrenwend et al., 2006; Kulka et al., 1990; Ramchand et al., 2010). Additionally, the impact of recent, large-scale man-made and natural disasters, such as the September 11, 2001, terrorist attacks and the Asian tsunami of December 2004, has been assessed in terms of large-scale population surveys. Although these studies typically do not use gold standard assessments to diagnose PTSD, they provide snapshot indices of PTSD symptomatology in trauma-exposed communities. For example, a phone survey of adult residents of Manhattan conducted 1 to 2 months after 9/11 found 7.5% of individuals to endorse symptoms suggestive of a PTSD diagnosis (Galea et al., 2002). This rate increased to 20% for individuals who lived in close proximity to the World Trade Center site. A study of people affected by the Asian tsunami used a multistaged, cluster, population-based mental health survey (specifically, the Short-Form Health Survey [SF-36]) to assess outcomes. Participants were displaced and nondisplaced persons in the Phang Nga province of Thailand, where more than 5,000 individuals were confirmed dead. The researchers found that 12% of displaced persons and 7% of nondisplaced persons evidenced PTSD symptoms 8 weeks after the tsunami (van Griensven et al., 2006). A follow-up survey 9 months after the tsunami demonstrated that the percentage of individuals reporting PTSD symptomatology had decreased to 7% of displaced persons and 3% of nondisplaced persons.

Undoubtedly, we will soon learn about any changes in prevalence rates given the shift to *DSM-5* criteria for PTSD. Although not using a true random sample, the National Stressful Events Survey collected data from a large and diverse sample recruited from an online panel of U.S. census-matched adults, and these data were used to compare *DSM-IV* and *DSM-5* rates of trauma exposure and PTSD status (Kilpatrick et al., 2013). According to this study, 89.7% of the sample reported lifetime exposure to at least one *DSM-5* Criterion A event (modal number of events was 3), suggesting high rates of lifetime trauma exposure. The percentage of individuals meeting *DSM-5* criteria tended to be lower than the percentage of those meeting *DSM-IV* criteria, but this difference was not consistently statistically significant (Kilpatrick et al., 2013). Other studies suggest that rates of diagnosis may be comparable across measures corresponding to *DSM-IV* and *DSM-5* criteria. For example, in a study of self-reported PTSD symptoms among U.S. soldiers, 13% screened positive for *DSM-IV* PTSD, while 12% screened positive for *DSM-5* criteria (Hoge, Riviere, Wilk, Herrell, & Weathers, 2014). However, in spite of general agreement in diagnostic status across measures ($k = 0.67$), 45% of soldiers had discordant results (i.e., meeting criteria for *DSM-IV* but not *DSM-5* criteria or meeting *DSM-5* criteria only). In another study using a gold-standard clinical interview in a sample of individuals hospitalized for a severe injury, rates of diagnosis were not significantly different across *DSM-IV* and *DSM-5* versions of the interview (O'Donnell et al., 2014).

SEX DIFFERENCES

There appears to be a sex difference in rates of PTSD, with women nearly three times as likely as men to have a lifetime diagnosis (9.7% to 3.6%; Kessler et al., 2005). This pattern was also observed in the aforementioned National Stressful Events Survey of *DSM-5* PTSD (Kilpatrick et al., 2013). In Hoge and colleagues' studies of men and women deployed to Iraq and Afghanistan, 23.6% of women reported mental health concerns compared with 18.6% of the men (Hoge, Auchterlonie, & Milliken, 2006). A meta-analysis of sex differences in risk for PTSD demonstrated that, consistent with the summarized data discussed previously, although females are more likely than males to meet criteria for PTSD, they are less likely to have experienced potentially traumatic events (Tolin & Foa, 2006). Moreover, even when type of trauma is controlled, women still appear to exhibit higher rates of PTSD, suggesting that risk of exposure to particular types of trauma only partially explains the differential PTSD rates in men and women. A number of explanations for this difference have been offered, including biological, psychological, and sociocultural points of view (Kimerling, Ouimette, & Wolfe, 2002). However, in a recent study of 340 female and 252 male veterans who had been deployed to Iraq or Afghanistan, Vogt et al. (2011), using standardized measures rather than screening tools, found no sex differences in the overall number of traumatic events during deployment or in rates of PTSD. The men had experienced more combat, but the women had experienced more perceived threat and other types of trauma, such as sexual assault. The same findings are reported by Street, Gradus, Giasson, Vogt, and Resick (2013) from 2,000 men and women who were deployed to Iraq or Afghanistan. These researchers found that 20% of each sex had probable PTSD.

COMORBIDITY AND PERSONALITY

Posttraumatic stress disorder is associated with very high rates of comorbidity. Brown, Di Nardo, Lehman, and Campbell (2001) examined comorbidity patterns of 1,126 community outpatients and found that PTSD had the highest and most diverse rate of comorbid disorders (over 90%), with the most frequent comorbid disorder being major depressive disorder (77%), followed by generalized anxiety disorder (38%) and alcohol abuse/dependence (31%). Studies of military veterans have found rates of comorbidity from 50% to 80% (Kulka et al., 1990; Orsillo et al., 1996). Thus, the question of why comorbid conditions are so common in PTSD arises. Recent research on the dimensional nature of psychopathology may provide an explanation along with an understanding of the function of the comorbid symptoms in managing PTSD intrusion and arousal.

Psychopathology and personality researchers have examined the latent dimensions of internalizing and externalizing that underlie adult disorders. A series of factor analytic studies have determined that comorbid disorders fall along these dimensions (e.g., Cox, Clara, & Enns, 2002; Krueger, McGue, & Iacono, 2001), such that substance abuse disorders and antisocial personality load on the externalizing dimension, while mood and anxiety disorders load on the internalizing dimension. Widiger and Simonsen (2005) have proposed a hierarchical structure to personality disorders as well, with internalization and externalization at the highest level of this structure. Immediately beneath these higher-order dimensions are three to five broad domains of personality functioning, followed by personality trait constructs, and at the lowest level the more behaviorally specific diagnostic criteria.

Studies have examined whether the internalizing-externalizing model is relevant to patterns of posttraumatic psychopathology (e.g., Miller, Fogler, Wolf, Kaloupek, & Keane, 2008; Miller & Resick, 2007), particularly with regard to explanations for the high levels of comorbidity among those with PTSD or the consideration of *complex PTSD*. Miller and colleagues have evidence of internalizing and externalizing subtypes of PTSD in both male and female samples totaling over 1,000 subjects through a series of cluster analytic studies of personality inventories (Miller, Greif, & Smith, 2003; Miller, Kaloupek, Dillon, & Keane, 2004; Miller & Resick, 2007). Across these three studies, Miller and colleagues found that there are people who score low on both internalizing and externalizing who could be conceptualized as displaying a subtype of simple PTSD. A second subtype, externalizing, is characterized by the tendency to outwardly express distress through antagonistic interactions with others, blaming others, and coping through acting out. Individuals in this subgroup endorsed elevated levels of anger and aggression, substance-related disorders, and Cluster B personality disorder features. They described themselves as impulsive, with little regard for the consequences of their actions, easily upset, and chronically stressed. On measures of personality disorder symptoms, they described themselves as tending toward manipulative, exhibitionistic, and unconventional behavior. Externalizers described themselves as being emotionally labile, overactive, fearless, and feeling chronically betrayed and mistreated by others. In both studies of veterans, in which data on pre-military characteristics were available, those with externalizing tendencies reported higher rates of pre-military delinquency, suggesting the influence of externalizing personality traits was present prior to the trauma.

The third subtype, the internalizing subtype, is characterized by the tendency to direct posttraumatic distress inwardly through shame, self-defeating and self-deprecating beliefs, anxiety, avoidance, depression, and withdrawal. Across the three studies, people in this subtype reported the highest levels of PTSD and reported high rates of comorbid major depression and panic disorder, schizoid and avoidant personality disorder features, and personality profiles defined by high negative emotionality combined with low positive emotionality. Members of this subtype also described themselves as unenthusiastic, uninspired, easily fatigued, and lacking interests. They endorsed having few friends, being aloof and distant from others, preferring to spend time alone, having a restricted range of emotions in interpersonal settings, and experiencing feelings of social inhibition, inadequacy, and hypersensitivity to negative evaluation. These findings suggest that the internalizing-externalizing subtypes of psychopathology, originally developed to account for covariation among broad classes of mental disorders (cf. Krueger, Caspi, Moffitt, & Silva, 1998; Krueger et al., 2001), are relevant to the understanding of the heterogeneity of PTSD comorbidity. These profiles suggest that different underlying personality processes may influence later presentation of psychopathology.

Again, more research on *DSM-5* comorbidity is underway; however, initial research suggests similar patterns of association between PTSD and commonly co-occurring disorders. The aforementioned study comparing *DSM-IV* and *DSM-5* versions of a PTSD self-report measure found that the two versions of the measure had nearly identical associations with major depression, generalized anxiety, and alcohol misuse (Hoge et al., 2014). Likewise, PTSD comorbidity with depression, assessed using a structured interview format among severe injury survivors, was not significantly different when using *DSM-IV* versus *DSM-5* criteria (O'Donnell et al., 2014). Thus, there is little evidence so far to suggest that the move from *DSM-IV* to *DSM-5* symptoms results in differential comorbidity rates, but future epidemiological studies will shed more light on this topic and provide more conclusive findings.

In sum, epidemiological research on trauma and PTSD has consistently found that exposure to trauma is a common experience. Prevalence rates of PTSD in the general U.S. population are about 7% for a lifetime diagnosis, but increase substantially (up to 20% to 30%) when examining specific trauma-exposed groups. War veterans, rape victims, and victims of natural and man-made disasters have been the most frequently studied populations. Increasing attention by the research community to the effects of global events and more sophisticated rapid assessment techniques have allowed a better understanding of the development and maintenance of PTSD symptomatology in trauma survivors.

Biological Factors

A number of neurobiological systems have been implicated in the pathophysiology of PTSD, including alterations in the noradrenergic, hypothalamic-pituitary-adrenal (HPA) axis and the gamma-aminobutyric acid (GABA)/glutamate, serotonin, and dopamine systems.

NORADRENERGIC SYSTEM

A number of studies, using various methodologies, have provided compelling evidence for increased noradrenergic activity in traumatized humans with PTSD (e.g., Friedman & Southwick, 1995; Southwick et al., 1999; Yehuda et al., 1998; Young & Breslau, 2004). Heightened norepinephrine reactivity to pharmacological and behavioral challenge appears to be a more important marker of PTSD than high tonic or baseline levels of norepinephrine sampled at a single point in time (Blanchard, Kolb, Prins, Gates, & McCoy, 1991; McFall, Murburg, Ko, & Veith, 1990; Southwick et al., 1993). Moreover, the presence of comorbid depression appears to be an important moderator of the association between heightened noradrenergic output and PTSD. For example, Yehuda et al. (1998) found that combat veterans with PTSD but without comorbid depression had higher mean norepinephrine levels at nearly every time point compared with combat veterans with PTSD and comorbid depression, subjects with depression alone, and healthy controls.

Neuropeptide Y (NPY) is simultaneously released with norepinephrine during stress provocation and acts as an endogenous antiadrenergic, thereby having anxiolytic- and cognitive-enhancing effects. In men undergoing military survival training involving high levels of uncontrollable stress, Morgan, Wang, and Southwick (2000) and Morgan et al. (2001) found a significant positive association between NPY release and superior performance in mock training situations, as well as a significant negative relationship between NPY and symptoms of dissociation. Compared with healthy controls, PTSD patients have also been found to exhibit low baseline levels of NPY and blunted NPY responses to yohimbine stimulation (Rasmusson et al., 2000).

HYPOTHALAMIC-PITUITARY-ADRENAL (HPA) AXIS

Corticotrophin-releasing factor (CRF) promotes the release of norepinephrine from the locus coeruleus as well as the release of corticotrophin (ACTH) from the pituitary gland, which then promotes release of cortisol and other glucocorticoids from the adrenal cortex. Vietnam veterans with PTSD have been shown to have elevated resting levels of cerebrospinal fluid CRF (Baker et al., 1999; Bremner et al., 1997), and enhanced hypothalamic release of CRF (Yehuda, 2002).

Although excessive HPA dysregulation is consistently associated with trauma exposure and PTSD, there have been inconsistent results surrounding the nature of HPA dysfunction. Low urinary cortisol output has been found in male combat veterans and male and postmenopausal female Holocaust survivors. Conversely, high cortisol output has been found most consistently in premenopausal women and children with PTSD (e.g., Heim et al., 2000; Lipschitz, Rasmusson, & Yehuda, 2003; Rasmusson, Vasek, & Lipschitz, 2004; Rasmusson, Vythilingam, & Morgan, 2003; Young & Breslau, 2004). The inconsistency in these findings is likely related to other clinical and methodological factors associated with cortisol output and its measurement, including sex hormones, diagnostic comorbidity (especially depression or dissociation), age at trauma exposure, substance use, medications, exercise, and ethnicity or genetic factors (Rasmusson et al., 2004).

Dehydroepiandrosterone (DHEA) is another adrenal steroid that is released in concert with cortisol in the face of stress. In a sample of premenopausal women with PTSD, Rasmusson et al. (2003) found an inverse relationship between DHEA reactivity and severity of PTSD symptoms. In the study of military members undergoing Special Forces training mentioned earlier, Morgan et al. (2004) found a negative relationship between the ratio of DHEAS (the sulfated version of DHEA) to cortisol and dissociation. They also found a positive correlation between the DHEAS-cortisol ratio and better behavioral performance in this sample.

There have been a few studies on allotetrahydrodeoxycorticosterone and allopregnanolone in PTSD; these are neuroactive steroids that positively modulate the effects of GABA (see the following discussion) and produce anxiolytic, sedative, and analgesic effects. In a study of premenopausal women with PTSD who were in the follicular phase of the menstrual cycle, CSF allopregnanolone levels in the PTSD subjects were less than 40% of those in the nontraumatized healthy subjects (Rasmusson, Pinna, & Paliwal, 2006). The allopregnanolone-to-DHEA ratio in these subjects was also negatively associated with reexperiencing and depressive symptoms in the PTSD participants (Rasmusson et al., 2006).

GAMMA-AMINOBUTYRIC ACID (GABA)

Gamma-aminobutyric acid (GABA) is the brain's primary inhibitory neurotransmitter, which functions to counter excitatory glutamatergic synaptic transmission. Bremner et al. (2000) found that benzodiazepine receptor density and/or affinity was reduced in the medial prefrontal cortex among patients with PTSD compared with controls in a sample of accident victims. Vaiva and colleagues (2004) reported significantly lower plasma GABA levels in subjects who developed PTSD compared with subjects who did not.

SEROTONIN (5H-T)

Among individuals with PTSD, a resting state has been associated with decreased platelet serotonin uptake (Arora, Fichtner, O'Connor, & Crayton, 1993; Bremner, Southwick, & Charney, 1999); blunted prolactin response to d-fenfluramine (Davis, Clark, Kramer, Moeller, & Petty, 1999); and exaggerated panic/anxiety and heart rate reactions to a serotonergic probe, meta-chlorophenylpiperazine (Southwick et al., 1997), relative to non-PTSD controls. Fichtner, Arora, O'Connor, and Crayton (1994) also found that PTSD patients who responded best to the medication paroxetine were those with the highest pretreatment platelet affinity for the drug.

DOPAMINE

Excessive dopamine release may play a role in the hyperarousal, hypervigilance, and brief psychotic states sometimes observed in individuals with PTSD. Surprisingly little research has focused on dopamine in comparison with the neurotransmitters previously reviewed. Elevated urinary and plasma dopamine concentrations have been found among PTSD subjects (Hamner & Diamond, 1993; Lemieux & Coe, 1995; Yehuda et al., 1994).

BRAIN STRUCTURES

Brain regions implicated in PTSD are also associated with fear conditioning and extinction, including the amygdala, the medial prefrontal cortex (mPFC), the anterior cingulate cortex (ACC), and the hippocampus. Across a number of studies, investigators have found a positive association between PTSD severity and increased amygdala responsivity, such that individuals with PTSD demonstrate hyperresponsivity to both trauma-related and trauma-unrelated emotional material (see Shin, Rauch, & Pitman, 2006, for a review). In contrast, PTSD symptom severity is negatively related to mPFC responsivity. Among those with PTSD, the mPFC prefrontal cortex appears to be smaller and hyporesponsive (Shin et al., 2006). A related, adjacent brain structure, the medial orbitofrontal cortex (mOFC), has also been implicated in PTSD, such that individuals with PTSD demonstrate decreased mOFC activity, corresponding to a failure to inhibit anxiety responses (see Milad & Rauch, 2007, for a review). Thus, both the amygdala and portions of the prefrontal cortex (PFC) appear to be consistently affected in PTSD, and a reciprocal relationship has been observed between these regions (Shin et al., 2006). Likewise, it is theorized that, among individuals with PTSD, the ACC fails to inhibit amygdala hyperactivity. A recent meta-analysis of magnetic resonance imaging (MRI) studies revealed a reduction in bilateral amygdala volume for individuals with PTSD relative to healthy controls but no significant reduction compared to trauma-exposed controls (O'Doherty, Chitty, Saddiqui, Bennett, & Lagopoulos, 2015). They also found significant bilateral volume reductions in the ACC among individuals with PTSD relative to healthy controls as well as trauma-exposed controls.

Finally, there appears to be decreased hippocampal volume among individuals with PTSD relative to control subjects without PTSD, including both PTSD-negative trauma-exposed and trauma-unexposed controls, although the evidence has been mixed (e.g., O'Doherty et al., 2015; Shin et al., 2006). Interestingly, this abnormality may represent a vulnerability factor for, rather than a consequence of, PTSD based on a study reporting reduced hippocampal volume among individuals with PTSD and their trauma-unexposed twins (Gilbertson et al., 2002). By contrast, in a recent meta-analysis, Woon and Hedges (2008) reported reduced hippocampal volume among adults with childhood maltreatment-related PTSD, whereas children with maltreatment-related PTSD did not evidence analogous hippocampal volume deficits, suggesting that trauma exposure or PTSD might disrupt hippocampal development. More research is certainly warranted in this area.

Cognitive and Emotional Factors

PTSD pathology is dominated by disruptions in cognition or memory, which are reflected in the *DSM-5* criteria. The symptoms that comprise the B criterion include the hallmark symptoms of recurrent and intrusive recollections of the event, dreams about the event, and flashbacks. One of the C criteria is avoidance of trauma-related thoughts and images. Within the D criterion are items about amnesia for the event and persistent and exaggerated negative beliefs about oneself, others, or the world as well as erroneous self-blame and blame of others. The E arousal criterion includes difficulty concentrating, which could reflect problems of attention, as well as arousal. Theorists and researchers have noted that traumatized people have problems with both remembering and forgetting traumatic events, and that cognitive processes feature prominently in individuals' attempts to cope with intrusive memories and emotions.

Cognitions can be considered as cognitive processes or cognitive content. Cognitive processes include attempts to cope with intrusive recollections of the event (e.g., thought suppression, overaccommodation) or attentional bias to direct attention to potential danger cues. Cognitive content includes specific beliefs that become maladaptive ("because one person assaulted me, that means no one can be trusted") or the outcomes of cognitive or memory processes such as amnesia for the event or fragmented memory. Most recent theories of PTSD have incorporated cognition, along with considerations of arousal, emotions, and avoidance (Cahill & Foa, 2007). Some theorists have focused specifically on memory processes in PTSD (Brewin, 2007; Brewin, Dalgleish, & Joseph, 1996; Dalgleish, 2004).

The study of memory in PTSD began with the observations of flashbacks, intrusive memories, amnesia, and fragmented memory among those with PTSD. In order to account for some of these phenomena, as well as to incorporate extant theories, Brewin et al. (1996) proposed a dual representation theory of PTSD, in which memories of a traumatic experience are thought to be stored in two ways: 1) autobiographical memories of the experience, referred to as verbally accessible memories (VAM), which include information the individual attended to before, during, and after the traumatic event with sufficient conscious processing to be transferred to long-term memory, and 2) situationally accessible memories (SAM), which contain extensive nonconscious and nonverbal information about the traumatic event that cannot be deliberately accessed or easily altered. These latter memories can, however, be triggered in the form of flashbacks, nightmares, or intrusive images. Brewin et al. also propose two types of emotional reactions: primary emotions, conditioned during the traumatic event (e.g., fear, helplessness, horror), and secondary emotions that result from post hoc consideration of the traumatic event (e.g., anger, shame, sadness). Brewin et al. propose that successful emotional processing of a traumatic event requires the activation of both VAM and SAM. Resolution of schema conflicts occurs through a conscious search for meaning during activation of SAM and VAM, resulting in an integrated view of the trauma.

Ehlers and Clark (2000) have focused on the apparent paradox of memory in PTSD, such that someone with PTSD may have trouble intentionally accessing his or her memory of the event but have involuntary intrusions of parts of it. Ehlers and Clark noted that anxiety disorders, within a cognitive framework, are focused on future danger, while PTSD appears to be focused on an event in the past. They resolve this discrepancy by suggesting that people with PTSD are processing their traumatic events in idiosyncratic ways that produce an appraisal of serious current threat. Ehlers and Clark propose that because the memory encoded at the time of the trauma is poorly elaborated and integrated with other memories with regard to details, context of time, sequence, and so forth, this might explain why people with PTSD may have poor autobiographical memory and yet may be triggered to have memory fragments that have a here-and-now quality (no time context) or may not have appropriate posttrauma appraisals (e.g., "I did not die"). Ehlers and Clark also propose that like the emotional processing models, strong associative learning is paired with fear responses and can generalize.

In response to the perceptions of threat, people with PTSD adopt various maladaptive coping strategies, depending on their appraisals. For example, people who believe they will go crazy if they think about the traumatic event will attempt to avoid thoughts about the trauma and will try to keep their minds occupied with other things as much as they can. Someone who believes that he or she must figure out why the traumatic event happened to keep it from happening again will ruminate about how it could have been prevented. Those who think that the traumatic event was punishment for prior actions may become immobilized and unable to make decisions. These maladaptive strategies, most often avoidance behaviors, may (a) increase symptoms, (b) prevent change in negative appraisals, or (c) prevent change in the trauma memory.

Social-cognitive theorists have observed that traumatic events dramatically alter basic beliefs about the self, the world, and others. These theorists tend to focus on the content of altered cognitions and the processes by which trauma victims integrate traumatic events into their overall conceptual systems, either by assimilating the information into existing schemas or by altering existing schemas to accommodate the new information (Hollon & Garber, 1988). Janoff-Bulman (1992) focused primarily on three major assumptions that may be shattered in the face of a traumatic event: personal invulnerability, the world as a meaningful and predictable place, and the self as positive or worthy. McCann, Sakheim, and Abrahamson (1988) proposed six major areas of functioning, either self- or other-focused, that can be disrupted by traumatic victimization: agency, safety, trust, power/control, esteem, and intimacy. This theory suggests that difficulties with adaptation following traumatic events result if previously positive schemas (basic assumptions or conceptual systems) are disrupted by the experience or if previous negative schemas are seemingly confirmed by the experience.

In a similar vein, Resick (1992) has proposed that when traumatic events conflict with prior beliefs, the people affected have three possibilities: altering their interpretations of the event in an attempt to maintain previously held beliefs (assimilation), altering their beliefs just enough to accommodate the new information (accommodation), or changing their beliefs drastically (overaccommodation). Examples of these three processes would be for someone who was attacked by a friend to think, "It's all my fault; I must have caused him to do this" (assimilation), "There must be something wrong with him that he would betray me this way" (accommodation), or "This means that I can't trust anyone" (overaccommodation). Those people who have histories of traumatic events are particularly prone to overaccommodation, and use experiences with disparate events as mounting proof of an extreme belief (McCann & Pearlman, 1990).

As part of a larger emotional processing theory (see the following discussion), Foa and her colleagues (Cahill & Foa, 2007; Foa & Rothbaum, 1998) have proposed that cognitions of people with PTSD fall into two classes: one, that the world is dangerous, and two, that the person himself or herself is completely incompetent. They propose that danger cognitions emanate from the large number of stimulus representations that can activate the mental fear structure that is thought to underlie PTSD. Incompetence beliefs are generated from erroneous mental representations of how the person behaved during the trauma and from subsequent symptoms.

RESEARCH ON COGNITIVE PROCESSES

There is evidence supporting the fragmentation of trauma memories, cognitive avoidance by way of thought suppression, and an attentional bias toward threat cues. Regarding fragmentation and content of memory for traumatic events, research has shown that recovery from a trauma event involves organizing and streamlining the traumatic memory (e.g., Foa & Kozak, 1986; Foa & Riggs, 1993; Rachman, 1980). Consistent with this notion, research has shown that trauma narratives that are disorganized are associated with increased PTSD symptom severity (e.g., Foa, Molnar, & Cashman, 1995; Jones, Harvey, & Brewin, 2007; Zoellner, Alvarez-Conrad, & Foa, 2002). Importantly, Jones et al. (2007) found that the disorganization of trauma narratives did not distinguish participants who had suffered a traumatic brain injury during the traumatic event from those who had not. Therefore, the disorganization findings for trauma narratives do not appear to be merely the result of cognitive deficits associated with traumatic brain injury (e.g., physical assault, combat injury, motor vehicle accident).

Cognitive theories of PTSD have also emphasized the importance of memory vividness and accessibility (Brewin, 1996), and research has found that sections of trauma narratives that are reflective of a flashback contain more sensory words compared with other sections of the narrative (e.g., Brewin, 1996; Hellawell & Brewin, 2004). Foa and Kozak's (1986) emotional processing theory also suggests that effectively accessing a trauma memory should result in greater usage of words representing negative emotion and trauma-associated sensory content. Consistent with this theory, trauma narratives of PTSD individuals contain more sensory details and negative emotion content compared with narratives of trauma survivors who do not develop PTSD (Hellawell & Brewin, 2004; Jones et al., 2007; Zoellner et al., 2002).

Thought-suppression paradigms have been used to examine the role of cognitive avoidance in the maintenance of PTSD symptoms (Davies & Clark, 1998; Harvey & Bryant, 1998; McNally & Riccardi, 1996). A rebound effect, an increase in thoughts after initial suppression, was assumed to parallel what naturally occurs when trauma survivors try to avoid intrusive trauma-related thoughts. In studies of recent trauma survivors with and without acute stress disorder (Harvey & Bryant, 1998) and in longer-term samples of women with or without PTSD (Shipherd & Beck, 1999), the rebound effect has been demonstrated in those with stress-related disorders compared with those without those disorders. These findings were replicated when comparing motor vehicle accident survivors with and without PTSD (Shipherd & Beck, 2005). Together, these studies support the theories that emphasize the role of cognitive avoidance as a maintaining factor in PTSD.

A modified Stroop paradigm has been used to study selective processing in people with or without PTSD by asking participants to name the color of words that do or don't relate to their trauma. Studies have demonstrated that people with PTSD are slower at naming the color of trauma-related words compared to positive words, general threat words, and neutral words. This Stroop effect has been demonstrated in a variety of trauma populations, including war veterans (Litz et al., 1996; McNally, English, & Lipke, 1993; McNally, Kaspi, Riemann, & Zeitlin, 1990), sexual assault survivors (Foa, Feske, Murdock, Kozak, & McCarthy, 1991), survivors of a ferry disaster (Thrasher, Dalgleish, & Yule, 1994), childhood sexual abuse survivors (Bremner et al., 2004; Field et al., 2001), motor vehicle accident survivors (Beck, Freeman, Shipherd, Hamblen, & Lackner, 2001; Bryant & Harvey, 1995), and child and adolescent trauma survivors (Freeman & Beck, 2000; Moradi, Taghavi, Neshat Doost, Yule, & Dalgleish, 1999).

RESEARCH ON COGNITIVE CONTENT

There is also evidence regarding the relationship between cognitive content disturbance and PTSD. Strong correlations have been found between maladaptive beliefs regarding safety, trust, esteem, or intimacy and PTSD symptoms among survivors of child sexual abuse (Wenninger & Ehlers, 1998). Using the same scale, the Personal Beliefs and Reactions Scale (PBRS; Resick, Schnicke, & Markway, 1991), Owens and Chard (2001) found similar findings among 53 adult survivors of child sexual abuse. PTSD severity was correlated with cognitive distortions on all seven subscales. Kubany (1994) specifically examined guilt cognitions among combat veterans and battered women and found that guilt cognitions correlated highly with several different PTSD measures. In the development of a short form of the PBRS, called the Posttraumatic Maladaptive Beliefs Scale (PMBS; Vogt, Shipherd, & Resick, 2012), maladaptive cognitions were found to be significantly correlated with PTSD severity on the Clinician-Administered PTSD Scale (CAPS) in a sample of 294 women with histories of interpersonal trauma.

Dunmore, Clark, and Ehlers (1999) examined 92 assault victims with or without PTSD in a cross-sectional study and found that those diagnosed with PTSD reported more mental defeat, mental planning, mental confusion, and detachment during the traumatic event. They also reported more negative appraisals of their initial posttrauma symptoms, a more negative perception of others' responses, a lower positive perception of others' responses, and a greater perception of perceived permanent damage. Furthermore, they reported a greater impact on their posttrauma beliefs. When those who had recovered from their PTSD and those who had persistent PTSD were compared, the important cognitive variables associated with persistence of PTSD were mental defeat, mental confusion, negative appraisals of emotions and symptoms, negative responses from others, and the belief they had permanently changed and had altered beliefs posttrauma. In a related longitudinal study, Dunmore, Clark, and Ehlers (2001) examined assault victims within 4 months and then again at 6 and 9 months postcrime. They also found that cognitive variables were predictive of PTSD at 6 or 9 months postcrime either directly or indirectly, mediated by initial PTSD.

There have been a growing number of studies that have examined cognitions as a mechanism of change in PTSD treatment. Gallagher and Resick (2012) examined hopelessness as both an outcome and a mediator of change in PTSD among women who had rape as their index event. Participants assigned to cognitive processing therapy (CPT; Resick & Schnicke, 1993), a therapy directly targeting problematic cognitions in PTSD, had larger pre-post reductions in hopelessness than those assigned to prolonged exposure (PE; Foa, Hearst, Dancu, Hembree, & Jaycox, 1994), and changes in hopelessness predicted changes in PTSD symptoms in CPT participants more so than in PE participants. Gilman, Schumm, and Chard (2012) also examined hope (rather than hopelessness, with a different measure than Gallagher and Resick used) in veterans seeking treatment for PTSD. Measures of PTSD symptoms, depression, and hope were gathered across the course of treatment in a residential program. Gilman et al. (2012) found that higher levels of hope midtreatment were associated with reductions in PTSD and depression from mid- to posttreatment, and not the other way around, thus supporting that hope is a change mechanism toward symptom reduction.

Schumm, Dickstein, Walter, Owens, and Chard (2015) conducted a cross-lagged panel analysis from pretreatment to midtreatment to posttreatment CPT among male and female veterans to determine the longitudinal relationship between cognitions (negative beliefs about self, negative beliefs about the world, and self-blame), PTSD, and depression. They found significant improvements in all the scales over the course of treatment. They also found that that pre- to midtreatment change in self-blame and negative beliefs about the self positively predicted and temporally preceded mid- to posttreatment change in PTSD symptomatology. They also found that changes in negative beliefs about the self preceded changes in depression but that pre- to midtreatment changes in depression preceded changes in self-blame and PTSD. These findings support the idea that improvement in negative cognitions is an important mechanism of change in PTSD.

EMOTIONAL FACTORS

The emotion that has received the lion's share of theoretical and research attention in PTSD is fear. Prior to *DSM-5*, PTSD had been classified as an anxiety disorder; thus theories regarding fear and anxiety have been applied to PTSD. There is ample evidence that fear and anxiety play a large role in PTSD. However, clinicians and researchers have long noted that people with PTSD also have serious problems with anger, shame, and guilt (e.g., Andrews, Brewin, Rose, & Kirk, 2000; Henning & Frueh, 1997; Kubany, 1994; Leskela, Dieperink, & Thuras, 2002; Riggs, Dancu, Gershuny, Greenberg, & Foa, 1992; Wong & Cook, 1992).

Brewin, Andrews, and Rose (2000) found that in addition to fear, emotions of helplessness or horror experienced within 1 month of the crime were predictive of PTSD status 6 months later. Also, shame and anger predicted later PTSD status, even after controlling for intense emotions of fear, helplessness, and horror. Pitman, Orr, Forgue, and Altman (1990) also found that combat veterans with PTSD reported experiencing a range of emotions other than fear while listening to individualized traumatic scripts. In fact, veterans with PTSD were no more likely to report experiencing fear than other emotions. Similarly, in a study examining responses at the time of the trauma, Rizvi and colleagues (Rizvi, Kaysen, Gutner, Griffin, & Resick, 2008) have demonstrated that rape victims reported a wide range of emotional responses during the rape and that emotions other than fear (e.g., sadness, humiliation, and anger) were more predictive of later PTSD symptomatology than was fear.

Ramage and colleagues (2016) noted that emotions like disgust, guilt, shame, or sadness, which may be more common during traumas involving traumatic loss or moral injury, engage different neural systems than fear, which may be more common during traumas involving threat to personal safety. In support of this position, Ramage et al. (2016) found evidence of neural markers for potential "subtypes" of PTSD based on the nature of the worst traumatic event. They compared U.S. soldiers with PTSD resulting from danger-based traumas (e.g., personal exposure to threat of death or serious injury) to soldiers with PTSD resulting from non-danger-based traumas (e.g., exposure to aftermath of violence, traumatic loss, moral injury), as well as to combat-exposed soldiers without PTSD and non-combat controls. In support of this theory, they found different patterns of neuronal activity in the amygdala and precuneus among those with danger- versus non-danger-based traumas.

Behavioral Factors

Avoidance behaviors were identified early in the study of trauma (e.g., Keane, Fairbank, Caddell, Zimering, & Bender, 1985; Kilpatrick et al., 1985). The first theories of reactions to trauma, and subsequently PTSD, were based on a two-factor theory (Mowrer, 1947), which proposed that anxiety is first acquired through classical conditioning in which an unconditioned stimulus (the traumatic event) becomes associated with other stimuli, which then elicit conditioned emotional responses. However, instead of extinguishing in the absence of further traumatic events, the person escapes or avoids the conditioned stimuli in an attempt to stop the negative emotional response. The avoidance behavior is negatively reinforced by the short-term reduction in anxiety but ultimately causes the initial anxious reaction to be maintained through the second factor of operant conditioning.

Avoidance behaviors have been implicated in maintenance of PTSD symptoms in more modern theories as well. A theory regarding the development of fear networks in PTSD has been offered by Foa and her colleagues (e.g., Cahill & Foa, 2007; Foa & Kozak, 1985, 1986), following upon the work of Lang (1979). In this theory, it is suggested that following traumatic events, a pathological fear structure develops that is composed of feared stimuli, responses, and meaning elements. The fear structure is activated by stimuli in the environment that match elements of the fear structure. When activated, cognitive, behavioral, and arousal anxiety reactions result. If the situation were in fact dangerous, it would be an effective program for escape or avoidance. However, a pathological fear network triggers false alarms because of the generalization of stimuli to nondangerous cues (Jones & Barlow, 1990). Fear elicits escape and avoidance behavior and subsequent emotional numbing. Resick and Schnicke (1992) have also suggested that avoidance is an important element in the maintenance of PTSD and have suggested that many of the symptoms and disorders that develop along with PTSD may develop as attempts to avoid the intrusive images and strong emotions. However, they have emphasized that fear is not the only emotion being avoided; many traumatic events elicit anger, sadness, guilt, and horror, which are overwhelming. These emotions, too, may trigger escape, avoidance, and numbing.

Evidence for a fear network and activation/extinction of fear comes from two sources. Physiological reactivity to trauma cues is associated with PTSD (Keane, Kolb, et al., 1998; Shalev, Orr, Peri, & Schreiber, 1992; Tarrier et al., 2002), and this reactivity changes as a function of successful treatment (Blanchard et al., 2003; Boudewyns & Hyer, 1990). In a study of physiological reactivity comparing treatment responders with nonresponders, Griffin, Resick, and Galovski (2006) found that patients who responded to treatment exhibited overall decreases in physiological responding from pretreatment to posttreatment, whereas those who did not benefit from treatment showed no such change. Rather than assessing physiological activation, Foa, Riggs, Massie, and Yarczower (1995) examined facial expressions during the first prolonged exposure session and found that greater facial displays of fear, assumed to reflect emotional engagement, were predictive of positive treatment outcomes.

Environmental Factors

By definition, external environmental factors play a key role in PTSD. Criterion A requires a traumatic stressor. Interestingly, not all stressors have equal effects, which provided support for the idea that PTSD is not just a conditioned response to a fear-inducing situation. In the National Comorbidity Study, Kessler et al. (1995) found that the more personally directed events, such as rape, molestation, assault, and combat, were more likely to result in PTSD than more impersonal events, such as disasters or accidents, even though the latter were far more common. In fact, rape was the single event most likely to result in PTSD among both men and women. There is also a dose-response relationship such that the more traumatic events one experiences, the more likely one is to develop PTSD (e.g., Fairbank, Keane, & Malloy, 1983; Foy, Carroll, & Donahoe, 1987; March, 1993; Rodriguez, Vande-Kemp, & Foy, 1998).

IMPORTANCE OF SOCIAL SUPPORT AND ADDITIONAL LIFE STRESS

Among risk factors for the development or maintenance of PTSD, social support has emerged as one of the most important variables. A number of studies have found that lack of social support is a risk factor for PTSD among people exposed to trauma (e.g., Keane, Scott, Chavoya, Lamparski, & Fairbank, 1985; King, King, Foy, Keane, & Fairbank, 1999; Solomon & Mikulincer, 1990). Brewin, Andrews, and Valentine (2000) conducted a meta-analysis of 77 studies to evaluate risk factors for PTSD. They examined 14 predictors of PTSD that were typically examined in these studies, including various demographics, psychiatric and trauma history, trauma severity, lack of social support, and additional life stress. They looked at 11 studies that measured lack of social support and 8 studies that assessed additional life stressors. They found that factors occurring during or after the trauma (trauma severity, lack of social support, additional life stress) had stronger effects on PTSD than pretrauma factors. Lack of social support had the strongest effect size across studies, and additional life stressors demonstrated the second-highest effect size in the Brewin, Andrews, and Valentine (2000) meta-analysis.

INTIMATE RELATIONSHIPS AND PTSD

An external or interpersonal factor associated with PTSD is intimate relationship dysfunction. Epidemiological studies indicate that those with PTSD are as likely as those without PTSD to be married, but both men and women with PTSD are substantially more likely to divorce, and divorce multiple times, following onset of the disorder (Kessler, Walters, & Forthofer, 1998). PTSD has also been found to be associated with relationship discord, domestic violence, sexual dysfunction, and mental health problems in the partners of those with PTSD (e.g., Monson, Fredman, & Dekel, 2010; Taft, Watkins, Stafford, Street, & Monson, 2011). Avoidance and numbing symptoms of PTSD have been specifically implicated in relationship satisfaction (Riggs, Byrne, Weathers, & Litz, 1998), and the hyperarousal symptoms have been associated with violence perpetration (Byrne & Riggs, 1996). Most of the research in this area has been cross-sectional, which does not allow for conclusions about the directionality of this association. However, there is likely a reciprocal relationship between intimate relationship functioning and PTSD, wherein each may serve to facilitate or exacerbate the other (Monson, Price, & Ranslow, 2005).

CONSERVATION OF RESOURCES

Another way in which trauma interacts with the environment to interfere with recovery from PTSD is through the loss of resources. For example, if people have severe PTSD such that they do not sleep and cannot concentrate at work, they may lose their jobs. Without a job, they may lose social and family support. Hobfoll (1989, 1991) has proposed a theory of stress called conservation of resources (COR) that he has subsequently applied to, and tested with, traumatic stress. The underlying tenet of COR is that people "will strive to obtain, retain, and protect what they value" (Hobfoll, 1991, p. 187). Stress occurs when resources are threatened or lost, or when resources don't increase adequately following their initial investment. Hobfoll examines four types of resources: conditions (e.g., stable marriage or work), objects (e.g., housing, car), personal characteristics (e.g., self-efficacy, skills), and energies, such as credit or insurance. Because the expenditure of resources to offset losses may deplete the person's resources, loss spirals may result.

According to COR theory, traumatic stress results in sudden and rapid loss of resources and the resources that are most valued (e.g., trust in self and others, perception of control, sense of well-being). Furthermore, traumatic events make excessive demands, for which people have little experience and therefore fewer strategies for coping. Because the demands of traumatic stressors are excessive, there is typically no amount of resources that would prevent an initial reaction. However, those who possess abundant personal, social, and financial resources would be expected to recover more quickly, whereas those who are already facing additional life stressors or whose resources are depleted by the trauma may face loss spirals and a downward trajectory of functioning.

Assessment

Given the high prevalence of traumatic events in the general population, as well as the shame and guilt that often accompanies certain types of trauma, assessment of PTSD requires care and sensitivity. The first task of a comprehensive assessment is to determine whether a life event meets the requirement of a traumatic stressor (Criterion A). Following this, the presence and severity of the 20 associated symptoms that comprise Criteria B to E must be determined. Interviews are considered the most reliable and valid method for assessing PTSD; however, a number of self-report questionnaires have been developed that may provide a valid, yet quicker and less costly alternative to an interview (Monson et al., 2014). These measures are summarized in the following section; however, it should be noted that there have been a limited number of studies examining the psychometric properties of the more newly developed measures corresponding to *DSM-5* criteria.

ASSESSMENT OF TRAUMATIC EVENTS

In order to determine whether the diagnosis of PTSD is plausible, the first step in assessment is to identify traumatic events that the individual experienced in his or her lifetime. This history can be extraordinarily difficult to obtain, depending on the experiences and the level of shame, self-blame, or embarrassment the person may be suffering. For example, although individuals may have little trouble disclosing that they experienced a natural disaster like a hurricane or tornado, rape or child sexual abuse victims may have greater difficulty spontaneously disclosing what happened to them. This inhibition of disclosure is also consistent with general patterns of avoidance of trauma-related reminders or cues (i.e., symptoms of avoiding talking about or thinking about what occurred).

Kilpatrick (1983) has suggested several other reasons victims might not be forthcoming with this information, including fear of a negative reaction to disclosure, especially if previous disclosure has resulted in disbelief or blame. The terminology used in the assessment can have an impact on disclosure as well. For example, many trauma victims may not recognize or label their experiences as "trauma," "rape," or "assault," especially if the perpetrator was known to them, or if the experience was one suffered by many, such as combat or a natural disaster. Therefore, it is important for the assessor to use sensitive language and, early in the assessment, be more willing to include false positives for traumatic events than risk losing important information. Later questioning can reduce the error of being overly inclusive.

An alternative to this relatively lengthy approach to assessing past traumas is to use a self-report measure, such as a checklist, to acquire initial information that can then be explored further through interview. There are a number of such checklists that can be used as a springboard for further inquiry. One such measure, the Life Events Checklist for DSM-5 (LEC-5; Weathers et al., 2013b) has been updated to correspond to events that may qualify as *DSM-5* Criterion A events. The LEC-5 can be used alone or in conjunction with PTSD symptom measures, such as the Clinician-Administered PTSD Scale for DSM-5 (CAPS-5; Weathers et al., 2013a) or the PTSD Checklist for DSM-5 (PCL-5; Weathers et al., 2013, discussed later). Other scales to assess for traumatic events include the Traumatic Stress Schedule (Norris, 1990), the Trauma History Questionnaire (THQ; Green, 1996), the Traumatic Life Events Questionnaire (TLEQ; Kubany, Leisen, Kaplan, Watson, et al., 2000), and the Traumatic Events Scale (Vrana & Lauterbach, 1994). With regard to combat in particular, the Combat Exposure Scale (Keane, Fairbank, Caddell, & Zimering, 1989) has been used widely to assess the degree of combat exposure. Although these are useful tools that can be administered to shorten the overall diagnostic interview, clinicians are discouraged from relying on them exclusively, without follow-up questions, due to the possibility of misreporting or lack of understanding on the part of the individual answering the questions. That is, an individual's endorsing an event on a checklist doesn't necessarily indicate that this event would meet criteria for a traumatic event. With the exception of the Combat Exposure Scale, most of these measures assess a number of different types of potentially traumatic events, including accidents, natural and man-made disasters, sexual assault, child abuse, and physical assault.

Diagnostic Interviews

A number of interviews exist that allow a clinician to make a diagnosis of PTSD and also to assess its overall severity. The measure often considered to be the gold standard diagnostic assessment for PTSD is the Clinician-Administered PTSD Scale for DSM-5 (CAPS-5; Weathers et al., 2013a). This semistructured interview provides a diagnostic decision and also produces a severity score. The CAPS-5 also includes assessment for the dissociative subtype of PTSD new to *DSM-5*. Although the CAPS-5 has not yet been thoroughly researched, the predecessor to the CAPS-5 (the CAPS for DSM-IV; Blake et al., 1995) has a large body of research demonstrating its reliability and validity across a wide variety of populations (see Weathers, Keane, & Davidson, 2001, for a review). Because of these strengths, the CAPS/CAPS-5 is probably the most widely used diagnostic interview for PTSD (Weathers et al., 2001; Weathers, Ruscio, & Keane, 1999). The Structured Clinical Interview for DSM-5 (SCID-5; First, Williams, Karg, & Spitzer, 2015) is a semistructured interview for a variety of Axis I disorders including PTSD. Different versions of the SCID-5 are available, including versions for clinical or research use. The SCID-5 was developed for use by experienced clinicians and assesses the presence or absence of all the symptoms of PTSD, thus yielding a decision about diagnosis. However, the SCID does not assess for frequency or severity of individual symptoms, and it is only possible to obtain a count of number of symptoms (in addition to a diagnosis).

The Diagnostic Interview Schedule (DIS; Robins, Helzer, Croughan, & Ratcliff, 1981) is a structured interview that has the advantage of requiring less training and experience than the CAPS-5 and SCID-5. As with the SCID, one can make a diagnosis of PTSD with the DIS, but one cannot assess its level of severity. However, to date, a version for *DSM-5* has not been released.

Finally, the PTSD Symptom Scale–Interview for DSM-5 (PSSI-5; Foa, McLean, Zang, Zhong, Rauch, et al., 2015) is a semistructured interview that provides a diagnostic determination as well as an estimate of symptom severity. Initial research has provided support for the reliability and validity of the PSSI-5 (Foa, McLean, Zang, Zhong, Rauch, et al., 2015), and its predecessor, the PSS-I (Foa, Riggs, Dancu, & Rothbaum, 1993), has been widely used and has also demonstrated strong psychometric properties.

SELF-REPORT MEASURES

A large number of self-report scales for PTSD have been developed, many with excellent psychometric properties. One potential problem with using a self-report measure for PTSD is that the measure often has to rely on the participant's judgment about what constitutes a traumatic event. In addition, some were developed with specific trauma populations in mind and thus may be appropriate for only a certain subset of individuals or may require knowledge about the traumatic event prior to administration. As with any self-report measure, it is important to recognize potential limitations in diagnosis or assessment of symptom severity. However, these limitations can be overcome in part by using self-report measures in conjunction with a structured interview. In this capacity, the self-report measures can be used as a quick screening tool or to demonstrate changes in symptomatology over time.

Two self-report measures with strong psychometric properties that have been updated to the current criteria are the PTSD Checklist for DSM-5 (PCL-5; Weathers, Litz, et al., 2013) and the Posttraumatic Diagnostic Scale for DSM-5 (PDS-5; Foa, McLean, Zang, Zhong, Powers, et al., 2015). Both of these measures can be scored dimensionally to assess global severity or used to make a provisional diagnosis of PTSD by summing the number of symptoms meeting criteria in each PTSD cluster or by using a cutoff score. Other measures include the Mississippi Scale for Combat-Related PTSD (Keane, Cadell, & Taylor, 1988), the Purdue PTSD Scale–Revised (Lauterbach & Vrana, 1996), the Impact of Event Scale–Revised (IES-R; Weiss & Marmar, 1997), and the Distressing Event Questionnaire (DEQ; Kubany, Leisen, Kaplan, & Kelly, 2000), although these measures have not been updated to reflect *DSM-5* PTSD criteria.

Two additional measures of PTSD have been empirically derived from other existing scales. Posttraumatic stress disorder subscales have been derived from the Symptom Checklist-90-R (SCL-90-R; Derogatis, 1983) from different sets of items for female crime victims (Saunders, Arata, & Kilpatrick, 1990) and for combat veterans (Weathers et al., 1999). The Keane-PTSD Scale (PK) of the Minnesota Multiphasic Personality Inventory (MMPI) and MMPI-2 has been used successfully to discriminate Vietnam combat veterans with and without PTSD (Keane, Malloy, & Fairbank, 1984; Weathers & Keane, 1999).

In response to the more recent need to screen mass numbers of people for PTSD after combat or disasters, or in primary care medical settings when time is limited, brief PTSD screens may be used (e.g., the Primary Care PTSD Screen [PC-PTSD]; Prins et al., 2004). Studies have not validated this measure according to the *DSM-5* criteria, though.

Finally, of all these measures, it should be noted that few trauma-related scales include scales to assess response bias. One notable exception is the Trauma Symptom Inventory (TSI; Briere, 1995). For forensic purposes, in which response bias may be of particular concern, the assessor may wish to include the TSI or administer the MMPI-2, which contains the PK scale as well as validity subscales. In addition to clinical scales, the TSI includes subscales assessing tendencies to overendorse unusual or bizarre symptoms, to respond in an inconsistent or random manner, and to deny symptoms others commonly endorse. The clinical scales include PTSD-related scales that assess issues such as intrusive experiences, defensive avoidance, and anxious arousal, as well as subscales that measure frequently observed problems with depression, anger, dissociation, tension-reduction behaviors, and disruptions in self-perception and sexual functioning. Unfortunately, the TSI does not assess exposure to specific traumatic events, thus requiring the clinician to establish the presence of a Criterion A event prior to administration.

PHYSIOLOGICAL ASSESSMENT

Given that physiological reactivity to trauma cues is one of the criteria of the disorder, a comprehensive assessment of PTSD should include psychophysiological testing, especially when the validity of the diagnosis for a particular individual is questioned. A number of studies have shown that Vietnam veterans with PTSD are consistently more physiologically reactive to combat imagery than Vietnam veterans without PTSD (Keane, Kaloupek, & Kolb, 1998; Keane, Kolb, et al., 1998; Pitman et al., 1990; Pitman, Orr, Forgue, de Jong, & Claiborn, 1987). Similar differences between PTSD and non-PTSD individuals have been found in motor vehicle accident survivors (Blanchard, Hickling, Buckley, & Taylor, 1996) and childhood sexual abuse victims (Orr et al., 1998).

A number of factors can affect physiological reactivity, and these must be taken into account when assessing the validity of psychophysiological findings. For example, the presence of psychotropic drugs, especially benzodiazepines and beta-adrenergic blockers, can affect an individual's response. Furthermore, it has been demonstrated that antisocial characteristics can suppress levels of psychophysiological responding (Miller, Kaloupek, & Keane, 1999). In addition to those people who do not physiologically respond, for various reasons, there appear to be some who have an alternative physiological response to trauma cues, which must also be taken into account (e.g., dissociation; see Griffin et al., 1997).

Treatment

As reviewed below, there are a variety of psychosocial and biological treatments that are efficacious in the treatment of PTSD. Moreover, there have been recent efforts to use psychopharmacological interventions to facilitate the psychosocial treatments.

PSYCHOSOCIAL TREATMENT

There have now been over 75 randomized controlled trials (RCTs) of psychotherapy for PTSD (see Watts et al., 2013, for a meta-analysis). Early trials compared active treatment to wait-list control, whereas later trials have compared different psychotherapies to one another or to therapies controlling for the nonspecific elements of any good psychotherapy. More recent efforts have been aimed at comparing the additive value of different types of interventions and at determining the essential elements of a given therapy using dismantling designs. The research suggests that psychotherapy is effective for the treatment of PTSD, with meta-analyses indicating large effect sizes overall ($g = 1.14$; Watts et al., 2013). Cognitive-behavioral therapy (CBT) has the most evidence supporting its efficacy and has demonstrated the largest effect size ($g = 1.26$; Watts et al., 2013). There are several other types of therapies with growing evidence of efficacy based on RCTs.

Cognitive-Behavioral Therapy

As noted above, CBT has the strongest support and is therefore considered the frontline treatment approach for PTSD. Therapies in this category vary in terms of the degree of focus on exposure, cognitive restructuring, and skill building. A number of RCTs have established the efficacy of behavioral exposure to trauma-related material in the treatment of PTSD compared to a wait-list control condition. The exposure interventions come in the form of exposure to the trauma memory, as in imaginal exposure, or through exposure to trauma-related stimuli in the environment, that is, in vivo exposure. One of the most thoroughly researched exposure therapies is prolonged exposure (PE; Foa, Hearst, Dancu, Hembree, & Jaycox, 1994), which includes both imaginal and in vivo exposure techniques. PE is built on emotional processing theory (e.g., Cahill & Foa, 2007), discussed earlier, which suggests that, for recovery from trauma to occur, the affected person must be able to activate his or her trauma memory, block the negative reinforcement that occurs with escape and avoidance behavior, habituate to anxiety, and disconfirm erroneous beliefs. As anxiety diminishes, the person learns that he or she can tolerate fear and anxiety, and begins to change his or her incompetence beliefs. Through exposure to both trauma memories, as well as real-life situations, the person also learns to discriminate true danger cues from false alarms and past experiences from the present. PE also addresses the cognition and memory issues theorized to underlie PTSD by helping patients organize their trauma memory in a coherent way. Consistent with this aim, Foa, Riggs, et al. (1995) found that decreases in disorganization of the trauma narrative from pretreatment to posttreatment were correlated with successful treatment with PE. PE has been shown to be efficacious in the treatment of PTSD across many studies (see Powers, Halpern, Farenschak, Gillihan, & Foa, 2010, for a meta-analysis).

Similarly, several trials have established the efficacy of different forms of cognitive therapy that have not included behavioral (i.e., in vivo) exposure interventions in the treatment of PTSD (Bryant, Moulds, & Guthrie, 2003; Marks, Lovell, Noshirvani, Livanou, & Thrasher, 1998; Resick et al., 2008; Tarrier et al., 1999). Based in part on the social-cognitive and information processing theories of PTSD discussed earlier, cognitive processing therapy (CPT; Resick, Monson, & Chard, in press); Resick & Schnicke, 1993) targets unhelpful and inaccurate ways of thinking that occur following trauma, including assimilation and over-accommodation, using predominantly cognitive approaches with progressive worksheets to teach the clients to become their own therapists. CPT also specifically targets five cognitive content areas discussed earlier that tend to be affected in PTSD: safety, trust, power/control, esteem, and intimacy. CPT has established efficacy in the treatment of PTSD and depression in a variety of traumatized populations (see Lenz, Bruijn, Serman, & Bailey, 2014, for a meta-analysis). As noted earlier, investigators found support for the proposed mechanism of CPT, such that changes in trauma-related cognitions (i.e., self-blame and negative beliefs about the self) preceded and predicted changes in PTSD later in treatment (Schumm et al., 2015).

Both CPT and PE are considered trauma-focused therapies, in that they involve talking about the patient's traumatic event. There are a few non-trauma-focused cognitive-behavioral therapies that have been found to be more efficacious than wait-list control conditions. For example, Stress Inoculation Therapy (SIT) without any trauma-specific interventions has been shown to be efficacious in the treatment of PTSD (Foa et al., 1999). Present-centered therapy (PCT), which was originally conceived to be a control condition with a focus on current problem solving to manage PTSD symptoms, has had good results in several trials and is now considered to be an evidence-based treatment. In three of five trials reviewed, it performed as well as the evidence-based treatment comparisons (see Frost, Laska, & Wampold, 2014, for a meta-analysis).

In head-to-head trials comparing different forms of CBT, very few differences between the therapies in their ability to treat PTSD have generally emerged. For example, in the Resick, Nishith, Weaver, Astin, and Feuer (2002) trial, there were no statistical differences between CPT and PE in PTSD symptoms at any assessment point, including PTSD and depression at a long-term follow-up (Resick et al., 2008). There have been a few potentially important differences between these treatments found at follow-up assessments and in the treatment of comorbid conditions. In Foa's early trial comparing PE and SIT, there were no differences between the two treatments at posttreatment assessment; however, starting at 3-month follow-up, there was an advantage of PE over SIT in treating PTSD symptoms (Foa, Rothbaum, Riggs, & Murdock, 1991). At the 5-year follow-up of their trial comparing imaginal exposure and cognitive therapy, Tarrier and Sommerfield (2004) found an advantage of cognitive therapy over imaginal exposure in maintaining diminished PTSD symptoms. With regard to conditions often co-occurring with PTSD, Resick et al. (2002) found statistical advantages of CPT over PE in trauma-related guilt and more recently with hopelessness (Gallagher & Resick, 2012) and suicidal ideation over the long term (Gradus, Suvak, Wisco, Marx, & Resick, 2013).

The latest generation of studies examining specific cognitive and behavioral interventions and their combinations in the treatment of PTSD generally suggests that interventions with a singular element are as efficacious as those with combined elements. Findings supporting this conclusion come from Foa et al.'s (1999) study comparing PE to SIT and to their combination (PE/SIT), and Foa et al.'s (2005) study comparing PE to PE plus cognitive therapy. Similarly, in Resick et al.'s (2008) dismantling study comparing full CPT with the written trauma account–only element of CPT (Writing Accounts [WA]) and the cognitive therapy–only element of CPT (CPT-C), there were no differences at posttreatment or 6-month follow-up assessment. However, Resick et al. (2008) also found that the CPT-C version led to faster symptom improvement during treatment, differed significantly from full CPT version until the exposure component was completed, and differed from the WA condition until the 6-month follow-up. Thus, the written accounts did not add benefit to the cognitive therapy–only protocol.

An exception to the trend of equivalent efficacy in singular and combined therapies comes from Bryant et al.'s (2003) study revealing advantages to combined imaginal exposure and cognitive restructuring over imaginal exposure alone. An additional caveat to the conclusion that therapies with a singular element are equally as efficacious as combined therapies is that studies heretofore have equated the amount of time spent in treatment sessions for each therapy, for methodological reasons. Therefore, it is difficult to determine whether additional elements delivered with extra time might yield more efficacious treatment.

A study of CPT by Galovski and colleagues (Galovski, Blain, Mott, Elwood, & Houle, 2012) tested the question of whether adding more sessions would improve outcomes for those who had heretofore been considered treatment nonresponders with fixed-length treatments. Galovski et al. defined a treatment completer as a client who had reached a good end-state functioning on both PTSD and depression self-report measures according to mutual agreement by the therapist and the client and the independent interview of PTSD by a blind assessor. The researchers found that 58% of the participants needed fewer than the 12 sessions called for by the CPT protocol (mean number of sessions was 7.5 among early completers), 8% needed exactly 12 sessions, and 26% reached good end-state functioning with 13 to 18 sessions (mean number of sessions was 15.2 in this group). When given extra sessions, all but two of the participants no longer had PTSD by the 3-month follow-up.

More recently, researchers have expanded the evidence base for existing frontline treatments by demonstrating their effectiveness in new populations and through different delivery modalities. For example, there have been studies examining group-administered CPT-C with both veterans and active military members (Morland, Hynes, Mackintosh, Resick & Chard, 2011; Resick et al., 2015). Morland and colleagues (2011) compared group CPT-C delivered in person to group CPT-C delivered via telehealth in a sample of veterans and found that these treatments were equally effective. Resick et al. (2015) compared group-administered CPT-C to group-administered PCT among a sample of active military members and found that, while both produced significant reductions in PTSD symptoms, CPT-C was significantly better than PCT. More importantly, CPT-C produced reductions in depression while PCT did not. Taken together, these findings suggest that CPT-C is an effective treatment for veterans and military personnel, even when delivered in group format or via telehealth.

Finally, some new studies are looking at the effects of CBT on other areas of functioning. Galovski, Elwood, Blain, and Resick (2014) found that improvement in PTSD led to improvements in trait anger and control over anger. Iverson et al. (2011) examined the subset of women who were victims of intimate partner violence (IPV) in the Resick et al. (2008) dismantling study. They found that reductions in PTSD symptoms were associated with lower rates of IPV at the 6-month follow-up. Gradus et al. (2013)

examined suicidal ideation from the Resick et al. (2002) comparison of CPT and PE, and found that while suicidal ideation was decreased for both groups, there was a significantly greater decrease among those who received CPT through the long-term follow-up. Wachen, Jimenez, Smith, and Resick (2014) examined long-term functional outcomes from the Resick et al. (2002) comparison of CPT with PE. They found that both treatments had long-term benefits for overall functioning, social/leisure activities, the family unit, and economic adjustment. The poorer functioning at posttreatment and beyond found in some group members was associated with depression rather than PTSD. Finally, Shnaider et al. (2014) examined psychosocial functioning in a finer-grained way using the Resick et al. (2008) data. Overall, all domains of psychosocial functioning improved over treatment and were maintained at follow-up. On the PTSD symptom cluster level, improvements in hyperarousal were associated with psychosocial outcomes overall and in the specific areas of daily living and household tasks, whereas improvements in emotional numbing were associated with psychosocial outcomes in the nonfamily relationships domain.

Eye Movement Desensitization and Reprocessing

Eye movement desensitization and reprocessing (EMDR; Shapiro, 1989b) is another treatment used with individuals with PTSD, although the proposed mechanism of the treatment has been a source of controversy. The goal of EMDR is to help the patient process trauma-related information, but a unique aspect of the treatment is the use of side-to-side eye movements (or other forms of stimulation such as hand tapping or auditory stimuli) that are theorized to help enhance information processing (e.g., Shapiro & Maxfield, 2002). Several studies have shown that eye movement desensitization and reprocessing (EMDR) is more effective than wait-list control conditions in the treatment of PTSD (e.g., Rothbaum, 1997; Wilson, Becker, & Tinker, 1995), and a trial comparing EMDR with PE found no differences between the two groups in their efficacy in treating PTSD (Rothbaum, Astin, & Marsteller, 2005), although the sample size might have been too small to detect anything but large differences. Although EMDR may lead to improvements in PTSD symptoms, there is much debate surrounding the active ingredients of EMDR that are considered responsible for improvements (see Davidson & Parker, 2001, for a meta-analysis of these and other relevant questions). RCTs in which patients have received the treatment with and without the manipulation of eye movements, or with eye movements versus other irrelevant movements, have yielded no evidence supporting the specific efficacy of eye movements (e.g., Devilly & Spence, 1999; Pitman et al., 1996). These results have led many to conclude that the active ingredients of EMDR are really cognitive-behavioral in nature, because EMDR includes elements of exposure as well as cognitive reappraisal, which have been shown to be effective without eye movements (Monson et al., 2014).

Other Therapies with Controlled Evidence

Several other therapies have been shown to be efficacious relative to wait-list and other control conditions. Brief eclectic psychotherapy (BEP) combines cognitive-behavioral and psychodynamic approaches and includes five basic elements: (1) psychoeducation about PTSD, (2) imaginal exposure, (3) writing tasks and memorabilia aimed at uncovering difficult feelings, (4) meaning and integration, and (5) farewell ritual. It has been shown to be efficacious compared with wait-list control conditions in samples of police officers (Gersons, Carlier, & Lamberts, 2000) and outpatients with a range of traumas (Lindauer, Vlieger, & Jalink, 2005). A more recent RCT by an independent research group also found favorable results for BEP as compared with a minimal attention control condition (Schnyder, Muller, Maercker, & Wittman, 2011). In another RCT comparing BEP with EMDR, there was no significant difference in outcomes; however, those in the EMDR condition exhibited faster recovery (Nijdam, Gersons, Reitsma, de Jongh, & Olff, 2012). To date, no published studies have involved a direct comparison of BEP to CBT. Thus, further research is needed to evaluate this treatment relative to current frontline approaches.

Narrative exposure therapy (NET; Schauer, Neuner, & Elbert, 2005) involves patients providing a detailed chronological report of their own biographies, with a special focus on traumatic experiences. This report is recorded in written form and read during sessions with the goal of developing a coherent narrative of the traumatic event and the habituation of emotional responses to reminders of the traumatic event. There have been two controlled trials of NET showing it to be efficacious compared with psychoeducation and supportive counseling in survivors of political detention (Bichescu, Neuner, Schauer, & Elbert, 2007) and refugees (Neuner, Schauer, Klaschik, Karunakara, & Elbert, 2004). Other narrative writing interventions also exist (e.g., "interapy," "written disclosure," "expressive writing," "written exposure therapy,") that vary greatly as to the number and content of the writing prompts and the degree of therapist involvement. Authors of a recent review suggest that more rigorous research is needed to evaluate these interventions and their mechanisms before they can be recommended for treatment of PTSD, but they may be promising options, particularly for individuals who may not have access to evidence-based, trauma-focused treatment (Sloan, Sawyer, Lowmaster, Wernick, & Marx, 2015).

Finally, cognitive-behavioral conjoint therapy for PTSD (CBCT; Monson & Fredman, 2012) is a 15-session, manualized therapy delivered in a conjoint format with the goals of simultaneously improving PTSD and its comorbid symptoms while also improving interpersonal relationship functioning. The rationale for this approach is that PTSD has been consistently associated with problematic interpersonal relations, and these factors have a reciprocal effect on one another. Therefore, the treatment simultaneously targets PTSD symptoms and relationship functioning. Three uncontrolled trials and a recent wait-list controlled trial with a range of traumatized individuals have documented improvements in PTSD symptoms on a par with individual evidence-based therapies for PTSD, as well as significant improvements in intimate relationship functioning (Monson et al., 2011, 2012; Monson, Schnurr, Stevens, & Guthrie, 2004; Schumm, Fredman, Monson, & Chard, 2013). Improvements in partners' psychological functioning have also been found (e.g., Monson, Stevens, & Schnurr, 2005). Follow-up studies reveal that those with greater pretreatment relationship distress (Shnaider et al., 2015) and significant others who are more accommodating of their partners' PTSD symptoms (Fredman et al., 2016) are especially likely to profit from the treatment. Improvements in various PTSD clusters and trauma-related cognitions with CBCT support the theory underlying the treatment (Macdonald, Pukay-Martin, Wagner, Fredman, & Monson, in press).

Extensions to Younger Patients

Although a lengthy discussion of child treatment is beyond the scope of this chapter, it is worth mentioning that analogous evidence-based treatments also exist for children and adolescents with PTSD (e.g., Allen & Kronenberg, 2014). For example, trauma-focused cognitive-behavioral therapy (TF-CBT; Cohen, Mannarino, & Deblinger, 2006;) is a well-established, evidence-based treatment for children and adolescents that involves psychoeducation, parenting skills, relaxation, affective modulation, cognitive coping and processing, trauma narrative, in vivo mastery of trauma reminders, conjoint child-parent sessions, and enhancing future safety and development (see Lenz & Hollenbaugh, 2015, for a meta-analysis). Child-parent psychotherapy (CPP; Lieberman & Van Horn, 2005) is another evidence-based treatment for children ages 0 to 5 that focuses on the caregiver-child attachment with the overall goal of supporting healthy child development (Allen & Kronenberg, 2014). Finally, parent-child interaction therapy (PCIT; Eyeberg & Funderburk, 2011) is an evidence-based parent training intervention originally developed for behavioral problems among children ages 2 to 7, but its application has been expanded to address parent-child interactions in families that have experienced violence with the goal of reducing child behavior problems, caregiver distress, and the potential for child abuse (Allen & Kronenberg, 2014; Herschell & McNeil, 2005). In addition to these child-specific treatments, some of the better-established treatments initially developed for adults have also demonstrated success when applied to younger patient populations. For example, CPT and PE have each been found to be effective in adolescent populations (e.g., Ahrens & Rexford, 2002; Foa, McLean, Capaldi, & Rosenfield, 2013).

PSYCHOPHARMACOLOGICAL TREATMENT

There are currently two medications, both in the class of antidepressants, that have received indications from the U.S. Food and Drug Administration (FDA) for the treatment of PTSD: sertraline and paroxetine. Both of these medications are selective serotonin reuptake inhibitors (SSRIs), the class of medications considered to be the front-line pharmacological treatment for PTSD in various clinical practice guidelines. While SSRIs have generally been effective in the treatment of PTSD (a recent meta-analysis found a pooled effect size for SSRIs in the medium range), not all are equally effective (Watts et al., 2013). For example, Watts et al. (2013) found significant effects for paroxetine, fluoxetine, and sertraline but not citalopram. Other medications have also yielded variable results in the treatment of PTSD.

Other Antidepressants

In meta-analyses of RCTs for PTSD, researchers have found that, in addition to SSRIs, venlafaxine, a serotonin-norepinephrine reuptake inhibitor (SNRI), also has strong support (Hoskins et al., 2015; Ipser & Stein, 2012; Watts et al., 2013). According to a meta-analysis by Watts et al. (2013), tricyclic antidepressants (TCAs), monoamine oxidase inhibitors (MAOIs), and other antidepressants (i.e., bupropion, nefazodone, and mirtazapine) had small, nonsignificant effects and therefore have less support for their use than SSRIs and venlafaxine.

Antiadrenergics (Drugs Acting on the Epinephrine and Norepinephrine Systems)

In a meta-analysis of randomized, double-blind, placebo-controlled trials evaluating prazosin for the treatment of sleep disturbance among individuals with PTSD, results were promising, with medium to large effect sizes (Khachatryan, Groll, Booij, Sepehry, & Schütz, 2015). While the results appear favorable for prazosin's effect on sleep symptoms, the results are mixed on its effects on other PTSD symptoms (e.g., Bernardy & Friedman, 2015). By contrast, a single RCT of guanfacine found no superiority over placebo in veterans with PTSD and a number of side effects associated with the drug's use; thus, these results do not support the use of guanfacine in the treatment of PTSD (Neylan et al., 2006). In addition, there was some initial evidence that propranolol is not only an efficacious treatment for PTSD (e.g., Famularo, Kinscherff, & Fenton, 1988) but also an effective prophylactic agent to prevent acutely traumatized individuals from later PTSD (e.g., Pitman et al., 2002; Vaiva et al., 2003). However, the authors of a recent meta-analysis found inconsistent results across five studies and concluded that propranolol after trauma exposure did not appear to reduce the incidence of PTSD (Argolo, Cavalcanti-Ribeiro, Netto, & Quarantini, 2015), and it is therefore not recommended as an acute intervention (Bernardy & Friedman, 2015).

Mood Stabilizers and Anticonvulsants

Research on the use of mood stabilizers/anticonvulsants for PTSD has been mixed. Watts et al. (2013) reported that anticonvulsants were overall ineffective in the treatment of PTSD but reported a pooled significant effect for topiramate as monotherapy and augmentation across three RCTs. One small RCT of lamotrigine found improvements in the reexperiencing and avoidance symptoms of PTSD (Hertzberg et al., 1999). A large RCT of tiagabine found no differences from placebo (Davidson, Brady, Mellman, Stein, & Pollack, 2007). Similarly, no differences between divalproex and placebo were found in an RCT (Davis et al., 2008).

GABA-ergic Agonists (Antianxiety Medication)

In a systematic review and meta-analysis on benzodiazepines for PTSD, the authors concluded that benzodiazepines are largely ineffective in the treatment of PTSD and that their risks most likely outweigh any potential benefits (Guina, Rossetter, DeRhodes, Nahhas, & Welton, 2015). Thus, it is recommended that providers avoid benzodiazepines as a treatment for PTSD given the availability of other, more promising options.

Atypical Antipsychotics

A few RCTs have investigated atypical antipsychotics as monotherapy or added to augment another treatment with mixed results. In a meta-analysis, Watts et al. (2013) found risperidone (but not olanzapine) to have a significant effect and to be superior to placebo; however, Bernardy and Friedman (2015) noted that there is insufficient evidence to support the use of risperidone for monotherapy or adjunctive therapy and highlighted potential side effects as a deterrent to this treatment approach.

Augmentation With Partial NMDA Agonist

D-cycloserine (DCS) is a partial NMDA glutamatergic receptor agonist that has positive effects on memory deficits in elderly volunteers (Jones, Wesnes, & Kirby, 1991) and Alzheimer's disease patients (Schwartz, Hashtroudi, Herting, Schwartz, & Deutsch, 1996). For PTSD, DCS has primarily been examined as a drug to augment the effects of other interventions. It is also thought that DCS may augment exposure therapies by enhancing extinction, but results across studies have been inconsistent. For example, an initial placebo-controlled trial of DCS as an adjunct to PE found no overall enhancement of treatment effects, but those individuals with more severe pretreatment PTSD symptoms that needed more sessions had more symptom reduction when receiving DCS compared with placebo (de Kleine, Hendriks, Kusters, Broekman, & van Minnen, 2012). Another placebo-controlled trial with Iraq and Afghanistan veterans found that exposure therapy plus DCS produced worse outcomes than exposure therapy plus placebo (Litz et al., 2012). In a sample of individuals with PTSD secondary to the World Trade Center attacks in New York, those receiving DCS plus virtual reality exposure therapy showed greater improvements in PTSD symptoms, depression, sleep, and anger than those receiving exposure plus placebo (Difede et al., 2014). Finally, in another study with Iraq and Afghanistan veterans with military trauma PTSD, DCS fared no better than placebo on treatment outcomes when added to virtual reality exposure therapy, but the DCS-treated group exhibited reduced cortisol and startle reactivity (Rothbaum et al., 2014).

TREATMENT SUMMARY

Several efficacious pharmacological and psychosocial treatments are available that are capable of ameliorating the symptoms of PTSD for many individuals. We are aware of only one published head-to-head trial comparing medications and psychotherapy in the treatment of PTSD, and that trial compared EMDR to fluoxetine (van der Kolk et al., 2007). EMDR yielded greater symptom reductions that were better sustained over time compared with fluoxetine. These results, favoring psychotherapy over medications for PTSD, are consistent with meta-analyses comparing medications and psychotherapies generally (Van Etten & Taylor, 1998; Watts et al., 2013). It is also important to note that discontinuation of medication is associated with relapse of PTSD symptoms (e.g., Martenyi, Brown, Zhang, Koke, & Prakash, 2002), whereas long-term follow-up of patients in PTSD psychotherapy trials indicates maintenance of gains across different types of therapy (e.g., Resick, Williams, et al., 2012; Schnurr et al., 2007; Tarrier & Sommerfield, 2004).

Future studies that examine the combination and sequencing of current evidence-based medication and psychosocial treatments (e.g., Rothbaum et al., 2006), as well as the use of medications that might potentiate the effects of psychotherapy for PTSD, are needed to increase the percentage of individuals who respond to treatment. Moreover, there is room for psychosocial and pharmacological treatment innovations for the approximately 50% of individuals in intention-to-treat samples who do not have a remission in their PTSD diagnosis as a result of treatment. Several psychotherapies for PTSD in development have at least uncontrolled trial data supporting their efficacy, including such therapies as imagery rescripting (Smucker, Dancu, Foa, & Niederee, 1995), interapy (Lange, Rietdijk, & Hudcovicova, 2003), virtual reality exposure (Rothbaum, Hodges, & Ready, 2001), acceptance and commitment therapy (Walser & Hayes, 2006), behavioral activation therapy (Jakupcak et al., 2006), and cognitive-behavioral conjoint therapy for PTSD (Monson et al., 2012). Thus, while cognitive and exposure-based therapies like CPT and PE are the most effective treatments for PTSD, patients who do not benefit from these treatments, or who refuse them, have other potential treatment options, and ongoing research will likely continue to identify ways to improve treatment response through enhancements to existing treatments as well as the development of new treatments. Likewise, there are new drugs in development that are theoretically likely to improve PTSD symptoms, such as the corticotrophin-releasing factor antagonist antalarmin, which has been shown to reduce stress-induced fearful behavior in preclinical studies (Friedman & Davidson, 2007). There are also existing drugs, like hydrocortisone, a glucocorticoid, or mifepristone (RU-486), which blocks glucocorticoid receptors, that might be considered with new indications if diminished or excessive cortisol levels (respectively) prove to be consistently associated with the disorder (Friedman & Davidson, 2007). Finally, ketamine is another medication currently under investigation. A recent study provided initial evidence for a rapid reduction in symptoms following ketamine infusion in a sample of chronic PTSD patients, although most patients retained significant PTSD symptoms at a 1-week follow-up (Feder et al., 2014). Furthermore, this treatment was in some cases associated with adverse effects including temporary dissociative symptoms and blood pressure elevation. Thus, these new avenues of treatment approaches will require replication and further study.

Summary and Future Directions

Over the past four decades of study on the effects and treatment of traumatic stress, we have made great gains in understanding posttraumatic responses and recovery. We now understand that most people experience traumatic events in their lives that are of sufficient magnitude to trigger serious posttraumatic responses. Nevertheless, with time, the majority of people go on to recover from these events. However, there does appear to be a limit to how much trauma people can absorb, as demonstrated by a strong dose-response relationship. The more traumas that people experience, the more difficulty they will have returning to healthy and balanced functioning without some type of assistance. A person's biological makeup and alterations of biology that occur as a result of trauma will interact with memory, cognition, emotions, and behavior to promote or interfere with recovery. The external environment also has an important effect on recovery or maintenance of PTSD symptoms. Positive and sufficient social support, lack of negative reactions (which has a disproportionate influence compared with good support), and sufficient resources are important in recovery. Additional life stressors such as family adjustment problems and problems with work or housing can all complicate and delay, or prevent, recovery. One only has to look at situations like Hurricane Katrina or Sandy, with the prolonged duration of each event and each area's slow recovery, or the wars in Iraq and Afghanistan, with their multiple deployments of military personnel into highly volatile and unpredictable violence, to understand how continued environmental instability prevents the return to homeostasis.

Fortunately, we have treatments that work with the majority of people with PTSD (40% to 80% have been found to fully remit, depending on the population and sampling method). Although there is no specific PTSD medication thus far that is as effective as psychotherapy, many medications can provide some relief for some symptoms. Both cognitive therapy and exposure treatments are effective, and unlike some other disorders, there is little evidence of relapse over time. However, because PTSD is maintained over time by avoidance and numbing, people often refuse to seek treatment even when they know it is available, and they may exhibit rather high dropout rates (20% to 40%). Also, because PTSD is often accompanied by other disorders, treatment may be complicated by substance abuse, chronic pain, severe depression, and personality disorders. The wars in Iraq and Afghanistan highlight the problem of head injury and PTSD; this may have been an unidentified complication in other cases of PTSD in which head injuries are common, such as domestic violence, child abuse, and motor vehicle accidents.

Challenges have included the incorporation of what we have learned about PTSD into current diagnostic schemes (e.g., *DSM-5*) as we move forward in ICD-11. Although most current theories of PTSD are concerned with memory, emotions, and cognition, there was very little mention of these in the *DSM-IV* diagnostic criteria. Because PTSD has been categorized with the anxiety disorders, most of the research and treatment focus has been on fear and anxiety to the exclusion of other important emotions, such as anger, sadness, shame, or horror. There is sufficient research on these topics to indicate that they may interfere with recovery and predict poorer outcome with treatment than fear and anxiety do. The new criteria for *DSM-5* include emotions and cognitions and will most likely spur more research on these topics.

Research on treatment is beginning to push into areas of comorbidity, and is questioning the current wisdom of treating comorbid conditions separately and sequentially. Research on systems of delivery such as telehealth or internet-based therapies is currently under way. Research on dissemination of evidence-based treatments is also under way, with a growing understanding that books and workshops are not sufficient to train clinicians; built-in follow-up supports and actual system change may be needed. The best way to train clinicians to use evidence-based treatments with fidelity in regular practice remains an open question. It is clear that implementing trauma treatment can be a difficult undertaking for therapists. Specific PTSD treatment elements are challenging to master, whether they require effectively engaging patients in imaginal exposure or identifying the impact of trauma on a patient's belief system. Furthermore, trauma therapists must be able to hear details of traumatic events including violent and horrific acts and also remain objective when dealing with moral transgressions such as acts of violence perpetrated during war. Such work is particularly difficult when therapists have their own traumatic experiences. Thus, for both mastering the nuances of individual protocols and remaining attuned to personal reactions and managing one's own stress, trauma therapists benefit from feedback and consultation.

Finally, there is a great deal of research currently being conducted on the underlying biology of PTSD, including neurotransmitters, hormones, and brain structures, which will fuel our understanding of the interaction of biology, individual differences, and environment in PTSD over the next decade.

References

Ahrens, J., & Rexford, L. (2002). Cognitive processing therapy for incarcerated adolescents with PTSD. *Journal of Aggression, Maltreatment & Trauma*, 6(1), 201–216.

Allen, B., & Kronenberg, M. (Eds.). (2014). *Treating traumatized children: A casebook of evidence-based therapies*. New York, NY: Guilford Press.

American Psychiatric Association. (1980). *Diagnostic and statistical manual of mental disorders* (3rd ed.). Washington, DC: Author.

American Psychiatric Association. (1987). *Diagnostic and statistical manual of mental disorders* (3rd ed., text rev.). Washington, DC: Author.

American Psychiatric Association. (1994). *Diagnostic and statistical manual of mental disorders* (4th ed.). Washington, DC: Author.

American Psychiatric Association. (2013). *Diagnostic and statistical manual of mental disorders* (5th ed.). Washington, DC: Author.

Andrews, B., Brewin, C. R., Philpott, R., & Stewart, L. (2007). Delayed onset posttraumatic stress disorder: A systematic review of the evidence. *American Journal of Psychiatry*, 164, 1319–1326.

Andrews, B., Brewin, C. R., Rose, S., & Kirk, M. (2000). Predicting PTSD symptoms in victims of violent crime: The role of shame, anger, and childhood abuse. *Journal of Abnormal Psychology*, 109, 69–73.

Argolo, F. C., Cavalcanti-Ribeiro, P., Netto, L. R., & Quarantini, L. C. (2015). Prevention of posttraumatic stress disorder with propranolol: A meta-analytic review. *Journal of Psychosomatic Research*, 79(2), 89–93.

Arora, R. C., Fichtner, C. G., O'Connor, F., & Crayton, J. W. (1993). Paroxetine binding in the blood platelets of post-traumatic stress disorder patients. *Life Sciences*, 53, 919–928.

Baker, D. G., West, S. A., Nicholson, W. E., Ekhator, N. N., Kasckow, J. W., Hill, K. K., ... Geracioti, T. D., Jr. (1999). Serial CSF corticotropin-releasing hormone levels and adrenocortical activity in combat veterans with posttraumatic stress disorder. *American Journal of Psychiatry*, 156, 585–588.

Beck, J. G., Freeman, J. B., Shipherd, J. C., Hamblen, J. L., & Lackner, J. M. (2001). Specificity of Stroop interference in patients with pain and PTSD. *Journal of Abnormal Psychology*, 110, 536–543.

Beckham, J. C., Feldman, M. E., & Kirby, A. C. (1998). Atrocities exposure in Vietnam combat veterans with chronic posttraumatic stress disorder: Relationship to combat exposure, symptom severity, guilt, and interpersonal violence. *Journal of Traumatic Stress*, 11, 777–785.

Bernardy, N. C., & Friedman, M. J. (2015). Psychopharmacological strategies in the management of posttraumatic stress disorder (PTSD): What have we learned? *Current Psychiatry Reports*, 17(4), 1–10.

Bichescu, D., Neuner, F., Schauer, M., & Elbert, T. (2007). Narrative exposure therapy for political imprisonment–related chronic posttraumatic stress disorder and depression. *Behaviour Research and Therapy*, 45, 2212–2220.

Blake, D. D., Weathers, F. W., Nagy, L. M., Kaloupek, D. G., Gusman, F. D., Charney, D. S., & Keane, T. M. (1995). The development of a clinician-administered PTSD scale. *Journal of Traumatic Stress*, 8, 75–90.

Blanchard, E. B., Hickling, E. J., Buckley, T. C., & Taylor, A. E. (1996). Psychophysiology of posttraumatic stress disorder related to motor vehicle accidents: Replication and extension. *Journal of Consulting and Clinical Psychology*, 64, 742–751.

Blanchard, E. B., Hickling, E. J., Malta, L. S., Jaccard, J., Devineni, T., Veazey, C. H., & Galovski, T. E. (2003). Prediction of response to psychological treatment among motor vehicle accident survivors with PTSD. *Behavior Therapy*, 34, 351–363.

Blanchard, E. B., Kolb, L. C., Prins, A., Gates, S., & McCoy, G. C. (1991). Changes in plasma norepinephrine to combat-related stimuli among Vietnam veterans with posttraumatic stress disorder. *Journal of Nervous and Mental Disease*, 179, 371–373.

Boudewyns, P. A., & Hyer, L. (1990). Physiological response to combat memories and preliminary treatment outcome in Vietnam veteran PTSD patients treated with direct therapeutic exposure. *Behavior Therapy*, 21, 63–87.

Bremner, J. D., Innis, R. B., Southwick, S. M., Staib, L., Zoghbi, S., & Charney, D. S. (2000). Decreased benzodiazepine receptor binding in prefrontal cortex in combat-related posttraumatic stress disorder. *American Journal of Psychiatry*, 157, 1120–1126.

Bremner, J. D., Licinio, J., Darnell, A., Krystal, J. H., Owens, M. J., & Southwick, S. M., ... Charney, D. S.

(1997). Elevated CSF corticotropin-releasing factor concentrations in posttraumatic stress disorder. *American Journal of Psychiatry, 154*, 624–629.

Bremner, J. D., Southwick, S., & Charney, D. (1999). The neurobiology of posttraumatic stress disorder: An integration of animal and human research. In P. A. Saigh & J. D. Bremner (Eds.), *Posttraumatic stress disorder: A comprehensive text* (pp. 103–143). Boston, MA: Allyn & Bacon.

Bremner, J. D., Vermetten, E., Vythilingam, M., Afzal, N., Schmahl, C., Elzinga, B., & Charney, D. S. (2004). Neural correlates of the classic color and emotional Stroop in women with abuse-related posttraumatic stress disorder. *Biological Psychiatry, 55*, 612–620.

Brewin, C. R. (1996). Theoretical foundations of cognitive-behavioral therapy for anxiety and depression. *Annual Review of Psychology, 47*, 33–57.

Brewin, C. R. (2007). Remembering and forgetting. In M. J. Friedman, T. M. Keane, & P. A. Resick (Eds.), *Handbook of PTSD: Science and practice* (pp. 116–134). New York, NY: Guilford Press.

Brewin, C. R., Andrews, B., & Rose, S. (2000). Fear, helplessness, and horror in posttraumatic stress disorder: Investigating DSM-IV criterion A2 in victims of violent crime. *Journal of Traumatic Stress, 13*, 499–509.

Brewin, C. R., Andrews, B., & Valentine, J. D. (2000). Meta-analysis of risk factors for posttraumatic stress disorder in trauma-exposed adults. *Journal of Consulting and Clinical Psychology, 68*, 748–766.

Brewin, C. R., Dalgleish, T., & Joseph, S. (1996). A dual representation theory of posttraumatic stress disorder. *Psychological Review, 103*, 670–686.

Briere, J. (1995). *The Trauma Symptom Inventory (TSI): Professional manual.* Odessa, FL: Psychological Assessment Resources.

Brown, T. A., Di Nardo, P. A., Lehman, C. L., & Campbell, L. A. (2001). Reliability of *DSM-IV* anxiety and mood disorders: Implications for the classification of emotional disorders. *Journal of Abnormal Psychology, 119*, 49–58.

Bryant, R. A., & Harvey, A. G. (1995). Processing threatening information in posttraumatic stress disorder. *Journal of Abnormal Psychology, 104*, 537–541.

Bryant, R. A., Moulds, M. L., & Guthrie, R. M. (2003). Imaginal exposure alone and imaginal exposure with cognitive restructuring in treatment of posttraumatic stress disorder. *Journal of Consulting and Clinical Psychology, 71*, 706–712.

Byrne, C. A., & Riggs, D. S. (1996). The cycle of trauma: Relationship aggression in male Vietnam veterans with symptoms of posttraumatic stress disorder. *Violence and Victims, 11*, 213–225.

Cahill, S. P., & Foa, E. B. (2007). Psychological theories of PTSD. In M. J. Friedman, T. M. Keane, & P. A. Resick (Eds.), *Handbook of PTSD: Science and practice* (pp. 55–77). New York, NY: Guilford Press.

Cohen, J. A., Mannarino, A. P., & Deblinger, E. (2006). *Treating trauma and traumatic grief in children and adolescents.* New York, NY: Guilford Press.

Cox, B. J., Clara, I. P., & Enns, M. W. (2002). Posttraumatic stress disorder and the structure of common mental disorders. *Depression and Anxiety, 15*, 168–171.

Dalgleish, T. (2004). Cognitive approaches to posttraumatic stress disorder: The evolution of multirepresentational theorizing. *Psychological Bulletin, 130*, 228–260.

Davidson, J. R., Brady, K., Mellman, T. A., Stein, M. B., & Pollack, M. H. (2007). The efficacy and tolerability of tiagabine in adult patients with post-traumatic stress disorder. *Journal of Clinical Psychopharmacology, 27*(1), 85–88. doi: 10.1097/JCP.0b013e31 802e5115

Davidson, P. R., & Parker, K. C. H. (2001). Eye movement desensitization and reprocessing (EMDR): A meta-analysis. *Journal of Consulting and Clinical Psychology, 69*(2), 305–316.

Davies, M. I., & Clark, D. M. (1998). Thought suppression produces a rebound effect with analogue posttraumatic intrusions. *Behaviour Research and Therapy, 36*, 571–582.

Davis, L., Clark, D., Kramer, G., Moeller, F., & Petty, F. (1999). D-fenfluramine challenge in posttraumatic stress disorder. *Biological Psychiatry, 45*, 928–930.

Davis, L. L., Davidson, J. R., Ward, L. C., Bartolucci, A., Bowden, C. L., & Petty, F. (2008). Divalproex in the treatment of posttraumatic stress disorder: A randomized, double-blind, placebo-controlled trial in a veteran population. *Journal of Clinical Psychopharmacology, 28*(1), 84–88. doi: 10.1097/JCP.0b013e3 18160f83b

de Kleine, R. A., Hendriks, G. J., Kusters, W. J., Broekman, T. G., & van Minnen, A. (2012). A randomized placebo-controlled trial of D-cycloserine to enhance exposure therapy for posttraumatic stress disorder. *Biological Psychiatry, 71*(11), 962–968. doi: 10.1016/j.biopsych.2012.02.033

Derogatis, L. R. (1983). *SCL-90-R: Administration, scoring and procedures manual–II*. Towson, MD: Clinical Psychometric Research.

Devilly, G. J., & Spence, S. H. (1999). The relative efficacy and treatment distress of EMDR and a cognitive-behavior trauma treatment protocol in the amelioration of posttraumatic stress disorder. *Journal of Anxiety Disorders, 13*, 131–157.

Difede, J., Cukor, J., Wyka, K., Olden, M., Hoffman, H., Lee, F. S., & Altemus, M. (2014). D-cycloserine augmentation of exposure therapy for post-traumatic stress disorder: A pilot randomized clinical trial. *Neuropsychopharmacology, 39*(5), 1052–1058.

Dohrenwend, B. P., Turner, J. B., Turse, N. A., Adams, B. G., Koenen, K. C., & Marshall, R. (2006). The psychological risks of Vietnam for U.S. veterans: A revisit with new data and methods. *Science, 313*, 979–982.

Dunmore, E., Clark, D. M., & Ehlers, A. (1999). Cognitive factors involved in the onset and maintenance of posttraumatic stress disorder (PTSD) after physical or sexual assault. *Behaviour Research and Therapy, 37*, 809–829.

Dunmore, E., Clark, D. M., & Ehlers, A. (2001). A prospective investigation of the role of cognitive factors in persistent posttraumatic stress disorder (PTSD) after physical or sexual assault. *Behaviour Research and Therapy, 39*, 1063–1084.

Ehlers, A., & Clark, D. M. (2000). A cognitive model of posttraumatic stress disorder. *Behaviour Research and Therapy, 38*, 319–345.

Eyeberg, S. M., & Funderburk, B. (2011). *Parent-child interaction therapy protocol*. Gainesville, FL: PCIT International.

Fairbank, J. A., Keane, T. M., & Malloy, P. F. (1983). Some preliminary data on the psychological characteristics of Vietnam veterans with posttraumatic stress disorder. *Journal of Consulting and Clinical Psychology, 51*, 912–919.

Famularo, R., Kinscherff, R., & Fenton, T. (1988). Propranolol treatment for childhood posttraumatic stress disorder, acute type. *American Journal of Diseases of Children, 142*, 1244–1247.

Feder, A., Parides, M. K., Murrough, J. W., Perez, A. M., Morgan, J. E., Saxena, S., & … Charney, D. S. (2014). Efficacy of intravenous ketamine for treatment of chronic posttraumatic stress disorder: A randomized clinical trial. *JAMA Psychiatry, 71*(6), 681–688. doi: 10.1001/jamapsychiatry.2014.62

Fichtner, C., Arora, R., O'Connor, F., & Crayton, J. (1994). Platelet paroxetine binding and fluoxetine pharmacotherapy in posttraumatic stress disorder: Preliminary observations on a possible predictor of clinical treatment response. *Life Sciences, 54*, 39–44.

Field, N. P., Classen, C., Butler, L. D., Koopman, C., Zarcone, J., & Spiegel, D. (2001). Revictimization and information processing in women survivors of childhood sexual abuse. *Journal of Anxiety Disorders, 15*, 459–469.

First, M. B., Williams, J. B. W., Karg, R. S., & Spitzer, R. L. (2015). *Structured Clinical Interview for DSM-5 Disorders, Clinician Version (SCID-5-CV)*. Arlington, VA: American Psychiatric Association.

Foa, E. B., Dancu, C. V., Hembree, E. A., Jaycox, L. H., Meadows, E. A., & Street, G. P. (1999). A comparison of exposure therapy, stress inoculation training, and their combination for reducing posttraumatic stress disorder in female assault victims. *Journal of Consulting and Clinical Psychology, 67*, 194–200.

Foa, E. B., Feske, U., Murdock, T. B., Kozak, M. J., & McCarthy, P. R. (1991). Processing of threat-related information in rape victims. *Journal of Abnormal Psychology, 100*, 156–162.

Foa, E. B., Hearst, D. E., Dancu, C. V., Hembree, E., & Jaycox, L. H. (1994). *Prolonged exposure (PE) manual*. Unpublished manuscript. Medical College of Pennsylvania, Eastern Pennsylvania Psychiatric Institute.

Foa, E. B., Hembree, E. A., Cahill, S. P., Rauch, S. A., Riggs, D. S., Feeny, N. C., & Yadin, E. (2005). Randomized trial of prolonged exposure for post-traumatic stress disorder with and without cognitive restructuring: Outcome at academic and community clinics. *Journal of Consulting and Clinical Psychology, 73*, 953–964.

Foa, E. B., & Kozak, M. J. (1985). Treatment of anxiety disorders: Implications for psychopathology. In A. H. Tuma & J. D. Maser (Eds.), *Anxiety and the anxiety disorders* (pp. 421–452). Hillsdale, NJ: Erlbaum.

Foa, E. B., & Kozak, M. J. (1986). Emotional processing of fear: Exposure to corrective information. *Psychological Bulletin, 99*, 20–35.

Foa, E. B., McLean, C. P., Capaldi, S., & Rosenfield, D. (2013). Prolonged exposure vs supportive counseling for sexual abuse–related PTSD in adolescent girls: A randomized clinical trial. *JAMA, 310*(24), 2650–2657.

Foa, E. B., McLean, C. P., Zang, Y., Zhong, J., Powers, M. B., Kauffman, B. Y., … Knowles, K.

(2015). Psychometric properties of the Posttraumatic Diagnostic Scale for DSM-5 (PDS-5). *Psychological Assessment*. Advance online publication. doi: 10.1037/pas0000258

Foa, E. B., McLean, C. P., Zang, Y., Zhong, J., Rauch, S., Porter, K., ... Kauffman, B. Y. (2015). Psychometric properties of the Posttraumatic Stress Disorder Symptom Scale Interview for DSM–5 (PSSI–5). *Psychological Assessment*. Advance online publication. doi: 10.1037/pas0000259

Foa, E. B., Molnar, C., & Cashman, L. (1995). Change in rape narratives during exposure therapy for posttraumatic stress disorder. *Journal of Traumatic Stress*, *8*, 675–690.

Foa, E. B., & Riggs, D. S. (1993). Posttraumatic stress disorder in rape victims. In J. Oldham, M. B. Riba, & A. Tasman (Eds.), *American Psychiatric Press review of psychiatry* (pp. 273–303). Washington, DC: American Psychiatric Press.

Foa, E. B., Riggs, D. S., Dancu, C. V., & Rothbaum, B. O. (1993). Reliability and validity of a brief instrument for assessing post-traumatic stress disorder. *Journal of Traumatic Stress*, *6*, 459–473.

Foa, E. B., Riggs, D. S., Massie, E. D., & Yarczower, M. (1995). The impact of fear activation and anger on the efficacy of exposure treatment for posttraumatic stress disorder. *Behavior Therapy*, *26*, 487–499.

Foa, E. B., & Rothbaum, B. O. (1998). *Treating the trauma of rape: Cognitive-behavioral therapy for PTSD*. New York, NY: Guilford Press.

Foa, E. B., Rothbaum, B. O., Riggs, D. S., & Murdock, T. B. (1991). Treatment of posttraumatic stress disorder in rape victims: A comparison between cognitive-behavioral procedures and counseling. *Journal of Consulting and Clinical Psychology*, *59*, 715–723.

Foy, D. W., Carroll, E. M., & Donahoe, C. P. (1987). Etiological factors in the development of PTSD in clinical samples of Vietnam combat veterans. *Journal of Clinical Psychology*, *43*, 17–27.

Fredman, S. J., Pukay-Martin, N. D., Macdonald, A., Wagner, A. C., Vorstenbosch, V., & Monson, C. M. (2016). Partner accommodation moderates treatment outcomes for couple therapy for PTSD. *Journal of Consulting and Clinical Psychology*, *84*, 79–87. doi: 10.1037/ccp0000061

Freeman, J. B., & Beck, J. G. (2000). Cognitive interference for trauma cues in sexually abused adolescent girls with posttraumatic stress disorder. *Journal of Clinical Child Psychology*, *29*, 245–256.

Friedman, M. J., & Davidson, J. R. (2007). Pharmacotherapy for PTSD. In M. J. Friedman, T. M. Keane, & P. A. Resick (Eds.), *Handbook of PTSD: Science and practice* (pp. 376–405). New York, NY: Guilford Press.

Friedman, M. J., Resick, P. A., Bryant, R. A., & Brewin, C. R. (2011). Considering PTSD for *DSM-5*. *Depression and Anxiety*, *28*(9), 750–769. doi: 10.1002/da.20767

Friedman, M. J., & Southwick, S. M. (1995). Towards pharmacotherapy for post-traumatic stress disorder. In M. J. Friedman, D. S. Charney, & A. Y. Deutch (Eds.), *Neurobiological and clinical consequences of stress* (pp. 465–482). Philadelphia, PA: Lippincott-Raven.

Frost, N. D., Laska, K. M., & Wampold, B. E. (2014). The evidence for present-centered therapy as treatment for posttraumatic stress disorder. *Journal of Traumatic Stress*, *27*(1), 1–8.

Galea, S., Ahern, J., Resnick, H., Kilpatrick, D., Bucuvalas, M., Gold, J., & Vlahov, D. (2002). Psychological sequelae of the September 11 terrorist attacks in New York City. *New England Journal of Medicine*, *346*, 982–987.

Gallagher, M. W., & Resick, P. A. (2012). Mechanisms of change in cognitive processing therapy and prolonged exposure therapy for PTSD: Preliminary evidence for the differential effects of hopelessness and habituation. *Cognitive Therapy and Research*, *36*, 750–755. doi: 10.1007/s10608-011-9423-6

Galovski, T. E., Blain, L. M., Mott, J. M., Elwood, L., & Houle, T. (2012). Manualized therapy for PTSD: Flexing the structure of cognitive processing therapy. *Journal of Consulting and Clinical Psychology*, *80*, 968–981. doi: 10.1037/a0030600

Galovski, T., E., Elwood, L. S., Blain, B. M., & Resick, P. A. (2014). Changes in anger in relationship to responsivity to PTSD treatment. *Psychological Trauma: Theory, Research, Practice, and Policy*, *6*(1), 56–64. doi: 10.1037/a0031364

Gersons, B. P. R., Carlier, I. V. E., & Lamberts, R. D. (2000). Randomized clinical trial of brief eclectic psychotherapy for police officers with posttraumatic stress disorder. *Journal of Traumatic Stress*, *13*, 333–347.

Gilbertson, M. W., Shenton, M. E., Ciszewski, A., Kasai, K., Lasko, N. B., Orr, S. P., & Pitman, R. K. (2002). Smaller hippocampal volume predicts pathologic vulnerability to psychological trauma. *Nature Neuroscience*, *5*(11), 1242–1247.

Gilman, R., Schumm, J. A., & Chard, K. M. (2012). Hope as a change mechanism in the treatment of posttraumatic stress disorder. *Psychological Trauma: Theory, Research, Practice, and Policy, 4*(3), 270–277. doi: 10.1037/a0024252

Gradus, J. L., Suvak, M. K., Wisco, B. E., Marx, B. P., & Resick, P. A. (2013). Treatment of posttraumatic stress disorder reduces suicidal ideation. *Depression and Anxiety, 30*, 1046–1053.

Green, B. L. (1996). Trauma History Questionnaire. In B. H. Stamm (Ed.), *Measurement of stress, trauma, and adaptation* (pp. 366–369). Lutherville, MD: Sidran.

Griffin, M. G., Resick, P. A., & Galovski, T. E. (2006, November). *Psychobiological assessment following cognitive behavioral treatment for PTSD in rape and physical assault survivors.* Paper presented at the Psychobiology and Treatment of PTSD symposium, International Society for Traumatic Stress Studies, Hollywood, CA.

Griffin, M. G., Resick, P. A., & Mechanic, M. B. (1997). Objective assessment of peritraumatic dissociation: Psychophysiological indicators. *American Journal of Psychiatry, 154*(8), 1081–1088.

Guina, J., Rossetter, S. R., DeRhodes, B. J., Nahhas, R. W., & Welton, R. S. (2015). Benzodiazepines for PTSD: A systematic review and meta-analysis. *Journal of Psychiatric Practice, 21*(4), 281–303.

Gutner, C., Rizvi, S. L., Monson, C. M., & Resick, P. A. (2006). Changes in coping strategies, relationship to the perpetrator, and posttraumatic stress disorder in female crime victims. *Journal of Traumatic Stress, 19*, 813–823.

Hamner, M., & Diamond, B. (1993). Elevated plasma dopamine in posttraumatic stress disorder: A preliminary report. *Biological Psychiatry, 33*, 304–306.

Harvey, A. G., & Bryant, R. A. (1998). The effect of attempted thought suppression in acute stress disorder. *Behaviour Research and Therapy, 36*, 583–590.

Heim, C., Newport, D. J., Heit, S., Graham, Y. P. Wilcox, M., Bonsall, R., ... Nemeroff, C. B. (2000). Pituitary-adrenal and autonomic responses to stress in women after sexual and physical abuse in childhood. *JAMA, 284*, 592–597.

Hellawell, S. J., & Brewin, C. R. (2004). A comparison of flashbacks and ordinary autobiographical memories of trauma: Content and language. *Behaviour Research and Therapy, 42*, 1–12.

Henning, K. R., & Frueh, B. C. (1997). Combat guilt and its relationship to PTSD symptoms. *Journal of Clinical Psychology, 53*, 801–808.

Herschell, A. D., & McNeil, C. B. (2005). Theoretical and empirical underpinnings of parent-child interaction therapy with child physical abuse populations. *Education & Treatment of Children, 28*(2), 142–162.

Hertzberg, M. A., Butterfield, M. I., Feldman, M. E., Beckham, J. C., Sutherland, S. M., Connor, K. M., & Davidson, J. R. (1999). A preliminary study of lamotrigine for the treatment of posttraumatic stress disorder. *Biological Psychiatry, 45*, 1226–1229.

Hobfoll, S. E. (1989). Conservation of resources: A new attempt at conceptualizing stress. *American Psychologist, 44*, 513–524.

Hobfoll, S. E. (1991). Traumatic stress: A theory based on rapid loss of resources. *Anxiety Research, 4*, 187–197.

Hoge, C. W., Auchterlonie, J. L., & Milliken, C. S. (2006). Mental health problems, use of mental health services, and attrition from military service after returning from deployment to Iraq or Afghanistan. *JAMA, 295*, 1023–1032.

Hoge, C. W., Riviere, L. A., Wilk, J. E., Herrell, R. K., & Weathers, F. W. (2014). The prevalence of post-traumatic stress disorder (PTSD) in US combat soldiers: A head-to-head comparison of DSM-5 versus DSM-IV-TR symptom criteria with the PTSD checklist. *Lancet Psychiatry, 1*(4), 269–277.

Hollon, S. D., & Garber, J. (1988). Cognitive therapy. In L. Y. Abramson (Ed.), *Social cognition and clinical psychology: A synthesis* (pp. 204–253). New York, NY: Guilford Press.

Hoskins, M., Pearce, J., Bethell, A., Dankova, L., Barbui, C., Tol, W. A., ... Bisson, J. I. (2015). Pharmacotherapy for post-traumatic stress disorder: Systematic review and meta-analysis. *British Journal of Psychiatry, 206*(2), 93–100.

Ipser, J. C., & Stein, D. J. (2012). Evidence-based pharmacotherapy of post-traumatic stress disorder (PTSD). *International Journal of Neuropsychopharmacology, 15*(06), 825–840.

Iverson, K. M., Gradus, J. L., Resick, P. A., Suvak, M. K., Smith, K. F., & Monson, C. M. (2011). Cognitive-behavioral therapy for PTSD and depression symptoms reduces risk for future intimate partner violence among interpersonal trauma survivors. *Journal of Consulting and Clinical Psychology, 79*, 193–202.

Jakupcak, M., Roberts, L., Martell, C., Mulick, P., Michael, S., Reed, R., … McFall, M. (2006). A pilot study of behavioral activation for veterans with posttraumatic stress disorder. *Journal of Traumatic Stress*, *19*, 387–391.

Janoff-Bulman, R. (1992). *Shattered assumptions: Towards a new psychology of trauma*. New York, NY: Free Press.

Jones, C., Harvey, A. G., & Brewin, C. R. (2007). The organisation and content of trauma memories in survivors of road traffic accidents. *Behaviour Research and Therapy*, *45*, 151–162.

Jones, J. C., & Barlow, D. H. (1990). The etiology of posttraumatic stress disorder. *Clinical Psychology Review*, *10*, 299–328.

Jones, R. W., Wesnes, K. A., & Kirby, J. (1991). Effects of NMDA modulation in scopolamine dementia. *Annals of the New York Academy of Sciences*, *640*, 241–244.

Keane, T. M., Caddell, J. M., & Taylor, K. L. (1988). Mississippi Scale for Combat-Related Posttraumatic Stress Disorder: Three studies in reliability and validity. *Journal of Consulting and Clinical Psychology*, *56*, 85–90.

Keane, T. M., Fairbank, J. A., Caddell, J. M., & Zimering, R. T. (1989). Implosive (flooding) therapy reduces symptoms of PTSD in Vietnam combat veterans. *Behavior Therapy*, *20*, 245–260.

Keane, T. M., Fairbank, J. A., Caddell, J. M., Zimering, R. T., & Bender, M. E. (1985). A behavioral approach to assessing and treating posttraumatic stress disorder in Vietnam veterans. In C. R. Figley (Ed.), *Trauma and its wake* (pp. 257–294). New York, NY: Brunner/ Mazel.

Keane, T. M., Kaloupek, D. G., & Kolb, L. C. (1998). VA Cooperative Study #334: I. Summary of findings on the psychological assessment of PTSD. *PTSD Research Quarterly*, *9*, 1–4.

Keane, T. M., Kolb, L. C., Kaloupek, D. G., Orr, S. P., Blanchard, E. B., Thomas, R. G., … Lavori, P. W. (1998). Utility of psychophysiology measurement in the diagnosis of posttraumatic stress disorder: Results from a Department of Veterans Affairs cooperative study. *Journal of Consulting and Clinical Psychology*, *66*, 914–923.

Keane, T. M., Malloy, P. F., & Fairbank, J. A. (1984). Empirical development of an MMPI subscale for the assessment of combat-related posttraumatic stress disorder. *Journal of Consulting and Clinical Psychology*, *52*, 888–891.

Keane, T. M., Scott, W. O., Chavoya, G. A., Lamparski, D. M., & Fairbank, J. A. (1985). Social support in Vietnam veterans with posttraumatic stress disorder: A comparative analysis. *Journal of Consulting and Clinical Psychology*, *53*, 95–102.

Kessler, R. C., Berglund, P., Demler, O., Jin, R., Merikangas, K. R., & Walters, E. E. (2005). Lifetime prevalence and age-of-onset distributions of DSM-IV disorders in the National Comorbidity Survey Replication. *Archives of General Psychiatry*, *62*, 593–602.

Kessler, R. C., Sonnega, A., Bromet, E., Hughes, M., & Nelson, C. B. (1995). Posttraumatic stress disorder in the National Comorbidity Survey. *Archives of General Psychiatry*, *52*, 1048–1060.

Kessler, R. C., Walters, E. E., & Forthofer, M. A. (1998). The social consequences of psychiatric disorders: III. *Probability of marital stability. American Journal of Psychiatry*, *155*, 1092–1096.

Khachatryan, D., Groll, D., Booij, L., Sephery, A. A., & Schütz, C. G. (2015). Prazosin for treating sleep disturbances in adults with posttraumatic stress disorder: A systematic review and meta-analysis of randomized controlled trials. *General Hospital Psychiatry*. Advance online publication. doi: 10.1016/ j.genhosppsych.2015.10.007

Kilpatrick, D. G. (1983). Rape victims: Detection, assessment and treatment. *Clinical Psychologist*, *36*, 92–95.

Kilpatrick, D. G., Best, C. L., Veronen, L. J., Amick, A. E., Villeponteaux, L. A., & Ruff, G. A. (1985). Mental health correlates of criminal victimization: A random community survey. *Journal of Consulting and Clinical Psychology*, *53*, 866–873.

Kilpatrick, D. G., Resnick, H. S., Milanak, M. E., Miller, M. W., Keyes, K. M., & Friedman, M. J. (2013). National estimates of exposure to traumatic events and PTSD prevalence using DSM-IV and DSM-5 criteria. *Journal of Traumatic Stress*, *26*(5), 537–547.

Kimerling, R., Ouimette, P. C., & Wolfe, J. (Eds.). (2002). *Gender and PTSD*. New York, NY: Guilford Press.

King, D. W., King, L. A., Foy, D. W., Keane, T. M., & Fairbank, J. A. (1999). Posttraumatic stress disorder in a national sample of female and male Vietnam veterans: Risk factors, war-zone stressors, and resilience-recovery variables. *Journal of Abnormal Psychology*, *108*, 164–170.

Krueger, R. F., Caspi, A., Moffitt, T. E., & Silva, P. A. (1998). The structure and stability of common mental disorders (*DSM-III-R*): A longitudinal-epidemiological study. *Journal of Abnormal Psychology*, *107*, 216–227.

Krueger, R. F., McGue, M., & Iacono, W. G. (2001). The higher-order structure of common DSM mental disorders: Internalization, externalization, and their connections to personality. *Personality and Individual Differences*, *30*, 1245–1259.

Kubany, E. S. (1994). A cognitive model of guilt typology in combat-related PTSD. *Journal of Traumatic Stress*, *7*, 3–19.

Kubany, E. S., Leisen, M. B., Kaplan, A. S., & Kelly, M. P. (2000). Validation of a brief measure of posttraumatic stress disorder: The Distressing Event Questionnaire (DEQ). *Psychological Assessment*, *12*, 197–209.

Kubany, E. S., Leisen, M. B., Kaplan, A. S., Watson, S. B., Haynes, S. N., Owens, J. A., & Burns, K. (2000). Development and preliminary validation of a brief broad-spectrum measure of trauma exposure: The Traumatic Life Events Questionnaire. *Psychological Assessment*, *12*, 210–224.

Kulka, R. A., Schlenger, W. E., Fairbank, J. A., Hough, R. L., Jordan, B. K., Marmar, C. R., & Weiss, D. S. (1990). *Trauma and the Vietnam War generation: Report of findings from the National Vietnam Veterans Readjustment Study*. New York, NY: Brunner/Mazel.

Lang, P. J. (1979). A bio-informational theory of emotional imagery. *Psychophysiology*, *16*, 495–512.

Lange, A., Rietdijk, D., & Hudcovicova, M. (2003). Interapy: A controlled randomized trial of the standardized treatment of posttraumatic stress through the Internet. *Journal of Consulting and Clinical Psychology*, *71*, 901–909.

Lanius, R. A., Brand, B., Vermetten, E., Frewen, P. A., & Spiegel, D. (2012). The dissociative subtype of posttraumatic stress disorder: Rationale, clinical and neurobiological evidence, and implications. *Depression and Anxiety*, *29*(8), 701–708. doi: 10.1002/da.21889

Lauterbach, D., & Vrana, S. R. (1996). Three studies on the reliability and validity of a self-report measure of posttraumatic stress disorder. *Assessment*, *3*, 17–25.

Lemieux, A. M., & Coe, C. L. (1995). Abuse-related posttraumatic stress disorder: Evidence for chronic neuroendocrine activation in women. *Psychosomatic Medicine*, *57*, 105–115.

Lenz, S., Bruijn, B., Serman, N. S., & Bailey, L. (2014). Effectiveness of cognitive processing therapy for treating posttraumatic stress disorder. *Journal of Mental Health Counseling*, *36*(4), 360.

Lenz, A. S., & Hollenbaugh, K. M. (2015). Meta-analysis of trauma-focused cognitive behavioral therapy for treating PTSD and co-occurring depression among children and adolescents. *Counseling Outcome Research and Evaluation*, *6*(1), 18–32.

Leskela, J., Dieperink, M., & Thuras, P. (2002). Shame and posttraumatic stress disorder. *Journal of Traumatic Stress*, *15*, 223–226.

Lieberman, A. F., & Van Horn, P. (2005). *Don't hit my mommy!: A manual for child-parent psychotherapy with young witnesses of family violence*. Washington, DC: Zero to Three Press.

Lindauer, R. J. L., Vlieger, E.-J., & Jalink, M. (2005). Effects of psychotherapy on hippocampal volume in out-patients with post-traumatic stress disorder: An MRI investigation. *Psychological Medicine*, *35*, 1421–1431.

Lipschitz, D. S., Rasmusson, A. M., & Yehuda, R. (2003). Salivary cortisol responses to dexamethasone in adolescents with posttraumatic stress disorder. *Journal of the American Academy of Child & Adolescent Psychiatry*, *42*, 1301–1317.

Litz, B. T., Salters-Pedneault, K., Steenkamp, M. M., Hermos, J. A., Bryant, R. A., Otto, M. W., & Hofmann, S. G. (2012). A randomized placebo-controlled trial of D-cycloserine and exposure therapy for posttraumatic stress disorder. *Journal of Psychiatric Research*, *46*(9), 1184–1190.

Litz, B. T., Weathers, F. W., Monaco, V., Herman, D. S., Wulfsohn, M., Marx, B., & Keane, T. M. (1996). Attention, arousal, and memory in posttraumatic stress disorder. *Journal of Traumatic Stress*, *9*, 497–518.

Macdonald, A., Pukay-Martin, N. D., Wagner, A., Fredman, S. J., & Monson, C. M. (In press). Improvements in PTSD symptom clusters and trauma-related cognitions in a randomized controlled trial of cognitive-behavioral couple therapy for PTSD. *Journal of Family Psychology*.

March, J. S. (1993). What constitutes a stressor? The "criterion A" issue. In J. R. T. Davidson & E. B. Foa (Eds.), *DSM-IV and beyond* (pp. 37–54). Washington, DC: American Psychiatric Press.

Marks, I., Lovell, K., Noshirvani, H., Livanou, M., & Thrasher, S. (1998). Treatment of posttraumatic stress disorder by exposure and/or cognitive restructuring: A controlled study. *Archives of General Psychiatry*, *55*, 317–325.

Martenyi, F., Brown, E. B., Zhang, H., Koke, S. C., & Prakash, A. (2002). Fluoxetine v. placebo in prevention of relapse in post-traumatic stress disorder. *British Journal of Psychiatry, 181*, 315–320.

McCann, I. L., & Pearlman, L. A. (1990). *Psychological trauma and the adult survivor: Theory, therapy, and transformation.* New York, NY: Brunner/Mazel.

McCann, I. L., Sakheim, D. K., & Abrahamson, D. J. (1988). Trauma and victimization: A model of psychological adaptation. *Counseling Psychologist, 16*, 531–594.

McFall, M. E., Murburg, M. M., Ko, G. N., & Veith, R. C. (1990). Autonomic responses to stress in Vietnam combat veterans with posttraumatic stress disorder. *Biological Psychiatry, 27*, 1165–1175.

McNally, R. J., English, G. E., & Lipke, H. J. (1993). Assessment of intrusive cognition in PTSD: Use of the modified Stroop paradigm. *Journal of Traumatic Stress, 6*, 33–41.

McNally, R. J., Kaspi, S. P., Riemann, B. C., & Zeitlin, S. B. (1990). Selective processing of threat cues in posttraumatic stress disorder. *Journal of Abnormal Psychology, 99*, 398–402.

McNally, R. J., & Riccardi, J. N. (1996). Suppression of negative and neutral thoughts. *Behavioural and Cognitive Psychotherapy, 24*, 17–25.

Milad, M. R., & Rauch, S. L. (2007). The role of the orbitofrontal cortex in anxiety disorders. *Annals of the New York Academy of Sciences, 1121*(1), 546–561.

Miller, M. W., Fogler, J., Wolf, E. J., Kaloupek, D. G., & Keane, T. M. (2008). The internalizing and externalizing structure of psychiatric comorbidity in combat veterans. *Journal of Traumatic Stress, 21*, 58–65.

Miller, M. W., Greif, J. L., & Smith, A. A. (2003). Multidimensional Personality Questionnaire profiles of veterans with traumatic combat exposure: Externalizing and internalizing subtypes. *Psychological Assessment, 15*, 205–215.

Miller, M. W., Kaloupek, D. G., Dillon, A. L., & Keane, T. M. (2004). Externalizing and internalizing subtypes of combat-related PTSD: A replication and extension using the PSY-5 scales. *Journal of Abnormal Psychology, 113*, 636–645.

Miller, M. W., Kaloupek, D. G., & Keane, T. M. (1999, October). *Antisociality and physiological hyporesponsivity during exposure to trauma-related stimuli in patients with PTSD.* Poster presented at the 39th Annual Meeting of the Society for Psychophysiological Research, Granada, Spain.

Miller, M. W., & Resick, P. A. (2007). Internalizing and externalizing subtypes in female sexual assault survivors: Implications for the understanding of complex PTSD. *Behavior Therapy, 38*, 58–71.

Monson, C. M., & Fredman, S. J. (2012). *Cognitive-behavioral conjoint therapy for PTSD.* New York, NY: Guilford Press.

Monson, C. M., Fredman, S. J., Adair, K. C., Stevens, S. P., Resick, P. A., Schnurr, P. P., … Macdonald, A. (2011). Cognitive-behavioral conjoint therapy for PTSD: Pilot results from a community sample. *Journal of Traumatic Stress, 24*, 97–101.

Monson, C. M., Fredman, S. J., & Dekel, R. (2010). Posttraumatic stress disorder in an interpersonal context. In J. G. Beck (Ed.), *Interpersonal processes in the anxiety disorders: Implications for understanding psychopathology and treatment* (pp. 179–208). Washington, DC: American Psychological Association.

Monson, C. M., Fredman, S. J., Macdonald, A., Pukay-Marin, N. D., Resick, P. A., & Schnurr P. P. (2012). Effect of cognitive-behavioral couple therapy for PTSD: A randomized controlled trial. *JAMA, 308*, 700–709.

Monson, C. M., Friedman, M., & La Bash, H. A. J. (2014). A psychological history of PTSD. In M. J. Friedman, T. M. Keane, & P. A. Resick (Eds.), *Handbook of PTSD: Science and practice* (pp. 60–78). New York, NY: Guilford Press.

Monson, C. M., Price, J. L., & Ranslow, E. (2005). Treating combat PTSD through cognitive processing therapy. *Federal Practitioner, 22*, 75–83.

Monson, C. M., Schnurr, P. P., Stevens, S. P., & Guthrie, K. A. (2004). Cognitive-behavioral couple's treatment for posttraumatic stress disorder: Initial findings. *Journal of Traumatic Stress, 17*, 341–344.

Monson, C. M., Stevens, S. P., & Schnurr, P. P. (2005). Cognitive-behavioral couple's treatment for posttraumatic stress disorder. In T. A. Corales (Ed.), *Focus on posttraumatic stress disorder research* (pp. 245–274). Hauppague, NY: Nova Science.

Moradi, A. R., Taghavi, M. R., Neshat Doost, H. T., Yule, W., & Dalgleish, T. (1999). Performance of children and adolescents with PTSD on the Stroop colour-naming task. *Psychological Medicine, 29*, 415–419.

Morgan, C. A., III, Hazlett, G., Wang, S., Richardson, E. G., Jr., Schnurr, P., & Southwick, S. M. (2001). Symptoms of dissociation in humans experiencing acute, uncontrollable stress: A prospective investigation. *American Journal of Psychiatry, 158*, 1239–1247.

Morgan, C. A., III, Southwick, S., Hazlett, G., Rasmusson, A., Hoyt, G., Zimolo, Z., & Charney, D. (2004). Relationships among plasma dehydro-epiandrosterone sulfate and cortisol levels, symptoms of dissociation, and objective performance in humans exposed to acute stress. *Archives of General Psychiatry, 61*, 819–825.

Morgan, C. A., III, Wang, S., & Southwick, S. M. (2000). Plasma neuropeptide-Y concentrations in humans exposed to military survival training. *Biological Psychiatry, 47*, 902–909.

Morland, L. A., Hynes, A. K., Mackintosh, M., Resick, P. A., & Chard, K. M. (2011). Group cognitive processing therapy delivered to veterans via telehealth: A pilot cohort. *Journal of Traumatic Stress, 24*(4), 465–469.

Mowrer, O. H. (1947). On the dual nature of learning—a re-interpretation of "conditioning" and "problem-solving." *Harvard Educational Review, 14*, 102–148.

Neuner, F., Schauer, M., Klaschik, C., Karunakara, U., & Elbert, T. (2004). A comparison of narrative exposure therapy, supportive counseling, and psychoeducation for treating posttraumatic stress disorder in an African refugee settlement. *Journal of Consulting and Clinical Psychology, 72*, 579–587.

Neylan, T. C., Lenoci, M., Samuelson, K. W., Metzler, T. J., Henn-Haase, C., Hierholzer, R. W., ... Marmar, C. R. (2006). No improvement of posttraumatic stress disorder symptoms with guanfacine treatment. *American Journal of Psychiatry, 163*(12), 2186–2188. doi: 10.1176/appi.ajp.163.12.2186

Nijdam, M. J., Gersons, B. P. R., Reitsma, J. B., de Jongh, A., & Olff, M. (2012). Brief eclectic psychotherapy v. eye movement desensitization and reprocessing therapy for post-traumatic stress disorder: Randomised controlled trial. *British Journal of Psychiatry, 200*(3), 224–231.

Norris, F. H. (1990). Screening for traumatic stress: A scale for use in the general population. *Journal of Applied Social Psychology, 20*, 1704–1718.

Norris, F. H. (1992). Epidemiology of trauma: Frequency and impact of different potentially traumatic events on different demographic groups. *Journal of Consulting and Clinical Psychology, 60*, 409–418.

O'Doherty, D. M., Chitty, K. M., Saddiqui, S., Bennett, M. R., & Lagopoulos, J. (2015). A systematic review and meta-analysis of magnetic resonance imaging measurement of structural volumes in posttraumatic

stress disorder. *Psychiatry Research: Neuroimaging, 232*(1), 1–33. doi: 10.1016/j.pscychresns.2015 .01.002

O'Donnell, M. L., Alkemade, N., Nickerson, A., Creamer, M., McFarlane, A. C., Silove, D., ... Forbes, D. (2014). Impact of the diagnostic changes to post-traumatic stress disorder for DSM-5 and the proposed changes to ICD-11. *British Journal of Psychiatry, 205*(3), 230–235.

Orr, S. P., Lasko, N. B., Metzger, L. J., Berry, N. J., Ahern, C. E., & Pitman, R. K. (1998). Psychophysiologic assessment of women with posttraumatic stress disorder resulting from childhood sexual abuse. *Journal of Consulting and Clinical Psychology, 66*, 906–913.

Orsillo, S. M., Weathers, F. W., Litz, B. T., Steinberg, H. R., Huska, J. A., & Keane, T. M. (1996). Current and lifetime psychiatric disorders among veterans with war zone–related posttraumatic stress disorder. *Journal of Nervous and Mental Disease, 184*, 307–313.

Owens, G. P., & Chard, K. M. (2001). Cognitive distortions among women reporting childhood sexual abuse. *Journal of Interpersonal Violence, 16*, 178–191.

Pitman, R. K., Orr, S. P., Altman, B., Longpre, R. E., Poiré, R. E., & Macklin, M. L. (1996). Emotional processing during eye movement desensitisation and reprocessing therapy of Vietnam veterans with chronic posttraumatic stress disorder. *Comprehensive Psychiatry, 37*, 419–429.

Pitman, R. K., Orr, S. P., Forgue, D. F., & Altman, B. (1990). Psychophysiologic responses to combat imagery of Vietnam veterans with posttraumatic stress disorder versus other anxiety disorders. *Journal of Abnormal Psychology, 99*, 49–54.

Pitman, R. K., Orr, S. P., Forgue, D. F., de Jong, J., & Claiborn, J. M. (1987). Psychophysiologic assessment of posttraumatic stress disorder imagery in Vietnam combat veterans. *Archives of General Psychiatry, 44*, 970–975.

Pitman, R. K., Sanders, K. M., Zusman, R. M., Healy, A. R., Cheema, F., Lasko, N. B., ... Orr, S. P. (2002). Pilot study of secondary prevention of posttraumatic stress disorder with propranolol. *Biological Psychiatry, 51*, 189–192.

Powers, M. B., Halpern, J. M., Ferenschak, M. P., Gillihan, S. J., & Foa, E. B. (2010). A meta-analytic review of prolonged exposure for posttraumatic stress disorder. *Clinical Psychology Review, 30*, 635–641.

Prins, A., Ouimette, P., Kimerling, R., Camerond, R. P., Hugelshofer, D. S., Shaw-Hegwer, J., ... Sheikh, J. I. (2004). The Primary Care PTSD Screen (PC-PTSD): Development and operating characteristics. *Primary Care Psychiatry, 9,* 9–14.

Rachman, S. (1980). Emotional processing. *Behaviour Research and Therapy, 18,* 51–60.

Ramage, A. E., Litz, B. T., Resick, P. A., Woolsey, M. D., Dondanville, K. A., Young-McCaughan, S., ... the STRONG STAR Consortium. (2016). Regional cerebral glucose metabolism differentiates danger- and non-danger-based traumas in post-traumatic stress disorder. *Social Cognitive and Affective Neuroscience.* Advance online publication. doi: 10.1093/scan/nsv102

Ramchand, R., Schell, T. L., Karney, B. R., Osilla, K. C., Burns, R. M., & Caldarone, L. B. (2010). Disparate prevalence estimates of PTSD among service members who served in Iraq and Afghanistan: Possible explanations. *Journal of Traumatic Stress, 23*(1), 59–68. doi: 10.1002/jts.20486

Rasmusson, A. M., Hauger, R. L., Morgan, C. A., III, Bremner, J. D., Southwick, S. M., & Charney, D. S. (2000). Low baseline and yohimbine stimulated plasma neuropeptide Y (NPY) levels in combat-related PTSD. *Biological Psychiatry, 47,* 526–539.

Rasmusson, A. M., Pinna, G., & Paliwal, P. (2006). Decreased cerebrospinal fluid allopregnanolone levels in women with posttraumatic stress disorder. *Biological Psychiatry, 60,* 704–713.

Rasmusson, A. M., Vasek, J., & Lipschitz, D. S. (2004). An increased capacity for adrenal DHEA release is associated with decreased avoidance and negative mood symptoms in women with PTSD. *Neuropsychopharmacology, 29,* 1546–1557.

Rasmusson, A. M., Vythilingam, M., & Morgan, C. A., III, (2003). The neuroendocrinology of posttraumatic stress disorder: New directions. *CNS Spectrums, 8,* 651–667.

Resick, P. A. (1992). Cognitive treatment of a crime-related post-traumatic stress disorder. In R. D. Peters, R. J. McMahon, & V. L. Quinsey (Eds.), *Aggression and violence throughout the life span* (pp. 171–191). Newbury Park, CA: Sage.

Resick, P. A., Monson, C. M., & Chard, K. M. (In press). *Cognitive processing therapy for PTSD: A comprehensive manual.* New York, NY: Guilford Press.

Resick, P. A., Nishith, P., Weaver, T. L., Astin, M. C., & Feuer, C. A. (2002). A comparison of cognitive processing therapy, prolonged exposure and a waiting condition for the treatment of posttraumatic stress disorder in female rape victims. *Journal of Consulting and Clinical Psychology, 70,* 867–879.

Resick, P. A., & Schnicke, M. K. (1992). Cognitive processing therapy for sexual assault victims. *Journal of Consulting and Clinical Psychology, 60,* 748–756.

Resick, P. A., & Schnicke, M. K. (1993). *Cognitive processing therapy for rape victims: A treatment manual.* Newbury Park, CA: Sage.

Resick, P. A., Schnicke, M. K., & Markway, B. G. (1991, November). *The relation between cognitive content and PTSD.* Paper presented at the 25th Annual Convention of the Association for the Advancement of Behavioral Therapy, New York, NY.

Resick, P. A., Uhlmansiek, M. O., Clum, G. A., Galovski, T. E., Scher, C. D., & Young-Xu, Y. (2008). A randomized clinical trial to dismantle components of cognitive processing therapy for posttraumatic stress disorder in female victims of interpersonal violence. *Journal of Consulting and Clinical Psychology, 76,* 243–258.

Resick, P. A., Wachen, J. S., Mintz, J., Young-McCaughan, S., Roache, J. D., Borah, A. M., ... Peterson, A. L. (2015). A randomized clinical trial of group cognitive processing therapy compared with group present-centered therapy for PTSD among active duty military personnel. *Journal of Consulting and Clinical Psychology, 83*(6), 1058–1068.

Resick, P. A., Williams, L. F., Suvak, M. K., Monson, C. M., & Gradus, J. L. (2012). Long-term outcomes of cognitive-behavioral treatments for posttraumatic stress disorder among female rape survivors. *Journal of Consulting and Clinical Psychology, 80*(2), 201–210. doi: 10.1037/a0026602

Riggs, D. S., Byrne, C. A., Weathers, F. W., & Litz, B. T. (1998). The quality of the intimate relationships of male Vietnam veterans: Problems associated with posttraumatic stress disorder. *Journal of Traumatic Stress, 11,* 87–101.

Riggs, D. S., Dancu, C. V., Gershuny, B. S., Greenberg, D., & Foa, E. B. (1992). Anger and post-traumatic stress disorder in female crime victims. *Journal of Traumatic Stress, 5,* 613–625.

Rizvi, S. L., Kaysen, D., Gutner, C. A., Griffin, M. G., & Resick, P. A. (2008). Beyond fear: The role of peritraumatic responses in posttraumatic stress and depressive symptoms among female crime victims. *Journal of Interpersonal Violence, 23,* 853–868.

Robins, L. N., Helzer, J. E., Croughan, J., & Ratcliff, K. S. (1981). National Institute of Mental Health

Diagnostic Interview Schedule: Its history, characteristics, and validity. *Archives of General Psychiatry*, *38*, 381–389.

Rodriguez, N., Vande-Kemp, H., & Foy, D. W. (1998). Posttraumatic stress disorder in survivors of childhood sexual and physical abuse: A critical review of the empirical research. *Journal of Child Sexual Abuse*, *7*, 17–45.

Rothbaum, B. O. (1997). A controlled study of eye movement desensitisation and reprocessing in the treatment of posttraumatic stress disordered sexual assault victims. *Bulletin of the Menninger Clinic*, *61*, 317–334.

Rothbaum, B. O., Astin, M. C., & Marsteller, F. (2005). Prolonged exposure versus eye movement desensitization and reprocessing (EMDR) for PTSD rape victims. *Journal of Traumatic Stress*, *18*, 607–616.

Rothbaum, B. O., Cahill, S., Foa, E., Davidson, J., Compton, J., Connor, K., ... Hahn, C. G. (2006). Augmentation of sertraline with prolonged exposure in the treatment of posttraumatic stress disorder. *Journal of Traumatic Stress*, *19*, 625–638.

Rothbaum, B. O., & Foa, E. B. (1993). Subtypes of posttraumatic stress disorder and duration of symptoms. In J. R. T. Davidson & E. B. Foa (Eds.), *Posttraumatic stress disorder: DSM-IV and beyond* (pp. 23–35). Washington, DC: American Psychiatric Press.

Rothbaum, B. O., Foa, E. B., Riggs, D. S., & Walsh, W. (1992). Posttraumatic stress disorder in rape victims: A prospective examination of posttraumatic stress disorder and rape victims. *Journal of Traumatic Stress*, *5*, 455–475.

Rothbaum, B. O., Hodges, L. F., & Ready, D. (2001). Virtual reality exposure therapy for Vietnam veterans with posttraumatic stress disorder. *Journal of Clinical Psychiatry*, *62*, 617–622.

Rothbaum, B. O., Price, M., Jovanovic, T., Norrholm, S. D., Gerardi, M., Dunlop, B., ... Ressler, K. J. (2014). A randomized, double-blind evaluation of D-cycloserine or alprazolam combined with virtual reality exposure therapy for posttraumatic stress disorder (PTSD) in Iraq and Afghanistan war veterans. *American Journal of Psychiatry*, *171*(6), 640–648.

Saunders, B. E., Arata, C. M., & Kilpatrick, D. G. (1990). Development of a crime-related posttraumatic stress disorder scale for women within the Symptom Checklist-90-Revised. *Journal of Traumatic Stress*, *3*, 439–448.

Schauer, M., Neuner, F., & Elbert, T. (2005). *Narrative exposure therapy: A short-term intervention for traumatic stress disorders after war, terror, or torture*. Ashland, OH: Hogrefe & Huber.

Scheeringa, M. S., Myers, L., Putnam, F. W., & Zeanah, C. H. (2012). Diagnosing PTSD in early childhood: An empirical assessment of four approaches. *Journal of Traumatic Stress*, *25*(4), 359–367. doi: 10.1002/jts.21723

Scheeringa, M. S., Zeanah, C. H., & Cohen, J. A. (2011). PTSD in children and adolescents: Toward an empirically based algorithm. *Depression and Anxiety*, *28*, 770–782.

Schnurr, P. P., Friedman, M. J., Engel, C. C., Foa, E. B., Shea, T., Chow, B. K., ... Bernardy, N. (2007). Cognitive behavioral therapy for posttraumatic stress disorder in women: A randomized controlled trial. *JAMA*, *297*, 820–830.

Schnyder, U., Muller, J., Maercker, A., & Wittman, L. (2011). Brief eclectic psychotherapy for PTSD: A randomized controlled trial. *Journal of Clinical Psychiatry*, *72*(4), 564–566.

Schumm, J. A., Dickstein, B. D., Walter, K. H., Owens, G. P., & Chard, K. M. (2015). Changes in posttraumatic cognitions predict changes in posttraumatic stress disorder symptoms during cognitive processing therapy. *Journal of Consulting and Clinical Psychology*, *83*(6), 1161–1166.

Schumm, J. A., Fredman, S. J., Monson, C. M., & Chard, K. M. (2013). Cognitive-behavioral conjoint therapy for PTSD: Initial findings for Operations Enduring and Iraqi Freedom male combat veterans and their partners. *American Journal of Family Therapy*, *41*(4), 277–287.

Schwartz, B. L., Hashtroudi, S., Herting, R. L., Schwartz, P., & Deutsch, S. I. (1996). D-cycloserine enhances implicit memory in Alzheimer patients. *Neurology*, *46*, 420–444.

Shalev, A. Y., Orr, S. P., Peri, T., & Schreiber, S. (1992). Physiologic responses to loud tones in Israeli patients with posttraumatic stress disorder. *Archives of General Psychiatry*, *49*, 870–875.

Shapiro, F. (1989b). Eye movement desensitization: A new treatment for post-traumatic stress disorder. *Journal of Behavior Therapy & Experimental Psychiatry*, *20*, 211–217.

Shapiro, F., & Maxfield, L. (2002). Eye movement desensitization and reprocessing (EMDR): Information processing in the treatment of trauma. *Journal of Clinical Psychology*, *58*(8), 933–946.

Shin, L. M., Rauch, S. L., & Pitman, R. K. (2006). Amygdala, medial prefrontal cortex, and hippocampal function in PTSD. *Annals of the New York Academy of Sciences, 1071*(1), 67–79.

Shipherd, J. C., & Beck, J. G. (1999). The effects of suppressing trauma-related thoughts on women with rape-related posttraumatic stress disorder. *Behaviour Research and Therapy, 37*, 99–112.

Shipherd, J. C., & Beck, J. G. (2005). The role of thought suppression in posttraumatic stress disorder. *Behavior Therapy, 36*, 277–287.

Shnaider, P., Pukay-Martin, N. D., Sharma, S., Jenzer, T., Fredman, S. J., Macdonald, A., & Monson, C. M. (2015). A preliminary examination of the effects of pre-treatment relationship satisfaction on treatment outcomes in cognitive-behavioral conjoint therapy for PTSD. *Couple and Family Psychology: Research and Practice, 4*, 229–238.

Shnaider, P., Vorstenbosch, V., Macdonald, A., Wells, S. Y., Monson, C. M., & Resick, P. A. (2014). Associations between functioning and PTSD symptom clusters in a dismantling trial of cognitive processing therapy in female interpersonal violence survivors. *Journal of Traumatic Stress, 27*, 526–534. doi: 10.1002/jts.21954

Sloan, D. M., Sawyer, A. T., Lowmaster, S. E., Wernick, J., & Marx, B. P. (2015). Efficacy of narrative writing as an intervention for PTSD: Does the evidence support its use? *Journal of Contemporary Psychotherapy, 45*(4), 215–225.

Smucker, M. R., Dancu, C., Foa, E. B., & Niederee, J. (1995). Imagery rescripting: A new treatment for survivors of childhood sexual abuse suffering from posttraumatic stress. *Journal of Cognitive Psychotherapy, 9*(1), 3–17.

Solomon, Z., & Mikulincer, M. (1990). Life events and combat-related posttraumatic stress disorder: The intervening role of locus of control and social support. *Military Psychology, 2*, 241–256.

Southwick, S. M., Bremner, J. D., Rasmusson, A., Morgan, C. A., III, Arnsten, A., & Charney, D. S. (1999). Role of norepinephrine in the pathophysiology and treatment of posttraumatic stress disorder. *Biological Psychiatry, 46*, 1192–1204.

Southwick, S. M., Krystal, J. H., Bremner, J. D., Morgan, C. A., Nicolaou, A. L., Nagy, L. M., ... Charney, D. S. (1997). Noradrenergic and serotonergic function in posttraumatic stress disorder. *Archives of General Psychiatry, 54*, 749–758.

Southwick, S. M., Krystal, J. H., Morgan, C. A., Johnson, D., Nagy, L. M., Nicolaou, A., ... Charney, D. S. (1993). Abnormal noradrenergic function in posttraumatic stress disorder. *Archives of General Psychiatry, 50*, 266–274.

Street, A. E., Gradus, J. L., Giasson, H. L., Vogt, D., & Resick, P. A. (2013). Gender differences among veterans deployed in support of the wars in Afghanistan and Iraq. *Journal of General Internal Medicine, 28*(2), 556–562.

Taft, C. T., Watkins, L. E., Stafford, J., Street, A. E., & Monson, C. M. (2011). Posttraumatic stress disorder and intimate relationship functioning: A meta-analysis. *Journal of Consulting and Clinical Psychology, 79*, 22–33.

Tarrier, N., Pilgrim, H., Sommerfield, C., Faragher, B., Reynolds, M., Graham, E., & Barrowclough, C. (1999). A randomized trial of cognitive therapy and imaginal exposure in the treatment of chronic posttraumatic stress disorder. *Journal of Consulting and Clinical Psychology, 67*, 13–18.

Tarrier, N., & Sommerfield, C. (2004). Treatment of chronic PTSD by cognitive therapy and exposure: 5 year follow-up. *Behavior Therapy, 35*, 231–246.

Tarrier, N., Sommerfield, C., Connell, J., Deakin, B., Pilgrim, H., & Reynolds, M. (2002). The psychophysiological responses to PTSD patients: Habituation, responses to stressful and neutral vignettes and association with treatment outcome. *Behavioral and Cognitive Psychotherapy, 30*, 129–142.

Thrasher, S., Dalgleish, T., & Yule, W. (1994). Information processing in post-traumatic stress disorder. *Behaviour Research and Therapy, 32*, 247–254.

Tolin, D. F., & Foa, E. B. (2006). Sex differences in trauma and posttraumatic stress disorder: A quantitative review of 25 years of research. *Psychological Bulletin, 132*, 959–992.

Vaiva, G., Ducrocq, F., Jezequel, K., Averland, B., Lestavel, P., Brunet, A., & Marmar, C. R. (2003). Immediate treatment with propranolol decreases posttraumatic stress disorder two months after trauma. *Biological Psychiatry, 54*, 947–949.

Vaiva, G., Thomas, P., Ducrocq, F., Fontaine, M., Boss, V., & Devos, P., ... Goudemand, M. (2004). Low posttrauma GABA plasma levels as a predictive factor in the development of acute posttraumatic stress disorder. *Biological Psychiatry, 55*, 250–254.

van der Kolk, B., Spinazzola, J., Blaustein, M., Hopper, J., Hopper, E., Korn, D., & Simpson, W. B. (2007). A randomized clinical trial of eye movement desensitization and reprocessing (EMDR), fluoxetine, and pill placebo in the treatment of posttraumatic stress disorder: Treatment effects and long-term mainte-nance. *Journal of Clinical Psychiatry*, *68*, 37–46.

Van Etten, M. L., & Taylor, S. (1998). Comparative efficacy of treatment for posttraumatic stress disorder: A meta-analysis. *Clinical Psychology and Psychotherapy*, *5*, 126–144.

van Griensven, F., Chakkraband, M. L., Thienkrua, W., Pengjuntr, W., Lopes Cardozo, B., Tantipiwatanaskul, P., & Tappero, J. W. (2006). Mental health problems among adults in tsunami-affected areas in southern Thailand. *JAMA*, *296*, 537–548.

Vogt, D., Shipherd, J., & Resick, P. A. (2012). Posttraumatic maladaptive beliefs scale: Evolution of the personal beliefs and reactions scale. *Assessment*, *19*(3), 308–317.

Vogt, D., Vaughn, R., Glickman, M. E., Schultz, M., Drainoni, M. L., Elwy, R., & Eisen, S. (2011). Gender differences in combat-related stressors and their association with postdeployment mental health in a nationally representative sample of U.S. OEF/OIF veterans. *Journal of Abnormal Psychology*, *120*(4), 797–806. doi: 10.1037/a0023452

Vrana, S., & Lauterbach, D. (1994). Prevalence of traumatic events and post-traumatic psychological symptoms in a nonclinical sample of college students. *Journal of Traumatic Stress*, *7*, 289–302.

Wachen, J. S., Jimenez, S., Smith, K., & Resick, P. A. (2014). Long-term functional outcomes of women receiving cognitive processing therapy and prolonged exposure. *Psychological Trauma: Theory, Research, Practice, and Policy*, *6*(Suppl. 1), S58–S65. doi: 10.1037/a0035741

Walser, R. D., & Hayes, S. C. (2006). Acceptance and commitment therapy in the treatment of posttraumatic stress disorder: Theoretical and applied issues. In V. M. R. Follette & I. Josef (Eds.), *Cognitive-behavioral therapies for trauma* (2nd ed., pp. 146–172). New York, NY: Guilford Press.

Watts, B. V., Schnurr, P. P., Mayo, L., Young-Xu, Y., Weeks, W. B., & Friedman, M. J. (2013). Meta-analysis of the efficacy of treatments for posttraumatic stress disorder. *Journal of Clinical Psychiatry*, *74*(6), e551–e557. doi: 10.4088/JCP.12r08225

Weathers, F. W., Blake, D. D., Schnurr, P. P., Kaloupek, D. G., Marx, B. P., & Keane, T. M. (2013a). *The Clinician-Administered PTSD Scale for DSM-5 (CAPS-5)*. Interview available from the National Center for PTSD at www.ptsd.va.gov

Weathers, F. W., Blake, D. D., Schnurr, P. P., Kaloupek, D. G., Marx, B. P., & Keane, T. M. (2013b). *The Life Events Checklist for DSM-5 (LEC-5)*. Instrument available from the National Center for PTSD at www.ptsd.va.gov

Weathers, F. W., & Keane, T. M. (1999). Psychological assessment of traumatized adults. In P. A. Saigh & J. D. Bremner (Eds.), *Posttraumatic stress disorder: A comprehensive text* (pp. 219–247). Boston, MA: Allyn & Bacon.

Weathers, F. W., Keane, T. M., & Davidson, J. R. (2001). Clinician-administered PTSD scale: A review of the first ten years of research. *Depression and Anxiety*, *13*, 132–156.

Weathers, F. W., Litz, B. T., Keane, T. M., Palmieri, P. A., Marx, B. P., & Schnurr, P. P. (2013). *The PTSD Checklist for DSM-5 (PCL-5)*. Scale available from the National Center for PTSD at www.ptsd.va.gov

Weathers, F. W., Ruscio, A. M., & Keane, T. M. (1999). Psychometric properties of nine scoring rules for the Clinician-Administered Posttraumatic Stress Disorder Scale. *Psychological Assessment*, *11*, 124–133.

Weiss, D. S., & Marmar, C. R. (1997). The Impact of Event Scale—Revised. In J. P. Wilson & T. M. Keane (Eds.), *Assessing psychological trauma and PTSD* (pp. 399–411). New York, NY: Guilford Press.

Wenninger, K., & Ehlers, A. (1998). Dysfunctional cognitions and adult psychological functioning in child sexual abuse survivors. *Journal of Traumatic Stress*, *11*, 281–300.

Widiger, T. A., & Simonsen, E. (2005). Alternative dimensional models of personality disorder: Finding a common ground. *Journal of Personality Disorders*, *19*, 110–130.

Wilson, S. A., Becker, L. A., & Tinker, R. H. (1995). Eye movement desensitisation and reprocessing (EMDR) treatment for psychologically traumatized individuals. *Journal of Consulting and Clinical Psychology*, *63*, 928–937.

Wolf, E. J., Lunney, C. A., Miller, M. W., Resick, P. A., Friedman, M. J., & Schnurr, P. P. (2012). The dissociative subtype of PTSD: A replication and extension. *Depression and Anxiety*, *29*(8), 679–688. doi: 10.1002/da.21946

Wong, M. R., & Cook, D. (1992). Shame and its contribution to PTSD. *Journal of Traumatic Stress*, *5*, 557–562.

Woon, F. L., & Hedges, D. W. (2008). Hippocampal and amygdala volumes in children and adults with childhood maltreatment-related posttraumatic stress disorder: A meta-analysis. *Hippocampus*, *18*(8), 729–736.

Yehuda, R. (2002). Current status of cortisol findings in post-traumatic stress disorder. *Psychiatric Clinics of North America, 2,* 341–348.

Yehuda, R., Giller, E. L., Southwick, S. M., Kahana, B., Boisneau, D., Ma, X., & Mason, J. W. (1994). Relationship between catecholamine excretion and PTSD symptoms in Vietnam combat veterans and holocaust survivors. In M. M. Murburg (Ed.), *Catecholamine function in post-traumatic stress disorder: Emerging concepts* (pp. 203–220). Washington, DC: American Psychiatric Press.

Yehuda, R., Siever, L. J., Teicher, M. H., Levengood, R. A., Gerber, D. K., Schmeidler, J., & Yang, R. K. (1998). Plasma norepinephrine and 3-methoxy-4-hydroxyphenylglycol concentrations and severity of depression in combat posttraumatic stress disorder and major depressive disorder. *Biological Psychiatry, 44,* 56–63.

Young, E. A., & Breslau, N. (2004). Cortisol and catecholamines in posttraumatic stress disorder: An epidemiologic community study. *Archives of General Psychiatry, 61*(4), 394–401. doi: 10.1001/archpsyc.61.4.394

Zoellner, L. A., Alvarez-Conrad, J., & Foa, E. B. (2002). Peritraumatic dissociative experiences, trauma narratives, and trauma pathology. *Journal of Traumatic Stress, 15,* 49–57.

Chapter 7

Depressive Disorders

W. Edward Craighead, Daniel N. Klein, Charles F. Gillespie,
Lorie A. Ritschel, and Katherine E. Phillips

Descriptions of individuals suffering from depressive disorders have been remarkably similar for centuries, though the designation of specific criteria for diagnosis of these disorders has been relatively recent. Descriptions of depression exist in literary references across the world and throughout history; one of the very earliest examples is the biblical description of Job's depression.

In U.S. history, a number of well-known individuals from all walks of life have suffered from depression. These include Abraham Lincoln, who suffered at least two depressive episodes; William James, one of the founders of psychology and the primary force in establishing it as a discipline at Harvard University in the 1890s; actors such as Anne Hathaway, Jon Hamm, and Brad Pitt; J. K. Rowling, author of the world-renowned Harry Potter book series; astronaut Buzz Aldrin, who was the second human to walk on the moon; television personalities such as Drew Carey, David Letterman, and newscaster Mike Wallace; musicians such as Beyoncé Knowles, Bruce Springsteen, and Sheryl Crow; and athletes such as Delonte West, an NBA basketball player, and Amanda Beard, a gold-medal-winning Olympic swimmer. Although each had a somewhat different experience and course of the disorder, the symptoms and defining characteristics were remarkably similar.

It is fairly common to hear someone remark, "I am so depressed," because almost everyone has experienced a sad mood, one of the primary indicators of clinical depression. Most often, however, this comment describes transient feelings of sadness, dysphoria, or disappointment that dissipate within a fairly brief period of time. At clinical levels, the symptoms of both major depressive disorder (MDD) and persistent depressive disorder (PDD or chronic depression) are clearly distinguishable from the transient dysphoric states that most people are experiencing when they somewhat casually refer to themselves as "depressed." The feelings of sadness and anhedonia indicative of clinical depression are of much greater intensity, depth, and duration and are more encompassing than the typical negative mood states accompanying the more casual complaint of being "depressed." Furthermore, clinical depression, by definition, is disruptive to the individual's life and environment, including characteristic patterns of behavioral, cognitive, emotional, and biological dysfunction far beyond the level of disruption caused by blue, sad, or depressed transient mood states, even when this dysphoric mood state might continue for several days.

In addition to extraordinary personal and family suffering, depression also produces significant societal burdens, such as an increased use of social and medical services (Marcus & Olfson, 2010). There are also enormous financial costs for its treatment and for lost productivity due to impairment at work or absenteeism (Bruffaerts et al., 2012; Greenberg, Fournier, Sisitsky, Pike, & Kessler, 2015). In fact, when considered among all diseases, depressive disorders rank first among disorders responsible for the global disease burden with all concomitant economic costs to society, and it also ranks first among the disabilities of 15- to 44-year-old U.S. citizens (Greenberg et al., 2015; World Health Organization [WHO], 2015). Furthermore, depression, especially recurrent or chronic depression, is very strongly related to suicide attempts and completions (Mościcki, 2001; WHO, 2015), particularly when depressed individuals reach a state of hopelessness regarding the disorder or not finding a way to overcome it. This chapter focuses on *major depressive disorder* (MDD), the most prevalent form of depression, and *persistent depressive disorder* (PDD), which accounts for almost 30% of all cases of depressive disorders (Murphy & Byrne, 2012).

Symptoms and Diagnostic Criteria

Depression (formerly called melancholia) was first described in a systematic fashion by the Greek physician Hippocrates (ca. 460 to 377 BCE). He based his naturalistic classification system on the writings of Greek philosophers such as Thales, who had lived about a century earlier. At that point in history, Greek philosophers posited that the basic elements of the world comprised earth, air, fire, and water. Hippocrates maintained that each of these elements was represented in the body by one of four humors—yellow bile, black bile, phlegm, and blood. In a healthy person these humors were maintained in balance, but disease occurred when the humors were out of balance. Melancholia, it was hypothesized, resulted from the presence of too much black bile. This "scientific" view of human disease was distinct from earlier, more religious interpretations. Eventually, the great Greek physician Galen (128 to ca. 200 CE) successfully interpreted this model in such a fashion as to make it palatable to the Christian religion, so it found some favor through the Middle Ages.

In relatively modern times, the German psychiatrist Emil Kraepelin (1856–1926) first used the word *depression* to characterize his clinical observations of patients being treated in German hospitals where he served as chief psychiatrist. In the sixth edition of his *Textbook of Psychiatry* (1899), Kraepelin described both "dementia praecox" and "manic-depressive insanity" (see Decker, 2004). These disorders roughly correspond to current diagnoses of schizophrenia (dementia praecox) and bipolar disorder (manic-depressive insanity). Depression continued to be viewed as one end of the manic-depressive continuum for much of the 20th century. The major exceptions to this were Adolf Meyer's more psychosocially based description of a "depressive reaction" to negative life experiences, and the psychodynamic descriptions of depression by Abraham (1911) and Freud (1917/1950). Even within these alternative conceptual frameworks, the descriptions of the phenomenology of depression remained essentially identical to the clinical characterization of depression articulated by Kraepelin. Over the course of the last half of the 20th century, empirical data and theoretical developments led to the separation and specific distinctions of depression and manic-depressive disorders. Consequently, criteria for MDD and PDD were developed and presented formally as psychiatric diagnoses in the American Psychiatric Association's *Diagnostic and Statistical Manual of Mental Disorders*—first as a depressive reaction and manic depressive illness, depressed type (*DSM-II*; American Psychiatric Association [APA], 1968) and then as major depressive disorder and dysthymic disorder, a conglomeration of earlier constructs of neurotic depression and depressive personality, respectively (*DSM-III*; APA, 1980). In the *DSM-IV* (APA, 1994), the primary clinical forms of depression were major depressive disorder (with categorizations for both single episode and recurrent or chronic cases), dysthymia, and depressive episodes as they occur in the context of bipolar disorder. The *DSM-5* (APA, 2013a) includes major depressive disorder (MDD) as one of the depressive disorders, and there were no significant changes from *DSM-IV* in the primary criteria for MDD. *DSM-5* also combined two previous diagnoses—dysthymic disorder and major depressive episode, chronic subtype—under a single rubric labeled persistent depressive disorder (PDD). The other depressive disorders include disruptive mood regulation disorder (included in an attempt to reduce the number of children perhaps inappropriately diagnosed with bipolar disorder—see Chapter 8), premenstrual dysphoric disorder, substance- or medication-induced depressive disorder, depressive disorder due to another medical condition, and other specified and unspecified depressive disorders (see APA, 2013a). In this chapter, we focus solely on MDD and PDD.

MAJOR DEPRESSIVE DISORDER

DSM-5 identifies nine symptoms of depression, and a formal diagnosis is made when a person meets at least five of the nine symptoms (see Figure 7.1). Of those five, the person must endorse one or both of the following symptoms: (1) dysphoric mood (sad, empty, or tearful) and/or (2) anhedonia, or the loss of interest or pleasure in almost all activities (APA, 2013a). In addition, the individual must also experience at least four additional symptoms (three if both dysphoric mood and anhedonia are present), as shown in Figure 7.1. Finally, the person must report experiencing marked distress or a decrease in functioning for at least 2 weeks during which these symptoms were present for most of the day, for more days than not. Notably, a person can meet criteria for MDD without exhibiting all the listed symptoms, and different people may have different combinations of the symptoms, resulting in a variety of presentations of the disorder. Although we follow the *DSM-5* diagnostic system, perhaps the rapidly increasing view is that depression is not a single disorder but rather comprises heterogeneous disorders, a view that influences the writing at various places throughout this chapter.

When diagnosing MDD, it is important to consider other problems that might cause an individual to experience depression. In particular, *DSM-5* specifies that when the depressive symptoms are substance-induced (either by prescription medications or by recreational drugs) or are directly attributable to a general medical illness, then MDD is not the appropriate primary diagnosis. For example, a person with hypothyroidism may meet all the criteria for MDD (the symptoms of the two disorders demonstrate substantial overlap); however, in this case hypothyroidism may better account for the presence of these symptoms than MDD and therefore should be the primary diagnosis. Of course, it is entirely possible for a person to meet criteria for *both* hypothyroidism and MDD, which

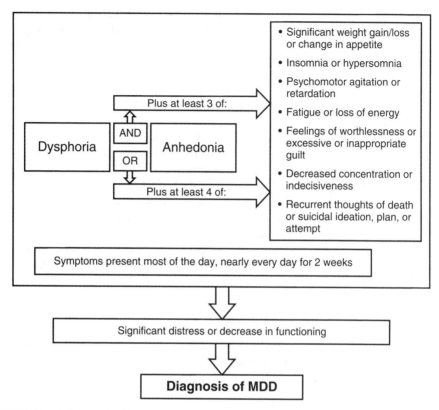

FIGURE 7.1 A Schematic Illustration of the Diagnostic Criteria for Major Depression

underscores the importance of conducting thorough diagnostic assessments that include questions about related medical illnesses, substances that can cause or mimic depression, and other possible primary *DSM* disorders.

There are a number of additional diagnostic elements called *specifiers* that need to be incorporated into a clinical assessment of MDD. First, the clinician indicates whether this is a single (i.e., first) episode of major depression or a recurrent form of depression. A second important specifier is the level of depression severity. Specifically, a major depressive episode may be characterized as mild, moderate, or severe; when assigning a "severe" specifier, the clinician also indicates whether psychotic features are part of the clinical presentation. Other depression specifiers that have potential implications for treatment decisions include the following:

1. *Chronic MDD*, in which depression occurs continuously and without remission for at least 2 years. In the *DSM-5*, chronic MDD has been consolidated with dysthymia into PDD, which is explained further in this chapter.

2. *Atypical MDD*, which characterizes approximately 15% of depressed patients and is marked by mood reactivity (i.e., mood brightens in response to positive events or potential positive events), hypersomnia, extended fatigue, heightened sensitivity to criticism, and a significant increase in appetite and weight gain.

3. *Peripartum (formerly postpartum) MDD*, in which a major depressive episode occurs during pregnancy or within the 4 weeks following delivery. It is estimated that 3% to 6% of pregnancies include a depressive episode either during or in the month following pregnancy (APA, 2013a).

Two other specifiers, melancholia and seasonal pattern, retain the *DSM-IV* terminology but do not appear to be of great clinical significance. That is, knowing that a person may be more vulnerable to depression onset in the fall (or even another season) might help in earlier identification of an episode, but the data for differing treatments based on either of these specifiers are meager, and there are no data to suggest that a fundamentally differential course of treatment is warranted.

DSM-5 added two new specifiers for MDD (APA, 2013a). For patients who meet criteria for MDD and who endorse at least three symptoms of a manic or hypomanic episode but who do not meet the full criteria for bipolar disorder, the specifier "with mixed features" can appropriately be added. This specifier is intended to allow the clinician to note the presence of symptoms that are of clinical significance with regard to the potential future emergence of a manic or hypomanic episode. In addition, the clinician may add the specifier "with anxious distress" for those individuals who display considerable overlap between symptoms of depression and anxiety. This specifier was added based on the body of literature that has emerged over the past several decades and indicates that the presence of anxiety in the course of MDD can affect treatment decisions and prognosis. Finally, *DSM-5* has removed the *DSM-IV* bereavement exclusion criterion that applied when the disorder occurred within 2 months of a significant loss. *DSM-5* encourages the clinician to make a differential diagnosis between bereavement and MDD.

PERSISTENT DEPRESSIVE DISORDER

Chronic depression can take a number of forms that vary in their pattern of severity over time. *DSM-IV* (APA, 1994) used the separate diagnostic labels of dysthymic disorder and major depressive episode, chronic. As noted, these categories were combined under the rubric of *persistent depressive disorder* (PDD) in *DSM-5* (APA, 2013b). *DSM-5* identifies six symptoms of depression typically seen in patients with PDD. A formal diagnosis is made when a person meets at least two of six symptoms accompanied by the occurrence of a depressed mood for most of the day, for more days than not, for at least 2 years. The six symptoms include poor appetite or overeating, insomnia or hypersomnia, low energy or fatigue, low self-esteem, poor concentration or difficulty making decisions, and feelings of hopelessness. A minimum of two symptoms must be present consistently throughout the 2-year duration; in addition the patient must report that the symptoms have never remitted for more than 2 months during the 2-year period. Finally, the person must report experiencing marked distress or impairment in social, occupational, or other important areas of functioning. The amalgamation of the *DSM-IV* diagnoses of dysthymia and chronic major depressive episode as PDD in *DSM-5* was based on research indicating that there are virtually no differences between patients with each of these conditions on comorbidity, psychosocial functioning, depressive cognitions, coping style, early adversity, family history, and treatment response (McCullough et al., 2000, 2003).

DSM-5 includes a number of diagnostic specifiers that need to be incorporated into a clinical assessment of PDD. The clinician can use these specifiers to note the severity, age of onset and state of remission. As is the case with MDD, a diagnosis of PDD can include specifiers of anxious distress, mixed features, and melancholic features, among others. More specific to the PDD diagnosis are four specifiers that indicate the course of the chronic depression. These are

- *Pure dysthymic syndrome*, which indicates that full criteria for MDD have not been met in the previous 2 years.
- *Persistent depressive episode*, which indicates full criteria for major depressive episode have been met at some point in the preceding 2-year period.
- *Intermittent major depressive episode, with current episode*, which is designed to capture individuals who are currently in a nonchronic major depressive episode.
- *Intermittent major depressive episode, without current episode*, which indicates that the full criteria for a nonchronic major depressive episode were previously met at some point in the preceding 2 years.

DISTINCTION BETWEEN CHRONIC AND NONCHRONIC DEPRESSION

Despite their similarities, there are a number of differences between PDD and MDD that support their separation. Given the recent *DSM-5* changes outlined above, little research has been done looking specifically at differences between MDD and the recently defined PDD. However, there is a substantial literature comparing individuals with dysthymic disorder and major depressive episode, chronic, to those with nonchronic MDD. Given the substantial overlap between PDD and what was formerly labeled as dysthymia and major depressive episode, chronic, we will use the term *chronic depression* to encompass all PDD diagnoses in summarizing the data comparing chronic and nonchronic depression.

Persons with chronic depression have greater comorbidity with anxiety, substance use, and personality disorders than persons with nonchronic MDD (Blanco et al., 2010; Gilmer et al., 2005; Klein, Shankman, Lewinsohn, Rohde, & Seeley, 2004; Pepper et al., 1995; Sang et al., 2011). In addition, chronic depression is associated with more extreme normal-range personality traits, such as higher neuroticism and lower extraversion (Hirschfeld, Klerman, Andreasen, Clayton, & Keller, 1986; Klein, Taylor, Dickstein, & Harding, 1988; Sang et al., 2011); lower self-esteem (Blanco et al., 2010); higher levels of at least some depressive cognitive biases (Klein et al., 1988; Riso et al., 2003); higher levels of experiential avoidance (Barnhofer Brennan, Crane, Duggan, & Williams, 2014), and greater suicidality (Garvey, Tollefson, & Tuason,1986; Gilmer et al., 2005; Holm-Denoma, Berlim, Fleck, & Joiner, 2006; Klein, Shankman, & Rose, 2006). Compared to persons with nonchronic MDD, individuals with chronic depression also report having experienced greater early adversity, maladaptive parenting, and childhood emotional abuse (Barnhofer et al., 2014; Fisher et al., 2013; Lizardi et al., 1995; Wiersma et al., 2011), and are more likely to have a family history of depression among first-degree relatives (Blanco et al., 2010; Klein et al., 1995; Klein, Shankman, Lewinsohn, Rohde, & Seeley, 2004; Sang et al., 2011). Chronic depression aggregates specifically in families;

the relatives of probands with chronic depression have significantly higher rates of chronic depression than the relatives of patients with nonchronic MDD (Klein et al., 1995; Klein, Shankman, et al., 2004; Mondimore et al., 2006). Consistent with its definition, chronic depression predicts a more persistent course and poorer outcomes than nonchronic MDD (Rhebergen et al., 2009). For example, in a 10-year follow-up study, patients with chronic depression had a significantly higher level of depressive symptomatology, spent a significantly greater portion of the follow-up meeting criteria for a depressive disorder (i.e., a significantly smaller proportion recovered from all depressive disorders during the follow-up period), and had a greater number of suicide attempts and hospitalizations than patients with nonchronic MDD. Moreover, the distinction between chronic and nonchronic depression was very stable over time (Klein et al., 2006). Finally, patients with forms of chronic depression that include periods of major depression have lower response and remission rates following intensive treatment than patients with nonchronic MDD (Köhler et al., 2015) and are more likely to profit from a combination of antidepressant medications and psychotherapy (Craighead & Dunlop, 2014). Thus, despite PDD being closely related to classic episodic MDD, the two conditions appear to differ in significant ways. Interestingly, although PDD is thought of as symptomatically milder, the cumulative burden of persistent depressive symptoms and impaired functioning is substantial and can be greater than that of episodic MDD (Blanco et al., 2010; Gilmer et al., 2005; Hellerstein, Agosti, Bosi, & Black, 2010; Leader & Klein, 1996).

Given the differences between PDD and MDD, a final question concerns whether the two groups differ qualitatively or by only degree. The specificity of familial aggregation (Klein et al., 1995; Mondimore et al., 2006) and stability over time (Klein et al., 2006) raise the possibility of qualitative differences. Klein and Kotov (2016) directly addressed the issue of whether chronicity lies on a continuum or manifests natural boundaries in a 10-year follow-up of depressed outpatients. They found strong and consistent evidence for a nonlinear relationship between degree of chronicity during the first 30 months of follow-up and symptoms and psychosocial functioning at the 10-year follow-up, supporting the existence of qualitatively distinct subgroups. Moreover, when the course data were used to generate empirically defined persistent and nonpersistent subgroups, the two groups differed on most of the features previously reported to distinguish chronic and nonchronic depression. In light of these differences, it appears worthwhile to search for etiological and pathophysiological differences between PDD and nonchronic MDD. Unfortunately, there is a paucity of research on this topic.

Prevalence

Prevalence of MDD

Major depressive disorder is one of the most commonly diagnosed psychiatric disorders among adults, with U.S. lifetime prevalence rates of approximately 17%. Prevalence rates are between 20% and 25% for women and from 9% to 12% for men; point prevalence rates are approximately 6% for women and 3% for men (Kessler, Chiu, Demler, & Walters, 2005). In keeping with these prevalence statistics women, starting in adolescence, are 1.5 to 3 times more likely than men to experience MDD (Hankin et al., 1998).

Prevalence of MDD shows variability among different racial and ethnicity groups in the United States. Lifetime prevalence rates of depression are highest among Native Americans (19.2%), while lifetime prevalence rates among African Americans and Asian Americans are lower at 8.9% and 8.8%, respectively. Hispanic/Latino Americans generally experience a 9.6% lifetime prevalence of MDD, but the rates are higher among certain Latino subgroups (i.e., Puerto Ricans) and among U.S.-born, English-language-proficient, and third-generation Latinos (Alegría et al., 2007; Hasin, Goodwin, Stinson, & Grant, 2005; Alderete, Vega, Colody, & Aguilar-Gaxiola, 1999).

Although it is a debated issue (see Costello, Erkanli, & Angold, 2006), the prevalence of MDD and depressive symptoms appears to have increased among recent birth cohorts (Fergusson, Horwood, Ridder, & Beautrais, 2005; Twenge et al., 2010; Twenge, 2015) and in the population in general (Hidaka, 2012), which suggests that the lifetime prevalence may ultimately be higher for current younger cohorts. The age at which the first episode of MDD occurs also has been decreasing, such that peak years for first onset currently are between 15 and 29 years of age, with the peak onset for females being even earlier at 15 to 20 (Fergusson et al., 2005; Weissman et al., 2006). At least one half of these individuals with early onset will experience subsequent depressive episodes, and a substantial minority will go on to experience chronic depression (Mueller et al., 1999; Rohde, Lewinsohn, Klein, Seeley, & Gau, 2012). Thus, MDD is a major health problem for which it is important to develop a better understanding and interventions.

PREVALENCE OF PDD

Epidemiological studies of nationally representative samples in the United States have reported 12-month prevalence rates of dysthymic disorder (now PDD) that range from 0.5% to 2.5%; lifetime prevalence has ranged from 0.9% to 6.4% (Blanco et al., 2010; Kessler et al., 1994; Kessler, Berglund, Demler, Jin, & Walters, 2005; Riolo, Nguyen, Greden, & King, 2005). The World Mental Health Surveys indicate that rates of what is now termed PDD are higher in developed countries than in developing countries (Gureje, 2011).

In the only published epidemiological study of chronic MDD, Blanco et al. (2010) reported 12-month and lifetime prevalence rates of 1.5% and 3.1%, respectively. Finally, Murphy and Byrne (2012) recently reported that among a nationally representative Australian sample, the lifetime prevalence of all forms of chronic depression combined was 4.6%.

The prevalence of PDD is almost two times greater among women than men (Blanco et al., 2010; Kessler et al., 1994). PDD is associated with lower income; data on the effects of race, ethnicity, and education are inconsistent (Blanco et al., 2010; Riolo et al., 2005).

Psychological Models of Depression

Depression is frequently thought of as a disturbance of mood or emotion (Engel & DeRubeis, 1993); however, not everyone who meets criteria for depression reports feeling sad. Although the diagnostic criteria require the presence of either a sad mood or loss of interest or pleasure, the remaining criteria are related to changes in behavior, physiology, or cognition (APA, 2013a). The *DSM-5* criteria for MDD—which must be present most of the day nearly every day during a 2-week period—can be broadly categorized as follows:

Emotional Symptoms of Depression
- Depressed mood

Behavioral or Physiological Symptoms of Depression
- Markedly diminished interest or pleasure in all, or almost all, activities (anhedonia)
- Significant weight loss (when not dieting) or weight gain, or a significant increase or decrease in appetite
- Insomnia or hypersomnia
- Psychomotor agitation or retardation
- Fatigue or loss of energy

Cognitive Symptoms of Depression
- Feelings of worthlessness or excessive or inappropriate guilt
- Diminished ability to think or concentrate, or indecisiveness
- Recurrent thoughts of death, recurrent suicidal ideation without a specific plan, or a suicide attempt or a specific plan for committing suicide

The symptoms of PDD are similar to MDD, except that they must be present most of the day more days than not for a 2-year period, and there are additional cognitive symptoms (feelings of hopelessness and poor self-esteem). Some of the MDD symptoms (e.g., psychomotor agitation and recurrent thoughts of death, among others), however, are not included in the symptom criteria for PDD.

It is possible to receive a diagnosis of PDD and MDD simply by endorsing predominantly behavioral, biological, or cognitive symptoms. Because both behaviors and cognitions play such important roles in the etiology and maintenance of depression, it is critical to understand both categories of dysfunctions for research and clinical purposes, so we now turn to an overview of the major behavioral (including interpersonal behaviors), cognitive, and biological theories and research regarding depression.

Behavioral Models of Depression

The 1960s and 1970s were marked by the development and expansion of behavioral models of the etiology and maintenance of depression (e.g., Ferster, 1965, 1966, 1973; Lewinsohn, 1974). Skinner (1953) previously had proposed that depression is related to a reduction in behaviors that elicit positive reinforcement from the environment. Ferster elaborated on Skinner's ideas and postulated that three proximal causes were likely to contribute to a depressive shift in affect. First, infrequent positive reinforcement is likely to lead to an overall decline in behaviors. Second, behaviors are further inhibited by the presence of anxiety. Third, unexpected changes in environmental stimuli (including interpersonal interactions and human relationships) decrease the frequency of behaviors.

In other words, people tend to withdraw in the absence of positive reinforcement and when anxiety or unexpected environmental changes occur. Ferster (1973) also posited that a decrease in positive environmental reinforcement is likely to result in a narrowing of an individual's behavioral repertoire in an effort to prevent further loss of positive reinforcement. Within this framework, depression is caused by behavioral inhibition and maintained through a process of avoidance or escape (negative reinforcement).

Lewinsohn and colleagues (Lewinsohn, 1974; Lewinsohn & Gotlib, 1995; Lewinsohn, Youngren, & Grosscup, 1979) further refined Ferster's work with a focus on schedules of positive reinforcement. Lewinsohn agreed with his behavioral predecessors that depression develops when individuals experience a low rate of positive reinforcement for their behavior. He extended previous conceptualizations by positing that the rate of positive reinforcement is contingent upon three elements: (1) the number of reinforcing activities in which an individual engages, (2) the amount of positive reinforcement that the environment is able to provide, and (3) the skillfulness of the individual in eliciting reinforcement from the environment (i.e., social and interpersonal skills deficiencies are fundamentally related to low rates of environmental reinforcement). Lewinsohn further hypothesized that, in addition to low rates of positive reinforcement, depression could be caused by elevated rates of aversive experiences or events.

Some scholars theorized that depression results from the interaction of cognitive and behavioral difficulties. For example, Pyszcynski and Greenberg (1987) concurred with early behaviorists that depression is related to decreases in environmental reinforcement. They posited, additionally, that cognitive and emotional changes initiate and perpetuate behavioral changes in depression. Specifically, they hypothesized that onset and maintenance of depression are predicated upon a loss of a source of self-esteem that is followed by an increase in self-focused attention (see Mor & Winquist, 2002). They suggested that this process increases the salience of the lost source of esteem as well as the negative affect induced by the loss. The resulting self-criticism interferes with social performance, which the individual perceives as validation of the self-criticism. As a result, self-criticism and negative affect increase, thereby perpetuating the cycle.

Taken together, these behavioral theories called attention to the importance of both positive and negative reinforcement in the etiology and maintenance of depression. The question, then, is how these models translate into observable human behaviors. The next section describes the clinical presentation of the behavioral symptoms of depression and the empirical evidence supporting behavioral theories of depression.

BEHAVIORAL DEFICITS IN MDD

Three symptom classes commonly found in depression are anhedonia, amotivation, and avoidance. Together, they weave a vicious web that perpetuates depressive episodes. As individuals lose interest in activities that previously brought them pleasure (anhedonia), they subsequently lose the desire to continue to attempt those activities (amotivation). As energy and motivation decrease, individuals often prefer not to engage in activities or spend time with other people because these activities (a) require energy they do not have and (b) are no longer rewarding. Depressed individuals, consequently, find greater satisfaction in doing nothing (avoidance). As a result, amotivation and avoidance are targeted as primary behavioral deficits in the behavioral treatment of depression.

Amotivation and Anhedonia

One of the most commonly reported symptoms of depression is a loss of motivation or ability to carry out the necessary tasks of one's life. Many depressed individuals know what they need to do; they simply lack the motivation or energy to engage in tasks of living. For example, it is not unusual for patients to report that they have difficulty getting out of bed and going to work or school. They also may be neglecting activities at home, such as washing the dishes or cleaning the house. In more extreme cases, they may not even attend to personal tasks such as exercise, dressing, or showering. Completing small tasks often has the effect of helping patients build self-efficacy (Bandura, 1977) or mastery, increasing the likelihood that they will receive positive reinforcement from their environment. Patients are, therefore, encouraged to engage in behaviors despite their lack of motivation, under the assumption that motivation will follow activity rather than the inverse.

Neuropsychological research suggests that behavioral symptoms in depression are related to deficits in the behavioral activation system. Gray (1987) proposed that behavior is largely monitored by two systems: the behavioral activation system (BAS), which is responsive to reward cues, and the behavioral inhibition system (BIS), which is responsive to punishment cues (i.e., the BAS is behavior generating, whereas the BIS is behavior inhibiting). Applying Gray's model, Davidson (1992) posited that an underactive BAS is related to reductions in positive emotion and motivation. These reductions, in turn, are risk factors for depression (see Bijttebier, Beck, Claes, & Vandereycken, 2009, for a review). Davidson (1992, 1998) proposed a model suggesting that behavioral activation is modulated by activity in the left prefrontal cortex, while behavioral inhibition (or withdrawal) is modulated by activity in the right prefrontal cortex. Several studies have supported this hypothesis (see McFarland, Shankman, Tenke, Bruder, & Klein, 2006, for a review). The treatment section of this chapter presents more details regarding behavioral interventions.

Avoidance and Passivity

Emotions and emotional states frequently can be identified by the behavioral patterns that accompany them. For example, if an individual desires to hit another person, one typically infers the person is feeling angry. Or if an individual runs away from a particular situation (e.g., a burning building), it would be reasonable to assume that he is feeling fear. Similarly, sadness has a behavioral correlate: to isolate oneself.

Avoidance has long been recognized as a common consequence of depression and may possibly play an even larger role in depression than the more commonly studied deficits in approach (Ferster, 1973; Manos, Kanter, & Busch, 2010). For depressed individuals, avoidance functions to minimize distress, thereby becoming a negative reinforcer. For example, if a patient calls in sick to work because he would rather lie in bed all day, he feels better in the moment because he does not have to go to work and interact with others. In this way, calling in sick (avoidance) has been reinforced as a solution to the experience of dread about work.

The consequences of avoidant behaviors, however, are twofold. First, avoidance is a passive, short-term strategy that often results in ever-mounting long-term difficulties. For example, repeatedly calling in sick is likely to cause problems with coworkers and bosses, and the patient may soon face disciplinary action or termination for repeated absences. Thus, ongoing avoidance typically creates a new set of problems to be solved. The second consequence of avoidance is that it reduces the opportunity for depressed individuals to encounter positive reinforcement in their environment (see Dimidjian, Martell, Addis, & Herman-Dunn, 2008); that is, it is hard to be told that you are doing a good job at work if you are not even going to work! It is also difficult to derive pleasure from friendly interactions when friends are avoided. This combination of negative reinforcement and lack of positive reinforcement fuels the cycle of avoidant behavior, and depressed individuals become more and more withdrawn and increasingly depressed (Martell, Addis, & Jacobson, 2010). As time goes on, an individual's behavioral repertoire narrows further until passivity is the dominant behavioral response (Dimidjian et al., 2008). Avoidance and inhibition are both related to BIS activation (Trew, 2011); higher BIS sensitivity is commonly found in depressed samples and changes in this sensitivity have been found to predict changes in depression over time (Bijttebier et al., 2009; Kasch, Rottenberg, Arnow, & Gotlib, 2002; Brown, 2007).

Cognitive Models of Depression

Although depressed individuals experience different combinations of symptoms, most people who are suffering from depression report some type of cognitive disturbance. During the 1970s, there was a veritable explosion of research regarding cognitive theories of depression. The following sections review the relevant cognitive models that continue to guide current research regarding the major cognitive deficits present in depression (for more extensive reviews, see Joormann & Quinn, 2014; Kircanski, Joormann, & Gotlib, 2012; Snyder, 2013).

BECK'S COGNITIVE MODEL

Beck's cognitive theory of depression (Beck, 1968, 1976; Beck, Rush, Shaw, & Emery, 1979) grew out of his experiences working with depressed patients who often made personally evaluative statements that were negatively biased. His model comprises three components: negative self-statements, cognitive errors, and underlying schemas or core beliefs. In this model, the combination of information processing deficits (cognitive errors) and enduring negative cognitive patterns (schemas/core beliefs) contributes to the development and maintenance of depression (see Figure 7.2). That is, Beck postulates that the processes and ways that people think about a situation are critical elements in the development of depression. Furthermore, cognitive behavior therapy (CBT) focuses on teaching patients to change these statements, processes, and beliefs so they become more adaptive and the more positive views are internalized.

Automatic Thoughts

Automatic thoughts are the words that go through one's mind frequently in response to an event. They are considered automatic because one does not have to work to generate these thoughts; rather, they arise spontaneously without effort. Beck and colleagues (1979) noted that depressed individuals tend to have *negative* automatic thoughts or self-statements. These thoughts may be about themselves, the world, and the future (frequently referred to as the cognitive triad). Although depressed individuals generally

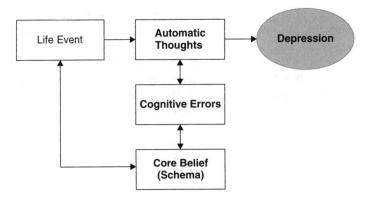

FIGURE 7.2   A Graphic View of Beck's Cognitive Model of Depression

are aware of these thoughts, they often are unaware that their thoughts contain errors or distortions and that these automatic thoughts serve to maintain or exacerbate negative mood. Consider a situation in which you are walking down the hallway at work and you pass by a colleague who does not acknowledge you. Assuming that you are not depressed, you might say something to yourself like, "Tom must be awfully busy today," or, "I wonder what Tom was reading—he looked like he was really into it." According to Beck's model, a depressed individual would be more likely to have the automatic thought, "Tom probably didn't acknowledge me because he doesn't like me. Nobody does—I'm not a very likable person. I guess I'll never fit in or have friends." Hence, the depressed individual tells himself that he is inherently unlikable (negative view of self), that he does not fit in (negative view of the world), and that this condition will last indefinitely (negative view of the future). In this example, the depressed individual is aware of his thoughts but does not seem to question them as invalid. Rather, he believes them to be true. For someone vulnerable to depression, the emotional response is similar to what it would be if the distorted automatic thoughts were actually true.

Cognitive Distortions

A central tenet of Beck's cognitive theory of depression is that the thinking of a depressed individual is not only negatively biased and automatic, but also fraught with cognitive errors. According to Beck, these errors are activated by continuous negative self-statements or they derive from the individual's self-schema or core beliefs. Some examples of cognitive errors are (adapted from J. S. Beck, 1995):

- *All-or-nothing thinking*: viewing things in black-and-white terms, rather than as occurring on a continuum.
  - *Example*: "I got only a B on that test. What a total failure."
- *Arbitrary inference*: drawing negative conclusions in the absence of corroborating evidence.
  - *Example*: "My husband always comes home late from work; he must be having an affair."

- *Overgeneralization*: drawing conclusions that far exceed the bounds of the current situation.
  - *Example*: "I don't get along with my neighbor. I'll never get along with anyone."
- *Selective abstraction*: concentrating on one detail about a situation and ignoring others, thereby not seeing the whole picture.
  - *Example*: "My teacher took 2 points off my essay. I'm a terrible writer."
- *Magnification/minimization*: tending to unreasonably magnify the negative aspects of a person or situation and minimize the positive aspects.
  - *Example*: "Who cares that I got a good overall performance evaluation? I got a 'needs improvement' in one area."
- *Personalization*: believing that external events happen because of one's own inherent inadequacy, weakness, or other flaw; disregarding contradictory evidence.
  - *Example*: "That person just cut me off in traffic because he thinks I'm a bad driver."
- *Emotional reasoning*: thinking something must be true because of the strength of the feeling behind the thought.
  - *Example*: "I know my boyfriend says I'm a great person with lots of great qualities, but I just feel like an awful, worthless person."

As is evident in these examples, these kinds of cognitive processing errors function to screen out positive information and to bias negative or neutral information in a negative way.

Core Beliefs

Sacco and Beck (1995) noted that the cognitive theory of depression is predicated on a diathesis-stress model. Depressogenic schemas begin to develop early in life (diathesis) and in most cases are latent until they are activated by life events (usually negative and stressful) and after that serve as a filter for incoming information. Hence, depressogenic schemas ultimately predispose individuals to depression because they increase the likelihood of cognitive errors and negative self-statements or automatic thoughts and result in negative emotional states. In addition to the cognitive triad, Beck postulated that depressed individuals also show a stable negative cognitive *pattern* when interpreting environmental information. As described, these patterns are based on an individual's fundamental beliefs or assumptions—schemas—that he holds about himself.

Humans use various schemas to organize incoming data and to enhance processing speed in everyday life. For example, if you are sitting in a booth and someone hands you a menu and gives you silverware, your "restaurant schema" will be activated, and you will have a certain set of expectations about what will happen next (e.g., a person will soon come to the table and ask you what you want to eat and drink). Hence, schemas can effectively streamline cognitive processing by consolidating mental effort. In depression, however, people often hold fundamental beliefs about themselves that are far less innocuous. For example, a depressed individual might believe she is unlovable, that she must be perfect, or that she is worthless. Hence, all incoming information is organized according to these schemas, which results in cognitive distortions or errors when basic beliefs are not accurate reflections of reality.

LEARNED HELPLESSNESS MODEL AND EXPLANATORY STYLE

The learned helplessness theory (Peterson, Maier, & Seligman, 1993; Seligman, 1975), which developed within a behavioral learning framework, proposed that individuals become depressed because they view their situations as futile, and they view themselves as unable to bring about changes in these situations. The authors of this theory posited that people begin to experience feelings of helplessness in situations where outcomes are perceived to be independent of behavior. In essence, people give up trying when they have determined that an aversive situation is unlikely to change no matter what they do. Further, Seligman specifically hypothesized that helplessness was related to the motivational, emotional, behavioral, and cognitive deficits often seen in depression (see Engel & DeRubeis, 1993).

As Seligman and his colleagues refined the research on learned helplessness, they began to explore the concept of attributional styles. Specifically, they posited that the crux of helplessness did not develop because people perceived there was no relationship between their actions and situational outcomes; rather, it was the way people explained this lack of a contingency to themselves that was crucial (Abramson, Metalsky, & Alloy, 1989; Seligman, Abramson, Semmel, & von Baeyer, 1979).

According to the revised model of learned helplessness (Abramson et al., 1989; Abramson, Seligman, & Teasdale, 1978), three essential belief dimensions are considered in regard to the preponderance of depressive symptoms: internal-external; global-specific, or stable-unstable. People may make attributions about causality that run the gamut from "not at all my fault" to "completely my fault." Abramson et al. (1978) refer to these attributions as external or internal styles. For example, the student from a previous example may attribute her test failure to her teacher by saying, "That teacher is so unfair" (external style). Alternatively, she may blame herself for her failure by saying, "I am so stupid" (internal style). The second dimension refers to the specificity or universality of a belief. For example, on the one hand, an individual who gets into a fender bender may say to herself, "I am a terrible driver" (specific style); on the other hand, she may say, "I am always terrible at everything" (global style). Finally, stable-unstable refers to the extent to which an individual believes that a problem is either temporary or permanent. Someone who recently went through the breakup of a relationship may say, "This is hard, but I learned a lot that will help me in my next relationship" (unstable style). Alternatively, she may say, "I will be alone for the rest of my life" (stable style).

Abramson and colleagues (1989) found that the most depressed individuals have explanatory styles for negative events that are internal, global, and stable. In the relationship example, this individual might say to herself, "This breakup is all my fault. If only I weren't so annoying and clingy, I wouldn't have to be alone forever." As a corollary, depressed individuals attribute positive events to causes that are external, unstable, and specific (Seligman et al., 1979). For example, a student might say, "Oh sure, I passed this test, but that's only because the teacher made this one so easy. It is only one test, and I will not be so successful next time."

HOPELESSNESS THEORY OF DEPRESSION

Abramson, Metalsky, and Alloy (1989) published an updated and refined version of learned helplessness called the hopelessness theory of depression. They hypothesized that *hopelessness depression* is a subtype of depression wherein hopelessness is "an expectation that highly desired outcomes will not occur or that highly aversive outcomes will occur coupled with an expectation that no response in one's repertoire will change the likelihood of occurrence" (Abramson et al., 1989, p. 359). They viewed hopelessness as a proximal, sufficient cause of depression; in other words, if hopelessness is present, symptoms of depression likely will be present as well.

Hopelessness theory posits that depression is more likely to occur when (a) negative events that are important to the individual are attributed to global and stable causes, (b) these negative events are predicted to lead to additional negative consequences, and (c) the individual makes a causal attribution about the relationship between the negative event and his or her inherent deficiencies (Abramson et al., 2002; Alloy, Abramson, Whitehouse, et al., 2006; Liu, Kleiman, Nestor, & Cheek, 2015).

In summary, these cognitive theories emphasize the importance of the contributions of thoughts, attributions, and schemas to the etiology and maintenance of depression. What, however, do the data say about the contributions of distorted thinking to mood disturbance?

COGNITIVE DEFICITS IN DEPRESSION

The common thread in the cognitive theories of depression is that depression is associated with disturbances in cognitive processes. Specifically, cognitive models have proposed that the thinking of depressed individuals tends to be negatively biased (Sacco & Beck, 1995). When compared to nondepressed controls, empirical support for the hypothesized negative bias in depressed individuals has been obtained for memory processes (e.g., Hamilton & Gotlib, 2008; Hertel & Brozovich, 2010; Joormann, Teachman, & Gotlib, 2009; Mathews & MacLeod, 2005), attentional processes (e.g., Gotlib et al., 2004; Koster, De Raedt, Leyman, & De Lissnyder, 2010), and most aspects of executive functioning (Snyder, 2013). Data also indicate higher negative content in thoughts about the self, the world, the future, and life in general (Blackburn, Jones, & Lewin, 2011; Kleiman, Liu, Riskind, & Hamilton, 2015).

Information Processing, Learning, and Memory

Cognitive distortions and negative attentional and memory biases are thought to play a major role in the development of negative cognitions (Sacco & Beck, 1995). All of the aforementioned cognitive theories of depression posit that a major vulnerability to depression occurs when depressed individuals orient toward negatively biased self-referential information. This is the primary premise behind Beck's theory of schemas (1967, 1987) and has long been observed in depressed individuals (see Ingram, Miranda, & Segal, 1998). Alloy and Abramson (1999) found that individuals considered to be at higher risk (HR) for depression were more strongly oriented toward negative self-referential adjectives (e.g., "failure," "useless") than were individuals with lower risk (LR) for depression. In addition, HR individuals were less strongly oriented toward positive self-referential adjectives (e.g., "worthy," "competent") compared to LR individuals. Additionally, depressed individuals have been found to show preferential orientation and maintenance of attention (looking for longer) toward images of sad faces (Duque & Vázquez, 2015; Fritzsche et al., 2010). Currently depressed individuals also demonstrate similar preferential attention (Mogg, Bradley, Williams, & Mathews, 1993; Teachman, Joormann, Steinman, & Gotlib, 2012).

Many studies have found that depressed individuals demonstrate negative interpretation biases (Foland-Ross & Gotlib, 2012). Initially, Butler and Mathews (1983) found that when presented with a social situation and options of possible interpretations, depressed patients more often choose the negative interpretation option. This finding has been replicated and elaborated (Nunn, Mathews, & Trower, 1997; Voncken, Bögels, & Peeters, 2007). For example, depressed individuals are more likely to show negative interpretation biases when hearing ambiguous words (e.g., die/dye, weak/week) and when endorsing associations between ambiguous sentences and negative descriptors (Mogg, Bradbury, & Bradley, 2006). Evidence for negative interpretation biases in depressed patients also comes from emotion recognition tasks, where studies have shown that depressed patients are slower and less accurate in recognizing neutral facial emotions (Bourke, Douglas, & Porter, 2010; Dalili, Penton-Voak, Harmer, & Munafò, 2015; Gollan, Pane, McCloskey, & Coccaro, 2008; Leppänen, Milders, Bell, Terriere, & Hietanen, 2004).

Multiple studies have shown that memory processes, both verbal and visual, are affected in the course of depression (Austin, Mitchell, & Goodwin, 2001). In addition, depressed individuals frequently show deficits in learning and episodic memory (McDermott & Ebmeier, 2009). In some studies, depressed individuals show more negative bias in recognition memory and event recall (Joormann et al., 2009) as well as in autobiographical memory (Williams et al., 2007); in other words, these individuals are more likely to remember bad experiences rather than good experiences. Additionally, depressed individuals show more overgeneralization in their autobiographical memory recall (Williams et al., 2007). Although this is thought to be efficacious in minimizing the affect associated with negative autobiographical memories (Foland-Ross & Gotlib, 2012), overgeneralized memory has been correlated with rumination, cognitive deficits, and longer durations of depressive episodes (Raes et al., 2005; Watkins & Teasdale, 2001, 2004). Depressed individuals recall more negative feedback and less positive feedback when compared to nondepressed individuals (Nelson & Craighead, 1977; Ridout, Astell, Reid, Glen, & O'Carroll, 2003); other studies, however, have shown that anxiety may be an important component in the recall of feedback. For example, Kennedy and Craighead (1988) found that both depressed and anxious individuals and nondepressed and anxious individuals are more accurate in their recall of *negative* feedback than nondepressed-nonanxious people. The distortion of recall of *positive* feedback, however, seemed to be a function of depression, with depressed individuals consistently recalling having received less positive feedback than they, in fact, had received; whereas, anxious-nondepressed individuals and nonanxious-nondepressed individuals accurately recalled positive feedback.

Clinically, these data are relevant to the treatment of depression because research has shown that memory functioning is imperative for the regulation of negative affect (Joormann, Yoon, & Siemer, 2010). First, given that depressed individuals interpret and recall information and events with a negative bias, they also are likely to report this information to therapists as though it is factual. Clearly, this presents a dilemma for the clinician; although the patient is not purposefully withholding information, it is possible that she still is not presenting a complete picture due to the memory deficits associated with her depression. *In addition, clinicians should understand that attentional biases are compounded by negative memory biases.* Depressed individuals are not only more likely to orient toward negative stimuli in their environments but also more likely to recall negative information than positive information. Taken together, these data highlight three important clinical points: (1) information presented in therapy may be distorted by impaired attentional and memory processes; (2) the therapist will likely need to inquire directly about positive experiences that may have occurred; and (3) shifts in the proportion of positive to negative events that are reported in therapy should be carefully tracked, as they may be indicative of clinical progress.

Rumination

According to response styles theory (RST; Nolen-Hoeksema, 1987), rumination involves self-focused attention accompanied by a repetitive focus on negative emotional causes, symptoms, and consequences (for a review, see Olatunji, Naragon-Gainey, & Wolitzky-Taylor, 2013; Smith & Alloy, 2009). Depressed individuals who ruminate will often report that they have difficulty disengaging from thoughts about their symptoms (e.g., "I cry all the time and can't seem to stop") or about possible causes of their depression (e.g., "If only my marriage hadn't ended"). Individuals with ruminative response styles also report focusing on potential consequences of their depression (e.g., "If I continue to stay home in bed, I'm probably going to lose my job"). They report feeling "stuck" with their depressive thoughts and unable to focus their attention on anything else.

After studying students' reactions to the 1989 Loma Prieta earthquake in the San Francisco Bay area, Nolen-Hoeksema and Morrow (1991) concluded that rumination is more aptly classified as a response style rather than as a symptom of depression. Indeed, even ruminating about daily struggles is related to increased distress and sadness (Wood, Saltzberg, Neale, Stone, & Rachmiel, 1990). Other investigators have shown that rumination mediates both the relationship between risk factors for depression (e.g., negative cognitive style, prior history of depression) and the onset of a major depressive episode (Spasojevic & Alloy, 2001). Rumination also mediates the relationship between impaired cognitive control of emotional information (which facilitates negative interpretation and memory biases) and depressive symptoms (Demeyer, De Lissnyder, Koster, & De Raedt, 2012).

Although ruminative thoughts are similar in form and function to the automatic thoughts described by Beck and colleagues (1979), they differ in style. Both automatic and ruminative thoughts are often depressogenic; however, rumination is a repetitive pattern of thinking that is characterized by a failure to disengage attention from thought content. This repetitious style differentiates rumination from automatic thoughts, which may have a profound effect on mood but are often time-limited occurrences (Nolen-Hoeksema, 1991). In addition, the grist for the cognitive-behavioral mill lies in the distortions in depressive thinking; that is, automatic thoughts include cognitive errors. Ruminative thoughts, however, are often accurate reflections of reality (Nolen-Hoeksema, Morrow, & Fredrickson, 1993).[1] For example, there is some truth to the thought, "If I continue to stay home from work because I am so depressed, I will probably get fired." Note also that ruminative individuals spend a considerable amount of time thinking about their symptoms and possible

---

[1] Some findings suggest that depressed individuals have a more realistic appraisal of reality than nondepressed individuals (i.e., depressive realism); however, empirical support for this theory is equivocal (Moore & Fresco, 2007).

consequences, leaving little opportunity for those individuals to be distracted from their negative mood.

Rumination is a passive rather than active problem-solving strategy (Nolen-Hoeksema, 2000) that exhausts cognitive resources and interferes with problem-solving and decision-making processes (Riso et al., 2003: van Randenborgh, de Jong-Meyer, & Hüffmeier, 2010). The individual's thought content is centered on the symptoms and consequences of depression rather than on how to alleviate those symptoms. Several studies have shown that people who endorse a ruminative thinking style are less likely than nonruminators to engage in active problem solving (e.g., Donaldson & Lam, 2004).

The processes and outcomes of ruminative thought patterns are similar to the previously discussed information processing problems. Joormann and colleagues (2010) found that self-reported rumination was associated with diminished abilities to shift attention from negative stimuli and to identify neutral stimuli (indication of negative attentional biases). Individuals who ruminate also show distortions of memories, present-day interpretations of events, and projections about their futures (see Lyubomirsky & Tkach, 2004). These progressive distortions via rumination lead to an increased sense of hopelessness and decreased problem-solving abilities (Nolen-Hoeksema, 2002). Since the initial description of RST, a number of studies have shown that rumination is a useful predictor of both the onset of depressive episodes and the intensity of depressive symptoms (Olatunji et al., 2013; Robinson & Alloy, 2003; Spasojevic & Alloy, 2001).

Studies of the neural circuitry of depressed individuals have found rumination to be positively correlated with increased amygdala activation (Mandell, Siegle, Shutt, Feldmiller, & Thase, 2014). This finding is in line with similar findings that amygdala hyperactivity in response to negative stimuli and amygdala hypoactivity in response to positive stimuli may be hallmarks of depression (Young, Siegle, Bodurka, & Drevets, 2015).

Attentional Deficits

It has been shown that mood is related to attentional biases regarding emotional expression on human faces (Gotlib et al., 2004; Fritzsche et al., 2010; Woody, Owens, Burkhouse, & Gibb, 2015). Depressed individuals have a stronger bias than nondepressed individuals toward sad rather than angry, neutral, or happy faces. In addition, Gotlib and colleagues (2004) found that symptom severity in depression was related to a tendency to look away from happy faces. Some evidence suggests that such attentional biases continue even when depression has remitted (Fritzsche et al., 2010; Joormann & Gotlib, 2007; Timbremont & Braet, 2004). Similarly, data show that depressed individuals are more strongly oriented toward unhappy faces in their environment. Hence, a depressed patient may report that "it just seems like everyone around me is sad—I probably make everyone else miserable." Gotlib and colleagues (2004) demonstrated that it may be that the depressed person in this example failed to notice all the happy, neutral, or angry people around him and oriented instead to the other sad people in his environment. Again, this individual is not purposefully misrepresenting her experience in the world (i.e., "poor me"); rather, she is experiencing a common cognitive pattern characteristic of MDD.

Neuroscience has recently begun to identify patterns of neural dysregulation and connectivity associated with attention and depression (Craske, 2014; Snyder, 2013). As with rumination, further understanding of neural activity associated with attentional biases may inform the modification of current interventions or the development of novel treatments for MDD.

Negative Cognitive Style

All cognitive models of depression posit that people who encounter negative life events and who go on to develop depression are more likely to have a negative cognitive style than their nondepressed counterparts.

Alloy and Abramson (1999) spearheaded research efforts regarding negative cognitive style and depression in the Temple–Wisconsin Cognitive Vulnerabilities to Depression (CVD) project. They have proposed that similar to Beck's theory, individuals with negative cognitive styles, compared to individuals without negative cognitive styles, are at greater risk for developing depression in the face of negative life events. In the Temple–Wisconsin CVD project, college freshmen with no history of Axis I pathology were screened for the presence of negative cognitive styles. Those who showed evidence of a negative cognitive style were considered to be at high risk (HR) for depression, while those without a negative cognitive style were considered to be at low risk (LR) for depression. Students with negative cognitive styles were significantly more likely to have a lifetime history of depressive episodes as well as greater prior recurrences of depressive episodes (Alloy & Abramson, 1999; Alloy et al., 2000; Alloy, Abramson, Whitehouse, et al., 2006; Alloy et al., 1999). Another compelling finding showed that a negative cognitive style in previously never depressed students predicted both first onset and recurrence of MDD (Alloy, Abramson, Walshaw, & Neeren, 2006; Alloy, Abramson, Whitehouse, et al., 2006). These findings lend critical support to the hypothesis that negative cognitive style increases vulnerability to depression.

Other studies have shown that negative cognitive styles are related to a greater number of depressive episodes, more intense episodes, and more chronic depressive episodes than are experienced by individuals without a negative cognitive style (Haeffel et al., 2003; Iacoviello, Alloy, Abramson, Whitehouse, & Hogan, 2006; Perveen, 2015).[2] In addition, negative cognitive style has been shown to be associated with past depressive episodes even after controlling for current depressive symptoms (Abela, Stolow, Zhang, & McWhinnie, 2012) and also has been shown to predict increases in number of symptoms during current episodes (Iacoviello et al., 2006), particularly in the face of high stressors (Meyer, Gudgeon, Thomas, & Collerton, 2010). It should be noted, however, that virtually all of these studies have excluded or failed to assess Axis II symptomatology, which is significant because when Axis II symptomatology and negative cognitive style are accounted for simultaneously, most of the predictive power is attributable to the Axis II symptoms rather than to cognitive style (Craighead, Sheets, Craighead, & Madsen, 2011; Ilardi & Craighead, 1999). Gender may also play an important role in the relationship between cognitive style and depression. In a study of stress and depression in a youth sample, Rood, Roelofs, Bögels, and Meesters (2012) found that negative cognitive style in the areas of achievement and appearance was more strongly related to depression in girls than in boys, whereas negative cognitive style in the interpersonal sphere was related to depression in both genders.

---

[2] See Gibb (2002) for a review of the etiology of negative cognitive styles.

Cognitive Deficits in Chronic Depression

Given the central role of cognitive theories in depression, there has been surprisingly little research on the role of cognitive variables in chronic depression. McCullough and colleagues (1994) found that a nonclinical sample with chronic depression exhibited more stable and global attributions for negative events and less stable attributions for positive events than healthy controls. Similarly, Riso and colleagues (2003) reported that patients with chronic depression exhibited more stable and global attributions for negative events, a higher level of dysfunctional attitudes, a more ruminative response style, and higher scores on a measure of maladaptive schemas and core beliefs than did healthy controls.

In one of the few studies addressing the nature of the relationship between cognitive variables and chronic depression, Arnow, Spangler, Klein, and Burns (2004) modeled the associations among rumination, distraction, and depressive symptomatology over the course of 12 weeks in a large sample of patients with double depression (simultaneous MDD and dysthymia) and chronic major depression. A model positing that depression and rumination are both caused by the same factors provided a better fit to the data than models positing that rumination causes subsequent depression or that depression causes subsequent rumination.

Biological Models of Depression

Major depressive disorder is characterized by complex genetics and diverse symptomatology suggestive of the disruption of a variety of neural systems within the central nervous system (CNS). The neural system disruptions participate in the regulation of mood, sleep, motivation, energy balance, and cognition (Krishnan & Nestler, 2010). In addition to disrupted functioning of the CNS, other organ systems, including the endocrine and immune systems, are dysregulated in patients with MDD; this also contributes to depressive pathophysiology within the CNS. This portion of the chapter provides a brief and selected overview of relevant genetic and other biological research.

GENETICS OF DEPRESSION

MDD, like other stress-related psychiatric disorders, is in part a heritable disorder (for reviews, see Levinson, 2006; Dunn et al, 2014; Ressler & Smoller, 2016). Based on data from twin studies, heritability estimates for MDD range from 40% to 50%. Adoption studies also support the notion of a substantial genetic risk for MDD; quantitatively, the relative risk ratio for major depression probands is 2 to 3 times the population base rate. Risk for MDD is also increased by exposure to detrimental environmental factors such as childhood abuse and neglect or other forms of early-life stress that promote depression vulnerability (Caspi et al., 2003; Nemeroff, 2016).

Like many disorders, MDD is a clinical syndrome that likely evolves from the differential contribution of multiple, variably penetrant genes with differing modes of inheritance. The expression of these genes is multiply influenced by environmental exposures, epigenetic processes, and architectural genomic changes such as chromosomal rearrangement or copy number variation. Consequently, MDD is best termed a complex genetic disorder. The term *complex* serves to differentiate the pattern of genetic contribution in complex genetic disorders from that observed in classic genetic diseases such as Huntington's disease or phenylketonuria; the latter are often referred to as Mendelian[3] disorders—disorders in which mutations of a single gene are completely or largely responsible for the presence of the disease. Alternatively, in the context of complex genetic disorders, additive and multiplicative models of genetic risk are best used to estimate the genetic contribution to depression.

Genetic association methods have been used extensively to evaluate a large number of candidate genes whose allelic variants are thought to predict differences in risk for MDD or depressive symptomatology, either as genetic main effects or in concert with influences from the environment (reviewed in Heim & Binder, 2012; Sharma, Powers, Bradley, & Ressler, 2016; Sun, Kennedy, & Nestler, 2013). In some cases, these variants are single nucleotide polymorphisms (SNPs) that may have an identified function, such as alteration of either gene expression or the structure of the protein for which the gene codes. Some of the better-known genes that have been implicated in depression include the serotonin transporter gene (5-HTTLPR), the brain-derived neurotrophic factor gene (BDNF), the glucocorticoid receptor chaperone protein gene (FKBP5), and the type 1 corticotrophin-releasing hormone receptor gene (CRHR1). Although solid findings have emerged from well-designed candidate gene studies of genetic effects on risk for MDD, there are also a large number of genetic studies whose findings have failed replication and whose design issues limit interpretation or comparison of the experimental findings with other studies. Current efforts to identify depression-related genes have moved from candidate gene association studies to genome-wide association studies (GWAS). GWAS allow for the investigation of genetic variation across the entire genome (Psychiatric GWAS Consortium Coordinating Committee, 2009).

In contrast to traditional association studies, GWAS candidate genes are selected based on whether a gene variant is associated with a phenotypic outcome, such as the presence or absence of MDD or the severity of depressive symptoms. Very strict significance levels are set to control for Type I statistical error because a very large number of SNPs are generally being tested in GWAS. Ideally, gene variants that achieve genome-wide significance will be selected for hypothesis-driven follow-up studies designed to evaluate the biological effects of that particular gene variant. An advantage of the atheoretical GWAS approach is that selection of candidate genes is not limited by the biological plausibility or implausibility of a candidate gene; thus, the entire genome may be investigated. However, results from extant studies have provided limited advances to the understanding of the pathogenesis of MDD. Although a number of novel candidate genes that *may* influence MDD have been identified, definitive findings of large components of genetic variance associated with MDD have not yet emerged.

Other genetic studies are attempting to identify larger gene variant–specific effects on MDD risk through the use of "intermediate phenotypes" to investigate particular depression symptom components, such as anhedonia or mood reactivity (Leuchter, Hunter, Krantz, & Cook, 2014; Hornung & Heim, 2015). This approach holds promise for illnesses such as MDD because it allows for the investigation of specific phenotypes that are representative of a syndromal component of an illness (e.g., anhedonia); such

---

[3] Named in honor of the Augustinian monk Gregor Johann Mendel (1822–1884).

components are more likely to be affected by a particular gene variant to a greater degree than is the overall MDD syndrome. Given the extensive symptom overlap among depression, anxiety, and even psychotic disorders, the use of intermediate phenotypes also enables transdiagnostic genetic investigation of psychiatric symptoms such as anhedonia (a core symptom of both MDD and schizophrenia) that may lead to novel and unanticipated insights into the role of genes in the etiology and treatment of psychiatric disorders.

NEUROCHEMISTRY OF DEPRESSION

Since the 1950s, a large body of research has investigated the role of monoamine neurotransmitter systems in the pathogenesis of psychiatric disorders. These studies have provided the intellectual foundation for later investigation into the psychobiology of depressive symptomatology and MDD in particular.

As originally formulated, the monoamine hypothesis of depression posited that MDD was caused by a deficiency in central nervous system concentration or receptor function of the catecholamine neurotransmitter norepinephrine (NE) or the indoleamine neurotransmitter serotonin (5-HT). The monoamine hypothesis was derived in part from pharmacological interventions and clinical observations of their effects on mood. For example, reserpine, initially used as an antihypertensive agent, was found to produce depressive symptoms in many patients receiving it as part of their treatment for hypertension. By extension, the depressogenic effects of reserpine were hypothesized to be due to its capacity to deplete monoamines from CNS neurons. Similarly, the mood-elevating action of monoamine oxidase inhibitors (MAOIs), which prolong the actions of monoamines within the synapse by preventing their catabolism by monoamine oxidase, was discovered by the chance observation of the antidepressant effects of the MAOI iproniazid. Although iproniazid was originally developed to treat tuberculosis, it was observed to alleviate symptoms of depression in patients with comorbid tuberculosis and MDD. Collectively, these early research findings on the relationship between monoamine activity in the CNS and mood stimulated further investigation into the relationship between neurotransmitter activity within the central nervous system and MDD. In the subsections that follow, key findings related to 5-HT and NE in patients with MDD are selectively reviewed as are more recent research findings with brain-derived neurotrophic factor (BDNF), all of which have informed the current view of the relationship between neurochemistry and MDD.

Serotonin and Depression

Serotonin (5-hydroxytryptamine, or 5-HT) is an indoleamine neurotransmitter synthesized from the amino acid tryptophan in the neurons of the rostral and caudal raphe nuclei of the brain stem. Neural fibers originating from the raphe are widespread and project through a variety of forebrain structures, including the hypothalamus, amygdala, basal ganglia, thalamus, hippocampus, cingulate cortex, and prefrontal cortex (Azmitia & Gannon, 1986). Following release from synaptic terminals, 5-HT is removed from extracellular fluid by the serotonin transporter (SERT), located on cells' presynaptic terminal, and is either repackaged into synaptic vesicles or degraded by monoamine oxidase (MAO).

Several lines of evidence suggest that deficiencies in 5-HT signaling play a role in depression and suicide (Owens & Nemeroff, 1994). Low cerebrospinal fluid (CSF) concentrations of the principal 5-HT metabolite, 5-hydroxyindoleacetic acid (5-HIAA), have been consistently observed in patients with MDD and among individuals who complete suicide, particularly by violent means. Consistent with the finding of low CSF concentrations of 5-HIAA in patients with MDD, functional brain imaging studies also have identified reduced levels of the serotonin transporter in the raphe nuclei of patients with MDD. In addition, imaging studies of MDD patients who have completed suicide show increased density of 5-HT_2 receptors on platelets and in the frontal cortex. Although the association between indices of reduced 5-HT turnover and impulsive violent suicide has been consistently replicated, this finding does not appear to be specific to depressive disorders, which suggests that low levels of CNS 5-HT may be a marker for a nonspecific aversive motivational state rather than depression per se. With regard to treatment response, reduction in platelet 5-HT_2 receptor binding is associated with clinical improvement among patients treated with antidepressants (Biegon et al., 1987), and a large body of clinical data supports the efficacy of selective serotonin reuptake inhibitors (SSRIs; e.g., fluoxetine, paroxetine, citalopram, sertraline, and escitalopram) in the treatment of depression (Nemeroff, 2007). Finally, the experimental depletion of tryptophan (the amino acid precursor from which serotonin is synthesized) rapidly precipitates recurrence of depression among patients whose MDD had previously remitted when treated with SSRIs (Smith, Fairburn, & Cowen, 1997).

Norepinephrine and Depression

Norepinephrine (NE) is a catecholamine neurotransmitter synthesized from the amino acid tyrosine by neurons of the locus coeruleus and, to a lesser extent, by neurons of the lateral tegmental fields of the midbrain. Projections originating from the locus coeruleus innervate a variety of forebrain structures, including the cerebral cortex, thalamus, cerebellar cortex, hippocampus, hypothalamus, and amygdala (Moore & Bloom, 1979). NE acts through activation of alpha and beta adrenergic receptors. Following release, NE is taken up on the presynaptic element by the norepinephrine transporter (NET) and is either repackaged into synaptic vesicles or degraded by MAO.

As with 5-HT, experimental findings related to NE (e.g., concentrations in the CNS, experimental depletion, and antidepressant efficacy) collectively implicate NE in the pathophysiology and treatment of depression (Ressler & Nemeroff, 2001). Elevated CSF concentrations of the major NE metabolite (3-methoxy-4-hydroxyphenylglycol, or MHPG) have been consistently observed for many years among depressed patients (Schildkraut, 1965). In addition to studies that have identified CNS pools of NE metabolites, it has also been found that NE and its metabolites are increased in the plasma and urine of depressed patients (Roy, Pickar, DeJong, Karoum, & Linnoila, 1988). Finally, SSRI treatment of patients with depression results in decreased concentrations of CSF MHPG (Sheline, Bardgett, & Csernansky, 1997), and treatment of depressed patients with tricyclic antidepressants (TCAs) results in decreased plasma (Charney, Heninger, Sternberg, & Roth, 1981) and urinary (Linnoila et al., 1986) metabolites of NE.

Among depressed patients who have had a therapeutic response to treatment with an antidepressant such as desipramine (which works predominantly to increase NE within the CNS), the experimental depletion of NE precipitates relapse of depression

(Charney, 1998). This suggests that a state of relative NE deficiency may play a role in the production of depressive symptomatology. Taking this approach a step further, the experimental depletion of catecholamine neurotransmitters (which depletes NE as well as dopamine) in euthymic, unmedicated patients with a history of depression has also been shown to precipitate relapse of depressive symptoms (Berman et al., 1999). Although not used as often as SSRIs, a large body of clinical data supports the efficacy of NE reuptake inhibitors (e.g., reboxetine, desipramine) in treating depression (Nemeroff, 2007).

Brain-Derived Neurotrophic Factor and Depression

Brain-derived neurotrophic factor (BDNF) is a neuropeptide neurotransmitter that plays a substantial role in the regulation of neuronal survival, differentiation, and function within the developing and adult central nervous system. It also performs important regulatory roles in short- and long-term synaptic plasticity, the cellular processes whereby connections between neurons are altered. These effects appear to be driven in part by activity of the tyrosine kinase B receptor (TrkB) through which BDNF acts. Functionally, BDNF appears to be important in episodic as well as emotion-related memory. Clinical research with humans has identified a functional polymorphism (Val66Met) within the BDNF gene that affects hippocampal function and episodic memory (Duncan, Hutchison, Carey, & Craighead, 2009; Egan et al., 2003) as well as function of the hypothalamic-pituitary-adrenal axis in depressed patients (Schüle et al., 2006).

The complex relationship that exists between stress and mood disorders may be mediated in part by the activity of BDNF and other neurotrophic factors (Duman & Monteggia, 2006; Schmidt & Duman, 2007; Sharma, da Costa e Silva, Soares, Carvalho, Quevedo, 2016); this may provide an opportunity for the development of novel antidepressants (Berton & Nestler, 2006; though also see Groves, 2007). Using rodent models, stress has been found to decrease BDNF expression within the hippocampus, using a variety of paradigms including restraint (Smith, Makino, Kvetnansky, & Post, 1995), maternal deprivation (Roceri, Hendriks, Racagni, Ellenbroek, & Riva, 2002), and social defeat (Tsankova et al., 2006). Increased hippocampal BDNF-like immunoreactivity, an index of BDNF protein levels, has been observed in depressed patients treated with antidepressants (Chen, Dowlatshahi, MacQueen, Wang, & Young, 2001). Serum BDNF is also lower in depressed patients (Shimizu et al., 2003), and it appears to normalize with antidepressant treatment (Gonul et al., 2005).

NEUROENDOCRINOLOGY OF DEPRESSION

Complementing the literature on neurochemical disturbances in patients with MDD is a large body of research examining abnormal function of the endocrine system in depressed patients. Excess secretion of cortisol (Carpenter & Bunney, 1971) and its metabolites (Sachar, Hellman, Fukushima, & Gallagher, 1970) was first observed nearly 50 years ago in depressed patients.

Hypothalamic-Pituitary-Adrenal (HPA) Axis

The prominence of depression and anxiety in the clinical presentation of patients with endocrinopathies affecting the hypothalamic-pituitary-adrenal (HPA) axis (e.g., Cushing's disease; Dorn et al., 1997) in conjunction with the observation of increased secretion of cortisol in healthy patients exposed to stress contributed to the development of a diathesis-stress model of depression. This model hypothesizes that individual predisposition to excess reactivity of the neural and endocrine stress response systems plays a central role in susceptibility to depression. The presence of acute or prolonged stress in vulnerable individuals plays a significant role in both the onset and relapse of certain forms of depression (Brown, Varghese, & McEwen, 2004). This diathesis-stress model highlights the interaction of life events, cognitive styles, and neurobiology in the etiology of MDD.

Functional Organization of the HPA Axis

The discovery of corticotrophin-releasing factor (CRF; Vale, Spiess, Rivier, & Rivier, 1981) greatly accelerated research into the biology of stress, and it helped clarify the organization of the HPA axis, a collection of neural and endocrine structures that function collectively to facilitate the adaptive response to stress. Parvocellular neurons of the paraventricular nucleus (PVN) within the hypothalamus project to the median eminence, where they secrete CRF into the primary plexus of blood vessels that comprise the hypothalamo-hypophyseal portal system (Swanson, Sawchenko, Rivier, & Vale, 1983). The secreted CRF is then transported to the anterior pituitary gland, where it activates CRF receptors on pituitary corticotrophs, resulting in increased secretion of adrenocorticotrophic hormone (ACTH). The ACTH released from the anterior pituitary into the systemic circulation subsequently stimulates the production and release of cortisol from the adrenal cortex. As HPA axis activity increases, cortisol levels increase and feedback inhibition increases; this reduces activation of the HPA axis and limits excess secretion of glucocorticoids, thereby effectively dampening the stress response (Jacobson & Sapolsky, 1991).

In addition to its neuroendocrine role of regulating activity of the HPA axis, CRF also functions as a neurotransmitter in coordinating the behavioral, autonomic, endocrine, and immune responses to stress (Arborelius, Owens, Plotsky, & Nemeroff, 1999). Behavioral changes (disturbed sleep, diminished food intake, reduced grooming, decreased reproductive behavior, and enhanced fear-conditioning) similar to those observed in humans with depression occur following central administration of CRF in rodents and primates (Owens & Nemeroff, 1991). Pretreatment with CRF receptor antagonists reduces the experimental induction of these physiological changes within behavioral stress paradigms (Gutman, Owens, Skelton, Thrivikraman, & Nemeroff, 2003).

Depression and Pathophysiology of the HPA Axis

The dexamethasone suppression test (DST), originally designed to aid in the diagnosis of Cushing's disease, was one of the first endocrine challenge tests studied in psychiatric patients. Dexamethasone acts at the level of the anterior pituitary corticotrophs to reduce the secretion of ACTH; this results in a decrease in the synthesis and release of cortisol from the adrenal cortex. Failure to suppress plasma cortisol concentrations after dexamethasone administration suggests impaired feedback regulation and hyperactivity of the HPA axis. The DST is useful as a clinical index of HPA axis activity. It consists of the administration of a low dose (1 mg) of the synthetic glucocorticoid dexamethasone at 11:00 ~PM, followed by measurement of plasma cortisol concentrations at two or three time points the following day.

A large percentage of drug-free patients with major depression fail to suppress secretion of cortisol following administration of dexamethasone, a finding known as dexamethasone nonsuppression (DST-NS; Carroll, Martin, & Davies, 1968). This suggested that DST-NS might be a biological marker for depression (Carroll, 1982). DST-NS status and hypercortisolemia (i.e., high concentrations of cortisol in the bloodstream) are both common in depression, although they are not universal. Meta-analyses have revealed that DST-NS status is most commonly found in patients with psychotic depression or mixed bipolar states (Evans & Nemeroff, 1983). DST-NS status also generally predicts a more severe course of MDD (Arana, Baldessarini, & Orsteen, 1985). However, the greatest contribution of the DST was to serve as an impetus for subsequent studies exploring the underlying pathophysiology of the HPA axis in depression.

Considerable data support the hypothesis that the dysregulation of the HPA axis observed in depression is a state, rather than a trait, phenomenon. In this context, state dependence implies the presence of pathophysiological phenomena that are related to a particular phase of depression rather than being constitutively present (i.e., trait based). Among depressed patients who secrete abnormally high amounts of cortisol into the bloodstream (i.e., hypercortisolemia), plasma cortisol levels (Sachar et al., 1970), DST-NS status (Arana et al., 1985), blunting of the ACTH response to CRF infusion (Amsterdam et al., 1988), hypersecretion of CRF (Nemeroff, Bissette, Akil, & Fink, 1991), and adrenal hypertrophy (Rubin, Phillips, Sadow, & McCracken, 1995) all normalize following resolution of clinical symptoms.

There appear to be a variety of ways in which the presence of depression is reflected in altered functioning of the HPA axis. For example, patients with psychotic depression demonstrate hyperactivity of the HPA axis along with the highest rates of nonsuppression on the dexamethasone suppression test (Schatzberg et al., 1983), whereas depressed patients without psychosis may have either decreased or normal activity of the HPA axis (Posener et al., 2000). Alternatively, patients who have a history of childhood adversity show elevated secretion of ACTH and cortisol in response to a laboratory stress test as well as abnormal responses to neuroendocrine challenge tests, whereas those without such history do not (for a review, see Gillespie & Nemeroff, 2007).

PSYCHONEUROIMMUNOLOGY OF DEPRESSION

Inflammation is another key component of the adaptive response to stress. Stress stimulates the body's inflammatory response so it may appropriately respond to injury and contamination by infectious agents. The principal way that this occurs is by the stress-induced secretion by white blood cells of small peptides known as proinflammatory cytokines that stimulate the development of inflammation (Glaser & Kiecolt-Glaser, 2005). The relationship between the HPA axis and systemic inflammation may be especially pertinent in view of the findings that patients with a history of early-life stress have an impaired capacity to regulate the HPA axis in the presence of psychosocial stress (Nemeroff, 2016); this suggests that control of the inflammatory response (as a consequence of HPA axis dysregulation) may be impaired as well.

Research evidence indicates that systemic inflammation may play a key role in the etiology of some depressions (see Haroon, Raison, & Miller, 2012; Kiecolt-Glaser, Derry, & Fagundes, 2015; Miller & Raison, 2016). This may be due in part to the body's inability to regulate short-term physiological reactions to stress (e.g., inflammation and HPA activation) following exposure to stressful circumstances in susceptible individuals. Administration of proinflammatory cytokines to laboratory animals results in a syndromal pattern of behavioral and neurovegetative symptoms known as sickness behavior that is similar to the pattern of signs of depression in human patients and includes psychomotor slowing, fatigue, elevated pain sensitivity, disrupted sleep, and anxiety (Remus & Dantzer, 2016). Clinical research in humans has identified an array of proinflammatory cytokines, including interleukin-6 (IL-6), IL-1, and tumor necrosis factor-alpha (TNF-α) and inflammatory markers such as CRP that are associated with the presence of depression (Young, Bruno, & Pomara, 2014).

Inflammatory cytokines appear to exert their effects on mood and behavior through a variety of biological mechanisms (Pace & Miller, 2009; Miller, Haroon, Raison, & Felger, 2013). Inflammatory cytokines influence the metabolism of monoamine neurotransmitters (especially 5-HT) and also are capable of dampening the activity of the HPA axis. Cytokine-mediated alteration of monoamine metabolism and effects on HPA axis function correlate significantly with the presence of depressive symptoms.

Inflammation may be particularly relevant to three populations of depressed patients: individuals with treatment-resistant depression (Strawbridge et al., 2015), chronic medical illness comorbid with depression (Evans et al., 2005), and depression associated with early-life stress (Nemeroff, 2016). In some patients, exposure to trauma or stressful childhood experiences may be a variable connecting risk for depression, chronic medical illness, and inflammation (Nusslock & Miller, 2015). For example, patients with histories of childhood trauma have an elevated risk for depression that is often chronic in course (Nemeroff, 2016), and they also have elevated risk for a variety of common, chronic, and progressive medical diseases, including coronary artery disease (Goodwin & Stein, 2004).

An Integrative Model of Depression

It is important to understand the psychological and biological research within the context of an overall interactive and developmental conceptual model of depression. In Figure 7.3, we present a schematic representation of a model that incorporates the various aspects of depression outlined in this chapter. The reviewed empirical data fit within this theoretical framework that also serves heuristically to guide future research and clinical intervention.

The diathesis-stress model has been noted in several places in this chapter. Within this integrative model, the diathesis may be biological (e.g., genetic or involving neural connectivity) or psychological (e.g., behavioral, cognitive, emotional). Importantly, the key concept is that the diathesis is neither unidimensional nor singular in its etiological role. Rather, it may include more than one variable in any of the domains categorized as individual variables.

The schematic representation is best viewed as a snapshot or static description of what, in fact, is a dynamic and interacting set of variables within and across domains. In this model, the various depressive symptoms categorized earlier in this chapter occur within an environmental context. As children grow and develop, they are continually interacting with their environment, which includes a multitude of dynamic, causative factors that reciprocally influence the children across all individual domains. As Bandura (1969)

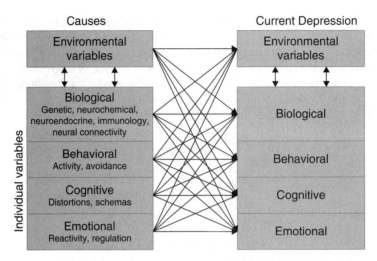

FIGURE 7.3   A Graphic View of an Integrative Model of Depression

articulated, the external environment influences the person, but it is a two-way street in that the person has a reciprocal impact on the environment. This process of transactional development affects those variables both within and outside the individual. Furthermore, within the individual there are interactive processes across the various domains. For example, emotion regulation is an important variable in the development of depression and other disorders. On the one hand, emotional arousal and subsequent regulation may be a bottom-up process in that it may originate in the limbic system. On the other hand, research has shown that emotions may also be regulated via top-down processing that originates in the frontal areas of the brain (see Ochsner & Gross, 2007). Unraveling these processes and increasing understanding of their interrelationships will be essential to enhance the prevention and treatment of MDD.

It is posited that each environmental and individual variable is multidimensional and transactional in its impact, both causing and ameliorating MDD. Hence, antidepressant medications directly affect neurobiology and, by extension, affect cognitions, emotions, and behaviors (i.e., bottom-up processing). Conversely, CBT directly targets cognitions and behaviors and indirectly affects neurobiological pathways associated with MDD (i.e., top-down processing; McGrath et al., 2013; Yoshimura et al., 2014). Thus, this model implies that a clinician may intervene in any of the domains depicted in Figure 7.3 and expect to have an impact on most or all other domains. The impact of the intervention may be most directly observed within the same domain (e.g., a CBT therapist may see the greatest and most immediate change in depressogenic cognitions such as rumination), but each domain impacts the other domains. In contrast to unidimensional causative models of MDD, this approach underscores both the interactive and developmental aspects of all domains of human functioning. Consequently, it is essential to study MDD from a multi-disciplinary approach in order to elucidate the significant etiological and treatment pathways. It further underscores the importance of identifying which types of interventions may be most effective for which patterns of empirically determined subtypes of MDD.

Assessment of Depression

A variety of instruments have been developed to diagnose major depressive disorder and to gauge the severity of depressive symptoms. We review the interviews, self-report measures, and clinical rating scales most commonly used in clinical practice and in research studies of MDD.

CLINICAL INTERVIEWS

The Structured Clinical Interview for DSM-5 Disorders, Clinician Version (SCID-5-CV; First, Williams, Karg, & Spitzer, 2015) is a semistructured interview that helps clinicians and researchers systematically inquire about possible disorder symptomatology based on updated *DSM-5* criteria. The interviewer asks a series of questions and elicits examples that allow diagnostic determinations to be made. This instrument allows the assessment of both current and lifetime diagnoses. Up-to-date information about the SCID-5-CV is available at www.scid5.org.

The SCID is generally regarded as the "gold standard" in assessing psychopathology (Shear et al., 2000). Reliability for categorical constructs (such as diagnostic status for MDD) is reported in terms of the kappa statistic, which assesses the agreement between independent raters while correcting for chance agreement. Kappa scores range from 0 (no agreement between two raters) to 1.00 (perfect agreement); thus higher scores indicate a greater degree of agreement. Viera and Garrett (2005) suggested that levels of agreement may be slight (kappa ranges .21 to .40), fair (.41 to .60), moderate (.61 to .80), or substantial (.81 to .99). Kappa ratings for MDD across several studies have ranged from moderate (.61) to substantial (.93), with typical kappa scores being about .80 (First & Gibbon, 2004). Validity ratings for the SCID have been more difficult to establish, owing to the fact that no other gold standard exists for diagnosing DSM disorders. Using Spitzer's best-estimate diagnosis technique, the SCID was superior to standard clinical intake interviews in two studies (Basco et al., 2000; Kranzler et al., 1995).

The Longitudinal Interval Follow-up Evaluation (LIFE; Keller et al., 1987) is a semistructured interview created to assess the longitudinal course of *DSM-IV* (*also applicable to DSM-5 criteria*) disorders, including MDD. Specific dates of onset, remission, relapse, and recurrence are recorded, which makes the LIFE the most appropriate measure for conducting longitudinal or treatment outcome studies of MDD. The LIFE was designed to be administered every 6 months; if, however, a patient or research participant misses an interview, information for the missing period can be collected at the next scheduled interview. High interrater reliability has been demonstrated for the interview (Keller et al., 1987), which takes 30 to 60 minutes to administer.

SELF-REPORT MEASURES

The most widely used self-report measure is the Beck Depression Inventory–II (BDI-II) (Beck, Steer, & Brown, 1996), which can be administered to patients aged 13 to 80 years. The BDI-II is a 21-item instrument that measures the intensity of both cognitive and somatic/affective symptoms of depression. The BDI-II demonstrates high internal consistency across a wide variety of populations (average coefficient $\alpha = .91$). It also has high convergent validity, demonstrating strong correlations with the Hamilton Rating Scale for Depression ($r = .71$), with the Beck Hopelessness Scale ($r = .68$), and with previous versions of the BDI ($r = .93$) (Dozois & Covin, 2004).

Another well-known self-report measure is the Center for Epidemiologic Studies Depression Scale (CES-D; Radloff, 1977). The CES-D is a 20-item measure that was designed for use as a screening measure in the general population; it was *not* designed as a diagnostic instrument, nor was it intended as a way to measure the severity of depressive symptomology in patients who meet criteria for MDD, although it is sometimes used for that purpose. The CES-D has demonstrated high internal consistency in the general population ($\alpha = .85$) and in patient samples ($\alpha = .90$) (Radloff, 1977).

The Patient Health Questionnaire (PHQ-9; Kroenke, Spitzer, & Williams, 2001) is a briefer self-report assessment measure for depression. It is a 9-item scale originally designed to assess depressive symptoms in primary care settings. The 9 items were adapted from the *DSM* diagnostic criteria for depressive disorders (Kroenke & Spitzer, 2002). The PHQ-9 has shown high internal consistency in primary care settings ($\alpha = 0.83$ and 0.92 at baseline and end of treatment, respectively) (Cameron, Crawford, Lawton, & Reid, 2008).

CLINICAL RATING SCALES OF MDD SEVERITY

The Hamilton Rating Scale for Depression (HAM-D; Hamilton, 1960) is a 17-item, clinician-administered interview designed to measure intensity of MDD (i.e., it is not intended to be a diagnostic instrument). There are various longer versions of the HAM-D, but the 17-item version is the most frequently used. The HAM-D demonstrates good internal consistency (average coefficient $\alpha = .78$) as well as interrater reliability (range = .70 to .96; Kovak, 2004).[4] The HAM-D correlates highly with the BDI-II as well as the Montgomery-Asberg Depression Rating Scale (MADRS; Kovak, 2004). The HAM-D is especially useful for detecting change in participants' levels of depression over time, which makes it particularly attractive for research purposes.

The Quick Inventory of Depression Symptomatology (QIDS; Rush et al., 2003) is available as both a clinician-administered scale (QIDS-C) and as a self-report measure (QIDS-SR). The QIDS is a 16-item measure designed to assess symptom severity across the nine *DSM-5* symptom domains. The QIDS has demonstrated high internal consistency ($\alpha = .87$), and scores on the QIDS-SR are highly correlated with scores on the HAM-D ($r = .86$) (Rush et al., 2003).

ASSESSMENT OF PDD

PDD can be challenging to diagnose. It is easy to overlook, as clinicians tend to focus on more acute periods of depressive symptoms and miss milder periods of depression that may precede or follow it. In addition, many patients experiencing PDD, especially those with an early onset, consider dysphoria to be normal or a part of their "usual self," so

---

[4] It is important to note that these ratings are affected by the interviewer's level of training, and the numbers reported here include studies that used raters who were not highly trained.

they fail to report it to clinicians or to consider that it may be an appropriate target for treatment (Akiskal, 1983). Residual depressive symptoms are also overlooked as patients and clinicians focus on improvement since the initiation of treatment.

To assess and diagnose PDD, clinicians must take a careful history of the patient's past course of depression. If the patient has a history of nonchronic major depressive episodes, it is critical to explore the presence of milder depression before and after the MDD episodes. It is often helpful to construct a life chart or time line, with the patient graphing his or her level of depression over time (McCullough et al., 1996). It is also critical to explain to the patient that depression can exist at varying levels of severity, and that it is important to describe the milder as well as the more severe periods. Unfortunately, these procedures have not been incorporated into the standard versions of widely used diagnostic instruments.

Many structured diagnostic interviews assessed dysthymic disorder (for *DSM-III, III-R*, and *IV*) only if currently present, and failed to collect information on a past history of chronic depression. Moreover, many of these instruments instructed interviewers to skip the dysthymia section if the respondent had multiple or lengthy major depressive episodes in the past 2 years. Thus, previous studies likely underestimated the prevalence of both lifetime and current chronic depression. Fortunately, this has been rectified in the *DSM-5* SCID, which assesses both current and past PDD.

Most widely used depression rating scales and self-report inventories can be useful in assessing symptom severity and monitoring treatment response in PDD. However, they have some limitations when applied to chronic depressive conditions. For example, the widely used 17- and 21-item versions of the HAM-D do not assess many of the most common symptoms in PDD (e.g., cognitive symptoms; Keller et al., 1995). Thus, it is advisable to use modified and longer versions of the HAM-D that include helplessness, hopelessness, worthlessness, and reversed vegetative features to assess persistent depression. In addition, the HAM-D assesses patients' symptoms with reference to differences from their "normal" or "usual" state. However, for many patients with early-onset chronic depressions, their normal or usual state may be depressed. Consequently, symptoms may be overlooked if questions are phrased in terms of change or worsening from the usual state. To address these problems, Mason and colleagues (1995) developed the Cornell Dysthymia Rating Scale, which has greater content validity, a broader range of symptom severity, and greater sensitivity to change than does the HAM-D (Hellerstein, Batchelder, Lee, & Borisovskaya, 2002).

The General Behavior Inventory (GBI; Depue, Krauss, Spoont, & Arbisi, 1989) was explicitly developed to screen for chronic depressive and bipolar mood disorders. It assesses symptoms on a trait basis, rather than during a recent, discrete time period. The GBI has good psychometric properties and exhibits relatively good concordance with interview-based diagnoses in community and clinical samples and in adolescents and adults (Danielson, Youngstrom, Findling, & Calabrese, 2003; Depue et al., 1989; Klein, Dickstein, Taylor, & Harding, 1989).

Treatment of Depression

There are psychosocial and somatic treatments for MDD and PDD. Several types of psychosocial interventions have been employed in the treatment of depression; however, most clinical research has examined the effectiveness of behavioral, cognitive behavioral, and interpersonal treatments. Although a thorough review of these and other interventions for depression is beyond the scope of this chapter, we review briefly the evidence for behavior therapy (BT), cognitive behavior therapy (CBT), and interpersonal psychotherapy (IPT).[5]

BEHAVIORAL TREATMENTS

Historically, behavioral interventions for depression focused on decreasing unpleasant events and increasing pleasant activities, largely by teaching patients to increase behaviors likely to generate positive reinforcement from the environment (Craighead, Craighead, Ritschel, & Zagoloff, 2013). Multiple interventions based on this principle have demonstrated empirical success, beginning with Lewinsohn, Sullivan, and Grosscup's (1980) 12-session program (Lewinsohn & Gotlib, 1995). Lewinsohn's original formulation has been augmented with the addition of social skills training (Becker, Heimberg, & Bellack, 1987), self-monitoring and self-reinforcement (Antonuccio, Ward, & Tearnan, 1991), and problem solving (Nezu, Nezu, & Perri, 1989).

From the 1980s through the late 1990s, behavioral treatments were overshadowed by increased research regarding cognitive-behavioral interventions. However, Jacobson and colleagues (1996) found that the behavioral components of CBT (i.e., activity scheduling, reducing avoidance, increasing positive events) produced outcomes equal to the full package of CBT (i.e., behavioral principles plus cognitive restructuring and schema modification). More recently, Dimidjian and colleagues (2006) presented a manualized version of this intervention called behavioral activation (BA). BA builds on the principles of the older behavior therapies by emphasizing the link between avoidance and depression. Behavioral activation aims to augment an individual's behavioral repertoire to increase opportunities for environmental positive reinforcement. In one study, BA was equal to antidepressant medication and superior to CBT in the treatment of severely depressed patients (Dimidjian et al., 2006). Although more research is needed, preliminary findings are encouraging. Multiple meta-analyses have found support for behavioral treatments for MDD (Cuijpers, van Straten, & Warmerdam, 2007; Ekers, Richards, & Gilbody, 2008; Mazzucchelli, Kane, & Rees, 2009; Chartier & Provencher, 2013). These findings suggest that (a) behavioral symptoms of depression can and should be evaluated and targeted in the course of treatment, (b) alleviating behavioral deficits in depressed individuals has an impact on overall mood, and (c) further research is needed to determine which treatments work for which patients.

BA has also shown recent promise as an effective treatment for depressed adolescents (Dimidjian & McCauley, 2016). An RCT by McCauley and colleagues (2015), comparing a 14-session BA protocol modified for use with adolescents to "evidence-based practice for depression" (a condition meant to replicate standard care offered at academically affiliated clinic settings, which included CBT and IPT), found BA to be both an effective and a feasible treatment for depressed adolescents. Positive treatment effects were recently reported in a within subjects study in which over half of the depressed sample were fully remitted by the end of 19 weeks of BA treatment (Ritschel, Ramirez, Cooley, & Craighead, 2016).

---

[5] For thorough reviews regarding the effectiveness of psychological interventions for depression, see Craighead, Johnson, Carey, and Dunlop (2015), pp. 331–408.

COGNITIVE BEHAVIOR THERAPY (CBT)

CBT (Beck et al., 1979) is a short-term (16 to 20 sessions over 12 to 16 weeks) structured treatment that aims to teach patients to identify their automatic self-thoughts and their relationship to feelings, recognize and correct cognitive errors, and change underlying core beliefs about themselves. In the final sessions of CBT, the focus of therapy shifts to consolidating gains to help prevent future depressive episodes.

CBT has been empirically subjected to more than 80 controlled clinical trials (Cuijpers et al., 2013), and numerous studies have documented its effectiveness in treating depression (see Hollon et al., 2014; Craighead, Johnson, Carey, & Dunlop, 2015). Results comparing CBT to antidepressant medications, however, have been equivocal. Several studies have found that CBT and medications are equally efficacious in the treatment of depression (for a review, see Craighead et al., 2015). The most notable exception to this finding is the National Institute of Mental Health Treatment of Depression Collaborative Research Project (TDCRP), which found medications to be superior to CBT in the treatment of depressed outpatients (Elkin et al., 1989). Concerns about the TDCRP have been noted, and additional studies have since been conducted comparing medications to CBT; these studies have failed to find differences between the two interventions (DeRubeis et al., 2005; also see Vittengl, Clark, Dunn, & Jarrett, 2007).

INTERPERSONAL PSYCHOTHERAPY (IPT)

IPT is a short-term (12–16 weeks), weekly treatment (Klerman, Weissman, Rounsaville, & Chevron, 1984) that emphasizes the reciprocity between the biological and psychological underpinnings of depression. It is rooted in the idea that interpersonal relationships play a large role in the onset and maintenance of depression and focuses on identifying and amending lapses in interpersonal functioning that actively contribute to depression (Craighead et al., 2015).

IPT has been tested as a treatment for depression in more than 60 studies, including more than 30 RCTs. IPT has been widely found to be an effective treatment for depression versus control conditions (Cuijpers, Donker, Weissman, Ravitz, & Cristea, 2016). Although the results of the TDCRP study (previously noted in this chapter) are equivocal, secondary analysis found IPT and medication with clinical management to be comparably effective in treating severely depressed patients. More recently, IPT has shown promise when integrated into nontraditional approaches, and with treating patients with pathology outside of MDD (Donker et al., 2013; Elkin et al., 1995; Elkins, Gibbons, Shea, & Shaw, 1996; Markowitz, Lipsitz, & Milrod, 2014). Recent studies have found IPT to be effective in reducing depressive symptoms when implemented via a self-guided format on an internet platform (Donker et al., 2013).

SOMATIC TREATMENTS

The observation that the induction of seizure activity was useful in the treatment of psychiatric illness was first noted among asylum patients treated with convulsion-inducing chemical agents such as camphor and then later with metrazole and insulin (Fink, 2001). The subsequent development of electrical methods of seizure induction and technical refinements to its application (Loo, Schweitzer, & Pratt, 2006) led to modern electro-convulsive therapy (ECT).

Since that time, clinical options for the biological treatment of depression have grown extensively. The serendipitous discovery of the first antidepressants, the monoamine oxidase inhibitors (MAOIs), during the course of drug treatment for tuberculosis, led over time to the development of additional empirically validated antidepressant medications (Slattery, Hudson, & Nutt, 2004). In parallel, other somatic treatments for depression have been developed. These include newer brain stimulation paradigms such as transcranial magnetic stimulation (Camprodon, 2016; Rotenberg, Horvath, & Pascual-Leone, 2014) and deep brain stimulation (Riva-Posse, Holtzheimer, Garlow, & Mayberg, 2013).

At present, antidepressant medications are the most common somatic treatment employed for depression (for a review, see Rocha, Fuzikawa, Riera, & Hara, 2012). Several classes of antidepressant medications exist for the treatment of MDD (Prendes-Alvarez, Schatzberg, & Nemeroff, 2015). With respect to class, these medications include the monoamine oxidase inhibitors (MAOIs; e.g., phenelzine, tranylcypromine, selegiline); tricyclic antidepressants (TCAs; e.g., imipramine, desipramine, clomipramine, amitriptyline); selective serotonin reuptake inhibitors (SSRIs; e.g., fluoxetine, sertraline, paroxetine, citalopram, escitalopram, fluvoxamine); dual serotonin and norepinephrine reuptake inhibitors (SNRIs; e.g., venlafaxine and duloxetine); and the other types of antidepressants (e.g., trazodone, bupropion, nefazodone, mirtazapine, vilazodone, and vortioxetine). In addition, a wide variety of additional medications may be used in conjunction with antidepressants as augmentation strategies to optimize antidepressant response (Fava & Rush, 2006). Examples of augmenting medications include lithium carbonate, valproic acid, lamotrigine, atypical antipsychotic medications (e.g., ziprasidone, risperidone, olanzapine, aripiprazole, quetiapine, and brexpiprazole), thyroid agents (e.g., triiodothyronine), psychostimulants (e.g., dextroamphetamine, lisdexamfetamine, and methylphenidate), and anxiolytic medications (e.g., buspirone).

The common thread linking the various classes of currently available antidepressants is activity directed toward alteration of monoamine neurotransmitter activity, primarily serotonin and norepinephrine (Slattery et al., 2004). Most antidepressants were presumed to work by altering synaptic concentrations of monoamines, and although they do that, it is now believed that the mechanism of action is more complex.

The key advances that have been made with respect to antidepressant pharmacology have been substantial improvement in safety and tolerability (Prendes-Alvarez et al., 2015). For example, the use of MAOIs requires particular dietary restrictions that, if disregarded, may result in a potentially life-threatening elevation of blood pressure known as a hypertensive crisis; TCAs, as a drug class, and lithium carbonate are both potentially lethal in overdose; and particular TCAs as well as lithium carbonate sometimes have burdensome dose-dependent side-effect profiles as well. Despite these issues, MAOIs, TCAs, and lithium (in the case of bipolar depression) may produce remission of depressive symptoms in instances when many other medications do not; thus, they remain core elements of the antidepressant armamentarium.

A major current focus of clinical trials research in depression is the derivation of treatment algorithms to guide effective implementation of antidepressant therapy, such as with the Sequenced Treatment Alternatives to Relieve Depression (STAR*D) trial (Rush et al., 2006; Thase et al., 2007) and the integration of psychological and pharmacological treatments for depression (Craighead & Dunlop, 2014). In addition, the discovery of biological predictors of treatment response (Binder et al., 2004; Ising et al., 2007), differential treatment moderators identifying who will respond to CBT as opposed to antidepressants (McGrath et al., 2013), and treatment-emergent symptoms such as suicidal ideation (Laje et al., 2007) and adverse effect burden (Hu et al., 2007) are additional major areas of investigation.

TREATMENT OF PDD

There are few direct comparisons of treatment response between chronic and nonchronic depressions, and the results are inconsistent (Gilmer et al., 2008; Sung et al., 2012; Thase et al., 1994). However, indirect evidence suggests that PDD may require somewhat different approaches to treatment. For example PDD may require a longer duration of pharmacotherapy (Koran et al., 2001) and may be more likely than nonchronic MDD to benefit from combined pharmacotherapy and psychotherapy (Keller et al., 2000). This is in line with recent findings that patients with chronic depression show lower response and remission rates as well as prolonged courses of treatment as compared to MDD patients (Köhler et al., 2015).

ACUTE-PHASE TREATMENT

Recent meta-analyses (Cuijpers et al., 2010; Kriston, von Wolff, Westphal, Hölzel, & Härter, 2014; Levkovitz, Tedeschini, & Papakostas, 2011; von Wolff, Hölzel, Westphal, Härter, & Kriston, 2013) suggest that antidepressant medication is superior to placebo in the treatment of chronic depression. The major classes of antidepressants appear to be equivalent, although dropout rates are higher for TCAs than for SSRIs (von Wolff et al., 2013). As the placebo response rate is lower in chronic than nonchronic depressions, individuals with chronic depression experience greater specific benefits from active treatment (Levkovitz et al., 2011).

In Cuijpers and colleagues' (2010) meta-analysis, psychotherapy was significantly more efficacious than control conditions (e.g., placebo, treatment as usual, nonspecific treatment, wait list), although the effect size was small. However, pharmacotherapy was significantly more efficacious than psychotherapy, although this difference was derived entirely from studies focusing on dysthymic disorder; there was no difference for more severe forms of chronic depression. Examination of length of treatment indicated that a minimum of 18 sessions of psychotherapy is needed for optimal effects.

The two best-studied approaches to psychotherapy in chronic depression are the cognitive behavioral analysis system of psychotherapy (CBASP; McCullough, 2000), and IPT (Markowitz, 1998). CBASP, which was specifically designed for chronic depression, uses behavioral, cognitive, and interpersonal techniques to help patients become more effective in their social environments and develop better social problem-solving skills. CBASP is showing increasing promise in yielding high rates of remission as both an outpatient and inpatient treatment option for chronic depression (Swan et al., 2014; Brakemeier et al.,

2015). IPT is a short-term, psychodynamically inspired therapy that focuses on current interpersonal problems such as interpersonal conflicts, change in an important social role, grief, and social isolation/skills deficits. In one of the few head-to-head comparisons of different psychotherapy approaches for chronic depression, Schramm et al. (2011) found that CBASP produced a significantly higher remission rate than IPT, although the two treatments did not differ on change in HAM-D or effects 1 year posttreatment.

Finally, the combination of psychotherapy and pharmacotherapy appears to be significantly more efficacious than either monotherapy, particularly for double depression and chronic MDD (Cuijpers et al., 2010). This contrasts with studies of MDD in general, where combination treatment is generally not more effective than psychotherapy or medication alone (Craighead & Dunlop, 2014), though the combination may be more effective for severe and perhaps for severe-chronic MDD (Hollon et al., 2014).

Common factors that cut across specific forms of therapy, such as the therapeutic alliance, also play a significant role in fostering change with chronically depressed patients (Klein et al., 2003; Arnow et al., 2013). Similarities in both therapists' and patients' reports of the alliance have been associated with more reductions in some depressed symptoms in chronically depressed patients (Laws et al., 2016). In a comparison of the effects of common and specific factors in CBASP, Santiago and colleagues (2005) reported that they had additive effects in predicting outcome, with common factors accounting for somewhat more variance than specific factors.

On balance, it appears that antidepressant medication may be somewhat more efficacious than psychotherapy in treating PDD. However, some forms of psychotherapy, or psychotherapy administered with sufficient intensity, may be as effective as pharmacotherapy. Given the broad range of treatment options available, an important question is whether there are predictors of differential treatment response to help guide treatment selection. Unfortunately, few predictors of differential response to different medications or to pharmacotherapy versus psychotherapy have been identified. However, Nemeroff et al. (2003) found that CBASP produced a significantly higher rate of remission than pharmacotherapy in the subgroup of chronically depressed patients with a history of childhood adversity. Several studies have reported that patients' preferences for psychotherapy versus pharmacotherapy had a significant impact on their outcomes (Kocsis et al., 2009; Steidtmann et al., 2013). Moreover, Steidtmann and colleagues (2013) found that patients who had not shown improvement with psychotherapy during the first 8 weeks of treatment were unlikely to remit with continued therapy.

CONTINUATION AND MAINTENANCE TREATMENT

Due to the high risk of relapse and recurrence (Klein et al., 2006), continuation and maintenance pharmacotherapy is an important consideration for patients with chronic depression. The continuation phase consists of the first 4 to 6 months of treatment after recovery; the maintenance phase consists of treatment after that point. Several double-blind, placebo-discontinuation studies have demonstrated that continuation treatment (Koran et al., 2001) and maintenance treatment (Keller et al., 1998; Kocsis et al., 1996) of patients who have recovered from chronic depression are associated with a significantly lower risk of relapse or recurrence than placebo. There are fewer studies of the efficacy of psychotherapy in preventing relapse and recurrence in chronic depression. However, Klein, Santiago, and colleagues (2004) reported that psychotherapy can be an effective maintenance phase treatment. Chronically depressed patients who responded to acute and continuation treatment were randomly assigned to continue to receive either one session of CBASP per month or assessment only for 12 months. Patients who received maintenance CBASP had a significantly lower risk of recurrence than patients who were assigned to the assessment-only condition.

TREATMENT SUMMARY

BA, CBT, and IPT as well as antidepressant medications attenuate the symptoms for many sufferers of MDD, and CBASP, IPT, and medications are effective in the treatment of PDD. Many empirical questions remain, however. How should treatments be selected—can we determine which treatments work best for which patients? Which treatments produce the most enduring effects? What are the mechanisms of action of the psychosocial and pharmacological interventions? When are combination therapies (i.e., psychotherapy plus medication) indicated? These and other questions are under investigation, and results from these studies will inform a new generation of research and treatment.

Summary and Future Directions

Depression is a prevalent and debilitating disorder resulting in suffering at the individual, family, and societal levels. It can be reliably diagnosed, even though it is a heterogeneous disorder with multiple etiological pathways. In this chapter, we have described the psychological, genetic, and neurobiological characteristics and possible etiologies of depression, and how the extant effective treatments have been derived and implemented.

It is now widely recognized that depressive disorders often exhibit a chronic course. Indeed, chronic depressions account for at least one third of the cases of mood disorders in clinical settings, and this prevalence has been reflected with the re-categorization of chronic depression under the single PDD diagnosis in the *DSM-5* (APA, 2013a). Despite this important acknowledgment, much more research is needed in the realm of PDD. Now that research has made it clear that chronic depression differs from nonchronic depression in a number of important respects, more systematic studies need to be done to elucidate the etiopathogenetic and neurobiological factors underlying chronic depression, as well as to create and assess more efficacious treatment regimes and PDD-specific assessment measures.

Clearly, great advances have been made in the evolution of clinical science research regarding depression. It seems that the most significant future questions need to address how the multiple pathways of the etiology of the disorder interact in the development of MDD. Though efficacious treatments have been developed, results still indicate that only about 30% to 35% of depressed patients completely remit from their episode when treated; work is needed to better understand the disorder so a greater percentage of the patients suffering from depression will be successfully treated. Clinical scientific development has reached the point where we can ask which patients respond best to which treatment (see McGrath et al., 2013); this should provide badly needed evidence to guide clinical intervention. The dissemination of efficacious treatments to a wider range of the population is essential; dissemination will most likely advance by the development of more sophisticated and more easily used contemporary technologies, such as those used by the Improving Access to Psychological Therapies initiative in the United Kingdom (Clark, 2011). Finally, it is extremely important to extend programs designed to prevent the initial episode of major depression.

References

Abela, J. R. Z., Stolow, D., Zhang, M., & McWhinnie, C. M. (2012). Negative cognitive style and past history of major depressive episodes in university students. *Cognitive Therapy and Research, 36*, 219–227. doi: 10.1007/s10608-010-9334-y

Abraham, K. (1911). Notes on the psychoanalytic investigation and treatment of manic-depressive insanity and allied conditions. In D. Bryan & A. Strachey (Eds.), *Selected papers on psychoanalysis* (pp. 137–156). New York, NY: Basic Books.

Abramson, L. Y., Alloy, L. B., Hankin, B. L., Haeffel, G. J., MacCoon, D. G., & Gibb, B. E. (2002). Cognitive vulnerability-stress models of depression in a self-regulatory and psychobiological context. In I. H. Gotlib & C. L. Hammen (Eds.), *Handbook of depression* (pp. 268–294). New York, NY: Guilford Press.

Abramson, L. Y., Metalsky, G. I., & Alloy, L. B. (1989). Hopelessness depression: A theory-based subtype of depression. *Psychological Review, 96*, 358–372. doi: 10.1037/0033-295X.96.2.358

Abramson, L. Y., Seligman, M. E. P., & Teasdale, J. (1978). Learned helplessness in humans: Critique and reformulation. *Journal of Abnormal Psychology, 87*, 49–74. doi: 10.1037/0021-843X.87.1.49

Akiskal, H. S. (1983). Dysthymic disorder: Psychopathology of proposed chronic depressive subtypes. *American Journal of Psychiatry, 140*(1), 11–20.

Alderete, E., Vega, W. A., Kolody, B., & Aguilar-Gaxiola, S. (1999). Depressive symptomatology: Prevalence and psychosocial risk factors among Mexican migrant farmworkers in California. *Journal of Community Psychology, 27*(4), 457–471.

Alegría, M., Mulvaney-Day, N., Torres, M., Polo, A., Cao, Z., & Canino, G. (2007). Prevalence of psychiatric disorders across Latino subgroups in the United States. *American Journal of Public Health, 97*(1), 68–75.

Alloy, L. B., & Abramson, L. Y. (1999). The Temple–Wisconsin Cognitive Vulnerability to Depression (CVD) Project: Conceptual background, design, and methods. *Journal of Cognitive Psychotherapy, 13*, 227–262.

Alloy, L. B., Abramson, L. Y., Hogan, M. E., Whitehouse, W. G., Rose, D. T., Robinson, M. S., ... Lapkin, J. B. (2000). The Temple–Wisconsin Cognitive Vulnerability to Depression Project: Lifetime history of Axis I psychopathology in individuals at high and low cognitive risk for depression. *Journal of Abnormal Psychology, 109*(3), 403–418.

Alloy, L. B., Abramson, L. Y., Walshaw, P. D., & Neeren, A. M. (2006). Cognitive vulnerability to unipolar and bipolar mood disorders. *Journal of Social and Clinical Psychology, 25*, 726–754. doi: 10.1521/jscp.2006.25.7.726

Alloy, L. B., Abramson, L. Y., Whitehouse, W. G., Hogan, M. E., Panzarella, C., & Rose, D. T. (2006). Prospective incidence of first onsets and recurrences of depression in individuals at high and low cognitive risk for depression. *Journal of Abnormal Psychology, 115*, 145–156. doi: 10.1037/0021-843X.115.1.145

Alloy, L. B., Abramson, L. Y., Whitehouse, W. G., Hogan, M. E., Tashman, N. A., Steinberg, D. L., ... Donovan, P. (1999). Depressogenic cognitive styles: Predictive validity, information processing and personality characteristics, and developmental origins. *Behaviour Research and Therapy, 37*, 503–531. doi: 10.1016/S0005-7967(98)00157-0

American Psychiatric Association. (1968). *Diagnostic and statistical manual of mental disorders* (2nd ed.). Washington, DC: Author.

American Psychiatric Association. (1980). *Diagnostic and statistical manual of mental disorders* (3rd ed., rev.). Washington, DC: Author.

American Psychiatric Association. (1994). *Diagnostic and statistical manual of mental disorders* (4th ed.) Washington, DC: Author.

American Psychiatric Association. (2013a). *Diagnostic and statistical manual of mental disorders* (5th ed.). Washington, DC: Author.

American Psychiatric Association. (2013b). *Highlights of changes from DSM-IV-TR to DSM-5*. Washington, DC: Author.

Amsterdam, J. D., Maislin, G., Winokur, A., Berwish, N., Kling, M., & Gold, P. (1988). The oCRH stimulation test before and after clinical recovery from depression. *Journal of Affective Disorders, 14*, 213–222. doi: 10.1016/0165-0327(88)90037-7

Antonuccio, D. O., Ward, C. H., & Tearnan, B. H. (1991). The behavioral treatment of unipolar depression in adult outpatients. In M. Hersen, R. M. Eisler, & P. M. Miller (Eds.), *Progress in behavior modification* (Vol. 24, pp. 152–191). Newbury Park, CA: Sage.

Arana, G. W., Baldessarini, R. J., & Orsteen, M. (1985). The dexamethasone suppression test for diagnosis and prognosis in psychiatry: Commentary and review. *Archives of General Psychiatry, 42,* 1193–1204. doi: 10.1001/archpsyc.1985.01790350067012

Arborelius, L., Owens, M. J., Plotsky, P. M., & Nemeroff, C. B. (1999). The role of corticotropin-releasing factor in depression and anxiety disorders. *Journal of Endocrinology, 160,* 1–12. doi: 0022 –0795/99/0160–0001

Arnow, B. A., Steidtmann, D., Blasey, C., Manber, R., Constantino, M. J., Klein, D. N., … Kocsis, J. H. (2013). The relationship between the therapeutic alliance and treatment outcome in two distinct psychotherapies for chronic depression. *Journal of Consulting and Clinical Psychology, 81*(4), 627–638.

Arnow, B. A., Spangler, D., Klein, D. N., & Burns, D. D. (2004). Rumination and distraction among chronic depressives in treatment: A structural equation analysis. *Cognitive Therapy and Research, 28,* 67–83.

Austin, M. P., Mitchell, P., & Goodwin, G. M. (2001). Cognitive deficits in depression. *British Journal of Psychiatry, 178*(3), 200–206.

Azmitia, E. C., & Gannon, P. J. (1986). Anatomy of the serotonergic system in the primate and sub-primate brain. *Advances in Neurology, 43,* 407–468.

Bandura, A. (1969). *Principles of behavior modification.* New York, NY: Holt, Rinehart & Winston.

Bandura, A. (1977). Self-efficacy: Toward a unifying theory of behavioral change. *Psychological Review, 84,* 191–215. doi: 10.1037/0033-295X.84.2.191

Barnhofer, T., Brennan, K., Crane, C., Duggan, D., & Williams, J. M. G. (2014). A comparison of vulnerability factors in patients with persistent and remitting lifetime symptom course of depression. *Journal of Affective Disorders, 152,* 155–161.

Basco, M. R., Bostic, J. Q., Davies, D., Rush, A. J., Witte, B., Hendrickse, W. A., & Barnett, V. (2000). Methods to improve diagnostic accuracy in a community mental health setting. *American Journal of Psychiatry, 157,* 1599–1605. doi: 10.1176/appi.ajp .157.10.1599

Beck, A. T. (1967). *Depression: Clinical, experimental, and theoretical aspects.* New York, NY: Harper & Row.

Beck, A. T. (1968). *Depression: Causes and treatment.* Philadelphia: University of Pennsylvania Press.

Beck, A. T. (1976). *Cognitive therapy and the emotional disorders.* New York, NY: International Universities Press.

Beck, A. T. (1987). Cognitive models of depression. *Journal of Cognitive Psychotherapy, 1,* 5–37.

Beck, J. S. (1995). *Cognitive therapy: Basics and beyond.* New York, NY: Guilford Press.

Beck, A. T., Rush, A. J., Shaw, B. F., & Emery, G. (1979). *Cognitive therapy of depression.* New York, NY: Guilford Press.

Beck, A. T., Steer, R. A., & Brown, G. K. (1996). *Beck Depression Inventory manual* (2nd ed.). San Antonio, TX: Psychological Corporation.

Becker, R. E., Heimberg, R. G., & Bellack, A. S. (1987). *Social skills training treatment for depression.* Elmsford, NY: Pergamon Press.

Berman, R. M., Narasimhan, M., Miller, H. L., Anand, A., Cappiello, A., Oren, D. A., … Charney, D. S. (1999). Transient depressive relapse induced by catecholamine depletion: Potential phenotypic vulnerability marker? *Archives of General Psychiatry, 56,* 395–403. doi: 10.1001/archpsyc.56.5.395

Berton, O., & Nestler, E. J. (2006). New approaches to antidepressant drug discovery: Beyond monoamines. *Nature Reviews Neuroscience, 7,* 137–151. doi: 10.1038/nrn1846

Biegon, A., Weizman, A., Karp, L., Ram, A., Tiano, S., & Wolff, M. (1987). Serotonin 5-HT2 receptor binding on blood platelets—a peripheral marker for depression? *Life Science, 41,* 2485–2492. doi: 10.1016/0024-3205(87)90675-8

Bijttebier, P., Beck, I., Claes, L., & Vandereycken, W. (2009). Gray's Reinforcement Sensitivity Theory as a framework for research on personality–psychopathology associations. *Clinical Psychology Review, 29*(5), 421–430.

Binder, E. B., Salyakina, D., Lichtner, P., Wochnik, G. M., Ising, M., Putz, B., … Muller-Myhsok, B. (2004). Polymorphisms in FKBP5 are associated with increased recurrence of depressive episodes and rapid response to antidepressant treatment. *Nature Genetics, 36,* 1319–1325. doi: 10.1038/ng1479

Blackburn, I. M., Jones, S., & Lewin, R. J. P. (2011). Cognitive style in depression. *British Journal of Clinical Psychology, 25,* 241–251. doi: 10.1111/ j.2044-8260.1986.tb00704.x

Blanco, C., Okuda, M., Markowitz, J. C., Liu, S. M., Grant, B. F., & Hasin, D. S. (2010). The epidemiology of chronic major depressive disorder and dysthymic disorder: Results from the National Epidemiologic Survey on Alcohol and Related Conditions. *Journal of Clinical Psychiatry, 71*(12), 1645–1656.

Bourke, C., Douglas, K., & Porter, R. (2010). Processing of facial emotion expression in major depression: A review. *Australian and New Zealand Journal of Psychiatry, 44*(8), 681–696.

Brakemeier, E. L., Radtke, M., Engel, V., Zimmermann, J., Tuschen-Caffier, B., Hautzinger, M., … Normann, C. (2015). Overcoming treatment resistance in chronic depression: A pilot study on outcome and feasibility of the cognitive behavioral analysis system of psychotherapy as an inpatient treatment program. *Psychotherapy and Psychosomatics, 84*(1), 51–56.

Brown, E. S., Varghese, F. P., & McEwen, B. S. (2004). Association of depression with medical illness: Does cortisol play a role? *Biological Psychiatry, 55,* 1–9. doi: 10.1016/S0006-3223(03)00473-6

Brown, T. A. (2007). Temporal course and structural relationships among dimensions of temperament and *DSM-IV* anxiety and mood disorder constructs. *Journal of Abnormal Psychology, 116*(2), 313.

Bruffaerts, R., Vilagut, G., Demyttenaere, K., Alonso, J., AlHamzawi, A., Andrade, L. H., … Kessler, R. C. (2012). Role of common mental and physical disorders in partial disability around the world. *British Journal of Psychiatry, 200*(6), 454–461.

Butler, G., & Mathews, A. (1983). Cognitive processes in anxiety. *Advances in Behaviour Research and Therapy, 5*(1), 51–62.

Cameron, I. M., Crawford, J. R., Lawton, K., & Reid, I. C. (2008). Psychometric comparison of PHQ-9 and HADS for measuring depression severity in primary care. *British Journal of General Practice, 58*(546), 32–36.

Camprodon, J. A. (2016). Transcranial magnetic stimulation. In *Psychiatric Neurotherapeutics* (pp. 165–186). New York, NY: Springer.

Carpenter, W. T., & Bunney, W. E. (1971). Adrenal cortical activity in depressive illness. *American Journal of Psychiatry, 128,* 31–40.

Carroll, B. J. (1982). Use of the dexamethasone suppression test in depression. *Journal of Clinical Psychiatry, 43,* 44–50.

Carroll, B. J., Martin, F. I., & Davies, B. (1968). Pituitary-adrenal function in depression. *Lancet, 1,* 1373–1374. doi: 10.1016/S0140-6736(68)92072-2

Caspi, A., Sugden, K., Moffitt, T. E., Taylor, A., Craig, I. W., Harrington, H., … Poulton, R. (2003). Influence of life stress on depression: Moderation by a polymorphism in the 5-HTT gene. *Science, 301*(5631), 386–389.

Charney, D. S. (1998). Monoamine dysfunction and the pathophysiology and treatment of depression. *Journal of Clinical Psychiatry, 59*(Suppl. 14), 11–14.

Charney, D. S., Heninger, G. R., Sternberg, D. E., & Roth, R. H. (1981). Plasma MHPG in depression: Effects of acute and chronic desipramine treatment. *Psychiatry Research, 5,* 217–229.

Chartier, I. S., & Provencher, M. D. (2013). Behavioural activation for depression: Efficacy, effectiveness and dissemination. *Journal of Affective Disorders, 145*(3), 292–299.

Chen, B., Dowlatshahi, D., MacQueen, G. M., Wang, J. F., & Young, L. T. (2001). Increased hippocampal BDNF immunoreactivity in subjects treated with antidepressant medication. *Biological Psychiatry, 50,* 260–265. doi: 10.1016/S0006-3223(01)01083-6

Clark, D. M. (2011). Implementing NICE guidelines for the psychological treatment of depression and anxiety disorders: The IAPT experience. *International Review of Psychiatry, 23*(4), 318–327.

Costello, E. J., Erkanli, A., & Angold, A. (2006). Is there an epidemic of child or adolescent depression? *Journal of Child Psychology and Psychiatry, 47,* 1263–1271. doi: 10.1111/j.1469-7610.2006.01682.x

Craighead, W. E., Craighead, L. W., Ritschel, L. A., & Zagoloff, A. (2013). Behavior therapy and cognitive-behavioral therapy. In I. B. Weiner, G. Stricker, & T. A. Widiger (Eds.), *Handbook of psychology: Vol. 8. Clinical psychology* (2nd ed., pp. 291–319). Hoboken, NJ: Wiley.

Craighead, W. E., & Dunlop, B. W. (2014). Combination psychotherapy and antidepressant medication treatment for depression: For whom, when, and how. *Annual Review of Psychology, 65,* 267–300.

Craighead, W. E., Johnson, B. N., Carey, S., & Dunlop, B. W. (2015). Psychosocial treatments for major depressive disorder. In P. E. Nathan & J. M. Gorman (Eds.), *A guide to treatments that work* (pp. 381–408). New York, NY: Oxford University Press.

Craighead, W. E., Sheets, E. S., Craighead, L. W., & Madsen, J. W. (2011). Recurrence of MDD: A prospective study of personality pathology and cognitive distortions. *Personality Disorders: Theory, Research, and Treatment, 2*(2), 83.

Craske, M. G. (2014). Introduction to special issue: How does neuroscience inform psychological treatment? *Behaviour Research and Therapy, 62,* 1–2.

Cuijpers, P., Berking, M., Andersson, G., Quigley, L., Kleiboer, A., & Dobson, K. S. (2013). A meta-analysis of cognitive-behavioural therapy for adult depression, alone and in comparison with other treatments. *Canadian Journal of Psychiatry*, *58*(7), 376.

Cuijpers, P., Donker, T., Weissman, M. M., Ravitz, P., & Cristea, I. A. (2016). Interpersonal psychotherapy for mental health problems: A comprehensive meta-analysis. *American Journal of Psychiatry*, *173*(7), 680–687.

Cuijpers, P., van Straten, A., Schuurmans, J., van Oppen, P., Hollon, S. D., & Andersson, G. (2010). Psychotherapy for chronic major depression and dysthymia: A meta-analysis. *Clinical Psychology Review*, *30*, 51–62. doi: 10.1016/j.cpr.2009.09.003

Cuijpers, P., van Straten, A., & Warmerdam, L. (2007). Behavioral activation treatments of depression: A meta-analysis. *Clinical Psychology Review*, *27*, 318–326. doi: 10.1016/j.cpr.2006.11.001

Dalili, M. N., Penton-Voak, I. S., Harmer, C. J., & Munafò, M. R. (2015). Meta-analysis of emotion recognition deficits in major depressive disorder. *Psychological Medicine*, *45*(6), 1135–1144.

Danielson, C. K., Youngstrom, E. A., Findling, R. L., & Calabrese, J. R. (2003). Discriminative validity of the General Behavior Inventory using youth report. *Journal of Abnormal Child Psychology*, *31*, 29–39. doi: 10.1023/A:1021717231272

Davidson, R. J. (1992). Anterior cerebral symmetry and the nature of emotion. *Brain and Cognition*, *20*, 125–151.

Davidson, R. J. (1998). Affective style and affective disorders: Perspectives from affective neuroscience. *Cognition and Emotion*, *12*, 307–330. doi: 10.1080/026999398379628

Decker, H. S. (2004). The psychiatric works of Emil Kraepelin: A many-faceted story of modern medicine. *Journal of the History of Neuroscience*, *13*, 248–276.

Demeyer, I., De Lissnyder, E., Koster, E. H., & De Raedt, R. (2012). Rumination mediates the relationship between impaired cognitive control for emotional information and depressive symptoms: A prospective study in remitted depressed adults. *Behaviour Research and Therapy*, *50*(5), 292–297.

Depue, R. A., Krauss, S., Spoont, M. R., & Arbisi, P. (1989). General Behavior Inventory identification of unipolar and bipolar affective conditions in a nonclinical university population. *Journal of Abnormal Psychology*, *98*, 117–126. doi: 10.1037/0021-843X.98.2.117

DeRubeis, R. J., Hollon, S. D., Amsterdam, J. D., Shelton, R. C., Young, P. R., Salomon, R. M., ... Gallop, R. (2005). Cognitive therapy vs. medications in the treatment of moderate to severe depression.

Archives of General Psychiatry, *62*, 409–416. doi: 10.1001/archpsyc.62.4.409

Dimidjian, S., Hollon, S. D., Dobson, K. S., Schmaling, K. B., Kohlenberg, R. J., Addis, M. E., ... Jacobson, N. S. (2006). Randomized trial of behavioral activation, cognitive therapy, and antidepressant medication in the acute treatment of adults with major depression. *Journal of Consulting and Clinical Psychology*, *74*, 658–670. doi: 10.1037/0022-006X .74.4.658

Dimidjian, S., Martell, C. R., Addis, M. E., & Herman-Dunn, R. (2008). Behavioral activation for depression. In D. H. Barlow (Ed.), *Clinical handbook of psychological disorders: A step-by-step treatment manual* (4th ed., pp. 328–364). New York, NY: Guilford Press.

Dimidjian, S., & McCauley, E. (2016). Modular, scalable, and personalized: Priorities for behavioral interventions for adolescent depression. *Clinical Psychology: Science and Practice*, *23*(1), 58–61.

Donaldson, C., & Lam, D. (2004). Rumination, mood and social problem-solving in major depression. *Psychological Medicine*, *34*, 1309–1318. doi: 10.1017/S0033291704001904

Donker, T., Batterham, P. J., Warmerdam, L., Bennett, K., Bennett, A., Cuijpers, P., ... Christensen, H. (2013). Predictors and moderators of response to internet-delivered interpersonal psychotherapy and cognitive behavior therapy for depression. *Journal of Affective Disorders*, *151*(1), 343–351.

Dorn, L. D., Burgess, E. S., Friedman, T. C., Dubbert, B., Gold, P. W., & Chrousos, G. P. (1997). The longitudinal course of psychopathology in Cushing's syndrome after correction of hypercortisolism. *Journal of Clinical Endocrinology & Metabolism*, *82*, 912–919. doi: 10.1210/jc.82.3.912

Dozois, D. J. A., & Covin, R. (2004). The Beck Depression Inventory (BDI-II), Beck Hopelessness Scale (BHS), and Beck Scale for Suicide Ideation (BSS). In M. J. Hilsenroth & D. L. Segal (Eds.), *Comprehensive handbook of psychological assessment* (pp. 50–69). Hoboken, NJ: Wiley.

Duman, R. S., & Monteggia, L. M. (2006). A neurotrophic model for stress-related mood disorders. *Biological Psychiatry*, *59*, 1116–1127. doi: 10.1016/j.biopsych.2006.02.013

Dunn, E. C., Brown, R. C., Dai, Y., Rosand, J., Nugent, N. R., Amstadter, A. B., & Smoller, J. W. (2014). Genetic determinants of depression: Recent findings and future directions. *Harvard Review of Psychiatry*, *23*(1), 1–18.

Duncan, L. E., Hutchison, K. E., Carey, G., & Craighead, W. E. (2009). Variation in brain-derived neurotrophic factor (BDNF) gene is associated with symptoms of depression. *Journal of Affective Disorders, 115*, 215–219.

Duque, A., & Vázquez, C. (2015). Double attention bias for positive and negative emotional faces in clinical depression: Evidence from an eye-tracking study. *Journal of Behavior Therapy and Experimental Psychiatry, 46*, 107–114.

Egan, M. F., Kokima, M., Callicott, J. H., Goldberg, T. E., Kolachana, B. S., Bertolino, A., … Weinberger, D. R. (2003). The BDNF val66met polymorphism affects activity dependent secretion of BDNF and human memory and hippocampal function. *Cell, 112*, 257–269.

Ekers, D., Richards, D., & Gilbody, S. (2008). A meta-analysis of randomized trials of behavioural treatment of depression. *Psychological Medicine, 38*(05), 611–623.

Elkin, I., Gibbons, R. D., Shea, M. T., & Shaw, B. F. (1996). Science is not a trial (but it can sometimes be a tribulation). *Journal of Consulting and Clinical Psychology, 64*, 92–103.

Elkin, I., Gibbons, R. D., Shea, M. T., Sotsky, S. M., Watkins, J. T., Pilkonis, P. A., & Hedeker, D. (1995). Initial severity and differential treatment outcome in the National Institute of Mental Health Treatment of Depression Collaborative Research Program. *Journal of Consulting and Clinical Psychology, 63*(5), 841.

Elkin, I., Shea, M. T., Watkins, J. T., Imber, S. D., Sotsky, S. M., Collins, J. F., … Parloff, M. B. (1989). National Institute of Mental Health Treatment of Depression Collaborative Research Program: General effectiveness of treatments. *Archives of General Psychiatry, 46*, 971–982. doi: 10.1001/archpsyc.1989.01810110013002

Engel, R. A., & DeRubeis, R. J. (1993). The role of cognition in depression. In K. S. Dobson & P. C. Kendall (Eds.), *Psychopathology and cognition* (pp. 83–119). San Diego, CA: Academic Press.

Evans, D. L., Charney, D. S., Lewis, L., Golden, R. N., Gorman, J. M., Krishnan, K. R., … Valvo, W. J. (2005). Mood disorders in the medically ill: Scientific review and recommendations. *Biological Psychiatry, 58*, 175–189. doi: 10.1016/j.biopsych.2005.05.001

Evans, D. L., & Nemeroff, C. B. (1983). The dexamethasone suppression test in mixed bipolar disorder. *American Journal of Psychiatry, 140*, 615–617.

Fava, M., & Rush, A. J. (2006). Current status of augmentation and combination treatments for major depressive disorder: A literature review and a proposal for a novel approach to improve practice. *Psychotherapy and Psychosomatics, 75*, 139–153. doi: 10.1159/000091771

Fergusson, D. M., Horwood, J., Ridder, E. M., & Beautrais, A. L. (2005). Subthreshold depression in adolescence and mental health outcomes in adulthood. *Archives of General Psychiatry, 62*, 66–72. doi: 10.1001/archpsyc.62.1.66

Ferster, C. B. (1965). Classification of behavioral pathology. In L. Krasner & L. P. Ullmann (Eds.), *Research in behavior modification* (pp. 6–26). New York, NY: Holt, Rinehart & Winston.

Ferster, C. B. (1966). Animal behavior and mental illness. *Psychological Record, 16*, 345–356.

Ferster, C. B. (1973). A functional analysis of depression. *American Psychologist, 28*, 857–870. doi: 10.1037/h0035605

Fink, M. (2001). Convulsive therapy: A review of the first 55 years. *Journal of Affective Disorders, 63*, 1–15. doi: 10.1016/S0165-0327(00)00367-0

First, M. B., & Gibbon, M. (2004). The Structured Clinical Interview for DSM-IV Axis I Disorders (SCID-I) and the Structured Clinical Interview for DSM-IV Axis II Disorders (SCID-II). In M. J. Hilsenroth & D. L. Segal (Eds.), *Comprehensive handbook of psychological assessment* (pp. 134–143). Hoboken, NJ: Wiley.

First, M. B., Williams, J. B. W., Karg, R. S., & Spitzer, R. L. (2015). *User's guide for the Structured Clinical Interview for DSM-5 Disorders, Research Version (SCID-5-RV)*. Arlington, VA: American Psychiatric Association.

Fisher, H. L., Cohen-Woods, S., Hosang, G. M., Korszun, A., Owen, M., Craddock, N., … Uher, R. (2013). Interaction between specific forms of childhood maltreatment and the serotonin transporter gene (5-HTT) in recurrent depressive disorder. *Journal of Affective Disorders, 145*(1), 136–141.

Foland-Ross, L. C., & Gotlib, I. H. (2012). Cognitive and neural aspects of information processing in major depressive disorder: An integrative perspective. *Frontiers in Psychology, 3*, 489.

Freud, S. (1950). Mourning and melancholia. In *Collected papers* (Vol. 4.). London, England: Hogarth Press. (Original work published 1917)

Fritzsche, A., Dahme, B., Gotlib, I. H., Joormann, J., Magnussen, H., Watz, H., … von Leupoldt, A. (2010). Specificity of cognitive biases in patients with current depression and remitted depression and in patients with asthma. *Psychological Medicine, 40*(5), 815–826.

Garvey, M. J., Tollefson, G. D., & Tuason, V. B. (1986). Is chronic primary major depression a distinct depression subtype? *Comprehensive Psychiatry, 27,* 446–448. doi: 10.1016/0010-440X(86)90032-5

Gibb, B. E. (2002). Childhood maltreatment and negative cognitive styles: A quantitative and qualitative review. *Clinical Psychology Review, 22*(2), 223–246.

Gillespie, C. F., & Nemeroff, C. B. (2007). Corticotropin-releasing factor and the psychobiology of early life stress. *Current Directions in Psychological Science, 16,* 85–89. doi: 10.1111/j.1467-8721.2007.00481.x

Gilmer, W. S., Gollan, J. K., Wisniewski, S. R., Howland, R. H., Trivedi, M. H., Miyahara, S., ... Rush, A. J. (2008). Does the duration of index episode affect the treatment outcome of major depressive disorder? A STAR*D report. *Journal of Clinical Psychiatry, 69,* 1246–1256.

Gilmer, W. S., Trivedi, M. H., Rush, A. J., Wisniewski, S. R., Luther, J., Howland, R. H., ... Alpert, J. (2005). Factors associated with chronic depressive episodes: A preliminary report from the STAR-D project. *Acta Psychiatrica Scandinavica, 112,* 425–433. doi: 10.1111/j.1600-0447.2005.00633.x

Glaser, R., & Kiecolt-Glaser, J. K. (2005). Stress-induced immune dysfunction: Implications for health. *National Review of Immunology, 5,* 243–251. doi: 10.1038/nri1571

Gollan, J. K., Pane, H. T., McCloskey, M. S., & Coccaro, E. F. (2008). Identifying differences in biased affective information processing in major depression. *Psychiatry Research, 159*(1), 18–24.

Gonul, A. S., Akdeniz, F., Taneli, F., Donat, O., Eker, C., & Vahip, S. (2005). Effect of treatment on serum brain-derived neurotrophic factor levels in depressed patients. *European Archives of Psychiatry and Clinical Neuroscience, 255,* 381–386. doi: 10.1007/s00406-005-0578-6

Goodwin, R. D., & Stein, M. B. (2004). Association between childhood trauma and physical disorders among adults in the United States. *Psychological Medicine, 34,* 509–520. doi: 10.1017/S003329170300134X

Gotlib, I. H., Kasch, K. L., Traill, S., Joormann, J., Arnow, B. A., & Johnson, S. L. (2004). Coherence and specificity of information-processing biases in depression and social phobia. *Journal of Abnormal*

Psychology, 113, 386–398. doi: 10.1037/0021-843X.113.3.386

Gray, J. A. (1987). *The psychology of fear and stress* (2nd ed.). New York, NY: Cambridge University Press.

Greenberg, P. E., Fournier, A. A., Sisitsky, T., Pike, C. T., & Kessler, R. C. (2015). The economic burden of adults with major depressive disorder in the United States (2005 and 2010). *Journal of Clinical Psychiatry, 76*(2), 155–162.

Groves, J. O. (2007). Is it time to reassess the BDNF hypothesis of depression? *Molecular Psychiatry, 12,* 1079–1088. doi: 10.1038/sj.mp.4002075

Gureje, O. (2011). Dysthymia in a cross-cultural perspective. *Current Opinion in Psychiatry, 24,* 67–71.

Gutman, D. A., Owens, M. J., Skelton, K. H., Thrivikraman, K. V., & Nemeroff, C. B. (2003). The corticotropin-releasing factor$_1$ receptor antagonist R121919 attenuates the behavioral and endocrine responses to stress. *Journal of Pharmacological and Experimental Therapy, 304,* 874–880. doi: 10.1124/jpet.102.042788

Haeffel, G. J., Abramson, L. Y., Voelz, Z. R., Metalsky, G. I., Halberstadt, L., Dykman, B. M., ... Alloy, L. B. (2003). Cognitive vulnerability to depression and lifetime history of Axis I psychopathology: A comparison of negative cognitive styles (CSQ) and dysfunctional attitudes (DAS). *Journal of Cognitive Psychotherapy, 17,* 3–22. doi: 10.1891/jcop.17.1.3.58269

Hamilton, J. P., & Gotlib, I. H. (2008). Neural substrates of increased memory sensitivity for negative stimuli in major depression. *Biological Psychiatry, 63*(12), 1155–1162.

Hamilton, M. (1960). A rating scale for depression. *Journal of Neurology, Neurosurgery, and Psychiatry, 23*(1), 56.

Hankin, B. L., Abramson, L. Y., Moffitt, T. E., Silva, P. A., McGee, R., & Angell, K. E. (1998). Development of depression from preadolescence to young adulthood: Emerging gender differences in a 10-year longitudinal study. *Journal of Abnormal Psychology, 107*(1), 128.

Haroon, E., Raison, C. L., & Miller, A. H. (2012). Psychoneuroimmunology meets neuropsychopharmacology: Translational implications of the impact of inflammation on behavior. *Neuropsychopharmacology, 37*(1), 137–162.

Hasin, D. S., Goodwin, R. D., Stinson, F. S., & Grant, B. F. (2005). Epidemiology of major depressive disorder: Results from the National Epidemiologic Survey on Alcoholism and Related Conditions. *Archives of General Psychiatry, 62*(10), 1097–1106.

Heim, C., & Binder, E. B. (2012). Current research trends in early life stress and depression: Review of human studies on sensitive periods, gene–environment interactions, and epigenetics. *Experimental Neurology, 233*(1), 102–111.

Hellerstein, D. J., Agosti, V., Bosi, M., & Black, S. R. (2010). Impairment in psychosocial functioning associated with dysthymic disorder in the NESARC study. *Journal of Affective Disorders, 127,* 84–88. doi: 10.1016/j.jad.2010.04.013

Hellerstein, D. J., Batchelder, S. T., Lee, A., & Borisovskaya, M. (2002). Rating dysthymia: An assessment of the construct and content validity of the Cornell Dysthymia Rating Scale. *Journal of Affective Disorders, 71*(1), 85–96.

Hertel, P. T., & Brozovich, F. (2010). Cognitive habits and memory distortions in anxiety and depression. *Current Directions in Psychological Science, 19*(3), 155–160.

Hidaka, B. H. (2012). Depression as a disease of modernity: Explanations for increasing prevalence. *Journal of Affective Disorders, 140,* 205–214. doi: 10.1016/j.jad.2011.12.036

Hirschfeld, R. M. A., Klerman, G. L., Andreasen, N. C., Clayton, P. J., & Keller, M. B. (1986). Psychosocial predictors of chronicity in depressed patients. *British Journal of Psychiatry, 148,* 648–654. doi: 10.1192/bjp.148.6.648

Hollon, S. D., DeRubeis, R. J., Fawcett, J., Amsterdam, J. D., Shelton, R. C., Zajecka, J.,...Gallop, R. (2014). Effect of cognitive therapy with antidepressant medications vs antidepressants alone on the rate of recovery in major depressive disorder: A randomized clinical trial. *JAMA Psychiatry, 71*(10), 1157–1164.

Holm-Denoma, J. M., Berlim, M. T., Fleck, M. P. A., & Joiner, T. E. (2006). Double depression in adult psychiatric outpatients in Brazil: Distinct from major depression? *Psychiatry Research, 144,* 191–196. doi: 10.1016/j.psychres.2005.06.011

Hornung, O. P., & Heim, C. M. (2015, February 17). Gene–environment interactions and intermediate phenotypes: Early trauma and depression. *Frontiers in Endocrinology.* doi: 10.3389/fendo.2014.00014

Hu, X. Z., Rush, A. J., Charney, D., Wilson, A. F., Sorant, A. J., Papanicolaous, G. J.,...Lipsky, R. H. (2007). Association between a functional serotonin transporter promoter polymorphism and citalopram treatment in adult outpatients with major depression. *Archives of General Psychiatry, 64,* 783–792. doi: 10.1001/archpsyc.64.7.783

Iacoviello, B. M., Alloy, L. B., Abramson, L. Y., Whitehouse, W. G., & Hogan, M. E. (2006). The course of depression in individuals at high and low cognitive risk for depression: A prospective study. *Journal of Affective Disorders, 93,* 61–69. doi: 10.1016/j.jad.2006.02.012

Ilardi, S. S., & Craighead, W. E. (1999). The relationship between personality pathology and dysfunctional cognitions in previously depressed adults. *Journal of Abnormal Psychology, 108,* 51–57. doi: 10.1037/0021-843X.108.1.51

Ingram, R. E., Miranda, J., & Segal, Z. V. (1998). *Cognitive vulnerability to depression.* New York, NY: Guilford Press.

Ising, M., Horstmann, S., Kloiber, S., Lucae, S., Binder, E. B., Kern, N.,...Holsboer, F. (2007). Combined dexamethasone/corticotropin releasing hormone test predicts treatment response in major depression—a potential biomarker? *Biological Psychiatry, 62,* 47–54. doi: 10.1016/j.biopsych.2006.07.039

Jacobson, L., & Sapolsky, R. (1991). The role of the hippocampus in feedback regulation of the hypothalamic-pituitary-adrenocortical axis. *Endocrine Reviews, 12,* 118–134. doi: 10.1210/edrv -12-2-118

Jacobson, N. S., Dobson, K. S., Truax, P. A., Addis, M. E., Koerner, K., Gollan, J. K.,...Prince, S. E. (1996). A component analysis of cognitive-behavioral treatment for depression. *Journal of Consulting and Clinical Psychology, 64,* 295–304. doi: 10.1037/0022 -006X.64.2.295

Joormann, J., & Gotlib, I. H. (2007). Selective attention to emotional faces following recovery from depression. *Journal of Abnormal Psychology, 116*(1), 80.

Joormann, J., & Quinn, M. E. (2014). Cognitive processes and emotion regulation in depression. *Depression and Anxiety, 31*(4), 308–315.

Joormann, J., Teachman, B. A., & Gotlib, I. H. (2009). Sadder and less accurate? False memory for negative material in depression. *Journal of Abnormal Psychology, 118*(2), 412.

Joormann, J., Yoon, K. L., & Siemer, M. (2010). Cognition and emotion regulation. In A. M. Kring & D. M. Sloan (Eds.), *Emotion regulation and psychopathology: A transdiagnostic approach to etiology and treatment* (pp. 174–203). New York, NY: Guilford Press.

Kasch, K. L., Rottenberg, J., Arnow, B. A., & Gotlib, I. H. (2002). Behavioral activation and inhibition systems and the severity and course of depression. *Journal of Abnormal Psychology*, *111*(4), 589.

Keller, M. B., Klein, D. N., Hirschfeld, R. M. A., Kocsis, J. H., McCullough, J. P., Miller, I., … Shea, T. (1995). Results of the DSM-IV mood disorders field trial. *American Journal of Psychiatry*, *152*, 843–849.

Keller, M. B., Kocsis, J. H., Thase, M. E., Gelenberg, A. J., Rush, A. J., Koran, L., … Harrison, W. (1998). Maintenance phase efficacy of sertraline for chronic depression: A randomized controlled trial. *JAMA*, *280*, 1665–1672. doi: 10.1001/jama.280.19.1665

Keller, M. B., Lavori, P. W., Friedman, B., Nielsen, E., Endicott, J., McDonald-Scott, P., & Andreasen, N. C. (1987). The Longitudinal Interval Follow-up Evaluation: A comprehensive method for assessing outcome in prospective longitudinal studies. *Archives of General Psychiatry*, *44*, 540–548. doi: 10.1001/archpsyc.1987.01800180050009

Keller, M. B., McCullough, J. P., Klein, D. N., Arnow, B., Dunner, D. L., Gelenberg, A. J., … Zajacka, J. (2000). A comparison of nefazodone, the cognitive behavioral-analysis system of psychotherapy, and their combination for the treatment of chronic depression. *New England Journal of Medicine*, *342*, 1462–1470. doi: 10.1056/NEJM200005183422001

Kennedy, R., & Craighead, W. E. (1988). Differential effects of depression and anxiety on recall of feedback in a learning task. *Behavior Therapy*, *19*, 437–454. doi: 10.1016/S0005-7894(88)80015-7

Kessler, R. C., Berglund, P., Demler, O., Jin, R., & Walters, E. E. (2005). Lifetime prevalence and age of onset distributions of DSM-IV disorders in the National Comorbidity Study Replication. *Archives of General Psychiatry*, *62*, 593–602. doi: 10.1001/archpsyc.62.6.593

Kessler, R. C., Chiu, W. T., Demler, O., & Walters, E. E. (2005). Prevalence, severity, and comorbidity of 12-month DSM-IV disorders in the National Cormorbidity Survey Replication. *Archives of General Psychiatry*, *62*, 617–627. doi: 10.1001/archpsyc.62.6.617

Kessler, R. C., McGonagle, K. A., Zhao, S., Nelson, C. B., Hughes, M., Eshleman, S., … Kendler, K. S. (1994). Lifetime and 12-month prevalence of DSM-III-R psychiatric disorders in the United States: Results from the National Comorbidity Survey. *Archives of General Psychiatry*, *51*(1), 8–19.

Kiecolt-Glaser, J. K., Derry, H. M., & Fagundes, C. P. (2015). Inflammation: Depression fans the flames and feasts on the heat. *American Journal of Psychiatry*, *172*(11), 1075–1091.

Kircanski, K., Joormann, J., & Gotlib, I. H. (2012). Cognitive aspects of depression. *Wiley Interdisciplinary Reviews: Cognitive Science*, *3*(3), 301–313.

Kleiman, E. M., Liu, R. T., Riskind, J. H., & Hamilton, J. L. (2015). Depression as a mediator of negative cognitive style and hopelessness in stress generation. *British Journal of Psychology*, *106*(1), 68–83.

Klein, D. N., Dickstein, S., Taylor, E. B., & Harding, K. (1989). Identifying chronic affective disorders in outpatients: Validation of the General Behavior Inventory. *Journal of Consulting and Clinical Psychology*, *57*, 106–111. doi: 10.1037/0022-006X.57.1.106

Klein, D. N., & Kotov, R. (2016). Persistence of depression in a 10-year prospective study: Evidence for a qualitatively distinct subtype. *Journal of Abnormal Psychology*, *125*, 337–348.

Klein, D. N., Riso, L. P., Donaldson, S. K., Schwartz, J. E., Anderson, R. L., Ouimette, P. C., … Aronson, T. A. (1995). Family study of early-onset dysthymia: Mood and personality disorders in relatives of outpatients with dysthymia and episodic major depression and normal controls. *Archives of General Psychiatry*, *52*, 487–496.

Klein, D. N., Santiago, N. J., Vivian, D., Arnow, B. A., Blalock, J. A., Dunner, D. L., … Keller, M. B. (2004). Cognitive-behavioral analysis system of psychotherapy as a maintenance treatment for chronic depression. *Journal of Consulting and Clinical Psychology*, *72*, 681–688. doi: 10.1037/0022-006X.72.4.681

Klein, D. N., Schwartz, J. E., Santiago, N. J., Vivian, D., Vocisano, C., Castonguay, L. G., … Keller, M. B. (2003). Therapeutic alliance in depression treatment: Controlling for prior change and patient characteristics. *Journal of Consulting and Clinical Psychology*, *71*(6), 997–1006.

Klein, D. N., Shankman, S. A., Lewinsohn, P. M., Rohde, P., & Seeley, J. R. (2004). Family study of chronic depression in a community sample of young adults. *American Journal of Psychiatry*, *161*, 646–653. doi: 10.1176/appi.ajp.161.4.646

Klein, D. N., Shankman, S. A., & Rose, S. (2006). Ten-year prospective follow-up study of the naturalistic course of dysthymic disorder and double depression. *American Journal of Psychiatry*, *163*, 872–880.

Klein, D. N., Taylor, E. B., Dickstein, S., & Harding, K. (1988). Primary early-onset dysthymia: Comparison with primary non-bipolar, non-chronic major depression on demographic, clinical, familial, personality, and socioenvironmental characteristics and short-term outcome. *Journal of Abnormal Psychology, 97*, 387–398. doi: 10.1037/0021-843X.97.4.387

Klerman, G. L., Weissman, M. M., Rounsaville, B. J., & Chevron, E. S. (1984). *Interpersonal psychotherapy of depression.* New York, NY: Basic Books.

Kocsis, J. H., Friedman, R. A., Markowitz, J. C., Leon, A. C., Miller, N. L., Gniwesch, L., ... Parides, M. (1996). Maintenance therapy for chronic depression: A controlled clinical trial of desipramine. *Archives of General Psychiatry, 53*, 769–774. doi: 10.1001/archpsyc.1996.01830090013002

Kocsis, J. H., Leon, A. C., Markowitz, J. C., Manber, R., Arnow, B., Klein, D. N., & Thase, M. E. (2009). Patient preference as a moderator of outcome for chronic depression treated with nefazodone, cognitive behavioral analysis system of psychotherapy, or their combination. *Journal of Clinical Psychiatry, 70*, 354–361. doi: 10.4088/JCP.08m04371

Köhler, S., Wiethoff, K., Ricken, R., Stamm, T., Baghai, T. C., Fisher, R., ... Adli, M. (2015). Characteristics and differences in treatment outcome of inpatients with chronic vs. episodic major depressive disorders. *Journal of Affective Disorders, 173*, 126–133.

Koran, L. M., Gelenberg, A. J., Kornstein, S. G., Howland, R. H., Friedman, R. A., DeBattista, C., ... Keller, M. B. (2001). Sertraline versus imipramine to prevent relapse in chronic depression. *Journal of Affective Disorders, 65*, 27–36. doi: 10.1016/S0165-0327(00)00272-X

Koster, E. H., De Raedt, R., Leyman, L., & De Lissnyder, E. (2010). Mood-congruent attention and memory bias in dysphoria: Exploring the coherence among information-processing biases. *Behaviour research and therapy, 48*(3), 219–225.

Kovak, K. A. (2004). The Hamilton Depression Rating Scale (HAMD). In M. J. Hilsenroth & D. L. Segal (Eds.), *Comprehensive handbook of psychological assessment* (pp. 87–98). Hoboken, NJ: Wiley.

Kraepelin, E. (1899). *Psychiatrie: Ein Lehrbuch* (6th ed.). Leipzig, Germany: Barth.

Kranzler, H. R., Kadden, R., Burleson, J., Babor, T. F., Apter, A., & Rounsaville, B. J. (1995). Validity of psychiatric diagnoses in patients with substance use disorders—is the interview more important than the interviewer? *Comprehensive Psychiatry, 36*, 278–288. doi: 10.1016/S0010-440X(95)90073-X

Krishnan, V., & Nestler, E. J. (2010). Linking molecules to mood: New insight into the biology of depression. *American Journal of Psychiatry, 167*(11), 1305–1320.

Kriston, L., von Wolff, A., Westphal, A., Hölzel, L. P., & Härter, M. (2014). Efficacy and acceptability of acute treatments for persistent depressive disorder: A network meta-analysis. *Depression and Anxiety, 31*(8), 621–630.

Kroenke, K., & Spitzer, R. L. (2002). The PHQ-9: A new depression diagnostic and severity measure. *Psychiatric Annals, 32*(9), 509–515.

Kroenke, K., Spitzer, R. L., & Williams, J. B. (2001). The PHQ-9: Validity of a brief depression severity measure. *Journal of General Internal Medicine, 16*(9), 606–613.

Laje, G., Paddock, S., Manji, H., Rush, A. J., Wilson, A. F., Charney, D., & McMahon, F. J. (2007). Genetic markers of suicidal ideation emerging during citalopram treatment of major depression. *American Journal of Psychiatry, 109*, 6444–6450. doi: 10.1176/appi.ajp.2007.06122018

Laws, H. B., Constantino, M. J., Sayer, A. G., Klein, D. N., Kocsis, J. H., Manber, R., ... Arnow, B. A. (2016). Convergence in patient-therapist therapeutic alliance ratings and its relation to outcome in chronic depression treatment. *Psychotherapy Research.* Advance online publication. doi: 10.1080/10503307.2015.1114687

Leader, J. B., & Klein, D. N. (1996). Social adjustment in dysthymia, double depression, and episodic major depression. *Journal of Affective Disorders, 37*, 91–101. doi: 10.1016/0165-0327(95)00076-3

Leppänen, J. M., Milders, M., Bell, J. S., Terriere, E., & Hietanen, J. K. (2004). Depression biases the recognition of emotionally neutral faces. *Psychiatry Research, 128*(2), 123–133.

Leuchter, A. F., Hunter, A. M., Krantz, D. E., & Cook, I. A. (2014). Intermediate phenotypes and biomarkers of treatment outcome in major depressive disorder. *Dialogues in Clinical Neuroscience, 16*(4), 525.

Levinson, D. F. (2006). The genetics of depression: A review. *Biological Psychiatry, 60*(2), 84–92.

Levkovitz, Y., Tedeschini, E., & Papakostas, G. I. (2011). Efficacy of antidepressants for dysthymia: A meta-analysis of placebo-controlled randomized trials. *Journal of Clinical Psychiatry, 72*, 509–514. doi: 10.4088/JCP.09m05949blu

Lewinsohn, P. M. (1974). A behavioral approach to depression. In R. J. Friedman & M. Katz (Eds.),

The psychology of depression: Contemporary theory and research (pp. 157–178). Oxford, England: Wiley.

Lewinsohn, P. M., & Gotlib, I. H. (1995). Behavioral therapy and treatment of depression. In E. E. Beckham & W. R. Leber (Eds.), *Handbook of depression* (2nd ed., pp. 352–375). New York, NY: Guilford Press.

Lewinsohn, P. M., Sullivan, J. M., & Grosscup, S. J. (1980). Changing reinforcing events: An approach to the treatment of depression. *Psychotherapy: Theory, Research, & Practice, 17*, 322–334. doi: 10.1037/h0085929

Lewinsohn, P. M., Youngren, M. A., & Grosscup, S. J. (1979). Reinforcement and depression. In R. A. Dupue (Ed.), *The psychobiology of depressive disorders: Implications for the effects of stress* (pp. 291–316). New York, NY: Academic Press.

Linnoila, M., Guthrie, S., Lane, E. A., Karoum, F., Rudorfer, M., & Potter, W. Z. (1986). Clinical norepinephrine metabolism: How to interpret the numbers. *Psychiatry Research, 17*, 229–239. doi: 10.1016/0165-1781(86)90051-X

Liu, R. T., Kleiman, E. M., Nestor, B. A., & Cheek, S. M. (2015). The Hopelessness Theory of Depression: A quarter-century in review. *Clinical Psychology: Science and Practice, 22*(4), 345–365.

Lizardi, H., Klein, D. N., Ouimette, P. C., Riso, L. P., Anderson, R. L., & Donaldson, S. K. (1995). Reports of the childhood home environment in early-onset dysthymia and major depression. *Journal of Abnormal Psychology, 104*, 132–139. doi: 10.1037/0021 -843X.104.1.132

Loo, C. K., Schweitzer, I., & Pratt, C. (2006). Recent advances in optimizing electroconvulsive therapy. *Australian and New Zealand Journal of Psychiatry, 40*, 632–638. doi: 10.1111/j.1440-1614 .2006.01862.x

Lyubomirsky, S., & Tkach, C. (2004). The consequences of dysphoric rumination. In C. Papageorgiou & A. Wells (Eds.), *Depressive rumination: Nature, theory, and treatment* (pp. 21–42). Chichester, England: Wiley.

Mandell, D., Siegle, G. J., Shutt, L., Feldmiller, J., & Thase, M. E. (2014). Neural substrates of trait ruminations in depression. *Journal of Abnormal Psychology, 123*(1), 35.

Manos, R. C., Kanter, J. W., & Busch, A. M. (2010). A critical review of assessment strategies to measure the behavioral activation model of depression. *Clinical Psychology Review, 30*(5), 547–561.

Marcus, S. C., & Olfson, M. (2010). National trends in the treatment for depression from 1998 to 2007. *Archives of General Psychiatry, 67*(12), 1265–1273.

Markowitz, J. C. (1998). *Interpersonal psychotherapy for dysthymic disorder*. Washington, DC: American Psychiatric Press.

Markowitz, J. C., Lipsitz, J., & Milrod, B. L. (2014). Critical review of outcome research on interpersonal psychotherapy for anxiety disorders. *Depression and Anxiety, 31*(4), 316–325.

Martell, C. R., Addis, M. E., & Jacobson, N. S. (2001). *Depression in context: Strategies for guided action.* New York, NY: W. W. Norton.

Mason, B. J., Kocsis, J. H., Leon, A. C., Thompson, S., Frances, A. J., Morgan, R. O., & Parides, M. K. (1995). Assessment of symptoms and change in dysthymic disorder. In J. H. Kocsis & D. N. Klein (Eds.), *Diagnosis and treatment of chronic depression* (pp. 73–88). New York, NY: Guilford Press.

Mathews, A., & MacLeod, C. (2005). Cognitive vulnerability to emotional disorders. *Annual Review of Clinical Psychology, 1*, 167–195.

Mazzucchelli, T., Kane, R., & Rees, C. (2009). Behavioral activation treatments for depression in adults: A meta-analysis and review. *Clinical Psychology: Science and Practice, 16*(4), 383–411.

McCauley, E., Gudmundsen, G., Schloredt, K., Martell, C., Rhew, I., Hubley, S., & Dimidjian, S. (2015). The Adolescent Behavioral Activation Program: Adapting behavioral activation as a treatment for depression in adolescence. *Journal of Clinical Child & Adolescent Psychology, 45*(3), 1–14.

McCullough, J. P. (2000). *Treatment for chronic depression: Cognitive behavioral analysis system of psychotherapy.* New York, NY: Guilford Press.

McCullough, J. P., Klein, D. N., Keller, M. B., Holzer, C. E., Davis, S. M., Kornstein, S. G., … Harrison, W. M. (2000). Comparison of *DSM-III-R* chronic major depression and major depression superimposed on dysthymia (double depression): A study of the validity and value of differential diagnosis. *Journal of Abnormal Psychology, 109*, 419–427. doi: 10.1037/0021-843X.109.3.419

McCullough J. P., Jr., Klein, D. N., Borian, F. E., Howland, R. H., Riso, L. P., Keller, M. B., & Banks, P. L. (2003). Group comparisons of *DSM-IV* subtypes of chronic depression: Validity of the distinctions, part 2. *Journal of Abnormal Psychology, 112*(4), 614.

McCullough, J. P., Kornstein, S. G., McCullough, J. P., Belyea-Caldwell, S., Kaye, A. L., Roberts, W. C., …

Kruus, L. K. (1996). Differential diagnosis of chronic depressive disorders. *Psychiatric Clinics of North America*, *19*(1), 55–71.

McCullough, J. M., McCune, K. J., Kaye, A. L., Braith, J. A., Friend, R., Roberts, W. C., … Hampton, C. (1994). One-year prospective replication study of an untreated sample of community dysthymia subjects. *Journal of Nervous and Mental Disease*, *182*, 396–401. doi: 10.1097/00005053-199407000-00005

McDermott, L. M., & Ebmeier, K. P. (2009). A meta-analysis of depression severity and cognitive function. *Journal of Affective Disorders*, *119*(1), 1–8.

McFarland, B. R., Shankman, S. A., Tenke, C. E., Bruder, G. E., & Klein, D. N. (2006). Behavioral activation system deficits predict the six-month course of depression. *Journal of Affective Disorders*, *91*, 229–234. doi: 10.1016/j.jad.2006.01.012

McGrath, C., Kelley, M. E., Holtzheimer, P. E., Dunlop, B. W., Craighead, W. E., Franco, A. R., … Mayberg, H. S. (2013). Toward a neuroimaging treatment selection biomarker for major depressive disorder. *JAMA Psychiatry*, *70*(8), 821–829. doi: 10.1001/jamapsychiatry.2013.143

Meyer, T. D., Gudgeon, E., Thomas, A. J., & Collerton, D. (2010). Cognitive style and depressive symptoms in elderly people: Extending the empirical evidence for the cognitive vulnerability–stress hypothesis. *Behaviour Research and Therapy*, *48*(10), 1053–1057.

Miller, A. H., Haroon, E., Raison, C. L., & Felger, J. C. (2013). Cytokine targets in the brain: Impact on neurotransmitters and neurocircuits. *Depression and Anxiety*, *30*(4), 297–306.

Miller, A. H., & Raison, C. L. (2016). The role of inflammation in depression: From evolutionary imperative to modern treatment target. *Nature Reviews Immunology*, *16*(1), 22–34.

Mogg, K., Bradbury, K. E., & Bradley, B. P. (2006). Interpretation of ambiguous information in clinical depression. *Behaviour Research and Therapy*, *44*(10), 1411–1419.

Mogg, K., Bradley, B. P., Williams, R., & Mathews, A. (1993). Subliminal processing of emotional information in anxiety and depression. *Journal of Abnormal Psychology*, *102*(2), 304.

Mondimore, F. M., Zandi, P. P., MacKinnon, D. F., McInnis, M. G., Miller, E. B., Crowe, R. P., … Potash, J. B. (2006). Familial aggregation of illness chronicity in recurrent, early-onset major depression pedigrees. *American Journal of Psychiatry*, *163*(9), 1554–1560.

Moore, R. Y., & Bloom, F. E. (1979). Central catecholamine neuron systems: Anatomy and physiology of the norepinephrine and epinephrine systems. *Annual Review of Neuroscience*, *2*, 113–168. doi: 10.1146/annurev.ne.02.030179.000553

Moore, M. T., & Fresco, D. M. (2007). Depressive realism and attributional style: Implications for individuals at risk for depression. *Behavior Therapy*, *38*(2), 144–154.

Mor, N., & Winquist, J. (2002). Self-focused attention and negative affect: A meta-analysis. *Psychological Bulletin*, *128*, 638–662. doi: 10.1037/0033-2909.128.4.638

Mościcki, E. K. (2001). Epidemiology of completed and attempted suicide: Toward a framework for prevention. *Clinical Neuroscience Research*, *1*, 310–323. doi: 10.1016/S1566-2772(01)00032-9

Mueller, T. I., Leon, A. C., Keller, M. B., Solomon, D. A., Endicott, J., Coryell, W., … Maser, J. D. (1999). Recurrence after recovery from major depressive disorder during 15 years of observational follow-up. *American Journal of Psychiatry*, *156*, 1000–1006.

Murphy, J. A., & Byrne, G. J. (2012). Prevalence and correlates of the proposed DSM-5 diagnosis of chronic depressive disorder. *Journal of Affective Disorders*, *139*(2), 172–180.

Nelson, R. E., & Craighead, W. E. (1977). Selective recall of positive and negative feedback, self-control behaviors, and depression. *Journal of Abnormal Psychology*, *86*, 379–388. doi: 10.1037/0021-843X.86.4.379

Nemeroff, C. B. (2007). The burden of severe depression: A review of diagnostic challenges and treatment alternatives. *Journal of Psychiatric Research*, *41*, 189–206. doi: 10.1016/j.jpsychires.2006.05.008

Nemeroff, C. B. (2016). Paradise lost: The neurobiological and clinical consequences of child abuse and neglect. *Neuron*, *89*(5), 892–909.

Nemeroff, C. B., Bissette, G., Akil, H., & Fink, M. (1991). Neuropeptide concentrations in the cerebrospinal fluid of depressed patients treated with electroconvulsive therapy: Corticotrophin-releasing factor, beta-endorphin, and somatostatin. *British Journal of Psychiatry*, *158*, 59–63. doi: 10.1192/bjp.158.1.59

Nemeroff, C. G., Heim, C. M., Thase, M. E., Klein, D. N., Rush, A. J., Schatzberg, A. F., … Keller, M. B.

(2003). Differential responses to psychotherapy versus pharmacotherapy in the treatment for patients with chronic forms of major depression and childhood trauma. *Proceedings of the National Academy of Sciences*, *100*, 14293–14296. doi: 10.1073/pnas.2336126100

Nezu, A. M., Nezu, C. M., & Perri, M. G. (1989). *Problem-solving therapy for depression: Theory, research, and clinical guidelines.* New York, NY: Wiley.

Nolen-Hoeksema, S. (1987). Sex differences in unipolar depression: Evidence and theory. *Psychological Bulletin*, *101*, 259–282. doi: 10.1037/0033-2909.101.2.259

Nolen-Hoeksema, S. (1991). Responses to depression and their effects on the duration of the depressive episode. *Journal of Abnormal Psychology*, *100*, 569–582.

Nolen-Hoeksema, S. (2000). The role of rumination in depressive disorders and mixed anxiety/depressive symptoms. *Journal of Abnormal Psychology*, *109*, 504–511. doi: 10.1037/0021-843X.109.3.504

Nolen-Hoeksema, S. (2002). Gender differences in depression. In I. H. Gotlib & C. L. Hammen (Eds.), *Handbook of depression* (pp. 492–510). New York, NY: Guilford Press. doi: 10.1111/1467-8721.00142

Nolen-Hoeksema, S., & Morrow, J. (1991). A prospective study of depression and posttraumatic stress symptoms after a natural disaster: The 1989 Loma Prieta earthquake. *Journal of Personality and Social Psychology*, *61*(1), 115–121.

Nolen-Hoeksema, S., Morrow, J., & Fredrickson, B. L. (1993). Response styles and the duration of episodes of depressed mood. *Journal of Abnormal Psychology*, *102*, 20–28. doi: 10.1037/0021-843X.102.1.20

Nunn, J. D., Mathews, A., & Trower, P. (1997). Selective processing of concern-related information in depression. *British Journal of Clinical Psychology*, *36*(4), 489–503.

Nusslock, R., & Miller, G. E. (2015). Early-life adversity and physical and emotional health across the lifespan: A neuroimmune network hypothesis. *Biological Psychiatry*, *80*(1), 23–32.

Ochsner, K. N., & Gross, J. J. (2007). The neural architecture of emotion regulation. In J. J. Gross (Ed.), *Handbook of emotion regulation* (pp. 87–109). New York, NY: Guilford Press.

Olatunji, B. O., Naragon-Gainey, K., & Wolitzky-Taylor, K. B. (2013). Specificity of rumination in anxiety and depression: A multimodal meta-analysis.

Clinical Psychology: Science and Practice, *20*(3), 225–257.

Owens, M. J., & Nemeroff, C. B. (1991). Physiology and pharmacology of corticotropin-releasing factor. *Pharmacological Review*, *43*, 425–473.

Owens, M. J., & Nemeroff, C. B. (1994). Role of serotonin in the pathophysiology of depression: Focus on the serotonin transporter. *Clinical Chemistry*, *40*, 288–295.

Pace, T. W., & Miller, A. H. (2009). Cytokines and glucocorticoid receptor signaling; Relevance to major depression. *Annals of the New York Academy of Sciences*, *1179*(1), 86–105.

Pepper, C. M., Klein, D. N., Anderson, R. L., Riso, L. P., Ouimette, P. C., & Lizardi, H. (1995). Axis II comorbidity in dysthymia and major depression. *American Journal of Psychiatry*, *152*, 239–247.

Perveen, S. (2015). Relationship between negative cognitive style and depression among university students. *Online Journal of New Horizons in Education*, *5*(4), 74–83.

Peterson, C., Maier, S. F., & Seligman, M. E. P. (1993). *Learned helplessness: A theory for the age of personal control.* New York, NY: Oxford University Press. doi: 10.1002/9780470479216.corpsy0500

Posener, J. A., DeBattista, C., Williams, G. H., Chmura-Kraemer, H., Kalehzan, B. M., & Schatzberg, A. F. (2000). 24-Hour monitoring of cortisol and corticotropin secretion in psychotic and nonpsychotic major depression. *Archives of General Psychiatry*, *44*, 434–440. doi: 10.1001/archpsyc.57.8.755

Prendes-Alvarez, S., Schatzberg, A. F., & Nemeroff, C. B. (2015). Pharmacological treatments for unipolar depression. In P. E. Nathan & J. M. Gorman (Eds.), *A guide to treatments that work* (pp. 327–354). New York, NY: Oxford University Press.

Psychiatric GWAS Consortium Coordinating Committee. (2009). Genomewide association studies: History, rationale, and prospects for psychiatric disorders. *American Journal of Psychiatry*, *166*(5), 540–556.

Pyszcynski, T., & Greenberg, J. (1987). Self-regulatory perseveration and the depressive self-focusing style: A self-awareness theory of reactive depression. *Psychological Bulletin*, *102*, 122–138. doi: 10.1037/0033-2909.102.1.122

Radloff, L. S. (1977). The CES-D scale: A self-report depression scale for research in the general population. *Applied Psychology Measurement*, *1*, 385–401. doi: 10.1177/014662167700100306

Raes, F., Hermans, D., Williams, J. M. G., Demyttenaere, K., Sabbe, B., Pieters, G., & Eelen, P. (2005). Reduced specificity of autobiographical memory: A mediator between rumination and ineffective social problem-solving in major depression? *Journal of Affective Disorders, 87*(2), 331–335.

Remus, J. L., & Dantzer, R. (2016, April). Inflammation models of depression in rodents: Relevance to psychotropic drug discovery. *International Journal of Neuropsychopharmacology.* doi: 10.1093/ijnp/pyw028

Ressler, K. J., & Nemeroff, C. B. (2001). Role of norepinephrine in the pathophysiology of neuropsychiatric disorders. *CNS Spectrums, 6,* 663–666, 670. doi: 10.1016/S0006-3223(99)00127-4

Ressler, K. J., & Smoller, J. W. (2016). Impact of stress on the brain: Pathology, treatment and prevention. *Neuropsychopharmacology, 41*(1), 1.

Rhebergen, D., Beekman, A. T. F., de Graaf, R., Nolen, W. A., Spijker, J., Hoogendijk, W. J., & Penninx, B. W. J. H. (2009). The three-year naturalistic course of major depressive disorder, dysthymic disorder and double depression. *Journal of Affective Disorders, 115,* 450–459. doi: 10.1016/j.jad.2008.10.018

Ridout, N., Astell, A., Reid, I., Glen, T., & O'Carroll, R. (2003). Memory bias for emotional facial expressions in major depression. *Cognition & Emotion, 17*(1), 101–122.

Riolo, S. A., Nguyen, T. A., Greden, J. F., & King, C. A. (2005). Prevalence of depression by race/ethnicity: Findings from the National Health and Nutrition Examination Survey III. *American Journal of Public Health, 95,* 998–1000.

Riso, L. P., du Toit, P. L., Blandino, J. A., Penna, S., Darcy, S., Duin, J. S., … Ulmer, C. S. (2003). Cognitive aspects of chronic depression. *Journal of Abnormal Psychology, 112,* 72–80. doi: 10.1037/0021-843X.112.1.72

Ritschel, L. A., Ramirez, C. L., Cooley, J. L., & Edward Craighead, W. (2016). Behavioral activation for major depression in adolescents: Results from a pilot study. *Clinical Psychology: Science and Practice, 23*(1), 39–57. doi: 10.1111/cpsp.12140

Riva-Posse, P., Holtzheimer, P. E., Garlow, S. J., & Mayberg, H. S. (2013). Practical considerations in the development and refinement of subcallosal cingulate white matter deep brain stimulation for treatment-resistant depression. *World Neurosurgery, 80*(3–4), e25–e34.

Robinson, M. S., & Alloy, L. B. (2003). Negative cognitive styles and stress-reactive rumination interact to predict depression: A prospective study. *Cognitive Therapy and Research, 27,* 275–292. doi: 10.1023/A:1023914416469

Roceri, M., Hendriks, W., Racagni, G., Ellenbroek, B. A., & Riva, M. A. (2002). Early maternal deprivation reduces the expression of BDNF and NMDA receptor subunits in rat hippocampus. *Molecular Psychiatry, 7,* 606–616. doi: 10.1038/sj.mp.4001036

Rocha, F., Fuzikawa, C., Riera, R., & Hara, C. (2012). Combination of antidepressants in the treatment of major depressive disorder: A systematic review and meta-analysis. *Journal of Clinical Psychopharmacology, 32,* 278–281. doi: 10.1097/JCP.0b013e318248581b

Rohde, P., Lewinsohn, P. M., Klein, D. N., Seeley, J. R., & Gau, J. M. (2012). Key characteristics of major depressive disorder occurring in childhood, adolescence, emerging adulthood, and adulthood. *Clinical Psychological Science, 1,* 1–12. doi: 10.1177/2167702612457599

Rood, L., Roelofs, J., Bögels, S. M., & Meesters, C. (2012). Stress-reactive rumination, negative cognitive style, and stressors in relationship to depressive symptoms in non-clinical youth. *Journal of Youth and Adolescence, 41*(4), 414–425.

Rotenberg, A., Horvath, J. C., & Pascual-Leone, A. (2014). The transcranial magnetic stimulation (TMS) device and foundational techniques. In A. Rotenberg, J. C. Horvath, & A. Pascual-Leone (Eds.), *Transcranial magnetic stimulation* (pp. 3–13). New York, NY: Humana Press.

Roy, A., Pickar, D., DeJong, J., Karoum, F., & Linnoila, M. (1988). Norepinephrine and its metabolites in cerebrospinal fluid, plasma, and urine: Relationship to hypothalamic-pituitary-adrenal axis function in depression. *Archives of General Psychiatry, 45,* 849–857. doi: 10.1001/archpsyc.1988.01800330081010

Rubin, R. T., Phillips, J. J., Sadow, T. F., & McCracken, J. T. (1995). Adrenal gland volume in major depression: Increase during depressive episode and decrease with successful treatment. *Archives of General Psychiatry, 52,* 213–218. doi: 10.1001/archpsyc.1995.03950150045009

Rush, A. J., Bernstein, I. H., Trivedi, M. H., Carmody, T. J., Wisniewski, S., Mundt, J. C., … Fava, M. (2006). An evaluation of the Quick Inventory of Depressive Symptomatology and the Hamilton

Rating Scale for Depression: A sequenced treatment alternatives to relieve depression trial report. *Biological Psychiatry, 59*, 493–501. doi: 10.1016/j.biopsych.2005.08.022

Rush, A. J., Trivedi, M. H., Ibrahim, H. M., Carmody, T. J., Arnow, B., Klein D. N., ... Keller, M. B. (2003). The 16-item Quick Inventory of Depressive Symptomatology, clinician rating, and self-report: A psychometric evaluation in patients with chronic major depression. *Biological Psychiatry, 54*, 573–583. doi: 10.1016/S0006-3223(02)01866-8

Sacco, W. P., & Beck, A. T. (1995). Cognitive theory and therapy. In E. E. Beckham & W. R. Leber (Eds.), *Handbook of depression* (pp. 329–351). New York, NY: Guilford Press.

Sachar, E. J., Hellman, L., Fukushima, D. K., & Gallagher, T. F. (1970). Cortisol production in depressive illness: A clinical and biochemical clarification. *Archives of General Psychiatry, 23*, 289–298. doi: 10.1001/archpsyc.1970.01750040001001

Sang, W., Li, Y., Su, L., Yang, F., Wu, W., Shang, X., ... Li, K. (2011). A comparison of the clinical characteristics of Chinese patients with recurrent major depressive disorder with and without dysthymia. *Journal of Affective Disorders, 135*, 106–110. doi: 10.1016/j.jad.2011.06.051

Santiago, N. J., Klein, D. N., Vivian, D., Arnow, B. A., Blalock, J. A., Kocsis, J. H., ... Keller, M. B. (2005). The therapeutic alliance and CBASP-specific skill acquisition in the treatment of chronic depression. *Cognitive Therapy and Research, 29*, 803–817. doi: 10.1007/s10608-005-9638-5

Schatzberg, A. F., Rothschild, A. J., Stahl, J. B., Bond, T. C., Rosenbaum, A. H., Lofgren, S. B., ... Cole, J. O. (1983). The dexamethasone suppression test: Identification of subtypes of depression. *American Journal of Psychiatry, 140*, 88–91.

Schildkraut, J. J. (1965). The catecholamine hypothesis of affective disorders: A review of supporting evidence. *American Journal of Psychiatry, 122*, 509–522.

Schmidt, H. D., & Duman, R. S. (2007). The role of neurotrophic factors in adult hippocampal neurogenesis, antidepressant treatments and animal models of depressive-like behavior. *Behavioural Pharmacology, 18*, 391–418. doi: 10.1097/FBP.0b013e3282ee2aa8

Schramm, E., Zobel, I., Dykierek, P., Kech, S., Brakemeier, E. L., Külz, A., & Berger, M. (2011). Cognitive behavioral analysis system of psychotherapy versus interpersonal psychotherapy for early-onset chronic depression: A randomized pilot study. *Journal of Affective Disorders, 129*, 109–116. doi: 10.1016/j.jad.2010.08.003

Schüle, C., Zill, P., Baghai, T. C., Eser, D., Zwanzger, P., Wenig, N., ... Bondy, B. (2006). Brain-derived neurotrophic factor Val66Met polymorphism and dexamethasone/CRH test results in depressed patients. *Psychoneuroendocrinology, 31*, 1019–1025. doi: 10.1016/j.psyneuen.2006.06.002

Seligman, M. E. P. (1975). *Helplessness: On depression, development, and death*. San Francisco, CA: Jossey-Bass.

Seligman, M. E. P., Abramson, L. Y., Semmel, A., & von Baeyer, C. (1979). Depressive attributional style. *Journal of Abnormal Psychology, 88*, 242–247. doi: 10.1037/0021-843X.93.2.235

Sharma, A. N., da Costa e Silva, B. F. B., Soares, J. C., Carvalho, A. F., & Quevedo, J. (2016). Role of trophic factors GDNF, IGF-1 and VEGF in major depressive disorder: A comprehensive review of human studies. *Journal of Affective Disorders, 197*, 9–20.

Sharma, S., Powers, A., Bradley, B., & Ressler, K. J. (2016). Gene × environment determinants of stress- and anxiety-related disorders. *Annual Review of Psychology, 67*, 239–261.

Shear, M. K., Greeno, C., Kang, J., Ludewig, D., Frank, E., Swartz, H. A., & Hanekamp, M. (2000). Diagnosis of nonpsychotic patients in community clinics. *American Journal of Psychiatry, 157*, 581–587.

Sheline, Y. I., Bardgett, M. E., & Csernansky, J. G. (1997). Correlated reductions in cerebrospinal fluid 5–HIAA and MHPG concentrations after treatment with selective serotonin reuptake inhibitors. *Journal of Clinical Psychopharmacology, 17*, 11–14.

Shimizu, E., Hashimoto, K., Okamura, N., Koike, K., Komatsu, N., Kumakiri, C., ... Iyo, M. (2003). Alterations of serum levels of brain-derived neurotrophic factor (BDNF) in depressed patients with or without antidepressants. *Biological Psychiatry, 54*, 70–75. doi: 10.1016/S0006-3223(03)00181-1

Skinner, B. F. (1953). *Science and human behavior*. New York, NY: Macmillan.

Slattery, D. A., Hudson, A. L., & Nutt, D. J. (2004). The evolution of antidepressant mechanisms. *Fundamental & Clinical Pharmacology, 18*, 1–21. doi: 10.1111/j.1472-8206.2004.00195.x

Smith, J. M., & Alloy, L. B. (2009). A roadmap to rumination: A review of the definition, assessment, and conceptualization of this multifaceted construct. *Clinical Psychology Review, 29*(2), 116–128.

Smith, K. A., Fairburn, C. G., & Cowen, P. J. (1997). Relapse of depression after rapid depletion of tryptophan. *Lancet, 349*, 915–919. doi: 10.1016/S0140 -6736(96)07044-4

Smith, M. A., Makino, S., Kvetnansky, R., & Post, R. M. (1995). Stress and glucocorticoids affect the expression of brain-derived neurotrophic factor and neurotrophin-3 mRNAs in the hippocampus. *Journal of Neuroscience, 15*, 1768–1777.

Snyder, H. R. (2013). Major depressive disorder is associated with broad impairments on neuropsychological measures of executive function: A meta-analysis and review. *Psychological Bulletin, 139*(1), 81.

Spasojevic, J., & Alloy, L. B. (2001). Rumination as a common mechanism relating depressive risk factors to depression. *Emotion, 1*, 25–37. doi: 10.1037/1528 -3542.1.1.25

Steidtmann, D., Manber, R., Blasey, C., Markowitz, J. C., Klein, D. N., Rothbaum, B. O., ... Arnow, B. A. (2013). Detecting critical decision points in psychotherapy and psychotherapy + medication for chronic depression. *Journal of Consulting and Clinical Psychology, 81*, 783–792.

Strawbridge, R., Arnone, D., Danese, A., Papadopoulos, A., Vives, A. H., & Cleare, A. J. (2015). Inflammation and clinical response to treatment in depression: A meta-analysis. *European Neuropsychopharmacology, 25*(10), 1532–1543.

Sun, H., Kennedy, P. J., & Nestler, E. J. (2013). Epigenetics of the depressed brain: Role of histone acetylation and methylation. *Neuropsychopharmacology, 38*(1), 124–137.

Sung, S. C., Haley, C. L., Wisniewski, S. R., Fava, M., Nierenberg, A. A., Warden, D., ... Rush, A. J. (2012). The impact of chronic depression on acute and long-term outcomes in a randomized trial comparing selective serotonin reuptake inhibitor monotherapy versus each of 2 different antidepressant medication combinations. *Journal of Clinical Psychiatry, 73*, 967–976. doi: 10.4088/JCP.11m07043

Swan, J. S., MacVicar, R., Christmas, D., Durham, R., Rauchhaus, P., McCullough, J. P., & Matthews, K. (2014). Cognitive Behavioural Analysis System of Psychotherapy (CBASP) for chronic depression: Clinical characteristics and six month clinical outcomes in an open case series. *Journal of Affective Disorders, 152*, 268–276.

Swanson, L. W., Sawchenko, P. E., Rivier, J., & Vale, W. W. (1983). Organization of ovine corticotropin-releasing factor immunoreactive cells and fibers in the rat brain: An immunohistochemical study. *Neuroendocrinology, 36*, 165–186. doi: 10.1159/000123454

Teachman, B. A., Joormann, J., Steinman, S. A., & Gotlib, I. H. (2012). Automaticity in anxiety disorders and major depressive disorder. *Clinical Psychology Review, 32*(6), 575–603.

Thase, M. E., Friedman, E. S., Biggs, M. M., Wisniewski, S. R., Trivedi, M. H., Luther, J. F., ... Rush, A. J. (2007). Cognitive therapy versus medication in augmentation and switch strategies as second-step treatments: A STAR*D report. *American Journal of Psychiatry, 164*, 739–752. doi: 10.1176/appi.ajp.164.5.739

Thase, M. E., Reynolds, C. F., Frank, E., Simons, A. D., Garamoni, G. D., McGeary, J., ... Cahalane, J. F. (1994). Response to cognitive-behavioral therapy in chronic depression. *Journal of Psychotherapy Practice and Research, 3*, 204–214.

Timbremont, B., & Braet, C. (2004). Cognitive vulnerability in remitted depressed children and adolescents. *Behaviour Research and Therapy, 42*, 423–437. doi: 10.1016/S0005-7967(03)00151-7

Trew, J. L. (2011). Exploring the roles of approach and avoidance in depression: An integrative model. *Clinical Psychology Review, 31*(7), 1156–1168.

Tsankova, N. M., Berton, O., Renthal, W., Kumar, A., Neve, R. L., & Nestler, E. J. (2006). Sustained hippocampal chromatin regulation in a mouse model of depression and antidepressant action. *Nature Neuroscience, 9*, 519–525. doi: 10.1038/nn1659

Twenge, J. M. (2015). Time period and birth cohort differences in depressive symptoms in the US, 1982–2013. *Social Indicators Research, 121*(2), 437–454.

Twenge, J. M., Gentile, B., DeWall, C., Ma, D., Lacefield, K., & Schurtz, D. R. (2010). Birth cohort increases in psychopathology among young Americans, 1938–2007: A cross-temporal meta-analysis of the MMPI. *Clinical Psychology Review, 30*, 145–154. doi: 10.1016/j.cpr.2009.10.005

Vale, W., Spiess, J., Rivier, C., & Rivier, J. (1981). Characterization of 41–residue ovine hypothalamic peptide that stimulates secretion of corticotropin and beta-endorphin. *Science, 213*, 1394–1397. doi: 10.1126/science.6267699

van Randenborgh, A., de Jong-Meyer, R., & Hüffmeier, J. (2010). Decision making in depression:

Differences in decisional conflict between healthy and depressed individuals. *Clinical Psychology & Psychotherapy, 17*(4), 285–298.

Viera, A. J., & Garrett, J. M. (2005). Understanding interobserver agreement: The kappa statistic. *Family Medicine, 37,* 360–363.

Vittengl, J. R., Clark, L. A., Dunn, T. W., & Jarrett, R. B. (2007). Reducing relapse and recurrence in unipolar depression: A comparative meta-analysis of cognitive therapy's effects. *Journal of Consulting and Clinical Psychology, 75,* 475–488. doi: 10.1037/0022-006X.75.3.475

Voncken, M. J., Bögels, S. M., & Peeters, F. (2007). Specificity of interpretation and judgemental biases in social phobia versus depression. *Psychology and Psychotherapy: Theory, Research and Practice, 80*(3), 443–453.

von Wolff, A., Hölzel, L. P., Westphal, A., Härter, M., & Kriston, L. (2013). Selective serotonin reuptake inhibitors and tricyclic antidepressants in the acute treatment of chronic depression and dysthymia: A systematic review and meta-analysis. *Journal of Affective Disorders, 144,* 7–15.

Watkins, E., & Teasdale, J. D. (2001). Rumination and overgeneral memory in depression: Effects of self-focus and analytic thinking. *Journal of Abnormal Psychology, 110*(2), 353.

Watkins, E., & Teasdale, J. D. (2004). Adaptive and maladaptive self-focus in depression. *Journal of Affective Disorders, 82*(1), 1–8.

Weissman, M. M., Wickramaratne, P., Nomura, Y., Warner, V., Pilowsky, D., & Verdeli, H. (2006). Offspring of depressed parents: 20 years later. *American Journal of Psychiatry, 163*(6), 1001–1008.

Wiersma, J. E., van Oppen, P., van Schaik, D. J., van der Does, A. J., Beekman, A. T., & Penninx, B. W. (2011). Psychological characteristics of chronic depression: A longitudinal cohort study. *Journal of Clinical Psychiatry, 72,* 288–294. doi: 10.4088/JCP.09m05735blu

Williams. J. M. G., Barnhofer, T., Crane, C., Hermans, D., Raes, F., Watkins, E., & Dalgleish, T. (2007). Autobiographical memory specificity and emotional disorder. *Psychological Bulletin, 133,* 122–148. doi: 10.1037/0033-2909.133.1.122

Wood, J. V., Saltzberg, J. A., Neale, J. M., Stone, A. A., & Rachmiel, T. B. (1990). Self-focused attention, coping responses, and distressed mood in everyday life. *Journal of Personality and Social Psychology, 58,* 1027–1036. doi: 10.1037/0022-3514.58.6.1027

Woody, M. L., Owens, M., Burkhouse, K. L., & Gibb, B. E. (2015). Selective attention toward angry faces and risk for major depressive disorder in women: Converging evidence from retrospective and prospective analyses. *Clinical Psychological Science, 4*(2), 206–215. doi: 10.1177/2167702615581580

World Health Organization. (2016). Suicide attempt surveillance. http://www.who.int/mental_health/suicide-prevention/en

Yoshimura, S., Okamoto, Y., Onoda, K., Matsunaga, M., Okada, G., Kunisato, Y., … Yamawaki, S. (2014). Cognitive behavioral therapy for depression changes medial prefrontal and ventral anterior cingulate cortex activity associated with self-referential processing. *Social Cognitive and Affective Neuroscience, 9*(4), 487–493.

Young, J. J., Bruno, D., & Pomara, N. (2014). A review of the relationship between proinflammatory cytokines and major depressive disorder. *Journal of Affective Disorders, 169,* 15–20.

Young, K. D., Siegle, G. J., Bodurka, J., & Drevets, W. C. (2015). Amygdala activity during autobiographical memory recall in depressed and vulnerable individuals: Association with symptom severity and autobiographical overgenerality. *American Journal of Psychiatry.* Advance online publication. doi: 10.1176/appi.ajp.2015.15010119

Chapter 8

Bipolar Disorder

DAVID J. MIKLOWITZ AND SHERI L. JOHNSON

The endless questioning finally ended. My psychiatrist looked at me, there was no uncertainty in his voice. "Manic-depressive illness." I admired his bluntness. I wished him locusts on his lands and a pox upon his house. Silent, unbelievable rage. I smiled pleasantly. He smiled back. The war had just begun.

—Kay Redfield Jamison, *An Unquiet Mind* (1995)

Bipolar disorder (BD) is a highly debilitating psychiatric illness that may affect as many as 1 in every 25 persons (Merikangas et al., 2007, 2011). People with the disorder have highly disruptive episodes, frequent recurrences, and severe psychosocial impairments, even when not symptomatic. The illness typically has its onset in adolescence, and even late childhood in some people—much earlier than was once thought.

BD represents a conundrum on many fronts: how to reliably diagnose it and distinguish it from "near-neighbor" disorders; to what extent the timing of recurrences can be reliably predicted; what the relative contributions of genetic, biological, and psychosocial factors are at various phases of development; and what the roles of medications and psychotherapy are in acute and maintenance treatment of BD. Nonetheless, the outlook for people with BD is more optimistic than ever before because of notable advances in research on its diagnosis, etiology, prognosis, and treatment.

This chapter discusses current research findings in BD. Relative to similar chapters that might appear in medical texts, this chapter emphasizes the role of psychosocial variables as predictors of recurrence, and psychosocial interventions as adjunctive to pharmacotherapy. Special emphasis is placed on knowledge gained from research on psychosocial stressors and randomized trials of psychotherapy, which have proliferated in the past decade. We conclude with recommendations for the next generation of research on this disorder.

Description of the Disorder

Bipolar disorder has been recognized as a psychiatric condition since at least 400 B.C., when described by Hippocrates in his medical texts. Although formal diagnostic systems did not come into wide use until the 1950s, our current operational definitions of the depressed and manic phases of this illness bear a striking similarity to Hippocrates' original descriptions of melancholia and mania. This section describes the current requirements for a bipolar diagnosis and its various subtypes, and presents a case example.

Symptoms and *DSM* Criteria

Bipolar disorder is characterized by severe changes in mood, thinking, and behavior, from extreme highs to lows. In its most classic presentation, mania and depression alternate in distinctive episodes that can last anywhere from a few days to a year or more. According to the *Diagnostic and Statistical Manual of Mental Disorders, Fifth Edition* (*DSM-5*; American Psychiatric Association [APA], 2013), people in manic episodes experience elated, expansive, or irritable mood (Criterion A) plus increased goal-directed activity. At least three of the following Criterion B symptoms must also be present (four if the mood is only irritable): inflated self-esteem (grandiosity), decreased need for sleep, racing thoughts or flight of ideas, rapid or pressured speech, reckless and impulsive behavior (e.g., indiscreet sexual liaisons, spending sprees, reckless driving), increased energy, and distractibility. Manic episodes are defined by symptoms lasting at least 1 week; evidence of functional impairment (deterioration in family, work, or social functioning); or, if lasting less than 1 week, the need for hospitalization or emergency treatment. Although most of these criteria are virtually identical to those in *DSM-IV-TR* (APA, 2000), a significant change is that increased goal-directed activity is now given Criterion A status, along with elevated or irritable mood. This change may increase the identification of persons who have difficulty describing changes in their mood states but can give examples of changes in their behavior (see www.dsm5.org).

Hypomanic episodes are defined by symptoms of shorter duration (i.e. 4 or more days) and noticeable changes in behavior that do not meet the *DSM* definition of functional impairment. The changes in behavior, mood, or energy must be noticeable to others, but the symptoms do not cause undue financial, emotional, or practical damage (e.g., precipitate divorce). In practice, this distinction between salience and functional impairment can be hard to make and may contribute to low reliabilities of the mania-hypomania distinction. Depressive phases are defined by the criteria used for major depressive disorder: intense sadness and/or loss of interests (anhedonia), with the following associated symptoms: insomnia or hypersomnia, psychomotor agitation or retardation, changes in weight or appetite, loss of energy, difficulty concentrating or making decisions, feelings of worthlessness or guilt, hopelessness, worry, and suicidal ideation or behavior. To qualify for the diagnosis, individuals must have at least five of these symptoms for at least 2 weeks.

DSM-IV required a separate designation of "mixed" episodes, in which fully syndromal manic and depressive episodes occur simultaneously (i.e., severely irritable mood along with racing thoughts, decreased need for sleep, suicidal thoughts, feelings of worthlessness, and insomnia for a minimum of 1 week). Mixed states are associated with a more debilitating course of illness, with earlier onset and greater levels of comorbidity with anxiety and substance use disorders (Swann et al., 2012). Many clinicians reported that the *DSM-IV* mixed episode criteria were too strict; in practice, they reported seeing patients who have fully syndromal presentations of one pole and subsyndromal presentations of the other. In an analysis of 1,044 medication visits among patients who were in a hypomanic episode, "mixed hypomania" was present in 57% of visits and was particularly common among women. *DSM-5* no longer has a category called mixed episodes. Mixed is now a broad course specifier, to be applied when three or more subthreshold symptoms from the opposite pole occur during a manic, depressive, or hypomanic episode (First, 2010). It remains to be seen whether this revision of mixed episodes improves clinical utility.

BIPOLAR SUBTYPES

Individuals with BD who have at least one manic episode are diagnosed with bipolar I disorder, and those with recurrent major depression and at least one hypomanic episode are diagnosed with bipolar II disorder. Persons need not have had a depressive episode to have bipolar I disorder. Unipolar mania is commonly reported within community studies of mania, affecting 25% to 33% of those diagnosed with bipolar I disorder (Miklowitz & Johnson, 2006). Indeed, in the National Comorbidity Survey Replication (NCS-R), 1.7% of U.S. adolescents had experienced a manic episode without depression (Merikangas et al., 2012). Nonetheless, most patient samples are characterized by high rates of depression, perhaps because depression is related to more aggressive help-seeking (Calabrese, Hirschfeld, Frye, & Reed, 2004). Interestingly, in a 20-year follow-up of patients who had been treated for unipolar mania, the majority (20/27, or 74%) had at least one episode of depression during follow-up (Solomon et al., 2003). Thus, there is controversy concerning whether unipolar mania is stable over the life course or whether most bipolar I patients, if followed long enough, eventually develop a depressive episode.

There are important distinctions in the naturalistic courses of bipolar I and bipolar II disorders. In a study involving a 10-year follow-up, only about 1 in 10 patients with bipolar II disorder eventually developed a full manic or mixed episode and could then be diagnosed with bipolar I (Coryell et al., 1995). Because bipolar II disorder is defined by recurrent depressive episodes (whereas bipolar I disorder does not have a depression-related criterion), patients with bipolar II disorder spend the majority of their weeks ill in depressive rather than hypomanic states (with a ratio of 37 weeks to 1), whereas the ratio of depressed versus manic weeks in bipolar I disorder is about 3:1 (Judd et al., 2002). Patients with bipolar II disorder are also more likely to be "rapid cyclers" (i.e., to have four or more illness episodes in a single year) than are patients with bipolar I disorder (Schneck et al., 2004). This difference may reflect that the diagnostic criteria for bipolar II disorder require the occurrence of at least two distinct episodes (major depression and hypomania), whereas bipolar I disorder can be diagnosed from a single manic episode.

DSM-5 provides criteria for at least two broader bipolar spectrum diagnoses. *Cyclothymia* is characterized by 2 or more years of switching between hypomanic and depressive symptoms that do not meet the full criteria for a hypomanic or a major depressive episode. Cyclothymic disorder appears to have a younger age at onset than major depressive disorder or bipolar II disorder (Van Meter, Youngstrom, Demeter, & Findling, 2013). *DSM-5* also includes the diagnosis of "bipolar disorder not elsewhere classified" (formerly called "bipolar disorder not otherwise specified" [NOS]), or simply "unclassified bipolar disorder," for people with brief and recurrent manic or hypomanic phases that fall short of the duration criteria for manic or hypomanic episodes. The multisite Course and Outcome of Bipolar Youth (COBY) study offered the following definition of bipolar disorder NOS: a distinct period of abnormally elevated, expansive, or irritable mood plus two (three if irritable mood only) *DSM-IV* symptoms of mania that caused a change in functioning, lasted for at least 1 day, and was present for a total of at least 4 days in a person's lifetime (Axelson et al., 2011; Birmaher et al., 2009). The COBY study found that 54% of childhood/adolescent patients who began with a bipolar NOS diagnosis and who had a family history of mania in at least one first- or second-degree relative "converted" to bipolar I or II disorder within a 4- to 5-year time frame. In some cases, conversion simply meant developing manic or hypomanic episodes that lasted a few days longer than previously, but crossed the threshold into syndromal bipolar I or II disorder.

PHENOMENOLOGY OF THE MANIC SYNDROME

In *DSM-5*, the cardinal symptoms of mania are still euphoria and/or irritability, although increased activity is now a cardinal symptom as well. Other common "B" symptoms of mania include accelerated thought processes, pressured speech, inflated self-esteem, and decreased need for sleep. A meta-analysis of seven studies examining the characteristics of mania among youth (ages 5–18) (Kowatch, Youngstrom, Danielyan, & Findling, 2005) revealed that the most common symptoms were increased energy, distractibility, and pressured speech. Approximately 80% of youth showed irritability and grandiosity, whereas 70% had elated mood, decreased need for sleep, or racing thoughts. Less frequent symptoms included hypersexuality and psychotic symptoms. Thus, most children with mania have symptoms that also characterize adults with mania.

CASE EXAMPLE

Mania is not necessarily experienced as a pleasurable state in either children or adults. It can be experienced as an angry, depressed, unfocused, "tired but wired," and suicidal state.

Robert, age 45, managed a landscape architecture firm. According to his girlfriend, Jessie, his most recent manic episode began when, over a weeklong period, he became increasingly "expressive," impulsive, and loud, and "took on a physical dominance stance." For example, he screamed inappropriately at the coach while watching his daughter's basketball game, and "barked" orders at the waitress in a restaurant. He agreed that he was being "hyper" but also believed that he was seeing things more clearly than ever before. Things deteriorated when Robert, angry that his 21-year-old son, Brian, had not returned his phone calls, confronted Brian at the art supply store where he worked. A shouting match laden with obscenities ensued, and Brian's boss almost fired him.

In the next couple of days, Robert became frenetic. He became highly irritable and fixated on ideas about a musical career, even though he had only recently begun taking guitar lessons. He slept less and less. Toward the end of the week he impulsively moved out of the house he shared with Jessie and into his office. One night, he called her in a state of panic, saying that either he was dying or he might kill himself—he was unsure which. Jessie called the police, who found him lying on the floor of his office and staring at the ceiling. He was admitted to the hospital and stayed for 2 weeks (from Miklowitz, 2008).

EPIDEMIOLOGY

The World Health Organization's World Mental Health Survey Initiative, a study of 61,392 adults in 11 countries, found that an estimated 0.6% of the general population meet lifetime *DSM-IV* criteria for bipolar I disorder, 0.4% meet criteria for bipolar II disorder, and 1.4% meet criteria for subthreshold bipolar disorder. According to this study, the United States had the highest rates of BD, with prevalence estimates of 1.0% for bipolar I disorder, 1.1% for bipolar II disorder, and 2.4% for subthreshold BD (Merikangas et al., 2011). In the Netherlands, a lifetime history of cyclothymia (a form of subthreshold BD) characterized 4.2% of the population (Regeer et al., 2004). By contrast, major depressive disorder is at least 4 times more prevalent than BD or cyclothymia (17.5% lifetime prevalence in the United States; Kessler, Berglund, Demler, Jin, & Walters, 2005).

Data are becoming increasingly available on the prevalence of BD in youth. In a U.S. community sample of 10,123 adolescents (ages 13–18), 2.5% met lifetime *DSM-IV* criteria for bipolar I or II disorders, with double the prevalence in older adolescents (ages 15–18) compared to younger adolescents (Merikangas et al., 2012). The rate may be as high as 6% in treatment-seeking samples of children (Youngstrom, Findling, Youngstrom, & Calabrese, 2005).

In a meta-analysis of 12 studies of youth ages 7 to 21 across the world (*N* = 16,222), the rate of bipolar spectrum disorder was 1.8%, and did not differ significantly across countries (Van Meter, Moreira, & Youngstrom, 2011). Data were not presented on the separate cross-national rates of threshold versus subthreshold BD, however.

AGE AT ONSET

There is considerable variability in age at onset from study to study, depending on whether onset is defined as the first syndromal manic episode, the first depressive episode, or the first onset of any mood symptoms. In the World Health Organization study, the mean age at onset of bipolar I disorder (defined as the first manic/hypomanic or depressive episode) was 18.4 years; for bipolar II it was 20.0 years, and for subthreshold bipolar disorder, 21.9 years (Merikangas et al., 2011). Another large-scale study found that between 50% and 67% of bipolar I and II patients reported onset before age 18, and between 15% and 28% before age 13 (Perlis et al., 2004). Earlier age at onset (i.e., prior to age 17) is associated with rapid cycling and other negative illness course features in adulthood (Coryell et al., 2003; Schneck et al., 2004; Suppes et al., 2001).

The age of onset of mood disorders is getting younger in successive birth cohorts. In the NCS-R, Kessler et al. (2005) reported that the lifetime risk of bipolar I or II disorders in 18- to 29-year-olds was 22 times higher than in persons over 60. It is likely that more recent birth cohorts place a greater value on self-expression and disclosure than previous generations did, and they may be correspondingly more likely to report mood disorder symptoms.

The decreasing age of onset of BD may also in part reflect the less distinctive boundary between pre-illness and illness states in our current nomenclature. In the Pittsburgh Bipolar Offspring Study (BIOS), children of bipolar parents ($N = 391$) and children of healthy parents ($N = 248$) were evaluated at an average age of 11.9 years and followed prospectively over 7 years (Axelson et al., 2015). Overall, bipolar I or II disorder developed in 8.4% of the offspring of bipolar parents and 0.8% of the offspring of healthy parents, but high-risk offspring also had an increased risk for attention-deficit/hyperactivity disorder (ADHD) (30.7% compared with 18.2%), anxiety disorders (39.9% vs. 21.8%), and substance misuse disorders (20.0% vs. 10.1%). The age at onset of the first manic or hypomanic episode in BIOS was much younger than in earlier studies (mean = 13.4 years vs. 17–19 years). The strongest predictor of a bipolar I manic onset in offspring followed over 7 years was the presence of a subthreshold manic episode in childhood (i.e., prior to age 12).

SUICIDALITY

In studies that follow patients who have been hospitalized for bipolar disorder, rates of completed suicide are up to 15 times greater than in the general population (Harris & Barraclough, 1997; Jamison & Baldessarini, 1999) and 4 times greater than among patients with major depressive disorder (Brown, Beck, Steer, & Grisham, 2000). In a 40- to 44-year follow-up of 406 mood disorder inpatients (unipolar, bipolar I, and bipolar II), Angst, Angst, Gerber-Werder, and Gamma (2005) found that 11% had died by suicide. It is less clear how frequent suicide is in people with BD who have never been hospitalized. Risk factors for completed suicide include younger age, recent illness onset, male gender, prior suicide attempts, a family history of suicide, comorbid alcohol or substance abuse, rapid cycling course, social isolation, anxious mood, and "impulsive aggression" (Angst et al., 2005; Bridge, Goldstein, & Brent, 2006; Fawcett, Golden, & Rosenfeld, 2000; Jamison, 2000; Marangell et al., 2006).

Adolescents with BD are at particularly high risk for suicidal ideation, suicide attempts, and nonsuicidal self-injury. A study of 413 youth with BD (mean age 12.6) found that 18% had made at least one attempt in the prior 5 years; of these attempters, 41% had made multiple attempts (Goldstein et al., 2012). Not surprisingly, patients with recent severe depression were more likely to think about or attempt suicide than were those who were clinically stable.

Little is known about how to treat suicidality in bipolar disorder. Angst et al. (2005) found that patients who were treated with lithium, antipsychotics, or antidepressants— particularly in combination regimens—had a lower suicide rate than those who were not. In a sample of 20,638 health plan members (aged 14 years or older) who had BD, lithium was more effective than divalproex sodium (Depakote) in reducing suicide attempts and completions (Goodwin et al., 2003). A meta-analysis of 48 randomized trials of lithium in both bipolar and major depressive patients revealed that lithium was more effective than placebo in reducing the overall number of suicides, but did not affect rates of deliberate self-injury. The mechanisms by which lithium reduces suicide risk are unknown, although reductions in recurrence rates, impulsiveness, and aggression are possible candidates (Cipriani, Hawton, Stockton, & Geddes, 2013).

COMORBID DISORDERS

More than 95% of persons diagnosed with bipolar disorder have a lifetime history of other psychiatric disorders. In the NCS-R, the highest 1-year associations were observed between mania/hypomania and anxiety disorders (62.9%), behavior disorders (ADHD and oppositional defiant disorder, 44.8%), and substance use disorders (36.8%) (Merikangas et al., 2007). Children and adult BD patients with comorbid disorders have poorer long-term prognoses than do those without comorbid disorders (e.g., Masi et al., 2004; Otto et al., 2006). Adolescents and young adults with bipolar disorder and comorbid ADHD have a threefold greater risk (3.0% versus 1.1%) of making a suicide attempt than those without this comorbidity (Lan et al., 2015).

The comorbidity of bipolar disorder and ADHD in children is between 60% and 90%, even when overlapping symptoms are not included (Kim & Miklowitz, 2002). Differentiation of the two disorders usually requires a careful diagnostic evaluation, information from multiple informants (e.g., parents, teachers), and longitudinal observation of the course of illness. Risk for substance use disorders is 5 times greater in bipolar adolescents than in healthy adolescents (Wilens et al., 2004). Anxiety disorders, which occur in approximately 44% of children with bipolar disorder, are often diagnosed before the onset of a mood disorder in children of parents with bipolar disorder (Masi et al., 2004; Sala et al., 2010).

IMPAIRMENT IN PSYCHOSOCIAL FUNCTIONING

The majority of patients with BD experience significant impairment in work, social, and family functioning after illness episodes (Altshuler et al., 2006; Fagiolini et al., 2005; Gitlin, Mintz, Sokolski, Hammen, & Altshuler, 2011). In a Stanley Foundation Bipolar Network study of 253 adult patients with bipolar disorder, only about one in three worked full-time outside of the home. More than half (57%) were unable to work or worked only in sheltered settings (Suppes et al., 2001). In a community sample, people with bipolar disorder were approximately 4 times more likely to experience disability compared to the general population, and were at greater risk for divorce than those diagnosed with unipolar depression (Mitchell, Slade, & Andrews, 2004).

A remarkable feature of bipolar spectrum disorders is the wide range of functioning, with some individuals doing quite well and others struggling with core domains of life such as employment and relationships. A variety of variables are associated with life functioning, including subsyndromal depressive symptoms following a manic episode (Gitlin et al., 2011) and cognitive dysfunction (Altshuler, Bearden, Green, van Gorp, & Mintz, 2008). In one study, the presence of a supportive relationship was the best predictor of successful employment (Hammen, Gitlin, & Altshuler, 2000).

The relationship between functional impairment and symptoms appears to be bidirectional. Even low levels of post-episode residual symptoms are associated with delays in functional recovery (e.g., Gitlin et al., 2011). Equally important, failure to recover one's premorbid functioning after an episode is associated with earlier symptomatic recurrences over 1 year (Weinstock & Miller, 2010).

MANIA AND CREATIVITY

Mania has been described as a highly productive, creative state of exuberance (Jamison, 2005). Many historical figures in the arts, literature, and politics are believed to have had bipolar disorder—Vincent Van Gogh, Ernest Hemingway, and Winston Churchill are examples (Jamison, 1993). The unaffected first-degree relatives of those with bipolar disorder demonstrate higher creativity than do the affected relatives, and persons with bipolar II disorder achieve higher levels of creativity than do those with bipolar I disorder (Johnson, Murray, et al., 2012; Richards, Kinney, Lunde, Benet, & Merzel, 1988). Children diagnosed with bipolar disorder and children who are the offspring of bipolar parents score higher on a measure related to creativity than healthy control children (Simeonova, Chang, Strong, & Ketter, 2005). Creativity, along with other positive aspects of BD, has been proposed as an outcome variable that is particularly meaningful to patients (Michalak et al., 2016).

This profile of findings suggests that fully syndromal manic episodes are not the cause of elevated creativity. Bipolar disorder and risk for mania have been related to several traits that could promote increased creativity, including positive affective traits (e.g., optimism), impulsivity, and increased ambition (Johnson, Murray, et al., 2012). Some research suggests that heightened ambition may promote greater creative accomplishment in patients with BD (Johnson et al., 2015; Ruiter & Johnson, 2015). More research is needed on the mechanisms linking bipolar disorder to creativity.

Etiology, Risk Factors, and Protective Factors: The Biopsychosocial Perspective

Modern perspectives view the expression of bipolar symptoms as the result of a continuous interaction between genetic vulnerability, neurobiological dysregulation, and environmental events. Evidence for the main effects of genetic and biological factors on bipolar onset or course, along with evidence for the psychological and environmental factors that appear to interact with them, is presented here.

GENETIC STUDIES

Bipolar disorder is among the most heritable of disorders. Heritability estimates from twin studies are as high as .85 to .93 (Kieseppa, Partonen, Haukka, Kaprio, & Lonnquist, 2004; McGuffin et al., 2003). At least a dozen studies have examined the risk of bipolar disorder among first-degree relatives of those with bipolar disorder, with estimates ranging from 5% to 12%, and between 20% and 25% when all forms of mood disorder in first-degree relatives are considered (Smoller & Finn, 2003). A meta-analysis of 17 studies suggested that children of BD parents are at a fourfold increased risk of affective disorders compared to children of parents without a psychiatric diagnosis (Lapalme, Hodgins, & LaRoche, 1997).

Molecular genetic studies have indicated multiple loci as relevant to bipolar disorder, but relatively few of these have been replicated. CACNA1C, ODZ4, and NCAN have been replicated in large-scale studies (Craddock & Sklar, 2013; Sullivan, Daly, & O'Donovan, 2012). In the single largest genetic study of psychiatric disorders (Cross Disorder Group of the Psychiatric Genomics Consortium, 2013), which contained 33,332 patients with a variety of disorders (6,990 with bipolar disorder) and 27,888 controls, there was moderate evidence for genes that had been previously identified as associated with schizophrenia or bipolar disorder: a locus near MIR137; TCF4, the MHC region on chromosome 6; and SYNE1. There was also a role for calcium channel signaling genes in all five disorders under examination (autism spectrum disorders, ADHD, bipolar disorder, major depressive disorder, and schizophrenia). The overall evidence suggests an aggregated small effect of a large number of genes (*risk variants*), with weak differences among diagnoses.

Modern genetic studies are identifying *quantitative phenotypes* in the neurocognitive, neuroanatomical, or behavioral domains that may be associated with bipolar disorder (Fears et al., 2014). In this methodology one examines, for example, the genetic correlates of activation in specific neural circuits or in the volume or thickness of brain structures thought to be relevant to mood regulation. Identifying genetically correlated brain changes, however, raises considerable challenges related to sample size. One innovative method for studying quantitative phenotypes is to examine extended pedigrees in cultures in which family members tend to stay in the same general location. One multinational study examined two genetically isolated populations—in the Central Valley of Costa Rica and the Antioquia region of Colombia—and included 738 individuals, 181 of whom had bipolar I disorder. The authors examined 169 phenotypes (e.g., structural changes in prefrontal cortex) and determined that 31% of these phenotypes were genetically linked to bipolar disorder. Certain phenotypes (e.g., cortical thickness in prefrontal and temporal regions) were promising candidate traits for genetic mapping in bipolar disorder based on degree of heritability. Quantitative trait methods may eventually identify genetic loci related to the disease (Fears et al., 2014).

Another line of genetic investigation has examined the offspring of parents with BD who do and do not respond well to lithium. Grof, Duffy, Alda, and Hajek (2009) posited that children of lithium responders develop the illness in a predictable series of stages, starting with nonspecific sleep disturbance and anxiety in childhood, followed by major depression during the postpubescent period, and finally fully syndromal mania. These predictions do not appear to be consistent with those of the Pittsburgh Bipolar Offspring Study that found that children of bipolar parents often develop subthreshold mania before depression, with an average age of onset of 12 (Axelson et al., 2015). Nonetheless, we are now in a better position than in the past to consider familial drug responses as moderators of genetic susceptibility in children, given the fact that the current generation of parents developed BD after lithium and other mood stabilizers became available.

GENETIC VULNERABILITIES OF BIPOLAR DISORDER SHARED WITH DEPRESSION AND SCHIZOPHRENIA

Among the first-degree relatives of BD probands, there is an increased risk of major depressive disorders (Smoller & Finn, 2003) as well as schizophrenia. A key question is the extent of overlap in the phenotypes and genotypes for these disorders. One twin study found that the heritabilities for unipolar depression and mania were modestly correlated, but 71% of the genetic liability to mania was distinct from that of depression (McGuffin et al., 2003). A polymorphism in the serotonin transporter promotor region (5-HTTLPR) has been documented across at least some studies of BD (Levinson, 2006), and it has been documented as a risk factor for unipolar depression in the context of childhood adversity and life events (Caspi et al., 2003; Kendler, Kuhn, Vittum, Prescott, & Riley, 2005; Taylor et al., 2005). In a meta-analysis of 54 studies, the effect of 5-HTTLPR as a moderator in the stress-depression relationship was stronger for childhood maltreatment than for life events (Karg, Burmeister, Shedden, & Sen, 2011).

In parallel, researchers have begun to examine overlap in the genetic risk of schizophrenia and BD. In regard to schizophrenia, the monozygotic twins of persons with schizophrenic disorder are at an increased risk for mania (8.2%) as well as schizophrenia (40.8%). Likewise, the monozygotic twins of manic patients are at an increased risk for schizophrenia (13.6%) and mania (36.4%) (Cardno, Rijsdijk, Sham, Murray, & McGuffin, 2002).

Of the genetic regions hypothesized to be involved in BD, several appear to overlap with those proposed to increase risk for schizophrenia (Sullivan et al., 2012; Cross Disorder Group of the Psychiatric Genomics Consortium, 2013). Greater overlap in gene loci may be found for forms of bipolar disorder that show certain psychotic features. For example, a genome-wide association study found overlap in gene variants among persons with bipolar disorder who had mood-incongruent psychotic delusions or hallucinations (i.e., with no clear content related to sadness or elation) and persons with schizophrenia (Goes et al., 2012).

Eventually, genetic research may identify regions that increase vulnerability to both bipolar disorder and schizophrenia; that risk will not be defined only on the basis of symptom profiles or pathological behaviors. However, the methods for translating information about gene loci into preventive interventions have not been clarified.

NEUROTRANSMITTER DYSREGULATION

Over the past decade, models of neurotransmitter disturbance in BD have shifted from a focus on absolute levels of neurotransmitters to an emphasis on the overall functioning of cellular systems. Bipolar disorder may involve impairments in the plasticity of synapses and receptors and disturbances in intracellular signaling cascades (the functioning of molecules inside neurons that mediate signal transduction) rather than the amount of dopamine or serotonin (Manji, 2009). Increasingly sophisticated technologies facilitate examining facets of the system that contribute to overall functioning, such as the binding of neurotransmitters to receptors or individual differences in sensitivity to pharmacological challenges.

Although we focus on dopamine, serotonin, and glutamate dysfunctions, these likely interact with deficits in other neurotransmitter systems, such as γ-aminobutyric acid (GABA) and substance P, to produce symptoms of mood disorders (e.g., Stockmeier, 2003). We do not focus on norepinephrine here—although norepinephrine levels have been found to be increased during mania and diminished during depression, it is less clear whether changes in norepinephrine levels are a product or a cause of mood symptoms (Thase, Jindal, & Howland, 2002).

Dopamine

Theories of BD have long placed emphasis on the dopaminergic pathways involved in reward sensitivity (Depue, Collins, & Luciana, 1996; Hestenes, 1992), including the nucleus accumbens and the ventral tegmentum (Naranjo, Tremblay, & Busto, 2001). In this model, mania is a highly reward-driven state. Current theory suggests that dopamine function is enhanced during mania and diminished during depression (Cousins, Butts, & Young, 2009). Among people without BD, dopaminergic agonists have been found to trigger manic symptoms such as increased mood, energy, and talkativeness (Sax & Strakowski, 2001; Willner, 1995). Manic symptoms in response to amphetamine are more pronounced among people with BD than among people without BD, probably because amphetamine increases the bioavailability of dopamine as well as other catecholamines (Anand et al., 2000). People diagnosed with BD demonstrate increased behavioral response (as measured with symptoms on mania rating scales) to amphetamines compared to those diagnosed with schizophrenia (Anand et al., 2000).

In a phenomenon known as *behavioral sensitization*, most individuals demonstrate a rapid increase in motor activity from the first to the second exposure to amphetamines. Persons with first-episode psychosis and BD fail to show this shift from first to second exposure, perhaps indicating that dopaminergic receptors have already developed increased sensitivity (Strakowski, Sax, Setters, & Keck, 1996; Strakowski, Sax, Setters, Stanton, & Keck, 1997). This is consistent with the hypothesis (discussed below under "Goal Dysregulation") that BD is characterized by greater sensitivity to reward, as mediated by changes in the regulation of dopaminergic reward pathways. People with euthymic bipolar disorder show larger shifts in reward-seeking behavior than those with no bipolar disorder when administered a dopamine agonist (Burdick, Braga, Gopin, & Malhotra, 2014).

Serotonin

Substantial evidence suggests that BD is related to diminished function of the serotonin system. As serotonin constrains other neurotransmitter systems, deficits in the function of the serotonin system are believed to allow greater variability in the function of dopamine. Neuroimaging studies indicate that mood disorders are generally associated with decreased sensitivity of the serotonin receptors (Stockmeier, 2003).

Research has examined how people respond to fluctuations in serotonin, induced by either depleting or augmenting of tryptophan, the precursor to serotonin. Persons with a positive family history of BD display more cognitive deficits after serotonin-depletion and serotonin-augmentation procedures than persons without a positive family history of BD do (Sobcazk, Honig, Schmitt, & Riedel, 2003; Sobczak et al., 2002). The psychomimetic effects of drugs like LSD that stimulate the action of serotonin receptors may also suggest a role for serotonergic dysregulation in BD.

Glutamate

Glutamate is well established as a major excitatory neurotransmitter that plays a key role in the plasticity of dendrites, axons, and synapses (Chen, Henter, & Manji, 2010). Across paradigms, researchers have found evidence for changes in glutamate function within bipolar disorder. In postmortem tissue samples, elevated levels of glutamate have been found in prefrontal cortical regions of patients with BD (Hashimoto, Sawa, & Iyo, 2007).

In a single-photon emission computed tomography (SPECT) study, there was evidence for glutamate receptor dysfunction although no changes in absolute glutamate levels (Sanacora, Zarate, Krystal, & Manji, 2008).

Inflammatory Cytokines

It is well established that cytokines and cytokine inducers lead to behaviors associated with depression, including changes in sleep, anhedonia, and decreased activity. Patients with MDD can be distinguished from healthy volunteers by higher levels of proinflammatory cytokines (Miller, Maletic, & Raison, 2009). Persons diagnosed with bipolar disorder appear to have irregularities in immunological processes as well. A meta-analysis of 30 studies concluded that adults with BD could be distinguished from healthy volunteers on concentrations of interleukin-4 (IL-4), IL-10, soluble IL-2 and IL-6 receptors, recombinant tumor necrosis factor-alpha (TNF-α), soluble TNF receptor 1 (sTNFR1), and an IL-1 receptor antagonist (Modabbernia, Taslimi, Brietzke, & Ashrafi, 2013). These differences, however, were less consistent when comparing euthymic (rather than acutely symptomatic) patients to controls. For example, Brietzke et al. (2009) found that the proinflammatory cytokines IL-2, IL-4, and IL-6 were increased among symptomatic bipolar adults compared to control subjects, but only increased levels of IL-4 distinguished euthymic patients with BD from controls.

Less is known about whether increased levels of inflammatory activity normalize with medication treatments. Kim et al. (2004) found that at the time of hospital admission, medication-free patients with mania could be distinguished from healthy controls on elevated levels of interferon gamma (IFN-y, a cytokine that is central to immune reactions to viral and bacterial infections) and IL-4, and lower levels of transforming growth factor–beta 1 (TGF-β1, a protein that controls cell growth and proliferation). Interestingly, TGF-β1 levels increased significantly from admission to a reassessment after 8 weeks of mood stabilizer treatment. Lithium treatment was associated with normalization of inflammatory markers in one small open trial (Boufidou, Nikkolaou, Alevizios, Liappas, & Christodoulou, 2004). Thus, mood state and medication status may account for a proportion of the variance in inflammatory states among patients with BD.

NEURAL CORRELATES OF BIPOLAR DISORDER

A growing body of research has mapped the brain regions involved in emotional reactivity and regulation among healthy individuals (Phillips, Drevets, Rauch, & Lane, 2003; Strakowski et al., 2012). For example, the amygdala is involved in identifying the significance of emotionally relevant stimuli of both negative and positive valence (Aggleton, 2000). Signals from the amygdala activate relevant structures involved in emotion processing and planning, such as the hippocampus, which is hypothesized to facilitate encoding and retrieval of emotion-relevant memories, and the prefrontal cortex (PFC), which appears to be involved in the regulation of emotion (Ochsner & Gross, 2005).

Not surprisingly, these same regions have been implicated in the pathophysiology of BD. Bipolar I disorder is associated with hyperactivity in the amygdala in positron-emission tomography (PET) studies (Kruger, Seminowicz, Goldapple, Kennedy, & Mayberg, 2003), as well as in functional magnetic resonance imaging (fMRI) studies of activity during cognitive or emotional tasks (for a review, see Phillips & Swartz, 2014).

Several investigators (Altshuler & Townsend, 2012; Keener & Phillips, 2007) have described bipolar disorder as involving impairments in the cortical and subcortical structures and circuits that subserve emotional salience and response inhibition, collectively known as an *emotional control* circuit. In a review of studies, Altshuler and colleagues (e.g., Townsend & Altshuler, 2012) showed that the amygdala is hyperactivated in manic states, shows variable activity in depression, and is normally activated during euthymic mood. Also relevant to this circuit is the anterior cingulate cortex, which is less activated during mania compared to euthymia. Several studies also indicate that those with BD show increased striatal activation in response to emotion stimuli as compared to controls. Reduced ventrolateral PFC activity is also shown across manic, depressed, and euthymic states, and may be a traitlike characteristic of bipolar disorder.

Several studies indicate that BD is characterized by reduced resting state connectivity of the amygdala and prefrontal regions (Strakowski et al., 2012). For example, functional connectivity between the perigenual anterior cingulate cortex and amygdala is compromised in BD during remission (Wang et al., 2009). One model posits that chronic ventrolateral PFC hypoactivation may lead to abnormal modulatory control of the limbic structures, which may partially explain why patients with BD have mood instability and hyperreactivity to events even when in relative remission (Townsend & Altshuler, 2012). Diminished activity of the PFC and related cortical regions might interfere with the ability to inhibit emotions and to conduct effective planning and goal pursuit in the context of emotion.

A recent meta-analysis of functional MRI studies indicated that hyperactivation of the basal ganglia is common among BD patients (Chen, Suckling, Lennox, Ooi, & Bullmore, 2011). Although early studies suggested that this activation was related to manic symptoms (Blumberg et al., 1999; Caligiuri et al., 2003), the body of evidence suggests that hyperactivation is observed across manic, euthymic, and depressive states (Chen et al., 2011). Hence, bipolar disorder may be associated with abnormal activity of a neural circuit involving (a) elevated sensitivity of regions relevant to emotionality (e.g., the amygdala) and reward sensitivity (e.g., the basal ganglia) and (b) diminished activity in regions relevant for emotion regulation (e.g., regions such as the ventrolateral PFC).

Future neuroimaging studies may clarify whether abnormal activity in these circuits distinguishes BD from unipolar depression, and whether these circuits are impaired before the onset of the disorder. A novel strategy for addressing the latter question comes from studies of youth at risk for BD (i.e., those with a family history of mania who show subthreshold mania or hypomania from a young age; e.g., Axelson et al., 2015). Youth with BD and youth at risk for BD show decreased dorsolateral PFC activity and increased amygdala or posterior cingulate activity when viewing fearful faces (Chang et al., 2004; Garrett et al., 2014; Olsavsky et al., 2012).

Psychosocial Variables as Predictors of the Course of Bipolar Disorder

By the end of the 1980s, it was relatively well established that genetic models of BD did not explain the enormous heterogeneity in the course of the illness over time (Prien & Potter, 1990). Several studies established that psychosocial stress variables were robust predictors of the course of the disorder. For example, Ellicott, Hammen, Gitlin, Brown, and Jamison (1990) found that BD patients with high levels of life events were at 4.5 times greater risk for relapse within 2 years than were patients with medium or low levels of life events, even when the focus of the analyses was on life events that were not caused by the person. Intriguingly, life events have also been found to predict the onset of mood disorders among the adolescent children of parents with BD (Hillegers et al., 2004; Wals et al., 2005).

Psychosocial stressors can include chronic environmental adversities, such as high levels of expressed emotion (EE: such as criticism, hostility, or emotional overinvolvement) attitudes in parents of symptomatic offspring. Miklowitz, Goldstein, Nuechterlein, Snyder, and Mintz (1988) found that young adult inpatients with mania discharged to parents who were rated high on EE or who showed high levels of affective negativity during parent-to-patient interactions were at 94% risk for relapse within 9 months. This figure compares to a 17% risk of relapse among patients discharged to parents who were low on both EE attitudes and affective negativity during interactions.

Although these early studies established the predictive value of psychosocial variables, they did not address key issues such as the effects of stress on manic versus depressive symptoms. Recent research has systematically examined how psychosocial variables— childhood adversity, sleep/schedule disruption, and life events—influence the onset or course of depression and mania within BD.

CHILDHOOD ADVERSITY

A significant amount of research has examined early adversity experiences (i.e., sexual, physical, or emotional abuse) in bipolar disorder. On the whole, rates of early adversity appear to be extremely high among persons with BD. In addition, there is substantive evidence that early adversity relates to a worse course of disorder. In one review of 19 studies, childhood abuse—and particularly, physical abuse—was related to early illness onset, substance abuse, and suicidality in BD (Daruy-Filho, Brietzke, Lafer, & Grassi-Oliveira, 2011).

In longitudinal research, traumatic events have been found to increase the risk of chronic stress within BD, which in turn increases the risk of depressive symptoms (Gershon, Johnson, & Miller, 2013). One cross-sectional study (Dienes, Hammen, Henry, Cohen, & Daley, 2006) found that patients who reported severe early adversity (i.e., parental neglect or sexual/physical abuse) reported less stress prior to illness recurrences and an earlier age at onset of BD than patients who reported no early adversity.

In a reanalysis of data from the National Epidemiologic Survey on Alcohol and Related Conditions relating to 811 individuals with a lifetime history of mania, childhood adversity (physical and sexual maltreatment) was associated with a higher risk of first-onset mania and a higher risk of recurrent manic episodes in adulthood. Moreover, stressful events that occurred in the year before the study's baseline assessment (e.g., financial hardships) were more closely associated with onsets or recurrences of mania among genetically at-risk individuals with a history of childhood adversity than they were among those without childhood adversity. This pattern suggests that childhood adversity may potentiate the effects of stressful events on manic onset or recurrence (Gilman et al., 2015).

In considering the meaning of interactions between family history, childhood adversity, and stress, we need to rule out competing explanations, such as that individuals from more genetically prone families are more likely to be exposed to childhood adversity; stressful events in the year prior to an illness episode may partially reflect the person's prodromal behavior in the progression to mania (e.g., increasingly manic overspending leads to financial ruin); and the degree to which memories of parental affective disorder can be distinguished from memories of childhood adversity. While these issues have been well considered in the life events field, this type of issue is generally less well addressed in the available studies of early adversity.

SLEEP AND SCHEDULE DISRUPTION

Much has been learned in the past 25 years about the role of sleep in cognitive and emotional functioning in healthy individuals, and much of this knowledge is relevant to bipolar disorder. For example, sleep deprivation has been found to interfere with recalibrating the sensitivity of dopamine receptors (Ebert, Feistel, Barocks, Kaschka, & Pirner, 1994), diminish functional activation of the prefrontal cortex to emotionally relevant cues (Walker, 2011), and heighten reactivity to negative stimuli (Gujar, McDonald, Nishida, & Walker, 2011) and reward stimuli (Gujar, Yoo, Hu, & Walker, 2010).

Wehr, Sack, and Rosenthal (1987) hypothesized that sleep deprivation might mediate the effects of life events on episodes of BD, noting that life events often interfere with the ability to sleep (e.g., transmeridian flights, childbirth, etc.). This theory was expanded to a fuller conceptualization of circadian rhythm disruptions by Ehlers and colleagues (Ehlers, Frank, & Kupfer, 1988; Ehlers, Kupfer, Frank, & Monk, 1993). In the elaborated model, environmental and interpersonal influences serve the role of timekeepers ("social *zeitgebers*"), whereas other social influences ("social *zeitstorers*") disrupt the ability of the BD person to maintain daily rhythms (e.g., a job with shifting work hours). Ehlers and colleagues also suggested that social rhythm disruptions (e.g., to daily routines, social plans, and sleep-wake cycles) might predict symptoms above and beyond the role of disruptions specific to sleep.

In an early study of the social rhythm stability hypothesis in BD, Malkoff-Schwartz et al. (1998) conducted interviews with patients to assess life events before their most recent illness episode. Patients reported more life events that disrupted social rhythms in the 8 weeks before mania recurrences than in the 8 weeks before depressive recurrences. These results remained consistent in a replication with an enlarged sample (Malkoff-Schwartz et al., 2000). Such findings provide one more potential mechanism for understanding how life events affect the onset of mania.

Patients with BD show greater variability in their circadian patterns of activity, as measured using actigraphy, than do controls, even during interepisode periods (Harvey, Schmidt, Scarna, Semler, & Goodwin, 2005; Jones, Hare, & Evershed, 2005; McKenna, Drummond, & Eyler, 2014). Similar profiles have been observed in a study of parents with bipolar disorder and their children with early-onset mood disorders (Jones, Tai, Evershed, Knowles, & Bentall, 2006). Self-ratings of instability in social rhythms also were found to predict the onset of mood episodes among undergraduates with high scores on measures of subsyndromal depressive and manic symptoms (Shen, Alloy, Abramson, & Sylvia, 2008).

In a recent meta-analysis of nine studies (412 participants) using actigraphy to assess sleep patterns in BD, people with remitted BD showed longer sleep duration and lower sleep efficiency than controls (Geoffroy et al., 2015). Daily fluctuations in sleep quality may trigger more negative mood among those with BD than among those with no mood disorder (Gershon et al., 2012).

Once manic states are present, many people with BD show diminished sleep at night, as assessed using actigraphy (Gonzalez, Tamminga, Tohen, & Suppes, 2014; Salvatore et al., 2008; Wehr, Sack, & Rosenthal, 1987). Empirical research has shown that sleep deprivation is also a potent predictor of manic symptoms (Barbini et al., 1998; Murray & Harvey, 2010). In an 18-month naturalistic study of more modest sleep changes, diminished time sleeping predicted next-day increases in manic symptoms (Leibenluft, Albert, Rosenthal, & Wehr, 1996). Intriguingly, exposure to bright light, which can change circadian rhythms, has been shown to trigger manic symptoms (Benedetti, Barbini, Colombo, & Smeraldi, 2007).

Taken together, the evidence is growing that BD may be characterized by a vulnerability of the sleep and circadian rhythm system, such that even at baseline, people show less distinct and regular routines. As people become manic, profound reductions in sleep and circadian rhythms may occur. Bidirectional effects appear likely, in that (a) sleep deprivation can trigger manic symptoms, (b) life events involving schedule disruption are common before manic episodes, and (c) manic symptoms can foster a more chaotic lifestyle and sleep-wake pattern. It is less clear how depression is tied to problems with this system. Later in this chapter, we describe an intervention geared toward addressing sleep-wake cycle disruptions (interpersonal and social rhythm therapy [IPSRT]).

NEGATIVE LIFE EVENTS AND DEPRESSION WITHIN BIPOLAR DISORDER

The symptomatology and neurobiology of unipolar and of BD depression have many strong parallels (Cuellar, Johnson, & Winters, 2005). Thus, it is not surprising that many of the psychosocial predictors of unipolar depression also predict the course of BD depression. Predictors of bipolar depressive recurrences or symptoms include low self-ratings of perceived social support (Johnson, Winett, Meyer, Greenhouse, & Miller, 1999); high ratings of parental EE from clinical interviews (Kim & Miklowitz, 2004; Miklowitz, Biuckians, & Richards, 2006; Yan, Hammen, Cohen, Daley, & Henry, 2004); and high scores on self-ratings of neuroticism (Heerlein, Richter, Gonzalez, & Santander, 1998; Lozano & Johnson, 2001).

In considering the role of life events in bipolar disorder, it is important for investigators to use interview-based methods that exclude life events caused by symptoms (Johnson, 2005a). Three cross-sectional studies that used interview-based methods found that negative life events were equally common before episodes of either bipolar or unipolar depression (Malkoff-Schwartz et al., 2000; Pardoen et al., 1996; Perris, 1984). Prospective interview-based studies suggest that stressful life events lengthen the time to recovery from a depressive episode and predict increases in bipolar depression over several months (Johnson, 2005a).

A small number of studies have considered specific forms of life stressors. Life events involving danger and loss have been found to predict increases in depression over time (Hosang, Uher, Maughan, McGuffin, & Farmer, 2012). Kim, Miklowitz, Biuckians, and

Mullen (2007) followed 38 adolescents with BD who were enrolled in a randomized treatment trial. Adolescents who experienced more chronic stress in family and romantic relationships during follow-up also experienced more sustained depressive symptoms over time. Negative life events have not been found to predict increases in manic symptoms, but they do predict the depressive symptoms within mixed (depressive and manic) episodes.

One study examined whether life events predicted the onset of bipolar disorder among offspring of parents with BD. A cumulative count of the number of severe life events over the past 5 years was related to risk of bipolar onset (Hillegers et al., 2004). Events occurring within the previous 14 months were also associated with a greater risk of bipolar disorder onset within this sample (Wals et al., 2005).

Few studies have examined the mechanisms by which negative life events are associated with bipolar depression. In traditional cognitive theories of depression, the effects of stress on depression are magnified by negative cognitive biases (Beck, Rush, Shaw, & Emery, 1987). Negative cognitive styles have been documented in BD as well, particularly among persons with more severe depressive symptoms (Cuellar et al., 2005). That is, cognitions appear to be more negative during depressive periods compared with well periods (Knowles, Tai, Christensen, & Bentall, 2005; Thomas & Bentall, 2002), and among those with more severe depressive histories (Alloy, Reilly-Harrington, Fresco, Whitehouse, & Zechmeister, 1999). Negative cognitive styles and low self-esteem predict increases in depression over time (Johnson & Fingerhut, 2004; Johnson, Meyer, Winett, & Small, 2000). However, we do not have data from clinical samples indicating that negative events are more potent in eliciting depression in the presence of negative cognitive biases in BD.

Theories of "kindling" (Post & Weiss, 1998) postulate a significant role for stress in the early phases of BD. In these models, later episodes of illness are generated autonomously, with one episode begetting the next. However, studies have not consistently found that life events are more potent in provoking initial episodes than later episodes of BD (Bender & Alloy, 2011; Hammen & Gitlin, 1997; Hlastala et al., 2000).

GOAL DYSREGULATION AND MANIA

Two major models have clarified the behavioral and neural mechanisms underlying recurrences of mania: goal dysregulation (emphasizing reward sensitivity) and sleep or schedule disruption. As described earlier, it has long been hypothesized that BD relates to dysregulation in reward pathways. People diagnosed with BD have been shown to have greater activation of the nucleus accumbens (thought to play a role in reward and pleasure) during reward anticipation than do those with no mood disorder (Nusslock et al., 2012). As a consequence, people with BD may be more reactive to rewards and successes in their environment (Johnson, 2005b). Across more than a dozen studies, people with a history of mania and students vulnerable to mania describe themselves as more reward sensitive, or more likely to be strongly motivated by reward cues (Johnson, Edge, Holmes, & Carver, 2012; Meyer, Johnson, & Carver, 1999).

Elevated reward sensitivity has been found to predict a more severe course of mania among those diagnosed with bipolar I disorder (Meyer, Johnson, & Winters, 2001; Salavert et al., 2007). Reward sensitivity predicted the conversion to threshold bipolar I or II disorder among college students with subthreshold hypomanic traits (Alloy, Urošević, et al., 2012). In a longitudinal study of adolescents at risk for BD, EEG indices suggestive of heightened reward sensitivity predicted conversion from bipolar spectrum disorder to bipolar I disorder (Nusslock et al., 2012).

Johnson, Sandrow, et al. (2010) hypothesized that excess reward sensitivity may heighten reactivity to success, such that manic symptoms would be more likely after life events involving goal attainment. In a longitudinal study of bipolar I patients, goal-attainment life events predicted increases in manic but not depressive symptoms, even after controlling for baseline manic symptoms and excluding life events that could have been caused by these symptoms. These findings were replicated in another bipolar I sample (Johnson et al., 2008) and a sample of college students with subthreshold BD (Nusslock, Abramson, Harmon-Jones, Alloy, & Hogan, 2007).

A key focus for future research involves identifying which components of reward processing are most related to the course of BD (Johnson, Edge, et al., 2012). To date, critical components of reward sensitivity include highly ambitious goal setting and increases in confidence and energy after receipt of rewards. Regarding the first domain, people with BD endorse highly ambitious life goals, and ambitious goal setting is associated with a more severe course of mania (Johnson, Eisner, & Carver, 2009; Johnson, Fulford, & Carver, 2012). Highly ambitious goal setting also predicts the onset of BD in vulnerable adolescents (Alloy, Bender, et al., 2012).

Other studies have elucidated cognitive processes that shift in response to reward. These include tendencies to attend to and process information in a more positive manner (Eich, Macaulay, & Lam, 1997; Lembke & Ketter, 2002; Murphy et al., 1999) and an increase in confidence (Johnson, Edge, et al., 2012). There are also distinct behavioral shifts after success that are more pronounced for those with BD than for those without the disorder; for example, more active goal pursuit after making initial progress toward a goal (Fulford, Johnson, Llabre, & Carver, 2012). Although one might expect that increases in positive thinking, confidence, and goal pursuit after an initial success would be adaptive, longitudinal evidence suggests that increases in goal engagement (setting new goals and spending time pursuing goals) predict increases in manic symptoms in bipolar I disorder over several months (Lozano & Johnson, 2001).

In sum, goal attainments and successes appear to inspire bursts of confidence, which then fuel increased goal engagement in BD. Excessive goal engagement may accelerate the development of manic symptoms (Johnson, 2005b). Intervening to encourage self-regulation when patients with BD experience successes may be a key self-management tool to prevent the escalation of mania following a goal attainment life event.

Diagnostic Assessment

Bipolar disorder is diagnosed using clinical interviews. There are no biological or genetic tests that consistently distinguish patients with BD from patients with other psychiatric disorders. In this section, we review research on interview and questionnaire methods used to diagnose or chart the symptomatic course of BD.

STRUCTURED INTERVIEWS

Most clinicians rely directly on the history offered by the patient or family members in structured or semistructured diagnostic interviews. Some clinicians are reluctant to diagnose BD unless they actually see the patient in a manic or hypomanic state. Other clinicians eschew use of structured interviews, believing them to be stilted or overly formalized.

The most prominent diagnostic interview in the United States is the Structured Diagnostic Interview for DSM, now in its fifth edition (SCID-5; First, Williams, Karg, & Spitzer, 2016). The Schedule for Affective Disorders and Schizophrenia (SADS) is also a commonly used interview. Both the SCID and the SADS have achieved excellent inter-rater reliability and validity for the diagnosis of bipolar I disorder (Rogers, Jackson, & Cashel, 2001; Williams et al., 1992). Both are time-consuming, however, and some researchers are now using the Mini International Neuropsychiatric Interview (Sheehan et al., 1998), which simply requires patients to respond with "yes" or "no" to various questions about current and previous symptom states. The chance for false negative responses, however, increases in a yes/no format.

For patients under the age of 18, either the "Kiddie" Schedule for Affective Disorders and Schizophrenia, Present and Lifetime Version (K-SADS-PL; Chambers et al., 1985; Kaufman et al., 1997) or the Washington University K-SADS (Geller et al., 2002) is preferred. In childhood samples, parent report is generally more reliable than child report, but most studies obtained K-SADS data from both parent and child (Youngstrom, Findling, & Calabrese, 2004; Youngstrom, Findling, Calabrese, Gracious, et al., 2004).

Even with structured interviews, the diagnosis of bipolar II disorder or cyclothymic disorder can be quite difficult. When interviewers rate the same tapes, reliability estimates for bipolar II disorder are inadequate for the SADS in some studies (Keller et al., 1981; Kessler et al., 2006), but not all studies (e.g., Simpson et al., 2002). Disagreements between rater pairs often occur because the second rater diagnoses the person with another form of bipolar spectrum disorder, such as bipolar I disorder or bipolar disorder NOS (e.g., Kessler et al., 2006). In the field trials leading up to the publication of *DSM-5*, test-retest reliability was "fair" for bipolar I disorder in adults, averaging 0.52 across sites. It was also 0.52 at the one site that examined child/adolescent bipolar I and bipolar II patients, although the separate coefficient for bipolar II disorder was only .40 (Regier et al., 2013). Overdiagnosis of BD is particularly common when distinguishing between BD and borderline personality disorder (Zimmerman et al., 2010).

To gain a thorough assessment of the disorder and its subsyndromal forms, structured diagnostic assessments like the SCID should be supplemented by self-report questionnaires, family history interviews, and life charting (time line records of the frequency, severity, and timing of prior episodes; e.g., Leverich & Post, 1998). However, any of these self-report measures can yield questionable information when patients are highly symptomatic. It is critical to gather additional input from family members or other caregivers.

QUESTIONNAIRE MEASURES OF RISK FOR BIPOLAR DISORDER

As described earlier, structured clinical interviews do not fare well in identifying the milder forms of BD. Subsyndromal or spectrum forms of bipolar disorder—notably cyclothymia or hyperthymia—may precede the onset of fully syndromal bipolar disorder (Akiskal et al., 2005). Several investigators have attempted to capture these spectrum conditions with self-report questionnaires measuring tendencies toward highly positive mood states or excessive mood variability.

The Temperament Evaluation of Memphis, Pisa, Paris, and San Diego—Autoquestionnaire Version (TEMPS-A) yields five factors with high internal consistency: cyclothymic (0.91), depressive (0.81), irritable (0.77), hyperthymic (0.76), and anxious (0.67) (Akiskal et al., 2005). Moreover, in a prospective study using a questionnaire measure adapted from the TEMPS-A cyclothymic scale for children, baseline cyclothymic-hypersensitive TEMPS-A scores predicted the onset of bipolar disorder in a 2-year follow-up of clinically depressed youth (Kochman et al., 2005).

The Hypomanic Personality Scale (HPS), a self-report instrument for measuring hypomanic temperaments among college students, predicted the onset of bipolar spectrum disorders over 13 years in one study (Kwapil et al., 2000). Among high scorers on the HPS, 77.5% reported a history of hypomanic episodes (Eckblad & Chapman, 1986). A recent study of the HPS validated these findings. In a 3-year follow-up of 112 college students who had taken the HPS, 13 developed new bipolar spectrum disorders. In total, 58% of participants scoring in the upper quartile of the HPS had bipolar spectrum disorders at follow-up. However, the HPS also predicted domains that are not specific to bipolar disorder, such as impulsivity, substance use disorders, psychosocial impairment, and borderline traits (Walsh, DeGeorge, Barrantes-Vidal, & Kwapil, 2015).

The 79-item General Behavior Inventory (GBI; Depue, Kleinman, Davis, Hutchinson, & Krauss, 1985) measures hyperthymia, dysthymia, or biphasic/cyclothymic temperaments, reflecting difficulty with mood and energy regulation. High GBI scores were associated with psychosocial impairment in a 19-month follow-up of adolescents (Klein & Depue, 1984). Among teens with depression, higher scores on the depression subscale of the GBI were associated with bipolar disorder at 5-year follow-up (Reichart et al., 2005). A 10-item parent-rated version of the GBI had strong discriminant validity for identifying bipolar and unipolar disorders in children (Youngstrom, Frazier, Demeter, Calabrese, & Finding, 2008).

There has been a considerable amount of interest in the Mood Disorders Questionnaire (MDQ) as a potential epidemiological screening instrument (Hirschfeld et al., 2000). The MDQ is a brief true/false questionnaire regarding lifetime manic episodes. Significant questions have been raised about false positive diagnoses with the MDQ. In a study of 534 psychiatric outpatients assessed using the SCID, borderline personality disorder was diagnosed 4 times as often in an MDQ positive group as in an MDQ negative group. Of the 98 patients who scored positively on the MDQ, 24% had bipolar disorder and 28% had borderline personality disorder (Zimmerman et al., 2010). Thus, it seems unlikely that the MDQ has enough diagnostic specificity to justify its use in epidemiological studies, although it may help to identify patients who should receive a more in-depth evaluation.

ASSESSMENT OF LONGITUDINAL OUTCOME

Studies focused on recovery or recurrence often use the Longitudinal Interval Follow-up Evaluation (LIFE; Keller et al., 1987). The LIFE is a semistructured interview given to the patient at 3- to 6-month intervals. The 1 to 6 ratings of psychiatric status are given for each week of follow-up and cover the severity of mania, hypomania, major depression, delusions, hallucinations, and comorbid disorders (e.g., anxiety, ADHD). From these ratings, the timing, duration, and frequency of recoveries and recurrences can be tabulated.

An adolescent version (A-LIFE) of the LIFE was used in the Course and Outcome of Bipolar Youth study (Birmaher et al., 2009), with interrater reliabilities (intraclass correlations) of $\geq.80$ for mood disorder ratings. Moreover, among youth with subthreshold bipolar disorder, weekly ratings on the A-LIFE enabled investigators to clarify the progression to fully syndromal bipolar I or II disorder over a 5-year period (Axelson et al., 2011).

Instruments like the A-LIFE are quite time intensive for both patient and research staff, and require that patients (and often their caregivers) travel to a clinic and invest 1 to 2 hours, incurring travel expenses in the process. Unless the investigator or clinician has funds to cover travel expenses and compensation, these costs can be unwieldy. An alternative is an electronic short-messaging service, such as the Oxford University True Colours self-rating system, which cues patients every week to fill out self-rating scales of mania and depression (Bopp et al., 2010). Collecting data on mood over several months may capture some of the more subtle forms of mood variation that are forgotten when patients attempt to recall mood episodes for the LIFE. The True Colours system provided the primary outcome in a study of psychoeducation for bipolar disorder (Bilderbeck et al., in press). This method is not without its bugs, but it is possible that similar methods will gradually replace face-to-face interviews for capturing mood fluctuations and relapses of BD.

Treatment: Pharmacotherapy

Considerable strides have been made in the drug treatment of bipolar disorder within the past 2 decades. Drug treatment serves at least three purposes: (1) to stabilize an acute manic, depressed, or mixed/cycling episode; (2) to prevent relapse (maintenance pharmacotherapy); and (3) to reduce the severity of symptoms and to improve functioning between episodes. For detailed discussion of drug treatment of bipolar depression and mania in adults and children, the reader is referred to comprehensive reviews (Delbello & Kowatch, 2006; Goldberg, 2004; Kowatch, Fristad, et al., 2005; Miklowitz & Gitlin, 2015).

During the past decade, the most significant change in pharmacological treatment for bipolar disorder has been the increasing use of anticonvulsant and antipsychotic medications. Although lithium and divalproex sodium continue to be the mainstays of treatment, psychiatrists increasingly are using lamotrigine (an anticonvulsant) or atypical antipsychotics (olanzapine, risperidone, quetiapine, ziprasidone, aripiprazole, asenapine, lurasidone, or paliperidone) to control acute manic or mixed episodes, alleviate depressive symptoms, and prevent recurrences. The increased popularity of anticonvulsants and atypical antipsychotics is generally attributed to their more tolerable side effect profiles. In fact, these agents have side effect profiles *different* from lithium, as elaborated next.

TREATMENT OF ACUTE MANIA AND LONG-TERM PROPHYLAXIS

Approximately 60% to 70% of patients with bipolar disorder improve on lithium during a manic episode, although not all responders fully remit (Goldberg, 2004). Lithium can be difficult to tolerate; patients experience sedation, weight gain, tremors of the hands, stomach irritation, thirst, and kidney clearance problems. Divalproex sodium is a second mood stabilizer often used to control manic episodes, but it generally has more benign side effects (Bowden et al., 1994; Kowatch et al., 2000). The side effects of divalproex can include stomach pain, nausea, weight gain, elevated liver enzymes, and lowering of blood platelet counts.

A large-scale randomized community effectiveness trial, the Oxford University BALANCE study, raises questions about the long-term prophylaxis afforded by divalproex. In a study of 330 outpatients randomly assigned to lithium, divalproex, or the combination, the combination approach and lithium alone were both more effective in relapse prevention than divalproex alone. These findings suggest that lithium has an advantage over divalproex in delaying recurrences (BALANCE investigator and collaborators, 2010).

Olanzapine, an atypical antipsychotic medication, appears to have strong antimanic properties and may be particularly useful for mixed episodes or rapid cycling (Frazier et al., 2001; Gonzalez-Pinto et al., 2002; Tohen et al., 2000). Its prophylaxis against recurrences of mania or mixed episodes is as good as or better than lithium or divalproex (Tohen et al., 2003; Tohen, Greil, et al., 2005; Tohen, Kryzhanovskaya, et al., 2005). However, concerns about olanzapine side effects, including weight gain and the metabolic syndrome (abdominal obesity, elevated blood pressure, abnormal blood lipids, glucose intolerance), have made physicians favor other antipsychotics for treating mania, especially if the medication is going to be used in maintenance treatment.

Quetiapine and risperidone (second-generation antipsychotics) appear to be associated with intermediate risk of weight gain and metabolic dysfunction, whereas aripiprazole and ziprasidone are of lowest risk (Newcomer, 2007). Quetiapine is increasingly used to control manic symptoms in adolescents, either alone or in combination with divalproex (Delbello et al., 2006; Delbello, Schwiers, Rosenberg, & Strakowski, 2002).

TREATMENT OF DEPRESSION

Although many clinicians use antidepressants in combination with mood stabilizers to control bipolar depressive episodes, it is not clear that they are effective (Ghaemi, Lenox, & Baldessarini, 2001). The multisite randomized Systematic Treatment Enhancement Program for Bipolar Disorder (STEP-BD) trial (Sachs et al., 2007) found that patients receiving mood stabilizers plus bupropion or paroxetine did not stabilize any faster than patients receiving mood stabilizers plus placebo, nor were they any more likely to have treatment-emergent affective switches. In contrast, findings of a multisite naturalistic study found that bipolar depressed patients who were stabilized on mood stabilizers in combination with selective serotonin reuptake inhibitors (SSRIs) were less likely to relapse into depression and no more likely to develop mania or rapid cycling if they continued antidepressants for 6 months after remission, when compared to patients who discontinued antidepressants (Altshuler et al., 2003).

One trial found that combining lithium and divalproex is as effective in treating bipolar depression as combining mood stabilizers with an SSRI, raising the question of whether antidepressants are worth the risk of more frequent mood cycles (Young et al., 2000). However, in one small study of 17 depressed patients with bipolar II disorder who had previously failed lithium therapy, patients could be stabilized with antidepressants alone without significant increases in manic symptoms (Amsterdam, Wang, & Shults, 2010).

Current treatment guidelines for bipolar depression recommend adding antidepressants to mood stabilizers or atypical antipsychotics when other agents have failed (e.g., Kowatch, Fristad, et al., 2005; Yatham et al., 2005; Goodwin & Consensus Group of the British Association for Psychopharmacology, 2009).

Other options for bipolar depression, mania, and rapid cycling include quetiapine (Delbello & Kowatch, 2006) and lamotrigine (Malhi, Adams, & Berk, 2009). Quetiapine appears to be more effective than lithium as an antidepressant but not as an antimanic agent (Goodwin et al., 2004). Quetiapine can cause dizziness and sleepiness as well as weight gain. Lamotrigine was more effective than inositol or risperidone for patients with bipolar depression who had failed at least two prior antidepressant trials (Nierenberg et al., 2006). In a meta-analysis of lamotrigine trials, Geddes, Calabrese, and Goodwin (2009) found that effect sizes relative to placebo or other treatments were consistently higher when patients were in the upper 50% of the depressive severity continuum. Concerns about a serious skin rash that in a small number of patients can progress into Stevens-Johnson syndrome—a potentially fatal dermatological condition—has made clinicians cautious about the use of lamotrigine.

Lurasidone (Latuda), a second generation antipsychotic, appears to be effective as monotherapy in alleviating bipolar depressive symptoms when compared to placebo (Loebel et al., 2014). There have been no trials yet to determine whether lurasidone should be a first-line treatment for bipolar depression or an adjunctive when clinical response is incomplete. The side effects for lurasidone—nausea, restlessness, and sedation—are somewhat less disturbing than those of other second generation antipsychotics.

Finally, the combination of olanzapine and fluoxetine (Prozac)—usually called OFC or Symbyax—has a strong record of stabilizing both mania and depression (Tohen et al., 2003). However, OFC has not come into wide use. Physicians are usually reluctant to prescribe medicines that contain two compounds, because it is difficult to change the dosage of one agent without also changing the other.

MEDICATION NONADHERENCE

Perhaps the biggest limitation to mood stabilizers is the high rate of nonadherence among patients who are expected to take them continuously. Between 40% and 60% of patients are fully or partially nonadherent with mood stabilizer regimens in the year after a manic episode (Colom et al., 2000; Keck, McElroy, Strakowski, Bourne, & West, 1997; Strakowski et al., 1998). Rates of noncompliance in community mental health clinics are especially high; one study estimated that patients took lithium for an average of only 2 to 3 months (Johnson & McFarland, 1996). Rates of nonadherence among adolescents with BD are similar to those observed in adults: 65% reported inconsistency with medications during the first year of treatment after a manic episode (Delbello, Hanseman, Adler, Fleck, & Strakowski, 2007). Rapid discontinuation of lithium places patients at considerably higher risk for recurrence and suicide (Suppes, Baldessarini, Faedda, Tondo, & Tohen, 1993; Tondo & Baldessarini, 2000).

Nonadherence is due, at least in part, to a desire to re-create high periods and to resentment of having one's moods controlled by medications (Jamison, Gerner, & Goodwin, 1979). Difficulties with accepting the disorder and high rates of denial of the disorder also contribute to medication inconsistency or discontinuation (Greenhouse,

Meyer, & Johnson, 2000). Other studies have emphasized the contributory role of side effects, comorbid personality disorders, substance or alcohol abuse disorders, and more severe, recurrent forms of the illness (Colom et al., 2000).

Treatment: Psychotherapy

Given the high rates of recurrence among bipolar patients, even when maintained on optimal pharmacotherapy, investigators are increasingly looking to combine pharmacotherapy with psychotherapy. Early trials of cognitive-behavioral therapy (Cochran, 1984) and family therapy (Clarkin et al., 1990) had shown positive benefits in enhancing medication compliance, reducing recurrences, and improving functioning among bipolar patients. More recently, treatments have become manual-based and disorder-specific. Four forms of psychotherapy have emerged as effective in the long-term maintenance of bipolar disorder. Each of these treatments includes a significant focus on psychoeducation, although the length and format vary considerably. Recent studies on these modalities are reviewed here (for a comprehensive review, see Geddes & Miklowitz, 2013).

PSYCHOEDUCATIONAL APPROACHES

A study conducted at the University of Barcelona, Spain (Colom et al., 2003), assessed the efficacy of psychoeducational and support groups among 120 adult patients with bipolar I disorder who had been in remission for at least 6 months. All patients received mood-stabilizing medications. One group received 21 weekly sessions of structured group psychoeducation and the other received 21 unstructured, nondidactic group sessions. At the end of 2 years, fewer of the group psychoeducation patients (67%) than of the control patients (92%) had relapsed, and fewer had been hospitalized. Patients in group psychoeducational treatment were also more likely to maintain lithium levels within the therapeutic range (Colom et al., 2005). The results remained significant at a 5-year follow-up (Colom et al., 2009).

Bauer and colleagues (2006) tested a *collaborative care management* (CCM) program for bipolar patients ($N = 306$) treated at 11 participating U.S. Department of Veterans Affairs sites. The intervention centered on a group psychoeducational treatment to improve patients' self-management skills, but also included enhanced access to care through a nurse coordinator and medication practice guidelines for the treating psychiatrist. Patients were followed over 3 years. Those patients in the collaborative care management program spent fewer weeks in manic episodes than patients who received continued care as usual. They also showed greater improvements in social functioning, quality of life, and treatment satisfaction. The CCM treatment did not have an effect on mean levels of manic and depressive symptoms over the 3-year period. Dismantling studies will be necessary to determine the unique contribution of the group psychoeducation to the effectiveness of the full CCM program.

Extending this work to a group health network, Simon, Ludman, Bauer, Unutzer, and Operskalski (2006) randomly assigned 441 patients who were part of a prepaid group health plan to a 2-year multicomponent care management intervention or to treatment as usual (TAU). Patients were in various clinical states. Care management consisted of pharmacotherapy, telephone-based monitoring, interdisciplinary care planning, relapse prevention planning, and group psychoeducational treatment. Over 2 years, patients in the program had significantly lower mania scores and spent less time in manic or hypomanic episodes than those in the TAU group, but there were no effects on depressive symptoms. The results were strongest for patients who were symptomatic at baseline.

Perry, Tarrier, Morriss, McCarthy, and Limb (1999) examined a 7- to 12-session individual psychoeducational treatment and medication in comparison with routine care and medication. Psychoeducational sessions instructed patients how to identify early warning signs of recurrence and obtain emergency medical intervention. The investigators observed a 30% reduction in manic relapses, a longer time before manic relapse, and enhanced social functioning in the relapse prevention condition. The intervention was not associated with time to depressive relapse. Thus, a brief relapse prevention intervention may be a cost-effective way of delaying manic recurrences.

There have been recent attempts to test the effects of psychoeducationally oriented clinics on the relapse/remission course of BD. Kessing et al. (2014) randomly assigned 158 patients to treatment in a specialized outpatient mood disorder clinic that integrated pharmacotherapy with group psychoeducation, or to a standard care outpatient clinic. There was an interaction between treatment and age: those patients who were between 18 and 25 years old benefited more than those over the age of 26 from the integrated intervention than from standard treatment in terms of likelihood of rehospitalization. The younger patients also took more mood stabilizers and antipsychotics than the older group. This study may indicate that younger, more recent-onset patients may benefit more from psychoeducation than older and highly recurrent patients, and may be more likely to commit to a pharmacological regimen when treated in a specialty setting.

Studies that examine treatments at the clinic level rather than the individual patient level may be quite informative for community dissemination. Ideally, in replication studies, investigators should stratify participants on age before randomly assigning to clinics.

FAMILY INTERVENTION APPROACHES

Miklowitz and Goldstein (1990, 1997; Miklowitz, 2008) designed a family-focused treatment (FFT) for recently ill patients with BD. This approach is based on the idea that improving knowledge about bipolar disorder, reducing high EE attitudes, and enhancing communication will reduce relapse rates. It also involved the first use of a relapse prevention drill—a well-known technique in the substance dependence literature (e.g., Marlatt, 1985)—for bipolar disorder. The treatment involves three stages: psychoeducation for the patient and family members about BD (e.g., identifying and learning to intervene early with prodromal symptoms of relapse), communication-enhancement training, and problem-solving skills training.

In a randomized trial, the Colorado Treatment Outcome study, FFT was combined with standard pharmacotherapy and compared with a brief psychoeducation control (two sessions of family psychoeducation plus crisis intervention sessions as needed over 9 months) (Miklowitz, George, Richards, Simoneau, & Suddath, 2003). Patients had bipolar I disorder ($N = 101$) and were recruited during or shortly after a manic, mixed, or depressive episode. Over a 2-year follow-up, patients in FFT were 3 times more likely to complete the study without relapsing (52% versus 17%) and had longer periods of stability without relapse (73.5 weeks versus 53.2 weeks). They also had greater improvements over time in depression, lower mania symptoms, and better adherence to medications than patients in the comparison group. Patients in FFT demonstrated more improved communication with their relatives than patients in the control treatment did. Moreover, improved communication was associated with alleviation of mood symptoms over 1 year (Simoneau, Miklowitz, Richards, Saleem, & George, 1999).

Rea and colleagues (2003) compared FFT plus pharmacotherapy to an equally intensive (21-session) individually focused patient treatment plus pharmacotherapy for bipolar I patients after hospitalization for a manic episode ($N = 53$). In the first study year, no treatment differences were observed in relapse or rehospitalization rates. Over a 1- to 2-year posttreatment follow-up, however, patients in FFT had much lower rates of rehospitalization (12%) and symptomatic relapse (28%) than patients in individual therapy (60% rehospitalization and 60% relapse). There were no differences between the groups in medication regimens or adherence over 2 years.

In a two-site randomized controlled trial (RCT), Miklowitz et al. (2008) assigned 58 adolescent bipolar patients to either a developmentally appropriate version of FFT (FFT-A) plus pharmacotherapy or a three-session "enhanced care" (EC) psychoeducational treatment plus pharmacotherapy. Adolescent patients met *DSM-IV* diagnostic criteria for bipolar I, bipolar II, or BD not otherwise specified. Over 2 years, adolescents in FFT-A had more rapid time to recovery from initial depressive symptoms, less time in depressive states, and greater stabilization of depressive symptoms than adolescents in EC. A secondary analysis of this trial revealed that adolescents in high expressed emotion families showed greater reductions in both mania and depression if they received FFT-A than if they received EC. Thus, when choosing candidates for FFT-A in community settings, adolescents with higher parent-offspring criticism and conflict may show the biggest treatment-associated improvements (Miklowitz et al., 2009).

A second trial involving three study sites and 145 adolescents with BD I or II (Miklowitz et al., 2014), however, did not replicate the first. Adolescents in FFT-A and the 3-session EC comparator did not differ in time to recovery from their index episode of mania or depression, or in time to recurrence over 2 years. The presence of a comorbid anxiety disorder was the strongest predictor of recurrences in this study. A secondary analysis revealed a strong effect of stage of treatment: during the 1-year posttreatment phase, adolescents in FFT-A had significantly lower mania symptom scores than those in EC. These results are similar to those of the Rea et al. (2003) study of young adult patients with BD, which indicated a greater protective effect of FFT-A in the year following the 9-month FFT program than the 9-month individual therapy program displayed in the year after. Possibly, families need time to absorb the communication, problem-solving, and relapse prevention skills before implementation of these skills exerts a protective influence on the course of the disorder.

FFT has been manualized for children *at risk* for bipolar disorder as well: those with a family history of mania who present with major depression, bipolar disorder not elsewhere classified, or cyclothymic disorder. In a 1-year RCT, 40 high-risk children (ages 9–17) with MDD or bipolar disorder NOS were randomly assigned to either 12 sessions of FFT high-risk version (FFT-HR) or a 1- or 2-session education control (Miklowitz et al., 2013). About 60% of the children were taking psychotropic medications as well. All participants had at least one first-degree relative with bipolar I or II disorder, as revealed by direct interview. The participants in FFT-HR demonstrated more rapid recovery from their initial mood symptoms, more weeks in remission from mood symptoms, and more improvement in hypomania symptoms over 1 year than participants in the education control. Once again, the largest treatment effect sizes were among children in high expressed emotion families

FFT is only one approach to family intervention. Other investigators have examined treatment protocols that are more suited to younger bipolar patients. Multiple family groups (Fristad, Verducci, Walters, & Young, 2009) and a 12-session integrated program of individual CBT and FFT sessions known as RAINBOW (West et al., 2014) were both found to be effective in randomized trials for children with bipolar spectrum disorders (age 12 or under). Considerable work has been published on the factors that moderate or mediate these interventions (e.g., Fristad & MacPherson, 2014).

COGNITIVE-BEHAVIORAL THERAPY

Several major trials of cognitive-behavioral therapy (CBT) have been conducted. It is worth noting, as background, that several CBT manuals have been developed and published, and these manuals vary in their content.

Lam and colleagues (2003; Lam, Hayward, Watkins, Wright, & Sham, 2005) compared 6 months of CBT (12 to 18 sessions, plus two booster sessions after 6 months) with pharmacotherapy to treatment as usual with pharmacotherapy for 103 bipolar patients who had been in remission for at least 6 months. At 1 year, relapse rates were 44% in the CBT condition and 75% in the usual care condition. Patients in CBT also spent fewer days in illness episodes. One year to 30 months after treatment, CBT no longer prevented relapse relative to usual care but did continue to show a positive influence on mood and days spent in episodes. The effects of CBT were stronger on depression than on mania.

A UK multicenter trial conducted across five sites ($N = 253$) (Scott et al., 2006) compared 22 sessions of CBT plus medication to treatment as usual plus medication. The goal of this study was to examine the effectiveness of CBT when administered across a broader range of treatment settings. The patients had been in various clinical states before entry into the trial. A total of 60% of the patients had a recurrence during the 18-month follow-up, but no effects of CBT versus treatment as usual on time to recurrence were found. A post hoc analysis revealed that patients with fewer than 12 prior episodes had fewer recurrences if treated with CBT than with treatment as usual, whereas the opposite pattern was apparent among patients with 12 or more prior episodes. It is not clear whether patients with fewer than 12 episodes were less ill/episodic, younger, or had been ill for fewer years than patients with 12 or more episodes. Moreover, a meta-analysis of randomized trials (prior to 2009) did not find a moderating effect of number of prior episodes on treatment response (Lam, Burbeck, Wright, & Pilling, 2009).

In a four-site Canadian trial (Parikh et al., 2012), 204 patients were randomly assigned to 20 weekly sessions of CBT or to six group psychoeducation sessions with pharmacotherapy. Results showed no group differences in relapse or symptom severity over 72 weeks. Given that the six group psychoeducation sessions cost an average of $180 per patient whereas the 20 sessions of CBT cost $1,200 per patient, group treatment was the more cost-effective alternative in this study.

Meyer and Hautzinger (2012) examined 76 patients in a variety of clinical states who were randomly assigned to CBT plus pharmacotherapy (20 therapy sessions over 9 months) or a comparably intensive individual supportive therapy plus pharmacotherapy.

Thus, the design was similar to the study by Rea et al. (2003) for FFT. Over 33 months, there were no differences between the groups in relapse or time to relapse.

In sum, findings regarding CBT have been mixed, with not all trials demonstrating effects above other active treatments or usual care across participants. CBT does appear to be more effective for bipolar patients who have had fewer episodes and is unlikely to produce positive clinical outcomes among patients who have experienced 12 or more episodes. It is difficult to evaluate whether the stronger effects of CBT in the Lam et al. (2005) study were due to differences in patient characteristics, treatment manuals, or the nature of the comparison condition (treatment as usual).

Interpersonal and Social Rhythm Therapy

As discussed previously, one model suggests that BD symptoms are triggered by disruptions in daily routines and sleep-wake cycles. Frank (2005) developed the interpersonal and social rhythm therapy (IPSRT) as a means to alter this pathway to recurrence. IPSRT begins during or shortly following an acute illness episode and includes techniques to stabilize social rhythms and resolve interpersonal problems that preceded the episode. Patients learn to track their daily routines and sleep-wake cycles and to identify events (e.g., job changes, transatlantic travel) that may provoke changes in these routines.

In the Pittsburgh Maintenance Therapies study (Frank et al., 2005), acutely ill patients ($N = 175$) were randomly assigned to one of two weekly psychosocial treatments in combination with medication management: IPSRT or individual clinical management. Clinical management was focused on symptom control and medication adherence. Once patients were stabilized, they were randomly reassigned to IPSRT or individual clinical management (ICM) for a 2-year maintenance phase. Thus, four treatment strategies were formed. The 2-year recurrence rates were as follows: 41% for IPSRT followed by IPSRT, 41% for IPSRT followed by ICM, 28% for ICM followed by ICM, and 63% for ICM followed by IPSRT, suggesting that switching treatments was less effective for patients than simply continuing with the treatment assigned at their first randomization. However, IPSRT in the acute phase was associated with longer time before recurrence in the maintenance phase than was ICM. Moreover, IPSRT was most effective in delaying recurrences in the maintenance phase when patients succeeded in stabilizing their daily routines and sleep-wake cycles during the acute phase, suggesting that regularity of social and circadian rhythms may mediate the clinical effects of this treatment. IPSRT during the maintenance phase, however, was not superior to ICM in delaying recurrences.

In a small-scale acute treatment trial, 25 unmedicated patients with bipolar II depression were randomly assigned to a regimen of quetiapine or IPSRT (without medicines) (Swartz, Frank, & Cheng, 2012). Response rates, reductions in mean depression scores, and dropout rates were equal in the two treatments over 12 weeks. It is difficult to determine whether the lack of differences in time to stabilization indicates equal effectiveness, but it does raise the question of whether some bipolar II depressed patients can be treated with psychotherapy alone.

A study of IPSRT in New Zealand (Inder et al., 2015) examined 100 adolescent to young adult patients (ages 15–36), who were randomly assigned to 26 to 78 weeks of IPSRT treatment or to standard "specialty supportive care" (SSC), both given with medications. Over the interval, both groups improved in depressive symptoms, manic symptoms, and social functioning. However, there were no group differences. Thus, it is unclear whether the degree of change was attributable to nonspecific elements of the two treatments, the effects of pharmacotherapy, or different causal processes that led to the same overall outcome.

THE STEP-BD STUDY

In the early 2000s, little was known about what forms of psychotherapy were most effective for BD. Only single trials existed on the major forms of treatment. One study compared the effectiveness of psychotherapies found to be effective in single-site trials. The Systematic Treatment Enhancement Program for Bipolar Disorder (STEP-BD) (Miklowitz, Otto, Frank, Reilly-Harrington, Wisniewski, et al., 2007) examined the effectiveness of IPSRT, FFT, and CBT (30 sessions over 9 months) compared to a three-session psychoeducational control intervention (collaborative care, or CC). (The study did not test group psychoeducation as an additional modality, which in retrospect seems unfortunate.) BD I and II patients ($N = 293$), who began in a major depressive episode, were treated at 15 STEP-BD sites. All patients received pharmacotherapy with at least one mood stabilizer and often adjunctive atypical antipsychotics, antidepressants, or anxiolytics.

Over 1 year, patients in the intensive therapy conditions were more likely to recover from depression (64%) and recovered more rapidly (mean 169 days) than patients in CC (52%, 279 days, respectively). One-year rates of recovery, which did not statistically differ across the intensive therapy groups, were 77% for FFT, 65% for IPSRT, and 60% for CBT. Patients in the intensive therapies were also more likely to remain well in any given month of the 12-month study than patients in CC (Miklowitz, Otto, Frank, Reilly-Harrington, Wisniewski, et al., 2007). Additionally, patients in intensive therapy had better overall functioning, relationship functioning, and life satisfaction over time than patients in CC over 1 year (Miklowitz, Otto, Frank, Reilly-Harrington, Kogan, et al., 2007). The effects of intensive therapy on recovery were strongest among patients with comorbid anxiety disorders (Deckersbach et al., 2014).

The STEP-BD program suggests that intensive psychotherapy is a vital part of the effort to stabilize episodes of depression and enhance functioning in bipolar disorder. Possibly, the emphasis on pharmacological maneuvering to combat mood dysregulation has obscured the potential role of psychotherapy in addressing life stressors associated with depression. Given that bipolar patients often spend up to one third of their lives in states of depression (Judd et al., 2002) and that mood-stabilizing medications are generally more effective in controlling mania than depression (Keck, McElroy, Richtand, & Tohen, 2002), the integration of pharmacological and psychosocial treatments seems increasingly important.

Summary and New Directions

Patients with bipolar disorders experience a highly recurrent course of illness with substantial psychosocial impairment. Although considerable advances have been made in understanding the diagnostic boundaries, etiology, prognostic factors, and pharmacological and psychosocial treatment of the illness, much remains to be learned.

GENETIC AND NEUROBIOLOGICAL MARKERS OF RISK

A family history of BD clearly puts people at risk for the illness, but genetic markers with disease specificity have not been identified. Certain genetic loci appear promising as candidates for identifying persons at risk. Ongoing efforts are directed at (a) identifying genes that overlap between bipolar disorder and schizophrenia, and (b) identifying quantitative traits relevant to genetic risk that distinguish those with bipolar disorder from comparison groups.

Changes in the regulation of dopaminergic reward pathways and a decreased sensitivity of serotonin receptors have been implicated in bipolar mood symptoms, with newer work implicating glutamate and inflammatory cytokines as well. Serotonin deficits may contribute to a general dysregulation of emotion systems that increases vulnerability to a wide range of disorders (Carver, Johnson, & Joormann, 2009). Further research will be necessary to determine the exact nature and diagnostic specificity of these neurotransmitter system dysfunctions, and the degree to which such dysfunctions are evident during euthymic as well as symptomatic states.

PSYCHOSOCIAL PREDICTORS OF SYMPTOMS

Similar to recurrent major depressive disorder, bipolar disorder is characterized by pathology in the brain systems involved in emotion regulation. Early adversity may lead to greater disruption of brain regions involved in regulating emotions (Hanson et al., 2013), and for the person already vulnerable to BD, may intensify the risk of a range of negative outcomes and course parameters. The psychosocial variables that trigger unipolar depression, such as negative life events and high EE in caregivers, exert a major influence on the depressive course of bipolar disorder. But what are the unique predictors of mania? Patients whose bipolar disorder is in remission have high sensitivity to reward and ambitious goal setting; once they begin to experience successes, they may develop cognitions that contain overly optimistic biases (Johnson, 2005b). Relatedly, excess goal engagement appears to predict increases in mania.

Sleep deprivation has also been found to predict manic symptoms. Life events that disrupt social rhythms are more common before manic recurrences than before depressive recurrences. Nonetheless, a growing body of research suggests that sleep and circadian rhythms are disrupted during remission, and may be relevant for understanding depression as well (e.g. Cardoso et al., 2015).

OPTIMAL TREATMENT REGIMENS FOR BIPOLAR PATIENTS

Pharmacotherapy trials have become more sophisticated, and increasing evidence points to the utility of anticonvulsants and atypical antipsychotics in stabilizing depression and mania. Few of these trials have considered long-term maintenance, however. We do not know, for example, whether bipolar patients are best maintained on combination therapy or on monotherapy. Changes have occurred in the thinking about bipolar II disorder. For example, some patients with bipolar II may be treatable with antidepressants alone (Amsterdam et al., 2010). Bipolar II patients in a depressive episode may stabilize just as rapidly with psychotherapy alone as with atypical antipsychotics alone (Swartz et al., 2012). The idea of treating certain forms of bipolar disorder without medication runs against the grain of current psychiatric practice, but the clinical trial data do not justify long-term medication maintenance in every case.

Randomized controlled trials indicate that adding psychotherapy onto medication helps stabilize the disorder and prevent recurrences. It is not clear whether the effect sizes for adjunctive psychotherapy are the same for manic as for depressive symptoms, whether the polarity of the episode at entry into treatment is an important determinant of treatment outcomes, or what the role of comorbid anxiety disorders is in determining response to psychosocial treatments. The next generation of psychosocial research should examine treatment moderators to determine the conditions under which psychotherapies are more and less successful.

In the mental health literature, investigators are increasingly using practical trial designs in which treatment regimens are not set in stone and clinicians have the flexibility to change strategies when patients do not respond adequately. A recent example is the STAR*D trial that tested algorithms for using SSRIs and/or cognitive therapy for depression (Rush, 2007). Studies have only begun to study the effectiveness of algorithms for the drug treatment of bipolar disorder. Likewise, investigators could propose treatment-staging strategies that combine psychopharmacology with psychotherapy, such as treating bipolar depressed patients to remission with mood stabilizers and atypical antipsychotics and then determining whether adding a psychosocial intervention enables quicker discontinuation of the adjunctive agent.

PREVENTION OF ONSET

The potential application of psychosocial interventions to the prevention of the onset of bipolar disorder has considerable promise. Bipolar disorder can be conceptualized within a developmental psychopathology framework: how do bipolar symptoms emerge over time as a function of risk and protective processes within the genetic, biological, social, familial, and cultural domains, and how might one intervene in these developmental pathways to maximize protection and minimize risk (Miklowitz & Cicchetti, 2006)? These interventions may be both psychosocial and pharmacological. Prevention of the onset of the first manic episode may mean fewer or less severe mood symptoms over time, less risk of suicide, and enhanced psychosocial functioning.

Chang, Howe, Gallelli, and Miklowitz (2006) have offered the following hypothesis regarding how early intervention might stave off the onset of full bipolar disorder. Areas of the prefrontal cortex, along with other structures in the limbic system, suffer neurodegeneration after repeated episodes of bipolar illness. The stress of repeated episodes may interfere with prefrontal mood regulation, which may lead to increased cycling and increasing resistance to pharmacological interventions. Pharmacological or psychosocial preventive interventions (i.e., those administered before the first full manic episode) that interfere with neurodegeneration and successfully restore healthy prefrontal neural circuitry and neuronal integrity would, theoretically, reduce the vulnerable person's chances of having a full onset of BD. One study has shown that early intervention with FFT may reduce symptom severity in symptomatic children who have a first-degree relative with bipolar I disorder (Miklowitz et al., 2013). Future studies may establish whether early interventions that help ameliorate current symptoms have downstream effects that contribute to the prevention of the full bipolar syndrome.

Prevention of Suicide

Finally, few psychosocial interventions have addressed the prevention of suicide in BD, despite the fact that it is an exceptionally high-risk illness. Given that some psychosocial interventions have greater effects on depression than on mania and can enhance life satisfaction, it follows that they may also reduce suicidal risk. One small trial ($N = 20$) found that, in adolescents with bipolar spectrum disorders, dialectical behavior therapy was associated with greater improvements in suicidal thinking and lower levels of depressive symptoms than an active therapy control over 1 year (Goldstein et al., 2014).

These questions have not been addressed in studies that are adequately powered by sample sizes or lengths of follow-up. Thus, suicide prevention is a key area for investigation in the next generation of psychosocial research on bipolar disorder.

References

Aggleton, J. P. (2000). *The amygdala: A functional analysis* (2nd ed.). Oxford, England: Oxford University Press.

Akiskal, H. S., Mendlowicz, M. V., Jean-Louis, G., Rapaport, M. H., Kelsoe, J. R., Gillin, J. C., & Smith, T. L. (2005). TEMPS-A: Validation of a short version of a self-rated instrument designed to measure variations in temperament. *Journal of Affective Disorders*, *85*(1–2), 45–52.

Alloy, L. B., Bender, R. E., Whitehouse, W. G., Wagner, C. A., Liu, R. T., Grant, D. A., … Abramson, L. Y. (2012). High behavioral approach system (BAS) sensitivity, reward responsiveness, and goal-striving predict first onset of bipolar spectrum disorders: A prospective behavioral high-risk design. *Journal of Abnormal Psychology*, *121*(2), 339–351.

Alloy, L. B., Reilly-Harrington, N., Fresco, D. M., Whitehouse, W. G., & Zechmeister, J. S. (1999). Cognitive styles and life events in subsyndromal unipolar and bipolar disorders: Stability and prospective prediction of depressive and hypomanic mood swings. *Journal of Cognitive Psychotherapy*, *13*, 21–40.

Alloy, L. B., Urošević, S., Abramson, L. Y., Jager-Hyman, S., Nusslock, R., Whitehouse, W. G., & Hogan, M. E. (2012). Progression along the bipolar spectrum: A longitudinal study of predictors of conversion from bipolar spectrum conditions to bipolar I and II disorders. *Journal of Abnormal Psychology*, *121*(1), 16–27.

Altshuler, L. L., Bearden, C., Green, M., van Gorp, W., & Mintz, J. (2008). A relationship between neurocognitive impairment and functional impairment: A pilot study. *Psychiatry Research*, *157*, 289–293.

Altshuler, L. L., Post, R. M., Black, D. O., Keck, P. E. Jr., Nolen, W. A., Frye, M. A., … Mintz, J. (2006). Subsyndromal depressive symptoms are associated with functional impairment in patients with bipolar disorder: Results of a large, multisite study. *Journal of Clinical Psychiatry*, *67*(10), 1551–1560.

Altshuler, L., Suppes, T., Black, D., Nolen, W. A., Keck, P. E., Jr., Frye, M. A., … Post, R. M. (2003). Impact of antidepressant discontinuation after acute bipolar depression remission on rates of depressive relapse at 1-year follow-up. *American Journal of Psychiatry*, *160*, 1252–1262.

Altshuler, L. L., & Townsend, J. D. (2012). Functional brain imaging in bipolar disorder. In S. M. Strakowski (Ed.), *The bipolar brain: Integrating neuroimaging and genetics* (pp. 53–77). New York, NY: Oxford University Press.

American Psychiatric Association. (2000). *Diagnostic and statistical manual of mental disorders* (4th ed., text rev.). Washington, DC: Author.

American Psychiatric Association. (2013). *Diagnostic and statistical manual of mental disorders* (5th ed.). Washington, DC: Author.

Amsterdam, J. D., Wang, G., & Shults, J. (2010). Venlafaxine monotherapy in bipolar type II depressed patients unresponsive to prior lithium monotherapy. *Acta Psychiatrica Scandinavica*, *121*(3), 201–208.

Anand, A., Verhoeff, P., Seneca, N., Zoghbi, S. S., Seibyl, J. P., Charney, D. S., & Innis, R. B. (2000). Brain SPECT imaging of amphetamine-induced dopamine release in euthymic bipolar disorder patients. *American Journal of Psychiatry*, *157*, 1109–1114.

Angst, J., Angst, F., Gerber-Werder, R., & Gamma, A. (2005). Suicide in 406 mood-disordered patients with and without long-term medication: A 40 to 44 years' follow-up. *Archives of Suicide Research*, *9*(3), 279–300.

Axelson, D. A., Birmaher, B., Strober, M. A., Goldstein, B. I., Ha, W., Gill, M. K., … Keller, M. B. (2011). Course of subthreshold bipolar disorder in youth: Diagnostic progression from bipolar disorder not otherwise specified. *Journal of the American Academy of Child & Adolescent Psychiatry*, *50*(10), 1001–1016.

Axelson, D. A., Goldstein, B., Goldstein, T., Monk, K., Yu, H., Hickey, M. B., … Birmaher, B. (2015). Diagnostic precursors to bipolar disorder among offspring of parents with bipolar disorder: A longitudinal study. *American Journal of Psychiatry*, *172*(7), 638–646.

BALANCE investigators and collaborators, Geddes, J. R., Goodwin, G. M., Rendell, J., Azorin, J. M., Cipriani, A., Ostacher, M. J., … Juszczak, E. (2010). Lithium plus valproate combination therapy versus monotherapy for relapse prevention in bipolar I disorder (BALANCE): A randomised open-label trial. *Lancet*, *375*(9712), 385–395.

Barbini, B., Colombo, C., Benedetti, F., Campori, E., Bellodi, L., & Smeraldi, E. (1998). The unipolar-bipolar dichotomy and the response to sleep deprivation. *Psychiatry Research, 79,* 43–50.

Bauer, M. S., McBride, L., Williford, W. O., Glick, H., Kinosian, B., Altshuler, L., ... Cooperative Studies Program 430 Study Team. (2006). Collaborative care for bipolar disorder: Part II. Impact on clinical outcome, function, and costs. *Psychiatric Services, 57,* 937–945.

Beck, A. T., Rush, A. J., Shaw, B. F., & Emery, G. (1987). *Cognitive therapy of depression.* New York, NY: Guilford Press.

Bender, R. E., & Alloy, L. B. (2011). Life stress and kindling in bipolar disorder: Review of the evidence and integration with emerging biopsychosocial theories. *Clinical Psychology Review, 31*(3), 383–398.

Benedetti, F., Barbini, B., Colombo, C., & Smeraldi, E. (2007). Chronotherapeutics in a psychiatric ward. *Sleep Medicine Review, 11,* 509–522.

Bilderbeck, A. C., Atkinson, L. Z., McMahon, H. C., Voysey, M., Simon, J., Price, J., ... Goodwin, G. M. (In press). Psychoeducation and online mood tracking for patients with bipolar disorder: A randomised controlled trial. *Journal of Affective Disorders.* doi: 10.1016/j.jad.2016.06.064

Birmaher, B., Axelson, D., Goldstein, B., Strober, M., Gill, M. K., Hunt, J., ... Keller, M. B. (2009). Four-year longitudinal course of children and adolescents with bipolar spectrum disorders: The Course and Outcome of Bipolar Youth (COBY) study. *American Journal of Psychiatry, 166*(7), 795–804.

Blumberg, H. P., Stern, E., Ricketts, S., Martinez, D., de Asis, J., White, T., ... Silbersweigh, D. A. (1999). Rostral and orbital prefrontal cortex dysfunction in the manic state of bipolar disorder. *American Journal of Psychiatry, 156,* 1986–1988.

Bopp, J. M., Miklowitz, D. J., Goodwin, G. M., Stevens, W., Rendell, J. M., & Geddes, J. R. (2010). The longitudinal course of bipolar disorder as revealed through weekly text-messaging. *Bipolar Disorders, 12*(3), 327–334.

Boufidou, F., Nikkolaou, C., Alevizios, B., Liappas, I. A., & Christodoulou, G. N. (2004). Cytokine production in bipolar affective disorder patients under lithium treatment. *Journal of Affective Disorders, 82,* 309–313.

Bowden, C. L., Brugger, A. M., Swann, A. C., Calabrese, J. R., Janicak, P. G., Petty, F., ... The Depakote Mania Study Group. (1994). Efficacy of divalproex vs lithium and placebo in the treatment of mania: The Depakote Mania Study Group. *JAMA, 271,* 918–924.

Bridge, J. A., Goldstein, T. R., & Brent, D. A. (2006). Adolescent suicide and suicidal behavior. *Journal of Child Psychology and Psychiatry, 47*(3–4), 372–394.

Brietzke, E., Stertz, L., Fernandes, B. S., Kauer-Sant'anna, M., Mascarenhas, M., Escosteguy, V. A., ... Kapczinski, F. (2009). Comparison of cytokine levels in depressed, manic and euthymic patients with bipolar disorder. *Journal of Affective Disorders, 116*(3), 214–217. doi: 10.1016/j.jad.2008.12.001

Brown, G. K., Beck, A. T., Steer, R. A., & Grisham, J. R. (2000). Risk factors for suicide in psychiatric outpatients: A 20-year prospective study. *Journal of Consulting and Clinical Psychology, 68*(3), 371–377.

Burdick, K. E., Braga, R. J., Gopin, C. B., & Malhotra, A. K. (2014). Dopaminergic influences on emotional decision making in euthymic bipolar patients. *Neuropsychopharmacology, 39,* 274–282.

Calabrese, J. R., Hirschfeld, R.M.A., Frye, M. A., & Reed, M. L. (2004). Impact of depressive symptoms compared with manic symptoms in bipolar disorder: Results of a U.S. community-based sample. *Journal of Clinical Psychiatry, 65,* 1499–1504.

Caligiuri, M. P., Brown, G. G., Meloy, M. J., Eberson, S. C., Kindermann, S. S., Frank, L. R., ... Lohr, J. B. (2003). An fMRI study of affective state and medication on cortical and subcortial regions during motor performance in bipolar disorder. *Psychiatry Research: Neuroimaging, 123,* 171–182.

Cardno, A. G., Rijsdijk, F. V., Sham, P. C., Murray, R. M., & McGuffin, P. (2002). A twin study of genetic relationships between psychotic symptoms. *American Journal of Psychiatry, 159,* 539–545.

Cardoso, T. A., Campos, M. T., Reyes, A. N., Zeni, C. P., Souza, L. D., da Silva, R. A., & Jansen, K. (2015). Biological rhythm and bipolar disorder: Twelve-month follow-up of a randomized clinical trial. *Journal of Nervous and Mental Disease, 203*(10), 792–797.

Carver, C. S., Johnson, S. L., & Joormann, J. (2009). Two-mode models of self-regulation as a tool for conceptualizing effects of the serotonin system in normal behavior and diverse disorders. *Current Directions in Psychological Science, 18*(4), 195–199.

Caspi, A., Sugden, K., Moffitt, T., Taylor, A., Craig, I. W., Harrington, H., ... Poulton, R. (2003). Influence of life stress on depression: Moderation by a polymorphism in the 5-HTT gene. *Science, 301,* 386–390.

Chambers, W. J., Puig-Antich, J., Hirsch, M., Paez, P., Ambrosini, P. J., Tabrizi, M. A., … Davies, M. (1985). The assessment of affective disorders in children and adolescents by semi-structured interview: Test-retest reliability of the Schedule for Affective Disorders and Schizophrenia for School-Age Children, Present Episode Version. *Archives of General Psychiatry, 42,* 696–702.

Chang, K., Adleman, N. E., Dienes, K., Simeonova, D. J., Menon, V., & Reiss, A. (2004). Anomalous prefrontal-subcortical activation in familial pediatric bipolar disorder: A functional magnetic resonance imaging investigation. *Archives of General Psychiatry, 61*(8), 781–792.

Chang, K., Howe, M., Gallelli, K., & Miklowitz, D. (2006). Prevention of pediatric bipolar disorder: Integration of neurobiological and psychosocial processes. *Annals of the New York Academy of Sciences, 1094,* 235–247.

Chen, C.-H., Suckling, J., Lennox, B. R., Ooi, C., & Bullmore, E. T. (2011). A quantitative meta-analysis of fMRI studies in bipolar disorder. *Bipolar Disorders, 13,* 1–15.

Chen, G., Henter, I. D., & Manji, H. K. (2010). Presynaptic glutamatergic dysfunction in bipolar disorder. *Biological Psychiatry, 67*(11), 1007–1009.

Cipriani, A., Hawton, K., Stockton, S., & Geddes, J. R. (2013). Lithium in the prevention of suicide in mood disorders: Updated systematic review and meta-analysis. *British Medical Journal, 346.* doi: 10.1136/bmj.f3646

Clarkin, J. F., Glick, I. D., Haas, G. L., Spencer, J. H., Lewis, A. B., Peyser, J., … Lestelle, V. (1990). A randomized clinical trial of inpatient family intervention: V. Results for affective disorders. *Journal of Affective Disorders, 18,* 17–28.

Cochran, S. D. (1984). Preventing medical noncompliance in the outpatient treatment of bipolar affective disorders. *Journal of Consulting and Clinical Psychology, 52,* 873–878.

Colom, F., Vieta, E., Martínez-Arán, A., Reinares, M., Benabarre, A., & Gastó, C. (2000). Clinical factors associated with treatment noncompliance in euthymic bipolar patients. *Journal of Clinical Psychiatry, 61,* 549–555.

Colom, F., Vieta, E., Martínez-Arán, A., Reinares, M., Goikolea, J. M., Benabarre, A., … Corominas, J.

(2003). A randomized trial on the efficacy of group psychoeducation in the prophylaxis of recurrences in bipolar patients whose disease is in remission. *Archives of General Psychiatry, 60,* 402–407.

Colom, F., Vieta, E., Sánchez-Moreno, J., Martínez-Arán, A., Reinares, M., Goikolea, J. M., & Scott, J. (2005). Stabilizing the stabilizer: Group psychoeducation enhances the stability of serum lithium levels. *Bipolar Disorders, 7*(Suppl. 5), 32–36.

Colom, F., Vieta, E., Sánchez-Moreno, J., Palomino-Otiniano, R., Reinares, M., Goikolea, J. M., … Martínez-Arán, A. (2009). Group psychoeducation for stabilised bipolar disorders: 5-year outcome of a randomised clinical trial. *British Journal of Psychiatry, 194*(3), 260–265.

Coryell, W., Endicott, J., Maser, J. D., Keller, M. B., Leon, A. C., & Akiskal, H. S. (1995). Long-term stability of polarity distinctions in the affective disorders. *American Journal of Psychiatry, 152,* 385–390.

Coryell, W., Solomon, D., Turvey, C., Keller, M., Leon, A. C., Endicott, J., … Mueller, T. (2003). The long-term course of rapid-cycling bipolar disorder. *Archives of General Psychiatry, 60,* 914–920.

Cousins, D. A., Butts, K., & Young, A. H. (2009). The role of dopamine in bipolar disorder. *Bipolar Disorders, 11*(8), 787–806.

Craddock, N., & Sklar, P. (2013). Genetics of bipolar disorder. *Lancet, 381*(9878), 1654–1662.

Cross Disorder Group of the Psychiatric Genomics Consortium. (2013). Identification of risk loci with shared effects on five major psychiatric disorders: A genome-wide analysis. *Lancet, 381*(9875), 1371–1379.

Cuellar, A., Johnson, S. L., & Winters, R. (2005). Distinctions between bipolar and unipolar depression. *Clinical Psychology Review, 25,* 307–339.

Daruy-Filho, L., Brietzke, E., Lafer, B., & Grassi-Oliveira, R. (2011). Childhood maltreatment and clinical outcomes of bipolar disorder. *Acta Psychiatrica Scandinavica, 124*(6), 427–434. doi: 10.1111/j.1600-0447.2011.01756.x

Deckersbach, T., Peters, A., Sylvia, L., Urdahl, A., Magalhães, P.V.S., Otto, M. W., … Nierenberg, A. (2014). Do comorbid anxiety disorders moderate the effects of psychotherapy for bipolar disorder? Results from STEP-BD. *American Journal of Psychiatry, 171*(2), 178–186.

Delbello, M. P., Hanseman, D., Adler, C. M., Fleck, D. E., & Strakowski, S. M. (2007). Twelve-month outcome of adolescents with bipolar disorder following first-hospitalization for a manic or mixed episode. *American Journal of Psychiatry, 164*(4), 582–590.

Delbello, M. P., & Kowatch, R. (2006). Pharmacological interventions for bipolar youth: Developmental considerations. *Development and Psychopathology, 18*(4), 1231–1246.

Delbello, M. P., Kowatch, R. A., Adler, C. M., Stanford, K. E., Welge, J. A., Barzman, D. H., ... Strakowski, S. M. (2006). A double-blind randomized pilot study comparing quetiapine and divalproex for adolescent mania. *Journal of the American Academy of Child & Adolescent Psychiatry, 45*(3), 305–313.

Delbello, M. P., Schwiers, M. L., Rosenberg, H. L., & Strakowski, S. M. (2002). A double-blind, randomized, placebo-controlled study of quetiapine as adjunctive treatment for adolescent mania. *Journal of the American Academy of Child & Adolescent Psychiatry, 41*, 1216–1223.

Depue, R. A., Collins, P. F., & Luciana, M. (1996). A model of neurobiology–environment interaction in developmental psychopathology. In M. F. Lenzenweger & J. J. Haugaard (Eds.), *Frontiers of developmental psychopathology* (pp. 44–77). New York, NY: Oxford University Press.

Depue, R. A., Kleinman, R. M., Davis, P., Hutchinson, M., & Krauss, S. P. (1985). The behavioral high-risk paradigm and bipolar affective disorder: VII. Serum free cortisol in nonpatient cyclothymic subjects selected by the General Behavior Inventory. *American Journal of Psychiatry, 142*, 175–181.

Dienes, K. A., Hammen, C., Henry, R. M., Cohen, A. N., & Daley, S. E. (2006). The stress sensitization hypothesis: Understanding the course of bipolar disorder. *Journal of Affective Disorders, 95*(1–3), 43–49.

Ebert, D., Feistel, H., Barocks, A., Kaschka, W. P., & Pirner, A. (1994). SPECT assessment of cerebral dopamine D2 receptor blockade in depression before and after sleep deprivation. *Biological Psychiatry, 35*, 880–885.

Eckblad, M., & Chapman, L. J. (1986). Development and validation of a scale for hypomanic personality. *Journal of Abnormal Psychology, 95*, 214–222.

Ehlers, C. L., Frank, E., & Kupfer, D. J. (1988). Social *zeitgebers* and biological rhythms: A unified approach to understanding the etiology of depression. *Archives of General Psychiatry, 45*, 948–952.

Ehlers, C. L., Kupfer, D. J., Frank, E., & Monk, T. H. (1993). Biological rhythms and depression: The role of *zeitgebers* and *zeitstorers. Depression, 1*, 285–293.

Eich, E., Macaulay, D., & Lam, R. W. (1997). Mania, depression, and mood dependent memory. *Cognition and Emotion, 11*, 607–618.

Ellicott, A., Hammen, C., Gitlin, M., Brown, G., & Jamison, K. (1990). Life events and the course of bipolar disorder. *American Journal of Psychiatry, 147*, 1194–1198.

Fagiolini, A., Kupfer, D. J., Masalehdan, A., Scott, J. A., Houck, P. R., & Frank, E. (2005). Functional impairment in the remission phase of bipolar disorder. *Bipolar Disorders, 7*, 281–285.

Fawcett, J., Golden, B., & Rosenfeld, N. (2000). *New hope for people with bipolar disorder*. Roseville, CA: Prima Health.

Fears, S. C., Service, S. K., Kremeyer, B., Araya, C., Araya, X., Bejarano, J., ... Bearden, C. E. (2014). Multisystem component phenotypes of bipolar disorder for genetic investigations of extended pedigrees. *JAMA Psychiatry, 71*(4), 375–387.

First, M. B. (2010). DSM-5 proposals for mood disorders: A cost-benefit analysis. *Current Opinion in Psychiatry, 24*(1), 1–9.

First, M. B., Williams, J.B.W., Karg, R. S., &, Spitzer, R. L. (2016). *Structured Clinical Interview for DSM-5 Disorders–Clinician Version (SCID-5-CV)*. New York, NY: Biometrics Research Department, New York State Psychiatric Institute.

Frank, E. (2005). *Treating bipolar disorder: A clinician's guide to interpersonal and social rhythm therapy*. New York, NY: Guilford Press.

Frank, E., Kupfer, D. J., Thase, M. E., Mallinger, A. G., Swartz, H. A., Fagiolini, A. M., ... Monk, T. (2005). Two-year outcomes for interpersonal and social rhythm therapy in individuals with bipolar I disorder. *Archives of General Psychiatry, 62*(9), 996–1004.

Frazier, J. A., Biederman, J., Tohen, M., Feldman, P. D., Jacobs, T. G., Toma, V., ... Nowlin, Z. M. (2001). A prospective open-label treatment trial of olanzapine monotherapy in children and adolescents with bipolar disorder. *Journal of Child and Adolescent Psychopharmacology, 11*, 239–250.

Fristad, M. A., & MacPherson, H. A. (2014). Evidence-based psychosocial treatments for child and adolescent bipolar spectrum disorders. *Journal of Child and Adolescent Psychology, 43*(3), 339–355. doi: 10.1080/15374416.2013.822309

Fristad, M. A., Verducci, J. S., Walters, K., & Young, M. E. (2009). Impact of multifamily psychoeducational psychotherapy in treating children aged 8 to 12 years with mood disorders. *Archives of General Psychiatry, 66*(9), 1013–1021.

Fulford, D., Johnson, S. L., Llabre, M. M., & Carver, C. S. (2012). Pushing and coasting in dynamic goal pursuit: Coasting is attenuated in bipolar disorder. *Psychological Sciences*, *21*(7), 1021–1027.

Garrett, A. S., Miklowitz, D. J., Howe, M. E., Singh, M. K., Acquaye, T. K., Hawkey, C. G., … Chang, K. D. (2015). Changes in brain activation following psychotherapy for youth with mood dysregulation at familial risk for bipolar disorder. *Progress in Neuro-Psychopharmacology & Biological Psychiatry*, *56*, 215–220.

Geddes, J. R., Calabrese, J. R., & Goodwin, G. M. (2009). Lamotrigine for treatment of bipolar depression: Independent meta-analysis and meta-regression of individual patient data from five randomised trials. *British Journal of Psychiatry*, *194*(1), 4–9.

Geddes, J. R., & Miklowitz, D. J. (2013). Treatment of bipolar disorder. *Lancet*, *381*(9878), 1672–1682.

Geller, B., Zimerman, B., Williams, M., DelBello, M. P., Bolhofner, K., Craney, J. L., … Nickelsburg, M. J. (2002). DSM-IV mania symptoms in a prepubertal and early adolescent bipolar disorder phenotype compared to attention deficit hyperactive and normal controls. *Journal of Child and Adolescent Psychopharmacology*, *12*, 11–25.

Geoffroy, P. A., Scott, J., Boudebesse, C., Lajnef, M., Henry, C., Leboyer, M., … Etain, B. (2015). Sleep in patients with remitted bipolar disorders: A meta-analysis of actigraphy studies. *Acta Psychiatrica Scandinavica*, *131*(2), 89–99. doi: 10.1111/acps.12367

Gershon, A., Johnson, S. L., & Miller, I. (2013). Chronic stressors and trauma: Prospective influences on the course of bipolar disorder. *Psychological Medicine*, *43*(12), 2583–2592. doi: 10.1017/S0033291713000147

Gershon, A., Thompson, W. K., Eidelman, P., McGlinchey, E. L., Kaplan, K. A., & Harvey, A. G. (2012). Restless pillow, ruffled mind: Sleep and affect coupling in interepisode bipolar disorder. *Journal of Abnormal Psychology*, *121*(4), 863–873. doi: 10.1037/a0028233

Ghaemi, S. N., Lenox, M. S., & Baldessarini, R. J. (2001). Effectiveness and safety of long-term antidepressant treatment in bipolar disorder. *Journal of Clinical Psychiatry*, *62*, 565–569.

Gilman, S. E., Ni, M. Y., Dunn, E. C., Breslau, J., McLaughlin, K. A., Smoller, J. W., & Perlis, R. H. (2015). Contributions of the social environment to first-onset and recurrent mania. *Molecular Psychiatry*, *20*(3), 329–336.

Gitlin, M. J., Mintz, J., Sokolski, K., Hammen, C., & Altshuler, L. L. (2011). Subsyndromal depressive symptoms after symptomatic recovery from mania are associated with delayed functional recovery. *Journal of Clinical Psychiatry*, *72*(5), 692–697.

Goes, F. S., Hamshere, M. L., Seifuddin, F., Pirooznia, M., Belmonte-Mahon, P., Breuer, R., … Potash, J. B. (2012, October). Genome-wide association of mood-incongruent psychotic bipolar disorder. *Translational Psychiatry*, *2*.

Goldberg, J. F. (2004). The changing landscape of psychopharmacology. In S. L. Johnson & R. L. Leahy (Eds.), *Psychological treatment of bipolar disorder* (pp. 109–138). New York, NY: Guilford Press.

Goldstein, T. R., Fersch-Podrat, R. K., Rivera, M., Axelson, D. A., Merranko, J., Yu, H., … Birmaher, B. (2014). Dialectical behavior therapy (DBT) for adolescents with bipolar disorder: Results from a pilot randomized trial. *Journal of Child and Adolescent Psychopharmacology*. Advance online publication. doi: 10.1089/cap.2013.0145

Goldstein, T. R., Ha, W., Axelson, D. A., Goldstein, B. I., Liao, F., Gill, M. K., … Birmaher, B. (2012). Predictors of prospectively examined suicide attempts among youth with bipolar disorder. *Archives of General Psychiatry*, *69*(11), 1113–1122.

Gonzalez, R., Tamming, C. A., Tohen, M., & Suppes, T. (2014). The relationship between affective state and the rhythmicity of activity in bipolar disorder. *Journal of Clinical Psychiatry*, *75*(4), e317–322.

Gonzalez-Pinto, A., Tohen, M., Lalaguna, B., Pérez-Heredia, J. L., Fernandez-Corres, B., Gutierrez, M., … Micó, J. A. (2002). Treatment of bipolar I rapid cycling patients during dysphoric mania with olanzapine. *Journal of Clinical Psychopharmacology*, *22*, 450–454.

Goodwin, F. K., Fireman, B., Simon, G. E., Hunkeler, E. M., Lee, J., & Revicki, D. (2003). Suicide risk in bipolar disorder during treatment with lithium and divalproex. *JAMA*, *290*, 1467–1473.

Goodwin, G. M., Bowden, C. L., Calabrese, J. R., Grunze, H., Kasper, S., White, R., … Leadbetter, R. (2004). A pooled analysis of 2 placebo-controlled 18-month trials of lamotrigine and lithium maintenance in bipolar I disorder. *Journal of Clinical Psychiatry*, *65*, 432–441.

Goodwin, G. M., & Consensus Group of the British Association for Psychopharmacology. (2009). Evidence-based guidelines for treating bipolar disorder: Revised second edition—recommendations from the British Association for Psychopharmacology. *Journal of Psychopharmacology, 23*(4), 346–388.

Greenhouse, W. J., Meyer, B., & Johnson, S. L. (2000). Coping and medication adherence in bipolar disorder. *Journal of Affective Disorders, 59*(3), 237–241.

Grof, P., Duffy, A., Alda, M., & Hajek, T. (2009). Lithium response across generations. *Acta Psychiatrica Scandinavica, 120*(5), 378–385.

Gujar, N., McDonald, S. A., Nishida, M., & Walker, M. P. (2011). A role for REM sleep in recalibrating the sensitivity of the human brain to specific emotions. *Cerebral Cortex, 21*(1), 115–123.

Gujar, N., Yoo, S. S., Hu, P., & Walker, M. P. (2010). The unrested resting brain: Sleep deprivation alters activity within the default-mode network. *Journal of Cognitive Neuroscience, 22*(8), 1637–1648.

Hammen, C., & Gitlin, M. J. (1997). Stress reactivity in bipolar patients and its relation to prior history of the disorder. *American Journal of Psychiatry, 154*, 856–857.

Hammen, C., Gitlin, M., & Altshuler, L. (2000). Predictors of work adjustment in bipolar I patients: A naturalistic longitudinal follow-up. *Journal of Consulting and Clinical Psychology, 68*, 220–225.

Hanson, J. L., Adluru, N., Chung, M. K., Alexander, A. L., Davidson, R. J., & Pollak, S. D. (2013). Early neglect is associated with alterations in white matter integrity and cognitive functioning. *Child Development, 84*(5), 1566–1578.

Harris, E. C., & Barraclough, B. (1997). Suicide as an outcome for mental disorders: A meta-analysis. *British Journal of Psychiatry, 170*, 205–208.

Harvey, A. G., Schmidt, D. A., Scarna, A., Semler, C. N., & Goodwin, G. M. (2005). Sleep-related functioning in euthymic patients with bipolar disorder, patients with insomnia, and subjects without sleep problems. *American Journal of Psychiatry, 162*, 50–57.

Hashimoto, K., Sawa, A., & Iyo, M. (2007). Increased levels of glutamate in brains from patients with mood disorders. *Biological Psychiatry, 62*(11), 1310–1316.

Heerlein, A., Richter, P., Gonzalez, M., & Santander, J. (1998). Personality patterns and outcome in depressive and bipolar disorders. *Psychopathology, 31*, 15–22.

Hestenes, D. (1992). A neural network theory of manic-depressive illness. In D. S. Levine & S. J. Leven (Eds.), *Motivation, emotion, and goal direction in neural networks* (pp. 209–257). Hillsdale, NJ: Erlbaum.

Hillegers, M. H., Burger, H., Wals, M., Reichart, C. G., Verhulst, F. C., Nolen, W. A., & Ormel, J. (2004). Impact of stressful life events, familial loading and their interaction on the onset of mood disorders. *British Journal of Psychiatry, 185*, 97–101.

Hirschfeld, R. M., Williams, J. B., Spitzer, R. L., Calabrese, J. R., Flynn, L., Keck, P. E., Jr., & Zajecka, J. (2000). Development and validation of a screening instrument for bipolar spectrum disorder: The Mood Disorder Questionnaire. *American Journal of Psychiatry, 157*, 1873–1875.

Hlastala, S. A., Frank, E., Kowalski, J., Sherrill, J. T., Tu, X. M., Anderson, B., & Kupfer, D. J. (2000). Stressful life events, bipolar disorder, and the "kindling model." *Journal of Abnormal Psychology, 109*, 777–786.

Hosang, G. M., Uher, R., Maughan, B., McGuffin, P., & Farmer, A. E. (2012). The role of loss and danger events in symptom exacerbation in bipolar disorder. *Journal of Psychiatry Research, 46*(12), 1584–1589.

Inder, M. L., Crowe, M. T., Luty, S. E., Carter, J. D., Moor, S., Frampton, C. M., & Joyce, P. R. (2015). Randomized, controlled trial of Interpersonal and Social Rhythm Therapy for young people with bipolar disorder. *Bipolar Disorders, 17*(2), 128–138.

Jamison, K. R. (1993). *Touched with fire: Manic-depressive illness and the artistic temperament.* New York, NY: Maxwell Macmillan International.

Jamison, K. R. (1995). *An unquiet mind.* New York, NY: Knopf.

Jamison, K. R. (2000). Suicide and bipolar disorder. *Journal of Clinical Psychiatry, 61*(Suppl. 9), 47–56.

Jamison, K. R. (2005). *Exuberance: The passion for life.* New York, NY: Vintage.

Jamison, K. R., & Baldessarini, R. J. (1999). Effects of medical interventions on suicidal behavior. *Journal of Clinical Psychiatry, 60*(Suppl. 2), 4–6.

Jamison, K. R., Gerner, R. H., & Goodwin, F. K. (1979). Patient and physician attitudes toward lithium: Relationship to compliance. *Archives of General Psychiatry, 36*, 866–869.

Johnson, R. E., & McFarland, B. H. (1996). Lithium use and discontinuation in a health maintenance organization. *American Journal of Psychiatry, 153*, 993–1000.

Johnson, S. L. (2005a). Life events in bipolar disorder: Towards more specific models. *Clinical Psychology Review, 25*(8), 1008–1027.

Johnson, S. L. (2005b). Mania and dysregulation in goal pursuit. *Clinical Psychology Review, 25*, 241–262.

Johnson, S. L., Cuellar, A., Ruggero, C., Perlman, C., Goodnick, P., White, R., & Miller, I. (2008). Life events as predictors of mania and depression in bipolar I disorder. *Journal of Abnormal Psychology, 117,* 268–277.

Johnson, S. L., Edge, M. D., Holmes, M. K., & Carver, C. S. (2012). The behavioral activation system and mania. *Annual Review of Clinical Psychology, 8,* 143–167.

Johnson, S. L., Eisner, L., & Carver, C. S. (2009). Elevated expectancies among persons diagnosed with bipolar disorders. *British Journal of Clinical Psychology, 48,* 217–222.

Johnson, S. L., & Fingerhut, R. (2004). Negative cognitions predict the course of bipolar depression, not mania. *Journal of Cognitive Psychotherapy, 18,* 149–162.

Johnson, S. L., Fulford, D., & Carver, C. S. (2012). The double-edged sword of goal engagement: Consequences of goal pursuit in bipolar disorder. *Clinical Psychology and Psychotherapy, 19*(4), 352–362.

Johnson, S. L., Meyer, B., Winett, C., & Small, J. (2000). Social support and self-esteem predict changes in bipolar depression but not mania. *Journal of Affective Disorders, 58,* 79–86.

Johnson, S. L., Murray, G., Fredrickson, B., Youngstrom, E. A., Hinshaw, S., Bass, J. M., ... Salloum, I. (2012). Creativity and bipolar disorder: Touched by fire or burning with questions? *Clinical Psychology Review, 32*(1), 1–12.

Johnson, S. L., Murray, G., Hou, S., Staudenmaier, P. J., Freeman, M. A., Michalak, E. E., & CREST-BD. (2015). Creativity is linked to ambition across the bipolar spectrum. *Journal of Affective Disorders, 178,* 160–164. doi: 10.1016/j.jad.2015.02.021

Johnson, S. L., Sandrow, D., Meyer, B., Winters, R., Miller, I., Solomon, D., & Keitner, G. (2000). Increases in manic symptoms following life events involving goal attainment. *Journal of Abnormal Psychology, 109,* 721–727.

Johnson, S. L., Winett, C. A., Meyer, B., Greenhouse, W. J., & Miller, I. (1999). Social support and the course of bipolar disorder. *Journal of Abnormal Psychology, 108,* 558–566.

Jones, S. H., Hare, D. J., & Evershed, K. (2005). Actigraphic assessment of circadian activity and sleep patterns in bipolar disorder. *Bipolar Disorders, 7,* 176–186.

Jones, S. H., Tai, S., Evershed, K., Knowles, R., & Bentall, R. (2006). Early detection of bipolar disorder: A pilot familial high-risk study of parents with bipolar disorder and their adolescent children. *Bipolar Disorders, 8,* 362–372.

Judd, L. L., Akiskal, H. S., Schettler, P. J., Endicott, J., Maser, J., Solomon, D. A., ... Keller, M. B. (2002). The long-term natural history of the weekly symptomatic status of bipolar I disorder. *Archives of General Psychiatry, 59,* 530–537.

Karg, K., Burmeister, M., Shedden, K., & Sen, S. (2011). The serotonin transporter promoter variant (5-HTTLPR), stress, and depression meta-analysis revisited: Evidence of genetic moderation. *Archives of General Psychiatry, 5,* 444–454.

Kaufman, J., Birmaher, B., Brent, D., Rao, U., Flynn, C., Moreci, P., ... Ryan, N. (1997). Schedule for affective disorders and schizophrenia for school-age children-present and lifetime version (K-SADS-PL): Initial reliability and validity data. *Journal of the American Academy of Child & Adolescent Psychiatry, 36,* 980–988.

Keck, P. E., Jr., McElroy, S. L., Richtand, N., & Tohen, M. (2002). What makes a drug a primary mood stabilizer? *Molecular Psychiatry, 7*(Suppl. 1), S8–S14.

Keck, P. E., Jr., McElroy, S. L., Strakowski, S. M., Bourne, M. L., & West, S. A. (1997). Compliance with maintenance treatment in bipolar disorder. *Psychopharmacology Bulletin, 33,* 87–91.

Keener, M. T., & Phillips, M. L. (2007). Neuroimaging in bipolar disorder: A critical review of current findings. *Current Psychiatry Reports, 9*(6), 512–520.

Keller, M. B., Lavori, P. W., Friedman, B., Nielsen, E., Endicott, J., McDonald-Scott, P., & Andreasen, N. C. (1987). The Longitudinal Interval Follow-up Evaluation: A comprehensive method for assessing outcome in prospective longitudinal studies. *Archives of General Psychiatry, 44,* 540–548.

Keller, M. B., Lavori, P. W., McDonald-Scott, P., Scheftner, W. A., Andreasen, N. C., Shapiro, R. W., & Croughan, J. (1981). Reliability of lifetime diagnoses and symptoms in patients with current psychiatric disorder. *Journal of Psychiatry Research, 16,* 229–240.

Kendler, K. S., Kuhn, J. W., Vittum, J., Prescott, C. A., & Riley, B. (2005). The interaction of stressful life events and a serotonin transporter polymorphism in the prediction of episodes of major depression: A replication. *Archives of General Psychiatry, 62*(5), 529–535.

Kessing, L. V., Hansen, H. V., Christensen, E. M., Dam, H., Gluud, C., Wetterslev, J., & The Early Intervention Affective Disorders (EIA) Trial Group. (2014). Do young adults with bipolar disorder benefit from early intervention? *Journal of Affective Disorders*, *152–154*, 403–408. doi: 10.1016/j.jad.2013.10.001

Kessler, R. C., Akiskal, H. S., Angst, J., Guyer, M. H., Hirschfeld, R. M., Merikangas, K. R., & Stang, P. E. (2006). Validity of the assessment of bipolar spectrum disorders in the WHO CIDI 3.0. *Journal of Affective Disorders*, *96*(3), 259–269.

Kessler, R. C., Berglund, P., Demler, O., Jin, R., & Walters, E. E. (2005). Lifetime prevalence and age-of-onset distributions of DSM-IV disorders in the National Comorbidity Survey Replication. *Archives of General Psychiatry*, *62*, 593–602.

Kieseppa, T., Partonen, T., Haukka, J., Kaprio, J., & Lonnquist, J. (2004). High concordance of bipolar I disorder in a nationwide sample of twins. *American Journal of Psychiatry*, *161*, 1814–1821.

Kim, E. Y., & Miklowitz, D. J. (2002). Childhood mania, attention deficit hyperactivity disorder, and conduct disorder: A critical review of diagnostic dilemmas. *Bipolar Disorders*, *4*, 215–225.

Kim, E. Y., & Miklowitz, D. J. (2004). Expressed emotion as a predictor of outcome among bipolar patients undergoing family therapy. *Journal of Affective Disorders*, *82*, 343–352.

Kim, E. Y., Miklowitz, D. J., Biuckians, A., & Mullen, K. (2007). Life stress and the course of early-onset bipolar disorder. *Journal of Affective Disorders*, *99*(1), 37–44.

Kim, Y. K., Myint, A. M., Lee, B. H., Han, C. S., Lee, S. W., Leonard, B. E., & Steinbusch, H. W. (2004). T-helper types 1, 2, and 3 cytokine interactions in symptomatic manic patients. *Psychiatry Research*, *129*(3), 267–272.

Klein, D. N., & Depue, R. A. (1984). Continued impairment in persons at risk for bipolar disorder: Results of a 19-month follow-up. *Journal of Abnormal Psychology*, *93*, 345–347.

Knowles, R., Tai, S., Christensen, I., & Bentall, R. (2005). Coping with depression and vulnerability to mania: A factor analytic study of the Nolen-Hoeksema (1991) Response Styles Questionnaire. *British Journal of Clinical Psychology*, *44*, 99–112.

Kochman, F. J., Hantouche, E. G., Ferrari, P., Lancrenon, S., Bayart, D., & Akiskal, H. S. (2005). Cyclothymic temperament as a prospective predictor of bipolarity and suicidality in children and adolescents with major depressive disorder. *Journal of Affective Disorders*, *85*(1–2), 181–189.

Kowatch, R. A., Fristad, M., Birmaher, B., Wagner, K. D., Findling, R. L., Hellander, M., & Child Psychiatric Workgroup on Bipolar Disorder. (2005). Treatment guidelines for children and adolescents with bipolar disorder. *Journal of the American Academy of Child & Adolescent Psychiatry*, *44*(3), 213–235.

Kowatch, R. A., Suppes, T., Carmody, T. J., Bucci, J. P., Hume, J. H., Kromelis, M., ... Rush, A. J. (2000). Effect size of lithium, divalproex sodium, and carbamazepine in children and adolescents with bipolar disorder. *Journal of the American Academy of Child & Adolescent Psychiatry*, *39*, 713–720.

Kowatch, R. A., Youngstrom, E. A., Danielyan, A., & Findling, R. L. (2005). Review and meta-analysis of the phenomenology and clinical characteristics of mania in children and adolescents. *Bipolar Disorders*, *7*(6), 483–496.

Kruger, S., Seminowicz, S., Goldapple, K., Kennedy, S. H., & Mayberg, H. S. (2003). State and trait influences on mood regulation in bipolar disorder: Blood flow differences with an acute mood challenge. *Biological Psychiatry*, *54*, 1274–1283.

Kwapil, T. R., Miller, M. B., Zinser, M. C., Chapman, L. J., Chapman, J., & Eckblad, M. (2000). A longitudinal study of high scorers on the hypomanic personality scale. *Journal of Abnormal Psychology*, *109*, 222–226.

Lam, D. H., Burbeck, R., Wright, K., & Pilling, S. (2009). Psychological therapies in bipolar disorder: The effect of illness history on relapse prevention— a systematic review. *Bipolar Disorders*, *11*(5), 474–482.

Lam, D. H., Hayward, P., Watkins, E. R., Wright, K., & Sham, P. (2005). Relapse prevention in patients with bipolar disorder: Cognitive therapy outcome after 2 years. *American Journal of Psychiatry*, *162*, 324–329.

Lam, D. H., Watkins, E. R., Hayward, P., Bright, J., Wright, K., Kerr, N., ... Sham, P. (2003). A randomized controlled study of cognitive therapy of relapse prevention for bipolar affective disorder: Outcome of the first year. *Archives of General Psychiatry*, *60*, 145–152.

Lan, W. H., Bai, Y. M., Hsu, J. W., Huang, K. L., Su, T. P., Li, C. T., ... Chen, M. H. (2015). Comorbidity of ADHD and suicide attempts among adolescents and young adults with bipolar disorder: A nationwide longitudinal study. *Journal of Affective Disorders, 176,* 171–175.

Lapalme, M., Hodgins, S., & LaRoche, C. (1997). Children of parents with bipolar disorder: A meta-analysis of risk for mental disorders. *Canadian Journal of Psychiatry, 42,* 623–631.

Leibenluft, E., Albert, P. S., Rosenthal, N. E., & Wehr, T. A. (1996). Relationship between sleep and mood in patients with rapid-cycling bipolar disorder. *Psychiatry Research, 63,* 161–168.

Lembke, A., & Ketter, T. (2002). Impaired recognition of facial emotion in mania. *American Journal of Psychiatry, 159,* 302–304.

Leverich, G. S., & Post, R. M. (1998). Life charting of affective disorders. *CNS Spectrums, 3,* 21–37.

Levinson, D. F. (2006). The genetics of depression: A review. *Biological Psychiatry, 60,* 84–92.

Loebel, A., Cucchiaro, J., Silva, R., Kroger, H., Hsu, J., Sarma, K., & Sachs, G. (2014). Lurasidone monotherapy in the treatment of bipolar I depression: A randomized, double-blind, placebo-controlled study. *American Journal of Psychiatry, 171*(2), 160–168.

Lozano, B. L., & Johnson, S. L. (2001). Can personality traits predict increases in manic and depressive symptoms? *Journal of Affective Disorders, 63,* 103–111.

Malhi, G. S., Adams, D., & Berk, M. (2009). Medicating mood with maintenance in mind: Bipolar depression pharmacotherapy. *Bipolar Disorders, 11*(Suppl. 2), 55–76.

Malkoff-Schwartz, S., Frank, E., Anderson, B. P., Hlastala, S. A., Luther, J. F., Sherrill, J. T., … Kupfer, D. J. (2000). Social rhythm disruption and stressful life events in the onset of bipolar and unipolar episodes. *Psychological Medicine, 30,* 1005–1016.

Malkoff-Schwartz, S., Frank, E., Anderson, B., Sherrill, J. T., Siegel, L., Patterson, D., … Kupfer, D. J. (1998). Stressful life events and social rhythm disruption in the onset of manic and depressive bipolar episodes: A preliminary investigation. *Archives of General Psychiatry, 55,* 702–707.

Manji, H. (2009). The role of synaptic and cellular plasticity cascades in the pathophysiology and treatment of mood and psychotic disorders. *Bipolar Disorders, 11*(Suppl. 1), 2–3.

Marangell, L. B., Bauer, M., Dennehy, E. B., Wisniewski, S. R., Allen, M., Miklowitz, D. J., … Thase, M. E. (2006). Prospective predictors of suicide and suicide attempts in 2000 patients with bipolar disorders followed for 2 years. *Bipolar Disorders, 8*(5, Pt. 2), 566–575.

Marlatt, G. A. (1985). *Relapse prevention.* New York, NY: Guilford Press.

Masi, G., Perugi, G., Toni, C., Millepiedi, S., Mucci, M., Bertini, N., & Akiskal, H. S. (2004). Obsessive-compulsive bipolar comorbidity: Focus on children and adolescents. *Journal of Affective Disorders, 78,* 175–183.

McGuffin, P., Rijsdijk, F., Andrew, M., Sham, P., Katz, R., & Cardno, A. (2003). The heritability of bipolar affective disorder and the genetic relationship to unipolar depression. *Archives of General Psychiatry, 60,* 497–502.

McKenna, B. S., Drummond, S. P., & Eyler, L. T. (2014). Associations between circadian activity rhythms and functional brain abnormalities among euthymic bipolar patients: A preliminary study. *Journal of Affective Disorders, 164,* 101–106.

Merikangas, K. R., Akiskal, H. S., Angst, J., Greenberg, P. E., Hirschfeld, R.M.A., Petukhova, M., & Kessler, R. C. (2007). Lifetime and 12-month prevalence of bipolar spectrum disorder in the National Comorbidity Survey Replication. *Archives of General Psychiatry, 64*(5), 543–552.

Merikangas, K. R., Cui, L., Kattan, G., Carlson, G. A., Youngstrom, E. A., & Angst, J. (2012). Mania with and without depression in a community sample of US adolescents. *Archives of General Psychiatry, 69*(9), 943–951.

Merikangas, K. R., Jin, R., He, J. P., Kessler, R. C., Lee, S., Sampson, N. A., … Zarkov, Z. (2011). Prevalence and correlates of bipolar spectrum disorder in the World Mental Health Survey Initiative. *Archives of General Psychiatry, 68*(3), 241–251.

Meyer, B., Johnson, S. L., & Carver, C. S. (1999). Exploring behavioral activation and inhibition sensitivities among college students at-risk for bipolar-spectrum symptomatology. *Journal of Psychopathology and Behavioral Assessment, 21,* 275–292.

Meyer, B., Johnson, S. L., & Winters, R. (2001). Responsiveness to threat and incentive in bipolar disorder: Relations of the BIS/BAS scales with symptoms. *Journal of Psychopathology and Behavioral Assessment, 23,* 133–143.

Meyer, T. D., & Hautzinger, M. (2012). Cognitive behaviour therapy and supportive therapy for bipolar disorders: Relapse rates for treatment period and 2-year follow-up. *Psychological Medicine, 42*(7), 1429–1439.

Michalak, E. E., Jones, S., Lobban, F., Algorta, G. P., Barnes, S. J., Berk, L., ... CREST-BD. (2016). Harnessing the potential of community-based participatory research approaches in bipolar disorder. *International Journal of Bipolar Disorders, 4*(1), 4.

Miklowitz, D. J. (2008). *Bipolar disorder: A family-focused treatment approach* (2nd ed.). New York, NY: Guilford Press.

Miklowitz, D. J., Axelson, D. A., Birmaher, B., George, E. L., Taylor, D. O., Schneck, C. D., ... Brent, D. A. (2008). Family-focused treatment for adolescents with bipolar disorder: Results of a 2-year randomized trial. *Archives of General Psychiatry, 65*(9), 1053–1061.

Miklowitz, D. J., Axelson, D. A., George, E. L., Taylor, D. O., Schneck, C. D., Sullivan, A. E., ... Birmaher, B. (2009). Expressed emotion moderates the effects of family-focused treatment for bipolar adolescents. *Journal of the American Academy of Child & Adolescent Psychiatry, 48*, 643–651.

Miklowitz, D. J., Biuckians, A., & Richards, J. A. (2006). Early-onset bipolar disorder: A family treatment perspective. *Development and Psychopathology, 18*(4), 1247–1265.

Miklowitz, D. J., & Cicchetti, D. (2006). Toward a lifespan developmental psychopathology perspective on bipolar disorder. *Development and Psychopathology, 18*(4), 935–938.

Miklowitz, D. J., George, E. L., Richards, J. A., Simoneau, T. L., & Suddath, R. L. (2003). A randomized study of family-focused psychoeducation and pharmacotherapy in the outpatient management of bipolar disorder. *Archives of General Psychiatry, 60*, 904–912.

Miklowitz, D. J. & Gitlin, M. J. (2015). *Clinician's guide to bipolar disorder: Integrating psychopharmacology with psychotherapy.* New York, NY: Guilford Press.

Miklowitz, D. J., & Goldstein, M. J. (1990). Behavioral family treatment for patients with bipolar affective disorder. *Behavior Modification, 14*, 457–489.

Miklowitz, D. J., & Goldstein, M. J. (1997). *Bipolar disorder: A family-focused treatment approach.* New York, NY: Guilford Press.

Miklowitz, D. J., Goldstein, M. J., Nuechterlein, K. H., Snyder, K. S., & Mintz, J. (1988). Family factors and the course of bipolar affective disorder. *Archives of General Psychiatry, 45*, 225–231.

Miklowitz, D. J., & Johnson, S. L. (2006). The psychopathology and treatment of bipolar disorder. *Annual Review of Clinical Psychology, 2*, 199–235.

Miklowitz, D. J., Otto, M. W., Frank, E., Reilly-Harrington, N. A., Kogan, J. N., Sachs, G. S., ... Wisniewski, S. R. (2007). Intensive psychosocial intervention enhances functioning in patients with bipolar depression: Results from a 9-month randomized controlled trial. *American Journal of Psychiatry, 164*(9), 1–8.

Miklowitz, D. J., Otto, M. W., Frank, E., Reilly-Harrington, N. A., Wisniewski, S. R., Kogan, J. N., ... Sachs, G. S. (2007). Psychosocial treatments for bipolar depression: A 1-year randomized trial from the Systematic Treatment Enhancement Program. *Archives of General Psychiatry, 64*, 419–427.

Miklowitz, D. J., Schneck, C. D., George, E. L., Taylor, D. O., Sugar, C. A., Birmaher, B., ... Axelson, D. A. (2014). Pharmacotherapy and family-focused treatment for adolescents with bipolar I and II disorders: A 2-year randomized trial. *American Journal of Psychiatry, 171*(6), 658–667.

Miklowitz, D. J., Schneck, C. D., Singh, M. K., Taylor, D. O., George, E. L., Cosgrove, V. E., ... Chang, K. D. (2013). Early intervention for symptomatic youth at risk for bipolar disorder: A randomized trial of family-focused therapy. *Journal of the American Academy of Child & Adolescent Psychiatry, 52*(2), 121–131.

Miller, A. H., Maletic, V., & Raison, C. L. (2009). Inflammation and its discontents: The role of cytokines in the pathophysiology of major depression. *Biological Psychiatry, 65*, 732–741.

Mitchell, P. B., Slade, T., & Andrews, G. (2004). Twelve-month prevalence and disability of DSM-IV bipolar disorder in an Australian general population survey. *Psychological Medicine, 34*(5), 777–785.

Modabbernia, A., Taslimi, S., Brietzke, E., & Ashrafi, M. (2013). Cytokine alterations in bipolar disorder: A meta-analysis of 30 studies. *Biological Psychiatry, 74*(1), 15–25. doi: 10.1016/j.biopsych.2013.01.007

Murphy, F. C., Sahakian, B. J., Rubinsztein, J. S., Michael, A., Rogers, R. D., Robbins, T. W., & Paykel, E. S. (1999). Emotional bias and inhibitory control processes in mania and depression. *Psychological Medicine, 29*, 1307–1321.

Murray, G., & Harvey, A. (2010). Circadian rhythms and sleep in bipolar disorder. *Bipolar Disorders, 12*, 459–472.

Naranjo, C. A., Tremblay, L. K., & Busto, U. E. (2001). The role of the brain reward system in depression. *Progress in Neuro-Psychopharmacology & Biological Psychiatry, 25*, 781–823.

Newcomer, J. W. (2007). Metabolic considerations in the use of antipsychotic medications: A review of recent evidence. *Journal of Clinical Psychiatry, 68*(Suppl. 1), 20–27.

Nierenberg, A. A., Ostacher, M. J., Calabrese, J. R., Ketter, T. A., Marangell, L. B., Miklowitz, D. J., … Sachs, G. S. (2006). Treatment-resistant bipolar depression: A STEP-BD equipoise randomized effectiveness trial of antidepressant augmentation with lamotrigine, inositol, or risperidone. *American Journal of Psychiatry, 163*(2), 210–216.

Nusslock, R., Abramson, L. Y., Harmon-Jones, E., Alloy, L. B., & Hogan, M. E. (2007). A goal-striving life event and the onset of hypomanic and depressive episodes and symptoms: Perspective from the behavioral approach system (BAS) dysregulation theory. *Journal of Abnormal Psychology, 116*(1), 105–115.

Nusslock, R., Harmon-Jones, E., Alloy, L. B., Urosevic, S., Goldstein, K. E., & Abramson, L. Y. (2012). Elevated left-frontal cortical prospectively predicts conversion to bipolar I disorder. *Journal of Abnormal Psychology, 121*(3), 592–601.

Ochsner, K. N., & Gross, J. J. (2005). The cognitive control of emotion. *Trends in Cognitive Sciences, 9*, 242–249.

Olsavsky, A. K., Brotman, M. A., Rutenberg, J. G., Muhrer, E. J., Deveney, C. M., Fromm, S. J., … Leibenluft, E. (2012). Amygdala hyperactivation during face emotion processing in unaffected youth at risk for bipolar disorder. *Journal of the American Academy of Child & Adolescent Psychiatry, 51*(3), 294–303.

Otto, M. W., Simon, N. M., Wisniewski, S. R., Miklowitz, D. J., Kogan, J., Reilly-Harrington, N. A., … Pollack, M. H. (2006). Prospective 12-month course of bipolar disorder in outpatients with and without comorbid anxiety disorders. *British Journal of Psychiatry, 189*, 20–25.

Pardoen, D., Bauewens, F., Dramaix, M., Tracy, A., Genevrois, C., Staner, L., & Mendlewicz, J. (1996). Life events and primary affective disorders: A one-year prospective study. *British Journal of Psychiatry, 169*, 160–166.

Parikh, S. V., Zaretsky, A., Beaulieu, S., Yatham, L. N., Young, L. T., Patelis-Siotis, I., … Streiner, D. L. (2012). A randomized controlled trial of psychoeducation or cognitive-behavioral therapy in bipolar disorder: A Canadian Network for Mood and Anxiety Treatments (CANMAT) study. *Journal of Clinical Psychiatry, 73*(6), 803–810.

Perlis, R. H., Miyahara, S., Marangell, L. B., Wisniewski, S. R., Ostacher, M., Delbello, M. P., … STEP-BD Investigators. (2004). Long-term implications of early onset in bipolar disorder: Data from the first 1000 participants in the Systematic Treatment Enhancement Program for Bipolar Disorder (STEP-BD). *Biological Psychiatry, 55*, 875–881.

Perris, H. (1984). Life events and depression: Part 2. Results in diagnostic subgroups and in relation to the recurrence of depression. *Journal of Affective Disorders, 7*, 25–36.

Perry, A., Tarrier, N., Morriss, R., McCarthy, E., & Limb, K. (1999). Randomised controlled trial of efficacy of teaching patients with bipolar disorder to identify early symptoms of relapse and obtain treatment. *British Medical Journal, 16*, 149–153.

Phillips, M. L., Drevets, W. C., Rauch, S. L., & Lane, R. (2003). Neurobiology of emotion perception II: Implications for major psychiatric disorders. *Biological Psychiatry, 54*, 515–528.

Phillips, M. L., & Swartz, H. A. (2014). A critical appraisal of neuroimaging studies of bipolar disorder: Toward a new conceptualization of underlying neural circuitry and a road map for future research. *American Journal of Psychiatry, 171*(8), 829–843.

Post, R. M., & Weiss, S.R.B. (1998). Sensitization and kindling phenomena in mood, anxiety, and obsessive-compulsive disorders: The role of serotonergic mechanisms in illness progression. *Biological Psychiatry, 44*, 193–206.

Prien, R. F., & Potter, W. Z. (1990). NIMH Workshop report on treatment of bipolar disorder. *Psychopharmacology Bulletin, 26*, 409–427.

Rea, M. M., Tompson, M., Miklowitz, D. J., Goldstein, M. J., Hwang, S., & Mintz, J. (2003). Family focused treatment vs. individual treatment for bipolar disorder: Results of a randomized clinical trial. *Journal of Consulting and Clinical Psychology, 71*, 482–492.

Regeer, E. J., ten Have, M., Rosso, M. L., Hakkaart-van Roijen, L., Vollebergh, W., & Nolen, W. A. (2004). Prevalence of bipolar disorder in the general population: A reappraisal study of the Netherlands Mental Health Survey and Incidence Study. *Acta Psychiatrica Scandinavica, 110*, 374–382.

Regier, D. A., Narrow, W. E., Clarke, D. E., Kraemer, H. C., Kuramoto, J., Kuhl, E. A., & Kupfer, D. J. (2013). DSM-5 field trials in the United States and Canada: Part II. Test-retest reliability of selected categorical diagnoses. *American Journal of Psychiatry, 170*(1), 59–70.

Reichart, C. G., van der Ende, J., Wals, M., Hillegers, M. H., Nolen, W. A., Ormel, J., & Verhulst, F. C. (2005). The use of the GBI as predictor of bipolar disorder in a population of adolescent offspring of parents with a bipolar disorder. *Journal of Affective Disorders, 89*(1–3), 147–155.

Richards, R., Kinney, D. K., Lunde, I., Benet, M., & Merzel, A. P. (1988). Creativity in manic-depressives, cyclothymes, their normal relatives, and control subjects. *Journal of Abnormal Psychology, 97*, 281–288.

Rogers, R., Jackson, R. L., & Cashel, M. (2001). The Schedule for Affective Disorders and Schizophrenia (SADS). In R. Rogers (Ed.), *Handbook of diagnostic and structural interviewing* (pp. 84–102). New York, NY: Guilford Press.

Ruiter, M., & Johnson, S. L. (2015). Mania risk and creativity: A multi-method study of the role of motivation. *Journal of Affective Disorders, 170*, 52–58. doi: 10.1016/j.jad.2014.08.049

Rush, A. J. (2007). STAR*D: What have we learned? *American Journal of Psychiatry, 164*(2), 201–204.

Sachs, G. S., Nierenberg, A. A., Calabrese, J. R., Marangell, L. B., Wisniewski, S. R., Gyulai, L., ... Thase, M. E. (2007). Effectiveness of adjunctive antidepressant treatment for bipolar depression. *New England Journal of Medicine, 356*(17), 1711–1722.

Sala, R., Axelson, D. A., Castro-Fornieles, J., Goldstein, T. R., Ha, W., Liao, F., ... Birmaher, B. (2010). Comorbid anxiety in children and adolescents with bipolar spectrum disorders: Prevalence and clinical correlates. *Journal of Clinical Psychiatry, 71*(10), 1344–1350.

Salavert, J., Caseras, X., Torrubia, R., Furest, S., Arranz, B., Duenas, R., & San, L. (2007). The functioning of the behavioral activation and inhibition systems in bipolar I euthymic patients and its influence in subsequent episodes over an eighteen-month period. *Personality and Individual Differences, 42*(7), 1323–1331.

Salvatore, P., Ghidini, S., Zita, G., De Panfilis, C., Lambertino, S., Maggini, C., & Baldessarini, R. J. (2008). Circadian activity rhythm abnormalities in ill and recovered bipolar I disorder patients. *Bipolar Disorders, 10*(2), 256–265.

Sanacora, G., Zarate, C. A., Krystal, J., & Manji, H. K. (2008). Targeting the glutamatergic system to develop novel improved therapeutics for mood disorders. *Nature Reviews and Drug Discovery, 7*(5), 426–437.

Sax, K. W., & Strakowski, S. M. (2001). Behavioral sensitization in humans. *Journal of Addictive Diseases, 20*, 55–65.

Schneck, C. D., Miklowitz, D. J., Calabrese, J. R., Allen, M. H., Thomas, M. R., Wisniewski, S. R., ... Sachs, G. S. (2004). Phenomenology of rapid cycling bipolar disorder: Data from the first 500 participants in the Systematic Treatment Enhancement Program for Bipolar Disorder. *American Journal of Psychiatry, 161*, 1902–1908.

Scott, J., Paykel, E., Morriss, R., Bentall, R., Kinderman, P., Johnson, T., ... Hayhurst, H. (2006). Cognitive behaviour therapy for severe and recurrent bipolar disorders: A randomised controlled trial. *British Journal of Psychiatry, 188*, 313–320.

Sheehan, D. V., Lecrubier, Y., Sheehan, K. H., Amorim, P., Janavs, J., Weiller, E., ... Dunbar, G. C. (1998). The Mini-International Neuropsychiatric Interview (M.I.N.I.): The development and validation of a structured diagnostic psychiatric interview for DSM-IV and ICD-10. *Journal of Clinical Psychiatry, 59*(Suppl. 20), 22–33.

Shen, G. H., Alloy, L. B., Abramson, L. Y., & Sylvia, L. G. (2008). Social rhythm regularity and the onset of affective episodes in bipolar spectrum individuals. *Bipolar Disorders, 10*(4), 520–529.

Simeonova, D. I., Chang, K. D., Strong, C., & Ketter, T. A. (2005). Creativity in familial bipolar disorder. *Journal of Psychiatric Research, 39*(6), 623–631.

Simon, G. E., Ludman, E. J., Bauer, M. S., Unutzer, J., & Operskalski, B. (2006). Long-term effectiveness and cost of a systematic care program for bipolar disorder. *Archives of General Psychiatry, 63*(5), 500–508.

Simoneau, T. L., Miklowitz, D. J., Richards, J. A., Saleem, R., & George, E. L. (1999). Bipolar disorder and family communication: Effects of a psychoeducational treatment program. *Journal of Abnormal Psychology, 108*, 588–597.

Simpson, S. G., McMahon, F. J., McInnis, M. G., MacKinnon, D. F., Edwin, D., Folstein, S. E., & DePaulo, J. R. (2002). Diagnostic reliability of bipolar II disorder. *Archives of General Psychiatry, 59*, 746–750.

Smoller, J. W., & Finn, C. T. (2003). Family, twin, and adoption studies of bipolar disorder. *American Journal of Medical Genetics: Part C. Seminars in Medical Genetics, 123*(1), 48–58.

Sobcazk, S., Honig, A., Schmitt, J.A.J., & Riedel, W. J. (2003). Pronounced cognitive deficits following an intravenous L-tryptophan challenge in first-degree relatives of bipolar patients compared to healthy controls. *Neuropsychopharmacology, 28*, 711–719.

Sobczak, S., Riedel, W. J., Booij, L., aan het Rot, M., Deutz, N.E.P., & Honig, A. (2002). Cognition following acute tryptophan depletion: Difference between first-degree relatives of bipolar disorder patients and matched healthy control volunteers. *Psychological Medicine, 32*, 503–515.

Solomon, D. A., Leon, A. C., Endicott, J., Coryell, W. H., Mueller, T. I., Posternak, M. A., & Keller, M. B. (2003). Unipolar mania over the course of a 20-year follow-up study. *American Journal of Psychiatry, 160*, 2049–2051.

Stockmeier, C. A. (2003). Involvement of serotonin in depression: Evidence from postmortem and imaging studies of serotonin receptors and the serotonin transporter. *Journal of Psychiatric Research, 37*, 357–373.

Strakowski, S. M., Adler, C. M., Almeida, J., Altshuler, L. L., Blumberg, H. P., Chang, K. D., ... Townsend, J. D. (2012). The functional neuroanatomy of bipolar disorder: A consensus model. *Bipolar Disorders, 14*(4), 313–325.

Strakowski, S. M., Keck, P. E., Jr., McElroy, S. L., West, S. A., Sax, K. W., Hawkins, J. M., ... Bourne, M. L. (1998). Twelve-month outcome after a first hospitalization for affective psychosis. *Archives of General Psychiatry, 55*, 49–55.

Strakowski, S. M., Sax, K. W., Setters, M. J., & Keck, P. E., Jr. (1996). Enhanced response to repeated d-amphetamine challenge: Evidence for behavioral sensitization in humans. *Biological Psychiatry, 40*, 827–880.

Strakowski, S. M., Sax, K. W., Setters, M. J., Stanton, S. P., & Keck, P. E., Jr. (1997). Lack of enhanced behavioral response to repeated d-amphetamine challenge in first-episode psychosis: Implications for a sensitization model of psychosis in humans. *Biological Psychiatry, 42*, 749–755.

Sullivan, P. F., Daly, M. J., & O'Donovan, M. (2012). Genetic architectures of psychiatric disorders: The emerging picture and its implications. *Nature Reviews Genetics, 13*, 537–551. doi: 10.1038/nrg3240

Suppes, T., Baldessarini, R. J., Faedda, G. L., Tondo, L., & Tohen, M. (1993, September–October). Discontinuation of maintenance treatment in bipolar disorder: Risks and implications. *Harvard Review of Psychiatry, 1*, 131–144.

Suppes, T., Leverich, G. S., Keck, P. E., Nolen, W. A., Denicoff, K. D., Altshuler, L. L., ... Post, R. M. (2001). The Stanley Foundation Bipolar Treatment Outcome Network: II. Demographics and illness characteristics of the first 261 patients. *Journal of Affective Disorders, 67*, 45–59.

Swann, A. C., Lafer, B., Perugi, G., Frye, M. A., Bauer, M., Bahk, W. M., ... Suppes, T. (2012). Bipolar mixed states: An International Society for Bipolar Disorders task force report of symptom structure, course of illness, and diagnosis. *American Journal of Psychiatry, 170*(1), 31–42.

Swartz, H. A., Frank, E., & Cheng, Y. (2012). A randomized pilot study of psychotherapy and quetiapine for the acute treatment of bipolar II depression. *Bipolar Disorders, 14*(2), 211–216.

Taylor, W. D., Steffens, D. C., Payne, M. E., MacFall, J. R., Marchuk, D. A., Svenson, I. K., & Krishnan, K. R. (2005). Influence of serotonin transporter promoter region polymorphisms on hippocampal volumes in late-life depression. *Archives of General Psychiatry, 62*(5), 537–544.

Thase, M. E., Jindal, R., & Howland, R. H. (2002). Biological aspects of depression. In C. L. Hammen & I. H. Gotlib (Eds.), *Handbook of depression* (pp. 192–218). New York, NY: Guilford Press.

Thomas, J., & Bentall, R. (2002). Hypomanic traits and response styles to depression. *British Journal of Clinical Psychology, 41*, 309–314.

Tohen, M., Greil, W., Calabrese, J. R., Sachs, G. S., Yatham, L. N., Oerlinghausen, B. M., ... Bowden, C. L. (2005). Olanzapine versus lithium in the maintenance treatment of bipolar disorder: A 12-month, randomized, double-blind, controlled clinical trial. *American Journal of Psychiatry, 162*, 1281–1290.

Tohen, M., Jacobs, T. G., Grundy, S. L., McElroy, S. L., Banov, M. C., Janicak, P. G., ... Breier, A. (2000). Efficacy of olanzapine in acute bipolar mania: A double-blind, placebo-controlled study. The Olanzapine HGGW Study Group. *Archives of General Psychiatry, 57*, 841–849.

Tohen, M., Kryzhanovskaya, L., Carlson, G., Delbello, M. P., Wozniak, J., Kowatch, R., ... Biederman, J. (2005). Olanzapine in the treatment of acute mania in adolescents with bipolar I disorder: A 3-week randomized double-blind placebo-controlled study. *Neuropsychopharmacology, 30*(Suppl. 1), 176.

Tohen, M., Vieta, E., Calabrese, J., Ketter, T. A., Sachs, G., Bowden, C., ... Breier, A. (2003). Efficacy of olanzapine and olanzapine-fluoxetine combination in the treatment of bipolar I depression. *Archives of General Psychiatry, 60,* 1079–1088.

Tondo, L., & Baldessarini, R. J. (2000). Reduced suicide risk during lithium maintenance treatment. *Journal of Clinical Psychiatry, 61*(Suppl. 9), 97–104.

Townsend, J., & Altshuler, L. L. (2012). Emotion processing and regulation in bipolar disorder: A review. *Bipolar Disorders, 14*(4), 326–339.

Van Meter, A. R., Moreira, A. L., & Youngstrom, E. A. (2011, May 31). Meta-analysis of epidemiologic studies of pediatric bipolar disorder. *Journal of Clinical Psychiatry.* Advance online publication. doi: 10.4088/JCP.10m06290

Van Meter, A., Youngstrom, E. A., Demeter, C., & Findling, R. L. (2013). Examining the validity of cyclothymic disorder in a youth sample: Replication and extension. *Journal of Abnormal Child Psychology, 41*(3), 367–378.

Walker, M. P. (2011). The role of sleep in cognition and emotion. *Annals of the New York Academy of Sciences, 1156,* 168–197.

Wals, M., Hillegers, M.H.J., Reichart, C. G., Verhulst, F. C., Nolen, W. A., & Ormel, J. (2005). Stressful life events and onset of mood disorders in children of bipolar parents during 14-month follow-up. *Journal of Affective Disorders, 87,* 253–263.

Walsh, M. A., DeGeorge, D. P., Barrantes-Vidal, N., & Kwapil, T. R. (2015). A 3-year longitudinal study of risk for bipolar spectrum psychopathology. *Journal of Abnormal Psychology, 124*(3), 486–497.

Wang, F., Kalmar, J. H., He, Y., Jackowski, M., Chepenik, L. G., Edmiston, E. E., … Blumberg, H. P. (2009). Functional and structural connectivity between the perigenual anterior cingulate and amygdala in bipolar disorder. *Biological Psychiatry, 66*(5), 516–521.

Wehr, T. A., Sack, D. A., & Rosenthal, N. E. (1987). Sleep reduction as a final common pathway in the genesis of mania. *American Journal of Psychiatry, 144,* 210–214.

Weinstock, L. M., & Miller, I. W. (2010). Psychosocial predictors of mood symptoms 1 year after acute phase treatment of bipolar I disorder. *Comprehensive Psychiatry, 51*(5), 497–503.

West, A. E., Weinstein, S. M., Peters, A. T., Katz, A. C., Henry, D. B., Cruz, R. A., & Pavuluri, M. N. (2014). Child- and family-focused cognitive-behavioral therapy for pediatric bipolar disorder: A randomized clinical trial. *Journal of the American Academy of Child & Adolescent Psychiatry, 53*(11), 1168–1178.

Willner, P. (1995). Sensitization of dopamine D-sub-2- or D-sub-3-type receptors as a final common pathway in antidepressant drug action. *Clinical Neuropharmacology, 18* (Suppl. 1), S49–S56.

Wilens, T. E., Biederman, J., Kwon, A., Ditterline, J., Forkner, P., Moore, H., … Faraone, S. V. (2004). Risk of substance use disorders in adolescents with bipolar disorder. *Journal of the American Academy of Child & Adolescent Psychiatry, 43*(11), 1380–1386.

Williams, J.B.W., Gibbon, M., First, M. B., Spitzer, R. L., Davies, M., Borus, J., … Wittchen, H.-U. (1992). The Structured Clinical Interview for the DSM-III-R (SCID): II. Multisite test-retest reliability. *Archives of General Psychiatry, 49,* 630–636.

Willner, P. (1995). Sensitization of dopamine D-sub-2- or D-sub-3-type receptors as a final common pathway in antidepressant drug action. *Clinical Neuropharmacology, 18*(Suppl. 1), S49–S56.

Yan, L. J., Hammen, C., Cohen, A. N., Daley, S. E., & Henry, R. M. (2004). Expressed emotion versus relationship quality variables in the prediction of recurrence in bipolar patients. *Journal of Affective Disorders, 83,* 199–206.

Yatham, L. N., Kennedy, S. H., O'Donovan, C., Parikh, S., MacQueen, G., McIntyre, R., … Canadian Network for Mood and Anxiety Treatments. (2005). Canadian Network for Mood and Anxiety Treatments (CANMAT) guidelines for the management of patients with bipolar disorder: Consensus and controversies. *Bipolar Disorders, 7*(Suppl. 3), 5–69.

Young, L. T., Joffe, R. T., Robb, J. C., MacQueen, G. M., Marriott, M., & Patelis-Siotis, I. (2000). Double-blind comparison of addition of a second mood stabilizer versus an antidepressant to an initial mood stabilizer for treatment of patients with bipolar depression. *American Journal of Psychiatry, 157,* 124–126.

Youngstrom, E. A., Findling, R. L., & Calabrese, J. R. (2004). Effects of adolescent manic symptoms on agreement between youth, parent, and teacher ratings of behavior problems. *Journal of Affective Disorders, 82*(Suppl. 1), S5–S16.

Youngstrom, E. A., Findling, R. L., Calabrese, J. R., Gracious, B. L., Demeter, C., DelPorto-Bedoya, D., & Price, M. (2004). Comparing the diagnostic accuracy of six potential screening instruments for bipolar disorder in youths age 5 to 17 years. *Journal of the American Academy of Child & Adolescent Psychiatry, 43*, 847–858.

Youngstrom, E. A., Findling, R. L., Youngstrom, J. K., & Calabrese, J. R. (2005). Towards an evidence-based assessment of pediatric bipolar disorder. *Journal of Clinical Child & Adolescent Psychology, 34*(3), 433–448.

Youngstrom, E. A., Frazier, T. W., Demeter, C., Calabrese, J. R., & Findling, R. L. (2008). Developing a 10-item mania scale from the Parent General Behavior Inventory for children and adolescents. *Journal of Clinical Psychiatry, 69*(5), 831–839.

Zimmerman, M., Galione, J. N., Ruggero, C. J., Chelminski, I., Young, D., Dalrymple, K., & McGlinchey, J. B. (2010). Screening for bipolar disorder and finding borderline personality disorder. *Journal of Clinical Psychiatry, 71*(9), 1212–1217.

Chapter 9

Sleep-Wake Disorders

Lu Dong, Jennifer C. Kanady, and Allison G. Harvey

W e spend approximately one third of our lives sleeping. Although the study of human sleep is a relatively young science and many fascinating mysteries remain to be solved, there have been great advances in knowledge about the function of sleep. For example, it is increasingly evident that sleep has a critical role in many domains of health (Zee & Turek, 2006) and psychological functioning (Walker & Stickgold, 2006). Great advances in knowledge have also been made relating to the nature and treatment of sleep disorders. Moreover, sleep disturbance is a characteristic of psychiatric disorders and, as we discuss below, can play a critical role in the maintenance of several disorders (Harvey, 2008a). In this chapter we focus on insomnia, as it is the most common sleep disorder.

Insomnia is a chronic difficulty that involves a predominant complaint of dissatisfaction with sleep quantity or quality, accompanied by problems in getting to sleep, maintaining sleep, or early awakening with an inability to return to sleep (American Psychiatric Association [APA], 2013). It is a prevalent problem, reported by approximately 10% of the population (Ohayon & Reynolds, 2009; Roth et al., 2011). The consequences are severe and may include impairments in the quality of life (Léger et al., 2012), poor cognitive performance in such areas as concentration and memory (Fortier-Brochu, Beaulieu-Bonneau, Ivers, & Morin, 2012), higher rates of work absenteeism, decreased job performance, increased rates of work-related accidents, and increased use of medical services (Léger, Guilleminault, Bader, Lévy, & Paillard, 2002). Sleep deprivation has detrimental effects on many domains of health (Zee & Turek, 2006), including the immune system, the neuroendocrine system, and the cardiovascular system (Dinges, Rogers, & Baynard, 2005). Given the prevalence and associated impairments, the cost of sleep disorders to society is enormous (Martin, Aikens, & Chervin, 2004).

Sleep Basics

Human sleep can be divided into (a) nonrapid eye movement (NREM) sleep that can be subdivided into three stages (N1 or sleep onset, N2, and N3 or slow-wave sleep) through which sleep progressively deepens; and (b) rapid eye movement (REM) sleep. In adult humans, sleep begins in NREM and progresses through the NREM stages. The first REM occurs approximately 80 to 100 minutes later. Thereafter, each NREM-REM cycle spans approximately 90 minutes. Stage N3 dominates early in the night and N2 and REM sleep lengthen during the latter half of the night (Carskadon & Dement, 2011). NREM sleep is thought to be important for conservation of energy and restoration and is associated with the most rapid cell division in some tissues as well as with increased protein synthesis (Kryger, Roth, & Dement, 2011). The functions of REM sleep are understood to include a role in learning, unlearning of irrelevant information, memory consolidation, emotional memory and information processing, and emotion regulation (Walker, 2011).

Sleep Across Development

From a developmental perspective, total sleep time varies substantially across the age range. In newborns, average total sleep time is approximately 16 to 18 hours, organized into 3- to 4-hour sleep periods across the 24-hour cycle. The average amount of sleep obtained by a 5-year-old is 11.1 hours and in a 9-year-old is 10.2 hours (Hoban, 2004). In adolescence, nighttime sleep reduces from an average of 9 hours at age 13 to 7.9 hours in 16-year-olds (Hoban, 2004). In young adults, average nighttime sleep varies between 7 and 9 hours and in the middle adult years between 6 and 8 hours. There are also alterations in sleep architecture over the course of development. Newborn infants are thought to start sleep with REM and then to move into NREM, with each REM-NREM cycle lasting about 50 minutes (Carskadon & Dement, 2011). In newborns, REM and NREM phases are called *active* and *quiet* sleep, respectively, because of the difficulty in differentiating sleep stages at this age. Whereas at birth approximately 50% of sleep is spent in active sleep, once a child is 2 years of age this percentage has reduced to 20% to 30% of total sleep time. Between the ages of 6 and 11, the amount of N3 sleep reduces and N2 sleep increases (Hoban, 2004).

Across the adolescent years, the "adult" sleep cycle length becomes established, with N3 further decreasing in length, accompanied by increases in N2 sleep (Carskadon & Dement, 2011). During the adolescent years, there is a delay in circadian phase and a corresponding delay in sleep onset, often shifting past midnight to the early morning hours (Carskadon, 2002; Tate, Richardson, & Carskadon, 2002). This has been attributed to a number of influences, which include a tendency toward increasing autonomy in deciding what time to go to bed, which coincides with both a natural biological delay in the circadian cycle plus irregularity in the sleep schedule associated with psychosocial stress and social activities (Carskadon, 2002; Hoban, 2004).

Description of the Disorder

We begin this section by describing the symptoms of insomnia. Then, we discuss several insomnia case examples, the history of insomnia, and the epidemiology of insomnia.

DESCRIPTION OF SYMPTOMS AND CRITERIA

There are three main classification systems for sleep disorders: the third edition of the *International Classification of Sleep Disorders* (ICSD-3; American Academy of Sleep

Medicine, 2014), the Research Diagnostic Criteria (RDC) (Edinger et al., 2004), and the fifth edition of the *Diagnostic and Statistical Manual of Mental Disorders* (*DSM-5*; APA, 2013). In keeping with the other chapters in this book, we focus on the *DSM-5* criteria; however, readers are encouraged to consult the ICSD-3 manual and the RDC criteria for further information about the other two nosologies commonly used in clinical and research settings. In the *DSM-5*, there are several differences in the classifications of sleep disorders compared to the fourth edition of the *Diagnostic and Statistical Manual of Mental Disorders* (*DSM-IV-TR*; APA, 2000). These differences include the elimination of the diagnosis of "primary insomnia" and the use of the diagnosis of "insomnia disorder" instead (Reynolds & Redline, 2010). Because insomnia can be associated with a wide range of medical illnesses and psychiatric disorders, the *DSM-5* distinguishes between insomnia disorder with and without mental health, physical health, and sleep disorder comorbidities.

Using the *DSM-5*, a diagnosis of insomnia may be given when there is a predominant complaint of dissatisfaction with sleep quantity or quality, including trouble with falling asleep, staying asleep, or early-morning awakening with an inability to return to sleep. These sleep difficulties must be present for at least 3 nights per week for more than 3 months and be associated with daytime impairment. These sleep difficulties must not be attributable to substance use or better explained by another sleep-wake disorder or co-existing medical or psychiatric conditions.

Quantitative criteria have been used to supplement the diagnostic criteria. The quantitative criteria for insomnia require that self-reported sleep onset latency (SOL) and/or wakefulness after sleep onset (WASO) must be equal to or longer than 30 minutes for at least 3 nights per week over a period of at least 6 months (Lichstein, Durrence, Taylor, Bush, & Riedel, 2003). Readers are also referred to Buysse, Ancoli-Israel, Edinger, Lichstein, and Morin (2006), who offer additional quantitative criteria for insomnia.

CASE EXAMPLES

Insomnia Without Comorbidity

Susan had never been a sound sleeper, but over the past 5 years insomnia had caused her significant distress and difficulty coping during the day, so much so that she took early retirement from her job as a preschool teacher. Susan could never predict whether she would sleep poorly. When she did sleep poorly, she suffered from a combination of difficulty getting to sleep at the beginning of the night (on a bad night taking between 40 minutes and 2 hours to get to sleep) and experiencing six or more awakenings over the course of the night, each varying from 10 minutes to 2 hours in duration. Following a night of poor sleep, Susan would spend much of the next day sleeping or resting.

Insomnia That Is Comorbid With Another Psychiatric Disorder

Jerry had just dropped out of his third year as an undergraduate at university because of episodes of mania and depression. He was diagnosed with bipolar disorder. He experienced insomnia between episodes, and it worsened approximately 2 weeks prior to a relapse. Jerry was aware of the damage each episode caused in his life, and knew that sleep disturbance was an early warning signal of an impending episode, so he had come to fear and worry about poor sleep. He no longer had a social life in the evening owing to his attempts to ensure a good night of sleep. He would nap during the day to try to guarantee getting enough sleep. Some days he would not get out of bed at all. Jerry concluded that he should get more than 10 hours of sleep per night to avoid episodes of mania and depression, and if he did not get 10 hours he would become worried and preoccupied with his sleep.

Insomnia That Is Comorbid With a Medical Problem

Gemma's sleep difficulties led her to resign her job as a bank manager 3 months prior to coming for treatment. Gemma thought that her sleep difficulties were due to a urinary tract disorder (which she had been told was called "irritable bladder"). This problem caused her to get up between five and eight times each night to go to the bathroom. After getting back into bed, she found it hard to get to sleep and would worry about the consequences of the disturbed sleep on her health and her ability to cope the next day. She had had two surgeries in an attempt to correct the bladder problem. These had not helped. Although Gemma felt that this medical problem was the major contributor to her insomnia, she came for treatment primarily because of her worry about her sleep. Interestingly, a treatment focused on Gemma's anxiety about sleep, with a special focus on monitoring the need to urinate, substantially reduced the number of bathroom visits during the night.

BRIEF HISTORY OF INSOMNIA

Jacobson's presentation of progressive muscle relaxation treatment in 1934 was the first approach to treating insomnia. The primary rationale for this treatment, and for many others that followed, was that heightened arousal disturbed sleep and predisposed individuals to a host of medical problems (Jacobson, 1934). Progressive muscle relaxation, as well as some of the treatments developed subsequently, was couched in the prevailing notion that insomnia was always secondary to other medical or psychiatric illnesses, a view that was prevalent through the 1960s.

During the rise of behaviorist thinking in the 1960s and 1970s, sleep disturbance came to be seen as a result of conditioning, where the bedroom environment and heightened arousal became associated with insomnia, leading to a learned sleep disturbance (e.g., Bootzin, 1979). As a correlate to this theoretical shift, empirical work began to focus more specifically on primary, rather than secondary, insomnia. In the 1980s, biofeedback, which requires patients to learn to monitor their electromyography or sensory-motor rhythm levels, became a popular treatment for insomnia. In a review of nonpharmacological treatments of sleep disturbance published in the 1990s, Chesson and colleagues (1999) listed biofeedback as an efficacious treatment option. However, the growing popularity of cognitive-behavioral therapy (CBT) as well as the time-consuming nature of biofeedback has rendered the latter significantly less popular as a contemporary intervention. Currently, cognitive behavioral theoretical and treatment approaches are the most commonly accepted and practiced modalities (Chesson et al., 1999; Morin, Bootzin, et al., 2006; Morin, Hauri, et al., 1999). These approaches are discussed in greater detail later.

EPIDEMIOLOGY

Insomnia is one of the most common health complaints in the general population (Ohayon & Reynolds, 2009). It is estimated that approximately one third of the general population worldwide reports significant symptoms of insomnia. Depending on the diagnostic criteria used, the prevalence estimates of insomnia range from 3.9% to 22.1% with about 10% meeting criteria for *DSM-IV* criteria (Ohayon & Reynolds, 2009; Roth et al., 2011). The 1-year incidence estimates of insomnia range from 7% to 15% (LeBlanc et al., 2009; Morphy, Dunn, Lewis, Boardman, & Croft, 2007). The course of insomnia is often chronic, with a median duration of 3 years (Pillai, Roth, & Drake, 2015). Longitudinal epidemiological studies of insomnia suggest that about 60% to 74% of patients with insomnia had been suffering for at least 1 year (Morin et al., 2009; Morphy et al., 2007; Pillai et al., 2015) and about half still had insomnia 3 years later (Morin et al., 2009). Insomnia is also common and chronic among adolescents, with an estimated prevalence of 10.7% for *DSM-IV* insomnia and a median age of onset of 11 years (Johnson, Roth, Schultz, & Breslau, 2006).

Age and sex are among the important factors influencing the prevalence of insomnia. Although insomnia symptoms, particularly sleep fragmentation, are more common in older adults (Ohayon, Carskadon, Guilleminault, & Vitiello, 2004), the prevalence of insomnia symptoms decreases with age, with older adults reporting less daytime impairment or distress than younger adults (Ohayon et al., 2004; Roth et al., 2011). Age also appears to influence insomnia phenotypes, such that sleep onset insomnia (i.e., trouble falling asleep) is more common among younger adults, whereas sleep maintenance problems (i.e., trouble staying asleep) are more common in middle-aged and older adults (Pillai et al., 2015). Moreover, insomnia is more prevalent in women than in men. Gonadal steroid effects are thought to be a potential reason for the sex difference that begins at puberty (Johnson et al., 2006) and becomes more apparent around and after menopause (Zhang & Wing, 2006).

For older adults, insomnia is often accompanied by medical illnesses, which may complicate issues of assessment and treatment, further compounding burden and cost (Morin, LeBlanc, Daley, Gregoire, & Mérette, 2006). In a large epidemiological study, Ford and Kamerow (1989) found that an approximately 50% comorbidity rate between insomnia and other psychiatric or medical illnesses. Other studies have yielded a rate as high as 75% (Lichstein, 2000). In cases of comorbid insomnia, additional empirical and clinical attention may be especially important as there is a cyclical influence of sleep disturbance on medical or psychiatric illnesses, with worsening sleep problems leading to a decline in general health, and the maintenance of daytime health problems and distress worsening sleep problems (Harvey, 2008a; Smith, Huang, & Manber, 2005).

Genetic epidemiological studies suggest the importance of genetic influences on insomnia. Family studies indicate that insomnia aggregates in families (Drake, Scofield, & Roth, 2008), with 30% to more than 70% of individuals with insomnia reporting a positive family history (Dauvilliers et al., 2005; Harvey, Gehrman, & Espie, 2014). Twin studies suggest insomnia is moderately heritable, with heritability estimates between 30% and 60% (Heath, Kendler, Eaves, & Martin, 1990; Watson, Goldberg, Arguelles, & Buchwald, 2006). Specific molecular genetic risk factors contributing to insomnia remain unclear. There is some evidence from candidate gene studies suggesting a potential link between individual differences in sleep-wake regulation and a common variant in the period circadian clock 3 (PER3) among healthy humans (Viola et al., 2007). In the literature on the role of serotonin in sleep regulation, another candidate gene study found a link between primary insomnia and a common variant on the 5-HT transporter (5-HT) gene (SLC6A4) (Deuschle et al., 2010). Replications of these findings are needed.

Models of Insomnia

We begin this section by discussing an influential overarching framework, the Spielman model. We then move on to describe a sample of the behavioral, cognitive, hyperarousal, neurocognitive, and hybrid models of insomnia.

THREE-FACTOR MODEL

The *three-factor model*, also called the *three-P model*, is a diathesis-stress model. According to Spielman, Caruso, & Glovinsky (1987), acute, or short-term, insomnia occurs as a result of predisposing factors (e.g., traits) and precipitating factors (e.g., life stressors). This acute form can then develop into a chronic or longer-term disorder as a result of perpetuating factors (e.g., poor coping strategies such as unhelpful beliefs/thoughts and behavior). Predisposing factors (such as a tendency to worry) constitute a vulnerability for insomnia, and this vulnerability remains across the life of the disorder. Precipitating factors trigger acute insomnia, but their influence tends to wane over time. In contrast, perpetuating factors take hold and serve to maintain insomnia; these include behaviors (e.g., extending time spent in bed trying to sleep more, taking naps) and/or thoughts (e.g., fear of sleeplessness, excessive worries about daytime consequences) developed to cope with insomnia.

BEHAVIORAL STIMULUS CONTROL MODEL

An important behavioral model is the stimulus control model (Bootzin, 1972). It is based on the conditioning principle that insomnia occurs when the bed or bedroom ceases to be paired specifically with sleep and instead becomes paired with many possible responses (e.g., being awake and anxious about not sleeping). As is described later in this chapter, this theory has led to the development of an intervention with strong efficacy (Morin, Bootzin, et al., 2006).

COGNITIVE MODEL

One cognitive model of insomnia aims to specify the cognitive processes that serve to perpetuate insomnia (Harvey, 2002). According to this conceptualization, insomnia is maintained by a cascade of cognitive processes that operate at night and during the day. The equal emphasis on the nighttime and daytime processes is an important feature of this model. The key cognitive processes that comprise the cascade are (a) worry and rumination, (b) selective attention and monitoring, (c) misperception of sleep and daytime deficits, (d) dysfunctional beliefs about sleep (based on Morin, 1993), and (e) counterproductive safety behaviors that serve to maintain beliefs. Many of the specific predictions generated by this model have been empirically tested, leading to refinement of the model (Harvey, 2005) and a new cognitive therapy treatment approach that has support from an open trial (Harvey, Sharpley, Ree, Stinson, & Clark, 2007) and a comparative efficacy RCT of cognitive therapy, behavior therapy, and cognitive-behavioral therapy (A. G. Harvey et al., 2014).

HYPERAROUSAL MODELS

The hypothesis that physiological hyperarousal serves to perpetuate insomnia has attracted interest for several decades, since the classic work of Monroe (1967), in which significantly increased physiological activation (increased rectal temperature, heart rate, basal skin resistance, and aphasic vasoconstrictions) was found 30 minutes before and during sleep in persons with insomnia as compared to good sleepers. Additionally, in a series of elegant studies, Bonnet and Arand (1992) experimentally induced a chronic physiological activation via caffeine intake in good sleepers. The caffeine resulted in decreased sleep efficiency and increased daytime fatigue. In addition, Bonnet and Arand (1995) measured whole body VO_2, which was conceptualized as an index of hyperarousal, at intervals across the day and during sleep. VO_2 was consistently elevated at all measurement points in insomnia patients relative to the good sleepers. The authors concluded that the 24-hour increase in metabolic rate observed may be an important factor that maintains insomnia.

NEUROCOGNITIVE MODEL

The neurocognitive model (Perlis, Giles, Mendelson, Bootzin, & Wyatt, 1997; Perlis, Merica, Smith, & Giles, 2001) extends the behavioral model by explicitly allowing for the possibility that conditioned arousal may act as a perpetuating factor. The concept of arousal is expressed in terms of somatic, cognitive, and cortical arousal.

Somatic arousal corresponds to measures of metabolic rate, *cognitive arousal* typically refers to mental constructs like worry and rumination, and *cortical arousal* refers to the level of cortical activation (but may also include all CNS arousal). Cortical arousal, it is hypothesized, occurs as a result of classical conditioning and allows abnormal levels of sensory and information processing and also long-term memory formation. These phenomena, in turn, are directly linked to sleep continuity disturbance and/or sleep state misperception. Specifically, enhanced sensory processing (detection of a stimulus and potentially the emission of a startle and/or orienting response) around sleep onset and during NREM sleep is thought to make the individual particularly vulnerable to perturbation by environmental stimuli (e.g., a noise outside on the street), which interferes with sleep initiation and/or maintenance. Enhanced information processing (detection of, and discrimination between, stimuli and the formation of a short-term memory of the stimulating event) during NREM sleep may blur the phenomenological distinction between sleep and wakefulness. That is, one cue for "knowing" that one is asleep is the lack of awareness for events occurring during sleep. Enhanced information processing may therefore account for insomnia patients' tendency to misperceive sleep indexed by polysomnography (PSG) as wakefulness.

Finally, enhanced long-term memory (detection of, and discrimination between, stimuli and recollection of a stimulating event hours after its occurrence) around sleep onset and during NREM sleep may interfere with the subjective experience of sleep initiation and duration. Normally, individuals cannot recall information from periods immediately prior to sleep, during sleep, or during brief arousals from sleep. An enhanced ability to encode and retrieve information in insomnia would be expected to influence judgments about sleep latency, wakefulness after sleep onset, and sleep duration.

HOMEOSTATIC AND CIRCADIAN INFLUENCES

The two-process model of sleep regulation (Borbély, 1982) proposes that sleep and wakefulness are dependent on a homeostatic process and a sleep-wake independent circadian process (Achermann & Borbély, 2011). Sleep homeostasis influences sleep propensity; that is, sleep homeostasis results in an increased tendency to sleep when a person has been sleep deprived, and a decreased tendency to sleep after having had a substantial amount of sleep. The circadian rhythm is an internal biological clock that is responsible for oscillations of melatonin, cortisol, temperature, and other biological functions, with one complete oscillation of about 24 hours (Lack & Bootzin, 2003). Some, but not all, studies have found impaired sleep homeostasis in persons with insomnia (e.g., Besset, Villemin, Tafti, & Billiard, 1998; Stepanski, Zorick, Roehrs, & Roth, 2000).

There is a similar lack of consensus in the research about whether circadian rhythm abnormalities play a role in insomnia. Environmentally induced phase shifts, such as those occurring as a result of shift work or jet lag, can cause acute insomnia, which in some cases can lead to chronic insomnia, per the earlier-discussed Spielman model (Perlis, Smith, & Pigeon, 2005). There is also evidence that the earlier-discussed hyperarousal may not be a 24-hour issue for some but rather may fluctuate according to circadian influences (Perlis et al., 2005).

HYBRID MODELS

At least three models have been proposed that incorporate a range of levels of explanation (e.g., behavioral, physiological) and across various points of the disorder (e.g., precipitating factors, perpetuating factors). These will now be described.

Morin's (1993) cognitive behavioral model of insomnia incorporates cognitive, temporal, and environmental variables as both precipitating and perpetuating factors. Morin places hyperarousal as the key precipitating factor of insomnia. The hyperarousal can be cognitive-affective, behavioral, or physiological. Stimulus conditioning can then exacerbate this arousal. For example, a person may associate temporal (e.g., bedtime routines) and environmental (e.g., the bedroom setting) stimuli with fear of being unable to sleep. Worry and rumination may then result. Additional perpetuating factors may ensue, including, as in the cognitive model, daytime fatigue, worry and emotional distress about sleep loss, and maladaptive habits (e.g., excessive time in bed). Thus, hyperarousal may serve as a trigger, but a multitude of factors perpetuate the negative cycle, including sleeplessness itself.

Lundh's (1998) cognitive behavioral model of insomnia also considers cognitive and physiological arousal, as well as stressful life events, as factors. However, Lundh's model proposes sleep-interpreting processes as additional factors. Sleep-interpreting processes are thoughts about sleep, including perceptions about sleep onset latency, total sleep time, and sleep quality; thoughts about sleep quantity requirements and the consequences of not meeting these requirements; the ways in which variations in sleep quality are explained; and the degree to which negative aspects of daily functioning are attributed to poor sleep. Thus, a central tenet of this model is that individuals' cognitions and perceptions about their poor sleep and their consequent daytime functioning play key roles in maintaining insomnia. Morin's and Lundh's cognitive behavioral models of insomnia add to the cognitive model of insomnia by also taking into account problematic behaviors associated with sleep problems, in addition to maladaptive thought processes.

Espie's (2002) psychobiological inhibition model posits that insomnia is a disorder of the automaticity of homeostatic and circadian processes. That is, in good sleepers, these two processes naturally default to good sleep and can adjust to some variability, but in persons with insomnia, the central problem is with inhibition of de-arousal processes critical to good sleep. The attention-intention-effort pathway (Espie, Broomfield, MacMahon, Macphee, & Taylor, 2006) extends this model by providing an explanation of how insomnia develops and what critical factors maintain it. More specifically, this pathway suggests that sleep-wake automaticity is inhibited by selectively attending to sleep, by explicitly intending to sleep, and by introducing effort into the sleep engagement process.

THE ROLE OF EMOTION

Though there is currently limited empirical research on the role of emotion in insomnia, it is intuitive that an individual's emotion regulation ability is likely to play a role in whether he or she can cognitively and physiologically down-regulate in order to sleep. One study that is consistent with this hypothesis has been reported by Morin, Rodrigue, and Ivers (2003), who found that persons with insomnia rate the impact of daily minor stressors and the intensity of major negative life events higher than good sleepers. Also, persons with insomnia were found to use more emotion-oriented coping strategies and have greater pre-sleep arousal than good sleepers. A path model showed that emotion-focused coping negatively affected sleep by increasing both the impact of stress and the pre-sleep arousal. Hence, this study suggests a detrimental impact of emotional arousal on sleep.

It seems likely that emotion regulation and sleep are bidirectionally related (Harvey, 2008a). The previous paragraph made the case that emotion regulation difficulty makes it difficult to get to sleep, and there is evidence that sleep quality impacts emotion and mood the next day. For example, in a meta-analysis of 19 studies of sleep deprivation (Pilcher & Huffcutt, 1996), mood was more negatively affected than either cognitive performance or motor performance. Also, Dinges et al. (1997) restricted the sleep of healthy participants to 5 hours per night for 1 week and found that mood disturbance progressively increased throughout the week.

Two studies examined the sleep-and-mood cycle in bipolar disorder, whose main feature is difficulty in emotion regulation. One study found that mood regulation impairment, especially in regulating positive emotional stimuli, may contribute to disturbance in sleep onset latency (Talbot, Hairston, Eidelman, Gruber, & Harvey, 2009). In another study, compared to healthy controls, individuals with interepisode bipolar disorder and insomnia experienced both elevated sleep disturbance and more negative mood. Further, sleep disturbance was associated with daytime negative mood, whereas evening negative mood was associated with subsequent sleep disturbance and positive mood was associated with better sleep (Talbot et al., 2012). These results indeed support the bidirectional relationship between the dysfunctions in mood and sleep.

ENVIRONMENTAL FACTORS

The relation between environment and insomnia is another understudied area. One aspect of the environment, the interpersonal context of sleep, may be an important contributor to insomnia. In fact, for many couples, sleep problems and relationship problems co-occur, and the association between sleep and relationships is likely to be bidirectional and reciprocal (Troxel, Robles, Hall, & Buysse, 2007). There is evidence that sleeping arrangement (e.g., sleeping with a partner) has significant effects on sleep measures: attachment insecurity in couples was associated with poor subjective sleep quality; while marital harmony was prospectively linked with fewer self-reported sleep problems (for a review, see Troxel et al., 2007). Interestingly, there is also evidence suggesting that sleep disturbance and sleep disorders have a negative impact on the functioning of a couple's relationship (Troxel et al., 2007) and on the degree, nature, and resolution of relationship conflict (Gordon & Chen, 2013).

Additionally, increased technology and busier schedules may have an effect on insomnia. These effects may be particularly profound in adolescence. A study of sleep habits in 7th through 12th graders found that 45% of adolescents report getting insufficient sleep on school nights and 28% complain they often feel "irritable and cranky" as a result of getting too little sleep (Carskadon, Mindell, & Drake, 2006). Technology options (TV, movies, video games, the Internet, music, cell phones, and text messaging) and busier schedules (increased homework, part-time employment, and increased time spent on sports and other extracurricular activities) contribute to delays in bedtimes in adolescents. Yet, it is known that during the adolescent years the need for sleep increases. A meta-analysis of risk factors for sleep disturbance in adolescents found that video gaming; phone, computer, and internet use; and evening light were related to delayed bedtimes in teens (Bartel, Gradisar, & Williamson, 2015).

Assessment of Disorder

The assessment of insomnia varies depending on whether it is being done in a clinical or research context. This next section focuses on the assessment of insomnia for clinical purposes. The clinical assessment of insomnia typically includes a clinical interview and self-report measures of insomnia symptoms and sleep diaries. Objective measures, such as polysomnography and actigraphy, may be included as part of the assessment to rule out other sleep disorders but are not routinely recommended (Littner et al., 2003; Morgenthaler et al., 2007). Subjective and objective measures of sleep are described below.

The clinical interview to assess insomnia often includes the following domains (Morin et al., 2015): (a) insomnia symptoms, including age of onset, current symptoms, frequency and course of symptoms, and perceived daytime consequences; (b) factors influencing insomnia symptoms, including history of insomnia treatment and its efficacy, factors that improve insomnia, factors that exacerbate insomnia (e.g., stress), and factors that maintain insomnia (e.g., sleep incompatible thoughts/behaviors); (c) health, including comorbid medical or psychiatric illnesses, other sleep disorders, pain, and pharmacological considerations (e.g., medications that have sedating/activating effects); and (d) family, social, and work concerns, including sleep-incompatible behaviors that are work- or family-related, family history of insomnia, and stressful life events. It is crucial not only to thoroughly assess nighttime symptoms but also to focus on the 24-hour impact of insomnia (e.g., daytime consequences). Conceptual models (reviewed above) may be used to guide the clinical assessment and inform the case conceptualization and treatment planning. Buysse et al. (2006) made additional important recommendations for the assessment of insomnia (e.g., definition, diagnosis, and measures of sleep and insomnia). These recommendations are particularly important to consider when evaluating insomnia in a research study (Buysse et al., 2006).

ASSESSMENT OF SUBJECTIVELY PERCEIVED SLEEP

As is evident from the *DSM-5* criteria, insomnia is defined subjectively. Thus, three levels of self-reported sleep data are collected from patients during an assessment for insomnia. First, a clinical sleep history is taken to assess the individual for the diagnostic criteria and the presence of comorbid problems. Information gathered includes the duration, frequency, and severity of nighttime sleep disturbances, including estimates of the key sleep parameters: sleep onset latency (SOL), number of awakenings after sleep onset (NWAKE), total amount of time awake after sleep onset (WASO), total sleep time (TST), and an estimate of sleep quality (SQ). Information about the onset and duration of the insomnia and the type of symptoms (i.e., sleep onset, sleep maintenance, or early morning awakening problems, or combinations of these) is collected. A description of the daytime correlates and consequences of insomnia is key. In addition, obtaining information about medications (prescription and over-the-counter) and screening for the presence of comorbid psychiatric disorder and medical problems (including other sleep disorders) are also important.

Second, one or more validated questionnaire measures can be used to index the presence and severity of sleep disturbance (e.g., Pittsburgh Sleep Quality Index; Buysse, Reynolds, Monk, Berman, & Kupfer, 1989), insomnia (e.g., Insomnia Severity Index; Bastien, Vallieres, & Morin, 2001), and daytime sleepiness (e.g., Stanford Sleepiness Scale; Hoddes, Zarcone, Smythe, Phillips, & Dement, 1973). Third, asking the patient to complete a sleep diary each morning as soon as possible after waking for 2 weeks provides prospective estimates of sleep. Many clinicians think of the sleep diary as their best friend. A sleep diary provides a wealth of information, including night-to-night variability in sleeping difficulty and sleep-wake patterns, and can be used to determine the presence of circadian rhythm problems, such as a delayed sleep phase or an advanced sleep phase. Also, sleep diaries reduce several problems associated with retrospective reporting, such as answering on the basis of saliency (i.e., the worst night) or recency (i.e., last night) (Smith, Nowakowski, Soeffing, Orff, & Perlis, 2003). Interestingly, the "enhanced awareness" of sleep patterns facilitated by diary keeping can reduce anxiety over sleep loss and thus contribute to better sleep (Morin, 1993, p. 71).

There are many sleep diary versions. Carney et al. (2012) developed a consensus sleep diary based on expert agreement and qualitative patient input. These authors proposed that all sleep diary versions should contain "core" sleep questions in order to adequately address the sleep problem. As shown in Figure 9.1, core sleep questions that should be addressed by a sleep diary include the following: (a) What time did you get into bed? (b) What time did you try to go to sleep? (c) How long did it take you to fall asleep? (d) How many times did you wake up, not counting your final awakening? (e) In total, how long did these awakenings last? (f) What time was your final awakening? (g) What time did you get out of bed for the day? (h) How would you rate the quality of your sleep (on a scale from "poor" to "very good")? and (i) Do you have any additional comments pertaining to your sleep? (Carney et al., 2012). These core questions align nicely with previous suggestions about recommended sleep diary parameters (Buysse et al., 2006).

Consensus Sleep Diary-Core ID/Name:_____

Today's date	Sample 4/5/11	9/13/13	9/14/13	9/15/13	9/16/13	9/17/13	9/18/13	9/19/13
1. What time did you get into bed?	10:15 p.m.	11 p.m.	11 p.m.	11 p.m.	11 p.m.	11 p.m.	1 a.m.	2:30 a.m.
2. What time did you try to go to sleep?	11:30 p.m.	12:30 a.m.	1:30 a.m.	12 a.m.	12:30 a.m.	11 p.m.	1 a.m.	2:30 a.m.
3. How long did it take you to fall asleep?	55 min.	5 min.	10 min.	15 min.	10 min.	10 min.	5 min.	1 min.
4. How many times did you wake up, not counting your final awakening?	3 times	1 time	2 times	1 time	0 times	0 times	0 times	0 times
5. In total, how long did these awakenings last?	1 hour 10 min.	3 min.	12 min.	10 min.	0 min.	0 min.	0 min.	0 min.
6. What time was your final awakening?	6:35 a.m.	10:15 a.m.	5:15 a.m.	8:30 a.m.	5:15 a.m.	9:15 a.m.	10:00 a.m.	10:30 a.m.
7. What time did you get out of bed for the day?	7:20 a.m.	10:30 a.m.	5:15 a.m.	8:30 a.m.	5:20 a.m.	9:30 a.m.	10:15 a.m.	11:00 a.m.
8. How would you rate the quality of your sleep?	☐ Very poor ☑ Poor ☐ Fair ☐ Good ☐ Very good	☐ Very poor ☐ Poor ☐ Fair ☑ Good ☐ Very good	☐ Very poor ☑ Poor ☐ Fair ☐ Good ☐ Very good	☐ Very poor ☐ Poor ☐ Fair ☑ Good ☐ Very good	☐ Very poor ☑ Poor ☐ Fair ☐ Good ☐ Very good	☐ Very poor ☐ Poor ☑ Fair ☐ Good ☐ Very good	☐ Very poor ☐ Poor ☐ Fair ☑ Good ☐ Very good	☐ Very poor ☐ Poor ☐ Fair ☑ Good ☐ Very good
9. Comments (if applicable)	I have a cold		I have a morning class		I have a morning class			

FIGURE 9.1   Sleep Diary Instructions: Core Questions (from Carney et al., 2012, fig. 1) with Sample Responses

Additional sleep diary questions can also be included. For example, questions pertaining to alcohol and caffeine use, medication use, napping and/or exercise might be helpful in further analyzing the sleep problem. Last, some sleep patients prefer different sleep diary formats (e.g., clock diagram on which the participants indicate their bedtime and rise time); therefore, a practitioner can tailor the sleep diary to adhere to the patient's preference (Carney et al., 2012).

OBJECTIVE ESTIMATES

The gold standard measure of sleep is polysomnography (PSG). PSG is used to classify sleep into the aforementioned stages. It involves placing surface electrodes on the scalp and face to measure electrical brain activity (electroencephalogram, EEG), eye movement (electro-oculogram, EOG), and muscle tone (electromyogram, EMG). The data obtained are used to classify each epoch of data by sleep stage and by sleep cycles (NREM and REM). Disadvantages associated with PSG include its expense, discomfort for participants, and labor-intensive nature. According to the Standards of Practice Committee of the American Academy of Sleep Medicine guidelines, PSG is *not* needed for the routine assessment of insomnia (Littner et al., 2003). However, PSG is useful for diagnostic clarification in instances of treatment failure or when a patient is suspected of having a sleep-related breathing disorder or periodic limb movement disorder (Littner et al., 2003).

Actigraphy is an alternative means of providing an objective estimate of sleep. Actigraphs are small wrist-worn devices that contain a sensor, a processor, and memory storage. The sensor samples physical motion, and the processor translates it into numerical digital data, summarizing the frequency of motions into epochs of specified time duration and storing the summary in memory. These data are then downloaded to a computer and analyzed to generate various sleep parameters. Because the body becomes more quiescent during sleep, actigraphy can be used to differentiate between periods of wakefulness and periods of sleep, but not different stages of sleep. According to the Standards of Practice Committee guidelines, actigraphy yields acceptably accurate estimates of sleep patterns in healthy adults and patients with sleep disorders (Morgenthaler et al., 2007). Although not required for the assessment of insomnia, actigraphy is indicated as a method for measuring circadian rhythm patterns or sleep disturbance in individuals with insomnia, including those with comorbid depression. Actigraphy is also a useful tool for evaluating the response to treatment in insomnia patients (Morgenthaler et al., 2007).

Interventions

In this section, we introduce both nonpharmacological and pharmacological interventions for treating adult insomnia, as well as comparisons between these two types of intervention. We also briefly discuss treatment adherence and treatment for comorbid insomnia.

CBT-I

A number of treatments are available to address insomnia in adults. Most of the research to date has focused on cognitive-behavioral therapy for insomnia (CBT-I) and psychopharmacological interventions, each of which is described in the following pages. Four to 10 weekly sessions of CBT-I are typically needed to administer its various components (described in this section). The primary goal of CBT-I is to address the cognitive and behavioral maintaining mechanisms involved in perpetuating sleep disturbance. A second important goal is to teach coping techniques that patients can use in instances of residual sleep difficulty. CBT-I is currently considered the treatment of choice for insomnia. It is a multicomponent treatment that is typically comprised of one or more of the following components: stimulus control; sleep restriction; sleep hygiene education; paradoxical intention; relaxation therapy, including imagery training; and cognitive restructuring for unhelpful beliefs about sleep. Each of these components is now described.

Stimulus Control

The rationale for stimulus control therapy lies in the notion that insomnia is a result of conditioning that occurs when the bed becomes associated with inability to sleep. As described by Bootzin, Epstein, and Wood (1991), stimulus control requires patients to (a) set a regular sleep schedule, with a consistent waking time and no daytime naps; (b) go to bed and stay in bed only when sleepy and when sleep is imminent (this requires individuals to leave the bed if they are not falling asleep and to return to bed only when they are feeling very sleepy); and (c) eliminate from the bedroom all sleep-incompatible activities (like upsetting conversations, problem solving, and watching TV).

Sleep Restriction

Sleep restriction therapy, as developed by Spielman and colleagues (Spielman, Saskin, & Thorpy, 1987), rests on the general premise that time in bed should be limited in order to maximize the sleep drive and so that the association between the bed and sleeping is strengthened. This behavioral treatment begins with a reduction of time spent in bed so that time in bed is equivalent to the time the patient estimates he or she spends sleeping. For instance, if an individual thinks he or she gets approximately 6 hours of sleep per night, but usually spends about 2 additional hours trying to get to sleep, the sleep restriction therapy would begin by limiting his or her time spent in bed to 6 hours. This initial reduction in time spent in bed is intended to heighten a person's homeostatic sleep drive (Perlis & Lichstein, 2003). Following this restriction, sleep gradually becomes more efficient, at which point time spent in bed is gradually increased to reach an optimal sleep efficiency. Sleep efficiency is defined as the total sleep time divided by time in bed multiplied by 100. The goal is to increase sleep efficiency to more than 85% to 90%.

Sleep Hygiene Education

Information about sleep and sleep-incompatible behaviors, and the daytime consequences of sleep disturbance, is often given to inform patients of basic steps to improve their sleep. Interventions focused on sleep hygiene are behavioral in nature and target sleep-incompatible routines. Factors typically addressed in sleep hygiene interventions include alcohol, tobacco, and caffeine use; diet; exercise; and the bedroom environment (Morin & Espie, 2003). Although sleep hygiene education is typically included as one component of CBT-I, its use as the sole intervention in treating insomnia has not been empirically supported (Morin, Bootzin, et al., 2006).

Paradoxical Intention

In paradoxical intention therapy, patients are instructed to stay awake for as long as possible. The aim is to reduce performance anxiety related to sleep (e.g., Espie & Lindsay, 1985). Paradoxical intention therapy aims to replace the tendency to actively try to get to sleep, a strategy that is often employed by individuals struggling with insomnia. Because employing an active focus and strategy to induce sleep is actually sleep incompatible (Espie, 2002), paradoxical intention places patients in the role of passive observer, thereby decreasing anxiety and increasing the likelihood of sleep onset (Ascher & Efran, 1978).

Relaxation Therapy

Patients are taught to implement a variety of exercises while in the relaxation therapy session. They are then encouraged to practice these exercises as much as they can between sessions, but the emphasis is on practice during the day (as opposed to using them only at night in an effort to get to sleep). Practice is essential and is often aided by a tape of the relaxation instructions that the patient can use at home. Morin and Espie (2003) make a number of recommendations to maximize the effectiveness of relaxation therapy. Specifically, in choosing among the available relaxation techniques, they suggest a focus on imagery training, breathing exercises, and the release of muscle tension. Additionally, they note that while patients are generally receptive to relaxation therapy, it is important for them to understand that relaxation serves to set a context in which sleep is more likely to occur, and is not supposed to automatically induce sleep, as a sleep medication does.

Cognitive Therapy

The formal cognitive therapy component of CBT-I, traditionally administered in one session, involves altering faulty beliefs about sleep by education and discussion about sleep requirements, the biological clock, and the effects of sleep loss on sleep-wake functions (e.g., Edinger, Wohlgemuth, Radtke, Marsh, & Quillian, 2001). More recently, a different approach has been developed. Derived from the cognitive theory of insomnia described earlier (Harvey, 2002), this approach aims to reverse cognitive maintaining processes such as worry and rumination about sleep (e.g., Harvey, 2005). Importantly, in a recent study, interventions targeting the cognitive maintaining processes were integrated into CBT-I. This study compared the efficacy of CBT-I to behavior therapy (BT) and to (the enhanced version of) cognitive therapy (CT) components alone (A. G. Harvey et al., 2014). Details of this study are discussed in the next section.

EVIDENCE FOR CBT-I COMPONENTS

A number of randomized controlled trials (RCTs) have compared one or more components of CBT-I to each other and/or to placebo. In a recent review of CBT-I, the Standards of Practice Committee of the American Academy of Sleep Medicine found CBT-I to be highly effective and to have sustainable gains over long-term follow-up for 24 months in adult and older adult samples (Morin, Bootzin, et al., 2006). This review used the American Psychological Association criteria for well-supported empirically based treatments (Chambless & Hollon, 1998) and concluded that these criteria are met by stimulus control, paradoxical intention, relaxation, and sleep restriction approaches, and the administration of multiple components in the form of CBT-I. The sleep hygiene education intervention alone was not found to be effective as a treatment for insomnia.

Cognitive therapy for insomnia is a promising new approach, but RCTs are still needed for it to meet APA criteria for an empirically supported treatment.

Since the publication of the Standards of Practice Committee guidelines, an RCT has compared the efficacy of eight-session, individual behavior therapy (BT), cognitive therapy (CT), and full cognitive-behavioral therapy (CBT) for chronic insomnia (A. G. Harvey et al., 2014). BT includes a combination of stimulus control and sleep restriction strategies. CT targets a broad range of cognitive maintaining mechanisms, such as sleep-related worries, unhelpful beliefs, and attentional processes (based on Harvey, 2002; Harvey et al., 2007), and is considered an enhanced version of the CT traditionally included in CBT-I. Full CBT consists of a combination of BT and the enhanced version of CT. Results suggest that full CBT was associated with greatest and sustained improvement. Both BT and CT were effective, with a rapid but less sustained effect for BT and a delayed but sustained effect for CT. Hence, full (i.e., enhanced) CBT is the treatment of choice, although it should be noted that full CBT had more session time (approximately 75 minutes each session) relative to CT and BT (approximately 45–60 minutes each session). Perhaps BT is easier to implement but needs the help of a therapist for "coaching," while changes to cognitive processes in CT may be initially harder to achieve but once achieved are similar to forming habits. These different trajectories of change raise the interesting possibility of distinct mechanisms of change through behavioral versus cognitive processes (A. G. Harvey et al., 2014).

TREATMENT ADHERENCE

This chapter has described powerful, successful interventions for treating insomnia. However, to make sure these interventions have the greatest possible impact on people's lives, we need to make sure that the patient engages in the treatment process. In a study of treatment adherence in patients with chronic insomnia (Hebert, Vincent, Lewycky, & Walsh, 2010), the strongest predictors of treatment adherence were perceived behavioral control, social support, and intention to complete the program.

There are multiple ways in which a clinician can enhance treatment adherence. To be successful, an intervention needs to include the following three components: (1) the clinician needs to adequately explain the treatment process, (2) the patient needs to understand the treatment process, and (3) the patient needs to implement what he or she learns during treatment (Lichstein & Riedel, 1994). First, patients may be discouraged from previous unsuccessful treatment attempts. The practitioner should take the time to motivate the patient to try again (Morin, 1993). Second, it is important to schedule activities during the newly created wake time of the sleep restriction component. This helps to motivate the patient to stay out of bed (Morin, 1993). Third, concrete examples and written instructions aid the patient in remembering what was discussed during sessions (Chambers & Alexander, 1992). Fourth, it is important to explain the rationale for the treatment components and to coach the patient in their implementation (Sloan et al., 1993).

TREATMENT OF COMORBID INSOMNIA

In the past, it had often been assumed that insomnia that is comorbid with another psychiatric or medical disorder could not be successfully treated if the primary condition with which it was associated was not treated first. Although it is certainly true that cases of comorbid insomnia present additional challenges, the evidence suggests that such insomnia does respond to treatment when it is treated with CBT-I, even if the psychiatric or medical disorder is not under control. For example, in an RCT comparing CBT-I to an active control condition (in this case, stress management) in older adults suffering from a range of chronic illnesses (such as osteoarthritis and pulmonary disease), CBT-I was associated with a significant improvement in 8 out of 10 sleep measures compared to the control condition (Rybarczyk, Lopez, Schelble, & Stepanski, 2005; for similar examples across a range of psychiatric and medical conditions, see Smith et al., 2005). Notably, Smith et al. (2005) concluded that treatment effects are generally moderate to large for CBT-I when given to patients with medical and psychiatric illnesses. These effects are comparable to treatment effects for primary insomnia.

Two recent pilot RCTs provided further evidence that CBT-I can be highly effective for improving sleep in patients with severe psychiatric illnesses. Freeman et al. (2015) reported a pilot RCT that compared the eight-session CBT-I plus standard care (i.e., medication and contact with the clinical team) to standard care alone to treat sleep problems in patients with persistent delusions and hallucinations. Compared to standard care alone, the CBT-I plus standard care group led to a reduction in insomnia with large effect sizes at posttreatment, providing support for the use of CBT-I in treating sleep problems in patients with psychotic experiences. The treatment effect was equivocal for psychotic symptoms (Freeman et al., 2015). Another recent pilot RCT provided support for treating insomnia using an eight-session, bipolar disorder–specific modification of CBT-I (CBTI-BP) in interepisode bipolar disorder I patients (Harvey et al., 2015). Compared with psychoeducation (PE; providing information without facilitating behavior change), the CBTI-BP was associated with greater sleep improvement, with small to medium effect sizes at posttreatment, including reduced insomnia severity ratings and higher rates of insomnia remission. Both CBTI-BP and PE led to improved sleep, although sleep improved more in CBTI-BP than in PE. Importantly, compared to PE, CBTI-BP was associated with a significantly lower relapse rate for hypomania/mania and fewer days in an episode through 6-month follow-up. These studies add to the emerging literature suggesting that CBT-I improves not only sleep outcome but also the symptoms of comorbid psychiatric illnesses (Harvey et al., 2015).

PHARMACOLOGICAL INTERVENTIONS

Several different classes of medications may be used to treat insomnia, including benzodiazepines, nonbenzodiazepines, antihistamines, melatonin receptor agonists, and antidepressants (for reviews, see Krystal, 2011; Morin et al., 2015; Walsh & Roth, 2011). The term *hypnotics* is used to refer to medications whose primary purpose is to induce sleep. Among the hypnotics, benzodiazepine receptor agonists (BzRAs) are currently the only pharmacological interventions with adequate scientific support (National Institutes of Health [NIH], 2005), and they are generally recommended as first-line hypnotics for treating chronic insomnia (Walsh & Roth, 2011). Although not all BzRAs have a chemical structure similar to that of benzodiazepines, the primary action mechanism involves the inhibition of gamma-aminobutyric acid (GABA) through the occupation of benzodiazepine receptors.

All benzodiazepines have been shown to improve sleep, compared to placebo, in controlled clinical trials (Holbrook, Crowther, Lotter, Cheng, & King, 2000; Kupfer & Reynolds, 1997). Additionally, all BzRAs at appropriate doses lead to a decrease in sleep onset latency, and all BzRAs, with the exception of zaleplon, have also been shown to increase total sleep time (Nowell et al., 1997; Walsh & Roth, 2011). Although the bulk of these studies were conducted over a short period of time (typically no longer than 35 days), two trials raise the possibility that longer-term treatment may also be effective for some individuals with insomnia (Krystal et al., 2003; Perlis, McCall, Krystal, & Walsh, 2004). However, neither of these studies included a follow-up to evaluate whether the benefits to sleep were sustained after treatment ceased.

Although there is little risk of overdose or severe adverse effects, pharmacological interventions for insomnia do carry some risk of daytime residual effects (such as memory disturbance or anterograde amnesia), as well as risks of tolerance and dependence (Krystal, 2009). When used on a regular and prolonged basis, rebound insomnia is a common problem associated with discontinuation. Even short-term use can result in several days of rebound insomnia following discontinuation. However, discontinuation from the newer hypnotic medications (e.g., zolpidem and eszopiclone) is associated with fewer withdrawal symptoms (Morin & Espie, 2003).

A number of antidepressants, most commonly trazodone, amitriptyline, mirtazapine, and doxepin, have been used off label to treat insomnia, although they are used at lower doses than for treatment of depression (Krystal, 2009; Morin et al., 2015). The mechanisms of action, safety profiles, and efficacy for hypnotics are known. In contrast, there are minimal data on the risk-benefit ratio of antidepressants in the treatment of insomnia. In sum, BzRAs have the most extensive efficacy and safety data in the treatment of insomnia. Adequate evidence for using other medications (such as antidepressants) is not currently available (Walsh & Roth, 2011).

PSYCHOLOGICAL VERSUS PHARMACOLOGICAL INTERVENTIONS

It is important for clinicians to conduct a thorough efficacy and cost-benefit analysis for the different available treatment options in order to determine the best course of action in addressing insomnia. Primarily, a choice of CBT-I, pharmacology, or a combination of the two must be made.

A meta-analysis of 21 RCTs of CBT-I (primarily stimulus control and sleep restriction therapies) and pharmacological (BzRA) treatments for primary insomnia concluded that effects for the two treatment modalities are comparable in the short term, but CBT-I is more effective in decreasing sleep onset latency (Smith et al., 2002). Additionally, a study by Sivertsen et al. (2006) compared CBT-I, zopiclone, and placebo. The results clearly favored CBT-I, which resulted in improved short- and long-term functioning relative to zopiclone on three out of the four outcome measures. Moreover, for most outcomes zopiclone was no better than placebo. Because longer-term posttreatment follow-ups are often not included in studies of pharmacological interventions, questions concerning efficacy after treatment has ceased cannot yet be answered.

Addressing the issue of whether a combined pharmacological and CBT-I approach is indicated, Morin, Colecchi, Stone, Sood, and Brink (1999) compared pharmacological treatment alone (temazepam, with an initial dosage of 7.5 mg and a maximum dosage of 30 mg per night), CBT-I alone (delivered in eight weekly sessions), temazepam plus CBT-I (combination treatment), and placebo medication as treatments for insomnia in older adults. All three active treatments were associated with short-term clinical gains, while placebo was not. However, only individuals who received CBT-I were found to sustain treatment gains over time (up to 24-month follow-up). The combination treatment was associated with some sustained gains, but treatment efficacy became more variable over follow-up than in the CBT-I-alone group. Additionally, study participants, their significant others, and their treating clinicians rated the CBT-I to be more effective than and preferable to pharmacotherapy alone (Morin, Colecchi, et al., 1999).

Brief Overview of Other Sleep Disorders

Although a full description of other sleep disorders and their treatment is beyond the scope of this chapter, we provide a brief description of each of the other major sleep disorders here. The presence of one of these disorders is an exclusionary criterion for an insomnia disorder (APA, 2013). Thus, their presence should be assessed in all insomnia cases. Each of these disorders is relatively common and can have serious consequences for the health and daytime functioning of the sufferer. For further information on these disorders, we refer the reader to Kryger, Roth, and Dement (2011).

SLEEP APNEA

Transient closure of the upper airway during sleep is associated with disruption to sleep. The nighttime symptoms of sleep apnea can include snoring, pauses in breathing during sleep, shortness of breath during sleep, choking during sleep, headaches on waking, and difficulty getting breath or breathlessness on waking. The adverse outcomes include daytime sleepiness and cardiovascular problems.

RESTLESS LEGS SYNDROME

The symptoms of restless legs syndrome (RLS) are a sensation of an urge to move the limbs (usually legs) and a feeling of restlessness because of sensations in the limbs (usually legs). The sensations start or get worse when resting, relaxing, or first going to bed. A clear circadian pattern must be present.

PERIODIC LIMB MOVEMENT DISORDER

The hallmark feature of periodic limb movement disorder (PLMD) is repetitive episodes of limb movements during sleep, usually the legs. The movements are associated with a partial or full awakening.

CIRCADIAN RHYTHM DISORDERS

There are two main circadian rhythm disorders: advanced phase (common among older adults), which involves falling asleep early and waking up early, and delayed sleep phase (common among adolescents), which involves not being able to fall asleep until the early hours in the morning and sleeping well into the next day.

NARCOLEPSY

This is a disorder characterized by excessive sleepiness. Episodes of short uncontrollable naps during the day are typical. Often the nap is associated with cataplexy (loss of muscle tone triggered by strong emotion), sleep paralysis, or hypnogogic hallucinations.

HYPERSOMNIA

Unlike the sleep disorders discussed previously in this section, a diagnosis of hypersomnia is not an exclusionary criterion for a diagnosis of insomnia. Hypersomnia is a sleep disorder characterized by prolonged nighttime sleep episodes, excessive daytime sleepiness, and frequent napping. Hypersomnia has been associated with emotional disturbance, increased interpersonal problems (Roberts, Roberts, & Chen, 2001), a greater likelihood of substance abuse, and future incidence of major depressive episodes (Breslau, Roth, Rosenthal, & Andreski, 1996). Cognitive behavioral strategies discussed earlier are very adaptable to treatment of hypersomnia (Kaplan & Harvey, 2009). See Kaplan and Harvey (2009) for a comprehensive review.

Summary and Future Directions

The most common sleep disorder is chronic insomnia. This chapter provides a description of the disorder, an overview of the various theories of the factors that predispose an individual to developing insomnia, the factors that precipitate insomnia, and those that perpetuate insomnia. In addition, it presents an overview of the assessment and treatment of insomnia and a brief introduction to other sleep disorders. Although humans spend approximately one third of their lives sleeping, sleep is a relatively new topic of scientific study, and there are a myriad of mysteries and questions about the function of sleep and sleep disorders that are yet to be answered. The results that have emerged to date clearly document that sleep is critical for the health and well-being of humans throughout the age ranges. As such, it is a domain that holds a large number of exciting opportunities for future research. Before closing we draw attention to three of the many interesting questions that remain to be answered relating to chronic insomnia and the role of sleep in other psychiatric and medical disorders.

SLEEP INTERVENTION FOR CHILDREN AND ADOLESCENTS

Given the evidence for the efficacy and effectiveness of CBT-I for both adults and older adults, the downward extension of developmentally appropriate CBT-I components for adolescents and children has been of recent interest. There is a small but growing evidence base reporting on the effectiveness of using CBT-I components with children and adolescents who suffer from sleep disturbance (Bootzin & Stevens, 2005; de Bruin, Oort,

Bögels, & Meijer, 2014; Gradisar, Dohnt, et al., 2011; Gradisar, Gardner, & Dohnt, 2011; Owens, France, & Wiggs, 1999; Paine & Gradisar, 2011; Sadeh, 2005; Schlarb, Liddle, & Hautzinger, 2010). Moreover, a transdiagnostic intervention has recently been developed to treat sleep and circadian problems in children and adolescents (TranS-C-Youth; Harvey, 2016). This intervention draws on relevant components from three evidence-based interventions: (1) components from CBT-I to increase homeostatic pressure to sleep (stimulus control and sleep restriction) and reduce arousal (cognitive therapy); (2) components from the delayed sleep phase type (DSPT) to gradually move bedtime earlier (planned sleep modification) and get exposure to natural sunlight; and (3) components from interpersonal and social rhythm therapy (IPSRT) to stabilize daily rhythms (e.g., physical and social activities) and sleep-wake schedules. The developer of TranS-C-Youth adopted a transdiagnostic approach, with the result that this treatment can be used for sleep problems in multiple psychiatric disorders. This intervention is currently being tested in a large community sample of youth (ages 10–18) who have evening preference and are "at risk" in one or more domains (e.g., cognitive, behavioral, emotional) of their lives.

IMPROVEMENT OF TREATMENT

There is no doubt that CBT-I is an effective treatment, as indicated by several meta-analyses (Morin & Culbert, 1994; Murtagh & Greenwood, 1995; Smith et al., 2002) and reviews conducted by the Standards of Practice Committee of the American Academy of Sleep Medicine (Chesson et al., 1999; Morin, Bootzin, et al., 2006; Morin, Hauri, et al., 1999). However, the field is not as yet at a point where patients can be offered a maximally effective psychological treatment, as indicated by (a) the significant subset of patients who do not improve following CBT-I (19% to 26%), (b) the average overall improvement being in the range of 50% to 60% (Morin, Culbert, & Schwartz, 1994; Murtagh & Greenwood, 1995), and (c) the fact that only a minority of patients reach a high end state (i.e., become good sleepers) (Harvey & Tang, 2003). Furthermore, the widely held assumption that a treatment that addresses sleep will also effectively address the daytime consequences of insomnia has not yet been supported (Means, Lichstein, Epperson, & Johnson, 2000). In fact, there is some evidence that aspects of the daytime impairment suffered by patients with insomnia are independent of nighttime sleep and are instead associated with the subjective perception of inadequate sleep (Neitzert Semler & Harvey, 2005). Hence, treatment development efforts that improve outcome and target daytime symptoms are an important direction for the future.

COMORBIDITY

The comorbidity between chronic insomnia and other psychiatric or medical conditions has been widely recognized (NIH, 2005; Buysse, 2005). The cause-effect relationship may be difficult to establish, and therefore it is likely that treating insomnia may alleviate symptoms of the comorbid condition. Morin and colleagues (Morin, Bootzin, et al., 2006) as well as Smith and colleagues (2005) suggest that improvement in sleep following CBT-I treatment has great potential to facilitate improvement in medical and psychological symptoms of the so-called primary psychiatric or medical disorder. In fact, data suggest that treating comorbid sleep disturbance improves symptoms in PTSD (Germain, Shear, Hall, & Buysse, 2007), chronic pain (Currie, Wilson, Pontefract, & deLaplante, 2000), depression (Manber et al., 2008), and anxiety (Belleville, Cousineau, Levrier, & St-Pierre-Delorme, 2011), and also positive symptoms in psychotic patients (Freeman et al., 2015). Moreover, in terms of sleep in bipolar disorder (Harvey, 2008b, 2011), as discussed above, treating sleep disturbance with CBT-I during interepisode periods of bipolar disorder may prevent relapse into a mood episode and increase quality of life (Harvey et al., 2015). Hence, this is clearly an exciting direction for future exploration, and more research on other comorbid medical and psychological symptoms/disorders is needed. Theoretically, this links back to issues covered earlier in this chapter that sleep likely has a mood and emotion regulatory role as well as a role in bodily repair and immune system functioning. Hence, sleep disturbance is likely to contribute to the exacerbation of symptoms in psychiatric and medical disorders, and the treatment of sleep disturbance may be critical for full recovery.

References

Achermann P., & Borbély, A. A. (2011). Sleep homeostasis and models of sleep regulation. In M. H. Kryger, T. Roth, & W. C. Dement (Eds.), *Principles and practice of sleep medicine* (5th ed., pp. 431–444). Saint Louis, MO: Elsevier Saunders.

American Academy of Sleep Medicine. (2014). *International Classification of Sleep Disorders: Diagnostic and coding manual* (3rd ed.). Westchester, IL: Author.

American Psychiatric Association. (2000). *Diagnostic and statistical manual of mental disorders* (4th ed., text rev.). Washington, DC: Author.

American Psychiatric Association. (2013). *Diagnostic and statistical manual of mental disorders* (5th ed.). Washington, DC: Author.

Ascher, L. M., & Efran, J. (1978). Use of paradoxical intention in a behavioral program for sleep onset insomnia. *Journal of Consulting and Clinical Psychology*, *46*, 547–550.

Bartel, K. A., Gradisar, M., & Williamson, P. (2015). Protective and risk factors for adolescent sleep: A meta-analytic review. *Sleep Medicine Reviews*, *21*, 72–85.

Bastien, C. H., Vallieres, A., & Morin, C. M. (2001). Validation of the Insomnia Severity Index as an outcome measure for insomnia research. *Sleep Medicine*, *2*, 297–307.

Belleville, G., Cousineau, H., Levrier, K., & St-Pierre-Delorme, M.-È. (2011). Meta-analytic review of the impact of cognitive-behavior therapy for insomnia on concomitant anxiety. *Clinical Psychology Review*, *31*(4), 638–652.

Besset, A., Villemin, E., Tafti, M., & Billiard, M. (1998). Homeostatic process and sleep spindles in patients with sleep-maintenance insomnia: Effect of partial (21 h) sleep deprivation. *Electroencephalography and Clinical Neurophysiology*, *107*(2), 122–132.

Bonnet, M. H., & Arand, D. L. (1992). Caffeine use as a model of acute and chronic insomnia. *Sleep*, *15*, 526–536.

Bonnet, M. H., & Arand, D. L. (1995). 24-Hour metabolic rate in insomniacs and matched normal sleepers. *Sleep*, *18*(7), 581–588.

Bootzin, R. R. (1972). Stimulus control treatment for insomnia. *Proceedings of the American Psychological Association*, *7*, 395–396.

Bootzin, R. R. (1979). Effects of self-control procedures for insomnia. *American Journal of Clinical Biofeedback*, *2*, 70–77.

Bootzin, R. R., Epstein, D., & Wood, J. M. (1991). Stimulus control instructions. In P. J. Hauri (Ed.), *Case studies in insomnia* (pp. 19–28). New York, NY: Plenum Press.

Bootzin, R. R., & Stevens, S. J. (2005). Adolescents, substance abuse, and the treatment of insomnia and daytime sleepiness. *Clinical Psychology Review*, *25*(5), 629–644.

Borbély, A. A. (1982). A two process model of sleep regulation. *Human Neurobiology*, *1*, 195–204.

Breslau, N., Roth, T., Rosenthal, L., & Andreski, P. (1996). Sleep disturbance and psychiatric disorders: A longitudinal epidemiological study of young adults. *Biological Psychiatry*, *39*, 411–418.

Buysse, D. J. (2005). Insomnia state of the science: An evolutionary, evidence-based assessment. *Sleep*, *28*(9), 1045–1046.

Buysse, D., Ancoli-Israel, S., Edinger, J. D., Lichstein, K. L., & Morin, C. M. (2006). Recommendations for a standard research assessment of insomnia. *Sleep*, *29*, 1155–1173.

Buysse, D. J., Reynolds, C. F., Monk, T. H., Berman, S. R., & Kupfer, D. J. (1989). The Pittsburgh Sleep Quality Index: A new instrument for psychiatric practice and research. *Psychiatry Research*, *28*, 193–213.

Carney, C. E., Buysse, D. J., Ancoli-Israel, S., Edinger, J. D., Krystal, A. D., Lichstein, K. L., & Morin, C. M. (2012). The consensus sleep diary: Standardizing prospective sleep self-monitoring. *Sleep*, *35*, 287–302.

Carskadon, M. A. (2002). Factors influencing sleep patterns of adolescents. In M. A. Carskadon (Ed.), *Adolescent sleep patterns: Biological, social, and psychological influences* (pp. 4–26). New York, NY: Cambridge University Press.

Carskadon, M. A., & Dement, W. C. (2011). Normal human sleep: An overview. In M. H. Kryger, T. Roth, & W. C. Dement (Eds.), *Principles and practice of sleep medicine* (5th ed., pp. 16–26). Saint Louis, MO: Elsevier Saunders.

Carskadon, M. A., Mindell, J. A., & Drake, C. (2006). *2006 Sleep in America poll*. The National Sleep Foundation. Retrieved from http://www .sleepfoundation.org/hottopics/index.php?secid-16&id=392

Chambers, M. J., & Alexander, S. D. (1992). Assessment and prediction of outcome for a brief behavioral insomnia treatment program. *Journal of Behavior Therapy and Experimental Psychiatry, 23*, 289–297.

Chambless, D. L., & Hollon, S. D. (1998). Defining empirically supported theories. *Journal of Consulting and Clinical Psychology, 1*, 7–18.

Chesson, A. L., Jr., Anderson, W. M., Littner, M., Davila, D., Hartse, K., Johnson, S., ... Rafecas, J. (1999). Practice parameters for the nonpharmacologic treatment of chronic insomnia. An American Academy of Sleep Medicine report. Standards of Practice Committee of the American Academy of Sleep Medicine. *Sleep, 22*, 1128–1133.

Currie, S. R., Wilson, K. G., Pontefract, A. J., & deLaplante, L. (2000). Cognitive-behavioral treatment of insomnia secondary to chronic pain. *Journal of Consulting and Clinical Psychology, 68*, 407–416.

Dauvilliers, Y., Morin, C., Cervena, K., Carlander, B., Touchon, J., Besset, A., & Billiard, M. (2005). Family studies in insomnia. *Journal of Psychosomatic Research, 58*(3), 271–278.

de Bruin, E. J., Oort, F. J., Bögels, S. M., & Meijer, A. M. (2014). Efficacy of internet and group-administered cognitive behavioral therapy for insomnia in adolescents: A pilot study. *Behavioral Sleep Medicine, 12*(3), 235–254.

Deuschle, M., Schredl, M., Schilling, C., Wüst, S., Frank, J., Witt, S. H., ... Schulze, T. G. (2010). Association between a serotonin transporter length polymorphism and primary insomnia. *Sleep, 33*(3), 343–347.

Dinges, D. F., Pack, F., Williams, K., Gillen, K. A., Powell, J. W., Ott, G. E., ... Pack, A. I. (1997). Cumulative sleepiness, mood disturbance, and psychomotor vigilance performance decrements during a week of sleep restricted to 4–5 hours per night. *Sleep, 20*, 267–277.

Dinges, D. F., Rogers, N. L., & Baynard, M. D. (2005). Chronic sleep deprivation. In M. H. Kryger, T. Roth, & W. C. Dement (Eds.), *Principles and practice of*

sleep medicine (4th ed., pp. 67–76). Philadelphia, PA: Elsevier Saunders.

Drake, C. L., Scofield, H., & Roth, T. (2008). Vulnerability to insomnia: The role of familial aggregation. *Sleep Medicine, 9*(3), 297–302.

Edinger, J. D., Bonnet, M. H., Bootzin, R. R., Doghramji, K., Dorsey, C. M., Espie, C. A., ... American Academy of Sleep Medicine Work Group. (2004). Derivation of research diagnostic criteria for insomnia: Report of an American Academy of Sleep Medicine Work Group. *Sleep, 27*, 1567–1596.

Edinger, J. D., Wohlgemuth, W. K., Radtke, R. A., Marsh, G. R., & Quillian, R. E. (2001). Cognitive behavioral therapy for treatment of chronic primary insomnia: A randomized controlled trial. *JAMA, 285*, 1856–1864.

Espie, C. A. (2002). Insomnia: Conceptual issues in the development, persistence, and treatment of sleep disorder in adults. *Annual Review of Psychology, 53*, 215–243.

Espie, C. A., Broomfield, N. M., MacMahon, K. M., Macphee, L. M., & Taylor, L. M. (2006). The attention-intention-effort pathway in the development of psychophysiologic insomnia: A theoretical review. *Sleep Medicine Reviews, 10*, 215–245.

Espie, C. A., & Lindsay, W. R. (1985). Paradoxical intention in the treatment of chronic insomnia: Six case studies illustrating variability in therapeutic response. *Behaviour Research and Therapy, 23*, 703–709.

Ford, D. E., & Kamerow, D. B. (1989). Epidemiologic study of sleep disturbances and psychiatric disorders: An opportunity for prevention? *JAMA, 262*, 1479–1484.

Fortier-Brochu, É., Beaulieu-Bonneau, S., Ivers, H., & Morin, C. M. (2012). Insomnia and daytime cognitive performance: A meta-analysis. *Sleep Medicine Reviews, 16*(1), 83–94.

Freeman, D., Waite, F., Startup, H., Myers, E., Lister, R., McInerney, J., ... Yu, L.-M. (2015). Efficacy of cognitive behavioural therapy for sleep improvement in patients with persistent delusions and hallucinations (BEST): A prospective, assessor-blind, randomised controlled pilot trial. *Lancet Psychiatry, 2*(11), 975–983.

Germain, A., Shear, M. K., Hall, M., & Buysse, D. J. (2007). Effects of a brief behavioral treatment for PTSD-related sleep disturbances: A pilot study. *Behaviour Research and Therapy, 45*, 627–632.

Gordon, A. M., & Chen, S. (2013). The role of sleep in interpersonal conflict: Do sleepless nights mean worse fights? *Social Psychological & Personality Science, 5*(2), 168–175.

Gradisar, M., Dohnt, H., Gardner, G., Paine, S., Starkey, K., Menne, A., ... Trenowden, S. (2011). A randomized controlled trial of cognitive-behavior therapy plus bright light therapy for adolescent delayed sleep phase disorder. *Sleep, 34*(12), 1671–1680.

Gradisar, M., Gardner, G., & Dohnt, H. (2011). Recent worldwide sleep patterns and problems during adolescence: A review and meta-analysis of age, region, and sleep. *Sleep Medicine, 12*(2), 110–118.

Harvey, A. G. (2002). A cognitive model of insomnia. *Behaviour Research and Therapy, 40*, 869–894.

Harvey, A. G. (2005). A cognitive theory of and therapy for chronic insomnia. *Journal of Cognitive Psychotherapy, 19*, 41–60.

Harvey, A. G. (2008a). Insomnia, psychiatric disorders, and the transdiagnostic perspective. *Current Directions in Psychological Science, 17*, 299–303.

Harvey, A. G. (2008b). Sleep and circadian rhythms in bipolar disorder: Seeking synchrony, harmony, and regulation. *American Journal of Psychiatry, 165*, 820–829.

Harvey, A. G. (2011). Sleep and circadian functioning: Critical mechanisms in the mood disorders? *Annual Review of Clinical Psychology, 7*, 297–319.

Harvey, A. G. (2016). A transdiagnostic intervention for youth sleep and circadian problems. *Cognitive and Behavioral Practice, 23*(3), 341–355. doi: 10.1016/j.cbpra.2015.06.001

Harvey, A. G., Bélanger, L., Talbot, L., Eidelman, P., Beaulieu-Bonneau, S., Fortier-Brochu, É., ... Morin, C. M. (2014). Comparative efficacy of behavior therapy, cognitive therapy, and cognitive behavior therapy for chronic insomnia: A randomized controlled trial. *Journal of Consulting and Clinical Psychology, 82*(4), 670–683.

Harvey, A. G., Sharpley, A., Ree, M. J., Stinson, K., & Clark, D. M. (2007). An open trial of cognitive therapy for chronic insomnia. *Behaviour Research and Therapy, 45*, 2491–2501.

Harvey, A. G., Soehner, A. M., Kaplan, K. A., Hein, K., Lee, J., Kanady, J., ... Buysse, D. J. (2015). Treating insomnia improves mood state, sleep, and functioning in bipolar disorder: A pilot randomized controlled trial. *Journal of Consulting and Clinical Psychology, 83*(3), 564–577.

Harvey, A. G., & Tang, N.K.J. (2003). Cognitive behavior therapy for insomnia: Can we rest yet? *Sleep Medicine Reviews, 7*, 237–262.

Harvey, C. J., Gehrman, P., & Espie, C. A. (2014). Who is predisposed to insomnia: A review of familial aggregation, stress-reactivity, personality and coping style. *Sleep Medicine Reviews, 18*(3), 217–227.

Heath, A. C., Kendler, K. S., Eaves, L. J., & Martin, N. G. (1990). Evidence for genetic influences on sleep disturbance and sleep pattern in twins. *Sleep, 13*(4), 318–335.

Hebert, E. A., Vincent, N., Lewycky, S., & Walsh, K. (2010). Attrition and adherence in the online treatment of chronic insomnia. *Behavioral Sleep Medicine, 8*(3), 141–150.

Hoban, T. F. (2004). Sleep and its disorders in children. *Seminars in Neurology, 24*, 327–340.

Hoddes, E., Zarcone, V., Smythe, H., Phillips, R., & Dement, W. C. (1973). Quantification of sleepiness: A new approach. *Psychophysiology, 10*, 431–436.

Holbrook, A. M., Crowther, R., Lotter, A., Cheng, C., & King, D. (2000). The diagnosis and management of insomnia in clinical practice: A practical evidence-based approach. *Canadian Medical Association Journal, 162*, 216–220.

Jacobson, E. (1934). *Progressive relaxation.* Chicago, IL: University of Chicago Press.

Johnson, E. O., Roth, T., Schultz, L., & Breslau, N. (2006). Epidemiology of DSM-IV insomnia in adolescence: Lifetime prevalence, chronicity, and an emergent gender difference. *Pediatrics, 117*(2), e247–e256.

Kaplan, K. A., & Harvey, A. G. (2009). Hypersomnia across mood disorders: A review and synthesis. *Sleep Medicine Reviews, 13*, 275–285.

Kryger, M. H., Roth, T., & Dement, W. C. (Eds.). (2011). *Principles and practice of sleep medicine* (5th ed.). Philadelphia, PA: Elsevier Saunders.

Krystal, A. D. (2009). A compendium of placebo-controlled trials of the risks/benefits of pharmacological treatments for insomnia: The empirical basis for U.S. clinical practice. *Sleep Medicine Reviews, 13*, 265–274.

Krystal, A. D. (2011). Pharmacologic treatment: Other medications. In M. H. Kryger, T. Roth, & W. C. Dement (Eds.), *Principles and practice of sleep medicine* (5th ed., pp. 916–930). Philadelphia, PA: Elsevier Saunders.

Krystal, A. D., Walsh, J. K., Laska, E., Caron, J., Amato, D. A., Wessel, T., & Roth, T. (2003). Sustained efficacy of eszopiclone over 6 nights of nightly treatment: Results of a randomized, double-blind, placebo-controlled study in adults with chronic insomnia. *Sleep, 26,* 793–799.

Kupfer, D. J., & Reynolds, C. F., 3rd. (1997). Management of insomnia. *New England Journal of Medicine, 336,* 341–346.

Lack, L. C., & Bootzin, R. B. (2003). Circadian rhythm factors in insomnia and their treatment. In M. L. Perlis & K. L. Lichstein (Eds.), *Treating sleep disorders: Principles and practice of behavioral sleep medicine* (pp. 305–343). Hoboken, NJ: Wiley.

LeBlanc, M., Mérette, C., Savard, J., Ivers, H., Baillargeon, L., & Morin, C. M. (2009). Incidence and risk factors of insomnia in a population-based sample. *Sleep, 32*(8), 1027–1037.

Léger, D., Guilleminault, C., Bader, G., Lévy, E., & Paillard, M. (2002). Medical and socio-professional impact of insomnia. *Sleep, 25*(6), 625–629.

Léger, D., Morin, C. M., Uchiyama, M., Hakimi, Z., Cure, S., & Walsh, J. K. (2012). Chronic insomnia, quality-of-life, and utility scores: Comparison with good sleepers in a cross-sectional international survey. *Sleep Medicine, 13*(1), 43–51.

Lichstein, K. (2000). Secondary insomnia. In K. Lichstein & C. Morin (Eds.), *Treatment of late-life insomnia* (pp. 297–319). Thousand Oaks, CA: Sage.

Lichstein, K. L., Durrence, H. H., Taylor, D. J., Bush, A. J., & Riedel, B. W. (2003). Quantitative criteria for insomnia. *Behaviour Research and Therapy, 41,* 427–445.

Lichstein, K. L., & Riedel, B. W. (1994). Behavioral assessment and treatment of insomnia: A review with an emphasis on clinical application. *Behavior Therapy, 25,* 659–688.

Littner, M., Hirshkowitz, M., Kramer, M., Kapen, S., Anderson, W. M., Bailey, D., ... Standards of Practice Committee. (2003). Practice parameters for using polysomnography to evaluate insomnia: An update. *Sleep, 26*(6), 754–760.

Lundh, L.-G. (1998). Cognitive-behavioural analysis and treatment of insomnia. *Scandinavian Journal of Behaviour Therapy, 27,* 10–29.

Manber, R., Edinger, J. D., Gress, J. L., San Pedro-Salcedo, M. G., Kuo, T. F., & Kalista, T. (2008). Cognitive behavioral therapy for insomnia enhances depression outcome in patients with comorbid major depressive disorder and insomnia. *Sleep, 31,* 489–495.

Martin, S. A., Aikens, J. E., & Chervin, R. D. (2004). Toward cost-effectiveness analysis in the diagnosis and treatment of insomnia. *Sleep Medicine Reviews, 8,* 63–72.

Means, M. K., Lichstein, K. L., Epperson, M. T., & Johnson, C. T. (2000). Relaxation therapy for insomnia: Nighttime and daytime effects. *Behaviour Research and Therapy, 38,* 665–678.

Monroe, L. J. (1967). Psychological and physiological differences between good and poor sleepers. *Journal of Abnormal Psychology, 72,* 255–264.

Morgenthaler, T., Alessi, C., Friedman, L., Owens, J., Kapur, V., Boehlecke, B., ... American Academy of Sleep Medicine. (2007). Practice parameters for the use of actigraphy in the assessment of sleep and sleep disorders: An update for 2007. *Sleep, 30*(4), 519–529.

Morin, C. M. (1993). *Insomnia: Psychological assessment and management.* New York, NY: Guilford Press.

Morin, C. M., Bélanger, L., LeBlanc, M., Ivers, H., Savard, J., Espie, C. A., ... Grégoire, J.-P. (2009). The natural history of insomnia. *Archives of Internal Medicine, 169*(5), 447.

Morin, C. M., Bootzin, R. R., Buysse, D. J., Edinger, J. D., Espie, C. A., & Lichstein, K. L. (2006). Psychological and behavioral treatment of insomnia: An update of recent evidence (1998–2004). *Sleep, 29,* 1396–1406.

Morin, C. M., Colecchi, C., Stone, J., Sood, R., & Brink, D. (1999). Behavioral and pharmacological therapies for late-life insomnia. *JAMA, 281,* 991–999.

Morin, C. M., & Culbert, P. (1994). Nonpharmacological interventions for insomnia: A meta-analysis of treatment efficacy. *American Journal of Psychiatry, 151*(8), 1172–1180.

Morin, C. M., Culbert, J. P., & Schwartz, S. M. (1994). Nonpharmacological interventions for insomnia: A meta-analysis of treatment efficacy. *American Journal of Psychiatry, 151,* 1172–1180.

Morin, C. M., Drake, C., Harvey, A. G., Krystal, A. D., Manber, R., Riemann, D., & Spiegelhalder, K. (2015). Insomnia disorder. *Nature Reviews Disease Primers.* doi: 10.1038/nrdp.2015.26

Morin, C. M., & Espie, C. A. (2003). *Insomnia: A clinical guide to assessment and treatment.* New York, NY: Kluwer Academic/Plenum Publishers.

Morin, C. M., Hauri, P. J., Espie, C. A., Spielman, A. J., Buysse, D. J., & Bootzin, R. R. (1999). Non-pharmacologic treatment of chronic insomnia: An

American Academy of Sleep Medicine review. *Sleep*, *22*, 1134–1156.

Morin, C. M., LeBlanc, M., Daley, M., Gregoire, J. P., & Mérette, C. (2006). Epidemiology of insomnia: Prevalence, self-help treatments, consultations, and determinants of help-seeking behaviors. *Sleep Medicine*, *7*(2), 123–130.

Morin, C. M., Rodrigue, S., & Ivers, H. (2003). Role of stress, arousal, and coping skills in primary insomnia. *Psychosomatic Medicine*, *65*, 259–267.

Morphy, H., Dunn, K. M., Lewis, M., Boardman, H. F., & Croft, P. R. (2007). Epidemiology of insomnia: A longitudinal study in a UK population. *Sleep*, *30*(3), 274–280.

Murtagh, D.R.R., & Greenwood, K. M. (1995). Identifying effective psychological treatments for insomnia: A meta-analysis. *Journal of Consulting and Clinical Psychology*, *63*(1), 79–89.

National Institutes of Health. (2005). National Institutes of Health State of the Science Conference statement on manifestations and management of chronic insomnia in adults, June 13–15, 2005. *Sleep*, *28*, 1049–1057.

Neitzert Semler, C., & Harvey, A. G. (2005). Misperception of sleep can adversely affect daytime functioning in insomnia. *Behaviour Research and Therapy*, *43*, 843–856.

Nowell, P. D., Mazumdar, S., Buysse, D. J., Dew, M. A., Reynolds, C. F., 3rd, & Kupfer, D. J. (1997). Benzodiazepines and zolpidem for chronic insomnia: A meta-analysis of treatment efficacy. *JAMA*, *278*, 2170–2177.

Ohayon, M. M., Carskadon, M. A, Guilleminault, C., & Vitiello, M. V. (2004). Meta-analysis of quantitative sleep parameters from childhood to old age in healthy individuals: Developing normative sleep values across the human lifespan. *Sleep*, *27*(7), 1255–1273.

Ohayon, M. M., & Reynolds, C. F. (2009). Epidemiological and clinical relevance of insomnia diagnosis algorithms according to the DSM-IV and the International Classification of Sleep Disorders (ICSD). *Sleep Medicine*, *10*(9), 952–960.

Owens, J. L., France, K. G., & Wiggs, L. (1999). Behavioural and cognitive-behavioural interventions for sleep disorders in infants and children: A review. *Sleep Medicine Reviews*, *3*, 281–302.

Paine, S., & Gradisar, M. (2011). A randomised controlled trial of cognitive-behaviour therapy for behavioural insomnia of childhood in school-aged children. *Behaviour Research and Therapy*, *49*(6–7), 379–388.

Perlis, M. L., Giles, D. E., Mendelson, W. B., Bootzin, R. R., & Wyatt, J. K. (1997). Psychophysiological insomnia: The behavioural model and a neurocognitive perspective. *Journal of Sleep Research*, *6*, 179–188.

Perlis, M. L., & Lichstein, K. L. (Eds.). (2003). *Treating sleep disorders: Principles and practice of behavioral sleep medicine*. Hoboken, NJ: Wiley.

Perlis, M. L., McCall, W. V., Krystal, A. D., & Walsh, J. K. (2004). Long-term, non-nightly administration of zolpidem in the treatment of patients with primary insomnia. *Journal of Clinical Psychiatry*, *65*, 1128–1137.

Perlis, M. L., Merica, H., Smith, M. T., & Giles, D. E. (2001). Beta EEG activity and insomnia. *Sleep Medicine Reviews*, *5*, 363–374.

Perlis, M. L., Smith, M. T., & Pigeon, W. R. (2005). Etiology and pathophysiology of insomnia. In M. H. Kryger, T. Roth, & W. C. Dement (Eds.), *Principles and practice of sleep medicine* (4th ed., pp. 714–725). Philadelphia, PA: Elsevier Saunders.

Pilcher, J. J., & Huffcutt, A. I. (1996). Effects of sleep deprivation on performance: A meta-analysis. *Sleep*, *19*, 318–326.

Pillai, V., Roth, T., & Drake, C. L. (2015). The nature of stable insomnia phenotypes. *Sleep*, *38*(1), 127–138.

Reynolds, C. F., & Redline, S. (2010). The DSM-V sleep-wake disorders nosology: An update and an invitation to the sleep community. *Sleep*, *33*, 10–11.

Roberts, R. E., Roberts, C. R., & Chen, I. G. (2001). Functioning of adolescents with symptoms of disturbed sleep. *Journal of Youth and Adolescence*, *30*, 1–18.

Roth, T., Coulouvrat, C., Hajak, G., Lakoma, M. D., Sampson, N. A., Shahly, V., … Kessler, R. C. (2011). Prevalence and perceived health associated with insomnia based on DSM-IV-TR; International Statistical Classification of Diseases and Related Health Problems, Tenth Revision; and Research Diagnostic Criteria/International Classification of Sleep Disorders, Second Edition criteria: Results from the America Insomnia Survey. *Biological Psychiatry*, *69*(6), 592–600.

Rybarczyk, B., Lopez, M., Schelble, K., & Stepanski, E. (2005). Home-based video CBT for comorbid geriatric insomnia: A pilot study using secondary data analyses. *Behavioral Sleep Medicine*, *3*, 158–175.

Sadeh, A. (2005). Cognitive-behavioral treatment for childhood sleep disorders. *Clinical Psychology Review, 25,* 612–628.

Schlarb, A. A., Liddle, C. C., & Hautzinger, M. (2010). A multimodal program for treatment of insomnia in adolescents: A pilot study. *Nature and Science of Sleep, 3,* 13.

Sivertsen, B., Omvik, S., Pallesen, S., Bjorvatn, B., Havik, O. E., Kvale, G., ... Nordhus, I. H. (2006). Cognitive behavioral therapy vs zopiclone for treatment of chronic primary insomnia in older adults: A randomized controlled trial. *JAMA, 295,* 2851–?

Sloan, E. P., Hauri, P., Bootzin, R., ... Stevenson, M., & Shapiro, C. M. ... and bolts of behavioral therapy fo... *of Psychosomatic Research, 37,* ...

Smith, L. J., Nowakowski, S., ... H. J., & Perlis, M. L. (200...) of sleep. In M. L. Perlis & ... *Treating sleep disorders: Pri... ...ctice of behavioral sleep medicine* (pp. ...) Hoboken, NJ: Wiley.

Smith, M. T., Huang, M. I., & Manber, R. (2005). Cognitive behavior therapy for chronic insomnia occurring within the context of medical and psychiatric disorders. *Clinical Psychology Review, 25,* 559–592.

Smith, M. T., Perlis, M. L., Park, A., Smith, M. S., Pennington, J., Giles, D. E., & Buysse, D. J. (2002). Comparative meta-analysis of pharmacotherapy and behavior therapy for persistent insomnia. *American Journal of Psychiatry, 159*(1), 5–11.

Spielman, A. J., Caruso, L. S., & Glovinsky, P. B. (1987). A behavioral perspective on insomnia treatment. *Psychiatric Clinics of North America, 10,* 541–553.

Spielman, A. J., Saskin, P., & Thorpy, M. J. (1987). Treatment of chronic insomnia by restriction of time in bed. *Sleep, 10,* 45–56.

Stepanski, E. J., Zorick, F., Roehrs, T., & Roth, T. (2000). Effects of sleep deprivation on daytime sleepiness in primary insomnia. *Sleep, 23,* 215–219.

Talbot, L. S., Hairston, I. S., Eidelman, P., Gruber, J., & Harvey, A. G. (2009). The effect of mood on sleep onset latency and REM sleep in interepisode bipolar disorder. *Journal of Abnormal Psychology, 118*(3), 448–458.

Talbot, L. S., Stone, S., Gruber, J., Hairston, I. S., Eidelman, P., & Harvey, A. G. (2012). A test of the bidirectional association between sleep and mood in bipolar disorder and insomnia. *Journal of Abnormal Psychology, 121*(1), 39–50.

Tate, B. A., Richardson, G. S., & Carskadon, M. A. (2002). Maturational changes in sleep-wake timing: Longitudinal studies of the circadian activity rhythm ... diurnal rodent. In M. A. Carskadon (Ed.), *Ado... ...ep patterns: Biological, social, and psy- ...uences* (pp. 40–49). New York, NY: ...sity Press.

...oles, T. F., Hall, M., & Buysse, D. J. ...arital quality and the marital bed: Examin- ...he covariation between relationship quality and ...leep. *Sleep Medicine Reviews, 11*(5), 389–404.

...iola, A. U., Archer, S. N., James, L. M., Groeger, J. A., Lo, J.C.Y., Skene, D. J., ... Dijk, D. J. (2007). PER3 polymorphism predicts sleep structure and waking performance. *Current Biology, 17*(7), 613–618.

Walker, M. P. (2011). The role of sleep in neurocognitive function. In C. M. Morin & C. A. Espie (Eds.), *The Oxford handbook of sleep and sleep disorders* (pp. 110–130). New York, NY: Oxford University Press.

Walker, M. P., & Stickgold, R. (2006). Sleep, memory, and plasticity. *Annual Review of Psychology, 57,* 139–166.

Walsh, J. K., & Roth, T. (2011). Pharmacological treatment of insomnia: Benzodiazepine receptor agonists. In M. H. Kryger, T. Roth, & W. C. Dement (Eds.), *Principles and practice of sleep medicine* (5th ed., pp. 905–915). Saint Louis, MO: Elsevier Saunders.

Watson, N. F., Goldberg, J., Arguelles, L., & Buchwald, D. (2006). Genetic and environmental influences on insomnia, daytime sleepiness, and obesity in twins. *Sleep, 29*(5), 645–649.

Zee, P. C., & Turek, F. W. (2006). Sleep and health: Everywhere and in both directions. *Archives of Internal Medicine, 166,* 1686–1688.

Zhang, B., & Wing, Y.-K. (2006). Sex differences in insomnia: A meta-analysis. *Sleep, 29*(1), 85–93.

Chapter 10

Schizophrenia and the Psychosis Spectrum

ARTHUR T. RYAN, HANAN D. TROTMAN, VIJAY A. MITTAL,
KEVIN D. TESSNER, AND ELAINE F. WALKER

I can't find the words to describe it. Schizophrenia is like a disconnect. My thoughts and my feelings are not connected. I'm not connected with other people. I don't understand them and they don't understand me. It is like life is just passing me by, and it is out of my control. My mind is out of my control and it is frightening.

—Schizophrenia patient

The preceding words are from a man in his 40s who was diagnosed with schizophrenia during his 20s. *Schizophrenia* is a brain disorder whose symptoms typically show up by young adulthood and continue as a chronic condition, albeit waxing and waning over time. It has affected nearly every aspect of this man's life, including making friends, getting married, and holding down a job. This chapter will attempt to explain how this complex and often misunderstood illness can have such pervasive effects upon those who suffer from it.

Schizophrenia falls into the broader category of psychotic disorders. The defining symptoms of psychotic disorders involve a disconnect from reality. Psychotic symptoms include hallucinations (perceiving things that aren't there), delusions (strange fixed beliefs that are not amenable to change despite exposure to contradictory evidence), disorganized and illogical thinking, and bizarre behavior. Schizophrenia is probably the disorder most closely associated with psychotic symptoms in the minds of clinicians and the general public alike. Other psychotic disorders include bipolar I disorder, major depressive disorder with psychotic features, and delusional disorder. As this chapter will go on to explain, however, schizophrenia's psychotic symptoms are just one component of this complex and often misunderstood disease.

Symptoms and Diagnostic Criteria

The modern conceptualization of schizophrenia divides its symptoms into three major categories. The names of some of these categories may be confusing at first, but once one understands the underlying logic, the categories can help to sensibly organize schizophrenia's wide array of symptoms. The three categories are positive symptoms, negative symptoms, and cognitive symptoms.

Positive symptoms are the defining feature of psychotic disorders. Positive symptoms are the set of symptoms typically referred to as *psychotic* symptoms: that is, those symptoms that involve a clear break with reality. As noted, these symptoms may occur within the context of schizophrenia or other *psychotic disorders*, or they may be triggered by other causes, such as heavy metal poisoning. The term *positive symptoms* is used because these symptoms add on to regular, everyday experience: in other words, they are experiences that individuals with psychotic symptoms have that most other people do not experience in their day-to-day lives. Hallucinations are one kind of positive symptom: they are perceptual experiences that occur without an external stimulus. Some examples of hallucinations are hearing voices when no one is speaking, seeing shadowy figures, and smelling gasoline when none is present. Individuals who do not have schizophrenia or any other illness do occasionally experience hallucinations (Tien, 1991). However, individuals with schizophrenia who experience hallucinations often have delusional beliefs associated with those hallucinations (e.g., they believe they hear voices because a radio has been surgically implanted into their brain), which is generally not true of hallucinations experienced by people without psychotic illness (e.g., they hear the footsteps of a deceased loved one coming in the door, and they believe their mind is playing tricks on them). The most common hallucinations in schizophrenia are auditory hallucinations, but hallucinations can occur in all other sensory modalities (visual, tactile, olfactory, and gustatory; Behrendt & Young, 2004).

Delusions are another kind of positive symptom. They are fixed false beliefs that are not common in an individual's cultural milieu and are not amenable to change even when confronted with conflicting evidence. Delusions can take a wide variety of forms. One particularly common type of delusion is a paranoid delusion. Paranoid delusions involve a belief that one or more people are trying to harm the individual even though there is no evidence to support that belief. For example, a person may start to believe that her husband of many years is trying to poison her. Or, as occurred in the case of Nobel Prize–winning mathematician John Nash, an individual may believe that a huge conspiracy has been organized against him and may start to see everyday events as being tied into this conspiracy (e.g., someone's coughing at a bus stop is interpreted as a secret signal being communicated to other agents in the area). As one might imagine, paranoid delusions can wreak terrible damage upon a person's social life and his or her ability to function in the workplace.

Paranoid delusions are by no means the only kind of delusions that occur in schizophrenia. Other common delusions include those of thought insertion (e.g., people are inserting thoughts into my head), thought broadcasting (e.g., people can hear my thoughts), grandiose delusions (e.g., I am a particularly famous person, possibly even a historical or fictional character such as Napoleon or Superman), control delusions (e.g., my body and actions are controlled by an external force), and bizarre delusions (delusions that are patently absurd; e.g., my stomach has been replaced with a swimming pool). It is important to keep the distinction between hallucinations and delusions clear. Delusions are false beliefs, whereas hallucinations are false perceptual experiences that may or may not be accompanied by false beliefs. So, on the one hand, if someone interprets a man's coughing as a secret message, that is a delusion: the man really is coughing, it is just the individual's beliefs about the coughing that are atypical. On the other hand, if someone hears a voice in her head that she interprets as hearing another person's thoughts, that is a hallucination with an associated delusional belief.

Disorganized thoughts and behavior are another kind of positive symptom. Disorganized thinking is often diagnosed on the basis of disorganized speech. Elyn Saks, a University of Southern California law professor, writes movingly of her experience with schizophrenia in *The Center Cannot Hold* (2008). Professor Saks gives examples of her own disorganized speech and thought throughout the book. In response to her doctor asking if anything was wrong with her, Saks responded: "There's cheese and there's whizzes, I'm a cheese whiz. It has to do with effort and subliminal choice. Vertigo and killing" (Saks, 2008, p. 191). Later, after her doctor said that Saks's friends were worried about her, Saks responded: "Oh, they're nice. Do you like spice? I ate it thrice. They're all hurting me! They're hurting me and I'm scared!" (Saks, 2008, p. 191). As one can see, the individual sentences may be grammatical and even seemingly relevant to the topic at hand, but they are also often nonsensical or contradictory.

Disorganized behavior involves behavior that is disconnected from the physical reality around the person and seems random or dangerous. Returning to Saks again, she describes how she stood up and announced, "Let's go out on the roof!" in the middle of a study session at the Yale Law School library, and she promptly did just that without any clear reason for doing so (Saks, 2008, p. 1). Disorganized behavior may sometimes be driven by underlying delusions (e.g., an individual might say "let's go out on the roof" because he believes that CIA agents are in pursuit), but sometimes disorganized behavior has no clear rationale, delusional or otherwise.

Catatonia refers to a subset of disorganized behaviors that have been classified into a distinct subcategory because they appear to be linked in their presentation and neural underpinnings (Taylor & Fink, 2003). Similar to other disorganized behavior, catatonia involves behavior that is not a response to what is happening in a person's environment: this behavior may take the form of immobility (e.g., waxy flexibility, where individuals with catatonia maintain whatever body position they are left in), or purposeless, repetitive behavior (e.g., repeating the same pattern of facial expressions over and over). While historically associated with schizophrenia, catatonic symptoms can be present in a wide variety of psychotic disorders.

In contrast to positive symptoms, *negative symptoms* involve the diminution of a part of the normal psychological experience that most people have (Kirkpatrick, Fenton, Carpenter, & Marder, 2006). The following are some specific examples of negative symptoms. Reduced emotional experience is the reduced ability to imagine or experience emotional extremes. Avolition is a decrease in motivated, self-directed behavior: individuals may no longer seek out opportunities to engage with other people, may refrain from tasks they used to enjoy, and may even spend significant amounts of time sitting around doing nothing in particular. Alogia is a decreased amount of speech output. Diminished emotional expressiveness is a decreased production of facial expressions associated with emotions. Anhedonia is a decrease in the ability to experience pleasurable sensations or imagine experiencing pleasure in response to remembered situations (Gard, Kring, Gard, Horan, & Green, 2007). When one examines the wide variety of negative symptoms that exist, it is apparent that they can affect nearly every aspect of a person's life: engaging in meaningful work, socializing with others, and experiencing pleasure and satisfaction in those activities. Unsurprisingly then, the severity of negative symptoms has been found to predict poor functioning even more strongly than the severity of positive symptoms (Strauss et al., 2013).

The third set of symptoms associated with schizophrenia are perhaps the most subtle but nonetheless may be the most impairing: these are the *cognitive symptoms*. People with schizophrenia can have a wide variety of problems with attention (Nuechterlein, Luck, Lustig, & Sarter, 2009). They can have difficulty ignoring distractors in the environment (e.g., focusing on a conversation in a noisy room), persisting in a task that requires extended attention (e.g., reading a paragraph without drifting off into thoughts about something else), and inhibiting automatic behavior (e.g., stopping themselves from pressing the gas pedal when the light turns green when another car is still in the intersection). Individuals with schizophrenia also have difficulty with performing simple mental tasks quickly (e.g., sorting mail by last name). They often have impaired working memory (e.g., difficulty doing mental math) as well as longer-term verbal memory (e.g., difficulty remembering a list of grocery items while shopping). People with schizophrenia also show difficulties in social cognition: that is, thinking specifically related to social information (e.g., identifying facial expressions). As one can tell from even this brief synopsis of cognitive impairments in schizophrenia, cognitive symptoms affect nearly every aspect of domestic, occupational, academic, and social life. While not as obvious as paranoid delusions or a lack of facial expressions, the pervasiveness of cognitive symptoms means that deficits in this area are often the best predictors of whether or not someone with schizophrenia will be able to function well in everyday life (Bowie, Reichenberg, Patterson, Heaton, & Harvey, 2006).

In day-to-day living with schizophrenia, symptoms from these different categories can overlap and reinforce one another. For example, someone with schizophrenia might no longer spend time with her friends because she is afraid they are plotting against her (positive symptom), because she can't imagine having a good time if she did hang out with them (negative symptom), and because when she does hang out with them, she finds it difficult to follow their conversation (cognitive symptom). Nonetheless, this division of schizophrenia symptoms into categories is useful because symptoms within each of the three categories do tend to have some important similarities (e.g., how responsive they are to medication and when they first appear in the course of the illness).

It is also worth noting that individuals with schizophrenia often suffer from a variety of other diagnosable mental disorders, both before and after the onset of schizophrenia (Buckley, Miller, Lehrer, & Castle, 2009). Individuals with schizophrenia are more likely to suffer from depression, anxiety, obsessive-compulsive, and neurodevelopmental and learning disorders than people in the general population. The rate of substance use disorders among individuals with schizophrenia is particularly high; as many as 47% of individuals with schizophrenia meet lifetime *DSM* criteria for a substance use disorder

(Buckley et al., 2009). These disorders add to the already heavy burden of schizophrenia itself.

The symptoms of schizophrenia do not generally stay at a constant intensity across the entire lifespan of an individual with schizophrenia. Positive symptoms in particular often come in waves, sometimes referred to as psychotic episodes, that wax and wane over an individual's life (Andreasen et al., 2005). This fluctuating intensity of positive symptoms is present even among individuals who never take medications to treat their positive symptoms, suggesting that the fluctuations are not simply due to individuals taking and then not taking their medications over time. Positive symptoms can fluctuate even in individuals who take their medication regularly, sometimes necessitating dosage adjustments or temporary hospitalizations for individuals whose symptoms were previously well controlled by the exact same dose of medication. In the long run, positive symptoms often, though not always, decline in severity as an individual ages. The mathematician John Nash provides a good example of this. Nash suffered from uncontrolled positive symptoms of schizophrenia until they slowly remitted when he was in his sixties (Nasar, 2011). In contrast to positive symptoms, negative symptoms and cognitive symptoms tend to be more stable, both in the short run and over a person's lifespan (Harvey, Koren, Reichenberg, & Bowie, 2006).

HOW TO DIFFERENTIATE SYMPTOMS OF SCHIZOPHRENIA FROM SYMPTOMS OF OTHER PSYCHOTIC DISORDERS

One way to better understand schizophrenia and other psychotic disorders is to learn about the process of making a differential diagnosis between schizophrenia and other psychotic disorders. Recall that positive symptoms (e.g., hallucinations) can occur in bipolar I disorder and other psychotic disorders, so the presence of positive symptoms itself does not differentiate between schizophrenia and other psychotic disorders. Furthermore, the presence of depression or manic symptoms cannot be used to rule out the diagnosis of schizophrenia, as the majority of people with schizophrenia will have at least one major mood episode during their lifetime (Buckley et al., 2009). The negative and cognitive symptoms of schizophrenia also often mimic the symptoms of a mood episode, further complicating the distinction. So how does one make the distinction between schizophrenia and other psychotic disorders? This chapter will now explore this issue, using the symptom criteria laid out in the fifth edition of the *Diagnostic and Statistical Manual of Mental Disorders* (*DSM-5*) as a guide (American Psychiatric Association, 2013).

Let us start with differentiating between schizophrenia and bipolar I disorder. First, to be diagnosed with bipolar I disorder, an individual has to have had at least one manic episode. So if there is no evidence of a manic episode, that eliminates the possibility of bipolar I disorder. Second, psychotic symptoms in bipolar disorder occur nearly exclusively during mood episodes, that is, during diagnosable manic or depressive episodes. So if psychotic symptoms occur predominantly outside of mood episodes, then the person does not have bipolar I disorder. The logic is similar when diagnosing someone with major depressive disorder with psychotic features: the psychotic symptoms should only occur during major depressive episodes. So if someone has psychotic symptoms frequently outside of major depressive or manic episodes, can one definitively diagnose that individual with schizophrenia? Not quite yet. There is a third potential diagnosis that lies between schizophrenia and mood disorders with psychotic features: schizoaffective disorder. To be diagnosed with schizoaffective disorder, an individual needs to (a) have had distinct mood episodes that included psychotic symptoms, (b) have had psychotic symptoms that occurred for 2 weeks or longer *outside* of mood episodes, and (c) have experienced mood episodes during a majority of the time since the onset of the disorder. Essentially then, schizoaffective disorder is differentiated from schizophrenia by the existence of prominent mood episodes that occur for the majority of the illness. It is differentiated from bipolar I disorder and major depressive disorder with psychotic features by the requirement of having 2 weeks or longer of psychotic symptoms outside of a mood episode.

As one might imagine, these diagnostic distinctions can be difficult to make in clinical and even research settings and often require making educated guesses for any particular individual. This overlap probably reflects that (a) schizophrenia is not one disease with a single underlying cause, and (b) schizophrenia, schizoaffective disorder, bipolar I disorder, and major depressive disorder with psychotic features are not unique or completely independent disorders that can be perfectly separated from one another (O'Donovan, Craddock, & Owen, 2009). However, the diagnostic distinctions are still important to make as useful clinical information can nonetheless be derived from even imperfect diagnostic distinctions; for example, psychotic symptoms in bipolar I disorder often respond to lithium while those in schizophrenia generally do not (Zemlan, Hirschowitz, Sautter, & Garver, 1984).

Accurate schizophrenia diagnosis also requires distinguishing between other *schizophrenia spectrum* disorders and miscellaneous mental disorders with psychotic features. *Schizotypal personality disorder, paranoid personality disorder*, and *schizoid personality disorder* can be roughly thought of as attenuated versions of schizophrenia with emphases on different symptom clusters (positive symptoms, paranoia, and negative/cognitive symptoms, respectively). In fact, the symptom criteria for schizotypal personality disorder were initially developed by researchers who interviewed family members of individuals with schizophrenia (Spitzer, Endicott, & Gibbon, 1979). These family members tended to have attenuated versions of the symptoms of schizophrenia. Schizotypal, paranoid, and schizoid personality disorders are often grouped together under the label "Cluster A personality disorders," as they tend to occur together at higher rates in families, especially in families of individuals with schizophrenia (Erlenmeyer-Kimling et al., 1995). A key way to distinguish between schizophrenia and Cluster A personality disorders is that individuals with schizophrenia have had full-blown psychotic symptoms during at least some portion of their illness. In contrast, positive symptoms in Cluster A personality disorders tend not to rise to the severity of full-blown delusions or hallucinations. For example, someone with paranoid personality disorder may chronically doubt the faithfulness of his romantic partners without any rational evidence of their infidelity, but he would not believe that all of his romantic partners are secretly CIA agents who plan to assassinate him. The diagnostic distinction between schizophrenia and Cluster A personality disorders is important to make because Cluster A personality disorders are associated with less impairment than schizophrenia (Siever & Davis, 2004) and have different recommended treatments.

Delusional disorder is yet another form of psychotic disorder. Delusional disorder's psychotic symptoms are usually restricted to one or more delusions, in contrast to the often multiple psychotic symptoms that occur in schizophrenia. Delusional disorder's delusions are occasionally accompanied by nonprominent hallucinations relevant to the delusions (e.g., an individual who has the delusion that a microchip has been installed under her skin may have the tactile hallucination of feeling the microchip moving underneath her skin). Individuals with delusional disorder tend to be less functionally impaired than individuals with schizophrenia (Marneros, Pillmann, & Wustmann, 2012), and the disease tends to occur much later in life: for example, when individuals are in their 50s (Wustmann, Pillmann, & Marneros, 2011).

Brief psychotic disorder differs from schizophrenia in that the psychotic symptoms occur for only a brief time (i.e., less than 1 month), resolve on their own, and once they resolve, the individual returns to a normal level of functioning. This diagnostic distinction is important to make because the prognoses of schizophrenia and brief psychotic disorder are (almost by definition) quite different (Pillmann, Haring, Balzuweit, Blöink, & Marneros, 2002). *Schizophreniform disorder* lies somewhere between brief psychotic disorder and schizophrenia. Schizophreniform disorder is only diagnosed when a person has had symptoms of schizophrenia that have lasted at least 1 month but no longer than 6 months. If all symptoms (including residual symptoms) spontaneously resolve within 6 months, the individual will never be diagnosed with schizophrenia and will simply have a history of schizophreniform disorder. If the symptoms persist beyond 6 months, then the schizophreniform diagnosis is changed to a schizophrenia diagnosis. As with brief psychotic disorder, one of the main reasons that schizophreniform disorder exists as a diagnosis is that it is associated with a significantly better prognosis than that of schizophrenia (Mojtabai, Susser, & Bromet, 2003). As one might expect, however, researchers have found a variety of biological and clinic similarities between schizophrenia, brief psychotic disorder, schizophreniform disorder, schizoaffective disorder, Cluster A personality disorders, and delusional disorder: thus the term *schizophrenia spectrum disorders* (Siever & Davis, 2004).

A few other mental disorders can feature psychotic symptoms and are worth reviewing before this chapter moves on to other topics. Substance- or medication-induced psychotic disorder and psychotic disorder due to another medical condition are differentiated from schizophrenia because their psychotic symptoms have an identifiable organic cause. This distinction is important to make because the psychotic symptoms in these conditions can sometimes be alleviated by eliminating the psychosis-inducing substance or by treating the underlying organic problem (Pego-Reigosa & Isenberg, 2008). For example, in steroid-induced psychosis, the patient's medication dose can be lowered to alleviate the symptoms (Ross & Cetas, 2012).

Several other mental disorders in the *DSM* can include delusional beliefs. Obsessive-compulsive disorder (OCD) can be associated with delusional beliefs related to obsessions or compulsions (O'Dwyer & Marks, 2000). For example, an individual with OCD might have the delusion that she will die of an infection if she does not wash her hands 15 times a day despite repeated assurances by physicians that she will not. Body dysmorphic disorder, which is categorized as an obsessive-compulsive related disorder, can be associated with delusional beliefs about the person's body that result in severe impairment (Phillips, Menard, & Fay, 2006). For example, a 6-foot-tall male individual may be so convinced that he is grotesquely short that he withdraws from school so that others will not see him and seeks out dangerous surgery to increase his height. Anorexia nervosa can also include delusional beliefs about whether the individual is of normal weight:

these delusional beliefs can eventually lead to death through starvation (Steinglass, Eisen, Attia, Mayer, & Walsh, 2007). Neurocognitive disorders, including Alzheimer's disease, frontotemporal dementia, and Lewy body dementia, can also present with prominent psychotic symptoms (Ballard et al., 1995). Because of this, it is especially important to rule out neurocognitive disorders when an elderly individual reports experiencing psychotic symptoms for the first time later in life (McKeith et al., 2005). As can be seen from this review, psychotic symptoms are not unique to schizophrenia or mood disorders with psychotic features. Instead, schizophrenia is a disorder that shares some similarities with other psychotic disorders, yet also has unique clinical and biological features.

Signs and Symptoms That Precede the Onset of Schizophrenia

Many diseases are preceded by an identifiable set of signs or symptoms that occur before the cardinal symptoms necessary to diagnose the condition appear. These preceding symptoms are known as the disease's *prodrome*, from the Greek *pro-* ("before") and *dromos* ("running"). For example, months or years before developing the cardinal motor symptoms of Parkinson's disease, individuals may experience anosmia (i.e., loss of the sense of smell), depression, and sleepwalking (Postuma et al., 2012). Studying these prodromal symptoms can give researchers clues to what causes a disease and perhaps eventually help them to detect the disease before its symptoms fully manifest.

Schizophrenia and other psychotic disorders are often preceded by identifiable prodromal symptoms. These include subclinical positive symptoms (e.g., increased suspiciousness), negative symptoms (e.g., mild anhedonia), cognitive problems (e.g., increased difficulty with attention), and problems with functioning (e.g., decreased academic performance; Lencz, Smith, Auther, Correll, & Cornblatt, 2004). The psychosis prodrome is usually first apparent in adolescence and can last anywhere from a few weeks to several years. Researchers are now attempting to predict the development of schizophrenia by finding out which prodromal symptoms reliably precede the illness. This chapter will describe research into the psychosis prodrome in a later section.

Illness Course and Prognosis

Schizophrenia is usually first diagnosed when individuals are between 20 and 29 years old, striking just when young adults are starting the key tasks of building their independent lives (DeLisi, 1992). Critical developmental milestones of gaining independence from parents, developing romantic relationships, pursuing educational goals, and starting a career are often disrupted at this critical stage. Only 20% to 30% of individuals with schizophrenia are able to live independently and/or maintain a job (Grebb & Cancro, 1989). Another 20% to 30% of individuals with schizophrenia have persistent moderate symptoms and impairment, while the remaining 50% experience severe impairment for the remainder of their lives. A 15-year study of individuals with schizophrenia found that only about 40% had one or more periods of recovery (Harrow, Grossman, Jobe, & Herbener, 2005). Overall, individuals with schizophrenia have poorer clinical and functional prognoses than individuals with other psychotic and most nonpsychotic mental disorders.

Several factors have been established as valid predictors of better or worse outcomes for individuals diagnosed with schizophrenia. Individuals with an acute onset of positive symptoms have a better prognosis than those with an insidious (gradual) onset of positive symptoms (Davidson & McGlashan, 1997). There is some evidence that the longer psychotic symptoms go without treatment, the worse the prognosis (Harris et al., 2005). Being male and having an early age of onset, poor premorbid functioning, more severe negative symptoms negative symptoms, and a family history of schizophrenia are all associated with a poorer prognosis (Breier, Schreiber, Dyer, & Pickar, 1991). In addition, some environmental factors seem to contribute to a worse prognosis. Individuals with schizophrenia who live in homes where family members express high levels of criticism, hostility, or emotional overinvolvement are more likely to relapse (Rosenfarb, Bellack, & Aziz, 2006). Similarly, exposure to psychosocial stressors (e.g., the death of a parent) has been found to exacerbate schizophrenia symptoms (Horan et al., 2005).

Prevalence and Epidemiological Factors

Schizophrenia appears to be a universal human scourge. While research has shown some interesting variations in the prevalence of schizophrenia in different subpopulations, the broad fact remains that schizophrenia's lifetime prevalence is between 0.5% and 1% across markedly different cultures, nations, and times (Saha, Chant, Welham, & McGrath, 2005).

More recently, there is evidence to suggest that the use of certain recreational drugs can be a risk factor for developing schizophrenia. To the surprise of many scientists—as well as the general public—there is evidence that marijuana use, especially chronic use, can contribute to risk for psychosis (Moore et al., 2007). Both retrospective and prospective studies support this relationship. Although the mechanisms involved are not yet known, there is reason to suspect that the principal active ingredient of cannabis—D-9-tetrahydrocannabinol (D-9-THC)—increases risk for psychosis by augmenting dopamine neurotransmission and stress hormone release (D'Souza et al., 2005).

On average, individuals with schizophrenia die about 15 years earlier than individuals without the disorder (Healy et al., 2012). This increased mortality is probably due to several factors, including chronic health conditions such as heart disease and poorly controlled diabetes. Increased rates of suicide also partly explain this increased mortality. It has been estimated that 25% to 50% of individuals with schizophrenia attempt suicide and 4% to 13% die by suicide (Meltzer, 2001). For comparison, about 4% of the general U.S. population attempts suicide (Weissman et al., 1999) and about 1.5% of all deaths are due to suicide (Xu, Murphy, Kochanek, & Bastian, 2016). Risk factors associated with suicide in individuals with schizophrenia include having more severe depressive symptoms, being male, engaging in substance abuse, having an earlier age of onset, and suffering recent traumatic events (Gómez-Durán, Martin-Fumadó, & Hurtado-Ruíz, 2012). Clearly then, schizophrenia is a health crisis not only because of the chaos and suffering it wreaks upon individuals and their families but also because it leads to the premature death of thousands of individuals every year.

Biological, Psychological, Behavioral, and Environmental Factors

As noted earlier in the chapter, schizophrenia is not a unidimensional illness characterized solely by psychotic symptoms. Schizophrenia often has profound effects on cognitive, emotional, and social aspects of the human psyche. Researchers have thus attempted to study schizophrenia through a wide variety of experimental lenses. This section reviews what different kinds of experimental research have revealed about this multifaceted illness.

COGNITIVE DEFICITS

As noted earlier, people with schizophrenia have impairments in a wide variety of cognitive domains. The cognitive abilities affected range from basic sensory processing to abstract thinking (Mesholam-Gately, Giuliano, Goff, Faraone, & Seidman, 2009). Given how common and pervasive these cognitive deficits are, some investigators have argued that such deficits are the core defining feature of schizophrenia (Elvevag & Goldberg, 2000), or, at least, that they closely reflect its underlying neurobiology (Allen, Griss, Folley, Hawkins, & Pearlson, 2009). This claim is supported by the fact that cognitive deficits are the best predictor of how well individuals with schizophrenia will function in their personal, academic, and occupational lives (Bowie et al., 2006).

Some of the cognitive deficits in schizophrenia are detected at the very earliest stages of sensory information processing. Schizophrenia patients are slower in the initial processing of visual stimuli (Silverstein & Keane, 2011). This slower and more error-prone initial processing of visual stimuli means that individuals with schizophrenia will take longer and make more mistakes when completing tasks that require visual perception: that is, a huge proportion of tasks in everyday life. For example, individuals with schizophrenia often have trouble with reading fluently and some of this difficulty appears to stem from problems with basic visual perception (Revheim et al., 2006).

Another basic sensory process that is impaired in individuals with schizophrenia is sensory gating. Sensory gating is the neurological process of filtering out redundant or unnecessary stimuli in the environment, and more specifically, of habituation to repeated exposure to the same sensory stimulus (Potter, Summerfelt, Gold, & Buchanan, 2006). This inhibition of responsiveness to repetitive stimulation helps individuals to block out irrelevant stimuli: for example, to ignore the hum of an air conditioner while focusing on a friend's conversation. Researchers have documented biological correlates of this deficit using electroencephalogram (EEG) measures. During sensory gating tasks, individuals with schizophrenia show measureable abnormalities in their P50 waveforms, a pattern of electrical activity associated with successful sensory gating (Bramon, Rabe-Hesketh, Sham, Murray, & Frangou, 2004).

In the realm of higher-level cognitive functions, individuals with schizophrenia show deficits in verbal and spatial memory and abstract reasoning (Caspi et al., 2003). Individuals with schizophrenia also show deficits in executive functioning, a broad category of cognitive abilities that includes holding things in working memory, planning, responding flexibly, and inhibiting responses (Minzenberg, Laird, Thelen, Carter, & Glahn, 2009). Deficits in executive functioning are of particular interest to researchers because they may contribute to anosognosia, the striking lack of insight that many individuals with schizophrenia have into the fact that they suffer from psychotic symptoms (Shad, Tamminga, Cullum, Haas, & Keshavan, 2006).

In addition to deficits in basic sensory processing and higher-level cognitive abilities, individuals with schizophrenia also show deficits in social cognition: that is, in thinking about social phenomena. Studies of social cognition in individuals with schizophrenia have consistently demonstrated impairments in the ability to comprehend and solve social problems (Penn, Waldheter, Perkins, Mueser, & Lieberman, 2005). Furthermore, individuals with schizophrenia are less accurate in their ability to label facial expressions of emotion (Bigelow et al., 2006). These social cognitive deficits may contribute to the well-documented impairments in social functioning that are common among individuals with schizophrenia.

ENVIRONMENTAL AND SOCIOCULTURAL FINDINGS

The current scientific consensus is that psychosocial factors can act as stressors that trigger or worsen schizophrenia's symptoms in vulnerable individuals (Walker & Diforio, 1997). Just as stress exposure can trigger or exacerbate physical illnesses (Sapolsky, 2004), stress may increase the risk of psychotic episodes and worsen functional outcomes in schizophrenia and other psychotic disorders (Trotman et al., 2014).

Both correlational and treatment studies have shown that persistent social stress can worsen the course of schizophrenia and, conversely, that decreasing persistent social stress can reduce the severity of schizophrenia symptoms (Holtzman et al., 2013). Negative expressed emotion is an interpersonal communication style characterized by critical, negative, or emotionally overinvolved speech patterns. Individuals with schizophrenia living in families characterized by high levels of negative expressed emotion have worse symptoms and are more likely to require hospitalization in the future (Miklowitz, 2004). However, it is important to clearly state that this finding does *not* mean that schizophrenia is caused by stressful family communication. Schizophrenia is a disease of the brain, and family members who support their loved ones with schizophrenia are engaged in a supremely challenging and praiseworthy endeavor. What this research does suggest, however, is that there are specific communication strategies that families can employ to improve the symptoms of individuals with schizophrenia, in the same way that family members of individuals with diabetes can employ some nutritional strategies to improve their loved ones' health. This possibility has been confirmed by trials that have shown that psychosocial therapies that improve family communication patterns can decrease rates of hospitalization and positive symptoms among individuals with schizophrenia (Mueser, Deavers, Penn, & Cassisi, 2013).

GENETIC VULNERABILITY

Vulnerability to schizophrenia is heritable (Schulze et al., 2014). Behavioral genetics studies utilizing twin, adoption, and family history methods have all shown that the risk for schizophrenia is elevated in individuals who have a biological relative with the illness. The evidence is also conclusive that the more closely related a relative with schizophrenia is, the greater the risk (Sullivan, Kendler, & Neale, 2003).

Monozygotic (MZ) twins share all of their genes with their co-twin, and 30% to 50% of MZ co-twins of individuals with schizophrenia will also go on to develop schizophrenia (Cardno & Gottesman, 2000). Dizygotic (DZ) twins share only about half of their genes with their co-twin, and 12% to 17% of DZ co-twins of individuals with schizophrenia go on to develop the illness. Adoption studies also provide evidence that the tendency for schizophrenia to run in families is due to genetic factors, rather than being caused by shared environmental stressors (e.g., mentally ill parents). Adoptees whose biological parents have schizophrenia are more likely to develop schizophrenia than adoptees whose biological parents do not have schizophrenia (Heston, 1966). Similarly, biological relatives of schizophrenia-afflicted adoptees are more likely to have schizophrenia than their nonbiological relatives.

What can one conclude from this pattern of findings? First, the more an individual's genome resembles the genome of a family member with schizophrenia, the more likely that individual is to develop schizophrenia. However, one can also conclude that schizophrenia is not completely determined by inherited genes. If this were the case, we should expect a 100% concordance rate in MZ twins. This is clearly not the case, so schizophrenia's etiology must be more complicated than a purely genetic one.

Inherited genetic vulnerabilities for schizophrenia can interact with environmental factors. For example, some studies have shown that the increased risk for schizophrenia in adopted children whose biological parents have schizophrenia is only significant when those children have been adopted into families rated as dysfunctional (Tienari et al., 1994). Thus, to really increase the risk for developing schizophrenia, a child needed to have both a genetic vulnerability (e.g., a biological mother with schizophrenia) as well as psychosocial stressors (i.e., a dysfunctional home environment).

Although researchers initially hoped to find a single gene or small number of genes that explained risk for schizophrenia, findings from behavioral and molecular genetic studies of schizophrenia have led to the conclusion that the disorder involves many genes—with no single gene or allele having a major impact on risk status (O'Donovan et al., 2009). Studies have also shown both unique and shared risk genes for schizophrenia and other psychotic disorders (Riley & Kendler, 2006). Linkage and candidate gene association studies have provided some evidence for the involvement of several chromosomal regions as well as some specific genes that may account for a small proportion of the risk for schizophrenia. The latter include genes that code for hormones, nerve growth factors, and serotonin and dopamine receptors (Mowry & Nancarrow, 2001).

Does the fact that inherited genes alone are insufficient to explain risk for schizophrenia mean that genetics does not have an important role to play in understanding schizophrenia? No. The role of genetics research in schizophrenia is likely to be similar to the role of genetics research in cancer (Cheetham, Gruhl, Mattick, & Dinger, 2013). Genetics obviously plays an important role in many cancers. The relationship between genetics and cancer isn't simple, however. Specific genetic markers are associated with one kind of cancer and not another, environmental factors (e.g., cigarette smoking) interact with cancer risk genes, and so on, in a complex web of findings. When we finally understand the genetics of schizophrenia, the picture is likely to be similarly complicated.

In the past two decades, researchers have begun using genome-wide approaches to study the genetics of schizophrenia. This research involves large-scale studies that scan markers across the entire genome to understand the heritable variance in schizophrenia. Genome-wide approaches initially met with limited success. However, more recent studies using larger sample sizes and advanced statistical approaches that focus on more fine-grained markers have identified areas of the genome where genetic differences are reliably associated with increased risk for schizophrenia (Schizophrenia Working Group of the Psychiatric Genomics Consortium, 2014).

As strange as it may sound, genetic vulnerability doesn't necessarily entail inheriting genes present in one's parents' DNA. Schizophrenia may result from multiple rare genetic variants that can arise from spontaneous de novo mutations (i.e., mutations not present in the parents' DNA). One good example of a de novo genetic vulnerability is 22q11.2 deletion syndrome. In 22q11.2 deletion syndrome, a person's genetic code lacks a long section of DNA on the 22nd chromosome. Most of the time, however, neither parent of a person with 22q11.2 deletion syndrome has this length of DNA missing. So where did this gap in the genetic code come from? This gap is caused by an error during the copying process that creates a germ cell (sperm or egg cell) that will form the basis of the child's genetic code. The 22q11.2 deletion syndrome often leads to a variety of physical signs, including structural anomalies of the face, head, and heart. Of relevance to the current chapter, 30% of individuals with 22q11.2 deletion syndrome will develop schizophrenia or another psychotic disorder in their lifetime, a 30-fold increase over the general population (Gothelf et al., 2007). To date, 22q11.2 is the strongest genotypic predictor of schizophrenia.

Another recent advance in genetics is the burgeoning field of epigenetics. Epigenetics is the study of potentially heritable changes in gene expression that are not due to changes in the DNA sequence. A brief metaphor may be helpful here. Imagine the DNA code as dozens of instruction manuals on a wall in a factory. Normally, a person walks up to the wall, takes a binder off the shelf, reads the instructions, and does what the instructions tell her to do: turn on this machine, turn off that machine, put these parts into boxes, and so forth. Epigenetic modification would be like writing "DO NOT READ" in big red letters on the cover of one of the binders. Has the text of the instruction manual been modified? No. Are those instructions less likely to be read and carried out? Yes. Epigenetic modification of DNA often works in a similar way. Sections of DNA are made less likely to be transcribed into RNA by transcription factors (i.e., the workers who now ignore the instruction manual).

Unlike an individual's genetic code, nonrandom epigenetic changes can be made throughout an individual's lifespan. To continue the metaphor, while you can't rewrite one of the factory's instruction manuals, you can put "DO NOT READ" on the cover or strike it out when you like. Scientists once thought that any epigenetic changes made during a person's lifetime were reset when her or his genetic code was copied to form a new egg or sperm cell: that is, when the instruction manuals were copied, any "DO NOT READ" signs were ignored and not copied. However, research has shown that epigenetic changes acquired during a person or animal's lifetime can sometimes be passed down to their offspring; that is, sometimes "DO NOT READ" is indeed copied onto the new manual along with the original instructions. Rats who are trained to fear a certain smell have epigenetic changes in genes associated with smell perception, and those changes can be found in their offspring (Dias & Ressler, 2014). Parents who are exposed to famine have children who have epigenetic changes on genes related to metabolism and food storage, changes that can be passed down even to their grandchildren (Handel, Ebers, & Ramagopalan, 2010). Scientists have shown that stress, toxins, hormones, and a variety of other factors can modify epigenetic instructions.

Schizophrenia researchers have been interested in whether epigenetic modification can be used to help explain how a pair of individuals with the same genetic code (i.e., a pair of monozygotic twins) can be discordant for schizophrenia. Could the difference between the co-twins be a difference in their epigenetic profiles? Returning to our metaphor, could it be that one twin has "DO NOT READ" printed on an important brain development instruction manual and the other twin does not? Scientists have found some evidence that suggests that differences in epigenetic instructions may indeed help to explain schizophrenia discordance in monozygotic twins. Schizophrenia discordant monozygotic twin pairs are more likely to have different epigenetic profiles than schizophrenia concordant twin pairs (Dempster et al., 2011). Scientists have also started to analyze the epigenetic profiles themselves and have shown that some kinds of epigenetic profiles are more common among individuals who develop schizophrenia (Furrow, Christiansen, & Feldman, 2011). Time will tell how much epigenetics contributes to the development of schizophrenia, but for now, this is a promising area of research.

ABNORMALITIES IN BRAIN STRUCTURE AND FUNCTION

Since the beginning of the 20th century, writers in the field of psychopathology have suspected that schizophrenia involved some kind of abnormality in the brain (Bleuler, 1911). However, it was not until the advent of neuroimaging techniques that solid empirical data were available to support this hypothesis. As described below, research on schizophrenia has revealed abnormalities in the brain's anatomy, neurotransmitters, and functional activity.

Early computerized axial tomography (CAT) brain scans of individuals with schizophrenia showed evidence of enlarged brain ventricles (i.e., cerebrospinal fluid–filled cavities in the brain; Dennert & Andreasen, 1983). These cavities are a normal part of a healthy brain: the cerebrospinal fluid plays an important role in moving organic debris away from the brain and performing other biological functions. However, when these ventricles are abnormally enlarged, it can be a sign that the brain has shrunk and the ventricles have expanded to fill the vacated space, as is seen in some neurodegenerative conditions (Adams, Fisher, Hakim, Ojemann, & Sweet, 1965).

As new brain scanning techniques were developed, findings of enlarged ventricles in schizophrenia were replicated and additional abnormalities were detected (Henn & Braus, 1999). Magnetic resonance imaging (MRI) revealed decreased frontal, temporal, and whole brain volume among individuals with schizophrenia (Olabi et al., 2011). More fine-grained analyses demonstrated reductions in the size of structures such as the thalamus and hippocampus: these changes appear to be progressive and are present prior to the onset of psychotic symptoms (Chan, Di, McAlonan, & Gong, 2011). In fact, of all the regions studied, the hippocampus is the one that most consistently differentiates individuals with schizophrenia from healthy controls (Adriano, Caltagirone, & Spalletta, 2011).

A landmark study of monozygotic twins discordant for schizophrenia was the first to demonstrate that brain abnormalities are not solely attributable to genetic factors (Suddath, Christison, Torrey, Casanova, & Weinberger, 1990). When compared to their healthy identical co-twins, twins with schizophrenia were found to have smaller temporal lobes, with the hippocampal region showing the most dramatic reduction in volume. Other studies have replicated reduced brain volume among schizophrenia-afflicted twins (Borgwardt et al., 2010). These studies support the idea that brain abnormalities observed in schizophrenia are at least partially due to environmental factors that interfere with prenatal brain development rather than the result of genetic risk alone.

Functional MRI allows researchers to measure the rate of blood flow within brain regions, which is correlated with the level of activity in those brain regions. Functional MRI findings in individuals with schizophrenia indicate that brain activity in the frontal cortex is reduced, particularly during working memory tasks (Brown & Thompson, 2010). There is also evidence that brain activity related to processing emotional stimuli is different in individuals with schizophrenia, with reduced medial temporal responses to emotional stimuli as compared to healthy controls (Whalley et al., 2012).

A newer advance in imaging, diffusion tensor imaging (DTI), measures the strength and direction of water diffusion in white matter. Diffusion of water in white matter is not equal in all directions. In a healthy brain, water flows more regularly along pathways of myelinated neurons. In an unhealthy brain (e.g., one with compromised myelinated pathways), water doesn't flow along these paths as regularly. One can think of an unhealthy brain as having a lot of leaky pipes, with water seeping out along the length of the pipes rather that flowing straight through them. Scientists can take images of the brain using an MRI scanner to see how much water is flowing along pipes (myelinated pathways) and how much water is moving around randomly to get an idea of how intact the brain's myelinated pathways are overall.

Functional anisotropy (FA) is a way of mathematically summarizing how organized water flow in the brain is on average. People with schizophrenia show functional anisotropy reductions: that is, more water is flowing around randomly (Scheel, Prokscha, Bayerl, Gallinat, & Montag, 2013). These reductions may be indicative of axonal damage and demyelination, the leaky pipes of our previous metaphor. Reduced functional anisotropy is also apparent in individuals who are at high risk of developing schizophrenia, suggesting that this problem precedes the onset of full-blown psychosis (Karlsgodt, Niendam, Bearden, & Cannon, 2009).

Despite a plethora of research findings indicating the presence of abnormalities in the brains of individuals with schizophrenia, there is no evidence that any specific abnormality is unique to schizophrenia or characterizes the brains of all individuals with schizophrenia. It is likely that the abnormalities observed in schizophrenia are signs of disturbed neurodevelopment that leads to schizophrenia-prone neurocircuitry. Given the current evidence, one can certainly conclude that there are one or more ways in which neurodevelopment can go wrong and leave someone with a brain predisposed to developing schizophrenia. However, researchers have not yet been able to figure out what specific final wiring states are necessary to develop schizophrenia and why those specific wiring states lead to the symptoms of schizophrenia.

However, this doesn't mean that researchers lack hypotheses about what some of those schizophrenia-prone brain wiring states might be. One schizophrenia-prone brain wiring state might be abnormal connectivity *between* brain regions, as opposed to abnormal wiring *within* a particular brain region (Schmitt, Hasan, Gruber, & Falkai, 2011). In this model, it is not a poorly functioning hippocampus that causes someone to develop schizophrenia. It is something wrong with the way the hippocampus talks with the frontal cortex, the frontal cortex talks with the basal ganglia, and so on that causes someone to develop schizophrenia. This theory is consistent with the earlier described findings of reduced functional anisotropy among individuals with schizophrenia: those "leaky pipes" are not properly transferring information between different areas of the brain and these errors in communication might be an underlying cause of the symptoms of schizophrenia.

NEUROTRANSMITTER ABNORMALITIES

The idea that schizophrenia involves an abnormality in the function of neurotransmitters has a long history. Dopamine is used in many areas of the brain and is a key neurotransmitter in the circuits that link cortical brain regions (e.g., those responsible for higher brain functions like planning) with subcortical brain regions (e.g., those responsible for basic emotions, like pleasure; Jentsch, Roth, & Taylor, 2000). Theories about dopamine have played the most enduring role in research into the biochemical basis of schizophrenia symptoms.

Initial support for the role of dopamine in schizophrenia was based on two key pieces of evidence: (1) drugs that reduce dopamine activity diminish psychotic symptoms, and (2) drugs that increase dopamine activity exacerbate or trigger psychotic symptoms (Carlsson et al., 2001). It was eventually confirmed that antipsychotic drugs produce their effect by blocking dopamine receptors, especially the D2 subtype of dopamine receptor.

Each neurotransmitter in the brain has multiple types of receptors that are sensitive to that neurotransmitter and perform different functions. For example, some dopamine receptors might cause a neuron to be more likely to fire when they detect dopamine, while other kinds of dopamine receptors might initiate long-term changes in the way a cell works. D2 receptors are one kind of dopamine receptor in the brain.

D2 receptors are especially prevalent in the more primitive subcortical regions of the brain, suggesting that these regions are important for understanding the neurobiology of psychotic symptoms. Whereas newer antipsychotic drugs act on neurotransmitter systems other than dopamine (Gründer, Hippius, & Carlsson, 2009), even these newer drugs still have effects that eventually lead to decreased dopamine activity, suggesting that all current antipsychotic medications require some change be made to dopamine signaling in the brain.

It is not only drugs that block dopamine signaling that demonstrate the link between dopamine and psychotic symptoms. Drugs that *increase* dopamine signaling in the brain can cause or worsen psychotic symptoms. Stimulants such as cocaine and amphetamine work by increasing dopamine activity (Boileau et al., 2006). Thus, cocaine and amphetamine can also cause psychotic symptoms and movement abnormalities in individuals with schizophrenia, even at relatively low doses (Weiner, Rabinstein, Levin, Weiner, & Shulman, 2001) and even in individuals without schizophrenia at higher doses (Brady, Lydiard, Malcolm, & Ballenger, 1991).

Given the success of dopamine-blocking drugs in treating the symptoms of schizophrenia, researchers hoped that they would be able to find excessive dopamine in the brains of individuals with schizophrenia. If researchers could find this hypothesized excessive dopamine, then they could say that schizophrenia was an illness of "too much dopamine in the brain." Unfortunately, however, dopamine concentrations were not found to be markedly elevated in the brains of individuals with schizophrenia (Davis, Kahn, Ko, & Davidson, 1991). Thus, researchers went back to the drawing board. If it wasn't excessive dopamine, maybe individuals with schizophrenia had too many dopamine receptors, meaning that the brains of individuals with schizophrenia were too sensitive to whatever amount of dopamine that was present. When investigators tested this, they did indeed find that individuals with schizophrenia have increased numbers of dopamine receptors in some areas of the brain (Howes & Kapur, 2009). However, this finding was not strong or reliable enough to conclude that schizophrenia is a disorder of "excessive dopamine sensitivity." Further complicating the issue, individuals with schizophrenia appear to have dopamine signaling *deficits* in certain areas of the brain associated with effortful control and long-term planning: for example, the prefrontal cortex (Okubo et al., 1997). Thus, researchers had to abandon a simple "too much dopamine" hypothesis of schizophrenia. While theories designating dopamine as the single cause of schizophrenia seem untenable, the modern consensus is that dopamine remains an important piece of the schizophrenia symptom puzzle.

Another important line of evidence suggests that glutamate, an excitatory neurotransmitter, may play a role in the pathology of schizophrenia. This research has studied the effects of drugs that block glutamate receptors in the brain. Just as there are different types of dopamine receptors in the brain (D1, D2, etc.), there are different kinds of glutamate receptors in the brain. One type of glutamate receptor is called the N-methyl-D-aspartic acid (NMDA) receptor. Several drugs, such as phencyclidine (PCP) and ketamine, block NMDA receptors and prevent them from sensing glutamate; these drugs are thus called NMDA antagonists. The interesting thing about NMDA antagonists is that they produce schizophrenia-like symptoms in people who use them (Coyle & Tsai, 2004). In fact, NMDA antagonists induce symptoms that are even more schizophrenia-like than the symptoms induced by stimulants: NMDA antagonists cause negative and cognitive symptoms in addition to positive symptoms. Conversely, drugs that improve NMDA receptor functioning can reduce negative symptoms and improve cognitive functioning in individuals with schizophrenia, though the evidence for this particular finding is more mixed (Menniti et al., 2013).

It is important to note that the finding that NMDA antagonists cause schizophrenia-like symptoms does not mean that the dopamine hypothesis of positive symptoms has been proven wrong. There are reciprocal connections between dopamine circuits and glutamate circuits in the brain (Del Arco & Mora, 2009). Thus, dysregulation of glutamate circuits can cause problems in dopamine circuits and vice versa (Kantrowitz & Javitt, 2010). More broadly speaking, all neurotransmitter systems interact in varied ways and at multiple levels in the brain's neural architecture (Mora, Segovia, & Del Arco, 2008). Thus, the final description of neurotransmitter abnormalities in schizophrenia is certainly going to be a complex one when it is fully articulated.

PRENATAL AND OBSTETRICAL FACTORS

The fact that more than 50% of monozygotic co-twins of individuals with schizophrenia do not develop the illness clearly illustrates the importance of nongenetic factors in schizophrenia's etiology. The prenatal period has received greater attention in recent years as a period that might offer ways to explain this finding. Obstetrical complications are abnormalities that occur during pregnancy or labor. There is extensive evidence that obstetrical complications have an adverse impact on the developing fetal brain and may contribute to schizophrenia vulnerability. Individuals with schizophrenia are more likely to have a history of obstetrical complications (O'Donnell, O'Connor, & Glover, 2009). These schizophrenia-related obstetrical complications include preeclampsia (high maternal blood pressure and large amounts of protein in the mother's urine) and fetal hypoxia (lack of oxygen to the fetus).

Another prenatal event that has been linked to increased risk for schizophrenia is maternal viral infection. Researchers have found elevated risk for schizophrenia among individuals born shortly after a flu epidemic or after being prenatally exposed to rubella (Brown, 2006). The critical period of exposure appears to be between the fourth and sixth months of pregnancy. The findings from research on prenatal viral infection might help explain the season-of-birth effect in schizophrenia. A disproportionate number of individuals with schizophrenia are born during the winter months (Narita et al., 2000). This may reflect seasonal exposure to viral infections, which are most common in late fall and early winter. Thus, the fetus would have been exposed to infection during the second trimester, a critical period for fetal brain development. Disruptions during this stage may give rise to brain abnormalities that confer vulnerability to schizophrenia.

Indirect support for the relationship between second-trimester fetal insult (i.e., a damaging event in the second trimester) and schizophrenia also comes from the observation that many individuals with schizophrenia show subtle physical abnormalities in body features, referred to as minor physical anomalies (Compton & Walker, 2009). Parts of the head, limbs, and the central nervous system all originate in the same germinal layer of fetal tissue (i.e., the ectoderm) during this same period of fetal development. The presence of minor physical abnormalities is thus assumed to be an outward manifestation of abnormal central nervous system development. Exposure to nutritional deficiency during the first trimester is also linked with an increased risk for schizophrenia (Susser, Brown, & Gorman, 1999).

Studies of rodents and nonhuman primates have shown that prenatal maternal stress can interfere with fetal brain development and is associated with elevated glucocorticoid (i.e., stress hormone) release and hippocampal abnormalities in offspring (Coe et al., 2003). Along the same line, in humans there is evidence that stressful events during pregnancy are associated with greater risk for schizophrenia and other mental disorders in adult offspring. Researchers have found higher rates of schizophrenia in the offspring of women whose spouses died during their pregnancies (Huttunen, 1989) and among the offspring of women who were exposed to a military invasion during their pregnancies (van Os & Selten, 1998). It is likely that prenatal stress triggers the release of maternal stress hormones, which can disturb fetal neurodevelopment (Welberg & Seckl, 2001).

One of the chief questions confronting researchers is whether obstetric complications act independently to increase risk for schizophrenia or produce their effects by interacting with genetic vulnerability. One possibility is that the genetic vulnerability for schizophrenia involves an increased sensitivity to prenatal factors that interfere with fetal neurodevelopment (Walshe et al., 2005). For examples, individuals with certain immune system genotypes may be more sensitive to the adverse effects of prenatal exposure to maternal viral infection (Brown, 2006). This and related questions are currently an active area of research.

LONGITUDINAL FINDINGS

There is compelling evidence that signs of vulnerability to schizophrenia are present long before the illness is diagnosed. Most of these signs are subtle and do not reach the level of severity necessary to make a clinical diagnosis. Nonetheless, when compared to children with healthy adult outcomes, children who later develop schizophrenia manifest deficits in multiple domains. In some of these domains, the deficits are apparent as early as infancy. This chapter will classify these pre-schizophrenia signs and symptoms into two categories: (1) premorbid symptoms, which are often subtle and occur long before the onset of the illness, and (2) prodromal symptoms, which more immediately precede the onset of psychotic symptoms. Both categories of signs and symptoms are described in the following paragraphs.

Children who later develop schizophrenia tend to perform worse than their healthy siblings and classmates on measures of cognitive functioning. This is reflected in lower intelligence and achievement test scores as well as in poorer grades in school (Cornblatt et al., 2012). Children who later develop schizophrenia also show abnormalities in social behavior. They are less responsive in social situations, exhibit less positive emotion (Walker, Grimes, Davis, & Smith, 1993), show abnormalities in gestural behavior (Mittal et al., 2006), and have poorer social adjustment compared with children who have healthy adult outcomes (Ang & Tan, 2004).

In a series of studies examining home movies of children who went on to develop schizophrenia, researchers employed frame-by-frame analysis to determine whether behavioral characteristics seen in these videos could predict which children would go on to develop schizophrenia and which would not (Walker et al., 1993). The researchers found that children who later developed schizophrenia showed more negative facial expressions of emotion than their healthy siblings as early as the first year of life, thereby indicating that the vulnerability for schizophrenia is subtly manifested in very early social interactions. The children who went on to develop schizophrenia also showed higher rates of motor abnormalities and delays, such as atypical hand gestures, lateness in walking, and so forth (Walker, 1994).

This chapter has already reviewed substantial evidence that schizophrenia does not emerge out of nowhere in adolescence or young adulthood. While positive symptoms do not typically emerge until young adult life, subtle signs of abnormal neurodevelopment can be seen at birth and in early childhood. However, the fact remains that the most striking symptoms of schizophrenia (i.e., hallucinations and delusions) do not emerge until young adulthood for most individuals. So how can it be that genetic and obstetrical problems, present at birth, take so long to cause positive symptoms? Examining the longitudinal development of schizophrenia's signs and symptoms has given researchers hints as to what biological mechanisms might underlie this strange pattern.

As previously described, prodromal and psychotic level positive symptoms often emerge during adolescence and young adulthood. Maturational increases in dopamine activity during adolescence have been cited as a potential factor accounting for this age of onset for positive symptoms (Benes, 2003). In addition, following the onset of puberty, significant developmental changes in brain structure and function may contribute to an increased likelihood of abnormal brain development. In particular, adolescence is a time of rapid pruning (i.e., selective destruction) of excess neural connections. This cutting away of excess brain connections is key for producing the gains in cognitive ability and self-control that occur during adolescence (Paolicelli et al., 2011). However, in individuals who go on to develop schizophrenia, this pruning process may go too far and leave them with schizophrenia-prone brains that contain aberrant connectivity in dopamine-related brain circuits (Cannon, 2015). This possibility has been supported by excellent recent research that showed evidence for aberrant pruning activity at multiple levels of analysis, including the levels of genes, proteins, and neural circuitry (Sekar et al., 2016).

As noted earlier, the onset of schizophrenia is often preceded by weeks, months, or even years of increasing clinical symptoms that often resemble attenuated versions of the full-blown symptoms of schizophrenia: for example, social withdrawal and suspiciousness that doesn't rise to the level of paranoia. Drawing from retrospective observations of the prodromal period, researchers attempted to design a set of criteria that would predict whether someone would develop a psychotic illness within a few months or years: that is, determine whether an individual is currently experiencing a schizophrenia prodrome that will eventually develop into schizophrenia. A team of Australian researchers were eventually able to do just that; they developed a set of criteria that identified individuals who had a 30% to 40% chance of developing schizophrenia within the next 2 years (Yung & Nelson, 2011). This high-risk profile has been given different names over time, including at-risk mental states (ARMS), ultra-high-risk (UHR) state, and the clinical high-risk (CHR) state. We will use the term *clinical high-risk state*, but remember that these terms generally refer to the same or very similar things: a set of clinical criteria that identifies individuals at high risk for developing schizophrenia within a few years.

Clinical high-risk (CHR) individuals show some of the same abnormalities observed in individuals with schizophrenia. For example, CHR individuals evince motor abnormalities, cognitive deficits, and psychosocial impairment intermediate between those found in individuals with schizophrenia and in healthy controls (Fusar-Poli et al., 2013). CHR individuals also have increased levels of cortisol, a stress hormone, and other biological abnormalities similar to those found among individuals with schizophrenia (Salokangas et al., 2012).

The clinical high-risk state was considered for inclusion in the *DSM-5* under the name "attenuated psychosis syndrome." Several reasons were presented to support this inclusion (Fusar-Poli & Yung, 2012). First, the symptoms of the CHR state are often distressing and are associated with impairments in social and occupational functioning. Some clinicians wanted to be able to diagnose the condition so that they could provide treatments to individuals with the CHR state while billing medical insurance companies for those services. Second, the CHR state does indeed predict an increased likelihood of developing schizophrenia, which can be important information for a clinician to have when deciding on a treatment plan for a patient. However, other clinicians and researchers argued that including attenuated psychosis syndrome in *DSM-5* was ill advised as it would lead to clinicians assuming that CHR individuals would develop schizophrenia when most CHR individuals will not in fact develop schizophrenia (remember that 60% or more of CHR individuals do not develop a psychotic illness). Those opposing the inclusion also noted that standard treatments for psychotic illness did not appear to prevent the onset of psychotic symptoms and were associated with significant side effects. In the end, a compromise decision was made to place attenuated psychosis syndrome in the "Conditions for Further Study" section of *DSM-5* and to wait for more research to be conducted before deciding whether or not to include the syndrome in the main text of future editions of the *DSM*.

Models of Schizophrenia

Theories attempting to explain psychosis have been documented since antiquity (Evans, McGrath, & Milns, 2003). However, most researchers now agree that no single cause can explain all cases of schizophrenia, let alone psychotic disorders more generally (Jablensky, 2006). Thus, our final understanding of schizophrenia is likely to resemble our modern understanding of cancer. In the case of cancer, we know that (a) there are many distinct kinds of cancer; (b) although there are similar mechanisms and symptoms across different kinds of cancers, no single biological mechanism can be used to fully explain all kinds of cancer; and (c) no single treatment or preventive measure will be effective in preventing or treating all kinds of cancer. Similarly, schizophrenia researchers generally agree that (a) the collection of symptoms we label schizophrenia constitutes not a single disease with a single cause but rather a syndrome with multiple causes; (b) schizophrenia is a behavioral manifestation of brain dysfunction; (c) the etiology of schizophrenia involves an interplay between genetic and environmental factors, including psychosocial stressors; (d) multiple developmental pathways lead to the onset of schizophrenia; (e) overlap exists among the genetic and environmental factors that confer risk for schizophrenia and other psychotic disorders; and (f) brain maturational processes play a role in schizophrenia's etiology.

Figure 10.1 summarizes a contemporary diathesis-stress model of schizophrenia. This model proposes that diathesis (i.e., vulnerability) for schizophrenia comes from both genetic (e.g., inherited genetic risk and genetic mutations) and acquired (e.g., environmental) factors (Walker, Mittal, & Tessner, 2008). Genetic risk factors are assumed to

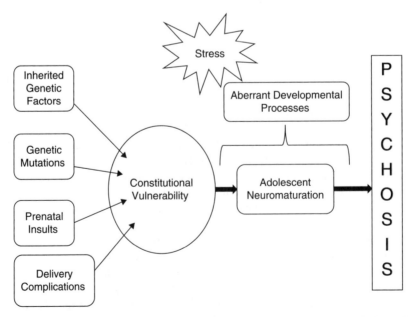

FIGURE 10.1   A Diathesis-Stress Model of the Etiology of Schizophrenia and Other Psychotic Disorders

confer vulnerability by altering structural and functional characteristics of the brain. Acquired risk factors can result from delivery complications (e.g., oxygen deprivation during pregnancy) that compromise fetal brain development. Whatever the combination of genetic and environmental factors that leads a particular brain to be vulnerable to developing schizophrenia, the model assumes that a diathesis for schizophrenia is, in most cases, present at birth.

The diathesis-stress model posits that being born with a diathesis for schizophrenia (i.e., a schizophrenia-prone brain), does not mean that that a person is guaranteed to develop schizophrenia during his or her lifetime. The diathesis-stress model argues that developing schizophrenia typically involves both a diathesis for schizophrenia and one or more stressors that occur after the individual is born. These stressors cause the underlying vulnerability (i.e., the schizophrenia-prone brain) to become apparent in the form of schizophrenia symptoms. Importantly though, a person may go through life with a diathesis and never manifest the symptoms of schizophrenia if he or she is never exposed to a critical volume of stressors. Finally, it is worth noting that a diathesis for schizophrenia is not an all or nothing attribute. An individual may possess an extreme diathesis for schizophrenia and thus be essentially guaranteed to develop the disorder in even the most propitious of circumstances (e.g., good childhood nutrition, a positive family environment, no stressors beyond the normal challenges of growing up). Conversely, an individual may have only a very mild diathesis for schizophrenia and thus might develop the symptoms of schizophrenia only within the context of extreme biological or psychosocial stress (e.g., extreme childhood malnutrition, chronic cannabis exposure, and multiple head traumas).

The neural diathesis-stress model also posits biological mechanisms through which exposure to stress can trigger or exacerbate psychotic symptoms. Specifically this model focuses on the hypothalamic-pituitary-adrenal axis, one of the major biological systems subserving the stress response. This system governs the secretion of the stress hormone cortisol, which, in turn, can alter the function of neurons and neurotransmitters, such as dopamine. In the case of dopamine, the effect of cortisol is to augment its release (Wand et al., 2007). Thus, stress exposure and elevated cortisol can act to increase dopamine activity and thereby increase the likelihood of psychotic symptoms in vulnerable individuals.

A parallel with cancer can be drawn that helps to explain risk for schizophrenia within a diathesis-stress model. Lifetime risk for lung cancer is very low for individuals who do not smoke cigarettes: about 0.2% among men who do not smoke (Eldridge, 2016). Regular cigarette smoking dramatically increases the rate of lung cancer to about 24% in men. However, that means that 75% of male regular smokers will not develop lung cancer. Developing lung cancer thus generally requires both a diathesis (e.g., a genetic or other predisposition toward developing lung cancer) and a stressor (e.g., regular smoking). The corresponding percentages are certainly different in the case of schizophrenia, but the principle of diathesis-stress is the same.

Assessment

For both the individual experiencing her first psychotic symptoms and her loved ones, the first episode of psychosis is a time of confusion, uncertainty, and suffering. A good initial diagnostic evaluation is an important opportunity to provide the individual and her loved ones with a way to understand what is going on and some initial strategies for what they can do to improve the situation.

A number of measures exist to help a clinician make the diagnosis of schizophrenia. One such measure is the Structured Clinical Interview for DSM-5 Disorders (SCID-5; First, Williams, Karg, & Spitzer, 2016). The SCID-5 is a structured diagnostic interview that queries individuals about their experiences to determine whether they meet criteria for schizophrenia or other mental disorders. Within the *DSM-5* system, clinicians are also encouraged to provide numerical ratings for schizophrenia's individual symptom domains (e.g., delusions and negative symptoms) to better communicate the specific nature of an individual's symptoms.

Beyond making the diagnosis of schizophrenia itself, other important clinical information should be collected during initial and subsequent assessments. Given the high rate of suicide among individuals with schizophrenia, it is important to assess the risk of self-harm and violence (McGirr et al., 2006). Also, a medical examination is typically conducted to rule out other illnesses that can cause or exacerbate psychotic symptoms (Richards & Gurr, 2000). This examination includes a review of the individual's medical history, a physical examination, and laboratory tests. While the majority of schizophrenia-like presentations cannot be attributed to an identifiable organic condition (e.g., most people with schizophrenia do not show obvious abnormalities on brain scans), it is important to have a medical examination to rule out reversible causes of psychosis.

Researchers have also developed more detailed measures to assess the many individual symptoms of schizophrenia and provide more objective guidelines for rating their severity. The gold standard measure for this purpose is the Positive and Negative Syndrome Scale (PANSS) for schizophrenia (Kay, Fiszbein, & Opler, 1987). Another important rating scale is the Abnormal Involuntary Movement Scale (AIMS; Munetz & Benjamin, 1988), which allows clinicians to monitor for signs of important medication-related side effects, which will be described later in this chapter.

Several structured interviews have also been developed to identify individuals at clinical high risk for developing schizophrenia. These structured interviews also produce symptom ratings to indicate how severe an individual's attenuated symptoms are. The two most prominent interviews are the Comprehensive Assessment of At-Risk Mental States (CAARMS; Yung et al., 2005) and the Structured Interview for Prodromal Syndromes (SIPS; Miller et al., 2002).

Treatment

There are currently no biological or psychotherapeutic cures for schizophrenia. However, a combination of medication and other interventions can often control the positive symptoms of schizophrenia and significantly improve the prognosis of someone afflicted with the illness.

The treatment of schizophrenia can be divided into three phases: acute, stabilization, and maintenance (Sadock, Sadock, Ruiz, & Kaplan, 2009). In the acute phase, the goal of treatment is to reduce the severity of symptoms; this usually involves the administration of medication to control positive symptoms. In the stabilization phase, the goal is to consolidate treatment gains and help the patient attain a stable living situation. Finally, during the maintenance phase, when the symptoms are in partial or complete remission, the goal is to reduce residual symptoms, prevent relapse, and improve functioning.

ANTIPSYCHOTIC MEDICATION

The mainstay biological treatment of schizophrenia is antipsychotic medication. First introduced in the 1950s, antipsychotic medications had an enormous impact on the lives of people afflicted with schizophrenia. Many individuals' positive symptoms were brought under control for the first time, and some people who had lived in psychiatric hospitals for the majority of their adult lives were able to return to living in the community. These early medications are now referred to as *typical antipsychotics*: chlorpromazine (Thorazine) is a well-known example of this class. As mentioned earlier, typical antipsychotics are dopamine antagonists; that is, they work by blocking dopamine receptors, especially D2 receptors. Unfortunately, since typical antipsychotics also block dopamine receptors in areas of the brain associated with coordinating physical movement, typical antipsychotics can have the side effect of causing problems with motor functioning. These motor side effects are called *extrapyramidal symptoms*. They are named after one of the movement circuits in the brain that is disrupted (Miyamoto, Duncan, Marx, & Lieberman, 2004). Extrapyramidal symptoms include bradykinesia (slowed movements), tremor, akathisia (an extremely uncomfortable desire to move constantly), and facial masking (little or no facial expression). One might notice that some of these symptoms resemble those of Parkinson's disease. This is no coincidence, as typical antipsychotics block the same dopamine receptors that are destroyed in Parkinson's disease. Luckily, extrapyramidal symptoms can usually be reversed by lowering the dosage of antipsychotic medication or changing to a new medication. However, clinicians often have to balance preventing movement side effects with maintaining a high enough dose to treat the positive symptoms of schizophrenia.

There is a second, potentially permanent set of motor side effects that can be caused by antipsychotic medication. This second type of motor side effect is called tardive dyskinesia. It is important to understand the difference between extrapyramidal symptoms and tardive dyskinesia, as tardive dyskinesia is caused by a mechanism that is essentially the opposite of the one that causes extrapyramidal symptoms. In response to detecting that motor areas in the brain are not receiving the expected amount of dopamine signaling, the brain tries to generate extra dopamine receptors in those areas (Casey, 2000). That way, the motor areas in the brain can be more sensitive to the little bit of dopamine that is getting through the antipsychotic blockade. The problem is that these extra dopamine receptors eventually lead to the misfiring of neurons in motor areas of the brain, which, in turn, causes abnormal movements: these abnormal movements are the symptoms of tardive dyskinesia. The abnormal movements include involuntary lip puckering, tongue thrusting, and (in more severe cases) movements involving the entire torso. These symptoms can be permanent because the extra receptors do not go away once the antipsychotic medication is discontinued. Clinicians use the Abnormal Involuntary Movement Scale (AIMS) to catalogue and measure involuntary movements over time so that the antipsychotic medication prescriber can identify and address any involuntary movement symptoms early and prevent the development of permanent tardive dyskinesia symptoms (Gharabawi et al., 2005).

Even though typical antipsychotic medications were a huge success for the medical and pharmaceutical community, they had obvious limitations. Namely, they treated only the positive symptoms of schizophrenia and carried the risk of movement disorders. This spurred pharmaceutical companies to keep working on new kinds of antipsychotic medications. In the late 1980s, a new generation of antipsychotic medications was introduced; these are now generally referred to as *atypical antipsychotics*. These medications are dopamine antagonists, like the typical antipsychotics, but they also affect other neurotransmitter systems, including serotonin. Atypical antipsychotics were indeed an improvement in some ways over the typical antipsychotics as they have a lower risk of inducing movement disorders and are often better tolerated by patients (Gianfrancesco, Rajagopalan, Sajatovic, & Wang, 2006). However, atypical antipsychotics did not turn out to be the miracle drugs that patients and clinicians hoped they would be. First, atypical antipsychotics can still induce movement disorders, though research generally suggests that they do so at a lower rate than typical antipsychotics (Rummel-Kluge et al., 2012). Second, many atypical antipsychotics carry a substantial risk of causing *metabolic syndrome*, which includes substantial weight gain (sometimes dozens of pounds); the onset or worsening of diabetes mellitus; and lipid abnormalities (Newcomer, 2005). Third, most atypical antipsychotics turned out to be no more effective than typical antipsychotics in treating the positive symptoms of schizophrenia. One exception to this is the atypical antipsychotic clozapine, which has been shown to be effective in treating some individuals with schizophrenia whose positive symptoms have not responded to any other antipsychotic medication. However, in a small minority of individuals, clozapine can cause a severe side effect that includes the destruction of an important type of immune cell throughout the body, so individuals who use it must get regular blood tests to monitor for this side effect (Nielsen, Correll, Manu, & Kane, 2013). Fourth, like typical antipsychotics, atypical antipsychotics have little to no effect on the nonpositive symptoms of schizophrenia: that is, cognitive impairments, mood problems, and negative symptoms (Swartz et al., 2007). While atypical antipsychotics have not turned out to be everything they were hoped to be, their demonstrated efficacy in treating the positive symptoms of schizophrenia combined with their lower probability of inducing motor side effects has made them the essential first-line treatment for schizophrenia.

Given the efficacy of atypical antipsychotics in treating the positive symptoms of schizophrenia, there was some initial hope that low-dose antipsychotics could prevent the onset of schizophrenia in individuals at clinical high risk (CHR) for schizophrenia. Unfortunately though, initial studies showed that, at best, atypical antipsychotics reduce attenuated positive symptoms in CHR individuals and perhaps *delay* the onset of full-blown psychotic symptoms while CHR individuals take the medication. However, once CHR individuals stop taking atypical antipsychotic medication, they become as likely to develop psychotic symptoms as they would have been had they not taken the antipsychotic medication in the first place (Addington & Heinssen, 2012). To summarize then, the evidence suggests that atypical antipsychotics *cannot* be used to permanently prevent the development of full-blown schizophrenia in CHR individuals. Given the significant side effects of atypical antipsychotic medications (e.g., weight gain and diabetes), the choice of whether to use atypical antipsychotics with a particular CHR individual is a hotly debated risk-benefit calculation and probably best determined by a cautious and well-informed clinician who works closely with each patient to weigh the risks and benefits for that particular individual.

PSYCHOSOCIAL TREATMENTS

Although antipsychotic medication is the crucial first step in the treatment of schizophrenia, there is substantial evidence that psychosocial interventions can also be beneficial for both the individual suffering from schizophrenia and his or her family. It is generally agreed that the optimal treatment approach is one that combines medication and psychosocial interventions. In fact, family and patient psychoeducation should begin as early as the initial assessment (Gadelha, Noto, & de Jesus Mari, 2012). Research supports the use of family psychoeducation therapy—which includes psychoeducational and behavioral components—in treatment programs for schizophrenia (Bustillo, Lauriello, Horan, & Keith, 2001). Family psychoeducation therapy is an evidence-based practice that is included in the schizophrenia Patient Outcomes Research Team (PORT) guidelines for schizophrenia treatment (Dixon et al., 2010). In addition to improving family members' knowledge of schizophrenia, family psychoeducation therapy reduces patient relapse and hospitalization rates by as much as 50% (Lucksted, McFarlane, Downing, & Dixon, 2012).

Comprehensive programs for supporting an individual's transition back into the community have also been effective in enhancing recovery and reducing relapse. One such program, called assertive community treatment (ACT), was originally developed in the 1970s by researchers in Madison, Wisconsin (Udechuku et al., 2005). Assertive community treatment is a comprehensive treatment approach for the seriously mentally ill living in the community. Patients are assigned to a multidisciplinary team (nurse, case manager, general physician, and psychiatrist) that has a fixed caseload and a high staff-to-patient ratio. The team delivers all services to the patient when and where he or she needs them and is available to the patient at all times. Services include home delivery of medication, monitoring of physical and mental health status, in vivo social skills training, and frequent contact with family members. Studies suggest that assertive community treatment can reduce time spent in a hospital, improve housing stability, and increase patient and family satisfaction with treatment. Recent studies have shown that assertive community treatment, especially when focused on finding and treating individuals during their first episode of psychosis, results in net cost savings for the local health care system (Rosenheck et al., 2016). The increased cost of delivering the service is offset by reduced hospitalizations and incarcerations among individuals who receive it.

Social skills training seeks to improve the overall functioning of individuals with schizophrenia by teaching the skills necessary to perform daily living activities, function in the workplace, and develop interpersonal relationships (Bustillo et al., 2001). Social skills training programs make use of behavioral techniques, including modeling, rehearsal, and reinforcement. Recent research indicates that social skills training improves social competence and treatment compliance, as compared to structured leisure activities or treatment as usual, resulting in lower social disability and lower dropout among individuals who receive social skills training (Rus-Calafell, Gutiérrez-Maldonado, Ortega-Bravo, Ribas-Sabaté, & Caqueo-Urízar, 2013). However, it remains unclear to what extent this improvement in social competence translates into better functioning in the community (Pilling et al., 2002). The 2009 PORT schizophrenia treatment guidelines recommend that social skills training be accompanied by strategies to increase real-world use of the skills obtained in therapy (Dixon et al., 2010). Because the rate of competitive employment for the severely mentally ill is low (Lehman et al., 2002), vocational rehabilitation has also been a major focus of many treatment programs. Some evidence suggests that supported employment programs produce better results than traditional vocational rehabilitation programs: nonetheless, job retention remains a significant problem.

Cognitive-behavioral therapy (CBT) for schizophrenia draws on the tenets of cognitive therapy that were originally developed by Beck and Ellis (Beck, 1976; Ellis, 1980). CBT theory posits that dysfunctional cognitions can contribute to specific psychotic symptoms (Naeem, Kingdon, & Turkington, 2005). Individual CBT emphasizes a collaborative relationship between patient and therapist, with the start of therapy focusing on establishing and developing a therapeutic alliance without challenging or reinforcing delusional beliefs (Mueser et al., 2013). Clinicians will then often provide psychoeducation regarding schizophrenia and the influence of stress upon symptoms. Clinicians normalize the client's symptoms as a way to reduce the sense of isolation common among individuals with schizophrenia. Clinicians will then often employ traditional CBT techniques, such as examining the antecedents, beliefs, and consequences relevant to the client's psychotic symptoms. The goal of therapy is generally not to get clients to conclude that their beliefs are delusional. Instead, the primary goal is to reduce symptom severity and associated distress by helping clients develop more effective coping strategies (e.g., distraction techniques to make auditory hallucinations less distressing; Dickerson, 2000). Recent reviews suggest that CBT is effective in reducing symptom severity in schizophrenia patients (Mueser et al., 2013), though its effects are mild to moderate and it must generally be combined with effective antipsychotic medication treatment. There have also been a few early studies of acceptance and commitment therapy for psychosis (Bach, Gaudiano, Hayes, & Herbert, 2013), but at this time there is too little research to draw reliable conclusions about its effectiveness.

Another psychosocial intervention that has shown promising results is cognitive remediation. Cognitive remediation is similar to interventions used with individuals who have neurological problems following a stroke (Wykes, Huddy, Cellard, McGurk, & Czobor, 2011). Individuals with schizophrenia practice over and over again on tasks that require attention, short-term memory, and other cognitive abilities that are impaired in schizophrenia. Over time, their performance on these tasks improves, and it is hoped that this improved performance then translates to everyday tasks that require concentration and memory. While research has clearly shown that individuals with schizophrenia can improve on laboratory measures of cognitive ability, evidence for if, when, and to what extent this leads to improved performance on real-world tasks is more mixed and is an active area of research (Bowie, McGurk, Mausbach, Patterson, & Harvey, 2012).

To summarize then, psychosocial interventions have a significant role to play in the treatment of schizophrenia. Recent meta-analyses have generally shown that targeted psychosocial interventions (e.g., CBT for psychosis), when added to medication treatment as usual, result in moderate gains in symptom control and on measures of functioning. Better still are intensive, specialized, multidisciplinary programs that provide assertive outreach treatment, evidence-based interventions tailored to patient needs, low-dose atypical antipsychotic regimens, manualized cognitive-behavioral strategies, individualized crisis management plans, family counseling, and/or psychoeducation. These "total package" programs have been shown to reduce relapse rates and days of hospitalization (Alvarez-Jimenez et al., 2011). While these programs might seem to be expensive and difficult to implement, recent research has shown that they are cost effective in the long run, suggesting that they should be implemented in far more locations than they currently are (Rosenheck et al., 2016).

Summary and Future Directions

Decades of research have documented the tremendous personal and social cost of schizophrenia and other psychotic disorders. Although the cause of schizophrenia has not yet been definitively identified, substantial progress has been made in understanding schizophrenia's precursors and underlying mechanisms. We now know that the early assumption that schizophrenia was a single disorder that involved only one or a few etiological factors was inaccurate. Instead, researchers now agree that schizophrenia is a syndrome with multiple causes and that some of these involve complex interactions among genetic and environmental factors.

What does the future hold for the understanding and treatment of schizophrenia? First, it is likely that research efforts will gradually identify more genetic and bioenvironmental factors that contribute to schizophrenia. In the process, it is likely that subgroups of patients characterized by the same etiological processes will be identified. Second, our understanding of the brain dysfunction that gives rise to psychotic symptoms will increase. Advances in neuroimaging have made it possible to explore the brain from the level of gross anatomy to the microscopic level of receptor function. It is likely that the neural circuits associated with psychotic symptoms can be disrupted at multiple points via different neurotransmitter systems. This information will play a major role in the development of novel treatments. Third, advances will be made in our understanding of the way environmental factors—from prenatal complications to postnatal stress exposure—can trigger the expression of latent vulnerability to schizophrenia. Advances in this area will set the stage for efforts at prevention, including public health strategies aimed at the general population and preventive interventions for at-risk individuals. Finally, scientific progress in understanding adolescent brain development will likely move the field forward (Walker & Bollini, 2002). The fact that the overwhelming majority of individuals who are diagnosed with a major mental disorder, including both psychotic and mood disorders, experience a clinical decline that begins within years after the onset of puberty highlights the importance of understanding the role of adolescent brain development in the etiology of psychotic disorders.

References

Adams, R. D., Fisher, C. M., Hakim, S., Ojemann, R. G., & Sweet, W. H. (1965). Symptomatic occult hydrocephalus with normal cerebrospinal-fluid pressure. *New England Journal of Medicine*, *273*(3), 117–126. doi: 10.1056/NEJM196507152730301

Addington, J., & Heinssen, R. (2012). Prediction and prevention of psychosis in youth at clinical high risk. *Annual Review of Clinical Psychology*, *8*(1), 269–289. doi: 10.1146/annurev-clinpsy-032511-143146

Adriano, F., Caltagirone, C., & Spalletta, G. (2011). Hippocampal volume reduction in first-episode and chronic schizophrenia: A review and meta-analysis. *Neuroscientist*, *18*(2), 180–200. doi: 10.1177/1073858410395147

Allen, A. J., Griss, M. E., Folley, B. S., Hawkins, K. A., & Pearlson, G. D. (2009). Endophenotypes in schizophrenia: A selective review. *Schizophrenia Research*, *109*(1–3), 24–37. doi: 10.1016/j.schres.2009.01.016

Alvarez-Jimenez, M., Gleeson, J. F., Henry, L. P., Harrigan, S. M., Harris, M. G., Amminger, G. P., ... McGorry, P. D. (2011). Prediction of a single psychotic episode: A 7.5-year, prospective study in first-episode psychosis. *Schizophrenia Research*, *125*(2–3), 236–246. doi: 10.1016/j.schres.2010.10.020

American Psychiatric Association. (2013). *Diagnostic and statistical manual of mental disorders* (5th ed.). Washington, DC: Author.

Andreasen, N. C., Carpenter, W. T., Kane, J. M., Lasser, R. A., Marder, S. R., & Weinberger, D. R. (2005). Remission in schizophrenia: Proposed criteria and rationale for consensus. *American Journal of Psychiatry*, *162*(3), 441–449. doi: 10.1176/appi.ajp.162.3.441

Ang, Y. G., & Tan, H. Y. (2004). Academic deterioration prior to first episode schizophrenia in young Singaporean males. *Psychiatry Research*, *121*(3), 303–307. doi: 10.1016/S0165-1781(03)00257-9

Bach, P., Gaudiano, B. A., Hayes, S. C., & Herbert, J. D. (2013). Acceptance and commitment therapy for psychosis: Intent to treat, hospitalization outcome and mediation by believability. *Psychosis*, *5*(2), 166–174. doi: 10.1080/17522439.2012.671349

Ballard, C. G., Saad, K., Patel, A., Gahir, M., Solis, M., Coope, B., & Wilcock, G. (1995). The prevalence and phenomenology of psychotic symptoms in dementia sufferers. *International Journal of Geriatric Psychiatry*, *10*(6), 477–485. doi: 10.1002/gps.930100607

Beck, A. T. (1976). *Cognitive therapy and the emotional disorders*. Oxford, England: International Universities Press.

Behrendt, R. P., & Young, C. (2004). Hallucinations in schizophrenia, sensory impairment, and brain disease: A unifying model. *Behavioral and Brain Sciences*, *27*(6), 771–830. doi: 10.1017/S0140525X04000184

Benes, F. M. (2003). Why does psychosis develop during adolescence and early adulthood? *Current Opinion in Psychiatry*, *16*(3), 317–319.

Bigelow, N. O., Paradiso, S., Adolphs, R., Moser, D. J., Arndt, S., Heberlein, A., ... Andreasen, N. C. (2006). Perception of socially relevant stimuli in schizophrenia. *Schizophrenia Research*, *83*(2–3), 257–267. doi: 10.1016/j.schres.2005.12.856

Bleuler, E. (1911). *Dementia praecox or the group of schizophrenias* (J. Zinkin, Trans.). New York, NY: International Universities Press.

Boileau, I., Dagher, A., Leyton, M., Gunn, R. N., Baker, G. B., Diksic, M., & Benkelfat, C. (2006). Modeling sensitization to stimulants in humans: An [^{11}C]raclopride/positron emission tomography study in healthy men. *Archives of General Psychiatry*, *63*(12), 1386–1395. doi: 10.1001/archpsyc.63.12.1386

Borgwardt, S. J., Picchioni, M. M., Ettinger, U., Toulopoulou, T., Murray, R., & McGuire, P. K. (2010). Regional gray matter volume in monozygotic twins concordant and discordant for schizophrenia. *Biological Psychiatry*, *67*(10), 956–964. doi: 10.1016/j.biopsych.2009.10.026

Bowie, C. R., McGurk, S. R., Mausbach, B., Patterson, T. L., & Harvey, P. D. (2012). Combined cognitive remediation and functional skills training for schizophrenia: Effects on cognition, functional competence, and real-world behavior. *American Journal of Psychiatry*, *169*(7), 710–718. doi: 10.1176/appi.ajp.2012.11091337

420

Bowie, C. R., Reichenberg, A., Patterson, T. L., Heaton, R. K., & Harvey, P. D. (2006). Determinants of real-world functional performance in schizophrenia subjects: Correlations with cognition, functional capacity, and symptoms. *American Journal of Psychiatry, 163*(3), 418–425. doi: 10.1176/appi.ajp.163.3.418

Brady, K. T., Lydiard, R. B., Malcolm, R., & Ballenger, J. C. (1991). Cocaine-induced psychosis. *Journal of Clinical Psychiatry, 52*(12), 509–512.

Bramon, E., Rabe-Hesketh, S., Sham, P., Murray, R. M., & Frangou, S. (2004). Meta-analysis of the P300 and P50 waveforms in schizophrenia. *Schizophrenia Research, 70*(2–3), 315–329. doi: 10.1016/j.schres.2004.01.004

Breier, A., Schreiber, J. L., Dyer, J., & Pickar, D. (1991). National Institute of Mental Health longitudinal study of chronic schizophrenia: Prognosis and predictors of outcome. *Archives of General Psychiatry, 48*(3), 239–246.

Brown, A. S. (2006). Prenatal infection as a risk factor for schizophrenia. *Schizophrenia Bulletin, 32*(2), 200–202. doi: 10.1093/schbul/sbj052

Brown, G. G., & Thompson, W. K. (2010). Functional brain imaging in schizophrenia: Selected results and methods. In N. R. Swerdlow (Ed.), *Behavioral neurobiology of schizophrenia and its treatment* (pp. 181–214). New York, NY: Springer. Retrieved from http://link.springer.com/chapter/10.1007/7854_2010_54

Buckley, P. F., Miller, B. J., Lehrer, D. S., & Castle, D. J. (2009). Psychiatric comorbidities and schizophrenia. *Schizophrenia Bulletin, 35*(2), 383–402. doi: 10.1093/schbul/sbn135

Bustillo, J. R., Lauriello, J., Horan, W. P., & Keith, S. J. (2001). The psychosocial treatment of schizophrenia: An update. *American Journal of Psychiatry, 158*(2), 163–175. doi: 10.1176/appi.ajp.158.2.163

Cannon, T. D. (2015). How schizophrenia develops: Cognitive and brain mechanisms underlying onset of psychosis. *Trends in Cognitive Sciences, 19*(12), 744–756. doi: 10.1016/j.tics.2015.09.009

Cardno, A. G., & Gottesman, I. I. (2000). Twin studies of schizophrenia: From bow-and-arrow concordances to Star Wars Mx and functional genomics. *American Journal of Medical Genetics, 97*(1), 12–17. doi: 10.1002/(SICI)1096-8628(200021)97:1<12::AID-AJMG3>3.0.CO;2-U

Carlsson, A., Waters, N., Holm-Waters, S., Tedroff, J., Nilsson, M., & Carlsson, M. L. (2001). Interactions between monoamines, glutamate, and GABA in schizophrenia: New evidence. *Annual Review of Pharmacology and Toxicology, 41*(1), 237–260.

Casey, D. E. (2000). Tardive dyskinesia: Pathophysiology and animal models. *Journal of Clinical Psychiatry, 61*(Suppl. 4), 5–9.

Caspi, A., Reichenberg, A., Weiser, M., Rabinowitz, J., Kaplan, Z., Knobler, H., … Davidson, M. (2003). Cognitive performance in schizophrenia patients assessed before and following the first psychotic episode. *Schizophrenia Research, 65*(2–3), 87–94. doi: 10.1016/S0920-9964(03)00056-2

Chan, R.C.K., Di, X., McAlonan, G. M., & Gong, Q. (2011). Brain anatomical abnormalities in high-risk individuals, first-episode, and chronic schizophrenia: An activation likelihood estimation meta-analysis of illness progression. *Schizophrenia Bulletin, 37*(1), 177–188. doi: 10.1093/schbul/sbp073

Cheetham, S. W., Gruhl, F., Mattick, J. S., & Dinger, M. E. (2013). Long noncoding RNAs and the genetics of cancer. *British Journal of Cancer, 108*(12), 2419–2425. doi: 10.1038/bjc.2013.233

Coe, C. L., Kramer, M., Czéh, B., Gould, E., Reeves, A. J., Kirschbaum, C., & Fuchs, E. (2003). Prenatal stress diminishes neurogenesis in the dentate gyrus of juvenile rhesus monkeys. *Biological Psychiatry, 54*(10), 1025–1034. doi: 10.1016/S0006-3223(03)00698-X

Compton, M. T., & Walker, E. F. (2009). Physical manifestations of neurodevelopmental disruption: Are minor physical anomalies part of the syndrome of schizophrenia? *Schizophrenia Bulletin, 35*(2), 425–436. doi: 10.1093/schbul/sbn151

Cornblatt, B. A., Carrión, R. E., Addington, J., Seidman, L., Walker, E. F., Cannon, T. D., … Lencz, T. (2012). Risk factors for psychosis: Impaired social and role functioning. *Schizophrenia Bulletin, 38*(6), 1247–1257. doi: 10.1093/schbul/sbr136

Coyle, J. T., & Tsai, G. (2004). NMDA receptor function, neuroplasticity, and the pathophysiology of schizophrenia. *International Review of Neurobiology, 59*, 491–515.

Davidson, L., & McGlashan, T. H. (1997). The varied outcomes of schizophrenia. *Canadian Journal of Psychiatry, 42*(1), 34–43.

Davis, K. L., Kahn, R. S., Ko, G., & Davidson, M. (1991). Dopamine in schizophrenia: A review and reconceptualization. *American Journal of Psychiatry, 148*(11), 1474–1486. doi: 10.1176/ajp.148.11.1474

Del Arco, A., & Mora, F. (2009). Neurotransmitters and prefrontal cortex–limbic system interactions: Implications for plasticity and psychiatric disorders. *Journal of Neural Transmission*, *116*(8), 941–952. doi: 10.1007/s00702-009-0243-8

DeLisi, L. E. (1992). The significance of age of onset for schizophrenia. *Schizophrenia Bulletin*, *18*(2), 209–215. doi: 10.1093/schbul/18.2.209

Dempster, E. L., Pidsley, R., Schalkwyk, L. C., Owens, S., Georgiades, A., Kane, F., ... Mill, J. (2011). Disease-associated epigenetic changes in monozygotic twins discordant for schizophrenia and bipolar disorder. *Human Molecular Genetics*, *20*(24), 4786–4796. doi: 10.1093/hmg/ddr416

Dennert, J. W., & Andreasen, N. C. (1983). CT scanning and schizophrenia: A review. *Psychiatric Developments*, *1*(1), 105–122.

Dias, B. G., & Ressler, K. J. (2014). Parental olfactory experience influences behavior and neural structure in subsequent generations. *Nature Neuroscience*, *17*(1), 89–96. doi: 10.1038/nn.3594

Dickerson, F. B. (2000). Cognitive behavioral psychotherapy for schizophrenia: A review of recent empirical studies. *Schizophrenia Research*, *43*(2–3), 71–90. doi: 10.1016/S0920-9964(99)00153-X

Dixon, L. B., Dickerson, F., Bellack, A. S., Bennett, M., Dickinson, D., Goldberg, R. W., ... Kreyenbuhl, J. (2010). The 2009 schizophrenia PORT psychosocial treatment recommendations and summary statements. *Schizophrenia Bulletin*, *36*(1), 48–70. doi: 10.1093/schbul/sbp115

D'Souza, D. C., Abi-Saab, W. M., Madonick, S., Forselius-Bielen, K., Doersch, A., Braley, G., ... Krystal, J. H. (2005). Delta-9-tetrahydrocannabinol effects in schizophrenia: Implications for cognition, psychosis, and addiction. *Biological Psychiatry*, *57*(6), 594–608. doi: 10.1016/j.biopsych.2004.12.006

Eldridge, L. (2016, February 11). *What percentage of smokers get lung cancer, anyway?* Verywell. Retrieved March 5, 2016, from http://lungcancer.about.com/od/Lung-Cancer-And-Smoking/f/Smokers-Lung-Cancer.htm

Ellis, A. (1980). Rational-emotive therapy and cognitive behavior therapy: Similarities and differences. *Cognitive Therapy and Research*, *4*(4), 325–340. doi: 10.1007/BF01178210

Elvevag, B., & Goldberg, T. E. (2000). Cognitive impairment in schizophrenia is the core of the disorder.

Critical Reviews in Neurobiology, *14*(1), 1–21. doi: 10.1615/CritRevNeurobiol.v14.i1.10

Erlenmeyer-Kimling, L., Squires-Wheeler, E., Adamo, U. H., Bassett, A. S., Cornblatt, B. A., Kestenbaum, C. J., ... Gottesman, I. I. (1995). The New York High-Risk Project: Psychoses and cluster A personality disorders in offspring of schizophrenic parents at 23 years of follow-up. *Archives of General Psychiatry*, *52*(10), 857–865.

Evans, K., McGrath, J., & Milns, R. (2003). Searching for schizophrenia in ancient Greek and Roman literature: A systematic review. *Acta Psychiatrica Scandinavica*, *107*(5), 323–330. doi: 10.1034/j.1600-0447.2003.00053.x

First, M., Williams, J. B. W., Karg, R. S., & Spitzer, R. L. (2016). *Structured Clinical Interview for DSM-5 Disorders, Clinician Version (SCID-5-CV)*. Arlington, VA: American Psychiatric Association.

Furrow, R. E., Christiansen, F. B., & Feldman, M. W. (2011). Environment-sensitive epigenetics and the heritability of complex diseases. *Genetics*, *189*(4), 1377–1387. doi: 10.1534/genetics.111.131912

Fusar-Poli, P., Borgwardt, S., Bechdolf, A., Addington, J., Riecher-Rössler, A., Schultze-Lutter, F., ... Yung, A. (2013). The psychosis high-risk state: A comprehensive state-of-the-art review. *JAMA Psychiatry*, *70*(1), 107–120. doi: 10.1001/jamapsychiatry.2013.269

Fusar-Poli, P., & Yung, A. R. (2012). Should attenuated psychosis syndrome be included in DSM-5? *Lancet*, *379*(9816), 591–592. doi: 10.1016/S0140-6736(11)61507-9

Gadelha, A., Noto, C. S., & de Jesus Mari, J. (2012). Pharmacological treatment of schizophrenia. *International Review of Psychiatry*, *24*(5), 489–498.

Gard, D. E., Kring, A. M., Gard, M. G., Horan, W. P., & Green, M. F. (2007). Anhedonia in schizophrenia: Distinctions between anticipatory and consummatory pleasure. *Schizophrenia Research*, *93*(1), 253–260.

Gharabawi, G. M., Bossie, C. A., Lasser, R. A., Turkoz, I., Rodriguez, S., & Chouinard, G. (2005). Abnormal Involuntary Movement Scale (AIMS) and Extrapyramidal Symptom Rating Scale (ESRS): Cross-scale comparison in assessing tardive dyskinesia. *Schizophrenia Research*, *77*(2–3), 119–128. doi: 10.1016/j.schres.2005.03.008

Gianfrancesco, F. D., Rajagopalan, K., Sajatovic, M., & Wang, R. (2006). Treatment adherence among patients with schizophrenia treated with atypical and typical antipsychotics. *Psychiatry Research*, *144*(2–3), 177–189. doi: 10.1016/j.psychres.2006 .02.006

Gómez-Durán, E. L., Martin-Fumadó, C., & Hurtado-Ruíz, G. (2012). Clinical and epidemiological aspects of suicide in patients with schizophrenia. *Actas Españolas Psiquiatría*, *40*(6), 333–345.

Gothelf, D., Feinstein, C., Thompson, T., Gu, E., Penniman, L., Van Stone, E., ... Reiss, A. L. (2007). Risk factors for the emergence of psychotic disorders in adolescents with 22q11.2 deletion syndrome. *American Journal of Psychiatry*, *164*(4), 663–669.

Grebb, J. A., & Cancro, R. (1989). Schizophrenia: Clinical features. In J. I. Kaplan & B. J. Sadock (Eds.), *Synopsis of psychiatry: Behavioral sciences, clinical psychiatry* (Vol. 5, pp. 757–777). Baltimore, MD: Williams & Wilkins.

Gründer, G., Hippius, H., & Carlsson, A. (2009). The "atypicality" of antipsychotics: A concept re-examined and re-defined. *Nature Reviews Drug Discovery*, *8*(3), 197–202. doi: 10.1038/nrd2806

Handel, A. E., Ebers, G. C., & Ramagopalan, S. V. (2010). Epigenetics: Molecular mechanisms and implications for disease. *Trends in Molecular Medicine*, *16*(1), 7–16. doi: 10.1016/j.molmed.2009.11.003

Harris, M. G., Henry, L. P., Harrigan, S. M., Purcell, R., Schwartz, O. S., Farrelly, S. E., ... McGorry, P. D. (2005). The relationship between duration of untreated psychosis and outcome: An eight-year prospective study. *Schizophrenia Research*, *79*(1), 85–93. doi: 10.1016/j.schres.2005.05.024

Harrow, M., Grossman, L. S., Jobe, T. H., & Herbener, E. S. (2005). Do patients with schizophrenia ever show periods of recovery? A 15-year multi-follow-up study. *Schizophrenia Bulletin*, *31*(3), 723–734.

Harvey, P. D., Koren, D., Reichenberg, A., & Bowie, C. R. (2006). Negative symptoms and cognitive deficits: What is the nature of their relationship? *Schizophrenia Bulletin*, *32*(2), 250–258. doi: 10.1093/schbul/sbj011

Healy, D., Le Noury, J., Harris, M., Butt, M., Linden, S., Whitaker, C., ... Roberts, A. P. (2012). Mortality in schizophrenia and related psychoses: Data from two cohorts, 1875–1924 and 1994–2010. *BMJ Open*, *2*(5), e001810. doi: 10.1136/bmjopen-2012-001810

Henn, F. A., & Braus, D. F. (1999). Structural neuroimaging in schizophrenia: An integrative view of neuromorphology. *European Archives of Psychiatry and Clinical Neuroscience*, *249*(Suppl. 4), 48–56.

Heston, L. L. (1966). Psychiatric disorders in foster home reared children of schizophrenic mothers. *British Journal of Psychiatry*, *112*(489), 819–825.

Holtzman, C. W., Trotman, H. D., Goulding, S. M., Ryan, A. T., MacDonald, A. N., Shapiro, D. I., ... Walker, E. F. (2013). Stress and neurodevelopmental processes in the emergence of psychosis. *Neuroscience*, *249*, 172–191. doi: 10.1016/j .neuroscience.2012.12.017

Horan, W. P., Ventura, J., Nuechterlein, K. H., Subotnik, K. L., Hwang, S. S., & Mintz, J. (2005). Stressful life events in recent-onset schizophrenia: Reduced frequencies and altered subjective appraisals. *Schizophrenia Research*, *75*(2), 363–374.

Howes, O. D., & Kapur, S. (2009). The dopamine hypothesis of schizophrenia: Version III—the final common pathway. *Schizophrenia Bulletin*, *35*(3), 549–562.

Huttunen, M. O. (1989). Maternal stress during pregnancy and the behavior of the offspring. In S. Doxiadis & S. Stewart (Eds.), *Early influences shaping the individual* (pp. 175–182). New York, NY: Plenum Press. Retrieved from http://link.springer .com/chapter/10.1007/978-1-4684-5634-9_15

Jablensky, A. (2006). Subtyping schizophrenia: Implications for genetic research. *Molecular Psychiatry*, *11*(9), 815–836.

Jentsch, J. D., Roth, R. H., & Taylor, J. R. (2000). Role for dopamine in the behavioral functions of the prefrontal corticostriatal system: Implications for mental disorders and psychotropic drug action. *Progress in Brain Research*, *126*, 433–453.

Kantrowitz, J., & Javitt, D. (2010). Thinking glutamatergically: Changing concepts of schizophrenia based upon changing neurochemical models. *Clinical Schizophrenia & Related Psychoses*, *4*(3), 189–200.

Karlsgodt, K. H., Niendam, T. A., Bearden, C. E., & Cannon, T. D. (2009). White matter integrity and prediction of social and role functioning in subjects at ultra-high risk for psychosis. *Biological Psychiatry*, *66*(6), 562–569.

Kay, S. R., Fiszbein, A., & Opler, L. A. (1987). The Positive and Negative Syndrome Scale (PANSS) for schizophrenia. *Schizophrenia Bulletin*, *13*(2), 261–276. doi: 10.1093/schbul/13.2.261

Kirkpatrick, B., Fenton, W. S., Carpenter, W. T., & Marder, S. R. (2006). The NIMH-MATRICS consensus statement on negative symptoms. *Schizophrenia Bulletin*, *32*(2), 214–219.

Lehman, A. F., Goldberg, R., Dixon, L. B., McNary, S., Postrado, L., Hackman, A., & McDonnell, K. (2002). Improving employment outcomes for persons with severe mental illnesses. *Archives of General Psychiatry, 59*(2), 165–172.

Lencz, T., Smith, C. W., Auther, A., Correll, C. U., & Cornblatt, B. (2004). Nonspecific and attenuated negative symptoms in patients at clinical high-risk for schizophrenia. *Schizophrenia Research, 68*(1), 37–48.

Lucksted, A., McFarlane, W., Downing, D., & Dixon, L. (2012). Recent developments in family psychoeducation as an evidence-based practice. *Journal of Marital and Family Therapy, 38*(1), 101–121.

Marneros, A., Pillmann, F., & Wustmann, T. (2012). Delusional disorders—are they simply paranoid schizophrenia? *Schizophrenia Bulletin, 38*(3), 561–568.

McGirr, A., Tousignant, M., Routhier, D., Pouliot, L., Chawky, N., Margolese, H. C., & Turecki, G. (2006). Risk factors for completed suicide in schizophrenia and other chronic psychotic disorders: A case–control study. *Schizophrenia Research, 84*(1), 132–143.

McKeith, I. G., Dickson, D. W., Lowe, J., Emre, M., O'Brien, J. T., Feldman, H., … The Consortium on DLB. (2005). Diagnosis and management of dementia with Lewy bodies: Third report of the DLB consortium. *Neurology, 65*(12), 1863–1872. doi: 10.1212/01.wnl.0000187889.17253.b1

Meltzer, H. Y. (2001). Treatment of suicidality in schizophrenia. *Annals of the New York Academy of Sciences, 932*(1), 44–60.

Menniti, F. S., Lindsley, C. W., Conn, P. J., Pandit, J., Zagouras, P., & Volkmann, R. A. (2013). Allosteric modulators for the treatment of schizophrenia: Targeting glutamatergic networks. *Current Topics in Medicinal Chemistry, 13*(1), 26–54.

Mesholam-Gately, R. I., Giuliano, A. J., Goff, K. P., Faraone, S. V., & Seidman, L. J. (2009). Neurocognition in first-episode schizophrenia: A meta-analytic review. *Neuropsychology, 23*(3), 315–336.

Miklowitz, D. J. (2004). The role of family systems in severe and recurrent psychiatric disorders: A developmental psychopathology view. *Development and Psychopathology, 16*(3), 667–688.

Miller, T. J., McGlashan, T. H., Rosen, J. L., Somjee, L., Markovich, P. J., Stein, K., & Woods, S. W. (2002). Prospective diagnosis of the initial prodrome for schizophrenia based on the Structured Interview for Prodromal Syndromes: Preliminary evidence of interrater reliability and predictive validity. *American Journal of Psychiatry, 159*(5), 863–865.

Minzenberg, M. J., Laird, A. R., Thelen, S., Carter, C. S., & Glahn, D. C. (2009). Meta-analysis of 41 functional neuroimaging studies of executive function in schizophrenia. *Archives of General Psychiatry, 66*(8), 811–822. doi: 10.1001/archgenpsychiatry.2009.91

Mittal, V. A., Tessner, K. D., McMillan, A. L., Delawalla, Z., Trotman, H. D., & Walker, E. F. (2006). Gesture behavior in unmedicated schizotypal adolescents. *Journal of Abnormal Psychology, 115*(2), 351–358.

Miyamoto, S., Duncan, G. E., Marx, C. E., & Lieberman, J. A. (2004). Treatments for schizophrenia: A critical review of pharmacology and mechanisms of action of antipsychotic drugs. *Molecular Psychiatry, 10*(1), 79–104. doi: 10.1038/sj.mp.4001556

Mojtabai, R., Susser, E. S., & Bromet, E. J. (2003). Clinical characteristics, 4-year course, and DSM-IV classification of patients with nonaffective acute remitting psychosis. *American Journal of Psychiatry, 160*(12), 2108–2115. doi: 10.1176/appi.ajp.160.12.2108

Moore, T.H.M., Zammit, S., Lingford-Hughes, A., Barnes, T.R.E., Jones, P. B., Burke, M., & Lewis, G. (2007). Cannabis use and risk of psychotic or affective mental health outcomes: A systematic review. *Lancet, 370*(9584), 319–328.

Mora, F., Segovia, G., & Del Arco, A. (2008). Glutamate–dopamine–GABA interactions in the aging basal ganglia. *Brain Research Reviews, 58*(2), 340–353.

Mowry, B., & Nancarrow, D. (2001). Molecular genetics of schizophrenia. *Clinical and Experimental Pharmacology and Physiology, 28*(1–2), 66–69. doi: 10.1046/j.1440-1681.2001.03399.x

Mueser, K. T., Deavers, F., Penn, D. L., & Cassisi, J. E. (2013). Psychosocial treatments for schizophrenia. *Annual Review of Clinical Psychology, 9*(1), 465–497. doi: 10.1146/annurev-clinpsy-050212-185620

Munetz, M. R., & Benjamin, S. (1988). How to examine patients using the Abnormal Involuntary Movement Scale. *Psychiatric Services, 39*(11), 1172–1177. doi: 10.1176/ps.39.11.1172

Naeem, F., Kingdon, D., & Turkington, D. (2005). Cognitive behaviour therapy for schizophrenia in patients with mild to moderate substance misuse problems. *Cognitive Behaviour Therapy, 34*(4), 207–215.

Narita, K., Sasaki, T., Akaho, R., Okazaki, Y., Kusumi, I., Kato, T., … Tokunaga, K. (2000). Human leukocyte antigen and season of birth in Japanese patients with schizophrenia. *American Journal of Psychiatry, 157*(7), 1173–1175. doi: 10.1176/appi.ajp.157.7.1173

Nasar, S. (2011). *A beautiful mind.* New York, NY: Simon & Schuster.

Newcomer, J. W. (2005). Second-generation (atypical) antipsychotics and metabolic effects. *CNS Drugs, 19*(1), 1–93.

Nielsen, J., Correll, C. U., Manu, P., & Kane, J. M. (2013). Termination of clozapine treatment due to medical reasons: When is it warranted and how can it be avoided? *Journal of Clinical Psychiatry, 74*(6), 603–613. doi: 10.4088/JCP.12r08064

Nuechterlein, K. H., Luck, S. J., Lustig, C., & Sarter, M. (2009). CNTRICS final task selection: Control of attention. *Schizophrenia Bulletin, 35*(1), 182–196. doi: 10.1093/schbul/sbn158

O'Donnell, K., O'Connor, T. G., & Glover, V. (2009). Prenatal stress and neurodevelopment of the child: Focus on the HPA axis and role of the placenta. *Developmental Neuroscience, 31*(4), 285–292.

O'Donovan, M. C., Craddock, N. J., & Owen, M. J. (2009). Genetics of psychosis: Insights from views across the genome. *Human Genetics, 126*(1), 3–12.

O'Dwyer, A.-M., & Marks, I. (2000). Obsessive-compulsive disorder and delusions revisited. *British Journal of Psychiatry, 176*(3), 281–284. doi: 10.1192/bjp.176.3.281

Okubo, Y., Suhara, T., Suzuki, K., Kobayashi, K., Inoue, O., Terasaki, O., … Toru, M. (1997). Decreased prefrontal dopamine D1 receptors in schizophrenia revealed by PET. *Nature, 385*(6617), 634–636. doi: 10.1038/385634a0

Olabi, B., Ellison-Wright, I., McIntosh, A. M., Wood, S. J., Bullmore, E., & Lawrie, S. M. (2011). Are there progressive brain changes in schizophrenia? A meta-analysis of structural magnetic resonance imaging studies. *Biological Psychiatry, 70*(1), 88–96. doi: 10.1016/j.biopsych.2011.01.032

Paolicelli, R. C., Bolasco, G., Pagani, F., Maggi, L., Scianni, M., Panzanelli, P., … Dumas, L. (2011). Synaptic pruning by microglia is necessary for normal brain development. *Science, 333*(6048), 1456–1458.

Pego-Reigosa, J. M., & Isenberg, D. A. (2008). Psychosis due to systemic lupus erythematosus: Characteristics and long-term outcome of this rare manifestation of the disease. *Rheumatology, 47*(10), 1498–1502. doi: 10.1093/rheumatology/ken260

Penn, D. L., Waldheter, E. J., Perkins, D. O., Mueser, K. T., & Lieberman, J. A. (2005). Psychosocial treatment for first-episode psychosis: A research update. *American Journal of Psychiatry, 162*(12), 2220–2232.

Phillips, K. A., Menard, W., & Fay, C. (2006). Gender similarities and differences in 200 individuals with body dysmorphic disorder. *Comprehensive Psychiatry, 47*(2), 77–87. doi: 10.1016/j.comppsych.2005.07.002

Pilling, S., Bebbington, P., Kuipers, E., Garety, P., Geddes, J., Martindale, B., … Morgan, C. (2002). Psychological treatments in schizophrenia: Meta-analyses of randomized controlled trials of social skills training and cognitive remediation. *Psychological Medicine, 32*(5), 783–791.

Pillmann, F., Haring, A., Balzuweit, S., Blöink, R., & Marneros, A. (2002). The concordance of ICD-10 acute and transient psychosis and DSM-IV brief psychotic disorder. *Psychological Medicine, 32*(3), 525–533. doi: 10.1017/S0033291702005408

Postuma, R. B., Aarsland, D., Barone, P., Burn, D. J., Hawkes, C. H., Oertel, W., & Ziemssen, T. (2012). Identifying prodromal Parkinson's disease: Pre-motor disorders in Parkinson's disease. *Movement Disorders, 27*(5), 617–626. doi: 10.1002/mds.24996

Potter, D., Summerfelt, A., Gold, J., & Buchanan, R. W. (2006). Review of clinical correlates of P50 sensory gating abnormalities in patients with schizophrenia. *Schizophrenia Bulletin, 32*(4), 692–700.

Revheim, N., Butler, P. D., Schechter, I., Jalbrzikowski, M., Silipo, G., & Javitt, D. C. (2006). Reading impairment and visual processing deficits in schizophrenia. *Schizophrenia Research, 87*(1–3), 238–245. doi: 10.1016/j.schres.2006.06.022

Richards, C. F., & Gurr, D. E. (2000). Psychosis. *Emergency Medicine Clinics of North America, 18*(2), 253–262.

Riley, B., & Kendler, K. S. (2006). Molecular genetic studies of schizophrenia. *European Journal of Human Genetics, 14*(6), 669–680.

Rosenfarb, I. S., Bellack, A. S., & Aziz, N. (2006). Family interactions and the course of schizophrenia in African American and White patients. *Journal of Abnormal Psychology, 115*(1), 112–120.

Rosenheck, R., Leslie, D., Sint, K., Lin, H., Robinson, D. G., Schooler, N. R., ... Kane, J. M. (2016). Cost-effectiveness of comprehensive, integrated care for first episode psychosis in the NIMH RAISE early treatment program. *Schizophrenia Bulletin. Advance online publication.* doi: 10.1093/schbul/sbv224

Ross, D. A., & Cetas, J. S. (2012). Steroid psychosis: A review for neurosurgeons. *Journal of Neuro-Oncology, 109*(3), 439–447. doi: 10.1007/s11060-012-0919-z

Rummel-Kluge, C., Komossa, K., Schwarz, S., Hunger, H., Schmid, F., Kissling, W., ... Leucht, S. (2012). Second-generation antipsychotic drugs and extrapyramidal side effects: A systematic review and meta-analysis of head-to-head comparisons. *Schizophrenia Bulletin, 38*(1), 167–177. doi: 10.1093/schbul/sbq042

Rus-Calafell, M., Gutiérrez-Maldonado, J., Ortega-Bravo, M., Ribas-Sabaté, J., & Caqueo-Urízar, A. (2013). A brief cognitive–behavioural social skills training for stabilised outpatients with schizophrenia: A preliminary study. *Schizophrenia Research, 143*(2), 327–336.

Sadock, B. J., Sadock, V. A., Ruiz, P., & Kaplan, H. I. (Eds.). (2009). *Kaplan & Sadock's comprehensive textbook of psychiatry* (9th ed.). Philadelphia, PA: Wolters Kluwer Health/Lippincott Williams & Wilkins.

Saha, S., Chant, D., Welham, J., & McGrath, J. (2005). A systematic review of the prevalence of schizophrenia. *PLOS Medicine, 2*(5), e141. doi: 10.1371/journal.pmed.0020141

Saks, E. R. (2008). *The center cannot hold: My journey through madness.* New York, NY: Hachette Books.

Salokangas, R.K.R., Nieman, D. H., Heinimaa, M., Svirskis, T., Luutonen, S., From, T., ... The EPOS Group. (2012). Psychosocial outcome in patients at clinical high risk of psychosis: A prospective follow-up. *Social Psychiatry and Psychiatric Epidemiology, 48*(2), 303–311. doi: 10.1007/s00127-012-0545-2

Sapolsky, R. M. (2004). *Why zebras don't get ulcers* (3rd ed.). New York, NY: Holt Paperbacks.

Scheel, M., Prokscha, T., Bayerl, M., Gallinat, J., & Montag, C. (2013). Myelination deficits in schizophrenia: Evidence from diffusion tensor imaging. *Brain Structure and Function, 218*(1), 151–156.

Schizophrenia Working Group of the Psychiatric Genomics Consortium. (2014). Biological insights from 108 schizophrenia-associated genetic loci. *Nature, 511*(7510), 421–427. doi: 10.1038/nature13595

Schmitt, A., Hasan, A., Gruber, O., & Falkai, P. (2011). Schizophrenia as a disorder of disconnectivity. *European Archives of Psychiatry and Clinical Neuroscience, 261*(2), 150–154.

Schulze, T. G., Akula, N., Breuer, R., Steele, J., Nalls, M. A., Singleton, A. B., ... McMahon, F. J. (2014). Molecular genetic overlap in bipolar disorder, schizophrenia, and major depressive disorder. *World Journal of Biological Psychiatry, 15*(3), 200–208.

Sekar, A., Bialas, A. R., de Rivera, H., Davis, A., Hammond, T. R., Kamitaki, N., ... McCarroll, S. A. (2016). Schizophrenia risk from complex variation of complement component 4. *Nature, 530*(7589), 177–183. doi: 10.1038/nature16549

Shad, M. U., Tamminga, C. A., Cullum, M., Haas, G. L., & Keshavan, M. S. (2006). Insight and frontal cortical function in schizophrenia: A review. *Schizophrenia Research, 86*(1), 54–70.

Siever, L. J., & Davis, K. L. (2004). The pathophysiology of schizophrenia disorders: Perspectives from the spectrum. *American Journal of Psychiatry, 161*(3), 398–413. doi: 10.1176/appi.ajp.161.3.398

Silverstein, S. M., & Keane, B. P. (2011). Perceptual organization impairment in schizophrenia and associated brain mechanisms: Review of research from 2005 to 2010. *Schizophrenia Bulletin, 37*(4), 690–699. doi: 10.1093/schbul/sbr052

Spitzer, R. L., Endicott, J., & Gibbon, M. (1979). Crossing the border into borderline personality and borderline schizophrenia: The development of criteria. *Archives of General Psychiatry, 36*(1), 17–24.

Steinglass, J. E., Eisen, J. L., Attia, E., Mayer, L., & Walsh, B. T. (2007). Is anorexia nervosa a delusional disorder? An assessment of eating beliefs in anorexia nervosa. *Journal of Psychiatric Practice, 13*(2), 65–71. doi: 10.1097/01.pra.0000265762.79753.88

Strauss, G. P., Horan, W. P., Kirkpatrick, B., Fischer, B. A., Keller, W. R., Miski, P., ... Carpenter, W. T. (2013). Deconstructing negative symptoms of schizophrenia: Avolition–apathy and diminished expression clusters predict clinical presentation and functional outcome. *Journal of Psychiatric Research, 47*(6), 783–790.

Suddath, R. L., Christison, G. W., Torrey, E. F., Casanova, M. F., & Weinberger, D. R. (1990). Anatomical abnormalities in the brains of monozygotic twins discordant for schizophrenia. *New England Journal of Medicine, 322*(12), 789–794.

Sullivan, P. F., Kendler, K. S., & Neale, M. C. (2003). Schizophrenia as a complex trait: Evidence from a meta-analysis of twin studies. *Archives of General Psychiatry, 60*(12), 1187–1192.

Susser, E. S., Brown, A. S., & Gorman, J. M. (Eds.). (1999). *Prenatal exposures in schizophrenia.* Washington, DC: American Psychiatric Press.

Swartz, M. S., Perkins, D. O., Stroup, T. S., Davis, S. M., Capuano, G., Rosenheck, R. A., ... Lieberman, J. A.; CATIE Investigators. (2007). Effects of antipsychotic medications on psychosocial functioning in patients with chronic schizophrenia: Findings from the NIMH CATIE study. *American Journal of Psychiatry, 164*(3), 428–436. doi: 10.1176/ajp .2007.164.3.428

Taylor, M. A., & Fink, M. (2003). Catatonia in psychiatric classification: A home of its own. *American Journal of Psychiatry, 160*(7), 1233–1241.

Tien, A. Y. (1991). Distribution of hallucinations in the population. *Social Psychiatry and Psychiatric Epidemiology, 26*(6), 287–292. doi: 10.1007/ BF00789221

Tienari, P., Wynne, L. C., Moring, J., Lahti, I., Naarala, M., Sorri, A., ... Kaleva, M. (1994). The Finnish Adoptive Family Study of Schizophrenia: Implications for family research. *British Journal of Psychiatry. Supplement, 164*(23), 20–26.

Trotman, H. D., Holtzman, C. W., Walker, E. F., Addington, J. M., Bearden, C. E., Cadenhead, K. S., ... McGlashan, T. H. (2014). Stress exposure and sensitivity in the clinical high-risk syndrome: Initial findings from the North American Prodrome Longitudinal Study (NAPLS). *Schizophrenia Research, 160*(1–3), 104–109. doi: 10.1016/j.schres.2014 .09.017

Udechuku, A., Olver, J., Hallam, K., Blyth, F., Leslie, M., Nasso, M., ... Burrows, G. (2005). Assertive community treatment of the mentally ill: Service model and effectiveness. *Australasian Psychiatry, 13*(2), 129–134.

van Os, J., & Selten, J.-P. (1998). Prenatal exposure to maternal stress and subsequent schizophrenia. The May 1940 invasion of The Netherlands. *British Journal of Psychiatry, 172*(4), 324–326.

Walker, E. F. (1994). Developmentally moderated expressions of the neuropathology underlying schizophrenia. *Schizophrenia Bulletin, 20*(3), 453–480.

Walker, E. F., & Bollini, A. M. (2002). Pubertal neurodevelopment and the emergence of psychotic symptoms. *Schizophrenia Research, 54*(1), 17–23.

Walker, E. F., & Diforio, D. (1997). Schizophrenia: A neural diathesis-stress model. *Psychological Review, 104*(4), 667.

Walker, E. F., Grimes, K. E., Davis, D. M., & Smith, A. J. (1993). Childhood precursors of schizophrenia: Facial expressions of emotion. *American Journal of Psychiatry, 150*(11), 1654–1660. doi: 10.1176/ajp.150.11.1654

Walker, E. F., Mittal, V., & Tessner, K. (2008). Stress and the hypothalamic pituitary adrenal axis in the developmental course of schizophrenia. *Annual Review of Clinical Psychology, 4,* 189–216. doi: 10.1146/annurev.clinpsy.4.022007.141248

Walshe, M., McDonald, C., Taylor, M., Zhao, J., Sham, P., Grech, A., ... Murray, R. M. (2005). Obstetric complications in patients with schizophrenia and their unaffected siblings. *European Psychiatry, 20*(1), 28–34.

Wand, G. S., Oswald, L. M., McCaul, M. E., Wong, D. F., Johnson, E., Zhou, Y., ... Kumar, A. (2007). Association of amphetamine-induced striatal dopamine release and cortisol responses to psychological stress. *Neuropsychopharmacology, 32*(11), 2310–2320. doi: 10.1038/sj.npp.1301373

Weiner, W. J., Rabinstein, A., Levin, B., Weiner, C., & Shulman, L. M. (2001). Cocaine-induced persistent dyskinesias. *Neurology, 56*(7), 964–965.

Weissman, M. M., Bland, R. C., Canino, G. J., Greenwald, S., Hwu, H.-G., Joyce, P. R., ... Yeh, E.-K. (1999). Prevalence of suicide ideation and suicide attempts in nine countries. *Psychological Medicine, 29*(1), 9–17.

Welberg, L. A., & Seckl, J. R. (2001). Prenatal stress, glucocorticoids and the programming of the brain. *Journal of Neuroendocrinology, 13*(2), 113–128.

Whalley, H. C., Papmeyer, M., Sprooten, E., Lawrie, S. M., Sussmann, J. E., & McIntosh, A. M. (2012). Review of functional magnetic resonance imaging studies comparing bipolar disorder and schizophrenia. *Bipolar Disorders, 14*(4), 411–431.

Wustmann, T., Pillmann, F., & Marneros, A. (2011). Gender-related features of persistent delusional disorders. *European Archives of Psychiatry and Clinical Neuroscience, 261*(1), 29–36.

Wykes, T., Huddy, V., Cellard, C., McGurk, S. R., & Czobor, P. (2011). A meta-analysis of cognitive remediation for schizophrenia: Methodology and effect sizes. *American Journal of Psychiatry, 168*(5), 472–485. doi: 10.1176/appi.ajp.2010.10060855

Xu, J., Murphy, S., Kochanek, K., & Bastian, B. (2016). Deaths: Final data for 2013. *National Vital Statistics Reports, 64*(2).

Yung, A. R., & Nelson, B. (2011). Young people at ultra high risk for psychosis: A research update.

Early Intervention in Psychiatry, 5(Suppl. 1), 52–57. doi: 10.1111/j.1751-7893.2010.00241.x

Yung, A. R., Yuen, H. P., McGorry, P. D., Phillips, L. J., Kelly, D., Dell'Olio, M., … Buckby, J. (2005). Mapping the onset of psychosis: The Comprehensive Assessment of At-Risk Mental States. *Australian and New Zealand Journal of Psychiatry, 39*(11–12), 964–971. doi: 10.1111/j.1440-1614.2005.01714.x

Zemlan, F. P., Hirschowitz, J., Sautter, F. J., & Garver, D. L. (1984). Impact of lithium therapy on core psychotic symptoms of schizophrenia. *British Journal of Psychiatry, 144*(1), 64–69.

Chapter 11

Alcohol Use Disorder

Lara A. Ray, Kelly E. Courtney, ReJoyce Green,
and Guadalupe A. Bacio

This chapter provides a comprehensive overview of alcohol use disorders, and also brief descriptions of other substance use disorders. First, we review the history of alcohol use disorders in the United States and across Western societies. Second, we review diagnostic considerations, including research and clinical questions as the field adapts to the fifth edition of the *Diagnostic and Statistical Manual of Mental Disorders* (*DSM-5*). Third, we discuss a theoretical conceptualization of alcoholism based on a biopsychosocial model of psychiatric disorders, and present a review of psychosocial and biological factors thought to influence the etiology of alcohol use disorders. Finally, we briefly discuss empirically supported treatment approaches for alcohol use disorders, including psychosocial and pharmacological interventions.

History

Even after the legalization of alcohol in the United States in the mid-1930s, societal and political views on alcohol consumption have varied considerably throughout the years. After the drug-friendly culture of the 1960s and early 1970s, the end of the 20th century saw increased public concern about heavy alcohol and drug use and underage drinking (McCrady, 2001). The drinking age was increased to 21 again, after it had been lowered to 18 during the Vietnam War era, and the government started increasing its efforts to stop illegal alcohol and drug use. But not only the government was concerned about underage drinking; increased deaths from drunk driving were receiving increased public attention. Groups such as Mothers Against Drunk Driving helped promote stricter drunk driving laws. Moreover, binge drinking and deaths resulting from alcohol on college campuses have received increased news media attention for several years now, with a recent study suggesting approximately a 3% per 100,000 increase in alcohol-related, unintentional injury deaths from 1998 to 2005 among college students (Hingson, Zha, & Weitzman, 2009). As a result, the implementation of programs to reduce underage drinking is now a major priority for most colleges in the United States (McCrady, 2001). It appears that society has taken two opposing approaches to dealing with alcohol use: a conservative attitude that promotes more punishment for irresponsible alcohol use (especially any alcohol use by underage individuals), and a more liberal approach that focuses primarily on reducing the harm that may be caused by alcohol use.

As the perspectives on alcohol use have shifted throughout the years, the treatment modalities for alcohol use disorders have likewise changed. Until the mid-1930s, individuals who did not have the financial means to pay for inpatient treatment at a private hospital were forced to use state hospitals, rescue missions, jails, the Salvation Army, or public ministries. Alcoholics Anonymous (AA), which was founded in 1935 by two alcohol-dependent individuals—Bill Wilson, a stock speculator, and Dr. Bob Smith, a medical doctor—provided the first community-based approach to supporting the recovery of alcohol-dependent individuals, regardless of their financial status, by offering free, peer-delivered group treatment to all comers. For many years, AA has offered one of the few outpatient treatment approaches that individuals could turn to for help with alcohol problems. In addition, the AA approach was also the first to combine religion, medicine, and the help of sponsors (individuals with a history of recovery from alcohol problems who were committed to helping others stay sober). AA has since become a well-known and highly utilized organization, with more than 100,000 groups in more than 150 countries, and with approximately 2 million members worldwide (Alcoholics Anonymous, 2006). From the perspective of psychology, AA and the other self-help groups that were developed following the AA model (e.g., Narcotics Anonymous, Cocaine Anonymous) have been criticized for their emphasis on individuals' powerlessness over addiction, and for the spiritual focus of their 12-step program. As a response to these criticisms, alternative self-help groups have evolved that are based on more rational and humanistic approaches. Abstinence-based programs such as Self-Management and Recovery Training (SMART) and self-help groups emphasizing moderation in drinking (e.g., Moderation Management, or MM) promote the use of cognitive-behavioral principles within a self-help environment to help individuals achieve desired outcomes. One of the best known of these alternative self-help programs is Rational Recovery (RR; Trimpey, 1992). Rational Recovery emphasizes self-empowerment and the individual's ability to replace harmful behaviors with healthier choices. The process of achieving sobriety using the Rational Recovery framework involves education and awareness, and the recognition of instances when the old brain (i.e., the addicted part of the brain) may try to "tempt" the new brain. Currently, research evaluating the effectiveness of RR is based primarily on self-reports about patients' sobriety, with little backing from research using randomized controlled trials—the type of research that has recently become available for 12-step facilitation approaches (Project MATCH Research Group, 1997). Nevertheless, limited results suggest that RR may be comparable to (Galanter, Egelko, & Edwards, 1993) or possibly more effective than (Schmidt, Carns, & Chandler, 2001) AA-type treatments, and thus that RR may constitute a viable self-help alternative. There is, however, little research investigating other variables important in understanding the effectiveness of self-help treatment in general, such as defensiveness, resistance to recovery, and denial (Schmidt et al., 2001). Because of its low cost and accessibility, self-help is likely to remain a core element of treatment, and more research using objective measures, as well as multiple outcome variables, is needed to evaluate the effectiveness of self-help programs.

Throughout the past 20 years, treatment of alcohol use disorders has evolved primarily from two approaches: rehabilitation and harm reduction. Examples of the rehabilitative approach are employee assistance programs (EAPs) and the provision of education classes for individuals who have been convicted of drunk driving or other alcohol offenses (e.g., underage drinking). Rehabilitative programs are based on the belief that treatment is a better alternative to punishment, and that abstinence-based treatment will increase a person's chances of returning to his baseline of productive functioning in society (McCrady, 2001). Conversely, harm-reduction models are based on the belief that human beings are going to continue to engage in behaviors that are potentially dangerous. The goal of these models is to reduce alcohol intake and to minimize harm by providing individuals with safer ways to engage in such risky behaviors (e.g., by using designated drivers). Individuals are encouraged to make changes in their use of alcohol that do not have to be as radical as complete and sustained abstinence. Controlled drinking, for example, is one approach thought to promote a decrease in risky alcohol use behaviors and, as a result, a decrease in the negative consequences of drinking. Although the harm-reduction model remains widely debated, there is a great deal of research supporting its effectiveness and efficacy in the treatment *and* prevention of alcohol problems (Witkiewitz & Marlatt, 2006).

The issue of abstinence versus moderation as alternative treatment goals remains a highly debated topic. The more traditional approach contends that abstinence is the only acceptable goal, given the progressive nature of an alcohol use disorder. The goal of abstinence remains the standard clinical practice for alcoholism treatment in the United States. However, drinking moderation has been introduced as an alternative to abstinence in some programs. This approach is typically criticized when suggested as an option for treating severe use disorders but has been better accepted as an alternative for the treatment of mild use disorders (formally referred to as *alcohol abuse*). The empirical findings suggest that having individuals select their treatment goal (i.e., abstinence or controlled drinking) may increase compliance and improve outcomes (Öjehegan & Berglund, 1989; Orford & Keddie, 1986). A recent study looked at three different drinking goals offered within either a cognitive-behavioral intervention or a medical management only framework: abstinence, conditional abstinence (i.e., allowing for occasional use), and controlled drinking (Bujarski, O'Malley, Lunny, & Ray, 2013). Analyses revealed that those with an abstinence goal had overall better outcomes, followed by those with a conditional abstinence goal and then those with a controlled drinking goal. Interestingly, a treatment × drinking goal interaction emerged such that the benefit of cognitive behavioral intervention over medical management was only evident for those individuals who reported controlled drinking as a goal (Bujarski et al., 2013).

Some experts have argued in favor of abstinence as a preferred treatment goal (McCrady, 1992), and have suggested that selecting moderation as a goal may reinforce a person's distorted view that alcohol is important to his functioning and therefore should not be given up (McCrady, 2001). In line with this conceptualization, researchers found that health care providers were more likely to strongly recommend abstinence than controlled drinking for individuals with a greater severity of alcohol problems and greater social support (Cox, Rosenberg, Hodgins, Macartney, & Maurer, 2004). Interestingly, recent research has found that the level of impaired control over drinking predicted outcome in a moderation-oriented treatment, such that patients who scored higher on impaired control were less likely to have been successful in a moderation-oriented treatment program at 6-month follow-up (Heather & Dawe, 2005). In a different study, controlled drinking was found to be more appropriate for individuals who were younger, showed lower levels of dependence and withdrawal, had a history of being able to drink in moderation, had no medical or psychological problems likely to be exacerbated by continued drinking, and did not have a family history positive for alcoholism (Rosenberg, 1993). These findings are consistent with the clinical impression that moderation-oriented approaches may be appropriate for individuals with overall lower severity alcohol use disorders. As noted by McCrady (2001), clinicians should consider any initial drinking goal (abstinence or moderation) as tentative, given that goals may need to be reevaluated during the course of therapy. Thus, individuals who are not succeeding in their efforts to drink in moderation need to reconsider their drinking goal and reevaluate the extent of their alcohol problems. Such persons may not be able to recover from alcohol addiction without embracing abstinence as their goal.

The diagnosis of alcohol use disorders has changed significantly over the years, a process reflected in the various editions of the *DSM*. In the first edition of the *Diagnostic and Statistical Manual of Mental Disorders* (*DSM-I*; American Psychiatric Association [APA], 1952), alcoholism was classified as a personality disorder, reflecting the notion that alcoholism stemmed from an addictive personality. More than 20 years later, Edwards and Gross (1976) published an influential paper describing alcohol dependence syndrome (ADS), which led to a major shift in the way substance use disorders were conceptualized. Specifically, Edwards and Gross (1976) emphasized the salience that a given substance of abuse was occupying in a person's life, thereby expanding the concept of dependence to various substances—many of which did not have clinically relevant withdrawal syndromes or tolerance (e.g., cannabis). As a result, in the third edition of the *Diagnostic and Statistical Manual of Mental Disorders* (*DSM-III*; APA, 1980), the diagnosis of alcohol problems was based heavily on the notion that multiple substances of abuse could lead to a dependence syndrome, based on their impact on one's life and functioning. Importantly, up through *DSM-II*, only diagnostic labels and brief descriptions of the major illnesses had been provided. It was not until the *DSM-III* that specific diagnostic criteria were provided for substance use disorders, an approach that found rapid acceptance in the United States and internationally (Hasin et al., 2003). The use of specific diagnostic criteria in the *DSM-III* was predated and heavily influenced by the Feighner diagnostic criteria (Feighner et al., 1972) for alcohol dependence, which had been developed mainly for research purposes. An important change implemented in *DSM-III* was the distinction between *abuse* and *dependence*. According to *DSM-III*, alcohol abuse was characterized by a pattern of pathological alcohol use, impairment in social or occupational functioning, and duration of disturbance of at least 1 month. *DSM-III-R* (APA, 1987) and *DSM-IV* (APA, 1994) expanded the characterization of alcohol abuse by providing a more concrete operational definition of the abuse criteria, which in turn increased the reliability of the alcohol abuse diagnosis.

In *DSM-III*, alcohol dependence required that either the tolerance or the withdrawal criterion had been met. However, in *DSM-III-R* this was no longer a necessary requirement for the diagnosis of alcohol dependence. Furthermore, *DSM-III-R* established a specific definition for the tolerance criterion, quantifying the increase in the amount of drinking necessary to achieve a level of intoxication or desired effect: that is, intake must be at least 50% higher to demonstrate tolerance. However, *DSM-IV* dropped that concept and suggested that tolerance needed to be established on a case-by-case basis. The *DSM-IV* expanded on the *DSM-III-R* definition for tolerance by introducing the concept that a casual user's behavior could be impaired with the same level of blood alcohol at which an individual with alcohol dependence might function adequately. With the recently released fifth edition of the *DSM* (*DSM-5*; APA, 2013), the diagnosis of and criteria for alcohol abuse and dependence have once again received a significant overhaul. However, the notion of tolerance and withdrawal as sufficient, yet not necessary, symptoms of the disorder remains (assuming the substance in question is not prescribed by a physician).

In summary, the changes in the definition of alcohol abuse and dependence and of alcohol use disorder across versions of the *DSM* over the years highlight the history of the alcohol use disorder conceptualization and reflect societal views of alcohol use. Specifically, the field started with a conceptualization of alcohol dependence that was based largely on personality traits and the idea of an addictive personality, but that view has evolved into the current conceptualization of alcohol use disorder, which emphasizes the interplay between the biological and psychological processes that lead to significant impairments in functioning as a result of excessive alcohol use.

Diagnosis

According to the *Diagnostic and Statistical Manual of Mental Disorders, Fifth Edition* (*DSM-5*), the diagnosis of an *alcohol use disorder* necessitates the experience of a problematic pattern of alcohol use leading to clinically significant impairment or distress, as manifested by at least 2 of 11 specified symptoms, occurring within a 12-month period (APA, 2013). (See Table 11.1 for a list of the criteria.) The *DSM-5* criterion set includes the symptoms formerly subsumed under substance abuse and substance dependence in the *DSM-IV*, with some minor, yet important variations. The two most notable changes include the removal of "legal problems" and the addition of "drug craving" to the symptom list. The American Psychiatric Association (APA), publishers of the *DSM*, noted that the removal of "legal problems" was based on the observation of distinct variations in international as well as local U.S. jurisdiction standards (APA, 2012), making this symptom highly unreliable and not suitable for diagnostic purposes. The addition of "craving" as a symptom represents an effort to increase consistency between the *DSM-5* and the International Classification of Diseases (ICD-10; World Health Organization, 2010), as well as an acknowledgment of the vast amount of scientific research highlighting the importance of craving in the perpetuation of the disorder. In treatment settings, moderate to intense cravings are reported by substantial proportions of patients (Oslin, Cary, Slaymaker, Colleran, & Blow, 2009; Yoon, Kim, Thuras, Grant, & Westermeyer, 2006), and the amelioration of craving is a frequent treatment target (Pavlick, Hoffmann, & Rosenberg, 2009). A longitudinal study of alcoholism course and chronicity found that craving was associated with the highest relative risk of all ICD-10 criteria for *DSM-IV* alcohol dependence (de Bruijn, Van Den Brink, de Graaf, & Vollebergh, 2005). Further, craving has been consistently found to predict substance consumption in multiple laboratory studies (Leeman, Corbin, & Fromme, 2009; Leeman, O'Malley, White, & McKee, 2010; MacKillop & Lisman, 2005; O'Malley, Krishnan-Sarin, Farren, Sinha, & Kreek, 2002), and represents a translational phenotype (Sinha & Li, 2007), thus highlighting its potential utility in identifying alcohol use disorders.

Importantly, the withdrawal and intoxication symptoms presented in the *DSM-5* are unique to each substance of abuse, and they are based largely on the pharmacological

TABLE 11.1   *DSM-5* Criteria for Alcohol Use Disorder

In *DSM-IV*, the criteria for alcohol abuse	Recurrent alcohol use resulting in a failure to fulfill major role obligations at work, school, or home.
	Recurrent alcohol use in situations in which it is physically hazardous.
	Continued alcohol use despite having persistent or recurrent social or interpersonal problems caused or exacerbated by the effects of alcohol.
In *DSM-IV*, the criteria for alcohol dependence	Tolerance, the need for greater amounts of the alcohol to achieve the same intoxication level or desired effect, or a markedly diminished effect with continued use of the same amount of alcohol.
	Withdrawal, the physiological and cognitive maladaptive symptoms that occur when the blood concentration of alcohol declines after prolonged and heavy use of alcohol.
	Alcohol is often taken in larger amounts and/or over longer periods of time than intended.
	Persistent desire or unsuccessful efforts to stop or cut down alcohol use.
	Increased amount of time is spent consuming, obtaining, or recovering from the effects of alcohol.
	Important occupational, social, or recreational activities are given up or reduced because of alcohol use.
	Alcohol consumption continues despite the knowledge of having persistent or recurrent physiological and psychological difficulties (e.g., blackouts, depression, worsening of an ulcer).
New criterion added in *DSM-5*	Craving or strong desire to use alcohol.
Severity Rating	Mild = 2 to 3 symptoms met.
	Moderate = 4 to 5 symptoms met.
	Severe = 6 to 11 symptoms met.

and behavioral effects of each substance when it is acutely present (i.e., intoxication) or acutely absent (i.e., withdrawal). The following alcohol withdrawal symptoms are specified in *DSM-5*: (a) autonomic hyperactivity (e.g., sweating or racing heart); (b) increased hand tremor; (c) insomnia; (d) nausea or vomiting; (e) transient visual, tactile, or auditory hallucinations or illusions; (f) psychomotor agitations; (g) anxiety; and (h) seizures. The *DSM-5* provides a distinct diagnosis for alcohol withdrawal syndrome, which is separate from alcohol use disorder; for a diagnosis of withdrawal syndrome, at least two of these symptoms must be met and those symptoms must cause clinically significant distress or impairment in functioning and must not be due to a general medical condition or be better accounted for by another mental disorder.

The decision in *DSM-5* to move to a single diagnosis of substance use disorder represents a significant shift from the previous distinction between substance abuse and substance dependence as defined in *DSM-IV*. This change was based on the overall goal of simplifying the diagnostic process for clinicians from having to remember two sets of criteria to having to remember only one ("DSM-5 to Include Controversial Changes," 2012), and most importantly, on a sizeable amount of research suggesting that substance use disorders are more adequately represented by a continuum of severity (Saha, Chou, & Grant, 2006; Martin, Chung, Kirisci, & Langenbucher, 2006). Thus, the *DSM-5* diagnosis requires the specification of a severity level (i.e., mild, moderate, or severe), based on the total number of criteria met (see Table 11.1). However, consistent with the polythetic nature of the *DSM*, any combination of two of the symptoms described is necessary and sufficient for a diagnosis of an alcohol use disorder. As a result, one individual may exhibit psychological difficulties after alcohol consumption and may drink in larger amounts than planned, thus arriving at an alcohol use disorder diagnosis, while another patient may experience tolerance and an inability to quit drinking, and receive the same diagnosis. This is an example of how our current nosology system allows clinicians to assign the same diagnosis to a variety of presentations of the same syndrome, which reflects the phenotypic heterogeneity, discussed further below, which is problematic from a behavioral genetics viewpoint.

In addition to the severity specifiers, the *DSM-5* suggests that remission and environmental specifiers be used when appropriate. Because individuals are at particularly high risk for relapse in the first 12 months after symptoms remit, the *DSM-5* distinguishes between early remission and sustained remission. Early remission is specified when none of the criteria for alcohol use disorder have been met for at least 3 months but for less than 12 months (with the exception of the craving criterion); whereas sustained remission is used when none of the criteria for alcohol use disorder have been met at any time during a period of 12 months or longer (again with the exception of the craving criterion). A controlled environment specifier is used to indicate the individual is currently in an environment where access to alcohol is restricted (e.g., a treatment facility).

In addition to alcohol, the *DSM-5* lists a number of other substance use disorders, each of which is diagnosed separately based on the substance being used (tobacco, cannabis, hallucinogens, inhalants, opioids, sedatives, hypnotics, anxiolytics, stimulants, caffeine, and other or unknown substances). Although the focus of this chapter is on alcohol use disorders, it is important to note that nearly all substance use disorders outlined in the *DSM-5* are diagnosed based on the same general set of criteria as outlined in Table 11.1. Thus, the overarching theme of loss of control, failure to fulfill obligations, continued use despite problems, and so forth, appear to capture the nature of a use disorder, despite differences in the specific substance used.

Nevertheless, there are unique diagnostic features for each substance use disorder. For example, smoking behaviors indicative of tobacco use disorder include smoking more cigarettes per day over time, smoking within the first 30 minutes of waking, and waking at night to smoke (Baker, Breslau, Covey, & Shiffman, 2012; Piper, McCarthy, & Baker, 2006). The *DSM-5* diagnostic features of post-abstinence withdrawal symptoms for tobacco use disorder are due largely to nicotine deprivation. These symptoms are presumably more severe in those smoking cigarettes or using smokeless tobacco as opposed to those using nicotine medication, due to the increased levels and quicker onset of nicotine that accompany cigarette smoking (APA, 2013). Tobacco withdrawal can occur in daily and nondaily smokers, and withdrawal symptoms include clinically significant changes in mood, such as irritability, anxiety, or depressed mood (APA, 2013).

Cannabis use disorder tends to develop over an elongated period of time, with patterns of cannabis use that slowly increase in amount and frequency (APA, 2013). Cannabis is generally one of the first substances adolescents try, along with alcohol and tobacco, and cannabis use prior to the age of 15 is a strong predictor for developing cannabis use disorder in young adulthood (Fergusson, Boden, & Horwood, 2006). Among adults, symptoms of cannabis use disorder include daily cannabis use and failed repeated cessation attempts, while milder adult cases can parallel adolescent cases in which cannabis use is less frequent but persists despite significant consequences (APA, 2013).

Opioid use disorder represents a distinct substance use disorder that requires careful diagnostic consideration from the clinician, as abuse of opioids can arise in individuals who are prescribed opioid medications for pain-related medical conditions. Symptoms of opioid use disorder include compulsive self-administration of opioid substances that are not prescribed for any medical reason or are used in exorbitant amounts for the particular medical condition (APA, 2013). Opioid withdrawal can cause anxiety and restlessness, along with physiological symptoms of dilated pupils, rhinorrhea, and nausea (APA, 2013). Lastly, stimulant use disorder can involve a range of abused stimulants, with the most common being amphetamines, methamphetamines, and cocaine. Features specific to stimulant withdrawal include disturbances in sleep patterns and increased daytime sleepiness (APA, 2013). Of note, the tolerance symptom specifies that this symptom does not count toward the required number when that substance is prescribed by a physician.

Prevalence

Alcohol use is highly prevalent worldwide. According to the World Health Organization (WHO), alcohol is the third largest risk factor for disability and disease, and the fourth leading preventable cause of death (WHO, 2010; Stahre, Roeber, Kanny, Brewer, & Zhang, 2014). As many as 90% of the U.S. population have had some experiences with alcohol during their lives, and a great number of those have developed one or more problems related to alcohol. Alcohol use disorders constitute a frequently occurring psychiatric problem. The lifetime prevalence of *DSM-IV* alcohol dependence (the more severe diagnosis) is approximately 12.5% in the general population, whereas the point prevalence is approximately 3.8%—suggesting that about 3.8% of the adult population in the United States meet the criteria for alcohol dependence in a single year (Hasin, Stinson, Ogburn, & Grant, 2007). *DSM-IV* alcohol abuse (the less severe diagnosis), which was given in cases where alcohol use causes significant interference in one or more domains of functioning, affects approximately 4% to 5% of the adult population in the United States (Grant et al., 2004). The 2014 National Survey on Drug Use and Health (NSDUH) revealed that 71.0% of adults had reported consuming alcohol in the past year, and 6.7% had reported engaging in heavy drinking in the past month (Substance Abuse and Mental Health Services Administration [SAMHSA], 2014a, 2014b).

Findings from a major epidemiological study, the National Epidemiologic Survey on Alcohol and Related Conditions (NESARC) conducted between 2001 and 2002 by the National Institute on Alcohol Abuse and Alcoholism (Dawson et al., 2005), indicated that the prevalence of *DSM-IV* alcohol dependence in the general population of adults in the United States was 3.81%—with a higher incidence of the disorder among males

(5.42%) as compared to females (2.32%). Results from the second wave of this study (NESARC-II), conducted between 2004 and 2005, indicated that 77.54% of current drinkers who did not have an alcohol use disorder during the first wave continued to drink without developing an alcohol use disorder. Of those who reported only past-year alcohol abuse during the first wave, 14.01% had developed alcohol dependence, and of those who had dependence during the first wave, 36.34% remained dependent at the second wave (National Institutes of Health [NIH], 2010). The proportion of individuals remaining dependent from one wave to the next did vary by age, such that those between the ages of 45 and 64 exhibited the highest rate of remaining alcohol dependent (44.10%), followed by 38.34% of individuals between the ages of 25 and 44, and 31.78% between the ages of 18 and 24 (NIH, 2010). Results from the third wave (NESARC-III), conducted between 2012 and 2013, when compared to the first wave, revealed an overall increase in the proportion of past-year drinkers (from 65.4% to 72.7%), with a substantial decrease in lifetime abstainers (from 17.30% to 11.10%) (Dawson, Goldstein, Saha, & Grant, 2015). Females had nearly twice the increase in the proportion of past-year drinking (from 59.6% to 69.0%) compared to males (from 71.8% to 76.7%; Dawson et al., 2015). Additionally, there was a 20% increase in the prevalence of greater than monthly heavy episodic drinking, which was defined as 5+ or 4+ drinks (for men and women respectively) (Dawson et al., 2015). Results from the National Health Interview Survey revealed that 29.8% of men, in comparison to 18.6% of women, had at least one heavy drinking day in the past year (Clarke, Ward, Freeman, & Schiller, 2015).

Results from the third wave of NESARC revealed the prevalence of alcohol use disorder as determined by the *DSM-5*, which combines alcohol abuse and dependence criteria into a single category with the subclassifications of mild, moderate, and severe. The prevalence of 12-month and lifetime *DSM-5* alcohol use disorder was 13.9% and 29.1%, respectively, with higher rates among males (17.6% and 36.0%, respectively) than among females (10.4% and 22.7%, respectively) (Grant et al., 2015). The mean age of alcohol use disorder onset was 26.2 years, and this decreased with increasing disorder severity to 23.9 years for severe alcohol use disorder (Grant et al., 2015). While nearly 20% of those with lifetime alcohol use disorder sought help or treatment, the mean age of first treatment was 29.4 years, indicating a 3-year gap between onset and treatment (Grant et al., 2015). Taken together, results from the most recent epidemiological study of alcohol use disorders suggest that 13.9% of the adult population in the United States suffer from an alcohol use disorder in a given year, totaling 32.6 million individuals (Grant et al., 2015). These figures clearly underscore the significance of alcohol use disorders as an important public health concern, and they are corroborated by studies estimating that the economic cost of alcohol abuse and dependence was $249 billion for 2010 (Sacks, Gonzales, Bouchery, Tomedi, & Brewer, 2015), representing an astounding but preventable financial burden.

ALCOHOL USE DISORDER CROSS-CULTURALLY

Patterns of alcohol use and misuse vary cross-culturally. Although most of the relevant literature is limited to simple descriptions of alcohol use patterns in different cultures, these studies highlight the importance of examining cultural factors influencing alcohol use and, ultimately, alcohol pathology. Accordingly, various studies have examined differences among ethnic/racial groups in the United States as well as worldwide. Results from epidemiological U.S. population studies have revealed stable high-risk subgroups for alcohol use disorders. These subgroups include whites, Native Americans, and males (Grant et al., 2015). Native Americans have the highest risk for alcohol dependence (Delker, Brown, & Hasin, 2015). Although the exact rates vary by tribe, Native American drinkers report high rates of alcohol-related health problems, including mortality (Beals, Novins, Whitsell, Mitchell, & Manson, 2005).

Asian Americans, African Americans, and Hispanics in the United States exhibit lower rates of lifetime alcohol use disorders than their white non-Hispanic counterparts do (Grant et al., 2015). However, ethnic/racial differences in alcohol use disorders continue to change with the evolving sociocultural context. For example, it remains unknown why African Americans and Hispanics, who tend to be of lower socioeconomic status, are at lower risk for alcohol use disorders than their white non-Hispanic counterparts, given the socioeconomic disparities between these groups and the strong association between lower socioeconomic status and poor health (Link & Phelan, 2002; Phelan, Link, & Tehranifar, 2010).

Furthermore, African Americans, Asian Americans, and Hispanics are heterogeneous groups that vary culturally. Nativity, or place of birth, has been identified as a strong predictor of alcohol use and misuse. Paradoxically, individuals who are born outside the United States and then immigrate to the United States seem to have a lower risk for alcohol use disorders than their U.S.-born counterparts, despite the fact that the former seemingly encounter more risk factors than the latter (Caetano, Clark, & Tam, 1998; Vega & Sribney, 2011). This pattern has come to be commonly known as the *immigrant paradox* (Vega & Sribney, 2011). However, the mechanisms that account for these differences are yet to be identified.

Worldwide cross-cultural comparisons of drinking behaviors typically describe cultural factors that could account for the observed differences in drinking patterns across cultures. For example, a comparison of drinking habits in Finnish and Canadian samples found a higher prevalence of binge drinking in Finnish men (Cunningham & Mäkelä, 2003). The study authors discussed these observed differences in the context of the cultural view of alcohol as an intoxicant in Finland, a society in which there is a higher cultural acceptance of drunkenness (Cunningham & Mäkelä, 2003). A study comparing alcohol problems in Germany and the United States found that at matched drinking levels, more Americans reported alcohol-related problems than Germans did. The authors hypothesized that those differences in problem endorsement may reflect greater cultural ambivalence about the use of alcohol in the United States (Bloomfield, Greenfield, Kraus, & Augustin, 2002). A recent examination of the literature on the associations between culture and alcohol use highlighted how the transition from casual indigenous societies to regulated Western societies adds additional stressors that appear to result in increases in alcohol consumption as a form of coping (Castro, Barrera, Mena, & Aguirre, 2014).

Cross-cultural differences in the relationship between alcohol use and gender are well documented in the literature (de Lima, Dunn, Novo, Tomasi, & Reisser, 2003; Grant et al., 2004; Schmid et al., 2003; Wilsnack, Vogeltanz, Wilsnack, & Harris, 2000). Grant and colleagues (2004) identified that young adult African American females and Asian American males showed a sharp increase in prevalence rates for alcohol dependence between 1992 and 2002. Similarly, rates of alcohol abuse increased among Latino males, African American males, and Asian females in this 10-year span (Grant et al., 2004). Wilsnack and colleagues (2000), reporting on data from the International Research Group on Gender and Alcohol, examined gender differences in 10 countries. The main findings were that women and men differed little in the likelihood of current drinking versus abstaining, but men reported significantly higher drinking frequencies, quantities, and rates of heavy drinking. The authors proposed that gender roles may magnify biological differences in pharmacological responses to alcohol and that gender differences in drinking may be impacted by culturally bound constructs such as gender roles (Wilsnack et al., 2000). In short, these findings underscore the complex nature of the relationship between cultural factors and alcohol use. Based on the results of this large epidemiological study of alcohol use disorders, Grant and colleagues (2004) argued for new prevention programs designed with the observed gender and racial/ethnic differences in mind, as well as early prevention efforts for youth.

Although most cross-cultural studies have focused on comparing alcohol use among various cultures and countries, a few studies have examined moderators and mediators of the effects of culture on alcohol use and abuse. In examining ethnic/cultural groups in the United States, acculturation-related processes such as adopting drinking behaviors consistent with the majority, host culture continue to be explored as potential mediators of differences in alcohol use disorders between whites and ethnic minorities in the United States (Caetano et al., 1998). An examination of female American Indian parents and caretakers revealed that historical loss (i.e., trauma/loss experienced by earlier generations) mediated the effects of discrimination on past-year alcohol abuse, while enculturation did not mediate or moderate the effect of discrimination (Les Whitbeck, Chen, Hoyt, & Adams, 2004). In addition, studies have also focused on examining beliefs about the use and effects of alcohol in various cultures. In attempting to capture belief systems and "drinking cultures," a number of typologies for cultural views of drinking have been proposed. These typologies include distinctions between "wet" and "dry" cultures, where the primary factor is whether alcohol use is integrated into daily life—for example, whether there is acceptance of having wine with meals. This typology refers primarily to European societies, especially those in Mediterranean cultures (Room, 1998). Another model, proposed by Partanen (1991), consists of a two-dimensional typology with the following two axes: (1) engagement with alcohol, and (2) serious drinking. According to this typology, cultural views of alcohol should be analyzed in both domains. An additional typology for alcohol culture is Levine's distinction between temperance and nontemperance cultures (Levine, 1992). The distinction is based on both religion (temperance cultures are mostly Protestant) and societal position toward alcohol (e.g., temperance cultures are highly concerned about alcohol misuse and are often active in combating alcoholism). Studies have found that temperance cultures consume less alcohol and have more AA groups (Peele, 1993, 1997).

Finally, a few studies have attempted to understand cultural factors associated with alcohol use by examining cognitive factors, such as alcohol expectancies (Lindman, Sjöholm, & Land, 2000), and other cultural factors, such as the role of the family (Bjarnason et al., 2003; Johnson & Johnson, 1999). Regarding alcohol expectancies, results from a large cross-cultural comparison revealed that expectations of increased positive affect when drinking were influenced by culture, in addition to the direct pharmacological effects of alcohol (Lindman et al., 2000).

In summary, most cross-cultural studies to date have focused on comparing drinking patterns and alcohol misuse cross-culturally, while a few studies have begun to examine factors that mediate or moderate the relationship between culture and alcohol use.

These efforts represent an important step toward increasing our understanding of the role of cultural factors in the initiation, progression, and maintenance of alcohol use disorders.

DEVELOPMENTAL CONSIDERATIONS

Alcohol use typically starts in early adolescence and escalates during late adolescence (ages 16 to 20), which is the period of highest risk for alcohol use disorders (Brown et al., 2008; Hasin et al., 2007). School-based surveys indicate that by 12th grade, 72% of adolescents report having drunk alcohol, 55% report having been drunk, and 25% report binge drinking in the past 2 weeks (Johnston, O'Malley, Bachman, & Schulenberg, 2010). In fact, starting to drink before age 15 increases the risk for developing alcohol dependence later in life (Windle et al., 2008). A recent cross-national examination of adolescent alcohol use found a decrease in weekly alcohol use in North America and Europe that was theorized to be due to changes in social norms or an increased recognition of the harmful effects of alcohol and utilization of associated preventive strategies (de Looze et al., 2015). Among U.S. college students, the prevalence of alcohol problems is high and increasing, with studies suggesting that the prevalence of binge drinking (i.e., consuming five or more drinks on a single occasion) among college students is 37.9% within the past month (SAMHSA 2014c), and that approximately 20% of U.S. college students met the criteria for an alcohol use disorder (Bianco et al., 2008).

Gender differences in alcohol use emerge in late adolescence/early adulthood. Specifically, males and females report comparable drinking rates during early adolescence but males report drinking more often and in greater quantities compared to females as they transition to adulthood (Windle, Mun, & Windle, 2005). These gender differences appear to be consistent across ethnic/racial groups in the United States.

Ethnic/racial differences in drinking patterns among adolescents reflect those of adult populations, as described above. These ethnic/racial differences, however, may vary with age. According to the most recent Monitoring the Future (MFT) survey estimates, by the 8th grade, Latino teens report higher prevalence rates of binge drinking (10.8%) in the past 2 weeks than non-Hispanic white (7.1%) and African American (5.3%) adolescents. However, by the 12th grade, non-Hispanic white teens report the highest rates of binge drinking (27.6%) compared to Latino (22.1%) and African American (13.1%) adolescents. Likewise, non-Hispanic white youth report higher rates of getting drunk (31.6%) than Latino (20.5%) and African American (14.7%) adolescents.

Given that using alcohol during adolescence is a risk behavior and elevates the probability of developing an alcohol use disorder later in life, many studies have been devoted to identifying risk and protective factors for adolescent alcohol use. On the one hand, one of the most robust risk factors for drinking alcohol in adolescence is the peer context. Specifically, associating with substance-using peers (Brown et al., 2008; Spear, 2000) increases the probability of underage drinking across ethnic groups (Bacio, Mays, & Lau, 2013; Wood, Read, Mitchell, & Brand, 2004). On the other hand, the family context remains important throughout adolescence. The relationships that adolescents have with their families influence the types of behaviors in which they engage. For example, a decrease in parental monitoring during adolescence has been associated with increased risk for alcohol use (Barnes, Reifman, Farrell, & Dintcheff, 2000), whereas parental involvement has been found to attenuate the relationship between peer use and adolescent alcohol use (Wood et al., 2004).

Similarly, cross-cultural studies of alcohol use among adolescents have highlighted important cultural factors influencing the initiation and maintenance of alcohol use, as well as the development of alcohol-related problems. A recent study comparing alcohol use among adolescents in the United States and in Puerto Rico found higher rates of alcohol use among U.S. youth (Warner, Canino, & Colón, 2001). Interestingly, there were also significant differences in the symptoms endorsed, in that youth from Puerto Rico were more likely to report "failure to fulfill obligations." The authors hypothesized that these findings may reflect differences in familial attachment between the two cultures (Warner et al., 2001). A larger study examining alcohol use among 15-year-olds in 22 European and North American countries found significant geographical differences in adolescent drinking patterns, with higher drinking levels in the Nordic countries (Schmid et al., 2003). It was hypothesized that geographical location served as a proxy for drinking culture. The authors also noted that gender differences in alcohol use were greater in male-dominated drinking cultures marked by more classic gender roles (Schmid et al., 2003). Interestingly, analyses of a multicultural sample of adolescents in the United States suggested that *DSM-IV* symptom endorsement patterns and the diagnosis of alcohol use disorders varied as a function of ethnicity and gender (Wagner, Lloyd, & Gil, 2002).

Furthermore, cross-cultural studies of the family system and adolescent alcohol use revealed that the adverse effects of living in a nonintact family on drinking behaviors were greater in societies with higher alcohol availability and where adolescent heavy drinking was more common (Bjarnason et al., 2003). These results are consistent with the hypothesized role of the family in influencing the negative meaning of alcohol, which in turn is thought to delay the initiation of drinking and reduce alcohol use (Johnson & Johnson, 1999).

The National Institute on Alcohol Abuse and Alcoholism (NIAAA) strongly advocates for developing prevention programs to delay drinking initiation before age 15 in an effort to prevent alcohol use disorders. Despite the fact that many prevention and intervention programs have been developed over the years, much work still needs to be done to effectively address adolescent alcohol use and incorporate cultural components when necessary.

Theory

A *theory* is a conceptualization of a phenomenon of interest. It represents an attempt to capture and summarize empirical findings into a cohesive set of rules that can be used to generate hypotheses. Theories may vary widely in scope (e.g., broad versus narrow) and focus (e.g., focus on the social bases of behavior versus focus on biological processes). In contemporary psychology, theories have become increasingly circumscribed. Nevertheless, theories are essential to fulfill the scientific purpose of "connecting empirical relations with statements of mechanisms and processes" (Kazdin, 2002, p. 127). In short, we want to make sense of the world by understanding the *why* and *how* of phenomena, and theories represent our attempts to do so.

The overarching framework adopted throughout this chapter for examining specific theories about factors influencing the development and maintenance of alcohol use disorders is a *biopsychosocial model* of psychiatric disorders. Specifically, the biopsychosocial model applied to alcohol use disorders posits that the etiology of alcoholism represents a complex interplay between *psychosocial* factors (e.g., cognitions, personality traits, and environmental variables such as peer groups and norms) and *biological* factors (e.g., genetics and neurobiology). This section of this chapter discusses important psychosocial and biological factors thought to influence the development and maintenance of alcohol use disorders, working within the premise that these factors interplay in the development of the complex and heterogeneous phenomenon known as an *alcohol use disorder*. As with all complex diseases, alcoholism can be thought of as a clinical outcome resulting from a combination of many risk factors, both biological and psychosocial. Importantly, the alcohol-dependent population represents a spectrum of individuals arriving at the diagnosis through diverse pathways and displaying different sets of symptoms.

PSYCHOSOCIAL FACTORS

In recent years, a number of psychological theories of alcohol use and abuse have been developed by focusing on specific factors relevant to alcohol use and alcohol use disorders. These theoretical frameworks represent attempts to conceptualize the phenomenon of alcohol use disorders and to explain why some individuals become dependent on alcohol and by which mechanisms (i.e., how). It has become increasingly clear that individuals may develop alcohol-related problems by various mechanisms resulting from a complex interaction among multiple, and often interrelated, psychosocial and biological factors. In this section we discuss some of the more widely researched psychosocial factors and their related theories. These conceptual models examine the complex pathways to alcohol use disorders from diverse vantage points, which in turn further highlight the phenotypic complexity of addictive behaviors.

Expectancy theory provides an explanation for a broad range of psychological phenomena, and it is often used to integrate psychological processes with their underlying biological mechanisms. Expectancy refers to processes within the nervous system that use neurobiological and cognitive residues of previous experience to guide future behavior. It is thought that the activation of an expectancy template can directly initiate a behavioral sequence previously associated with a recognized stimulus. Such a template can directly activate an affective experience. In a more indirect fashion, activation of expectancy can elicit a behavior that is associated with, or results from, the activation of an affective state. For example, persons may become more socially outgoing because they are affectively aroused.

The cognitive processes associated with expectancies are theorized to influence all behaviors and have been applied to understanding drinking and alcohol dependence (Brown, Goldman, Inn, & Anderson, 1980; Del Boca, Darkes, Goldman, & Smith, 2002). In this application, information that reflects the reinforcement value of alcohol acquired as a function of biological, psychological, or environmental risk variables is viewed as being stored as memory templates (Goldman & Darkes, 2004). The memory systems that retain this information are conceptualized as a kind of information-based buffer. Once acquired, these templates have the capacity to influence alcohol use and its associated behavioral patterns over widely varying periods of time. In short, alcohol expectancy refers to information that reflects the reinforcement value of alcohol, is stored as memory templates, and can influence alcohol use.

Although most research has focused on alcohol expectancies as moderators of drinking risk, some theorists argue that alcohol expectancies may serve as a mediator of alcohol use risk (Goldman, Del Boca, & Darkes, 1999). Expectancy theory is one of the most widely researched and empirically supported psychological theories of alcohol misuse. Results have largely and consistently supported an association between alcohol expectancies and drinking behaviors, such that higher positive expectancies regarding the effects of alcohol are strong predictors of heavier alcohol use. Importantly, expectancy theory has often been integrated into models that take into account additional risk factors for alcohol misuse, such as peer influences, personality constructs, and genetic factors (Del Boca et al., 2002; Schuckit et al., 2006; Zamboanga, Schwartz, Ham, Jarvis, & Olthuis, 2009). The role of alcohol expectancies has also been examined in adolescence, with Cranford, Zucker, Jester, Puttler, and Fitzgerald (2010) demonstrating how early adolescent alcohol expectancies, coupled with different aspects of parental alcohol involvement, independently predict middle adolescence drinking behavior. Recent work using functional magnetic resonance imaging (fMRI) has suggested that decreased inhibitory neural processing may be associated with more positive and less negative alcohol outcome expectancies (Anderson, Schweinsburg, Paulus, Brown, & Tapert, 2005). In conclusion, expectancy theory represents an advanced cognitive model of alcohol use with strong empirical support from a wide array of research methodologies. Expectancies represent information processing systems that are proximally related to alcohol use patterns and capture the incentive value of drinking, which in turn is best conceptualized as a dynamic and unfolding process.

The central tenet of the *tension-reduction theory* of alcohol use is the assertion that individuals drink alcohol because of its ability to reduce tension. This theory was initially influenced by the drive reduction theory of the 1940s (Hull, 1943), which emphasized motivational aspects underlying drinking. Although there is significant intuitive appeal to the notion that individuals drink to reduce tension, an early review by Cappell and Herman (1972) suggested that empirical support for the theory was limited. A related theory, developed in the 1980s, focused on the stress-response dampening (SRD) effects of alcohol (Levenson, Sher, Grossman, Newman, & Newlin, 1980; Sher & Levenson, 1982). The SRD model focused on refining the operational definition and laboratory manipulation of stressors (e.g., electric shock, public speaking task) and examining individual differences in the stress-response dampening effects of alcohol, making it a more focused and testable theory (Greeley & Oei, 1999). As stated by Greeley and Oei (1999) in reviewing the empirical support for the tension-reduction theory, "the general consensus has been that alcohol, at certain dosages, is capable of reducing some signs of tension in some humans, under certain contextual conditions" (p. 23).

More recent work on the tension-reduction model and related theories emphasizes understanding the pharmacological and neurobiological mechanisms by which alcohol may dampen a stress response, as well as the individual and contextual differences that may moderate those effects. Examples of such moderators include hostility (Zeichner, Giancola, & Allen, 1995), anxiety sensitivity (Stewart, Karp, Pihl, & Peterson, 1997), gender (Sinha, Robinson, & O'Malley, 1998), and the type of social situation (Armeli et al., 2003) or life stressor (Hart & Fazaa, 2004). Further, genetic predispositions to stress reactivity, via variations in HPA axis genes, have been looked at as possible mediators of the effects of stress on alcohol consumption (Clarke et al., 2007). Thus, alcohol-induced stress reduction may be especially salient for those individuals with genetically determined heightened stress reactivity. In short, the tension-reduction theory and its most widely researched offshoot, the SRD model, identify alcohol's ability to reduce tension and stress reactivity as central to the motivation to drink and the development of alcohol-related problems. Recent work on these theories has focused on understanding the pharmacological mechanisms by which alcohol may reduce tension and the genetic predispositions to heightened stress reactivity, and on describing potential moderators of a heightened stress-dampening response.

Personality theory has been applied to alcohol use disorders for many years. The notion that personality played a causal role in alcoholism had so much intuitive appeal that many past studies sought to identify the alleged "alcoholic personality." As noted earlier, alcoholism was classified as a personality disorder in the first edition of the *DSM*. An examination of personality motives in relation to risky behaviors found that a high degree of neuroticism, along with a high degree of impulsivity or extraversion, predicted an increased reliance on alcohol use as a coping method (Cooper, Agocha, & Sheldon, 2000). Over the past 5 decades, researchers have shown that although personality traits may account for some of the variance in vulnerability to alcohol use disorders, personality characteristics are not necessarily a core component of the disorder and there is clearly not a specific personality dimension that can reliably predict alcoholism (Sher, Trull, Bartholow, & Vieth, 1999).

Recent research has focused on the role of personality in the etiology of alcohol use disorders, and on establishing a causal link between personality traits and the development of alcohol pathology. In addition, personality characteristics have been used to identify possible subtypes of alcohol dependence. For example, Cloninger's (1987) model of Type 1 and Type 2 alcoholics suggests that the first group is marked by an early onset of alcoholism and by antisocial personality traits, whereas the latter group is characterized by a late onset of problems and a tendency toward negative emotionality. A related typology was proposed by Babor (1996), who recommended parsing the alcohol dependence phenotype into either Type A or Type B. The Type A alcohol-dependent cluster is characterized by later onset, fewer childhood risk factors, less severe dependence, fewer alcohol-related problems, and less psychopathological dysfunction; whereas the Type B cluster is characterized by childhood risk factors, familial alcoholism, early onset of alcohol-related problems, greater severity of dependence, polydrug use, a more chronic treatment history, greater psychopathological dysfunction, and more life stress (Babor et al., 1992). Results from a randomized clinical trial based on the A and B typology found that Type A alcoholics did better in group psychotherapy and more poorly with coping skills training, whereas Type B alcoholics had better outcomes with the coping skills treatment and did worse with interactional group therapy; these results maintained at 2-year follow-up (Litt, Babor, Del Boca, Kadden, & Cooney, 1992). A more recent review of the clinical subtyping of alcohol use disorders found mixed results in terms of construct, concurrent, and predictive validity of these classifications and concluded that further research is needed before these typologies could be useful in clinical practice (Babor & Caetano, 2006).

In addition to the clinical subtypes developed largely on the basis of personality characteristics, several studies to date have suggested a relationship—at times causal in nature—between certain personality traits and alcohol use disorders. The personality dimension of impulsivity/disinhibition appears to be the one most relevant to an individual's risk for developing an alcohol use disorder (Finn, Earleywine, & Pihl, 1992). Recent findings suggest, however, that impulsivity is not a unitary construct. In a sample of problem drinkers, the impulsive decision-making dimension of impulsivity was found to be more predictive of alcohol use and alcohol pathology than were measures of response inhibition, risky decision making, and self-reported risk attitudes (Courtney et al., 2012). Further, a recent neuroimaging study examined individuals with stimulant dependence and their unaffected siblings while they performed a task of inhibitory control (i.e., the stop signal task). The results indicated that abnormalities in frontostriatal brain systems were implicated in self-control in both stimulant-dependent individuals and their biological siblings who had no history of chronic drug abuse (Ersche et al., 2012). This work highlights the diverse ways in which personality characteristics, and their complex facets, can relate to alcohol use outcomes. To clarify these relationships, personality researchers in the addictions field have begun to integrate personality constructs with parallel lines of research on behavioral genetics, cognitive neuroscience, stress and coping, pharmacological responses to alcohol, and developmental theories.

Social learning theory (SLT) emphasizes learning from social environments and also cognitions as important determinants of behavior. SLT is a general theory of human behavior whose most notable proponent is Albert Bandura (1977, 1986). SLT has heavily influenced the cognitive-behavioral approach to alcohol use disorders (Dimeff & Marlatt, 1995; Marlatt & Gordon, 1985). Applying SLT to the study of alcoholism often entails focusing on three aspects of behavior: social-environmental variables, coping skills, and cognitive factors (Maisto, Carey, & Bradizza, 1999).

Social environmental variables include situational factors that may be associated (i.e., paired) with alcohol use; these are generally conceptualized as triggers. Coping skills, in turn, involve the patient's ability to cope with stressful events without reverting to the use of alcohol. This approach has been emphasized in cognitive-behavioral interventions for alcoholism that focus on building skills such as drinking refusal skills and ways of coping with urges and with negative thoughts and feelings. SLT also highlights two cognitive factors thought to be relevant for the development and maintenance of alcoholism: self-efficacy and outcome expectancies. Self-efficacy refers to belief in one's ability to enact a given behavior or obtain a certain outcome. Abstinence self-efficacy has been found to be a strong predictor of treatment outcome for alcohol use disorders (Ilgen, McKellar, & Tiet, 2005). Alcohol expectancies—one's beliefs about the consequences of alcohol use—have received extensive empirical support for their role in alcohol use disorders (for details, see the previous section on expectancy theory).

One important application of SLT has been the conceptualization of the relapse process (Marlatt & Gordon, 1985). In brief, this model conceptualizes lapses as resulting from the patient's lack of skills for coping with high-risk situations, which leads to low levels of self-efficacy beliefs about his or her ability to cope with stressful situations and expectancies that alcohol use will help him or her cope effectively with situations in the future. Relapse represents an important theoretical and clinical issue in alcohol use disorders. Recent research on relapse has attempted to develop multivariate models that can account for both distal and proximal factors likely to influence the relapse process, in order to capture its complex nature. For example, distal factors found to predict relapse include less active coping efforts, lower self-efficacy, higher craving, and lower participation in self-help groups and treatment (McKay, Franklin, Patapis, & Lynch, 2006). Proximal factors are personal characteristics and experiences likely to trigger a particular relapse episode. The understanding of proximal factors in relapse has been improved by recent advances in assessment methods, such as ecological momentary assessment (EMA), that allow for near real-time assessments of the circumstances surrounding a relapse episode. Studies of proximal relapse factors using EMA suggested that greater anxiety predicted higher alcohol use later in the day, especially among men (Swendsen et al., 2000). More recently, Marlatt's original taxonomy of relapse precipitants has been updated as the Marlatt-Witkiewitz model of relapse. In particular, this model emphasizes the dynamic interplay between distal and proximal risk factors in determining relapse (Witkiewitz & Marlatt, 2007). Using sophisticated quantitative methods, such as stochastic catastrophe models, Witkiewitz and Marlatt (2007) elegantly demonstrate that complex models fit the relapse data better than traditional linear or logistic models of relapse do. An important implication of this model is to challenge the notion that any drinking should be considered a treatment failure, when instead a more complete and dynamic picture of the relapse process can be used to define a range of successful outcomes beyond complete abstinence. For an in-depth review of the relapse literature see Maisto and Connors (2006) and the special issue of *Clinical Psychology Review* edited by Connors and Maisto (2006) In short, SLT emphasizes social environments, coping skills, and cognitions as important determinants of behavior, and SLT concepts have been widely applied to the current cognitive-behavioral conceptualization and related treatment models for alcohol use disorders.

BIOLOGICAL FACTORS

As noted previously, alcoholism is a complex disorder resulting from the interplay between biological and psychosocial factors (for reviews on the neurobiology of addiction, see Kalivas & Volkow, 2005; Volkow & Li, 2005). Although several neurotransmitter systems are activated by alcohol administration, initial models in the literature focused on the role of mesolimbic dopamine and the stimulatory and reinforcing effects of alcohol (Littleton & Little, 1994; Samson & Harris, 1992). Both alcohol consumption and alcohol cue exposure prior to drinking increase dopamine activity in the nucleus accumbens (NAC), suggesting that prior learning and anticipation of reinforcement activates a dopamine response that is isomorphic to the effect of alcohol on mesolimbic dopamine activation (Weiss, Lorang, Bloom, & Koob, 1993). An important question that has only been partially answered is how alcohol might influence mesolimbic dopamine activity. Some researchers have suggested that the consumption of alcohol triggers the release of endogenous opioids, which may mediate mesolimbic dopamine activity (Gianoulakis, 1993; Gianoulakis, de Waele, & Thavundayil, 1996; Schuckit & Smith, 1996; Volpicelli, Pettinati, McLellan, & O'Brien, 2001). In fact, a recent study using positron-emission tomography (PET) was the first to demonstrate the release of endogenous opioids in the orbitofrontal cortex and nucleus accumbens following alcohol administration in humans (Mitchell et al., 2012). The release of endogenous opioids is also thought to inhibit gamma-aminobutyric acid (GABA) interneurons that subsequently release dopaminergic neurons from inhibition (Kalivas & Stewart, 1991). This notion is consistent with a study demonstrating that the administration of ethanol increased dopamine activity in the NAC, and that naltrexone—a mu-opioid receptor antagonist—reduced dopaminergic activity in the NAC (Benjamin, Grant, & Pohorecky, 1993). In conjunction, these studies highlight the multiple neurotransmitter systems underlying the pharmacological and behavioral effects of alcohol.

One of the early theories regarding biological mechanisms that influence the development of alcohol dependence was the *psychostimulant theory of addiction*. According to this psychomotor stimulant theory of addiction, substances with high abuse potential—including alcohol—have the ability to produce psychomotor stimulation. This theory further proposes that the stimulatory and rewarding effects of a vast range of addictive substances share an underlying biological mechanism (Wise & Bozarth, 1987). Consequently, individuals who experience greater alcohol-induced reward are thought to be more likely to develop alcohol problems. Specifically, Wise and Bozarth (1987) based their theory on three major assertions: (1) that all addictive substances produce psychomotor stimulation, (2) that the stimulant effects of these addictive substances share a common biological mechanism, and (3) that the stimulant effects of these substances produce their positive reinforcement. Importantly, the common neural pathway involved in the stimulant and reinforcing properties of several substances—including alcohol—is thought to be mediated by mesocorticolimbic dopamine activity in the reward circuitry in the brain.

Although early models of addiction focused on dopamine and the stimulatory and reinforcing effects of alcohol and drugs, subsequent biological models shifted the focus from reward to incentive salience and craving (Berridge & Robinson, 2003; Robinson & Berridge, 1993, 2001). These models suggest that activation along mesolimbic dopamine substrates is critical to the development of the motivational and appetitive properties of tobacco, alcohol, and other drugs. The models also suggest that the mechanisms that serve the motivational properties of alcohol and other drugs may be distinct from those that mediate reward. This assertion led to a biological conceptualization of alcohol craving, which has recently been articulated as an incentive sensitization model of craving. This model stipulates that mesolimbic dopamine activation influences the motivational and appetitive properties of alcohol and drug use by controlling the attribution of incentive salience to neural representations of alcohol-related stimuli (Berridge & Robinson, 1998; Robinson & Berridge, 1993; Wise, 1988). Thus, the acquisition and sensitization of incentive salience (i.e., craving) for substances of abuse—including alcohol—is produced by repeated drug/alcohol ingestion and the associated release of dopamine. After these pathways have become sensitized, the expression of incentive salience (i.e., craving) can be activated by the release of dopamine that is initiated in response to drug cues or priming doses of the drug itself (de Wit, 1996; Stewart, de Wit, & Eikelboom, 1984).

A recent biological model of alcohol dependence that is more broadly focused is known as the *allostatic model of dependence* (Koob, 2003; Koob & LeMoal, 2001, 2005). This model is an important development because it is one of the first models to integrate the neurobiology of the acute rewarding effects of alcohol and drugs with mechanisms related to the negative reinforcement associated with alcohol withdrawal and the influence of stress. Conceptually, the development of an alcohol use disorder is characterized as an allostatic process that involves changes in reward and stress circuits that become dysregulated with repeated exposure to alcohol. More specifically, this process putatively involves alterations of corticotrophin-releasing factor (CRF) and neuropeptide Y (NPY) in the central nucleus of the amygdala and bed nucleus of the stria terminalis. In turn, these changes confer vulnerability to relapse among alcohol-dependent patients. One of the primary advantages of this model is that it integrates a considerable amount of data on the molecular, cellular, and neuronal changes associated with the pathophysiology of alcoholism.

In brief, the basic neuroscience of addiction has provided compelling evidence of the neural and behavioral bases of key addiction mechanisms, such as the transition from goal-directed to habitual drug taking; the development of incentive salience; the neuroadaptive processes underlying tolerance and withdrawal (including protracted withdrawal); and brain damage from drug use as well as recovery from such damage during prolonged abstinence. Although considerable research has yet to be done to effectively translate these findings to help patients suffering from addictive disorders, insights from neuroscience are being incorporated into clinical research and practice. Thus, a new direction in the clinical psychology of addiction is the integration of basic neuroscience models into clinical science. This approach, termed *clinical neuroscience of addiction*, has the potential to use basic science findings to inform clinical practice and vice versa (Ray, 2012).

Finally, no discussion of the biological factors underlying alcohol use disorders would be complete without considering the role of *behavioral genetics*. Although behavioral genetics research does not offer a complete model for understanding alcoholism, the role of genetic factors in the etiology of the disorder is well established (Dick & Beirut, 2006). One of the most important contributions of genetic research is the demonstration that genetic factors account for a significant proportion of the variability in alcohol use disorders, with recent heritability estimates—based on twin and adoption studies—of approximately 50% to 60% (Heath et al., 1997). In addition, twin studies have shown that a number of alcohol-related traits, or phenotypes, are also heritable—such as alcohol sensitivity (Health & Martin, 1991; Viken, Rose, Morzoati, Christian, & Li, 2003), alcohol metabolism (Martin et al., 1985), and alcohol use (Koopmans & Boomsma, 1996). More recent behavioral genetics research has focused on identifying specific genes underlying individual differences in vulnerability to the development of an alcohol use disorder. In light of such efforts, the identification of more narrow behavioral phenotypes—or endophenotypes—for alcoholism has received increased attention (Hines, Ray, Hutchison, & Tabakoff, 2005), as is the case for most psychiatric disorders (Burmeister, 1999; Gottesman & Gould, 2003). To be useful, an endophenotype must be narrowly defined, readily identifiable, and related to the disorder of interest (Hutchison, McGeary, Smolen, Bryan, & Swift, 2002). When used correctly, endophenotypes for psychiatric disorders are expected to increase the power to detect specific genes underlying the risk for a given disorder. Endophenotypes are thought to be more closely linked to specific neurobiological processes than are full psychiatric syndromes, which are often quite heterogeneous phenotypes (Burmeister, 1999; Gottesman & Gould, 2003). Importantly, clinicians should recognize that alcoholism represents a disorder of complex genetics, such that no single gene is likely to fully explain its genetic liability. As stated by McGue (1999), future research on behavioral genetics of alcoholism should focus on processes intervening between genetic effects and behavior as well as mechanisms by which environmental factors may interact with an individual's genetic predisposition and contribute to the behavioral outcome currently classified as alcoholism.

Treatment

It is estimated that approximately 700,000 individuals receive treatment for alcohol use disorders on any given day (Fuller & Hiller-Sturmhofel, 1999), with most patients receiving care on an outpatient basis. This reflects a trend in alcohol treatment, which has largely moved from primarily residential and inpatient programs to intensive outpatient treatment programs, preceded by brief hospitalization for detoxification when needed. In 2014, the National Survey on Drug Use and Health revealed that approximately 8.9% of adults who needed treatment received that treatment at a specialized facility (SAMHSA, 2014d). The most common treatment modalities are detoxification, behavioral treatments—including AA and 12-step facilitation—pharmacotherapy, and brief primary care interventions (Fuller & Hiller-Sturmhofel, 1999). Most treatment-seeking patients receive some form of psychosocial intervention for alcohol use disorder. Pharmacotherapies are less commonly used; however, the development of new and more efficacious medications for alcohol use disorders has received increased research attention over the past decade. Notably, recent analyses based on the National Epidemiologic Survey on Alcohol and Related Conditions suggest that the vast majority (85%) of individuals who meet lifetime criteria for an alcohol use disorder never receive formal treatment or participate in self-help groups (Cohen, Feinn, Arias, & Kranzler, 2007).

PSYCHOSOCIAL TREATMENTS

Most psychosocial treatments available for alcohol use disorders are highly eclectic and have not been evaluated for efficacy. Empirically supported psychosocial treatments for alcohol use disorders are described in the following list:

- *Brief interventions* focus on providing feedback, negotiating behavioral change, and promoting some form of follow-up. These interventions are often delivered by health care professionals to opportunistic samples. Meta-analyses have concluded that brief interventions are superior to no treatment controls but should not replace specialist-delivered extended treatment approaches (Moyer, Finney, Swearingen, & Vergun, 2002).

- Motivational interviewing, or *motivational enhancement therapy* (MET), focuses on enhancing individuals' motivation and commitment to change by adopting an empathetic and nonconfrontational therapeutic manner (Miller & Rollnick, 2002). Results of a recent meta-analysis have supported its efficacy (Vasilaki, Hosier, & Cox, 2006).

- *Cognitive-behavioral therapies* (CBT) focus on teaching skills for coping with drinking urges, including identifying triggers and preventing relapses (Monti, Kadden, Rohsenow, Cooney, & Abrams, 2002). CBT for alcohol use disorders has received empirical support over no treatment or minimal treatment control conditions (Carroll, 1996).

- *Behavioral marital therapy* (BCT) treats the substance-abusing person along with his or her spouse to ensure the spouse's support. A sobriety contract is negotiated, communication skills are taught, and positive alternative activities are scheduled. BCT has been found to be superior to individual treatment in enhancing motivation to seek treatment, increasing abstinence, and improving relationship functioning (O'Farrell & Fals-Stewart, 2003). BCT has also been found to reduce domestic violence and emotional problems in the treated couple's children.

- *Behavioral treatments* for alcohol use disorders generally take the form of the community reinforcement approach (CRA) and contingency management (CM) programs. Behavioral treatments operate on the assumption that alcohol use is reinforcing and that in order to decrease alcohol use its reinforcing value must decrease while alternative sources of reinforcement must increase. Controlled studies have found support for this approach in the treatment of alcohol use disorders (Smith, Meyers, & Delaney, 1998).

- *Cue-exposure (CE) therapy* focuses on repeated exposure to alcohol cues to produce a decrease in alcohol craving and an increase in self-efficacy for coping with urges and high-risk situations. CE treatment has received some empirical support in comparisons to cognitive-behavioral approaches (Loeber, Croissant, Heinz, Mann, & Flor, 2006; Rohsenow et al., 2001) and in conjunction with pharmacotherapies (Monti et al., 2001). However, other studies suggest that CE does not significantly add to CBT approaches (Kavanagh et al., 2006).

- *Twelve-step therapies*, which are based on the philosophy of Alcoholics Anonymous (AA), are the most widely used resource for individuals with alcohol problems. They promote the goal of long-term complete abstinence and generally discourage the use of any psychiatric medications (Rychtarik, Connors, Dermen, & Stasiewicz, 2000), although this attitude appears to be changing over time. This latter aspect can be problematic and needs to be specifically addressed in the treatment of individuals with comorbid disorders that benefit from medications.

- *Mindfulness-based therapies* are based on meditation/mindfulness techniques adapted to Western psychology (from their Buddhist roots) to increase and promote awareness of the "here and now." Mindfulness is used to cope with urges such as craving. For example, Mindfulness-Based Relapse Prevention (Witkiewitz, Marlatt, & Walker, 2005) helps individuals cope with craving by increasing their awareness of their initial response to craving in a nonjudgmental manner such that this awareness facilitates their ability to modify their response. Although preliminary findings suggest that this approach may be promising, further research needs to be conducted to establish its efficacy.

In short, many psychosocial treatment approaches have received some empirical support for treating alcohol use disorders, but no one treatment has emerged as highly successful in treating this complex problem.

A large multisite study of outpatient treatments for alcohol use disorders, called Project MATCH, attempted to identify specific patient characteristics that might predict which patients would respond better to a particular treatment. Project MATCH compared the efficacy of three widely used psychosocial treatments: cognitive-behavioral therapy (CBT), motivational enhancement therapy (MET), and 12-step facilitation (TSF) (Project MATCH Research Group, 1997, 1998). In addition, Project MATCH compared two types of enrollment into the study. One group of patients was enrolled directly into a traditional outpatient service, but the other group was enrolled into the study as an aftercare program, immediately following discharge from inpatient treatment for alcoholism. Results from Project MATCH revealed only small differences between the three psychosocial treatment modalities at 1-year follow-up, such that TSF patients were more likely to remain abstinent at 1-year follow-up than CBT and MET patients (Project MATCH Research Group, 1997). One hypothesis is that patients assigned to TSF may have done slightly better because they would have been encouraged to continue attending AA meetings once the intervention ended. However, by 3-year follow-up, drinking outcomes for all of the three treatment groups were similar, with about 30% of all patients reporting total abstinence in follow-up months 37 to 39 (Project MATCH Research Group, 1998). Type of enrollment showed a moderate effect as somewhat more (35%) of the patients in the aftercare condition were found to be continuously abstinent from alcohol 1 year following treatment, compared to 20% of patients in the outpatient condition (Project MATCH Research Group, 1998). Perhaps those individuals just coming out of inpatient care were more highly motivated to take advantage of the outpatient treatment.

Results from Project MATCH lent only moderate support to the hypothesis that matching individuals to treatment on the basis of patient variables might improve outcomes. Only 4 of the possible 21 matches were found to improve treatment outcomes for alcohol use disorder, with initial client level of anger being the most consistent moderator of treatment response. Specifically, individuals who initially scored higher in anger fared better in MET as compared to CBT and TSF, whereas individuals who scored lower in anger did better after CBT and TSF treatment than in MET. Additionally, at 3-year follow-up there was a significant effect of the individual's pretreatment drinking social network, such that individuals whose social networks were more supportive of drinking responded better to TSF treatment than to MET. In summary, results from Project MATCH as well as the recent literature on psychosocial treatment for alcoholism make it clear that alternative, more effective psychosocial approaches to treating alcohol use disorders are still needed.

PHARMACOLOGICAL TREATMENT

Pharmacotherapy for alcohol use disorder is used less often than psychosocial interventions. Aside from detoxification treatment, when pharmacological agents are often used to manage withdrawal symptoms, few community programs combine pharmacotherapy and psychosocial interventions to treat alcohol use disorder. The limited use of pharmacotherapy is due, in part, to the relative lack of effective pharmacological options to treat alcohol use disorders. Specifically, the only pharmacotherapies currently approved by the Food and Drug Administration (FDA) for the treatment of alcohol dependence are disulfiram (Antabuse), naltrexone, acamprosate, and Vivitrol—an injectable, longer acting form of naltrexone (Petrakis, 2006; Pettinati & Rabinowitz, 2006).

Naltrexone is perhaps the most studied of these medications. Shortly after two initial trials suggested that naltrexone resulted in significantly fewer drinking days and lower rates of relapse (a 23% relapse rate for naltrexone versus a 54% relapse rate for placebo) after 3 months of treatment (O'Malley, 1992; Volpicelli, Altermana, Hayahida, & O'Brien, 1992), naltrexone was advanced as one of the more promising pharmacological interventions for decreasing alcohol consumption and treating alcohol dependence (Litten, Allen, & Fertig, 1996; Schuckit & Smith, 1996). These findings also suggested that the effects of naltrexone were more prominent among individuals who consumed alcohol during the trial, with a 95% relapse rate among placebo-treated individuals versus a 50% relapse rate among naltrexone-treated patients (Volpicelli et al., 1992). These initial results have been largely supported by more recent trials of naltrexone that generally demonstrate beneficial effects on heavy drinking rates, particularly among those who are compliant with the medication (Anton et al., 1999; Chick et al., 2000; Monterosso et al., 2001; Monti et al., 2001; Morris, Hopwood, Whelan, Gardner, & Drummond, 2001). However, support for naltrexone is not consistent. A few trials, including a large multisite trial, have reported no significant outcome differences between naltrexone and placebo-treated patients (e.g., Krystal, Cramer, Krol, Kirk, & Rosenheck, 2001; Kranzler, Modesto-Lowe, & Van Kirk, 2000). Moreover, the effect sizes of previous findings are often modest, even when they reach statistical significance. In sum, studies of naltrexone to date suggest only a modest effect on the reduction of alcohol use among treatment-seeking individuals with alcohol use disorder.

Ondansetron and topiramate are two recent pharmacotherapies currently under study that show promise for the treatment of alcohol use disorder. Ondansetron is a 5-HT3 antagonist that has demonstrated effectiveness, relative to placebo, in the reduction of drinking among early-onset alcoholics (Johnson, Ait-Daoud, & Prihoda, 2000). Although the mechanism of action is unclear, it has been speculated that ondansetron might address the serotonergic dysfunction thought to characterize early-onset *DSM-IV* alcohol dependence (Johnson & Ait-Daoud, 2000; Johnson et al., 2000). In addition, it has been suggested that ondansetron might reduce craving for alcohol, possibly through the influence of 5-HT3 projections to mesolimbic dopaminergic connections in the midbrain (Johnson et al., 2000; Johnson & Ait-Daoud, 2000). Topiramate is an anticonvulsant medication that was only recently tested with alcohol-dependent patients. This trial found that topiramate reduced drinking and alcohol craving over a 12-week treatment period (Johnson et al., 2003). The effects of topiramate were not limited to early-onset alcoholism, as was the case with ondansetron. The mechanism of action of topiramate, however, remains unclear. In general, topiramate reduces neuronal excitability through inhibition at glutamate AMPA/kainate receptors and L-type calcium channels. This could conceivably decrease the distress of protracted withdrawal. Topiramate also facilitates brain GABA function and may even increase GABA levels. Both of these effects (i.e., glutamate blockade and GABA facilitation) can reduce or inhibit mesolimbic DA activity. It has been suggested that topiramate may indirectly influence midbrain dopaminergic activity, thereby reducing craving (Johnson et al., 2003). Two additional medications that have shown promise are quetiapine (Monnelly, Ciraulo, Knapp, LoCastro, & Sepulveda, 2004) and olanzapine (Hutchison et al., 2003, 2006). Both of these medications may show promise, in part, because of their ability to reduce craving by targeting mesocorticolimbic dopamine function.

In brief, randomized clinical trials have provided sufficient evidence of the efficacy, albeit modest efficacy, of acamprosate, naltrexone, and Vivitrol for the treatment of alcoholism (Kranzler et al., 2000; Mann, 2004; Myrick, Brady, & Malcolm, 2001; Schaffer & Naranjo, 1998). However, much additional work is needed to identify psychosocial predictors of medication compliance and efficacy (Kranzler et al., 2000), expand knowledge of dosing issues (Mason, 1996), improve the dissemination of research findings to clinicians in the field (Meza & Kranzler, 1996), examine the combined effects of psychosocial and pharmacotherapy treatments (McCaul & Petry, 2003), and investigate the role of genetic factors in predicting treatment response to pharmacotherapies as one way to potentially match patients to treatments (Hutchison et al., 2006; Ray & Hutchison, 2007).

Consistent with the goal of advancing the treatment of alcohol use disorders by combining pharmacotherapies and psychotherapies, NIAAA conducted a large multisite trial of naltrexone, acamprosate, or placebo in combination with a behavioral intervention (combined behavioral intervention, or CBI) or medication management (COMBINE Study Research Group, 2003a, 2003b). In this project, a CBI was designed to combine several elements of empirically supported treatments previously tested in Project MATCH, such as motivation enhancement therapy, cognitive-behavioral therapy, and facilitation of involvement in mutual-help groups (Miller, 2004). Results from the COMBINE study found that patients receiving medical management (MM) with naltrexone, CBI, or both fared better on drinking outcomes, whereas acamprosate showed no evidence of efficacy, either with or without CBI. No combination of medications produced better efficacy than MM with naltrexone or MM with CBI (Anton et al., 2006). The authors concluded that naltrexone with medical management could be most easily delivered in health care settings, thus serving patients with alcohol use disorder who might otherwise not receive treatment.

A pharmacogenetic study within the COMBINE project examined whether a single nucleotide polymorphism (SNP) in the mu-opioid receptor (OPRM1) gene, the Asn40Asp SNP, predicted clinical response to naltrexone, an opioid antagonist. Results indicated that if treated with MM and naltrexone, 87.1% of Asp40 carriers had a good clinical outcome, compared with only 54.8% of individuals with the Asn40/Asn40 genotype (odds ratio, 5.75; confidence interval, 1.88 to 17.54), while, if treated with placebo, 48.6% of Asp40 carriers and 54.0% of individuals with the Asn40/Asn40 genotype had a good clinical outcome (Anton et al., 2008). These findings are consistent with controlled laboratory studies suggesting that individuals with this polymorphism of the OPRM1 gene had a stronger hedonic response to alcohol in the lab (Ray & Hutchison, 2004; Ray et al., 2013), in the natural environment (Ray et al., 2010), and in the scanner when measuring dopamine release to alcohol administration (Ramchandani et al., 2011). Further, controlled studies suggest that naltrexone attenuates the rewarding effects of alcohol more strongly among Asp40 carriers (Ray & Hutchison, 2007; Ray et al., 2012; Setiawan et al., 2011). As reviewed in detail elsewhere (Ray, Chin, & Miotto, 2010), the naltrexone × OPRM1 gene interaction is a prime example of pharmacogenetics in the field of alcoholism, and serves more broadly as an example of the potential for genetics to allow more personalized medicine for psychiatric disorders.

Summary and Future Directions

Alcohol use disorders are multifaceted in their etiology, maintenance, and relapse processes. Research reviewed in this chapter has underscored the complex nature of alcohol use disorders that are currently best accounted for by a biopsychosocial model, which proposes that alcohol pathology results from the interplay between biological and psychosocial variables. The factors contributing to the etiology and development of alcohol problems appear to differ among individuals, such that patients may arrive at an alcohol use disorder diagnosis through multiple pathways that are heavily influenced by culture. Likewise, within a given patient, the factors contributing to the initial development of alcohol use disorder may be different from the factors maintaining the disorder or subserving a relapse. The historical, cultural, developmental, diagnostic, theoretical, and treatment considerations reviewed in this chapter clearly speak to the complexity of the alcohol addiction phenomenon. Importantly, the research reviewed here also highlights the progress of the field over the past several decades, as marked by an increased understanding of the psychological and biological factors underlying alcohol problems. This knowledge has been used to inform the most recent *DSM-5* diagnostic scheme and to guide the development of more effective treatments. However, current rates of recovery are modest even for the best available medications and psychosocial treatments. Future progress in the field hinges on our ability as clinicians and researchers to capture the complexity of alcohol use disorders in ways that are both cognizant of the empirical literature in our field and sensitive to each patient's presenting problems. Research and clinical work is needed to integrate various aspects of the biopsychosocial model and investigate its complexity in ways that capture the full picture of alcohol use disorders. Thus, a clinical neuroscience approach to the etiology and treatment of alcohol use disorders represents a critical direction in our field. To that end, clinical psychologists have an important role to play in the translational science of addiction. Clinical expertise in the phenomenology of addiction is essential to the success of such pursuits. Training the next generation of clinical scientists and practitioners to integrate their knowledge about psychopathology with an understanding of the underlying neural mechanisms of very complex behaviors, such as alcoholism, represents both a challenge and a tremendous opportunity for the field of clinical psychology.

References

Alcoholics Anonymous. (2006). *AA at a glance.* Retrieved from http://www.alcoholics-anonymous .org

American Psychiatric Association. (1952). *Diagnostic and statistical manual of mental disorders.* Washington, DC: Author.

American Psychiatric Association. (1980). *Diagnostic and statistical manual of mental disorders* (3rd ed.). Washington, DC: Author.

American Psychiatric Association. (1987). *Diagnostic and statistical manual of mental disorders* (3rd ed., rev.). Washington, DC: Author.

American Psychiatric Association. (1994). *Diagnostic and statistical manual of mental disorders* (4th ed.). Washington, DC: Author.

American Psychiatric Association. (2012). *APA corrects* New York Times *article on changes to DSM-5's substance use disorders.* Retrieved from http:// syp4550.socworld.com/docs/APA_DSM-5_NYT.pdf

American Psychiatric Association. (2013). *Diagnostic and statistical manual of mental disorders* (5th ed.). Washington, DC: Author.

Anderson, K. G., Schweinsburg, A., Paulus, M. P., Brown, S. A., & Tapert, S. (2005). Examining personality and alcohol expectancies using functional magnetic resonance imaging (fMRI) with adolescents. *Journal of Studies on Alcohol, 66,* 323–331.

Anton, R. F., Moak, D. H., Waid, L. R., Latham, P. K., Malcom, R. J., & Dias, J. K. (1999). Naltrexone and cognitive behavioral therapy for the treatment of out-patient alcoholics: Results of a placebo-controlled trial. *American Journal of Psychiatry, 156,* 1758–1764.

Anton, R. F., O'Malley, S. S., Ciraulo, D. A., Cisler, R. A., Couper, D., Donovan, D. M., ... Longabaugh, R. (2006). Combined pharmacotherapies and behavioral interventions for alcohol dependence: The COMBINE study: A randomized controlled trial. *JAMA, 295*(17), 2003–2017.

Anton, R. F., Oroszi, G., O'Malley, S., Couper, D., Swift, R., Pettinati, H., & Goldman, D. (2008). An evaluation of μ-opioid receptor (OPRM1) as a predictor of naltrexone response in the treatment of alcohol dependence: Results from the Combined Pharmacotherapies and Behavioral Interventions for Alcohol Dependence (COMBINE) study. *Archives of General Psychiatry, 65*(2), 135–144.

Armeli, S., Tennen, H., Todd, M., Carney, M. A., Mohr, C., Affleck, G., & Hromi, A. (2003). A daily process examination of the stress-response dampening effects of alcohol consumption. *Psychology of Addictive Behaviors, 17,* 266–276.

Babor, T. F. (1996). The classification of alcoholics: Typology theories from the 19th century to the present. *Alcohol Health and Research World, 20,* 6–17.

Babor, T. F., & Caetano, R. (2006). Subtypes of substance dependence and abuse: Implications for diagnostic classification and empirical research. *Addiction, 101*(Suppl. 1), 104–110.

Babor, T. F., Hofmann, M., Del Boca, F. K., Hesselbrock, V., Meyer, R. E., Dolinsky, Z. S., & Rounsaville, B. (1992). Types of alcoholics: I. Evidence for an empirically derived typology based on indicators of vulnerability and severity. *Archives of General Psychiatry, 49,* 599–608.

Bacio, G. A., Mays, V. M., & Lau, A. S. (2013). Drinking initiation and problematic drinking among Latino adolescents: Explanations of the immigrant paradox. *Psychology of Addictive Behaviors, 27*(1), 14.

Baker, T. B., Breslau, N., Covey, L., & Shiffman, S. (2012). DSM criteria for tobacco use disorder and tobacco withdrawal: A critique and proposed revisions for DSM-5. *Addiction, 107*(2), 263–275.

Bandura, A. (1977). *Social learning theory.* Englewood Cliffs, NJ: Prentice-Hall.

Bandura, A. (1986). *Social foundations of thought and action: A social cognitive theory.* Englewood Cliffs, NJ: Prentice-Hall.

Barnes, G. M., Reifman, A. S., Farrell, M. P., & Dintcheff, B. A. (2000). The effects of parenting on the development of adolescent alcohol misuse: A six-wave latent growth model. *Journal of Marriage and the Family, 62,* 175–186.

Beals, J., Novins, D. K., Whitsell, N. P., Mitchell, C. M., & Manson, S. M. (2005). Prevalence of mental disorders and mental health services in two American Indian reservation populations: Mental health disparities in the national context. *American Journal of Psychiatry, 15*(1).

Benjamin, D., Grant, E. R., & Pohorecky, L. A. (1993). Naltrexone reverses ethanol-induced dopamine release in the nucleus accumbens in awake, freely moving rats. *Brain Research*, *621*, 137–140.

Berridge, K. C., & Robinson, T. E. (1998). What is the role of dopamine in reward: Hedonic impact, reward learning, or incentive salience? *Brain Research Reviews*, *28*, 309–369.

Berridge, K. C., & Robinson, T. E. (2003). Parsing reward. *Trends in Neuroscience*, *26*, 507–513.

Bianco, C., Okuda, M., Wright, C., Hasin, D. S., Grant, B. F., Liu, S. M., & Olfson, M. (2008). Mental health of college students and their non–college-attending peers: Results from the National Epidemiologic Study on Alcohol and Related Conditions. *Archives of General Psychiatry*, *65*(12), 1429–1437.

Bjarnason, T., Andersson, B., Choquet, M., Elekes, Z., Morgan, M., & Rapinett, G. (2003). Alcohol culture, family structure and adolescent alcohol use: Multilevel modeling of frequency of heavy drinking among 15–16 year old students in 11 European countries. *Journal of Studies on Alcohol*, *64*, 200–208.

Bloomfield, K., Greenfield, T. K., Kraus, L., & Augustin, R. (2002). A comparison of drinking patterns and alcohol-use-related problems in the United States and Germany, 1995. *Substance Use & Misuse*, *37*, 399–428.

Brown, S. A., Goldman, M. S., Inn, A., & Anderson, L.R. (1980). Expectations of reinforcement from alcohol: Their domain and relation to drinking problems. *Journal of Consulting and Clinical Psychology*, *48*, 419–426.

Brown, S. A., McGue, M., Maggs, J., Schulenberg, J., Hingson, R., Swartzwelder, S., ... Winters, K. C. (2008). A developmental perspective on alcohol and youths 16 to 20 years of age. *Pediatrics*, *121*, S290–S310.

Bujarski, S., O'Malley S, S., Lunny, K., & Ray, L. A. (2013). The effects of drinking goal on treatment outcome for alcoholism. *Journal of Consulting and Clinical Psychology*, *81*(1), 13–22.

Burmeister, M. (1999). Basic concepts in the study of diseases with complex genetics. *Biological Psychiatry*, *45*, 522–532.

Caetano, R., Clark, C. L., & Tam, T. (1998). Alcohol consumption among racial/ethnic minorities: Theory and research. *Alcohol Research and Health*, *22*(4), 233–241.

Cappell, H., & Herman, C. P. (1972). Alcohol and tension reduction: A review. *Journal of Studies on Alcohol*, *33*, 33–64.

Carroll, K. M. (1996). Relapse prevention as a psychosocial treatment: A review of controlled clinical trials. *Experimental and Clinical Psychopharmacology*, *4*, 46–54.

Castro, F. G., Barrera, M., Jr., Mena, L. A., & Aguirre, K. M. (2014). Culture and alcohol use: Historical and sociocultural themes from 75 years of alcohol research. *Journal of Studies on Alcohol and Drugs, Supplement* (*17*), 36–49.

Chick, J., Anton, R., Checinski, K., Croop, R., Drummond, D. C., Farmer, R., ... Peters, T. (2000). A multicentre, randomized, double-blind, placebo-controlled trial of naltrexone in the treatment of alcohol dependence or abuse. *Alcohol and Alcoholism*, *35*(6), 587–593.

Clarke, T. K., Treutlein, J., Zimmermann, U. S., Kiefer, F., Skowronek, M. H., Rietschel, M., ... Schumann, G. (2007). Review: HPA-axis activity in alcoholism: Examples for a gene–environment interaction. *Addiction Biology*, *13*, 1–14.

Clarke, T. C., Ward, B. W., Freeman, G., & Schiller, J. S. (2015, September). *Early release of selected estimates based on data from the January–March 2015 National Health Interview Survey*. Atlanta, GA: National Center for Health Statistics.

Cloninger, C. R. (1987). Neurogenetic adaptive mechanisms in alcoholism. *Science*, *236*, 410–416.

Cohen, E., Feinn, R., Arias, A., & Kranzler, H. (2007). Alcohol treatment utilization: Findings from the National Epidemiologic Survey on Alcohol and Related Conditions. *Drug and Alcohol Dependence*, *86*, 214–221.

COMBINE Study Research Group. (2003a). Testing combined pharmacotherapies and behavioral interventions in alcohol dependence: Rationale and methods. *Alcoholism: Clinical and Experimental Research*, *27*, 1107–1122.

COMBINE Study Research Group. (2003b). Testing combined pharmacotherapies and behavioral interventions in alcohol dependence (The COMBINE Study): A pilot feasibility study. *Alcoholism: Clinical and Experimental Research*, *27*, 1123–1131.

Connors, G. J., & Maisto, S. A. (Eds.). (2006). Relapse in the addictive behaviors [Special issue]. *Clinical Psychology Review*, *26*(2).

Cooper, M. L., Agocha, V. B., & Sheldon, M. S. (2000). A motivational perspective on risky behaviors: The role of personality and affect regulatory processes. *Journal of Personality, 68*(6), 1059–1088.

Courtney, K. E., Arellano, R., Barkley-Levenson, E., Gálvan, A., Poldrack, R. A., MacKillop, J., ... Ray, L. A. (2012). The relationship between measures of impulsivity and alcohol misuse: An integrative structural equation modeling approach. *Alcoholism: Clinical and Experimental Research, 36*(6), 923–931.

Cox, W. M., Rosenberg, H., Hodgins, C.H.A., Macartney, J. I., & Maurer, K. A. (2004). United Kingdom and United States healthcare providers' recommendations of abstinence versus controlled drinking. *Alcohol and Alcoholism, 39*(2), 130–134.

Cranford, J. A., Zucker, R. A., Jester, J. M., Puttler, L. I., & Fitzgerald, H. E. (2010). Parental alcohol involvement and adolescent alcohol expectancies predict alcohol involvement in male adolescents. *Psychology of Addictive Behaviors, 24*(3), 386.

Cunningham, J. A., & Mäkelä, P. (2003). Comparing drinking patterns in Finland and Ontario (Canada). *Contemporary Drug Problems, 30*, 685–699.

Dawson, D. A., Goldstein, R. B., Saha, T. D., & Grant, B. F. (2015). Changes in alcohol consumption: United States, 2001–2002 to 2012–2013. *Drug and Alcohol Dependence, 148*, 56–61.

Dawson, D. A., Grant, B. F., Stinson, F. S., Chou, P. S., Huang, B., & Ruan, W. J. (2005). Recovery from DSM-IV alcohol dependence: United States, 2001–2002. *Addiction, 100*, 281–292.

de Bruijn, C., Van Den Brink, W., de Graaf, R., & Vollebergh, W. A. (2005). Alcohol abuse and dependence criteria as predictors of a chronic course of alcohol use disorders in the general population. *Alcohol and Alcoholism, 40*, 441–446.

de Lima, M. S., Dunn, J., Novo, I. P., Tomasi, E., & Reisser, A.A.P. (2003). Gender differences in the use of alcohol and psychotropics in a Brazilian population. *Substance Use & Misuse, 38*, 51–65.

de Looze, M., Raaijmakers, Q., Ter Bogt, T., Bendtsen, P., Farhat, T., Ferreira, M., ... Simons-Morton, B. (2015). Decreases in adolescent weekly alcohol use in Europe and North America: Evidence from 28 countries from 2002 to 2010. *European Journal of Public Health, 25*(Suppl. 2), 69–72.

de Wit, H. (1996). Priming effects with drugs and other reinforcers. *Experimental and Clinical Psychopharmacology, 4*, 5–10.

Del Boca, F. K., Darkes, J., Goldman, M. S., & Smith, G. T. (2002). Advancing the expectancy concept via the interplay between theory and research. *Alcoholism: Clinical and Experimental Research, 26*, 926–935.

Delker, E., Brown, Q., & Hasin, D. (2015). Epidemiological studies of substance dependence and abuse in adults. *Current Behavioral Neuroscience Reports, 2*(1), 15–22.

Dick, D. M., & Beirut, L. J. (2006). The genetics of alcohol dependence. *Current Psychiatry Reports, 8*, 151–157.

Dimeff, L. A., & Marlatt, G. A. (1995). Relapse prevention. In R. H. Hester & W. R. Miller (Eds.), *Handbook of alcoholism treatment approaches* (pp.176–194). Needham Heights, MA: Allyn & Bacon.

DSM-5 to include controversial changes to criteria for substance use disorders. (2012, July). *Journal of Studies on Alcohol and Drugs, 73*. Retrieved from http://alcoholstudies.rutgers.edu/news/JSADpress/JSADJuly12_DSM.pdf

Edwards, G., & Gross, M. M. (1976). Alcohol dependence: Provisional description of a clinical syndrome. *British Medical Journal, 1*(6017), 1058–1061.

Ersche, K. D., Jones, P. S., Williams, G. B., Turton, A. J., Robbins, T. W., & Bullmore, E. T. (2012). Abnormal brain structure implicated in stimulant drug addiction. *Science, 335*(6068), 601–604.

Feighner, J. P., Robins, E., Guze, S. B., Woodruff, R. A. J., Winokur, G., & Munoz, R. (1972). Diagnostic criteria for use in psychiatric research. *Archives of General Psychiatry, 26*, 57–63.

Fergusson, D. M., Boden, J. M., & Horwood, L. J. (2006). Cannabis use and other illicit drug use: Testing the cannabis gateway hypothesis. *Addiction, 101*(4), 556–569.

Finn, P. R., Earleywine, M., & Pihl, R. O. (1992). Sensation seeking, stress reactivity, and alcohol dampening discriminate the density of a family history of alcoholism. *Alcoholism: Clinical and Experimental Research, 16*, 585–590.

Fuller, R. K., & Hiller-Sturmhofel, S. (1999). Alcoholism treatment in the United States: An overview. *Alcohol Research & Health, 23*, 69–77.

Galanter, M., Egelko, S., & Edwards, H. (1993). Rational recovery: Alternative to AA for addiction. *American Journal of Drug and Alcohol Abuse, 19*, 499–510.

Gianoulakis, C. G. (1993). Endogenous opioids and excessive alcohol consumption. *Journal of Psychiatry and Neuroscience, 18*, 148–156.

Gianoulakis, C. G., de Waele, J. P., & Thavundayil, J. (1996). Implication of the endogenous opioid system in excessive ethanol consumption. *Alcohol, 13*, 19–23.

Goldman, M. S., & Darkes, J. (2004). Alcohol expectancy multiaxial assessment: A memory network-based approach. *Psychological Assessment, 16*, 4–15.

Goldman, M. S., Del Boca, F. K., & Darkes, J. (1999). Alcohol expectancy theory: The application of cognitive neuroscience. In K. E. Leonard & H. T. Blane (Eds.), *Psychological theories of drinking and alcoholism* (pp. 203–246). New York, NY: Guilford Press.

Gottesman, I. I., & Gould, T. D. (2003). The endophenotype concept in psychiatry: Etymology and strategic intentions. *American Journal of Psychiatry, 160*, 636–645.

Grant, B. F., Dawson, D. A., Stinson, F. S., Chou, S. P., Dufour, M. C., & Pickering, R. P. (2004). The 12-month prevalence and trends in DSM-IV alcohol abuse and dependence: United States, 1991–1992 and 2001–2002. *Drug and Alcohol Dependence, 74*, 223–234.

Grant, B. F., Goldstein, R. B., Saha, T. D., Chou, S. P., Jung, J., Zhang, H., … Hasin, D. S. (2015). Epidemiology of DSM-5 alcohol use disorder: Results from the National Epidemiologic Survey on Alcohol and Related Conditions III. *JAMA Psychiatry, 72*(8), 757–766.

Greeley, J., & Oei, T. (1999). Alcohol and tension reduction. In K. E. Leonard & H. T. Blane (Eds.), *Psychological theories of drinking and alcoholism* (pp. 14–53). New York, NY: Guilford Press.

Hart, K. E., & Fazaa, N. (2004). Life stress events and alcohol misuse: Distinguishing contributing stress events from consequential stress events. *Substance Use & Misuse, 39*, 1319–1339.

Hasin, D. S., Schuckit, M. A., Martin, C. S., Grant, B. F., Bucholz, K. K., & Helzer, J. E. (2003). The validity of the DSM-IV alcohol dependence: What do we know and what do we need to know? *Alcoholism: Clinical and Experimental Research, 27*, 244–252.

Hasin, D. S., Stinson, F. S., Ogburn, E., & Grant, B. F. (2007). Prevalence, correlates, disability, and comorbidity of DSM-IV alcohol abuse and dependence in the United States: Results from the National Epidemiologic Survey on Alcohol and Related Conditions. *Archives of General Psychiatry, 64*, 830–842.

Heath, A. C., Bucholz, K. K., Madden, P. A., Dinwiddie, S. H., Slutske, W. S., Bierut, L. J., … Martin, N. G. (1997). Genetic and environmental contributions to alcohol dependence risk in a national twin sample: Consistency of findings for women and men. *Psychological Medicine, 27*, 1381–1391.

Heath, A. C., & Martin, A. G. (1991). Intoxication after an acute dose of alcohol: An assessment of its association with alcohol consumption patterns by using twin data. *Alcoholism: Clinical and Experimental Research, 15*, 122–128.

Heather, N., & Dawe, S. (2005). Level of impaired control predicts outcome of moderation-oriented treatment for alcohol problems. *Addiction, 100*, 945–952.

Hines, L., Ray, L. A., Hutchison, K. E., & Tabakoff, B. (2005). Alcoholism: The dissection for endophenotypes. *Dialogues in Clinical Neuroscience, 7*, 153–163.

Hingson, R. W., Zha, W., Weitzman, E. R. (2009). Magnitude of and trends in alcohol-related mortality and morbidity among U.S. college students ages 18–24, 1998–2005. *Journal of Studies on Alcohol and Drugs, Supplement* (16), 12–20.

Hull, C. L. (1943). *Principles of behavior*. New York, NY: Appleton-Century-Crofts.

Hutchison, K. E., McGeary, J., Smolen, A., Bryan, A., & Swift, R. M. (2002). The DRD4 VNTR polymorphism moderates craving after alcohol consumption. *Health Psychology, 21*, 139–146.

Hutchison, K. E., Ray, L. A., Sandman, E., Rutter, M. C., Peters, A., & Swift, R. (2006). The effect of olanzapine on craving and alcohol consumption. *Neuropsychopharmacology, 31*, 1310–1317.

Hutchison, K. E., Wooden, A., Swift, R. M., Smolen, A., McGeary, J., & Adler, L. (2003). Olanzapine reduces craving for alcohol: A DRD4 VNTR polymorphism by pharmacotherapy interaction. *Neuropsychopharmacology, 28*, 1882–1888.

Ilgen, M., McKellar, J., & Tiet, Q. (2005). Abstinence self-efficacy and abstinence 1 year after substance use disorder treatment. *Journal of Consulting and Clinical Psychology, 73*, 1175–1180.

Johnson, B. A., & Ait-Daoud, N. (2000). Neuropharmacological treatments for alcoholism: Scientific basis and clinical findings. *Psychopharmacology, 149*, 327–344.

Johnson, B. A., Ait-Daoud, N. & Prihoda, T. J. (2000). Combining ondansetron and naltrexone effectively treats biologically predisposed alcoholics: From hypotheses to preliminary clinical evidence. *Alcoholism: Clinical and Experimental Research, 24*, 737–742.

Johnson, B. A., O'Malley, S. S., Ciraulo, D. A., Roache, J. D., Chambers, R. A., Sarid-Segal, O., & Couper, D. (2003). Dose-ranging kinetics and behavioral pharmacology of naltrexone and acamprosate, both alone and combined, in alcohol dependent subjects. *Journal of Clinical Psychopharmacology, 23*, 281–293.

Johnson, P. B., & Johnson, H. L. (1999). Cultural and familial influences that maintain the negative meaning of alcohol. *Journal of Studies on Alcohol, 13*, 79–83.

Johnston, L. D., O'Malley, P. M., Bachman, J. G., & Schulenberg, J. E. (2010). *Monitoring the future national results on adolescent drug use: Overview of key findings, 2009.* Bethesda, MD: National Institute on Drug Use.

Kalivas, P. W., & Stewart, J. (1991). Dopamine transmission in the initiation and expression of drug-and stress-induced sensitization of motor activity. *Brain Research Reviews, 16*, 223–244.

Kalivas, P. W., & Volkow, N. D. (2005). The neural basis of addiction: A pathology of motivation and choice. *American Journal of Psychiatry, 162*, 1403–1413.

Kavanagh, D. J., Sitharthan, G., Young, R. M., Sitharthan, T., Saunders, J. B., Shockley, N., & Giannopoulos, V. (2006). Addition of cue exposure to cognitive-behaviour therapy for alcohol misuse: A randomized trial with dysphoric drinkers. *Addiction, 101*, 1106–1116.

Kazdin, A. E. (2002). *Research design in clinical psychology* (4th ed.). Boston, MA: Allyn & Bacon.

Koob, G. F. (2003). Neuroadaptive mechanisms of addiction: Studies on the extended amygdala. *European Neuropsychopharmacology, 13*, 442–452.

Koob, G. F., & LeMoal, M. (2001). Drug addiction, dysregulation of reward, and allostasis. *Neuropsychopharmacology, 24*, 97–129.

Koob, G. F., & LeMoal, M. (2005). Plasticity of reward neurocircuitry and the "dark side" of drug addiction. *Nature Neuroscience, 8*, 1442–1444.

Koopmans, J. R., & Boomsma, D. L. (1996). Familial resemblances in alcohol use: Genetic or cultural transmission? *Journal of Studies on Alcohol, 57*, 19–28.

Kranzler, H. R., Modesto-Lowe, V., & Van Kirk, J. (2000). Naltrexone vs. nefazedone for treatment of alcohol dependence: A placebo-controlled trial. *Neuropsychopharmacology, 22*, 493–503.

Krystal, J. H., Cramer, J. A., Krol, W. F., Kirk, G. F., & Rosenheck, R. A. (2001). Naltrexone in the treatment of alcohol dependence. *New England Journal of Medicine, 345*, 1734–1739.

Leeman, R. F., Corbin, W. R., & Fromme, K. (2009). Craving predicts within session drinking behavior following placebo. *Personality and Individual Differences, 46*, 693–698.

Leeman, R. F., O'Malley, S. S., White, M. A., McKee, S. A. (2010). Nicotine and food deprivation decrease the ability to resist smoking. *Psychopharmacology, 212*, 25–32.

Les Whitbeck, B., Chen, X., Hoyt, D. R., & Adams, G. W. (2004). Discrimination, historical loss and enculturation: Culturally specific risk and resiliency factors for alcohol abuse among American Indians. *Journal of Studies on Alcohol, 65*(4), 409–418.

Levenson, R. W., Sher, K. J., Grossman, L. M., Newman, J., & Newlin, D. B. (1980). Alcohol and stress-response dampening: Pharmacological effects, expectancy, and tension reduction. *Journal of Abnormal Psychology, 89*, 528–538.

Levine, H. G. (1992). Temperance cultures: Alcohol as a problem in Nordic and English-speaking cultures. In M. Lader, G. Edwards, & C. Drummond (Eds.), *The nature of alcohol and drug-related problems* (pp. 16–36). New York, NY: Oxford University Press.

Lindman, R. E., Sjöholm, B. A., & Lang, A. R. (2000). Expectations of alcohol-induced positive affect: A cross-cultural comparison. *Journal of Studies on Alcohol, 61*, 681–687.

Link, B. G., & Phelan, J. C. (2002). McKeown and the idea that social conditions are fundamental causes of disease. *American Journal of Public Health, 92*(5), 730–732.

Litt, M. D., Babor, T. F., Del Boca, F. K., Kadden, R. M., & Cooney, N. L. (1992). Types of alcoholics: II. Application of an empirically derived typology to treatment matching. *Archives of General Psychiatry, 49*, 609–614.

Litten, R. Z., Allen, J., & Fertig, J. (1996). Pharmacotherapies for alcohol problems: A review of research with focus on developments since 1991. *Alcoholism: Clinical and Experimental Research, 20*, 859–876.

Littleton, J., & Little, H. (1994). Current concepts of ethanol dependence. *Addiction, 89*, 1397–1412.

Loeber, S., Croissant, B., Heinz, A., Mann, K., & Flor, H. (2006). Cue exposure in the treatment of alcohol dependence: Effects on drinking outcome, craving and self-efficacy. *British Journal of Clinical Psychology, 45*, 515–529.

MacKillop, J., & Lisman, S. A. (2005). Reactivity to alcohol cues: Isolating the role of perceived availability. *Experimental and Clinical Psychopharmacology, 13*, 229.

Maisto, S. A., Carey, K. B., & Bradizza, C. M. (1999). Social learning theory. In K.E. Leonard & H. T. Blane (Eds.), *Psychological theories of drinking and alcoholism* (pp. 106–163). New York, NY: Guilford Press.

Maisto, S. A., & Connors, G. J. (2006). Relapse in the addictive behaviors: Integration and future directions. *Clinical Psychology Review, 26*, 229–231.

Mann, K. (2004). Pharmacotherapy of alcohol dependence: A review of the clinical data. *CNS Drugs, 18*, 485–504.

Marlatt, G. A., & Gordon, J. R. (1985). *Relapse prevention*. New York, NY: Guilford Press.

Martin, C. S., Chung, T., Kirisci, L., & Langenbucher, J. W. (2006). Item response theory analysis of diagnostic criteria for alcohol and cannabis use disorders in adolescents: Implications for the *DSM-V. Journal of Abnormal Psychology, 115*, 807–814.

Martin, N. G., Oakeshott, J. G., Gibson, J. B., Starmer, G. A., Perl, J., & Wilks, A. V. (1985). A twin study of psychomotor and physiological responses to an acute dose of alcohol. *Behavior Genetics, 15*, 305–347.

Mason, B. J. (1996). Doing issues in the pharmacotherapy of alcoholism. *Alcoholism: Clinical and Experimental Research, 20*, 10–16.

McCaul, M. E., & Petry, N. M. (2003). The role of psychosocial treatment in pharmacotherapy for alcoholism. *American Journal of Addictions, 12*, S41–S52.

McCrady, B. S. (1992). A reply to Peele: Is this how you treat your friends? *Addictive Behaviors, 17*, 67–72.

McCrady, B. S. (2001). Alcohol use disorders. In D. H. Barlow (Ed.), *Clinical handbook of psychological disorders* (pp. 376–433). New York, NY: Guilford Press.

McGue, M. (1999). Behavioral genetic models of alcoholism and drinking. In K. E. Leonard & H. T. Blane (Eds.), *Psychological theories of drinking and*

alcoholism (pp. 372–421). New York, NY: Guilford Press.

McKay, J. R., Franklin, T. R., Patapis, N., & Lynch, K. G. (2006). Conceptual, methodological, and statistical issues in the study of relapse. *Clinical Psychology Review, 26*, 109–127.

Meza, E., & Kranzler, H. R. (1996). Closing the gap between alcoholism research and practice: The case for pharmacotherapy. *Psychiatric Service, 47*, 917–920.

Miller, W. R. (Ed.). (2004). Combined behavioral intervention manual: A clinical research guide for therapists treating people with alcohol dependence. *COMBINE Monograph Series, 1* (NIH 04-5288). Bethesda, MD: National Institute on Alcohol Abuse and Alcoholism.

Miller, W. R., & Rollnick, S. (2002). Motivational interviewing: Preparing people for change. *Journal of Studies of Alcohol, 63*, 776–777.

Mitchell, J. M., O'Neil, J. P., Janabi, M., Marks, S. M., Jagust, W. J., & Fields, H. L. (2012). Alcohol consumption induces endogenous opioid release in the human orbitofrontal cortex and nucleus accumbens. *Science Translational Medicine, 4*(116), 116ra6.

Monnelly, E. P., Ciraulo, D. A., Knapp, C., LoCastro, J., & Sepulveda, I. (2004). Quetiapine for treatment of alcohol dependence. *Journal of Clinical Psychopharmacology, 24*, 532–535.

Monterosso, J. R., Flannery, B. A., Pettinati, H. M., Oslin, D. W., Rukstalis, M., O'Brien, C. P., & Volpicelli, J. R. (2001). Predicting treatment response to naltrexone: The influence of craving and family history. *American Journal on Addictions, 10*(3), 258–268.

Monti, P. M., Kadden, R. M., Rohsenow, D. J., Cooney, N. L., & Abrams, D. B. (2002). *Treating alcohol dependence: A coping skills training guide* (2nd ed.). New York, NY: Guilford Press.

Monti, P. M., Rohsenow, D. J., Swift, R. M., Gulliver, S. B., Colby, S. M., Mueller, T. I., … Asher, M. K. (2001). Naltrexone and cue exposure with coping and communication skills training for alcoholics: Treatment process and 1-year outcomes. *Alcoholism: Clinical and Experimental Research, 25*(11), 1634–1647.

Morris, P. L., Hopwood, M., Whelan, G., Gardner, J., & Drummond, E. (2001). *Addiction, 96*, 1565–1573.

Moyer, A., Finney, J. W., Swearingen, C. E., & Vergun, P. (2002). Brief interventions for alcohol problems: A meta-analytic review of controlled investigations in treatment-seeking and non-treatment-seeking populations. *Addiction*, *97*, 279–292.

Myrick, H., Brady, K. T., & Malcolm, R. (2001). New developments in the pharmacotherapy of alcohol dependence. *American Journal of Addictions*, *10*, 3–15.

National Institutes of Health. (2010). *Alcohol epidemiologic data reference manual: Vol 8, No. 2. Alcohol use and alcohol use disorders in the United States, a 3-year follow-up: Main findings from the 2004–2005 wave 2 National Epidemiologic Survey on Alcohol and Related Conditions (NESARC)* (NIH Publication No. 10-7677). Rockville, MD: National Institute on Alcohol Abuse and Alcoholism.

O'Farrell, T. J., & Fals-Stewart, W. (2003). Alcohol abuse. *Journal of Marital and Family Therapy*, *29*, 121–146.

Öjehegan, A., & Berglund, M. (1989). Changes of drinking goals in a two-year outpatient alcoholic treatment program. *Addictive Behaviors*, *14*, 1–10.

O'Malley, S. S., Jaffe, A. J., Chang, G., Schottenfeld, R. S., Meyer, R. E., & Rounsaville, B. (1992). Naltrexone and coping skills therapy for alcohol dependence. *Archives of General Psychiatry*, *49*, 881–887.

O'Malley, S. S., Krishnan-Sarin, S., Farren, C., Sinha, R., & Kreek, M. (2002). Naltrexone decreases craving and alcohol self-administration in alcohol-dependent subjects and activates the hypothalamo-pituitary-adrenocortical axis. *Psychopharmacology (Berlin)*, *160*, 19–29.

Orford, J., & Keddie, A. (1986). Abstinence or controlled drinking in clinical practice: A test of the dependence and persuasion hypotheses. *British Journal of Addiction*, *81*, 495–504.

Oslin, D. W., Cary, M., Slaymaker, V., Colleran, C., & Blow, F. C. (2009). Daily ratings measures of alcohol craving during an inpatient stay define subtypes of alcohol addiction that predict subsequent risk for resumption of drinking. *Drug and Alcohol Dependence*, *103*, 131–136.

Partanen, J. (1991). *Sociability and intoxication: Alcohol and drinking in Kenya, Africa and the modern world*. Helsinki, Finland: Finnish Foundation for Alcohol Studies, Vol. 39.

Pavlick, M., Hoffmann, E., & Rosenberg, H. (2009). A nationwide survey of American alcohol and drug craving assessment and treatment practices. *Addiction Research & Theory*, *17*, 591–600.

Peele, S. (1993). The conflict between public health goals and the temperance mentality. *American Journal of Public Health*, *83*, 805–810.

Peele, S. (1997). Utilizing culture and behavior in epidemiological models of alcohol consumption and consequences for Western nations. *Alcohol and Alcoholism*, *32*, 51–64.

Petrakis, I. L. (2006). A rational approach to the pharmacotherapy of alcohol dependence. *Journal of Clinical Psychopharmacology*, *26*, S3–S12.

Pettinati, H. M., & Rabinowitz, A. R. (2006). Choosing the right medication for the treatment of alcoholism. *Current Psychiatry Reports*, *8*, 383–388.

Phelan, J. C., Link, B. G., & Tehranifar, P. (2010). Social conditions as fundamental causes of health inequalities: Theory, evidence, and policy implications. *Journal of Health and Social Behavior*, *51*(Suppl.), S28–S40.

Piper, M. E., McCarthy, D. E., & Baker, T. B. (2006). Assessing tobacco dependence: A guide to measure evaluation and selection. *Nicotine & Tobacco Research*, *8*(3), 339–351.

Project MATCH Research Group. (1997). Matching alcoholism treatment to client heterogeneity: Project MATCH posttreatment drinking outcomes. *Journal of Studies on Alcohol*, *58*, 7–29.

Project MATCH Research Group. (1998). Matching alcoholism treatments to client heterogeneity: Project MATCH three-year drinking outcomes. *Alcoholism: Clinical and Experimental Research*, *22*, 1300–1311.

Ramchandani, V. A., Umhau, J., Pavon, F. J., Ruiz-Velasco, V., Margas, W., Sun, H., … Schwandt, M. L. (2011). A genetic determinant of the striatal dopamine response to alcohol in men. *Molecular Psychiatry*, *16*(8), 809–817.

Ray, L. A. (2012). Clinical neuroscience of addiction: Applications to psychological science and practice. *Clinical Psychology: Science and Practice*, *19*(2), 154–166.

Ray, L. A., Barr, C. S., Blendy, J. A., Oslin, D., Goldman, D., & Anton, R. F. (2012). The role of the Asn40Asp polymorphism of the mu opioid receptor gene (OPRM1) on alcoholism etiology and treatment: A critical review. *Alcoholism: Clinical and Experimental Research*, *36*(3), 385–394.

Ray, L. A., Bujarski, S., MacKillop, J., Courtney, K. E., Monti, P. M., & Miotto, K. (2013). Subjective response to alcohol among alcohol-dependent individuals: Effects of the mu-opioid receptor (OPRM1) gene and alcoholism severity. *Alcoholism: Clinical and Experimental Research*, *37*, E116–E124.

Ray, L. A., Chin, P. F., & Miotto, K. (2010). Naltrexone for the treatment of alcoholism: Clinical findings, mechanisms of action, and pharmacogenetics. *CNS & Neurological Disorders—Drug Targets*, *9*, 13–22.

Ray, L. A., & Hutchison, K. E. (2004). A polymorphism of the μ-opioid receptor gene (OPRM1) and sensitivity to the effects of alcohol in humans. *Alcoholism: Clinical and Experimental Research*, *28*(12), 1789–1795.

Ray, L. A., & Hutchison, K. E. (2007). Effects of naltrexone on alcohol sensitivity and genetic moderators of medication response: A double-blind placebo-controlled study. *Archives of General Psychiatry*, *64*(9), 1069–1077.

Ray, L. A., Miranda, R., Jr., Tidey, J. W., McGeary, J. E., MacKillop, J., Gwaltney, C. J., ... Monti, P. M. (2010). Polymorphisms of the mu-opioid receptor and dopamine D4 receptor genes and subjective responses to alcohol in the natural environment. *Journal of Abnormal Psychology*, *119*(1), 115–125.

Robinson, T. E., & Berridge, K. C. (1993). The neural basis of drug craving: An incentive sensitization theory of addiction. *Brain Research Reviews*, *18*, 247–291.

Robinson, T. E., & Berridge, K. C. (2001). Incentive-sensitization and addiction. *Addiction*, *96*, 103–114.

Rohsenow, D. J., Monti, P. M., Rubonis, A. V., Gulliver, S. B., Colby, S. M., Binkoff, J. A., & Abrams, D. B. (2001). Cue exposure with coping skills training and communication skills training for alcohol dependence: 6- and 12-month outcomes. *Addiction*, *96*, 1161–1174.

Room, R. (1998). Drinking patterns and alcohol-related social problems: Frameworks for analysis in developing societies. *Drug and Alcohol Review*, *17*, 389–398.

Rosenberg, H. (1993). Prediction of controlled drinking by alcoholics and problem drinkers. *Psychological Bulletin*, *113*, 129–139.

Rychtarik, R. G., Connors, G. J., Dermen, K. H., & Stasiewicz, P. R. (2000). Alcoholics Anonymous and the use of medications to prevent relapse: An anonymous survey of member attitudes. *Journal of Studies on Alcohol*, *61*, 134–138.

Sacks, J. J., Gonzales, K. R., Bouchery, E. E., Tomedi, L. E., & Brewer, R. D. (2015). 2010 national and state costs of excessive alcohol consumption. *American Journal of Preventive Medicine*, *49*(5), e73–e79.

Saha, T. D., Chou, S. P., & Grant, B. F. (2006). Toward an alcohol use disorder continuum using item response theory: Results from the National Epidemiologic Survey on Alcohol and Related Conditions. *Psychological Medicine*, *36*, 931–941.

Samson, H. H., & Harris, R. A. (1992). Neurobiology of alcohol abuse. *Trends in Pharmacological Sciences*, *13*, 206–211.

Schaffer, A., & Naranjo, C. A. (1998). Recommended drug treatment strategies for the alcoholic patient. *CNS Drugs*, *56*, 571–585.

Schmid, H., Bogt, T. T., Godeau, E., Hublet, A., Dias, S. F., & Fotiou, A. (2003). Drunkenness among young people: A cross-national comparison. *Journal of Studies on Alcohol*, *64*, 650–661.

Schmidt, E. A., Carns, A., & Chandler, C. (2001). Assessing the efficacy of rational recovery in the treatment of alcohol/drug dependence. *Alcoholism Treatment Quarterly*, *19*, 97–106.

Schuckit, M. A., & Smith, T. L. (1996). An 8-year follow-up of 450 sons of alcoholic and control subjects. *Archives of General Psychiatry*, *53*, 202–210.

Schuckit, M. A., Windle, M., Smith, T. L., Hesselbrock, V., Ohannessian, C., Averna, S., ... Sher, K. J. (2006). Searching for the full picture: Structural equational modeling in alcohol research. *Alcoholism: Clinical and Experimental Research*, *26*, 194–202.

Setiawan, E., Pihl, R. O., Cox, S. M., Gianoulakis, C., Palmour, R. M., Benkelfat, C., & Leyton, M. (2011). The effect of naltrexone on alcohol's stimulant properties and self-administration behavior in social drinkers: Influence of gender and genotype. *Alcoholism: Clinical and Experimental Research*, *35*(6), 1134–1141.

Sher, K. J., & Levenson, R. W. (1982). Risk for alcoholism and individual differences in the stress-response dampening of alcohol. *Journal of Abnormal Psychology*, *91*, 350–367.

Sher, K. J., Trull, T. J., Bartholow, B. D., & Vieth, A. (1999). Personality and alcoholism: Issues, methods, and etiological processes. In K. E. Leonard & H. T. Blane (Eds.), *Psychological theories of drinking and alcoholism* (pp. 54–105). New York, NY: Guilford Press.

Sinha, R., & Li, C. (2007). Imaging stress- and cue-induced drug and alcohol craving: Association with relapse and clinical implications. *Drug and Alcohol Review*, *26*, 25–31.

Sinha, R., Robinson, J., & O'Malley, S. (1998). Stress response dampening: Effects of gender and family history of alcoholism and anxiety disorders. *Psychopharmacology, 137*, 311–320.

Smith, J. E., Meyers, R. J., & Delaney, H. D. (1998). Community reinforcement approach with homeless alcohol-dependent individuals. *Journal of Consulting and Clinical Psychology, 66*, 541–548.

Spear, L. P. (2000). The adolescent brain and age-related behavioral manifestations. *Neuroscience and Biobehavioral Review, 24*(4), 417–463.

Stahre, M., Roeber, J., Kanny, D., Brewer, R. D., & Zhang, X. (2014). Contribution of excessive alcohol consumption to deaths and years of potential life lost in the United States. *Preventing Chronic Disease, 11*, E109.

Stewart, J., de Wit, H., & Eikelboom, R. (1984). Role of unconditioned and conditioned drug effects in the self-administration of opiates and stimulants. *Psychological Review, 91*, 251–268.

Stewart, S. H., Karp, J., Pihl, R. O., & Peterson, R. A. (1997). Anxiety sensitivity and self-reported reasons for drug use. *Journal of Substance Abuse, 9*, 223–240.

Substance Abuse and Mental Health Services Administration. (2014a). Table 2.41B—Alcohol use in lifetime, past year, and past month among persons aged 18 or older, by demographic characteristics: Percentages, 2013 and 2014. In *Results from the 2014 National Survey on Drug Use and Health: Detailed tables*. Retrieved from http://www.samhsa.gov/data/sites/default/files/NSDUH-DetTabs2014/NSDUH-DetTabs2014.htm#tab2-41b

Substance Abuse and Mental Health Services Administration. (2014b). Table 2.46B—Alcohol use, binge alcohol use, and heavy alcohol use in the past month among persons aged 18 or older, by demographic characteristics: Percentages, 2013 and 2014. In *Results from the 2014 National Survey on Drug Use and Health: Detailed tables*. Retrieved from http://www.samhsa.gov/data/sites/default/files/NSDUH-DetTabs2014/NSDUH-DetTabs2014.htm#tab2-46b

Substance Abuse and Mental Health Services Administration. (2014c). Table 6.89B—Binge alcohol use in the past month among persons aged 18 to 22, by college enrollment status and demographic characteristics: Percentages, 2013 and 2014. In *Results from the 2014 National Survey on Drug Use and Health: Detailed tables*. Retrieved from http://www.samhsa.gov/data/sites/default/files/NSDUH-DetTabs2014/NSDUH-DetTabs2014.htm#tab6-89b

Substance Abuse and Mental Health Services Administration. (2014d). Table 5.49A—Need for and receipt of treatment at a specialty facility for an alcohol problem in the past year among persons aged 18 or older, by demographic characteristics: Numbers in thousands and percentages, 2013 and 2014. In *Results from the 2014 National Survey on Drug Use and Health: Detailed tables*. Retrieved from http://www.samhsa.gov/data/sites/default/files/NSDUH-DetTabs2014/NSDUH-DetTabs2014.htm#tab5-49a

Swendsen, J. D., Tennen, H., Carney, M. A., Affleck, G., Willard, A., & Hromi, A. (2000). Mood and alcohol consumption: An experience sampling test of the self-medication hypothesis. *Journal of Abnormal Psychology, 109*, 198–204.

Trimpey, J. (1992). *The small book*. New York, NY: Delacorte.

Vasilaki, E. I., Hosier, S. G., & Cox, W. M. (2006). The efficacy of motivational interviewing as a brief intervention for excessive drinking: A meta-analytic review. *Alcohol and Alcoholism, 41*, 328–335.

Vega, W. A., & Sribney, W. M. (2011). Understanding the Hispanic Health Paradox through a multigeneration lens: A focus on behavior disorders. *Nebraska Symposium on Motivation, 57*, 151–168.

Viken, R. J., Rose, R. J., Morzoati, S. L., Christian, J. C., & Li, T.-K. (2003). Subjective intoxication in response to alcohol challenge: Heritability and covariation with personality, breath alcohol level, and drinking history. *Alcoholism: Clinical and Experimental Research, 27*, 795–803.

Volkow, N., & Li, T. K. (2005). The neuroscience of addiction. *Nature Neuroscience, 8*, 1429–1430.

Volpicelli, J. R., Altermana, A. I., Hayahida, M., & O'Brien, C. P. (1992). Naltrexone in the treatment of alcohol dependence. *Archives of General Psychiatry, 49*, 876–880.

Volpicelli, J. R., Pettinati, H. M., McLellan, A., & O'Brien, C. P. (2001). *Combining medication and psychosocial treatments for addictions: The BRENDA approach*. New York, NY: Guilford Press.

Wagner, E. F., Lloyd, D. A., & Gil, A. G. (2002). Racial/ethnic and gender differences in the incidence and onset age of DSM-IV alcohol use disorder symptoms among adolescents. *Journal of Studies on Alcohol, 63*, 609–619.

Warner, L. A., Canino, G., & Colón, H. M. (2001). Prevalence and correlates of substance use disorders among older adolescents in Puerto Rico and the United States: A cross-cultural comparison. *Drug and Alcohol Dependence, 63,* 229–243.

Weiss, F., Lorang, M. T., Bloom, F. E., & Koob, G. F. (1993). Oral alcohol self-administration stimulates dopamine release in the rat nucleus accumbens: Genetic and motivational determinants. *Journal of Pharmacology and Experimental Therapeutics, 267,* 250–258.

Wilsnack, R. W., Vogeltanz, N. D., Wilsnack, S. C., & Harris, T. R. (2000). Gender differences in alcohol consumption and adverse drinking consequences: Cross-cultural patterns. *Addiction, 95,* 251–265.

Windle, M., Mun, E. Y., & Windle, R. C. (2005). Adolescent-to-young adulthood heavy drinking trajectories and their prospective predictors. *Journal of Studies on Alcohol, 66*(3), 313–322.

Windle, M., Spear, L. P., Fuligni, A. J., Angold, A., Brown, J. D., Pine, D., ... Dahl, R. E. (2008). Transitions into underage and problem drinking: Developmental processes and mechanisms between 10 and 15 years of age. *Pediatrics, 121*(Suppl. 4), S273–S289.

Wise, R. A. (1988). The neurobiology of craving: Implications for the understanding and treatment of addiction. *Journal of Abnormal Psychology, 97,* 118–132.

Wise, R. A., & Bozarth, M. A. (1987). A psychomotor stimulant theory of addiction. *Psychological Review, 94,* 469–492.

Witkiewitz, K., & Marlatt, G. A. (2006). Overview of harm reduction treatments for alcohol problems. *International Journal of Drug Policy, 17,* 285–294.

Witkiewitz, K., & Marlatt, G. A. (2007). Modeling the complexity of post-treatment drinking: It's a rocky road to relapse. *Clinical Psychology Review, 27*(6), 724–738.

Witkiewitz, K., Marlatt, G. A., & Walker, D. (2005). Mindfulness-based relapse prevention for alcohol and substance use disorders. *Journal of Cognitive Psychotherapy, 19*(3), 211–228.

Wood, M. D., Read, J. P., Mitchell, R. E., & Brand, N. H. (2004). Do parents still matter? Parent and peer influences on alcohol involvement among recent high school graduates. *Psychology of Addictive Behaviors, 18*(1), 19–30.

World Health Organization. (2010). Mental and behavioural disorders due to psychoactive substance use (F10–F19). In *International statistical classification of diseases and related health problems 10th revision (ICD-10)*. Geneva: Author.

Yoon, G., Kim, S. W., Thuras, P., Grant, J. E., & Westermeyer, J. (2006). Alcohol craving in outpatients with alcohol dependence: Rate and clinical correlates. *Journal of Studies on Alcohol and Drugs, 67,* 770.

Zamboanga, B. L., Schwartz, S. J., Ham, L. S., Jarvis, L. H., & Olthuis, J. V. (2009). Do alcohol expectancy outcomes and valuations mediate peer influences and lifetime alcohol use among early adolescents? *Journal of Genetic Psychology, 170,* 359–376.

Zeichner, A., Giancola, P. R., & Allen, J. D. (1995). Effects of hostility on alcohol stress-response dampening. *Alcoholism: Clinical and Experimental Research, 19,* 977–983.

Chapter 12

Eating Disorders

LINDA W. CRAIGHEAD, MARGARET A. MARTINEZ, KELLY L. KLUMP, JAMES LOCK, AND NINA KIRZ

Disordered eating can take a variety of forms, with the *core problem behaviors* that lead to a diagnosis of an eating disorder identified as (a) restrictive eating (low intake and/or restricted range of food types), (b) binge eating (loss of control), and (c) compensatory behaviors. Important *cognitive and affective features* that go along with these behaviors include pathologically high levels of concern about weight and shape and their control, excessive fear of weight gain, feeling "fat" despite being in the normal weight range, and maladaptive beliefs about eating, exercise, and desired body weight. A related feature includes distress about repeatedly eating more than intended, but this is also characteristic of many individuals worried about weight and thus does not distinguish those with clinically significant disorders. Problematic eating behavior can, but does not necessarily, impact weight and it is notable that weight is featured as a required diagnostic criterion in only one of the three clinical presentations that are the focus of this chapter: anorexia nervosa (AN). Bulimia nervosa (BN) and binge eating disorder (BED) have no weight criteria but both require binge eating; they are differentiated by the presence or absence of compensatory behaviors.

Prior to the introduction of the current diagnostic system, the fifth edition of the *Diagnostic and Statistical Manual of Mental Disorders* (*DSM-5*) (American Psychiatric Association [APA], 2013), AN and BN were the only specified eating disorder (ED) diagnoses. Often individuals with these diagnoses were put together and referred to as a sample with Eating Disorders. The *DSM-5* maintained the historical distinction between AN and BN, which is based primarily on weight, but it greatly expanded the scope of eating disorder diagnoses. These changes were needed because more than half the individuals presenting for eating concerns failed to meet criteria for AN or BN. In *DSM-5*, BED has been added as a distinct diagnosis and the criteria for AN and BN have been modified to be more inclusive. In addition, the category Other Specified Feeding or Eating Disorder (OSFED) was added, which identifies subthreshold variants of AN, BN, and BED, as well as the syndromes called *purging disorder* and *night-eating syndrome*. The hope is that these changes will facilitate research to improve our understanding of different developmental pathways, encourage earlier detection and diagnosis, and promote the development of effective strategies that target specific presenting patterns. Note that the *DSM-5* OSFED category also includes three disorders not discussed in this chapter; these are pica (the eating of non-nutritive substances), and rumination disorder, which were previously listed under disorders of early infancy and childhood, and the newly created avoidant and restrictive food intake disorder.

Within the current diagnostic system, it is an even greater challenge to describe and explain the pathology of individuals with eating disorders when considered as a "unitary group"; that group may now include individuals as different in presentation as a chronically low weight person who restricts severely and never overeats and a morbidly obese individual for whom the distinction between overeating and binge eating is not so clear and for whom obesity is the urgent problem. Despite this significant range of presentations, recent theories of eating disorders have emphasized the substantial similarities among the eating syndromes. Fairburn's transdiagnostic theory (Fairburn, Cooper, & Shafran, 2003) identifies the centrality of overvaluation of eating, shape, and weight and their control across the range of eating pathology. Fairburn postulates that variations in eating symptomatology are all expressions of this overvaluation and argues that the mechanism of this core belief must be targeted in treatment. This transdiagnostic view of eating disorders is supported by data demonstrating similarities in risk factors (Bakalar, Shank, Vannucci, Radin, & Tanofsky-Kraff, 2015; Hilbert et al., 2014), genetic mechanisms (Bulik et al., 2007), neurobiological processes (Uher et al., 2004), and maintaining factors (Stice, 2002), as well as data showing significant diagnostic crossover over time (Stice, Marti, & Rohde, 2013). However, there are critical differences both between and within the three eating disorders discussed in this chapter. After reviewing the evidence marshaled to make recommendations for *DSM-5*, Keel, Brown, Holland, and Bodell (2012) concluded that this evidence supported the utility of broad distinctions among AN, BN, and BED. These authors suggested that the field may find a differentiated diagnostic system more useful in researching etiology, even if a transdiagnostic model turns out to be useful clinically in developing and prescribing treatments. Our intention in this chapter is to highlight differences in presenting pathology within the broad category of eating disorders while also identifying the significant similarities in risk factors and in certain core features that have important implications, particularly in terms of prevention and early intervention. The reader is also encouraged to bear in mind that at the individual level, there is significant variety in presentation within any given diagnostic group.

Diagnostic Criteria and Clinical Presentation

As noted above, there are both substantial similarities and important distinctions between the three eating disorders. This section is designed to provide clinicians with the information necessary to identify, differentiate, and diagnosis AN, BN, and BED.

ANOREXIA NERVOSA (AN)

Anorexia nervosa is the earliest of the eating disorders to be described in the medical literature and remains the most serious of them in terms of physical sequelae and morbidity. A French physician (Lasègue, 1883) and a British physician (Gull, 1874) independently described an illness, primarily affecting girls and young women, that consisted of severe weight loss, amenorrhea, constipation, and restlessness, without evidence of any organic pathology. Gull first used the term *anorexia nervosa*, but the syndrome, which was relatively uncommon, did not receive widespread attention. Psychoanalytic thinking was predominant until the 1950s, and within that view, AN was thought of as a fear of oral impregnation (Thoma, 1967). Psychiatrist Hilde Bruch, who published her pioneering work in the 1970s (Bruch, 1973, 1978), was the first to identify the core issues of low self-esteem, limited self-concept, and distorted body image, which remain central to current formulations of AN. Crisp (1997) developed a related formulation of AN as an effort to avoid difficulties associated with physical maturation and emotional and familial problems—often experienced with the onset of adolescence. Theories about family psychopathology related to intrusiveness and overcontrol as contributors to the psychological vulnerability of adolescents who developed AN were advanced by Minuchin, Rosman, and Baker (1978) and Selvini Palazzoli (1974). Currently, there are multiple theories about AN, but none have taken over as the most prominent or widely accepted model because empirical support for the models remains limited. However, most theories continue to place at least some emphasis on issues of individuation and family processes because adolescence is the most typical age of onset. Theories that would explain more adult onset are not as well developed. In addition, most theories place AN within a biopsychosocial framework that includes recognition of the roles of genetic vulnerability, individual differences in pre-illness personality traits, the family context, and the larger social context that supports the thin ideal. In the treatment section, interventions that have emerged from theories about etiology and the resistance to weight restoration—that typically persists despite increasing recognition of the negative consequences of the low weight—are described.

The current diagnostic criteria for AN, as well as for BN and BED, are outlined in Table 12.1; Figure 12.1 provides a diagnostic flowchart for making a differential eating disorder diagnosis. The primary symptom that distinguishes individuals with a diagnosis of AN from those with BN or BED is restriction of intake leading to a significantly low weight that is less than minimally normal or (in children or adolescents) less than minimally expected. Additional required symptoms include an intense fear of gaining weight *or* of becoming fat *or* persistent behavior that interferes with weight gain (in the context of low weight), and also body-image disturbance, overconcern with weight/shape, *or* lack of recognition of the medical seriousness of low weight. The *DSM-IV* (APA, 1994) had required 3 consecutive months of amenorrhea in postmenarcheal females, but that criterion has been eliminated; it was not consistently useful and was not applicable to all individuals. The *DSM-5* retains the *DSM-IV* distinction between two subtypes of AN—restricting and binge eating/purging—although the evidence supporting these subtypes as clinically discrete entities is controversial (e.g., Olatunji et al., 2012). Some evidence suggests that patients with the binge/purge subtype have a more complicated course and are more likely to have comorbid problems with depression, substance abuse, and personality disorders (Le Grange, Fitzsimmons-Craft, et al., 2014). No differences in recovery rates or psychopathology (Eddy et al., 2002) have been clearly established. Over a more chronic course, the distinction becomes less useful due to the crossing over that often occurs between the subtypes.

In clinical presentation, the most salient feature of AN is the clear and unwavering *behavioral refusal to obtain or maintain weight acceptable for height and health*. This

TABLE 12.1 Diagnostic Criteria for *DSM-5* Eating Disorders

Anorexia Nervosa	Bulimia Nervosa	Binge Eating Disorder
A. Significantly low body weight resulting from restricted energy intake relative to expenditure. B. Fear of weight gain or of possibility of being overweight or behavior that maintains low weight. C. Body-image disturbance, overvaluation of shape or weight, or denial of severity of low weight. *Specify whether* **Restricting type:** individual does not engage in any binge eating or purging; weight loss is the product of dieting and/or excessive exercise only. **Binge eating/purging type:** individual engages in recurrent instances of binge eating or purging over the past 3 months.	A. Repeated episodes of binge eating in which the individual 　1. Eats in a distinct episode an unusually large amount of food relative to what would be consumed by most individuals. 　2. Experiences a sense of loss of control over eating. B. Repeated episodes of behaviors intended to compensate for overeating and avoid weight gain, such as vomiting, inappropriate use of laxatives/diuretics/other medications, fasting, or excessive energy. C. Binge eating and purging behaviors occur on average at least once a week for 3 months. D. Individual displays overvaluation of shape or weight. E. Individual does not meet criteria for anorexia nervosa.	A. Repeated episodes of binge eating in which the individual 　1. Eats in a distinct episode an unusually large amount of food relative to what would be consumed by most individuals. 　2. Experiences a sense of loss of control over eating. B. Episodes of binge eating are characterized by at least 3 of the following: 　1. Increased rate of eating. 　2. Eating beyond the point of fullness. 　3. Eating in the absence of physical hunger. 　4. Eating alone out of embarrassment. 　5. Feelings of disgust, depression, or guilt after episodes of binge eating. C. Binge eating causes significant distress. D. Binge eating occurs on average at least once a week for 3 months. E. The individual does not meet criteria for either AN or BN.

Source: Based on *DSM-5*.

behavior is particularly perplexing when it occurs in the context of an otherwise relatively nonproblematic and often high-achieving adolescent. The initiation of dieting may occur after an identifiable trigger such as being called fat by a peer or sibling or the initiation of efforts to lose weight for a special occasion may escalate to maladaptive levels. Often these behaviors appear initially innocuous, even consistent with age-appropriate developmental concerns about appearance; however, over time, these behaviors take on an urgent and insistent nature while other important social and emotional pursuits are deferred or avoided all together. Over time, the weight loss becomes an end in and of itself and spirals

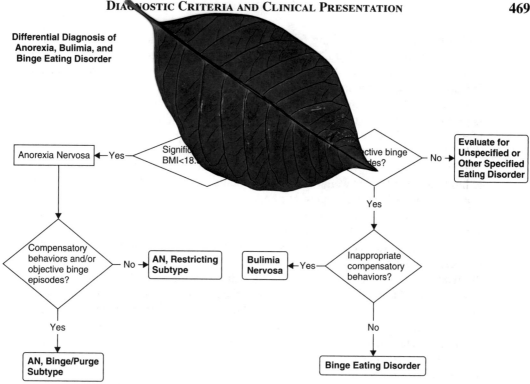

Differential Diagnosis of Anorexia, Bulimia, and Binge Eating Disorder

Anorexia Nervosa ←Yes— Signifi... BMI<18...

...ctive binge ...des? —No→ Evaluate for Unspecified or Other Specified Eating Disorder

Yes

Compensatory behaviors and/or objective binge episodes? —No→ AN, Restricting Subtype

Bulimia Nervosa ←Yes— Inappropriate compensatory behaviors?

Yes

AN, Binge/Purge Subtype

No

Binge Eating Disorder

FIGURE 12.1 Diagnostic Flowchart for AN, BN, and BED.

out of the patient's control, a process hypothesized to be under the control of dorsostriatal stimulus-response learning systems in the brain (Foerde, Steinglass, Shohamy, & Walsh, 2015; Walsh, 2013). Many patients firmly believe the behavior is within their control until they try to stop, at which point they sometimes realize that their symptoms actually control them. The behaviors that illustrate this refusal include a highly restrictive and selective eating pattern, excessive exercise, and in some cases purging behaviors.

Restrictive behaviors take a variety of forms, some of which are characteristic of eating disorders more generally. However, intentional dieting that results in an unhealthy low weight is the hallmark of AN. Hours may be spent calculating calories and planning meals. Converting to vegetarianism in the context of dieting can be an early sign of disordered eating. Only certain foods come to be seen as safe to consume, and the list of permissible foods typically becomes smaller over time until often a patient eats the exact same thing every day. Some patients drink excessive amounts of water to control hunger, while others will consume very little water because it appears to increase their weight or makes them feel bloated. They may weigh themselves frequently and may feel the day is ruined if their weight has not decreased. Exercise may initially be fairly normal in quantity and quality, but *compulsive exercise* patterns develop where attempts to interrupt the behavior are met with extreme resistance (Davis & Kaptein, 2006). The patient may feel he or she must exercise in order to be allowed to eat, or may exercise after meals to burn off the calories consumed. Some patients will not miss a day despite illness or injury and will forgo almost any other activity to ensure they can exercise. Some individuals exercise at such a high level (e.g., training for a marathon or participation in intensive sports) that their caloric intake may actually be in the normal range. This presentation is referred to clinically as *exercise anorexia*. Such individuals refuse to eat "unhealthy" foods and to increase calories sufficiently to achieve or maintain a healthy weight. Alternatively, some individuals with AN may not engage in intense physical activity but may instead spend large amounts of time standing or fidgeting, behaviors that they appear to engage in more often than healthy controls do and that may contribute to relapse (Gianini et al., 2015).

Individuals who restrict and/or overexercise may also engage in other, more *harmful weight-loss behaviors*. Purging behaviors develop in 15% to 20% of cases as an attempt to limit the potential for weight gain. AN patients may purge after eating normal or even small amounts of food and may not endorse loss of control over eating (although the extreme dieting often triggers feelings of loss of control). Patients may also abuse laxatives, diuretics, or enemas that lead to dehydration rather than true weight loss, and they may abuse medications, such as improper use of insulin in diabetics. The "feeling of decreased weight" or having a "flat stomach" provides temporary reassurance against the fear of weight gain. Research indicates that purging is fairly ineffective because a large portion of the calories are actually absorbed before the patient is able to vomit them up (Kaye, Weltzin, Hsu, McConaha, & Bolton, 1993), and these unhealthy weight-loss behaviors are believed to be associated with long-term weight gain, rather than weight loss (Neumark-Sztainer, Wall, Story, & Standish, 2012). Over time, the experiences of starvation, exercise, and even purging behaviors become self-reinforcing and are experienced as a source of support and comfort for the person with AN.

The psychological basis for these weight-loss behaviors is usually considered to be an intense fear of fat or of gaining weight. The triggers for the development of this specific type of anxiety and fear are extremely variable but commonly include the onset of puberty, development of an extreme health or nutrition focus, being teased about weight or appearance, initiating social or academic transitions (e.g., starting middle school or high school), emergence of a medical illness that initiates weight loss, attempting to improve athletic performance, and experiences of physical and sexual abuse. The fear of weight gain and fat is relieved—albeit temporarily—by the various weight-loss–inducing behaviors. This is accomplished both directly (because the behaviors lead to weight loss and that reduces the anxiety and fear) and indirectly (by providing a focus for the obsessive worry that accompanies these fears). Regardless, the behaviors are strongly reinforced, which is believed to help explain their persistence in spite of some negative consequences, and the strong resistance to giving them up. It is notable that the previous (*DSM-IV*) requirement for weight phobia was eliminated in *DSM-5*. Behavior that interferes with weight gain is now sufficient to warrant the diagnosis, regardless of the reasons given for that behavior. Individuals diagnosed with AN in non-Western countries are less likely to report fear of fatness as the main motivation for their weight loss, as are younger adolescents and preadolescents (Nicholls & Bryant-Waugh, 2003). Interestingly, in the context of the transdiagnostic emphasis on the centrality of overconcern with weight and its control, Strober, Freeman, and Morrell (1999) reported that patients without weight phobia (the fear of fatness) were less likely to have a chronic course or engage in binge eating, and more likely to be fully weight-recovered at a 10- to 15-year follow-up.

Another important psychological aspect of AN is the disturbance in the appreciation of current body weight and shape, leading to an overestimation of body size relative to true body size. This body-image distortion likely results from a consistent and persistent overfocus on the body as a whole or on specific parts of the body (e.g., thighs, buttocks, cheeks) in an attempt to assess the success of efforts to lose weight or fat. Initially, this focus may be a source of limited reassurance, much in the way that constant checking of weight on a scale may be, because changes can be seen and measured. However, over time, the hyperfocus on the body leads to greater and greater distortions and misperceptions. This can also lead to a severe distortion in evaluating the medical consequences of being severely underweight. This denial of the seriousness of malnutrition is a major source of treatment avoidance and represents a significant psychological hazard for successful weight restoration.

The result of the interaction among the psychological factors of fear, distortion, and denial and the behaviors precipitating extreme weight loss is *physiological malnutrition.* A commonly used figure for determining malnutrition in adults is a body mass index (BMI) of 17.5 or below, or a body weight that is 85% or less of ideal body weight (IBW). Notably, the *DSM-5* gives these weight cut-points as examples, not absolutes, though many clinicians and researchers appear to treat them as such. Individuals who are overweight before the onset of illness may lose substantial weight and demonstrate severe thoughts, behaviors, and medical consequences but not reach the state of physiological starvation characteristic of AN. In *DSM-5* these individuals are considered subclinical or atypical cases of AN (within the OSFED category). Importantly, in children and adolescents the weight cut-points are particularly likely to be misleading as growth and pubertal status greatly affect these types of norms. Younger patients may be growth-retarded due to malnutrition, so consideration of their prior growth curve data must also be taken into consideration.

Malnutrition affects most organ systems, as the body responds to manage a starvation state and conserves energy by cutting back on all but the most essential functions. Blood flow to the periphery is decreased, leading to cold extremities. Skin becomes dry and hair falls out, while the body becomes coated with lanugo, a fine downy hair meant to conserve warmth. Menstruation stops or becomes irregular, and fertility is impaired. Along with these hormonal changes, calcium is lost from the bones, leading to osteopenia or in severe cases to osteoporosis. In children who are still growing, growth can be slowed or stopped. Heart and brain function are preserved for as long as possible but eventually the cardiac muscle weakens, leading to low heart rate, low blood pressure, and possible death. Brain scans have shown shrinkage of the brain during the illness that reverses with weight restoration (Lázaro et al., 2013; Mainz, Schulte-Rüther, Fink, Herpertz-Dahlmann, & Konrad, 2012). Of all these complications, the only one known to definitely persist after weight restoration is osteoporosis, the severity of which depends on the duration of the illness.

Case Example: Anorexia Nervosa

Lisa is a 17-year-old female who reports, "According to other people, I'm not eating safely." About 6 months ago she decided to "lose a few pounds" for her junior prom. She is 5 feet 5 inches tall, and initially wanted to decrease her weight from 130 pounds to 120 pounds. She initiated her dieting by eating what she described as "healthier": she cut out junk food, desserts, and fast food, and limited her portion sizes. She also started an exercise routine of running 3 miles and doing 100 sit-ups and 100 pushups every day.

Her weight dropped to 120 pounds by prom, but she still felt overweight. She cut more and more foods from her diet until she was eating mostly fruits and vegetables and was skipping lunch at school. She kept careful track of calories and tried not to eat more than 500 kcal/day. Her parents noticed that she was losing too much weight and tried to keep her from exercising, but Lisa felt too guilty about "all those calories just sitting there" and was afraid of gaining weight. She started secretly doing jumping jacks and running in place in her room at night. She thought about trying to throw up her food, but she did not like the idea because it seemed dirty and messy. As her weight decreased further she became more and more irritable, especially when her parents tried to encourage her to eat. Her menses ceased, she felt cold all the time, and her hair started falling out. She stopped spending time with friends because she was worried they would comment on her not eating, and because she just did not have the energy to go out. Her parents became concerned enough to bring her to the pediatrician, who found that her weight was down to 100 pounds and her heart rate was 42 beats per minute. She was admitted to the hospital, which Lisa thought was completely unnecessary. She was furious at being made to gain weight in the hospital as she felt her thighs were still "huge."

BULIMIA NERVOSA (BN)

Liddell and Scott (1972) note that the term *boulimos*—meaning a great deal of (or ravenous) hunger—was used by several early Greek authors, including the physician Galen. The term came to refer both to hunger and to the overeating that extreme hunger triggers. James (1743) described cases of atypical preoccupation with food and overeating, including a variant, caninus appetite, that involved overeating followed by vomiting. In the modern era, Stunkard (1959) drew attention to clinically significant patterns of eating large amounts when he described a binge eating syndrome in some individuals. These patients, some of whom were overweight, would report high levels of hunger, would seek out food, and would typically not stop eating until physically uncomfortable. Vomiting was sometimes induced but often served as a means to relieve abdominal pain rather than specifically to prevent weight gain. These patients reported guilt, remorse, and self-contempt related to their failure to control their eating behavior. This work broadened thinking about eating by considering that failures to stop eating after normal amounts might be due to decreased sensations of satiety instead of (or in addition to) being a consequence of excessive hunger resulting from dieting. This distinction continues to be useful in understanding that pathways to objective binge eating may develop in the absence of severe restriction or weight loss, as is more often the case in BED than in BN.

Attention was directed toward purging behaviors following a publication by Boskind-Lodahl and White (1978) that described a variant of AN found among normal weight women that was considered particularly difficult to treat and that these authors called "bulimarexia." Russell (1979) described similar cases but used the term "bulimia nervosa," and it was this term that was adopted when BN was formally recognized as a distinct diagnosis in the *DSM-III-R* (APA, 1987). The cognitive and affective features associated with normal weight individuals who purge are strikingly similar to those found in individuals with AN. Crossover from BN to a full diagnosis of AN is not common, but crossover to subclinical AN occurs with some frequency (i.e., high levels of restriction remain even when purging stops). The acceptance of BN as an "eating disorder" far earlier than the acceptance of BED may have been due to the perception that that merely eating large amounts was a problem for weight (i.e. obesity) but not a form of "disordered" eating. Behavioral interventions for obesity were evolving during this time within the framework of health psychology rather than within the framework of eating disorder treatment.

Fairburn, Marcus, and Wilson (1993) proposed a model to explain the persistence (i.e., maintenance) of BN that explicitly identified excessive dieting as the proximal cause of purging behaviors and identified overconcern with weight and shape (and their control) as the more distal feature driving dieting and purging behaviors. This model does not directly address etiology, but risk factor models such as those proposed by Stice (2002) identify a number of societal, family, and other variables that likely contribute to the development and maintenance of this overconcern with weight and shape. The stronger than expected short-term effectiveness, particularly for recent onset cases, of cognitive-behavioral therapy (CBT) treatment provided strong support for this conceptualization of BN. In this model, dieting behaviors are targeted first and then the cognitive dysfunction is addressed. Other theories of BN emerged subsequently that placed more emphasis on interpersonal difficulties, personality vulnerabilities, and the role of emotion regulation, and these issues have largely been incorporated into Fairburn's more recent work. The original CBT for BN model was expanded to create the transdiagnostic model (Fairburn & Bohn, 2005; Fairburn et al., 2003), which has been proposed as a useful way to understand the important common pathology across eating disorders while providing a sufficiently flexible approach to treatment that the basic strategies can be tailored to address a wide range of problematic ED behaviors. Treatment also addresses weight issues (underweight or obesity) when needed.

The diagnostic criteria for bulimia nervosa (BN) center around the presence of recurrent *objective binge episodes* (OBEs) and the various compensatory behaviors such as vomiting, laxative use, fasting, or excessive exercise that are intended to minimize the impact of the binges (i.e., to prevent weight gain). OBEs are defined as eating more than most people would eat in a similar situation and in a discrete period of time (e.g., 2 hours) and with a sense of loss of control over eating (i.e., feeling unable to control what or how much food is consumed). Assessing loss of control can be problematic as some individuals have difficultly reporting on their experience, and many in fact "plan" when they are going to binge eat. Episodes in which loss of control is endorsed but where normal or even small portions are reported are labeled *subjective binge episodes* (SBEs); these are common but do not count toward the frequency criterion required for diagnosis. The clinical guideline for determining large amounts is a portion at least 3 times the typical portion size for that food. The caloric value reported by Bartholome, Raymond, Lee, Peterson, and Warren (2006) for an objective binge episode averaged 1,900 calories and for a subjective binge episode about 700 calories. The OBEs and compensatory behaviors may be closely linked in time, forming a distinct binge/purge episode that is easily identifiable, but that is not necessarily the case. OBEs and compensatory behaviors are required to occur at least once per week for 3 months for a diagnosis of BN; these criteria represent a decrease from those in the *DSM-IV* (twice per week for 6 months), allowing less severe and more recent onset cases to be diagnosed. Individuals who do not meet the weight criterion for AN but who purge only after SBEs or solely as a deliberate weight control strategy are diagnosed with purging disorder (which is in the OSFED category). This pattern is clinically significant as it may persist over considerable periods of time or may serve as a pathway to either AN or BN.

Clearly identifiable binge/purge episodes typically occur when the individual is alone, and evenings are especially high-risk times (Deaver, Miltenberger, Smyth, Meidinger, & Crosby, 2003; Stein et al., 2007). The behaviors are quite secretive and are usually associated with high levels of shame and embarrassment. Individuals with BN typically restrict their food intake, often severely, between binge/purge episodes. Many individuals binge primarily on the foods they otherwise restrict (e.g., high-fat, high-calorie foods such as pastries or ice cream), whereas others binge on whatever is available or eat large quantities of healthy foods. Individuals with BN frequently skip meals in an attempt to limit total intake and many feel at risk for bingeing or overeating whenever they do eat. Both type and amount of food may be severely limited by a set of rigid rules (e.g., no fat, no processed foods, no meat, no food after dinner or eating only at specified times). The most typical BN pattern is little or no breakfast or lunch, with intake postponed to as late as possible in the day. Early in the course of the disorder, binges are often unplanned (normal eating turns into overeating and then bingeing and purging). As the pattern crystallizes, it becomes more common that individuals fight the urge to binge and purge. As they struggle to resist urges, they become very vulnerable, particularly when they are alone and have the opportunity to binge and purge. When the urge to binge escalates, the person typically plans to binge/purge at a time when he or she will not be detected. Some individuals then experience a period of relief from their urges and can refrain for several days.

Common triggers for bingeing and purging include emotions (both positive and negative), lapses in self-awareness, interpersonal stressors, the presence of tempting food, feeling that a dieting rule has been broken, body-image dissatisfaction, and skipping meals or getting extremely hungry (Engelberg, Steiger, Gauvin, & Wonderlich, 2007; Kjelsås, Børsting, & Gudde, 2004; Lavender et al., 2015; Vanderlinden, Grave, Vandereycken, & Noorduin, 2001). Eating-disordered behaviors often serve to distract individuals from unpleasant emotions, to comfort or soothe individuals, to numb unpleasant emotions, or to provide a sense of control. However, after bingeing and purging, individuals typically report feeling intense guilt and shame. Although binge episodes are intended to relieve negative mood, mood often worsens following them (Hilbert & Tuschen-Caffier, 2007). In chronic cases, the binge/purge pattern has become so well established it may feel more like a habit than a conscious response to current distress, and for some, the episodes are not particularly distressing. Many individuals maintain some level of purging over long periods of time based on the maladaptive belief that it is necessary to prevent weight gain. These individuals do not typically present for treatment until there is a significant worsening of binge and purge symptoms (Hepworth & Paxton, 2007; Mond et al., 2009), some life event makes the behaviors more difficult to maintain, or a significant other confronts them and provides the motivation to change. Most individuals become very distressed whenever they do decide to stop and realize they feel powerless to do so. Due to the high levels of distress that accompany binge/purge symptoms, in addition to intense fears that their compensatory strategies may be failing, individuals with bulimia are more likely to seek treatment voluntarily than are those with AN (Fairburn & Harrison, 2003; Klein & Walsh, 2004; Polivy & Herman, 2002).

Individuals with BN are typically within the normal weight range (APA, 2013; Fairburn & Harrison, 2003), although many are at the higher end of that range, which they consider to be overweight/fat. Regardless of their actual weight, these individuals either want to be considerably thinner or are convinced that they will gain weight if they stop their compensatory behaviors. Thus, while individuals with BN are highly motivated to stop binge eating and lose weight, most are ambivalent about stopping or even moderating their compensatory behaviors (especially exercise). When individuals first start purging, the behavior is often associated with some weight loss, but its utility in this regard is usually short-lived. It turns out that purging and laxative abuse are both fairly ineffective weight control strategies as substantial portions of calories are still retained by the body (Kaye, Weltzin, Hsu, McConaha, & Bolton, 1993). The frequency of binge eating typically escalates as motivation to eat moderately is undermined by having options to compensate, and normal appetite regulation is increasingly disrupted.

Medical complications arise most often from the purging behaviors—for example, self-induced vomiting and laxative abuse (Guarda, Redgrave, & Dressler, 2012; Mehler, 2010)—especially at high levels of use. In a moderately severe case, the frequency of purging is limited to a few times a week, but in the most severe cases, an individual may purge several times a day or purge after any food is eaten. Extended episodes that include multiple periods of eating and then purging are not uncommon. Individuals with BN may develop fluid or electrolyte abnormalities (leading to potentially fatal arrhythmias), esophageal complications, gastrointestinal (GI) symptoms, renal system problems, menstrual irregularities, and thyroid dysfunction (Mehler, 2010). Medical complications related to prolonged laxative abuse, another common form of purging, include reflex constipation and the loss of normal colonic function (cathartic colon syndrome; Mehler, 2010). However, many individuals show few medical indicators for extended periods of time. Russell's sign (scarring or calluses on the tops of the hands from repeatedly inducing vomiting), dental problems (dental enamel erosion, gum disease), and enlarged parotid glands (chipmunk-like cheeks) are often the only obvious signs of chronic vomiting. It is useful for dentists to ask about purging when atypical dental problems are evident. Laboratory tests (for salivary amylase) can be used as an indicator of inflammation of the parotid glands, and positive results may mean the person is purging; but this test is not a specific indicator, so it is not widely used. BN is very difficult to detect early in the course of the disorder if a person is motivated to hide the problem. Social difficulties related to atypical eating patterns, social isolation, unexplained absences, secretive behavior, missing food (or money), and excessive bathroom use are often the more observable signs that a person's problems have reached clinically significant levels.

Decreased stomach motility can contribute to patients' complaints that they feel very full after eating normal or small amounts of food (making it more difficult to resist urges to purge). Some data suggest that individuals with BN have blunted postprandial cholecystokinin (CCK) release, which may contribute to their difficulty in feeling satisfied with normal amounts of food (Hannon-Engel, 2011), although data are mixed (Hannon-Engel, Filin, & Wolfe, 2013; Rigamonti et al., 2014). Failure to consistently replicate blunted CCK response in individuals with BN may be related to type of food consumed. For example, protein may increase production of CCK, which may in turn contribute to increased feelings of fullness after eating protein-rich foods (Potier, Darcel, & Tomé, 2009).

Over time, some individuals identify certain methods of eating (or types of foods) that make it easier to self-induce vomiting. Using those strategies may escalate the frequency of both bingeing and purging. Some individuals find they are able to induce vomiting simply by flexing their stomach muscles. In contrast, others find that inducing vomiting becomes more and more difficult over time. A few individuals resort to using ipecac to induce vomiting, a method that is medically very dangerous as it can cause irreversible damage to heart muscle tissue. Individuals with diabetes are at particular risk for medical problems as they may misuse their medication as a form of compensatory behavior. Many women with BN seek treatment from a medical doctor for related medical conditions and weight concerns before they seek psychological treatment for the disorder (Crow & Peterson, 2003; Mitchell & Crow, 2006; Mond, Hay, Rodgers, & Owen, 2007). Some data suggest that individuals with BN fail to seek treatment due to shame and embarrassment in addition to stigma, reluctance to tell parents, lack of financial resources, and failure to perceive BN as a treatable problem (Evans et al., 2012).

BINGE EATING DISORDER (BED)

Cultural norms have long supported a variety of forms of overeating (even to the point of discomfort) as part of celebrations of the harvest or other social events. The degree to which "overeating" has always been considered normative complicates the definition of binge eating. Psychology's adoption of the term *binge eating* in the context of diagnosing a mental illness/disorder evolved over time, and it requires endorsement of loss of control, which does not entirely correspond to the term *binge* as it is used by the general public. This requirement is more problematic to diagnose in BED than in BN, where the presence of overtly problematic compensatory behaviors easily distinguishes the pattern as pathological. Because eating large amounts is normative, many individuals fail to identify the experience of loss of control as a psychiatric problem or to seek treatment, even though highly effective treatments for BED are available. Eating large amounts is often viewed as a "problem" only when the person is also overweight, and weight loss is often the only goal of individuals with BED. However, interventions are only modestly effective for weight loss even when binge eating is eliminated first, leaving most individuals dissatisfied. When abstinence from binge eating fails to significantly affect weight, motivation to maintain the normalized patterns can be undermined; however, a return to dieting can increase vulnerability to relapse of the binge eating.

Stunkard, Grace, and Wolff (1955) may be best credited with drawing modern-day researchers' attention to the phenomenon of binge eating as distinct from either purging behaviors or obesity. They first described a night-eating syndrome (NES), which they conceptualized as a deficit within the satiety regulation system. These patients did not report high levels of hunger during the day but ate a lot at night (often waking up during the night to eat). They had extreme difficulty in stopping eating as long as food was available but they did not seem highly motivated to seek out food. This syndrome did not receive significant attention until more recently, perhaps due to its relatively low base rate, but it is now described as one option under the OSFED category and is viewed as distinct from BED, although there are many similarities. It has been particularly interesting from a theoretical viewpoint to note that while BED responds well to a variety of psychosocial interventions designed to reduce dieting and moderate overconcern with weight, NES responds better to antidepressant medication, suggesting it may have a different etiology.

A pattern of eating large amounts without compensating became the focus of significant research attention in the 1980s and 1990s, as clinicians noted normal or overweight individuals presenting for eating disorder treatment who were like individuals with BN in terms of chaotic eating patterns and associated cognitive and affective features but whose compensatory behaviors were not clearly unhealthy. In addition, as behavior therapy (BT) for obesity became broadly accepted as the most effective psychosocial treatment for weight loss, clinicians noted the presence of BN-like features in some participants. When present, those features were often associated with poorer response to the straightforward BT obesity interventions that focused on reducing intake (though not skipping meals) and were less likely to address problematic cognitions and emotional eating. Criteria for binge eating disorder were developed for the *DSM-IV*, and BED was identified in that edition as a "condition requiring further study"; notably, overweight was not included as a criterion. Subsequent research made it clear that BED was much more prevalent than initially thought and was different from BN in some important ways. Thus, in *DSM-5,* BED was elevated to the status of a distinct diagnosis. To be consistent with the revised criteria for BN, the required frequency and length of time was set at one binge episode per week for 3 months which was lower than the original frequency of two binge episodes per week for 6 months established in *DSM-IV-TR* (APA, 2000). With this change, more individuals will meet criteria for BED; the fact that binge eating is a risk factor for obesity (which has serious health consequences and is quite resistant to treatment) supports the decision to identify and treat BED as early as possible.

As noted earlier, the cognitive model originally developed by Fairburn for BN evolved into a transdiagnostic model which applies to BED; this is now perhaps the most widely accepted formulation of BED. This model clearly identifies binge eating as a response to periods of restricting or dieting, even when total intake is not abnormally low and even when significant weight is not lost. However, it is notable that a significant minority of those with BED report that binge eating developed before any efforts to diet (Haiman & Devlin, 1999; Marcus, Moulton, & Greeno, 1995). However initiated, binge eating can lead to weight gain, and worry about overweight status (or the possibility of weight gain) may well initiate dieting, which could then exacerbate binge eating. Craighead (Allen & Craighead, 1999; Craighead & Allen, 1995) proposed that a history of chronic overeating leads to decreased awareness and responsivity to natural satiety cues, which increases vulnerability to eating in response to cues other than hunger (including emotions and food stimuli) as well as failing to stop until food is gone or one becomes very uncomfortable. This pathway is one explanation of how binge eating (or obesity) might develop before efforts to diet. Other models of maladaptive eating(Leehr et al., 2015; Munsch, Meyer, Quartier, & Wilhelm, 2012) heavily emphasize the role of eating as a way to regulate emotions, noting that individuals may use either restriction (i.e., not eating) or overeating as ways to cope with intense negative emotions. As individuals come to rely more heavily on eating as a form of emotion regulation, nonpathological eating may escalate to overeating and ultimately to binge eating. Many individuals do in fact endorse binge eating as a way to "numb out," providing anecdotal support for this hypothesis. Regardless of how binge eating starts, it seems likely that it is the overconcern with weight and its control that distinguishes the trajectory to BED from the less pathological trajectory in which overeating may lead to weight gain (which may be distressing or impair health) but not to the development of BED.

Criteria for the diagnosis of BED require objective binge episodes (once per week for the past 3 months) and specify that individuals cannot meet the BN criteria for compensatory behaviors, even though they may well diet and exercise to some degree. For a diagnosis of BED, the OBEs must be characterized by three of the following five descriptors: eating more rapidly than normal; eating until uncomfortably full; eating large amounts when not hungry; eating alone due to embarrassment; and feeling disgusted, depressed, or very guilty after overeating. These descriptors have been added to help distinguish the problematic eating pattern of BED from the less pathological overeating that is problematic primarily because it contributes to obesity. While the binge behavior must be reported as distressing, the BED criteria *do not require the display of overconcern with weight/shape* that is a requirement for BN. There are some data to suggest that the presence of overconcern with weight/shape in BED may be associated with more severe pathology and poorer long-term outcome (Grilo, Masheb, & White, 2010; Grilo, White, Gueorguieva, Wilson, & Masheb, 2013). Some individuals do not meet full criteria for BED in spite of a significant diet history and distress about weight because they no longer endorse loss of control; these individuals have been described as "burnt out dieters." In the current system, these individuals could be diagnosed as subclinical BED (under the OSFED category).

In clinical presentation, the majority of individuals with BED are overweight (with approximately half reaching the level designated as obese), and these individuals often have appropriate concerns about their weight related to actual medical problems or the potential for such problems. Individuals with BED are typically more invested in the goal of weight loss than in achieving abstinence from binge eating, so any individuals with BED have difficulty accepting the normalized eating strategies needed to reduce binge eating and accepting binge abstinence with no or modest weight loss as a positive outcome of treatment. Those with BED give a variety of reasons for their lack of progression to the inappropriate compensatory behaviors characteristic of BN. These reasons include social and health concerns, inability to fast or to self-induce vomiting, and aversion to vomiting and/or exercise. Individuals with BED who are in the normal weight range present differently from overweight or obese individuals with BED and in many ways seem more similar to those with BN in terms of cognitions, fears of weight gain, and unrealistically low ideal weights (Goldschmidt et al., 2011). These individuals often cross over between BN and BED, as illustrated in the case example below. Since overweight status poses special challenges for treatment, some studies limit the treatment sample to those designated as overweight BED. Some research compares obese BED samples to samples labeled as having "nonbingeing obesity" to investigate differences between these groups that may be relevant to understanding the pathology and treatment of BED.

Individuals presenting for the treatment of BED may report a fairly clear onset of binge eating, typically triggered by significant life stressors; however, binge eating is more commonly a long-term pattern that includes episodes of overeating not marked by loss of control. The pattern often has no clear onset, waxes and wanes in relation to situational factors, and has usually been problematic for many years as individuals have struggled to manage their weight before they seek treatment for help with weight loss.

These individuals may be best characterized as chronic, excessively concerned, distressed, and unsuccessful dieters. They report less restrictive eating between binge episodes than those with BN, so they typically have less clearly delineated episodes of binge eating. Binges may be difficult to distinguish from overeating, especially when a "grazing" pattern is present (i.e., when an individual snacks over an extended period of time, such as all afternoon or evening, yet the overall amount consumed is objectively large and the person endorses loss of control). Currently, some approaches to treatment suggest labeling binges loosely as small, medium, or large, because reducing the size of binges is often a more useful or acceptable initial goal than abstinence from binge eating.

Urgent medical problems associated with binge eating are relatively uncommon but individuals may report significant GI distress. However, individuals with BED are at risk for the development of obesity and its complications (e.g., metabolic syndrome) (Mitchell, 2015). The risk for metabolic complications in obese men with BED appears to be higher than for obese females with the disorder (Udo et al., 2014).

Case Example: Bulimia Nervosa and Binge Eating Disorder

Anne, a 20-year-old Caucasian woman, is a junior in college majoring in exercise physiology. She is an only child who lives at home while attending a large state university. Anne reports she has always worried about her weight and has felt "large," particularly in relation to her slightly thin mother who eats junk food and does not exercise. Anne was not objectively overweight as a child, but she was always muscular and on the high side of normal weight. She does not remember exactly when she started feeling loss of control with eating, but she started purging as part of her efforts to lose weight around seventh grade. At that point she would have met criteria for BN, but she was never assessed or treated.

Anne told her mother about purging when she was in high school, but her mother just told her to stop and threatened severe consequences if she did not, including removing access to her car. Anne stopped purging for about a year but continued to binge at least once a week; at some point during that year she would have met criteria for BED. She gradually gained weight and reached her highest-ever weight, which was unacceptable to her. At that point, Anne decided to focus on being healthy and became involved in intensive competitive fitness training at a local gym. Her trainer did not want her to count calories or to lose weight but prescribed a high-protein training diet. Anne followed these guidelines rigidly and started to purge whenever she ate something off-limits. Initially, she lost 35 pounds, but she never went below a BMI of 19 and so never met criteria for AN. She was not able to maintain her lowest weight as her binge eating and purging escalated.

Anne has been stable for the past year at a BMI of 24 but has very low body fat due to her intensive exercise. She says she is fairly satisfied with her current weight and shape but also says her ideal weight would be 30 pounds thinner. She dresses attractively and has a supportive, long-term romantic relationship. Anne reports thinking about eating, weight, and shape about 80% of the day, and says these thoughts are highly distressing, are difficult to stop, and interfere with concentration. Despite the fact that she eats mostly healthy foods, whenever she does eat anything she considers unhealthy or eats too much, which occurs about four times a week, she feels compelled to purge, as she is unwilling to gain any weight. Anne finds it easy to purge by simply tensing her stomach. She cannot tolerate the feeling of a very full stomach, so if she is eating out, she will often leave the table to go purge in the middle of the meal and then go back and eat the rest of her meal. Episodes that most clearly meet criteria for OBEs typically occur when she is alone at home with access to food. She then typically purges multiple times in a single episode.

Anne has not told anyone about her purging over the past few years and came to treatment only after her boyfriend confronted her in a supportive way. After trying unsuccessfully to stop on her own for 6 weeks, she sought treatment. She states she is not willing to stop her training, even though it requires a few weeks of very restricted intake, called "cutting," prior to the periodic competitions. She believes she can stop purging while maintaining her planned career as a trainer. She is very embarrassed by the fact that she is responsible for training other people in healthy eating and exercise habits yet isn't able to do this herself. She really wants to be a responsible and healthy role model.

Epidemiology

In addition to differences in clinical presentation, the three EDs also differ in prevalence, course, and patterns of comorbidity. This section is designed to provide clinicians with basic information on the epidemiology of eating disorders.

PREVALENCE

Prior to the publication of the *DSM-5*, there was concern that prevalence rates of eating disorders would rise substantially with the relative loosening of the diagnostic criteria for anorexia nervosa and bulimia nervosa and the formal recognition of binge eating disorder. However, the limited data available at present demonstrate that while prevalence rates have risen slightly from *DSM-IV-TR* AN and BN (as was intended, in order to reclassify individuals with subthreshold versions), the increases have not been as dramatic as feared. The data available suggest that the prevalence of AN using *DSM-5* criteria is comparable to or slightly higher than previous estimates using *DSM-IV-TR* criteria. Most estimates for point prevalence of AN are under 1% of the population, while rates of atypical AN (i.e., AN with a significant weight loss but not to the point of being underweight) are around 2.8% (Stice et al., 2013). Prevalence estimates vary depending on the population studied (i.e., community versus clinical samples). In their sample of U.S. adolescent girls, Stice and colleagues (2013) found the lifetime prevalence of AN to be 0.8%; similarly, in a large population study of Australians, Hay and colleagues (Hay, Girosi, & Mond, 2015) found the point prevalence of AN to be 0.8%. The prevalence of AN among high-risk adolescents (i.e., those who already demonstrate some atypical eating behaviors or elevated concern with weight/shape/eating) appears to be higher, with a point prevalence of 1.2% and a lifetime prevalence of 1.7% (Smink, van Hoeken, Oldehinkel, & Hoek, 2014). Approximately 5% to 10% of patients with AN are male, although the true incidence in males may be higher as males are less likely to come to clinical attention and may present with different symptom profiles (Striegel-Moore et al., 2009).

Prevalence estimates for BN using *DSM-5* criteria are slightly higher than those using *DSM-IV-TR* criteria (Trace et al., 2011). Several recent studies estimate the lifetime prevalence of BN to be around 0.6% to 2.6% of females (Hay et al., 2015; Stice et al., 2013), with lower rates in males. As with AN, the prevalence of subthreshold BN across both genders is higher, with a lifetime prevalence of 4.4%, and the prevalence of any binge eating symptoms is higher still, around 5.7% (Hudson, Hiripi, Pope Harrison, & Kessler, 2007). Women in late adolescence or early adulthood (ages 18–24) continue to be at the highest risk for onset of BN (APA, 2013; Currin, Schmidt, Treasure, & Jick, 2005; Hudson et al., 2007).

Prevalence rates for BED are higher than those for AN and BN. In community samples of adolescents and adults, prevalence rates for BED using *DSM-5* criteria are around 2% to 5% (Hay et al., 2015; Smink et al., 2014; Stice et al., 2013). These estimates are only slightly higher than those using *DSM-IV-TR* criteria (Hudson, Coit, Lalonde, & Pope Harrison, 2010; Trace et al., 2011). The prevalence of BED among individuals seeking weight-loss interventions is substantially higher (≈30%) (Marek, Ben-Porath, Ashton, & Heinberg, 2014; Vinai et al., 2015). Prevalence in other countries may be slightly lower (Kessler et al., 2013; Smink, van Hoeken, & Hoek, 2012). The majority of patients with BED presenting for treatment are women. However, in community samples the rates of BED are more similar for males and females (55–65% female, 45–35% male) (Hay et al., 2015; Marek et al., 2014; Vinai et al., 2015), and additional data suggest that unlike in AN and BN, clinical presentations are overwhelmingly similar in males and females with BED (Udo et al., 2014). This discrepancy in the gender breakdown of BN versus BED provides some support for the hypothesis that binge eating (eating large amounts) may be associated with certain biological vulnerabilities, whereas patterns involving compensatory behaviors may be more culture-bound.

Although eating disorders were initially thought to be more prevalent among white females from higher-income families, current data suggest that eating disorders are prevalent across ethnicities and socioeconomic groups. Internationally, rates of eating disorders and the public health burden of these disorders have increased substantially in recent years, particularly among cultures "in transition" toward more Westernized standards of living (Pike, Dunne, & Addai, 2013). Furthermore, within the United States, increasing attention is being paid to the occurrence of eating pathology and disorders in racial and ethnic minority groups and among immigrants. Data suggest that eating disorders (and in particular those that involve binge eating) are not uncommon among racial and ethnic minorities, although minority individuals are significantly less likely to present for treatment (Jennings, Kelly-Weeder, & Wolfe, 2015; Marques et al., 2010; Pike et al., 2013). Together, these data challenge popular notions of eating disorders as culturally limited disorders and highlight the need for culturally sensitive treatments.

COURSE

Eating disorders often start with dieting or exercising to lose just a little weight during early adolescence (Rohde, Stice, & Marti, 2015). Age of onset varies across the three disorders, but the typical onset is late adolescence or early adulthood. Diagnostic crossover is also extremely common (Stice et al., 2013) and becomes even more so when the course of illness is extended. The peak age of onset of anorexia nervosa in females appears to be bimodal, at 14 and 18 years of age, but onset of the disorder is increasingly seen in individuals as young as 7 years old and also among older adults into middle age (Pike et al., 2013). It is notable that most adolescents developing AN do not (at least initially) eat objectively large amounts and many fewer purge (Peebles, Wilson, & Lock, 2006), though if they remain ill for several years, the likelihood of adopting those behaviors increases (Eddy et al., 2008). Among those diagnosed with AN, relapse rates are high and vary with age of onset and BMI: prognosis is better in younger individuals and in those with higher BMIs, highlighting the need for early intervention (Ackard, Richter, Egan, & Cronemeyer, 2014; Franko et al., 2013; Treasure & Russell, 2011). Rapid response to treatment (i.e., weight gain early in treatment) is a powerful predictor of treatment outcome, particularly among adolescents (Doyle, Le Grange, Loeb, Doyle, & Crosby, 2010; Le Grange, Accurso, Lock, Agras, & Bryson, 2014). Prognosis worsens with duration of illness (Franko et al., 2013; Von Holle et al., 2008); the disorder assumes a chronic course in approximately one third of affected individuals (Fichter, Quadflieg, & Hedlund, 2006). It is perhaps because of the propensity to develop a chronic and unrelenting course, that AN in particular is associated with some of the highest mortality rates of any psychiatric illness (Arcelus, Mitchell, Wales, & Nielsen, 2011; Smink et al., 2012).

For bulimia nervosa and binge eating disorder, the typical age at which individuals meet full criteria or present for treatment is somewhat later, in late adolescence or early adulthood (APA, 2013; Hudson et al., 2007). However, the age of onset of objective binge eating varies widely and is often quite young (e.g., "I can't even remember when I didn't binge"). Furthermore, data from longitudinal studies suggest that, once started, binge eating can persist well into adulthood (Neumark-Sztainer, Wall, Larson, Eisenberg, & Loth, 2011).

Studies suggest that as many as one third of individuals with BN are not detected by health care professionals (Keski-Rahkonen et al., 2009), and an even smaller minority of affected individuals—only about 6%—receive mental health treatment (Hoek, 2006). When treatment is sought, the average length of illness at presentation is about 5 years (Mitchell, Hatsukami, Eckert, & Pyle, 1985). In community samples, approximately 15% to 20% of those with BN reported an earlier episode of AN (Favaro, Ferrara, & Santonastaso, 2003), whereas in clinical samples, the percentage of those with past AN increases to around one third (Eddy et al., 2007). Herzog et al. (1999) found that over a 7-year period, 16% of women with restricting AN developed BN, but only 7% of women with BN developed AN—providing some support for the argument that while restricting AN may have a chronic course, it can be an early phase that evolves to include binge eating or compensatory behaviors or there is crossover to BN or BED as individuals become weight restored. Prior history of AN among individuals with BN is associated with poorer long-term outcome and higher risk of relapse (Eddy et al., 2007; Keski-Rahkonen et al., 2009). A personal or family history of obesity prior to any eating disorder is also important information as some data suggest it is associated with adverse outcomes such as increased latency to seek treatment (e.g., Lebow, Sim, & Kransdorf, 2014), which may occur because experience with obesity tends to reify maladaptive beliefs about eating and weight and to reduce motivation to normalize eating behaviors.

Once established, both BN and BED may show a chronic course; it may comprise a number of discrete periods of illness, often initiated by life transitions or stressors (APA, 2013). Approximately one half of individuals with bulimia will achieve recovery, whether or not their illness has been detected (Keski-Rahkonen et al., 2009). However, about one third will continue to be chronically symptomatic (Keel & Brown, 2010; Keski-Rahkonen et al., 2009; Steinhausen & Weber, 2009). Even among those who fully recover from BN, relapse rates are high; approximately one third relapse during follow-up periods (Herzog et al., 1999; Keel, Mitchell, Miller, Davis, & Crow, 1999). Characteristics associated with poor prognosis include increased duration of illness, higher frequency of purging behaviors, and greater weight suppression (Keel & Heatherton, 2010; Steinhausen & Weber, 2009). Across all EDs, early response to treatment is the best predictor of positive long-term outcome, as demonstrated in a recent review and meta-analysis (Vall & Wade, 2015).

Comorbidity

Eating disorders are frequently comorbid with several other forms of psychopathology, including mood, anxiety, substance use, and personality disorders (Hudson et al., 2007). Mood disorders, especially major depression and dysthymia, are common among those with EDs, with estimates ranging from 36% to 80% (Halfon et al., 2015; Hudson et al., 2007; Swanson, 2011). Comorbid anxiety disorders are also extremely prevalent, with estimates ranging between 65% and 75% (Gadalla & Piran, 2008; Swinbourne et al., 2012), and in many cases, the anxiety disorders predate the onset of eating pathology (Swinbourne et al., 2012). Obsessive-compulsive disorder (OCD) and social phobia are two of the most common comorbid anxiety disorders (Kaye, Bulik, Thornton, Barbarich, & Masters, 2004; Swinbourne et al., 2012). Comorbid substance use disorders are also common, particularly among individuals who binge eat and purge (Fouladi et al., 2015; Grilo, White, & Masheb, 2009).

Despite similarities in patterns of comorbidity across AN, BN, and BED, there are some critical distinctions. For instance, posttraumatic stress disorder appears to be the only anxiety disorder that occurs significantly more often in BN and BED than in AN (Kaye et al., 2004; Mitchell, Mazzeo, Schlesinger, Brewerton, & Smith, 2011). Additionally, depression is less likely to predate the onset of AN than that of BN, suggesting that depressive symptomatology in AN may likely be a product of the state of starvation (O'Brien & Vincent, 2003), whereas depression may be a risk factor for BN (Stice, Burton, & Shaw, 2004) and perhaps BED. There are also some data to suggest that the relationship between duration of illness and comorbidity may vary across the eating disorders: some recent data suggest that the frequency of comorbid conditions in AN may increase with duration of illness (Bühren et al., 2014). It is worth noting that symptoms of certain comorbid conditions that start after the onset of an eating disorder (i.e., depression and OCD) sometimes resolve with improved nutrition, although some residual symptoms may remain (Mattar, Thiébaud, Huas, Cebula, & Godart, 2012). However, in follow-up studies a significant minority of patients continue to have anxiety and depressive disorders even after recovery from the acute symptoms of the eating disorder (Lock, Couturier, & Agras, 2006; Steinhausen, 2002).

Personality disorders are also frequently comorbid with eating disorders, with estimates ranging from 27% to 93% (Cassin & von Ranson, 2005). However, personality pathology among individuals with active eating disorders may be at least in part a sequela of eating pathology (Rø, Martinsen, Hoffart, Sexton, & Rosenvinge, 2005), a hypothesis supported by prospective data demonstrating that personality disorder pathology reduces with resolution of eating pathology (Rø et al., 2005; Vrabel, Rø, Martinsen, Hoffart, & Rosenvinge, 2009). Variations in personality disorder comorbidity across the eating disorders have been widely replicated and support the notion that there may be distinct personality profiles for individuals with different eating disorder symptoms and diagnoses

(Thompson-Brenner & Westen, 2005; Turner et al., 2014; Westen & Harnden-Fischer, 2001). Individuals with purely restricting behaviors are generally described as more constricted and overcontrolled and they have higher rates of avoidant, dependent, and obsessive compulsive personality disorder, whereas individuals with bingeing and/or purging behaviors are more often described as impulsive and affectively dysregulated and they have higher rates of borderline personality disorder (Cassin & von Ranson, 2005).

Neurobiology

The study of the neurobiology of eating disorders is an emerging area with the potential to improve our understanding of the biological underpinnings of eating behavior. Current avenues of exploration include the investigation of neurotransmitters and the use of neuroimaging techniques to examine certain structural and functional aspects of the brain as possible contributors to eating disorders.

Serotonin has been the most popular neurotransmitter targeted for investigation so far, as 5-HT systems are involved in mood and obsessiveness, appetite regulation, and impulse control. Patients with AN have been found to have low levels of 5-HT metabolites in the cerebrospinal fluid and abnormal hormonal response to 5-HT specific challenges. However, specific abnormalities in the serotonin system have not been identified.

Interest is developing in the dopaminergic neurotransmitter system. Preference for and overconsumption of palatable food has been conceptualized as reward-seeking behavior that might share neurobiological pathways with other reward-based disorders (e.g., substance use disorders; Berridge, 2009). Data thus far suggest overactivity in opioid systems (Nathan & Bullmore, 2009; Nathan et al., 2012; Stice, Spoor, Bohon, Veldhuizen, & Small, 2008; Stice, Spoor, Ng, & Zald, 2009) and dopaminergic systems (Gearhardt et al., 2011; Schienle, Schafer, Hermann, & Vaitl, 2009; Stice, Yokum, Burger, Epstein, & Small, 2011; Wang et al., 2011) is present that is similar to what is observed in individuals with substance use disorders. Nonetheless, research showing underactivity of dopaminergic pathways in acute BN and BED (Bello & Hajnal, 2010; Bohon, Stice, & Spoor, 2009) highlights the need to consider stage of illness. It has been proposed that an overly responsive reward system increases initial risk for binge eating, but once binge eating develops, chronic overconsumption of palatable food results in down-regulation and hyposensitivity of the system, such that more reward is needed to achieve the same effect (Berridge, 2009). Clearly, additional animal studies and longitudinal work are needed to disambiguate initial risk from maintenance factors. Interestingly, hypersensitivity of the dopaminergic system has also been suggested as an explanation for the extreme reactions of patients with AN to novel stimuli (Kaye, Strober, & Jimerson, 2008).

Recent studies support the notion that there is a neural basis for eating disorders (Trummer, Eustacchio, Unger, Tillich, & Flaschka, 2002; Uher et al., 2004; Ward, Tiller, Treasure, & Russell, 2000). There is a fairly substantial brain imaging literature for AN—including positron-emission tomography (PET) and single-photon emission computed tomography (SPECT) studies—that shows regional differences in metabolism and neurotransmitter (usually receptor) alterations, and there are also fMRI studies demonstrating differences in activation response to stimuli (usually food). However, these studies have been done only on adults and are generally small scale and variable in terms of patient subtypes, state of illness, and regional neuroanatomy examined (Frank et al., 2002; Kaye, Grendall, & Strober, 1998; Kaye, Strober, & Jimerson, 2008; Uher et al., 2004). Neuroimaging generally reveals decreased brain mass and enlarged sulci in patients in the acute malnourished phase of the disorder. This is thought to be either the direct effect of malnutrition or the effect of increased cortisol on brain tissue, and it seems in most (but not all) studies to resolve with weight restoration, as found in a recent review (Frank, 2015). SPECT studies have shown unilateral hypoperfusion (or inadequate blood supply) in specific areas of the brain in most patients with AN—most commonly in the temporal lobe—that seems to persist after recovery. Rastram, Bjure, and Vestergren (2001) found decreased blood flow to the temporal lobe in 14 of 21 patients 7 years after recovery, with no correlation between blood flow and BMI or IQ. Chowdhury, Gordon, and Lask (2003) found unilateral hypoperfusion correlated with eating disorder psychopathology and not with BMI. Lask (2006) found decreased temporal blood flow to correlate with eating disorder psychopathology and impaired executive functioning, and no correlation between blood flow and BMI, mood, or length of illness. On the 3-year follow-up, this investigator found that persistent hypoperfusion in 86% of the sample was associated with persistent eating disorder psychopathology and persistent cognitive impairment (visuospatial processing and memory, and cognitive inhibition) (Lask, 2006). Lask hypothesized that this unilateral hypoperfusion represented a preexisting deficit— likely either genetic or due to perinatal insult—that predisposed patients to develop AN. A study comparing adolescents with restrictive AN, AN binge/purge subtype adolescents and adolescents with BN, and normally developing adolescents found evidence of differences in activation during a test of behavioral inhibition (the go/no-go task) (Lock, Garrett, Beenhakker, & Reiss, 2011). Adolescents with BN displayed increased activation in the dorsolateral prefrontal cortex and anterior cingulate gyrus compared to adolescents with AN and normally developing adolescents without an eating disorder. These data provide evidence of a neural basis located in the frontostriatal circuit that is differentiated by disorder type (Marsh, Maia, & Peterson, 2009).

Further, data supportive of a variety of neurocognitive alterations in AN and BN patients are increasing (Godley, Tchanturia, MacLeod, & Schmidt, 2001; Tchanturia, Brecelj, et al., 2004; Tchanturia, Morris, et al., 2004; Tchanturia, Morris, Surguladze, & Treasure, 2002; Tchanturia, Serpell, Troop, & Treasure, 2001). These include problems with attention, executive functioning, divided attention, working memory, response inhibition, and mental inflexibility. These variables, among others, are likely not only to play a role in the etiology and maintenance of ED symptoms but also to have an impact on treatment response. Attention problems can make it difficult to participate in most psychological treatments. Problems with working memory are likely to inhibit insight-oriented therapies and cognitive therapies, and mental inflexibility may increase resistance to new ideas and behaviors proposed across a variety of treatments.

Risk Factors

At this point, the exact cause (or causes) of eating disorders is unknown. However, a large body of research suggests various risk factors associated with the development and maintenance of eating pathology. This literature is briefly summarized here.

BODY DISSATISFACTION

Body dissatisfaction is a consistent and robust risk factor for eating pathology, as well as a maintenance factor (Bakalar et al., 2015; Lilenfeld, Wonderlich, Riso, Crosby, & Mitchell, 2006; Stice, 2002). One recent prospective study found that among adolescent girls, low self-esteem and increased BMI were significant predictors of increased body dissatisfaction over a 1-year period (Wojtowicz & von Ranson, 2012). In addition to its direct impact on eating pathology, body dissatisfaction can lead to dieting and negative affect, which can in turn further exacerbate eating disorder symptoms (Stice, 2002; Stice & Shaw, 2002). It is also hypothesized that other causal factors affect eating pathology through body dissatisfaction (Polivy & Herman, 2002). For example, increased sociocultural pressure to be thin and elevated thin ideal internalization lead to increases in body dissatisfaction (Stice, 2002), which in turn directly increases eating pathology. Recent data suggest that it is through the mediating effects of body surveillance—the tendency to constantly evaluate one's shape and compare it to others' or to one's ideal—that internalization of the thin ideal leads to body dissatisfaction and may increase the risk of disordered eating behavior (Fitzsimmons-Craft et al., 2012).

DIETING

Elevated dieting and dietary restraint prospectively predict the onset of disordered eating symptoms, including binge eating, level of bulimic pathology, and negative affect (Bakalar et al., 2015; Jacobi, Hayward, de Zwaan, Kraemer, & Agras, 2004; Stice, 2002; Stice, Presnell, & Spangler, 2002). In addition, self-reported dieting is a maintenance factor for bulimic pathology (Stice, 2002), in that binge eating arises in response to rigid, stringent efforts at dietary control (Fairburn et al., 2003). Evidence suggests that dieting may result, in part, from body dissatisfaction (Polivy & Herman, 2002; Stice, 2002), so that it serves as an attempt to fix the weight and body problem. The most comprehensive meta-analysis of risk factors for eating disorders demonstrates that successful caloric deprivation (dieting) does not lead to increased eating disorder symptoms (Stice, 2002), suggesting that unsuccessful dieting or struggles with dieting may be more problematic than the actual restriction per se.

INTEROCEPTIVE AWARENESS

Interoceptive awareness refers to the ability to identify internal sensations, including both physiological and emotional states. Women with eating disorders report poor interoceptive awareness (Jacobi et al., 2004), and this inability to identify internal sensations prospectively predicts onset of eating disorder symptoms (Killen et al., 1996; Leon, Fulkerson, Perry, & Early-Zald, 1995). Some research suggests that even after recovery these women continue to struggle with identifying their internal states (Lilenfeld et al., 2006). However, specific intervention to train appetite awareness has been shown to improve awareness of internal hunger and satiety cues (Allen & Craighead, 1999; Craighead & Allen, 1995).

WEIGHT

Individuals with higher premorbid body mass were found to be at increased risk for perceived pressure to be thin, body dissatisfaction, and dieting, although higher initial body mass did not predict either negative affect or eating pathology (Stice, 2002). Thus, it seems that body weight influences other risk factors for eating pathology, rather than being a direct risk factor itself. It is of note that in a 10-year longitudinal study of adolescents, the use of unhealthy weight control behaviors was predictive of an increase in BMI (Neumark-Sztainer et al., 2012), which may perpetuate dieting and disordered eating. Additional research is needed to more clearly establish the mechanisms by which premorbid weight contributes to later risk for eating disorders, particularly among individuals with BED, where being overweight often occurs early in life and precedes the initiation of any dieting efforts.

SOCIOCULTURAL PRESSURE TO BE THIN

With the obvious deluge of images of overly thin women in the mass media, one misperception is that eating disorders are largely due to misguided efforts (i.e., excessive dieting) to attain our culture's thin ideal. As noted above, it has been difficult to establish the degree to which dieting is a direct risk factor. Similarly, efforts to document a clear causal relationship between the level of media exposure and eating disorders have not shown consistent, strong effects. Rather, research suggests that the transmission of the thin ideal may be occurring more indirectly, given data that individuals who immigrate to a Western culture and those living in relatively more urban than rural areas are at increased risk for eating disorders (Becker, Keel, Anderson-Fye, & Thomas, 2004). Two points are worth noting here. First, individuals clearly differ in the extent to which they personally adopt the predominant culture's thin ideal. The degree of internalization of the thin ideal and the degree to which a person personally feels pressured by others to be thin appear to be more closely associated with the development of other risk factors (i.e., body dissatisfaction) and eating pathology than simply with degree of media exposure (Bakalar et al., 2015; Culbert, Racine, & Klump, 2015; Keel & Forney, 2013; Stice et al., 2002). Furthermore, while media exposure appears to increase the risk of body dissatisfaction and subsequent dieting as well as binge eating, particularly among individuals already at increased risk for disordered eating (Hausenblas et al., 2013), media exposure appears to play less of a role in maintaining already established eating disorder symptoms (Stice, 2002).

FAMILY

The family may serve as one of the important ways that the thin ideal is transmitted and internalized. The attitudes and behaviors of family members and peers, including feeding patterns, critical comments, weight-related teasing, and modeling of restrictive eating or other disordered eating behaviors, are powerful influences on the development of disordered eating (Bakalar et al., 2015; Kluck, 2008, 2010), more so than media exposure. It is also useful to note that parental obesity is a risk factor for eating disorders, and in particular binge eating disorder (Hilbert et al., 2014). While this could be a result of shared genetic vulnerability to obesity (or impulsivity), it may also reflect more subtle environmental influences. Individuals with overweight family members are more likely to have been exposed to negative societal attitudes toward obesity and thus may impose pressure to exercise or diet on themselves. Similarly, parents who are overweight or concerned about weight or eating may exert excessive and unhelpful pressure on children to be thin in order to prevent them from developing weight problems. Beyond transmitting the pressure of the thin ideal, family environment may also play a role by failing to teach adaptive eating behavior or coping skills to build self-esteem (which in turn could reduce risk for EDs). Families of individuals with eating disorders have been described as more chaotic, conflicted, and critical, and as lower in positive expressiveness, cohesion, and caring than other families (Stern et al., 1989). A negative family environment could increase anxiety and depression, which are in turn associated with the later development of eating disorders.

CHILDHOOD ABUSE

Physical abuse and sexual abuse have been hypothesized to be significant risk factors for disordered eating. However, evidence suggests that childhood abuse—while common among individuals who go on to develop eating disorders (Hilbert et al., 2014)—is a risk factor for general psychopathology as opposed to a risk factor specific to eating disorders (Hund & Espelage, 2005; Katerndahl, Burge, & Kellogg, 2005).

GENETIC RISK FACTORS

Twin studies have convincingly shown that genetic factors account for 50% or more of the variance in AN, BN, and BED in adulthood (Bulik et al., 2007; Bulik, Sullivan, Wade, & Kendler, 2000; Klump & Culbert, 2007; Suisman & Klump, 2011). With few exceptions, moderate-to-large heritabilities have been observed across the spectrum of threshold and subthreshold cases, and extend even to specific eating disorder symptoms. These results suggest that eating disorders exhibit heritabilities that are on a par with other illnesses considered to be biologically based.

An interesting developmental pattern of genetic effects has emerged, however. Developmental twin studies show that in females, overall levels of eating disorder symptoms exhibit no genetic influences before puberty, but significant genetic effects are observed from mid-puberty on (Klump, 2013). The magnitude of genetic effects remains stable after puberty into middle adulthood (Klump, Burt, McGue, Iacono, & Wade, 2010; Klump & Culbert, 2007), suggesting that all of the genetic risk becomes activated during puberty. However, in contrast to these findings in girls, results for male twins show no changes in genetic effects across pre- to early puberty, mid- to late puberty, or young adulthood. The heritability remains constant at approximately 50% in all age groups (Klump et al., 2012). These findings suggest that pubertal increases in genetic influences are specific to girls and point to the possibility that the ovarian hormones (estrogen and progesterone) that become activated during puberty and drive pubertal development in girls (e.g., breast development, increased adiposity) may be responsible.

Klump, Keel, Sisk, and Burt (2010) indirectly examined the extent to which estrogen activation may account for increased genetic risk by comparing the magnitude of genetic effects between female twins in relation to their levels of estradiol during puberty. Results confirmed hypotheses and showed stronger genetic effects in girls with high versus girls with low estrogen levels. Corroborating data have come from twin studies of males, which do not show effects of puberty on genetic risk for disordered eating (Klump et al., 2012). Boys do not experience increases in estrogen during puberty, as their pubertal development is driven primarily by increases in testosterone. Thus, these preliminary results support the notion that estrogen may account for pubertal difference in genetic risk for ED. Interestingly, however, new data suggest that the effects of hormones on genetic risk may not be confined to puberty (Klump et al., 2015). Longitudinal studies of adult twins show substantial changes in genetic risk for disordered eating (e.g., emotional eating, or the tendency to overconsume food when feeling sad, anxious, etc.) across the menstrual cycle, with increasing genetic influences during menstrual cycle phases characterized by high estradiol and progesterone levels (i.e., post-ovulation). These data underscore the likely importance of ovarian hormones for genetic risk across development and a need to understand how and why hormones activate genetic risk.

Molecular genetic studies have attempted to identify specific genes that might account for the heritability of eating disorders in post-puberty and high-risk hormonal phases, but these investigations have largely fallen short. Initial reports of significant associations between potential candidate genes—for example, the serotonin transporter gene (Calati, De Ronchi, Bellini, & Serretti, 2011) and the serotonin 2a receptor polymorphism (Gorwood, Kipman, & Foulon, 2003)—and eating disorders often go unreplicated in subsequent studies (Pinheiro et al., 2010). Methodological limitations contribute to the high rate of nonreplication, most notably small sample sizes, making it difficult to identify genes that are likely to have very small effects (Pinheiro et al., 2010). Because of the difficulties encountered thus far, researchers are focusing on amassing much larger samples that are sufficiently powered to detect significant effects (Boraska et al., 2014). The methodological approaches used to examine risk genes are also changing: instead of zeroing in on one candidate gene or set of genes, contemporary studies are conducting genome-wide association studies (GWAS) that examine hundreds of thousands of genes across the genome. These studies are atheoretical in the sense that no hypotheses are proposed a priori about specific genes that may confer risk; instead, all genes are examined for their potential association with eating disorders by comparing the frequency of gene variants in eating disorder cases versus controls. The atheoretical stance of these studies is predicated on the belief that genetic risk for eating disorders is comprised of thousands of genes of very small effect that would be difficult to isolate a priori based on existing theory or data. Instead, the focus is on amassing extremely large samples of cases and controls (i.e., tens of thousands) that have the power to detect even very small differences in gene frequencies and identify novel risk genes that may or may not have been on scientists' radar based on prior data.

To date, researchers conducting GWAS have focused on AN more than BN or BED, and results have been nonsignificant and/or inconclusive (see Boraska et al., 2014). It is clear that much larger sample sizes will be needed to identify significant risk genes using this approach, as GWAS of schizophrenia have required 50,000+ cases and controls to obtain significant results (Schizophrenia Working Group of the Psychiatric Genetics Consortium, 2014). However, global initiatives are under way to amass these types of samples, with researchers from around the world combining datasets for GWAS analyses. Thus, it is hoped that significant findings will be available soon.

Finally, an emerging area is the examination of gene-by-environment interactions in twin and molecular research. Initial findings are promising in suggesting that dieting (Racine, Burt, & Klump, 2011) and food restriction (Akkermann, Hiio, Villa, & Harro, 2011) increase genetic risk for eating disorder phenotypes, such that genetic effects are stronger in individuals who score high on these traits. Notably, another form of gene-by-environment interaction, epigenetics (i.e., heritable changes in gene expression that are not due to changes in the DNA sequence), is likely to become important. Initial results are promising (e.g., epigenetic regulation of dopamine genes; see Frieling et al., 2010) and may provide critical information about how ovarian hormones (e.g., by activation of gene expression during and after puberty) and environmental stressors (e.g., a history of abuse) may differentially predict eating disorder risk in individuals with the same genetic background and/or the same environmental risk profiles.

Nonetheless, despite these difficulties, there are some promising leads, as serotonin genes, such as the serotonin transporter gene (Calati, De Ronchi, Bellini, & Serretti, 2011) and the serotonin 2a receptor polymorphism (Gorwood, Kipman, & Foulon, 2003); neurotrophic factor genes, such as the brain-derived neurotrophic factor polymorphism (Nakazato, Hashimoto, Shimizu, Niitsu, & Iyo, 2012; Rask-Andersen, Olszewski, Levine, & Schiöth, 2010); estrogen receptor genes, such as the estrogen receptor beta gene (Rask-Andersen et al., 2010); and dopamine genes, such as the dopamine transporter gene and the COMT polymorphisms (Bello & Hajnal, 2010) have shown associations with AN, BN, and/or eating disorder symptoms that have been replicated in some (but not all) studies. An interesting observation is that most of these systems are regulated by estrogen (Becker, 2009; Ostlund, Keller, & Hurd, 2003) and therefore may contribute to the pubertal differences in genetic effects observed in the twin studies.

Assessment

Weight is typically assessed during a medical exam rather than in a clinical interview, but a variety of interview-based and self-report assessments are available that are used to confirm the presence of a specific ED diagnosis or to provide a more dimensional assessment of general eating pathology. The use of a standardized assessment tool is particularly useful when considering the cognitive and affective features, as these do not have clear cutoffs in the diagnostic criteria. Currently, the most widely used assessment for disordered eating behaviors (across all diagnoses) in adults is the semistructured, interviewer-administered Eating Disorder Examination (EDE; Cooper, Cooper, & Fairburn, 1989; Cooper & Fairburn, 1987; Fairburn & Cooper, 1993). The EDE is widely considered to be the "gold standard" in eating disorders assessment and can be used both as a measure of symptom severity and as a diagnostic tool. The EDE yields four subscale scores, assessing restraint, eating concern, shape concern, and weight concern, as well as two behavioral indexes that quantify the frequency of binge eating and methods of extreme weight control. Administration takes about 1 hour. Such an assessment is important to use in the research context, where highly reliable diagnoses are required, but it can also be useful in a clinical context, where its interview format allows for greater clarification of nuanced and complex eating disorder symptoms (e.g., binge eating, overconcern about weight). Furthermore, the interview ensures that many important constructs are assessed that might not show up in an unstructured format due to the secrecy and shame associated with many of the behaviors. However, the level of training required to achieve reliability and the burden for staff and patients are both sufficiently high that briefer methods are more typically used in clinical practice.

The Eating Disorders Assessment for DSM-5 (EDA-5; Sysko et al., 2015; Walsh, Attia, Glasofer, & Sysko, 2015) is a recent, interview-based assessment that was developed in part to address the shortcomings of existing interview-based measures, including poor interrater reliability and lack of *DSM-5* diagnostic items. In addition to a paper-and-pencil format, the interview is also available in the form of a computer-assisted interview, which has the potential to aid in administration and is freely available online (www.EDA5.org). Initial data demonstrate that diagnoses of AN, BN, and BED made by the EDA-5 were highly consistent with diagnoses made by the EDE and that the EDA-5 took significantly less time to administer. However, while these data suggest that the EDA-5 may be a useful tool in the diagnosis of eating disorders, this interview is primarily a diagnostic instrument; it does not provide measures of symptom severity to the same extent as other measures.

In addition to the aforementioned interview assessments, there are also a variety of self-report measures for general eating disorder symptoms. The 36-item, self-report version of the EDE, the EDE-Q (Fairburn & Beglin, 1994), is commonly used. Like its interview counterpart, the EDE-Q provides the basis for a possible diagnosis as well as the same four subscales. However, a recent factor analysis suggested that a three-factor solution is more appropriate for the EDE-Q (Peterson et al., 2007). Correlations between the interview and self-report versions are reasonable (Fairburn & Beglin, 1994), even though within-individual discrepancies were common, particularly in terms of frequency of types of binge episodes. It is not clear whether clients were more willing to disclose information in a self-report compared to an in-person interview or whether an interviewer was more likely to be able to elicit accurate information. Regardless, interviewer ratings and subjective self-reports of constructs such as overconcern and distress both convey useful information.

Continuous measures also allow for assessing degree of improvement more globally than simple frequency counts of specific behaviors do. Many of these measures contain multiple subscales that attempt to capture the wide range of important constructs associated with disordered eating. The Eating Disorder Inventory (EDI-3; Garner, 2005) and the Bulimia Test–Revised (Thelen, Farmer, Wonderlich, & Smith, 1991) are most commonly used in assessing outcome. In addition, very specific self-reports are available to assess narrower constructs that may be of interest—such as specific cognitions, body dissatisfaction, restraint, dietary intent, or food avoidance (see the review by Anderson & Paulosky, 2004). Body checking is a specific construct that has only recently been identified as an important aspect of eating disorders. The Body Checking Questionnaire (Reas, Whisenhunt, & Netemeyer, 2002) is a 23-item self-report of the frequency and nature of the relevant behaviors. However, these measures and other measures of eating pathology are not without limitations, including inconsistent factor structure and poor discriminant validity. Recently, a 45-item measure, the Eating Pathology Symptoms Inventory (EPSI;

Forbush et al., 2013), was developed to address these and other limitations. The EPSI is a self-report measure intended to assess a wide variety of symptoms, including those assessed by older measures (e.g., body dissatisfaction, restricting, purging, cognitive restraint) as well as those often overlooked by researchers and clinicians alike (e.g., muscle building). There are some data to demonstrate its construct and discriminant validity in a nonclinical sample (Forbush, Wildes, & Hunt, 2014); however, as this is still a relatively new measure, additional data are needed to demonstrate its diagnostic and predictive utility.

Assessment of eating disorders in children and adolescents is not well developed, but several inventories and interviews are available. There is a child version of the EDE (ChEDE) that has been found to be both reliable and valid for children ages 8 to 14 (Bryant-Waugh, Cooper, Taylor, & Lask, 1996). Additionally, the Children's Eating Attitudes Test (Ch-EAT; Garner & Garfinkel, 1979) has been used, and the use of a shorter, 26-item version of Ch-EAT was reported by Wallin, Kronovall, and Majewski (2000). Shapiro, Woolson, et al.'s (2007) report on the Children's Binge Eating Disorder Scale, a brief structured interview, suggests that this assessment might be more appropriate if one's purpose is just to assess the degree to which overeating has become problematic for a child.

In addition to self-reports, daily self-monitoring records (of food intake, binges, and purges) are frequently an important aspect of assessment as well as treatment. Monitoring of appetite rather than food intake (Craighead, 2006) is a relatively recent development that can provide additional clinically relevant information. For example, episodes of binge eating can be identified as responses to hunger violations (i.e., waited until very hungry to start eating) or as satiety violations (i.e., continued to eat past moderate sensations of stomach fullness, regardless of level of hunger prior to eating). This kind of specific assessment of behavioral patterns can be useful in treatment planning and in tracking changes in response to treatment. Self-monitoring avoids the difficulty of retrospective recall and has great face validity but is less useful in reflecting changes in attitudes and affect. Thus, both monitoring and self-reports continue to be important.

Interventions

As noted earlier, there has been a shift within the field of eating disorders toward a transdiagnostic view that emphasizes the similarities in pathology across anorexia nervosa, bulimia nervosa, and binge eating disorder. This shift has been particularly relevant in the realm of clinical intervention. Fairburn's transdiagnostic CBT for eating disorders (CBT-E; Fairburn, 2008), which originated as a treatment for BN, is currently the clearest example of a transdiagnostic protocol that has been evaluated. However, historically, clinicians who present themselves as "ED specialists" have always used a range of approaches and usually apply their particular eclectic blend fairly broadly in treating individuals across the full range of symptoms. Within specialized ED inpatient or residential programs, the general programming is rarely disorder-specific, although individuals may receive particular interventions (e.g., exposure protocols for comorbid obsessive-compulsive features). Our intention in this chapter is to familiarize the reader with the literature that provides the empirical basis for the most common treatment approaches. All these approaches were originally developed and evaluated to target specific ED diagnoses, and many have since been empirically evaluated in other ED populations, much as they have been used broadly in clinical practice. We focus primarily on psychosocial outpatient treatments, as this is the recommended level of care for most individuals with an eating disorder (National Collaborating Centre for Mental Health, 2004), but will also briefly discuss more intensive treatments and pharmacological interventions.

OUTPATIENT: TRANSDIAGNOSTIC TREATMENTS

The clearest example of a transdiagnostic approach that has been applied to AN, BN, and BED, as well as to subthreshold versions of these pathologies, is Fairburn and colleagues' enhanced form of CBT (CBT-E; Fairburn, 2008; Murphy, Straebler, Cooper, & Fairburn, 2010). The rationale for transdiagnostic treatment is that, while initially the focus is normalizing eating behaviors, ultimately the core cognitive features (i.e., overconcern with weight and shape) that maintain eating-related pathology across the spectrum must be addressed. A randomized trial of CBT-E applied to BN and BED (over 20 weeks) compared it to standard CBT and found both similarly effective in reducing eating disorder symptoms (Fairburn et al., 2009). However, evidence suggested some added benefits for the enhanced form for those individuals with more comorbid pathology. More recently, data have demonstrated the feasibility and efficacy of CBT-E for the treatment of AN in both adults and adolescents (for reviews of CBT-E for AN, see Dalle Grave, El Ghoch, Sartirana, & Calugi, 2016, and Galsworthy-Francis & Allan, 2014). For AN, CBT-E is extended to 40 weeks to allow greater time for weight restoration. Retention rates were above 50%, and completers demonstrated significant increases in weight and decreases in overall eating pathology. These results are considered to be quite positive as the treatment was relatively acceptable to this difficult-to-engage population.

The content of CBT-E includes the standard CBT that has accumulated the most evidence by far of any approach for treating BN and BED. Clients first engage in daily self-monitoring focused around what and when they are eating to facilitate careful examination of their eating patterns. Second, clients are strongly encouraged to adopt a structured plan of three meals and two snacks a day to replace the chaotic and unhelpful restraint strategies they have developed in their struggle to restrict intake. Third, clients learn to use behavioral analysis and problem solving to develop effective alternatives for bingeing and purging, and to engage in cognitive restructuring to address dysfunctional thought patterns and their underlying overconcern with weight and shape, both of which drive dietary restraint and other unhealthy behaviors. Therapy also addresses more individualized concerns and establishes plans to prevent relapse. Patients who respond well to the standard CBT (i.e., who achieve rapid change in core symptoms over the first 6 to 8 weeks) can continue with the standard approach; for those not responding adequately, three mechanisms that may be impeding progress are assessed and, when found to be present, can then be directly addressed with specific modules. The issues the modules deal with are severe clinical perfectionism, unconditional and pervasive low self-esteem, and significant difficulties with interpersonal relationships. The earliest version of CBT-E also included an optional module targeting emotion dysregulation, but this module is now incorporated into the core treatment because so many individuals with eating difficulties demonstrate substantial difficulties in mood regulation.

It is of note that clinical trials for CBT have been almost exclusively done with young adult women. What little is known about treatment for more diverse populations, including males and older women, suggests that the CBT treatment effect is quite robust and does not require significant modifications. Work by Lock (2005) and others (Dalle Grave, Calugi, Doll, & Fairburn, 2013; Schapman-Williams, Lock, & Couturier, 2006) demonstrates that CBT can also be successfully adapted for adolescents, although other treatments may be preferable for this population, as will be discussed below.

To address issues of accessibility and affordability, several CBT-based versions of self-help have been developed and evaluated (Mitchell, Agras, & Wonderlich, 2007). Generally, results from these studies indicate that self-help is somewhat (but not significantly) less effective than traditional therapy. However, abstinence rates are lower and dropout higher. Nonetheless, self-help is clearly more cost effective and is often the most viable first step when resources are limited. Recent data suggest that self-help delivered via the Internet is comparable to other modalities of self-help (e.g., bibliotherapy) (Wagner et al., 2013). Guided self-help fares somewhat better than pure self-help, and guidance provided by a mental health professional is somewhat more effective than guidance provided by other professionals (Wilson & Zandberg, 2012).

Other interventions that stem from CBT have also been applied broadly across a spectrum of ED symptoms. Appetite awareness training (AAT) was initially developed for BED to target the overeating directly in addition to the reduction of dieting (Allen & Craighead, 1999), but it has since been applied to BN and used in early interventions for problematic eating patterns (Craighead, 2006). The goal of the approach is to shift attention away from the typical overfocus on food type and to promote reliance instead on internal appetite cues (both hunger and fullness) to guide eating decisions, a strategy accomplished by centering the self-monitoring on hunger and fullness rather than food. Treatment based around appetite monitoring demonstrates a level of effectiveness similar to that of CBT, but appetite monitoring is reported as more acceptable and helpful than food monitoring by many individuals.

Dialectical behavior therapy (DBT), originally developed as a treatment for chronically suicidal adults with borderline personality disorder (Linehan, 1993), has been modified for eating disorders on the basis that problematic eating behaviors may be conceptualized as another manifestation of emotion dysregulation (see Safer, Telch, & Agras, 2001, for DBT for BN, and Telch, Agras, & Linehan, 2001, for DBT for BED; see also Hill, Craighead, & Safer, 2011, for DBT enhanced with appetite monitoring). As noted above, a focus on emotion regulation has already been incorporated into core CBT-E. More recently, a modification of DBT, now called Radically Open DBT (Lynch et al., 2013), is being studied as an intervention for individuals with AN (see also Chen et al., 2015). This development may turn out to be useful in understanding the personality differences that are hypothesized to characterize certain groups of individuals with EDs and may enhance acceptance of and response to treatment for some individuals (Martinez & Craighead, 2015). As described by Lynch (in press), over- and undercontrol are not conceptualized as opposite ends of a self-control continuum but as potentially useful labels to describe a set of biopsychosocial behaviors with similar genotypic/phenotypic features. This work highlights potential new directions that may further the development of transdiagnostic treatment or suggest ways to further personalize treatment even when treatment is provided within a larger transdiagnostic framework.

SPECIFIC TREATMENTS FOR AN

Given the substantial difficulties in getting individuals to accept or stay in treatment and the generally poor response to treatment for severe and enduring AN, the last few decades have seen an explosion of treatment development for this diagnosis. It is beyond the scope of this chapter to cover all these developments, so the reader is directed to recent reviews for more information (see Hay, Touyz, & Sud, 2012; Martinez & Craighead, 2015; and Watson & Bulik, 2013). A wide array of theoretical formulations have led to approaches as different as highly behavioral exposure therapy (Steinglass et al., 2010, 2014) and treatments that emphasize effective emotion regulation (Wildes, Marcus, Cheng, McCabe, & Gaskill, 2014). Specific treatments for AN target weight restoration first, and most of the available literature emphasizes evaluation of success in this domain. Shortening the length of time at low weight has been considered important to minimize health consequences. Additionally, as noted above, data suggest that the prognosis is better for those with higher BMIs, highlighting the need for early intervention (Treasure & Russell, 2011). The bigger issues of achieving long-term weight maintenance and improving quality of life are addressed within a wide range of approaches. Martinez and Craighead (2015) suggest that highly individualized treatment options may be needed for AN, as the first goal is to reduce resistance to engaging in treatment; taking personality-based individual differences into account may facilitate that first step. In that regard, it is interesting to note that while inpatient treatment clearly promotes the quickest weight restoration, it is less clear whether inpatient treatment is the most effective long-term strategy because failing to maintain one's weight after discharge is common. As noted above, current standards of care recommend outpatient treatment, so hospital inpatient care is usually short-term and based around medical stabilization. Residential care is recommended for individuals who have not responded adequately to several attempts at outpatient treatment.

Specific outpatient treatments for AN have been developed and evaluated primarily for the (more common) cases of adolescent onset. Prior to the 1970s, pathological family dynamics were believed to be a major cause of adolescent AN, and treatment generally focused on separating the adolescent from the family to promote individual development. Then structural and strategic schools of family therapy were developed that proposed that the family system could be harnessed to be a helpful force in resolving the dilemma of AN in the adolescent patient. These approaches stress family process, communication, and negotiation of adolescent developmental issues. The most well-established treatment for adolescents with AN is a family-based treatment (FBT) that is also referred to as the Maudsley method (named for the hospital in London where it was originally developed). FBT for AN in adolescents developed by Dare and Eisler has been studied in a series of randomized clinical trials (Lock, Le Grange, Agras, & Dare, 2001). In FBT, parents are empowered to restore the child's weight at home; brief hospitalization is used only for emergencies. The first phase is aimed at assisting parents to take charge of weight restoration in their adolescent with AN. This represents a significant shift from the way parents have typically been responding to the child. The second phase focuses on assisting the adolescent with taking back control of eating once healthy patterns have been reestablished under parental supervision. The third phase consists of an exploration of adolescent developmental issues, particularly as they may have been affected by AN. Principle features of the approach, which make it quite different from prior family work, are an agnostic view of the cause of AN—viewing the parents as the primary agent of change—and separation of the illness from the patient (externalization). Although the majority of the clinician's time is spent meeting with the family as a whole, a portion of each session is spent individually with the adolescent to ascertain her or his perspective on progress and to identify issues relevant to the overall family treatment. The body of literature evaluating the effectiveness of FBT relative to other treatments for adolescent AN suggests that family therapy is superior to other treatments, though most of the studies are small in scale (Le Grange & Lock, 2005); the data also clearly demonstrate that prognosis is improved in adolescent-onset AN, which highlights the utility of an empirically supported treatment for these individuals (Ackard et al., 2014; Franko et al., 2013). A relatively larger study comparing individual therapy (called Adolescent Focused Therapy, or AFT) to FBT found that the rates of recovery at 1-year follow-up (defined as normal EDE scores and weight greater than 95% of expected BMI percentile for age and gender) were more than twice those of individual therapy (FBT = 50%; individual therapy = 20%) (Lock et al., 2010). In addition, data from a large multisite study demonstrate that, relative to AFT, FBT produces weight gain faster, is associated with fewer days in the hospital, and has lower treatment costs (Agras et al., 2014). However, AFT remains an important option, as in a significant number of cases, parents are either unable or unwilling to take on the roles needed for FBT to work effectively. While a greater proportion of individuals receiving FBT in clinical trials achieve remission, longitudinal data suggest that adolescents who achieve remission with either FBT or AFT maintain these gains over a period of several years (Le Grange, Lock, et al., 2014).

For adults with AN, McIntosh et al. (2005) developed and evaluated a specialist supportive individual therapy (SSIT) that focuses on using the therapeutic relationship to promote adherence, and encouraging adequate nutritional intake and weight restoration through education, support, and clinical management. SSIT was originally devised as a control condition for use in randomized controlled trials comparing the efficacy of other treatment approaches, so it is not based on a specific theory of etiology or intervention. In the only trial reported, SSIT turned out to be superior to both CBT and interpersonal psychotherapy (IPT), raising the question of what the mechanism of change may be (McIntosh et al., 2005). A careful reading of the manual suggests that SSIT maintains a consistent focus on making behavioral changes in eating patterns within a supportive, motivation-enhancing therapeutic stance that appears to minimize patient resistance, perhaps by reducing fears of losing control over the process of weight restoration. In this trial, IPT was less effective than CBT, suggesting that a less directive, more client-focused approach is not a viable alternative treatment for adult AN, even though it has been effective for BN and BED, as described later. The common element in SSIT and CBT in the trial seemed to be their explicit focus on setting behavioral goals. It has been suggested that CBT's direct challenging of distorted cognitions may elicit greater client resistance in AN than it does in other presentations because the symptoms of AN are highly ego-syntonic (Garner & Bemis, 1982; Garner, Vitousek, & Pike, 1997). If this hypothesis is supported by subsequent research, it would provide guidance to clinicians regarding differential foci of treatment for disordered eating when low weight is the primary target. This hypothesis is consistent with the finding noted earlier that a version of DBT designed to work with the overcontrolled personality type characteristic of many with AN is showing considerable promise.

As pointed out earlier, there are several reliable predictors of good response to treatment in AN, despite the many challenges inherent in treating this disorder. These predictors are relatively higher initial BMI (Treasure & Russell, 2011), earlier age of onset (Ackard et al., 2014; Le Grange et al., 2012), and early response to intervention (Doyle et al., 2010; Le Grange, Accurso, et al., 2014; Turner, Marshall, Wood, Stopa, & Waller, 2016). Data suggest that individuals with these indicators are more likely to show improvement in weight, eating disorder psychopathology, and comorbid psychological pathology following treatment. There are also limited data suggesting that better social adjustment is associated with positive response to treatment, whereas being unemployed, on psychotropic medications, or diagnosed with the binge/purge subtype of AN is associated with poor outcome (Carter et al., 2012; Le Grange, Fitzsimmons-Craft, et al., 2014). However, the reader should be cautious about drawing causal inferences from these findings as all these data are correlational. Additionally, the majority of these studies investigated predictors of outcome in cognitive-behavioral treatments of AN (e.g., CBT-E, FBT); thus, these findings may not generalize to other treatments.

SPECIFIC TREATMENTS FOR BN

As noted earlier, cognitive-behavioral therapy (CBT) is well established as the first-line treatment for BN, either alone or in combination with medications (see the review by Wilson, Grilo, & Vitousek, 2007). Interpersonal psychotherapy (IPT) is a second established option (see Murphy, Straebler, Basden, Cooper, & Fairburn, 2012; Rieger et al., 2010). Outcomes for IPT at the end of time-limited treatment are not as positive as for CBT, but individuals receiving IPT continue to show improvement over the course of follow-up, so that by 1-year follow-up, individuals who received IPT are not significantly different from those who received CBT. A more recent treatment designed specifically for individuals with BN is integrative cognitive-affective therapy (ICAT; Wonderlich et al., 2014), which is similar to CBT in its focus on promoting regular eating patterns but which also offers a greater focus on the role of emotions in maintaining bulimic symptoms. In the only trial of ICAT to date, the treatment was found to produce improvements comparable to those of CBT-E for BN (Wonderlich et al., 2014). More recent data looking at moderators of treatment outcome suggest that this treatment may be a useful alternative to CBT-E for individuals with greater affective lability and/or stimulus seeking (Accurso et al., 2015).

For adolescents with BN, FBT is an effective option. As described above, FBT was initially designed for adolescents with AN, but two studies have utilized it with adolescents with BN and support its utility (Le Grange, Crosby, Rathouz, & Leventhal, 2007; Schmidt et al., 2007). The adaptation of this treatment for adolescents with BN reflects the general movement within the field toward more transdiagnostic approaches. The major adjustments when using FBT with adolescents with BN are related to developmental differences and symptom presentation differences. Adolescents with BN are often more accepting of the need for treatment than those with AN, more involved in adolescent social processes, more capable of contributing to their own treatment earlier, and more likely to have comorbid psychiatric problems, especially depression (Le Grange & Lock, 2007). Like CBT for adults with BN, FBT for adolescents with BN requires about 20 sessions. The adolescent is asked to engage his or her parents in initially helping him or her to manage binge eating and purging. Once this is accomplished, control over eating is gradually transferred back to the adolescent, and the second and third phases of FBT target more general adolescent processes believed to be important in returning to an age-appropriate developmental course and reducing risk for relapse. Indeed, some data suggest that FBT for adolescent BN (FBT-BN) may be superior to CBT for adolescents (CBT-A): following 18 sessions, the abstinence rate for teens receiving FBT-BN was 39%, whereas only 20% of adolescents receiving CBT-A achieved abstinence (Le Grange, Lock, Agras, Bryson, & Jo, 2015). However, the difference between the two treatments was no longer significant at the 12-month follow-up point. Interestingly, other evidence-based approaches for the treatment of BN, such as DBT, are now being integrated into the FBT framework, with good (albeit preliminary) results (Murray et al., 2015).

Perhaps the most important observation from the many studies of interventions for BN is that as in AN treatment, change early in treatment is consistently the best predictor of ultimate outcome (Fairburn, Agras, Walsh, Wilson, & Stice, 2004; Vall & Wade, 2015). Additional variables found to be associated with greater symptom reduction following treatment include higher weight and shape concern and higher dietary restraint; conversely, the presence of more severe depressive symptoms at baseline was associated with lesser reductions in bulimic symptoms at end of treatment (Accurso et al., 2015). Severity of bulimic symptoms has also been found to be predictive of poor response to treatment: Dicker and Craighead (2004) reported that baseline purging once a day or more best differentiated their partial and poor responders from those who attained abstinence by the end of treatment. In this study, extending weekly outpatient treatment beyond 24 weeks was of limited benefit in getting partial responders to remission, supporting the notion that higher levels of care may be needed for non-responders. Similarly, at least one study examining predictors of therapeutic outcome in self-help interventions for BN found that lower frequency of binge eating at baseline was associated with good outcome at both the end of treatment and the 18-month follow-up (Wagner et al., 2015).

Given that individuals with more severe symptoms are less likely to respond to standard outpatient psychotherapies, the question of how best to achieve remission in these individuals remains. It is unclear whether individuals who fail to respond to an initial course of outpatient psychotherapy are benefited by switching to another weekly psychosocial therapy. Increases in frequency or level of care of treatment (i.e., intensive outpatient or partial hospitalization programs) are currently the clinical recommendation if response to outpatient treatment is insufficient, yet there are virtually no data evaluating the efficacy (or cost effectiveness) of higher levels of care for the treatment of BN. Evaluation of treatment options for individuals with BN who respond poorly or not at all to standard outpatient treatments remains a critical avenue of future research.

SPECIFIC TREATMENTS FOR BED

Most of the treatments that were first used to treat bulimia nervosa (including CBT, DBT, AAT, and IPT) have also been successfully applied to binge eating disorder; remission rates (i.e., no OBEs in the past month) of 70% to 85% are typical (for reviews, see Amianto, Ottone, Abbate Daga, & Fassino, 2015, and Iacovino, Gredysa, Altman, & Wilfley, 2012). Of note, CBT for BED does not show the distinct short-term advantage over IPT that has been shown for BN (Hilbert et al., 2012). The response of BED to a range of treatments suggests a fairly nonspecific effect of treatment. The common element among the treatments seems to be that all address emotional eating in various ways, suggesting that improved emotion regulation may be more critical to success in treating BED than the reduction in excessive dieting that is so clearly needed for BN. Unfortunately, no treatments have led to substantial weight loss (on average), although there are some data to suggest that whatever weight is lost during treatment may be maintained for up to 4 years after treatment (Hilbert et al., 2012). The reason that stopping binge eating does not lead to weight loss is not clear, but it may be that calories previously consumed as binges become distributed more appropriately throughout the day so eating no longer feels out of control even though total intake is not reduced adequately to achieve weight loss. Recent data suggest that weight gain precedes treatment seeking among overweight individuals with BED, so whatever weight is lost during treatment may represent a return to baseline weight (Masheb, White, & Grilo, 2013).

For BED with comorbid obesity, behavioral weight loss (BWL) has been suggested as a viable option, although most studies find that the modest initial weight-loss advantage shown in BWL compared to CBT for BED is not maintained. In contrast, data do suggest that individuals who achieve abstinence from binge eating are more likely to lose some weight and maintain lower weight than those who maintain any level of binge eating (Wilfley et al., 2002; Wilson, Wilfley, Agras, & Bryson, 2010). Although this finding might suggest a sequenced treatment approach wherein individuals receive CBT to facilitate cessation of binge eating and then BWL to assist with weight loss, the data do not seem to support this model. Grilo, Masheb, Wilson, Gueorguieva, and White (2011) found that at the end of a 12-month follow-up, CBT alone was superior to either BWL or a sequential treatment combining CBT and BWL. Furthermore, Munsch, Meyer, and Biedert (2012) reported that CBT and BWL produced comparable reductions in binge frequency at the end of a 12-month follow-up period, suggesting that sequenced care may not be beneficial. Given the lack of meaningful weight loss observed with current treatments, treatments that combine elements of CBT-E with BWL and also treatments that target impulsivity are currently being evaluated (Palavras et al., 2015; Schag et al., 2015).

As with treatment for BN, access to services is of critical importance in treating BED. Many of the interventions that are clearly effective, including CBT, IPT and DBT, are not cost effective and/or are not always accessible. A growing body of literature documents the efficacy of guided self-help interventions for BED (Beintner, Jacobi, & Schmidt, 2014; Striegel-Moore et al., 2010; Wilson et al., 2010). Many self-help programs use Fairburn's book *Overcoming Binge Eating* (2013), and studies evaluating these programs have found them to be effective. Additionally, Internet-based self-help programs (e.g., Carrard et al., 2011; de Zwaan et al., 2012) are gaining in popularity due in large part to their feasibility, high acceptability, and low dropout rates (Beintner et al., 2014). Abbreviated versions of CBT offered in a group setting to enhance access to treatment have been studied and found to perform comparably to self-help interventions (Fischer, Meyer, Dremmel, Schlup, & Munsch, 2014). Together, these alternative modes of treatment have and will likely continue to benefit many individuals who might not otherwise have access to psychotherapy, including members of racial and ethnic minorities who could be referred to self-help programs by their primary care physician (Grilo et al., 2014; but see Thompson-Brenner et al., 2013, for a discussion of additional limitations of existing treatments for minority populations).

Much as with AN and BN, the most robust predictor of outcome for individuals receiving treatment for BED is rapid response to treatment, both in traditional treatment modalities (Munsch et al., 2012) and in self-help or pharmacological interventions (Grilo, White, Masheb, & Gueorguieva, 2015). Overvaluation of shape and weight has also been found to be associated with poor prognosis in several studies (Grilo, Masheb, & Crosby, 2012; Grilo et al., 2013). Additionally, higher levels of pathology at baseline appear to be associated with worse prognosis following treatment (Fischer et al., 2014; Thompson-Brenner et al., 2013). It is useful to note that all existing studies of predictors and moderators of response to treatment and long-term outcome have examined data from studies of CBT for the treatment of BED; there are at present no data as to the long-term efficacy of treatments such as IPT or DBT, the treatments that most directly address the interpersonal and emotional triggers for binges and thus may do the best at promoting long-term maintenance of treatment gains. Additionally, as mentioned above, effective treatment for the comorbid obesity common in BED remains elusive and likely awaits new developments in our understanding of and ability to treat obesity more successfully.

INPATIENT, DAY HOSPITAL, AND RESIDENTIAL TREATMENTS

Intensive treatment in hospital, day hospital, or residential programs is used for severe and/or chronic AN and, less frequently, for severe BN or BED. The approaches used are usually based on behavioral principles (meaning that they involve withholding and/or providing desired activities or privileges), and they target either weight restoration in the case of AN or cessation of bingeing and/or purging behaviors for individuals with BN or BED.

Although there is little evidence evaluating these treatment approaches, they remain a critical aspect of the continuum of care needed to deal with the urgencies that develop in the context of these challenging disorders due to malnutrition or other medical complications. They also provide respite care for families and providers when outpatient approaches are not perceived as making adequate progress. In the case of AN, weight gain can be achieved at a substantially faster rate (in the range of 3–5 lbs/wk) in these more controlled settings than is feasible on an outpatient basis (in the range of 1–2 lbs/wk); for a recent review of refeeding practices in AN, see Garber et al. (2015). However, there is substantial debate as to whether weight gain in this setting is well maintained and whether restored normal eating habits generalize to the same extent as with outpatient treatment. The single review summarizing the effectiveness of inpatient and outpatient care for AN concluded that outpatient treatment in a specialist eating disorder service was as effective as inpatient treatment among those who did not warrant emergency admission (Meads, Gold, & Burls, 2001); more recent reviews on this topic are ongoing (Hay et al., 2013). As outpatient care is significantly less expensive, reliance on such care is likely to increase, and it is to be hoped that more rigorous evaluation of the associated step-down and residential programs will be undertaken in the future (Lock, 2003; Striegel-Moore, Leslie, Petrill, Garvin, & Rosenheck, 2000).

Higher levels of care are used much less frequently for individuals with BN and BED. Indeed, there are few indications to warrant inpatient hospitalization for these individuals short of significant medical issues or other psychiatric comorbidity. For individuals with BN or BED, abstinence from bingeing and/or purging behaviors is achieved almost immediately upon admission into an inpatient or residential facility, where opportunities to engage in these disordered behaviors are limited. However, data regarding the relative long-term efficacy of inpatient versus outpatient interventions for BN and BED are lacking, which may be partially due to the infrequency with which higher levels of care are used for the treatment of these disorders.

Inpatient psychiatric treatment programs vary greatly but most involve a combination of nutritional rehabilitation, education, medical intervention, psychotherapeutic treatment, psychosocial rehabilitation, and family therapies. Longer-term residential care programs provide intensive services (24-hour programming) and stays are generally between 1 and 2 months. Objective and systematic data on the outcomes of patients treated in residential centers are rarely available, but reports from these proprietary programs themselves suggest that treatment promotes recovery, prevents relapse, and reduces the development of a chronic course of illness. Less-intensive day hospital programs for eating disorders are available for adults and older adolescent patients. These programs usually provide services 4 to 7 days per week and include supervised meals, therapeutic groups, and individual therapy (Olmsted, 2002). Intensive outpatient programs (IOPs) are even less intensive programs (e.g., 3 hours twice a week) and often serve a transitional role between hospital and outpatient care or serve when a step up from weekly individual treatment is needed, as might be the case when BN or BED is not responding adequately to standard weekly therapy. Because of the high cost and uncertain outcomes of these programs and also because of the dearth of recent data evaluating their efficacy, it is important that evaluation of all these levels of treatment for eating disorders be undertaken (Frisch, Franko, & Herzog, 2006).

PSYCHOPHARMACOLOGICAL AND BIOLOGICAL INTERVENTIONS

Medications, either alone or in combination with psychotherapy, are used frequently in the treatment of eating disorders, with varying levels of success and empirical support (for a review and clinical guidelines, see Aigner, Treasure, Kaye, & Kasper, 2011). A variety of medications have been tried in treating AN (Miniati et al., 2015). To date, none of them appears to be systematically useful. The use of fluoxetine—the one medication approved for the treatment of an eating disorder (BN)—has been suggested as being useful in preventing relapse after weight restoration, but studies suggest that it may not be as helpful as initially believed (Kaye et al., 2001; Walsh et al., 2006). More recently, the field has begun investigating atypical antipsychotic medications (in particular olanzapine and aripiprazole) which have gained popularity in clinical use for their ability to reduce obsessionality, delusional thinking, and hyperactivity and to facilitate weight gain in other populations. However, data examining their efficacy in the treatment of AN are discouraging: recent reviews and meta-analyses find little effect of these medications on the core symptoms of AN and note that existing studies are plagued by low sample sizes and high dropout rates (Dold, Aigner, Klabunde, Treasure, & Kasper, 2015; Miniati et al., 2015). Given these findings, many clinicians are beginning to examine the utility of antipsychotic medications in combination with antidepressants, rather than as monotherapy, with some promising results (Marzola et al., 2015). In the face of limited pharmacological options, there have been some preliminary examinations of the use of more invasive biological techniques in severe cases. Deep brain stimulation has shown some promise (Lipsman & Lozano, 2014), but its use in this population raises important ethical issues (Maslen, Pugh, & Savulescu, 2015). Additional data are certainly necessary to evaluate existing interventions and provide guidance for the treatment of this population.

For the treatment of BN, several antidepressants have demonstrated overall effectiveness equivalent to CBT alone. Fluoxetine in particular has received the most consistent empirical support and has received a denotation of grade A evidence from the World Federation of Societies of Biological Psychiatry (WFSBP) (Aigner et al., 2011). However, compared to CBT, a smaller proportion of individuals (20%) achieve complete abstinence by the end of treatment, and relapse following medication withdrawal is a significant problem (Hay & Claudino, 2012; McElroy, Guerdjikova, Mori, & O'Melia, 2012). Medication is equally effective whether or not the individual has diagnosable comorbid depression; therefore the mechanism through which it works remains unclear. Given these data, medication alone is not recommended for BN. However, medication combined with CBT is clinically indicated when comorbid depression is present or when an individual does not respond adequately to an initial trial of CBT (Mitka, 2011).

Several classes of psychotropic medications have been examined in the treatment of BED. At present, several antidepressant (e.g., citalopram/escitalopram and sertraline), anticonvulsant (e.g., topiramate), and antiobesity (e.g., orlistat) medications have been evaluated. Data summarized in several recent reviews (Brownley, Peat, La Via, & Bulik, 2015; Goracci et al., 2015; Reas & Grilo, 2015) suggest that these medications help to reduce binge eating and associated pathology and facilitate weight loss to varying degrees, but few people achieve full remission with medication alone. Recently, lisdexamfetamine dimesylate (LDX), a stimulant medication used for the treatment of attention-deficit/hyperactivity disorder (ADHD), was approved by regulatory bodies in the United States for the treatment of moderate to severe BED (U.S. Food and Drug Administration [FDA], 2015). Of note, LDX is indicated only for the treatment of binge eating, not for weight loss; the utility of LDX for weight loss in individuals with BED will likely be explored in future research. Future directions for the pharmacological treatment of BED include medications for the treatment of substance abuse (e.g., disulfiram, or Antabuse; Farci et al., 2014) and novel antiobesity agents recently approved or pending approval from the FDA (e.g., bupropion/naltrexone and phentermine/topiramate; Brownley et al., 2015; Goracci et al., 2015). It seems likely, however, that psychotherapy will remain a critical component of the treatment of BED, particularly given data showing that adding medications does not provide significant additional benefit above and beyond psychotherapeutic interventions for BED and that medication may confer vulnerability to relapse when withdrawn (Devlin, Goldfein, Petkova, Liu, & Walsh, 2012; Grilo, Crosby, Wilson, & Masheb, 2012). Additional work investigating predictors and moderators of response to medication versus psychotherapy will be critical in clarifying the future role of pharmacological interventions in the treatment of BED.

Summary and Future Directions

The story of eating disorders is one of constant evolution and change. In this field, a single syndrome gave way to two and now three distinct diagnoses, diagnostic criteria have narrowed and broadened over the course of time, and treatments found to be effective in treating one population (e.g., CBT for BN, FBT for AN) have been systematically adapted and applied successfully in the treatment of other diagnoses. For individuals suffering from eating disorders, diagnostic crossover and symptom fluctuation are almost the norm, which lends support to a dimensional or transdiagnostic approach to eating pathology (Olatunji et al., 2012). This chapter highlighted both the similarities and the differences in symptoms, course, prevalence, etiology, and response to treatment among the three specific eating disorders. The clear similarities across these disorders have encouraged the development of transdiagnostic approaches to their treatment, with good success. Establishing the relative merit of disorder-specific versus transdiagnostic treatments remains a critical question in the field of eating disorders, but it is clear that broad treatments able to address weight in addition to problematic eating behaviors and cognitions will be needed for AN and for those with BED who have comorbid obesity.

At this point in time, CBT is well established as a highly effective, first-line treatment for BN and BED, although none of the available approaches effectively treat the frequently comorbid obesity. IPT is a viable alternative to CBT for BN and BED. A variety of outpatient interventions, including transdiagnostic CBT, are promising for those with AN, but resistance to entering and/or engaging in treatment remains a significant challenge. For example, for adolescents with AN, FBT has strong empirical support but is not a viable option in many cases. Overall, AN remains less well understood from a theoretical perspective than the other presentations, and the more intensive treatment options often required in its treatment are, unfortunately, not being systematically evaluated. Research on AN in particular has been limited by the relatively low base rate, frequency of medical and psychiatric comorbidities, ambivalence about treatment, and poor participant retention. Across all the eating disorders, more work is needed to understand what characterizes those individuals who fail the first-line treatments. This approach was critical in the development and success of CBT-E (Cooper & Fairburn, 2011) and will likely continue to contribute to the advancement of eating disorder treatments.

Despite substantial similarities among the three disorders, critical distinctions remain in presentation and course, a fact that supports the continued need for specific diagnoses so that research can explore differences in etiology and developmental trajectories and determine whether specific neurobiological or genetic underpinnings account for these different trajectories. The extent to which specific diagnoses will track to specialized interventions remains an open question, although, at a minimum, specific strategies to address the need for weight gain in AN and weight loss in many cases of BED will be needed. Furthermore, developing infrastructures for the successful dissemination of treatments that have already been found effective is critical so that more patients with eating disorders can receive high-quality, affordable care in the community. Only when we have done this can we hope to mitigate the substantial burden imposed by these serious and challenging disorders.

References

Accurso, E. C., Wonderlich, S. A., Crosby, R. D., Smith, T. L., Klein, M. H., Mitchell, J. E., … Peterson, C. B. (2015). Predictors and moderators of treatment outcome in a randomized clinical trial for adults with symptoms of bulimia nervosa. *Journal of Consulting and Clinical Psychology*, Advance online publication. doi: 10.1037/ccp0000073

Ackard, D. M., Richter, S., Egan, A., & Cronemeyer, C. (2014). Poor outcome and death among youth, young adults, and midlife adults with eating disorders: An investigation of risk factors by age at assessment. *International Journal of Eating Disorders*, 47(7), 825–835. doi: 10.1002/eat.22346

Agras, W. S., Lock, J., Brandt, H., Bryson, S. W., Dodge, E., Halmi, K. A., … Woodside, B. (2014). Comparison of 2 family therapies for adolescent anorexia nervosa: A randomized parallel trial. *JAMA Psychiatry*, 71(11), 1279–1286.

Aigner, M., Treasure, J., Kaye, W., & Kasper, S. (2011). World Federation of Societies of Biological Psychiatry (WFSBP) guidelines for the pharmacological treatment of eating disorders. *World Journal of Biological Psychiatry*, 12(6), 400–443. doi: 10.3109/15622975.2011.602720

Akkermann, K., Hiio, K., Villa, I., & Harro, J. (2011). Food restriction leads to binge eating dependent on the effect of the brain-derived neurotrophic factor Val66Met polymorphism. *Psychiatry Research*, 185(1–2), 39–43.

Allen, H. N., & Craighead, L. W. (1999). Appetite monitoring in the treatment of binge eating disorder. *Behavior Therapy*, 30(2), 253–272.

American Psychiatric Association. (1987). *Diagnostic and statistical manual of mental disorders* (3rd ed., rev.). Washington, DC: Author.

American Psychiatric Association. (1994). *Diagnostic and statistical manual of mental disorders* (4th ed.). Washington, DC: Author.

American Psychiatric Association. (2000). *Diagnostic and statistical manual of mental disorders* (4th ed., text rev.). Washington, DC: Author.

American Psychiatric Association. (2013). *Diagnostic and statistical manual of mental disorders* (5th ed.). Washington, DC: Author.

Amianto, F., Ottone, L., Abbate Daga, G., & Fassino, S. (2015). Binge-eating disorder diagnosis and treatment: A recap in front of DSM-5. *BMC Psychiatry*, 15, 70. doi: 10.1186/s12888-015-0445-6

Anderson, D. A., & Paulosky, C. A. (2004). Psychological assessment of eating disorders and related features. In J. K. Thompson (Ed.), *Handbook of eating disorders and obesity* (pp. 112–129). Hoboken, NJ: Wiley.

Arcelus, J., Mitchell, A. J., Wales, J., & Nielsen, S. (2011). Mortality rates in patients with anorexia nervosa and other eating disorders: A meta-analysis of 36 studies. *Archives of General Psychiatry*, 68(7), 724. Retrieved from http://archpsyc.ama-assn.org/cgi/reprint/68/7/724.pdf

Bakalar, J. L., Shank, L. M., Vannucci, A., Radin, R. M., & Tanofsky-Kraff, M. (2015). Recent advances in developmental and risk factor research on eating disorders. *Current Psychiatry Reports*, 17(6), 585. doi: 10.1007/s11920-015-0585-x

Bartholome, L. T., Raymond, N. C., Lee, S. S., Peterson, C. B., & Warren, C. S. (2006). Detailed analysis of binges in obese women with binge eating disorder: Comparisons using multiple methods of data collection. *International Journal of Eating Disorders*, 36, 685–693.

Becker, A. E., Keel, P., Anderson-Fye, E. P., & Thomas, J. J. (2004). Genes and/or jeans? Genetic and socio-cultural contributions to risk for eating disorders. *Journal of Addictive Diseases*, 23, 81–103.

Becker, J. B. (2009). Sexual differentiation of motivation: A novel mechanism? *Hormones and Behavior*, 55(5), 646–654.

Beintner, I., Jacobi, C., & Schmidt, U. H. (2014). Participation and outcome in manualized self-help for bulimia nervosa and binge eating disorder—a systematic review and metaregression analysis. *Clinical Psychology Review*, 34(2), 158–176. doi: 10.1016/j.cpr.2014.01.003

Bello, N. T., & Hajnal, A. (2010). Dopamine and binge eating behaviors. *Pharmacology Biochemistry & Behavior*, 97(1), 25–33.

Berridge, K. C. (2009). "Liking" and "wanting" food rewards: Brain substrates and roles in eating disorders. *Physiology and Behavior*, 97, 537–550.

Bohon, C., Stice, E., & Spoor, S. (2009). Female emotional eaters show abnormalities in consummatory and anticipatory food reward: A functional magnetic resonance imaging study. *International Journal of Eating Disorders*, *42*(3), 210–221.

Boraska, V., Franklin, C. S., Floyd, J. A. B., Thornton, L. M., Huckins, L. M., Southam, L., ... Bulik, C. M. (2014). A genome-wide association study of anorexia nervosa. *Molecular Psychiatry*, *19*(10), 1085–1094.

Boskind-Lodahl, M., & White, W. C. (1978). The definition and treatment of bulimarexia in college women—a pilot study. *Journal of American College Health Association*, *27*(2), 84–97.

Brownley, K. A., Peat, C. M., La Via, M., & Bulik, C. M. (2015). Pharmacological approaches to the management of binge eating disorder. *Drugs*, *75*(1), 9–32. doi: 10.1007/s40265-014-0327-0

Bühren, K., Schwarte, R., Fluck, F., Timmesfeld, N., Krei, M., Egberts, K., ... Herpertz-Dahlmann, B. (2014). Comorbid psychiatric disorders in female adolescents with first-onset anorexia nervosa. *European Eating Disorders Review*, *22*(1), 39–44. doi: 10.1002/erv.2254

Bulik, C. M., Hebebrand, J., Keski-Rahkonen, A., Klump, K. L., Reichborn-Kjennerud, T., Mazzeo, S. E., & Wade, T. D. (2007). Genetic epidemiology, endophenotypes and eating disorder classification. *International Journal of Eating Disorders*, *40*(S3), S52–S60. Retrieved from http://onlinelibrary.wiley .com/store/10.1002/eat.20398/asset/20398_ftp.pdf?v =1&t=gzbi4y6f&s=b61860098c2f8b6a02f48a 033207f3fc1a5f30df

Bulik, C. M., Sullivan, P. F., Wade, T. D., & Kendler, K. S. (2000). Twin studies of eating disorders: A review. *International Journal of Eating Disorders*, *17*(3), 251–261.

Bruch, H. (1973). *Eating disorders: Obesity, anorexia nervosa, and the person within*. New York, NY: Basic Books.

Bruch, H. (1978). *The golden cage: The enigma of anorexia nervosa*. Cambridge, MA: Harvard University Press.

Bryant-Waugh, R., Cooper, P., Taylor, C., & Lask, B. (1996). The use of the eating disorders examination with children: A pilot study. *International Journal of Eating Disorders*, *19*, 391–397.

Calati, R., De Ronchi, D., Bellini, M., & Serretti, A. (2011). The 5-HTTLPR polymorphism and eating disorders: A meta-analysis. *International Journal of Eating Disorders*, *44*(3), 191–199.

Carrard, I., Crépin, C., Rouget, P., Lam, T., Golay, A., & Van der Linden, M. (2011). Randomised controlled trial of a guided self-help treatment on the Internet for binge eating disorder. *Behaviour Research and Therapy*, *49*(8), 482–491. doi: 10.1016/j.brat.2011.05.004

Carter, J. C., Mercer-Lynn, K. B., Norwood, S. J., Bewell-Weiss, C. V., Crosby, R. D., Woodside, D. B., & Olmsted, M. P. (2012). A prospective study of predictors of relapse in anorexia nervosa: Implications for relapse prevention. *Psychiatry Research*, *200*(2–3), 518–523. doi: 10.1016/j.psychres.2012 .04.037

Cassin, S. E., & von Ranson, K. M. (2005). Personality and eating disorders: A decade in review. *Clinical Psychology Review*, *25*, 895–916. doi: 10.1016/j.cpr .2005.04.012

Chen, E. Y., Segal, K., Weissman, J., Zeffiro, T. A., Gallop, R., Linehan, M. M., ... Lynch, T. R. (2015). Adapting dialectical behavior therapy for outpatient adult anorexia nervosa—a pilot study. *International Journal of Eating Disorders*, *48*(1), 123–132. doi: 10.1002/eat.22360

Chowdhury, U., Gordon, I., & Lask, B. (2003). Early onset anorexia nervosa: Is there evidence of limbic system imbalance. *International Journal of Eating Disorders*, *33*, 388–396.

Cooper, P. J., & Fairburn, C. G. (1987). The Eating Disorder Examination: A semi-structured interview for the assessment of the specific psychopathology of eating disorders. *International Journal of Eating Disorders*, *6*, 1–8.

Cooper, Z., Cooper, P. J., & Fairburn, C. G. (1989). The validity of the eating disorder examination and its subscales. *British Journal of Psychiatry*, *154*(6), 807–812.

Cooper, Z., & Fairburn, C. G. (2011). The evolution of "enhanced" cognitive behavior therapy for eating disorders: Learning from treatment nonresponse. *Cognitive and Behavioral Practice*, *18*(3), 394–402. doi: 10.1016/j.cbpra.2010.07.007

Craighead, L. W. (2006). *The appetite awareness workbook: How to listen to your body and overcome binge eating, overeating, and obsession with food*. Oakland, CA: New Harbinger.

Craighead, L. W., & Allen, H. N. (1995). Appetite awareness training: A cognitive behavioral intervention for binge eating. *Cognitive and Behavioral Practice*, *2*, 249–270.

Crisp, A. H. (1997). Anorexia nervosa as flight from growth: Assessment and treatment based on the model. In D. M. Garner & P. Garfinkel (Eds.), *Handbook of treatment for eating disorders* (pp. 248–277). New York, NY: Guilford Press.

Crow, S. J., & Peterson, C. B. (2003). The economic and social burden of eating disorders: A review. In M. Maj, K. Halmi, J. J. Lopez-Ibor, & N. Sartorius (Eds.), *Eating disorders* (pp. 383–396). Chichester, England: Wiley.

Culbert, K. M., Racine, S. E., & Klump, K. L. (2015). Research review: What we have learned about the causes of eating disorders—a synthesis of sociocultural, psychological, and biological research. *Journal of Child Psychology and Psychiatry, 56*(11), 1141–1164.

Currin, L., Schmidt, U., Treasure, J., & Jick, H. (2005). Time trends in eating disorder incidence. *British Journal of Psychiatry, 186*, 132–135.

Dalle Grave, R., Calugi, S., Doll, H. A., & Fairburn, C. G. (2013). Enhanced cognitive behaviour therapy for adolescents with anorexia nervosa: An alternative to family therapy? *Behaviour Research and Therapy, 51*(1), R9–R12.

Dalle Grave, R., El Ghoch, M., Sartirana, M., & Calugi, S. (2016). Cognitive behavioral therapy for anorexia nervosa: An update. *Current Psychiatry Reports, 18*(1), 2. doi: 10.1007/s11920-015-0643-4

Davis, C., & Kaptein, S. (2006). Anorexia nervosa with excessive exercise: A phenotype with close links to obsessive-compulsive disorder. *Psychiatry Research, 142*(2–3), 209–217. doi: 10.1016/j.psychres.2005.11.006

de Zwaan, M., Herpertz, S., Zipfel, S., Tuschen-Caffier, B., Friederich, H.-C., Schmidt, F., … Hilbert, A. (2012). INTERBED: Internet-based guided self-help for overweight and obese patients with full or subsyndromal binge eating disorder. A multicenter randomized controlled trial. *Trials, 13*(1), 220. doi: 10.1186/1745-6215-13-220

Deaver, C. M., Miltenberger, R. G., Smyth, J., Meidinger, A., & Crosby, R. (2003). An evaluation of affect and binge eating. *Behavior Modification, 27*, 578–599.

Devlin, M. J., Goldfein, J. A., Petkova, E., Liu, L., & Walsh, B. T. (2012). Cognitive behavioral therapy and fluoxetine for binge eating disorder: Two-year follow-up. *Obesity, 15*(7), 1702–1709.

Dicker, S., & Craighead, L. W. (2004). Appetite focused cognitive behavioral therapy in the treatment of binge eating with purging. *Cognitive Behavioral Practice, 11*(2), 213–221.

Dold, M., Aigner, M., Klabunde, M., Treasure, J., & Kasper, S. (2015). Second-generation antipsychotic drugs in anorexia nervosa: A meta-analysis of randomized controlled trials. *Psychotherapy and Psychosomatics, 84*(2), 110–116. Retrieved from http://www.karger.com/DOI/10.1159/000369978

Doyle, P. M., Le Grange, D., Loeb, K., Doyle, A. C., & Crosby, R. D. (2010). Early response to family-based treatment for adolescent anorexia nervosa. *International Journal of Eating Disorders, 43*(7), 659–662. doi: 10.1002/eat.20764

Eddy, K. T., Dorer, D. J., Franko, D. L., Tahilani, K., Thompson-Brenner, H., & Herzog, D. B. (2007). Should bulimia nervosa be subtyped by history of anorexia nervosa? A longitudinal validation. *International Journal of Eating Disorders, 40*(Suppl.), S67–S71. doi: 10.1002/eat.20422

Eddy, K. T., Dorer, D. J., Franko, D. L., Tahilani, K., Thompson-Brenner, H., & Herzog, D. B. (2008). Diagnostic crossover in anorexia nervosa and bulimia nervosa: Implications for DSM-V. *American Journal of Psychiatry, 165*, 245–250.

Eddy, K. T., Keel, P., Dorer, D., Delinsky, S., Franko, D., & Herzog, D. B. (2002). Longitudinal comparison of anorexia nervosa subtypes. *International Journal of Eating Disorders, 31*, 191–202.

Engelberg, M. J., Steiger, H., Gauvin, L., & Wonderlich, S. A. (2007). Binge antecedents in bulimic syndromes: An examination of dissociation and negative affect. *International Journal of Eating Disorders, 40*(6), 531–536.

Evans, E. J., Hay, P. J., Mond, J., Paxton, S. J., Quirk, F., Rodgers, B., … Sawoniewska, M. A. (2012). Barriers to help-seeking in young women with eating disorders: A qualitative exploration in a longitudinal community survey. *Eating Disorders, 19*(3), 270–285.

Fairburn, C. G. (2013). *Overcoming binge eating* (2nd ed.). New York, NY: Guilford Press.

Fairburn, C. G. (2008). *Cognitive behavior therapy and eating disorders*. New York, NY: Guilford Press. Retrieved from http://books.google.com/books?id=KRvAlB3l8-MC&printsec=frontcover&dq=cognitive+behavior+therapy+and+eating+disorders+fairburn+2008&hl=&cd=1&source=gbs_api

Fairburn, C. G., Agras, W. S., Walsh, B. T., Wilson, G. T., & Stice, E. (2004). Prediction of outcome in bulimia nervosa by early change in treatment. *American Journal of Psychiatry, 161*(12), 2322–2324. Retrieved from http://ajp.psychiatryonline.org/article.aspx?articleID=177234

Fairburn, C. G., & Beglin, S. J. (1994). Assessment of eating disorders: Interview or self-report questionnaire? *International Journal of Eating Disorders, 16*, 363–370.

Fairburn, C. G., & Bohn, K. (2005). Eating disorder NOS (EDNOS): An example of the troublesome "not otherwise specified" (NOS) category in DSM-IV. *Behaviour Research and Therapy, 43*, 691–701.

Fairburn, C. G., & Cooper, Z. (1993). The eating disorder examination (12th ed.). In C. G. Fairburn & G. T. Wilson (Eds.), *Binge eating: Nature, assessment, and treatment* (pp. 317–360). New York, NY: Guilford Press.

Fairburn, C. G., Cooper, Z., Doll, H. A., O'Connor, M. E., Bohn, K., Hawker, D. M., … Palmer, R. L. (2009). Transdiagnostic cognitive-behavioral therapy for patients with eating disorders: A two-site trial with 60-week follow-up. *American Journal of Psychiatry, 166*(3), 311–319.

Fairburn, C. G., Cooper, Z., & Shafran, R. (2003). Cognitive behaviour therapy for eating disorders: A "transdiagnostic" theory and treatment. *Behaviour Research and Therapy, 41*(5), 509–528. Retrieved from http://www.sciencedirect.com/science/article/pii/S0005796702000888

Fairburn, C. G., & Harrison, P. J. (2003). Eating disorders. *Lancet, 361*, 407–416.

Fairburn, C. G., Marcus, M. D., & Wilson, G. T. (1993). Cognitive-behavioral therapy for binge eating and bulimia nervosa: A comprehensive treatment manual. In C. G. Fairburn & G. T. Wilson (Eds.), *Binge eating: Nature, assessment, and treatment* (pp. 361–404). New York, NY: Guilford Press.

Farci, A. M. G., Piras, S., Murgia, M., Chessa, A., Restivo, A., Gessa, G. L., & Agabio, R. (2014). Disulfiram for binge eating disorder: An open trail. *Eating Behaviors, 16*, 84–87. doi: 10.1016/j.eatbeh.2014.10.008

Favaro, A., Ferrara, S., & Santonastaso, P. (2003). The spectrum of eating disorders in young women: A prevalence study in a general population sample. *Psychosomatic Medicine, 65*(4), 701–708. doi: 10.1097/01.PSY.0000073871.67679.D8

Fichter, M. M., Quadflieg, N., & Hedlund, S. (2006). Twelve-year course and outcome predictors of anorexia nervosa. *International Journal of Eating Disorders, 39*, 87–100. doi: 10.1002/eat.20215

Fischer, S., Meyer, A. H., Dremmel, D., Schlup, B., & Munsch, S. (2014). Short-term cognitive-behavioral therapy for binge eating disorder: Long-term efficacy and predictors of long-term treatment success. *Behaviour Research and Therapy, 58*, 36–42. doi: 10.1016/j.brat.2014.04.007

Fitzsimmons-Craft, E. E., Harney, M. B., Koehler, L. G., Danzi, L. E., Riddell, M. K., & Bardone-Cone, A. M. (2012). Explaining the relation between thin ideal internalization and body dissatisfaction among college women: The roles of social comparison and body surveillance. *Body Image, 9*(1), 43–49. doi: 10.1016/j.bodyim.2011.09.002

Foerde, K., Steinglass, J. E., Shohamy, D., & Walsh, B. T. (2015). Neural mechanisms supporting maladaptive food choices in anorexia nervosa. *Nature Neuroscience, 18*, 1571–1573. doi: 10.1038/nn.4136

Forbush, K. T., Wildes, J. E., & Hunt, T. K. (2014). Gender norms, psychometric properties, and validity for the Eating Pathology Symptoms Inventory. *International Journal of Eating Disorders, 47*(1), 85–91. doi: 10.1002/eat.22180

Forbush, K. T., Wildes, J. E., Pollack, L. O., Dunbar, D., Luo, J., Patterson, K., … Watson, D. (2013). Development and validation of the Eating Pathology Symptoms Inventory (EPSI). *Psychological Assessment, 25*(3), 859–878. doi: 10.1037/a0032639

Fouladi, F., Mitchell, J. E., Crosby, R. D., Engel, S. G., Crow, S., Hill, L., … Steffen, K. J. (2015). Prevalence of alcohol and other substance use in patients with eating disorders. *European Eating Disorders Review, 23*, 531–536. doi: 10.1002/erv.2410

Frank, G. (2015). Advances from neuroimaging studies in eating disorders. *CNS Spectrums, 20*(4), 391–400.

Frank, G., Kaye, W. H., Meltzer C. C., Price J. C., Greer P., McConaha C., & Skovira, K. (2002). Reduced 5-HT2A receptor binding after recovery from anorexia nervosa. *Biological Psychiatry, 52*, 896–906.

Franko, D. L., Keshaviah, A., Eddy, K. T., Krishna, M., Davis, M. C., Keel, P. K., & Herzog, D. B. (2013). Do mortality rates in eating disorders change over time? A longitudinal look at anorexia nervosa and bulimia nervosa. *American Journal of Psychiatry, 170*(8), 917–925. doi: 10.1176/appi.ajp.2013.12070868

Frieling, H., Römer, K. D., Scholz, S., Mittlebach, F., Wilhelm, J., de Zwaan, M., … Bleich, S. (2010). Epigenetic dysregulation of dopaminergic genes in eating disorders. *International Journal of Eating Disorders, 43*(7), 577–583.

Frisch, J., Franko, D., & Herzog, D. B. (2006). Residential treatment for eating disorders. *International Journal of Eating Disorders*, *39*, 434–439.

Gadalla, T., & Piran, N. (2008). Psychiatric comorbidity in women with disordered eating behavior: A national study. *Women & Health*, *48*(4), 467–484. doi: 10.1080/03630240802575104

Galsworthy-Francis, L., & Allan, S. (2014). Cognitive behavioural therapy for anorexia nervosa: A systematic review. *Clinical Psychology Review*, *34*(1), 54–72. doi: 10.1016/j.cpr.2013.11.001

Garber, A. K., Sawyer, S. M., Golden, N. H., Guarda, A. S., Katzman, D. K., Kohn, M. R., ... Redgrave, G. W. (2015). A systematic review of approaches to refeeding in patients with anorexia nervosa. *International Journal of Eating Disorders*. Advance online publication. doi: 10.1002/eat.22482

Garner, D. M. (2005). *Eating Disorder Inventory–3*. Lutz, FL: Psychological Assessment Resources.

Garner, D. M., & Bemis, K. (1982). A cognitive-behavioral approach to anorexia nervosa. *Cognitive Therapy and Research*, *6*(2), 123–150.

Garner, D. M., & Garfinkel, P. (1979). The Eating Attitude Test: An index of the symptoms of anorexia nervosa. *Psychological Medicine*, *9*, 273–279.

Garner, D. M., Vitousek, K. M., & Pike, K. M. (1997). Cognitive-behavioral therapy for anorexia nervosa. In D. M. Garner & P. E. Garfinkel (Eds.), *Handbook of treatment for eating disorders* (2nd ed., pp. 94–144). New York, NY: Guilford Press.

Gearhardt, A. N., Yokum, S., Orr, P. T., Stice, E., Corbin, W. R., & Brownell, K. D. (2011). Neural correlates of food addiction. *Archives of General Psychiatry*, *68*(8), 808–816.

Gianini, L. M., Klein, D. A., Call, C., Walsh, B. T., Wang, Y., Wu, P., & Attia, E. (2015). Physical activity and post-treatment weight trajectory in anorexia nervosa. *International Journal of Eating Disorders*. Advance online publication. doi: 10.1002/eat.22495

Godley, J., Tchanturia, K., MacLeod, A., & Schmidt, U. (2001). Future directed thinking in eating disorders. *British Journal of Clinical Psychology*, *40*, 281–296.

Goldschmidt, A. B., Le Grange, D., Powers, P., Crow, S. J., Hill, L. L., Peterson, C. B., ... Mitchell, J. E. (2011). Eating disorder symptomatology in normal-weight vs. obese individuals with binge eating disorder. *Obesity*, *19*(7), 1515–1518. doi: 10.1038/oby.2011.24

Goracci, A., di Volo, S., Casamassima, F., Bolognesi, S., Benbow, J., & Fagiolini, A. (2015). Pharmacotherapy of Binge-Eating Disorder. *Journal of Addiction Medicine*, *9*(1), 1–19. doi: 10.1097/ADM.0000000000000089

Gorwood, P., Kipman, A., & Foulon, C. (2003). The human genetics of anorexia nervosa. *European Journal of Pharmacology*, *480*(1–3), 163–170.

Grilo, C. M., Crosby, R. D., Wilson, G. T., & Masheb, R. M. (2012). 12-Month follow-up of fluoxetine and cognitive behavioral therapy for binge eating disorder. *Journal of Consulting and Clinical Psychology*, *80*(6), 1108–1113.

Grilo, C. M., Masheb, R. M., & Crosby, R. D. (2012). Predictors and moderators of response to cognitive behavioral therapy and medication for the treatment of binge eating disorder. *Journal of Consulting and Clinical Psychology*, *80*(5), 897–906. doi: 10.1037/a0027001

Grilo, C. M., Masheb, R. M., & White, M. A. (2010). Significance of overvaluation of shape/weight in binge-eating disorder: Comparative study with overweight and bulimia nervosa. *Obesity*, *18*(3), 499–504. doi: 10.1038/oby.2009.280

Grilo, C. M., Masheb, R. M., White, M. A., Gueorguieva, R., Barnes, R. D., Walsh, B. T., ... Garcia, R. (2014). Treatment of binge eating disorder in racially and ethnically diverse obese patients in primary care: Randomized placebo-controlled clinical trial of self-help and medication. *Behaviour Research and Therapy*, *58*, 1–9. doi: 10.1016/j.brat.2014.04.002

Grilo, C. M., Masheb, R. M., Wilson, G. T., Gueorguieva, R., & White, M. A. (2011). Cognitive-behavioral therapy, behavioral weight loss, and sequential treatment for obese patients with binge eating disorder: A randomized controlled trial. *Journal of Consulting and Clinical Psychology*, *79*(5), 675–685. doi: 10.1037/a0025049

Grilo, C. M., White, M. A., Gueorguieva, R., Wilson, G. T., & Masheb, R. M. (2013). Predictive significance of the overvaluation of shape/weight in obese patients with binge eating disorder: Findings from a randomized controlled trial with 12-month follow-up. *Psychological Medicine*, *43*(6), 1335–1344. doi: 10.1017/S0033291712002097

Grilo, C. M., White, M. A., & Masheb, R. M. (2009). DSM-IV psychiatric disorder comorbidity and its correlates in binge eating disorder. *International*

Journal of Eating Disorders, *42*(3), 228–234. doi: 10.1002/eat.20599

Grilo, C. M., White, M. A., Masheb, R. M., & Gueorguieva, R. (2015). Predicting meaningful outcomes to medication and self-help treatments for binge-eating disorder in primary care: The significance of early rapid response. *Journal of Consulting and Clinical Psychology*, *83*(2), 387–394.

Guarda, A. S., Redgrave, G. W., & Dressler, D. D. (2012). Eating disorders. In S. C. McKean, J. J. Ross, D. D. Dressler, D. J. Brotman, & J. S. Ginsberg (Eds.), *Principles and practice of hospital medicine* (pp. 1908–1914). New York, NY: McGraw-Hill.

Gull, W. (1874). Anorexia nervosa (apepsia hysterica, anorexia hysterica). *Transactions of the Clinical Society of London*, *7*, 222–228.

Haiman, C., & Devlin, M. J. (1999). Binge eating before the onset of dieting: A distinct subgroup of bulimia nervosa? *International Journal of Eating Disorders*, *25*(2), 151–157. doi: 10.1002/(SICI)1098-108X(199903)25:2<151::AID-EAT4>3.0.CO;2-5

Halfon, O., Bizouard, P., Loas, G., Corcos, M., Jeammet, P., & Flament, M. F. (2015). Mood disorders in eating disorder patients: Prevalence and chronology of ONSET. *Journal of Affective Disorders*, *185*, 115–122. doi: 10.1016/j.jad.2015.06.039

Hannon-Engel, S. (2011). Regulating satiety in bulimia nervosa: The role of cholecystokinin. *Perspectives in Psychiatric Care*, *48*(1), 34–40.

Hannon-Engel, S. L., Filin, E., & Wolfe, B. E. (2013). CCK response in bulimia nervosa and following remission. *Physiology & Behavior*, *122*, 56–61. doi: 10.1016/j.physbeh.2013.08.014

Hausenblas, H. A., Campbell, A., Menzel, J. E., Doughty, J., Levine, M., & Thompson, J. K. (2013). Media effects of experimental presentation of the ideal physique on eating disorder symptoms: A meta-analysis of laboratory studies. *Clinical Psychology Review*, *33*(1), 168–181. doi: 10.1016/j.cpr.2012.10.011

Hay, P. J., & Claudino, A. M. (2012). Clinical psychopharmacology of eating disorders: A research update. *International Journal of Neuropsychopharmacology*, *15*(4), 209–222. doi: 10.1017/S1461145711000460

Hay, P. J., Claudino, A. M., Smith, C. A, Touyz, S., Lujic, S., & Madden, S. (2013). Inpatient versus outpatient care, partial hospitalisation and wait-list for people with eating disorders. *Cochrane Database of Systematic Reviews*, *2013*(12), 1–26. doi: 10.1002/14651858.CD010827

Hay, P., Girosi, F., & Mond, J. (2015). Prevalence and sociodemographic correlates of DSM-5 eating disorders in the Australian population. *Journal of Eating Disorders*, *3*(1), 19. doi: 10.1186/s40337-015-0056-0

Hay, P. J., Touyz, S., & Sud, R. (2012). Treatment for severe and enduring anorexia nervosa: A review. *Australian and New Zealand Journal of Psychiatry*, *46*(12), 1136–1144. doi: 10.1177/00048674 12450469

Hepworth, N., & Paxton, S. J. (2007). Pathways to help-seeking in bulimia nervosa and binge eating problems: A concept mapping approach. *International Journal of Eating Disorders*, *40*(6), 493–504.

Herzog, D. B., Dorer, D. J., Keel, P. K., Selwyn, S. E., Ekeblad, E. R., Flores, A. T., … Keller, M. B. (1999). Recovery and relapse in anorexia and bulimia nervosa: A 7.5-year follow-up study. *Journal of the American Academy of Child & Adolescent Psychiatry*, *38*(7), 829–837.

Hilbert, A., Bishop, M. E., Stein, R. I., Tanofsky-Kraff, M., Swenson, A. K., Welch, R. R., & Wilfley, D. E. (2012). Long-term efficacy of psychological treatments for binge eating disorder. *British Journal of Psychiatry*, *200*(3), 232–237. doi: 10.1192/bjp.bp.110.089664

Hilbert, A., Pike, K. M., Goldschmidt, A. B., Wilfley, D. E., Fairburn, C. G., Dohm, F.-A., … Striegel Weissman, R. (2014). Risk factors across the eating disorders. *Psychiatry Research*, *220*, 500–506. doi: 10.1016/j.psychres.2014.05.054

Hilbert, A., & Tuschen-Caffier, B. (2007). Maintenance of binge eating through negative mood: A naturalistic comparison of binge eating disorder and bulimia nervosa. *International Journal of Eating Disorders*, *40*(6), 521–530.

Hill, D. M., Craighead, L. W., & Safer, D. L. (2011). Appetite-focused dialectical behavior therapy for the treatment of binge eating with purging: A preliminary trial. *International Journal of Eating Disorders*, *44*(3), 249–261.

Hoek, H. W. (2006). Incidence, prevalence and mortality of anorexia nervosa and other eating disorders. *Current Opinion in Psychiatry*, *19*, 389–394.

Hudson, J. I., Coit, C. E., Lalonde, J. K., & Pope Harrison, G. J. (2010). By how much will the proposed new DSM-5 criteria increase the prevalence of binge eating disorder? *International Journal of Eating Disorders*, *45*(1), 139–141. doi: 10.1002/eat.20890

Hudson, J. I., Hiripi, E., Pope Harrison, G. J., & Kessler, R. C. (2007). The prevalence and correlates of eating disorders in the National Comorbidity Survey Replication. *Biological Psychiatry*, *61*(3), 348–358. Retrieved from http://linkinghub.elsevier.com/retrieve/pii/S0006322306004744

Hund, A. R., & Espelage, D. L. (2005). Childhood sexual abuse, disordered eating, alexithymia, and general distress: A mediation model. *Journal of Consulting Psychology*, *52*, 559–573.

Iacovino, J. M., Gredysa, D. M., Altman, M., & Wilfley, D. E. (2012). Psychological treatments for binge eating disorder. *Current Psychiatry Reports*, *14*(4), 432–446.

Jacobi, C., Hayward, C., de Zwaan, M., Kraemer, H. C., & Agras, W. S. (2004). Coming to terms with risk factors for eating disorders: Application of risk terminology and suggestions for a general taxonomy. *Psychological Bulletin*, *130*, 19–65.

James, R. (1743). *A medical dictionary*. London, England: Osborne.

Jennings, K. M., Kelly-Weeder, S., & Wolfe, B. E. (2015). Binge eating among racial minority groups in the United States: An integrative review. *Journal of the American Psychiatric Nurses Association*, *21*(2), 117–125. doi: 10.1177/1078390315581923

Katerndahl, D., Burge, S., & Kellogg, N. (2005). Predictors of development of adult psychopathology in female victims of childhood sexual abuse. *Journal of Nervous and Mental Disease*, *193*, 258–264.

Kaye, W. H., Bulik, C. M., Thornton, L., Barbarich, N., & Masters, K. (2004). Comorbidity of anxiety disorders with anorexia and bulimia nervosa. *American Journal of Psychiatry*, *161*(12), 2215–2221. doi: 10.1176/appi.ajp.161.12.2215

Kaye, W. H., Grendall, K., & Strober, M. (1998). Serotonin neuronal function and selective serotonin reuptake inhibitor treatment in anorexia nervosa. *Biological Psychiatry*, *44*, 825–838.

Kaye, W. H., Nagata, T., Weltzin, T., Hsu, B., Sokol, M., McConaha, C., ... Deep, D. (2001). Double-blind placebo controlled administration of fluoxetine in restricting and restricting-purging type anorexia nervosa. *Biological Psychiatry*, *49*, 644–652.

Kaye, W., Strober, M., & Jimerson, D. (2008). The neurobiology of eating disorders. In D. S. Charney & E. J. Nestler (Eds.), *The neurobiology of mental illness* (3rd ed., pp. 1349–1369). New York, NY: Oxford University Press.

Kaye, W. H., Weltzin, T. E., Hsu, L. K. G., McConaha, C. W., & Bolton, B. (1993). Amount of calories retained after binge eating and vomiting. *American Journal of Psychiatry*, *150*, 969. Retrieved from http://journals.psychiatryonline.org/data/Journals/AJP/3600/969.pdf

Keel, P. K., & Brown, T. A. (2010). Update on course and outcome in eating disorders. *International Journal of Eating Disorders*, *43*(3), 195–204. Retrieved from http://www.ncbi.nlm.nih.gov/pubmed/20186717

Keel, P. K., Brown, T. A., Holland, L. A., & Bodell, L. P. (2012). Empirical classification of eating disorders. *Annual Review of Clinical Psychology*, *8*(1): 381–404.

Keel, P. K., & Forney, K. J. (2013). Psychosocial risk factors for eating disorders. *International Journal of Eating Disorders*, *46*(5), 433–439. doi: 10.1002/eat.22094

Keel, P. K., & Heatherton, T. F. (2010). Weight suppression predicts maintenance and onset of bulimic syndromes at 10-year follow-up. *Journal of Abnormal Psychology*, *119*(2), 268–275. doi: 10.1037/a0019190

Keel, P. K., Mitchell, J. E., Miller, K. B., Davis, T. L., & Crow, S. J. (1999). Long-term outcome of bulimia nervosa. *Archives of General Psychiatry*, *56*(1), 63–69.

Keski-Rahkonen, A., Hoek, H. W., Linna, M. S., Raevuori, A., Sihvola, E., Bulik, C. M., ... Kaprio, J. (2009). Incidence and outcomes of bulimia nervosa: A nationwide population-based study. *Psychological Medicine*, *39*(5), 823–831. doi: 10.1017/S0033291708003942

Kessler, R. C., Berglund, P. A., Chiu, W. T., Deitz, A. C., Hudson, J. I., Shahly, V., ... Xavier, M. (2013). The prevalence and correlates of binge eating disorder in the World Health Organization World Mental Health Surveys. *Biological Psychiatry*, *73*(9), 904–914. doi: 10.1016/j.biopsych.2012.11.020

Killen, J. D., Barr Taylor, C., Hayward, C., Farish Haydel, K., Wilson, D. M., Hammer, L., ... Strachowski, D. (1996). Weight concerns influence the development of eating disorders: A 4-year prospective study. *Journal of Consulting and Clinical Psychology*, *64*, 936–940.

Kjelsås, E., Børsting, I., & Gudde, C. B. (2004). Antecedents and consequences of binge eating episodes in women with an eating disorder. *Eating and Weight Disorders, 9*(1), 7–15.

Klein, D. A., & Walsh, B. T. (2004). Eating disorders: Clinical features and pathophysiology. *Physiology and Behavior, 81*, 359–374.

Kluck, A. S. (2008). Family factors in the development of disordered eating: Integrating dynamic and behavioral explanations. *Eating Behaviors, 9*(4), 471–483. doi: 10.1016/j.eatbeh.2008.07.006

Kluck, A. S. (2010). Family influence on disordered eating: The role of body image dissatisfaction. *Body Image, 7*(1), 8–14. doi: 10.1016/j.bodyim.2009.09.009

Klump, K. L., Burt, S. A., McGue, M., Iacono, W. G., & Wade, T. M. (2010). Age differences in genetic and environmental influences on weight and shape concerns. *International Journal of Eating Disorders, 43*(8), 679–688. doi: 10.1002/eat.20772

Klump, K. L., & Culbert, K. M. (2007). Molecular genetic studies of eating disorders: Current status and future directions. *Current Directions in Psychological Science, 16*(1), 37–41.

Klump, K. L., Culbert, K. M., Slane, J. D., Burt, S. A., Sisk, C. L., & Nigg, J. T. (2012). The effects of puberty on genetic risk for disordered eating: Evidence for sex difference. *Psychological Medicine, 42*(3), 627–638

Klump, K. L., Hildebrandt, B. A., O'Connor, S. M., Keel, P. K., Neale, M., Sisk, C. L., … Burt, S. A. (2015). Changes in genetic risk for emotional eating across the menstrual cycle: A longitudinal study. *Psychological Medicine, 45*(15), 3227–3237.

Klump, K. L., Keel, P. K., Sisk, C. L., & Burt, S. A. (2010). Preliminary evidence that estradiol moderates genetic influences on disordered eating attitudes and behaviors during puberty. *Psychological Medicine, 40*(10), 1745–1753.

Klump, K. L. (2013). Puberty as a critical risk period for eating disorders: A review of human and animal studies. *Hormones and Behavior, 64*(2), 399–410.

Lasègue, E. (1883). De l'anorexie hystérique. *Archives Générales de Medecine, 21*, 384–403.

Lask, B. (2006). Functional neuroimaging in early-onset anorexia nervosa. *International Journal of Eating Disorders, 37*, S49–S51.

Lavender, J. M., Utzinger, L. M., Cao, L., Wonderlich, S. A., Engel, S. G., Mitchell, J. E., & Crosby, R. D. (2015). Reciprocal associations between negative affect, binge eating, and purging in the natural environment in women with bulimia nervosa. *Journal*

of *Abnormal Psychology*. Advance online publication. doi: 10.1037/abn0000135

Lázaro, L., Andrés, S., Calvo, A., Cullell, C., Moreno, E., Plana, M. T., … Castro-Fornieles, J. (2013). Normal gray and white matter volume after weight restoration in adolescents with anorexia nervosa. *International Journal of Eating Disorders, 46*(8), 841–848. doi: 10.1002/eat.22161

Le Grange, D., Accurso, E. C., Lock, J., Agras, S., & Bryson, S. W. (2014). Early weight gain predicts outcome in two treatments for adolescent anorexia nervosa. *International Journal of Eating Disorders, 47*(2), 124–129.

Le Grange, D., Crosby, R., Rathouz, P. J., & Leventhal, B. L. (2007). A randomized comparison of family-based treatment and supportive psychotherapy for adolescent bulimia nervosa. *Archives of General Psychiatry, 64*(9), 1049–1056.

Le Grange, D., Fitzsimmons-Craft, E. E., Crosby, R. D., Hay, P., Lacey, H., Bamford, B., … Touyz, S. (2014). Predictors and moderators of outcome for severe and enduring anorexia nervosa. *Behaviour Research and Therapy, 56*, 91–98. doi: 10.1016/j.brat.2014.03.006

Le Grange, D., & Lock, J. (2005). The dearth of psychological treatment studies for anorexia nervosa. *International Journal of Eating Disorders, 37*, 79–81.

Le Grange, D., & Lock, J. (2007). *Treating bulimia nervosa in adolescents*. New York, NY: Guilford Press.

Le Grange, D., Lock, J., Accurso, E. C., Agras, S. W., Darcy, A., Forsberg, S., & Bryson, S. W. (2014). Relapse and remission at two- to four-year follow-up in two treatments for adolescent anorexia nervosa. *Journal of the American Academy of Child & Adolescent Psychiatry, 53*(11), 1162–1167.

Le Grange, D., Lock, J., Agras, W. S., Bryson, S. W., & Jo, B. (2015). Randomized clinical trial of family-based treatment and cognitive-behavioral therapy for adolescent bulimia nervosa. *Journal of the American Academy of Child & Adolescent Psychiatry, 54*(11), 886-894.

Le Grange, D., Lock, J., Agras, W. S., Moye, A., Bryson, S. W., Jo, B., & Kraemer, H. C. (2012). Moderators and mediators of remission in family-based treatment and adolescent focused therapy for anorexia nervosa. *Behaviour Research and Therapy, 50*(2), 85–92. doi: 10.1016/j.brat.2011.11.003

Lebow, J., Sim, L. A., & Kransdorf, L. N. (2014). Prevalence of a history of overweight and obesity in adolescents with restrictive eating disorders.

Journal of Adolescent Health, *56*(1), 19–24. doi: 10.1016/j.jadohealth.2014.06.005

Leehr, E. J., Krohmer, K., Schag, K., Dresler, T., Zipfel, S., & Giel, K. E. (2015). Emotion regulation model in binge eating disorder and obesity—a systematic review. *Neuroscience and Biobehavioral Reviews*, *49*, 125–34. doi: 10.1016/j.neubiorev.2014.12.008

Leon, G. R., Fulkerson, J. A., Perry, C. L., & Early-Zald, M. B. (1995). Prospective analysis of personality and behavioral vulnerabilities and gender influences in the later development of disordered eating. *Journal of Abnormal Psychology*, *104*, 140–149.

Liddell, H. G., & Scott, R. (1972). *Greek and English lexicon*. Oxford, England: Clarendon Press.

Lilenfeld, L. R. R., Wonderlich, S., Riso, L. P., Crosby, R., & Mitchell, J. (2006). Eating disorders and personality: A methodological and empirical review. *Clinical Psychology Review*, *26*, 299–320.

Linehan, M. M. (1993). *Cognitive-behavioral treatment of borderline personality disorder*. New York, NY: Guilford Press.

Lipsman, N., & Lozano, A. M. (2014). Targeting emotion circuits with deep brain stimulation in refractory anorexia nervosa. *Neuropsychopharmacology*, *39*(1), 250–251. doi: 10.1038/npp.2013.244

Lock, J. (2003). A health services perspective on anorexia nervosa. *Eating Disorders*, *11*, 197–208.

Lock, J. (2005). Adjusting cognitive behavior therapy for adolescents with bulimia nervosa: Results of case series. *American Journal of Psychotherapy*, *59*(3), 267–281.

Lock, J., Couturier, J., & Agras, W. S. (2006). Comparison of long-term outcomes in adolescents with anorexia nervosa treated with family therapy. *American Journal of Child and Adolescent Psychiatry*, *45*, 666–672.

Lock, J., Garrett, A., Beenhakker, J., & Reiss, A. (2011). Aberrant brain activation during a response inhibition task in adolescent eating disorder subtypes. *American Journal of Psychiatry*, *168*, 55–64.

Lock, J., Le Grange, D., Agras, W. S., & Dare, C. (2001). *Treatment manual for anorexia nervosa: A family-based approach*. New York, NY: Guilford Press.

Lock, J., Le Grange, D., Agras, W. S., Moye, A., Bryson, S. W., & Jo, B. (2010). A randomized clinical trial comparing family-based treatment to adolescent focused individual therapy for adolescents with

anorexia nervosa. *Archives of General Psychiatry*, *67*, 1025–1032.

Lynch, T. R. (In press). *Radically open dialectical behavior therapy for disorders of over-control*. New York, NY: Guilford Press.

Lynch, T. R., Gray, K. L. H., Hempel, R. J., Titley, M., Chen, E. Y., & O'Mahen, H. A. (2013). Radically open dialectical behavior therapy for adult anorexia nervosa: Feasibility and outcomes from an outpatient program. *BMC Psychiatry*, *13*(293), 1–17.

Mainz, V., Schulte-Rüther, M., Fink, G. R., Herpertz-Dahlmann, B., & Konrad, K. (2012). Structural brain abnormalities in adolescent anorexia nervosa before and after weight recovery and associated hormonal changes. *Psychosomatic Medicine*, *74*(6), 574–582. doi: 10.1097/PSY.0b013e31824ef10e

Marcus, M. D., Moulton, M. M., & Greeno, C. G. (1995). Binge eating onset in obese patients with binge eating disorder. *Addictive Behaviors*, *20*(6), 747–755. Retrieved from http://www.ncbi.nlm.nih.gov/pubmed/8820527

Marek, R. J., Ben-Porath, Y. S., Ashton, K., & Heinberg, L. J. (2014). Impact of using DSM-5 criteria for diagnosing binge eating disorder in bariatric surgery candidates: Change in prevalence rate, demographic characteristics, and scores on the Minnesota Multiphasic Personality Inventory-2 Restructured Form (MMPI-2-RF). *International Journal of Eating Disorders*, *47*(5), 553–557. doi: 10.1002/eat.22268

Marques, L., Alegria, M., Becker, A. E., Chen, C., Fang, A., Chosak, A., & Diniz, J. B. (2010). Comparative prevalence, correlates of impairment, and service utilization for eating disorders across US ethnic groups: Implications for reducing ethnic disparities in health care access for eating disorders. *International Journal of Eating Disorders*, *44*(5), 412–420. doi: 10.1002/eat.20787

Marsh, R., Maia, T., & Peterson B. (2009). Functional disturbances within frontostriatal circuits across multiple childhood psychopathologies. *American Journal of Psychiatry*, *166*, 664–674.

Martinez, M. A., & Craighead, L. W. (2015). Toward person(ality)-centered treatment: How consideration of personality and individual differences in anorexia nervosa may improve treatment outcome. *Clinical Psychology: Science and Practice*, *22*(3), 296–314.

Marzola, E., Desedime, N., Giovannone, C., Amianto, F., Fassino, S., & Abbate-Daga, G. (2015). Atypical antipsychotics as augmentation therapy in anorexia nervosa. *Plos One*, *10*(4), e0125569. doi: 10.1371/journal.pone.0125569

Masheb, R. M., White, M. A., & Grilo, C. M. (2013). Substantial weight gains are common prior to treatment-seeking in obese patients with binge eating disorder. *Comprehensive Psychiatry*, *54*(7), 880–884. doi: 10.1016/j.comppsych.2013.03.017

Maslen, H., Pugh, J., & Savulescu, J. (2015). The ethics of deep brain stimulation for the treatment of anorexia nervosa. *Neuroethics*, *8*, 215–230. doi: 10.1007/s12152-015-9240-9

Mattar, L., Thiébaud, M. R., Huas, C., Cebula, C., & Godart, N. (2012). Depression, anxiety and obsessive-compulsive symptoms in relation to nutritional status and outcome in severe anorexia nervosa. *Psychiatry Research*, *200*(2–3), 513–517. doi: 10.1016/j.psychres.2012.04.032

McElroy, S. L., Guerdjikova, A. I., Mori, N., & O'Melia, A. M. (2012). Current pharmacotherapy options for bulimia nervosa and binge eating disorder. *Expert Opinion on Pharmacotherapy*, *13*, 2015–2026. doi: 10.1517/14656566.2012.721781

McIntosh, V. W., Jordan, J., Carter, F. A., Luty, S. E., McKenzie, J. M., Bulik, C. M., ... Joyce, P. R. (2005). Three psychotherapies for anorexia nervosa: A randomized, controlled trial. *American Journal of Psychiatry*, *162*, 741–747.

Meads, C., Gold, L., & Burls, A. (2001). How effective is outpatient compared to inpatient care for treatment of anorexia nervosa? A systematic review. *European Eating Disorders Review*, *9*, 229–241.

Mehler, P. S. (2010). Medical complications of bulimia nervosa and their treatments. *International Journal of Eating Disorders*. Advance online publication. doi: 10.1002/eat.20825

Miniati, M., Mauri, M., Ciberti, A., Mariani, M. G., Marazziti, D., & Dell'Osso, L. (2015). Psychopharmacological options for adult patients with anorexia nervosa. *CNS Spectrums*, *21*, 134–142. doi: 10.1017/S1092852914000790

Minuchin, S., Rosman, B., & Baker, I. (1978). *Psychosomatic families: Anorexia nervosa in context*. Cambridge, MA: Harvard University Press.

Mitchell, J. E. (2015). Medical comorbidity and medical complications associated with binge-eating disorder. *International Journal of Eating Disorders*. Advance online publication. doi: 10.1002/eat.22452

Mitchell, J. E., Agras, S., & Wonderlich, S. (2007). Treatment of bulimia nervosa: Where are we and where are we going? *International Journal of Eating Disorders*, *40*(2), 95–101.

Mitchell, J. E., & Crow, S. (2006). Medical complications of anorexia nervosa and bulimia nervosa. *Current Opinion in Psychiatry*, *19*, 438–443.

Mitchell, J. E., Hatsukami, D., Eckert, E. D., & Pyle, R. L. (1985). Characteristics of 275 patients with bulimia. *American Journal of Psychiatry*, *142*, 482–485.

Mitchell, K. S., Mazzeo, S. E., Schlesinger, M. R., Brewerton, T. D., & Smith, B. N. (2011). Comorbidity of partial and subthreshold PTSD among men and women with eating disorders in the National Comorbidity Survey–Replication Study. *International Journal of Eating Disorders*, *45*(3), 307–315.

Mitka, M. (2011). Report weighs options for bulimia nervosa treatment. *JAMA*, *305*(9), 875.

Mond, J. M., Hay, P. J., Darby, A., Paxton, S. J., Quirk, F., Buttner, P., ... Rodgers, B. (2009). Women with bulimic eating disorders: When do they receive treatment for an eating problem? *Journal of Consulting and Clinical Psychology*, *77*(5), 835–844.

Mond, J. M., Hay, P. J., Rodgers, B., & Owen, C. (2007). Health service utilization for eating disorders: Findings from a community-based study. *International Journal of Eating Disorders*, *40*(5), 399–408.

Munsch, S., Meyer, A. H., & Biedert, E. (2012). Efficacy and predictors of long-term treatment success for Cognitive-Behavioral Treatment and Behavioral Weight-Loss-Treatment in overweight individuals with binge eating disorder. *Behaviour Research and Therapy*, *50*(12), 775–785. Retrieved from http://linkinghub.elsevier.com/retrieve/pii/S0005796712001362

Munsch, S., Meyer, A. H., Quartier, V., & Wilhelm, F. H. (2012). Binge eating in binge eating disorder: A breakdown of emotion regulatory process? *Psychiatry Research*, *195*(3), 118–124. Retrieved from http://linkinghub.elsevier.com/retrieve/pii/S0165178111005208

Murphy, R., Straebler, S., Basden, S., Cooper, Z., & Fairburn, C. G. (2012). Interpersonal psychotherapy for eating disorders. *Clinical Psychology & Psychotherapy*, *19*(2), 150–158.

Murphy, R., Straebler, S., Cooper, Z., & Fairburn, C. G. (2010). Cognitive behavioral therapy for eating disorders. *Psychiatric Clinics of North America*, *33*(3), 611–627.

Murray, S. B., Anderson, L., Cusack, A., Nakamura, T., Rockwell, R., Griffiths, S., & Kaye, W. H. (2015). Integrating family-based treatment and dialectical behavior therapy for adolescent bulimia nervosa: Preliminary outcomes of an open pilot trial. *Eating Disorders, 23*(4), 336–344. doi: 10.1080/10640266 .2015.1044345

Nakazato, M., Hashimoto, K., Shimizu, E., Niitsu, T., & Iyo, M. (2012). Possible involvement of brain-derived neurotrophic factor in eating disorders. *IUBMB Life, 64*(5), 355–361.

Nathan, P. J., & Bullmore, E. T. (2009). From taste hedonics to motivational drive: Central μ-opioid receptors and binge-eating behaviour. *International Journal of Neuropsychopharmacology, 12*(7), 995–1008.

Nathan, P. J., O'Neill, B. V., Mogg, K., Bradley, B. P., Beaver, J., Bani, M., ... Bullmore, E. T. (2012). The effects of the dopamine D₃ receptor antagonist GSK598809 on attentional bias to palatable food cues in overweight and obese subjects. *International Journal of Neuropsychopharmacology, 15*(2), 149–161.

National Collaborating Centre for Mental Health. (2004). *Eating disorders: Core interventions in the treatment and management of anorexia nervosa, bulimia nervosa, and related eating disorders.* Leicester, UK: British Psychological Society.

Neumark-Sztainer, D., Wall, M., Larson, N. I., Eisenberg, M. E., & Loth, K. (2011). Dieting and disordered eating behaviors from adolescence to young adulthood: Findings from a 10-year longitudinal study. *Journal of the American Dietetic Association, 111*(7), 1004–1011. doi: 10.1016/j.jada.2011.04.012

Neumark-Sztainer, D., Wall, M., Story, M., & Standish, A. R. (2012). Dieting and unhealthy weight control behaviors during adolescence: Associations with 10-year changes in body mass index. *Journal of Adolescent Health, 50*(1), 80–86. doi: 10.1016/ j.jadohealth.2011.05.010

Nicholls, D., & Bryant-Waugh, R. (2003). Children and adolescents. In J. L. Treasure, U. Schmidt, & E. van Furth (Eds.), *Handbook of eating disorders* (2nd ed., pp. 415–434). Chichester, England: Wiley.

O'Brien, K. M., & Vincent, N. K. (2003). Psychiatric comorbidity in anorexia and bulimia nervosa: Nature, prevalence, and causal relationships. *Clinical Psychology Review, 23*, 57–74.

Olatunji, B. O., Broman-Fulks, J. J., Ciesielski, B. G., Zawilinski, L. L., Shewmaker, S., & Wall, D. (2012). A taxometric investigation of the latent structure of eating disorders. *Psychiatry Research, 197*(1–2), 97–102.

Olmsted, M. (2002). Day hospital treatment of anorexia nervosa and bulimia nervosa. In C. G. Fairburn & K. Brownell (Eds.), *Eating disorders and obesity: A comprehensive review* (pp. 330–334). New York, NY: Guilford Press.

Ostlund, H., Keller, E., & Hurd, Y. L. (2003). Estrogen receptor gene expression in relation to neuropsychiatric disorders. *Annals of the New York Academy of Sciences, 1007*, 54–63.

Palavras, M. A., Hay, P., Touyz, S., Sainsbury, A., da Luz, F., Swinbourne, J., ... Claudino, A. (2015). Comparing cognitive behavioural therapy for eating disorders integrated with behavioural weight loss therapy to cognitive behavioural therapy-enhanced alone in overweight or obese people with bulimia nervosa or binge eating disorder: Study protocol for a randomised controlled trial. *Trials, 16*(1), 578. doi: 10.1186/s13063-015-1079-1

Peebles, R., Wilson, J., & Lock, J. (2006). How do children with eating disorders differ from adolescents with eating disorders at initial evaluation? *Journal of Adolescent Health, 39*, 800–805.

Peterson, C. B., Crosby, R. D., Wonderlich, S. A., Joiner, T., Crow, S. J., Mitchell, J. E., ... Le Grange, D. (2007). Psychometric properties of the Eating Disorder Examination-Questionnaire: Factor structure and internal consistency. *International Journal of Eating Disorders, 4*, 386–389.

Pike, K. M., Dunne, P. E., & Addai, E. (2013). Expanding the boundaries: Reconfiguring the demographics of the "typical" eating disordered patient. *Current Psychiatry Reports, 15*(11), 411. doi: 10.1007/s11920-013-0411-2

Pinheiro, A. P., Bulik, C. M., Thornton, L. M., Sullivan, P. F., Root, T. L., Bloss, C. S., ... Woodside, D. B. (2010). Association study of 182 candidate genes in anorexia nervosa. *American Journal of Medical Genetics Part B: Neuropsychiatric Genetics, 153B*(5), 1070–1080.

Polivy, J., & Herman, C. P. (2002). Causes of eating disorders. *Annual Review of Psychology, 53*, 187–213.

Potier, M., Darcel, N., & Tomé, D. (2009). Protein, amino acids and the control of food intake. *Current Opinion in Clinical Nutrition and Metabolic Care, 12*(1), 54–58.

Racine, S. E., Burt, S. A., & Klump, K. L. (2011). Dietary restraint moderates genetic risk for binge eating. *Journal of Abnormal Psychology, 120*, 119–128.

Rask-Andersen, M., Olszewski, P. K., Levine, A. S., & Schiöth, H. B. (2010). Molecular mechanisms underlying anorexia nervosa: Focus on human gene association studies and systems controlling food intake. *Brain Research, 62*(2), 147–164.

Rastram, M., Bjure, J., & Vestergren, E. (2001). Regional cerebral blood flow in weight-restored anorexia nervosa: A preliminary study. *Developmental Medicine and Child Neurology, 43*, 239–242.

Reas, D. L., & Grilo, C. M. (2015). Pharmacological treatment of binge eating disorder: Update review and synthesis. *Expert Opinion on Pharmacotherapy, 16*(10), 1–16. doi: 10.1517/14656566.2015.1053465

Reas, D. L., Whisenhunt, B., & Netemeyer, R. (2002). Development of the Body Checking Questionnaire: A self-report measure of body checking behaviors. *International Journal of Eating Disorders, 31*(3), 324–333.

Rieger, E., Van Buren, D. J., Bishop, M., Tanofsky-Kraff, M., Welch, R., & Wilfley, D. E. (2010). An eating disorder-specific model of interpersonal psychotherapy (IPT-ED): Causal pathways and treatment implications. *Clinical Psychology Review, 30*(4), 400–410.

Rigamonti, A. E., Sartorio, A., Scognamiglio, P., Bini, S., Monteleone, A. M., Mastromo, D., … Monteleone, P. (2014). Different effects of cholestyramine on postprandial secretions of cholecystokinin and peptide YY in women with bulimia nervosa. *Neuropsychobiology, 70*(4), 228–234. doi: 10.1159/000368160

Rø, Ø., Martinsen, E. W., Hoffart, A., Sexton, H., & Rosenvinge, J. H. (2005). The interaction of personality disorders and eating disorders: A two-year prospective study of patients with longstanding eating disorders. *International Journal of Eating Disorders, 38*(2), 106–111. doi: 10.1002/eat.20166

Rohde, P., Stice, E., & Marti, C. N. (2015). Development and predictive effects of eating disorder risk factors during adolescence: Implications for prevention efforts. *International Journal of Eating Disorders, 48*(2), 187–198. doi: 10.1002/eat.22270

Russell, G. (1979). Bulimia nervosa: An ominous variant of anorexia nervosa. *Psychological Medicine, 9*, 429–448.

Safer, D. L., Telch, C. F., & Agras, W. S. (2001). Dialectical behavior therapy for bulimia nervosa. *American Journal of Psychiatry, 158*(4), 632–634. Retrieved from http://www.ncbi.nlm.nih.gov/pubmed/11282700

Schag, K., Leehr, E. J., Martus, P., Bethge, W., Becker, S., Zipfel, S., & Giel, K. E. (2015). Impulsivity-focused group intervention to reduce binge eating episodes in patients with binge eating disorder: Study protocol of the randomised controlled IMPULS trial. *BMJ Open, 5*(12), e009445. doi: 10.1136/bmjopen-2015-009445

Schapman-Williams, A. M., Lock, J., & Couturier, J. (2006). Cognitive-behavioral therapy for adolescents with binge eating syndromes: A case series. *International Journal of Eating Disorders, 39*(3), 252–255.

Schienle, A., Schafer, A., Hermann, A., & Vaitl, D. (2009). Binge-eating disorder: Reward sensitivity and brain activation to images of food. *Biological Psychiatry, 65*(8), 654–661.

Schizophrenia Working Group of the Psychiatric Genetics Consortium. (2014). Biological insights from 108 schizophrenia-associated genetic loci. *Nature, 511*(7510), 421–427.

Schmidt, U., Lee, S., Beecham, J., Perkins, S., Treasure, J., Yi, I., … Eisler, I. (2007). A randomized clinical trial of family therapy and cognitive behavioral therapy guided self-care for adolescent bulimia nervosa and related conditions. *American Journal of Psychiatry, 164*, 591–598.

Selvini Palazzoli, M. (1974). *Self-starvation: From the intrapsychic to the transpersonal approach*. London, England: Chaucer.

Shapiro, J. R., Woolson, S. L., Hamer, R. M., Kalarchian, M. A., Marcus, M. D., & Bulik, C. M. (2007). Evaluating binge eating disorder in children: Development of the Children's Binge Eating Disorder Scale (C-BEDS). *International Journal of Eating Disorders, 40*, 82–89.

Smink, F. R. E., van Hoeken, D., & Hoek, H. W. (2012). Epidemiology of eating disorders: Incidence, prevalence and mortality rates. *Current Psychiatry Reports, 14*(4), 406–414. Retrieved from http://www.springerlink.com/index/10.1007/s11920-012-0282-y

Smink, F. R. E., van Hoeken, D., Oldehinkel, A. J., & Hoek, H. W. (2014). Prevalence and severity of DSM-5 eating disorders in a community cohort of adolescents. *International Journal of Eating Disorders, 47*(6), 610–619. doi: 10.1002/eat.22316

Stein, R. I., Kenardy, J., Wiseman, C. V., Dounchis, J. Z., Arnow, B. A., & Wilfley, D. E. (2007). What's driving the binge in binge eating disorder? A prospective examination of precursors and consequences.

International Journal of Eating Disorders, 40(3), 195–203.

Steinglass, J. E., Albano, A. M., Simpson, H. B., Wang, Y., Zou, J., Attia, E., & Walsh, B. T. (2014). Confronting fear using exposure and response prevention for anorexia nervosa: A randomized controlled pilot study. *International Journal of Eating Disorders, 47*(2), 174–180. doi: 10.1002/eat.22214

Steinglass, J. E., Sysko, R., Glasofer, D., Albano, A. M., Simpson, H. B., & Walsh, B. T. (2010). Rationale for the application of exposure and response prevention to the treatment of anorexia nervosa. *International Journal of Eating Disorders.* Advance online publication. doi: 10.1002/eat.20784

Steinhausen, H. C. (2002). The outcome of anorexia nervosa in the 20th century. *American Journal of Psychiatry, 159*(8), 1284–1293.

Steinhausen, H. C., & Weber, S. (2009). The outcome of bulimia nervosa: Findings from one-quarter century of research. *American Journal of Psychiatry, 166*(12), 1331–1341. Retrieved from http://www.ncbi.nlm.nih.gov/pubmed/19884225

Stern, S. L., Dixon, K. N., Jones, D., Lake, M., Nemzer, E., & Sansone, R. (1989). Family environment in anorexia nervosa and bulimia. *International Journal of Eating Disorders, 8*(1), 25–31. doi: 10.1002/1098-108X(198901)8:1<25::AID-EAT2260080104>3.0.CO;2-S

Stice, E. (2002). Risk and maintenance factors for eating pathology: A meta-analytic review. *Psychological Bulletin, 128*(5), 825–848. doi: 10.1037//0033-2909.128.5.825

Stice, E., Burton, E. M., & Shaw, H. (2004). Prospective relations between bulimic pathology, depression, and substance abuse: Unpacking comorbidity in adolescent girls. *Journal of Consulting and Clinical Psychology, 72*(1), 62–71. doi: 10.1037/0022-006X.72.1.62

Stice, E., Marti, C. N., & Rohde, P. (2013). Prevalence, incidence, impairment, and course of the proposed *DSM-5* eating disorders diagnoses in an 8-year prospective community study of young women. *Journal of Abnormal Psychology, 122*(2), 445–457. doi: 10.1037/a0030679

Stice, E., Presnell, K., & Spangler, D. (2002). Risk factors for binge eating onset in adolescent girls: A 2-year prospective investigation. *Health Psychology, 21*, 131–138.

Stice, E., & Shaw, H. E. (2002). Role of body dissatisfaction in the onset and maintenance of eating pathology: A synthesis of research findings. *Journal of Psychosomatic Research, 53*, 985–993.

Stice, E., Spoor, S., Bohon, C., Veldhuizen, M. G., & Small, D. M. (2008). Relation of reward from food intake and anticipated food intake to obesity: A functional magnetic resonance imaging study. *Journal of Abnormal Psychology, 117*(4), 924–935.

Stice, E., Spoor, S., Ng, J., & Zald, D. H. (2009). Relation of obesity to consummatory and anticipatory food reward. *Physiology and Behavior, 97*(5), 551–560.

Stice, E., Yokum, S., Burger, K. S., Epstein, L. H., & Small, D. M. (2011). Youth at risk for obesity show greater activation of striatal and somatosensory regions to food. *Journal of Neuroscience, 31*(12), 4360–4366.

Striegel-Moore, R. H., Leslie, D., Petrill, S. A., Garvin, V., & Rosenheck, R. A. (2000). One-year use and cost of inpatient and outpatient services among female and male patients with an eating disorder: Evidence from a national database of health insurance claims. *International Journal of Eating Disorders, 27*, 381–389.

Striegel-Moore, R. H., Rosselli, F., Perrin, N., DeBar, L., Wilson, G. T., May, A., & Kraemer, H. C. (2009). Gender difference in the prevalence of eating disorder symptoms. *International Journal of Eating Disorders, 42*(5), 471–474. doi: 10.1002/eat.20625

Striegel-Moore, R. H., Wilson, G. T., DeBar, L., Perrin, N., Lynch, F., Rosselli, F., & Kraemer, H. C. (2010). Cognitive behavioral guided self-help for the treatment of recurrent binge eating. *Journal of Consulting and Clinical Psychology, 78*(3), 312–321.

Strober, M., Freeman, A., & Morrell, W. (1999). Atypical anorexia nervosa: Separation from typical cases in course and outcome in a long-term prospective study. *International Journal of Eating Disorders, 25*, 135–142.

Stunkard, A. J. (1959). Eating patterns and obesity. *Psychiatric Quarterly, 33*, 284–295.

Stunkard, A. J., Grace, W. J., & Wolff, H. G. (1955). The night-eating syndrome: A pattern of food intake among certain obese patients. *American Journal of Medicine, 19*, 78–86.

Suisman, J. L., & Klump, K. L. (2011). Genetic and neuroscientific perspectives on body image. In T. F. Cash & L. Smolak (Eds.), *Body image: A handbook of science, practice, and prevention* (pp. 29–38). New York, NY: Guilford Press.

Swanson, S. A. (2011). Prevalence and correlates of eating disorders in adolescents: Results from the National Comorbidity Survey Replication Adolescent Supplement. *Archives of General Psychiatry, 68*(7), 714. doi: 10.1001/archgenpsychiatry.2011.22

Swinbourne, J., Hunt, C., Abbott, M., Russell, J., St Clare, T., & Touyz, S. (2012). The comorbidity between eating disorders and anxiety disorders: Prevalence in an eating disorder sample and anxiety disorder sample. *Australian and New Zealand Journal of Psychiatry, 46*(2), 118–131. doi: 10.1177/0004867411432071

Sysko, R., Glasofer, D. R., Hildebrandt, T., Klimek, P., Mitchell, J. E., Berg, K. C., ... Walsh, B. T. (2015). The eating disorder assessment for DSM-5 (EDA-5): Development and validation of a structured interview for feeding and eating disorders. *International Journal of Eating Disorders, 48*(5), 452–463. doi: 10.1002/eat.22388

Tchanturia, K., Brecelj, M., Sanchez, P., Morris, R., Rabe-Hesketh, S., & Treasure, J. L. (2004). An examination of cognitive flexibility in eating disorders. *Journal of the International Neuropsychological Society, 10*, 1–8.

Tchanturia, K., Morris, R., Brecelj Anderluh, M., Collier, D. A., Nikolau, V., & Treasure, J. L. (2004). Set shifting in anorexia nervosa: An examination before and after weight gain in full recovery and the relationship to childhood and adult OCDP traits. *Journal of Psychiatric Research, 38*(5), 545–552.

Tchanturia, K., Morris, R., Surguladze, S., & Treasure, J. L. (2002). An examination of perceptual and cognitive set shifting tasks in acute anorexia nervosa and following recovery. *Journal of Eating and Weight Disorders, 7*, 312–316.

Tchanturia, K., Serpell, L., Troop, N. A., & Treasure, J. L. (2001). Perceptual illusions in eating disorders: Rigid and fluctuating styles. *Journal of Behavior Therapy and Experimental Psychiatry, 32*, 107–115

Telch, C. F., Agras, W. S., & Linehan, M. M. (2001). Dialectical behavior therapy for binge eating disorder. *Journal of Consulting and Clinical Psychology, 69*(6), 1061. Retrieved from http://psycnet.apa.org/journals/ccp/69/6/1061/

Thelen, M. H., Farmer, J., Wonderlich, S., & Smith, M. (1991). A revision of the bulimia test: The BULIT-R. *Psychological Assessment, 3*, 119–124.

Thoma, H. (1967). *Anorexia nervosa.* New York, NY: International Universities Press.

Thompson-Brenner, H., Franko, D. L., Thompson, D. R., Grilo, C. M., Boisseau, C. L., Roehrig, J. P., ... Masheb, R. (2013). Race/ethnicity, education, and treatment parameters as moderators and predictors of outcome in binge eating disorder. *Journal of Consulting and Clinical Psychology, 81*(4), 710–721. doi: 10.1037/a0032946

Thompson-Brenner, H., & Westen, D. (2005). Personality subtypes in eating disorders: Validation of a classification in a naturalistic sample. *British Journal of Psychiatry, 186*, 516–524. doi: 10.1192/bjp.186.6.516

Trace, S. E., Thornton, L. M., Root, T. L., Mazzeo, S. E., Lichtenstein, P., Pedersen, N. L., & Bulik, C. M. (2011). Effects of reducing the frequency and duration criteria for binge eating on lifetime prevalence of bulimia nervosa and binge eating disorder: Implications for DSM-5. *International Journal of Eating Disorders, 45*(4), 531–536. doi: 10.1002/eat.20955

Treasure, J., & Russell, G. (2011). The case for early intervention in anorexia nervosa: Theoretical exploration of maintaining factors. *British Journal of Psychiatry, 199*(1), 5–7. doi: 10.1192/bjp.bp.110.087585

Trummer, M., Eustacchio, S., Unger, F., Tillich, M., & Flaschka, G. (2002). Right hemispheric frontal lesions as a cause for anorexia nervosa report of three cases. *Acta Neurochirurgica (Wien), 144*, 797–801.

Turner, B. J., Claes, L., Wilderjans, T. F., Pauwels, E., Dierckx, E., Chapman, A. L., & Schoevaerts, K. (2014). Personality profiles in eating disorders: Further evidence of the clinical utility of examining subtypes based on temperament. *Psychiatry Research, 219*(1), 157–165. doi: 10.1016/j.psychres.2014.04.036

Turner, H., Marshall, E., Wood, F., Stopa, L., & Waller, G. (2016). CBT for eating disorders: The impact of early changes in eating pathology on later changes in personality pathology, anxiety and depression. *Behaviour Research and Therapy, 77*, 1–6. doi: 10.1016/j.brat.2015.11.011

Udo, T., McKee, S. A., White, M. A., Masheb, R. M., Barnes, R. D., & Grilo, C. M. (2014). Sex differences in biopsychosocial correlates of binge eating disorder: A study of treatment-seeking obese adults in primary care setting. *General Hospital Psychiatry, 35*(6), 587–591. doi: 10.1016/j.genhosppsych.2013.07.010

Uher, R., Murphy, T., Brammer, M. J., Dalgleish, T., Phillips, M. L., Ng, V. W., ... Treasure, J. (2004).

Medial prefrontal cortex activity associated with symptom provocation in eating disorders. *American Journal of Psychiatry, 161*(7), 1238–1246.

U.S. Food and Drug Administration. (2015). FDA expands use of Vyvanse to treat binge-eating disorder. [Press release]. Retrieved from http://www.fda .gov/NewsEvents/Newsroom/PressAnnouncements/ ucm432543.htm.

Vall, E., & Wade, T. D. (2015). Predictors of treatment outcome in individuals with eating disorders: A systematic review and meta-analysis. *International Journal of Eating Disorders*. Advance online publication. doi: 10.1002/eat.22411

Vanderlinden, J., Grave, R. D., Vandereycken, W., & Noorduin, C. (2001). Which factors do provoke binge-eating? An exploratory study in female students. *Eating Behavior, 2*(1), 79–83.

Vinai, P., Da Ros, A., Speciale, M., Gentile, N., Tagliabue, A., Vinai, P., ... Cardetti, S. (2015). Psychopathological characteristics of patients seeking for bariatric surgery, either affected or not by binge eating disorder following the criteria of the DSM IV TR and of the DSM 5. *Eating Behaviors, 16*, 1–4. doi: 10.1016/j.eatbeh.2014.10.004

Von Holle, A., Pinheiro, P., Thornton, L. M., Klump, K. L., Berrettini, W. H., Brandt, H., ... Bulik, C. M. (2008). Temporal patterns of recovery across eating disorders subtype. *Australian and New Zealand Journal of Psychiatry, 42*(2), 108–117.

Vrabel, K. R., Rø, Ø., Martinsen, E. W., Hoffart, A., & Rosenvinge, J. H. (2009). Five-year prospective study of personality disorders in adults with long-standing eating disorders. *International Journal of Eating Disorders*. Advance online publication. doi: 10.1002/eat.20662

Wagner, G., Penelo, E., Nobis, G., Mayrhofer, A., Wanner, C., Schau, J., ... Karwautz, A. (2015). Predictors for good therapeutic outcome and drop-out in technology assisted guided self-help in the treatment of bulimia nervosa and bulimia like phenotype. *European Eating Disorders Review, 23*(2), 163–169. doi: 10.1002/erv.2336

Wagner, G., Penelo, E., Wanner, C., Gwinner, P., Trofaier, M.-L., Imgart, H., ... Karwautz, A. F. K. (2013). Internet-delivered cognitive-behavioural therapy v. conventional guided self-help for bulimia nervosa: Long-term evaluation of a randomised controlled trial. *British Journal of Psychiatry, 202*(2), 135–141. doi: 10.1192/bjp.bp.111.098582

Wallin, U., Kronovall, P., & Majewski, M. (2000). Body awareness therapy in teenage anorexia nervosa: Outcome after 2 years. *European Eating Disorders Review, 8*, 19–30.

Walsh, B. T. (2013). The enigmatic persistence of anorexia nervosa. *American Journal of Psychiatry, 170*(5), 477–484. doi: 10.1176/appi.ajp.2012 .12081074

Walsh, B. T., Attia, E., Glasofer, D. R., & Sysko, R. (Eds.). (2015). *Handbook of assessment and treatment of eating disorders*. Arlington, VA: American Psychiatric Publishing.

Walsh, B. T., Kaplan, A. S., Attia, E., Olmsted, M., Parides, M., Carter, J., ... Rockert, W. (2006). Fluoxetine after weight restoration in anorexia nervosa: A randomized clinical trial. *JAMA, 295*, 2605–2612.

Wang, G. J., Geliebter, A., Volkow, N. D., Telang, F. W., Logan, J., Jayne, M. C., ... Fowler, J. S. (2011). Enhanced striatal dopamine release during food stimulation in binge eating disorder. *Obesity, 19*(8), 1601–1608.

Ward, A., Tiller, J., Treasure, J. L., & Russell, C. (2000). Eating disorders: Psyche or soma? *International Journal of Eating Disorders, 27*, 279–287.

Watson, H. J., & Bulik, C. M. (2013). Update on the treatment of anorexia nervosa: Review of clinical trials, practice guidelines and emerging interventions. *Psychological Medicine, 43*(12), 2477–2500. doi: 10.1017/S0033291712002620

Westen, D., & Harnden-Fischer, J. (2001). Personality profiles in eating disorders: Rethinking the distinction between axis I and axis II. *American Journal of Psychiatry, 158*(4), 547–562. Retrieved from http://journals.psychiatryonline.org/article.aspx? Volume=158&page=547&journalID=13

Wildes, J. E., Marcus, M. D., Cheng, Y., McCabe, E. B., & Gaskill, J. A. (2014). Emotion acceptance behavior therapy for anorexia nervosa: A pilot study. *International Journal of Eating Disorders, 47*(8), 870–873. doi: 10.1002/eat.22241

Wilfley, D. E., Welch, R. R., Stein, R. I., Spurrell, E. B., Cohen, L. R., Saelens, B. E., ... Matt, G. E. (2002). A randomized comparison of group cognitive-behavioral therapy and group interpersonal psychotherapy for the treatment of overweight individuals with binge-eating disorder. *Archives of General Psychiatry, 59*(8), 713–721. Retrieved from http://www .ncbi.nlm.nih.gov/pubmed/12150647

Wilson, G. T., Grilo, C. M., & Vitousek, K. M. (2007). Psychological treatment of eating disorders. *American Psychologist*, *62*(3), 199–216.

Wilson, G. T., Wilfley, D. E., Agras, W. S., & Bryson, S. W. (2010). Psychological treatments of binge eating disorder. *Archives of General Psychiatry*, *67*(1), 1–8. Retrieved from http://archpsyc.jamanetwork.com.proxy.library.emory.edu/article.aspx?articleid=210525

Wilson, G. T., & Zandberg, L. J. (2012). Cognitive-behavioral guided self-help for eating disorders: Effectiveness and scalability. *Clinical Psychology Review*, *32*(4), 343–357.

Wojtowicz, A. E., & von Ranson, K. M. (2012). Weighing in on risk factors for body dissatisfaction: A one-year prospective study of middle-adolescent girls. *Body Image*, *9*(1), 20–30. doi: 10.1016/j.bodyim.2011.07.004

Wonderlich, S. A., Peterson, C. B., Crosby, R. D., Smith, T. L., Klein, M. H., Mitchell, J. E., & Crow, S. J. (2014). A randomized controlled comparison of integrative cognitive-affective therapy (ICAT) and enhanced cognitive-behavioral therapy (CBT-E) for bulimia nervosa. *Psychological Medicine*, *44*(03), 543–553. doi: 10.1017/S0033291713001098

Chapter 13

Sexual Dysfunctions

Cindy M. Meston and Amelia M. Stanton

exual problems are broadly defined as the inability to respond sexually or to experience sexual pleasure. In order for a sexual problem to be diagnosed as a sexual dysfunction, it must meet the criteria specified in the *Diagnostic and Statistical Manual of Mental Disorders, Fifth Edition* (*DSM-5*; American Psychiatric Association [APA], 2013); the individual also needs to report distress and should identify the problem as persistent and recurrent, occurring for a minimum of 6 months. In the *DSM-5*, sexual dysfunctions are also evaluated for severity and duration. For each disorder there are subtypes of lifelong versus acquired, and generalized versus situational. A *lifelong* disorder is one that has always been present. In contrast, an *acquired* disorder involves a loss of function that was previously unimpaired. A *generalized* sexual dysfunction is one in which the sexual problem occurs in all contexts regardless of stimulation, situation, or partner; a *situational* sexual disorder is one in which the problem occurs only in certain contexts, such as with specific partners, or while engaging in specific sexual activities.

Although people may complain of a variety of sexual concerns, the *DSM-5* recognizes only three major categories of sexual dysfunction: interest/arousal, orgasm, and pain. This chapter provides an overview of the definition, prevalence, etiology, assessment, and treatment of each of the sexual disorders described by the *DSM-5* that fall within these three categories.

Sexual Interest/Arousal Disorders

Sexual interest refers to the motivation to engage in sexual activity. Interest is commonly referred to as "desire," "sex drive," and "sexual appetite," and describes the sexual feelings motivating a person to seek some type of sexual activity, whether partnered or alone.

Sexual arousal is conceptualized as the second phase of the sexual response cycle and is defined by both physical and mental readiness for sexual activity. Physiological changes occur in the body to prepare for a sexual interaction (erection in males, vaginal swelling and lubrication in females).

FEMALE SEXUAL INTEREST/AROUSAL DISORDER

Definition, Diagnosis, and Prevalence

Female sexual interest/arousal disorder (FSIAD) is defined in the *DSM-5* as lack of, or significantly reduced, sexual interest/arousal. A woman must have three of the following six symptoms in order to receive the diagnosis: absent or reduced interest in sexual activity; absent or reduced sexual thoughts or fantasies; no or reduced initiation of sexual activity, and typically unreceptive to a partner's attempts to initiate; absent or reduced sexual excitement or pleasure in almost all or all sexual encounters; absent or reduced sexual interest/arousal in response to any internal or external sexual cues; and absent or reduced genital or nongenital sensations during sexual activity in all or almost all sexual encounters. These symptoms must cause clinically significant distress and have persisted for a minimum of 6 months. The disorder is specified by severity level and subtyped into lifelong versus acquired and generalized versus situational.

In past editions of the *DSM*, sexual interest and sexual arousal have been considered to be separate, though related, constructs. *DSM-IV-TR* (APA, 2000) described separate diagnoses for hypoactive sexual desire disorder (HSDD) and female sexual arousal disorder (FSAD). HSDD was characterized by the absence of sexual fantasies and lack of desire for sexual activity, and FSAD was characterized by continuous or recurrent inability to retain, or maintain, sufficient lubrication or swelling. The *DSM-5* sexual dysfunction subworkgroup cited evidence that desire and arousal could not be reliably distinguished in women (e.g., Brotto, Heiman, & Tolman, 2009). Other experts in the field disagree with this conceptualization (e.g., Clayton, DeRogatis, & Rosen, 2012), and the categorization of desire and arousal disorders into one diagnostic category in the *DSM-5* has led to substantial controversy in the field.

As FSIAD is new to the *DSM*, prevalence studies have not yet been published. However, previous work has examined the prevalence of low sexual interest (HSDD) and low sexual arousal (FSAD) in women. One of the most frequently cited prevalence studies found low sexual interest in 22% of women in the general U.S. population (Laumann, Paik, & Rosen, 1999). In a survey of women from 29 countries, rates of self-reported low sexual interest ranged from 26% to 43% (Laumann et al., 2005). For a clinical diagnosis of HSDD, which takes levels of distress into account, rates are lower and range from around 7% to 23%, depending on a woman's age, cultural background, and reproductive status.

Prevalence studies of sexual arousal problems in women have focused primarily on self-reported lack of vaginal lubrication. These studies have not always included all the information necessary to diagnose FSAD, as many did not inquire about distress or level of stimulation. Bancroft, Loftus, & Long, (2003) found that 31.2% of heterosexual women in the United States reported lubrication problems over the past month. For women living in the United Kingdom, the prevalence of persistent lubrication problems, lasting 3 months or more, ranged from 2.6% (Mercer et al., 2003) to 28% (Dunn, Croft, & Hackett, 1999). Research that does reference distress has found that many women reporting lubrication problems are not distressed by their lack of lubrication. Lubrication problems increase with age and menopausal status.

FACTORS ASSOCIATED WITH FEMALE SEXUAL INTEREST/ AROUSAL DISORDER

Since FSIAD is a new diagnostic category, we must rely on prior research to describe what is known about the causes and consequences of HSDD and FSAD (the prior diagnoses) in women. These elements are broken down into biological factors, including medical health, hormones, and medications, and psychological factors, including stress, relationships, comorbid mental illness, and history of sexual abuse.

Biological Factors

Endocrine levels are the most commonly discussed biological factor that may be related to *low sexual interest* in women. Lack of sexual desire has been associated with menopause, during which decreased ovarian function results in lower estrogen production. Epidemiological studies indicate that "surgical menopause" induced by oophorectomy (surgical removal of the ovaries), which causes a sharp drop in estradiol and testosterone, is a more prominent risk factor for HSDD than natural menopause, particularly among younger cohorts (Dennerstein, Koochaki, Barton, & Graziottin, 2006). Increased sexual desire has been found in women near the time of ovulation (e.g., Diamond & Wallen, 2011), and research has shown that decreased sexual desire occurs after chemical suppression of ovarian hormones (Schmidt & Rubinow, 2009).

Researchers have concluded that sex hormones, specifically androgens, estrogens, and progestins, affect female sexual interest and function, but there is still some uncertainty as to which hormones are most important. Androgens and estrogens govern the structure and function of the cervix, vagina, labia, and clitoris. With respect to sexual interest, androgens may be most influential, as they represent the immediate precursor to estrogen synthesis and thus affect sexual desire, mood, and energy. The concept of androgen insufficiency as a potential cause of low sexual desire in women is controversial. Researchers originally believed that androgen depletion occurred organically due to age-related decline in adrenal and ovarian androgen production; now, the field recognizes that the decline in androgen production begins in the early 20s, which means that it does not occur as a result of natural menopause. Though low androgen levels may contribute to hypoactive sexual desire in women, the lack of reference ranges for androgens in women has made it difficult to determine when a clinical insufficiency is present.

Evidence for a relationship between testosterone and women's sexual desire indicates that this hormone is correlated with solitary desire. In contrast to dyadic desire, or the desire to be sexual with another person, solitary desire is thought to be a "true" measure of desire, one that is less influenced by social context and more responsive to endogenous physiology. Several studies have indicated that higher levels of testosterone are associated with increased solitary desire (e.g., Van Anders, Brotto, Farrell, & Yule, 2009). In these same studies, dyadic desire showed no or negative correlation with testosterone. Masturbation, which is considered to be a behavioral index of solitary desire, has been linked to testosterone, such that women with low testosterone and high masturbation reported higher solitary desire than women with low testosterone and low masturbation (Van Anders, 2012).

There has also been recent interest in whether the hormonal changes caused by oral contraception use can lead to low sexual interest in women. Oral contraceptives involve a combination of estrogens and progesterone, and produce substantial increases in sex hormone-binding globulin, which can lower testosterone levels. It is possible that this decrease in testosterone could contribute to the low sexual desire reported by some women taking oral contraceptives. Research on the relationship between oral contraceptives and sexual desire has produced mixed results, with studies reporting that oral contraceptives increase, decrease, or do not change women's sexual desire. Despite the fact that oral contraceptives have been shown to decrease androgen levels, they have not been consistently associated with decreases in sexual desire. When McCall and Meston (2006) assessed cues for sexual desire, they determined that contraceptive use did not influence sexual desire in women with and without HSDD. Other studies have shown that oral contraceptives do have a negative impact on libido. For instance, a recent study of pre- and postmenopausal women revealed that women taking oral contraceptives had a significantly lower incidence of sexual thoughts and sexual interest compared to nonusers (Davison, Bell, LaChina, Holden, & Davis, 2008). In a study of over 1,000 German medical students, oral contraceptive users had significantly lower scores on the desire subscale of the Female Sexual Function Index (FSFI; Rosen et al., 2000) than did nonusers (Wallwiener et al., 2010); however, the causal nature of the relationship could not be determined. It is important to note that, for some women, the benefits derived from the use of oral contraception, such as freedom from a fear of pregnancy and a reduction in menstrual symptoms, may serve to enhance, rather than inhibit, sexual desire.

It is well known that many psychoactive medications affect sexual desire. There are both intraclass and interclass variations among antidepressants with respect to sexual dysfunction and particularly sexual desire. These variations are largely dependent on neurotransmitter receptor profiles and genetics. Selective serotonin reuptake inhibitors (SSRIs), used most commonly for treating depression and anxiety, increase serotonin levels and produce a variety of sexual side effects in both men and women including decreased desire. Sexual dysfunction secondary to SSRI use is believed to result, in part, from activation of the serotonin$_2$ receptor. Newer generations of antidepressants that act as antagonists (blockers) at the serotonin$_2$ receptor—for example, agomelatine (Valdoxan), bupropion (Wellbutrin), moclobemide (Amira), and reboxetine (Edronax)—are associated with fewer sexual side effects. Future research should seek to validate genetic factors associated with antidepressant medications. Doing so would enable personal genotyping and the development of individualized treatment approaches.

Research has shown that endocrine levels play a role in female *sexual arousal*. Specifically, estrogens influence the physiological function of tissues, including the lower genital tissues. That is, estrogens have vasodilatory and vasoprotective effects that govern blood flow into the vagina and the clitoris. Reductions in estradiol during menopause and lactation have been associated with reduced blood flow to the vaginal walls, resulting in reduced vaginal lubrication. One of the major biological changes that occurs during menopause is a decrease in circulating estrogen; that helps account for decreased lubrication and thus decreased genital arousal. Yet, there is no precise estrogen "cutoff" value that indicates whether a woman's level of estrogen is adequate for sexual arousal. In other words, it is hard to determine whether estrogen deficiency can be deemed a specific cause of sexual arousal problems.

Both the sympathetic and the parasympathetic nervous systems (SNS and PNS) play a role in genital arousal in women. Norepinephrine (NE) is the primary neurotransmitter involved in SNS communication, and when measured after exposure to a sexually arousing film, blood levels of NE are higher than pre-film levels (Exton et al., 2000). The spinal cord literature provides strong support for the role of the SNS in female sexual arousal. Women with spinal cord injuries between areas T11 and L2 in the spinal cord show a lack of lubrication during psychological sexual arousal (Sipski, Alexander, & Rosen, 1997). This region is associated with sympathetically mediated genital vasocongestion. That is, this is the area of the spinal cord where sympathetic nerves project to the genital region.

Laboratory studies have also provided evidence for the role of SNS involvement in women's sexual arousal. Meston and colleagues reported that moderate activation of the SNS using either exercise (Meston & Gorzalka, 1995, 1996a, 1996b) or ephedrine (Meston & Heiman, 1998) facilitated genital sexual arousal, and suppression of the SNS using clonidine inhibited genital arousal (Meston, Gorzalka, & Wright, 1997). A recent study proposed there is an optimal level of SNS arousal that is necessary for adequate genital arousal in women (Lorenz, Harte, Hamilton, & Meston, 2012). Lorenz and colleagues found that moderate increases in SNS activity were associated with higher physiological sexual arousal responses, while both very low and very high SNS activation were associated with lower levels of physiological sexual arousal. Similarly, low resting state heart rate variability has been associated with risk for sexual arousal problems (Stanton, Lorenz, Pulverman, & Meston, 2015). Heart rate variability is a noninvasive test of autonomic imbalance. Mechanisms that interfere with normal SNS activity, such as stress, can negatively impact a woman's ability to become sexually aroused.

Vascular and neurological problems (e.g., diabetes, pelvic vascular disorder, multiple sclerosis) often lead to sexual arousal concerns. Prescription drugs, especially SSRIs and SNRIs, may also decrease sexual arousal and vaginal lubrication in women (Frohlich & Meston, 2000). Some hormonal forms of contraceptives have been shown to reduce arousal.

Psychological Factors

Low sexual interest and/or arousal has also been linked with a number of psychosocial factors in both men and women. After controlling for age, relationship satisfaction, and sexual satisfaction, Murray and Milhausen (2012) found that relationship duration significantly predicted variance in sexual desire. Specifically, women's sexual desire decreased as relationship duration increased. Among married women, feelings of overfamiliarity and institutionalization of the relationship may lead to decreased desire. Daily hassles, such as worrying about children and paying the bills, and high-stress jobs are offenders for suppressing sexual desire, as are a multitude of relationship or partner-related issues. In regard to the latter, couples reporting sexual difficulties have been characterized by sex therapists as having less overall satisfaction within their relationships, an increased number of disagreements, more conflict resolution problems, and more sexual communication problems including discomfort with discussing sexual activities compared to couples without sexual problems. Warmth, caring, and affection within the relationship are undoubtedly linked to feelings of sexual desire. Beliefs and attitudes about sexuality acquired over the course of sexual development can influence sexual desire and sexual response across the lifespan. Women who internalize passive gender roles or negative attitudes toward sexuality may be at greater risk of experiencing sexual problems (Nobre & Pinto-Gouveia, 2006).

Societal factors may also contribute to low sexual interest and arousal. Sexual norms differ greatly by region and by culture. Women who are socialized to believe that being interested in sex is shameful often experience guilt and shame during sex, feelings that in turn have been associated with a number of sexual concerns.

McCall and Meston (2006) reported four distinct factors that serve as cues for sexual desire in women. These factors are emotional bonding cues (e.g., "feeling a sense of commitment from your partner"), erotic/explicit cues (e.g., "watching an erotic movie"), visual/proximity cues (e.g., "seeing/talking with someone famous"), and romantic/implicit cues (e.g., "having a romantic dinner with your partner"). Not surprisingly, when compared to sexually healthy women, women diagnosed with HSDD reported significantly fewer cues in each of these domains.

Psychological conditions most commonly associated with a lack of sexual interest include social phobia, obsessive-compulsive disorder, panic disorder, and mood disorders—depression in particular. It is feasible that sexuality becomes of secondary importance when an individual is experiencing substantial distress in other areas of his or her life. With regard to depression, it is feasible that rumination about negative events, a common cognitive aspect of depression, may contribute to the decrease in desire noted in depressed persons by leading to an exclusive focus on aspects of sexuality that are unpleasant. It is well known that people with depression are prone to interpret negative events as caused by stable, global causes, and this cognitive style could certainly negatively affect one's perception of sexuality.

A history of unwanted sexual experiences can also negatively affect sexual desire. Many, but not all, women with a history of childhood sexual abuse fear sexual intimacy, are likely to avoid sexual interactions with a partner, and are less receptive to sexual approaches from their partners (Rellini, 2008). Sexual self-schemas, cognitive generalizations about sexual aspects of the self that guide sexual behavior and influence the processing of sexually relevant information, have been shown to differ between women with and without a history of childhood sexual abuse (e.g., Meston, Rellini, & Heiman, 2006; Stanton, Boyd, Pulverman, & Meston, 2015). A high proportion of women with a history of childhood sexual abuse engage in risky sexual behaviors, such as sexual intercourse with strangers while intoxicated. It is unknown whether this behavior is a reflection of high levels of sexual desire, an inability to maintain or enforce physical boundaries, a compulsive act, emotional avoidance, or some combination of these reasons. Other studies have found that prior sexual abuse is associated with low sexual interest (e.g., Leonard & Follette, 2002).

Many of the factors affecting women's sexual desire noted earlier also affect women's sexual arousal. According to the dual-control model proposed by Bancroft and Janssen (2000), sexual arousal is the combination of both excitatory and inhibitory forces. Five main themes have been described as potential inhibitors or enhancers of sexual arousal for women aged 18 to 84 years: feelings about one's body, negative consequences of sexual activity (e.g., bad reputation, pregnancy), feeling desired and accepted by a sexual partner, feeling used by a sexual partner, and negative mood (Graham, Sanders, Milhausen, & Mcbride, 2004).

ASSESSMENT AND TREATMENT OF FEMALE SEXUAL INTEREST/AROUSAL DISORDER

Given that FSIAD is new to *DSM-5*, there are no assessment tools based on the new diagnostic criteria, and there are no published treatment studies that use the new criteria. Therefore, this section draws on the HSDD and FSAD literature.

Assessment

The assessment of sexual interest in women is difficult due to the subjective and complex nature of sexual desire. In her model of the female sexual response, Basson (2000) described the concept of receptive desire. She explained that, though many women do not seek out sexual activity, they respond sexually when approached by their partner. Basson was the first to suggest that level of responsiveness to sexual stimuli was indicative of desire in women. Assessing for low sexual desire may include inquiring about sexual thoughts, fantasies, and daydreams; examining the degree to which patients seek out sexually suggestive material; questioning how often patients have the urge to masturbate or engage in sensual self-touching; and determining level of motivation for partnered sexual activity. Overall, assessment of sexual desire needs to be carefully considered within the context of the dyadic relationship, and must take into consideration factors known to affect sexual functioning, such as the person's age, religion, culture; the length of the relationship; the partner's sexual function; and the context of the person's life.

In the assessment of sexual arousal, levels of physiological sexual arousal can be assessed indirectly by using a vaginal photoplethysmograph to assess vaginal blood engorgement, as well as by sonograms (pictures of internal organs derived from sound waves bouncing off organs and other tissues), thermograms (images derived from radiation in the long-infrared range of the electromagnetic spectrum), and fMRI (an imaging technique that tracks changes in blood concentration in inner organs) to assess blood engorgement in the genitals. However these techniques are more commonly used for research purposes than as clinical diagnostic tools.

Assessment of sexual interest and sexual arousal should comprise a complete sexual, medical, and psychosocial history, which can be obtained through standardized interviews and validated self-administered questionnaires. The clinician should explore the onset of the sexual problem, taking into account dates of surgeries, medication changes, and diagnoses of medical conditions. It is also important to assess the context of the problem, especially situations or cues that have stimulated sexual desire in the past. If a person reports specific cues for sexual desire, it should be determined whether they are now absent from his or her life, no longer of interest, or are now unacceptable for some reason. It is also imperative to explore the person's feelings about his or her current sexual partner to look for relationship factors that could be contributing to the sexual difficulties. Laboratory testing may be warranted, given the close relationship between androgens and sexual desire. A complete psychosocial history should include situational problems, relationship history, sexual problems of the partner, mood, sexual satisfaction, and psychological disorders.

Treatment

For women experiencing low sexual desire as a result of biologically-compromised natural levels of androgens, treatment with testosterone replacement therapy can be an effective option. Currently, no testosterone products have been approved by the U.S. Food and Drug Administration (FDA) for the treatment of low sexual desire in women. However, many clinicians prescribe "off-label" use of testosterone, in the form of patches or pills, for women with low sexual desire. One estimate suggests that 4.1 million prescriptions for off-label testosterone are made annually in the United States (Davis & Braunstein, 2012). The use of transdermal testosterone for reduced sexual desire in surgically menopausal women was approved by the European Medicines Agency in 2010, but has yet to be approved by the FDA or by Health Canada.

Other hormonal therapies for low sexual desire include estrogen treatment and tibolone therapy. Estrogen treatment is particularly efficacious for desire problems that stem from vulvovaginal atrophy. Given the established relationship between low levels of estrogen and atrophy, estrogen therapy is the first-line treatment for this particular condition (Tan, Bradshaw, & Carr, 2012). Tibolone is a 19-nortestosterone derivative and a selective tissue estrogenic activity regulator that is metabolized into metabolites with estrogenic, progestagenic, and androgenic properties (Brotto & Luria, 2014). Available in 90 countries (but not in the United States), tibolone therapy has been shown to increase sexual desire and lubrication. Nijland and colleagues (2008) demonstrated an overall improvement in sexual function in women receiving tibolone. There are some concerns, however, that tibolone may increase the risk of breast cancer recurrence (Kenemans et al., 2009) and stroke (Cummings et al., 2008) in older women.

Since the success of using PDE-5 inhibitors—for example, sildenafil (Viagra), tadalafil (Cialis), and vardenafil hydrochloride (Levitra)—to treat erectile dysfunction, researchers have attempted to find a comparable drug for women who are experiencing sexual desire or arousal problems. Flibanserin (Addyi) was approved by the FDA in 2015 after studies showed that the drug increased subjective reports of sexually satisfying events. Flibanserin acts on different neurotransmitters in the brain; the drug increases levels of norepinephrine and dopamine and reduces levels of serotonin.

There is some research on other nonhormonal, centrally acting investigational medications for low desire and arousal problems in women. Bupropion (Wellbutrin), sometimes used to counteract sexual dysfunction secondary to SSRI treatment, led to a modest improvement in sexual interest and arousal among nondepressed premenopausal women and among premenopausal women complaining of low sexual desire (Segraves, Clayton, Croft, Wolf, & Warnock, 2004).

Physiological aspects of low sexual arousal are most commonly treated with topical lubricants that help mask impairments in vaginal lubrication. They do not, however, enhance genital/clitoral blood flow or genital sensations that are often decreased, and they have not been shown to impact psychological sexual arousal. Evidence from limited placebo-controlled studies indicates that sildenafil (Viagra) increases genital engorgement in healthy, premenopausal women (Laan, Smith, Boolell, & Quirk, 2002), and in postmenopausal women with severe levels of genital arousal concerns (Basson & Brotto, 2003). Despite reports of increased physiological sexual arousal, studies in general have not found that these drugs positively impact a woman's psychological experience of sexual arousal. This suggests that, for women, psychological factors such as relationship satisfaction, mood state, and sexual scenarios may play a more important role in feelings of sexual desire and arousal than do physiological genital cues. If this is the case, drugs that target increasing vasocongestion are likely to be most effective in women with genital sexual arousal disorder whose primary complaint is decreased genital responding, experienced as decreases in lubrication and/or feelings of vaginal fullness or engorgement. This would most likely be women who are postmenopausal, who have undergone oophorectomy, or who suffer from arterial vascular problems. For some women, if a drug increases vaginal engorgement, to the extent that it is detected and labeled as a *sexual feeling*, this may also enhance their feelings of more general, psychological arousal.

Studies on vasodilator drugs for women have revealed a notable placebo effect on women's sexual arousal. That is, up to 40% of women in the placebo group of randomized clinical trials for sildenafil and other pharmacological agents reported significant improvements in sexual arousal. Nonspecific factors, such as expecting to improve, having contact with a sexuality professional, and monitoring sexual response, can exert a powerful influence on women's sexual arousal and satisfaction in general.

The EROS clitoral therapy device (Urometrics, St. Paul, Minnesota) is an FDA-approved treatment for women's sexual arousal concerns. This small, handheld device increases vasocongestion in the clitoral and labial region via a suction mechanism and has been reported to increase vaginal lubrication and sensation (Billups et al., 2001).

Psychological treatments for low desire include education about factors that affect sexual desire, couples exercises (e.g., scheduling times for physical and emotional intimacy), communication training (e.g., opening up about sexual issues and needs), cognitive restructuring of dysfunctional beliefs (e.g., a good sexual experience does not always end with an orgasm), sexual fantasy training (e.g., training people to develop and explore mental imagery), and sensate focus. *Sensate focus*, introduced by Masters and Johnson in the 1970s, is a behavioral technique in which couples learn to focus on the pleasurable sensations brought about by touching, while decreasing attention on goal-directed sex (e.g., orgasm). Recent research has also indicated that mindfulness-based approaches, which cultivate active awareness of the body and its sensations in a nonjudgmental and compassionate way, may be helpful for women with FSIAD (e.g., Brotto & Basson, 2014). By focusing on the physical sensations of sexual activity, instead of being preoccupied with sexual performance or current level of arousal, couples can learn to be present and to respond to their partner during the sexual situation. In the beginning stages of sensate focus couples are encouraged to touch each other's bodies and assess for sexual sensations but refrain from touching breasts or genitals, or engaging in intercourse. Over time, couples are encouraged to touch more and more increasingly erotic areas of the body in order to build organic desire, in preparation for intercourse. When desire has been fully heightened, intercourse is reintroduced as part of the sexual repertoire.

For women in satisfying relationships, treatment may include identifying potential distracting, negative thoughts and helping them to let go of these thoughts during sexual activity. Leiblum and Wiegel (2002) described four such types of distracting thoughts in women: myths and misconceptions (e.g., "women are not supposed to enjoy sex"), negative emotions, performance anxiety, and body image concerns (e.g., focusing on unattractive aspects of one's body). Behavioral techniques designed to help men and women explore their sexual likes and dislikes, alone or with their partners, can be used to help them associate sexual behaviors with positive affect and experiences. For individuals who are distracted by feelings of shame or embarrassment about their bodies, cognitive restructuring might involve helping them to identify their fears (e.g., a fear of rejection) and dysfunctional beliefs (e.g., "my partner thinks my body is not sexy") and then test the accuracy of these beliefs through a series of strategically designed behavioral experiments. The experiments aim to reduce avoidance behavior and provide corrective experiences to counteract dysfunctional beliefs. For example, a woman who keeps her clothing on during sex because she feels that her partner would reject her if he saw her naked would be encouraged to incrementally remove pieces of clothing, and test the reaction of her partner.

MALE HYPOACTIVE SEXUAL DESIRE DISORDER

Definition, Diagnosis, and Prevalence

Male hypoactive sexual desire disorder (MHSDD) is defined in the *DSM-5* as persistent or recurrently deficient sexual or erotic thoughts, fantasies, and desire for sexual activity. These symptoms must have persisted for a minimum of 6 months, and they must cause clinically significant distress. The disorder is specified by severity level and subtyped into lifelong versus acquired and generalized versus situational.

In past editions of the *DSM*, hypoactive sexual desire disorder was gender nonspecific and could therefore apply to either men or women. As sexual desire and arousal problems have been combined into a single disorder for women in *DSM-5*, MHSDD now accounts only for men. Other than the change from a gender-nonspecific disorder to a gender-specific disorder, there have not been any substantive alterations in the diagnostic criteria from *DSM-IV-TR* to *DSM-5*. One small change is worth noting. In *DSM-IV-TR*, hypoactive sexual desire disorder required "persistent" low interest in sex. The *DSM-5* now specifies that the symptoms be present for at least 6 months before a diagnosis can be conferred.

Low desire is less commonly the presenting clinical sexual complaint for men, who are more likely to present with erectile dysfunction. Cultural norms that often portray men as being ever desirous of sex may make it difficult for men to report low sexual desire to their physicians or their psychologists.

Most epidemiological studies have not inquired about the full set of diagnostic criteria for HSDD, making it difficult for researchers to determine accurate prevalence rates for the disorder. Research studies have asked men if they have a lack of interest in sex, but not whether the problem was consistent over a period of 6 months *and* distressing. One European study that examined the prevalence of distressingly low sexual interest in men over at least a 2-month period found that 14.4% of men reported a distressing lack of sexual desire lasting at least 2 months (Carvalheira, Traeen, & Štulhofer, 2014). Men between the ages of 30 and 39 were most likely to report low sexual interest.

Self-reported prevalence rates of problems with desire range from 4.8% in the United States (Laumann, Glasser, Neves, & Moreira, 2009) to 17% in the United Kingdom (Mercer et al., 2003). Desire problems appear to increase with age. In a sample of Swedish men between the ages of 66 and 74, 41% experienced low sexual desire (Fugl-Meyer & Fugl-Meyer, 1999). Prevalence rates typically decrease when studies examine *persistent* lack of interest in sexual activity. Among 40- to 80-year-old men in the United States, 4.8% reported an occasional lack of sexual desire, and 3.3% reported a frequent lack of sexual desire (Laumann et al., 2009).

Men in community samples are more likely to report desire problems than men in clinical samples. In community samples, reports of desire concerns exceed reports of erectile problems (e.g., Mercer et al., 2003). Men in clinical settings may feel more comfortable talking about erectile problems than desire problems, especially if they consider their problems to be biological rather than psychological in nature.

FACTORS ASSOCIATED WITH MALE HYPOACTIVE SEXUAL DESIRE DISORDER

Given that research has not yet examined factors associated with MHSDD as defined in *DSM-5*, our review will focus on the causes and consequences of low sexual interest (formerly HSDD). Historically, hormones have been the focus of biological research on low sexual desire in men. Recent studies have also investigated the relationship between neurological disorders and poor sex drive. Psychological causes of decreased interest in sexual activity seem to include relationship difficulties and certain mental health problems.

Biological Factors

Hormonal factors are often implicated in low sexual desire. In men for whom androgen levels have been suppressed, low testosterone levels have been associated with low levels of sexual interest (Bancroft, 2005). For these men, testosterone replacement has been shown to increase sexual desire; this is not the case for men with normal androgen levels (e.g., Corona, Rastrelli, Forti, & Maggi, 2011). Hypogonadism, diminished functional activity of the gonads, has been observed in 3% to7% of men between the ages of 30 and 69 and in 18% of men aged 70 and older (Araujo et al., 2007). This condition may account for the relationship between aging and low sexual interest. Hyperprolactinemia, defined as high levels of prolactin, and hypothyroidism have also been associated with low sexual desire in men.

Medications such as SSRIs and SNRIs have been linked to low sexual interest in men. Atypical antidepressants may have a lower incidence of reduced sexual desire (e.g., Clayton, Croft, & Handiwala, 2014).

Neurological disorders such as multiple sclerosis and medical conditions such as inflammatory bowel disease (IBD), Crohn's disease, ulcerative colitis, coronary disease, heart failure, renal failure, and HIV have all been linked with low sexual desire in men. However, decreased desire may result from the medications used to treat conditions like IBD, which have been shown to lower testosterone. It remains unclear whether decreases in desire are due to the conditions themselves, the medications used to treat the conditions, or the psychosocial stressors that often accompany the conditions. Further research in this area is warranted.

Psychological Factors

Many psychological factors have been associated with low sexual desire in men. These factors include relationship problems, concerns about one's own sexual performance, and comorbid psychological conditions, such as depression and anxiety. In a sample of male outpatients seeking treatment for sexual dysfunction, psychosocial symptoms were more predictive of low sexual interest than hormonal and other biological factors (Corona et al., 2004).

Relationship problems and interpersonal factors have been strongly associated with male sex drive. Men who have partners with low sexual desire are more likely to have sexual desire concerns than men who have partners without desire problems (McCabe & Connaughton, 2014). Desire problems have also been linked to not finding one's partner attractive and to long-term (more than 5 years) relationships (Carvalheira et al., 2014).

Individual factors, particularly mental health problems, have also been related to sexual desire problems in men. In a survey of male outpatients who sought treatment for sexual dysfunction, 43% of the men with a history of psychiatric symptoms reported moderate to severe loss of sexual desire (Corona et al., 2004). Many studies have highlighted the correlation between depression and low sexual desire (e.g., Carvalheira et al., 2014).

ASSESSMENT AND TREATMENT OF MALE HYPOACTIVE SEXUAL DESIRE DISORDER

Given that MHSDD is new to *DSM-5*, there are no assessment tools or treatment studies based on the new diagnostic criteria. However, there are many studies that focus independently on the assessment and treatment of low sexual desire in men. Treatment for MHSDD varies based on the etiology of the disorder, but the most common biological treatment centers on increasing testosterone levels. Though treatments targeting testosterone have been efficacious, they have recently been overprescribed and overused by men with normal testosterone levels. Psychosocial treatment for MHSDD includes cognitive and behavioral components, as well as attention to building strong communication between partners.

Assessment

Assessment for MHSDD should include private meetings with each member of the couple, as well as a couples meeting. Individual meetings with the male partner may reveal a number of diagnostic factors, including atypical arousal patterns that are not being met by his current partner, decreased attraction to his current partner, or a sexual affair that is satisfying his sexual needs outside of his current relationship.

In addition to meeting with both the individual and the couple, clinicians should also assess for changes in health status, life stressors, and relationship factors around the time that the male partner started to experience a lack of sexual interest. These factors may become the target of the clinician's treatment plan.

Clinicians should also consider the possibility that male patients presenting with complaints of low sexual desire may actually be suppressing their desires. This often occurs in men with long-standing heterosexual partners who either have had sexual relations with men or have fantasized about sexual relations with men during masturbation (Meana & Steiner, 2014). In such cases, the desire problem may be situational, such that the patient lacks desire in the context of his heterosexual relationship but experiences desire in other contexts (e.g., he may fantasize about engaging in sexual activity with a different partner).

Treatment

Treatment for low sexual desire in men should be etiologically oriented. If low testosterone level is determined to be the likely cause of MHSDD, biological treatment focuses primarily on increasing testosterone levels. As mentioned earlier, hypogonadism in males typically leads to low testosterone production, decreased sexual interest, and difficulties sustaining an erection. Testosterone replacement therapy can be delivered through the skin via an over-the-counter gel or patch, by injections, or by slow release pellets (Testopel) implanted under the skin. In a couple of studies, increasing testosterone levels has been shown to have beneficial effects on sexual motivations and sexual thoughts (Allan, Forbes, Strauss, & McLachlan, 2008; Wang et al., 2000).

There has been some concern about the overuse of testosterone gels, especially by men who have normal testosterone levels. There has been a marked increase in off-label prescriptions of testosterone, particularly transdermal testosterone, in most countries between 2000 and 2011. One of the likely causes of this increase may be the permissive U.S. and European guidelines for the prescription of testosterone, which promote the use of the drug for age-related functional androgen deficiency (Handelsman, 2013). In some countries, total testosterone prescribing exceeds the maximum amount that could be attributed to pathological androgen deficiency, which is known to occur in about 0.5% of men (Handelsman, 2010). In a study of older men randomly assigned to either daily application of testosterone gel or daily application of a placebo gel, men in the active condition had a greater frequency of cardiovascular, respiratory, and dermatological events compared to men in the control condition (Basaria et al., 2010). The incidence of adverse cardiovascular events in the testosterone group was significant enough to stop the trial before the completion of enrollment.

If low sexual desire is caused by elevated prolactin, another endocrinological disorder, or by depression, or anxiety, there are different biological treatment approaches to consider. Although organic hyperprolactinemia more frequently affects women than men, many psychotropic medications can cause increased prolactin in men. Treatment of other endocrinological disorders, such as hypothyroidism and hyperthyroidism, can increase sexual desire, as it is often compromised by these conditions. Depression and anxiety may also lead to decreased sexual desire in men. Treatment for depression often entails the use of antidepressants, which have been shown to impact sexual function in both men and women. If a depressed patient is already experiencing decreases in sexual desire before starting an antidepressant regimen, then his doctor should consider prescribing an antidepressant that has more mild effects on sexual function, such as mirtazapine (Remeron), bupropion (Wellbutrin), or an SNRI like duloxetine (Cymbalta) (Clayton et al., 2014).

It is also noteworthy that men with metabolic syndrome commonly report low sexual interest. If low sexual desire appears to be secondary to metabolic syndrome, then clinicians may recommend a combination of lifestyle changes, exercise, healthy diet, and testosterone replacement therapy (Glina, Sharlip, & Hellstrom, 2013).

Psychosocial treatment for MHSDD mirrors psychological treatment for FSIAD, as MHSDD and FSIAD share many causal psychological factors. Meana and Steiner (2014) provide a thorough overview of efficacious psychosocial treatments for MHSDD. Cognitive-affective-behavioral therapy is a treatment approach that combines cognitive, emotion-centered, and behavioral strategies. The cognitive component of the treatment includes identifying and challenging maladaptive thoughts and sexual scripts that interfere with sexual desire. Therapists may encourage patients with low desire to refocus on sexual stimuli, either before or during sexual activity. The emotional regulation aspect may help men decrease or control emotional reactivity with acceptance techniques like mindfulness. Acceptance techniques come into play in situations when patients may not be able to achieve the sexual function or level of desire that they wish. In these cases, learning to accept certain realities may have as positive an impact as changing what can be modified. Effective psychosocial treatment for MHSDD also includes different behavioral activation strategies, such as using sensate focus and optimizing the timing of sexual interactions, which help couples to refocus on sensuality and encourage them to prioritize sexual activity.

Cognitive-affective-behavioral therapy for MHSDD also includes relationship skills building and communication training, which are important for men who are having trouble talking about sexual preferences with their partners. The level of intimate connection between partners may be linked to sexual desire, so some treatment approaches highlight the importance of communication. Conflict resolution is an important part of communication training, as therapists may help their male patients with desire concerns by teaching them strategies to minimize blaming and encourage self-soothing. Another relational approach to treating sexual desire is the adoption of the Good Enough Sex (GES) model (McCarthy & Metz, 2008), which embraces the acceptance of individual and couple differences in the meaning and importance of sexual desire within the context of the relationship.

ERECTILE DISORDER

Definition, Diagnosis, and Prevalence

Erectile disorder (ED) is defined in the *DSM-5* as the recurrent inability to achieve an erection, the inability to maintain an adequate erection, and/or a noticeable decrease in erectile rigidity during partnered sexual activity. In order to meet the diagnostic criteria, these symptoms must have persisted for at least 6 months and must have occurred on at least 75% of occasions. The disorder can be specified by severity and subtyped as either generalized or situational.

Men of all ages occasionally have difficulty obtaining or maintaining an erection, but clinically diagnosable erectile disorder is more common after age 50. Among men younger than age 35, the prevalence of ED ranges from 7% to 10%. At least 18% of men over the age of 40, and more than 50% of men over the age of 60 report erectile problems. However, only 3.5% of them report consistent erectile problems (Laumann et al., 2005). It is important to note that, as age increases, men experience a number of normal physiological changes that affect erectile function. After age 60, there is a marked decrease in testosterone production, which impacts erectile ability. Elderly men produce less ejaculate than younger men, and orgasms become weaker and less frequent.

There are a number of factors beyond age that are associated with the prevalence of ED. Married men are less likely to report erectile problems compared to never married or divorced men (Laumann et al., 1999). Men with cardiovascular disease, diabetes, and metabolic syndrome are more likely to have ED than men without these diseases (Grover et al., 2006). Health factors such as smoking, obesity, and lack of exercise have been linked to higher prevalence of ED (Rosen, Miner, & Wincze, 2014).

FACTORS ASSOCIATED WITH ERECTION AND ERECTILE DYSFUNCTION

There has been a great deal of research on erectile dysfunction, identifying a number of key biological and psychological causes. Biological factors are related to changes in blood flow to the penis, and psychological factors involve anxiety and negative expectations for performance.

Biological Factors

Erection is caused by increased blood pressure in the corpora cavernosa via increased blood inflow and decreased blood outflow. In general, the likelihood of ED increases with different types of vascular disease, such as hyperlipidemia, coronary heart disease, and diabetes. The link between vascular problems and ED is so strong that ED is considered an early warning sign of vascular disease, especially in men under the age of 40 (e.g., Chew et al., 2010). Some researchers are in favor of viewing ED as a vascular disorder (e.g., Schouten et al., 2008).

Surgery, diabetes, alcoholism, infectious diseases such as HIV and other viral infections, and pelvic pathologies such as systemic lupus are all potential causes of ED. Drugs that decrease dopamine or reduce testosterone production are also implicated in ED. These include antihypertensive medications, antipsychotic drugs, anxiolytics, antiandrogens, anticholesterol agents, and drugs used to regulate heart rate. Antiparkinsonian medications increase dopamine and facilitate erection.

Psychological Factors

With respect to the different psychological factors that play a role in male sexual function, Perelman (2009) proposed the sexual tipping point model, defined as any one individual's characteristic threshold for the expression of a sexual response. Perelman suggested that an individual's sexual tipping point is determined by a variety of multidimensional factors that fall into two general categories, physiological or organic issues and psychosocial, cultural, and behavioral issues. Psychosocial issues that have been linked to ED include performance anxiety, spectatoring, a strong religious background that leads to guilt or strong avoidance behaviors, and a history of sexual trauma.

The major psychological contributors to ED as identified by Barlow's (1986) feedback model of sexual dysfunction are anxiety, negative expectations, and spectatoring. Men who are anxious about not being able to have an erection tend to focus on themselves and how they are performing more than on what gives them pleasure. This spectatoring increases anxiety, which, physiologically, inhibits the relaxation of the smooth muscles necessary for erection and, psychologically, leads to a negative mood state and a focus on negative expectancies. Since the result is impaired erectile responding, the man's fears of not being able to perform are confirmed, and he is likely to repeat the process in subsequent sexual situations. Performance anxiety is inherent in most cases of ED. As a man's penis is visible to both the man and his partner, the occurrence—or absence—of an erection is a known event, which increases focus on performance. According to Rosen and colleagues (2014), men experiencing performance anxiety will not only worry about erections during sexual activity but also engage in visual or tactile checking of the penis.

By contrast, men with normal erectile response approach sexual situations with positive expectancies and a focus on erotic cues. Consequently, they become aroused and are able to obtain and sustain an erection, which creates a positive feedback loop for future sexual encounters. Although spectatoring can be detrimental for men of any age, it appears to be particularly problematic in young men when they are first becoming sexually active. In the absence of sexual experience and a variety of sexual events in which to view evidence of their ability to attain an erection, these young men are particularly vulnerable to the influence of negative expectations about erectile performance.

Other psychosocial factors can contribute to the development and maintenance of ED. According to Nobre and Pinto-Gouveia (2009), men are likely to meet criteria for ED if they (a) endorse myths about male sexuality (e.g., "men always want to have sex"), (b) view themselves as incompetent, and (c) view their sexual problem as internal and stable over time. Mental health conditions, such as depression, generalized anxiety disorder, obsessive-compulsive disorder, and paraphilic disorders, have been linked to ED. In a survey of sexually healthy, college-aged men, Harte and Meston (2011) found a high incidence of off-label sildenafil (Viagra) use that was correlated with erectile dysfunction. They suggested that recreational sildenafil use among men without prior concerns about ED could lead to subsequent erectile problems by making users psychologically dependent on the drug for performance.

ASSESSMENT AND TREATMENT OF ERECTILE DYSFUNCTION

The assessment of erectile dysfunction is conducted via interview and may also include a physiological test. It is important for the assessor to determine the primary cause of the disorder, be it organic or psychogenic. Treatment approach will depend on the etiology of the erectile dysfunction, and the most common treatments include medication, individual psychotherapy, and lifestyle modifications.

Assessment

The psychological assessment of ED includes identifying the situation(s) surrounding the onset of ED and the beliefs that may have been formed at that time. Beliefs may be specific to the relationship (i.e., a feeling of inadequacy with one specific partner) or generalized to all sexual encounters. Clinicians can determine whether performance anxiety is present by assessing whether the patient is able to obtain an erection during situations where performance is not required, such as during sleep or masturbation.

In cases where ED is the result of a vascular problem, laboratory assessments that measure genital blood inflow and outflow during sexual stimulation may be helpful. Blood outflow can be measured by injecting an agent such as papaverine into the penile corpora cavernosa. The agent relaxes the smooth muscles at the base of the penis, which, in presence of normal blood outflow, produces penile erection even without sexual stimulation. When the drug fails to provide the expected erection, it is considered evidence for impairment in vascular mechanisms. Measurement of nocturnal penile erections, which are expected to increase during the REM sleep cycle in sexually healthy men, is another commonly used technique for assessing potential vascular causes of ED. Assays of free and bioavailable serum testosterone are used to rule out abnormal hormone levels.

Treatment

Biomedical treatments for ED include vacuum devices and constriction rings, intracavernosal injections, intraurethral pharmacotherapy, topical pharmacotherapy, oral pharmacotherapy, and penile implants. The first line of treatment is typically a form of PDE-5 inhibitor. As described earlier, erection is a vascular phenomenon caused by increased blood pressure in the penis due to increased blood inflow and decreased blood outflow. The increment of blood inflow is regulated by the relaxation of the smooth muscles surrounding the arterioles, a phenomenon that allows the arterioles to dilate. Smooth muscle relaxation has been attributed to an increase in parasympathetic activity, which causes a release of the neurotransmitters acetylcholine, vasoactive intestinal polypeptide, and nitric oxide. Nitric oxide causes a greater amount of cyclic guanosine monophosphate (cGMP) to be available in the smooth muscles, and this causes the smooth muscles to relax. Normally, cGMP is broken down by enzymes known as phosphodiesterases (PDEs). However, this may be circumvented by inhibiting the activity of these enzymes. Sildenafil (Viagra) and other drugs used to treat ED inhibit PDE type 5. In doing so, these drugs enhance the concentration of cGMP, allowing for greater smooth muscle relaxation and therefore improved erection. Detumescence (i.e., loss of erection) occurs with the release of catecholamines during orgasm and ejaculation. Sildenafil and other PDE-5 inhibitors have a success rate of at least 65% (Shamloul & Ghanem, 2013). These drugs are typically well tolerated by a variety of patients, and their side effects are generally mild.

Despite these drugs' success with facilitating erection, a recent study reported that about 50% of men with ED who began treatment with sildenafil stopped taking the medication (Carvalheira, Pereira, Maroco, & Forjaz, 2012). In this study, the majority of the men who stopped taking the drug (55.1%) discontinued it during the first 3 months of treatment, and the dropout rate was highest in men with diabetes. In the same study, a number of psychosocial factors, such as anxiety, negative emotions, and dysfunctional beliefs, were commonly cited reasons for discontinuation. It has been proposed that more comprehensive instruction at the beginning of pharmacological treatment as well as reeducation throughout the course of treatment might improve the rates of medication compliance.

When PDE-5 inhibitors fail to treat the erectile problem, clinicians typically recommend vacuum constriction devices, vasoactive gels, and intracavernosal injections. Vacuum devices typically consist of a tube that is placed over the penis, and a vacuum pump that draws blood into the penile arteries. A constriction ring is placed at the base of the penis to prevent blood outflow so that the erection is maintained until completion of the sexual act. Vasoactive gels can be produced in different dosage levels and with different mixtures of vasodilators, such as alprostadil (Muse), phentolamine (Regitine), and papaverine (Pavabid). These gels are inserted into the urethra and are typically effective within 15 minutes of insertion. Intracavernosal injections are the next line of treatment. Acting much like the gels, they are injected into the corpus cavernosum of the penis to induce erection. Although intracavernosal injections are effective in approximately 70% to 90% of patients, a large percentage of users discontinue treatment due to the inconvenience, cost, and/or invasiveness of treatment.

Penile implants are generally considered a last resort treatment technique, when tissue damage or deterioration is severe or when all other treatments have failed. This may be the case in men with severe diabetes mellitus or who have had radical prostatectomy. Implants can be hydraulic, semirigid, or soft silicone and consist of two or three cylinders placed in the space normally occupied by the spongy tissue in the penis. The patient's ability to ejaculate after the implant surgery remains intact; however, the implant does not restore sensitivity or sexual desire that may have been present prior to the onset of ED. Implant surgeries usually result in decreased penis size which may dissuade some men from undergoing surgery.

Researchers are investigating the application of gene therapy principles to the treatment of ED. Gene therapy offers hope for a potentially successful long-term treatment of ED, possibly even a cure for the disorder (Shamloul & Ghanem, 2013). Other new areas of ED treatment research include angiogenesis (Xie, Annex, & Donatucci, 2008), defined as the growth of new blood vessels from preexisting vasculature, and stem cell therapy (Bivalacqua et al., 2007).

Psychosocial treatments for ED include sensate focus techniques, increasing the level of erotic stimulation during sexual activity, sex education, and interpersonal therapy. Sensate focus is considered to be the cornerstone of sex therapy. Developed by Masters and Johnson (1970), sensate focus centers on heightening awareness of the sensations associated with sexual activity, rather than on the performance of the sexual act. In certain cases of ED, the patient may not be experiencing sufficient erotic stimulation to achieve an erection. This may be due to the environment or to a lack of variety or skill on the part of the male and/or his partner. Couples in long-standing relationships may have a routine, predictable approach to sexual activity and thus may be more vulnerable to erectile problems as well as decreased sexual interest. Sex education involves therapist guidance on the different aspects of sexual intercourse, and interpersonal therapy focuses on the relationship problems that may be driving psychogenic erectile dysfunction.

Lifestyle modifications can significantly improve erectile function. Studies have shown that targeting factors associated with erectile problems, such as smoking, obesity, alcohol consumption, and physical activity reduces the rate of sexual dysfunction. In a meta-analysis of over 700 men, Gupta and colleagues (2011) assessed the effects of lifestyle modification on the severity of erectile problems. They found that, regardless of PDE-5 use, the adoption of lifestyle modifications provided incremental benefits on erectile function. However, the combination of lifestyle modifications and PDE-5 inhibitors may more effectively improve erectile function than either method alone. In a randomized controlled trial that compared the use of a PDE-5 inhibitor alone with a PDE-5 inhibitor plus at least 3 hours of aerobic exercise per week, the combined approach was more effective in the treatment of ED (Maio, Saraeb, & Marchiori, 2010).

Orgasm Disorders

Orgasm disorders involve difficulties with the presence or absence of orgasm during sexual activity. This can include an inability to achieve orgasm and, in men, achieving orgasm too quickly. Orgasm disorders occur in both men and women; however, early ejaculation is the most common orgasm disorder in men, and an inability to attain orgasm is the most common orgasm disorder in women.

FEMALE ORGASMIC DISORDER

Definition, Diagnosis, and Prevalence

The *DSM-5* defines *female orgasmic disorder* (FOD) as reduced intensity, delay, infrequency, and/or absence of orgasm. These symptoms must persist for at least 6 months, and they may not be related to other physical or relational problems. The presence of distress related to these symptoms is necessary for a diagnosis of FOD. The *DSM-5* classification of FOD distinguishes between lifelong and acquired subtypes as well as between generalized and situational subtypes. Although not stated in the *DSM-5*, the clinical consensus is that a woman who can obtain orgasm during intercourse with manual stimulation but not intercourse alone would not meet criteria for clinical diagnosis unless she is distressed by the low frequency of her sexual response.

Operationalizing FOD is complicated by the fact that the field still lacks a clear consensus on the definition of the female orgasm. Indeed, one study cited more than 25 distinct definitions proposed by different authors (Mah & Binik, 2001). The following definition of female orgasm was derived by the committee on female orgasm and presented at the International Consultation on Urological Diseases in Official Relationship with the World Health Organization (WHO) in Paris in 2003:

> An orgasm in the human female is a variable, transient peak sensation of intense pleasure, creating an altered state of consciousness, usually accompanied by involuntary, rhythmic contractions of the pelvic, striated circumvaginal musculature often with concomitant uterine and anal contractions and myotonia that resolves the sexually-induced vasocongestion (sometimes only partially), usually with an induction of well-being and contentment. (Meston, Hull, Levin, & Sipski, 2004)

Orgasms are caused by erotic stimulation of both genital and nongenital zones of women's bodies. These areas include the clitoris, vagina, other areas of the vulva, and the breasts and nipples. Orgasm may also be caused by fantasy, mental imagery, and hypnosis. Orgasms can occur during sleep, precluding the necessity of consciousness for an orgasm to occur. Orgasms are not generally reported to occur spontaneously without at least some amount of physical or psychological sexual stimulation; however, some psychotropic drugs have been reported to induce spontaneous orgasms in women.

Women who are having difficulties with orgasm do not typically present with the same degree of distress that has been reported in men with ED. This may be because women, unlike men, are able to "fake" orgasm, thus rendering the performance anxiety seen in men unlikely.

Orgasm difficulties are the second most frequently reported sexual problems for women in the United States, with between 22% and 28% of women aged 18 to 59 years reporting they are unable to attain orgasm (Laumann, Michael, Gagnon, & Kolata, 1994). Young women (18 to 24 years) show lower rates of orgasm than older women for both orgasm with a partner and orgasm during masturbation. This is likely due to age-related differences in sexual experience. It is important to note that differences in research methodologies and diagnostic criteria make it difficult to accurately determine prevalence rates for FOD. In a review of 11 epidemiological studies, Graham (2010) found that the lowest prevalence rate of FOD was 3.5% when *DSM-III* criteria were used, and the highest rate was 34%, which was found when women were simply asked whether or not they had difficulties experiencing orgasm.

FACTORS ASSOCIATED WITH WOMEN'S ORGASM AND FOD

The female orgasm results from a complex interaction of biological, psychological, and cultural processes. Disruptions in any of these systems can affect a woman's ability to experience orgasm. The most common causes of the disorder are disturbances in the sympathetic nervous system; various types of chronic illness, particularly spinal cord injury; sexual guilt; anxiety; and relationship concerns.

Biological Factors

Impairments in the nervous system, endocrine system, or brain mechanisms involved in female orgasm may cause orgasmic dysfunction in some women. Disease, injury, and disruptions of the sympathetic or parasympathetic nervous systems have been identified as potential causes of orgasmic difficulties in women. Medical conditions that affect women's orgasmic ability include damage to the sacral/pelvic nerves, multiple sclerosis, Parkinson's disease, epilepsy, hysterectomy complications, vulvodynia, hypothalamus-pituitary disorders, kidney disease, fibromyalgia, and sickle-cell anemia. In general, women with spinal cord injuries in the sacral region (interfering with the sacral reflex arc of the spinal cord) have shown difficulty attaining orgasm. This is believed to be caused by interference with the vagus nerve, which has been shown to connect the cervix to the brain (Whipple, Gerdes, & Komisaruk, 1996).

Both vascular and nervous system problems have also been associated with orgasm difficulties. Vascular disease, such as diabetes mellitus and atherosclerosis, has been linked to orgasmic dysfunction. With respect to the nervous system, studies examining blood plasma levels of neuromodulators before, during, and after orgasm suggest that epinephrine and norepinephrine levels peak during orgasm in normally functioning women (e.g., Exton et al., 2000). With respect to the endocrine system, oxytocin levels are positively correlated with subjective intensity of orgasm among orgasmic women, and prolactin levels are elevated for up to 60 minutes following orgasm (for a review, see Meston & Frohlich, 2000). Studies in humans suggest that the paraventricular nucleus of the hypothalamus, an area of the brain that produces oxytocin, is involved in the orgasmic response (McKenna, 1999). Impairments in any of these systems could feasibly lead to FOD.

A number of psychotherapeutic drugs have been noted to affect the ability of women to attain orgasm. Drugs that increase serotonergic activity—for example, antidepressants, such as paroxetine (Paxil), fluoxetine (Prozac), and sertraline (Zoloft)—or decrease dopaminergic activity (e.g., antipsychotics) have been shown to affect orgasmic capacity (Meston, Levin, Sipski, Hull, & Heiman, 2004). Indeed about one third of women who take SSRIs report problems with orgasm (Stimmel & Gutierrez, 2006). These drugs can lead to delayed orgasm or a complete inability to reach orgasm. There is variability, however, in that some antidepressants have been associated with impaired orgasm more often than others. This seems to be related to the specific serotonin receptor subtype that is being activated. As noted earlier, drugs that inhibit serotonin activity at the serotonin$_2$ receptor—for example, nefazodone (Serzone) and cyproheptadine (Periactin)—cause fewer sexual side effects in women (for a review, see Meston, Levin, et al., 2004).

Recently, clinicians have reported that an increasing number of women believe that the structure of their genitalia may be contributing to difficulties with achieving or maintaining orgasm. This belief has contributed to an increase in genital plastic surgery, specifically labiaplasty (reduction of the size of the inner labia and the outer labia), vaginoplasty (rebuilding the vaginal canal and its mucous membrane), hymenoplasty (reconstruction of the hymen), perineoplasty (tightening or loosening of the perineal muscles and the vagina and/or correcting clinical defects of or damage to the vagina and the anus), and G-spot augmentation. A few studies have indicated that these surgeries resulted in increased sexual satisfaction (e.g., Goodman et al., 2010), but the little current evidence that supports these procedures failed to use standardized measures that formally assess for sexual dysfunction and did not include control groups. For these reasons, the American Congress of Obstetricians and Gynecologists, Committee on Gynecologic Practice (2007), and the

Society of Obstetricians and Gynaecologists of Canada, Clinical Practice Gynaecology Committee and Ethics Committee (2013), discourage physicians from performing genital plastic surgery.

Psychological Factors

The psychological factors associated with FOD include sexual guilt, anxiety related to sex, childhood loss or separation from the father, and relationship issues (for a review, see Meston, Hull, et al., 2004). Sexual guilt can affect orgasmic abilities by increasing anxiety and discomfort during sex and also by distracting a woman from what gives her pleasure. Women who strictly abide by the values of Western religions sometimes view sexual pleasure as a sin. Sins are later connected with a sense of shame and guilt, which could produce negative affect and cause distracting thoughts during sexual activities. Women who initiate and are more active participants during sexual activities report more frequent orgasms, most likely because being active allows women to assume positions that can provide a greater sense of sexual pleasure. More frequent masturbation and sexual activities are associated with more frequent orgasms. It is likely that women who engage in more sexual activities have a greater understanding of what gives them sexual pleasure and this can help them more easily reach orgasm. A romantic relationship in which the woman feels comfortable communicating her sexual needs may facilitate orgasmic capacity. Therefore, women experiencing relationship discord might be more at risk of orgasm problems than women who are satisfied with their relationships. However, only a small percentage of women are distressed by their anorgasmia (Graham, 2010).

Certain demographic factors such as age, education, and religion also provide clues to the psychological factors involved in FOD. As noted earlier, younger women, aged 18 to 24 years, are more likely than older women to report orgasm problems, during both masturbation and partnered sexual activity. It is possible that as women age they gain more sexual experience as well as become more aware of what their bodies need to attain orgasm. Women with lower levels of education reported more orgasm difficulties during masturbation than women with higher levels of education. Approximately 42% of women with a high school education report "always or usually" achieving orgasm during masturbation, compared to 87% of women with an advanced degree (Laumann et al., 1994). More educated women might hold more liberal views on sexuality and might be more likely to see their own pleasure as a goal of sexual activity.

A negative relation between high religiosity and orgasmic ability in women is frequently reported in the clinical literature. Possibly, the more religious a person is, the more likely she is to experience guilt during sexual activity. Guilt could impair orgasm via a number of cognitive mechanisms, in particular via distraction processes. A relationship between improved orgasmic ability and decreased sexual guilt has also been reported (Davidson & Moore, 1994). Laumann and colleagues (1994) found that a substantially higher proportion of women with no religious affiliation (79%) reported being orgasmic during masturbation compared with groups of religious women (53% to 67%).

In addition to specific demographics, it is also possible that overarching cultural notions of women's sexuality in general, and the value of women's sexual pleasure in particular, may also play a role in women's orgasmic capacity. Women who live in societies that value female orgasm tend to have more orgasms than women living in societies that discourage the concept of sexual pleasure for women (for a review, see Meston, Levin, et al., 2004).

Examples of societies that foster sexual pleasure for women and expect them to enjoy intercourse include the Mundugumor of Papua New Guinea and the Mangaians of the Cook Islands. Mangaian women are taught to have orgasms, hopefully two or three to each one of her male partner's, and to try to attain mutual orgasm. Mangaian males who are not able to give their partners multiple orgasms are looked down on. At the opposite end of the spectrum are societies that assume women will have no pleasure from coitus and that the female orgasm does not exist. The Arapesh of Papua New Guinea are such a society. In fact, they do not even have a word in their language for the female orgasm. It is feasible that women in societies that promote women's sexual pleasure are more likely to experiment and therefore learn about what facilitates their ability to have an orgasm. It may also be that in societies where sexual pleasure is discouraged, it may be shameful to admit to having an orgasm.

ASSESSMENT AND TREATMENT OF FOD

A doctor or psychologist familiar with the structure and function of orgasms should conduct the assessment of FOD. Depending on the etiology of the orgasm problem, a variety of both cognitive-behavioral and physical therapy techniques can be effective for increasing orgasmic capacity.

Assessment

Assessment of FOD involves a comprehensive sexual, medical, and psychosocial history similar to that used for assessing FSIAD. It is important for the clinician to determine whether the woman is unable to attain orgasm in all situations or just with a certain partner or during certain intercourse positions or sexual activities because this information may help to determine the most appropriate type of therapy.

Treatment

In general, sex therapy for FOD focuses on promoting healthy changes in attitudes and sexually relevant thoughts, decreasing anxiety, and increasing orgasmic ability and satisfaction. Sensate focus and systematic desensitization are used to treat FOD when anxiety seems to play a role. Sex education and communication skills training are often included as adjuncts to treatment. Kegel exercises (Kegel, 1952), which involve tightening and relaxing the pubococcygeus muscle, are also sometimes included as part of a treatment regime. Feasibly, they could help facilitate orgasm by increasing blood flow to the genitals, or by helping the woman become more aware of and comfortable with her genitals.

To date, the most efficacious treatment for FOD is directed masturbation (DM). This treatment uses cognitive-behavioral therapy techniques to educate a woman about her body and the sensations of manual self-stimulation. DM includes several stages that gradually build on one another. The first step of DM involves having the woman visually examine her nude body with the help of a mirror and diagrams of female genital anatomy. She is then instructed to explore her genitals using touch, with an emphasis on locating sensitive areas that produce feelings of pleasure. Once pleasure-producing areas are located, the woman is instructed to concentrate on manual stimulation of these areas and to increase the intensity and duration until "something happens." The use of topical lubricants, vibrators, and erotic videotapes is often incorporated into the exercises. Next, once the woman is able to attain orgasm alone, her partner is usually included in the sessions in order to desensitize her to displaying arousal and orgasm in his or her presence, and to educate the partner on how to provide her with effective stimulation.

Directed masturbation has been shown to effectively treat primary FOD when provided in a variety of formats, including individual, group, and couples therapy and also bibliotherapy (for a review, see Meston, 2006). A study of therapist-directed group therapy using DM reported a 100% success rate in treating primary FOD at 2-month follow-up (Heinrich, 1976). It has been proposed that DM is so effective because, in the early stages, it eliminates several factors that can impair orgasmic capacity, such as anxiety that may be associated with the presence of a partner. Since the exploration is focused on the woman's manual sexual stimulation, she is not dependent on her partner's sexual ability, or her ability to communicate her sexual needs to her partner until later in the treatment. Recent research has indicated that DM is particularly effective for women with primary FOD (Graham, 2014). It appears that DM can also be effective for women with secondary FOD who are uncomfortable touching their genitals, but in general, studies have found DM to be less effective for secondary FOD than for primary FOD. This may be because many women with secondary FOD only have trouble attaining orgasm with their partner. Therefore, treatments for secondary FOD typically focus on a couple's issues of communication, sexual skills, comfort, and trust.

If the etiology of the FOD appears to be related to anxiety about sex, then anxiety reduction techniques such as systematic desensitization and sensate focus may be useful. These strategies are often combined with sexual techniques training, DM, sex education, communication training, bibliotherapy, and Kegel exercises. As described earlier, Kegel exercises strengthen the pubococcygeus muscle, and are believed to facilitate orgasm by increasing the vascularity of the genitals. Supporting this technique, one study found a difference in the size of the pubococcygeus muscle between orgasmic and nonorgasmic women (Graber & Kline-Graber, 1979). Yet if anxiety is not the presenting cause of the orgasm problem, these techniques, while effective for desire and arousal problems, do not appear to be effective for treating orgasm problems (Meston, Levin, et al., 2004).

For women who have orgasm difficulties resulting from hysterectomy and oophorectomy, combined estrogen and testosterone therapy has been shown to enhance orgasmic ability (Shifren et al., 2000). A number of psychotherapeutic drugs have been used to try to eliminate orgasm problems that are secondary to antidepressant drug treatments. Results from placebo-controlled studies, to date, have failed to identify any drugs that enhance orgasmic ability better than placebo. However, one study indicated that exercise increases genital arousal in women taking either an SSRI or SNRI (Lorenz & Meston, 2012). As SSRIs are known to have greater SNS suppression compared to SNRIs, women taking SSRIs experienced significantly greater genital response postexercise than women taking SNRIs (Lorenz & Meston, 2012).

DELAYED EJACULATION

Definition, Diagnosis, and Prevalence

Delayed ejaculation (DE) is defined in *DSM-5* as a persistent difficulty or inability to achieve orgasm despite the presence of adequate desire, arousal, and stimulation. In order to be diagnosed with the disorder, patients must present with one of two symptoms: either a delay in or an infrequency of ejaculation on 75% to 100% of occasions for at least 6 months. The disorder can be specified as lifelong or acquired as well as generalized or situational. Most commonly, the term *delayed ejaculation* refers to a condition in which a man is unable to achieve orgasm with his partner, even though he is able to achieve and maintain an erection. Typically, men who present with DE are able to ejaculate during masturbation or sleep.

Researchers and clinicians alike agree that DE is not only the least common of the male sexual dysfunctions but also the least understood. A key concern that is often associated with DE but missed by clinicians is that partnered sexual activity may not be as exciting as masturbation. Techniques used during masturbation, such as rubbing the penis against different objects or rolling the penis between one's hands, may create an intense sense of friction that is otherwise elusive during sexual activity with a partner. In addition, masturbation may have a strong fantasy component, which again may be challenging to maintain when engaging in sexual intercourse with a partner.

It is important to note that men who are experiencing retrograde ejaculation do not meet the diagnostic criteria for DE. Retrograde ejaculation occurs when the ejaculatory fluid travels backward into the bladder rather than forward through the urethra. This may result from complications after prostate surgery or as a side effect of certain medications, particularly anticholinergic drugs.

The concept of a "delay" in ejaculation suggests that there are normative amounts of time in which ejaculation typically occurs. Only one study has addressed this question. Waldinger and Schweitzer (2005) measured intravaginal latency time in 500 heterosexual couples across five countries. They found that the median time was 5.4 minutes, the mean was 8 minutes, and the standard deviation was 7.1 minutes. Though these values are illuminating from a research perspective, it is noteworthy that the *DSM-5* does not include any objective measures of latency in the diagnostic criteria for the disorder, which makes it challenging to determine prevalence rates.

Prevalence rates of DE in the literature are low, usually 3% or lower. Researchers have suggested that the rate of DE will rise due to age-related ejaculatory decline (Perelman, 2003) as well as widespread use of SSRIs (Georgiadis et al., 2007), which have been implicated in increased ejaculation latency.

FACTORS ASSOCIATED WITH DELAYED EJACULATION

A number of biological and psychological factors have been shown to play an important role in delayed ejaculation. Biological factors include damage to the nerve pathways that facilitate ejaculation, chronic medical conditions, and potentially age. The various psychological etiologies of the disorder span from insufficient stimulation to assorted manifestations of "psychic conflict."

Biological Factors

During ejaculation, the efferent nerves that cause the release of semen and the closure of the bladder neck are sympathetic fibers that travel through the sympathetic ganglia and the peripheral pelvic nerves. Damage to any of these pathways may compromise ejaculation. Spinal cord injury is most likely to cause the nerve damage that results in DE.

Chronic medical conditions, such as multiple sclerosis and diabetes, are correlated with DE. Short-term, reversible medical conditions, including prostate infection, urinary tract infection, and substance abuse may also lead to symptoms of DE. Various psychopharmacological agents, including antipsychotics and antidepressants, may also lead to ejaculatory delay.

According to Segraves (2010), there is conflicting evidence regarding the effect of age on ejaculatory function. As DE is more common in older males, the disorder may be related to low penile sensitivity, which is associated with aging (e.g., Paick, Jeong, & Park, 1998). However, low penile sensitivity usually is not the primary cause of DE (Perelman, 2014). Rather, individual variability in the sensitivity of the ejaculatory reflex, which is exacerbated with age, may be driving the relationship between age and DE.

Psychological Factors

Recently, Althof (2012) reviewed the four leading psychological theories of DE. The first theory focuses on insufficient mental or physical stimulation (Masters & Johnson, 1970). Men with DE may have a diminished ability to experience penile sensations, as they have been shown to experience less sexual arousal than men without the disorder (Rowland, Keeney, & Slob, 2004). It is also possible that a lack of proper ambiance for sexual activity contributes to insufficient mental stimulation (Shull & Sprenkle, 1980).

The second theory that Althof (2012) mentions posits that DE is caused by a high frequency of masturbation or by a unique, idiosyncratic masturbatory style that differs greatly from the physical stimulation that occurs during vaginal penetration (e.g., Perelman & Rowland, 2006). Men with DE may experience a large disparity between the sensations that they experience when masturbating to a specific fantasy and the sensations that they experience during partnered sexual activity.

The third theory reviewed by Althof (2012) centers on "psychic conflict" as the root cause of DE. This theory was more common in the early stages of psychological treatment for DE, but some psychodynamically oriented therapists still conceptualize the disorder in terms of psychic conflict. Examples of psychic conflict include fear of loss of self due to loss of semen, fear that ejaculation may hurt the partner, fear of impregnating the partner, and guilt from a strict religious upbringing.

The final theory suggests that delayed ejaculation may be masking the presence of a desire disorder. In this case, the male may be overly concerned with pleasing his partner, and even when he is not aroused, may seek to ejaculate (Apfelbaum, 1989).

ASSESSMENT AND TREATMENT OF DELAYED EJACULATION

A medical doctor or clinical psychologist assesses for delayed ejaculation with an interview to determine ejaculation latency and to discuss the patient's reactions to this problem. The most common treatments incorporate behavioral techniques.

Assessment

Both physical and psychological assessment are necessary in order to gain a thorough understanding of the factors contributing to DE. To provide a thorough assessment, clinicians should conduct a genitourinary examination, check androgen levels, identify any physical anomalies, and assess any contributing neurological factors. Specific attention should be paid to the identification of urethral, prostatic, epididymal, and testicular infections (Corona, Jannini, Vignozzi, Rastrelli, & Maggi, 2012). Assessment of variables that improve or worsen performance in a given context may be informative, especially psychosocial factors like the use of fantasy during sex, anxiety during sexual activity, masturbatory patterns, and perceived partner attractiveness (Perelman, 2014).

Treatment

There has been limited success in the development and testing of pharmacological agents aimed at treating DE. Drugs that have been shown to be somewhat effective may only indirectly affect ejaculatory latency by altering other components of the sexual response cycle or by countering the effects of the drugs that led to the ejaculatory problem in the first place. In the future, alpha-1 adrenergic receptor agonists, such as imipramine, ephedrine, and midodrine, may play a role in the pharmacological treatment of DE. One study indicated that midodrine-facilitated ejaculation in men who were previously unable to ejaculate (Safarinejad, 2009), but further research is necessary. Other pharmacological agents, including yohimbine, buspirone (BuSpar), and oxytocin have been anecdotally associated with decreased ejaculation latency in men with DE. However, well-controlled studies with large sample sizes are needed to conclusively determine the effects of these drugs on ejaculation.

If the disorder is determined to be primarily psychological in origin, there are a number of psychosocial interventions that have been shown to effectively reduce ejaculation latency. Most sex therapists who treat DE rely on masturbatory retraining (Masters & Johnson, 1970) as a way to induce higher levels of arousal and help men rehearse for partnered sexual activity. This intervention may be particularly helpful for men who have grown accustomed to masturbating in idiosyncratic ways, such as with specific objects or under certain conditions. Masturbatory retraining typically entails introducing the patient to an alternative style of masturbation that mimics the sensations of partnered sexual activity. It may be that masturbation exercises, which progress from neutral to pleasurable sensations, remove the "demand aspects" of performance. If the disorder is derived from insufficient stimulation, therapists typically recommend vibrator stimulation, enhanced mental stimulation, and vigorous pelvic thrusting (Althof, 2012). For those who are experiencing DE due to heightened concern for the sexual pleasure of their partners, therapists encourage less focus on pleasing the partner and more attention to the self and the sensations experienced during sexual activity.

PREMATURE (EARLY) EJACULATION

Definition, Diagnosis, and Prevalence

Premature (early) ejaculation is defined in *DSM-5* as a persistent or recurrent pattern of ejaculation occurring during partnered sexual activity within about 1 minute following vaginal penetration and before the individual wishes it. Although the diagnosis may be applied to individuals who engage in nonvaginal sexual intercourse, specific duration criteria for such activities have not been established. In order to meet the diagnostic criteria, the problem must have persisted for at least 6 months, must be experienced on almost all or approximately all occasions of sexual activity, and must cause significant distress. The disorder may be specified by severity and can be categorized as lifelong or acquired and generalized or situational.

In recent years, there has been considerable disagreement about the definition, nature, and even the name of the disorder. The *DSM-5* sexual dysfunction subworkgroup changed the name of the disorder from "premature ejaculation" to "premature (early) ejaculation" due to criticism of the existing name, which some saw as pejorative. The diagnostic criteria of the disorder have also been critiqued, as researchers have argued that the time to ejaculation after penetration criterion oversimplifies, and may limit scientific understanding of the condition (e.g., Metz, Pryor, Nesvacil, Abuzzahab, & Koznar, 1997). Hong (1984) stated that premature (early) ejaculation might not warrant the term "dysfunction" unless it is extreme, "such as occurring before intromission."

Varying prevalence rates of the disorder have been reported, likely due to the lack of a universally accepted set of diagnostic criteria. It is important to note that there are currently no published epidemiological studies that assess the prevalence of premature (early) ejaculation as defined in *DSM-5*. However, many studies have assessed the prevalence of premature ejaculation concerns. Masters and Johnson (1970) identified premature (early) ejaculation as one of the most common male sexual dysfunctions. According to Laumann and colleagues (1994), premature (early) ejaculation is the most commonly reported sexual disorder in men, with approximately 30% of men in the United States reporting the condition in the previous year. Unlike ED, this condition has been estimated to affect younger men more than older men; prevalence estimates range from 40% of men under 40 years of age to about 10% of men over age 70. When the intravaginal ejaculation latency time criterion is used, however, prevalence rates are much lower, around 1% to 3% (Althof et al., 2010). In general, high rates of comorbidity are reported for premature (early) ejaculation and ED, with about one third of men who suffer from premature (early) ejaculation also experiencing ED.

FACTORS ASSOCIATED WITH PREMATURE (EARLY) EJACULATION

A number of factors have been shown to play an important role in both normal and premature ejaculation. Historically, premature ejaculation has been considered a psychological problem. But recent research has implicated a number of biological systems in the development and maintenance of the disorder, indicating that it may be important to focus on the physiological underpinnings of the ejaculatory process.

Biological Factors

During the first stage of ejaculation (sperm emission), sperm moves from the epididymis into the vas deferens. This process is controlled by the contraction of smooth muscles, which is generated by the sympathetic branch of the autonomic nervous system. After sperm emission, the individual has the subjective experience that ejaculation is "inevitable," known as the "point of inevitable ejaculation" or, more commonly, "the point of no return!" The striate muscles surrounding the spongious tissue and the cavernous tissue and in the pelvic floor contract rhythmically, causing ejaculation to occur. Usually, the subjective experience of orgasm is associated with the contractions of the striate muscles, and in most men, emission, ejaculation, and orgasm are interconnected. For a small portion of men, however, these phenomena are independent. For example, some men train themselves to have the subjective experience of orgasm without ejaculation and some men with premature (early) ejaculation experience emission without ejaculation.

The precise cause of premature (early) ejaculation is not known, but the most promising biological etiologies include malfunction of the serotonin receptors, genetic predisposition, and disruptions of the endocrine system. Waldinger, Rietschel, Nothen, Hengeveld, and Olivier (1998) noted that, in rodents, activation of one serotonin receptor speeds up ejaculation and activation of another serotonin receptor delays ejaculation. It is possible, then, that men who report symptoms of the disorder may have disturbances in central serotonergic neurotransmission, which could result in a lower threshold for sexual stimulation. Genetic predispositions may also play a role in the development of PE. In first-degree male relatives of Dutch men with lifelong PE, researchers found a high prevalence of PE (Waldinger, Rietschel, Nothen, Hengeveld, & Olivier, 1998). Similarly, a genetic study of Finnish male twins indicated that genetics accounts for 28% of the variance in PE (Jern et al., 2007). Recent research has confirmed the role of the endocrine system in the control of the ejaculatory reflex. Carani and colleagues (2005) found that 50% of men with hyperthyroidism also had PE. Indeed, the hormone thyrotropin, in addition to testosterone and prolactin, has been shown to play an independent role in the control of ejaculatory function (e.g., Corona et al., 2012).

PSYCHOLOGICAL FACTORS

Anxiety has been hypothesized to be one of the primary causes and maintaining factors for PE. Althof (2014) explained that three different mental phenomena related to PE can be characterized by the term *anxiety*. First, anxiety may reference a phobic response, such fear of the vaginal canal. Anxiety may also refer to an affective response, such as anger toward one's partner. Finally, anxiety may indicate performance concerns, such that a preoccupation with poor sexual performance leads to decreased sexual function and increased avoidance of sexual situations. Anxiety may have a reciprocal relationship with premature (early) ejaculation; specifically, performance anxiety may lead to problems with early ejaculation, and then those problems could increase performance anxiety (Althof et al., 2010). However, laboratory studies have generally not shown significant differences in levels of anxiety reported by men with and without PE.

One psychological variable that has been shown to distinguish men with PE from men without PE is perceived control over ejaculation. In an observational study of men with and without PE, Rosen and colleagues (2007) determined that subject-reported control over ejaculation and personal distress most strongly predicted a PE diagnosis. A greater understanding of the meaning men attribute to ejaculatory control may provide important insight into the psychological factors involved in this disorder.

Early learned experiences and lack of sensory awareness may also be important psychological factors that lead to PE. Masters and Johnson (1970) examined case histories of men with PE and found that many of these men had early sexual experiences during which they felt nervous and rushed. According to Masters and Johnson, these men learned to associate sex and sexual performance with speed and discomfort. Kaplan (1989) considered lack of sensory awareness to be the immediate cause of premature ejaculation. She believed that men with PE fail to develop sufficient awareness of their own level of arousal.

ASSESSMENT AND TREATMENT OF PREMATURE (EARLY) EJACULATION

A medical doctor or clinical psychologist assesses for premature (early) ejaculation with an interview to determine ejaculation latency and discuss reactions to this problem. The most common treatments are behavioral techniques that increase ejaculation latency.

Assessment

A thorough assessment of PE includes measuring three factors; length of time from penetration to ejaculation (ejaculation latency), subjective feelings of control over ejaculation, and personal and relational distress caused by the condition. Usually these dimensions of PE are assessed with retrospective self-reports provided by the patient. Sometimes the patient is asked to measure the time from insertion to ejaculation or to have his partner provide an estimate of his ejaculatory latency in order to increase measurement reliability.

Treatment

The most commonly used psychotherapy for increasing ejaculatory latency is an integration of psychodynamic, behavioral, and cognitive approaches. According to Althof (2014), the focus of psychotherapy for men with PE is to learn to control ejaculation while understanding the meaning of the symptom and the context in which the symptom occurs. Psychodynamically oriented therapists consider PE to be a metaphor for conflict in the relationship, while behavior-oriented therapists typically view the disorder as a conditioned response to certain interpersonal or environmental contexts. Common behavioral techniques for increasing ejaculatory latency are the squeeze technique developed by Masters and Johnson (1970) and the pause technique (Kaplan, 1989). The squeeze technique consists of engaging in sexual stimulation alone or with a partner for as long as possible before ejaculation. Before reaching the "point of inevitable ejaculation," the man is instructed to stop the activity and apply tactile pressure to the penile glans to decrease the urge to ejaculate but not to the point that he completely loses his erection. When the urge has subsided, the man resumes masturbation or intercourse stopping as many times as needed to delay ejaculation. The pause technique is similar to the squeeze technique with the exception that no pressure is applied to the penis. At times, clinicians may suggest using a PDE-5 inhibitor (e.g., sildenafil) along with these techniques so that the man can practice delaying ejaculation without worrying about maintaining an erection. Recent treatments combine these techniques and experimentation with new sexual positions that may reduce the propensity toward premature ejaculation. In one of the few well-controlled premature (early) ejaculation treatment studies, there was significant increase in ejaculation latency time among men treated with the squeeze technique compared to men in a wait-list control condition (de Carufel & Trudel, 2006).

Medical treatments include the use of topical anesthetics, such as prilocaine (Citanest) or lidocaine (Xylocaine), to diminish sensitivity; these are used in combination with condoms (to prevent the partner's genitals from being anesthetized). In men with lifelong PE, treatment with pharmacological antidepressants has been shown to increase the ejaculation latency and increase sexual pleasure and satisfaction. Selective serotonin reuptake inhibitors, such as sertraline (Zoloft), fluoxetine (Prozac), and paroxetine (Paxil), have most often been used to treat PE, because of their known side effects of delaying or inhibiting orgasm. These medications can be taken either daily or on demand 4 to 6 hours before sexual activity. Clinicians who treat men with PE have come to view the disorder as a "couple's problem" and recommend including the partner in treatment as much as possible to enhance both treatment compliance and treatment efficacy.

Dapoxetine (Priligy, Westoxetin), a rapid-acting SSRI with a short half-life, has been approved for treatment of premature (early) ejaculation in over 30 countries, but not in the United States. In clinical trials, dapoxetine taken before sexual activity was shown to significantly increase ejaculation latency compared to a pill placebo (Levine, 2006).

Sexual Pain Disorders

The *DSM-5* subworkgroup on sexual dysfunction combined the two sexual pain disorders identified in *DSM-IV-TR*, dyspareunia and vaginismus, into one disorder, called genito-pelvic pain/penetration disorder. In *DSM-IV-TR*, dyspareunia was defined as genital and/or pelvic pain, and vaginismus referred to an involuntary spasm or tightening of the pelvic muscles. The merging of dyspareunia and vaginismus emphasizes the multidimensional nature of genital pain, particularly in women.

GENITO-PELVIC PAIN/PENETRATION DISORDER

Definition, Diagnosis, and Prevalence

Genito-pelvic pain/penetration disorder (GPPPD) is defined in the *DSM-5* as persistent or recurrent difficulty with one or more of the following: (a) vaginal penetration during intercourse; (b) vulvovaginal or pelvic pain during vaginal intercourse or attempts at penetration; (c) fear or anxiety about vulvovaginal or pelvic pain in anticipation of, during, or as a result of vaginal penetration; and (d) tightening or tensing of the pelvic floor muscles during attempted vaginal penetration. At least one of these symptoms must have persisted for at least 6 months and must cause significant distress. The disorder can be specified by severity and as either lifetime or acquired.

The creation of the diagnosis of GPPPD came about partially as a response to arguments made by Binik (2010a), who questioned the logic of maintaining two separate diagnoses, given the high rates of comorbidity between difficulties with vaginal penetration and painful sexual intercourse. In a recent study of Portuguese women, 72.4% of women with a diagnosis of vaginismus reported symptoms of dyspareunia, and 47.7% of women with a diagnosis of dyspareunia reported symptoms of vaginismus (Peixoto & Nobre, 2013).

Binik (2010a) also argued in favor of a pain conceptualization, but the *DSM-5* subworkgroup decided to maintain the status of GPPPD as a sexual dysfunction. Kingsberg and Knudson (2011) have also questioned whether the disorder should be characterized as a pain disorder that interferes with sexual activity or as a sexual disorder predominately associated with pain. One study supports the pain conceptualization of GPPPD, as it indicated that nonpelvic chronic pain is associated with chronic genito-pelvic pain (Paterson, Davis, Khalifé, Amsel, & Binik, 2009). More research in this area is warranted.

Though the *DSM-IV-TR* diagnosis of dyspareunia applied to both males and females, male dyspareunia has been excluded from the *DSM-5* diagnostic criteria for GPPPD, likely due to a lack of empirical studies that address the condition. However, some research shows that males do occasionally suffer from localized or generalized pain during sexual activity. Clemens, Meenan, Rosetti, Gaos, and Calhoun (2005) suggested that the prevalence of male dyspareunia ranges from 5% to 15%. Researchers have established a term, *urological chronic pelvic pain syndrome* (UCPPS), that applies only to men, but it is not included in the *DSM-5* (Shoskes, Nickel, Rackley, & Pontari, 2009). Davis, Morin, Binik, Khalifé, and Carrier (2011) found that patterns of sensitivity and pelvic floor muscle function in men with UCPPS are similar to those of women who report problems with pelvic pain.

Painful intercourse and spasms of the pelvic floor muscle are frequently comorbid with sexual arousal problems in women. The genital changes that occur during sexual arousal, such as swelling and lubrication of the genitals facilitate penetrative intercourse. If these changes are absent but intercourse is still attempted, it can result in friction, tearing, and overstimulation of internal genital tissue that can lead to sexual pain. Therefore, some scientists believe that a lack of genital arousal may be a key antecedent to experiencing sexual pain and/or spasms.

As GPPPD is new to *DSM-5*, the prevalence of the disorder is currently unknown. Prevalence estimates do exist for dyspareunia and vaginismus. Rates of dyspareunia range from 2% to 7% in the general population of women (Peixoto & Nobre, 2013), from 6.5% to 45% in older women (van Lankveld et al., 2010), and from 14% to 34% in younger women (van Lankveld et al., 2010). With respect to vaginismus, prevalence rates are reported to be 5% to 6.6% (e.g., Fugl-Meyer et al., 2013), but higher rates of painful sexual intercourse have been noted in clinical settings and in countries where arranged marriages, polygamy, and/or widow inheritance are common (e.g., Amidu et al., 2010). Some women are at increased risk of genito-pelvic pain after giving birth. Paterson and colleagues (2009) found that 10% of women who experienced postpartum genito-pelvic pain continued to experience pain 1 year after childbirth. Risk factors for sexual pain include poor health, lower education, low family income, high stress, more frequent emotional problems, and the presence of urinary tract symptoms.

FACTORS ASSOCIATED WITH GENITO-PELVIC PAIN/ PENETRATION DISORDER

Research has identified the correlates of sexual pain in women (dyspareunia), including a number of medical conditions, as well as anxiety about sexual activity. Though not much is known about the correlates of painful, involuntary tensing of the pelvic floor muscles during attempted penetration (vaginismus), a robust association has been noted between vaginismus and anxiety. When sex is painful, women can build up anxiety around sex that works to exacerbate and maintain the pain associated with this disorder.

Biological Factors

Pain during sexual activity may result from a variety of medical conditions and anatomical complications. Superficial pain may be a symptom of dermatological disorders affecting the external genitalia, such as vaginal atrophy, anatomical variations, urinary tract infections, injury, and other diseases and infections of the vulva. Deep pain may result from uterine fibroids, endometriosis, urinary disease, and ovarian disease (for a review, see

Schultz et al., 2005). Pain may also stem from the treatment of gynecological and other cancers with pelvic radiation and chemotherapy (e.g., Fugl-Meyer et al., 2013).

One of the major causes of sexual pain at the superficial level is a biological disorder called provoked vestibulodynia (PVD; formerly called vulvar vestibulitis syndrome). This disorder is characterized by sensitivity to touch and pressure of the vulvar vestibule, a region bounded by the inner labia minora, the frenulum of the clitoris, and the lower portion of the vaginal opening. This touch and pressure evokes a sharp, burning pain. Generally, PVD is diagnosed by a gynecologist, who probes the vulvar vestibule with a cotton swab to determine the presence of pain sensations. Although the etiology of PVD is uncertain, it is believed to be at least partially caused by physiological sensitivity of the vulvar vestibule. Women with this disorder often have a history of yeast infections and may have had significant hormonal events in adolescence, including early onset of menstruation and early use of oral contraceptives (e.g., Farmer et al., 2011). PVD is the most common cause of premenopausal dyspareunia (Binik, 2010a). Related to superficial vaginal pain is vulvodynia, in which pain is not specific to the vulvar vestibule and not attributable to any other identifiable pathology. Another potential cause of superficial dyspareunia is vulvovaginal atrophy, the deterioration and reduction in flexibility and lubrication of the vaginal tissue that occurs with menopause. The vaginal symptoms reported by premenopausal women with PVD and postmenopausal women with vulvovaginal atrophy are markedly similar.

Causes of dyspareunia involving deep pain include uterine fibroids, urinary diseases such as uterine retroversion and uterine myomas, ovarian diseases such as ovarian remnant syndrome, adenomyosis, endometriosis, pelvic congestion syndrome, levator ani muscle myalgia, and irritable bowel syndrome. Sensitization of the neurons in the spinal cord and in parts of the brain has been postulated as the most likely cause of the deep type of dyspareunia. According to this theory, intense stimulation of peripheral tissue that occurs because of a physical trauma or repetitive abrasive stimulation can sensitize the neurons that bring the pain information to the brain. Consequently, the sensitized neurons require less stimulation to be activated, or they may even be activated without the presence of stimulation. Thus, the individual may feel pain after only a slight touch or even in the presence of no touch. Women with this type of dyspareunia often also report genital pain during nonsexual situations (Binik, 2010a).

Little research has focused on the biological factors associated with vaginismus. These involuntary spasms of the pelvic floor muscles may be due to genital malformations and/or poor general pelvic muscle control. As with dyspareunia, high rates of provoked PVD have been reported among women diagnosed with vaginismus (Binik, 2010b). The vaginal spasms that are associated with vaginismus may be a physiological response to intense pain during penetration; that is, the hypothesized vaginal spasm in vaginismus could be the body's automatic physical reaction to protect itself from anticipated pain. Associating pain with intercourse could lead to the avoidance of sexual activity often observed in women with vaginismus.

Psychological Factors

Fear of pain and anxiety associated with sexual activity have been proposed as both psychological symptoms and causes of sexual pain or dyspareunia. Compared to controls, women with dyspareunia exhibit a selective attentional bias toward pain stimuli, which is predicted by state and trait anxiety as well as fear of pain (Payne, Binik, Amsel, & Khalifé, 2005). Although anxiety appears to be a correlate of dyspareunia, not all women who experience sexual anxiety manifest the symptoms of sexual pain. Women with dyspareunia tend to fear sexual interactions and show more phobic anxiety about sexual activity than do women without sexual pain. It may be that after sexual pain has been experienced initially, anxiety about sexual activity maintains dyspareunia by increasing awareness for sexual pain. For example, women with PVD reported hypervigilance for sexual pain, and displayed an attentional bias toward pain-related stimuli on an emotional stressor task when compared to matched control women without PVD (Payne et al., 2005). In addition to anxiety, negative attitudes toward sexuality are correlated with dyspareunia.

Women with a history of abuse are more likely than nonabused women to experience genito-pelvic pain. Harlow and Stewart (2005) found that women who reported sexual pain were 4.1 times more likely to have a history of severe physical abuse and 6.5 times more likely to have a history of severe childhood sexual abuse compared to their nonabused counterparts. Fear of physical abuse has also been linked to experiencing genital pain (Landry & Bergeron, 2011), as has a history of abuse (Reissing, Binik, Khalifé, Cohen, & Amsel, 2004).

Depression and genito-pelvic pain are frequently linked in the literature; however, longitudinal studies have failed to find a direct relationship. It is likely that women who are more depressed are more likely to report pain in general and sexual pain in particular, but there is no evidence at this point that depression causes sexual pain or vice versa. Negative cognitions such as, "My partner will leave me," "I am a failure as a woman," and "I must be tearing inside," are commonly reported by women with sexual pain. From a relational point of view, women with dyspareunia report more pain when their relational distress increases, an indication that sexual pain may be partially associated with negative feelings between partners.

With respect to vaginismus, women who experience vaginal spasms report high levels of anxiety symptoms. It is unclear, however, whether anxiety plays a causal role in vaginismus, or whether the experience of the vaginal spasms contributes to increases in overall anxiety. Lower rates of positive attitudes toward one's sexuality have been observed in women who experience these spasms (Reissing et al., 2004). A lack of positive beliefs about one's sexuality may discourage a woman from seeking out positive sexual interactions and may contribute to avoidance of sexual activity.

ASSESSMENT AND TREATMENT OF GENITO-PELVIC PAIN/PENETRATION DISORDER

Assessment for GPPPD may include both an interview and a physical examination to identify areas where pain is experienced. The disorder is most often treated with cognitive-behavioral therapy or physical therapy methods that work on strengthening the pelvic floor and relaxing the vaginal muscles.

Assessment

The assessment of genito-pelvic pain should include an accurate description of the location, intensity, quality, duration, and time course of the pain; the degree of interference it has with sexuality; a summary of what elicits the pain (both sexual and nonsexual behaviors); and the meaning attributed to the pain. Pain is considered subjective and therefore is usually measured by a patient's self-report. Additional assessment by a gyne-cologist can help to identify the specific area(s) of the pain, as well as to take into account other potential gynecological issues that may be contributing to the pain. Assessment by a physical therapist may also be useful to confirm a diagnosis of GPPPD.

Treatment

The main treatments for genito-pelvic pain are cognitive-behavioral sex therapy/pain management, electromyographic feedback, and vestibulectomy. Topical anesthetics and other medications are also sometimes used to alleviate genital pain, but well-controlled studies examining their long-term effectiveness are currently lacking. Physical therapy with a focus on strengthening the pelvic floor through exercises, and enhancing flexibility with massage and stretching techniques have been used to treat sexual pain. Antidepres-sants and anticonvulsants have been used for pain relief, yet there are a limited number of clinical trials to support their efficacy.

The most current treatments for genito-pelvic pain combine cognitive-behavioral therapy to address education and faulty cognitions and physical therapy to strengthen and relax the vaginal muscles. Cognitive-behavioral sex therapy for dyspareunia generally includes educating the woman about sexual pain; the effect it has on sexual desire, arousal, and orgasm; and the factors that maintain the pain. Often cognitive restructuring exercises are used to help the woman identify faulty cognitions (e.g., "If I have sex my vagina may tear apart") and to replace them with more accurate beliefs (e.g., "My vagina is made of stretchable muscles that stretch out during intercourse"). These exercises aim to reduce the anxiety associated with sexual activity and encourage women to engage in nonpenetrative sexual activity to enhance sexual pleasure. Short-term group cognitive-behavioral therapy for PVD significantly reduced genital pain from pre- to posttreatment, with 39% of women endorsing great improvement or complete pain relief at the 6-month follow-up interval (Bergeron, Binik, Khalifé, Pagidas, & Glazer, 2001). Group cognitive-behavioral therapy and pain management for women with PVD also showed substantial reductions in genito-pelvic pain.

Electromyographic biofeedback has been used to treat genito-pelvic pain in women. Electromyography is a physiological response technique that records the electrical activity of skeletal muscles. The woman is trained to use the electromyography sensor to assess the tension in her pelvic muscles as she learns pelvic floor relaxation exercises. The exercises are practiced at home to reduce hypertonicity and increase the strength and flexibility of her pelvic floor. This technique was developed by Glazer, Rodke, Swencionis, Hertz, and Young (1995), who observed a relationship between PVD and abnormal responding of the pelvic floor musculature. Evidence suggests that electromyography and pelvic floor training significantly reduce sexual pain from PVD and may occasionally eliminate it altogether (e.g., Bergeron et al., 2001). Despite encouraging results from these trials of electromyography, success rates have varied considerably, calling for further study.

When physical therapy and psychological treatments have proven ineffective, there are also surgical treatment options. Vestibulectomy is an outpatient procedure that involves removal of vulvar vestibular tissue, and it has been shown to significantly reduce or com-pletely alleviate genital pain among the majority of recipients. If the genito-pelvic pain appears to have an etiology related to atrophy of the vaginal tissue, such as is common postmenopause, estrogen administration may help to rebuild vaginal tissue. The estrogens are usually administered via oral pharmacology or topical cream applied to the vagina.

Studies on the efficacy of estrogen treatment for dyspareunia related to atrophy of vaginal tissue have shown encouraging results (for a review, see Krychman, 2011).

Treatment for vaginismus, or involuntary spasms of the pelvic floor muscle, can include many of the same techniques used for treating dyspareunia, such as cognitive-behavioral therapy, electromyographic feedback, and vestibulectomy. As mentioned previously, cognitive-behavioral sex therapy focuses on educating the woman about her disorder; its potential impact on sexual desire, arousal, and orgasm; and potential elements that can maintain pain. Cognitive restructuring exercises and relaxation exercises like diaphragmatic breathing and progressive muscle relaxation are used to help the woman reduce her anxiety and avoidance of sexual activity.

Systematic desensitization has also been used to treat women who experience these painful pelvic spasms. In the context of sex therapy, systematic desensitization exercises are assigned for homework and entail relaxation coupled with gradual habituation to vaginal touch and penetration, usually beginning with the woman's fingers or artificial devices specifically designed for this purpose. Partners may also be incorporated into these exercises if desired. Despite the widespread use of systematic desensitization to treat this disorder, there is no empirical evidence that it is an effective treatment (Heiman & Meston, 1997). In a recent randomized clinical trial of cognitive-behavioral therapy for lifelong vaginismus that included systematic desensitization as a treatment component, women showed improvements in their ability to engage in penetrative intercourse (van Lankveld et al., 2006). However the efficacy of systematic desensitization alone is still unknown.

Summary and Future Directions

In summary, it is apparent that both biological and psychosocial factors play a prominent role in the etiology of sexual dysfunctions in men and women and must be carefully considered both in assessment and in treatment. The multidimensionality of sexuality calls for assessment and treatment strategies that account for all of the potential dimensions that are at play when an individual encounters sexual problems. All forms of sexual dysfunction occur in the context of a person's life. Consideration of that context, especially relational factors, can be used to guide treatment planning and recommendations.

In the lead-up to the publishing of the *DSM-5*, discussions of sexual dysfunction, especially with regard to women, became highly politicized and emotionally charged. The collapse of desire and arousal problems into one diagnostic category revealed tensions regarding the construct of female sexual desire, a construct that is sociopolitically loaded and challenging to tease apart in an objective fashion. In order to develop a more nuanced understanding of the relation between sexual desire and arousal in women, researchers and clinicians alike need to continue to delve into areas that may be controversial and uncomfortable.

The dramatic increase in medical approaches to the treatment of sexual problems has changed the landscape of sexual health research and treatment dissemination. It is evident that the future of the field will feature a large degree of multidisciplinary collaboration—among psychologists, psychiatrists, gynecologists, urologists, and primary care physicians—in order to continue to develop and refine research on the nature and treatment of sexual problems.

References

Allan, C. A., Forbes, E. A., Strauss, B.J.G., & McLachlan, R. (2008). Testosterone therapy increases sexual desire in ageing men with low-normal testosterone levels and symptoms of androgen deficiency. *International Journal of Impotence Research*, *20*(4), 396–401.

Althof, S. E. (2012). Psychological interventions for delayed ejaculation/orgasm. *International Journal of Impotence Research*, *24*, 131–136.

Althof, S. E. (2014). Treatment of premature ejaculation: Psychotherapy, pharmacotherapy, and combined therapy. In Y. M. Binik & K.S.K. Hall (Eds.), *Principles and practice of sex therapy* (5th ed., pp. 112–137). New York, NY: Guilford Press.

Althof, S. E., Abdo, C.H.N., Dean, J., Hackett, G., McCabe, M., McMahon, C. G., ... Tan, H. M. (2010). International Society for Sexual Medicine's guidelines for the diagnosis and treatment of premature ejaculation. *Journal of Sexual Medicine*, *7*(9), 2947–2969. doi: 10.1111/j.1743-6109.2010.01975.x

American Congress of Obstetricians and Gynecologists, Committee on Gynecologic Practice. (2007). *Vaginal "rejuvenation" and cosmetic vaginal procedures* (ACOG Committee Opinion No. 378). Washington, DC: American Congress of Obstetricians and Gynecologists.

American Psychiatric Association. (2000). *Diagnostic and statistical manual of mental disorders* (4th ed., text rev.). Washington, DC: Author.

American Psychiatric Association. (2013). *Diagnostic and statistical manual of mental disorders* (5th ed.). Washington, DC: Author.

Amidu, N., Owiredu, W.K.B.A., Woode, E., Addai-Mensah, O., Quaye, L., Alhassan, A., & Tagoe, E. A. (2010). Incidence of sexual dysfunction: A prospective survey in Ghanaian females. *Reproductive Biology and Endocrinology*, *8*, 106. doi: 10.1186/1477-7827-8-106

Apfelbaum, B. (1989). The diagnosis and treatment of retarded ejaculation. In S. R. Leiblum & R. C. Rosen (Eds.), *Principles and practice of sex therapy: Update for the 1990s* (pp. 168–206). New York, NY: Guilford Press.

Araujo, A. B., Esche, G. R., Kupelian, V., O'Donnell, A. B., Travison, T. G., Williams, R. E., ... McKinlay, J. B. (2007). Prevalence of symptomatic androgen deficiency in men. *Journal of Clinical Endocrinology and Metabolism*, *92*(11), 4241–4247. doi: 10.1210/jc.2007-1245

Bancroft, J. (2005). The endocrinology of sexual arousal. *Journal of Endocrinology*, *186*(3), 411–427. doi: 10.1677/joe.1.06233

Bancroft, J., & Janssen, E. (2000). The dual control model of male sexual response: A theoretical approach to centrally mediated erectile dysfunction. *Neuroscience and Biobehavioral Reviews*, *24*(5), 571–579. doi: 10.1016/S0149-7634(00)00024-5

Bancroft, J., Loftus, J., & Long, J. S. (2003). Distress about sex: A national survey of women in heterosexual relationships. *Archives of Sexual Behavior*, *32*(3), 193–208. doi: 10.1023/A:1023420431760

Barlow, D. H. (1986). Causes of sexual dysfunction: The role of anxiety and cognitive interference. *Journal of Consulting and Clinical Psychology*, *54*(2), 140–148. doi: 10.1037/0022-006X.54.2.140

Basaria, S., Coviello, A. D., Travison, T. G., Storer, T. W., Farwell, W. R., Jette, A. M., ... Bhasin, S. (2010). Adverse events associated with testosterone administration. *New England Journal of Medicine*, *362*(2), 109–122.

Basson, R. (2000). The female sexual response: A different model. *Journal of Sex & Marital Therapy*, *26*(1), 51–65.

Basson, R., & Brotto, L. A. (2003). Sexual psychophysiology and effects of sildenafil citrate in oestrogenised women with acquired genital arousal disorder and impaired orgasm: A randomised controlled trial. *BJOG: An International Journal of Obstetrics and Gynaecology*, *110*(11), 1014–1024. doi: 10.1111/j.1471-0528.2003.02438.x

Bergeron, S., Binik, Y. M., Khalifé, S., Pagidas, K., & Glazer, H. I. (2001). Vulvar vestibulitis syndrome: Reliability of diagnosis and evaluation of current diagnostic criteria. *Obstetrics and Gynecology*, *98*(1), 45–51. doi: 10.1016/S0029-7844(01)01389-8

Billups, K. L., Berman, L., Berman, J., Metz, M. E., Glennon, M. E., & Goldstein, I. (2001). A new non-pharmacological vacuum therapy for female sexual dysfunction. *Journal of Sex & Marital Therapy*, *27*(5), 435–441. doi: 10.1080/713846826

Binik, Y. M. (2010a). The DSM diagnostic criteria for dyspareunia. *Archives of Sexual Behavior*, *39*(2), 292–303. doi: 10.1007/s10508-009-9563-x

Binik, Y. M. (2010b). The DSM diagnostic criteria for vaginismus. *Archives of Sexual Behavior*, *39*(2), 278–291.

Bivalacqua, T. J., Deng, W., Kendirci, M., Usta, M. F., Robinson, C., Taylor, B. K., ... Kadowitz, P. J. (2007). Mesenchymal stem cells alone or ex vivo gene modified with endothelial nitric oxide synthase reverse age-associated erectile dysfunction. *American Journal of Physiology. Heart and Circulatory Physiology*, *292*(3), H1278–H1290. doi: 10.1152/ajpheart.00685.2006

Brotto, L. A., & Basson, R. (2014). Group mindfulness-based therapy significantly improves sexual desire in women. *Behavior Research and Therapy*, *57*, 43–54.

Brotto, L. A., Heiman, J. R., & Tolman, D. L. (2009). Narratives of desire in mid-age women with and without arousal difficulties. *Journal of Sex Research*, *46*(5), 387–398. doi: 10.1080/00224490902792624

Brotto, L., & Luria, M. (2014). Sexual interest/arousal disorder in women. In Y. M. Binik & K.S.K. Hall (Eds.), *Principles and practice of sex therapy* (5th ed., pp. 17–41). New York, NY: Guilford Press.

Carani, C., Isidori, A. M., Granata, A., Carosa, E., Maggi, M., Lenzi, A., & Jannini, E. A. (2005). Multicenter study on the prevalence of sexual symptoms in male hypo- and hyperthyroid patients. *Journal of Clinical Endocrinology and Metabolism*, *90*(12), 6472–6479. doi: 10.1210/jc.2005-1135

Carvalheira, A. A., Pereira, N. M., Maroco, J., & Forjaz, V. (2012). Dropout in the treatment of erectile dysfunction with PDE5: A study on predictors and a qualitative analysis of reasons for discontinuation. *Journal of Sexual Medicine*, *9*(9), 2361–2369. doi: 10.1111/j.1743-6109.2012.02787.x

Carvalheira, A., Traeen, B., & Štulhofer, A. (2014). Correlates of men's sexual interest: A cross-cultural study. *Journal of Sexual Medicine*, *11*(1), 154–164. doi: 10.1111/jsm.12345

Chew, K.-K., Finn, J., Stuckey, B., Gibson, N., Sanfilippo, F., Bremner, A., ... Jamrozik, K. (2010). Erectile dysfunction as a predictor for subsequent atherosclerotic cardiovascular events: Findings from a linked-data study. *Journal of Sexual Medicine*, *7*(1, Pt. 1), 192–202. doi: 10.1111/j.1743-6109.2009.01576.x

Clayton, A. H., Croft, H. A., & Handiwala, L. (2014). Antidepressants and sexual dysfunction: Mechanisms and clinical implications. *Postgraduate Medicine*, *126*(2), 91–99. doi: 10.3810/pgm.2014.03.2744

Clayton, A. H., DeRogatis, L. R., & Rosen, R. C. (2012). Intended or unintended consequences? The likely implications of raising the bar for sexual dysfunction diagnosis in the proposed DSM-V revisions: 1. For women with incomplete loss of desire or sexual receptivity. *Journal of Sexual Medicine*, *9*(8), 2027–2039.

Clemens, J. Q., Meenan, R. T., Rosetti, M. C. K., Gaos, S. Y., & Calhoun, E. A. (2005). Prevalence and incidence of interstitial cystitis in a managed care population. *Journal of Urology*, *173*(1), 98–102.

Corona, G., Jannini, E. A., Vignozzi, L., Rastrelli, G., & Maggi, M. (2012). The hormonal control of ejaculation. *Nature Reviews Urology*, *9*(9), 508–519. doi: 10.1038/nrurol.2012.147

Corona, G., Petrone, L., Mannucci, E., Ricca, V., Balercia, G., Giommi, R., ... Maggi, M. (2004). The impotent couple: Low desire. *International Journal of Andrology*, *28*(Suppl. 2), 46–52. doi: 10.1111/j.1365-2605.2005.00594.x

Corona, G., Rastrelli, G., Forti, G., & Maggi, M. (2011). Update in testosterone therapy for men (CME). *Journal of Sexual Medicine*, *8*(3), 639–654. doi: 10.1111/j.1743-6109.2010.02200.x

Cummings, S. R., Ettinger, B., Delmas, P. D., Kenemans, P., Stathopoulos, V., Verweij, P., ... Bilezikian. (2008). The effects of tibolone in older postmenopausal women. *New England Journal of Medicine*, *359*(7), 697–708.

Davidson, J. K., & Moore, N. B. (1994). Guilt and lack of orgasm during sexual intercourse: Myth versus reality among college women. *Journal of Sex Education and Therapy*, *20*(3), 153–174.

Davis, S. N., Morin, M., Binik, Y. M., Khalifé, S., & Carrier, S. (2011). Use of pelvic floor ultrasound to assess pelvic floor muscle function in urological chronic pelvic pain syndrome in men. *Journal of Sexual Medicine*, *8*(11), 3173–3180.

Davis, S. R., & Braunstein, G. D. (2012). Efficacy and safety of testosterone in the management of hypoactive sexual desire disorder in postmenopausal women. *Journal of Sexual Medicine*, *9*(4), 1134–1148.

Davison, S. L., Bell, R. J., LaChina, M., Holden, S. L., & Davis, S. R. (2008). Sexual function in well women: Stratification by sexual satisfaction, hormone use, and menopause status. *Journal of Sexual Medicine, 5*(5), 1214–1222.

de Carufel, F., & Trudel, G. (2006). Effects of a new functional-sexological treatment for premature ejaculation. *Journal of Sex & Marital Therapy, 32*(2), 97–114.

Dennerstein, L., Koochaki, P., Barton, I., & Graziottin, A. (2006). Hypoactive sexual desire disorder in menopausal women: A survey of Western European women. *Journal of Sexual Medicine, 3*, 212–222. doi: 10.1111/j.1743-6109.2006.00215.x

Diamond, L. M., & Wallen, K. (2011). Sexual minority women's sexual motivation around the time of ovulation. *Archives of Sexual Behavior, 40*(2), 237–246. doi: 10.1007/s10508-010-9631-2

Dunn, K. M., Croft, P. R., & Hackett, G. I. (1999). Association of sexual problems with social, psychological, and physical problems in men and women: A cross sectional population survey. *Journal of Epidemiology and Community Health, 53*(3), 144–148.

Exton, N. G., Truong, T. C., Exton, M. S., Wingenfeld, S. A., Leygraf, N., Saller, B., ... Schedlowski, M. (2000). Neuroendocrine response to film-induced sexual arousal in men and women. *Psychoneuroendocrinology, 25*(2), 187–199. doi: 10.1016/S0306-4530(99)00049-9

Farmer, M. A., Taylor, A. M., Bailey, A. L., Tuttle, A. H., MacIntyre, L. C., Milagrosa, Z. E., ... Mogil, J. S. (2011). Repeated vulvovaginal fungal infections cause persistent pain in a mouse model of vulvodynia. *Science Translational Medicine, 3*(101), 101ra91. doi: 10.1126/scitranslmed.3002613

Frohlich, P. F., & Meston, C. M. (2000). Evidence that serotonin affects female sexual functioning via peripheral mechanisms. *Physiology & Behavior, 71*(3-4), 383–393. doi: 10.1016/S0031-9384(00)00344-9

Fugl-Meyer, A. R., & Fugl-Meyer, K. S. (1999). Sexual disabilities, problems and satisfaction in 18–74 year old Swedes. *Scandinavian Journal of Sexology, 2*, 79–105.

Fugl-Meyer, K. S., Bohm-Starke, N., Damsted Petersen, C., Fugl-Meyer, A., Parish, S., & Giraldi, A. (2013). Standard operating procedures for female genital sexual pain. *Journal of Sexual Medicine, 10*(1), 83–93. doi: 10.1111/j.1743-6109.2012.02867.x

Georgiadis, J. R., Janniko, R., Reinders, A.A.T, Van der Graaf, F.H.C.E., Paans, A.M.J., & Kortekaas, R. (2007). Brain activation during human male ejaculation revisited. *Neuroreport, 18*(6), 553–557. doi: 10.1097/WNR.0b013e3280b10bfe

Glazer, H. I., Rodke, G., Swencionis, C., Hertz, R., & Young, A. W. (1995). Treatment of vulvar vestibulitis syndrome with electromyographic biofeedback of pelvic floor musculature. *Journal of Reproductive Medicine, 40*(4), 283–290.

Glina, S., Sharlip, I. D., & Hellstrom, W. J. (2013). Modifying risk factors to prevent and treat erectile dysfunction. *Journal of Sexual Medicine, 10*(1), 115–119. doi: 10.1111/j.1743-6109.2012.02816.x

Goodman, M. P., Placik, O. J., Benson, R. H., Miklos, J. R., Moore, R. D., Jason, R. A., ... Gonzalez, F. (2010). A large multicenter outcome study of female genital plastic surgery. *Journal of Sexual Medicine, 7*(4, Pt. 1), 1565–1577. doi: 10.1111/j.1743-6109.2009.01573.x

Graber, B., & Kline-Graber, G. (1979). Female orgasm: Role of pubococcygeus muscle. *Journal of Clinical Psychiatry, 40*(8), 348–351.

Graham, C. A. (2010). The DSM diagnostic criteria for female orgasmic disorder. *Archives of Sexual Behavior, 39*(2), 256–270.

Graham, C. A. (2014). Orgasm disorders in women. In Y. M. Binik & K.S.K. Hall (Eds.), *Principles and practice of sex therapy* (5th ed., pp. 89–111). New York, NY: Guilford Press.

Graham, C. A., Sanders, S. A., Milhausen, R. R., & Mcbride, K. R. (2004). Turning on and turning off: A focus group study of the factors that affect women's sexual arousal. *Archives of Sexual Behavior, 33*(6), 527–538. doi: 10.1023/B:ASEB.0000044737 .62561.fd

Grover, S. A., Lowensteyn, I., Kaouache, M., Marchand, S., Coupal, L., DeCarolis, E., ... Defoy, I. (2006). The prevalence of erectile dysfunction in the primary care setting: Importance of risk factors for diabetes and vascular disease. *Archives of Internal Medicine, 166*, 213–219.

Gupta, B. P., Murad, M. H., Clifton, M. M., Prokop, L., Nehra, A., & Kopecky, S. L. (2011). The effect of lifestyle modification and cardiovascular risk factor reduction on erectile dysfunction: A systematic review and meta-analysis. *Archives of Internal Medicine, 171*(20), 1797–1803. doi: 10.1001/archinternmed.2011.440

Handelsman, D. J. (2010). Androgen physiology, pharmacology and abuse. In L. J. DeGroot & J. L. Jameson (Eds.), *Endocrinology* (6th ed., pp. 2469–2498). Philadelphia, PA: Elsevier Saunders.

Handelsman, D. J. (2013). Global trends in testosterone prescribing, 2000–2011: Expanding the spectrum of prescription drug misuse. *Medical Journal of Australia, 199*, 548–551. doi: 10.5694/mja13.10111

Harlow, B. L., & Stewart, E. G. (2005). Adult-onset vulvodynia in relation to childhood violence victimization. *American Journal of Epidemiology, 161*(9), 871–880. doi: 10.1093/aje/kwi108

Harte, C. B., & Meston, C. M. (2011). Recreational use of erectile dysfunction medications and its adverse effects on erectile function in young healthy men: The mediating role of confidence in erectile ability. *Journal of Sexual Medicine, 9*(7), 1852–1859. doi: 10.1111/j.1743-6109.2012.02755.x

Heiman, J., & Meston, C. (1997). Evaluating sexual dysfunction in women. *Clinical Obstetrics and Gynecology, 40*(3), 616–629.

Heinrich, A. G. (1976). The effect of group and self-directed behavioral-educational treatment of primary orgasmic dysfunctions in females treated without their partners. *Dissertation Abstracts International, 37*(4-B).

Hong, L. K. (1984). Survival of the fastest: On the origin of premature ejaculation. *Journal of Sex Research, 20*(2), 109–122.

Jern, P., Santtila, P., Witting, K., Alanko, K., Harlaar, N., Johansson, A., … Sandnabba, K. (2007). Premature and delayed ejaculation: Genetic and environmental effects in a population-based sample of Finnish twins. *Journal of Sexual Medicine, 4*(6), 1739–1749. doi: 10.1111/j.1743-6109.2007.00599.x

Kaplan, H. S. (1989). *How to overcome premature ejaculation.* New York, NY: Brunner/Mazel.

Kegel, A. H. (1952). Stress incontinence and genital relaxation. *Ciba Clinical Symposia, 4*(2), 35–51.

Kenemans, P., Bundred, N. J., Foidart, J. M., Kubista, E., von Schoultz, B., Sismondi, P., … Beckmann, M. W. (2009). Safety and efficacy of tibolone in breast-cancer patients with vasomotor symptoms: A double-blind, randomised, non-inferiority trial. *Lancet Oncology, 10*(2), 135–146.

Kingsberg, S. A., & Knudson, G. (2011). Female sexual disorders: Assessment, diagnosis, and treatment. *CNS Spectrums, 16*(2), 49–62.

Krychman, M. L. (2011). Vaginal estrogens for the treatment of dyspareunia. *Journal of Sexual Medicine, 8*(3), 666–674. doi: 10.1111/j.1743-6109 .2010.02114.x

Laan, E., Smith, M. D., Boolell, M., & Quirk, F. (2002). Development of a sexual function questionnaire for clinical trials of female sexual dysfunction. *Journal of Women's Health & Gender-Based Medicine, 11*(3), 277–289.

Landry, T., & Bergeron, S. (2011). Biopsychosocial factors associated with dyspareunia in a community sample of adolescent girls. *Archives of Sexual Behavior, 40*(5), 877–889. doi: 10.1007/s10508-010-9637-9

Laumann, E. O., Glasser, D. B., Neves, R.C.S., & Moreira, E. D. (2009). A population-based survey of sexual activity, sexual problems and associated help-seeking behavior patterns in mature adults in the United States of America. *International Journal of Impotence Research, 21*(3), 171–178. doi: 10.1038/ijir.2009.7

Laumann, E. O., Michael, R. T., Gagnon, G. H., & Kolata, G. (1994). *Sex in America: A definitive survey.* Boston, MA: Little, Brown.

Laumann, E. O., Nicolosi, A., Glasser, D. B., Paik, A., Gingell, C., Moreira, E., & Wang, T. (2005). Sexual problems among women and men aged 40–80 y: Prevalence and correlates identified in the Global Study of Sexual Attitudes and Behaviors. *International Journal of Impotence Research, 17*(1), 39–57. doi: 10.1038/sj.ijir.3901250

Laumann, E. O., Paik, A., & Rosen, R. C. (1999). Sexual dysfunction in the United States. *JAMA, 281*(6), 537–545. doi: 10.1001/jama.281.6.537

Leiblum, S. R., & Wiegel, M. (2002). Psychotherapeutic interventions for treating female sexual dysfunction. *World Journal of Urology, 20*(2), 127–136.

Leonard, L. M., & Follette, V. M. (2002). Sexual functioning in women reporting a history of child sexual abuse: Review of the empirical literature and clinical implications. *Annual Review of Sex Research, 13*(1), 346–388.

Levine, L. (2006). Evaluation of withdrawal effects with dapoxetine in the treatment of premature ejaculation (PE). Poster presented at the meeting of the Sexual Medicine Society of North America.

Lorenz, T. A., Harte, C. B., Hamilton, L. D., & Meston, C. M. (2012). Evidence for a curvilinear relationship between sympathetic nervous system activation and women's physiological sexual arousal. *Psychophysiology, 49*(1), 111–117. doi: 10.1111/j.1469-8986 .2011.01285.x

Lorenz, T. A., & Meston, C. M. (2012). Acute exercise improves physical sexual arousal in women taking antidepressants. *Annals of Behavioral*

Medicine, 43(3), 352–361. doi: 10.1007/s12160-011 -9338-1

Mah, K., & Binik, Y. M. (2001). The nature of human orgasm: A critical review of major trends. *Clinical Psychology Review, 21*(6), 823–856. doi: 10.1016/ S0272-7358(00)00069-6

Maio, G., Saraeb, S., & Marchiori, A. (2010). Physical activity and PDE5 inhibitors in the treatment of erectile dysfunction: Results of a randomized controlled study. *Journal of Sexual Medicine, 7*(6), 2201–2208.

Masters, W. H., & Johnson, V. E. (1970). *Human sexual inadequacy*. Boston, MA: Little, Brown.

McCabe, M. P., & Connaughton, C. (2014). Psychosocial factors associated with male sexual difficulties. *Journal of Sex Research, 51*(1), 31–42. doi: 10.1080/00224499.2013.789820

McCall, K. M., & Meston, C. M. (2006). Cues resulting in desire for sexual activity in women. *Journal of Sexual Medicine, 3*(5), 838–852. doi: 10.1111/j .1743-6109.2006.00301.x

McCarthy, B., & Metz, M. E. (2008). The "Good Enough Sex" model. *Sexual and Relationship Therapy, 23*(3), 227–234.

McKenna, K. E. (1999). Orgasm. In M. A. Skinner (Ed.), *Encyclopedia of reproduction* (Vol. 3). San Diego, CA: Academic Press.

Meana, M., & Steiner, E. T. (2014). Sex therapy in transition: Are we there yet? In Y. M. Binik & K.S.K. Hall (Eds.), *Principles and practices of sex therapy* (5th ed., pp. 541–557). New York, NY: Guilford Press.

Mercer, C. H., Fenton, K. A., Johnson, A. M., Wellings, K., Macdowall, W., McManus, S., ... Erens, B. (2003). Sexual function problems and help seeking behaviour in Britain: National probability sample survey. *British Medical Journal, 327*(7412), 426–427. doi: 10.1136/bmj.327.7412.426

Meston, C. (2006). Female orgasmic disorder: Treatment strategies and outcome results. In I. Goldstein, C. M. Meston, S. Davis, & A. Traish (Eds.), *Women's sexual function and dysfunction: Study, diagnosis, and treatment*. Boca Raton, FL: CRC Press.

Meston, C. M., & Frohlich, P. F. (2000). The neurobiology of sexual function. *Archives of General Psychiatry, 57*(11), 1012–1030.

Meston, C. M., & Gorzalka, B. B. (1995). The effects of sympathetic activation on physiological and subjective sexual arousal in women. *Behavior Research and Therapy, 33*(6), 651–664.

Meston, C. M., & Gorzalka, B. B. (1996a). Differential effects of sympathetic activation on sexual arousal in sexually dysfunctional and functional women. *Journal of Abnormal Psychology, 105*(4), 582–591.

Meston, C. M., & Gorzalka, B. B. (1996b). The effects of immediate, delayed, and residual sympathetic activation on sexual arousal in women. *Behavior Research and Therapy, 34*(2), 143–148. doi: 10.1016/0005-7967(95)00050-X

Meston, C. M., Gorzalka, B. B., & Wright, J. M. (1997). Inhibition of subjective and physiological sexual arousal in women by clonidine. *Psychosomatic Medicine, 59*, 339–407.

Meston, C. M., & Heiman, J. R. (1998). Ephedrine-activated physiological sexual arousal in women. *Archives of General Psychiatry, 55*(7), 652–656.

Meston, C. M., Hull, E., Levin, R. J., & Sipski, M. (2004). Disorders of orgasm in women. *Journal of Sexual Medicine, 1*(1), 66–68.

Meston, C. M., Levin, R. J., Sipski, M. L., Hull, E. M., & Heiman, J. R. (2004). Women's orgasm. *Annual Review of Sex Research, 15*, 173–257. doi: 10.1080/ 10532528.2004.10559820

Meston, C. M., Rellini, A. H., & Heiman, J. R. (2006). Women's history of sexual abuse, their sexuality, and sexual self-schemas. *Journal of Consulting and Clinical Psychology, 74*(2), 229–36. doi: 10.1037/ 0022-006X.74.2.229

Metz, M. E., Pryor, J. L., Nesvacil, L. J., Abuzzahab, F., Sr., & Koznar, J. (1997). Premature ejaculation: A psychophysiological review. *Journal of Sex & Marital Therapy, 23*(1), 3–23.

Murray, S. H., & Milhausen, R. R. (2012). Sexual desire and relationship duration in young men and women. *Journal of Sex & Marital Therapy, 38*(1), 28–40. doi: 10.1080/0092623X.2011.569637

Nijland, E. A., Weijmar, S. W., Nathorst-Boos, J., Helmond, F. A., Van Lunsen, R. H., Palacios, S., ... Davis, S. R. (2008). Tibolone and transdermal E2/NETA for the treatment of female sexual dysfunction in naturally menopausal women: Results of a randomized active-controlled trial. *Journal of Sexual Medicine, 5*(3), 646–656.

Nobre, P. J., & Pinto-Gouveia, J. (2006). Dysfunctional sexual beliefs as vulnerability factors to sexual dysfunction. *Journal of Sex Research, 43*(1), 68–75. doi: 10.1080/00224490609552300

Nobre, P. J., & Pinto-Gouveia, J. (2009). Cognitive schemas associated with negative sexual events:

A comparison of men and women with and without sexual dysfunction. *Archives of Sexual Behavior*, *38*(5), 842–851. doi: 10.1007/s10508-008-9450-x

Paick, J. S., Jeong, H., & Park, M. S. (1998). Penile sensitivity in men with premature ejaculation. *International Journal of Impotence Research*, *10*(4), 247–250.

Paterson, L. Q., Davis, S. N., Khalifé, S., Amsel, R., & Binik, Y. M. (2009). Persistent genital and pelvic pain after childbirth. *Journal of Sexual Medicine*, *6*(1), 215–221.

Payne, K. A., Binik, Y. M., Amsel, R., & Khalifé, S. (2005). When sex hurts, anxiety and fear orient attention towards pain. *European Journal of Pain*, *9*(4), 427–436. doi: 10.1016/j.ejpain.2004.10.003

Peixoto, M., & Nobre, P. (2013). Prevalence of female sexual problems in Portugal: A community-based study. *Journal of Sexual Medicine*, *10*, 394.

Perelman, M. A. (2003). Sex coaching for physicians: Combination treatment for patient and partner. *International Journal of Impotence Research*, *15*(Suppl. 5), S67–S74. doi:10.1038/sj.ijir.3901075

Perelman, M. A. (2009). The sexual tipping point: A mind/body model for sexual medicine. *Journal of Sexual Medicine*, *6*(3), 629–632.

Perelman, M. A. (2014). Delayed ejaculation. In Y. M. Binik & K.S.K. Hall (Eds.), *Principles and practice of sex therapy* (5th ed., pp. 138–155). New York, NY: Guilford Press.

Perelman, M. A., & Rowland, D. L. (2006). Retarded ejaculation. *World Journal of Urology*, *24*(6), 645–652. doi: 10.1007/s00345-006-0127-6

Reissing, E. D., Binik, Y. M., Khalifé, S., Cohen, D., & Amsel, R. (2004). Vaginal spasm, pain, and behavior: An empirical investigation of the diagnosis of vaginismus. *Archives of Sexual Behavior*, *33*(1), 5–17. doi: 10.1023/B:ASEB.0000007458.32852.c8

Rellini, A. (2008). Review of the empirical evidence for a theoretical model to understand the sexual problems of women with a history of CSA. *Journal of Sexual Medicine*, *5*(1), 31–46.

Rosen, R., Brown, C., Heiman, J., Leiblum, S., Meston, C., Shabsigh, R., ... D'Agostino, R. (2000). The Female Sexual Function Index (FSFI): A multidimensional self-report instrument for the assessment of female sexual function. *Journal of Sex and Marital Therapy*, *26*(2), 191–208. doi: 10.1080/009262300278597

Rosen, R. C., McMahon, C. G., Niederberger, C., Broderick, G. A., Jamieson, C., & Gagnon, D. (2007). Correlates to the clinical diagnosis of premature ejaculation: Results from a large observational study of men and their partners. *Journal of Urology*, *177*(3), 1059–1064; discussion 1064. doi: 10.1016/j.juro.2006.10.044

Rosen, R. C., Miner, M. M., & Wincze, J. P. (2014). Erectile dysfunction: Integration of medical and psychological approaches. In Y. M. Binik & K.S.K. Hall (Eds.), *Principles and practice of sex therapy* (5th ed., pp. 61–88). New York, NY: Guilford Press.

Rowland, D. L., Keeney, C., & Slob, A. K. (2004). Sexual response in men with inhibited or retarded ejaculation. *International Journal of Impotence Research*, *16*(3), 270–274. doi: 10.1038/sj.ijir.3901156

Safarinejad, M. R. (2009). Midodrine for the treatment of organic anejaculation but not spinal cord injury: A prospective randomized placebo-controlled double-blind clinical study. *International Journal of Impotence Research*, *21*(4), 213–220.

Schmidt, P. J., & Rubinow, D. R. (2009). Sex hormones and mood in the perimenopause. *Annals of the New York Academy of Sciences*, *1179*, 70–85. doi: 10.1111/j.1749-6632.2009.04982.x

Schouten, B.W.V., Bohnen, A. M., Bosch, J.L.H.R., Bernsen, R.M.D., Deckers, J. W., Dohle, G. R., & Thomas, S. (2008). Erectile dysfunction prospectively associated with cardiovascular disease in the Dutch general population: Results from the Krimpen Study. *International Journal of Impotence Research*, *20*(1), 92–9. doi: 10.1038/sj.ijir.3901604

Schultz, W. W., Basson, R., Binik, Y. M., Eschenbach, D., Wesselmann, U., & Van Lankveld, J. (2005). Women's sexual pain and its management. *Journal of Sexual Medicine*, *2*(3), 301–316. doi: 10.1111/j.1743-6109.2005.20347.x

Segraves, R. T. (2010). Considerations for diagnostic criteria for erectile dysfunction in DSM V. *Journal of Sexual Medicine*, *7*(2, Pt. 1), 654–660.

Segraves, R. T., Clayton, A., Croft, H., Wolf, A., & Warnock, J. (2004). Bupropion sustained release (SR) for the treatment of hypoactive sexual desire disorder (HSDD) in nondepressed women. *Journal of Sex & Marital Therapy*, *27*(3), 303–316. doi: 10.1080/009262301750257155

Shamloul, R., & Ghanem, H. (2013). Erectile dysfunction. *Lancet*, *381*(9861), 153–165. doi: 10.1016/S0140-6736(12)60520-0

Shifren, J. L., Braunstein, G. D., Simon, J. A., Casson, P. R., Buster, J. E., Redmond, G. P., ...

Mazer, N. A. (2000). Transdermal testosterone treatment in women with impaired sexual function after oophorectomy. *New England Journal of Medicine*, *343*(10), 682–688. doi: 10.1097/00006254-20010 2000-00021

Shoskes, D. A., Nickel, J. C., Rackley, R. R., & Pontari, M. A. (2009). Clinical phenotyping in chronic prostatitis/chronic pelvic pain syndrome and interstitial cystitis: A management strategy for urologic chronic pelvic pain syndromes. *Prostate Cancer and Prostatic Diseases*, *12*, 177–183.

Shull, G. R., & Sprenkle, D. H. (1980). Retarded ejaculation reconceptualization and implications for treatment. *Journal of Sex & Marital Therapy*, *6*(4), 234–246.

Sipski, M. L., Alexander, C. J., & Rosen, R. C. (1997). Physiological parameters associated with sexual arousal in women with incomplete spinal cord injury. *Archives of Physical Medicine and Rehabilitation*, *78*, 305–313.

Society of Obstetricians and Gynaecologists of Canada, Clinical Practice Gynaecology Committee and Ethics Committee. (2013). *Female genital cosmetic surgery*. Ottawa, ON: Society of Obstetricians and Gynaecologists of Canada.

Stanton, A. M., Boyd, R. L., Pulverman, C. S., & Meston, C. M. (2015). Determining women's sexual self-schemas through advanced computerized text analysis. *Child Abuse & Neglect*, *46*, 78–88. doi: 10 .1016/j.chiabu.2015.06.003

Stanton, A. M., Lorenz, T. A., Pulverman, C. S., & Meston, C. M. (2015). Heart rate variability: A risk factor for female sexual dysfunction. *Applied Psychophysiology and Biofeedback*, *40*(3), 229–237. doi: 10.1007/s10484-015-9286-9

Stimmel, G., & Gutierrez, M. A. (2006). Sexual dysfunction and psychotropic medications. *CNS Spectrums*, *11*(8, Suppl. 9), 24–30.

Tan, O., Bradshaw, K., & Carr, B. R. (2012). Management of vulvovaginal atrophy-related sexual dysfunction in postmenopausal women: An up-to-date review. *Menopause*, *19*(1), 109–117.

Van Anders, S. M. (2012). Testosterone and sexual desire in healthy women and men. *Archives of Sexual Behavior*, *41*(6), 1471–1484. doi: 10.1007/ s10508-012-9946-2

Van Anders, S. M., Brotto, L. A., Farrell, J., & Yule, M. (2009). Associations among physiological and subjective sexual response, sexual desire, and salivary steroid hormones in healthy premenopausal women. *Journal of Sexual Medicine*, *6*, 739–751.

Van Lankveld, J., Granot, M., Schultz, W. W., Binik, Y. M., Wesselmann, U., Pukall, C. F., ... Achtrari, C. (2010). Women's sexual pain disorders. *Journal of Sexual Medicine*, *7*(1, Pt. 2), 615–631. doi: 10.1111/j.1743-6109.2009.01631.x

Van Lankveld, J. J., ter Kuile, M. M., de Groot, H. E., Melles, R., Nefs, J., & Zandbergen, M. (2006). Cognitive-behavioral therapy for women with lifelong vaginismus: A randomized waiting-list controlled trial of efficacy. *Journal of Consulting and Clinical Psychology*, *74*(1), 168–178.

Waldinger, M. D., Rietschel, M., Nothen, M. M., Hengeveld, M. W., & Olivier, B. (1998). Familial occurrence of primary premature ejaculation. *Psychiatric Genetics*, *8*(1), 37–40.

Waldinger, M. D., & Schweitzer, D. H. (2005). Retarded ejaculation in men: An overview of psychological and neurobiological insights. *World Journal of Urology*, *23*(2), 76–81.

Wallwiener, C. W., Wallwiener, L. M., Seeger, H., Muck, A. O., Bitzer, J., & Wallwiener, M. (2010). Prevalence of sexual dysfunction and impact of contraception in female German medical students. *Journal of Sexual Medicine*, *7*(6), 2139–2148.

Wang, C., Swerdloff, R. S., Iranmanesh, A., Dobs, A., Snyder, P. J., Cunningham, G., ... Berman, N. (2000). Transdermal testosterone gel improves sexual function, mood, muscle strength, and body composition parameters in hypogonadal men. *Journal of Clinical Endocrinology and Metabolism*, *85*(2), 2839–2853.

Whipple, B., Gerdes, C. A., & Komisaruk, B. R. (1996). Sexual response to self-stimulation in women with complete spinal cord injury. *Journal of Sex Research*, *33*(3), 231–240.

Xie, D., Annex, B. H., & Donatucci, C. F. (2008). Growth factors for therapeutic angiogenesis in hypercholesterolemic erectile dysfunction. *Asian Journal of Andrology*, *10*(1), 23–27. doi: 10.1111/j.1745-7262.2008.00372.x

Chapter 14

Borderline Personality Disorder

JILL M. HOOLEY AND SARA R. MASLAND

Borderline personality disorder (BPD) is a complex and challenging clinical problem. It is among the most severe forms of personality disorder that mental health professionals treat. Moreover, BPD is typically chronic, involves a high suicide rate, and is associated with significant distress. Thus, it warrants a great deal of attention from clinicians and researchers.

Unfortunately, the diagnosis of BPD is often regarded in a pejorative way by mental health professionals, some of whom view people with this disorder as manipulative and attention seeking, and they are therefore reluctant to accept them as patients. Yet few other groups of patients are in as much need of high-quality, thoughtful, and caring clinical care as those diagnosed with BPD. In this chapter, we illustrate some of the complexities of this disorder and the confusions that still surround it. We begin with a consideration of the clinical features of BPD and the symptoms that are at the heart of the *DSM* diagnosis.

Symptoms and Diagnostic Criteria

The suffering experienced by people with BPD is not easily captured in the summary list of *DSM-5* criteria (American Psychiatric Association [APA], 2013) shown in Table 14.1. BPD is a disorder characterized by profound emotional pain. As Zanarini and Frankenburg (1997) have noted, from the perspective of patients this pain is often perceived and described as being "the worst pain anyone has felt since the history of the world began." Other hallmarks of the disorder are instability and impulsivity. Indeed, BPD may be best understood as a disorder of "stable instability." There is instability in mood. This is reflected in inappropriate, intense anger or in periods of rapidly changing negative emotions, often in response to interpersonal stress. There is also instability in self-image: patients have difficulty in maintaining a sense of who they are and/or what they want from their lives, or in defining their goals and values. People with BPD also have highly unstable interpersonal relationships. The person they idolize in the morning may be the person they despise as the day draws to a close.

Impulsivity further characterizes the BPD sufferer. This is not carefree spontaneity. Rather, it is the kind of impulsivity that is potentially self-damaging and likely to create trouble. People with BPD frequently abuse alcohol or drugs, drive recklessly, or spend money that they do not have. They may engage in risky sexual behavior, gamble, or go on

TABLE 14.1   Clinical Features of Borderline Personality Disorder

Five or more of the following symptoms are required for the diagnosis of BPD:

1. Profound fears of abandonment (real or imagined). The person makes frantic and sometimes extreme efforts to avoid abandonment by others.

2. Interpersonal relationships that are both intense and unstable and that alternate between feelings of idealization and devaluation of the other person.

3. Identity disturbance characterized by a highly unstable sense of self or markedly disturbed self-image.

4. Impulsive behavior in at least two areas that have the potential to be self-damaging or to have harmful consequences (such as substance abuse, reckless driving, binge eating, unsafe sexual behavior, excessive spending).

5. Recurrent self-mutilating behavior or suicide threats, gestures, or suicidal behavior.

6. Highly reactive mood, leading to affective instability (e.g., intense negative affect such as depression, irritability, or anxiety that lasts a few hours or [rarely] a few days).

7. Persistent feelings of emptiness.

8. Intense or inappropriate anger that is difficult to control (e.g., constant feelings of anger, angry outbursts, or recurrent physical fights).

9. Brief periods of paranoid ideation or dissociative symptoms when under stress.

Source: Based on *DSM-5*.

eating binges. Unstable and strong emotions together with profound feelings of emptiness place people with BPD at high risk of engaging in other more direct forms of self-harm as well, such as cutting themselves with razor blades or burning themselves with cigarettes. Suicidal thoughts and behaviors are also common, especially in response to fears of being abandoned. Indeed, around 10% of patients with BPD will eventually take their own lives (Oldham, 2006). Simply put, the emotional pain that people with BPD experience is intense; managing their affective reactions to real or imagined slights or threats of abandonment presents patients, as well as their families, with serious challenges. In many cases, suicidal and self-injurious behaviors are used as strategies to regulate strong negative emotions, as in the following case example.

CASE EXAMPLE

CB is a 22-year-old single Hispanic woman who engages in nonsuicidal self-injury to manage feelings of anger, anxiety, and guilt. When she is angry at her boyfriend or another significant person in her life, she feels guilty for feeling angry; this leads to feelings of deep self-hatred, which she believes she cannot tolerate, and she begins to pinch her skin to feel physical pain that will distract her from these feelings. Sometimes the pinching leads to intense scratching until she draws blood. This provides a sense of relief from her emotions. The relief is experienced as "being back in control." CB describes two low-lethality suicide attempts, which she distinguishes from the nonsuicidal self-injury. On two separate occasions, on the anniversary of the death of her father, she became extremely angry at her boyfriend for not acknowledging the difficulty of the day for her.

She became hopeless, feeling that her boyfriend would never be able to understand her, and that she would always be unbearably sad about losing her father, and would be unable to get the help she needed to deal with it. She also felt there was something wrong with her for feeling this way. These thoughts led to a decision to take an overdose of her medication in order to kill herself. On both occasions, as soon as she took about 10 pills (not enough to cause lethal harm), she felt a sense of relief that at least she had done something to take control of her situation, and she no longer wished to die. She then fell asleep and had no other medical consequences from the overdose, and woke up feeling much better (adapted from Stanley & Brodsky, 2005, p. 54).

In addition to the clinical hallmarks of affective disturbances and impulsivity, people with BPD also show significant cognitive symptoms. We have already noted the presence of a disorganized and unstable self-image in BPD. In addition, in *DSM-IV* (APA, 1994), the ninth symptom, "brief paranoid ideas or severe dissociative symptoms related to stress," was added to the diagnostic criteria established in 1980. Approximately 75% of patients with BPD report paranoid ideas and/or dissociative episodes (Lieb et al., 2004; Skodol et al., 2002). More recent research, using experience sampling methods (which involve participants providing self-assessments when prompted by a beep from a digital device), indicates that people with BPD do indeed experience stress-related psychotic episodes (Glaser, Van Os, Thewissen, & Myin-Germeys, 2010; Stiglmayr et al., 2008).

Importantly, the cognitive symptoms of BPD differ significantly from the symptoms of patients with psychotic disorders or schizophrenia. For example, patients with BPD may have hallucinations, but they tend to have more insight than patients with psychosis and usually realize that these experiences are misperceptions. Moreover, when patients with BPD have paranoid ideas, these typically are not so firmly held that they reach delusional levels. Finally, the episodes of dissociation that are experienced by BPD patients are relatively brief and stress-related, often being experienced as a general feeling of estrangement.

HISTORY OF THE BORDERLINE DIAGNOSIS

Borderline personality disorder formally entered the diagnostic nomenclature in 1980 with the publication of *DSM-III*. However, the origins of the concept date back to the 1930s, when borderline patients were first described by the psychoanalyst Adolf Stern (1938). Stern's use of the term *borderline* was meant to reflect his view that the disorder did not fit well within the existing classification system, which was principally oriented around differentiating between neurosis and psychosis. Yet even today, many of the characteristics of the borderline patient that Stern described, including hypersensitivity, difficulties in reality testing, and negative reactions in therapy are recognizable to those familiar with the disorder.

Knight (1953) subsequently described a group of patients with severely impaired ego functions and primary process thinking, which is a type of thinking that reflects unconscious wishes and urges. Although others (e.g., Hoch & Polantin, 1949) had referred to such patients as suffering from "pseudo-neurotic schizophrenia," Knight used Stern's term, *borderline*. However, Knight considered the disorder to be on the border not just of neurosis but of both neurosis and psychosis. Knight observed that this group of patients had special needs in hospital settings and that failure to meet these needs could create tensions among staff members. Subsequently, the term *borderline* became used to describe atypical patients who were neither neurotic nor psychotic, but who were problematic to deal with when they were in the hospital (Gunderson, 2001).

The borderline diagnosis had been largely ignored from Stern's time until the late 1960s. After the psychoanalyst Otto Kernberg began to offer clinically rich and theoretically insightful perspectives on the disorder (Kernberg, 1967), interest began to increase. Around the same time, Grinker, Werble, and Drye (1968) published the first empirical study of the borderline syndrome.

A third key event was the highly influential literature review conducted by Gunderson and Singer (1975). This integrated the earlier descriptive efforts and attempted to provide diagnostic criteria for BPD. By 1980, the construct of borderline personality disorder was considered to be sufficiently well developed and valid to warrant inclusion in the most important revision of the diagnostic nomenclature—the *DSM-III* (APA, 1980; Spitzer, Endicott, & Gibbon, 1979; Spitzer, Forman, & Nee, 1979). BPD has since become the most researched of all the personality disorders.

One other historical note warrants mention. Just before BPD was added to the *DSM-III*, U.S. psychiatrists were polled about whether an alternative name for the disorder should be considered. More specifically, Spitzer, Endicott, and Gibbon (1979) proposed that the name "unstable personality disorder" be substituted. However, a majority of clinicians felt inclined to retain the familiar term, *borderline personality*.

As Paris (1999) has noted, however, this decision may have been a mistake. The term *borderline* is strongly linked to the psychoanalytic tradition. This may have led to the disorder being less accepted by clinicians from other perspectives. The term *borderline* is also inherently confusing because it is not immediately clear what *border* is being referred to. Indeed, Akiskal et al. (1985) have described *borderline* as "an adjective in search of a noun." These factors may have created resistance to accepting the disorder—resistance that, until relatively recently, was especially strong in Europe (e.g., Tyrer, 1999). Although BPD is now included in the ICD-10, the more descriptive term *emotionally unstable disorder* is used. This term has no psychoanalytic legacy or theoretical baggage, and from a clinical perspective, it also comes much closer to capturing some of the key elements of the disorder.

Many changes were originally proposed for personality disorders in the *DSM-5*. These included a major reconceptualization of personality pathology and the removal of several personality disorders from the diagnostic nomenclature. Although borderline personality was never in serious danger of being excluded, an early proposal to change the way that BPD was diagnosed (by matching patients to narrative prototypes) received severe criticism (Gunderson, 2010) because it represented such a radical shift from the *DSM-IV*. This proposal was subsequently discarded. Moreover, in the final days of the revision process a decision was made not to incorporate *any* of the changes that had been proposed by the Personality and Personality Disorders Work Group. These proposals had included a hybrid model of personality that incorporated both categorical and dimensional approaches and a focus on personality traits rather than on specific behavioral manifestations of these traits. Instead, an alternative *DSM-5* model for personality disorders now appears in Section III of the *DSM-5* manual—the section reserved for emerging measures and models. What this means is that, after years of meetings and countless hours of debate and discussion, the official *DSM-5* criteria for personality disorders are exactly the same as they were in *DSM-IV*.

Prevalence and Epidemiological Factors

With an estimated prevalence in the general population of 1% to 2% (Lenzenweger, Lane, Loranger, & Kessler, 2007) and a prevalence in outpatient samples of around 10% to 15% (Asnaani, Chelminski, Young, & Zimmerman, 2007; Hyman, 2002), BPD is far from a rare disorder. As we noted earlier, BPD is also associated with a high level of mortality from suicide. These factors, combined with the high propensity of patients with BPD to both utilize treatment resources (Bender et al., 2001; Zanarini, Frankenburg, Khera, & Bleichmar, 2001) and terminate treatment prematurely (Percudani, Belloni, Conti, & Barbui, 2002), make BPD a significant problem—both for those who suffer from it and for society in general.

It has long been accepted that BPD is more commonly found in women than in men, with women accounting for approximately 75% of cases (APA, 2000). There is also little support for the idea that this is the result of a gender bias in the diagnostic criteria (Jane, Oltmanns, South, & Turkheimer, 2007; Sharp et al., 2014), although this issue cannot be considered fully resolved (see Boggs et al., 2009). Rather, reported gender differences in the prevalence rates of BPD may be an artifact caused by samplings in clinical settings (Skodol & Bender, 2003). If women are more likely to seek treatment, prevalence estimates from clinical settings will naturally be biased in the direction of finding more females than males with the disorder.

Consistent with this idea, two representative, population-based studies, one conducted in Norway (Torgersen, Kringlen, & Cramer, 2001) and one conducted in the United States (Lenzenweger et al., 2007) have reported no gender differences in the prevalence of BPD. Further findings from community samples in Great Britain have even indicated that, in England, Scotland, and Wales, BPD is more prevalent in men (Coid, Yang, Tyrer, Roberts, & Ullrich, 2006). In light of these data, we believe there is no evidence to support the once commonly held assumption that there is a 3:1 female to male gender ratio in BPD.

HETEROGENEITY

BPD is a clinically heterogeneous disorder. The *DSM* lists nine symptoms, with five symptoms being necessary for the diagnosis. Because no one specific symptom is required, there are 126 different ways these symptoms can be combined to yield the same diagnostic outcome. This means that the BPD phenotype varies widely across those diagnosed with the disorder. The heterogeneity in BPD has prompted research into the "core aspects" of the disorder and has led to debate about its most important features.

Linehan (1993), for example, considers affective instability to be at the core of BPD. According to this view, it is the rapid mood changes, extreme reactivity to the environment, and dysthymic baseline mood that best characterize the disorder (Linehan, 1993). Bateman and Fonagy (2003), in contrast, have suggested that emotional instability is a secondary phenomenon that results from instability in the self-structure. Gunderson (1996) takes a more interpersonal perspective and highlights fear and intolerance of aloneness as central to the disorder. According to this perspective, the extreme fear of abandonment and the accompanying "frantic" efforts to avoid it are at the core of BPD. Still others, working from a more neurobiological framework, have asserted that disinhibition *and* general negative affectivity underlie borderline pathology (Siever & Davis, 1991; Trull, 2001). Finally, Zanarini, Frankenburg, Hennen, and Silk (2003) have noted that, even when other symptoms of the disorder remit, high levels of negative affectivity tend to remain in people with BPD. This suggests that a core aspect of the personality structure of those inclined to BPD may be an enduring dysphoria (see Westen, Bradley, & Shedler, 2005). In short, although BPD is the most common personality disorder found in clinical settings worldwide (Loranger et al., 1994; Torgersen et al., 2001; Widiger & Frances, 1989), it is far from being clearly conceptualized.

COMORBIDITY

Another important problem concerns comorbidity. Patients with BPD are much more likely to be co-diagnosed with other disorders than are psychiatric patients who do not have BPD (see Gunderson, 2001; Zanarini et al., 1998). In a representative clinical study, Zimmerman and Mattia (1999) conducted interviews with 409 psychiatric outpatients and compared the comorbid diagnoses of 59 patients who had BPD to the diagnoses of 305 patients who did not have BPD. A diagnosis of BPD was associated with higher rates of concurrent major depression (61%), dysthymia (12%), bipolar disorder (20%), eating disorders (17%), PTSD (36%), and substance abuse problems (14%). Recent findings from a large community sample also suggest that a majority of people with BPD meet criteria for a lifetime diagnosis of mood disorder (83%), anxiety disorder (85%), or substance use disorder (78%) (see Tomko, Trull, Wood, & Sher, 2014). One unusual feature of BPD is that it tends to be comorbid with both internalizing and externalizing disorders (Eaton et al., 2010).

The large overlap between BPD and mood disorders has led some to speculate that BPD is more appropriately regarded as a mood disorder variant (Akiskal, 2002; Akiskal et al., 1985; Sauer-Zavala & Barlow, 2014). However, this view is not widely endorsed (Choi-Kain & Gunderson, 2015; Gunderson & Phillips, 1991; Paris, 2004). Structural neuroimaging data show that although there is some overlap between the brain regions implicated in BPD and bipolar disorder, there are also important differences (Rossi et al., 2013). Functional neuroimaging data further indicate that, compared to healthy controls and to those diagnosed with dysthymia, people with BPD show a different pattern of neural activity when exposed to certain types of emotional stimuli (Hooley et al., 2010). These findings provide additional support for the idea that BPD is a distinct condition, different from chronic mood disorder. Nonetheless, it is highly likely that they share some common underlying vulnerabilities.

BPD is also highly comorbid with other personality disorders (e.g., antisocial personality disorder) (Lenzenweger et al., 2007; McGlashan et al., 2000; Tomko et al., 2014). High rates of comorbidity among personality disorders raise questions not only about the conceptualization of BPD itself but also about the conceptualization of personality disorders more broadly.

Current Theoretical Perspectives

It is important to state from the outset that the etiology of borderline personality disorder is still unknown. In this respect, BPD is like most other psychiatric conditions. Most prominent theorists, regardless of their orientation, highlight the roles of both biological vulnerabilities and environmental factors.

Psychodynamic Approaches

Working within the psychodynamic tradition, Kernberg (1975) presented one of the earliest theories of the pathogenesis of BPD. In this perspective, a high level of constitutional aggression in the child is regarded as a predisposing factor. This temperamental factor interferes with normal developmental processes such as the integration of different (positive and negative) perspectives of the self and others. Accordingly, memories of experiences with significant others are stored separately from each other as either good or bad (i.e., by affective valence) rather than being integrated (good *and* bad). In the face of environmental frustrations or failures in caretaking, "good" representations are threatened by strong negative feelings such as rage or hostile impulses. In Kernberg's conceptualization of "borderline personality organization"—which encompasses more than just the symptoms represented by the *DSM* diagnosis—patients have an unstable sense of self, together with the use of primitive (immature) defense mechanisms designed to protect these split representations of the self and others. At times, temporary problems in reality testing are apparent as the person experiences difficulty in determining what is real and what is imagined.

Another theorist whose ideas have been influential is Heinz Kohut (1971, 1977). As represented by Kohut, the tradition of self-psychology psychoanalytic theory emphasizes the importance of the caretaker's attunement to the needs of the child. This is not to say that caretakers have to be perfect. Rather, what is needed is what Winnicott (1953) referred to as "good enough mothering." Key components here are empathic responses that mirror the child's strengths and efforts to explore the world and that validate the child's sense of mastery. When caretakers are able to meet the child's needs in this way, the child is able to develop a stable sense of self and an ability to regulate self-esteem by drawing on an internal representation of the caretaker as a source of emotional comfort and soothing. In an unresponsive family environment, however, the child's angry emotions disrupt the development of a positive sense of self. In an application of this theory to BPD, Adler and Buie (Adler & Buie, 1979; Buie & Adler, 1982) have theorized that borderline patients lack the ability to call on memories of "good objects" (internal representations or images of nurturing and empathic caretakers) to provide self-soothing in times of distress. The absence of these images for people with BPD thus becomes an important factor in their inability to regulate their own emotions.

Behavioral Approaches

The most influential example of the cognitive-behavioral approach to understanding BPD is provided by the work of Marsha Linehan. According to Linehan's biosocial theory,

BPD results when biological or temperamental vulnerabilities interact with failures in the child's social environment, such that problems with emotion regulation are either created or exacerbated (Linehan, 1993). More specifically, problems such as a high level of sensitivity to negative emotions, high emotional reactivity, and a slow return to baseline after becoming emotionally aroused are thought to be precursors of the chronic problems with emotional regulation that are so characteristic of BPD. If the emotionally vulnerable person is able to manage these vulnerabilities successfully, all may be well. However, if the family environment does not provide the emotionally vulnerable child with the skills necessary to contain strong emotions, more severe emotional dysregulation (and a diagnosis of BPD) may be the result.

Within Linehan's model, the key environmental factor is an invalidating family environment. This is a concept that, although deeply rooted in the behavioral tradition, may have some overlap with the parental failures identified by Kohut and described in the psychoanalytic literature (e.g., inadequate acknowledgment of a child's emotional responses). Invalidation means that the child's communications of his or her actual internal experiences are met by responses on the part of the parents that are inappropriate, erratic, or otherwise out of touch with what is truly happening to the child (Fruzetti, Shenk, & Hoffman, 2005). For example, if the child sees something desirable to eat and says, "I'm hungry," an invalidating response from the parent might be to say, "No you aren't. You don't want to eat that." In other words, the child's experience of seeing the treat and wanting to eat it is dismissed and denied. In contrast, a validating response might involve the parent saying, "Yes, I know you want to eat that. But we will be having dinner very soon so I don't want you to spoil your appetite by eating that now." Notice that in neither instance does the child receive the treat—validation is not the same thing as gratification. However, in the second (validated) example, the child's internal experience of feeling hungry and wanting the treat is not ignored or rendered illegitimate.

There are many problems that are thought to stem from pervasive invalidation. These range from heightened emotional arousal immediately after being invalidated to a failure to learn how to accurately label one's own emotions. These difficulties, in turn, may create problems in managing emotions, and may also lead toward a tendency to self-invalidate (not trust one's own emotional responses). As we shall later see, some of the most important psychological treatments for BPD are designed to help patients learn some of the key skills that they failed to develop with regard to the appraisal and management of emotional events.

Biological Factors

BPD is perhaps best regarded as reflecting the interplay between biological vulnerabilities and environmental factors across development. This is important to keep in mind because new developments in research are making it increasingly clear that biological processes and psychosocial events can be separated only in the abstract. For example, different genotypes are associated with differential sensitivities to environmental stressors such as life events, child abuse, or maternal neglect (see Caspi et al., 2002; Gabbard, 2005). Other studies also support the conclusion that both nature *and* nurture play critical roles in such behaviors as impulsive aggression (Bennett et al., 2002; Higley, Suomi, &

Linnoila, 1991) and responsiveness to stress (Fish et al., 2004; Francis & Meaney, 1999). We encourage readers to keep in mind during later sections of this chapter that genes create differential sensitivities to environmental factors, that experiences turn some genes "on" while shutting other genes "off," and that psychosocial events can lead to changes in the neurobiology and neurochemistry of the brain (see Gabbard, 2005)

GENETICS

Family history studies of patients with BPD suggest that biological relatives have an increased prevalence of the disorder. Until recently, researchers relied solely on patients as the source of information and there was no direct assessment of the relatives themselves (see White, Gunderson, Zanarini, & Hudson, 2003 for a review). Studies that employ indirect assessment methods of this kind run the risk that people with BPD might exaggerate the extent to which their relatives showed elements of the disorder, thus inflating familiality estimates. Using an approach that involved direct interviews with people with BPD and their parents and siblings, Gunderson and colleagues (2011) reported a BPD prevalence of 14.1% in the relatives of individuals with BPD. This is considerably higher than the 4.9% prevalence of BPD in the relatives of participants who did not have BPD. In other words, BPD does show familial aggregation. Overall, people who have a family member with BPD have somewhere between a three- to fourfold increased risk of developing the disorder themselves (Gunderson et al., 2011).

The finding that a disorder runs in families does not necessarily mean that it is genetic. Many problems in children could arise as a consequence of being raised by a psychiatrically disturbed parent or from living in the chaotic family environment that might result from having a mentally ill sibling. To fully disentangle genetic from rearing effects, adoption studies are necessary. To date, no such studies have been conducted on the adopted-away offspring of women with BPD. However, using a twin sample, Torgersen and colleagues (2000) reported a concordance rate for BPD of 35% in monozygotic (MZ) twins compared with a concordance rate of 7% for dizygotic (DZ) twins. Other studies using even more sophisticated designs also support the idea that BPD has a heritable component (Distel et al., 2009).

But what is inherited? It is noteworthy that the family pedigrees of people with BPD also show increased prevalence rates of mood and anxiety disorders, impulse control disorders, and personality disorders such as antisocial PD (White et al., 2003; Zanarini, Barison, Frankenburg, Reich, & Hudson, 2009). It is also the case that the elements of BPD (e.g., affective instability) are more commonly found in the relatives of those with the disorder than is the diagnosis itself (Zanarini et al., 2004). What may therefore be inherited are traits that are linked to the neurobehavioral dimensions underlying a diagnosis of BPD (e.g., Depue & Lenzenweger, 2005). Heritability has been demonstrated for traits such as neuroticism, cognitive dysregulation, anxiety, and affective lability (Jang, Livesley, Vernon, & Jackson, 1996; Livesley, Jang, Jackson, & Vernon, 1993; Lubke et al., 2014). Impulsivity also appears to have a genetic component (see Goodman, New, & Siever, 2004). In other words, rather than inheriting the *DSM* disorder of BPD, it is much more likely that individuals inherit genetic propensities to exhibit traits that underlie the behavioral manifestations of BPD but that are also transdiagnostic.

For example, evidence is beginning to accumulate linking the serotonin transporter gene (5-HTT) with suicide and impulsivity, as well as with emotional lability (Bondy, Erfurth, deJonge, Kruger, & Meyer, 2000; Frankle et al., 2005; Hoefgen et al., 2005). Because these are characteristics of BPD, the serotonin transporter gene is now being investigated as a possible candidate gene for this disorder. Associations between certain aspects of the 5-HTT gene and BPD have been reported (Maurex, Zaboli, Öhman, Åsberg, & Leopardi, 2010; Ni et al., 2006). However, findings from other studies suggest that the link between the serotonin transporter gene and BPD is not likely to be straightforward (Pascual et al., 2008; Wagner, Baskaya, Lieb, Dahman, & Tadíc, 2009). The same is also true for other genes, such as MAO-A (monoamine oxidase A) and TPH-1 (tryptophan hydroxylase-1), that are involved in serotonin production and regulation. Despite some promising results indicating the importance of serotonergic genes for understanding BPD, meta-analysis results have been disappointing. In one meta-analytic study, no direct associations were found between any polymorphism and BPD (Calati, Gressier, Balestri, & Serretti, 2013). Similarly, a recent meta-analysis by Amad, Ramoz, Thomas, Jardri, and Gorwood (2014) found no association between the 5-HTT or TPH-1 genes and BPD. These same researchers have argued that we might best view genes as "susceptibility to environment genes" or "plasticity genes" rather than "vulnerability genes." That is, it may be more fruitful to consider that some genes may interact with both negative *and* positive aspects of the environment, and that the net effect of these interactions may determine how those genes are expressed.

Other candidate genes that have attracted the attention of researchers include the dopamine transporter gene (DAT1) as well as genes that code for dopamine reception production (such as DRD2 and DRD4). Dopamine is involved in the reward pathways of the brain. Cloninger (2000) has suggested that the trait of high novelty seeking, which is associated with BPD, may be related to altered dopaminergic function in the brain. The high levels of comorbidity between BPD and substance use disorders further support the hypothesized link between dopamine and BPD (Ebstein, Benjamin, & Belmaker, 2000).

Using a sample of depressed patients, Joyce and his colleagues (Joyce et al., 2009, Joyce, Stephenson, Kennedy, Mulder, & McHugh, 2014) have now replicated their earlier finding that the 9-repeat allele of the DAT1 gene is more likely to be found in depressed patients with BPD than in depressed patients who do not have BPD. This finding suggests that this polymorphism may be a risk factor for BPD. Other research reports significant associations between variants of the DRD2 and DRD4 dopamine receptor genes and the presence of BPD traits (Nemoda et al., 2010). These findings provide further support for the role of abnormalities in the dopamine system in the disorder. It is also intriguing to note that dopamine is an important neurotransmitter in psychotic disorders and that, when under stress, people with BPD sometimes experience transient psychotic episodes (Glaser et al., 2010).

A recent focus of research involves receptor genes for the neuropeptide oxytocin. A polymorphism of the oxytocin receptor gene (OXTR rs53576) has been shown to predict borderline pathology through an interaction with early family functioning (Hammen, Bower, & Cole, 2015). Only individuals with a specific polymorphism of this gene showed susceptibility to the effects of good versus poor family functioning.

With regard to the prediction of borderline pathology, the interaction between genes regulating oxytocin and environmental factors may also be moderated by gender. Cicchetti, Rogosch, Hecht, Crick, and Hetzel (2014) argue that a plasticity framework, in which genes influence the susceptibility of an individual to given environments (for better or worse), best explains the role of OXTR in predicting borderline pathology in boys. This means that OXTR polymorphisms predict the effects of both positive (protective) and negative (risk-conferring) environmental factors on boys. For girls, however, borderline pathology appears to be predicted by the interaction of specific polymorphisms with the experience of *negative* environmental stressors (child maltreatment in Cicchetti et al.'s 2014 study). In contrast to the situation with boys, OXTR polymorphisms did not predict the influence of positive environmental influences on girls. It is also noteworthy that this study also found that the "risk" alleles for boys and girls were opposite: homozygous major alleles (GG) conferred greater risk for borderline symptoms in boys. For girls it was combinations involving minor alleles (AG or AA) that conferred greater risk.

In summary, although there are many reasons to believe that genetic factors play an important role in BPD, nothing definitive can be said at this stage. To date, only two genome-wide association studies (GWAS) have been conducted and both have been limited by relatively small sample sizes (at least for genetic research). No reliable findings identifying specific genes for BPD have yet been found, although there are some preliminary leads (Witt et al., 2014). A focus on genetic transmission of BPD features, rather than the diagnosis itself, is likely to represent the most fruitful approach.

NEUROBIOLOGY

The high level of comorbidity between BPD and other disorders makes it difficult to evaluate the extent to which BPD has specific neurobiological correlates. It is also rather unlikely that the disorder itself has a distinct and specific neurobiological signature. More likely the various trait dimensions of BPD (e.g., impulsivity or anger and aggressiveness) are associated with underlying neurochemical or neuroanatomical dysregulations. Disturbances in serotonin, norepinephrine, and dopamine functioning have been implicated in BPD. There is also evidence of abnormalities in the hypothalamic-pituitary-adrenal (HPA) axis. In the following sections, we describe some of the key findings to date.

Neurotransmitters

As we have already noted, there are several reasons to believe that disturbances in the neurotransmitter serotonin might be implicated in BPD. Both animal and human studies have linked low levels of 5-hydroxyindoleacetic acid (5-HIAA), which is a major metabolite of serotonin, to higher levels of impulsive aggression (Coccaro, Siever, Klar, & Maurer, 1989; see also Goodman et al., 2004). A large literature has also linked low 5-HIAA in the cerebrospinal fluid (CSF) to suicide, especially violent forms of suicide (Åsberg, 1997). Moreover, rhesus monkeys with low levels of CSF 5-HIAA are also more inclined to consume alcohol when it is made available in experimental settings (Suomi, 2003). Because all of these behaviors are associated with BPD, it seems reasonable to expect that patients with the disorder might have disturbances in serotonergic function.

To test the serotonin hypothesis, Rinne, Westenberg, den Boer, and van den Brink (2000) administered a neuroendocrine challenge test to 12 women with BPD and 9 healthy control subjects. The neuroendocrine challenge involved the oral ingestion of m-CPP (meta-chlorophenylpiperazine), a serotonin agonist that acts on serotonin receptors to trigger the release of prolactin and cortisol. After receiving the m-CPP challenge, patients with BPD showed significantly lower levels of prolactin and cortisol in their blood than did the healthy controls. In particular, a history of physical and sexual abuse was highly and negatively correlated with the overall prolactin response. The results suggest that traumatic stress in childhood (which is reported by 20% to 75% of BPD patients; see Herman, Perry, & van der Kolk, 1989; Ogata et al., 1990; Salzman et al., 1993) may alter aspects of the serotonin system, perhaps at the level of the serotonin receptors.

Noradrenergic function may also be disturbed in BPD, possibly due to the link between norepinephrine function and aggression. Coccaro, Lee, and McClosky (2003) measured plasma levels of the major metabolite of norepinephrine (3-methoxy-4-hydroxyphenylglycol, or MHPG) in 30 males with personality disorders. Levels of MHPG were lower in the men who had BPD than in those who had other disorders. However, the strongest association was between MHPG levels and the life history of aggression that was reported by the subjects, with higher levels of aggressive behavior being associated with lower levels of MHPG. These findings suggest that norepinephrine may play an important role in modulating aggressive behaviors.

Simeon, Knutelska, Smith, Baker, and Hollander (2007) have also reported a positive correlation between levels of urinary norepinephrine and severity of dissociation (brief periods of detachment from reality) in a small sample of subjects ($n = 11$) with BPD. However, no differences were found between the BPD subjects and the controls with respect to baseline levels of urinary norepinephrine. To the extent that aggression and dissociation form part of the clinical picture of BPD, norepinephrine remains a neurotransmitter of interest to BPD researchers. However, understanding the role of norepinephrine in BPD is complicated by the high level of comorbidity between BPD and depression and the link between noradrenergic dysregulation and mood disorders (see Thase, Jindal, & Howland, 2002).

As already mentioned, an allele of the dopamine transporter gene is currently being explored as a possible candidate gene for BPD. Friedel (2004) has noted that antipsychotic medications, which act primarily via the blockade of dopamine receptors, often provide clinical benefits for BPD patients. Human and animal studies have further illustrated the importance of dopamine in emotion, impulsivity, and cognition (see Friedel, 2004), all of which are domains highly relevant to borderline pathology. Most of the current research on the role of dopamine dysfunction in BPD involves candidate genes, however, rather than the neurotransmitter directly. Many of these candidate genes are implicated in other disorders as well. In all probability, the etiology of BPD reflects biological mechanisms and pathways that are transdiagnostic, rather than specific to the disorder itself. This may also help us understand why there is so much comorbidity between BPD and a broad range of other psychiatric conditions.

Hormonal Systems

Other biological disturbances in BPD involve the hypothalamic-pituitary-adrenal (HPA) axis. The HPA axis, which is involved in stress regulation, has been widely studied in depression through the use of the dexamethasone suppression test (DST). This test involves administering an oral dose of dexamethasone, a synthetic glucocorticoid that acts via a feedback mechanism to suppress cortisol production. The "normal" response to the DST is a reduction in cortisol. In a naturalistic study, Lieb and colleagues (2004) collected a total of 32 saliva samples from 23 women with BPD who were not taking any medications and 24 matched healthy controls. Using the saliva samples, they measured cortisol levels in the two groups of women. Although far from conclusive, the data were suggestive of heightened adrenal activity in the BPD patients. When assessments from the first 2 days of the study were combined, total cortisol levels obtained in the first hour after awakening from sleep were significantly higher in the women with BPD than they were in the healthy women. Moreover, after receiving a dose of dexamethasone, women with BPD had a higher total daily level of cortisol compared to the healthy control women.

One problem with the Lieb et al. (2004) study, as well as with many other studies of HPA axis function in patients with BPD, is that the investigators did not assess comorbid PTSD. This is important, because 20% to 40% of patients with BPD also suffer from PTSD (see Gunderson & Sabo, 1993), and because PTSD is often associated with abnormalities in HPA axis function (see Rinne, de Kloet, et al., 2002). In a related vein, controlling for the possible effects of concurrent major depression is also necessary—again because major depressive disorder is highly comorbid with BPD (Corruble, Ginestet, & Guelfi, 1996), and because abnormal responses to a challenge with dexamethasone are often found in patients who are depressed. These problems make it difficult to interpret the existing data.

A large-scale study of HPA axis function in BPD, using a carefully diagnosed sample with full attention given to issues of comorbidity as well as exposure to trauma, is much needed. In fact, trauma may even be more important with regard to hyperresponsiveness of the HPA axis than BPD, major depressive disorder (MDD), or PTSD. When Rinne and colleagues (Rinne, de Kloet, et al., 2002) gave a combined dexamethasone/corticotrophin-releasing hormone (CRH) challenge to a sample of 39 patients with BPD, those who had experienced childhood abuse ($n = 24$) showed higher levels of cortisol and ACTH after the challenge than did those ($n = 15$) who had experienced little or no abuse in their childhoods. Importantly, these elevated responses were independent of BPD pathology; they were also unrelated to the presence of a comorbid diagnosis of PTSD or major depression (although patients with comorbid PTSD tended to have an attenuated ACTH response to the challenge whether or not they had a history of childhood abuse). Overall, Rinne, de Kloet, et al.'s data support the idea that sustained abuse early in life may lead to a hyperresponsiveness of ACTH release. This is consistent with research in women with histories of early childhood trauma (Heim et al., 2000). To the extent that many people with BPD report early and often chronic adverse life experiences, we might therefore expect to find evidence of hyperreactivity of the HPA axis in unselected samples of BPD patients.

Taken together, the evidence suggests that HPA axis functioning is abnormal in people with BPD (Zimmerman & Choi-Kain, 2009). Some of this may be due to comorbid PTSD or depression. Highly plausible, however, is that early childhood trauma (which, as will be seen later, is implicated in the development of BPD) may result in changes in the functioning of the HPA axis. BPD may therefore be associated with dysregulated HPA axis functioning in its own right. Nonetheless, the high degree of comorbidity between BPD and depression and PTSD (both of which are associated with HPA axis abnormalities) makes it challenging to confirm this hypothesis.

Oxytocin

As discussed earlier in relation to receptor genes, Oxytocin (OXT), sometimes referred to as the "love hormone" because of its role in attachment and social relationships, is now attracting the attention of BPD researchers. Oxytocin is a neuropeptide produced in the hypothalamus and the posterior pituitary gland. OXT has been shown to play an important role in parent-child attachment relationships (Feldman, Gordon, Influs, Gutbir, & Ebstein, 2013), which are often impaired for individuals with BPD. There is also some evidence that women with BPD have lower levels of plasma oxytocin, although the interplay of childhood maltreatment, oxytocin levels, and borderline pathology remains unclear (Bertsch, Schmidinger, Neumann, & Herpertz, 2013).

OXT has attracted attention because intranasally administered OXT increases trust and cooperation in healthy populations (Kosfeld, Heinrichs, Zak, Fischbacher, & Fehr, 2005; De Dreu, 2012; Keri & Kiss, 2011). Trust and cooperation are impaired in BPD. OXT is also implicated in attachment, another process known to be problematic for those with BPD. Findings such as these have led some to conclude that administering OXT might help individuals with BPD function better in their social relationships. Counter to expectations, however, work to date has shown that intranasal OXT administration actually *decreases* trust and cooperation for individuals with BPD (Bartz et al., 2010; Ebert et al., 2013). In contrast, other work has shown that OXT attenuates emotional dysphoria (Simeon et al., 2011), attentional avoidance of angry faces (Brune et al., 2013), and hypersensitivity to angry faces (Bertsch, Gamer, et al., 2013) in BPD.

Although it seems clear from genetic and behavioral studies that OXT is an important neuropeptide, its specific role in BPD, as well as its potential as a treatment agent, is much less clear. Herpertz and Bertsch (2015) have offered an organizing framework for further study, highlighting the effects of OXT on five biobehavioral mechanisms: attention bias to social cues, poor affect regulation, poor social reward experiences, maladaptive empathy, and abnormal pain processing. Further work is needed to understand specifically how OXT may interact with the neural circuits that underlie each of these mechanisms. Additionally, greater understanding of the interaction of OXT with vasopressin, a similar neuropeptide implicated in social behavior, is warranted.

NEUROIMAGING STUDIES OF BPD

Neuroimaging studies of BPD are a topic of considerable interest. Overall they suggest that patients with this disorder may have some abnormalities in limbic and prefrontal brain areas when compared to nonpatient controls (Krause-Utz, Winter, Niedtfeld, & Schmahl, 2014; Putnam & Silk, 2005). Such findings are of interest because prefrontal and limbic circuits are thought to be involved in emotion and emotion regulation (Davidson, 2002; LeDoux, 1996).

Structural Approaches

Structural imaging studies have shown a 13% to 21% reduction in the volume of the hippocampus and an 8% to 25% reduction in the volume of the amygdala in patients with BPD compared to controls (see Driessen et al., 2000; Nunes et al., 2009; Schmahl, Vermetten, Elzinga, & Bremner, 2003; Tebartz van Elst et al., 2003; O'Neill et al., 2013). In addition, some regions of the prefrontal cortex (PFC), including the dorsolateral prefrontal cortex (DLPFC), orbitofrontal cortex (OFC), and anterior cingulate cortex (ACC), have also been found to be reduced in volume. Tebartz van Elst et al. (2003) reported a 24% reduction in the left OFC and a 26% reduction in the right ACC in eight unmedicated female patients with BPD when compared to eight matched healthy controls (see also Chanen et al., 2008). Reduced volume of gray matter in the anterior cingulate cortex in 50 patients with BPD compared to 50 controls has also been reported by Hazlett and colleagues (2005). Moreover, reduced ACC volume appears to be correlated with self-injurious behaviors, impulsivity, and fears of abandonment (Whittle et al., 2009). Adolescents with BPD have also been shown to have a reduction in ACC volume, suggesting that it is present at an early stage of the disorder.

It is important to mention that decreased hippocampal volume is not a structural brain abnormality that is specific to BPD. Volume loss in the hippocampus has also been reported in other disorders, including unipolar and bipolar depression, schizophrenia, and PTSD (see Putnam & Silk, 2005). Decreased hippocampal volume in BPD may also, at least in part, be explained by comorbid PTSD (Rodrigues et al., 2011; Schmahl et al., 2009). Reductions in the volume of the DLPFC and OFC may also not be specific to BPD (Brunner et al., 2010). Researchers have observed a decrease in the volume of the orbitofrontal cortex in people with depression (Bremner, 2002) and obsessive-compulsive disorder (Szeszko et al., 1999). Although it is possible that reliable abnormalities in specific brain areas might eventually be linked to BPD, the data at this time are more suggestive than conclusive. Most likely is that the overall *pattern* of findings will prove to be more important than any particular abnormality in a given brain region.

White Matter Abnormalities.   Diffusion tensor imaging (DTI) is an imaging technique that can be used to examine the structure of white matter tracts in the brain. One tract that has been linked to emotion dysregulation is the uncinate fasciculus. This is the major white matter tract connecting the amygdala to the ACC and the PFC. In a recent study, individuals with BPD have been shown to have decreased structural integrity in the uncinate fasciculus (Lischke et al., 2015).

Although it is tempting to conclude that this might explain the emotional dysregulation that is characteristic of BPD, in the study just described, no significant correlations between structural alterations in the uncinate fasciculus and self-reported measures of depression, anxiety, or borderline symptoms were found. Nonetheless, these early findings are of considerable interest. White matter changes of the type reported are thought to result from myelin loss. Demyelination has been linked to inflammation, and inflammation often follows stressful life events. Stressful environmental events in early life are thought to play a major role in the development of BPD. It is also the case that BPD-specific differences in white matter tracts upon which emotion regulation relies have been identified as early as in adolescence (Maier-Hein et al., 2014). Taken together, findings such as these therefore provide some tantalizing clues about how environmental factors might set the stage for changes in brain structure and function that could later result in borderline pathology.

Functional Imaging

Positron-emission tomography (PET) approaches can be used to examine differences in resting brain activation in people with BPD compared to healthy controls or people with other forms of psychopathology. Several research groups have now reported that BPD is associated with lower metabolic activity in the OFC relative to comparison subjects (see Putnam & Silk, 2005). This is interesting because the OFC is a brain area thought to play a role in the regulation of emotion and responses to stress. It is also involved in impulse control (Berlin, Rolls, & Iversen, 2005) and may facilitate the inhibition of responses to external stimuli (Davidson, Putnam, & Larson, 2000).

Particularly interesting is the finding that when people with BPD are treated with fluoxetine, a selective serotonin reuptake inhibitor (SSRI) that is helpful in the treatment of depression and BPD, there is a significant increase in OFC metabolism at 12 weeks posttreatment (New et al., 2004). Treatment with fluoxetine (Prozac) also led BPD patients to report reduced levels of aggressive feelings and irritability. We have already noted the role of serotonin with respect to impulsivity, aggression, and suicidality (Oquendo & Mann, 2000). Taken together, these findings suggest that reduced serotonergic activity in brain areas such as the OFC may help us understand why high levels of impulsiveness and aggression may be commonly found in those who suffer from BPD.

Finally, we note that investigations that have used imaging methods to study the brain at work (i.e., PET and functional magnetic resonance imaging [fMRI] studies) have implicated some of the same brain regions identified in structural and resting brain investigations. For example, when people with BPD are exposed to aversive and neutral pictures they show increased activation in the amygdala compared to healthy controls (Herpertz et al., 2001). Following an aversive stimulus, patients with BPD also show temporally prolonged activation in the amygdala relative to healthy controls (Kamphausen et al., 2013). Increased amygdala activation relative to controls is also apparent when people with BPD view pictures of fearful, sad, or neutral faces (Donegan et al., 2003). Findings of increased amygdala activation are not entirely consistent, however. A meta-analysis by Ruocco, Amirthavasagam, Choi-Kain, and McMain (2013) suggests that, compared to controls, individuals with BPD may actually activate the amygdala to a *lesser* extent when exposed to negative stimuli. This could perhaps be due to the fact that amygdala volumes tend to be reduced by approximately 13% in people with BPD relative to controls (Ruocco, Amirthavasagam, & Zakzanis, 2012).

Other studies suggest differences in activation in such areas as the dorsolateral prefrontal cortex and anterior cingulate cortex in patients with BPD relative to controls when exposed to personalized abandonment scripts (Schmahl, Elzinga, et al., 2003) or during recall of personal memories of abandonment (Schmahl, Vermetten, et al., 2003). Overall, although results of individual studies are often inconsistent (possibly reflecting sample differences or differences in the task employed), they generally tend to support the idea that abnormalities in frontolimbic circuitry may underlie many of the key clinical features of BPD (Brendel, Stern, & Silbersweig, 2005; Salvador et al., 2014; Schmahl & Bremner, 2006).

More specifically, a major problem in BPD may be that there is a disconnection between activity in the prefrontal cortex and activity in the amygdala. This could be related to the white matter abnormalities we highlighted earlier. Although metabolic activity in these areas appears to be tightly coupled in healthy controls, the same degree of metabolic linkage is not found in people with BPD (New et al., 2007). This lack of functional connectivity may be one reason why emotion regulation is such a problem for those with this disorder.

Finally, we note that many of the brain regions and neural circuits that are implicated in BPD are also implicated in a broad range of other disorders. In other words, it would be unwise to assume that problems with frontolimbic connectivity are specific to BPD. Comorbidity issues also make it challenging to draw clear conclusions from the data in many studies. For these reasons, we can say little at the present time about unique ways in which brain structure and brain functioning are compromised in people with BPD.

Psychosocial Factors

Trauma and early life adversity are often reported by patients with BPD. Problems with attachment in close relationships are also common. These factors likely contribute to the disturbances in interpersonal functioning that are so characteristic of people with this disorder.

CHILDHOOD MALTREATMENT

The early lives of people with BPD are often characterized by high levels of trauma and adversity. Several studies have demonstrated that, compared to patients with other disorders, patients with BPD are significantly more likely to report experiencing physical abuse, sexual abuse, or neglect during childhood (Ogata et al., 1990; Weaver & Clum, 1993; Zanarini et al., 2000). Indeed, in a sample of 69 outpatients with BPD, only 4 (6.1%) reported that they had experienced *no* traumatic events in their childhoods, although this was true for the majority (61.5%) of the 109 psychiatrically healthy controls (Bandelow et al., 2005). Compared to the healthy controls, the early lives of the BPD patients involved significantly more maternal and paternal absences (i.e., mother in the hospital; father in jail), more discord between the parents, more experiences of being raised by other relatives or in a foster home, more physical violence in the family, and more sexual abuse during childhood.

One problem with almost all of the studies on the early life experiences of BPD patients is that they rely on retrospective reporting. Such data may be unreliable due to problems with recall or reporting biases. However, in an important longitudinal study, Johnson and colleagues (Johnson, Cohen, Brown, Smailes, & Bernstein, 1999) used records from the State of New York to collect data on documented cases of abuse or neglect in the lives of children from a representative sample of 639 families. Consistent with the findings of other studies, childhood maltreatment was significantly associated with increased levels of BPD symptoms later in life. More specifically, those who experienced early abuse or neglect were 7.73 times more likely to be diagnosed with BPD at a follow-up assessment than were those who did not experience such maltreatment. With its longitudinal design and its focus on verified cases of abuse, Johnson et al.'s study provides strong support for the link between traumatic or abusive experiences in early life and the subsequent development of BPD. A more recent study of children who were abused or neglected before the age of 11 (again documented by court records) provides additional support for this conclusion (Widom, Czaja, & Paris, 2009).

ATTACHMENT

Relationships are extremely problematic for people with BPD. Not only do they have problems in their relationships with others but they also have problems in their relationships with themselves. BPD is characterized by high levels of interpersonal impairment and extreme concern about abandonment. Also prominent are chronic feelings of emptiness, a lack of a sense of identity, self-harming behaviors, and an inability to self-soothe appropriately during times of distress.

Attachment theory provides a useful approach for conceptualizing this disorder (see Levy, 2005). Bowlby (1973) proposed that through the relationships and transactions that they have with their caregivers, infants develop mental representations of themselves and others and develop "internal working models" about interpersonal relationships. These are, essentially, sets of expectations about relationships that function to both organize personality development and shape the nature of relationships that are developed in the future (Levy, 2005). When an infant's needs are reliably met by an attentive and nurturing caretaker, he or she will come to regard others as reliable, responsive, and trustworthy. When an infant is raised by an abusive, neglectful, or emotionally disengaged caretaker, however, the working model of relationships that he or she develops is likely to be different, and may involve expectations of lack of care, unreliability, and unresponsiveness. Our internal working models may also shape how we perceive our social environments, influencing what we attend to and consider salient. In young children, secure attachment is characterized by using the mother as a "secure base" from which to explore the world and return to in times of stress. Attachment style is thought to have some continuity from childhood to adulthood, with securely attached children being more likely to create and maintain securely attached relationships in later life. According to Bowlby (1977, p. 206), childhood attachment influences the "later capacity to make affectional bonds as well as a whole range of adult dysfunctions." These dysfunctions include marital problems, difficulties with parenting, and personality disorders.

Given the apparent link between early life adversity and BPD, it should come as no surprise that people with this disorder show low rates of secure attachment when this is measured in adulthood. The vast majority of people with BPD are assessed (using interview-based or self-report methods) as insecurely attached, with only a minority (approximately 6% to 8%) being rated as having secure attachment patterns (see Levy, 2005). Although there is no specific style of insecure attachment that appears linked to BPD in empirical studies, problems with attachment may underlie many of the fundamental aspects of BPD. These problems may also help to explain why people with BPD are often extremely emotionally attached to safe and stable attachment objects such as stuffed animals, even in adulthood (Hooley & Wilson-Murphy, 2012).

It also warrants mention that real or misperceived rejection or invalidation in interpersonal events often serve as triggers for the emotional outbursts, impulsivity, and self-damaging behaviors that are so central to the BPD syndrome (Gurvits, Koenigsberg, & Siever, 2000; Yeomans & Levy, 2002). Bateman and Fonagy (2003) consider an inability to "mentalize" (i.e., to understand and interpret one's own mental states as well as those of others) to be fundamental to BPD and to be linked to failures in early attachment relationships. Finally, even when they are in therapy, patients with BPD find it much harder than other patients to sustain a mental representation of the therapist as helpful and the treatment relationship as caring and supportive (Bender et al., 2003). Simply stated, problems in early attachment relationships may set the stage for a broad range of relationship problems in later life.

Cognitive Factors

Trying to summarize the results of different studies of neurocognitive function in patients with borderline personality disorder is far from easy. Because of the polythetic nature of the *DSM-5* criteria, patients with the same diagnosis can show quite different clinical presentations. The interpretation of findings is further complicated by issues of comorbidity. As we have noted, many patients with BPD have a concurrent diagnosis of major depressive disorder. The extent to which the empirical findings are linked to BPD or simply reflect cognitive processing deficits associated with depression is therefore a source of concern. A third difficulty is that, in the typical research study, the majority of participants are taking medications. Although researchers usually try to control for this by noting the presence or absence of medications in a particular participant, it is rare that more detailed information about the class of medication, number of different medications, dosages, and duration of medication usage is provided (see Fertuck, Lenzenweger, Clarkin, Hoermann, & Stanley, 2006). Finally, the majority of these research studies have either involved only females or included very few males in their samples. We therefore know little about cognition in men with BPD.

There are many reasons to suspect that basic executive cognition and memory processes might be disrupted in BPD. The disorder itself involves unstable and dysregulated inhibitory control. This is readily apparent in the behavior, emotions, and cognitions of the BPD patient. Moreover, individuals with BPD and family members of these individuals report subjective difficulties with attention and memory (Ruocco, Lam, & McMain, 2014). Also, as we have already discussed, the results of neuroimaging studies have implicated abnormalities in the frontolimbic neurocircuitry in patients with the disorder. Reviews of executive neurocognitive functioning, memory, and BPD can be found elsewhere (see Fertuck et al., 2006; Unoka & Richman, 2016). In the sections below, we highlight some of the most important findings.

Executive Neurocognition

Executive neurocognition involves being able to delay or terminate a given response (cognitive or motor) for the purpose of achieving another goal or reward that is less immediate. There are several types of executive neurocognition. For example, when we make a conscious and deliberate effort to control our attention or motor behavior, we are engaging what is referred to as *interference control* (see Nigg, 2000). This method of control uses a neural system that relies on the connection between cortical (dorsolateral and orbitofrontal cortex) and subcortical (anterior cingulate) structures (see Fertuck et al., 2006). The Stroop task (Stroop, 1935) is an example of a test that taps this aspect of neuroexecutive function. It requires a person to name the color of the ink used to print a color word (e.g., saying the word "red" when the word "blue" is printed in red ink), and to suppress the tendency to simply read the word as printed.

Another form of executive neurocognition is *cognitive inhibition*. This is the ability to suppress information from working memory. An example of a task that requires effortful suppression is the "directed forgetting" task (see Bjork, 1989). In this task, subjects are presented with a list of words. After each word is presented, subjects see either an F (for forget) or an R (for remember). Subjects are instructed to remember words followed by an R and forget words followed by an F. However, at the end of the task, subjects are asked to recall all the words that were presented to them. Problems in cognitive inhibition can also be measured using implicit (unconscious) approaches involving negative priming tasks. Here, reaction times are assessed following negative or neutral primes (see Tipper, 1985). It is assumed that individuals who have more difficulty inhibiting negative information will be slower to respond after being exposed to negative primes.

A third type of executive neurocognition requires the person to inhibit an expected motor behavior or cognitive response in order to follow a different direction. This is termed *behavioral inhibition*. For example, in the go/no-go task (Casey et al., 1997), the subject is required to press a button when a particular (and frequent) stimulus such as an "X" appears. This is the "go" response. However, when another, less frequent stimulus is shown (e.g., the letter "Y"), the subject must refrain from pressing the button.

The final form of executive neurocognition is *motivational or affective inhibition*. This requires the purposeful interruption of a tendency or a behavior that results from a particular motivational-emotional state. For example, some forms of the Stroop task involve the use of emotional words (e.g., "angry"). In the emotional Stroop test, subjects typically take longer to name the ink color of emotional words than they do to name the color of ink used to print nonemotional words, such as "table." The emotional Stroop test is therefore thought to measure how well the subject can engage in affective inhibition. An example of a task that requires motivational inhibition is the passive avoidance task (Newman & Kosson, 1986). Here, subjects have to learn by trial and error whether responding to stimuli will lead to gaining or losing money. If the subject responds to a losing stimulus, this is considered to reflect a passive avoidance error (i.e., doing something that leads to a negative outcome). Failures to respond to a winning stimulus are considered to be errors of omission, where the subject misses out on a good outcome.

Inhibitory deficits are involved in inattention, impulsivity, and problems with affect regulation. The clinical presentation of BPD therefore makes it reasonable to expect that people with this disorder would show impairments on neurocognitive tasks requiring inhibition. Research suggests that patients with BPD do indeed show impairments on tasks that challenge inhibitory processes.

Posner et al. (2002) compared 39 BPD patients without comorbid mood disorder to 30 healthy controls on the Attention Network Task (ANT; Fan, McCandliss, Sommer, Raz, & Posner, 2002). This cognitive task, which measures interference control, taps three different aspects of attention. The first (alerting) is the ability to sustain an alert cognitive state, the second (orienting) is the ability to focus attention and select stimuli, and the third (conflict) is the capacity to decide among competing responses based on a predetermined organizing principle. Although the subjects with BPD performed similarly to the controls on the alerting and orienting components of the task, they showed impairments, relative to the controls, on the conflict task.

Impairments have also been found on tasks that require cognitive inhibition. Korfine and Hooley (2000) administered a directed forgetting task to healthy controls, and people diagnosed with BPD. Some of the BPD participants were hospital outpatients; others were drawn from a community sample. Participants were then exposed to borderline-salient words (e.g., "abandon," "enraged," "alone," "suicidal") as well as positive and neutral words. Even when they were specifically instructed to forget them, the BPD participants remembered more of the borderline-salient words than the controls did, suggesting that they were unable to inhibit material that was emotionally salient to them. In a subsequent replication of this general finding, Domes and colleagues (2006) have reported that, compared to healthy controls, unmedicated patients with BPD showed poorer inhibition of negative material on the directed forgetting task. This was true even though the negative words that they were exposed to were not so borderline specific. These findings suggest that one problem people with BPD have is that it is hard for them to suppress aversive material—even when they wish to do so.

As Korfine and Hooley (2000) note, it remains unclear whether findings such as these are driven by borderline pathology or by depression. Certainly, when level of depression is statistically controlled, main effects of BPD tend to become nonsignificant. However, main effects of depression are also rendered nonsignificant by the statistical control of BPD symptoms. Because mood disturbance is so fundamental to BPD, and because there is a strong relationship between depression and BPD in most people with the disorder, it may make little sense to covary depression out in studies of this kind. Nonetheless, there is a pressing need for this issue to be resolved through the use of comparison groups comprised of depressed (but non-BPD) participants.

BPD patients are also impaired on measures of behavioral inhibition. As we noted earlier, behavioral inhibition involves inhibiting a cognitive expectancy or motor behavior in order to follow a different directive or goal. Lenzenweger, Clarkin, Fertuck, and Kernberg (2004) have reported that BPD patients (without concurrent mood disorders) exhibit deficits in cognitive planning and set-shifting on the Wisconsin Card Sorting Test (WCST; Heaton, 1981). Problems in motivational inhibition (poorer performance on a decision-making task) have also been found in BPD subjects when compared to healthy controls (see Bazanis et al., 2002). People with BPD also show deficits on the go/no-go task, showing that they have difficulty learning when to respond (or not respond) to a stimulus (Leyton et al., 2001). This may be driven not by motor inhibition deficits but by decision-related deficits. There is evidence that the former may be dissociable from the latter, and that motor inhibition is intact in BPD (Barker et al., 2015). Decision making is, moreover, an area of major impairment in patients with BPD (Unoka & Richman, 2016). Impairments on the passive avoidance task (described above) have also been reported (Hochhausen, Lorenz, & Newman, 2002).

Finally, some (but not all) researchers have reported differences between healthy controls and participants with BPD on the emotional Stroop test (Arntz, Appels, & Sieswerda, 2000; Domes et al., 2006). These findings suggest that people with BPD may sometimes be less able than controls to inhibit interference from emotional words. Indeed, an emerging area of research involves the effect of affective context on cognitive processing. Growing evidence now suggests that negative information interferes with cognitive processes to a greater extent for individuals with BPD than it does for controls (e.g., Soloff, White, Omari, Ramaseshan, & Diwadkar, 2015).

Taken together, the pattern of results across domains is highly consistent with the idea that BPD is associated with deficits in executive cognition. More specifically, people with BPD often perform relatively poorly when they are engaged in tasks that make demands on inhibitory processes (see Fertuck et al., 2006). The more symptomatic patients are (e.g., having more severe symptoms, meeting more *DSM* criteria) and the more comorbid disorders they have, the less well they tend to do on these tasks (Fertuck, Lenzenweger, & Clarkin, 2005; Unoka & Richman, 2016).

Memory Systems

People with BPD appear to have some difficulties on conventional tests of memory. A recent meta-analysis has shown that BPD patients perform worse than controls on measures of both verbal and nonverbal memory (Unoka & Richman, 2016; see also Ruocco, 2005). Moreover, impairments in immediate and delayed memory have been linked to increased impulsivity (Seres, Unoka, Bodi, Aspan, & Keri, 2009).

The topic of autobiographical memory has been a focus of interest. The Autobiographical Memory Test (AMT; Williams & Broadbent, 1986) requires subjects to generate precise and specific memories to prompted words (e.g., "birthday"). A memory is considered to be specific if it references an occasion or an event and involves a time or a place (e.g., "for my birthday last year my friend and I went to dinner at Mario's"). Overgeneralized memories, which are characteristic of depressed patients, are hypothesized to occur as a way of avoiding the emotional turmoil that could result from more specific recall of negatively valenced emotional memories (see Renneberg, Theobald, Nobs, & Weisbrod, 2005).

Jones and colleagues (1999) initially reported that patients with BPD recalled more overgeneral (i.e., fewer specific) memories compared to controls. However, other investigators have failed to replicate this finding (Arntz, Meeren, & Wessell, 2002; Renneberg et al., 2005). Worthy of comment though, is that the BPD patients in the Renneberg et al. (2005) study retrieved more negative memories when prompted by the cue words than the controls did. This was also true of the depressed participants who were studied. Unlike the depressed participants, however, the BPD patients retrieved these more negative memories with a speed and a level of specificity that was comparable to that of the healthy controls. In other words, the BPD patients were rapidly able to access memories that were both specific and negative. Although the implications of this finding remain unclear, it is interesting to speculate whether such a retrieval style could play a role in the emotional turmoil that is so characteristic of BPD. Staying on an even keel emotionally may be much more difficult when negative memories are easily triggered and rapidly accessible.

Social Cognition

Social cognition is concerned with how we recognize, think about, and respond to social information in a variety of contexts. In other words, the focus is on stimuli that are related to social functioning. In light of the interpersonal difficulties that characterize people with BPD, it is hardly surprising that social cognition is now a topic of active research interest.

Neuroimaging research has revealed that, compared to healthy controls, female patients with BPD showed evidence of cortical thinning in specific brain regions related to social cognition (Bøen et al., 2014). Given this, and in light of the importance of early attachment experiences for developing the capacity for social cognition (see Bateman & Fonagy, 2003; Beeney et al., 2015), it is perhaps not surprising that a number of disturbances in social cognition have been observed in BPD.

Individuals with BPD attend more to negative cues during interactions with others (Lumsden, 1993). This may explain why, in young couples who are dating, the presence of BPD features predicts greater negative impact and more feelings of emotional loss in response to the behavior of romantic partners. This is the case whether the experience the partner initiates is positive or negative (Bhatia, Davila, Eubanks-Carter, & Burckell, 2013).

The tendency to appraise social interactions more negatively may be due in part to negative biases in facial emotion recognition. Although consistent results have been elusive, a recent meta-analysis finds no clear evidence to suggest that people with BPD differ from healthy controls in their ability to identify negative emotions (Mitchell, Dickens, & Picchioni, 2014). However, people with BPD do show a negative response bias. In other words, they tend to report negativity in neutral faces or in ambiguous facial stimuli.

Some of the inconsistency in the findings overall may stem from a lack of consideration of such factors as IQ and trauma history. Another variable that has not received appropriate consideration to date is the gender of the target face that is being viewed. Veague and Hooley (2014) have reported that, compared to healthy controls and women with trauma histories, women with BPD took longer to recognize the presence of happiness in male but not in female faces. BPD pathology was also linked to having a lower detection threshold for recognizing anger in male faces, although, again, no differences were noted when female faces were viewed. Finally, and consistent with the response bias findings reported by others (see Mitchell et al., 2014), participants with BPD were more likely to misidentify anger in male faces, seeing anger in completely neutral male faces or in male faces that contained no anger cues. This tendency was independent of participant's histories of abuse, and there was no similar misidentification when female faces were presented. Findings such as these suggest that enhanced or impaired emotion recognition may be moderated by whether the face being viewed is male or female. This is a variable that should be explored more fully in future research.

A new research direction centers on trait appraisal. Implicit trait appraisal is a primary shortcut allowing us to make quick, complex judgments about the traits or personality of others. Based entirely on facial characteristics, we make enduring judgments about a range of traits including dominance, likability, and competence (Todorov, Mandisodza, Goren, & Hall, 2005). Trait appraisal differs from emotion recognition in that it is concerned with how an individual ascribes personality characteristics, rather than emotional states, to a target individual.

Clinicians have long noted how difficult it is for individuals with BPD to trust others. Reflecting this, researchers have now begun to evaluate the process of trust or trustworthiness appraisal in BPD. Two types of paradigms are typically used: visual appraisal paradigms and trust games. Visual appraisal paradigms require the individual to view pictures of faces or videos and to judge, based only on limited information, how trustworthy the person is. Fertuck, Grinband, and Stanley (2013) showed individuals a series of faces that varied on either a fear or trust dimension. Respondents were simply asked to rate the trustworthiness of each face. Compared to controls, the BPD group rated the faces as less trustworthy. Importantly, this trust bias occurred independently of fear appraisal, indicating that less trustworthy faces are not simply those that evoke greater fear response.

Similar results have been found in individuals with subclinical borderline features (Miano, Fertuck, Arntz, & Stanley, 2013). Nicol, Pope, Sprengelmeyer, Young, and Hall (2013) found that relative to healthy controls, individuals with BPD rated faces as less trustworthy and less approachable. Approachability ratings were significantly correlated with childhood trauma within the BPD group, but trustworthiness ratings were not. Using a paradigm similar to that of Fertuck et al. (2013), with both facial and limited behavioral information available to subjects, Arntz and Veen (2001) found that individuals with BPD rated others more negatively in general when viewing short movie clips. Compared to healthy controls or to depressed patients, people with BPD also tend to rate others as more aggressive (Barnow et al., 2009).

What are the behavioral consequences of such negative impression formation? To explore this issue, researchers have used trust game paradigms. These require individuals not only to form initial impressions of others but then to cooperate with those others in the service of a common monetary goal. For example, Unoka, Seres, Aspan, Bodi, and Keri (2009) used a monetary investment paradigm in which individuals with BPD acted as investors who could choose to invest money in a trustee via the Internet. In this type of game, the investor and trustee are able to earn more money together through cooperative exchange than they would through conservative investment. Compared to control and depressed groups, the BPD group made smaller investments overall during the course of five trials, indicating less trust in the trustee. BPD participants also reported having less optimism about the outcome of the investment game right from the outset.

Similar findings were observed when the roles were reversed. Participants with BPD, acting as trustees rather than as investors, ruptured cooperation and trust by sending less money back to the investors (King-Casas et al., 2008). This shows that not only are individuals with BPD less trusting in these types of economic games but they are also less able to cooperate. In another, similar study, BPD participants rated their own behavior as less fair when a virtual trustee (an automated computer program displaying standardized images of the "trustee") played the trust game with a consistently neutral face, whereas control participants rated themselves as comparably fair regardless of the trustee's emotional facial cues (Franzen et al., 2011).

Biases in facial emotion perception as well as problems with trust appraisal may radically change how people with BPD experience their social worlds. Both are also likely to have important negative behavioral consequences. By approaching the world as if others are less trustworthy, people with PBD may set the stage for some of the interpersonal dysfunction that is so characteristic of their disorder.

Diagnosis and Assessment

The current *DSM* definition of BPD combines theoretical perspectives that are often quite different. There are also no *required* symptoms that must be present for the diagnosis to be made. This means that all nine symptoms are assumed to be of equal importance in the diagnosis of BPD. This clearly does not reflect the current debate about the "core aspects" of BPD.

Beyond this, however, many clinicians and researchers have reservations about whether personality disorders (including BPD) can even be classified in a categorical (e.g., *DSM*-like) fashion. Most personality researchers favor a dimensional (rather than categorical) view of personality disorders. Within this perspective, disorders of personality are theorized to occur along a continuum that includes normal personality functioning.

Some empirical evidence is consistent with this view. Using taxometric statistical procedures to analyze data from a clinical sample, Rothschild, Cleland, Haslam, and Zimmerman (2003) failed to find evidence of a distinct "borderline taxon" or categorical entity. Instead, the data suggested that BPD is better considered as a *dimensional* concept. To the extent that this is true, differences between people with and without the BPD diagnosis might therefore be more quantitative than qualitative, with people with BPD simply exhibiting more extreme forms of normal personality traits. In terms of the five-factor model of personality (Costa & McCrae, 1992), BPD can be viewed as reflecting high neuroticism and high openness, and low levels of both agreeableness and conscientiousness (see Few et al., 2016).

Not surprisingly, these issues have led to the development of a variety of different methods and techniques used to assess and diagnose BPD. In the following sections, we consider some of the most widely used approaches.

DIAGNOSTIC INTERVIEWS

Clinical approaches to assessment are based on the fundamental assumption that there is a known and accepted concept that exists to be assessed. Because of this, their form directly reflects the current definitions of the disorders that they assess. For BPD, the two most widely used clinical interviews are the Structured Clinical Interview for *DSM-IV* Personality Disorders (SCID-II; First, Gibbon, Spitzer, Williams, & Benjamin, 1997) and the Diagnostic Interview for Borderlines–Revised (DIB-R; Zanarini, Gunderson, Frankenburg, & Chauncey, 1989).

The SCID-II is an interview based on the current *DSM* criteria. Designed to be used by a trained interviewer, it can be used to assess all 11 of the personality disorders included in the *DSM*. The SCID-II has good sensitivity, specificity, validity, and interrater reliability (Jacobsberg, Perry, & Frances, 1995). Although the SCID-II does assess for the presence of *all* personality disorders, the subset of questions specific to BPD is often used on its own. Discriminant and criterion validity are fairly well established for the BPD section of the SCID-II, although this is not the case for diagnoses of all the disorders (Carcone, Tokarz, & Ruocco, 2015).

Unlike the SCID-II, the DIB-R (and its predecessor, the DIB) is focused solely on BPD. The original Diagnostic Interview for Borderlines (Gunderson, Kolb, & Austin, 1981) was developed to distinguish BPD from schizophrenia and major depressive disorder. Accordingly, the questions covered such domains as social adaptation, impulse action patterns, affects, psychosis, and interpersonal relations. The goal of the revision of the instrument was to improve its power to discriminate BPD from other personality disorders. To this end, questions about such symptoms as anxiety, odd thinking, quasi-psychotic thoughts, and concerns of abandonment were included. Indeed, these are the items that are more likely to discriminate BPD (Zanarini, Gunderson, & Frankenburg, 1990). The authors also adopted a standard duration of 2 years for all symptoms and established a predetermined scoring algorithm.

One measure of the success of this approach is that the DIB-R is now considered the best assessment instrument for distinguishing BPD from other personality disorders (Skodol et al., 2002). This semistructured interview produces scores on each of four scales: affect, cognition, impulsivity, and interpersonal relationships. The presence of BPD is then determined by a score of 8 or more on a 10-point scale. The DIB-R subscales map well onto the major behavioral patterns associated with BPD, including abandonment fears, demandingness and entitlement, treatment regressions, and the ability to arouse inappropriately close or hostile relationships during treatment. Perhaps the most important difference between the DIB-R and any of the measures based solely on *DSM* criteria is that the DIB-R, far from overidentifying cases of BPD, seems to identify a more homogeneous and severe subset of patients (Zanarini, Frankenburg, & Vujanovic, 2002).

There are several other interviews that, like the SCID-II, assess BPD according to the *DSM* diagnostic criteria. The Structured Interview for *DSM-IV* Personality Disorders (SIDP-IV: Pfohl, Blum, & Zimmerman, 1997) is popular because it incorporates both the *DSM-IV-TR* criteria and the ICD-10 criteria for personality disorders. This is also true of the International Personality Disorder Examination (IPDE; Loranger, 1999). However, a disadvantage of the IPDE is that it is the longest of all the semistructured interviews, and its criterion validity has not been well established empirically (Carcone et al., 2015).

Finally, there are two other assessment interviews that are reliable, based on *DSM* criteria, and can be used to provide a BPD diagnosis. The Personality Disorder Interview (PDI-IV; Widiger, Mangine, Corbitt, Ellis, & Thomas, 1995) and the Diagnostic Interview for Personality Disorders (DIPD-IV; Zanarini, Frankenburg, Chauncey, & Gunderson, 1987) both have good empirical support. However, they tend not to be used as often as the SCID-II, SIDP-IV, or IPDE.

SELF-REPORT QUESTIONNAIRES

The Personality Disorders Questionnaire (PDQ-4; Hurt, Hyler, Frances, Clarkin, & Brent, 1984) is a 99-item self-report instrument based on the *DSM-IV* criteria (which, as pointed out earlier, are the same as the *DSM-5* criteria). It contains items to assess each *DSM* personality disorder. Because it is brief, the PDQ is commonly used. It has shown good diagnostic agreement with the DIPD-IV (Zanarini et al., 2003). However, some have questioned its predictive and discriminant validity (de Reus, van den Berg, & Emmelkamp, 2013; Fossati et al., 1998).

MEASURING CHANGE IN BPD

The Zanarini Rating Scale for Borderline Personality Disorder (ZAN-BPD; Zanarini et al., 2003) is the only presently available measure that can be used to assess severity and *change* in borderline pathology. The items for this rating scale were adapted from the BPD module of the DIPD-IV, and converted so that each criterion is rated on a 0 to 4 scale and covers a 1-week time period. The rating points (0–4) in the scale were designed and anchored to consider both the severity and frequency of symptoms. The ZAN-BPD culminates in four sector scores that reflect the primary areas of dysfunction in BPD: affective (anger, emptiness, mood stability), cognitive (stress-related dissociation or paranoia, identity disturbance), impulsive (self-mutilation, suicide attempts, and other forms of impulsivity), and interpersonal (abandonment, unstable relationships). This clinician rating scale has achieved good convergent validity (scores correlate with the DIB-R, for example), discriminant validity (it accurately discriminates BPD from other disorders), and interrater reliability.

PSYCHOMETRIC ASSESSMENT APPROACHES TO BPD

A different approach to assessing borderline symptomatology is found in symptom and personality inventories that inquire about a broad range of possible pathology. Such measures can be used to help to determine *what* actually "makes up" the borderline construct. When people with BPD complete such measures, researchers can gain insight into the basic aspects of the disorder.

One such inventory is the Personality Assessment Inventory (PAI; Morey, 1991). This 344-question inventory, which is based on an interpersonal model of psychopathology, covers all *DSM* personality disorders. There are four BPD "feature" subscales in this measure; they probe affective instability, identity problems, negative relationships, and self-harming behavior. The PAI has shown good reliability and validity. It can also be used for diagnosing BPD because the BPD subscales incorporate all the *DSM* criteria.

The Schedule for Nonadaptive and Adaptive Personality–Second Edition (SNAP-2; Clark, 2009) is a 390-item self-report measure based on a dimensional model of personality disorders. Within this perspective, personality disorders are characterized as extreme forms of otherwise normal personality functioning. The SNAP has 10 diagnostic scales corresponding to the *DSM-IV* and *DSM-5* personality disorder diagnoses (including BPD), which are scored three ways: dimensionally, by number of criteria met, and dichotomously (whether or not the threshold for diagnosis was reached). Additionally, the SNAP-2 has 15 trait dimensional scales forming a three-factor structure of (1) negative emotionality (e.g., mistrust, aggression, self-harm), (2) positive emotionality (e.g., exhibitionism, entitlement), and (3) disinhibition (e.g., impulsivity versus workaholism/propriety). These trait scales have obvious relevance for researchers interested in BPD.

Like the SNAP, the Revised NEO Personality Inventory (NEO PI-R; Costa & McCrae, 1992) is based on a dimensional view of personality disorders, although in the case of the NEO the underlying basis is five-factor theory. Rather than being solely concerned with the abnormal traits characteristic of personality disorders, the NEO is designed to cover *both* normal and abnormal traits. The scores of patients with borderline personality disorder differ from community norms on all five factors (neuroticism, extraversion, openness, conscientiousness, and agreeableness) of the NEO. Problematically, the dimensions assessed by the NEO may not fully capture the clinical symptomatology seen in diagnosed patients with borderline personality disorder (Zweig-Frank & Paris, 1995). However, recent work has shown a high correlation between SCID-II derived borderline personality features and NEO PI-R traits, providing at least some initial evidence that the five-factor model may be useful for measuring the same underlying constructs as more specialized BPD assessment tools (Miller, Few, Lynam, & MacKillop, 2015). Changes in normal personality as conceptualized using a five-factor model also appear to track well with changes in borderline pathology over time (Wright, Hopwood, & Zanarini, 2015). Furthermore, a five-factor approach to borderline personality was recently shown to converge well with a variety of other measures of BPD, including the Personality Assessment Inventory–Borderline Features (PAI-BOR) scale. Bivariate twin modeling further suggested that assessment of BPD based on the five-factor model captures significant genetic variance in BPD liability (Few et al., 2016). Because five-factor measures of personality are typically easy to use and are widely available, they may hold promise for large epidemiological and genetic studies (Few et al., 2016).

Finally, it is appropriate to mention one psychometric measure that is specific to BPD. The Borderline Personality Inventory (BPI; Leichsenring, 1999) is based on Kernberg's psychodynamic formulation of the borderline diagnosis. Accordingly, the measure probes patient functioning in four discrete areas: identity diffusion, primitive defense mechanisms, reality testing, and fear of closeness. The BPI combines both categorical and dimensional aspects of personality; although it is dimensionally based, it *is* compatible with the *DSM-5* criteria for a BPD diagnosis. The construction of the scales in the BPI is rooted in factor analysis, and cutoff scores based on previous research are proposed.

CHALLENGES IN THE ASSESSMENT OF BPD

Clinical interviews were once thought to be the gold standard for diagnosing BPD (McDermut & Zimmerman, 2005), for several reasons. First, clinicians and researchers assumed that individuals with BPD might lack the insight or perspective-taking ability to accurately judge their own symptoms. Additionally, research has shown that many patients with BPD display certain "response styles that are associated with a distorted presentation of their psychological functioning" (Hopwood et al., 2008, p. 81; see also Lloyd, Overall, Kimsey, & Click, 1983).

A previous study found agreement between clinical interviews and self-report measures to be low (Zimmerman, 1994). This is thought to occur because concordance between BPD interviews is low (Hyler, Skodol, Oldham, Kellman, & Doidge, 1992), and because self-report methods usually yield higher base rates (e.g., Hunt & Andrews, 1992). It is thought that questionnaires in general tend to overdiagnose, and thus they are more typically recommended as screening tools, with clinical interviews remaining the standard for diagnosis (McDermut & Zimmerman, 2005).

However, a recent study (Hopwood et al., 2008) assessed the relative validity of a self-report measure of BPD (the PDQ-4, described earlier) and an interview measure of BPD (DIPD-IV, also described earlier) at the level of both diagnosis and individual criteria. The results supported the use of multiple methods (converging lines of evidence) in diagnosing BPD as being superior to each type of assessment used alone. For specific symptoms, sometimes one method performed better than the other; for example, the self-report measure better assessed experiential (nonobservable) symptoms such as identity disturbance or a feeling of chronic emptiness. However, the clinical interview performed better at assessing observable symptoms such as self-harm or impulsivity. It may be important, then, to weight the contributions of self-report and interview assessments differently, depending on the type of symptom a clinician is investigating.

One problem in the clinical or research assessment of BPD is that, as mentioned previously, BPD constitutes a pattern of comorbidity and symptom presentation that can be unstable (McGlashan et al., 2000, 2005). Additionally, the large number of measures that exist to assess BPD is inherently problematic and creates serious obstacles with respect to interpreting research findings. When different measures are used, different results are likely to be obtained. For this reason, some researchers (Pilkno[...] 1998; Shea, 1997) have advocated for the adoption of a commo[...] tionally, it has been suggested that a uniform assessment ba[...] treatment outcome. Although such an approach would ma[...] across studies, it is still unclear which of the current ins[...] for this purpose.

Clinical Course and Treatment

Treating patients who suffer from BPD is not easy. Patients o[...] sonal issues in the therapeutic relationship, leading to complicated [...] tional storms. Self-harming behaviors are common (60% to 80% of cases; see Bateman & Fonagy, 2003) and the mean number of lifetime suicide attempts in patients with BPD is 3.4 (Soloff, Lis, Kelly, Cornelius, & Ulrich, 1994). Moreover, as we have already noted, the 10% rate of completed suicide in BPD is alarmingly high (see Oldham, 2006). When all this is considered along with the tendency of BPD patients to drop out of treatment (Percudani et al., 2002), it is easy to see why the treatment of BPD patients is among the most challenging tasks that clinicians face.

CLINICAL OUTCOME

Despite the profound emotional pain that characterizes BPD sufferers and the turbulent nature of the treatment process, the long-term outcome of the disorder may be more benign than was previously assumed. Zanarini, Frankenburg, Reich, and Fitzmaurice (2012) conducted a 16-year follow-up study of a carefully diagnosed group of 290 patients with BPD who had initially received inpatient treatment. The researchers interviewed the patients every 2 years and collected data on their symptoms and levels of functioning. Dropout rates were remarkably low, with 231 participants from the original sample still remaining at the time of the 16-year follow up assessment. Importantly, the results showed that over the 16-year follow-up almost all (99%) of the patients with BPD showed significant reductions in their symptoms and entered remission for at least a 2-year period. What this means is that they no longer met criteria for a diagnosis of BPD during that time. It is also encouraging to note that the vast majority (78%) of patients had achieved lasting remissions (8 years or more) by the time of the 16-year follow-up. Perhaps unsurprisingly, given these high rates of remission, individuals with BPD also show decreasing rates of treatment utilization over time (Zanarini, Frankenburg, Reich, Conkey, & Fitzmaurice, 2015).

Compared to patients with other personality disorders, patients with BPD tend to be slower to achieve remission. By the time of the first follow-up assessment (conducted 2 years after hospitalization), only 35% were experiencing remission versus 88% of a comparison group of patients with other personality disorders. This may be because BPD represents such a severe form of personality disturbance. Predictors of a more rapid time to clinical remission included being younger, not having a history of childhood sexual abuse, and not having a family history of substance abuse disorders. Having a good recent work history, as well as having an agreeable temperament, scoring low on measures of neuroticism, and not having an anxious personality were also associated with patients getting better more rapidly (Zanarini, Frankenburg, Hennen, Reich, & Silk, 2006).

As might be expected, the number of patients who met criteria for recovery from BPD was lower than the number of patients who showed clinical remission. As defined in the Zanarini et al. studies (Zanarini, Frankenburg, Reich, & Fitzmaurice, 2010, 2012), recovery required good overall social or occupational functioning and only mild symptoms. Overall, 60% of patients were considered to have had at least a 2-year period of recovery and 40% to have had at least an 8-year recovery. Although these numbers are encouraging, they do suggest that sustained recovery from BPD is much less common than sustained remission (approximately 78%). In other words, for the majority of patients, having a lengthy period without clinically significant symptoms is a more likely outcome than having a lengthy period of generally good overall functioning (e.g., full-time work or school, or at least one emotionally sustaining close relationship). This is reflected in a recent review showing that although symptoms may improve over time, functional impairment may be more enduring (Biskin, 2015). Other work also suggests that interpersonal dysfunction may endure over time (Wright, Hallquist, Beeney, & Pilkonis, 2013).

There is also one characteristic of the family environment that warrants mention with regard to clinical outcome in BPD. Expressed emotion (EE) is a measure of the family environment that has been reliably linked to higher rates of relapse and poor clinical outcome in patients with schizophrenia, mood disorders, and other psychiatric conditions as well (see Hooley, 2007). Accordingly, when Hooley and Hoffman (1999) examined the clinical outcomes of patients with BPD over the course of a 1-year follow-up, they expected to find that EE was again predictive of a more unfavorable course of illness. However, this was not the case. The key elements of expressed emotion (criticism, hostility) did not predict worse outcomes in patients with BPD. Even more unexpected was the finding that patients with BPD fared *better* when their family members showed high levels of emotional overinvolvement (EOI), a component of EE that reflects high levels of protective attitudes, emotional concern, and anxiety, as well as self-sacrificing behavior on the part of family members.

In patients diagnosed with schizophrenia or mood disorders, EOI predicts worse clinical outcomes. This is thought to be because the intrusiveness of relatives high on EOI is stressful and overstimulating for these patients. Hooley and Hoffman (1999) hypothesized that, because of their fears of abandonment, people with BPD might process emotional overinvolvement in a different way, interpreting it as a positive rather than a negative stimulus. In a specific test of this hypothesis, Hooley et al. (2010) subsequently used fMRI to examine brain activation in participants with BPD, participants with dysthymia, and healthy controls during exposure to comments reflecting high levels of EOI. Specifically, they predicted that, compared to the other two groups, participants with BPD would show increased activation in the left prefrontal cortex when listening to EOI. This prediction was based on research showing that left prefrontal activation is associated with approach-related positive experiences and with reward processing (Pizzagalli, Sherwood, Henriques, & Davidson, 2005; Schaefer, Putnam, Benca, & Davidson, 2006). Consistent with this prediction, participants with BPD showed elevated left prefrontal activation to EOI relative to the controls and to the dysthymic participants. This is especially interesting in light of the finding that self-reports of the BPD participants suggested that they did not like hearing the EOI remarks. Nonetheless, below the radar, their brains were responding in a positive manner. Taken together, these results suggest that even though people with BPD may not overtly welcome expressions of concern or worry on the part of their family members, these expressions may actually be quite helpful for them.

PHARMACOLOGICAL APPROACHES

Medications are routinely used in the treatment of BPD. In a study of over 2,000 inpatients, Bridler et al. (2015) found that 90% were treated with some form of pharmacological intervention. Overall, 70% were treated with antipsychotics and/or antidepressants, 33% were treated with anticonvulsants, 30% with benzodiazepines, and 4% with lithium. More than half of these patients were treated with three or more concurrent medications.

Despite the widespread use of medications, there is a surprising paucity of randomized controlled trials attesting to their efficacy, and there is no routinely recommended medication. This is not to say that medications do not help some patients. However, their benefits are far more modest than would be expected, particularly in light of how often they are prescribed. Selective serotonin reuptake inhibitors (SSRIs) are commonly used to treat BPD. One rationale for using these medications is that many people with BPD are also depressed and these medications have demonstrated efficacy for depression. SSRIs also make sense when we consider the data linking aggression and suicide to low levels of serotonin (Åsberg, 1997). Open trial studies with small samples of patients have suggested that SSRIs may be helpful for patients with BPD (e.g., Cornelius, Soloff, Perel, & Ulrich, 1991). However, in efficacy studies, their benefits are often quite modest.

In a double-blind study, Rinne, van den Brink, Wouters, and van Dyck (2002) randomly assigned 38 women with BPD to either 6 weeks of SSRI treatment (fluvoxamine) or 6 weeks of treatment with placebo. At the end of the 6-week trial, half of the patients who had been given a placebo were switched to fluvoxamine (Luvox). All the patients (who were still blind to the type of treatment they were receiving) were then followed for a further 6 weeks. All the patients showed some clinical improvements after they entered the study. At the end of the 6-week period, patients in both the SSRI and the placebo condition showed improvements in anger and impulsivity, and there were no significant differences between the groups. However, patients who had been treated with fluvoxamine showed significantly more improvement in mood stability than did the patients who had received a placebo. These results suggest that treatment with an SSRI may help BPD patients experience fewer rapid mood shifts. However, even when they received the placebo, the patients with BPD still experienced clinical improvement.

Other medications in widespread use in the treatment of BPD include atypical antipsychotics such as olanzapine, clozapine, and risperidone. Again, most of these have been studied in the context of open trials, so more placebo-controlled studies are needed (see Markovitz, 2004). However, as a class, antipsychotic medications have been shown to have a beneficial effect on impulsivity and aggression (Nose, Cipriani, Biancosino, Grassi, & Barbui, 2006). Moreover, in a double-blind, placebo-controlled trial of olanzapine (Zyprexa), Zanarini and Frankenburg (2001) reported that the 19 female patients who were randomly assigned to receive olanzapine reported decreases in their levels of anxiety, paranoia, and interpersonal sensitivity, as well as anger/hostility, compared to the nine women who received a placebo. A placebo-controlled trial of the antipsychotic agent, aripiprazole, has also yielded promising preliminary results (Nickel et al., 2006).

Given that quetiapine is frequently prescribed, results of a recent double-blind, placebo-controlled trial are also encouraging. Black and colleagues (2014) randomly assigned 95 patients to one of three groups: low-dose quetiapine, moderate-dose quetiapine, or placebo. After 8 weeks of treatment and regardless of dose, patients who received quetiapine experienced more symptom improvement and faster treatment response. Overall, responders comprised 82% of individuals in the low-dose group, 74% in the moderate-dose group, and 48% in the placebo group.

Finally, we note that antiepileptic drugs are also now being used in the treatment of BPD. Mood stabilizers such as divalproex sodium have been shown to have beneficial effects on anger and mood instability in randomized controlled trials (Nose et al., 2006). However, they do not appear to alleviate such problems as impulsivity and aggression, or suicidality. Lithium has also been used in one small randomized clinical trial, although it was not associated with any improvements in mood or impulsivity (Links, Steiner, Boiago, & Irwin, 1990). There is also some evidence that lamotrigine may have beneficial effects for reducing affective lability, but more rigorous study in the context of BPD is needed (Bowen, Balbuena, & Baetz, 2014).

Considered together, these studies make it clear that medications do offer some benefits for patients. However, there is no medication that can be considered an adequate treatment for BPD. Medications help with some but not all of the symptoms of BPD. Recognizing this, we now turn our attention to some of the psychological approaches that are important in the treatment of this disorder.

PSYCHOLOGICAL APPROACHES

Perhaps the best-known treatment for BPD is dialectical behavior therapy (DBT). Developed by Marsha Linehan, this cognitive-behavioral approach involves weekly individual psychotherapy sessions as well as weekly skills training administered in a group format. Patients are also permitted to call their therapists for telephone consultations. The therapists attend weekly team consultation meetings to help them stay motivated and provide them with additional treatment skills (see Linehan et al., 2006).

DBT was specifically designed to treat patients with BPD, and research to date supports its efficacy for this disorder (Linehan, Armstrong, Suarez, Allman, & Heard, 1991; Linehan et al., 2006). In the most recent controlled trial, Linehan et al. (2006) randomly assigned patients either to DBT or to treatment with experts who had been nominated by community health leaders as being particularly skilled in the treatment of difficult patients. Patients in both groups received 1 full year of treatment and were then followed up for another year. Both groups of patients showed significant improvements in suicidal ideation and motivation to live. Both treatments were also successful in reducing patients' self-injurious behaviors. However, at the end of the 2 years the rate of suicide attempts in the patients who received DBT was significantly lower than the rate of suicide attempts in the patients who received treatment by the expert therapists (23.1% versus 46.0%). Patients assigned to DBT were also less likely to drop out of treatment, and less likely to require hospitalization than were the patients who did not receive DBT. These findings support the value of DBT, and highlight its particular benefits with regard to reducing suicide attempts (see also Panos, Jackson, Hasan, & Panos, 2014).

Although DBT is an extremely popular treatment, it is no longer the only empirically validated psychological approach. In recent years, several other treatment approaches have been developed, all of which are showing great promise. Working from a psychodynamic perspective, Bateman and Fonagy (2010) developed a new therapeutic approach called mentalization-based therapy (MBT). Based on attachment theory, mentalization uses the therapeutic relationship to help patients develop the skills they need to accurately understand their own feelings and emotions, as well as the feelings and emotions of others. Randomized controlled trials of mentalization-based therapy for BPD (Bateman & Fonagy, 1999, 2001, 2009) have revealed it to be an efficacious treatment. Moreover, many clinical improvements seem to be maintained even after an 8-year follow-up (Bateman & Fonagy, 2008). A randomized trial of MBT with self-harming adolescents (the majority of whom had BPD) has also demonstrated clear benefits compared to treatment as usual for both depression and self-harming behaviors over 1 year (Rossouw & Fonagy, 2012). Importantly, these clinical benefits were mediated by changes in mentalization. Further work by researchers who are unaffiliated with the treatment developers is now needed to more fully examine the effectiveness of this therapeutic approach.

Another promising, psychodynamically-oriented therapy is transference-focused psychotherapy, or TFP. Developed by Kernberg and his colleagues, this treatment approach uses the therapeutic relationship to help the patient understand and correct the distortions that occur in his or her perceptions of other people. Clarification, confrontation, and interpretation are key techniques here, with the transference relationship between the patient and the therapist being a central focus of interest (see Clarkin, Levy, Lenzenweger, & Kernberg, 2004). In a clinical trial, 90 patients with BPD were randomly assigned to receive either TFP, DBT, or supportive psychotherapy (Clarkin, Levy, Lenzenweger, & Kernberg, 2007). After 1 year of treatment, patients in all three groups showed significant clinical improvements in their levels of depression, anxiety, social adjustment, and overall functioning. Patients who received TFP and DBT also showed decreases in suicidality. One additional advantage of TFP relative to the other forms of treatment, however, was that it was also associated with a reduction in anger.

Other work has suggested a potential mechanism for the benefits that BPD patients experience in the course of TFP. In a small study of BPD patients, TFP was associated with increased activation in areas of the brain that putatively support cognitive control and decreases in areas thought to influence emotional reactivity (Perez et al., 2015). The same study also found that affective lability correlated with changes in frontolimbic function during a go/no-go task. Although limited by the small sample size of 10 patients, as well as by the lack of a comparison group, this is a promising development. This approach also highlights the importance of combining treatment studies with neuroimaging to better identify and understand mechanisms of change.

Other studies, while also supporting the clinical benefits of TFP, are further showing that schema-focused therapy (SFT) may be a valuable treatment for patients with BPD. Schema-focused cognitive therapy uses cognitive, behavioral, and also experiential techniques to explore and modify four schema modes (organized sets of schemas, or constellations, of underlying beliefs) that are thought to occur in BPD. These are the detached protector, punitive parent, abandoned/abused child, and angry/impulsive child modes. Patient and therapist work together in an effort to stop these dysfunctional schemas from controlling the patient's life. In a randomized trial, Giesen-Bloo et al. (2006) compared the effectiveness of TFP and SFT for 88 patients in community mental health centers. After 3 years of therapy, patients in both groups showed clinical improvement. More specifically, both treatments were associated with reductions in BPD symptoms, improvements in quality of life, and decreases in dysfunctional behaviors. In many cases, clinical improvements began to appear after 1 year of treatment. Of note, however, is that patients who received SFT showed significantly more clinical improvements on all measures (including borderline symptomatology, personality pathology, and quality of life) than did patients who received TFP. They were also significantly less likely to drop out of treatment and significantly more likely to recover. Cognitive analytic therapy (CAT; Ryle, 2005), a newer therapy that resembles SFT, has shown some initial promise (Clarke, Thomas, & James, 2013), and is worthy of further study.

Many of the treatments we have just described, including DBT, require significant and specialized clinical training to administer. However, a new approach called general psychiatric management (GPM; Gunderson & Links, 2014) may offer a more accessible alternative. GPM relies on six general principles (e.g., an active and nonreactive clinician style, support and validation, case management, and a collaborative agreement to monitor change and effectiveness of treatment) and can be learned fairly easily by individuals who are already clinically trained (Links, Ross, & Gunderson, 2015). Although research on GPM is still in its infancy, in a randomized, year-long, single-blind trial, results for GPM were comparable to DBT across several indices, including general measures of borderline symptoms, care utilization, depression, and distress (McMain et al., 2009). Improvements in self-injury, care utilization, depression, and borderline symptoms were also maintained at 2-year follow-up (McMain, Guimond, Streiner, Cardish, & Links, 2012).

Similarly, Systems Training for Emotional Predictability and Problem Solving (STEPPS; Blum, Bartels, St. John, & Pfohl, 2002) provides an easily-disseminated group addition to treatment as usual (TAU). STEPPS incorporates skills training (like DBT) and cognitive-behavioral therapy, as well as a systems approach. Although not designed to be used as a stand-alone treatment, STEPPS has been shown to provide incremental benefits when added to regular care (Blum et al., 2008). It is unclear how STEPPS might fare when compared to specialized treatments for BPD. However, most specialized treatments for BPD are difficult to disseminate and have significant training burdens. STEPPS may provide a way to reach a greater number of patients. Reflecting this, STEPPS is now widely used in the Netherlands (van Wel et al., 2006).

Within this climate of optimism, we wish to caution readers that not all therapeutic approaches have been found to provide significant benefits to patients with BPD.

Davidson et al. (2006) randomly assigned 106 patients with BPD to either TAU or TAU plus cognitive-behavioral therapy. In CBT, patients were helped to develop new and more adaptive beliefs about themselves as well as behavioral strategies that would improve their social and emotional well-being. Major targets of clinical intervention were patients' core beliefs as well as typical behaviors that got in the way of adaptive functioning. At the end of the 12-month treatment period (during which patients attended an average of 16 sessions), patients who had received CBT in addition to TAU were no better off than patients who had received only TAU on a broad range of outcomes measures. These included the presence or absence of suicide attempts, self-harming behaviors, depressed mood, and interpersonal and social functioning. Overall, the findings from this rigorously conducted trial are disappointing. They attest to the difficulties inherent in getting patients to engage in treatment, and suggest that for many patients, long-term intensive treatment may need to be provided for any real clinical gains to occur.

The increasing number of specific treatment interventions (each with its own acronym) makes treatment decisions inherently complex. Such diversity may also hinder coherence in our understanding of why and how treatments for BPD work. Paris (2015) argues that many of these treatments share important commonalities (e.g., most focus on emotion regulation and behavioral and interpersonal skills), and that an integrated treatment approach may be warranted. Ironically, the fact that we now have so many cooks in the kitchen may actually be limiting the development of more effective treatments for BPD.

Summary and Future Directions

Despite BPD being the most researched form of personality disorder, a full understanding of it remains elusive. Although we can reliably diagnose it, its core aspects are still the subject of debate. We also know little about its etiology, although it is almost certainly the result of the interaction of genetic, neurophysiological, psychological, and environmental factors. Finally, although medications and psychological treatments offer a great deal of help for BPD sufferers, we still have much to learn.

BPD is characterized by disturbances in a broad range of systems. This makes a full understanding of its nature both difficult and challenging. Genetic factors are likely to play an important role in the etiology of the disorder; early life experiences of abuse and trauma are also implicated. Yet many people who suffer from BPD do not have childhood histories of maltreatment. In some cases, it may simply be that genetic factors render patients especially sensitive to other, less malevolent (and common) forms of parental failure, such as invalidation or lack of empathic attunement. It is also possible that there is a pathway to BPD that is based primarily on genetic vulnerability and in which environmental factors play a more limited role.

Because biological and environmental factors are so inextricably linked, the clinical heterogeneity of BPD may actually be illustrating the range of outcomes that can result when temperamentally vulnerable individuals sustain damage from the psychosocial environment. Animal research has made it clear that adverse circumstances occurring during early development can have a permanent effect on the HPA axis, neurotransmitter systems, and cognitive functioning, as well as on attachment relationships and social adjustment (Fish et al., 2004; Oitzl, Workel, Fluttert, Frosch, & de Kloet, 2000). We need to learn more about the consequences of trauma and other forms of psychosocial damage on the developing brain. We also need to use genomic methods to further identify which genetic polymorphisms might be associated with differential reactivity to aversive early environments.

We believe that even the most complicated of clinical pictures can be assessed and connected back to basic psychological systems and processes (Lenzenweger & Hooley, 2003). Studying endophenotypes may be especially valuable in this endeavor. An endophenotype is a variable that can be measured or indexed and that is thought to lie along the pathway between the genotype and the disease (see Gottesman & Gould, 2003; Lenzenweger & Cicchetti, 2005). This could be a neurobiological, endocrinological, neuroanatomical, neuropsychological, or cognitive process. The rationale for studying endophenotypes (e.g., people who show problems with inhibitory processes on neuropsychological tests or people who have chronic high negative affect) rather than people with the disorder itself is that the endophenotype (because it is a simpler clue) may lead researchers closer to the genetic underpinnings of the disorder. Quite commonly used in schizophrenia research, the endophenotype concept, as Lenzenweger and Cicchetti (2005) note, may have much to offer those who wish to understand BPD.

We would like to end by making a call for more research in two key areas. The fact that our field knows so little about men with BPD is a major source of concern. Going forward, much more attention must be devoted to learning about the influence of gender on the disorder. Future research efforts also need to explore BPD in its earliest stages and identify the prodromal signs of the disorder. In all probability, the events that set the stage for the development of BPD happen early. If we can study these events and their biological and psychological sequelae closer in time to when they occur, we may gain much leverage in the research process. In so doing, we may also be better placed to reduce the years of suffering that people with BPD have to endure.

References

Adler, G., & Buie, D. H., Jr. (1979). Aloneness and borderline psychopathology: The possible relevance of child development issues. *International Journal of Psychoanalysis, 60,* 83–96.

Akiskal, H. S. (2002). The bipolar spectrum—the shaping of a new paradigm in psychiatry. *Current Psychiatry Reports, 4,* 1–3.

Akiskal, H. S., Chen, S. E., Davis, G. C., Puzantian, V. R., Kashgarian, M., & Bolinger, J. M. (1985). Borderline: An adjective in search of a noun. *Journal of Clinical Psychiatry, 46,* 41–48.

Amad, A., Ramoz, N., Thomas, P., Jardri, R., & Gorwood, P. (2014). Genetics of borderline personality disorder: Systematic review and proposal of an integrative model. *Neuroscience and Biobehavioral Reviews, 40,* 6–19.

American Psychiatric Association. (1980). *Diagnostic and statistical manual of mental disorders* (3rd ed.). Washington, DC: Author.

American Psychiatric Association. (1994). *Diagnostic and statistical manual of mental disorders* (4th ed.). Washington, DC: Author.

American Psychiatric Association. (2000). *Diagnostic and statistical manual of mental disorders* (4th ed., text rev.). Washington, DC: Author.

American Psychiatric Association. (2013). *Diagnostic and statistical manual of mental disorders* (5th ed.). Washington, DC: Author.

Arntz, A., Appels, C., & Sieswerda, S. (2000). Hypervigilance in borderline personality disorder: A test with the emotional Stroop paradigm. *Journal of Personality Disorders, 14*(4), 366–373.

Arntz, A., Meeren, M., & Wessel, I. (2002). No evidence for overgeneral memories in borderline personality disorder. *Behaviour Research and Therapy, 40*(9), 1063–1068.

Arntz, A., & Veen, G. (2001). Evaluations of others by borderline patients. *Journal of Nervous and Mental Disease, 189,* 513–521.

Åsberg, M. (1997). Neurotransmitters and suicidal behavior: The evidence from cerebrospinal fluid studies. *Annals of the New York Academy of Sciences, 836,* 158–181.

Asnaani, A., Chelminski, I., Young, D., & Zimmerman, M. (2007). Heterogeneity of borderline personality disorder: Do the number of criteria met make a difference? *Journal of Personality Disorders, 21,* 615–625.

Bandelow, B., Broocks, A., Hajak, G., Krause, J., Wedekind, D., & Rüther, E. (2005). Early traumatic life events, parental attitudes, family history, and birth risk factors in patients with borderline personality disorder and healthy controls. *Psychiatry Research, 134*(2), 169–179.

Barker, V., Romaniuk, L., Cardinal, R. N., Pope, M., Nicol, K., & Hall, K. (2015). Impulsivity in borderline personality disorder. *Psychological Medicine, 45*(9), 1955–1964.

Barnow, S., Stopsack, M., Grabe, H. J., Meinke, C., Spitzer, C., Kronmuller, K., & Sieswerda, S. (2009). Interpersonal evaluation bias in borderline personality disorder. *Behaviour Research and Therapy, 47,* 359–365.

Bartz, J., Simeon, D., Hamilton, H., Kim, S., Crystal, S., Braun, A., … Hollander, E. (2010). Oxytocin can hinder trust and cooperation in borderline personality disorder. *Social Cognitive and Affective Neuroscience.* Advance online publication. doi: 10.1093/scan/nsq085

Bateman, A. W., & Fonagy, P. (1999). Effectiveness of partial hospitalization in the treatment of borderline personality disorder: A randomized controlled trial. *American Journal of Psychiatry, 156,* 1563–1569.

Bateman, A. W., & Fonagy, P. (2001). Treatment of borderline personality disorder with psychoanalytically oriented partial hospitalization: An 18-month follow-up. *American Journal of Psychiatry, 158,* 36–42.

Bateman, A. W., & Fonagy, P. (2003). The development of an attachment-based treatment program for borderline personality disorder. *Bulletin of the Menninger Clinic, 67,* 187–211.

Bateman, A., & Fonagy, P. (2008). 8-year follow-up of patients treated for borderline personality disorder: Mentalization-based treatment versus treatment as usual. *American Journal of Psychiatry, 165,* 631–638.

Bateman, A. W., & Fonagy, P. (2009). Randomized controlled trial of outpatient mentalization-based treatment versus structured clinical management for borderline personality disorder. *American Journal of Psychiatry, 166,* 1355–1364.

Bateman, A. W., & Fonagy, P. (2010). Mentalization based treatment for borderline personality disorder. *World Psychiatry*, *9*, 11–15.

Bazanis, E., Rogers, R. D., Dowson, J. H., Taylor, P., Meux, C., Staley, C., … Sahakian, B. J. (2002). Neurocognitive deficits in decision-making and planning of patients with DSM-III-R borderline personality disorder. *Psychological Medicine*, *32*, 1395–1405.

Beeney, J. E., Stepp, S. D., Hallquist, M. N., Scott, L. N., Wright, A. G. C., Ellison, W. D., … Pilkonis, A. (2015). Attachment and social cognition in borderline personality disorder: Specificity in relation to antisocial and avoidant personality disorders. *Personality Disorders: Theory, Research, and Treatment*, *6*(3), 207–215.

Bender, D. S., Dolan, R. T., Skodol, A. E., Sanislow, C. A., Dyck, I. R., McGlashan, T. H., … Gunderson, J. G. (2001). Treatment utilization by patients with personality disorders. *American Journal of Psychiatry*, *158*, 295–302.

Bender, D. S., Farber, B. A., Sanislow, C. A., Dyck, I. R., Geller, J. D., & Skodol, A. E. (2003). Representations of therapists by patients with personality disorders. *American Journal of Psychotherapy*, *57*, 219–236.

Bennett, A. J., Lesch, K. P., Heils, A., Long, J. C., Lorenz, J. G., Shoaf, S. E., … Higley, J. D. (2002). Early experience and serotonin transporter gene variation interact to influence primate CNS function. *Molecular Psychiatry*, *7*, 118–122.

Berlin, H. A., Rolls, E. T., & Iversen, S. D. (2005). Borderline personality disorder: Impulsivity and the orbitofrontal cortex. *American Journal of Psychiatry*, *162*, 2360–2373.

Bertsch, K., Gamer, M., Schmidt, B., Schmidinger, I., Walther, S., Kastel, T., … Herpertz, S. C. (2013). Oxytocin and reduction of social threat hypersensitivity in women with borderline personality disorder. *American Journal of Psychiatry*, *170*(10), 1169–1177.

Bertsch, K., Schmidinger, I., Neumann, I. D., & Herpertz, S. C. (2013). Reduced plasma oxytocin levels in female patients with borderline personality disorder. *Hormones and Behavior*, *63*(3), 424–429.

Bhatia, V., Davila, J., Eubanks-Carter, C., & Burckell, L. A. (2013). Appraisals of daily romantic relationship experiences in individuals with borderline personality disorder features. *Journal of Family Psychology*, *27*(3), 519–524.

Biskin, R. S. (2015). The lifetime course of personality disorder. *Canadian Journal of Psychiatry*, *60*(7), 303–308.

Bjork, R. A. (1989). Retrieval inhibition as an adaptive mechanism in human memory. In H. L. Roediger & F. I. M. Craik (Eds.), *Varieties of memory and consciousness: Essays in honor of Endel Tulving* (pp. 309–330). Hillsdale, NJ: Erlbaum.

Black, D. W., Zanarini, M. C., Romine, A., Shaw, M., Allen, J., & Schulz, S. C. (2014). Comparison of low and moderate dosages of extended-release quetiapine in borderline personality disorder: A randomized, double-blind, placebo-controlled study. *American Journal of Psychiatry*, *171*(11), 1174–1182.

Blum, N., Bartels, N., St. John, D., & Pfohl, B. (2002). *STEPPS: Systems Training for Emotional Predictability and Problem Solving: Group treatment for borderline personality disorder*. Coralville, IA: Blum's Books.

Blum, N., St. John, D., Pfohl, B., Stuart, S., McCormick, B., Allen, J., … Black, D. W. (2008). Systems Training for Emotional Predictability and Problem Solving (STEPPS) for outpatients with borderline personality disorder: A randomized controlled trial and 1-year follow-up. *American Journal of Psychiatry*, *165*(4), 468–478.

Bøen, E., Westlye, L. T., Elvsashagen, T., Hummelen, B., Hol, P. K., Boye, B., … Malt, U. F. (2014). Regional cortical thinning may be a biological marker for borderline personality disorder. *Acta Psychiatrica Scandinavica*, *130*(3), 193–204.

Boggs, C. D., Morey, L. C., Skodol, A. E., Shea, M. T., Sanislow, C. A., Grilo, C. M., … Gunderson, J. G. (2009). Differential impairment as an indicator of sex bias in DSM-IV criteria for four personality disorders. *Personality Disorders: Theory, Research, and Treatment*, *S*(1), 61–68.

Bondy, B., Erfurth, A., deJonge, S., Kruger, M., & Meyer, H. (2000). Possible association of the short allele of the serotonin transporter promoter gene polymorphism (5-HTTLPR) with violent suicide. *Molecular Psychiatry*, *5*, 193–195.

Bowen, R. C., Balbuena, L., & Baetz, M. (2014). Lamotrigine reduces affective instability in depressed patients with mixed mood and anxiety disorders. *Journal of Clinical Psychopharmacology*, *34*(6), 747–749.

Bowlby, J. (1973). *Attachment and loss: Vol. 2. Separation*. New York, NY: Basic Books.

Bowlby, J. (1977). The making and breaking of affectional bonds: I. Aetiology and psychopathology in the light of attachment theory. *British Journal of Psychiatry, 130*, 201–210.

Bremner, J. D. (2002). Structural changes in the brain in depression and relationship to symptom recurrence. *CNS Spectrums, 7*, 129–130, 135–139.

Brendel, G. R., Stern, E., & Silbersweig, D. A. (2005). Defining the neurocircuitry of borderline personality disorder: Functional neuroimaging approaches. *Developmental Psychopathology, 17*, 1197–1206.

Bridler, R., Haberle, A., Muller, S. T., Cattapan, K., Grohmann, R., Toto, S., … Greil, W. (2015). Psychopharmacological treatment of 2195 in-patients with borderline personality disorder: A comparison with other psychiatric approaches. *Neuropsychopharmacology, 25*(6), 763–772.

Brune, M., Ebert, A., Kolb, M., Tas, C., Edel, M. A., & Roser, P. (2013). Oxytocin influences avoidant reactions to social threat in adults with borderline personality disorder. *Human Psychopharmacology, Clinical and Experimental, 28*(6), 552–561.

Brunner, R., Henze, R., Parzer, P., Kramer, J., Feigl, N., Lutz, K., … Stieltjes, B. (2010). Reduced prefrontal and orbitofrontal gray matter in female adolescents with borderline personality disorder: Is it disorder specific? *NeuroImage, 49*, 114–120.

Buie, D. H., & Adler, G. (1982). Definitive treatment of the borderline personality. *International Journal of Psychoanalytic Psychotherapy, 9*, 51–87.

Calati, R., Gressier, F., Balestri, M, & Serretti, A. (2013). Genetic modulation of borderline personality disorder: Systematic review and meta-analysis. *Journal of Psychiatric Research, 47*(10), 1275–1287.

Carcone, D., Tokarz, V. L., & Ruocco, A. C. (2015). A systematic review on the reliability and validity of semistructured diagnostic interviews for borderline personality disorder. *Canadian Psychology, 56*(2), 208–226.

Casey, B. J., Castellanos, F. X., Giedd, J. N., Marsh, W. L., Hamburger, S. D., Schubert, A. B., … Rapoport, J. L. (1997). Implication of right frontostriatal circuitry in response inhibition and attention-deficit/hyperactivity disorder. *Journal of the American Academy of Child & Adolescent Psychiatry, 36*, 374–383.

Caspi, A., McClay, J., Moffitt, T. E., Mill, J., Martin, J., Craig, I. W., … Poulton, R. (2002). Role of genotype in the cycle of violence in maltreated children. *Science, 297*, 851–854.

Chanen, A. M., Velakoulis, D., Carison, K., Gaunson, K., Wood, S. J., Yuen, H. P., … Pantelis, C. (2008). Orbitofrontal, amygdala and hippocampal volumes in teenagers with first-presentation borderline personality disorder. *Psychiatry Research: Neuroimaging, 163*, 116–125.

Choi-Kain, L. W., & Gunderson, J. G. (Eds.). (2015). *Borderline personality disorders and mood disorders: Comorbidity and controversy.* New York, NY: Springer.

Cicchetti, D., Rogosch, F. A., Hecht, K. F., Crick, N. R., & Hetzel, S. (2014). Moderation of maltreatment effects on childhood borderline personality symptoms by gender and oxytocin receptor and FK506 binding protein 5 genes. *Development and Psychopathology, 26*(3), 831–849.

Clark, L. A. (2009). *Schedule for Nonadaptive and Adaptive Personality–Second Edition (SNAP-2)* (2nd ed.). Minneapolis: University of Minnesota Press.

Clarke, S., Thomas, P., & James, K. (2013). Cognitive analytic therapy for personality disorders: Randomised controlled trial. *British Journal of Psychiatry, 202*(2), 129–134.

Clarkin, J. F., Levy, K. N., Lenzenweger, M. F., & Kernberg, O. F. (2004). The Personality Disorders Institute/Borderline Personality Disorder Research Foundation randomized control trial for borderline personality disorder: Rationale, methods, and patient characteristics. *Journal of Personality Disorders, 18*, 52–72.

Clarkin, J. F., Levy, K. N., Lenzenweger, M. F., & Kernberg, O. F. (2007). Evaluating three treatments for borderline personality disorder: A multiwave study. *American Journal of Psychiatry, 164*, 922–928.

Cloninger, C. R. (2000). Biology of personality dimensions. *Current Opinion in Psychiatry, 13*, 611–616.

Coccaro, E. F., Lee, R., & McClosky, M. (2003). Norepinephrine function in personality disorder: Plasma free MHPG correlates inversely with a life history of aggression. *CNS Spectrums, 8*, 731–736.

Coccaro, E. F., Siever, L. J., Klar, H. M., & Maurer, G. (1989). Serotonergic studies in patients with affective and personality disorders: Correlates with suicidal and impulsive aggressive behavior. *Archives of General Psychiatry, 46*, 587–599.

Coid, J., Yang, M., Tyrer, P. T., Roberts, A., & Ullrich, S. (2006). Prevalence and correlates of personality disorder in Great Britain. *British Journal of Psychiatry, 188*, 423–431.

Cornelius, J. R., Soloff, P. H., Perel, J. M., & Ulrich, R. F. (1991). A preliminary trial of fluoxetine in refractory borderline patients. *Journal of Clinical Psychopharmacology*, *11*(2), 116–120.

Corruble, E., Ginestet, D., & Guelfi, J. D. (1996). Comorbidity of personality disorders and unipolar major depression: A review. *Journal of Affective Disorders*, *37*, 157–170.

Costa, P. T., & McCrae, R. R. (1992). *Revised NEO Personality Inventory (NEO PI-R) and NEO Five-Factor Inventory (NEO-FFI) professional manual.* Odessa, FL: Psychological Assessment Resources.

Davidson, K., Norrie, J., Tyrer, P., Gumley, A., Tata, P., Murray, H., & Palmer, S. (2006). The effectiveness of cognitive behavior therapy for borderline personality disorder: Results from the borderline personality disorder study of cognitive therapy. *Journal of Personality Disorders*, *20*, 450–465.

Davidson, R. J. (2002). Anxiety and affective style: Role of prefrontal cortex and amygdala. *Biological Psychiatry*, *51*, 68–80.

Davidson, R. J., Putnam, K. M., & Larson, C. L. (2000). Dysfunction in the neural circuitry of emotion regulation—a possible prelude to violence. *Science*, *289*, 591–594.

De Dreu, C. K. W. (2012). Oxytocin modulates the link between adult attachment and cooperation through reduced betrayal aversion. *Psychoneuroendocrinology*, *32*, 871–880.

de Reus, R. J. M., van den Berg, J. F., & Emmelkamp, P. M. G. (2013). Personality Diagnostic Questionnaire 4+ is not useful as a screener in clinical practice. *Clinical Psychology & Psychotherapy*, *20*, 49–54.

Depue, R. A., & Lenzenweger, M. F. (2005). A neurobehavioral model of personality disturbance. In J. F. Clarkin & M. F. Lenzenweger (Eds.), *Major theories of personality disorder* (2nd ed., pp. 391–453). New York, NY: Guilford Press.

Distel, M. A., Rebollo-Mesa, I., Willemsen, G., Derom, C. A., Trull, T. J., Martin, N. G., & Boomsma, D. I. (2009). Familial resemblance of borderline personality disorder features: Genetic or cultural transmission? *PLoS ONE*, *4*(4).

Domes, G., Winter, B., Schnell, K., Vohs, K., Fast, K., & Herpertz, S. C. (2006). The influence of emotions on inhibitory functioning in borderline personality disorder. *Psychological Medicine*, *36*, 1163–1172.

Donegan, N. H., Sanislow, C. A., Blumberg, H. P., Fulbright, R. K., Lacadie, C., Skudlarski, P., … Wexler, B. E. (2003). Amygdala hyperreactivity in borderline personality disorder: Implications for emotional dysregulation. *Biological Psychiatry*, *54*, 1284–1293.

Driessen, M., Herrmann, J., Stahl, K., Zwaan, M., Meier, S., Hill, A., … Petersen, D. (2000). Magnetic resonance imaging volume of the hippocampus and the amygdala in women with borderline personality disorder and early traumatization. *Archives of General Psychiatry*, *57*, 1115–1122.

Eaton, N. R., Krueger, R. F., Keyes, K. M., Skodol, A. E., Markon, K. E., & Grant., B. F. (2010). Borderline personality disorder comorbidity: Relationship to the internalizing-externalizing structure of common mental disorders. *Psychological Medicine*, *41*, 1041–1050.

Ebert, A., Kolbe, M., Heller, J., Edel, M. A., Roser, P., & Brune, M. (2013). Modulation of interpersonal trust in borderline personality disorder by intranasal oxytocin and childhood trauma. *Social Neuroscience*, *8*(4), 305–313.

Ebstein, R. P., Benjamin, J., & Belmaker, R. H. (2000). Personality and polymorphisms of genes involved in aminergic neurotransmission. *European Journal of Pharmacology*, *410*, 205–214.

Fan, J., McCandliss, B. D., Sommer, T., Raz, M., & Posner, M. I. (2002). Testing the efficiency and independence of attentional networks. *Journal of Cognitive Neuroscience*, *3*(14), 340–347.

Feldman, R., Gordon, I., Influs, M., Gutbir, T., & Ebstein, R. P. (2013). Parental oxytocin and early caregiving jointly shape children's oxytocin response and social reciprocity. *Neuropharmacology*, *38*(7), 1154–1162.

Fertuck, E. A., Grinband, J., & Stanley, B. (2013). Facial trust appraisal negatively biased in borderline personality disorder. *Psychiatry Research*, *207*(3), 195–202.

Fertuck, E., Lenzenweger, M., & Clarkin, J. (2005) The association between attentional and executive controls in the expression of borderline personality disorder features: A preliminary study. *Psychopathology*, *38*(2), 75–81.

Fertuck, E. A., Lenzenweger, M. F., Clarkin, J. F., Hoermann, S., & Stanley, B. (2006). Executive neurocognition, memory systems, and borderline personality disorder. *Clinical Psychology Review*, *26*, 346–375.

Few, L. R., Miller, J. D., Grant, J. D., Maples, J., Trull, T. J., Nelson, E. C., … Agrawal, A. (2016). Trait-based assessment of borderline personality disorder using the NEO Five-Factor Inventory: Phenotypic and genetic support. *Psychological Assessment, 1,* 39–50.

First, M., Gibbon, M., Spitzer, R. L., Williams, J. B. W., & Benjamin, L. S. (1997). *User's guide for the Structured Clinical Interview for DSM-IV Axis II Personality Disorders.* Washington, DC: American Psychiatric Press.

Fish, E. W., Shahrokh, D., Bagot, R., Caldji, C., Bredy, T., Szyf, M., & Meaney, M. J. (2004). Epigenetic programming of stress responses through variations in maternal care. *Annals of the New York Academy of Sciences, 1036,* 167–180.

Fossati, A., Maffei, C., Bagnato, M., Donati, D., Donini, M., Fiorilli, M., ... Ansoldi, M. (1998). Brief communication: Criterion validity of the Personality Diagnostic Questionnaire–4+ (PDQ-4+) in a mixed psychiatric sample. *Journal of Personality Disorders, 12*(2), 172–178.

Francis, D. D., & Meaney, M. J. (1999). Maternal care and the development of stress responses. *Current Opinion in Neurobiology, 9,* 128–134.

Frankle, W. G., Lombardo, I., New, A. S., Goodman, M., Talbot, P. S., Huang, Y., ... Siever, L. J. (2005). Brain serotonin transporter distribution in subjects with impulsive aggressivity: A positron emission study with [^{11}C]McN 5652. *American Journal of Psychiatry, 162,* 915–923.

Franzen, N., Hagenhoff, M., Baer, N., Schmidt, A., Mier, D., Sammer, G., ... Lis, S. (2011). Superior "theory of mind" in borderline personality disorder: An analysis of interaction behavior in a virtual trust game. *Psychiatry Research, 187,* 224–233.

Friedel, R. O. (2004). Dopamine dysfunction in borderline personality disorder: A hypothesis. *Neuropsychopharmacology, 29,* 1029–1039.

Fruzzetti, A. E., Shenk, C., & Hoffman, P. D. (2005). Family interaction and the development of borderline personality disorder: A transitional model. *Development Psychopathology, 17,* 1007–1030.

Gabbard, G. O. (2005). Mind, brain, and personality disorders. *American Journal of Psychiatry, 162,* 648–655.

Giesen-Bloo, J., van Dyck, R., Spinhoven, P., van Tilberg, W., Dirksen, C., van Asselt, T., ... Arntz, A. (2006). Outpatient psychotherapy for borderline personality disorder: Randomized trial of schema-focused therapy vs transference focused psychotherapy. *Archives of General Psychiatry, 63,* 649–658.

Glaser, J. P., Van Os, J., Thewissen, V., & Myin-Germeys, I. (2010). Psychotic reactivity in borderline personality disorder. *Acta Psychiatrica Scandinavica, 121,* 125–134.

Goodman, M., New, A., & Siever, L. (2004). Trauma, genes, and the neurobiology of personality disorders. *Annals of the New York Academy of Sciences, 1032,* 104–116.

Gottesman, I. I., & Gould, T. D. (2003). The endophenotype concept in psychiatry: Etymology and strategic intentions. *American Journal of Psychiatry, 160,* 636–645.

Grinker, R., Werble, B., & Drye, R. (1968). *The borderline syndrome: A behavioral study of ego functions.* New York, NY: Basic Books.

Gunderson, J. G. (1996). The borderline patient's intolerance of aloneness: Insecure attachments and therapist availability. *American Journal of Psychiatry, 153*(6), 752–758.

Gunderson, J. G. (2001). *Borderline personality disorder: A clinical guide.* Washington, DC: American Psychiatric Publishing.

Gunderson, J. G. (2010). Revising the borderline diagnosis for DSM-V: An alternative proposal. *Journal of Personality Disorders, 24,* 694–708.

Gunderson, J. G., Kolb, J. E., & Austin, V. (1981). The diagnostic interview for borderline patients. *American Journal of Psychiatry, 138,* 896–903.

Gunderson, J. G., & Links, P. (2014). *Handbook of good psychiatric management for borderline personality disorder.* Arlington, VA: American Psychiatric Publishing.

Gunderson, J. G., & Phillips, K. A. (1991). A current view of the interface between borderline personality disorder and depression. *American Journal of Psychiatry, 48,* 967–975.

Gunderson, J. G., & Sabo, A. N. (1993). The phenomenological and conceptual interface between borderline personality and PTSD. *American Journal of Psychiatry, 150,* 19–27.

Gunderson, J. G., & Singer, M. (1975). Defining borderline patients: An overview. *American Journal of Psychiatry, 132,* 1–10.

Gunderson, J. G., Stout, R. L., McGlashan, T. H., Shea, M. T., Morey, L. C., Grilo, C. M., ... Skodol, A. E. (2011). Ten-year course of borderline personality disorder: Psychopathology and function from the Collaborative Longitudinal Personality Disorders Study. *Archives of General Psychiatry, 68*(8), 827–837.

Gurvits, I. G., Koenigsberg, H. W., & Siever, L. J. (2000). Neurotransmitter dysfunction in patients with borderline personality disorder. *Psychiatric Clinics of North America, 23*(1), 27–40.

Hammen, C., Bower, J. E., & Cole, S. W. (2015). Oxytocin receptor gene variation and differential susceptibility to family environment in predicting youth borderline symptoms. *Journal of Personality Disorders, 29*(2), 177–192.

Hazlett, E. A., New, A. S., Newmark, R., Haznedar, M. M., Lo, J. N., Speiser, L. J., … Buchsbaum, M. S. (2005). Reduced anterior and posterior cingulated gray matter in borderline personality disorder. *Biological Psychiatry, 58*, 614–623.

Heaton, R. K. (1981). *Wisconsin Card Sorting Test manual*. Odessa, FL: Psychological Assessment Resources.

Heim, C., Newport, C. J., Heit, S., Graham, Y. P., Wilcox, M., Bonsall, R., … Nemeroff, C. B. (2000). Pituitary, adrenal and autonomic responses to stress in women after sexual and physical abuse in childhood. *JAMA, 284*, 592–597.

Herman, J., Perry, J., & van der Kolk, B. (1989). Childhood trauma in borderline personality disorder. *American Journal of Psychiatry, 146*, 490–495.

Herpertz, S. C., & Bertsch, K. (2015). A new perspective on the pathophysiology of borderline personality disorder: A model of the role of oxytocin. *American Journal of Psychiatry, 172*(9), 840–851.

Herpertz, S. C., Dietrich, T. M., Wenning, B., Krings, T., Erberich, S. G., Willmes, K., … Sass, H. (2001). Evidence of abnormal amygdala functioning in borderline personality disorder: A functional MRI study. *Biological Psychiatry, 50*, 292–298.

Higley, J. D., Suomi, S. J., & Linnoila, M. (1991). CSF monoamine metabolite concentrations vary according to age, rearing, and sex, and are influenced by the stressor of social separation in rhesus monkeys. *Psychopharmacology, 103*, 551–556.

Hoch, P., & Polantin, P. (1949). Pseudo neurotic forms of schizophrenia. *Psychiatric Quarterly, 23*, 248–276.

Hochhausen, N., Lorenz, A., & Newman, J. (2002) Specifying the impulsivity of female inmates with borderline personality disorder. *Journal of Abnormal Psychology, 111*(3), 495–501.

Hoefgen, B., Schulze, T. G., Ohlraun, S., von Widdern, O., Hofels, S., Gross, M., … Rietschel, M. (2005). The power of sample size and homogenous sampling: Association between the 5-HTTLPR serotonin transporter polymorphism and major depressive disorder. *Biological Psychiatry, 57*, 247–251.

Hooley, J. M. (2007). Expressed emotion and relapse of psychopathology. *Annual Review of Clinical Psychology, 3*, 329–352. doi: 10.1146/annurev.clinpsy .2.022305.095236

Hooley, J. M., Gruber, S. A., Parker, H. A., Guillaumot, J., Rogowska, J., & Yurgelun-Todd, D. A. (2010). Neural processing of emotional overinvolvement in borderline personality disorder. *Journal of Clinical Psychiatry, 71*, 1017–1024.

Hooley, J. M., & Hoffman, P. D. (1999). Expressed emotion and clinical outcome in borderline personality disorder. *American Journal of Psychiatry, 156*, 1557–1562.

Hooley, J. M., & Wilson-Murphy, M. (2012). Adult attachment to transitional objects and borderline personality disorder. *Journal of Personality Disorders, 26*, 179–191.

Hopwood, C. J., Morey, L. C., Edelen, M. O., Shea, M. T., Grilo, C. M., Sanislow, C. A., … Skodol, A. E. (2008). A comparison of interview and self-report methods for the assessment of borderline personality disorder criteria. *Psychological Assessment, 20*, 81–85.

Hunt, C., & Andrews, G. (1992). Measuring personality disorder: The use of self-report questionnaires. *Journal of Personality Disorders, 6*, 125–133.

Hurt, S. W., Hyler, S. E., Frances, A., Clarkin, J. F., & Brent, R. (1984). Assessing borderline personality-disorder with self-report, clinical interview, or semistructured interview. *American Journal of Psychiatry, 141*(10), 1228–1231.

Hyler, S. E., Skodol, A. E., Oldham, J. M., Kellman, H. D., & Doidge, N. (1992). Validity of the Personality Diagnostic Questionnaire–Revised: A replication in an outpatient sample. *Comprehensive Psychiatry, 33*, 73–77.

Hyman, S. E. (2002). A new beginning for research on borderline personality disorder. *Biological Psychiatry, 51*, 933–935.

Jacobsberg, L., Perry, S., & Frances, A. (1995). Diagnostic agreement between the SCID-II screening questionnaire and the Personality Disorder Examination. *Journal of Personality Assessment, 65*(3), 428–433.

Jane, J. S., Oltmanns, T. F., South, S. C., & Turkheimer, E. (2007). Gender bias in diagnostic criteria for personality disorders: An item response theory analysis. *Journal of Abnormal Psychology, 116*, 166–175.

Jang, K. L., Livesley, W. J., Vernon, P. A., & Jackson, D. N. (1996). Heritability of personality disorder traits: A twin study. *Acta Psychiatrica Scandinavica, 94*, 438–444.

Johnson, J. G., Cohen, P., Brown, J., Smailes, E. M., & Bernstein, D. P. (1999). Childhood maltreatment increases risk for personality disorders during early adulthood. *Archives of General Psychiatry, 56*, 600–606.

Jones, B., Heard, H., Startup, M., Swales, M., Williams, J., & Jones, R. (1999). Autobiographical memory and dissociation in borderline personality disorder. *Psychological Medicine, 29*(6), 1397–1404.

Joyce, P. R., McHugh, P. C., Light, K. J., Rowe, S., Miller, A. L., & Kennedy, M. A. (2009). Relationships between angry-impulsive personality traits and genetic polymorphisms of the dopamine transporter. *Biological Psychiatry, 66*, 717–721.

Joyce, P. R., Stephenson, J., Kennedy, M., Mulder, R. T., & McHugh, P. C. (2014). The presence of both serotonin 1A reception (HTR1A) and dopamine transporter (DAD1) gene variants increase the risk of borderline personality disorder. *Frontiers in Genetics, 4.* doi: 10.3389/fgene.2013.00313.

Kamphausen, S., Schroder, P., Maier, S., Bader, K., Feige, B., Kaller, C., ... Tuscher, O. (2013). Medial prefrontal dysfunction and prolonged amygdala response during instructed fear processing in borderline personality disorder. *World Journal of Biological Psychiatry, 14*(4), 307–318.

Keri, S., & Kiss, I. (2011). Oxytocin response in a trust game and habituation of arousal. *Physiology and Behavior, 102*, 221–224.

Kernberg, O. (1967). Borderline personality organization. *Journal of the American Psychoanalytic Association, 15*, 641–675.

Kernberg, O. (1975). *Borderline conditions and pathological narcissism.* New York, NY: Aronson.

King-Casas, B., Sharp, C., Lomax-Bream, L., Lohrenz, T., Fonagy, P., & Montague, P. R. (2008). The rupture and repair of cooperation in borderline personality disorder. *Science, 321*, 806–810.

Knight, R. (1953). Borderline states. *Bulletin of the Menninger Clinic, 17*, 1–12.

Kohut, H. (1971). *The analysis of the self: A systematic approach to the treatment of narcissistic personality disorders.* New York, NY: International Universities Press.

Kohut, H. (1977). *The restoration of the self.* New York, NY: International Universities Press.

Korfine, L., & Hooley, J. (2000). Directed forgetting of emotional stimuli in borderline personality disorder. *Journal of Abnormal Psychology, 109*(2), 214–221.

Kosfeld, M., Heinrichs, M., Zak, P. J., Fischbacher, U., & Fehr, E. (2005). Oxytocin increases trust in humans. *Nature, 435*(2), 673–676.

Krause-Utz, A., Winter, D., Niedtfeld, & Schmahl, C. (2014). The latest neuroimaging findings in borderline personality disorder. *Current Psychiatry Reports, 16*, 438.

LeDoux, J. (1996). *The emotional brain: The mysterious underpinnings of emotional life.* New York, NY: Touchstone.

Leichsenring, F. (1999). Development and first results of the Borderline Personality Inventory: A self-report instrument for assessing borderline personality organization. *Journal of Personality Assessment, 73*, 45–63.

Lenzenweger, M. F., & Cicchetti, D. (2005). Toward a developmental psychopathology approach to borderline personality disorder. *Development and Psychopathology, 17*, 893–898.

Lenzenweger, M. F., Clarkin, J. F., Fertuck, E. A., & Kernberg, O. F. (2004). Executive neurocognitive functioning and neurobehavioral systems indicators in borderline personality disorder: A preliminary study. *Journal of Personality Disorders, 18*(5), 421–438.

Lenzenweger, M. F., & Hooley, J. M. (Eds.). (2003). *Principles of experimental psychopathology: Essays in honor of Brendan A. Maher.* Washington, DC: American Psychological Association.

Lenzenweger, M. F., Lane, M. C., Loranger, A. W., & Kessler, R. C. (2007). DSM-IV personality disorders in the National Comorbidity Survey Replication. *Biological Psychiatry, 62*(6), 553–564.

Levy, K. N. (2005). The implications of attachment theory and research for understanding borderline personality disorder. *Development and Psychopathology, 17*, 959–986.

Leyton, M., Okazawa, H., Diksic, D., Paris, J., Rosa, P., Mzengeza, S., ... Benkelfat, C. (2001). Brain regional α-[^{11}C]methyl-L-tryptophan trapping in impulsive subjects with borderline personality disorder. *American Journal of Psychiatry, 158*, 775–782.

Lieb, K., Rexhausen, J. E., Kahl, K. G., Schweiger, U., Philipsen, A., Hellhammer, D. M., & Bohus, M. (2004). Increased diurnal salivary cortisol in women with borderline personality disorder. *Journal of Psychiatric Research, 38,* 559–565.

Linehan, M. M. (1993). *Cognitive-behavioral treatment of borderline personality disorder: The dialectics of effective treatment.* New York, NY: Guilford Press.

Linehan, M. M., Armstrong, H. E., Suarez, A., Allman, D. A., & Heard, H. L. (1991). Cognitive-behavioral treatment of chronically parasuicidal borderline patients. *Archives of General Psychiatry, 48,* 1060–1064.

Linehan, M. M., Comtois, C. A., Murray, A. M., Brown, M. Z., Gallop, R. J., Heard, H. L., … Lindenboim, N. (2006). Two-year randomized controlled trial and follow-up of dialectical behavior therapy vs therapy by experts for suicidal behaviors and borderline personality disorder. *Archives of General Psychiatry, 63,* 757–766.

Links, P. S., Ross, J., & Gunderson, J. G. (2015). Promoting good psychiatric management for patients with borderline personality disorder. *Journal of Clinical Psychology, 71*(8), 753–763.

Links, P., Steiner, M., Boiago, I., & Irwin, D. (1990). Lithium therapy for borderline patients: Preliminary findings. *Journal of Personality Disorders, 2,* 14–20.

Lischke, A., Domin, M., Freyberger, H. J., Grabe, H. J., Mentel, R., Berhnheim, D., & Lotze, M. (2015). Structural alterations in white-matter tracts connecting (para-)limbic and prefrontal brain regions in borderline personality disorder. *Psychological Medicine, 45*(15), 3171–3180.

Livesley, W. J., Jang, K. L., Jackson, D. N., & Vernon, P. A. (1993). Genetic and environmental contributions to dimensions of personality disorder. *American Journal of Psychiatry, 150,* 1826–1831.

Lloyd, C., Overall, J. E., Kimsey, L. R., & Click, M. (1983). A comparison of the MMPI-168 profiles of borderline and nonborderline outpatients. *Journal of Nervous and Mental Disease, 171,* 207–215.

Loranger, A. W. (1999). *International Personality Disorder Examination (IPDE).* Odessa, FL: Psychological Assessment Resources.

Loranger, A. W., Sartorius, N., Andreoli, A., Berger, P., Buckheim, P., & Channabasavanna, S., … Regier, D. A. (1994). The International Personality Disorders Examination: The World Health Organization/Alcohol, Drug Abuse, and Mental Health Administration international pilot study of personality disorders. *Archives of General Psychiatry, 51,* 215–224.

Lubke, G. H., Laurin, C., Amin, N., Hottenga, J. J., Willemson, G., van Grootheest, G., … Boomsma, D. I. (2014). Genome-wide analysis of borderline personality features. *Molecular Psychiatry, 19*(8), 923–929.

Lumsden, E. A. (1993). Borderline personality disorder: A consequence of experiencing affect within a truncated time frame? *Journal of Personality Disorders, 7,* 265–274.

Maier-Hein, K. H., Brunner, R., Lutz, K., Henze, R., Parzer, P., Feigl, N., … Stieltjes, B. (2014). Disorder-specific white matter alterations in adolescent borderline personality disorder. *Biological Psychiatry, 75*(1), 81–88.

Markovitz, P. J. (2004). Recent trends in the pharmacotherapy of personality disorders. *Journal of Personality Disorders, 18,* 90–101.

Maurex, L., Zaboli, G., Öhman, A., Åsberg, M., & Leopardi, R. (2010). The serotonin transporter gene polymorphism (5-HTTLPR) and affective symptoms among women diagnosed with borderline personality disorder. *European Psychiatry, 25*(1), 19–25.

McDermut, W., & Zimmerman, M. (2005). Assessment instruments and standardized evaluation. In J. M. Oldham, A. E. Skodol, & D. S. Bender (Eds.), *Textbook of personality disorders* (pp. 89–101). Washington, DC: American Psychiatric Press.

McGlashan, T. H., Grilo, C. M., Sanislow, C. A., Ravelski, E., Morey, L. C., Gunderson, J. G., … Pagano, M. (2005). Two-year prevalence and stability of individual DSM-IV criteria for schizotypal, borderline, avoidant, and obsessive-compulsive personality disorders: Toward a hybrid model of Axis II disorders. *American Journal of Psychiatry, 162,* 883–889.

McGlashan, T. H., Grilo, C. M., Skodol, A. E., Gunderson, J. G., Shea, M. T., Morey, L. C., … Stout, R. L. (2000). The Collaborative Longitudinal Personality Disorders Study: Baseline Axis I/II and II/II diagnostic co-occurrence. *Acta Psychiatrica Scandinavica, 102,* 256–264.

McMain, S. F., Guimond, T., Streiner, D. L., Cardish, R. J., & Links, P. S. (2012). Dialectical behavior therapy compared with general psychiatric management for borderline personality disorder: Clinical outcomes and functioning over a 2-year follow-up. *American Journal of Psychiatry, 169*(6), 650–661.

McMain, S. F., Links, P. S., Gnam, W. H., Guimond, T., Cardish, R. J., Korman, L., & Streiner, D. L. (2009). A randomized trial of dialectical behavior therapy versus general psychiatric management for borderline personality disorder. *American Journal of Psychiatry, 166*(12), 1365–1374.

Miano, A., Fertuck, E. A., Arntz, A., & Stanley, B. (2013). Rejection sensitivity is a mediator between borderline personality disorder features and facial trust appraisal. *Journal of Personality Disorders, 27*, 442–456.

Miller, J. D., Few, L. R., Lynam, D. R., & MacKillop, J. (2015). Pathological personality traits can capture DSM-IV personality disorder types. *Personality Disorders: Theory, Research, and Treatment, 6*(1), 32–40.

Mitchell, A. E., Dickens, G. L., & Picchioni, M. M. (2014). Facial emotion processing in borderline personality disorder: A systematic review and meta-analysis. *Neuropsychology Review, 24*(2), 166–184.

Morey, L. C. (1991). *The Personality Assessment Inventory professional manual.* Odessa, FL: Psychological Assessment Resources.

Nemoda, Z., Lyons-Ruth, K., Szekely, A., Bertha, E., Faludi, G., & Sasvari-Szekely, M. (2010). Association between dopaminergic polymorphisms and borderline personality traits among at-risk young adults and psychiatric inpatients. *Behavioral and Brain Functions, 6*, 1–11.

New, A. S., Buchsbaum, M. S., Hazlett, E. A., Goodman, M., Koenigsberg, H. W., Lo, J., ... Siever, L. J. (2004). Fluoxetine increases metabolic rate in prefrontal cortex in impulsive aggression. *Psychopharmacology, 176*, 451–458.

New, A. S., Hazlett, E. A., Buchsbaum, M. S., Goodman, M., Mitelman, S. A., Newmark, R., ... Siever, L. J. (2007). Amygdala-prefrontal disconnection in borderline personality disorder. *Neuropsychopharmacology, 32*, 1629–1640.

Newman, J. P., & Kosson, D. S. (1986). Passive avoidance learning in psychopathic and nonpsychopathic offenders. *Journal of Abnormal Psychology, 95*, 257–263.

Ni, X., Chan, K., Bulgin, N., Sicad, T., Bismil, R., McMain, S., & Kennedy, J. L. (2006). Association between serotonin transporter gene and borderline personality disorder. *Journal of Psychiatric Research, 40*, 448–453.

Nickel, M. K., Muehlbacher, M., Nickel, C., Kettler, C., Pedrosa Gil, F., Bachler, E., ... Kaplan, P. (2006). Aripiprazole in the treatment of patients with borderline personality disorder: A double-blind, placebo-controlled study. *American Journal of Psychiatry, 163*, 833–838.

Nicol, K., Pope, M., Sprengelmeyer, R., Young, A., & Hall, J. (2013). Social judgment in borderline personality disorder. *PLoS ONE, 8*(11).

Nigg, J. T. (2000). On inhibition/disinhibition in developmental psychopathology: Views from cognitive and personality psychology and a working inhibition taxonomy. *Psychological Bulletin, 126*, 220–246.

Nose, M., Cipriani, A., Biancosino, B., Grassi, L., & Barbui, C. (2006). Efficacy of pharmacotherapy against core traits of borderline personality disorder: Meta-analysis of randomized controlled trials. *International Clinical Psychopharmacology, 21*(6), 345–353.

Nunes, P. M., Wenzel, A., Borges, K. T., Porto, C. R., Caminha, R. M., & Reis, D. O. (2009). Volumes of the hippocampus and amygdala in patients with borderline personality disorder: A meta-analysis. *Journal of Personality Disorders, 23*(4), 333–345.

Ogata, S. N., Silk, K. R., Goodrich, S., Lohr, N. E., Westen, D., & Hill, E. M. (1990). Childhood sexual and physical abuse in adult patients with borderline personality disorder. *American Journal of Psychiatry, 147*, 1008–1013.

Oitzl, M. S., Workel, J. O., Fluttert, M., Frosch, F., & de Kloet, E. R. (2000). Maternal deprivation affects behavior from youth to senescence: Amplification of individual differences in spatial learning and memory in senescent Brown Norway rats. *European Journal of Neuroscience, 12*, 3771–3780.

Oldham, J. M. (2006). Borderline personality disorder and suicidality. *American Journal of Psychiatry, 163*, 20–26.

O'Neill, A., D'Souza, A., Carballedo, A., Joseph, S., Kerskens, C., & Frodl, T. (2013). Magnetic resonance imaging in patients with borderline personality disorder: A study of volumetric abnormalities. *Psychiatry Research: Neuroimaging, 213*(1), 1–10.

Oquendo, M. A., & Mann, J. J. (2000). The biology of impulsivity and suicidality. *Psychiatric Clinics of North America, 23*, 11–25.

Panos, P. T., Jackson, J. W., Hasan, O., & Panos, A. (2014). Meta-analysis and systematic review assessing the efficacy of dialectical behavior therapy (DBT). *Research on Social Work Practice, 24*(2), 213–223.

Paris, J. (1999). Borderline personality disorder. In T. Millon, P. H. Blaney, & R. G. Davis (Eds.), *Oxford textbook of psychopathology* (628–652). New York, NY: Oxford University Press.

Paris, J. (2004). Borderline or bipolar? Distinguishing borderline personality disorder from bipolar spectrum disorders. *Harvard Review of Psychiatry, 12*, 140–145.

Paris, J. (2005). Recent advances in the treatment of borderline personality disorder. *Canadian Journal of Psychiatry, 50*, 435–441.

Paris, J. (2015). Applying the principles of psychotherapy integration to the treatment of borderline personality disorder. *Journal of Psychotherapy Integration, 25*(1), 13–19.

Pascual, J. P., Soler, J., Barrachina, J., Campins, M. J., Alvarez, E., & Pérez, V. (2008). Failure to detect an association between the serotonin transporter gene and borderline personality disorder. *Journal of Psychiatry Research, 42*, 87–88.

Percudani, M., Belloni, G., Conti, A., & Barbui, C. (2002). Monitoring community psychiatric services in Italy: Differences between patients who leave care and those who stay in treatment. *British Journal of Psychiatry, 180*, 254–259.

Perez, D. L., Vago, D. R., Pan, H., Root, J., Tuescher, O., Fuchs, B. H., … Stern, E. (2015). Frontolimbic neural circuit changes in emotional processing and inhibitory control associated with clinical improvement following transference-focused psychotherapy in borderline personality disorder. *Psychiatry and Clinical Neurosciences, 70*(1), 51–61.

Pfohl, B., Blum, N., & Zimmerman, M. (1997). *Structured Interview for DSM-IV Personality*. Washington, DC: American Psychiatric Press.

Pilknois, P. A. (1997). Measurement issues relevant to personality disorders. In H. H. Strupp, M. J. Lambert, & L. M. Horowitz (Eds.), *Measuring patient change in mood, anxiety, and personality disorders: Toward a core battery* (pp. 371–388). Washington, DC: American Psychological Association.

Pizzagalli, D. A., Sherwood, R. J., Henriques, J. B., & Davidson, R. J. (2005). Frontal brain asymmetry and reward responsiveness: A source-localization study. *Psychological Science, 16*, 805–813.

Posner, M. I., Rothbart, M. K., Vizueta, N., Levy, K., Evans, D. E., Thomas, K. M., … Kernberg, O. (2002). Mechanisms of borderline personality disorder. *Proceedings of the National Academy of Sciences of the United States of America, 99*, 16366–16370.

Putnam, K. M., & Silk, K. R. (2005). Emotion dysregulation and the development of borderline personality disorder. *Developmental Psychopathology, 17*, 899–925.

Regier, D. A., Kaelber, C. T., Rae, D. S., Farmer, M. E., Knauper, B., Kessler, R. C., & Norquist, G. S. (1998). Limitations of diagnostic criteria and assessment instruments for mental disorders: Implications for research and policy. *Archives of General Psychiatry, 55*, 109–115.

Renneberg, B., Theobald, E., Nobs, M., & Weisbrod, M. (2005). Autobiographical memory in borderline personality disorder and depression. *Cognitive Therapy and Research, 29*, 343–358.

Rinne, T., de Kloet, R., Wouters, L., Goekoop, J. G., DeRijk, R. H., & van den Brink, W. (2002). Hyperresponsiveness of hypothalamic-pituitary-adrenal axis to combined dexamethasone/corticotrophin-releasing hormone challenge in female borderline personality disorder subjects with a history of sustained childhood abuse. *Biological Psychiatry, 52*, 1102–1112.

Rinne, T., van den Brink, W., Wouters, L., & van Dyck, R. (2002). SSRI treatment of borderline personality disorder: A randomized, placebo-controlled clinical trial for female patients with borderline personality disorder. *American Journal of Psychiatry, 159*, 2048–2054.

Rinne, T., Westenberg, H. G. M., den Boer, J. A., & van den Brink, W. (2000). Serotonergic blunting to meta-chlorophenylpiperazine (m-CPP) highly correlates with sustained childhood abuse in impulsive and autoaggressive female borderline patients. *Biological Psychiatry, 47*, 548–556.

Rodrigues, E., Wenzel, A., Ribeiro, M. P., Quarantini, L. C., Miranda-Scippa, A., de Sena, E. P., & de Oliveira, I. R. (2011). Hippocampal volume in borderline personality disorder with and without comorbid posttraumatic stress disorder: A meta-analysis. *European Psychiatry, 26*, 452–456.

Rossi, R., Pievani, M., Lorenzi, M., Boccardi, M., Beneduce, R., Bignotti, S., … Frisoni, G. B. (2013). Structural brain features of borderline personality and bipolar disorders. *Psychiatry Research: Neuroimaging, 213*(2), 83–91

Rossouw, T. I., & Fonagy, P. (2012). Mentalization-based treatment for self-harm in adolescents: A randomized controlled trial. *Journal of the American Academy of Child & Adolescent Psychiatry, 51*(12), 1304–1313.

Rothschild, L., Cleland, C., Haslam, N., & Zimmerman, M. (2003). A taxometric study of borderline personality disorder. *Journal of Abnormal Psychology, 112*, 657–666.

Ruocco, A. C. (2005). The neuropsychology of borderline personality disorder: A meta-analysis and review. *Psychiatry Research, 137*, 191–202.

Ruocco, A. C., Amirthavasagam, S., Choi-Kain, L. W., & McMain, S. F. (2013). Neural correlates of negative emotionality in borderline personality disorder: An activation-likelihood-estimation meta-analysis. *Biological Psychiatry, 73*(2), 153–160.

Ruocco, A. C., Amirthavasagam, S., & Zakzanis, K. K. (2012). Amygdala and hippocampal volume reductions as candidate endophenotypes for borderline personality disorder: A meta-analysis of magnetic resonance imaging studies. *Psychiatry Research: Neuroimaging, 201*(3), 245–252.

Ruocco, A. C., Lam, J., & McMain, S. F. (2014). Subjective cognitive complaints and functional disability in patients with borderline personality disorder and their nonaffected first-degree relatives. *Canadian Journal of Psychiatry, 59*(6), 335–344.

Ryle, A. (2005). Cognitive analytic therapy. In J. C. Norcross & M. R. Goldfried (Eds.), *Handbook of psychotherapy integration* (2nd ed., pp. 196–217). New York, NY: Oxford University Press.

Salvador, R., Vega, D., Pascual, J. C., Marco, J., Canales-Rodriquez, E. J., Aguilar, S., ... Pomarol-Clotet, E. (2014). Converging medial frontal resting state and diffusion-based abnormalities in borderline personality disorder. *Biological Psychiatry, 79*(2), 107–116.

Salzman, J., Salzman, C., Wolfson, A., Albanese, A., Looper, J., Ostacher, M., ... Miyawaki, E. (1993). Association between borderline personality structure and history of childhood abuse in adult volunteers. *Comprehensive Psychiatry, 34,* 254–257.

Sauer-Zavala, S., & Barlow, D. H. (2014). The case for borderline personality disorder as an emotional disorder: Implications for treatment. *Clinical Psychology: Science and Practice, 21*(2), 118–138.

Schaefer, H. S., Putnam, K. M., Benca, R. M., & Davidson, R. J. (2006). Event-related functional magnetic resonance imaging measures of neural activity to positive social stimuli in pre- and post-treatment for depression. *Biological Psychiatry, 60,* 974–986.

Schmahl, C., Berne, K., Krause, A., Kleindienst, N., Valerius, G., Vermetten, E., & Bohus, M. (2009). Hippocampus and amygdala volumes in patients with borderline personality disorder with or without post-traumatic stress disorder. *Journal of Psychiatry & Neuroscience, 34*(4), 289–295.

Schmahl, C., & Bremner, J. D. (2006). Neuroimaging in borderline personality disorder. *Journal of Psychiatric Research, 40,* 419–427.

Schmahl, C. G., Elzinga, B. M., Vermetten, E., Sanislow, C., McGlashan, T. H., & Bremner, J. D. (2003). Neural correlates of memories of abandonment in women with and without borderline personality disorder. *Biological Psychiatry, 54,* 142–151.

Schmahl, C. G., Vermetten, E., Elzinga, B. M., & Bremner, J. D. (2003). Magnetic resonance imaging of hippocampal and amygdala volume in women with childhood abuse and borderline personality disorder. *Psychiatry Research, 122,* 193–198.

Seres, I., Unoka, Z., Bodi, N., Aspan, N., & Keri, S. (2009). The neuropsychology of borderline personality disorder: Relationship with clinical dimensions and comparison with other personality disorders. *Journal of Personality Disorders, 23*(6), 555–562.

Sharp, C., Michonski, J., Steinberg, L., Fowler, J. C., Frueh, B. C., & Oldham, J. M. (2014). An investigation of differential item functioning across gender of BPD criteria. *Journal of Abnormal Psychology, 123*(1), 231–236.

Shea, M. T. (1997). Core battery conference: Assessment of change in personality disorders. In H. H. Strupp, L. M. Horowitz, & M. J. Lambert (Eds.), *Measuring patient changes in mood, anxiety, and personality disorders: Toward a core battery* (pp. 389–400). Washington, DC: American Psychological Association.

Siever, L. J., & Davis, K. L. (1991). A psychobiological perspective on the personality disorders. *American Journal of Psychiatry, 148,* 1647–1658.

Simeon, D., Bartz, J., Hamilton, H., Crystal, S., Braun, A., Ketay, S., & Hollander, E. (2011). Oxytocin administration attenuates stress reactivity in borderline personality disorder: A pilot study. *Psychoneuroendocrinology, 36*(9), 1418–1421.

Simeon, D., Knutelska, M., Smith, L., Baker, B. R., & Hollander, E. (2007). A preliminary study of cortisol and norepinephrine reactivity to psychosocial stress in borderline personality disorder with high and low dissociation. *Psychiatry Research, 149,* 177–184.

Skodol, A. E., & Bender, D. S. (2003). Why are women diagnosed borderline more than men? *Psychiatric Quarterly, 74,* 349–360.

Skodol, A. E., Gunderson, J. G., Pfohl, B., Widiger, T. A., Livesley, W. J., & Siever, L. J. (2002). The borderline diagnosis I: Psychopathology, co-morbidity, and personality structure. *Biological Psychiatry, 51*(12), 936.

Soloff, P. H., Lis, J. A., Kelly, T., Cornelius, J., & Ulrich, R. (1994). Risk factors for suicidal behavior in borderline personality disorder. *American Journal of Psychiatry, 151,* 1316–1323.

Soloff, P. H., White, R., Omari, A., Ramaseshan, K., & Diwadkar, V. A. (2015). Affective context interferes with brain responses during cognitive processing in borderline personality disorder: fMRI evidence. *Psychiatry Research: Neuroimaging, 233*(1), 23–35.

Spitzer, R. L., Endicott, J., & Gibbon, M. (1979). Crossing the border into borderline personality and borderline schizophrenia: The development of criteria. *Archives of General Psychiatry, 36*, 17–34.

Spitzer, R. L., Forman, J. B. W., & Nee, J. (1979). DSM-III field trials: I. Initial inter-rater diagnostic reliability. *American Journal of Psychiatry, 136*, 815–817.

Stanley, B., & Brodsky, B. S. (2005). Suicidal and self-injurious behavior in borderline personality disorder: A self-regulation model. In J. G. Gunderson & P. D. Hoffman (Eds.), *Understanding and treating borderline personality disorder: A guide for professionals and families* (pp. 43–63). Washington, DC: American Psychiatric Publishing.

Stern, A. (1938). Psychoanalytic investigation of and therapy in the borderline group of neuroses. *Psychoanalytical Quarterly, 7*, 467–489.

Stiglmayr, C. E., Ebner-Priemer, U. W., Bretz, J., Behm, R., Mohse, M., Lammers, C. H., ... Bohus, M. (2008). Dissociative symptoms are positively related to stress in borderline personality disorder. *Acta Psychiatrica Scandinavica, 117*, 139–147.

Stroop, J. R. (1935). Studies of interference in serial verbal reactions. *Journal of Experimental Psychology, 18*, 643–662.

Suomi, S. J. (2003). Social and biological mechanisms underlying impulsive aggressiveness in rhesus monkeys. In B. B. Lahey, T. Moffitt, & A. Caspi (Eds.), *The causes of conduct disorder and severe juvenile delinquency* (pp. 345–362). New York, NY: Guilford Press.

Szeszko, P. R., Robinson, D., Alvir, J. M., Bilder, R. M., Lencz, T., Ashtari, M., ... Bogerts, B. (1999). Orbitofrontal and amygdala volume reductions in obsessive-compulsive disorder. *Archives of General Psychiatry, 56*, 913–919.

Tebartz van Elst, L., Hesslinger, B., Thiel, T., Geiger, E., Haegele, K., Lemieux, L., ... Ebert, D. (2003). Frontolimbic brain abnormalities in patients with borderline personality disorder: A volumetric magnetic resonance imaging study. *Biological Psychiatry, 54*, 163–171.

Thase, M. E., Jindal, R., & Howland, R. H. (2002). Biological aspects of depression. In I. H. Gotlib &

C. L. Hammen (Eds.), *Handbook of depression* (pp. 192–218). New York, NY: Guilford Press.

Tipper, S. P. (1985). The negative priming effect: Inhibitory priming by ignored objects. *Quarterly Journal of Experimental Psychology: Section A, Human Experimental Psychology, 37*, 571–590.

Todorov, A., Mandisodza, A., Goren, A., & Hall, C. (2005). Inferences of competence from faces predict election outcomes. *Science, 308*, 1623–1626.

Tomko, R. L., Trull, T. T., Wood, P. K., & Sher, K. J. (2014). Characteristics of borderline personality disorder in a community sample: Comorbidity, treatment utilization, and general functioning. *Journal of Personality Disorders, 28*(5), 734–750.

Torgersen, S., Kringlen, E., & Cramer, V. (2001). The prevalence of personality disorders in a community sample. *Archives of General Psychiatry, 58*, 590–596.

Torgersen, S., Lygren, S., Oien, P. A., Skre, I., Onstad, S., Edvardsen, J., ... Kringlen, E. (2000). A twin study of personality disorders. *Comprehensive Psychiatry, 41*, 416–425.

Trull, T. J. (2001). Structural relations between borderline personality disorder features and putative etiological correlates. *Journal of Abnormal Psychology, 110*, 471–481.

Tyrer, P. (1999). Borderline personality disorder: A motley diagnosis in need of reform. *Lancet, 354*(9196), 2095–2096.

Unoka, Z., & Richman, M. J. (2016). Neuropsychological deficits in BPD patients and the moderator effects of co-occurring mental disorders: A meta-analysis. *Clinical Psychology Review, 44*, 1–12.

Unoka, Z., Seres, I., Aspan, N., Bodi, N., & Keri, S. (2009). Trust game reveals restricted interpersonal transactions in patients with borderline personality disorder. *Journal of Personality Disorders, 23*(4), 399–409.

van Wel, B., Kockmann, I., Blum, N., Pfohl, B., Black, D. W., & Heesterman, W. (2006). STEPPS group treatment for borderline personality disorder in the Netherlands. *Annals of Clinical Psychiatry, 18*(1), 63–67.

Veague, H. B., & Hooley, J. M. (2014). Enhanced sensitivity and response bias for male anger in women with borderline personality disorder. *Psychiatry Research, 215*(3), 687–693.

Wagner, S., Baskaya, Ö., Lieb, K., Dahmen, N., & Tadić, A. (2009). The 5-HTTLPR polymorphism modulates the association of serious life events (SLE) and impulsivity in patients with borderline personality disorder. *Journal of Psychiatric Research, 43,* 1067–1072.

Weaver, T. L., & Clum, G. A. (1993). Early family environments and traumatic experiences associated with borderline personality disorder. *Journal of Consulting and Clinical Psychology, 61,* 1068–1075.

Westen, D., Bradley, R., & Shedler, J. (2005). *Refining the borderline construct: Diagnostic criteria and endophenotypes.* Unpublished manuscript.

White, C. N., Gunderson, J. G., Zanarini, M. C., & Hudson, J. I. (2003). Family studies of borderline personality disorder: A review. *Harvard Review of Psychiatry, 11,* 8–19.

Whittle, S., Chanen, A. M., Fornito, A., McGorry, P. D., Pantelis, C., & Yücel, M. (2009). Anterior cingulate volume in adolescents with first-presentation borderline personality disorder. *Psychiatry Research: Neuroimaging, 172,* 155–160.

Widiger, T. A., & Frances, A. (1989). Epidemiology, diagnosis, and co-morbidity of borderline personality disorder. In A. Tasman, R. E. Hales, & A. Frances (Eds.), *American Psychiatric Press review of psychiatry* (Vol. 8, pp. 8–24). Washington, DC: American Psychiatric Press.

Widiger, T. A., Mangine, S., Corbitt, E., Ellis, C., & Thomas, G. (1995). *Personality Disorder Interview-IV: A semi-structured interview for the assessment of personality disorders, professional manual.* Odessa, FL: Psychological Assessment Resources.

Widom, C. S., Czaja, S. J., & Paris, J. (2009). A prospective investigation of borderline personality disorder in abused and neglected children followed up into adulthood. *Journal of Personality Disorders, 23,* 433–446.

Williams, J. M. G., & Broadbent, K. (1986). Autobiographical memory in suicide attempters. *Journal of Abnormal Psychology, 95,* 144–149.

Winnicott, D. W. (1953). Transitional objects and transitional phenomena: A study of the first not-me possession. *International Journal of Psychoanalysis, 34,* 89–97.

Witt, S. H., Kleindienst, N., Frank, J., Treutlein, J., Muhleisen, T., Degenhardt, F., … Bohus, M. (2014). Analysis of genome-wide significant bipolar disorder genes in borderline personality disorder. *Psychiatric Genetics, 24,* 262–265.

Wright, A. G. C., Hallquist, M. N., Beeney, J. E., & Pilkonis, P. A. (2013). Borderline personality pathology and the stability of interpersonal problems. *Journal of Abnormal Psychology, 122*(4), 1094–1100.

Wright, A. G. C., Hopwood, C. J., & Zanarini, M. C. (2015). Associations between changes in normal personality traits and borderline personality disorder symptoms over 16 years. *Personality Disorders: Theory, Research, and Treatment, 6*(1), 1–11.

Yeomans, F. E., & Levy, K. N. (2002). An object relations perspective on borderline personality. *Acta Neuropsychiatrica, 14,* 76–80.

Zanarini, M. C., Barison, L. K., Frankenburg, F. R., Reich, D. B., & Hudson, J. I. (2009). Family history study of the familial coaggregation of borderline personality disorder with Axis I and nonborderline dramatic cluster Axis II disorders. *Journal of Personality Disorders, 23,* 357–369.

Zanarini, M. C., & Frankenburg, F. R. (1997). Pathways to the development of borderline personality disorder. *Journal of Personality Disorders, 11,* 93–104.

Zanarini, M. C., & Frankenburg, F. R. (2001). Olanzapine treatment of female borderline personality disorder patients: A double-blind, placebo-controlled pilot study. *Journal of Clinical Psychiatry, 62,* 849–854.

Zanarini, M. C., Frankenburg, F. R., Chauncey, D. L., & Gunderson, J. G. (1987). The Diagnostic Interview for Personality Disorders: Inter-rater and test-retest reliability. *Comprehensive Psychiatry, 28,* 467–480.

Zanarini, M. C., Frankenburg, F. R., Dubo, E. D., Sickel, A. E., Trikha, A., Levin, A., & Reynolds, V. (1998). Axis I co-morbidity of borderline personality disorder. *American Journal of Psychiatry, 155,* 1733–1739.

Zanarini, M. C., Frankenburg, F. R., Hennen, J., Reich, D. B., & Silk, K. S. (2006). Prediction of the 10-year course of borderline personality disorder. *American Journal of Psychiatry, 163,* 827.

Zanarini, M. C., Frankenburg, F. R., Hennen, J., & Silk, K. R. (2003). The longitudinal course of borderline psychopathology: 6-year prospective follow-up of the phenomenology of borderline personality disorders. *American Journal of Psychiatry, 160,* 274–283.

Zanarini, M. C., Frankenburg, F. R., Khera, G. S., & Bleichmar, J., (2001). Treatment histories of borderline inpatients. *Comprehensive Psychiatry, 42,* 144–150.

Zanarini, M. C., Frankenburg, F. R., Reich, D. B., Conkey, L. C., & Fitzmaurice, G. M. (2015). Treatment rates for patients with borderline personality disorder and other personality disorders: A 16-year study. *Psychiatric Services, 66*(1), 15–20.

Zanarini, M. C., Frankenburg, F. R., Reich, D. B., & Fitzmaurice, G. (2010). Time to attainment of recovery from borderline personality disorder and stability of recovery: A 10-year prospective follow-up study. *American Journal of Psychiatry, 167*, 663–667.

Zanarini, M. C., Frankenburg, F. R., Reich, D. B., & Fitzmaurice, G. (2012). Attainment and stability of sustained symptomatic remission and recovery among patients with borderline personality disorder and Axis II comparison subjects: A 16-year prospective follow-up study. *American Journal of Psychiatry, 169*(5), 476–483.

Zanarini, M. C., Frankenburg, F. R., Reich, D. B., Marino, M. F., Lewis, R. E., Williams, A. A., & Khera, G. S. (2000). Biparental failure in the childhood experiences of borderline patients. *Journal of Personality Disorders, 14*, 264–273.

Zanarini, M. C., Frankenburg, F. R., & Vujanovic, A. A. (2002). Inter-rater and test-retest reliability of the Revised Diagnostic Interview for Borderlines. *Journal of Personality Disorders, 16*, 270–276.

Zanarini, M. C., Frankenburg, F. R., Yong, L., Raviola, G., Bradford Reich, D., Hennen, J., ... Gunderson, J. G. (2004). Borderline psychopathology in the first-degree relatives of borderline and Axis II comparison probands. *Journal of Personality Disorders, 18*, 439–447.

Zanarini, M. C., Gunderson, J. G., & Frankenburg, F. R. (1990). Cognitive features of borderline personality disorder. *American Journal of Psychiatry, 147*(1), 57–63.

Zanarini, M. C., Gunderson, J. G., Frankenburg, F. R., & Chauncey, D. L. (1989). The Revised Diagnostic Interview for Borderlines: Discriminating BPD from other Axis II disorders. *Journal of Personality Disorders, 3*, 10–18.

Zimmerman, D. J., & Choi-Kain, L. W. (2009). The hypothalamic-pituitary-adrenal axis in borderline personality disorder: A review. *Harvard Review of Psychiatry, 17*, 167–183.

Zimmerman, M. (1994). Diagnosing personality disorders: A review of issues and research methods. *Archives of General Psychiatry, 51*, 225–245.

Zimmerman, M., & Mattia, J. I. (1999). Axis I diagnostic co-morbidity and borderline personality disorder. *Comprehensive Psychiatry, 40*, 245–251.

Zweig-Frank, H., & Paris, J. (1995). The five-factor model of personality in borderline and nonborderline personality disorders. *Canadian Journal of Psychiatry, 40*, 523–526.

Chapter 15

Psychopathy as Psychopathology

Key Developments in Assessment, Etiology, and Treatment

JENNIFER E. VITALE AND JOSEPH P. NEWMAN

The psychopathic individual is characterized by limited affective experiences, is known to act impulsively and often antisocially, but nevertheless seems calm and at ease in the presence of others. Although psychopathic individuals are clinically intriguing figures in their own right, their overrepresentation in criminal samples and their tendency toward impulsive and deviant behaviors provide strong and pragmatic motivation to understand the factors that underlie the psychopathy syndrome. In this chapter, we describe the traits associated with the syndrome, discuss developments in the measurement of the syndrome, and then consider the most prominent findings relevant to etiological models of psychopathy. Finally, we provide an overview of research on the treatment of psychopathy.

Diagnostic Criteria

Psychopathy has been referred to as "the elusive category" (Lewis, 1974), a clinical syndrome that is still often mentioned synonymously with general criminal behavior, sociopathy, and antisocial personality disorder. The personality style we now know as *psychopathy* appears throughout psychiatric history, under different labels, often as a subtype of other disorders. For example, today's psychopathic person would have been classified as one of Kraepelin's "morbid personalities," who were impulsive and antisocial as well as predisposed to deception; as one of Schneider's "affectionless" personalities, who lacked compassion and acted in a callous manner toward other individuals; or as one of Millon's (1981) "aggressive" personalities, who have a "faith only in themselves and ... [are] secure only when they are independent of those whom they fear may undo, harm, or humiliate them" (p. 181).

Historically, individuals in the field often trace the evolution of the concept of psychopathy to Pinel's *manie sans delire*, a syndrome characterized by an individual's repeated engagement in impulsive, destructive actions, in spite of intact reasoning (Pinel, 1806). This early, relatively objective conceptualization would later give way to conceptualizations of the syndrome that placed greater emphasis on moral considerations—hence Rush's (1812) "innate, preternatural moral depravity" (p. 112) and Prichard's (1835) "moral insanity." Although the labels have varied, what has been constant is nosologists' desire to classify this syndrome in such a way that it could be distinguished from other forms of mental illness and from general criminality.

It was such a desire that motivated Cleckley's (1941/1988) work *The Mask of Sanity*, which is now viewed as the seminal clinical description of the psychopathy syndrome. *The Mask of Sanity* provided detailed case histories and a set of specific criteria meant to distinguish the syndrome from the number of other disorders that had come to be included under the "psychopathy" label. Thus, through this work, Cleckley (1988) provided a means for distinguishing the "psychopath" from the "psychotic," the "psychoneurotic," the "mental defective," the "criminal," and the "alcoholic." *The Mask of Sanity* provided case descriptions of 15 psychopathic individuals and outlined 16 core traits of psychopathy formulated on the basis of these cases (see Table 15.1). Although later conceptualizations of the syndrome have, to different extents, attempted to encapsulate each of the criteria, the following six have most strongly influenced modern conceptualizations of the syndrome.

First, Cleckley (1988) described the "psychopath" as exhibiting "superficial charm and good intelligence" (p. 337). In his words, "The typical psychopath will seem particularly agreeable and make a distinctly positive impression when he is first encountered. . . . There

TABLE 15.1   Cleckley's Criteria for Psychopathy

Superficial charm and good "intelligence."

Absence of delusions and other signs of irrational thinking.

Absence of "nervousness" or psychoneurotic manifestations.

Unreliability.

Untruthfulness and insincerity.

Lack of remorse or shame.

Inadequately motivated antisocial behavior.

Poor judgment and failure to learn by experience.

Pathological egocentricity and incapacity for love.

General poverty in major affective reactions.

Specific loss of insight.

Unresponsiveness in general interpersonal relations.

Fantastic and uninviting behavior with drink and sometimes without.

Suicide rarely carried out.

Sex life impersonal, trivial, and poorly integrated.

Failure to follow any life plan.

Source: Cleckley, 1941/1988.

is nothing at all odd or queer about him and in every respect he tends to embody the concept of a well adjusted, happy person. . . . Sign of affectation or excessive affability are not characteristic. He looks like the real thing" (p. 338).

Second, the psychopathic individual is "lacking in remorse or shame" (p. 337). The psychopathic person does not express genuine contrition for the antisocial acts he or she commits, and often cannot even see the purpose in feeling such remorse. When remorse is expressed, it is often hollow, and rings false. As Cleckley wrote: "Usually he denies emphatically all responsibility and directly accuses others as responsible, but often he will go through an idle ritual of saying that much of his trouble is his own fault. . . . More detailed questioning about just what he blames himself for and why may show that a serious attitude is not only absent but altogether inconceivable to him" (p. 343).

Third, the psychopathic person engages in "inadequately motivated antisocial behavior" (p. 337). Among the behaviors Cleckley included in this category were minor infractions such as lies, cheating, and brawling, and also more serious offenses, such as theft, fraud, and forgery. According to Cleckley, however, the crucial factor was not necessarily the type or severity of the behavior itself, but the tendency to "commit such deeds in the absence of any apparent goal at all" (p. 343).

Fourth, the psychopathic person shows "poor judgment and failure to learn by experience" (p. 337). Despite the fact that these individuals are characterized by average intelligence, they nevertheless repeatedly make poor choices and evince poor judgment in their attempts at goal attainment. Further, although the individual may be able to explain "what went wrong" in a particular situation (i.e., what he did that may have led to the poor outcome), he seems incapable of using this knowledge in future situations, thereby exhibiting an inability to use prior experience to guide future behavior.

Fifth, the psychopathic person is characterized by "incapacity for love" (p. 337). Although he or she may be "capable of fondness, of likes, of dislikes ... [t]hese affective reactions are, however, always strictly limited in degree" (p. 348). This apparent inability to experience deep emotion or to connect emotionally with others is an important criterion for distinguishing the psychopathic individual from other antisocial individuals (e.g., Cooke, Michie, & Hart, 2006; Lykken, 1995).

The sixth characteristic is related to the fifth, and is the tendency for the psychopathic person to exhibit "general poverty in major affective reactions." Although the person may express himself in ways that suggest that he is experiencing affective reactions (e.g., a short temper, a declaration of affection), these expressions do not convey a sense of long-lasting, deep emotional experience. There is no "mature, wholehearted anger, true or consistent indignation, honest, solid grief, sustaining pride, deep joy, and genuine despair" (p. 348).

Like Cleckley, McCord and McCord (1964) provided rich descriptions of the psychopathic individual. Harkening back to figures such as Billy the Kid as early examples of a prototypical "psychopath," McCord and McCord placed great emphasis on defining characteristics such as aggression, impulsivity, excitement-seeking, guiltlessness, and "warped capacity for love." This last, also a core component of this syndrome described by Cleckley, receives particular emphasis. "Psychopaths," as Maslow (1951) writes, "have no love identifications with other human beings and can therefore hurt them or even kill them casually, without hate, and without pleasure" (p. 173).

Early versions of the *Diagnostic and Statistical Manual of Mental Disorders* (*DSM*) (e.g., American Psychiatric Association [APA], 1968) listed criteria for sociopathy and antisocial personality disorder that included characteristics such as selfishness, guiltlessness, callousness, and impulsivity, which overlapped in many ways with the Cleckley criteria. Despite this overlap, the *DSM* criteria were not meant to reflect the psychopathy syndrome described by Cleckley, and they were developed separately from the psychopathy literature. Thus, although psychopathy has often been used synonymously with sociopathy and antisocial personality disorder, this is a mistake. Most importantly, recent editions of the *DSM*, including the *DSM-5* (APA, 2013), have limited the criteria for antisocial personality disorder (ASPD) to more specific behavioral criteria (e.g., conduct disorder present before age 15, repeatedly performing acts that are grounds for arrest), thereby excluding many of the individuals who would be considered psychopathic using Cleckley's criteria. Second, emerging research suggests that the correlates of psychopathy and the correlates of ASPD are different in important ways (e.g., Verona, Sprague, & Sadeh, 2012).

ASSESSMENT OF PSYCHOPATHY

Like many psychological disorders, the assessment of psychopathy has had a complicated history, up to and including the present time. Although there has long been a consensus regarding certain core features of the syndrome, there has been less agreement regarding the best methods for assessing these features. Since the publication of Cleckley's book, the field has seen a number of measures developed to assess psychopathy. In the earliest years, clinicians relied on either case-based "psychopathy prototype" assessments (e.g., Hare, Frazelle, & Cox, 1978) or the use of self-report measures selected to capture the personality traits associated with the syndrome, such as the Socialization (So) subscale of the California Personality Inventory and the Psychopathic Deviate (Pd) scale of the Minnesota Multiphasic Personality Inventory (MMPI). However, these methods had definite limitations. In addition to poor diagnostic reliability, there was also a lack of uniformity in the field, as psychopathy findings based on one method were not necessarily generalizable to people assessed as psychopathic using another method.

Beginning in the 1980s and continuing into the present, the field has experienced two major developments in the assessment arena. The first is the development of Hare's psychopathy checklist and its many progeny (i.e., the Psychopathy Checklist–Revised, the Psychopathy Checklist: Screening Version, and the Psychopathy Checklist: Youth Version). The second is the increasing emphasis on the development of self-report measures that focus on psychopathy specifically (as opposed to more general personality traits) and that can be used with noninstitutionalized populations. Interestingly, in recent years many research investigators have returned to a conceptualization of psychopathy based on basic personality traits, and have begun to explore assessment tools reflecting this perspective (e.g., Widiger & Lynam, 1998).

THE PSYCHOPATHY CHECKLIST

In 1980, Hare developed the Research Scale for the Assessment of Psychopathy (also known as the Hare Psychopathy Checklist; Hare, 1980). Designed to capture the prototypical psychopathic person as conceptualized by Cleckley, the measure transformed

TABLE 15.2　Items on the Psychopathy Checklist–Revised

Glibness/superficial charm.

Grandiose sense of self-worth.

Need for stimulation.

Proneness to boredom.

Pathological lying.

Conning/manipulative.

Lack of remorse or guilt.

Shallow affect.

Callous/lack of empathy.

Parasitic lifestyle.

Poor behavioral controls.

Promiscuous sexual behavior.

Early behavior problems.

Lack of realistic, long-term goals.

Impulsivity.

Irresponsibility.

Failure to accept responsibility.

Many short-term marital relationships.

Juvenile delinquency.

Revocation of conditional release.

Criminal versatility.

Source: Hare, 1991, 2003.

Cleckley's 16 criteria into 22 items that could be scored using a semistructured interview and institutional file review. A revised version of the checklist, that deleted two items from the original scale, was published in 1991 (see Table 15.2). This Psychopathy Checklist–Revised (PCL-R) (Hare, 2003) quickly moved to the forefront of psychopathy assessment. Each item on the 20-item checklist can be scored, using an interview and file review, as 0, "not applicable to the individual"; 1, "applicable only to a certain extent"; or 2, "applicable to the individual." Scores range from 0 to 40, and although there is some taxometric evidence suggesting the scale indexes a continuous construct (e.g., Walters, Duncan, & Mitchell-Perez, 2007; Walters, Ermer, Knight, & Kiehl, 2015), a diagnostic cutoff of 30 is often used to define someone as a psychopathic individual in North American, male samples.

The development of the PCL-R provided a reliable method for assessing the psychopathy syndrome, and by providing a common metric for researchers and clinicians, it also facilitated much of the psychopathy research conducted from about 1990 to 2005. During this time period, researchers and clinicians were more likely to be called on to justify *not* using the PCL-R as their primary measure of psychopathy than vice versa. In the past decade, however, the assessment landscape has changed.

Although still at the forefront of psychopathy assessment, the PCL-R has been the subject of criticism. In response to certain of these limitations, the field has seen a new expansion in the development of alternative measures of the syndrome. Three interrelated controversies associated with use of the PCL-R can be identified as having been particularly influential in the development of alternative assessments. The first relates to the factor structure of the instrument and the related question of whether violence is a "core" feature of the psychopathy syndrome (e.g., Bishopp & Hare, 2008; Cooke et al., 2006). The second relates to the generalizability of the instrument to alternative samples, including incarcerated women and delinquent juveniles (e.g., Cooke & Michie, 1999; Kosson, Smith, & Newman, 1990; Verona & Vitale, 2005). The third is the concern that a focus on psychopathy as assessed by the PCL-R has kept researchers from developing measures of psychopathy for noninstitutionalized populations (e.g., Skeem, Polaschek, Patrick, & Lilienfeld, 2011), along with the related issue of the importance of studying the "successful" psychopathic individual.

PCL-R, Violence, and the Question of "Factors"

One of the PCL-R's clinical strengths is its power in predicting future dangerousness. High PCL-R scorers commit more violent criminal offenses than individuals with low scores and are more likely to recidivate in a violent manner than low scorers (see Hemphill, Templeman, Wong, & Hare, 1998; Olver & Wong, 2015, for reviews). In fact, on the basis of its associations with criminal recidivism and behavior, Hare (1998) has argued that PCL-R assessed psychopathy is "the single most important clinical construct in the criminal justice system," citing its usefulness in both risk assessments and treatment placements (see also Fulero, 1995).

Importantly, the crucial role that the PCL-R plays in the criminal justice system also highlights the ways in which PCL-R psychopathy departs from the construct first described by Cleckley. For example, although Cleckley (1988) included "inadequately motivated antisocial behavior" among his 16 criteria, criminal behavior (and specifically violent criminal behavior) was not viewed as a necessary component of the syndrome. Rather, Cleckley (1988) argued that "many persons showing the characteristics of those described here do commit major crimes and sometimes crimes of maximal violence. There are so many, however, who do not, that such tendencies should be regarded as the exception rather than as the rule" (p. 262).

The debate surrounding the association between psychopathy and violence is not new. In 1974, Lewis wrote: "reviews of the state of opinion about psychopathic personality ... reveal a preoccupation with the nosological status of the concept ... its forensic implications, its subdivisions, limits, [and] the propriety of identifying psychopathic personality with antisocial behavior" (pp. 137–138). Similarly, in 1981, Millon wrote: "50 years ago the same issues were in the forefront, notably whether the psychopathic personality was or was not synonymous with overt antisocial behavior" (p. 184).

This question continues to be among the most divisive arguments in the field today, as researchers and clinicians argue over the PCL-R's emphasis on antisocial behaviors and its inclusion of items assessing specific forms of criminal behavior (e.g., juvenile delinquency, criminal versatility, and revocation of conditional release). Critics of the measure have argued that such items are not necessary for diagnosing the syndrome originally conceptualized by Cleckley (Cooke et al., 2006), and they believe that the reliance on specific criminal behaviors overemphasizes this aspect of the syndrome at the expense of the personality traits theorized to lie at its core (Lilienfeld, 1994; Skeem et al., 2011).

This debate played out, in part, through a series of articles surrounding the analysis and interpretation of the PCL-R's factor structure. Initial exploratory factor analysis of the PCL-R revealed two correlated (.50) factors (Harpur, Hakstian, & Hare, 1988). The first, Factor 1, was dubbed the affective/interpersonal factor, as it included those items representing many of the deficient emotional and interpersonally manipulative characteristics of the syndrome (e.g., glib/superficial charm, manipulative, callous, shallow affect). The second, Factor 2, became known as the social deviance or impulsive/antisocial lifestyle factor on the basis of its inclusion of items measuring antisocial and criminal behavior (e.g., poor behavioral controls, impulsivity, and early behavioral problems).

In recent years, the two-factor conceptualization of the PCL-R has been repeatedly called into question. For example, Cooke and colleagues (2006) argued that analyses suggest that the two-factor solution represents a poor fit to the data, and they campaigned for a reconceptualization of the measure as comprising three factors: Factor 1 (interpersonal), Factor 2 (affective), and Factor 3 (lifestyle). The first two factors essentially divide the original Factor 1 into two components, interpersonal and affective. Importantly, this three-factor solution, although a significantly better fit to existing data than the traditional two-factor model (Cooke, Michie, Hart, & Clark, 2004), also excludes 7 PCL-R items. Cooke and colleagues have argued that this exclusion is necessary to purge the instrument of the specifically criminal behavior items that they believe are not core features of the syndrome (Cooke et al., 2006), an argument strongly refuted by Hare and colleagues (Hare, 2003; Neumann, Hare, & Newman, 2007).

Researchers continue to look for ways to address the concerns raised by the PCL-R's inclusion of overtly antisocial items. For example, researchers routinely conduct analyses to examine separately the contributions of those items associated with the interpersonal/affective components of the syndrome (i.e., Factor 1) versus the impulsive/antisocial items (i.e., Factor 2) when investigating the deficits underlying the syndrome (e.g., Patrick, Bradley, & Lang, 1993); this practice has revealed that external criteria often relate differentially to these factors (e.g., Hansen, Johnsen, Thornton, Waage, & Thayer, 2007; Vaidyanathan, Hall, Patrick, & Bernat, 2011).

Despite the existence of unique correlates of Factors 1 and 2, there are those who argue there is no good evidence to suggest that any one component of psychopathy is primary over any other component (e.g., Hare, 2003; Neumann et al., 2007), and that psychopathy is best conceptualized as a unidimensional construct. Essentially, this argument holds that the PCL-R as a whole best captures the syndrome originally described by Cleckley (1988), and that this "'whole' may be greater than the sum of the 'parts'" (Neumann et al., 2007). Thus, although psychopathy may have several components, it is best conceptualized as a "super-factor" (Neumann et al., 2007).

The factor debate reflects the larger disagreement regarding the nature of psychopathy and questions regarding the "core" features of the syndrome. It is clear that some in the field would like to separate serious criminal behaviors, worried that these items maintain a definition of psychopathy that excludes individuals with many of the same features who have not committed an explicitly criminal act (Lilienfeld & Andrews, 1996). Such individuals may actually be "commended and reinforced in a competitive society where tough hard-headed realism is admired as an attribute necessary for survival," and they may live on "the rugged side of the business, military, or political world" (Millon, 1981, pp. 181–182).

It is a key debate because understanding the core features of the disorder is crucial, not only for improving the ability to assess the syndrome reliably, and increasing understanding of the etiology of the syndrome, but also for clarifying how the syndrome may be expressed across populations. This debate is directly relevant to the next controversy, which involves the generalizability of psychopathy assessment, and the PCL-R especially, across groups.

Generalizability Across Groups

Much of the early PCL-R psychopathy research was limited by a reliance on samples of institutionalized, Caucasian, North American adult males. Fortunately, there has been more recent work that examines the expression and correlates of psychopathy in other specific groups, particularly female offenders and African American offenders (see Beryl, Chou, & Völlm, 2014; Verona & Vitale, 2005; and Sullivan & Kosson, 2006, for reviews).

The results in this area have not always been clear-cut. Specifically, although evidence supports the reliability of psychopathy assessments among female populations (e.g., Miller, Watts, & Jones, 2011; Salekin, Rogers, & Sewell, 1997; Vitale, Smith, Brinkley, & Newman, 2002) and across racial groups (e.g., Vachon, Lynam, Loeber, & Stouthamer-Loeber, 2012), the evidence for the generalizability of behavioral and etiologically relevant correlates of psychopathy across gender and race is more limited.

For example, several key deficits in emotion-related responding have not been demonstrated among African American offenders (e.g., Baskin-Sommers, Newman, Sathasivam, & Curtin, 2011) nor among female offenders (e.g., Anton, Baskin-Sommers, Vitale, Curtin, & Newman, 2012; Vitale, MacCoon, & Newman, 2011). Similarly, maladaptive response perseveration and poor passive avoidance learning, both well documented among psychopathic males, have not been reliably demonstrated by psychopathic females (e.g., Vitale & Newman, 2001). In addition, differences across gender in laboratory-based assessments have been found in studies of adolescents with high levels of psychopathy traits (e.g., Isen et al., 2010; Vitale et al., 2005; Wang, Baker, Gao, Raine, & Lozano, 2012). Finally, research suggests that psychopathy may be a less powerful predictor of recidivism in incarcerated female samples (Weizmann-Henelius, Virkkunen, Gammelgard, Eronen, & Putkonen, 2015)

The desire of the field to generalize psychopathy findings to alternate samples leads directly to the final challenge to the PCL-R, which is the inability to use the measure to assess psychopathy in noninstitutionalized populations. As a result of this key limitation, as well as the concerns surrounding the instrument's reliance on overt antisociality, there is a strong emphasis in the field on developing alternative measures of the psychopathy construct. The next section provides a brief overview of these alternative measures.

ALTERNATIVE MEASURES OF PSYCHOPATHY

Although the PCL-R has been the most commonly used assessment of psychopathy, other measures—some designed specifically to address limitations in the use of the PCL-R—have been developed over the past two decades. Some of these measures, such as the PCL: Screening Version (PCL:SV; Forth, Brown, Hart, & Hare, 1996), PCL: Youth

Version (PCL:YV; Forth, Kosson, & Hare, 2003), and the Self-Report Psychopathy scale (SRP, SRP-II, and SRP-III; e.g., Williams & Paulhus, 2004) are direct descendants of the PCL-R, designed to be used with specialized groups or in noninstitutional contexts.

For example, the PCL:SV was created as a way to assess psychopathy using less information and without formal criminal records; this increases its utility in psychiatric and noninstitutional settings (Forth et al., 1996). Generally, research suggests that the PCL:SV captures a syndrome similar to that identified by the PCL-R. The two measures are highly correlated (average correlation of .8) (Cooke, Michie, Hart, & Hare, 1999). The PCL:SV exhibits a factor structure and item functioning similar to that of the PCL-R (Hill, Neumann, & Rogers, 2004), and the PCL:SV is a good predictor of violent behavior (e.g., Douglas, Ogloff, Nicholls, & Grant, 1999; Skeem & Mulvey, 2001).

The PCL:YV is based on the assumption that the psychopathy syndrome observed among adults can be extended downward into adolescence. Although the items in the PCL:YV are based on the adult PCL-R, they have been modified to capture the syndrome as it might appear in adolescents aged 12 to 18 (Forth et al., 2003). Although there is some evidence for differential item functioning across gender (Tsang et al., 2015) and ethnicity (Tsang, Piquero, & Cauffman, 2014), other research using the PCL:YV has demonstrated reliability in both male and female samples (e.g., Bauer, Whitman, & Kosson, 2011). Research has also shown that the measure relates to criterion variables in ways that would be predicted based on PCL-R research with adults. For example, relative to adolescents with low scores, adolescents with high scores on the instrument commit a higher number of crimes and more violent crimes (Kosson, Cyterski, Steuerwald, Neumann, & Walker-Matthews, 2002). PCL:YV scores are also significantly inversely associated with familial attachment (Kosson et al., 2002).

Because the PCL:YV, like the PCL-R, requires a lengthy interview procedure, alternative measures of psychopathy for youth have been developed. For example, the Antisocial Process Screening Device (APSD; Frick & Hare, 2001) is a 20-item rating scale that can be used as a self-report measure or as a teacher and parent report measure. Research has shown that the APSD is associated with many of the personality traits and laboratory deficits exhibited by psychopathic adults. For example, high scores on the APSD delineate a group of individuals who exhibit higher rates of conduct problems and police contacts, and stronger family histories of antisocial behavior than groups characterized by lower scores do (Christian, Frick, Hill, Tyler, & Frazer, 1997; Fung, Gao, & Raine, 2010; Munoz & Frick, 2007; Pechorro et al., 2014). Higher scores on the APSD are also associated with decreased empathy, perspective taking, and fearfulness (Blair, Monson, & Frederickson, 2001).

Although items on the APSD tap the interpersonal (e.g., superficial charm, lack of empathy), emotional (e.g., shallow affect), and behavioral (e.g., reckless antisocial behaviors, impulsivity) characteristics of psychopathy, particular interest has emerged in the callous and unemotional traits assessed by the measure, because these appear to correlate most strongly with indices of psychopathy. For example, laboratory studies have demonstrated that adolescents characterized by the callous-unemotional traits, as assessed by the APSD, exhibit abnormal neural responses (e.g., Sebastian et al., 2012); performance deficits on a task requiring them to modify an initial reward-oriented response strategy in light of increasing rates of punishment (e.g., O'Brien & Frick, 1996); reduced interference on a picture-word Stroop test; and deficits in passive avoidance on a go/no-go task (Vitale et al., 2005)—although this latter finding was specific to male participants.

The Youth Psychopathic Traits Inventory (YPI; Andershed, Kerr, Statin, & Levander, 2002) and YPI–Child Version (YPI-CV) have been shown in some studies to relate to key correlates of psychopathy, including conduct problems and proactive aggression (Ručević, 2010; van Baardewijk, Vermeiren, Stegge, & Doreleijers, 2011), as well as self-reported antisocial attitudes and impulsivity (Campbell, Doucette, & French, 2009). However, the results are mixed, with other studies failing to find expected associations with criminal behavior or substance use (Colins, Andershed, & Pardini, 2015; Shepherd & Strand, 2015), and only weak evidence for the measure's ability to tap key features of psychopathy (i.e., callous-unemotional traits) (Oshukova et al., 2015). The scale shows moderate correlations with factors of the PCL:YV (Andershed, Hodgins, & Tengstrom, 2007), and correlates with other self-report measures of psychopathy (Cambell et al., 2009).

Although there appears to be good evidence, especially among males, that measures such as the PCL:YV, the APSD, and perhaps, the YPI-CV can assess a syndrome in adolescents similar to the psychopathy syndrome assessed in adults, there is considerable controversy regarding the assessment of psychopathy in youth. For example, there is not clear evidence that psychopathy assessments of adolescents have the same forensic utility as those made for adults (Cauffman, Kimonis, Dmitrieva, & Monahan, 2009). Others hold that a psychopathy label has become synonymous with increased dangerousness and poor treatment response (e.g., Edens, 2006; Lykken, 1995), beliefs that might hinder intervention attempts for youth. Further, because the psychopathy-like syndrome assessed among children and adolescents may reflect transient developmental processes, some have argued that it is inappropriate to use such a label in this group (e.g., Edens, Skeem, Cruise, & Cauffman, 2001; Skeem & Cauffman, 2003).

Nevertheless, there is clear evidence that many of the behaviors and performance abnormalities associated with adult psychopathy are apparent in youth, and there is emerging evidence for stability in psychopathic traits across childhood and adolescence (Lopez-Romero, Romero, & Villar, 2014). Further, those who use these measures note that ratings of items are based on the frequency, duration, and intensity of the attitudes and behaviors exhibited by the individual (Gretton, Hare, & Catchpole, 2004; Lynam, 1996), thereby decreasing the likelihood that scores will represent normal, transitory developmental processes. Consistent with this assertion, in community samples the mean PCL:YV score is low (i.e., a score of 5 out of a possible 40) (Forth et al., 2003), and assessments of juvenile psychopathy appear to be relatively stable across adolescence (e.g., Lynam et al., 2009; Neumann, Wampler, Taylor, Blonigen, & Iacono, 2011). On this basis, the counterargument is made that, by neglecting to examine psychopathy in adolescents, researchers, and clinicians may be giving up an important opportunity for examining the development of the syndrome across time and for designing interventions that might prevent the adolescent with psychopathic traits from becoming the adult with psychopathy (Frick, 1998; Lynam, 1996).

Just as investigators have sought new, more efficient ways to assess the psychopathy syndrome among adolescents, the field has developed more efficient alternative measures of the syndrome in adults. Thus, in addition to the PCL:SV and PCL:YV, Hare and colleagues (e.g., Hare, Harpur, & Hemphill, 1989; Williams, Paulhus, & Hare, 2007) have developed the Self-Report Psychopathy scale (SRP, SRP II, SRP-III) as a self-report measure of the syndrome in adult samples. The SRP-II and SRP-III are reliable (Neal & Sellbom, 2012) and relate in expected ways with correlates of the psychopathy syndrome, including scores on the PCL as well as measures of alcohol abuse, narcissism, empathy, Machiavellianism, agreeableness, and conscientiousness (e.g., Paulhus & Williams, 2002; Tew, Harkins, & Dixon, 2015; Zagon & Jackson, 1994; Watt & Brooks, 2012).

In addition to the direct progeny of the PCL-R, a number of self-report measures have developed relatively independently, in order to provide a means of assessing psychopathy in noninstitutionalized samples. These measures emphasize the traits associated with the syndrome, rather than emphasizing the numbers of disinhibited behaviors or criminal acts. Chief among these are the primary and secondary scales of Levenson's Self-Report Psychopathy Scale (SRPS; Levenson, Kiehl, & Fitzpatrick, 1995) and the Psychopathic Personality Inventory (PPI; Lilienfeld & Andrews, 1996).

The SRPS is a 26-item, self-report measure developed by Levenson et al. (1995). The scale has two components: the "primary" scale, which is positively correlated with disinhibition and boredom susceptibility and negatively correlated with harm avoidance on the Multidimensional Personality Questionnaire, and the "secondary" scale, which is associated with stress reactions. In a test of the validity of the SRPS, Brinkley, Schmitt, Smith, and Newman (2001) compared scores on the measure to PCL-R scores in an institutional sample. Results showed that the PCL-R was associated with the SRPS, and, more importantly, that the SRPS related in predictable ways to substance abuse, criminal versatility, and passive avoidance task performance. Similarly, additional research has found that SRPS scores relate in expected ways with a number of psychopathy correlates, including self-reported delinquency, low agreeableness, and performance on a go/no-go passive avoidance task (e.g., Lynam, Whiteside, and Jones, 1999; Sellbom, 2011).

Like the SRPS, the PPI was developed to emphasize the traits associated with psychopathy (Lilienfeld & Andrews, 1996). The PPI is a 187-item self-report measure with 8 subscales: Machiavellian Egocentricity, Coldheartedness, Social Potency, Carefree Nonplanfulness, Fearlessness, Impulsive Nonconformity, Blame Externalization, and Stress Immunity. Research shows that the PPI correlates with PCL-R total scores (Poythress, Edens, & Lilienfeld, 1998), and also with adult and childhood antisocial behavior, institutional misconduct (Edens, Poythress, Lilienfeld, & Patrick, 2008; Edens, Poythress, Lilienfeld, Patrick, & Test, 2008), measures of emotional empathy (Sandoval, Hancock, Poythress, Edens, & Lilienfeld, 2000), and self-report aggression and dominance (Edens, Poythress, & Watkins, 2001). The PPI has also been associated with abnormalities in affective startle responses (Anderson, Stanford, Wan, & Young, 2011) and in behavioral and neurological responses to incentives (Bjork, Chen, & Hommer, 2012).

Some have argued that these measures designed specifically to assess psychopathy are preferable to traditional self-report personality measures that may not fully capture the psychopathy syndrome (Lilienfeld, 2006). Others have held that traditional measures are entirely appropriate in the assessment of psychopathy. This argument reflects the emergence of alternative conceptualizations of psychopathy that are rooted strongly in personality traits.

Lynam and colleagues (e.g., Miller & Lynam, 2015; Lynam & Derefinko, 2006) have argued that psychopathy is best conceptualized according to the traditional five-factor model (FFM) of personality, and that psychopathy is easily captured by the traits and facets of personality measures like the NEO PI-R. According to the proponents of this approach, conceptualizing psychopathy in accordance with existing personality traits places the syndrome within the context of well-validated personality theory that is already strongly connected to research in diverse areas, including genetics, development, and neurobiology (Lynam & Derefinko, 2006).

Widiger and Lynam (1998) have suggested that each item of the PCL-R can be easily represented by facets within the FFM. For example, according to the authors, "glibness/superficial charm" is represented by low self-consciousness, and "shallow affect" by low warmth, low positive emotionality, low altruism, and low tender-mindedness. To test the validity of this profile, Miller, Lynam, Widiger, and Leukefeld (2001) asked psychopathy experts to generate a FFM profile of the prototypical psychopath on the basis of their understanding and knowledge of the syndrome. Importantly, the profile generated by these experts was similar to that generated by the theorists. Similarly, Derefinko and Lynam (2007) found support for conceptualizing psychopathy according to the FFM in a sample of drug abusers.

In subsequent research, Lynam and colleagues (Lynam & Widiger, 2001; Miller & Lynam, 2003) were able to calculate the Psychopathy Resemblance Index (PRI), which is a measure of the extent to which an individual resembles the FFM prototype. Research supports the argument that scores on the PRI do capture many of the qualities associated with psychopathy, as these scores are associated with an earlier age of onset of delinquency, greater criminal versatility, earlier drug use, and low internalizing problems (Miller et al., 2001). Among college students, PRI scores are associated with higher rates of substance abuse, aggression, riskier sex, and criminal versatility and are also predictive of performance on psychopathy-related laboratory tasks (i.e., the use of aggressive responses on a social-information task, and less willingness to delay gratification on a time-discounting task) (Miller & Lynam, 2003).

More recently, Lynam and colleagues (Lynam, Gaughan, et al., 2011; Lynam & Widiger, 2001; Miller & Lynam, 2003) have developed the Elemental Psychopathy Assessment (EPA), a self-report measure based on the five-factor personality model. The EPA scales assess the 18 traits that have been demonstrated to be associated with psychopathy, and in both forensic and college samples, scores on the EPA have been shown to correlate with existing psychopathy measures (i.e., SRP-III, PPI-R). They show expected associations with correlates of psychopathy, including aggressive social cognitions, antisocial personality features, and romantic infidelity (Miller, Gaughan, et al., 2011; Wilson, Miller, Zeichner, Lynam, & Widiger, 2011), and also alcohol use and antisocial behavior (Lynam et al., 2011).

Other researchers have put less emphasis on the five-factor personality model in their trait-based conceptualizations of psychopathy. For example, the triarchic personality model of psychopathy (Patrick, Fowles, & Krueger, 2009; Brislin, Drislane, Smith, Edens, & Patrick, 2015) places the three traits of meanness, disinhibition, and boldness at the core of the syndrome. Further, the Triarchic Psychopathy Measure (TriPM) was developed to assess these traits. Research using the triarchic conceptualization of psychopathy has found expected associations between measures of the core personality features and other measures of psychopathy and measures of psychopathy-related criteria, including antisocial behavior and self-reported empathy (Sellbom, Wygant, & Drislane, 2015), structural differences in the amygdala (Vieira et al., 2015), and deficits in emotion responses (Somma, Borroni, Drislane, & Fossati, 2015).

In recent years, the field has also been impacted by the conceptualization of psychopathy as part of the "Dark Triad" of personality: that is, narcissism, Machiavellianism, and psychopathy. Initially introduced in the early 2000s by Paulhus & Williams (2002), this domain has been the subject of a steady increase in research, reflecting the growing influence of this conceptualization (see Furnham, Richards, & Paulhus, 2013, for a review). In addition to exploring the negative consequences of these personality styles for those who exhibit them and for those around them (e.g., Crysel, Crosier, & Webster, 2013; Jones & Neria, 2015), Dark Triad researchers have also placed increasing emphasis on the ways in which the characteristics of the Dark Triad may have adaptive value in certain situations or contexts (e.g., Jonason, Duineveld, & Middleton, 2015). Although there are significant concerns regarding both the overall utility of the Dark Triad construct (Glenn & Sellbom, 2015) and the methods used to assess Dark Triad traits (Carter, Campbell, Muncer, & Carter, 2015), the Dark Triad will likely continue to influence personality-based discussions of the psychopathy syndrome.

ASSESSMENT CONCLUSIONS

One of the most advantageous outcomes of the development of the PCL-R and its progeny has been the unification of the field. Although some have cautioned that this unification may have come at the expense of the development of alternative measures, the benefit to clinical work and laboratory research of having a shared conceptualization of the psychopathy syndrome should not be underestimated (Hare, 1996). Further, the PCL-R has not entirely inhibited the development of alternative, non-PCL-based measures. In fact, in recent years alternative measures of the syndrome have proliferated, along with changes in many researchers' basic conceptualization of the construct. One of the most obvious results of these changes is a renewed interest in "defining" psychopathy as a construct, and the accompanying efforts to reconcile emerging theoretical and statistical inconsistencies across conceptualizations (e.g., Miller, Maples-Keller, & Lynam, 2015; Sellbom, Cooke, & Hart, 2015). In the absence of such analysis, it is unclear whether differences across samples and studies are the result of differences in the conceptualization of the construct or represent differences in the expression of the construct. This distinction may be particularly important depending upon whether a researcher is examining deviance-related correlates of the syndrome—which may be less likely to vary across diverse conceptualizations—or etiologically relevant correlates—the prediction of which may differ in important ways across the different conceptualizations being employed.

PREVALENCE OF PSYCHOPATHY

Because much of the research on psychopathy has been conducted in institutional settings, scientific understanding of the rates of the disorder in these samples is more advanced. For example, among samples of North American male offenders, the rates of psychopathy range from 15% to 49% (e.g., Herve, Mitchell, & Cooper, 2004; Salekin, Rogers,

Ustad, & Sewell, 1998). Similar rates have been found among forensic populations in Sweden (i.e., 23% to 32%) and Spain (18% to 38%). There does appear to be some variation within and between international samples. For example, rates in Scottish samples have been as low as 3% (Cooke & Michie, 1999), whereas among British samples, they have ranged from 4.5% in a prison sample to 47% in a psychiatric sample (see Sullivan & Kosson, 2006, for a review).

Rates tend to be lower in incarcerated female samples, with rates among incarcerated females as low as 9% to 20% (Lehman & Ittel, 2012; Salekin et al., 1997; Vitale et al., 2002). This range does not change much even when a lower diagnostic cutoff score of 25 is used (e.g., Lehman & Ittel, 2012).

More and more researchers are moving away from a diagnostic model that emphasizes cutoff scores and prevalence rates. Rather, the use of many of the alternative measures discussed in the previous section has shifted the emphasis toward the conceptualization of psychopathy as a continuous construct wherein individuals who might otherwise be categorized as "subclinical" for psychopathy are found to exhibit many of the underlying personality, affective, and behavioral characteristics of the traditional psychopathic individual. Nevertheless, for many in applied settings, the conceptualization of psychopathy as a discrete diagnostic entity is still common and likely has high practical utility.

Psychological Models and Somatic Factors

Conceptual and causal models of psychopathy emphasize both the emotional and cognitive characteristics associated with the syndrome. Although some approaches emphasize psychopathic individuals' deficits in fear and focus on associated abnormalities in amygdala functioning (e.g., Blair, 2006), an alternative approach is to consider the behavioral abnormalities associated with psychopathy as reflecting a response modulation deficit associated with abnormalities in attention processes (e.g., Gorenstein & Newman, 1980). Emerging findings in neuroimaging and genetics have further informed our understanding of the syndrome.

FEARLESSNESS, FEAR CONDITIONING, AND AMYGDALA ABNORMALITIES

Several theoretical formulations have emphasized fearlessness or insensitivity to punishment as underlying causes of the psychopathy syndrome (e.g., Fowles, 1980; Lykken, 1995). Early theories of psychopathy embraced Gray's (e.g., Gray & McNaughten, 2000) model of BIS/BAS functioning, which proposed three systems that served to regulate behavior: the fight/flight system (FFS), which responds to unconditioned or innately aversive stimuli; the behavioral activation system (BAS), described as sensitive to reward stimuli and likely to activate responses in the face of cues or conditioned stimuli signaling reward; and the behavioral inhibition system (BIS), described as sensitive to punishment stimuli and likely to inhibit ongoing responses in response to cues or conditioned stimuli signaling punishment or frustrative nonreward. Importantly, recent formulations of the model have deemphasized the idea that the BIS reflects generalized sensitivity to threat, and instead have suggested that the BIS is activated specifically under conditions of goal conflict (Gray & McNaughten, 2000).

Working from Gray's original model, Fowles (1980) proposed that the psychopathy syndrome, characterized as it was by impulsivity, callousness, and an absence of neurosis, was associated with deficits in the BIS. According to this formulation, a hyporeactive BIS, in conjunction with a normal BAS response, could result in the types of symptoms observed among psychopathic people. Specifically, these individuals would show the poor punishment learning and weak behavioral inhibition characteristic of the psychopathic individual (Fowles, 1980). Self-report data have supported this proposition, with those psychopathic individuals characterized by low levels of neurotic anxiety or those categorized as "primary" psychopathic individuals showing significantly lower scores on self-report measures of BIS functioning and punishment sensitivity (e.g., Broerman, Ross, & Corr, 2014; Newman, MacCoon, Vaughn, & Sadeh, 2005; Ross et al., 2007). Conversely, it was found that those individuals whose psychopathy symptoms were combined with high levels of trait anxiety or neuroticism (so-called secondary psychopathic individuals) were characterized not by deficits in the BIS but by hyperresponsivity of the BAS (Newman et al., 2005).

Early and current experimental data support the weak BIS formulation. For example, passive avoidance tasks, which require the individual to inhibit responses to previously punished stimuli, have reliably differentiated people with psychopathy from controls, with psychopathic individuals committing significantly more passive avoidance errors (e.g., Lykken, 1957; Newman & Kosson, 1986; Newman & Schmitt, 1998; Thornquist & Zuckerman, 1995). Similarly, on a card-playing task that requires the ability to modulate responses in the context of increasing punishment contingencies, psychopathic individuals play significantly more cards and lose significantly more money than controls (e.g., Newman, Patterson, & Kosson, 1987).

Physiological data also support the BIS hypothesis. For example, both psychopathic offenders and nonincarcerated individuals with high levels of psychopathic traits show decreased electrodermal responsivity in anticipation of an aversive event (Arnett, Howland, Smith, & Newman, 1993; Dindo & Fowles, 2011; Wang et al., 2012) and show abnormalities in eye-blink startle responses (Anderson et al., 2011; Levenston, Patrick, Bradley, & Lang, 2000; Patrick et al., 1993; Sutton, Vitale, & Newman, 2002). Specifically, research has demonstrated that exposure to aversive or unpleasant stimuli will potentiate an eye-blink startle response in controls. Psychopathic participants, however, show significantly reduced startle potentiation in response to these stimuli, although their startle response to pleasant stimuli does not differ from that of controls. Importantly, this finding has been linked most closely to the affective/interpersonal (i.e., Factor 1) features of psychopathy (Vaidyanathan et al., 2011).

Taken together, these self-report and laboratory data provide some evidence for deficient BIS functioning. However, other theorists have focused more on fearlessness as a trait and less on BIS functioning. For example, although Lykken's (1957, 1995) low-fear hypothesis dovetailed well with Fowles's (1980) emphasis on deficient BIS functioning, Lykken placed less emphasis on the particulars of Gray's model. Rather, Lykken (1995) proposed that the psychopathic individual is characterized by fearlessness, which impedes normal socialization and results in the cluster of symptoms characteristic of the syndrome (e.g., failure to learn from experience, lack of empathy, irresponsibility, manipulativeness). This proposal is based, in part, on the results of Lykken's highly influential 1957 study of conditioning and psychopathy. The results of this seminal study showed that the psychopathic individuals (designated on the basis of their similarity to Cleckley's prototype) had lower scores on a self-report measure of fearfulness (i.e., the Activity Preference Questionnaire), showed poor electrodermal conditioning relative to controls in a paradigm wherein electric shock served as the unconditioned stimulus (UCS), and also exhibited deficient passive avoidance performance (Lykken, 1957). Taken together, these data suggested deficient fear conditioning among psychopathic individuals, and served as the basis for Lykken's "low-fear" hypothesis.

Although there are data to support the weak-BIS and low-fear theories, Blair (2006) has criticized these traditional low-fear formulations on the basis of increasing specificity in the neurocognitive literature. Consequently, Blair (2006) emphasized the role of the amygdala in psychopathy and has focused primarily on punishment-based learning associated with this structure. Blair (2006) argued that psychopathic individuals should show abnormalities only on those tasks that involve the formation of associations between a conditioned stimulus and an unconditioned response (CS-UR) (e.g., a galvanic skin response to a stimulus previously associated with a shock); between a conditioned stimulus and an affect representation; and between a conditioned stimulus and the valenced sensory properties of the unconditioned stimulus associations (e.g., the visual appearance or smell of the unconditioned stimulus).

Consistent with Blair's proposal, psychopathic individuals have demonstrated deficits on tasks that preferentially involve these types of learning. For example, they show impairment on aversive conditioning tasks, which involve amygdala-specific learning (i.e., CS-UR and CS–affect representation associations) (Lykken, 1957; Rothemund et al., 2012). Further, there is evidence that, relative to controls, psychopathic participants show reduced amygdala activation during such aversive conditioning tasks (e.g., Veit et al., 2002), and that adolescents with high levels of psychopathic traits show relatively less amygdala responsiveness than controls on a passive avoidance task (Finger et al., 2011).

Differences in amygdala activation have also been noted in studies of both adults and juveniles with high versus low psychopathic traits (Glenn, Raine, & Schug, 2009; Jones, Laurens, Herba, Barker, & Viding, 2009; Marsh et al., 2008; White et al., 2012). Additionally, reductions in amygdala volume in both institutionalized and noninstitutionalized psychopathic individuals (e.g., Ermer, Cope, Nyalakanti, Calhoun, & Kiehl, 2012; Yang, Raine, Colletti, Toga, & Narr, 2010; Yang, Raine, Narr, Colletti, & Toga, 2009) and abnormalities in amygdala structure among psychopathic individuals (Boccardi et al., 2011) have been reported.

Paradigms using the fear-potentiated startle response to differentiate psychopathic individuals and controls also provide support for Blair's hypothesis. Because the amygdala is influential in the modulation of the startle response on such tasks (e.g., Davis, 2000), psychopathic individuals' deficient performance implicates this structure, providing further support that amygdala functioning is associated with the psychopathy syndrome.

Blair (2006) was also able to explain why psychopathic individuals show performance deficits on some tasks but not on others. For example, the low-fear and punishment insensitivity models for psychopathy have been criticized on the basis of psychopathic individuals' normal performance on punishment-only versions of the passive avoidance task. On this version of the task, participants are punished for responding to some stimuli and punished for *not* responding to other stimuli. Psychopathic participants' typical performance on such tasks suggests that, contrary to the punishment- and fear-based theories, psychopathic individuals do demonstrate adequate passive avoidance of punishment-related stimuli under certain conditions. To explain this discrepancy, Blair (2006) incorporated the theoretical formulations of Baxter and Murray (2002) that distinguished instrumental tasks that involve the amygdala (e.g., passive avoidance learning) from those instrumental learning tasks that do not (e.g., conditional learning and object discrimination). Specifically, according to Blair (2006), psychopathic individuals are not affected on the punishment-only task because this task requires the formation of stimulus-response associations, rather than CS–affect representation associations. In other words, because the punishment-only version of the passive avoidance task does not involve learning that requires the amygdala, psychopathic individuals are able to perform normally.

Although there is much evidence to support the low-fear and punishment-learning theories of psychopathy, this emphasis on emotion may result in an overly narrow focus. For example, the amygdala-based models of psychopathy have placed considerable emphasis on results showing differences in the activation and morphology of the amygdala between psychopathic individuals and individuals high in psychopathy traits relative to controls. However, it is important to recognize that differences in brain structure activation and morphology in psychopathy are not limited to the amygdala. For example, Finger and colleagues (2011) also noted decreased responsiveness in the orbitofrontal cortex and caudate, a finding consistent with that of Marsh et al. (2011). Similarly, Boccardi and colleagues (2011) found not only significant differences in amygdala structure between psychopathic individuals and controls but also significant reduction in orbitofrontal regions. Finally, research has found evidence for abnormal activation among both psychopathic and subclinical psychopathic individuals in several brain regions implicated in empathic responses to others' pain, including the anterior insula, inferior frontal gyrus, and mid- and anterior cingulate cortex (Decety, Skelley, & Kiehl, 2013; Seara-Cardosa, Viding, Lickley, & Sebastian, 2015).

This suggestion of more general abnormality is consistent with studies showing differences across psychopathic individuals and nonpsychopathic individuals in a variety of regions, including the dorsolateral prefrontal cortex (DLPFC; e.g., LaPierre, Braun, & Hodgins, 1995; Mitchell, Colledge, Leonard, & Blair, 2002), the orbitofrontal cortex (OFC; e.g., Ermer et al., 2012; LaPierre et al., 1995; Mitchell et al., 2002), and the medial frontal or anterior cingulate cortex (ACC; Ly et al., 2012; Munro et al., 2007; Veit et al., 2002). These findings are consistent with results showing that psychopathic individuals show deficits in performance on tasks involving OFC and ACC functioning (Blair et al., 2006). Further, beyond structural abnormalities, additional research is suggesting that abnormal connectivity between regions may be associated with psychopathy (Cohn et al., 2015; Ly et al., 2012; Motzkin, Newman, Kiehl, & Keonigs, 2011; Philippi et al., 2015).

Recently, Hamilton, Hiatt-Racer, and Newman (2015) have attempted to organize and reconcile these disparate findings within the framework of their proposed impaired integration (II) theory. According to the II theory, abnormalities in psychopathic individuals' neural connectivity interfere with their information integration. Specifically, the authors propose that psychopathy is characterized by decreased functioning of the salience and default mode networks, normal functioning in executive control networks, and less coordination between networks. Although further empirical evidence is needed to support the theory, it capitalizes on recent advancements in behavioral and neuroimaging data to present a coherent model for linking existing affective and cognitive models of psychopathy and offers a useful starting point for future research.

RESPONSE MODULATION AND ATTENTION

In addition to a focus on results specific to the amygdala, the traditional, amygdala-based models of psychopathy rely on laboratory tasks that emphasize valenced stimuli (e.g., the positive and negative visual stimuli presented as part of the acoustic startle paradigm, the punishment and reward stimuli used in passive avoidance tasks) as opposed to neutral stimuli. In an alternative line of investigation, Newman and colleagues (e.g., Hiatt, Schmitt, & Newman, 2004; Newman, Schmitt, & Voss, 1997; Vitale, Hiatt, Brinkley, & Newman, 2007) have used affectively and motivationally neutral tasks designed to examine attention processing among psychopathic people. On such tasks, psychopathic participants have reliably exhibited abnormalities in attention processing, particularly when stimuli are secondary or peripheral to their primary focus of selective attention (e.g., Hare & Jutai, 1988; Hiatt et al., 2004; Newman et al., 1997; Vitale et al., 2007).

Consistent with this emphasis, the response modulation hypothesis (RMH; Gorenstein & Newman, 1980; Newman & Baskin-Sommers, 2011) holds that abnormalities in selective attention undermine the ability of psychopathic individuals to consider contextual information that modulates the goal-directed behavior of others. In the most recent version of this model, Newman and Baskin-Sommers (2011) characterize the problem as an "attention bottleneck," which hampers the simultaneous processing of multiple channels of information. Thus, once attention is allocated to a specific goal, psychopathic individuals are less able to process the full range of affective and nonaffective stimuli, and their associated meanings, that normally provide an evaluative context for goal-directed behavior (MacCoon, Wallace, & Newman, 2004).

This focus on attention processing distinguishes the RMH from the low-fear and punishment-learning based models of psychopathy (e.g., Blair, 2006; Fowles, 1980; Lykken, 1995). Specifically, although the RMH predicts a situation-specific deficit, rather than a general deficit, in processing threat and other emotion cues, psychopathic individuals' failure to consider contextual information is not limited to affective information (Hiatt et al., 2004; Newman et al., 1997; Vitale et al., 2005; Wolf et al., 2011; Zeier, Maxwell, & Newman, 2009).

To evaluate the specificity of that aspect of the RMH, Newman and colleagues have conducted a series of studies that manipulate participants' focus of attention while measuring performance on tasks that are strongly associated with psychopathic behavior, including passive avoidance, electrodermal activity, fear-potentiated startle, and amygdala activation (see Newman & Baskin-Sommers, 2011, for a review). With regard to passive avoidance learning, for instance, the RMH predicts that psychopathic individuals will be relatively oblivious to inhibitory punishment cues when they are focused on responding to reward, but that they will use punishment cues to inhibit responding as well as nonpsychopathic individuals do when avoiding punishment is their primary goal. Consistent with these predictions, psychopathic offenders committed more passive avoidance errors than controls when avoiding punishment-involved learning to inhibit responses for reward, but their passive avoidance was as good or better than controls' avoidance was in a punishment-only version of the same task (i.e., when punishment cues were goal-relevant rather than peripheral to the primary focus of goal-directed behavior) (Newman & Kosson, 1986; Newman, Patterson, Howland, & Nichols, 1990; Newman & Schmitt, 1998). Thus, like Blair (2006), Newman and colleagues are able to reconcile the discrepant passive avoidance literature, although with an emphasis on the attentional demands of the task, rather than on the associations that must be formed.

Parallel findings have been obtained using fear-potentiated startle (FPS). Newman and colleagues (Baskin-Sommers, Curtin, & Newman, 2011; Newman, Curtin, Bertsch, & Baskin-Sommers, 2010) have used an instructed fear conditioning paradigm in which participants may receive electric shocks to their fingers when a red stimulus appears but not when a green stimulus appears. Further, participants' focus of attention is manipulated, such that participants are instructed to focus either on the color of each stimulus (red versus green) or on a characteristic of the stimulus unrelated to the shock (i.e., the presence of an uppercase or lowercase letter). Across diverse experiments, when FPS is measured in psychopathic versus nonpsychopathic participants, psychopathic offenders display significantly weaker FPS than controls, but only under the condition that directs their attention to the uppercase versus lowercase letters. When participants were instructed to focus on the red versus green color of the stimuli and respond accordingly, psychopathic offenders displayed as much or more FPS as controls. In other words, psychopathic participants' fear-related deficit in startle responding appeared and disappeared according to their focus of attention: when focused on threat-relevant information (i.e., the color associated with an electric shock) they displayed normal fear responses, but they displayed what appeared to be a profound fear deficit when the threat cues were peripheral to their goal-directed focus of attention (Baskin-Sommers et al., 2011; Newman et al., 2010).

According to the RMH, psychopathic individuals' insensitivity to punishment and other affectively significant cues is relatively specific to conditions in which the cues are peripheral to their goal-directed focus of attention. The RMH further predicts that these individuals should show insensitivity to potentially relevant but affectively neutral information under the same circumstances. To test this proposal, Newman and colleagues conducted a series of studies utilizing modified Stroop and flanker (e.g., Eriksen & Eriksen, 1974) tasks. In these tasks, participants are instructed to attend to a particular target stimulus and to make a response on the basis of the target. However, on each trial, the target stimulus appears with another stimulus that may be congruent (i.e., elicits the same response as the one associated with the target), incongruent (i.e., elicits a different response than the target), or neutral (has no implications for response selection). These characteristics allow researchers to measure the extent to which distracting peripheral cues interfere with goal-directed responses (i.e., engender interference). Interference is typically computed by subtracting response speed on neutral trials from response speed on incongruent trials. In contrast to most laboratory studies of psychopathology, which predict a performance deficit, the RMH predicts that psychopathic individuals will display superior performance (i.e., less interference), particularly on tasks that enable participants to readily distinguish between targets and distractors on the basis of spatial location or salient stimulus features.

In the first study to evaluate this hypothesis, Newman et al. (1997) used a computerized picture-word task. On this task, participants were presented with two consecutive pictures or words, and instructed to indicate whether the two pictures (or words) were conceptually related. On word trials, the first word was presented with a superimposed picture.

On picture trials, the first picture was presented with a superimposed word. On all trials, participants were instructed to ignore the superimposed (i.e., secondary context) stimulus. However, on half of the trials when the consecutively presented stimuli were conceptually unrelated, the superimposed picture (or word) was conceptually related to the second stimulus. In these trials, the correct response was "unrelated," but the response indicated by the secondary stimulus was incongruent with this response (e.g., the word "sweep" superimposed over a picture of a hat, followed by a picture of a broom). Among healthy participants, responses on these incongruent trials were reliably slower than responses to congruent trials (see Gernsbacher & Faust, 1991). Consistent with the performance of healthy participants, nonpsychopathic male offenders responded significantly more slowly on incongruent versus congruent trials (i.e., they showed interference). However, interference was virtually nonexistent in psychopathic male offenders, thus demonstrating significantly less sensitivity to the secondary stimulus among this group. This effect was subsequently replicated (e.g., Hiatt et al., 2004; Vitale et al., 2007).

Zeier and colleagues (2009) provided a conceptual replication of this study and, moreover, demonstrated the importance of attentional focus in determining the effect. In this study, participants viewed numbers (5, 8), letters (G, H), and neutral stimuli (#) within displays that always involved two of these stimuli (e.g., G and 5). Participants were instructed to press a button to indicate whether the target stimulus was a number or letter. The two stimuli were always presented to the left and right of a central fixation point that ultimately transformed into an arrow (< or >) designating the target location. In order to evaluate the importance of selective attention on psychopathy-related differences in sensitivity to incongruent information, the authors employed a cuing procedure that either allowed participants to predict the spatial location of the target before the target and distracter appeared or highlighted both stimulus locations. For instance, in one condition a rectangular box surrounded the location where the target would ultimately appear or appeared at both locations 100 milliseconds before the experimental display.

Consistent with RMH, when the boxes appeared at both locations, drawing attention to the target as well as the potentially distracting flanker stimulus, psychopathic offenders and controls displayed comparable amounts of interference. However, when the box cued the target location specifically, psychopathic offenders displayed significantly less interference than controls. Such findings again highlight that the hypothesized attention bottleneck associated with psychopathy may limit these individuals' processing of peripheral information. Though this characteristic may have enhanced their ability to ignore distraction, this advantage was counterbalanced by their failure to process peripheral information that may be crucial for regulating maladaptive responses. Recent research using alternative measures of attention allocation (e.g., box Stroop, gaze detection tasks) continues to provide support for the RMH (Baskin-Sommers & Newman, 2014; Dawel et al., 2015; Sethi et al., 2015).

An important consideration in evaluating the response modulation model is that many of the studies involved comparing low-anxious psychopathic individuals with a group of comparably low-anxious controls in order to test hypotheses concerning so-called primary psychopathy. Such distinctions have a long history in psychopathy research (e.g., Lykken, 1957) and continue to be emphasized today (e.g., Hicks, Markon, Patrick, Krueger, & Newman, 2004; Skeem et al., 2011). However, when interpreting such findings, it is important to bear in mind that not all individuals assessed as psychopathic using the

Psychopathy Checklist–Revised will fall into this group. It is also worth noting that the core evidence for the RMH, including abnormalities on the modified Stroop task (Hiatt et al., 2004), passive avoidance task (Newman & Kosson, 1986), and fear-potentiated startle tasks (Baskin-Sommers et al., 2011, Newman et al., 2010), has been found without restricting analyses to the low-anxious groups. Further research is needed to determine whether individuals categorized into the low- and high-anxious psychopathic subtypes should be conceptualized as having different disorders with distinct psychobiological correlates or as sharing a core psychobiological predisposition, the manifestation of which is importantly influenced by their levels of comorbid anxiety (see Brinkley, Newman, & Widiger, 2004; Lake, Baskin-Sommers, Li, Curtin, & Newman, 2011).

GENETICS

There are more than 100 studies examining the relative contributions of genetic and environmental factors to antisocial behavior. Generally, evidence supports a moderate contribution of each factor. For example, in a meta-analysis, Waldman and Rhee (2006) found moderate additive genetic ($a^2 = .32$), nonadditive genetic ($c^2 = .09$), shared environmental ($d^2 = .16$), and nonshared environmental ($e^2 = .43$) influences on antisocial behavior, and the best-fitting model included each of these four components ($\chi^2 = 1,394.46, df = 146, p < .001$; AIC = 1,102.46). Importantly, the studies included in this analysis focused primarily on antisocial behavior, and used diagnoses of ASPD or conduct disorder, criminal activity and delinquency, or self-reports of aggression as outcome variables. Although antisocial behavior is a component of psychopathy, the psychopathy syndrome is distinct from general criminality or antisociality (Cleckley, 1988). As a result, the meta-analysis only indirectly addresses the genetic basis of psychopathy. Fortunately, there is an emerging literature focused on examining the relative contribution of genetics to traits more specifically associated with the psychopathy syndrome.

In one study of adolescent monozygotic and dizygotic twin pairs, Larsson, Andershed, and Lichtenstein (2006) used the YPI to assess the affective, interpersonal, and behavioral components of the psychopathy syndrome. Their results indicated that for each of these three components of psychopathy, genetic[1] and nonshared environmental factors accounted for the majority of variance, with little or no influence from shared environmental factors. Further, because their sample included both males and females, the authors were able to test for gender differences in the relative influences of the factors. None were found, suggesting that there may not be significant differences in the heritability of psychopathic traits across gender (Larsson et al., 2006).

These data from Larsson et al. (2006) are consistent with Blonigen, Hicks, Kreuger, Patrick, and Iacono's (2006) analysis of 626 twin pairs from the Minnesota Twin Family Study. In this study, psychopathy was represented by the Fearless Dominance (representing a combination of the interpersonal and affective components of psychopathy) and Impulsive Antisociality (representing the behavioral component of psychopathy) subscales of the Multidimensional Personality Questionnaire (MPQ; Tellegen, 2000).

---

[1] The authors did not analyze additive and nonadditive genetic factors separately. Thus, these "genetic" contributions include both components.

As Larsson and colleagues (2006) had found, a model including additive genetic and nonshared environmental factors provided the best fit to the data, and there appeared to be no significant differences in the model fit across gender (Blonigen et al., 2006).

Using the Detachment and Antisocial subscales from the Minnesota Temperament Inventory to assess the affective and behavioral components of psychopathy, Taylor, Loney, Bobadilla, Iacono, and McGue (2003) examined the influence of genetic and shared and nonshared environmental factors in two samples of adolescent male twins (aged 16 to 18). As both Larsson et al. (2006) and Blonigen et al. (2006) found, the best-fitting model for both the affective and behavioral dimensions included additive genetic factors and nonshared environmental factors; there was little contribution from shared environmental factors (Taylor et al., 2003). This pattern of results has also been replicated by Bezdjian, Raine, Baker, and Lynam (2011), who used the Child Psychopathy Scale and found that genetic factors and nonshared environmental factors influenced psychopathy trait levels in males and females; as in previous research, shared environmental influences showed no influence.

Each of the preceding studies supports the importance of both genetic and nonshared environmental factors and the negligible influence of shared environmental factors. In this light, the distinction between shared and nonshared environmental influences becomes crucial for later investigation of the factors associated with psychopathy. Nonshared environmental factors are represented by the divergence of monozygotic twins whose shared environments are identical. One potentially potent nonshared environmental factor is peer relationships (Manke, McGuire, Reiss, Hetherington, & Plomin, 1995), which play an important role in adolescent development. Their importance to psychopathic personality, in particular, is highlighted by the finding that the level of psychopathic traits exhibited by an individual adolescent appears to be correlated with the levels of psychopathic traits exhibited by members of his or her peer friendship group (Andershed, Kerr, Stattin, & Engels, 2003, cited in Larsson et al., 2006).

The key role of genetic and nonshared environmental factors is further emphasized by a second meta-analysis of psychopathy-related studies, conducted by Waldman and Rhee (2006). Using only studies that included self-report measures of the interpersonal and affective traits associated with the psychopathy syndrome (e.g., the Psychopathic Deviate (Pd) subscale of the MMPI and MMPI-2) (Butcher, 1979; Butcher et al., 2001), the Minnesota Temperament Inventory (Taylor et al., 2003), and the Psychopathic Personality Inventory (Lilienfeld & Andrews, 1996) the authors found that a model including only additive genetic and nonshared environmental influences represented the best data fit ($\chi^2 = 45.77, df = 20, p < .001$; AIC = 5.77), with each component acting as a moderate influence ($a^2 = .49, e^2 = .51$).

Taken together, the preceding data provide good evidence for the roles of genetic and nonshared environmental factors in the development of the psychopathy syndrome. Further, these studies have also provided a means for examining the independence of the genetic contribution to each component of the syndrome. For example, Larsson and colleagues (2006) found that additive genetic and nonshared environmental factors were more important to the affective and impulsivity components than to the interpersonal component. Specifically, genetic factors accounted for 22% of the variance in the affective and impulsivity components of psychopathy, but only 1% of the variance in the interpersonal component. Similarly, nonshared environmental factors accounted for a greater proportion of the variance in the affective (45%) and impulsivity (28%) components compared to the interpersonal component (17%).

In their study using the MPQ subscales Fearless Dominance (FD) and Impulsive Antisociality (IA), Blonigen and colleagues (2006) examined the relative contributions of environmental and genetic factors to the separate development of these dimensions. To this end, the authors used data from two time points (ages 17 and 24). The authors partitioned the variance at age 24 into the variance contributed from the first time point (age 17) and the variance unique to this second time point. Thus, they were able to differentiate the influences of genetic and environmental factors on the stable proportion of variance and the genetic and environmental factors influencing the variance associated with change. Consistent with expectations for both dimensions, the stable proportion of variance in the traits was due primarily to additive genetic (FD $a^2 = .25$; IA $a^2 = .23$) rather than nonshared environmental factors (FD $e^2 = .12$; IA $e^2 = .07$); whereas, the proportion of variance associated with change was influenced by nonshared environmental factors (FD $e^2 = .45$; AI $e^2 = .44$) more than by additive genetic factors (FD $a^2 = .17$; IA $a^2 = .26$).

Research focusing on callous-unemotional traits in adolescents and children provides strong evidence for a genetic influence in the development of these traits, with an estimated 40% to 78% of the variation in CU traits attributable to genetic variation (see Viding & McCrory, 2012, for a review). Taken together, these data provide considerable evidence that psychopathy as it has been assessed in the preceding studies includes an additive genetic component. These data have opened new areas of investigation that attempt to characterize the precise nature of this influence. Some lines of investigation appear promising: for example, specificity of father-to-child transmission (Beaver, Rowland, Schwartz, & Nedelec, 2011); dopamine genes theorized to underlie attention-deficit/hyperactivity disorder (Waldman & Gizer, 2006), serotonergic genes associated with aggression and violence (Berman, Kavoussi, & Coccaro, 1997) and impulsivity (Sadeh et al., 2010); the MAOA gene, which is implicated in antisocial behavior, associated with childhood abuse (Tikkanen et al., 2011); and dopamine receptor gene variants associated with fear conditioning (Huertas et al., 2010). Yet, it is still too early to know which of these avenues—if any—will provide the best explanation for the psychopathy syndrome. In the meanwhile, alternative theories of psychopathy continue to flourish.

Treatment of Psychopathy

Historically, the prognosis for psychopathy has been poor, and most individuals in the field considered the syndrome to be relatively untreatable (e.g., Hare & Hart, 1993; Lykken, 1995). In recent years, however, research investigators have begun to look more critically at this issue, with many noting that the claim that psychopathy is "untreatable" may have been overstated. Further, researchers have argued that the potential for significant developments in the treatment of psychopathy exists, particularly as we increase our knowledge of the etiological factors that underlie the syndrome. This is particularly evident among younger samples and when alternative approaches to intervention and prevention are considered (Reidy et al., 2015; Viding & McCrory, 2012).

Ogloff, Wong, and Greenwood (1990) conducted one of the early and most influential treatment studies. They assessed psychopathic individuals' performance in a therapeutic community setting, and they found that these individuals were more likely to experience early discharge from the program, were less motivated, and showed less overall improvement (Ogloff et al., 1990). This study is particularly important because the authors used the early version of the Psychopathy Checklist to classify participants as psychopathic. As a result, in addition to ensuring a homogeneous psychopathic group for comparison purposes, the study is also directly relevant to current practice in the field, where the PCL-R is the clinical standard for assessment.

In a similar study, Rice, Harris, and Cormier (1992) examined psychopathic offenders' performance in an intensive therapeutic community contained within a maximum security prison. The treatment program was geared toward increasing empathy and responsibility for peers, and thus was primarily peer-operated. In a follow-up comparison, the authors compared 146 treated offenders with a matched comparison group of 146 untreated offenders on measures of recidivism. The results were consistent with those of Ogloff et al. (1990), in that psychopathic offenders did not appear to benefit from the therapeutic community program. Other studies provide similar evidence that psychopathic individuals may be resistant to treatment. Compared to nonpsychopathic participants, psychopathic participants in treatment demonstrate poor program adjustment and higher attrition (e.g., Berger, Rotermund, Vieth, & Hohnhorst, 2012; Hobson, Shine, & Roberts, 2000; Richards, Casey, & Lucente, 2003; Ogloff et al., 1990; Olver & Wong, 2009; Rice et al., 1992) and lower levels of therapeutic gain (Chakhssi, de Ruiter, & Berstein, 2010; Hughes, Hogue, Hollin, & Champion, 1997; Roche, Shoss, Pincus, & Ménard, 2011).

Although a number of studies point to the difficulty of treating psychopathy, the results of a meta-analysis conducted by Salekin (2002) suggested more reason for optimism than previously expected. In this analysis, when the proportion of treatment participants who would have been expected to improve without treatment was subtracted from the proportion of treatment participants who were judged to have improved, the mean rate of successful intervention was .62 across 42 treatment studies. There were several important limitations in this study: For example, the PCL-R was used to assess psychopathy in only four of the studies; several of the studies were also conducted in juvenile samples; and only a minority of the studies included aggressive or criminal behavior as one of the outcome variables. Nevertheless, the conclusion is consistent with the following subsequent research.

There are recent studies that suggest a potential for therapeutic gain, particularly among adolescents characterized by high levels of psychopathic traits. For example, Salekin, Tippey, and Allen (2012) found that a program designed to increase motivation, increase positive emotion, and decrease callousness in youth with conduct problems in a secure facility led to a significant decrease in psychopathy scores. Further, this finding held across all three psychopathy trait domains—callous/interpersonal, affective, and impulsivity. Similarly, in another study of children and adolescents, McDonald, Dodson, Rosenfield, and Jouriles (2011) found that an intervention aimed at altering mothers' harsh and inconsistent parenting led to a decrease in psychopathy trait scores in a sample of children experiencing high levels of conduct problems. Caldwell (2011) showed that changes in PCL:YV scores associated with treatment in a secure facility for adolescents were also associated with decreased general and violent reoffending. Finally, in a large study of civil psychiatric patients that included 72 individuals designated as psychopathic, Skeem, Monahan, and Mulvey (2002) found that psychopathy did not moderate the effects of treatment; that is, when reductions in violence were examined, psychopathic patients showed responses to treatment similar to nonpsychopathic patients.

In light of these findings, there are several alternatives. One is to de-emphasize treatments for psychopathic individuals that are geared toward building social skills or empathy, and instead to create behavior modification programs with the goal of reducing harm (i.e., criminal recidivism) caused by these individuals (Harris & Rice, 2006). A second possibility is to expand interventions for children and adolescents with psychopathic traits. Given the possibility that this group may be more likely to exhibit treatment gains, this would be a strategic use of resources. A third alternative is to turn to research on the etiology of psychopathy to devise treatment strategies better suited to the particular deficits demonstrated by this group (Wallace, Schmitt, Vitale, & Newman, 2000).

For example, Newman and colleagues (e.g., Newman, 1998; Wallace et al., 2000) have proposed that psychopathic individuals are characterized by a deficit in response modulation. Specifically, psychopathic individuals are proposed to be deficient in their ability to automatically redirect attention from the primary focus of their goal-directed behavior to the evaluation of secondary stimuli. Wallace and colleagues (2000) have argued that, on the basis of such a deficit, it would be unlikely that simply changing the content of psychopathic thought (e.g., teaching social skills and anger management, as in traditional cognitive therapy) would result in significant improvement in these individuals' behavior. This is because psychopathic individuals would be unable to benefit from changes in their thinking, that they could not subsequently access automatically in key situations, due to their response modulation deficit. Instead, the primary emphasis should be on developing and teaching strategies for compensating for the basic information processing deficit that makes accessing these cognitions so challenging (Wallace et al., 2000). In theory, such an approach would provide a means for psychopathic individuals to benefit more fully from other interventions they receive, thereby helping to "close the gap" in treatment response between individuals with and without psychopathy.

Consistent with the preceding suggestions, Baskin-Sommers, Curtin, and Newman (2015) examined the utility of taking a cognitive remediation approach to the treatment of psychopathy. In a cognitive remediation intervention, the emphasis is on training individuals in the particular cognitive skills—such as paying attention to contextual cues, sustained attention, and working memory—that underlie behavior (Klingberg, 2010; Wykes & van der Gaag, 2001). For example, in healthy adults, Klingberg and colleagues have shown that working memory training not only improves overall working memory capacity but also changes the functioning of dopamine neurotransmission and brain plasticity (McNab et al., 2009). Research examining the effects of cognitive remediation for disorders with known cognitive abnormalities, such as attention-deficit/hyperactivity disorder and schizophrenia, has been promising (Stevenson, Whitmont, Bornholt, Livesey, & Stevenson; 2002).

In their study, Baskin-Sommers, Curtin, and Newman (2015) designed a cognitive intervention that targeted the response modulation deficit associated with psychopathy, and they examined the efficacy of this intervention in a sample of incarcerated, adult male offenders. Participants in the study were 124 substance-dependent inmates who were classified as psychopathic or nonpsychopathic. Following pretesting on a set of tasks that assessed both response modulation–related and unrelated skills, participants were randomly assigned to one of two treatment conditions. In the psychopathy-specific "attention to context" condition, inmates participated in a 1-hour, computer-based training session once a week for 6 weeks that used three tasks targeting the RM deficit. Each task provided the participants with opportunities to practice attending to peripheral or nonsalient cues and noticing changes in contextual information (e.g., rule changes). In the non-psychopathy-specific control condition, participants also completed a 1-hour, computer-based training session once a week. However, in this control condition, the tasks were not selected to address specifically the RM deficit but were focused instead on providing practice in inhibiting behavior and regulating emotion reactions more generally.

Consistent with a cognitive remediation model, after 6 weeks of computerized training, psychopathic individuals in the attention to context (i.e., the psychopathy-specific) training group demonstrated significant improvement not only on the three training tasks but also on the RM-related tasks that had been used at pretesting. Conversely, psychopathic participants in the control condition showed no significant improvement over the course of training on the non-psychopathy-specific training tasks and showed significantly less improvement on the post-training RM tasks than those in the attention to context group.

Although these data represent only the first test of the efficacy of a cognitive remediation approach to psychopathy, given the apparently intractable nature of the deficits and the long-standing pessimism regarding treatability of psychopathy, these results represent a major step forward in the area of psychopathy treatment. Further, this study highlights the value of identifying, developing, and testing mechanism-based intervention, and the substantial potential for addressing psychopathic individuals' disinhibited and costly behavior by identifying and targeting the specific response modulation dysfunctions that characterize the disorder.

Summary and Future Directions

Societies throughout history have recognized the existence of the psychopathic personality. These individuals were distinguished by their fleeting, shallow interpersonal ties, their casual antisociality, and their sometimes explosive violence. Although a reliable classification system was a long time coming, the understanding that these individuals needed to be identified in order to prevent or at least limit their effects on society has also been long-standing. Today little is different. The individual commonly referred to as the "psychopath" is a drain on society's financial and emotional resources; psychopathic individuals commit a disproportionate number of crimes and comprise a significant proportion of our inmate populations.

Clinical descriptions of psychopathy have resulted in the development of reliable and valid measures of the syndrome across different populations. Early, disparate assessments gave way in the 1990s to more unified assessment relying on the PCL-R (Hare, 1991) and conceptually related measures (e.g., the PCL:YV and PCL:SV). More recently, the field has again seen the emergence of greater diversity in psychopathy assessments, as self-report measures such as the PPI (Lilienfeld & Andrews, 1996), the SRPS (Levenson et al., 1995), and the EPA (Miller et al., 2011) have been increasingly used and personality-based models have been emphasized.

Greater unification in the assessment of psychopathy has allowed research on the etiology of the syndrome to flourish and to enhance knowledge of the factors associated with this syndrome. Research has reliably demonstrated that there is a genetic component to the psychopathic personality (e.g., Waldman & Rhee, 2006). Research has also indicated that these individuals exhibit performance deficits that could be explained in terms of dispositional "fearlessness" (e.g., Lykken, 1995) or poor behavioral inhibition (e.g., Fowles & Dindo, 2006), or in terms of abnormalities in the functioning of the amygdala and associated structures (e.g., Blair, 2006). Still other lines of investigation have examined the attention processing of psychopathic individuals and have shown that these individuals appear deficient in their ability to initiate the relatively automatic shift in attention from the ongoing enactment of goal-directed behavior to contextual cues that would indicate that a behavior requires modulation (e.g., Hiatt & Newman, 2006).

Understanding the causal factors that underlie psychopathy may prove invaluable to the prevention and treatment of the syndrome. Currently, limited empirical data exists to suggest that psychopathic individuals will benefit from treatment (e.g., Harris & Rice, 2006). However, this conclusion may be challenged in the future, as interventions are expanded to new populations (i.e., adolescents). As etiological processes begin to inform interventions (e.g., Wallace et al., 2000), we may become better able to address the specific deficits associated with the psychopathy syndrome.

Moving forward in the field, research focused on the existing controversies and currently popular etiological theories will likely continue to dominate. Reliable assessment measures will be developed and applied in a variety of populations in order to reach a better understanding of the nature of the syndrome. We will better understand how the psychobiological processes associated with the characteristics of psychopathy develop into the full-blown syndrome. However, several new areas are also emerging, and they are likely to become increasingly important with the passage of time.

First, on the assessment front, researchers will be trying to determine whether it is best to conceptualize psychopathy as a discrete taxon or as a dimensional construct. Currently, there are competing claims regarding the best way to conceptualize the construct. In practice, this distinction may be made on the basis of anything from practical concerns to theoretical considerations. For example, when the PCL-R is used in clinical risk assessment, the designation "psychopathic" versus "nonpsychopathic" may be required, whereas in a study of the genetic contributions to psychopathy, the syndrome may be conceptualized in a dimensional, traitlike manner. The answer to the question of whether psychopathy is best conceptualized as a discrete category or as an extreme variation on normal personality may depend on whether the emphasis is on the behaviors, the traits, or the underlying psychobiological mechanisms associated with the syndrome (Brinkley et al., 2004).

Second, as a resolution is sought to the category-dimension question, we will likely see the emergence of subtypes of psychopathy. This would not be an altogether new development. Researchers and clinicians have long differentiated the "primary" from the "secondary," or "neurotic," psychopathic individual (e.g., Cleckley, 1941/1988; Karpman, 1941; Lykken, 1957), the latter being characterized by relatively higher levels of neuroticism or anxiety. Further, researchers have already moved forward by proposing and beginning to test the ways in which psychopathy might be usefully divided on the basis of symptom profile, etiological mechanism, or the presence of criminal behavior (e.g., Brinkley et al., 2004; Newman et al., 2005; Olver, Sewall, Sarty, Lewis, & Wong, 2015; Poythress & Skeem, 2006; Yildirim & Derksen, 2015). Such a development is consistent with the practice among other clinical disorders (e.g., schizophrenia), where subtypes representing different symptom profiles, different prognoses, and potentially different underlying psychobiological mechanisms have been differentiated from each other for clinical or research purposes. Although such a development may help to resolve many of the current controversies, it will inevitably lead to the question of whether each subtype can reasonably be considered "psychopathy." This fragmented future is near, as researchers and clinicians are already grappling with the challenge of understanding the complexities of research that has been generated using a variety of assessment measures, emphasizing disparate conceptualizations of the syndrome and applied across a multitude of samples. As consistencies in patterns of results accrue, these differences in assessment and conceptualization will become less problematic. However, in the presence of inconsistency and disagreement, such a diversity of measurement and conceptualization currently make it more difficult to reconcile discrepant findings.

Fortunately, recent research has demonstrated that certain treatments may be beneficial to individuals diagnosed as psychopathic. Among the most effective of these new interventions is cognitive remediation, which derives nicely from the basic evidence on the deficit processes associated with psychopathy. There is potential for the use of technology in applying cognitive remediation to possibly alleviate some of the primary deficiencies of psychopathy, a finding which bodes well for future dissemination of treatment results, provided the current findings are found to be robust.

References

American Psychiatric Association. (1968). *Diagnostic and statistical manual of mental disorders* (2nd ed.). Washington, DC: Author.

American Psychiatric Association. (2013). *Diagnostic and statistical manual of mental disorders* (5th ed.). Washington, DC: Author.

Andershed, H., Hodgins, S., & Tengstrom, A. (2007). Convergent validity of the Youth Psychopathic Traits Inventory (YPI): Association with the Psychopathy Checklist: Youth Version (PCL:YV). *Assessment, 14*, 144–154.

Andershed, H., Kerr, M., Stattin, H., & Levander, S. (2002). Psychopathic traits in non-referred youths: A new assessment tool. In E. Blaauw & L. Sheridan (Eds.), *Psychopaths: Current international perspectives* (pp. 131–158). The Hague, Netherlands: Elsevier.

Anderson, N. E., Stanford, M. S., Wan, L., & Young, K. A. (2011). High psychopathic trait females exhibit reduced startle potentiation and increased P3 amplitude. *Behavioral Sciences & the Law, 29*, 649–666.

Anton, M., Baskin-Sommers, A. R., Vitale, J., Curtin, J. J., & Newman, J. P. (2012). Differential effects of psychopathy and antisocial personality disorder symptoms on cognitive and fear processing in female offenders. *Cognitive, Affective, & Behavioral Neuroscience, 12*(4), 761–776.

Arnett, P. A., Howland, E. W., Smith, S. S., & Newman, J. P. (1993). Autonomic responsivity during passive avoidance in incarcerated psychopaths. *Personality and Individual Differences, 14*, 173–184.

Baskin-Sommers, A. R., Curtin, J. J., & Newman, J. P. (2011). Specifying the attentional selection that moderates the fearlessness of psychopathic offenders. *Psychological Science, 22*, 226–234.

Baskin-Sommers, A. R., Curtin, J. J., & Newman, J. P. (2015). Altering the cognitive-affective dysfunctions of psychopathic and externalizing offender subtypes with cognitive remediation. *Clinical Psychological Science, 3*, 45–57.

Baskin-Sommers, A. R., & Newman, J. P. (2014). Psychopathic and externalizing offenders display dissociable dysfunctions when responding to facial affect. *Personality Disorders: Theory, Research, and Treatment, 5*, 369–379.

Baskin-Sommers, A. R., Newman, J. P., Sathasivam, N., & Curtin, J. J. (2011). Evaluating the generalizability of a fear deficit in psychopathic African American offenders. *Journal of Abnormal Psychology, 120*, 71–78.

Bauer, D. L., Whitman, L. A., & Kosson, D. S. (2011). Reliability and construct validity of Psychopathy Checklist: Youth Version scores among incarcerated adolescent girls. *Criminal Justice and Behavior, 38*, 965–987.

Baxter, M. G., & Murray, E. A. (2002). The amygdala and reward. *Nature Reviews Neuroscience, 3*, 563–573.

Beaver, K. M., Rowland, M. W., Schwartz, J. A., & Nedelec, J. L. (2011). The genetic origins of psychopathic personality traits in adult males and females: Results from an adoption-based study. *Journal of Criminal Justice, 39*, 426–432.

Berger, K., Rotermund, P., Vieth, E. R., & Hohnhorst, A. (2012). The prognostic value of the PCL-R in relation to the SUD treatment ending. *International Journal of Law and Psychiatry, 35*, 198–201.

Berman, M. E., Kavoussi, R. J., & Coccaro, E. F. (1997). Neurotransmitter correlates of human aggression. In D. M. Stoff, J. Breiling, & J. D. Masur (Eds.), *Handbook of antisocial behavior* (pp. 305–313). New York, NY: Wiley.

Beryl, R., Chou, S., & Völlm, B. (2014). A systematic review of psychopathy in women within secure settings. *Personality and Individual Differences, 71*, 185–195.

Bezdjian, S., Raine, A., Baker, L. A., & Lynam, D. R. (2011). Psychopathic personality in children: Genetic and environmental contributions. *Psychological Medicine, 41*, 589–600.

Bishopp, D., & Hare, R. D. (2008). A multidimensional scaling analysis of the Hare PCL-R: Unfolding the structure of psychopathy. *Psychology, Crime & Law, 14*, 117–132.

Bjork, J. M., Chen, G., & Hommer, D. W. (2012). Psychopathic tendencies and mesolimbic recruitment by cues for instrumental and passively obtained rewards. *Biological Psychology, 89*, 408–415.

Blair, K. S., Newman, C., Mitchell, D. G. V., Richell, R. A., Leonard, A., Morton, J., & Blair, R. J. R.

(2006). Differentiating among prefrontal substrates in psychopathy: Neuropsychological findings. *Neuropsychology, 20*, 153–165.

Blair, R. J. R. (2006). Subcortical brain systems in psychopathy: The amygdala and associated structures. In C. Patrick (Ed.), *Handbook of psychopathy* (pp. 296–312). New York, NY: Guilford Press.

Blair, R. J. R., Monson, J., & Frederickson, N. (2001). Moral reasoning and conduct problems in children with emotional and behavioural difficulties. *Personality and Individual Differences, 31*, 799–811.

Blonigen, D. M., Hicks, B. M., Krueger, R. F., Patrick, C. J., & Iacono, W. G. (2006). Continuity and change in psychopathic traits as measured via normal-range personality: A longitudinal-biometric study. *Journal of Abnormal Psychology, 115*, 85–95.

Boccardi, M., Frisoni, G. B., Hare, R. D., Cavedo, E., Najt, P., Pievani, M., ... Tiihonen, J. (2011). Cortex and amygdala morphology in psychopathy. *Psychiatry Research: Neuroimaging, 193*, 85–92.

Brinkley, C. A., Newman, J. P., & Widiger, T. A. (2004). Two approaches to parsing the heterogeneity of psychopathy. *Clinical Psychology: Science and Practice, 11*, 69–94.

Brinkley, C. A., Schmitt, W. A., Smith, S. S., & Newman, J. P. (2001). Construct-validation of a self report psychopathy scale: Does Levenson's SRPS measure the same construct as Hare's PCL-R? *Personality and Individual Differences, 31*, 1021–1038.

Brislin, S. J., Drislane, L. E., Smith, S. T., Edens, J. F., & Patrick, C. J. (2015). Development and validation of triarchic psychopathy scales from the Multidimensional Personality Questionnaire. *Psychological Assessment, 27*, 838–851.

Broerman, R. L., Ross, S. R., & Corr, P. J. (2014). Throwing more light on the dark side of psychopathy: An extension of previous findings for the revised reinforcement sensitivity theory. *Personality and Individual Differences, 68*, 165–169.

Butcher, J. N. (Ed.). (1979). *New developments in the use of the MMPI*. Minneapolis: University of Minnesota Press.

Butcher, J. N., Graham, J. R., Ben-Porath, Y. S., Tellegen, A., Dahlstrom, W. G., & Kaemmer, B. (2001). *Minnesota Multiphasic Personality Inventory–2 (MMPI-2): Manual for administration, scoring, and interpretation* (rev. ed.). Minneapolis: University of Minnesota Press.

Caldwell, M. F. (2011). Treatment-related changes in behavioral outcomes of psychopathy facets in adolescent offenders. *Law and Human Behavior, 35*, 275–287.

Campbell, M. A., Doucette, N. L., & French, S. (2009). Validity and stability of the Youth Psychopathic Traits Inventory in a nonforensic sample of young adults. *Journal of Personality Assessment, 91*, 584–592.

Carter, G. L., Campbell, A. C., Muncer, S., & Carter, K. A. (2015). A Mokken analysis of the Dark Triad "Dirty Dozen": Sex and age differences in scale structures, and issues with individual items. *Personality and Individual Differences, 83*, 185–191.

Cauffman, E., Kimonis, E. R., Dmitrieva, J., & Monahan, K. C. (2009). A multimethod assessment of juvenile psychopathy: Comparing the predictive utility of the PCL:YV, YPI, and the NEO PRI. *Psychological Assessment, 21*, 528–542.

Chakhssi, F., de Ruiter, C., & Berstein, D. (2010). Change during forensic treatment in psychopathic versus nonpsychopathic offenders. *Journal of Forensic Psychiatry & Psychology, 21*, 660–682.

Christian, R. E., Frick, P. J., Hill, N. L., Tyler, A. L., & Frazer, D. (1997). Psychopathy and conduct problems in children: II. Implications for subtyping children with conduct problems. *Journal of the American Academy of Child & Adolescent Psychiatry, 36*, 233–241.

Cleckley, H. (1988). *The Mask of Sanity*. St. Louis, MO: Mosby. (Original work published 1941)

Cohn, M. D., Pape, L. E., Schmaal, L., van den Brink, W., van Wingen, D., Vermeiren, R. R. J. M., ... Popma, A. (2015). Differential relations between juvenile psychopathic traits and resting state network connectivity. *Human Brain Mapping, 36*, 2396–2405.

Colins, O. F., Andershed, H., & Pardini, D. A. (2015). Psychopathic traits as predictors of future criminality, intimate partner aggression, and substance use in young adult men. *Law and Human Behavior, 39*, 547–558.

Cooke, D., & Michie, C. (1999). Psychopathy across cultures: North America and Scotland compared. *Journal of Abnormal Psychology, 108*, 58–68.

Cooke, D. J., Michie, C., & Hart, S. D. (2006). Facets of clinical psychopathy: Towards clearer measurement. In C. Patrick (Ed.), *Handbook of psychopathy* (pp. 91–106). New York, NY: Guilford Press.

Cooke, D. J., Michie, C., Hart, S. D., & Clark, D. (2004). Reconstructing psychopathy: Clarifying the significance of antisocial and socially deviant behavior in the diagnosis of psychopathic personality disorder. *Journal of Personality Disorder*, *18*, 337–357.

Cooke, D. J., Michie, C., Hart, S. D., & Hare, R. D. (1999). Evaluating the Screening Version of the Hare Psychopathy Checklist–Revised: An item response theory analysis. *Psychological Assessment*, *11*, 3–13.

Crysel, L. C., Crosier, B. S., & Webster, G. D. (2013). The Dark Triad and risk behavior. *Personality and Individual Differences*, *54*, 35–40.

Davis, M. (2000). The role of the amygdala in conditioned and unconditioned fear and anxiety. In J. P. Aggleton (Ed.), *The amygdala: A functional analysis* (pp. 289–310). Oxford, England: Oxford University Press.

Dawel, A., McKone, E., O'Kearney, R., Sellbom, M., Irons, J., & Palermo, R. (2015). Elevated levels of callous unemotional traits are associated with reduced attentional cueing, with no specificity for fear or eyes. *Personality Disorders: Theory, Research, and Treatment*, *6*, 216–228.

Decety, J., Skelly, L. R., & Kiehl, K. A. (2013). Brain response to empathy-eliciting scenarios involving pain in incarcerated individuals with psychopathy. *JAMA Psychiatry*, *70*, 638–645.

Derefinko, K. J., & Lynam, D. R. (2007). Using the FFM to conceptualize psychopathy: A test using a drug abusing sample. *Journal of Personality Disorders*, *21*, 638–656.

Dindo, L., & Fowles, D. (2011). Dual temperamental risk factors for psychopathic personality: Evidence from self-report and skin conductance. *Journal of Personality and Social Psychology*, *100*, 557–566.

Douglas, K. S., Ogloff, J. R. P., Nicholls, T. L., & Grant, I. (1999). Assessing risk for violence among psychiatric patients: The HCR-20 violence risk assessment scheme and the Psychopathy Checklist: Screening Version. *Journal of Consulting and Clinical Psychology*, *67*, 917–930.

Edens, J. F. (2006). Unresolved controversies concerning psychopathy: Implications for clinical and forensic decision making. *Professional Psychology: Research and Practice*, *37*, 59–65.

Edens, J. F., Poythress, N. G., Lilienfeld, S. O., & Patrick, C. J. (2008). A prospective comparison of two measures of psychopathy in the prediction of institutional misconduct. *Behavioral Sciences & the Law*, *26*, 529–541.

Edens, J. F., Poythress, N. G., Lilienfeld, S. O., Patrick, C. J., & Test, A. (2008). Further evidence of the divergent correlates of the Psychopathic Personality Inventory factors: Prediction of institutional misconduct among male prisoners. *Psychological Assessment*, *20*, 86–91.

Edens, J. F., Poythress, N. G., & Watkins, M. M. (2001). Further validation of the Psychopathic Personality Inventory among offenders: Personality and behavioral correlates. *Journal of Personality Disorders*, *15*, 403–415.

Edens, J. F., Skeem, J. L., Cruise, K. R., & Cauffman, E. (2001). Assessment of "juvenile psychopathy" and its association with violence: A critical review. *Behavioral Sciences & the Law*, *19*, 53–80.

Eriksen, B. A., & Eriksen, C. W. (1974). Effects of noise letters upon the identification of a target letter in a nonsearch task. *Perception & Psychophysics*, *16*, 143–149.

Ermer, E., Cope, L. M., Nyalakanti, P. K., Calhoun, V. D., & Kiehl, K. A. (2012). Aberrant paralimbic gray matter in criminal psychopathy. *Journal of Abnormal Psychology*, *121*, 649–658.

Finger, E. A., Marsh, A. A., Blaire, K. S., Reid, M. E., Sims, C., Ng, P., … Blaire, R. J. (2011). Disrupted reinforcement signaling in the orbitofrontal cortex and caudate in youths with conduct disorder or oppositional defiant disorder and a high level of psychopathic traits. *American Journal of Psychiatry*, *168*, 152–162.

Forth, A. E., Brown, S. L., Hart, S. D., & Hare, R. D. (1996). The assessment of psychopathy in male and female noncriminals: Reliability and validity. *Personality and Individual Differences*, *20*, 531–543.

Forth, A. E., Kosson, D. S., & Hare, R. D. (2003). *The Psychopathy Checklist: Youth Version*. Toronto, ON: Multi-Health Systems.

Fowles, D. C. (1980). The three-arousal model: Implications of Gray's two-factor learning theory for heart rate, electrodermal activity, and psychopathy. *Psychophysiology*, *17*, 87–104.

Fowles, D. C., & Dindo, L. (2006). A dual-deficit model of psychopathy. In C. Patrick (Ed.), *Handbook of psychopathy* (pp. 14–34). New York, NY: Guilford Press.

Frick, P. J. (1998). Conduct disorders. In T. H. Ollendick & M. Hersen (Eds.), *Handbook of child psychopathology* (3rd ed., pp. 213–237). New York, NY: Plenum Press.

Frick, P. J., & Hare, R. D. (2001). *The Antisocial Process Screening Device*. Toronto, ON: Multi-Health Systems.

Fulero, S. M. (1995). Review of the Hare Psychopathy Checklist–Revised. In J. C. Conoley & J. C. Impara (Eds.), *Twelfth mental measurements yearbook* (pp. 453–454). Lincoln, NE: Buros Institute.

Fung, A. L., Gao, Y., & Raine, A. (2010). The utility of the child and adolescent psychopathy construct in Hong Kong, China. *Journal of Clinical Child & Adolescent Psychology, 39*, 134–140.

Furnham, A., Richards, S. C., & Paulhus, D. L. (2013). The dark triad of personality: A 10 year review. *Social and Personality Psychology Compass, 7*, 199–216.

Gernsbacher, M. A., & Faust, M. E. (1991). The mechanism of suppression: A component of general comprehension skill. *Journal of Experimental Psychology: Learning, Memory, and Cognition, 17*, 245–262.

Glenn, A. L., Raine, A., & Schug, R. A. (2009). The neural correlates of moral decision-making in psychopathy. *Molecular Psychiatry, 14*, 5–6.

Glenn, A. L., & Sellbom, M. (2015). Theoretical and empirical concerns regarding the Dark Triad as a construct. *Journal of Personality Disorders, 29*, 360–377.

Gorenstein, E. E., & Newman, J. P. (1980). Disinhibitory psychopathology: A new perspective and a model for research. *Psychological Review, 87*, 301–315.

Gray, J. A., & McNaughton, N. (2000). *The neuropsychology of anxiety* (2nd ed.). Oxford, England: Oxford University Press.

Gretton, H. M., Hare, R. D., & Catchpole, R. E. H. (2004). Psychopathy and offending from adolescence to adulthood: A 10-year follow-up. *Journal of Consulting and Clinical Psychology, 72*, 636–645.

Hamilton, R. K. B., Hiatt Racer, K., & Newman, J. P. (2015). Impaired integration in psychopathy: A unified theory of psychopathic dysfunction. *Psychological Review, 122*, 770–791.

Hansen, A. L., Johnsen, B. H., Thornton, D., Waage, L., & Thayer, J. F. (2007). Facets of psychopathy, heart rate variability and cognitive function. *Journal of Personality Disorders, 21*, 568–582.

Hare, R. D. (1980). A research scale for the assessment of psychopathy in criminal populations. *Personality and Individual Differences, 1*, 111–119.

Hare, R. D. (1991). *Manual for the Hare Psychopathy Checklist–Revised*. Toronto, ON: Multi-Health Systems.

Hare, R. D. (1996). Psychopathy: A clinical construct whose time has come. *Criminal Justice and Behavior, 23*, 25–54.

Hare, R. D. (1998). Psychopaths and their nature: Implications for the mental health and criminal justice systems. In T. Millon, E. Simonsen, M. Birket-Smith, & R. Davis (Eds.), *Psychopathy: Antisocial, criminal, and violent behavior* (pp. 188–212). New York, NY: Guilford Press.

Hare, R. D. (2003). *Manual for the Hare Psychopathy Checklist–Revised* (2nd ed.). Toronto, ON: Multi-Health Systems.

Hare, R. D., Frazelle, J., & Cox, D. N. (1978). Psychopathy and physiological responses to threat of an aversive stimulus. *Psychophysiology, 15*, 165–172.

Hare, R. D., Harpur, T. J., & Hemphill, J. D. (1989). *Scoring pamphlet for the Self-Report Psychopathy scale: SRP-II*. Unpublished manuscript, Simon Fraser University, Vancouver, BC.

Hare, R. D., & Hart, S. D. (1993). Psychopathy, mental disorder, and crime. In S. Hodgins (Ed.), *Mental disorder and crime* (pp. 104–115). Newbury Park, CA: Sage.

Hare, R. D., & Jutai, J. W. (1988). Psychopathy and cerebral asymmetry in semantic processing. *Personality and Individual Differences, 9*, 329–337.

Harpur, T. J., Hakstian, A. R., & Hare, R. D. (1988). Factor structure of the Psychopathy Checklist. *Journal of Consulting and Clinical Psychology, 56*, 741–747.

Harris, G. T., & Rice, M. E. (2006). Treatment of psychopathy: A review of empirical findings. In C. Patrick (Ed.), *Handbook of psychopathy* (pp. 555–572). New York, NY: Guilford Press.

Hemphill, J. F., Templeman, R., Wong, S., & Hare, R. D. (1998). Psychopathy and crime: Recidivism and criminal careers. In D. J. Cooke, A. E. Forth, & R. D. Hare (Eds.), *Psychopathy: Theory, research and implications for society* (pp. 375–399). Boston, MA: Kluwer Academic.

Herve, H., Mitchell, D., & Cooper, B. S. (2004). Psychopathy and unlawful confinement: An examination of perpetrator and event characteristics. *Canadian Journal of Behavioural Science, 36*, 137–145.

Hiatt, K. D., & Newman, J. P. (2006). Understanding psychopathy: The cognitive side. In C. Patrick (Ed.),

Handbook of psychopathy (pp. 334–352). New York, NY: Guilford Press.

Hiatt, K. D., Schmitt, W. A., & Newman, J. P. (2004). Stroop tasks reveal abnormal selective attention among psychopathic offenders. *Neuropsychology*, *18*, 50–59.

Hicks, B. M., Markon, K. E., Patrick, C. J., Krueger, R. F., & Newman, J. P. (2004). Identifying psychopathy subtypes on the basis of personality structure. *Psychological Assessment*, *16*, 276–288.

Hill, C. D., Neumann, C. S., & Rogers, R. (2004). Confirmatory factor analysis of the Psychopathy Checklist: Screening Version in offenders with Axis I disorders. *Psychological Assessment*, *16*, 90–95.

Hobson, J., Shine, J., & Roberts, R. (2000). How do psychopaths behave in a prison therapeutic community? *Psychology, Crime & Law*, *6*, 139–154.

Huertas, E., Ponce, G., Koeneke, M. A., Poch, C., España-Serrano, L., Palomo, T., … Hoenicka, J. (2010). The D2 dopamine receptor gene variant C957T affects human fear conditioning and aversive priming. *Genes, Brain, & Behavior*, *9*, 103–109.

Hughes, G., Hogue, T., Hollin, C., & Champion, H. (1997). First stage evaluation of a treatment programme for personality disordered offenders. *Journal of Forensic Psychiatry*, *8*, 515–527.

Isen, J., Raine, A., Baker, L., Dawson, M., Bezdjian, S., & Lozano, D. I. (2010). Sex-specific association between psychopathic traits and electrodermal reactivity in children. *Journal of Abnormal Psychology*, *119*, 216–225.

Jonason, P. K., Duineveld, J. J., & Middleton, J. P. (2015). Pathology, pseudopathology, and the Dark Triad of personality. *Personality and Individual Differences*, *78*, 43–47.

Jones, A. P., Laurens, K. R., Herba, C. M., Barker, G. J., & Viding, E. (2009). Amygdala hyporeactivity to fearful faces in boys with conduct problems and callous-unemotional traits. *American Journal of Psychiatry*, *166*, 95–102.

Jones, D. N., & Neria, A. L. (2015). The Dark Triad and dispositional aggression. *Personality and Individual Differences*, *86*, 360–364.

Karpman, B. (1941). On the need of separating psychopathy into two distinct clinical types: The symptomatic and the idiopathic. *Journal of Criminal Psychopathology*, *3*, 112–137.

Kosson, D. S., Cyterski, T. D., Steuerwald, B. L., Neumann, C. S., & Walker-Matthews, S. (2002). The reliability and validity of the Psychopathy Checklist:

Youth Version (PCL: YV) in nonincarcerated adolescent males. *Psychological Assessment*, *14*, 97–109.

Kosson, D. S., Smith, S. S., & Newman, J. P. (1990). Evaluating the construct validity of psychopathy in black and white male inmates: Three preliminary studies. *Journal of Abnormal Psychology*, *99*, 250–259.

Klingberg, T. (2010). Training and plasticity of working memory. *Trends in Cognitive Sciences*, *14*, 317–324.

Lake, A. J., Baskin-Sommers, A. R., Li, W., Curtin, J. J., & Newman, J. P. (2011). Evidence for unique threat-processing mechanisms in psychopathic and anxious individuals. *Cognitive, Affective, & Behavioral Neuroscience*, *11*, 451–462.

LaPierre, D., Braun, C. M. J., & Hodgins, S. (1995). Ventral frontal deficits in psychopathy: Neuropsychological test findings. *Neuropsychologia*, *33*, 139–151.

Larsson, H., Andershed, H., & Lichtenstein, P. (2006). A genetic factor explains most of the variation in psychopathic personality. *Journal of Abnormal Psychology*, *115*, 221–230.

Lehman, A., & Ittel, A. (2012). Aggressive behavior and measurement of psychopathy in female inmates of German prisons—a preliminary study. *International Journal of Law and Psychiatry*, *35*, 190–197.

Levenson, M. R., Kiehl, K. A., & Fitzpatrick, C. M. (1995). Assessing psychopathic attributes in a noninstitutionalized population. *Journal of Personality and Social Psychology*, *68*, 151–158.

Levenston, G. K., Patrick, C. J., Bradley, M. M., & Lang, P. J. (2000). The psychopath as observer: Emotion and attention in picture processing. *Journal of Abnormal Psychology*, *109*, 373–389.

Lewis, A. (1974). Psychopathic personality: A most elusive category. *Psychological Medicine*, *4*, 133–140.

Lilienfeld, S. O. (1994). Conceptual problems in the assessment of psychopathy. *Clinical Psychology Review*, *14*, 17–38.

Lilienfeld, S. O. (2006). The self-report assessment of psychopathy. In C. Patrick (Ed.), *Handbook of psychopathy* (pp. 107–132). New York, NY: Guilford Press.

Lilienfeld, S. O., & Andrews, B. P. (1996) Development and preliminary validation of a self-report measure of psychopathic personality traits in noncriminal populations. *Journal of Personality Assessment*, *66*, 488–524.

Lopez-Romero, L., Romero, E., & Villar, P. (2014). Assessing the stability of psychopathic traits:

Adolescent outcomes in a six-year follow-up. *Spanish Journal of Psychology, 17,* E97.

Ly, M., Motzkin, J. C., Philippi, C. L., Kirk, G. R., Newman, J. P., Kiehl, K. A., & Koenigs, M. (2012). Cortical thinning in psychopathy. *American Journal of Psychiatry, 169,* 743–749.

Lykken, D. T. (1957). A study of anxiety in the sociopathic personality. *Journal of Abnormal Psychology, 55,* 6–10.

Lykken, D. T. (1995). *The antisocial personalities.* Hillsdale, NJ: Erlbaum.

Lynam, D. R. (1996). Early identification of chronic offenders: Who is the fledgling psychopath? *Psychological Bulletin, 120,* 209–234.

Lynam, D. R., Charnigo, R., Moffitt, T. E., Raine, A., Loeber, R., & Stouthamer-Loeber, M. (2009). The stability of psychopathy across adolescence. *Development and Psychopathology, 21,* 1133–1153.

Lynam D. R., & Derefinko, K. J. (2006). Psychopathy and personality. In C. Patrick (Ed.), *Handbook of psychopathy* (pp. 133–155). New York, NY: Guilford Press.

Lynam, D. R., Gaughan, E. R., Miller, J. D., Miller, D. J., Mullins-Sweatt, S., & Widiger, T. A. (2011). Assessing the basic traits associated with psychopathy: Development and validation of the Elemental Psychopathy Assessment. *Psychological Assessment, 23,* 108–124.

Lynam, D. R., Whiteside, S., & Jones, S. (1999). Self-reported psychopathy: A validation study. *Journal of Personality Assessment, 73,* 110–132.

Lynam, D. R., & Widiger, T. A. (2001). Using the five factor model to represent the DSM-IV personality disorders: An expert consensus approach. *Journal of Abnormal Psychology, 110,* 401–412.

MacCoon, D., Wallace, J. F., & Newman, J. P. (2004). Self-regulation: Context-appropriate balanced attention. In R. F. Baumeister & K. D. Vohs (Eds.), *Handbook of self-regulation research* (pp. 422–444). New York, NY: Guilford Press.

Manke, B., McGuire, S., Reiss, D., Hetherington, E. M., & Plomin, R. (1995). Genetic contributions to adolescents' extrafamilial social interactions: Teachers, best friends, and peers. *Social Development, 4,* 238–256.

Marsh, A. A., Finger, E. C., Fowler, K. A., Jurkowitz, I. T. N., Schechter, J. C., Yu, H. H., … Blaire, R. J. R. (2011). Reduced amygdala-orbitofrontal connectivity during moral judgments in youths with disruptive behavior disorders and psychopathic traits. *Psychiatry Research: Neuroimaging, 194,* 279–286.

Marsh, A. A., Finger, E. C., Mitchell, D. G. V., Reid, M. E., Sims, C., Kosson, D. S., … Blaire, R. J. R. (2008). Reduced amygdala response to fearful expressions in children and adolescents with callous-unemotional traits and disruptive behavior disorders. *American Journal of Psychiatry, 165,* 712–720.

Maslow, A. H. (1951). *Principles of abnormal psychology: The dynamics of psychic illness.* New York, NY: Harper.

McCord, W., & McCord, J. (1964). *The psychopath: An essay on the criminal mind.* New York, NY: Van Nostrand.

McDonald, R., Dodson, M. C., Rosenfield, D., & Jouriles, E. N. (2011). Effects of parenting intervention on features of psychopathy in children. *Journal of Abnormal Child Psychology, 39,* 1013–1023.

McNab, F., Varrone, A., Jucaite, A., Bystritsky, P., Forssberg, H., & Klingberg, T. (2009). Change in cortical dopamine D1 receptor binding associated with cognitive training. *Science, 323,* 800–802.

Miller, J. D., Gaughan, E. T., Maples, J., Gentile, B., Lynam, D. R., & Widiger, T. A. (2011). Examining the construct validity of the Elemental Psychopathy Assessment. *Assessment, 18,* 106–114.

Miller, J. D., & Lynam, D. R. (2003). Psychopathy and the five factor model of personality: A replication and extension. *Journal of Personality Assessment, 81,* 168–178.

Miller, J. D., & Lynam, D. R. (2015). Understanding psychopathy using the basic elements of personality. *Social and Personality Psychology Compass, 9,* 223–237.

Miller, J. D., Lynam, D. R., Widiger, T. A., & Leukefeld, C. (2001). Personality disorders as extreme variants of common personality dimensions: Can the five factor model adequately represent psychopathy? *Journal of Personality, 69,* 253–276.

Miller, J. D., Maples-Keller, J. L., & Lynam, D. R. (2015). An examination of the three components of the Psychopathic Personality Inventory: Profile comparisons and tests of moderation. *Psychological Assessment.* Advance online publication. doi: 10.1037/pas0000221

Miller, J. D., Watts, A., & Jones, S. E. (2011). Does psychopathy manifest divergent relations with components of its nomological network depending on gender? *Personality and Individual Differences, 50,* 564–569.

Millon, T. (1981). *Disorders of personality: DSM-III, Axis II.* New York, NY: Wiley.

Mitchell, D. G. V., Colledge, E., Leonard, A., & Blair, R. J. R. (2002). Risky decisions and response reversal: Is there evidence of orbito-frontal cortex dysfunction in psychopathic individuals? *Neuropsychologia, 40,* 2013–2022.

Motzkin, J. C., Newman, J. P., Kiehl, K. A., & Koenigs, M. (2011). Reduced prefrontal connectivity in psychopathy. *Journal of Neuroscience, 31,* 17348–17357.

Munoz, L. C., & Frick, P. J. (2007). The reliability, stability, and predictive validity of the self-report version of the Antisocial Process Screening Device. *Scandinavian Journal of Psychology, 48,* 299–312.

Munro, G. E. S., Dywan, J., Hais, G. T., McKee, S., Unsal, A., & Segalowitz, S. J. (2007). ERN varies with degree of psychopathy in an emotion discrimination task. *Biological Psychology, 76,* 31–42.

Neal, T. M. S., & Sellbom, A. (2012). Examining the factor structure of the Hare Self-Report Psychopathy Scale. *Journal of Personality Assessment, 94,* 244–253.

Neumann, C. S., Hare, R. D., & Newman, J. P. (2007). The super-ordinate nature of psychopathy. *Journal of Personality Disorders, 21,* 102–117.

Neumann, C. S., Wampler, M., Taylor, J., Blonigen, D. M., & Iacono, W. G. (2011). Stability and invariance of psychopathic traits from late adolescence to young adulthood. *Journal of Research in Personality, 45,* 145–152.

Newman, J. P. (1998). Psychopathic behavior: An information processing perspective. In D. J. Cooke, A. E. Forth, & R. D. Hare (Eds.), *Psychopathy: Theory, research and implications for society* (pp. 81–104). Boston, MA: Kluwer Academic.

Newman, J. P., & Baskin-Sommers, A. R. (2011). Early selective attention abnormalities in psychopathy: Implications for self-regulation. In M. Posner (Ed.), *Cognitive neuroscience of attention* (pp. 421–440). New York, NY: Guilford Press.

Newman, J. P., Curtin, J. J., Bertsch, J. D., & Baskin-Sommers, A. R. (2010). Attention moderates the fearlessness of psychopathic offenders. *Biological Psychiatry, 67,* 66–70.

Newman, J. P., & Kosson, D. S. (1986). Passive avoidance learning in psychopathic and nonpsychopathic offenders. *Journal of Abnormal Psychology, 96,* 257–263.

Newman, J. P., MacCoon, D. G., Vaughn, L. J., & Sadeh, N. (2005). Validating a distinction between primary and secondary psychopathy with measures of Gray's BIS and BAS constructs. *Journal of Abnormal Psychology, 114,* 319–323.

Newman, J. P., Patterson, C. M., Howland, E. W., & Nichols, S. L. (1990). Passive avoidance in psychopaths: The effects of reward. *Personality and Individual Differences, 11,* 1101–1114.

Newman, J. P., Patterson, C. M., & Kosson, D. S. (1987). Response perseveration in psychopaths. *Journal of Abnormal Psychology, 96,* 145–148.

Newman, J. P., & Schmitt, W. A. (1998). Passive avoidance in psychopathic offenders: A replication and extension. *Journal of Abnormal Psychology, 107,* 527–532.

Newman, J. P., Schmitt, W. A., & Voss, W. (1997). Processing of contextual cues in psychopathic and nonpsychopathic offenders. *Journal of Abnormal Psychology, 106,* 563–575.

O'Brien, B. S., & Frick, P. J. (1996). Reward dominance: Associations with anxiety, conduct problems, and psychopathy in children. *Journal of Abnormal Child Psychology, 24,* 223–240.

Ogloff, J. R., Wong, S., & Greenwood, A. (1990). Treating criminal psychopaths in a therapeutic community program. *Behavioral Sciences & the Law, 8,* 181–190.

Olver, M. E., Sewall, L. A., Sarty, G. E., Lewis, K., & Wong, S. C. P. (2015). A cluster analytic examination and external validation of psychopathic offender subtypes in a multisite sample of Canadian federal offenders. *Journal of Abnormal Psychology, 124,* 355–371.

Olver, M. E., & Wong, S. C. P. (2009). Therapeutic responses of psychopathic sexual offenders: Treatment attrition, therapeutic change, and long-term recidivism. *Journal of Consulting and Clinical Psychology, 77,* 328–336.

Olver, M. E., & Wong, S. C. P. (2015). Short- and long-term recidivism prediction of the PCL-R and the effects of age: A 24-year follow-up. *Personality Disorders: Theory, Research, and Treatment, 6,* 97–105.

Oshukova, S., Kaltiala-Heino, R., Miettunen, K., Marttila, R., Tani, P., Aronen, E. T., … Lindberg, N. (2015). Self-reported psychopathic traits among non-referred Finnish adolescents: Psychometric properties of the Youth Psychopathic Traits Inventory and the Antisocial Process Screening Device. *Child and Adolescent Psychiatry and Mental Health, 9,* 15.

Patrick, C. J., Bradley, M. M., & Lang, P. J. (1993). Emotion in the criminal psychopath: Startle reflex modulation. *Journal of Abnormal Psychology, 102,* 82–92.

Patrick, C. J., Fowles, D. C., & Krueger, R. F. (2009). Triarchic conceptualization of psychopathy: Developmental origins of disinhibition, boldness, and meanness. *Development and Psychopathology, 21,* 913–938.

Paulhus, D. L., & Williams, K. M. (2002). The dark triad of personality: Narcissism, Machiavellianism, and psychopathy. *Journal of Research in Personality, 36,* 556–563.

Pechorro, P. S., Poiares, C. A., Vieira, R. X., Maroco, J., Nunes, C., & de Jesus, S. N. (2014). Psychological and behavioral adjustment in female youths with high or low psychopathic traits. *International Journal of Law and Psychiatry, 37,* 619–627.

Philippi, C. L., Pujara, M. S., Motzkin, J. C., Newman, J., Kiehl, K. A., & Koenigs, M. (2015). Altered resting-state functional connectivity in cortical networks in psychopathy. *Journal of Neuroscience, 35,* 6068–6078.

Pinel, P. (1806). *A treatise on insanity* (D. Davis, Trans.). New York, NY: Hafner.

Prichard, J. C. (1835). *A treatise on insanity.* London, England: Sherwood, Gilbert, & Piper.

Poythress, N. G., Edens, J. F., & Lilienfeld, S. O. (1998). Criterion-related validity of the Psychopathic Personality Inventory in a prison sample. *Psychological Assessment, 10,* 426–430.

Poythress, N. G., & Skeem, J. L. (2006). Disaggregating psychopathy: Where and how to look for subtypes. In C. Patrick (Ed.), *Handbook of psychopathy* (pp. 172–192). New York, NY: Guilford Press.

Reidy, D. E., Kearns, M. C., DeGue, S., Lilienfeld, S. O., Massetti, G., & Kiehl, K. A. (2015). Why psychopathy matters: Implications for public health and violence prevention. *Aggression and Violent Behavior, 24,* 214–225.

Richards, H. J., Casey, J. O., & Lucente, S. W. (2003). Psychopathy and treatment response in incarcerated female substance abusers. *Criminal Justice and Behavior, 30,* 251–276.

Rice, M. E., Harris, G. T., & Cormier, C. (1992). A follow-up of rapists assessed in a maximum security psychiatric facility. *Journal of Interpersonal Violence, 5,* 435–448.

Roche, M. J., Shoss, N. E., Pincus, A. L., & Ménard, K. S. (2011). Psychopathy moderates the relationship between time in treatment and levels of empathy in incarcerated male sexual offenders. *Sexual*

Abuse: A Journal of Research and Treatment, 23, 171–192.

Ross, S. R., Molto, J., Poy, R., Segarra, P., Pastor, M. C., & Montanes, S. (2007). Gray's model and psychopathy: BIS but not BAS differentiates secondary psychopathy in noninstitutionalized young adults. *Personality and Individual Differences, 43,* 1644–1655.

Rothemund, Y., Ziegler, S., Hermann, C., Gruesser, S. M., Foell, J., Patrick, C. J., & Flor, H. (2012). Fear conditioning in psychopaths: Event-related potentials and peripheral measures. *Biological Psychology, 90,* 50–59.

Ručević, S. (2010). Psychopathic personality traits and delinquent and risky sexual behaviors in Croatian sample of non-referred boys and girls. *Law and Human Behavior, 34,* 379–391.

Rush, B. (1812). *Medical inquiries and observations, upon the diseases of the mind.* Philadelphia, PA: Kimber and Richardson.

Sadeh, N., Javdani, S., Jackson, J. J., Reynolds, E. K., Potenza, M. N., Gelernter, J., … Verona, E. (2010). Serotonin transporter gene associations with psychopathic traits in youth vary as a function of socioeconomic resources. *Journal of Abnormal Psychology, 119,* 604–609.

Salekin, R. T. (2002). Psychopathy and therapeutic pessimisms: Clinical lore or clinical reality? *Clinical Psychology Review, 22,* 79–112.

Salekin, R. T., Rogers, R., & Sewell, K. W. (1997). Construct validity of psychopathy in a female offender sample: A multitrait-multimethod evaluation. *Journal of Abnormal Psychology, 106,* 576–585.

Salekin, R. T., Rogers, R., Ustad, K. L., & Sewell, K. W. (1998). Psychopathy and recidivism among female inmates. *Law and Human Behavior, 22,* 109–128.

Salekin, R. T., Tippey, J. G., & Allen, A. D. (2012). Treatment of conduct problem youth with interpersonal callous traits using mental models: Measurement of risk and change. *Behavioral Sciences & the Law, 30,* 470–486.

Sandoval, A. R., Hancock, D., Poythress, N., Edens, J., & Lilienfeld, S. (2000). Construct validity of the Psychopathic Personality Inventory in a correctional sample. *Journal of Personality Assessment, 74,* 262–281.

Seara-Cardoso, A., Viding, E., Lickley, R. A., & Sebastian, C. L. (2015). Neural responses to others' pain vary with psychopathic traits in healthy adult males. *Cognitive, Affective, & Behavioral Neuroscience, 15*, 578–588.

Sebastian, C. L., McCrory, E. J. P., Cecil, C. A. M., Lockwood, P. L., De Brito, S. A., Fontaine, N. M. G., & Viding, E. (2012). Neural responses to affective and cognitive theory of mind in children with conduct problems and varying levels of callous-unemotional traits. *JAMA Psychiatry, 69*, 814–822.

Sellbom, M. (2011). Elaborating on the construct validity of the Levenson Self-Report Psychopathy Scale in incarcerated and non-incarcerated samples. *Law and Human Behavior, 35*, 440–451.

Sellbom, M., Cook, D. J., & Hart, S. D. (2015). Construct validity of the Comprehensive Assessment of Psychopathic Personality (CAPP) concept map: Getting closer to the core of psychopathy. *International Journal of Forensic Mental Health, 14*, 172–180.

Sellbom, M., Wygant, D. B., & Drislane, L. E. (2015). Elucidating the construct validity of the psychopathic personality inventory triarchic scales. *Journal of Personality Assessment, 97*, 374–381.

Sethi, A., Gregory, S., Dell'Acqua, F., Thomas, E. P., Simmons, A., Murphy, D. G. M., ... Craig, M. C. (2015). Emotional detachment in psychopathy: Involvement of dorsal default-mode connections. *Cortex, 62*, 11–19.

Shepherd, S. M., & Strand, S. (2015). The utility of the Psychopathy Checklist: Youth Version (PCL:YV) and the Youth Psychopathic Trait Inventory (YPI)—is it meaningful to measure psychopathy in young offenders? *Psychological Assessment*. Advance online publication. doi: 10.1037/pas0000182

Skeem, J. L., & Cauffman, E. (2003). Views of the downward extension: Comparing the youth version of the Psychopathy Checklist with the Youth Psychopathic Traits Inventory. *Behavioral Sciences & the Law, 21*, 737–770.

Skeem, J. L., Monahan, J., & Mulvey, E. P. (2002). Psychopathy, treatment involvement, and subsequent violence among civil psychiatric patients. *Law and Human Behavior, 26*, 577–603.

Skeem, J. L., & Mulvey, E. P. (2001). Psychopathy and community violence among civil psychiatric patients: Results from the MacArthur Violence Risk Assessment Study. *Journal of Consulting and Clinical Psychology, 69*, 358–374.

Skeem, J. L., Polaschek, D. L. L., Patrick, C. J., & Lilienfeld, S. O. (2011). Psychopathic personality: Bridging the gap between scientific evidence and public policy. *Psychological Science in the Public Interest, 12*, 95–162.

Somma, A., Borroni, S., Drislane, L. E., & Fossati, A. (2015). Assessing the triarchic model of psychopathy in adolescence: Reliability and validity of the Triarchic Psychopathy Measure (TriPM) in three samples of Italian community-dwelling adolescents. *Psychological Assessment*. Advance online publication. doi: 10.1037/pas0000184

Stevenson, C. S., Whitmont, S., Bornholt, L., Livesey, D., & Stevenson, R. J. (2002). A cognitive remediation programme for adults with attention deficit hyperactivity disorder. *Australian and New Zealand Journal of Psychiatry, 36*, 610–616.

Sullivan, E. A., & Kosson, D. S. (2006). Ethnic and cultural variations in psychopathy. In C. Patrick (Ed.), *Handbook of psychopathy* (pp. 437–458). New York, NY: Guilford Press.

Sutton, S. K., Vitale, J. E., & Newman, J. P. (2002). Emotion among females with psychopathy during picture presentation. *Journal of Abnormal Psychology, 111*, 610–619.

Taylor, J., Loney, B. R., Bobadilla, L. Iacono, W. G., & McGue, M. (2003). Genetic and environmental influences on psychopathy trait dimensions in a community sample of male twins. *Journal of Abnormal Child Psychology, 31*, 633–645.

Tellegen, A. (2000). *Manual for the Multidimensional Personality Questionnaire*. Minneapolis: University of Minnesota Press.

Tew, J., Harkins, L., & Dixon, L. (2015). Assessing the reliability and validity of the Self-Report Psychopathy Scales in a UK offender population. *Journal of Forensic Psychiatry & Psychology, 26*, 166–184.

Thornquist, M. H., & Zuckerman, M. (1995). Psychopathy, passive avoidance learning, and basic dimensions of personality. *Personality and Individual Differences, 19*, 525–534.

Tikkanen, R., Auvinen-Lintunen, L., Ducci, F., Sjöberg, R. L., Goldman, D., Tiihonen, J., ... Virkkunen, M. (2011). Psychopathy, PCL-R, and MAOA genotype as predictors of violent reconvictions. *Psychiatry Research, 185*, 382–386.

Tsang, S., Piquero, A. R., & Cauffman, E. (2014). An examination of the Psychopathy Checklist: Youth Version (PCL:YV) among male adolescent offenders: An item response theory analysis. *Psychological Assessment, 26*, 1333–1346.

Tsang, S., Schmidt, K. M., Vincent, G. M., Salekin, R. T., Moretti, M. M., & Odgers, C. L. (2015). Assessing psychopathy among justice involved adolescents with the PCL:YV: An item response theory examination across gender. *Personality Disorders: Theory, Research, and Treatment, 6*, 22–31.

Vachon, D. D., Lynam, D. R., Loeber, R., & Stouthamer-Loeber, M. (2012). Generalizing the nomological network of psychopathy across populations differing on race and conviction status. *Journal of Abnormal Psychology, 121*, 263–269.

Vaidyanathan, U., Hall, J. R., Patrick, C. J., & Bernat, E. M. (2011). Clarifying the role of defensive reactivity deficits in psychopathy and antisocial personality using startle reflex methodology. *Journal of Abnormal Psychology, 120*, 253–258.

van Baardewijk, Y., Vermeiren, R., Stegge, H., & Doreleijers, T. (2011). Self-reported psychopathic traits in children: Their stability and concurrent and prospective association with conduct problems and aggression. *Journal of Psychopathology and Behavioral Assessment, 33*, 235–245.

Veit, R., Flor, H., Erb, M., Hermann, C., Lotze, M., Grodd, W., & Birbaumer, N. (2002). Brain circuits involved in emotional learning in antisocial behavior and social phobia in humans. *Neuroscience Letters, 328*, 233–236.

Verona, E., Sprague, J., & Sadeh, N. (2012). Inhibitory control and negative emotion processing in psychopathy and antisocial personality disorder. *Journal of Abnormal Psychology, 121*, 498–510.

Verona, E., & Vitale, J. E. (2005). Psychopathy in women: Assessment, manifestations, and etiology. In C. Patrick (Ed.), *Handbook of psychopathy* (pp. 415–436). New York, NY: Guilford Press.

Viding, E., & McCrory, E. J. (2012). Genetic and neurocognitive contributions to the development of psychopathy. *Development and Psychopathology, 24*, 969–983.

Vieira, J. B., Ferreira-Santos, F., Almeida, P. R., Barbosa, F., Marques-Teixeira, J., & Marsh, A. A. (2015). Psychopathic traits are associated with cortical and subcortical volume alterations in healthy individuals. *Social Cognitive and Affective Neuroscience, 10*, 1693–1704.

Vitale, J. E., Hiatt, K. D., Brinkley, C. A., & Newman, J. P. (2007). Abnormal selective attention in psychopathic female offenders. *Neuropsychology, 21*, 301–312.

Vitale, J. E., MacCoon, G. D., & Newman, J. P. (2011). Emotion facilitation and passive avoidance learning in psychopathic female offenders. *Criminal Justice and Behavior, 38*, 641–658.

Vitale, J. E., & Newman, J. P. (2001). Response perseveration in psychopathic women. *Journal of Abnormal Psychology, 110*, 644–647.

Vitale, J. E., Newman, J. P., Bates, J. E., Goodnight, J., Dodge, K. A., & Petit, G. S. (2005). Deficient behavioral inhibition and anomalous selective attention in a community sample of adolescents with psychopathic and low-anxiety traits. *Journal of Abnormal Child Psychology, 33*, 461–470.

Vitale, J. E., Smith, S. S., Brinkley, C. A., & Newman, J. P. (2002). The reliability and validity of the Psychopathy Checklist-Revised in a sample of female offenders. *Criminal Justice and Behavior, 29*, 202–231.

Waldman, I. D., & Gizer, I. R. (2006). The genetics of attention deficit hyperactivity disorder. *Clinical Psychology Review, 26*, 396–432.

Waldman, I. D., & Rhee, S. H. (2006). Genetic and environmental influences on psychopathy and antisocial behavior. In C. Patrick (Ed.), *Handbook of psychopathy* (pp. 205–228). New York, NY: Guilford Press.

Wallace, J. F., Schmitt, W. A., Vitale, J. E., & Newman, J. P. (2000). Experimental investigations of information processing deficiencies and psychopathy: Implications for diagnosis and treatment. In C. Gacono (Ed.), *Clinical and forensic assessment of psychopathy* (pp. 87–110). Hillsdale, NJ: Erlbaum.

Walters, G. D., Duncan, S. A., & Mitchell-Perez, K. (2007). The latent structure of psychopathy: A taxometric investigation of the Psychopathy Checklist–Revised in a heterogeneous sample of male inmates. *Assessment, 14*, 270–278.

Walters, G. D., Ermer, E., Knight, R. A., & Kiehl, K. A. (2015). Paralimbic biomarkers in taxometric analyses of psychopathy: Does changing the indicators change the conclusion? *Personality Disorders: Theory, Research, and Treatment, 6*, 41–52.

Wang, P., Baker, L. A., Gao, Y., Raine, A., & Lozano, D. I. (2012). Psychopathic traits and physiological responses to aversive stimuli in children aged 9–11 years. *Journal of Abnormal Child Psychology, 40*, 759–769.

Watt, B. D., & Brooks, N. S. (2012). Self-report psychopathy in an Australian community sample. *Psychiatry, Psychology and Law, 19*, 389–401.

Weizmann-Henelius, G., Virkkunen, M., Gammelgard, M., Eronen, M., & Putkonen, H. (2015). The PCL-R and violent recidivism in a prospective follow-up of a nationwide sample of female offenders. *Journal of Forensic Psychiatry & Psychology, 26,* 667–685.

White, S. F., Marsh, A. A., Fowler, K. A., Schechter, J. C., Adalio, C., Pope, K., ... Blair, R. J. R. (2012). Reduced amygdala response in youths with disruptive behavior disorders and psychopathic traits: Decreased emotional response versus increased top-down attention to nonemotional features. *American Journal of Psychiatry, 169,* 750–758.

Widiger, T. A., & Lynam, D. (1998). Psychopathy and the five-factor model of personality. In T. Millon, E. Simonsen, M. Birket-Smith, & R. Davis (Eds.), *Psychopathy: Antisocial, criminal, and violent behavior* (pp. 171–187). New York, NY: Guilford Press.

Williams, K. M., & Paulhus, D. L. (2004). Factor structure of the Self-Report Psychopathy scale (SRP-II) in non-forensic samples. *Personality and Individual Differences, 37,* 765–778.

Williams, K. M., Paulhus, D. L., & Hare, R. D. (2007). Capturing the four-factor structure of psychopathy in college students via self-report. *Journal of Personality Assessment, 88,* 205–219.

Wilson, L., Miller, J. D., Zeichner, A. Lynam, D. R., & Widiger, T. A. (2011). An examination of the validity of the elemental psychopathy assessment: Relations with other psychopathy measures, aggression, and externalizing behaviors. *Journal of Psychopathology and Behavioral Assessment, 33,* 315–322.

Wolf, R. C., Carpenter, R. W., Warren, C. M., Zeier, J. D., Baskin-Sommers, A. R., & Newman, J. P. (2012). Reduced susceptibility to the attentional blink in psychopathic offenders: Implications for the attention bottleneck hypothesis. *Neuropsychology, 26,* 102–109.

Wykes, T., & van der Gaag, M. (2001). Is it time to develop a new cognitive therapy for psychosis—cognitive remediation therapy (CRT)? *Clinical Psychology Review, 21,* 1227–1256.

Yang, Y., Raine, A., Colletti, P. Toga, A. W., & Narr, K. L. (2010). Morphological alterations in the prefrontal cortex and the amygdala in unsuccessful psychopaths. *Journal of Abnormal Psychology, 119,* 546–554.

Yang, Y., Raine, A., Narr, K. L., Colletti, P., & Toga, A. W. (2009). Localization of deformations within the amygdala in individuals with psychopathy. *Archives of General Psychiatry, 66,* 986–994.

Yildirim, B. O., & Derksen, J. L. (2015). Clarifying the heterogeneity in psychopathic samples: Towards a new continuum of primary and secondary psychopathy. *Aggression and Violent Behavior, 24,* 9–41.

Zagon, I., & Jackson, H. (1994). Construct validity of a psychopathy measure. *Personality and Individual Differences, 17,* 125–135.

Zeier, J. D., Maxwell, J. S., & Newman, J. P. (2009). Attention moderates the processing of inhibitory information in primary psychopathy. *Journal of Abnormal Psychology, 118,* 554–563.

Index